| KERUX COMMENTARIES |

ISAIAH
VOLUME 1: ISAIAH 1–39

KERUX COMMENTARIES

ISAIAH
VOLUME 1: ISAIAH 1–39

A Commentary for Biblical Preaching and Teaching

ROBERT B. CHISHOLM JR.
MICHAEL HONTZ

Isaiah, Volume 1: Isaiah 1–39: A Commentary for Biblical Preaching and Teaching

© 2025 by Robert B. Chisholm Jr. and Michael Hontz

Published by Kregel Ministry, an imprint of Kregel Publications, 2450 Oak Industrial Dr. NE, Grand Rapids, MI 49505-6020.

All rights reserved. No part of this book may be reproduced, stored in a retrieval system, or transmitted in any form or by any means—electronic, mechanical, photocopy, recording, or otherwise—without written permission of the publisher, except for brief quotations in printed reviews.

Unless otherwise indicated, the translations of the Scripture portions used throughout the commentary are the authors' own English rendering of the original biblical languages.

Scripture quotations marked ASV are from the American Standard Version. Public domain.

Scripture quotations marked ESV are taken from The ESV® Bible (The Holy Bible, English Standard Version®), © 2001 by Crossway, a publishing ministry of Good News Publishers. Used by permission. All rights reserved.

Scripture quotations marked HCSB are taken from the Holman Christian Standard Bible®, Copyright © 1999, 2000, 2002, 2003 by Holman Bible Publishers. Used by permission.

Scripture quotations marked KJV are from the King James Version. Public domain.

Scripture quotations marked NASB are taken from the (NASBR) New American Standard BibleR, Copyright © 1960, 1971, 1977, 1995, 2020 by The Lockman Foundation. Used by permission. All rights reserved. lockman.org.

Scripture quoted by permission. Quotations designated (NET) are from the NET Bible copyright ©1996, 2019 by Biblical Studies Press, L.L.C. http://netbible.com All rights reserved.

Scripture quotations marked NIV are taken from the Holy Bible, New International Version®, NIV®. Copyright © 1973, 1978, 1984, 2011 by Biblica, Inc.™ Used by permission of Zondervan. All rights reserved worldwide. www.zondervan.com. The "NIV" and "New International Version" are trademarks registered in the United States Patent and Trademark Office by Biblica, Inc.

Scripture quotations marked NLT are taken from the *Holy Bible*, New Living Translation, copyright © 1996, 2004, 2015 by Tyndale House Foundation. Used by permission of Tyndale House Publishers, Inc., Carol Stream, Illinois 60188. All rights reserved.

Scripture quotations marked NRSV are from the New Revised Standard Version Bible, copyright © 1989 by the National Council of the Churches of Christ in the United States of America. Used by permission. All rights reserved worldwide. https://www.friendshippress.org/pages/nrsvue-quick-faq

Italics in Scripture quotations indicate emphasis added by the authors.

All photos are under Creative Commons licensing, and contributors are indicated in the captions of the photos.

Maps on pages 44 and 46 are by A. D. Riddle. Used by permission.

Photos on pages 426 and 427 are by Michael Hontz. Used by permission.

Image of relief on page 235 is by Mary Harrsch, CC BY-SA 4.0 <https://creativecommons.org/licenses/by-sa/4.0>, via Wikimedia Commons.

The Hebrew font, NewJerusalemU, and the Greek font, GraecaU, are available from www.linguistsoftware.com/lgku.htm, +1-425-775-1130.

Library of Congress Cataloging-in-Publication Data

Names: Chisholm, Robert B., author. | Hontz, Michael, 1978– author.
Title: Commentary on Isaiah : a commentary for biblical preaching and
  teaching / Robert B. Chisholm Jr., Michael Hontz.
Description: First edition. | Grand Rapids, MI : Kregel Ministry, [2025] |
  Series: Kerux commentaries | Includes bibliographical references. |
  Contents: v. 1. 1-39—
Identifiers: LCCN 2024039914
Subjects: LCSH: Bible. Isaiah—Commentaries.
Classification: LCC BS1515.53 .C45 2025 | DDC 224/.107—dc23/eng/20241114
LC record available at https://lccn.loc.gov/2024039914

ISBN 978-0-8254-5845-3

Printed in China

25 26 27 28 29 / 5 4 3 2 1

Contents

Publisher's Preface to the Series / 7

Preface to Isaiah / 9

Exegetical Author's Acknowledgments / 11

Preaching Author's Acknowledgments / 12

Overview of All Preaching Passages / 13

Abbreviations / 35

Introduction to Isaiah 1–39 / 39

THE HOLY ONE OF ISRAEL PURIFIES HIS PEOPLE AND HIS ROYAL CITY (1–12)

The Lord Confronts His Rebellious People (1:1–20) / 57

Justice Demands Purification (1:21–31) / 77

Future Transformation (2:1–5) / 89

The Demise of Human Pride (2:6–22) / 99

Retribution, Vindication, Humiliation, and Restoration (3:1–4:6) / 113

A Vineyard in Ruins and Death Is Imminent (5:1–30) / 131

A Vision of the King (6:1–13) / 153

A Sign Child and Forfeited Blessing (7:1–8:10) / 171

A King Brings the Light of Deliverance (8:11–9:7) / 201

"His Hand Is Still Upraised": Persistent Judgment on Persistent Sin (9:8–10:4) / 225

The Lord Brings Down the Proud Assyrians (10:5–34) / 243

Justice, Peace, and Renewal (11:1–12:6) / 263

THE LORD REVEALS HIS SOVEREIGNTY THROUGH WORLDWIDE JUDGMENT (13–27)

Worldwide Judgment Focused on Babylon (13:1–14:27) / 285

Oracles Concerning Various Nations (14:28–23:18) / 309

Worldwide Judgment (24:1–23) / 359

The Restoration of Israel and the Vindication of the Righteous (25:1–27:13) / 379

JUDGMENT GIVES WAY TO SALVATION (28–35)

Judgment Overwhelms the Entire Land (28:1–29) / 411
Jerusalem's Coming Crisis and Transformation (29:1–24) / 431
Rebellion and Mercy (30:1–33) / 451
Genuine Security (31:1–32:20) / 469
The Mighty Warrior-king Delivers Zion (33:1–24) / 489
Devastating Judgment and Transformation (34:1–35:10) / 503

THE LORD DISPLAYS HIS SOVEREIGN POWER (36–39)

The Lord's Victory over the Assyrians (36:1–37:38) / 523
Hezekiah's New Lease on Life (38:1–22) / 545
Hezekiah Shows Off His Wealth (39:1–8) / 559

References / 569

PUBLISHER'S PREFACE TO THE SERIES

Since words were first uttered, people have struggled to understand one another and to know the main meaning in any verbal exchange.

The answer to what God is talking about must be understood in every context and generation; that is why Kerux (KAY-rukes) emphasizes text-based truths and bridges from the context of the original hearers and readers to the twenty-first-century world. Kerux values the message of the text, thus its name taken from the Greek *kērux*, a messenger or herald who announced the proclamations of a ruler or magistrate.

Biblical authors trumpeted all kinds of important messages in very specific situations, but a big biblical idea, grasped in its original setting and place, can transcend time. This specific, big biblical idea taken from the biblical passage embodies a single concept that transcends time and bridges the gap between the author's contemporary context and the reader's world. How do the prophets perceive the writings of Moses? How does the writer of Hebrews make sense of the Old Testament? How does Clement in his second epistle, which may be the earliest sermon known outside the New Testament, adapt verses from Isaiah and also ones from the Gospels? Or what about Luther's bold use of Romans 1:17? How does Jonathan Edwards allude to Genesis 19? Who can forget Martin Luther King Jr.'s "I Have a Dream" speech and his appropriation of Amos 5:24: "No, no, we are not satisfied, and we will not be satisfied until 'justice rolls down like waters, and righteousness like a mighty stream'"? How does a preacher in your local church today apply the words of Hosea in a meaningful and life-transforming way?

WHAT IS PRIME IN GOD'S MIND, AND HOW IS THAT EXPRESSED TO A GIVEN GENERATION IN THE UNITS OF THOUGHT THROUGHOUT THE BIBLE?

Answering those questions is what Kerux authors do. Based on the popular "big idea" preaching model, Kerux commentaries uniquely combine the insights of experienced Bible exegetes (trained in interpretation) and homileticians (trained in preaching). Their collaboration provides for every Bible book:

- A detailed introduction and outline
- A summary of all preaching sections with their primary exegetical, theological, and preaching ideas
- Preaching pointers that join the original context with the contemporary one
- Insights from the Hebrew and Greek text
- A thorough exposition of the text
- Sidebars of pertinent information for further background
- Appropriate charts and photographs
- A theological focus to passages

- A contemporary big idea for every preaching unit
- Present-day meaning, validity, and application of a main idea
- Creative presentations for each primary idea
- Key questions about the text for study groups

Many thanks to Jim Weaver, Kregel's former acquisitions editor, who conceived of this commentary series and further developed it with the team of Jeffrey D. Arthurs, Robert B. Chisholm, David M. Howard Jr., Darrell L. Bock, Roy E. Ciampa, and Michael J. Wilkins. We also recognize with gratitude the significant contributions of Dennis Hillman, Fred Mabie, Paul Hillman, Herbert W. Bateman IV, and Shawn Vander Lugt who have been instrumental in the development of the series. Finally, gratitude is extended to the two authors for each Kerux volume; the outside reviewers, editors, and proofreaders; and Kregel staff who suggested numerous improvements.

—*Kregel Publications*

PREFACE TO ISAIAH

Isaiah's reputation as the foremost prophet of the Old Testament is well deserved. In his prophetic vision, we see and hear our sovereign God revealing his glory and power. He is the "Holy One of Israel," seated in his palace receiving praise: "Holy, holy, holy is the LORD Almighty; the whole earth is full of his glory" (Isa. 6:3). We hear this same holy God declare: "I live in a high and holy place, but also with the one who is contrite and lowly in spirit" (Isa. 57:15). He is both transcendent and immanent. He is exalted in the heavens, yet also present with his people.

Isaiah's vision gives us the full scope of God's plan for his world and for his covenant people. This includes purifying judgment that paves the way for a glorious future for those who submit to God's authority and receive his mercy. The central figure in the outworking of the Lord's plan is the ideal Davidic king, whom we call Messiah. He will establish a kingdom of justice and peace. We also discover he is the suffering servant of the Lord, the agent of the Lord's salvation.

The Kerux commentary on Isaiah is divided into two volumes, the first covering chapters 1–39 and the second chapters 40–66. In chapters 1–39 Isaiah speaks to his eighth-century B.C. contemporaries, accusing them of breaking God's covenant and warning them of judgment. He announces the exile of the covenant community, but also foresees a time beyond exile when God will restore his covenant people to their land under the rule of the ideal Davidic king. God's judgment will also encompass the nations of the earth, but beyond judgment God will bring salvation to the nations and include them in his kingdom. In chapters 40–66 Isaiah, having predicted the exile, speaks to the future exiles, as if present with them. He gives a grand vision of God's sovereignty over history and his infinite superiority to the idol-gods of the pagan nations. The one true God knows the end from the beginning because he has the power to form the future.

As the exegetical author of this commentary, I apply the historical-grammatical method, which looks carefully at the prophet's historical and cultural context, as well as the words he has written in the original Hebrew text. Through footnotes and sidebars, I deal with technical issues where they are problematic or especially important. However, I avoid the temptation to be encyclopedic and to wander down rabbit trails. I seek to convey accurately the prophet's message, giving attention to the literary forms he uses and to his rhetorical strategy. I am also concerned to draw out the theological significance of the text, which becomes the foundation for my coauthor's applicational insights as the preaching author of this volume.

My target audience is not the academic guild, but rather pastors and teachers who have the important responsibility of teaching the Bible's message to the people whom God has entrusted to them. I seek to follow Peter's instruction: "If anyone speaks, let it be as one who speaks God's words" (1 Peter 4:7). My prayer is that this commentary helps pastors and teachers to carry out their task of proclaiming the whole counsel of God. If that happens, all the work that has gone into producing the commentary will be well worth it.

As this project has developed over several years, the publisher has adjusted its scope and form in some ways. One of those adjustments entails excluding some of the more detailed and technical comments that I included in an earlier draft of the commentary. However, the publisher has been kind enough to give me permission to distribute these additional comments on the text in an electronic form, free of charge. For those of you interested in receiving these comments please contact me at bchisholm@dts.edu or rbchiz@sbcglobal.net.

—Robert B. Chisholm Jr.
August 22, 2024

EXEGETICAL AUTHOR'S ACKNOWLEDGMENTS

*This commentary is dedicated to the memory of
my parents, Robert Bruce Chisholm and Ethel Potter Chisholm,
who trusted in Christ as their Savior in their thirties and never turned back,
serving him faithfully until they went to be with Him;
and to my paternal grandparents, William and Edna Chisholm,
who loved me unconditionally and encouraged me to read and study relentlessly,
and who in their declining years trusted in Christ as their Savior.*

A commentary project is a team effort. I want to thank Jim Weaver for envisioning the Kerux project and for inviting me to be a part of it. Jim embodies the Christlike virtues of kindness and humility; knowing him has enriched my life. I am thankful to Shawn Vander Lugt and the Kregel team, who have persistently pursued the vision of producing this series and have brought it to fruition. I am confident their efforts will have a positive impact on the evangelical community.

We all stand on the shoulders of those who have gone before us. I am thankful for my many teachers over the years who trained me in exegesis and theology. I am especially grateful to my first Hebrew teacher, Dr. James Battenfield, who invited and motivated me to pursue Old Testament studies, and to my mentor and friend, the late Prof. Donald Glenn, who patiently taught me how to approach and execute the exegetical-theological task. I hope that this commentary, at least in some small way, rewards their efforts.

I am thankful to Debra, my devoted wife of fifty years, for always encouraging me in my labor and inspiring me with her commitment to our Savior.

Finally, I praise King Jesus, who has saved me from my sins and has given me the privilege of serving him through a lifetime of teaching his people and preparing students for ministry in his church.

—Robert B. Chisholm Jr.
August 22, 2024

PREACHING AUTHOR'S ACKNOWLEDGMENTS

This commentary is dedicated to my Lord and Savior, Jesus Christ.

I would like to thank my wife Marta and my daughters, Ellie and Emmie, for their love and constant support. I am also thankful for my parents, Steve and Sue, who first introduced me to Jesus and who imperfectly but faithfully modeled Jesus to me throughout my life.

Additionally, I want to express my gratitude to former acquisitions editor Dr. Herb Bateman (who is also one of my former seminary professors) for inviting me to participate in this commentary series. I am grateful to him and to the whole team at Kregel for giving me this opportunity. Finally, I am very appreciative of Dr. Robert Chisholm for welcoming me to work with him in this commentary project. I feel greatly blessed to be able to partner with such an accomplished and respected scholar and author.

In His service,
Michael Hontz

OVERVIEW OF ALL PREACHING PASSAGES

Isaiah 1:1–20

EXEGETICAL IDEA
The Lord exposes disobedient Israel's hypocrisy and demands that they establish justice within the community so that they may experience forgiveness and escape judgment.

THEOLOGICAL FOCUS
No vital relationship with the Lord is possible apart from obedience to his commands concerning responsibilities to one's fellow human beings.

PREACHING IDEA
The Lord urges all rebels to return to their loving Father.

PREACHING POINTERS
Frank is sitting alone in his quiet house reminiscing about days gone by. Closing his eyes, he remembers how proud he was as the nurse handed him his daughter Marissa for the first time at the hospital and he cradled her in his arms. As she grew older, he can still hear her giggling at the funny faces he would make. He recalls the look on her face as she tore open her gifts on Christmas morning, her excitement the afternoon she finally learned to ride her bike on her own, and the hours the two of them spent playing basketball together in their driveway. Marissa was daddy's girl growing up, as the two of them had much in common. Today, however, things are very different. Marissa is all grown up now, and as many teenagers do she grew to resent many of the rules and restrictions Frank placed on her life. His pleas for her to consider the outcome of her choices went unheeded, and now Frank is forced to watch with deep heartache as his precious daughter bounces from one bad relationship to another and makes one destructive decision after the next.

Every parent can identify with the emotions of the father in this story. We can appreciate his deep sorrow over a beloved child who chooses to rebel and dismiss parental oversight to pursue a more alluring but destructive lifestyle. This story epitomizes the sentiment of Isaiah 1:2–20. God describes himself as a father grieving over his wayward daughter Israel. Despite his loving care for her, she has spurned his instructions in the pursuit of self-serving freedom. As such, this passage's intended illocutionary effect is to arouse emotion as much or more than to simply convey information. Such evocative imagery should cause the disobedient people of Judah, as well as disobedient Christ-followers today, to feel God's pain on their behalf and to recognize their need to repent and return to a submissive and obedient relationship with their loving and gracious Father.

Isaiah 1:21–31

EXEGETICAL IDEA
The Lord will replace Jerusalem's unjust, idolatrous leaders and populate the city with a godly remnant.

THEOLOGICAL FOCUS
When the Lord's covenant community is plagued by unjust and idolatrous leadership, he must purify it to bring his ideal to realization.

PREACHING IDEA
Leaders can make all the difference in the world.

PREACHING POINTERS
Between 1941 and 1945, Nazi Germany systematically murdered approximately six million Jews during what is now known as the Jewish Holocaust. It is arguably the darkest period of the last century. How is it that countless people sat by, either actively giving their consent or passively doing nothing, while so many horrific atrocities were being carried out against innocent people? While the answer to that question is undoubtedly complex and multifaceted, nobody can deny that a central component was the influential leadership of Adolf Hitler. This one man was instrumental in directing a nation's energies toward so much evil. And yet Hitler was only one man. He could never have accomplished all that he did without the support and consent of many otherwise normal German citizens.

Most people today look back and assume that, had they been living in Germany during this period of history, they would certainly have resisted and spoken out against this evil movement. And while a relative few would have strongly opposed Hitler's leadership had they lived through those horrific events, history is littered with political movements that resulted in large-scale brutality and carnage where a majority of citizens stood by and did nothing—or worse yet, actively participated. In reality, most people are followers. True leaders are a rare breed; virtuous leaders are even scarcer. In Isaiah 1, the prophet confronts Judah with her rebellion against Yahweh, particularly in the way that she dealt with and treated the weak and vulnerable. Isaiah 1:21–31 reveals that Judah wasn't always this way; she used to be a "faithful city," one known for its "righteousness" and "full of justice" for the oppressed (1:21). A central reason for this shift was the ungodly, self-serving leaders. Their influence evidently had a significantly negative impact—not only on the collective reputation of the nation, but also on the individual behavior of most of the people. This highlights emphatically how leaders can make all the difference in the world.

Isaiah 2:1–5

EXEGETICAL IDEA
Since all nations will someday recognize the Lord's authority, Isaiah urges God's people to obey the Lord in the here and now.

THEOLOGICAL FOCUS
Since all nations will seek the Lord's guidance and submit to his rule of peace, his people should preview that era by obeying his revealed moral will.

PREACHING IDEA
In the light of God's promise of a future kingdom, the best is yet to come!

PREACHING POINTERS
Global warming. Political corruption scandals. Skyrocketing national debt. Nuclear weapons proliferation. Mass shootings becoming commonplace. Riots and protests in the streets. Inner-city crime on the rise. Islamic terrorism. Growing rates of depression and mental illness. The breakdown of the nuclear family. A worldwide health pandemic. Human trafficking. The growing secularization of society. Everywhere we look, there seems to be justification for pessimism, anxiety, and hopelessness. Are there really solutions to all these problems? Even if there were, do we really trust the world's politicians to responsibly do the right thing?

The book of Isaiah begins with a similarly gloomy and negative view of life in Judah. Everywhere the prophet looked, there was reason for anger, skepticism, and feelings of futility: political corruption, religious compromise, oppression of the poor, cities burned and overrun by foreigners. We are inclined in our day to echo the sentiment of the prophet who longed for the good old days of the past (Isa. 1:21) as he contemplated the present plight of Jerusalem. It is precisely amid such pessimism and hopelessness that the message of Isaiah 2:1–5 strikes a stark, contrasting chord, inspiring optimism and hope. While so much is presently wrong with the world, all is not lost. The end of the story has not yet been written. Be reassured, the best is yet to come.

Isaiah 2:6–22

EXEGETICAL IDEA
Isaiah urges Israel not to trust in weak humans because the Lord is ready to bring devastating judgment, through which he will exalt himself and humiliate the proud.

THEOLOGICAL FOCUS
The Lord's people should trust in the Sovereign Lord, not in human beings or human-made gods, for the Lord will annihilate arrogant men and their false gods as he exalts himself through judgment.

PREACHING IDEA
God will judge the proud and destroy every idol.

PREACHING POINTERS
Some forms of pride are rather easy to detect – like the cruel classmate who publicly makes fun of another student's appearance, or the know-it-all coworker who routinely speaks to others in a condescending way, or the professional athlete who declares himself the greatest of all time during a press conference immediately following an impressive victory. Most people find behaviors such as these objectionable and even repulsive. This is especially true if we are the

student whose appearance is being belittled by our classmate or if we are a member of the athletic team whose defeat is being rubbed in by the pompous athlete on the opposing team.

However, pride takes other forms besides bragging and gloating over others. Many of these are more subtle, and thus are easier to overlook. One wise Christian writer defined pride as "the stubborn refusal to let God be God, with the corresponding ambition to take his place. It is the attempt to dethrone God and enthrone ourselves. . . . [Pride is] the pretense that we can manage without God or rival God" (Stott 1992, 111–12).

This definition aptly describes how Judah was behaving when the prophet confronted them with the message recorded in Isaiah 2:6–22. They were attempting to live independently of the Lord. Rather than look to him for guidance and direction, they had begun to turn to fortune tellers and mediums. Rather than trust in Yahweh for security and protection, Judah placed their hope in accumulated wealth, human armies, and fortified walls. They attempted to replace God with idols of their own making. In the same way that we take offense when arrogant people demean and belittle us, God is even more offended—and righteously so, when people he created live in ways that belittle his importance or dismiss their need of him. Thus God opposes the proud, and there is coming a day when he will judge the haughty and arrogant along with their false idols.

Isaiah 3:1–4:6

EXEGETICAL IDEA
The Lord's judgment targets Judah's unjust leaders, vindicates the righteous, and humiliates the proud women of Jerusalem. Following his purifying judgment, a remnant will experience agricultural blessing and the Lord's protection.

THEOLOGICAL FOCUS
The Lord punishes leaders who refuse to guide his people in his ways and take pride in status acquired at the expense of others. Yet his purifying judgment leads to the restoration of his blessing and protection.

PREACHING IDEA
Sin results in devastation. Nevertheless, God still offers hope.

PREACHING POINTERS
On the evening of December 10, 2021, a tornado system moved through Western Kentucky, leaving several towns with significant damage. One of the hardest-hit communities was the town of Mayfield. Among the establishments destroyed that night was Mayfield Consumer Products, a candle factory where 110 employees were working at that time. The storm caused the factory's roof to collapse, killing eight employees while injuring many others. In the aftermath of the storm, twenty-two people lost their lives in Mayfield alone, with hundreds more injured. In addition to the lives lost that day, many of the survivors lost their homes or businesses. As a result, many residents lost their jobs as well. In the aftermath of a disaster like this, people are left wondering: "How could this happen?" "Is there any reason at this point for hope?"

The imagery in Isaiah 3 records a similar sort of devastation like that after a natural disaster. It describes the city of Jerusalem immediately following a major military defeat, probably following a long siege. As a result, much of the city's walls and infrastructure have been demolished. Any wealth or valuables have been looted and stolen. Worst of all, most of the young men have either been killed or captured and deported by the enemy. Those left behind are forced to figure out how to carry on without anyone qualified to lead them. Isaiah reveals that this horrible outcome would come upon Judah because of the people's sin and God's subsequent judgment. They would be reaping what they had sown (3:9, 11). Nonetheless, God assures those who remain faithful to him, the righteous ones, that it would ultimately be well with them (3:10). The unit ends with imagery of hope as the righteous remnant of Israel is beautiful and glorious once again. The God who brought judgment will be the same one who purifies and restores his people. He will again become their savior and protector, a refuge and shelter from the storm and rain.

Isaiah 5:1–30

EXEGETICAL IDEA
The nation will be left desolate because it has failed to realize the Sovereign Lord's expectations and, despite his kindness, has violated his ethical standards by accumulating wealth through unjust means.

THEOLOGICAL FOCUS
The Lord powerfully intervenes and punishes his proud people with purifying judgment when they challenge his sovereignty by rejecting his word and perverting his standards of justice.

PREACHING IDEA
When people become wise in their own eyes and reject God's word, the consequences are painful and inevitable.

PREACHING POINTERS
We have all had an experience where we have uncovered spoiled food. Maybe it has begun to grow green mold or developed a putrid odor. Worse yet, maybe we didn't detect anything was wrong until we put some into our mouths and had a rude awakening on our taste buds. Yuck! Once it is discovered, there is only one thing to do with rotten food: throw it out.

Isaiah 5 compares Israel to a vineyard that Yahweh planted and tended. All along, his desire and expectation for his vineyard was that it would produce delicious grapes. However, when God went to check on the fruit, he discovered a harvest of sour grapes (5:2, 4). These grapes were totally unfit to eat. The reason for this was that Israel had embraced corrupt, unjust practices (5:7). They were acting in ways that seemed wise in their own eyes but showed disregard for God's laws (5:20–21, 24). In the process, they had replaced all that God called good and sweet with that which was evil and bitter (5:20). As a result, they had become sour to God, and he was about to spew them out of his mouth.

Isaiah 6:1–13

EXEGETICAL IDEA
Overwhelmed by God's holiness, Isaiah confessed his sinfulness, yet the Lord cleansed him and commissioned him to confront stubborn Israel with its sin.

THEOLOGICAL FOCUS
Recognizing God's holiness prompts one to confess sin and experiencing spiritual cleansing prompts one to carry out God's commission.

PREACHING IDEA
An encounter with the holy, sovereign God should lead us to repent of sin and humbly submit to God, resulting in our transformation.

PREACHING POINTERS
Metamorphic—in science, the word denotes rock that has undergone transformation by heat, pressure, or other natural agencies. However, the word can also denote some life-altering, transformative experience. On occasion, people will experience something so impactful it alters how they think or behave from that point forward. It could be a close call with death like a car accident or a heart attack that makes the brevity and uncertainty of life real. Maybe the birth of a child brings about a new sense of responsibility or purpose. Others may point to some religious or spiritual awakening within them that sparked a new and better direction for their lives. Whatever the experience, when its impact on an individual is a transformed life, we can rightly refer to it as a metamorphic event.

There may be no better word to describe the prophet's vision in Isaiah 6. Isaiah saw the Lord God, high and exalted in his temple. Angels surrounding him were declaring, "Holy, holy, holy is the Lord Almighty; the whole earth is full of his glory!" (6:3). One can only imagine the transformative impact such an experience would have on a person, to come face to face with the sovereign, holy creator of the universe. Understandably, Isaiah was overcome with a sense of his own sinfulness and unworthiness to be looking upon one so perfect and glorious. But his vision was accompanied by a calling. God sent him to go and speak on his behalf to the stubborn people of Israel. Despite assurances from God that his words would mostly fall on deaf ears, Isaiah nonetheless humbled himself before God and submitted to carry out the charge that he had been given.

Isaiah 7:1–8:10

EXEGETICAL IDEA
Isaiah made it clear that the covenant community should place their trust in the Lord's faithful promise of his protective presence, for a refusal to believe would turn potential blessing into divine discipline and tragic suffering.

THEOLOGICAL FOCUS
The Lord's people should place their trust in the Lord's faithful promise of his protective presence, for a refusal to believe can turn potential blessing into divine discipline and tragic suffering.

PREACHING IDEA
It is always wise to trust in God, for ultimate security is found only in him.

PREACHING POINTERS
When my wife was pregnant with our first child, a baby girl, we spent months thinking about what name we would give her. We considered several factors: Did we like the name? Did we like the shortened forms of her name that people would inevitably call her? How many other people did we know who shared that name? Would we name her after somebody in the family, or maybe somebody in the Bible? It didn't help that my wife and I had very different ideas of what names we liked and didn't like. At one point, we bought a book of possible names and just began to read through it together. Whenever a name seemed like a possibility, we highlighted it to consider for later. One name ended up sticking out to us both: Elliana. In addition to passing all the criteria we had set up ahead of time, the meaning of this name held significance to us. In Hebrew it means, "God has answered." We had been praying and trying to have a baby for a few years. We were beginning to wonder whether we were able to have children or not. Thus, this seemed the perfect name for our first baby girl.

Names are important. But few baby names were ever quite as consequential as the ones we encounter in Isaiah 7:1–8:10. This passage revolves around three different child names, each one intended to serve as an important message from God. The children themselves would serve as "signs" or object lessons to the nation of Judah that God's promises were sure, and that his word could be trusted regardless of the circumstances or the political climate of the day. While there was a significant temptation by the people of Judah and their king to look elsewhere for a sense of security and stability, God alone had the power to save and to protect. That truth is just as relevant today as it was more than 2,700 years ago. In a climate where there is much political turmoil, economic instability, and at times even religious hostility, it is always wise to trust in God, for ultimate security is found only in him.

Isaiah 8:11–9:7

EXEGETICAL IDEA
The righteous remnant within the covenant community must focus on the Lord as their source of security in an unsure world, for he will defeat Israel's enemies and establish a kingdom of justice and peace through a Davidic king.

THEOLOGICAL FOCUS
The Lord's people must focus on him when others are fearful and panicking, for the Lord controls his people's destiny and will establish a kingdom of justice and peace through the ideal Davidic king.

PREACHING IDEA
Amid political unrest, God's people must not fear but instead rest in the Lord and his promise of a glorious coming kingdom.

PREACHING POINTERS
One of our family's favorite home movies is one we recorded on the way back from a home improvement store. We had just purchased several plants for a landscaping project at our house. Among them was a small tree that we laid up the middle of the inside of our minivan. Our daughters at the time were five and two years old. For some reason, our two-year-old was terrified by the tree any time one of its branches moved. She had pushed her body away from the tree as far as she could in her car seat and looked out her window, refusing to look directly at the tree. But every ten seconds or so, she would turn her head just enough to glance at the tree with her peripheral vision. A branch would inevitably move, and she would cry out in fear with tears streaming down her eyes. Her older sister found this funny, and she laughed uncontrollably at her while my wife and I did everything we could to assure her that there was nothing to fear.

Whether it is a fear of plants, the dark, or maybe a harmless insect, children are prone to have misplaced fears. Isaiah 8:11–9:7 reveals that most adults similarly have misplaced fears. This can be especially true in the realm of politics. The people in Isaiah's day were afraid of the Israel-Syria coalition that threatened their livelihoods. God warned his people not to fear the things that the people in the broader culture feared. Rather, they were to fear the Lord alone above all else. If they would fear him, he would become a sanctuary for them from all the other things they were prone to fear. However, if they held onto their misplaced fears, God would be a stone of offense and a snare to them. In the end, only those whose hope and trust was anchored in Yahweh would experience the glorious, eternal government that the Lord's Messiah will ultimately set up at some point in the future.

Isaiah 9:8–10:4

EXEGETICAL IDEA
Culminating, devastating judgment was ready to fall on the northern kingdom (9:8–9 [HB 7–8]; 10:1–4) because the people had persisted in evil, despite the Lord's attempts to bring them to repentance.

THEOLOGICAL FOCUS
The Lord designs judgment to bring his people to repentance, but when they respond defiantly and persist in rebellion he must intensify his judgment.

PREACHING IDEA
Only by repentance will God's wrath be appeased.

PREACHING POINTERS
The eighteenth-century pastor and theologian Jonathan Edwards preached his most famous sermon, "Sinners in the Hands of an Angry God," about God's wrath and imminent hellfire judgment against the unrepentant. Responses to that message have unsurprisingly been mixed. While many praise it for its passion and vivid imagery, others have criticized Edwards's view of God as overly cruel and angry as he stands ready to unleash his fury against sinners. One such

critic was the satirical author Phyllis McGinley, who wrote a poem mocking the now-famous sermon titled "The Theology of Jonathan Edwards."[1]

It isn't popular to speak about God's wrath today, and it probably never has been. Even in the church, people would much rather hear sermons about God's love, mercy, and patience than to hear about his wrath and judgment. Many mistakenly assume that sermons about God's wrath and the reality of eternal hellfire is more of an invention by morbid or controlling preachers than an authentic biblical doctrine. However, passages like Isaiah 9:8 (HB 7)–10:4 reveal that God's wrath against sin and his coming judgment against sinners is a reality that needs to be embraced and responded to by people in every generation. For it is only when people repent of their sins that God's wrath will be appeased.

Isaiah 10:5–34

EXEGETICAL IDEA
The Lord would judge the arrogant Assyrians, because they did not acknowledge the Sovereign Lord but proudly attributed their success to their own strength.

THEOLOGICAL FOCUS
The Sovereign Lord sometimes uses proud nations to punish his people, but when these nations fail to acknowledge the Lord's sovereignty, the Lord judges them.

PREACHING IDEA
God opposes the proud but gives grace to the humble.

PREACHING POINTERS
Do you have many friends but not enough time to spend with all of them? If so, maybe it's time for you to make a few enemies. Consider the following advice:

Step 1: Work at being critical of others to their face. Better yet, be overly complimentary to people, but then scorch them behind their backs. Be sure to criticize them to enough people that you can be sure word will get back to them.
Step 2: Routinely ask people if they've gained weight recently.
Step 3: Ignore personal hygiene. Taking showers, using deodorant, and brushing your teeth are unnecessary. Remember, people throughout most of human history were unable to take advantage of these practices; there's no need for you to bother with them either.
Step 4: Routinely invade people's personal space. Be sure to stand no further than ten inches away from people when you talk to them. If you see them take a step back to create some room, be sure to step closer. This is especially effective when combined with step 3 above.

---

1   The poem can be read in its entirety online: http://www.amerlit.com/poems/POEMS%20McGinley,%20Phyllis%20The%20Theology%20of%20Jonathan%20Edwards%20(1957)%20wit.pdf.

Nobody wants to make enemies. Only a fool would go out of their way to make other people not like them. Even worse is to make oneself an enemy of God. The quickest way to make oneself God's enemy is by acting in arrogant pride. James 4:6 says, "God opposes the proud." Isaiah indicted Israel for its pride (9:8–10:4, see esp. 9:9). Next, God confronts Assyria for its arrogant pride, which arouses his anger and prompted him to be the Assyrians' enemy (10:5–34, see esp. vv. 12, 15, 33). As a result of God's discipline against them, a remnant from Judah will turn back to God in humility (10:20–22), prompting him to surround them once again with his grace (10:23–34). Thus we see that not only does God oppose the proud but he also gives grace to the humble (James 4:6; cf. Ps. 138:6; Prov. 3:34; Dan. 5:20–21; Luke 1:52; 1 Peter 5:5).

Isaiah 11:1–12:6

EXEGETICAL IDEA
The Lord would establish a kingdom of peace through a new David and restore his exiled people from bondage, demonstrating his power through a new exodus.

THEOLOGICAL FOCUS
The Sovereign Lord, who is committed to fulfilling his covenant promises, will establish his rule on earth through an ideal Davidic king, deliver his people from exile, and renew his relationship with them.

PREACHING IDEA
Only Jesus will usher in the world in which everybody wants to live.

PREACHING POINTERS
I recently saw a marketing campaign advertising vacation destinations in Mexico with the slogan "Best day ever!" The advertisement included a video loop that contained people involved in all sorts of fun and appealing activities. There was a family sitting together on a beautiful beach watching the sunset. A person was receiving a relaxing massage in another clip. There were images of beautiful wildlife. In other clips, people could be seen swimming in a large, resort-style pool or cruising through the ocean on a WaveRunner®. A family was enjoying a delicious meal at an outdoor restaurant while being serenaded with live music. Every scene was designed to arouse within the viewer a sense of longing to be somewhere other than where they currently were. The goal was that those who saw the advertisement would develop a vision of what could be, by way of their next vacation, in hopes that they would subsequently buy into this opportunity soon.

In many ways, this is the prophet's goal in Isaiah 11:1–12:6. He describes a world to his audience that is much better than the one they currently inhabit. What he describes to them, should they be among those who experience it, would be their "best day ever." Like the marketers of the ad campaign, God wants his people to recognize that their present reality is far from ideal. The reason for this is because of how sin has cursed their world and ruined their society. However, there is coming a day when God's Messiah will arrive. He will usher in a new world where all that is wrong will be judged and made right. Only those who buy into this future world now will have a place at the table when that time comes. Thus, God's people must remain faithful to him and committed to his promise of a coming kingdom age.

Isaiah 13:1–14:27

EXEGETICAL IDEA
The Lord will judge the world for its sin and arrogance, annihilating proud Babylon and restoring exiled Israel to its homeland.

THEOLOGICAL FOCUS
The Lord demonstrates his sovereignty over the world as he judges the arrogant king of Babylon, releases his people from exile, and restores them to their land.

PREACHING IDEA
At his appointed time, the sovereign God will deliver his people from the world's oppressive tyrants.

PREACHING POINTERS
Just wait! Those are two words that no child likes to hear. In truth, none of us like to be told to wait. It is often said that we live in an age of instant gratification. There aren't many things we have to wait on. We can cook a meal in minutes in the microwave. Voice assistant devices answer most of our questions in seconds. Mobile phones mean we must rarely wait to talk to most people. Amazon Prime has spoiled us to expect online orders to arrive in two days or less. We rarely even have to wait to watch most television shows or movies; many of them can be streamed whenever it's convenient for us. With smartphones and tablets, we don't even have to wait until we get home to binge-watch the next season of our favorite show.

Unfortunately for us, God's timetable of events often doesn't align with ours. We typically prefer God to intervene on our behalf *right now*. But often that just doesn't happen. This can be particularly frustrating as it relates to wicked world leaders who oppress and persecute God's followers. Those who are forced to endure persecution at the hands of tyrants such as Kim Jong-Un of North Korea or terrorist groups like al-Qaeda, al-Shabaab, or ISIS long to see God intervene in judgment to deliver them from their suffering. Together, believers across the world echo the question of the martyrs in Revelation 6:10: "How long, Sovereign Lord . . . until you judge the inhabitants of the earth and avenge our blood?" The answer to this question is found in Isaiah 13–14. While it does not provide a specific timetable, it does assure God's people that the Sovereign Lord has in fact purposed a day when he will judge every evil tyrant throughout every nation, resulting in the salvation of his people.

Isaiah 14:28–23:18

EXEGETICAL IDEA
The Lord would demonstrate his sovereignty over the nations by judging Philistia, Moab, Aram, Cush, Babylon, Dumah, Arabia, and Tyre. He would also punish Israel for trusting in an alliance with Aram, and Judah, whose arrogant royal official Shebna epitomized the nation's pride. However, someday the Lord will make Jerusalem secure through a just Davidic king.

THEOLOGICAL FOCUS
The Lord would judge the proud, idolatrous nations, as well as his covenant people Israel and Judah. God's people should look to him for security and blessing. Someday the Lord will make a descendant of David his king. This ideal Davidic ruler will establish a kingdom of justice and peace that will encompass the whole earth.

PREACHING IDEA
Though God must judge all nations for their sin and rejection of him, there is hope because of God's love for all and his promise to establish a worldwide kingdom.

PREACHING POINTERS
What comes to your mind when you hear the term "shock jock"? The term is generally applied to a broadcaster who is prone to push the limits of communication by saying things they know will be startling and offensive. It may not be an exaggeration to suggest that the prophet Isaiah was the very first shock jock—albeit a righteous one! Not only did he say many provocative things, but for three of those years Isaiah walked naked through the streets of Jerusalem as he loudly proclaimed the judgment that was coming upon Egypt and Cush (Isa. 20:2–4). Can you imagine the shock this would have caused to visitors who stumbled upon Isaiah for the first time? They must have been even more surprised, probably horrified, to discover that he was a well-known prophet of God.

In a very real way, God did intend to shock his people through the ministry of Isaiah. Over time, the inhabitants of Judah had come to admire the strength and wealth of some of their regional neighbors like Assyria and Egypt. As such, many assumed it was in their best interests to link their fortunes and future security to those nations. God wanted to wake his people up to the following realities concerning the nations: (1) All of these nations would eventually face judgment from God. (2) As such, it makes no sense for God's people to put their hope and confidence in human nations and groups. (3) Finally, Judah and Israel's great hope is the same as that of all the nations of the world. One day God will send a descendant of David who will establish a kingdom founded upon justice and righteousness for all.

Isaiah 24:1–23

EXEGETICAL IDEA
The Lord will judge the entire earth because of its violation of the "everlasting covenant," defeat all opposition, and establish his reign on Mount Zion.

THEOLOGICAL FOCUS
The Lord judges the nations when they break the everlasting covenant and then extends his rule to the entire earth.

PREACHING IDEA
God ushers in a glorious new world for his people by destroying the present corrupt earth, judging wicked humanity, and establishing his rule over the earth.

PREACHING POINTERS

Over the centuries, one of the tougher questions with which Christian theologians have wrestled is, "How can God send people to hell who reject him, but who have never had a chance to hear the gospel?" This is particularly troubling for those who live in regions of the world where there is no gospel witness at all. Basic fairness and justice would seem to require that a person only be held accountable for laws or standards of which they are aware. While aspects of this question remain difficult to answer, the Bible does teach universal accountability for sin based on general revelation, to which everyone has access (Ps. 19:1–6 [HB 2–7]; Rom. 1:18–20). All people should be able to deduce certain truths about God's existence and character from creation. Additionally, everyone has been hardwired with a conscience that informs them about God's righteous demands and their moral accountability before him (Rom. 2:12–16). Thus, the Scriptures teach that all humanity will be without excuse when they someday stand before God to give an account of their lives (Rom. 1:20).

Isaiah 24 contributes to the biblical doctrine of general accountability for sin. The prophet describes all humanity as having broken "the everlasting covenant" between them and God (Isa. 24:5). As such, they are guilty and deserving of judgment. In language reminiscent of the worldwide flood in the days of Noah, Isaiah warns of similar eschatological judgment against the world that will destroy the earth in its present corrupt form. God's judgment will pave the way for him to usher in his kingdom over a new, regenerated earth populated by the righteous.

Isaiah 25:1–27:13

EXEGETICAL IDEA
Judgment will dominate the immediate future, but the prophet looks beyond that as he focuses on Israel's restoration and the vindication of the righteous.

THEOLOGICAL FOCUS
The Lord will vindicate his covenant people by establishing his rule from Zion, defeating all enemies, reclaiming the exiles, and restoring his favor and blessing.

PREACHING IDEA
Believers celebrate their salvation as God defeats all their enemies, including death.

PREACHING POINTERS
Have you ever been to the funeral of a child or teenager who tragically died due to a natural disaster, some form of sickness, or a random act of violence? Maybe you knew a young serviceman or woman who died while serving our country in the prime of life. I (Mike) recently received word of some friends whose forty-year-old son just died from a brain tumor. Their only other child tragically died in infancy. One can only imagine the pain they are experiencing. At times like these, people inevitably begin to question God's goodness and his wisdom. Why would he allow this to happen? If he is all-loving and all-powerful, why wouldn't he do something to prevent these sorts of tragedies?

These are undeniably complex questions that require more than just a trite or simplistic answer, or worse yet, some shallow-sounding cliché. Nonetheless, the answer to these questions is addressed by God in these chapters. The deep longing of the human heart for the Lord to do something about the problem of death is provided here: "He will swallow up death forever. The Sovereign LORD will wipe away the tears from all faces" (Isa. 25:8). What a tremendous promise! Ever since the beginning of time, humanity has been suffering the anguish associated with sin in the form of sickness and eventual death. However, according to Isaiah, a time is coming when God will put an end to death forever. What's more, the bodies of those who have died long ago will be raised again as "the earth will give birth to her dead" (Isa. 26:19). The people of God will worship him and celebrate his salvation and gift of eternal life.

Isaiah 28:1–29

EXEGETICAL IDEA
The Lord's destructive judgment upon both Samaria and Judah will remove the covenant community's corrupt leaders and replace them with those who promote justice.

THEOLOGICAL FOCUS
The Lord, the people's only genuine source of security, judges corrupt leaders to establish justice in his covenant community.

PREACHING IDEA
The Lord alone can provide genuine security.

PREACHING POINTERS
In a 1943 paper entitled "A Theory of Human Motivation," Abraham Maslow (1943, 370–96) proposed a hierarchy of human needs. According to Maslow, the most basic of human needs are physiological—things such as breathing, food, water, and sleep. These things are necessary for life. Only one level above this on his proposed pyramid of needs are those related to human safety and security. While just a theory, Maslow's hierarchy of needs assumes that the more basic or essential a need is believed to be by an individual, the more it will likely impact their behavior. In other words, because food and water are needed to live, most people will do almost anything to get or maintain food and water. Similarly, because issues of safety and security are also very high on the spectrum of human needs, they too will naturally have a significant impact on many people's actions. Most people will go to great lengths in their life in order to feel safe and secure.

Isaiah 28 focuses on this issue of security. The prophet confronts the leaders of Israel and Judah regarding their misplaced faith as it related to whom/what they were trusting in for security. While Israel was trusting primarily in their capital city of Samaria to protect them in the event of a military attack, Judah's sense of security was tied to their "covenant with death," as the prophet referred to it. This was likely a reference to their alliance with Egypt. In reality, neither strong cities nor powerful military allies can provide ultimate protection, especially in the event that God decides to act in judgment against a people. As such, this passage explores the issue of security, including false sources of security. It reveals how, in the ultimate sense, the Lord alone provides genuine security.

Isaiah 29:1–24

EXEGETICAL IDEA
The Lord will bring a powerful army against Jerusalem, but then deliver the city from its attackers, demonstrating that he alone controls the city's destiny and is deserving of its trust. The Lord will restore his exiled people, prompting them to acknowledge his sovereignty as their spiritual vision is restored.

THEOLOGICAL FOCUS
The Lord demonstrates his sovereignty over the destiny of his people first by bringing a powerful army against Jerusalem, and then by mightily delivering the city from its attackers. Divine judgment has a positive goal: the spiritual transformation of the covenant community and their recognition of the Lord's sovereignty.

PREACHING IDEA
God directs hardships and discipline in his people's lives to bring about spiritual renewal and to demonstrate his trustworthiness.

PREACHING POINTERS
Mysterious. Unpredictable. Transcendent. Ineffable. These are just some of the words that come to mind when trying to describe the ways of God sometimes. The apostle Paul declares, "Oh, the depth of the riches of the wisdom and knowledge of God! How unsearchable his judgments, and his paths beyond tracing out!" (Rom. 11:33). There are many times when God's actions or inactions do not make much sense to us. We have all wrestled at times with thoughts such as, "If I were God, I would do this or that." For some who are skeptical or even cynical of Christianity, this is often a reason they give for withholding faith in him. If God is really loving and all-powerful, then why does he allow wicked people to carry out their nefarious plans?

While the answer to questions such as this are admittedly complex and elusive much of the time, passages such as Isaiah 29 confirm that God orchestrates some of the hardship in the world to accomplish his own sovereign plans. The existence of pain and suffering in the world does not serve as an indication that God is not in control of the world. Rather, pain and suffering function at some level as part of his sovereign plan. While on the surface it might appear strange that God would describe himself as the force behind the evil Assyrian army besieging and encircling his own people (29:2–3), in the end he will demonstrate himself to be both wise and loving even in this. God's sovereign actions will result in the just judgment of the Lord's enemies (29:20–21) as well as the salvation and spiritual renewal of his own people (29:17–19, 22–24).

Isaiah 30:1–33

EXEGETICAL IDEA
The Lord will punish those who seek help from Egypt and reject his authority, but he will extend his mercy to those who trust him as he defeats Assyria.

THEOLOGICAL FOCUS
The Sovereign Lord is the only source of security for his people.

PREACHING IDEA
The path of rebellion leads only to ruin, but repentance brings blessing and rejoicing.

PREACHING POINTERS
Every generation has a concept of what a rebel looks like. If one attended high school in the 1950s, they might imagine somebody in tight jeans with a white t-shirt, a black leather jacket, slicked back hair, and a cigarette behind his ear. If one was a child of the '60s, they may instead envision a marijuana-smoking hippie with long hair and a tie-dyed t-shirt. When I attended high school in the '90s, there was a subculture of people who identified themselves as goth and dressed in all black. Many of them dyed their hair black, wore black makeup, and embellished their faces and bodies with piercings and jewelry. These students personified rebellion in my day.

In Isaiah 30, the prophet confronts the "rebellious" (30:1, 9) people of Jerusalem. They chose to ignore his prophets' warnings against seeking help from foreign nations. Their refusal to trust in him was not just foolish but an act of rebellion. The people of Jerusalem thought they knew better than God and trusted their own wisdom more than his promises (30:12). Thus, God was going to have to judge them. However, because the Lord is such a patient and gracious God (30:18), he called on his people to repent, promising them that he waits expectantly for them to turn back to him (30:19). When they do, they would be greeted with salvation, blessings, and joy (30:15, 23–26, 29).

Isaiah 31:1–32:20

EXEGETICAL IDEA
After disciplining those who trusted in false sources of security, the Lord will deliver Zion from the Assyrian threat and provide just leadership, accompanied by renewed blessing and genuine security.

THEOLOGICAL FOCUS
The Lord protects and transforms his covenant community by defeating their enemy, establishing just leadership, and providing them with prosperity and security.

PREACHING IDEA
It is folly to trust in any saviors other than the Lord God.

PREACHING POINTERS
Government agencies generally don't have the best reputation for being quick, efficient, or reliable. This includes government agencies designed to respond immediately after a natural disaster or major crisis. Former president Ronald Reagan once humorously said, "The nine most terrifying words in the English language are: 'I'm from the government, and I'm here to help.'" Examples of this abound, such as the failures of both the local and federal governments leading

up to and following the flooding of New Orleans when Hurricane Katrina struck in 2005.[2] Then there's the failed response by FEMA to the massive destruction across Puerto Rico caused by Hurricane Maria in 2017.[3] These are just two of the many examples that highlight how poor governments typically are at rescuing the people who depend upon them during times of crisis.

In Isaiah 31–32, the prophet confronts the people of Judah for their foolishness in trusting the government of Egypt to protect them from the looming disaster of an Assyrian invasion. In the same way that governments today so often fail their people in times of crises, so too God warned Judah that Egypt would utterly fail to provide them with security and peace. Egypt was a "false savior." This passage highlights three separate false saviors, none of which could deliver them from harm nor provide them with the security they desired. Rather, as the prophet indicated, only God is a wholly sufficient savior. He alone is worthy of our confidence and devotion.

Isaiah 33:1–24

EXEGETICAL IDEA
In answer to prayer, the Lord will deliver and restore his favor to the covenant community, but only those who fear him and pursue righteousness will experience his blessings.

THEOLOGICAL FOCUS
The Lord, the mighty warrior-king, demonstrates his enduring commitment to those within the covenant community who fear and obey him.

PREACHING IDEA
God delivers those who appeal to him alone in faith based on his grace.

PREACHING POINTERS
People are naturally proud and want to be independent whenever possible. From an early age, children will often resist help from their parents, insisting they can do it themselves. Adults similarly take pride in their own work, especially when they can complete a task that most would have had to hire somebody else to do. Unfortunately, many people assume this same do-it-yourself, confident spirit of independence when it comes to things for which God has instructed us to trust in him alone. It is one thing to repair your own automobile or teach yourself to play a musical instrument without the help of a mechanic, tutor, or coach. It is altogether different when a person attempts to secure their own salvation apart from the Lord.

In Isaiah's time, this passage served to confirm God's gracious willingness to deliver his people from the threat of their enemy, the Assyrian king. However, Isaiah 33 becomes an ideal passage to preach about God's salvation from sin generally. In the same way that Hezekiah and the inhabitants of Jerusalem thought they could accomplish their own salvation apart from God, so too people throughout history have tried to accomplish their salvation on their

---

2 https://www.politico.com/story/2012/10/10-facts-about-the-katrina-response-081957.
3 https://newrepublic.com/article/149899/troubling-failure-americas-disaster-response.

own, usually through some form of moralism or good works. However, humans are utterly incapable of saving themselves from God's coming wrath against sin. It is only when people appeal to God alone in faith based on his grace that they will discover him to be their great deliverer.

Isaiah 34:1–35:10

EXEGETICAL IDEA
The Lord's anger ignites devastating judgment, but he will lead the godly home on "the Way of Holiness," transforming the desert and healing the handicapped.

THEOLOGICAL FOCUS
The Lord will punish the hostile nations for mistreating his people; he is committed to restoring his covenant people, but only the godly are allowed to experience the joy of this great transformation.

PREACHING IDEA
God's people should be encouraged by the promise of coming judgment, as it will be a day of both vengeance and salvation.

PREACHING POINTERS
From 2011 to 2014, the National Geographic Channel aired a reality television show called *Doomsday Preppers*. The show featured individuals or families who were so concerned about the possibility of a future catastrophic event that they were devoted toward preparing for that day. The participants expressed fear about different doomsday scenarios such as solar flares or a natural disaster such as an earthquake or meteorite. Others feared a global health pandemic, a nuclear war, or even the eventual effects of global warming. The results, though, looked about the same for each. They attempted to prepare for these potential events by stocking up on food and ammunition, and by making sure they had the knowledge and means to produce their own food, filter clean drinking water, and protect themselves against various threats.

There is much we don't know about the future. Nonetheless, the Bible does warn about a coming doomsday of sorts. However, God will initiate this day. It will be a day of his vengeance and wrath upon the sinful world that has rejected his rule over them. Isaiah 34 describes this event as resulting in great destruction and "slaughter" (34:2, 6) where the mountains are left flowing with human blood as dead corpses lie everywhere (34:3, 7). The luminaries in the sky fall to the earth while the sky rolls up like a scroll (34:4). The streams and soil are turned into burning pitch and sulfur (34:9). This destruction will leave cities and entire civilizations desolate (34:10, 12).

As horrible as this day will be for those who have rejected God, Isaiah 35 describes a wonderful coming day of salvation and transformation for God's people. In fact, the positive effects of this day are described in images that directly contrast with the negative effects upon God's enemies in chapter 34. Together, these chapters warn people to prepare adequately for this coming time.

Isaiah 36:1–37:38

EXEGETICAL IDEA
When the arrogant Assyrian king threatened Jerusalem, the Lord assured Hezekiah that he would deliver the city and humiliate the Assyrians.

THEOLOGICAL FOCUS
The Lord is sovereign over the destiny of nations and humiliates those who arrogantly challenge his authority.

PREACHING IDEA
God honors those who live for his glory, but those who defy his glory are doomed.

PREACHING POINTERS
People most naturally live for their own glory. Many of our daily actions are done out of concern to protect or enhance our own reputations. Our concern about what others think of us motivates much of what we do. We often calculate the things we say or don't say by whether it will make us look petty, arrogant, intelligent, whiny, cruel, or generous. It isn't uncommon at all to say something we don't really mean simply because it will make us look better than how we would be perceived if we were completely honest.

Many of the sins people struggle with are directly related to their desire to promote their own glory. Jealousy and covetousness flow out of a belief that I am as important or more important than that person. Lying is often viewed as a good option because we feel the need to protect our own honor by covering up some shameful truth about ourselves. Gossip is fueled by our desire to appear better than others. Yet we aren't nearly as tempted to speak ill of them in their presence because we don't want them to think ill of us. Many other examples could be offered to show that the default of all humans is to protect and promote their own glory and honor.

In contrast to this tendency is the Bible's admonition that we commit ourselves to live first and foremost for God's glory. In 1 Corinthians 10:31, believers are exhorted that in whatever they do, including when they eat and drink, they should live for God's glory. Thus, the calculus for our words and actions should always include how this will impact God's reputation. Isaiah 36–37 reveals just how important God's glory is to him. Just as Judah was at the brink of being conquered by the powerful Assyrian army, King Hezekiah appealed to the Lord for his help on the primary basis of God's own honor and reputation. In response to this, the Lord affirmed that he would act on Judah's behalf out of his concern for his own glory.

Isaiah 38:1–22

EXEGETICAL IDEA
Hezekiah's prayer prompts the Lord to give both the king and his royal city, Jerusalem, a reprieve. Hezekiah then thanks the Lord for sparing his life in response to his prayer.

THEOLOGICAL FOCUS
The Lord is willing to respond positively to the heartfelt petition of his people.

PREACHING IDEA
You are going to die, so turn to the Lord for salvation and set your house in order.

PREACHING POINTERS
Lately, you've not been feeling well. For the past six months or so, you've noticed that you have been fatigued more than usual. At first, you assumed it was just a matter of a busy schedule or just a sign that you're not as young as you used to be. You've always prided yourself on staying in shape, but having recently celebrated your forty-sixth birthday, you also realize that you're not twenty-five anymore either. However, when you begin to experience abdominal pain that you can't explain and that won't go away, you decide to have it checked out. The doctor runs a series of tests and schedules a follow-up appointment with you. When the diagnosis finally comes back a week later, it is even worse than you feared: you have stage four pancreatic cancer. Your options aren't promising. The doctor wants to begin an aggressive treatment immediately, but he also wants you to know that in all likelihood, your chances of surviving beyond six months are slim. As such, he urges you to set your house in order.

This is the scenario we encounter in Isaiah 38. King Hezekiah unexpectedly grew sick and was on the verge of death. When Isaiah the prophet came to visit with him, his message from the Lord was a solemn one: "Put your house in order, because you are going to die; you will not recover" (38:1). Like anyone else who experiences a moment like this, it likely engendered an array of negative emotions, including fear, anger, sadness, and regrets. Nonetheless, there is at least one significant blessing that results when one receives word that they are soon going to die. Unlike those who pass away from a heart attack or a car accident or some other totally unexpected occurrence, those who receive such news are provided the gift of knowing their time left on earth is short, and thus they can make whatever decisions are necessary to prepare themselves and their loved ones for their imminent passing. In a general sense, the realities of a relatively short life and a certain coming death are true of all people in every age. Because death is final and its implications are eternally impactful, it should motivate all of us to petition God for salvation and take to heart Isaiah's admonition to Hezekiah to put his house in order.

Isaiah 39:1–8

EXEGETICAL IDEA
Hezekiah shows off his wealth to the Babylonian messengers, prompting Isaiah to announce the Babylonian exile.

THEOLOGICAL FOCUS
As illustrated by Hezekiah's actions, there is a fine line between faith and failure.

PREACHING IDEA
Beware of pride and self-centeredness, which easily grow in the soil of God's blessings and success.

PREACHING POINTERS

It is human nature to forget things. The challenge to remember important things is a daily struggle. How did people ever make do without smartphones to remind them about all their important events and meetings? In the same way that humans routinely do not remember important dates and events, we are also prone to forget the spiritual lessons we've learned in the past. This was the case with King Hezekiah. He was just coming off a dramatic spiritual success story of God answering his prayer for healing and blessing him with the gift of fifteen more years of life (38:5). This was accompanied by a miracle where God turned back the sundial ten steps as proof that he had directly acted on Hezekiah's behalf (38:7–8). This happened in the context of God also miraculously delivering the entire city of Jerusalem from the powerful Assyrian army when his angel struck down 185,000 of them in one night (38:6; cf. 37:36–37).

These events must have had a huge impact on Hezekiah. He would have learned how powerful God is and why it is essential to look to him for Judah's defense and protection. He would also have learned the futility of political alliances with pagan nations. None of those alliances had helped him in the past. Only the Lord was able to deliver. Finally, he would have learned a lesson about the importance of God's glory, and why it is essential to maintain a proper posture toward him of humility and praise.

Nevertheless, Hezekiah seems to have forgotten every one of these lessons when the Babylonian envoys paid him a visit with gifts and flattery. Hezekiah used this opportunity to show off his own glory rather than to magnify the Lord for what he had done for him. Additionally, Hezekiah yet again appears to be enamored with the allure of a political alliance, this time with Babylon, rather than trusting in the protection afforded by the Lord. As such, this story reveals the importance of remembering the lessons we have learned rather than repeating the failures from our past.

ABBREVIATIONS

GENERAL ABBREVIATIONS

A.D.	in the year of our Lord (*anno Domini*)
B.C.	Before Christ
HB	Hebrew Bible
LXX	Septuagint

TECHNICAL ABBREVIATIONS

cf.	compare (*confer*)
e.g.	for example (*exempli gratia*)
etc.	and so forth, and the rest (*et cetera*)
i.e.	that is (*id est*)
mng.	meaning
v(v).	verse(s)

BIBLICAL SOURCES

Old Testament

Gen.	Genesis
Exod.	Exodus
Lev.	Leviticus
Num.	Numbers
Deut.	Deuteronomy
Josh.	Joshua
Judg.	Judges
Ruth	Ruth
1 Sam.	1 Samuel
2 Sam.	2 Samuel
1 Kings	1 Kings
2 Kings	2 Kings
1 Chron.	1 Chronicles
2 Chron.	2 Chronicles
Ezra	Ezra
Neh.	Nehemiah
Esther	Esther
Job	Job
Ps./Pss.	Psalm(s)
Prov.	Proverbs

Old Testament (continued)

Eccl.	Ecclesiastes
Song	Song of Songs
Isa.	Isaiah
Jer.	Jeremiah
Lam.	Lamentations
Ezek.	Ezekiel
Dan.	Daniel
Hos.	Hosea
Joel	Joel
Amos	Amos
Obad.	Obadiah
Jonah	Jonah
Micah	Micah
Nah.	Nahum
Hab.	Habakkuk
Zeph.	Zephaniah
Hag.	Haggai
Zech.	Zechariah
Malachi	Malachi

Abbreviations

New Testament

Matt.	Matthew
Mark	Mark
Luke	Luke
John	John
Acts	Acts
Rom.	Romans
1 Cor.	1 Corinthians
2 Cor.	2 Corinthians
Gal.	Galatians
Eph.	Ephesians
Phil.	Philippians
Col.	Colossians
1 Thess.	1 Thessalonians
2 Thess.	2 Thessalonians

New Testament (continued)

1 Tim.	1 Timothy
2 Tim.	2 Timothy
Titus	Titus
Philem.	Philemon
Heb.	Hebrews
James	James
1 Peter	1 Peter
2 Peter	2 Peter
1 John	1 John
2 John	2 John
3 John	3 John
Jude	Jude
Rev.	Revelation

PERIODICALS

ASTI	*Annual of the Swedish Theological Institute*
BA	*Biblical Archaeologist*
BBR	*Bulletin for Biblical Research*
Bib	*Biblica*
BSac	*Bibliotheca Sacra*
CBQ	*Catholic Biblical Quarterly*
CTJ	*Calvin Theological Journal*
CTR	*Criswell Theological Review*
HAR	*Hebrew Annual Review*
HBT	*Horizons in Biblical Theology*
HUCA	*Hebrew Union College Annual*
JBL	*Journal of Biblical Literature*
JBQ	*Jewish Bible Quarterly*
JETS	*Journal of the Evangelical Theological Society*
JNSL	*Journal of Northwest Semitic Languages*
JQR	*Jewish Quarterly Review*
JSOT	*Journal for the Study of the Old Testament*
OTE	*Old Testament Essays*
ResQ	*Restoration Quarterly*
SJT	*Scottish Journal of Theology*
TA	*Tel Aviv*
VT	*Vetus Testamentum*
WTJ	*Westminster Theological Journal*
ZAW	*Zeitschrift für die alttestamentliche Wissenschaft*

Abbreviations

SERIES

AB	Anchor (Yale) Bible
AnBib	Analecta Biblica
ANEM	Ancient Near Eastern Monographs
BECNT	Baker Exegetical Commentary on the New Testament
BibInt	Biblical Interpretation Series
BibOr	Biblica et Orientalia
BJSUCSD	Biblical and Judaic Studies from the University of California, San Diego
BZAW	Beihefte zur Zeitschrift für die alttestamentliche Wissenschaft
CBQMS	Catholic Biblical Quarterly Monograph Series
CC	Continental Commentaries
CHANE	Culture and History of the Ancient Near East
ConBOT	Coniectanea Biblica: Old Testament Series
FAT	Forschungen zum Alten Testament
FOTL	Forms of Old Testament Literature
HSM	Harvard Semitic Monographs
IBC	Interpretation: A Bible Commentary for Teaching and Preaching
ICC	International Critical Commentary
IRT	Issues in Religion and Theology
JSOTSup	Journal for the Study of the Old Testament Supplement Series
LAI	Library of Ancient Israel
LHBOTS	Library of Hebrew Bible/Old Testament Studies
NAC	New American Commentary
NCB	New Century Bible Commentary
NIBCOT	New International Bible Commentary: Old Testament
NICOT	New International Commentary on the Old Testament
NIVAC	NIV Application Commentary
OBT	Overtures to Biblical Theology
OTL	Old Testament Library
OTS	Old Testament Studies
RANE	Records of the Ancient Near East
RINAP	Royal Inscriptions of the Neo-Assyrian Period
SBLDS	Society of Biblical Literature Dissertation Series
SBLMS	Society of Biblical Literature Monograph Series
SHBC	Smith & Helwys Bible Commentary
SHCANE	Studies in the History and Culture of the Ancient Near East
SubBi	Subsidia Biblica
SVTG	Septuaginta: Vetus Testamentum Graecum Auctoritate Academiae Scientiarum Gottingensis editum
TOTC	Tyndale Old Testament Commentaries
VTSup	Supplements to Vetus Testamentum
WAW	Writings of the Ancient World
WBC	Word Biblical Commentary

REFERENCES

ANEP	Pritchard, James B., ed. *The Ancient Near East in Pictures: Relating to the Old Testament*. 2nd ed. with supplement. Princeton, NJ: Princeton University Press, 1969.
ANET	Pritchard, James B., ed. *Ancient Near Eastern Texts Relating to the Old Testament*. 3rd ed. Princeton, NJ: Princeton University Press, 1969.
ARAB	Luckenbill, Daniel David. *Ancient Records of Assyria and Babylonia*. 2 vols. Chicago: University of Chicago Press, 1926–1927.
BDB	Brown, Francis, S. R. Driver, and Charles A. Briggs. *The New Brown-Driver-Briggs-Gesenius Hebrew and English Lexicon*. Peabody, MA: Hendrickson, 1979.
CAD	Gelb, Ignace J., et al. *The Assyrian Dictionary of the Oriental Institute of the University of Chicago*. 21 vols. Chicago: Oriental Institute of the University of Chicago, 1956–2010.
COS	Hallo, William W., and K. Lawson Younger Jr., eds. *Context of Scripture*. 4 vols. Leiden: Brill, 1997–2016.
DHS	Davidson, A. B. *Hebrew Syntax*. 3rd ed. Edinburgh: T&T Clark, 1901.
GKC	Gesenius, Wilhelm. *Gesenius' Hebrew Grammar*. Edited by Emil Kautzsch. Translated by Arthur E. Cowley. 2nd ed. Oxford: Clarendon, 1910.
HALOT	Köhler, Ludwig, Walter Baumgartner, and Johann J. Stamm. *The Hebrew and Aramaic Lexicon of the Old Testament*. Translated and edited under the supervision of Mervyn E. J. Richardson. 2 vols. Leiden: Brill, 2001.
IBHS	Waltke, Bruce K., and Michael Patrick O'Connor. *An Introduction to Biblical Hebrew Syntax*. Winona Lake, IN: Eisenbrauns, 1990.
Joüon	Joüon, Paul. *A Grammar of Biblical Hebrew*. Translated and revised by T. Muraoka. 2 vols. SubBi 14. Rome: Pontifical Biblical Institute, 1993.
NDBT	Alexander, T. Desmond, Brian S. Rosner, D. A. Carson, and Graeme Goldsworthy, eds. *New Dictionary of Biblical Theology*. Downers Grove, IL: InterVarsity Press, 2000.
NIDOTTE	VanGemeren, Willem A., ed. *New International Dictionary of Old Testament Theology and Exegesis*. 5 vols. Grand Rapids: Zondervan, 1997.
TDOT	Botterweck, G. Johannes, Helmer Ringgren, and Heinz-Josef Fabry, eds. *Theological Dictionary of the Old Testament*. Translated by J. T. Willis, et al. 17 vols. Grand Rapids: Eerdmans, 1974–2021.

BIBLE TRANSLATIONS

ESV	English Standard Version
HCSB	Holman Christian Standard Bible
KJV	King James Version
NASB	New American Standard Bible
NET	New English Translation
NIV	New International Version
NLT	New Living Translation
NRSV	New Revised Standard Version

INTRODUCTION TO ISAIAH 1–39

> **OVERVIEW OF ISAIAH 1–39**
>
> **Author:** Isaiah
>
> **Date:** About 740–700 B.C.
>
> **Historical and Cultural Setting:** Judah
>
> **Literary Forms:** Judgment speech, salvation announcement, salvation portrayal, exhortation
>
> **Theological Emphases:** The Lord will fulfill his ideal for Israel by purifying his people through judgment and then restoring them to a renewed covenantal relationship. He will establish Jerusalem (Zion) as the center of his worldwide kingdom and reconcile the once hostile nations to himself.

AUTHORSHIP AND DATE OF ISAIAH 1–39

The book's heading identifies it as "The vision concerning Judah and Jerusalem that Isaiah son of Amoz saw during the reigns of Uzziah, Jotham, Ahaz and Hezekiah, kings of Judah."[1] Analogy with other prophetic books containing headings suggests that the heading pertains to the entire book of Isaiah.[2] The message is called a "vision" (חָזוֹן), which refers here to prophetic revelation (see Smith 2007, 98–99).

The focal point of this "vision" is "Judah and Jerusalem." In this regard, it is noteworthy that each of the main sections of chapters 1–35 ends with the restoration of

Painting of the Prophet Isaiah by Antonio Balestra

---

1   Unless indicated otherwise, biblical citations in introduction come from NIV11.
2   The New Testament citations of Isaiah by name come from throughout the book. See Matt. 3:3 (Isa. 40:3); 4:14–16 (Isa. 9:1); 8:17 (Isa. 53:4); 12:17 (Isa. 42:1–4); 13:14–15 (Isa. 6:9–10); 15:7–9 (Isa. 29:13); Mark 1:2–3 (Isa. 40:3); 7:6–7 (Isa. 29:13); Luke 3:4–6 (Isa. 40:3–5); 4:17–19 (Isa. 61:1–2); John 1:23 (Isa. 40:3); 12:38–41 (Isa. 53:1; 6:10); Acts 8:28–33 (Isa. 53:7–8); 28:25–27 (Isa. 6:9–10); Rom. 9:27–29 (Isa. 10:22–23; 1:9); 10:16 (Isa. 53:1), 20 (Isa. 65:1); 15:12 (Isa. 11:10).

the exiles to Zion/Jerusalem (12:6; 27:12–13; 35:10). Granted, at the surface (or locutionary) level, much of the material concerns foreign nations (see esp. the oracles in chs. 13–23) and the northern kingdom of Israel. However, even here the message is intended primarily for the people of Judah (see Oswalt 1986, 83), whose political and religious center was Jerusalem. At a deeper (illocutionary and perlocutionary) level, the oracles against the nations were relevant to the leaders and people of Judah. By affirming the Lord was sovereign over all nations, the oracles should have reminded Judah they did not need to fear foreign nations. They also served as a warning not to seek security through alliances with them. Additionally, the oracles should have encouraged and strengthened the faithful remnant by assuring them the Lord was in control of the world and was worthy of their continued trust. He was working out his plan for the nations and would eventually establish his kingdom, centered in Jerusalem.

The heading's list of kings indicates that Isaiah's ministry spanned at least forty years, probably longer. After a long reign, Uzziah died in 740 B.C. According to Isaiah 6:1, Isaiah received the vision and commission described there in the year of Uzziah's death. We are not told if the vision occurred before or after the king's death. While Isaiah is given a very specific commission in 6:9–13, it is possible he was functioning in a prophetic role prior to this. If so, the commission in chapter 6 may have marked a new direction or emphasis in Isaiah's ministry, but not necessarily his inaugural call to be a prophet (Milgrom 1964; Oswalt 1986, 80; Smith 2007, 26–28, 183–84). In this case, his ministry would have started a few or even several years before the king's death in 740 B.C. As for the end of Isaiah's prophetic career, Hezekiah's reign lasted until 686 B.C. Isaiah was very active in 701 B.C., when the Assyrians threatened Jerusalem, and shortly thereafter, when Babylonian envoys visited Hezekiah (see the discussion of the chronology of chs. 36–39 in the commentary below). But we cannot be certain how long Isaiah continued to function as a prophet after this. So, we can conclude from the book's heading that Isaiah prophesied during 740–700 B.C. at the least and perhaps a few (or even several) years before and/or after this period.

While the book's heading identifies Isaiah as its author, this does not demand that the prophet spoke or wrote every word in it. A robust view of biblical inspiration can and should make room for inspired additions. For example, most proponents of Mosaic authorship of Deuteronomy would acknowledge that the account of Moses's death at the end of the book comes from a later, albeit inspired, hand. In fact, the entire narrative frame of Deuteronomy may be from an editor. If so, the book is still essentially Mosaic in that the bulk of it contains his words. On a smaller scale, the final verses of Psalm 51, attributed to David in the psalm's heading, reflect the exilic period and were probably added by a later, inspired editor who was applying the ancient psalm's message to the circumstances of his own day. The addition has become part of the inspired final or canonical form of the psalm, much like the final verse ("When we've been there ten thousand years . . .") that was added to Newton's hymn "Amazing Grace." (For more on the concept of inspired updating of biblical texts, see Grisanti 2001.)

In the case of Isaiah, the authorship of the book's synoptic material is uncertain. Isaiah 2:2–4 is virtually identical to Micah 4:1–3. Isaiah and Micah were contemporaries. Did one of them borrow from the other? Except for Hezekiah's prayer (38:9–20), Isaiah 36–39 corresponds to 2 Kings 18:17–20:19. Is one dependent on the other or did they both draw on a common source, perhaps available in the nation's historical archives? The historical note of 37:38, which tells of Sennacherib's assassination in 681 B.C., postdates the reign of Hezekiah, which ended in 686, and therefore Isaiah's ministry (cf. 1:1), so it would have to be a later addition. Isaiah's words appear within these chapters (cf. 37:6–7, 21–35; 38:1, 5–8, 21; 39:3–7), yet the narrative framework mentions him by name. This stands in contrast to the autobiographical style used by the prophet in chapters 6 and 8. In addition to chapters 37–39, third-person references to Isaiah also occur in three of the book's headings (1:1; 2:1; 13:1) and within two narratives (7:3; 20:2–3).

It is possible that at least some of the synoptic material did not originate with Isaiah, but rather was integrated into the book by a later inspired editor. This may be the case as well with the headings in which he is mentioned and the narrative material that refers to him in the third person. Furthermore, it is also possible, perhaps even likely, that brief interpretive glosses appear here and there (such as in 37:38; see also the commentary below on 7:8).

This approach, which sees the book as essentially Isaianic with minimal redaction, stands in contrast to the higher-critical consensus that much of Isaiah 1–39 did not originate with the eighth-century prophet. According to the higher-critical approach, redactors added a great deal of material, making for a rather complicated literary history that sometimes ends up leaving relatively little to the prophet Isaiah. (In this regard, see Schultz's [2012, 248] critique of the redactional approach.) For example, Ronald Clements (1980, 2–8) sees traces of early Isaianic collections, which were supplemented by redaction in the time of Josiah and by additions during and after the exile. One can also detect the redactional work of so-called Deutero-Isaiah (the author of chs. 40–55). Otto Kaiser (1972, 1–8) proposes an even more complex development of eleven stages. He justifies his approach by arguing that modern western concepts of individual authorship were nonexistent in the ancient Near East (pp. 8–10). Consequently, redactors thought nothing of altering and reshaping prophetic sayings to contemporize the prophetic message.

Kaiser's notion that the concept of individual authorship is strictly a modern one is wrong, given the fact that all prophetic books have a heading attributing the book to an individual prophet. Furthermore, the prophets came as messengers of the covenant Lord to confront the people with their violation of the covenant and to warn them of the impending implementation of the covenant curses. Consequently, their messages, like the covenant itself, possess an inherent canonical, authoritative status. The kind of extensive revamping of the prophet's message proposed by redaction critics runs counter to this and makes the model inherently unlikely.

More recently, an emphasis on canonical arrangement of the material has led to a recognition that there is a "unity" of sorts (however one defines the term) in the final or canonical form of the text (see Williamson 2009, 26–30). Hugh Williamson explains that it was once the primary concern of redaction critics to separate authentic Isaianic material from secondary additions (p. 29). However, "Nowadays redaction critics nearly always work the other way around, seeking to first arrive at an understanding of the text as it currently stands (synchronic analysis) and then working back from that to the more hypothetical earlier stages (diachronic analysis)." However true this may be (and the change is welcome), the assumption remains that much of the material does not originate with Isaiah. No matter where redaction critics start and what trajectory they travel, in the end they are convinced the book is layered.

Redaction critics argue that close analysis of the text supports their model. But close inspection of their analyses, which are often pedantic and pedestrian, surfaces unproven assumptions (e.g., regarding predictive prophecy), conclusions that are only as valid as the questionable premises upon which they are constructed, methodological flaws at the literary-exegetical level, and insensitivity to the rhetorical dimension of messages that were constructed as "oral literature" in their original context. In the commentary below, I address several of these problems (see, e.g., 5:25; 6:11–12; 8:2; 11:1, 11–12; 18:7; 31:4; 34:5). Perhaps most problematic is redaction critics' assumption that the proposed editors did sloppy work and left such unsightly seams and glaring contradictions that a modern interpreter, despite being so far removed from the world of the text linguistically and culturally, can spot alleged sources and even pinpoint their time of origin! In the end, these outmoded redactional approaches are at best speculative and at worst akin to scholarly fiction. For a fuller discussion of authorship issues, see Block and Schultz (2015), Hays (2011), and Schultz (2004 and 2012).

HISTORICAL AND CULTURAL SETTING OF ISAIAH 1–39

Historical Setting

Under Jeroboam II (793–753 B.C.) Israel (the northern kingdom) prospered and expanded its borders. According to 2 Kings 14:28, Jeroboam made Damascus a vassal state. During this period Assyria was relatively weak. It went through a difficult time of political unrest and military defeat, during which a plague broke out. It was during this time that Jonah (a contemporary of Jeroboam II; see 2 Kings 14:25) visited Nineveh. To the south of Israel, Judah (the southern kingdom), led by Uzziah (792–740 B.C.) also experienced renewed prestige and influence.

Following the rise of Tiglath-pileser III (745–727 B.C.) to the throne of Assyria, the political situation in Israel and Judah changed abruptly. Tiglath-pileser retooled the Assyrian Empire as he conducted a series of military campaigns (see Tadmor and Yamada 2011; cf. *COS* 2.117:284–92). He made Rezin of Damascus, Menahem of Israel (752–742), and several other western kings pay tribute (2 Kings 15:19–20).

The Assyrian threat prompted Israel and Damascus to form an anti-Assyrian alliance. Pekah (740–732 B.C.), who had assassinated Menahem's son Pekahiah (742–740 B.C.), and Rezin tried to force Judah's King Ahaz (735–716 B.C.) to join their alliance, but he refused. In 735 B.C. they attacked Judah and threatened to replace Ahaz with a local ruler (called the "son of Tabeel" in Isa. 7:6; see 2 Kings 16:5–6; Isa. 7:1). The Lord, speaking through Isaiah, urged Ahaz to maintain political neutrality and to place his trust in the protection he promised. However, Ahaz enlisted the help of Tiglath-pileser and became his vassal (2 Kings 16:7–10).

Relief of Tiglath-Pileser III

Tiglath-pileser was heavily involved in the west during 734–732 B.C. In 732 B.C. he defeated Damascus and reduced it to a province (2 Kings 16:9). He then invaded and conquered Israel, dividing much of its territory into provinces. He set up Hoshea (732–722 B.C.), who assassinated Pekah, as a puppet king over a territorially reduced and greatly weakened Israelite state (2 Kings 15:29–30). (On Assyrian involvement in the west during this period, see Otzen 1977–1978 and 1979.)

Israel's days were numbered. During the reign of Shalmaneser V (727–722 B.C.), Hoshea embarked on an anti-Assyrian policy and enlisted the aid of Egypt. Shalmaneser attacked Israel, took Hoshea prisoner, besieged Samaria for three years before eventually taking the city in 722 B.C., and deported 27,500 Israelites (according to Assyrian records, *COS* 2.118D:295–96) to Assyria (2 Kings 17:3–6). Shalmaneser's successor Sargon II (722–705 B.C.) claimed to be the conqueror of Samaria (see *COS* 2.118D:295–96), but this claim is in part propagandistic. Sargon was probably a general in Shalmaneser's army when the city was taken.

Relief of King Sargon II and a Dignitary

With Israel out of the picture, Judah was now a neighbor of Assyria, which had reduced Israelite territory to provinces ruled by Assyrian governors. But changes were also taking place in Assyria, where Sargon II replaced Shalmaneser V as king. The change in rule prompted rebellions in the south and west, so Sargon, after solidifying his strength at home, had to stabilize his empire. In the south a coalition of Elamites and Chaldeans, led by Merodach-baladan (see 2 Kings 20:12), beat back the Assyrians at Der in 720 B.C. Sargon was not able to drive Merodach-baladan out of Babylon until 710 B.C.

In the west Sargon encountered a coalition that included forces from Damascus, Samaria, and Gaza, among others. In 720 B.C. Sargon defeated the rebels at Qarqar, swept through Philistia and went as far as the Egyptian border, forcing Judah to pay tribute. Sargon also brought the siege of Tyre, begun five years earlier by Shalmaneser, to a successful conclusion. After campaigning in the east for two years, Sargon was forced to put down another western rebellion in 717 B.C. In 712 B.C. he sent a force to the west again, this time to put down a rebellion by the king of Ashdod (see Isa. 20:1). (For inscriptions describing Sargon's campaigns, see *COS* 2.118:293–300.)

After Sargon's death in battle in 705 B.C., Sennacherib (704–681 B.C.) rose to the throne of Assyria. Rebellions broke out in the empire shortly after this. In 703 B.C. Merodach-baladan tried unsuccessfully to regain the throne of Babylon. In 701 B.C., in conjunction with his religious reforms and his attempt to revive the Davidic monarchy, Hezekiah of Judah (716–686 B.C.) allied with the kings of Sidon and Ashkelon and the leaders of Ekron in an attempt to overthrow Assyrian rule. (On Hezekiah's reforms and anti-Assyrian policies, see Borowski 1995, 148–55.) Sennacherib came west to put down the rebellion. The king of Sidon fled to Cyprus, the king of Ashkelon was carried away into exile, and the rebel leaders in Ekron were impaled. That left Judah.

Sennacherib's invasion of Judah consisted of two forces (Na'aman 1979, 61–86). The first advanced through central Judah and established a line of approach and supply through the northern Shephelah. This force captured

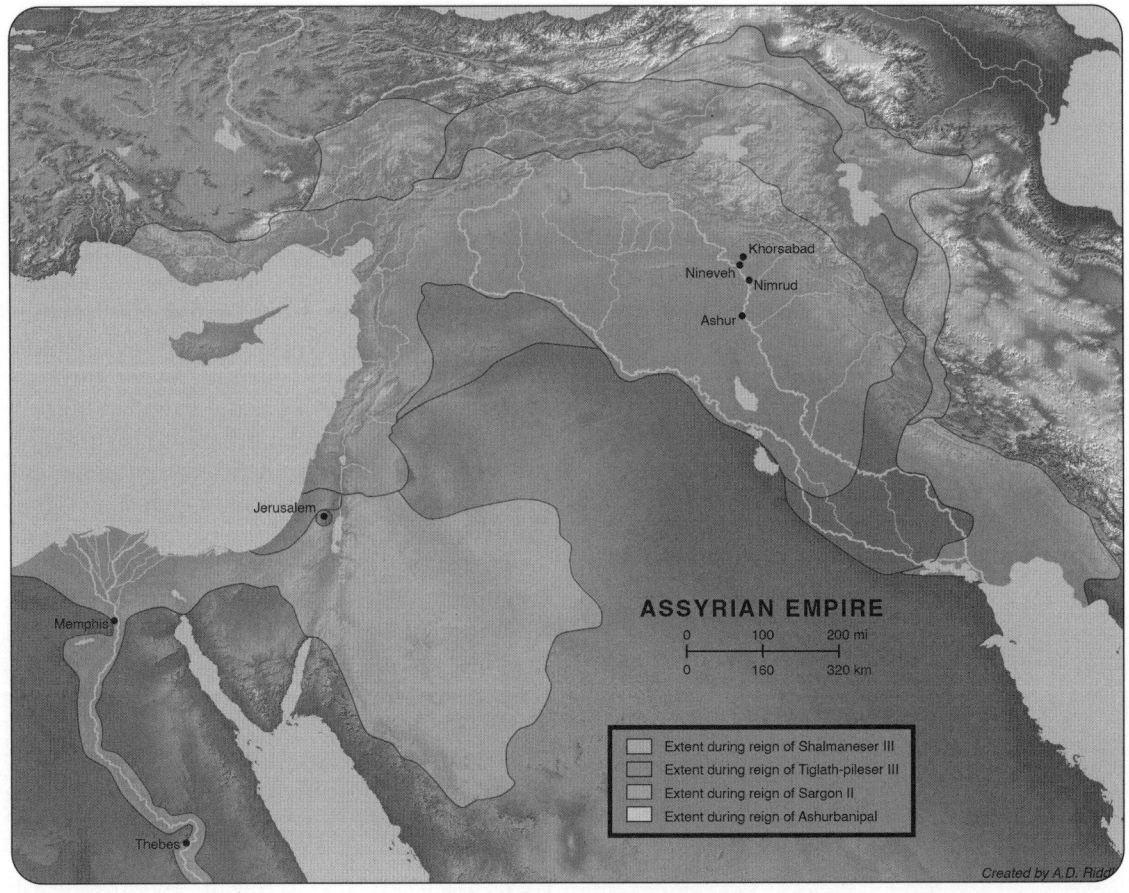

Map of the Assyrian Empire

Azekah, Gath, and the cities of the Shephelah, including Lachish. (On the siege of Lachish, see Ussishkin 1977, 28–60.) A second force moved from Lachish up to Jerusalem, destroying several towns along the way. In his annals Sennacherib describes his conquest of the land and his siege of Jerusalem. He boasts that he captured forty-six walled cities, took more than 200,000 captives, forced Hezekiah to pay a large amount of tribute, and trapped the Judahite king in his royal city "like a caged bird" (cf. *COS* 2.119B:303). Of course, the biblical account (see 2 Kings 18:17–19:35; Isa. 36–37) provides us with a more complete picture of what happened. Here we learn that the Lord destroyed 185,000 Assyrian soldiers, forcing Sennacherib to return to Assyria. Sennacherib does not record this disaster; this comes as no surprise, given his well-attested tendency to falsify history in his royal annals (Laato 1995, 198–226). Sennacherib does not claim to have taken Jerusalem or to have deposed Hezekiah. His silence in this case speaks volumes!

For the remainder of his reign Sennacherib was occupied with rebellions in the south. In 700 B.C. he defeated Merodach-baladan and his Elamite and Aramean allies. In 695–691 B.C. he campaigned against the Elamites, while in 689 B.C. he destroyed Babylon after besieging it for nine months. According to 2 Kings 19:37

(see also Isa. 37:38), two of Sennacherib's sons assassinated him while he worshiped in the temple of one of his gods and then escaped to Armenia. Sennacherib's son Esarhaddon (681–669 B.C.) took the Assyrian throne. (For inscriptions describing Sennacherib's campaigns, see Grayson and Novotny 2012 and 2014; *COS* 2.119:300–305.)

Isaiah prophesied events that took place beyond his lifetime. To understand how these prophecies were fulfilled, it is necessary to know what transpired in the Near East following the prophet's death. Sennacherib's successor Esarhaddon rebuilt Babylon, regaining the loyalty of the Babylonians and solidifying his rule in the south. In the west Esarhaddon maintained control of the Assyrian provinces and vassals, including Judah, now ruled by Hezekiah's son Manasseh, who is listed as one of Esarhaddon's subjects in one of the Assyrian king's inscriptions. Esarhaddon also campaigned against the Egyptians and even forced the princes of Lower Egypt to acknowledge his sovereignty.

Esarhaddon's successor, his son Ashurbanipal (668–627 B.C.), attempted to strengthen Assyrian control over Egypt. Toward the end of his father's reign, the Egyptians rebelled against Assyrian rule. After Ashurbanipal took the throne, he marched against Egypt and defeated the rebels. However, once the main army withdrew, the Egyptians did not cooperate with Assyrian occupational troops, which had to put down the uprising.

Sometime later, probably after 648 B.C., Manasseh rebelled against Assyrian rule. He was taken to Babylon in humiliation, but eventually was allowed to return to Jerusalem (see 2 Chron. 33:11–13). Manasseh was succeeded by his son Amon (643–641 B.C.), who was in turn succeeded by Josiah (641–609 B.C.). During Josiah's reign major political changes occurred in the Near East, as the Assyrian Empire collapsed, and the Babylonians and Egyptians rushed to fill the vacuum.

Ashurbanipal was succeeded by his son, Ashur-etil-ilani, who had to suppress two internal uprisings during his brief reign. During these internal struggles (if not before in some cases) Babylon, Judah, Phoenicia, and Media repudiated Assyrian rule. About 623 B.C. Sin-shar-ishkun seized the throne from his brother Ashur-etil-ilani, with the help of the Chaldean Nabopolassar who had already rebelled against Assyria in 626 B.C. Sin-shar-ishkun then broke off relations with Nabopolassar; Assyria and Babylon remained hostile until the demise of the former a few years later. In 615 B.C. the Medes under Cyaxares invaded Assyria, capturing the city of Assur. Cyaxares and Nabopolassar formed an alliance and defeated Nineveh in 612 B.C., an event described in the Babylonian Chronicle (*ANET*, 304–5) and prophesied by Nahum. Assyrian forces under Ashur-uballit, an officer of the king, regrouped in Harran.

In 609 B.C. the Egyptians, under Necho, who was trying to maintain the balance of power in the Near East, marched northward to aid the Assyrians. Josiah of Judah challenged him at Megiddo and was killed in battle (2 Kings 23:29–30). Judah now became an Egyptian vassal. In 609 B.C. Jehoahaz became king of Judah. He apparently rebelled against Egyptian rule, for Necho quickly replaced him with his brother Jehoiakim (609–598 B.C.; see 2 Kings 23:31–35).

In 605 B.C. the Egyptians and Babylonians, led by Nebuchadnezzar (605–562 B.C.), clashed at Carchemish (see Jer. 46:2). The Babylonians were victorious and Nebuchadnezzar marched southward into Judah, making Jehoiakim his vassal. When Jehoiakim rebelled in 601 B.C. (see 2 Kings 24:1), Nebuchadnezzar sent troops to the west, reestablished control of Judah, and claimed territory all the way to the Egyptian border (2 Kings 24:2, 7). In 598 B.C. Jehoiachin (598–597) succeeded Jehoiakim to the throne of Judah. Apparently, Judah rebelled at this time, for Nebuchadnezzar besieged Jerusalem, replaced Jehoiachin with Zedekiah, and deported

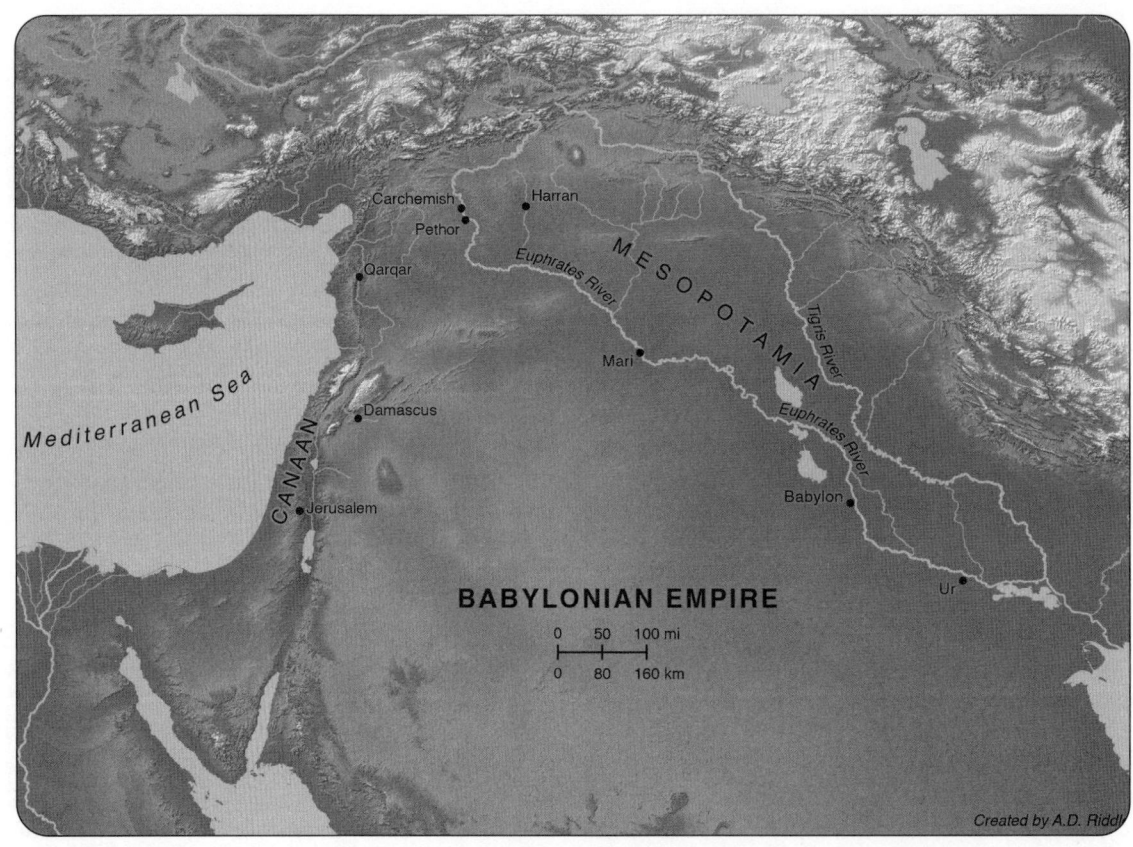

Map of the Babylonian Empire

many people, including Jehoiachin, to Babylon (see 2 Kings 24:10–17 and *ANET*, 305). Zedekiah (597–586 B.C.) remained loyal for a time but he, like his predecessors, eventually rebelled against Babylonian rule. In 588 B.C. Nebuchadnezzar besieged Jerusalem, which eventually capitulated in 586 B.C. The Babylonians sacked the city, burned the temple, and carried most of the people away into exile (2 Kings 25). The exiles would not return to their homeland until almost fifty years later, when the Persians, led by Cyrus, conquered Babylon (see *ANET*, 306–7) and allowed them to go back.

The Cultural Situation

Isaiah exposed and denounced the injustice and economic exploitation that were occurring in Israel and Judah during his time. The land occupied by Israel and Judah belonged to the Lord, who allotted it to the individual tribes as their inheritance (Lev. 25:23–24). He gave the people laws designed to ensure socioeconomic equilibrium. However, by Isaiah's time a royal military and judicial bureaucracy had developed in both Israel and Judah, just as the prophet Samuel had warned hundreds of years before (1 Sam. 8). As these bureaucracies expanded, they acquired more and more land and gradually commandeered the economic and legal systems. At various levels (including the local level), the system invited bribery, graft, and other dishonest practices.

The common people living outside the urban administrative centers—through confiscatory taxation, conscription, excessive interest rates, and other oppressive measures—were gradually disenfranchised and lost their landed property and, with it, their rights as citizens. "Big government" had radically disturbed the socioeconomic equilibrium envisioned in the covenant.

At the root of this societal disintegration was a lack of faith in the Lord's ability to protect his covenant community and a lack of respect for his moral authority as king. If God's people had really believed the Lord could protect them, they would not have asked for a king "like all the nations" in the first place, nor would the Judean monarchy have felt the need to build a military machine and accompanying bureaucracy to resist the Assyrians.

LITERARY FORMS IN ISAIAH 1–39

Isaiah used a variety of literary forms. The most widely used form in chapters 1–39 is the judgment speech, which typically contains two elements—the formal accusation (basis for judgment) and the formal announcement of judgment.[3] Within the announcement, there is often a reference to the Lord's intervention, accompanied by a description of its outcome. A subcategory of the judgment speech is the woe oracle (see Janzen 1972).[4] It is formally introduced with a pronouncement of woe (הוֹי), typically accompanied by an accusation (sometimes implicit in the description of the addressee) and announcement of judgment.

The prophet also included exhortations in his speeches at times.[5] Exhortations are marked by a formal appeal typically accompanied by a motivating statement, which can be a promise or a threat. Exhortations are invariably embedded within larger speeches.

Three different salvation genres appear (see Westermann 1991): (1) The salvation oracle, while more common in chapters 40–66, does appear twice in chapters 1–39 (10:24–34; 35:4). It begins with the reassurance formula, "fear not." (2) Salvation announcements focus on the act of divine intervention.[6] Basic elements of the genre include: an allusion to a lament or lamentable situation, a proclamation of salvation, and the goal of the saving intervention. (3) Salvation portrayals depict the aftermath of saving intervention.[7] According to Claus Westermann (1963, 208–9), salvation portrayals differ from announcements in two main ways. First, there is no direct connection literarily between a "concrete situation of distress and a concrete act of divine deliverance." Second, the portrayal presents an ideal eschatological picture in which the present order is radically transformed.

While these forms with their typical elements are discernible in Isaiah's prophecies, rhetorical criticism has demonstrated that the prophet often mixed, abridged, or expanded forms to produce a customized, unique message. Furthermore, he also combined various forms into one unified larger speech unit. Isaiah 5:8–30 provides a good example of this (see the commentary below for a more detailed analysis). From a form-critical perspective, this speech contains six oracles, each introduced by

---

3   See Westermann 1967, 129–88. Judgment speeches appear in chs. 1–39 in the following passages: 1:21–31; 2:6–21; 3:1–15; 3:16–4:1; 7:13–25; 8:5–8; 9:7–10:4; 13:2–22; 14:22–27, 28–32; 15:1–16:13; 17:1–14; 19:1–17; 20:1–6; 21:1–10, 11–12, 13–16; 22:1–14, 15–22; 23:1–18; 24:1–13, 17–23; 25:10–12; 26:20–21; 27:1; 28:7–13, 14–22; 29:13–14; 30:8–17; 32:9–14; 34:1–17; 37:22–29; 39:6–7.
4   Woe oracles appear in 1:4–9; 3:9–11; 5:8–30; 10:1–4, 5–19; 18:1–7; 28:1–4; 29:1–4, 15–24; 30:1–5; 31:1–3; 33:1–12.
5   Exhortations appear in 1:16–20; 2:5, 22; 7:4–9; 8:11–15, 19–22; 31:4–9; 33:13–16.
6   Salvation announcements appear in 10:20–23; 11:11–16; 14:1–21; 17:6–8; 26:19; 27:2–13; 29:5–8; 30:18–23, 27–33; 33:3–6; 37:30–35; 38:5–6.
7   Salvation portrayals appear in 2:2–4; 4:2–6; 8:23–9:6; 11:1–10; 19:18–25; 25:6–12; 28:5–6; 30:23–27; 32:1–8, 15–20; 33:17–24; 35:1–10.

הוֹי, "woe" (5:8–10, 11–17, 18–19, 20, 21, 22–30). A closer examination reveals some structural oddities. Woes 1 (vv. 8–10), 2 (vv. 13–17), and 6 (vv. 22–23, 24b) have both an accusation of guilt and an announcement of impending judgment, but woes 3–5 (vv. 18–19, 20, 21) have only an accusation. Redactional-critical explanations for the lack of structural symmetry reflect insensitivity to the prophet's rhetorical creativity. The omission of the announcements after woes 3–5 is by design. If woes 3–6 are combined, they form a powerful accusation (5:18–23, 24b), culminating in an overwhelming announcement of judgment (5:24a, 25–30). The clustering of woes 3–6 with no intervening announcement heightens the accusatory tone of the speech. Based on the pattern established in woes 1–2, one anticipates an announcement, but the delay creates a foreboding mood. One expects the announcement, when it does come, to be terrifying in the extreme, and the final announcement meets these expectations.

Rhetorical criticism also examines how speeches have been ordered and arranged in the final canonical form of the book. To what degree the prophet himself is responsible for the present arrangement of the book is uncertain. The macrostructure of chapters 1–12, 13–27, and 28–35 exhibits careful design with respect to the arrangement of the individual speeches (see the commentary below for detailed analyses). In each case, there is a discernible shift in emphasis from judgment to salvation, culminating in restoration from exile with Zion/Jerusalem as the focal point.

THEOLOGICAL FOCUS

The theological message of Isaiah 1–39 can be summarized as follows: *The Lord will fulfill his ideal for Israel by purifying his people through judgment and then restoring them to a renewed covenantal relationship. He will establish Jerusalem (Zion) as the center of his worldwide kingdom and reconcile the once hostile nations to himself.*[8]

The theological themes of chapters 1–39 can be conveniently arranged under two major headings that reflect the relational dimension of Isaiah's message: (1) God's relationship to his covenant people, and (2) God's relationship to the nations.

God's Relationship to His Covenant People

A Broken Covenant

First and foremost, the Lord is the Holy One of Israel, a title that appears twenty-five times in the book of Isaiah, twelve times in chapters 1–39. When Isaiah was commissioned as a prophet, he saw an overwhelming vision of the Lord, "the king" (6:5), seated on his royal throne with seraphs proclaiming, "Holy, holy, holy" (6:3). As the Holy One of Israel, set apart from sinful Israel, the Lord had full moral authority over his people. But Isaiah was very much aware that he lived among a community of sinners, who were destined to experience the judgment of the Lord of Armies, the mighty warrior-king (6:5). Once purified of his sin (6:6–7), Isaiah's prophetic mission was to confront the covenant community with its sin and to announce its impending judgment. But tragically and ironically, his message would serve to harden an already rebellious people and expedite their punishment. The more the prophet accused, exhorted, and warned, the more the message fell on deaf ears and blind eyes, hastening the arrival of devastating judgment and exile (6:8–13).

The background for Isaiah's accusations and announcements of judgment is the Mosaic covenant (see Exod. 24:1–8; 34:10–28; Deut. 29:1–32:47; Josh. 24:1–27). In this bilateral covenant Israel agreed to serve the Lord and follow his commandments. The Lord promised to reward obedience with agricultural prosperity and national security, but he

---

8 For a much fuller discussion of the theology of Isaiah, see Chisholm 1991.

also threatened to punish disobedience with destruction of crops, military defeat, and exile (see Lev. 26 and Deut. 28). Isaiah came as a specially commissioned messenger of Israel's covenant king to accuse the people of breaking the covenant, to call them to repentance, and to warn of impending judgment against those who refused to listen.

Isaiah accused the people of breaking God's covenant in various ways, including economic exploitation of others and its attendant religious hypocrisy, idolatry, misplaced trust in foreign alliances and their own national defense, and, more fundamentally, rejection of the Lord's authority.

Isaiah had much to say about the widespread exploitation of the poor that plagued the northern kingdom of Israel and the southern kingdom of Judah. Government bureaucrats enriched themselves by seizing property (5:8), instituting oppressive laws (10:1–2), and controlling the legal system (1:23; 5:23; 29:21). At the expense of the oppressed (3:15–16), they caroused from morning until evening (5:11–12, 22), while their wives proudly flaunted their beautiful clothes and expensive jewelry (3:16–23). From the Lord's perspective, this exploitation of the poor was tantamount to murder and bloodshed (1:15, 21; 4:4).

Like a farmer who plants a vineyard, the Lord established the covenant community. He expected them to produce the good grapes of justice and righteousness, but ironically they yielded only the wild grapes of bloodshed and cries of distress (5:1–7). The literary transformation of this song of the vineyard from a love song (cf. 5:1) to a harsh judgment speech (cf. esp. 5:5–7) highlights the Lord's sense of loss and disappointment.

Despite their mistreatment of their fellow Israelites, these oppressors had the audacity to bring the Lord offerings (1:11–15). The Lord rejected their religious rituals, pointing out that when they raised their bloodstained hands in prayer their hypocrisy was obvious. The Lord urged them to change their ways by promoting justice and defending the cause of the widow and orphan (1:16–17).

Isaiah also denounced idolatry (1:29) and other pagan religious practices, including divination (2:6) and spiritism (8:19). Rather than seeking guidance from their God, the people tried to contact the spirits of the dead. In the coming day of the Lord, idolaters would realize the futility of worshipping human-made images (2:8, 18–20; 17:8; 27:9; 31:7) and discard them like a menstrual rag (30:22).

The covenant community placed its faith in its own human-made weapons (2:7; 22:8) and fortifications. The northern kingdom was proud of its capital city Samaria (28:1). The people of Jerusalem refortified their city (22:8–11). However, these fortifications would not protect them against the Lord's "day of battering down walls" (22:5). The Assyrians captured Samaria in 722 B.C. (2 Kings 17:6) and were on the verge of conquering Jerusalem in 701 B.C. when the Lord miraculously delivered the city (2 Kings 18–19).

Because of their fear of the Assyrians, the leaders of Judah looked to other nations, especially the Egyptians, for assistance. Isaiah urged them to trust in the Lord alone, but the leaders were bent on allying with Egypt, thinking that Egyptian military might could protect them (30:1–7; 31:1). However, Egypt was destined for destruction (31:3). Isaiah reminded the people that security comes through God's power, not through soldiers and horses (31:3; cf. Exod. 15:1; Josh. 11:4–9; 2 Kings 6:14–17; Pss. 20:7 [HB 8]; 33:16–19; Prov. 21:31).

God's people rejected his authority by rejecting his prophetic word through Isaiah. They demanded that God's prophets bring them messages of salvation, rather than exhortations to holy living (Isa. 30:10–11). When Isaiah challenged Ahaz to trust in God's promise to David, the king rejected God's offer of a confirming sign (7:1–12).

Impending Judgment

The Lord warned that judgment would come upon the covenant community because of their rebellion. The Lord himself would regard them as his enemy and actively oppose them and their allies (1:24; 5:25; 9:19; 29:2–3; 31:3). They would become the objects of his warfare, just as Israel's enemies had been in earlier days (28:21). They would experience the day of the Lord, a day of "tumult and trampling and terror . . . of battering down walls and of crying out to the mountains" (22:5). Proud people would run for their lives, throwing their worthless human-made idols aside in their panic (2:10–21).

The Lord's instrument of judgment would be the Assyrian army. The Assyrians would come like a hail and windstorm against Samaria and trample it underfoot (28:2–3). They would then sweep through Judah like a flood (7:17; 8:6–8), marching relentlessly ahead, roaring like a lion, and causing a cloud of gloom and terror to descend upon the land (5:26–30). The Assyrians would besiege and terrorize Jerusalem (29:1–4). Though the Lord would miraculously deliver the city from their hands, he would eventually raise up another Mesopotamian power, the Babylonians, to conquer it (39:6–7). Through these foreigners the Lord would bring to pass the judgments threatened in the covenantal curse lists (see Lev. 26 and Deut. 28). The crops of the land would be destroyed (1:7; 5:5–6, 9–10; 6:11; 8:21) and the people killed or exiled (3:25; 5:13–14, 24–25; 6:12; 10:4; 39:7).

The Lord would reduce his people to a mere remnant. Besieged Jerusalem would be like an isolated hut in the middle of a field (1:9). The destruction would be so thorough that it would further reduce the remnant surviving the first wave of judgment (6:13). This remnant, likened to a lonely flagpole erected on a mountain (30:17), stands in stark contrast to the vast population promised in the Abrahamic covenant (10:22).

The judgment would be appropriate and just. Since the people worshipped foreign gods under "sacred oaks" and in gardens, they would become like an oak or garden deprived of water (1:29–30). Jerusalem's arrogant women would be humiliated, their luxurious clothing and jewelry replaced by captives' ropes and mourners' sackcloth (3:16–4:1). Those who dishonestly accumulated houses and lands would be deprived of their ill-gotten gains (5:8–10). Their carousing would come to an end as they died of hunger and thirst in exile (5:11–13). Ironically, they would become the main course at death's feast, while sheep would graze on the ruins of their banqueting halls (5:14, 17). The darkness of judgment would fall upon those who substituted darkness for light in the moral and ethical realm (5:20, 30). Those who mocked the prophet's words and complained that his message was too childlike would come face-to-face with foreign invaders, whose words would be unintelligible to them (28:9–13).

Despite its severity, the ultimate goal of God's judgment was to purify his people. Sin-filled Jerusalem was like good wine diluted by water or silver mixed with dross (1:22). The Lord's fiery judgment would burn away the dross and reestablish the city as a center of justice (1:25–27). By purging out the city's evildoers, the Lord would, as it were, wash away its bloodstains (4:4). These references to the purifying character of God's judgment are a guarantee of his commitment to his covenant people and lay the foundation for the shift from judgment to salvation in Isaiah's message.

Salvation

Israel's story would not end in judgment. The Lord's punishment of his people, while severe and devastating, was merely a necessary step in achieving his ideal for the covenant community. The miraculous deliverance of Jerusalem in 701 B.C., which forced the Assyrians to retreat to their homeland, became a reminder of the Lord's sovereignty over his people and the nations and a guarantee of Zion's ultimate exaltation. The Lord stopped short of wiping out his people like he had done to Sodom and Gomorrah (1:9). This historical remnant foreshadowed a future remnant that would return to the land from exile (10:21; 11:11, 16), populate a purified Jerusalem (4:3–6), experience the Lord's agricultural blessings (4:2), and trust in his strength (28:5).

The Lord's slaughter of the Assyrians outside Jerusalem's walls foreshadowed a time when he would deliver Zion from hostile foreign armies (17:12–14; 29:5–8; 30:27–33; 31:4–9). The vision of these texts, while rooted in the Assyrian crisis of 701 B.C., transcends that event, as the references to many nations (17:12–13; 29:5–8; 30:28) indicates. The association of the Assyrians' defeat with the messianic age (cf. 10:5–11:16 and 31:4–32:2) also indicates the typological nature of the former.

Zion would eventually experience a time of exaltation. Purified of evildoers (1:21–28), she would become a center of justice (2:2–4; 33:5) and enjoy the Lord's constant protection (4:5–6; 14:32; 25:1–5; 27:2–6; 33:17–24). As in the days of Moses, when a cloud and pillar of fire accompanied the people on their journey out of Egypt, there would be visible signs of God's protective presence (4:5). He would guard the city from enemies, just as a shelter guards one from scorching heat and driving rainstorms (4:6; 25:4–5). Though the covenant community had proven to be a fruitless vineyard (5:1–7), the Lord would make Zion a fruitful vineyard that would prosper under his protection and care (27:2–6).

At that time the entire covenant community would be transformed. The people would abandon idols and follow the Lord alone (17:7–8; 29:24; 30:22; 31:7). Wisdom (29:24; 32:5–8; 33:6), spiritual enlightenment (29:18; 30:20–21; 32:3–4; 35:8), justice (29:19–21; 32:1–2, 17–18; 33:5), and gratitude (25:9; 26:1–6) would characterize the renewed covenant community. Consequently, they would experience the Lord's abundant blessing (4:2; 29:17, 23; 30:23–25; 32:20; 35:1–2, 5–7).

The exiled people, including those of the northern kingdom, would experience a new exodus and return to their land (10:26; 11:11–12, 15–16; 14:1–3; 27:12–13). This redeemed community would praise the Lord for his salvation, just as Moses did at the Red Sea following Israel's deliverance from Egypt (cf. 12:1–2 with Exod. 15:2). However, in contrast to the time of Moses, when the wilderness became a place of rebellion and postponed blessing, the wilderness would blossom before the returning exiles (Isa. 35:1–10).

A key figure in Isaiah's vision of the restored covenant community is an ideal Davidic king who fulfills the Lord's promises to David. This coming king would be a mighty warrior who defeats Israel's enemies and inaugurates the culminating phase of salvation history. Out of the darkness of defeat, he would emerge like a bright light (8:22–9:2). As in "the day of Midian," when the Lord gave Gideon a decisive victory over the Midianite horde (Judg. 6–7), this king would defeat Israel's enemies (Isa. 9:4–5; cf. 10:26) and, as in the time of David, the united tribes of Israel would subdue the neighboring nations (11:13–14). This king's royal titles (9:6) depict him as an extraordinary military strategist who would be able to execute his plans because of divine enablement. His military ability would ensure the peace and prosperity of the covenant community.

The Lord's Spirit would enable this king to rule wisely (11:2). He would display extraordinary discernment, the ability to execute his decisions, and unwavering loyalty to the Lord. Consequently, his reign would be characterized by justice. He would judge based on truth, not superficial appearances or impressions (11:3). He would defend the cause of the oppressed and eliminate their evil oppressors (11:4). This transformation of human society would be mirrored by radical changes within the animal kingdom (11:6–8). Justice and peace would replace oppression and hostility throughout this king's realm (11:9).

God's Relationship to the Nations

Judgment

The theme of worldwide judgment occupies a good portion of chapters 1–39. The Lord would judge the various nations of ancient Israel's world, including the kingdoms of Egypt, Assyria, and Babylon, as well as the less prominent neighboring nations. This judgment would culminate with the final defeat of the hostile nations and the establishment of God's earthly kingdom on Zion. The oracles against the nations are a reminder that the Lord has absolute control over the nations and that his goal for Israel and the world will be realized. Consequently, it makes no sense for the Lord's people to fear or trust in the surrounding nations.

Egypt receives special attention in Isaiah's prophecies against the nations (cf. 18:1–20:6; 30:1–7; 31:1–3) because Judah was prone to form alliances with Egypt to protect themselves from the Assyrians. This policy was unwise, for the Lord would cause the Egyptians to wilt before the Assyrians (19:1, 4, 16). The Egyptian gods, wise men, civil leaders, and armies would be helpless before the Lord's attack (19:1, 3, 11–15; 31:1–3).

The Lord used Assyria as his instrument of judgment against his covenant community and the neighboring nations. The Assyrian king was nothing but a weapon in the hand of the Lord, but he taunted Jerusalem and even boasted that the Lord was unable to deliver his people from the powerful Assyrian army (10:5–14, 32; 36:4–20; 37:9–13, 24–25). He claimed to be the sovereign ruler of the world before whom the gods of the petty western states capitulated (cf. 36:18–20; 37:11–13). But once the Assyrians had served their purpose in the divine plan (cf. 10:12; 28:21), the Lord would punish Assyria for its hubris (10:5–34; 14:24–25; 30:27–33; 31:4–9).

The prophet uses several metaphors to describe the Lord's defeat of Assyria, including disease (10:16), fire (10:17; 30:27, 30, 33; 31:9), chopping of trees (10:18, 33–34), a flood (30:28), a rainstorm (30:30), and an attack by a raging lion (31:4). The use of this imagery is ironic, for the Assyrian kings used many of these metaphors in describing their conquests and exploits. Assyrian rulers boasted of chopping down the cedars of Lebanon (37:24), but in the day of the Lord's judgment the Assyrians, likened to the tall trees of Lebanon (10:34), would fall by the divine axe. Assyrian kings often portrayed themselves as raging lions, rushing floodwaters, and destructive fires, before which their enemies could not stand. However, in the day of judgment the Lord would unleash his anger like a lion, floodwaters, and fire against them. Just as the Assyrians sometimes put hooks into the noses of their captives, so the Lord would do to them (37:29). When all was said and done, the Lord would demonstrate that he, not the ruler of Assyria, was the most powerful warrior-king in the world. Isaiah 37:36–38 records the fulfillment of this prophecy of judgment. As the Assyrian army besieged Jerusalem, the angel of the Lord went out, and in one night destroyed the entire army. Sennacherib was forced to return home, where sometime later his own sons assassinated him as he worshipped in the temple of one of his gods.

The Chaldean empire of Babylon, Assyria's successor as the Near East's most powerful nation, would also experience God's judgment (13:1–14:23; 21:1–10). Though some question the authenticity of these judgment oracles and attribute them to a later exilic editor, their eighth-century origin can be adequately defended. Since Isaiah foresaw the Babylonian exile (39:6–7), it is quite natural that he would include Babylon within the scope of God's coming judgment upon the enemies of his people. In Isaiah's vision Babylon functions as a representative of all the hostile nations. His description of Babylon's fall (cf. 13:17–22; 14:23) transcends the historical fall of the city to the Medes and Persians and foreshadows the final judgment of the nations, prior to the establishment of God's earthly kingdom, as the cosmic tone of the language indicates (cf. 13:1–13; 14:26–27).

Like Babylon, Edom also serves a representative function in Isaiah's oracles against the nations. Isaiah 34 begins with a description of God's worldwide, cosmic judgment. The prophet then focuses on Edom, a nation with a long history of hostility toward Israel, despite the blood ties between them. The Lord's severe judgment of Edom is called his "day of vengeance" and "a year of retribution, to uphold Zion's cause" (34:8).

Isaiah's oracles against the nations culminate in a description of worldwide judgment that ushers in God's kingdom on earth. While several passages allude to and foreshadow the Lord's culminating victory over the nations (8:9–10; 13:1–14:27; 17:12–14; 29:58; 30:27–33; 31:49; 33:14; 34:1–17), chapters 24–27 give the most thorough and sustained treatment of this event.

Picking up on the cosmic tone and imagery of 13:1–13, Isaiah 24 pictures a curse devastating the whole earth (24:1–13) because the nations have violated "the everlasting covenant," a reference to God's covenant with Noah. The people of the earth have rebelled (24:16, 20) against the Noahic mandate to multiply and to respect God's image in humankind (Gen. 9:17) by indiscriminately shedding blood (cf. Isa. 26:21) and thereby polluting the land (Isa. 24:5). The focal point of God's judgment is an unnamed city characterized by strength and pride (24:10–12; 25:2; 26:56). The language echoes descriptions of Moab and Babylon, but since the fall of this city occurs in the context of worldwide disaster, it is representative of all the earth's strong cities.

Isaiah portrays the opposition to God as cosmic. God's enemies are specifically identified as "the powers in the heavens above and the kings on the earth below" (24:21), suggesting a spiritual-human coalition. The prophet utilizes ancient Near Eastern chaos imagery, as he depicts these rebels as the terrifying sea creature Leviathan (27:1). But the Lord subdues all those who oppose his plan and his authority.

The Lord would even destroy the ultimate enemy, death, and then celebrate his victory with a banquet on Zion, his royal mountain (25:68). Israel's return from exile would be a vivid demonstration of the Lord's authority over the realm of death. Separated from the Promised Land, the exiles were like lifeless corpses lying in the dust. However, the Lord would miraculously resurrect the nation and bring his people back to their land (26:19; 27:12–13; cf. Ezek. 37:1–14, which also employs resurrection imagery for the nation's restoration from exile). In contrast to their oppressors, who would be dead and gone forever (Isa. 26:14), the Lord's revived people would enjoy a new age of glory (26:15), highlighted by a literal resurrection of those who have died (26:19; cf. Dan. 12:2).

Reconciliation and Unification

Once the Lord established his worldwide kingdom in Zion, he would usher in an age of worldwide peace (cf. 11:10) and pure religious worship. Nations would acknowledge his sovereignty (18:7; 19:21; 23:18) and come to Jerusalem to receive his instruction and to submit their disputes to his mediation. With the all-wise, all-powerful God justly settling their disagreements, the once warring nations would forget about military preparations and devote their energies to more constructive pursuits (2:24). Even nations that were once archenemies would join in worshipping the Lord (19:23–25).

MACROSTRUCTURE AND OUTLINE OF ISAIAH 1–39

Macrostructure

Isaiah 1–39 contains four major literary units:

Chapters 1–12   Focus on Judah: The Lord purifies his covenant community through judgment, establishes his rule on earth from Zion, and restores his people from exile.

Chapters 13–27	Focus on the nations: The Lord judges the nations, establishes his rule on earth from Zion, and restores his people from exile.
Chapters 28–35	Focus on Judah: The Lord judges his people and their enemies, establishes his rule on earth from Zion, and restores his people from exile.
Chapters 36–39	Narrative bridge: The Lord delivers Jerusalem from the Assyrians, but announces his people will eventually be taken into exile to Babylon. This paves the way for chapters 40–66, where the Lord addresses the future exiles.

OUTLINE

THE HOLY ONE OF ISRAEL PURIFIES HIS PEOPLE AND HIS ROYAL CITY (ISAIAH 1–12)

- The Lord Confronts His Rebellious People (1:1–20)
- Justice Demands Purification (1:21–31)
- Future Transformation (2:1–5)
- The Demise of Human Pride (2:6–22)
- Retribution, Vindication, Humiliation, and Restoration (3:1–4:6)
- A Vineyard in Ruins and Death Is Imminent (5:1–30)
- A Vision of the King (6:1–13)
- A Sign Child and Forfeited Blessing (7:1–8:10)
- A King Brings the Light of Deliverance (8:11–9:7 [HB 6])
- "His Hand Is Still Upraised": Persistent Judgment on Persistent Sin (9:8 [HB 7]–10:4)
- The Lord Brings Down the Proud Assyrians (10:5–34)
- Justice, Peace, and Renewal (11:1–12:6)

THE LORD REVEALS HIS SOVEREIGNTY THROUGH WORLDWIDE JUDGMENT (ISAIAH 13–27)

- Worldwide Judgment Focused on Babylon (13:1–14:27)
- Oracles Concerning Various Nations (14:28–23:18)
- Worldwide Judgment (24:1–23)
- The Restoration of Israel and the Vindication of the Righteous (25:1–27:13)

JUDGMENT GIVES WAY TO SALVATION (ISAIAH 28–35)

- Judgment Overwhelms the Entire Land (28:1–29)
- Jerusalem's Coming Crisis and Transformation (29:1–24)
- Rebellion and Mercy (30:1–33)
- Genuine Security (31:1–32:20)
- The Mighty Warrior-King Delivers Zion (33:1–24)
- Devastating Judgment and Transformation (34:1–35:10)

THE LORD DISPLAYS HIS SOVEREIGN POWER (ISAIAH 36–39)

- The Lord's Victory over the Assyrians (36:1–37:38)
- Hezekiah's New Lease on Life (38:1–22)
- Hezekiah Shows Off His Wealth (39:1–8)

THE HOLY ONE OF ISRAEL PURIFIES HIS PEOPLE AND HIS ROYAL CITY (ISAIAH 1–12)

The main theme of Isaiah 1–12 is the Lord's purification of his covenant community. The Lord appears as the Holy One of Israel, the powerful warrior-king ("Lord of Armies") who determines the destiny of his people and their enemies (5:16; 6:1–13). Israel rejected the Holy One (1:4; 5:24), but they would eventually recognize his authority and return to him (10:24; 12:6).

The section oscillates between judgment and salvation (see the outline below). The theme of judgment dominates 1:2–10:4. In his role as warrior-king, the Lord brings disaster upon his people through the instrumentality of the Assyrians (cf. 1:9, 24; 2:12; 3:1, 15; 5:7, 9, 16, 24; 9:13, 19). Yet relatively brief glimpses of the coming restoration are strategically inserted (cf. 2:1–4; 4:2–6; 8:9–10; 9:1–7). In 10:5–12:6 salvation becomes the predominant theme, as the Lord of Armies defeats the Assyrians (10:16, 23–24, 26, 33), delivers his city, establishes a new David as king, and restores his exiled people.

Isaiah 1:1–20

EXEGETICAL IDEA
The Lord exposes disobedient Israel's hypocrisy and demands that they establish justice within the community so that they may experience forgiveness and escape judgment.

THEOLOGICAL FOCUS
No vital relationship with the Lord is possible apart from obedience to his commands concerning responsibilities to one's fellow human beings.

PREACHING IDEA
The Lord urges all rebels to return to their loving Father.

PREACHING POINTERS
Frank is sitting alone in his quiet house reminiscing about days gone by. Closing his eyes, he remembers how proud he was as the nurse handed him his daughter Marissa for the first time at the hospital and he cradled her in his arms. As she grew older, he can still hear her giggling at the funny faces he would make. He recalls the look on her face as she tore open her gifts on Christmas morning, her excitement the afternoon she finally learned to ride her bike on her own, and the hours the two of them spent playing basketball together in their driveway. Marissa was daddy's girl growing up, as the two of them had much in common. Today, however, things are very different. Marissa is all grown up now, and as many teenagers do she grew to resent many of the rules and restrictions Frank placed on her life. His pleas for her to consider the outcome of her choices went unheeded, and now Frank is forced to watch with deep heartache as his precious daughter bounces from one bad relationship to another and makes one destructive decision after the next.

Every parent can identify with the emotions of the father in this story. We can appreciate his deep sorrow over a beloved child who chooses to rebel and dismiss parental oversight to pursue a more alluring but destructive lifestyle. This story epitomizes the sentiment of Isaiah 1:2–20. God describes himself as a father grieving over his wayward daughter Israel. Despite his loving care for her, she has spurned his instructions in the pursuit of self-serving freedom. As such, this passage's intended illocutionary effect is to arouse emotion as much or more than to simply convey information. Such evocative imagery should cause the disobedient people of Judah, as well as disobedient Christ-followers today, to feel God's pain on their behalf and to recognize their need to repent and return to a submissive and obedient relationship with their loving and gracious Father.

THE LORD CONFRONTS HIS REBELLIOUS PEOPLE (1:1–20)

LITERARY STRUCTURE AND THEMES (1:1–20)

In this speech the Lord confronts rebellious Israel with their ingratitude and disobedience. The divine discipline they have already experienced is a warning signal to the disobedient and should motivate them to repentance. Their outward religious acts could not bring restoration. In fact, they only heighten the people's guilt by adding hypocrisy to their list of sins. The Lord demands that they cleanse away their sin by turning from evil and doing what is good. They must promote justice and defend the rights of the vulnerable and disadvantaged. If they willingly obey, they will once again experience the Lord's covenant blessings; but if they persist in their rebellion, they will perish.

This opening speech is marked out by the literary device of *inclusio*, in which a thematic bracket is placed around the literary unit. The statement "for the LORD has spoken" appears right after the opening summons (1:2), while the statement "for the mouth of the LORD has spoken" concludes the speech (Williamson 2006, 29). By placing the quotation formula at the beginning and end of the speech, the prophet emphasizes that he speaks with divine authority (Gitay 1983, 207–21; Willis 1984, 63–77).

Because of its legal tone, some label this first speech a covenant lawsuit. In the opening verses the prophet summons the ancient witnesses to the Lord's covenant with Israel and then quotes the Lord's complaint against his people (1:2–3). Using the form of a woe oracle, he then states the formal accusation (1:4). However, the speech cannot be reduced to the category of a mere lawsuit. The defendant is not simply accused, condemned, and sentenced. The speech is fundamentally a passionate appeal to repentance. The prophet tries to reason with his fellow Israelites, urging them to come to their senses before it is too late (1:5–9).

He then urges them to again hear the word of the Lord (1:10). The Lord's address to them has three parts: (1) He breaks down any potential defense by pointing out that their religious acts and rituals do not insulate them from divine judgment. On the contrary, their formalism adds hypocrisy to their list of sins (1:11–15). (2) He then appeals for change. The people must reject their oppressive policies and promote justice (1:16–17). (3) Finally, the Lord issues an ultimatum. They can obey and experience the Lord's blessing, or they can persist in their rebellion and be destroyed (1:18–20).

EXPOSITION (1:1–20)

Isaiah probably delivered this speech during the Assyrian invasion by Sennacherib in 701 B.C. (Claassen 1974, 1–17; Gray 1912, 12; Williamson 2006, 63) Even if we allow for a touch of hyperbole, this is the only event during Isaiah's time that comes close to satisfying the language of these verses. In his account of the invasion (see *COS* 2.119B:303), Sennacherib boasted that he "besieged forty-six" of Hezekiah's "walled cities and surrounding smaller towns, which were without number." He breached the walls, conquered the cities, and took captive 200,150 people, along with numerous livestock. Judah was on the verge of exile, which meant it would lose its national identity and the land the Lord had given them.

The Lord Confronts His Rebellious People (1:1–20)

- *Rebellious Children (1:1–3)*
- *Death Is Imminent (1:4–9)*
- *Meaningless Sacrifices (1:10–15)*
- *A Call to Repentance (1:16–17)*
- *Eat or Be Eaten (1:18–20)*

Rebellious Children (1:1–3)

1:1. Like rebellious children, the Lord's people have rejected his authority over them. Verse 1 is the heading for the entire book of Isaiah, explaining that Isaiah son of Amoz received this prophetic message (literally, "vision") concerning Judah and Jerusalem during the reigns of four kings, Uzziah, Jotham, Ahaz, and Hezekiah. For a detailed discussion of the historical background, see the introduction to the commentary above.

1:2a. The opening summons to the heavens and earth reflects the covenantal framework within which the Lord makes this appeal to Israel. Long before this, when Moses formalized the covenant agreement between the Lord and Israel, he invoked the heavens and earth as witnesses (Deut. 4:26; 30:19; 31:28; 32:1). The language reflects ancient Near Eastern idiom, but it appears to be mere personification in the context of the Mosaic covenant.[1] However, the appeal to the traditional covenant witnesses has the rhetorical effect of emphasizing that Israel's actions had not gone unnoticed. The reference is also a rhetorical cue that the Lord's accusation must be understood within the framework of his ancient, binding covenant demands. He held them accountable to the standard to which their forefathers had committed themselves many centuries before.

1:2b. The Lord's reference to his people as his "children" (or "sons") is also rooted in Deuteronomic covenantal idiom (cf. Deut. 14:1; 32:5, 20; see Roberts 2015, 20). By casting himself in the role of a father, the Lord highlights his protection and provision. Against this backdrop of fatherly care, his accusation of rebellion has extra force. He fulfilled his paternal responsibility, but his children have rewarded his commitment with disobedience. The verb translated "rebelled" (פָּשְׁעוּ) refers elsewhere to a subordinate party rebelling against a ruling authority (1 Kings 12:19; 2 Kings 1:1; 3:5, 7; 8:20, 22). In Israel's case this rebellion, which began very early in its history (Isa. 48:8), took the form of injustice (Isa. 1:15–17, 21–28; cf. 59:12–13) and idolatry (Isa. 1:29–30), both of which violated the fundamental principles of the covenant.

> *TRANSLATION ANALYSIS 1:2*
> For בָּנִים, "sons," ESV, HCSB, KJV, NIV, NLT, NRSV, and Tanakh have "children." This is certainly a valid way to translate the Hebrew masculine plural form (cf. Gen. 3:16; Exod. 21:5; 22:24 [HB 23]; Josh. 17:2 [which specifies that the "sons" are "male"]). See Gray 1912, 9. In this context the term appears to refer to all Israelites; note 1:4, where "sons" is parallel to "offspring," "people," and "nation."

1:3. The comparison to the ox and donkey highlights the spiritual insensitivity and dullness of the people. Even an ox can recognize its owner and a donkey can find its feeding trough. But Israel, in contrast to these brutish beasts of burden, has failed to recognize its master as the source of its blessings. The metaphor suggests that Israel's failure defies the basic laws of nature and reason. The nation's rejection of the Lord is both inexplicable and inexcusable.

The use of the verb "know" (יָדַע) has here the sense of "recognize, acknowledge," a nuance that is attested elsewhere and has a covenantal

---

1 On the ancient Near Eastern parallels, see *TDOT* 1:397. For ancient Near Eastern examples, see *COS* 2.18:105, 82:213. In these ancient Near Eastern treaties, the heavens and earth appear at the end of a long list of divine witnesses, a feature that is notably absent in biblical covenant formulary.

background (Roberts 2015, 20). For example, Eli's wicked sons "did not know" the Lord (1 Sam. 2:12); they refused to acknowledge his moral authority over their behavior. King Josiah, on the other hand, did "know" the Lord; he acknowledged the Lord's authority by obeying his policies regarding justice (Jer. 22:16).[2]

Death Is Imminent (1:4–9)

The Lord has begun to implement severe judgment.

1:4. The use of the interjection הוֹי, "woe," contributes powerfully to the rhetoric of the speech. This term was used in funeral laments (see 1 Kings 13:30; Jer. 22:18–19; 34:5; Amos 5:16). When used in prophetic judgment speeches, it carries the connotation of death and would certainly grab an audience's attention and convey urgency. By prefacing the formal accusation with this word, followed by "sinful nation," the prophet acts out Israel's funeral in advance, emphasizing that death is inevitable, if they do not repent.

> *TRANSLATION ANALYSIS 1:4 (NOTE 1)*
> The Hebrew word הוֹי is typically translated as an interjection, "ah" (ESV, KJV, NRSV, Tanakh), "oh" (HCSB, NLT), or "woe to" (NIV). These translations, while capturing the emotion of the prophet, miss the full significance of the word, which was used in funeral laments. NET "are as good as dead" seeks to bring out the force of the word more clearly.

The prophet depicts the guilt (עָוֹן) of Israel's sin as a heavy burden. Depending on the context, the word can refer to a sinful act (1 Sam. 20:1), the guilt such an action incurs (Job 33:9), or the punishment the deed deserves or receives (Gen. 4:13). In Isaiah 1:4 the word probably refers to Israel's guilt, which is like a heavy weight they carry (Young 1965, 45). Frequently in Isaiah the word refers to sinful deeds that incur guilt, prompt divine judgment (5:18; 13:11; 14:21; 22:14; 26:21; 30:13; 40:2; 43:24; 50:1; 53:5–6, 11; 57:17; 59:2–3, 12; 64:6–7; 65:7), and alienate the sinner from God (57:17; 59:2). Though predisposed to forgive sinners (6:7; 33:24; 64:9), God sometimes withholds forgiveness (22:14) or extends atonement only through purifying judgment (27:9; 40:2).

The prophet compares Israel to rebellious children who have rejected their father (cf. 1:2). To disregard his commands is to disrespect the very person and authority of the one who gives the commands. From the Lord's perspective, such failure to recognize his authority (cf. 1:3) is to abandon (עָזְבוּ) and reject (נִאֲצוּ) him. The use of these two verbs in proximity may reflect Deuteronomic idiom (cf. Deut. 31:16, 20). Apart from repentance, those who have abandoned the Lord will perish (see Isa. 1:28; 65:11–12).

> *TRANSLATION ANALYSIS 1:4 (NOTE 2)*
> The Hebrew text calls the rebellious children "offspring (of) wrongdoers" and "children (who) do wicked things." One might think "wrongdoers" is a genitive of source, indicating that their parents were wrongdoers. But in this context the Lord is viewed as their father. The parallelism, "children [in the absolute, not construct, form of the noun] (who) do wicked things," suggests that "wrongdoers" is appositional to "offspring," yielding, "offspring (who) are wrongdoers." For discussion see Wildberger 1991, 23 Young 1965, 46. Many English translations are ambiguous and capable of misleading the interpreter: KJV ("seed of evildoers"), ESV ("offspring of evildoers"), HCSB/NIV/*Tanakh* ("brood of evildoers"). The NLT ("evil people"), NRSV ("offspring who do evil"), and NET ("offspring who do wrong") provide greater clarity.

---

2   The apostle John draws on this Old Testament concept when he informs us that obedience to God's commands proves that one truly "knows" (i.e., acknowledges the moral authority of) God (1 John 2:3).

The form (*piel* stem) of the verb נִאֲצוּ highlights the serious nature of the crime. The *qal* stem of this verb is used of rejecting individuals (always human beings, not God personally) and wise advice, including God's counsel (Ps. 107:11). The *piel* stem is used with a variety of objects, including God himself (several times), his offerings (1 Sam. 2:17), his word (Isa. 5:24; Jer. 23:17), his people (Isa. 60:14), and his name (Ps. 74:10, 18). It appears that the *piel* is more common in contexts where God is rejected, whether directly or indirectly.

To emphasize the gravity of this rebellion, the prophet refers to the Lord as the "Holy One of Israel," a title that appears twenty-five times in Isaiah and depicts God as Israel's sovereign king who possesses moral authority over his covenant people. In Isaiah 6 the seraphim cry out "Holy, holy, holy," as they stand before the exalted king (6:3–5; cf. 43:15; 54:5). In 5:16 the Lord's holiness is associated with his exalted status as just king (cf. 57:15). The basic sense of the Hebrew word "holy" is "set apart, unique." The Lord is "set apart, unique" in the sense that he is the transcendent king who is infinitely superior to all would-be rivals (see 40:25). As such he dictates to those under his rule how they are to live. His moral and ethical standards reflect his essential nature, which is characterized by love and justice. (See 6:3 for further discussion.)

1:5–6. The prophet's rhetorical questions express his amazement that one so severely punished could persist in rebellion. Elsewhere in Isaiah, woe pronouncements (cf. 1:4) include an address with a built-in indictment, followed by an announcement of impending judgment (cf. 5:8–10, 11–17, 18–30; 10:1–4; 28:1–4; 29:1–4; 30:1–4; 31:1–3). But here it is apparent that judgment has already arrived, and death is even closer than usual (Janzen 1972, 57 n. 55).

The comparison of devastated Judah to a badly beaten body is highly effective rhetorically. One winces with pain at the detailed description of a bleeding body covered with multiple, gaping, untreated wounds. This description of Israel's pathetic condition emphasizes the need for an immediate decision and paves the way for the ultimatum of 1:18–20.

1:7–8. An invader (the Assyrians, see above) has devastated the land, leaving Jerusalem isolated (1:7–8). The land is in such ruin that it is close to total annihilation, the kind that destroyed Sodom and Gomorrah (cf. 1:9). Isaiah 1:7 specifically mentions burned cities and destroyed crops.

In 1:7 the prophet uses wordplay to characterize the judgment as well deserved. Twice he mentions "foreign invaders" (זָרִים). This echoes the final line of 1:4, which uses this same verbal root (זוּר) to describe how the people have turned away from the Lord. The repetition of the verb correlates the sin with the punishment. The people have treated the Lord as if he were a foreigner (or stranger) and so, appropriately, their punishment involves foreigners (or strangers). The homonym זוּר, "press out, treat" (BDB s.v. "זוּר" 266–67; GKC, 179 §67m) in 1:6 may contribute to the irony as well. Sinful Israel is battered, and their wounds are untreated (לֹא זֹרוּ). This is an appropriate punishment for those who have turned away (1:4, נָזֹרוּ) from the Lord (Chisholm 1987, 51).

In addition to wordplay, the prophet uses literary allusion in 1:7 to characterize the judgment. The reference to foreign invaders devouring the land (i.e., its crops; cf. Abernethy 2014, 29–34) echoes the covenant curses of Deuteronomy 28:33, 51, suggesting the judgment is the result of violating the Lord's covenant demands. The use of the word מַהְפֵּכָה, "overthrow" (cf. כְּמַהְפֵּכַת), echoes Deuteronomy 29:23, where the Lord warned that violation of the covenant would bring an "overthrow" comparable to Sodom and Gomorrah (cf. Amos 4:11). By using this term, the prophet indicates the people's sin has activated the covenant

The Lord Confronts His Rebellious People (1:1–20)

curses. This foreshadows his use of the Sodom and Gomorrah image in Isaiah 1:9–10.

The image of besieged and isolated Daughter Zion (i.e., Jerusalem), compared to a hut in a field (1:8), coincides with Sennacherib's claim that he, having conquered all of Judah's towns, "locked up" Hezekiah "within Jerusalem, his royal city, like a bird in a cage." He describes how he "surrounded" the city "with earthworks, and made it unthinkable for him to exit by the city gate." He also "cut off" from the land the cities he had "despoiled" and gave them to neighboring puppet kings (COS 2.119B:303).

TRANSLATION ANALYSIS 1:8
In 1:8a KJV and ESV have "Daughter of Zion," as if Zion had a daughter, but the genitive is appositional. A better translation is "Daughter Zion" (cf. HCSB, NET, NIV, NRSV). The NLT ("Beautiful Zion") and *Tanakh* ("Fair Zion") understand the genitive correctly but are overly interpretive.

In the last line of 1:8 the preposition "like" is used in the sense of "exactly like." Most translations are ambiguous, suggesting that Zion's experience was similar, but not identical, to the distress of a besieged city (cf. ESV, HCSB, NIV, NLT, NRSV, *Tanakh*). But the context suggests Zion was indeed isolated and under attack. The NET ("she is a besieged city") makes the point clear. This same use of the preposition occurs in the last line of 1:7, where the Hebrew has "like an overthrow by foreigners," i.e., "exactly like an overthrow by foreigners" (see HCSB, "a desolation demolished by foreigners").

1:9. The prophet uses the divine title יְהוָה צְבָאוֹת, traditionally, "Lord of Hosts," which is especially appropriate in this context. What is the referent of צְבָאוֹת within the title? Does it refer to earthly armies under the Lord's control (see 1 Sam. 17:45, as well as Isa. 13:4), or to his heavenly armies (sometimes associated with the stars of the heavens; see Josh. 5:13–15; Judg. 5:20; 2 Sam. 5:24; 1 Kings 22:19; 2 Kings 2:11–12; 6:17; Pss. 89:5–8 [HB 6–9]; 103:20–21; 148:2; Isa. 6:3, 5; 40:26; 45:12; Dan. 8:10–13)? Tryggve Mettinger argues that the title, at least at its most basic level, refers to the Lord's royal position at the head of the heavenly, angelic assembly, not to his role of military general per se:

> First, the Sabaoth name belongs to the temple milieu and refers to God as the heavenly King on his cherubim throne. Second, "Sabaoth" is linguistically related to the word *saba'* which itself designates the heavenly host, God's divine council. It is important to recognize that these two lines actually converge. *The Sabaoth name designates God as the heavenly King, and the element seba'ot directs our attention to the heavenly hosts around the throne of God.* These heavenly hosts have multiple functions: they sing the eternal praise of God in the heavenly sanctuary; they serve as members of God's heavenly government; and they carry out God's assignments on earth. (1988, 134–35, emphasis original)

The numerous instances where the title depicts the Lord as sovereign king, without any direct military connotation, support this.

However, at times the title seems to be associated with God's royal function of warrior-judge. When the context so dictates, it is legitimate to see the title as having a strong military connotation.[3] This is surely the case in Isaiah 1:9, where the context describes the devastation caused by an invading army. In such contexts, earthly armies, viewed as under the

---

3 Note esp. the use of the title in Pss. 24:10; 46:7–11 [HB 8–12]; 48:4–8 [HB 5–9]; 59:5 [HB 6]; 89:8–10 [HB 9–11]; Isa. 1:9; 2:12; 5:9, 16; 9:19; 10:16, 23, 26, 33; 13:4, 13; 14:22–27; 28:22; 31:4; Jer. 5:14–17; 6:6, 9; 9:7–11; 35:17; 38:17–18; Amos 3:13; 4:13; 5:14–16, 27; 6:8, 14; 9:5; Nah. 2:13; 3:5; Mal. 4:1–3.

Lord's sovereign direction, often seem to be in view.[4]

The comparison to Sodom and Gomorrah echoes the language of Deuteronomy 29:23, indicating that the covenant curses were descending upon the land. In biblical tradition these two cities epitomize total annihilation (cf. Isa. 13:19) and total depravity (cf. Isa. 3:9). The concepts are, of course, related, for it was the utter moral degradation of these cities (Gen. 13:13; 18:20–21) that led to their judgment (Gen. 19:13). If the land has experienced judgment that approximates the destruction of Sodom and Gomorrah, then it is reasonable to conclude that its sin also approximates their sin. The prophet indicates that such is the case in the next verse.

Meaningless Sacrifices (1:10–15)

The Lord exposes the guilt and hypocrisy of the people.

The people were engaged in formal worship. They brought sacrifices to the temple, were careful to observe religious feasts, and offered up prayers. They thought their rituals guaranteed the Lord's favor, but he was highly offended by their so-called worship because it was not undergirded by obedience to his commands pertaining to justice (cf. Isa. 1:16–17). By dismissing their religious efforts as mere hypocrisy, the Lord eliminated their religious fervor as a potential defense against his accusation.

1:10. In describing the destruction that has come upon the land, the prophet alludes to God's judgment upon Sodom and Gomorrah to emphasize the severity of what Judah was experiencing (1:9). In summoning the people to hear the Lord's word, he continues to exploit the ancient image. He sarcastically addresses Judah's leaders as the "rulers of Sodom" and the people as the "people of Gomorrah." This form of address, in the light of what follows, identifies Judah with Sodom and Gomorrah morally and ethically. It emphasizes the need for a swift and decisive response. To this point, the nation has been spared the destiny of the ancient twin cities (1:9), but its moral corruption, if not radically abandoned (cf. 1:16–17), is in danger of bringing final and complete destruction (cf. 1:20). It is time to pay attention to what the Lord has to say.

TRANSLATION ANALYSIS 1:10
For Hebrew תּוֹרָה (torah) in 1:10, the translations have "law" (KJV, NLT), "instruction" (HCSB, NIV, Tanakh), or "teaching" (ESV, NRSV). However, in this context none of these quite captures the correct nuance. The following speech mixes a hard-hitting accusation with a strong call to repentance. This is more than mere instruction or teaching; "corrective instruction" would better reflect the actual content of the word in this context (cf. NET "rebuke").

1:11. The Lord does not desire the many sacrifices the people are bringing to him (1:11). The verb שָׂבַע, "be satisfied, full," is often used of eating and/or drinking one's fill (*HALOT* s.v. "שָׂבַע" 1303; BDB s.v. "שָׂבַע" 959). Here sacrifices are viewed, in typical ancient Near Eastern fashion, as food for the deity. Accommodating his words to the thinking of the people, the Lord declares that he has received more than enough suet to eat and blood to drink.

1:12–14. The Lord uses very strong language in his denunciation of the people's cultic activity:

1. He describes their gathering to worship him as "trampling" his courtyards (1:12), like horses do a street or animals do a pasture (Ezek. 26:11; 34:18).

---

4 See, among others, 1 Sam. 17:45; Isa. 5:16, 24 (cf. 1:25–30); 13:2–5; 14:22; 28:22; Jer. 5:14–17; 6:3–6; 38:17–18; Amos 5:27; 6:8, 14; Nah. 2:13.

2. He calls their incense "detestable" (Isa. 1:13, תּוֹעֵבָה), a term used of idolatry and other sins that were especially repugnant in the Lord's sight (see Deut. 27:15). Ritually impure sacrifices were also considered detestable (see Deut. 17:1). However, in this case the people's incense was not detestable because of some ritual impurity, but due to their unethical behavior (see Prov. 21:27). Isaiah later uses this word to describe pagan idols and those who worship them (Isa. 41:24; 44:19).
3. The Lord also declares that he hates the people's festivals (1:14). The Hebrew text reads, "my soul hates." The Lord's "soul" (נֶפֶשׁ) is here the source of his emotions (cf. Jer. 12:7; Ezek. 23:18) from which, in this case, his hatred emanates. Only twice in the Old Testament is it said that God's soul "hates." According to Psalm 11:5, he hates "those who love violence." Here in Isaiah 1:14, he hates the hypocritical religious rituals of those who have spilled the blood of others (cf. 1:15). In both cases human violence is the catalyst for the expression of this divine emotion.
4. The Lord also states that he is "weary" of the people's festivals (1:14). God cannot literally be weary, but he uses such imagery to emphasize just how odious he considers the people's obsession with religious formalism.

1:15. While the Lord rejects the people's sacrifices, one might think that he would at least listen to their prayers, for prayer is a more personal and sincere form of worship. However, when the people spread out their hands (a typical prayer posture, especially when seeking divine favor), the Lord turns the other way and does not listen (1:15).

> **Spread Out Their Hands**
> The expression "spread out the hands" is used twelve times in the Old Testament. In ten cases the *qal* form of the verb is used; only here and in Jeremiah 4:31 is the verb in the *piel*. According to *IBHS* (406–7 §24.3.1), the *qal* "specifies the movement as an event," while the *piel* is resultative, indicating the movement is "at an end" or "terminal." Perhaps a better explanation is that the *piel* is pluralative, indicating repetition of the action. In this case it is likely rhetorical: the *qal* simply states the fact, while the *piel* draws attention to the repeated nature of the action. Jerusalem's sinners typically (and repeatedly) spread their bloodstained hands out to God. In Jeremiah 4:31 one can envision Zion, pictured as a mother in labor, repeatedly spreading out her hands with each new, more painful contraction.

The reason for this reaction is given in the final line of the verse: the people's hands are stained with shed blood. In the light of the preceding context (see 1:11), one might understand the referent as the sacrificial blood of animals that covered their hands and epitomized their empty ritualism. But the following context, which alludes to their acts of injustice, suggests that human blood is in view. By depriving the poor and destitute of proper legal recourse and adequate access to the economic system, the oppressors have, for all intents and purposes, killed their victims by subjecting them to abject poverty, hunger, and exploitation. The linguistic evidence also favors this interpretation. Elsewhere in Isaiah the plural form (דָּמִים) refers to human bloodshed (see 4:4; 9:5 [HB 4]; 26:21; 33:15). The singular form is used in 1:11, where animal blood is clearly in view (Gray 1912, 23; Williamson 2006, 98).

TRANSLATION ANALYSIS 1:15
The ESV, HCSB, KJV, NIV, and NRSV translate דָּמִים as "blood" without indicating that shed blood is in view. The NLT's "blood of innocent victims," while paraphrastic, captures the

meaning. *Tanakh*'s very interpretive "crime" is not vivid enough and fails to bring out the violent, murderous nature of their actions.

A Call to Repentance (1:16–17)
The Lord gives his people an opportunity to repent.

1:16. One might expect that the Lord, having demolished the people's defense and having established their guilt beyond reasonable doubt, would sentence them to be executed. But instead he calls them to repentance. He challenges them to cleanse themselves. The imagery of washing (1:16a) fits nicely with the last statement of 1:15: their hands are covered with the blood of their human victims; that blood needs to be washed away. This does not mean they should try to cover up or hide their evil deeds. They should cease doing evil (1:16b), transform their ethical behavior (1:17), and seek forgiveness (1:18).

As elsewhere in this speech, there may be an echo of Deuteronomic judgment language in 1:16. The phrase "sinful deeds" occurs in Deuteronomy 28:20, where Moses threatened that the nation's sinful deeds would result in their destruction. In that verse reference is also made to the people abandoning the Lord, a charge made by Isaiah earlier in this speech (Isa. 1:4).

1:17. The Lord demands that the people promote justice, which means they must protect the legal rights of those who are vulnerable in society.[5] This group includes the fatherless and the widow. The term יָתוֹם, traditionally translated "orphan," refers specifically to one who has lost a father, not necessarily to one who has lost both parents (see Exod. 22:24; Ps. 109:9, 12). In ancient Israelite society, the loss of one's father made one economically and legally vulnerable. To deprive the fatherless of justice was a heinous crime in the sight of God, worthy of severe judgment (see Deut. 27:19).

The word אַלְמָנָה often refers to a woman who has lost her husband through death (Gen. 38:11; Exod. 22:24; 2 Sam. 14:5; Pss. 78:64; 109:9; Ezek. 22:25). While it seems to refer to a widow as distinct from a divorcee (see Lev. 21:14; 22:13; Num. 30:9), in Isaiah 54:4 the "reproach of widowhood" appears to be the humiliation of being divorced. The husband in the metaphor is the Lord, who once divorced his "wife" Zion because she was barren, but he is now ready to restore her to the status of wife (see Isa. 54:1, 5–8). This text suggests the term "widow," at least in certain nonlegal contexts, may mean "husbandless," encompassing both widows and divorcees (Stassen 1994, 65). At any rate, in this ancient patriarchal culture, the loss of one's husband, whether by death or divorce, made one economically and legally vulnerable. To deprive such a woman of justice was a serious crime in the sight of God that deserved punishment (see Deut. 27:19).

---

5 The precise meaning of the third command in 1:17 is uncertain. ESV ("correct oppression") and HCSB ("correct the oppressor") appear to follow MT in making this a command about action to be taken against oppressors. However, KJV, NIV, NLT, and NRSV have "oppressed," while *Tanakh* has "wronged." The form חָמוֹץ occurs only here. It is usually interpreted as a noun meaning "oppressor" (*HALOT* s.v. "חָמוֹץ" 327). If MT is retained in Isaiah 1:17 and defined as "oppressor," then the *piel* of אשׁר would have to mean "set right, reprove, correct," a nuance it does not have elsewhere. Because of the morphological and semantic problems surrounding the traditional reading, some (see *BHS* n. a; Blenkinsopp 2000, 180) suggest revocalizing the consonantal text as חָמוּץ, "oppressed" (a passive participle). The passive reading has the support of the ancient versions (Williamson 2006, 81). One can then take the accompanying verb as אשׁר II. The factitive-delocutive *piel*, meaning "call/pronounce happy" (Gen. 30:13; Job 29:11; Ps. 72:17; Prov. 31:28; Song 6:9; Mal. 3:12, 15), would be metonymic here. Pronouncing the oppressed blessed implies acting on their behalf.

Eat or Be Eaten (1:18–20)

The people have two options before them: repent and live, or persist in sin and die.

1:18. The Lord brings his call to repentance to a climax by reiterating that forgiveness is available and by giving Israel two clear-cut options.[6] The red stains of sin could be transformed into white, as it were. The image of red sins in 1:18 echoes the language of 1:15, where the Lord accuses the people of having bloodstains on their hands. From the Lord's perspective, their evil deeds (symbolized by their hands) are as obvious as the color red. But this could change. If they washed and cleansed themselves, as it were, they could remove their evil deeds from the Lord's sight (1:16). In this case, washing and cleansing would take the form of rejecting evil and doing good, by promoting justice for the disadvantaged and vulnerable (1:17).

The traditional reading in line 1 is, "let us reason together" (cf. ESV, KJV; *Tanakh* has "let us reach an understanding"). This suggests the two parties should engage in a reasonable discussion about the issues raised by the Lord. But the term יָכַח may have a more formal, legal nuance here. In Job 23:7 the verb is used in this same stem (*niphal*) of an upright man presenting the case for his innocence, and in Genesis 20:16 it refers to Sarah being legally vindicated by receiving Abimelech's payment of restitution. Some translations attempt to bring out the legal dimension: "let us settle the matter" (NIV), "let us argue it out" (NRSV), "let's settle this" (NLT).[7]

The translations have "they shall be/become" (ESV, KJV, NIV, NRSV), "they will be" (HCSB), or "I will make" (NLT) in the apodoses of the conditional sentences in Isaiah 1:18, as if this were an unqualified promise of forgiveness. But the context indicates otherwise. Isaiah 1:16–17 call the people to repentance and 1:19–20 hold two options before the people—one promising restoration, the

---

6 There is some debate as to how the syntax of the conditional sentences should be understood. There are two major issues: (1) How are the protases, which have the conditional particle אִם, "if," followed by an imperfect verbal form, to be understood? They could express a hypothetical situation (as in 1:19–20), implying that the condition described was not the present reality. However, if so, this would imply that their sins were not actually as bad as the imagery of crimson/red suggests. Perhaps so, but 1:15–17 indicates their sin was highly offensive to God, and the imagery of 1:18 seems to echo the reference to their blood-stained hands (1:15). Thus, it seems likely that the protases of 1:18 reflect the reality of their present condition. (2) How are the statements in the apodoses to be understood? Though several translations give the impression these are unconditional assurances of forgiveness, this cannot be the case in this context. Forgiveness is held out as a possibility, but it is contingent on a positive response to the call to repentance in 1:16–17, as 1:19–20 makes clear (on the subjunctive sense of the verbs, see Smith 2007, 110; Watts 1985, 14–15; Williamson 2006, 114; Willis 1983, 45). Some commentators deny that forgiveness is in view, taking the apodoses as sarcastic questions (Culver 1969, 133–41; Kaiser 1972, 36, 38; Wildberger 1991, 56), ironic statements, or a quotation of an objection by the accused. For a summary and critique of these views, see Willis (1983, 40–42) as well as Sweeney (1996, 113). In this case, 1:18b denies the people can disguise their sins in court. However, the context both exhorts repentance and promises renewed blessing, albeit contingently. This implies the barrier of their sin could be overcome. Their guilt could be erased—a fact that is depicted vividly by the transformation of red to white. The image of washing (1:16) suggests transformation is a possibility. Proper behavior, as exhorted in 1:16–17 and described in 1:19, is the way in which the forgiveness depicted in 1:18 would be accomplished.

7 For a helpful discussion of the options, see Gray 1912, 27–28. He offers these options: "to reprove one another, to point out another's faults, to discuss with one another who is right and who is wrong." Willis (1983, 40) suggests "let us settle our differences." Roberts (2015, 24) offers "let us reach an agreement." Williamson (2006, 111–12) rejects the notion of a legal background here and prefers to see a family setting, "where all sorts of dispute occur from time to time." He translates, "let us settle our differences" (p. 103).

other destruction. So, the apodoses in 1:18 are better translated in a way that reflects the contingency that is clearly present here (see *Tanakh*, "they can turn white," and "they can become like fleece").[8]

1:19–20. The Lord sets two destinies before the people: If they are willing to respond positively to his appeal, then they can experience his covenantal blessing in the form of agricultural prosperity (1:19). But if they refuse his offer and persist in their rebellion, they will be devoured by the invader's sword (1:20).

The Lord emphasizes Israel's responsibility to make the right decision. Both אָבָה (1:19) and מֵאֵן (1:20) suggest volition: אָבָה, "to want, be willing" (*HALOT* s.v. "אָבָה" 3), is used of a subject desiring or consenting to act in a particular manner, while מֵאֵן, "refuse" (*HALOT* s.v. "מֵאֵן" 540), is used of one refusing to do so.[9] While ultimately sovereign over his people, the Lord would not coerce a decision. They would choose their destiny; the Lord would simply implement the consequences of that decision.

To respond positively means to "listen," that is, "obey" (שָׁמַע); to respond negatively means to rebel (מָרָה). There is no middle ground or other option.[10] The terminology may echo the law of the rebellious teenager in Deuteronomy 21:18–21. That law envisions a situation where a rebellious (מוֹרֶה) son (cf. Isa. 1:2, 4) does not obey (שָׁמַע) his parents and is executed in order that evil (רַע, cf. Isa. 1:16) will be eliminated. There may also be an allusion to Samuel's farewell address to Israel, in which he warned them that a refusal to obey (שָׁמַע)/decision to rebel (מָרָה) would prompt divine judgment (1 Sam. 12:14–15). Like the rebellious son envisioned by Moses, the people are on the brink of destruction. They are about to experience the judgment threatened by Samuel.

Obedience would bring the restoration of covenant blessing. The Lord specifically promises they would eat the "good of the land," a reference to abundant crops (cf. Jer. 31:12). Agricultural prosperity was one of the promised blessings of the covenant (cf. Deut. 28:2–14; 33:28). To highlight the correlation between positive act and consequence, the Lord uses wordplay—the verb "be willing" (תֹּאבוּ) sounds like the term "good" (טוּב; Miller 1982, 37).

The Lord also uses wordplay to contrast the two destinies that lay before Israel (Chisholm 1987, 46). If they repent, then they will "eat [אָכַל] the best of the land," for the Lord will restore his blessings to the land. However, if they refuse to change their sinful ways, they will be "devoured [or "eaten," אָכַל again] by the sword" of the invading enemy armies. As Patrick Miller (1982, 38) explains, reward and punishment "are made opposite sides of the same coin." He adds, "Both consequences involve eating, consuming." The wordplay may also encompass 1:7, where Isaiah describes invaders devouring (אָכַל) the land. If the people persist in sin, judgment will not stop with the crops; ultimately the people themselves will be devoured.

THEOLOGICAL FOCUS

The theological focus of this speech can be stated as follows: no vital relationship with the Lord is possible apart from obedience to his commands concerning responsibilities to one's fellow human beings. As the prophet develops this theological theme, several emphases emerge:

---

8   For a defense of this position see Willis (1983, 44–46), as well as Williamson (2006, 114–15, 117). Among those who see 1:18b as offering the possibility of forgiveness, some understand the verbs as having an obligatory or jussive force and interpret the statement as an exhortation to change. For a summary and critique, see Willis (1983, 42–43).
9   Usage in Deuteronomy 25:7, where negated אָבָה is equated with מֵאֵן, suggests the verbs are antonyms.
10 Usage elsewhere indicates that these terms are antonyms (cf. Deut. 1:43; 9:23; 21:18, 20; Josh. 1:18; 1 Sam. 12:14–15). In 1 Samuel 12:14 negated מָרָה is equated with שָׁמַע, while in the other texts negated שָׁמַע is equated with מָרָה.

The Lord Confronts His Rebellious People (1:1–20)

1. The covenant principle of retribution, with its correlation between sin and punishment

The covenantal background of this speech is apparent throughout. The prophet summons the ancient covenantal witnesses (1:2) and employs Deuteronomic covenantal language extensively.[11] The people are the Lord's children (1:2), but they have rejected him (1:4) and committed evil deeds (1:16), especially in their abuse of the vulnerable (1:17). For this reason, the covenant curses are being implemented before their very eyes (1:7). Using wordplay, the prophet makes it clear their punishment mirrors their deeds and is consequently just (1:7).

2. The delicate balance between divine sovereignty and human responsibility

The Lord's sovereignty is apparent throughout the speech. He is the Holy One of Israel, who sits exalted over his covenant people and possesses moral authority over them. He is the Lord of Armies, who has brought foreign invaders into the land as his instrument of judgment. He makes moral demands upon the people and controls their destiny.

Yet this sovereign king also appeals to his people and makes it clear that ultimately their decision will determine their destiny. While the sovereign God is certainly free to do as he desires and fully capable of doing as he desires, in fact he often grants people the freedom to act as they desire, even when their desires do not conform to his antecedent (or ideal) will. Matthew 23:37 is instructive, where the verb "to desire, will," is used of both Jesus's redemptive purpose for Jerusalem and, with a negative particle, for Jerusalem's refusal to accept that purpose. When the city willfully rejected God's antecedent will (that the city should repent and experience his salvation and protection), he had no choice but to implement judgment (his consequential will; Matt. 23:38–39). His consequential will in this case was his response to human sin and ran counter to his antecedent desire for his people, mirroring their rejection of the latter. In the case of Israel in Isaiah's time, the Lord expresses his antecedent will in 1:16–19, while the judgment of 1:20 expresses his consequential will.[12]

3. The delicate balance between divine forgiveness and justice

One also sees in this passage the delicate balance between divine forgiveness and justice. The Lord's justice demands that he punish evildoers for their violations of his standards. That justice is implemented in a fair and appropriate way (see theme 1 above). However, if the people turn from their evil ways and promote God's just standards, he will forgive their sins. Justice will be served, one way or the other. But God is not inflexible; he does not implement justice blindly. He gives violators an opportunity to change and escape the full force of his judgment. This divine predisposition to forgive is an important theme in the prophetic literature (see Isa. 55:7; Jer. 31:34; 33:8; Ezek. 18:23, 32; 33:11; Hos. 2:14–23 [Eng. 16–25]; Amos 5:14–15; Mic. 7:18–20). It becomes a dominant theme in Isaiah 40–55.

4. The priority of obedience over ritual

The Lord rejects the people's religious ritual because they are violating the ethical demands of the covenant (Isa. 1:11–17). As far back as the time of Samuel, the Lord made it clear that obedience to his commandments had priority over religious ritual (1 Sam. 15:22; cf. Jer. 7:21–26; Hos. 6:6). Moshe Greenberg perceptively identifies the premises of the Lord's argument in this speech:

> This vehement, unconditional repudiation of the whole of Israel's established worship has several premises: first, that

---

11 On linguistic parallels between Isaiah 1:2–20 and Deuteronomy 32, see Bergey 2003, 39–41.
12 On the "delicate balance . . . between human freedom and divine sovereignty" in 1:18, see Oswalt 1986, 102.

in all its forms, worship is, like prayer, a social transaction between persons, with no magical virtue or intrinsic efficacy. It rather is a gesture of submission and like all gestures a formality whose meaning depends ultimately on the total moral evaluation the recipient makes of the one who gestures; for the recipient to esteem the gesturer there must be some moral identification between them. (I should regard a gesture of good will made to me by my sworn enemy as a trick.) For worship to find favor in God's eyes, the worshipper must identify himself with ("know" in the biblical idiom; e.g., Jer. 22:15f) God in the one way possible for man—by imitating his moral conduct (compare Hos. 4:1f. and Jer. 9:23). Gestures of submission made by villains are an abomination to God. (1983, 55–56)

5. The priority of justice over sacrifice

This theme is closely related to the previous one, for it identifies the specific forms of ritual and obedience that are in view in this speech. The Lord rejects the people's sacrifices and prayers because they have neglected justice. The covenant demanded the latter. In fact, Moses reminded the people they had once been slaves, subject to the oppression of the Egyptians. For this reason, they must treat the vulnerable and disadvantaged kindly and justly (Deut. 24:17–18). The eighth-century prophets affirmed the centrality of justice (Hos. 12:6) and made it clear that justice had priority over sacrifices (Amos 5:21–24; Mic. 6:6–8).

This is not to say that Isaiah rejects the sacrificial system altogether. Despite the seemingly categorical tone of 1:11, a closer look at the Lord's words shows he is denouncing the sacrifices of a specific audience at a specific point in time. He is speaking to Sodom-Gomorrah-like people (1:10) who are experiencing God's judgment (1:4–9) despite frequenting his temple (1:12). The language of the text reflects this specificity: "the multitude of *your* sacrifices" (1:11), "when *you* come" (1:12), "who seeks this from *your* hands" (1:12, literal translation), "*your* new moon feasts and *your* appointed festivals" (1:14). In this context the statement in 1:11b generalizes about the Lord's attitude at a point in time and in a particular place. Though the Lord required sacrifices, they were not his priority (see 1 Sam. 15:22; Pss. 40:6 [HB 7]; 51:16–17 [HB 17–18]). Sacrifices were meaningful when offered by loyal, obedient followers, but were unacceptable when presented by disobedient hypocrites like those addressed here by Isaiah (Chisholm 2009, 261).

6. The foundational nature of love for others to a genuine relationship with God

This principle is fundamental to the previous two themes and the primary theological theme of this passage. Jesus made it clear that all the law can be summarized in the commands to love God and one's neighbor (Matt. 22:36–40; Mark 12:28–34; Luke 10:25–38). One cannot do the former without doing the latter. A meaningful relationship with God (the vertical plane) is not possible unless one obeys God's command to love one's fellow human beings in tangible, practical ways (the horizontal plane). So, James made caring for those who are vulnerable and needy (epitomized by the widow and fatherless) one of the twin pillars of genuine religion (James 1:27), because it fulfills the "royal law" of love for one's neighbor (2:8). Jesus taught that one should not expect to receive God's forgiveness, if one is not willing to forgive others (Matt. 6:14–15). Reconciling differences with a brother or sister must get priority over formal religious acts (Matt. 5:23–24). Withholding one's material goods from a needy brother is proof that one does not have a genuine relationship with God (1 John 3:17). Treating one's wife with disrespect can hinder one's prayer life (1 Peter 3:7). These examples illustrate the basic principle that obedience (to the royal law of love in a New

Testament context) has priority over sacrifice (or formal religious acts such as offerings and prayer in a New Testament context). In genuine biblical "religion," obedience is foundational to having a vital relationship with God, in contrast to pagan religion, which seeks such a relationship through religious formalism.

PREACHING AND TEACHING STRATEGIES

Exegetical and Theological Synthesis

Isaiah 1:1–20 confronts the people of God for their sin that has ultimately resulted in their becoming alienated from the God they claim to worship. In 1:2–10, the prophet uses a series of vivid images to express how God views sinful Judah. First, he likens them to rebellious teenagers who have forsaken their father and pursue their own way (1:2–4). Next, he compares them to a body that is bruised and injured from head to toe, and from the inside out (1:5–6). Finally, the prophet describes Judah in terms of a desolate, burned-up wasteland, like Sodom and Gomorrah after God rained down fiery sulfur as judgment against them (1:7–10; Gen. 19:23–28). The impact of these images is intended to wake God's people up to the severity of their sin against him. He intends to remove the façade of respectability and piety associated with a people who continue in their religious activity, but whose lives are lived in callous rebellion to many of the ethical and moral aspects of holiness.

The next section (Isa. 1:11–15) begins with a question, "The multitude of your sacrifices—What are they to me?" This question could be rephrased to say, "Would you like me to tell you what I think of your religious sacrifices and routines?" The verses that follow provide us with the answer to this question by way of a series of highly provocative statements indicating God's disgust with their offerings: "I have more than enough of [your sacrifices]" and "I have no pleasure in the blood of . . ." (1:11); "I cannot bear [them]" (1:13); "I hate [them] with all my being"; "They have become a burden to me"; and "I am weary of bearing them" (1:14). God makes it clear that he is not impressed with empty religious rituals. He is far more concerned about obedience and acts of righteousness than he is with sacrificial offerings (cf. Ps. 51:16–17 [HB 17–18]; Hos. 6:6; Amos 5:21–24; Mic. 6:6–8). In fact, God finds their observance of feast days and offering of animal sacrifices in the absence of general obedience to God and sincere love for others repulsive and offensive.

Thus, God calls them to change through a series of nine short and pointed imperatives, one right after the next, explaining what true repentance would look like (Isa. 1:16–17).[13] The prophet progresses from general exhortations like "wash and make yourselves clean" and "stop doing evil" to more specific appeals related to showing concern for the weak and oppressed in society. Commands such as "defend the oppressed," "take up the cause of the fatherless," and "plead the case of the widow" reveal that a primary point of sin and disobedience among the people of Judah was their neglect of the poor, weak, and vulnerable (cf. 1:23).

This leads to an invitation by God for the people to have their slate of wrongs wiped clean (Isa. 1:18). All they need to do is repent of their rebellion and begin to practice obedience toward God by acting justly toward their fellow Israelites. Not only will God forgive them, but he promises to bless them (1:19). Conversely, if they continue in their rebellion by taking advantage of the weak and vulnerable for their own advancement, they can expect severe judgment to follow (1:20).

---

13 The Hebrew of Isaiah 1:16–17 contains a total of nineteen words, nine of which are imperative verbs. Thus, the effect of moving very quickly from one command to the next is even more pronounced and dramatic in Hebrew than in English translations.

Preaching Idea
The Lord urges all rebels to return to their loving Father.

Contemporary Connections

What does it mean?
Calling all rebels to return to their loving Father first assumes that God is our Father. The Bible repeatedly uses the analogy of Yahweh as a loving Father. As Creator, God has generally revealed himself as the Father of all people (Mal. 2:10; 1 Cor. 8:6; Eph. 4:6). In a more particular sense, though, God describes himself as a father to those who are his covenant people, both in the Old Testament (Exod. 4:22; Jer. 31:9, 20; Hos. 11:1; Mal. 1:6) as well as in the New (Matt. 6:1, 9, 32; Rom. 8:14–16; Gal. 3:26; Eph. 5:1; 1 John 3:1).[14]

As their Father, God expects to be obeyed. In the same way that responsible, loving parents expect their children to obey them, so too God expects that his children will faithfully submit to his expressed will. A loving father establishes rules and boundaries for his children out of love to nurture and protect them. His rules are not arbitrary nor foolish; they are for the child's own good. Thus, it is out of love that rebellious children are called to repent of their stubborn, persistent disobedience, and return to a posture of humble submission under the protection of their wise and loving father.

Obedience to God remains a central theme for New Testament Christians as well. This is primarily lived out in the context of obedience to the teachings of Jesus. In fact, discipleship in the Great Commission is defined as obeying all that Jesus has commanded (Matt. 28:19–20). Jesus told his original band of disciples that if they loved him, they would keep his commandments (John 14:15). Understandably then, God calls his disobedient and wayward children to repent of their sins and their rebellion against him, both during Old Testament times as well as today (2 Tim. 2:22–26; Rev. 2:5, 16; 3:3, 19).

Is it true?
Are twenty-first-century churches occupied by a significant contingent of rebels in need of repentance? That seems like a harsh description of churchgoing, hymn-singing, tithe-giving church folks. Certainly, none of us is perfect, but "rebels"? That just sounds excessive. It should be remembered though, that Isaiah's audience consisted largely of people who regularly attended Sabbath worship (Isa. 1:12–13), offered *multitudes* of sacrifices to God (1:11–13), faithfully kept the appointed feasts and holy days (1:13–14), and lifted their hands in *many* expressions of prayer and praise to the Lord (1:15). These were respectable religious folks, not uncultured pagans who flaunted their disdain for God. Nor were these well-meaning but immature believers, those not yet educated in God's laws or expectations. These were "seasoned believers," well versed in the rituals and laws of their religious heritage. Nonetheless, their actions betrayed significant discontinuity between their external pretense of worship and their daily practices toward their fellow Israelites.

Unfortunately, many who fill the pews of modern churches today are not significantly different. God is not fooled by our façade of a well-pressed dress shirt and tie, or a vocabulary seasoned with Christian catchphrases, or even of hands raised high in passionate displays of worship. He isn't at all impressed by titles in front of our names or our developed skill in arguing complicated theological positions. Unlike man, God is not enamored with nor fooled by external shows of religiosity or piety. He sees through to the thoughts and intentions of the heart of each person (1 Sam. 16:7; 1 Chron. 28:9; Pss. 7:9 [HB 10]; 51:6 [HB 7]; 139:1–12; Jer. 11:20; 17:10; Heb. 4:12–13). God knows when we are living a lie. He is intimately aware of the

---

14 For God as Israel's father in Isaiah, see esp. Isa. 43:6–7; 63:8, 15–16; and 64:8.

subtle ways some Christians cheat on their taxes through technicalities or made-up numbers. He knows when we perpetually ignore the poor or disadvantaged because of our selfish greed in pursuit of some American Dream. He sees when we fail to come to the defense of the unpopular student who is being bullied or picked on. God hears every demeaning remark of idle gossip intended to tear down our fellow man or woman. He sees every lustful look, every internet search, and every immoral relationship. In other words, "No creature is hidden from his sight, but all are naked and exposed to the eyes of him to whom we must give account" (Heb. 4:13).

Many of us can identify at some level with the rebels who are confronted in Isaiah 1. There are times in our lives when we find that we have drifted away from obedience into doing our own thing. It isn't a matter of not knowing the right things that we should be doing; we simply want to follow our own hearts and do what feels good to us. Our hearts, coupled with deception from the Evil One, are disposed to drift toward selfish and disobedient autonomy from God. The hymn writer expressed well the tendency of us all when he wrote, "Prone to wander, Lord I feel it / Prone to leave the God I love" (Robert Robinson, "Come Thou Fount of Every Blessing," 1813, public domain).

Now what?
The good news is that despite our many failures, God still loves us. Psalm 103:13–14 says, "As a father shows compassion to his children, so the Lord shows compassion to those who fear him. For he knows our frame; he remembers that we are dust." Similarly, God says in Jeremiah 31:20, "Is Ephraim my dear son? Is he my darling child? For as often as I speak against him, I do remember him still. Therefore, my heart yearns for him; I will surely have mercy on him."

Repentance is something that all people need to be ready to practice. God's call for people to repent is a gesture of grace and mercy. Whereas he could simply act in judgment against those who rebel against him, he invites us to acknowledge our disobedience and commit to act in ways consistent with his character. In fact, repentance should be a regular part of the believer's life; it isn't just for the unbeliever who turns to God through Jesus for salvation at the moment of belief. Martin Luther began the Reformation by nailing ninety-five theses to the door of the Wittenberg Church in 1517. The very first thesis affirmed that Christ "willed the entire life of believers to be one of repentance."[15] In the same way that love relationships need to be rekindled on a regular basis, so too our love for Jesus should be routinely rekindled and our commitment to his lordship over us should be expressed with regularity.

When we are confronted with or are already aware of known sins, the appropriate response is to prayerfully repent. Additionally, though, it is helpful to devote a chunk of time every so often to simply search out our hearts before God and ask him to reveal any sins of commission or omission of which we are unaware or to which we have grown callous. Consider using a Scripture passage(s) centered around repentance as a model to help you express your own repentance in a meaningful prayer to God.[16] Additionally, consider using some spiritual life inventory or a checklist of possible sins to think through all of the areas of your life.[17]

---

15 Martin Luther, "Disputation of Doctor Martin Luther on the Power and Efficacy of Indulgences" (1517), thesis 1.
16 Some examples of repentance themed passages in Scripture are Neh. 1:4–11; Pss. 19:7–14 [HB 8–15]; 32; 51; and 143; Isa. 57:14–21; Dan. 9:1–19; James 4:4–10.
17 There are numerous checklists or inventories available for Christians to use as a rubric for self-evaluation and repentant prayer. One that I have used and appreciated is Neil Anderson's "The Steps to Freedom in Christ" (Anderson 2000, 207–57).

The Lord Confronts His Rebellious People (1:1–20)

Sample Repentance Inventory Checklist

Sins Related to How You Use Your Words
____ Have I engaged in conversations with others that were demeaning or unnecessarily specific in describing the faults or shortcomings of others?
____ Have I engaged in talk designed to pridefully promote myself (directly or subtly) or to draw attention to things that I accomplished in order to elicit acknowledgement or praise from others?
____ Have I unkindly and impatiently lashed out in anger with my words toward others, either in their presence or behind their backs?
____ Have I faithfully used my words as a tool to be an encouragement toward friends and family?
____ Have I faithfully used my words to offer praise and thanksgiving to God for the many blessings in my life?
____ Have I faithfully taken advantage of the opportunities that arise to point others toward Jesus?

Sins Related to How You Use Your Money
____ Have I been giving faithfully to support my local church?
____ Have I been sharing my resources with the poor or disadvantaged rather than hoarding my wealth and/or spending it all on myself and my family?
____ Have I been spending frivolously to find shallow satisfaction?
____ Am I overly preoccupied with earning/saving money?

Sins Related to How You Use Your Time/Energy
____ Have I made time for others (family/ministry/lost)?
____ Am I using the gifts God has given me to further his kingdom?
____ Have I spent too much time in leisure and entertainment to the neglect of other responsibilities?

Sins Related to How You Interact with Important Relationships
____ Have I been showing honor and respect toward my parents?
____ Have I been showing love and respect toward my spouse?
____ Have I been diligent in teaching and disciplining my children?
____ Have I been investing quality time with my family?
____ Have I been careful to show proper respect for my employer or others in authority over me at my place of work?
____ Have I been careful to reflect Christlikeness to my neighbors, coworkers, friends, and family?

Sins Related to How You Use Your Mind
____ Have I used my mind to entertain prideful thoughts of superiority to others, even if I haven't verbally expressed those attitudes?
____ Have I used my mind to entertain lustful thoughts about others, even if I haven't acted on those fantasies?
____ Have I used my mind to entertain thoughts of bitterness and hatred of others rather than forgiveness?
____ Have I used my mind to entertain thoughts of entitlement where I expect that God or others owe me in various ways?
____ Have I used my mind to entertain thoughts or emotions of fear and/or anxiety about my life, acting as though God were not good and sovereign over life?
____ Have I entertained attitudes of self-reliance where I have ignored or minimized my need of God and other people to accomplish all that God has called me to do?
____ Have I entertained false concepts about God that assumes him to be vindictive, controlling, unloving or arbitrary rather than kind, merciful, and loving as the Bible reveals him to be?
____ In areas of temptation, have I practiced taking every thought captive to obedience of Christ?
____ Have I sought to love God with all my mind through meditating on His Word and His attributes?

Sins Related to How You Use Your Physical Body
____ Have I misused my body in any way for sexual gratification outside the boundaries of a biblical marriage?
____ Have I overindulged in food to an unhealthy degree?
____ Have I overindulged in entertainment, games, or other leisure activities to the neglect of my responsibilities or investing myself in things with eternal value?
____ Have I used/misused drugs/alcohol in such a way so as to have lost or diminished control of my rational capacities?
____ Have I developed an inflated opinion of the importance of my outward, physical appearance or physique?

Sins Related to Your Relationship with God
____ Have I knowingly engaged in worshiping idols or false gods?
____ Have I sought out extra-biblical revelation through any form of divination such as a psychic, tarot card reading, or Ouija board?
____ Have I neglected the regular assembly with other believers in a local church?
____ Have I budgeted time for regular and consistent fellowship with God to talk to him in prayer and to read and meditate on his Word?

The Lord Confronts His Rebellious People (1:1–20)

Creativity in Presentation

Consider opening the sermon with a story (similar to the one under Preaching Pointers at the beginning of the chapter) about a parent whose son or daughter has walked away from them in rebellion. Try to make the story as real as possible, even if it is fictional. Include details about favorite memories the parent has about the child, goals and dreams the parent made for their son or daughter, and things they miss most now that they don't see them anymore (dinners, recreational activities together, holidays, family reunions, etc.). Encourage your audience to enter emotionally into the pain that this parent experiences every day of their lives. Make the connection that this is the sort of pain that God says he feels toward his children when they walk in perpetual rebellion against him.

Isaiah 1:3 draws a contrast between animals (oxen and donkeys) that know and obey the voice of their master with the people of Israel whose disobedience toward Yahweh reveals their lack of understanding. A modern example of an obedient animal can be found in the dog Skidboot, which won the $25,000 championship on Animal Planet's Pet Star competition in 2003. David Hartwig, the dog's owner, trained Skidboot to do many entertaining tricks. One example is where David throws the dog's favorite toy several feet away, but immediately tells the dog to wait. Only after the dog is told to ease up on the toy does he begin to slowly walk toward it. As he gets within a few feet, his eyes fixated on the toy, he slows to a stop. Hartwig then gives several other commands like "take a step" or "get closer" or "back up." Each time, Skidboot immediately obeys his master's command. Eventually, David tells the dog that he can touch the toy, but he can't get it, at which point the dog places his front paw onto the toy. Then, Hartwig says, "I'm gonna count to three. When I say 'three' you get that toy, but don't you get it until I say 'three.'" He then begins to count, "One, two (pause), four (with emphasis)." Surprisingly, the dog doesn't move. After a few more random numbers, David nonchalantly says "three" and Skidboot immediately and playfully grabs the toy. It would be most impactful to download and show the video of David Hartwig and Skidboot performing this act.

Share a time when you received a gift that you really didn't care for from somebody. Maybe it was a shirt or sweater that just wasn't your style. Or maybe it was a piece of art that you found to be gaudy or outdated. Now, imagine if when the person gave it to you, you decided to be brutally honest with them and ignored normal protocols of tact and graciousness, saying to them, "I hate this gift"; "I would never wear this sweater! I think it's downright ugly!"; or even, "You obviously don't know me very well if you think I would like or use something like this." So much for "It's the thought that counts." I'm sure that anyone who was spoken to in this way and whose gift was so disparaged would be utterly offended and hurt. This is precisely the tone and message of God to the people of Judah in regard to their ritual gifts/offerings to him. He doesn't mince words nor pretend that he is grateful for their effort, meager as it may be. God wants the people of Judah to *feel* the offense of their actions by his own strong and offensive response.

To conclude the message, the preacher might consider summarizing the parable by Jesus of the lost or prodigal son (Luke 15:11–32). There are many parallels between this story and the imagery the prophet Isaiah presents in this passage. In the parable, a son insults his father by demanding his inheritance early so that he can leave his father and go live for himself. The father reluctantly but graciously acquiesces to his request. In the process, the rebellious son ends up wasting everything on foolish living. Eventually he hits rock bottom and returns to his father repentantly, expecting his father to view him with some resentment and hold his past rebellion against him. To his great surprise, his father had been waiting expectantly with open arms for his return and ran to meet him. Not only did he welcome him home, but he threw a great party in celebration of the father-son relationship having been restored. This passage serves to highlight the deep love that God continues to have toward his children even when they have rebelliously and disrespectfully snubbed him in the past. It can serve as a great prelude into an invitation for the listeners in the room to prayerfully repent of known sins in their own lives, reminding them that the Lord graciously urges all rebels to return to their loving Father.

- The prophet gives an indictment against Israel's rebellion (1:1–9).

- The prophet highlights the irrelevance of Israel's religion (1:10–15).

- The prophet extends an invitation for Israel to repent (1:16–20).

DISCUSSION QUESTIONS

1. Assuming some in the group are parents: Have you ever experienced a teenage or adult son/daughter who rebelled significantly? What emotions did you feel, and how did you try to deal with them during that time?

2. What comes to your mind when you think of the word "rebel"? Is this a word you typically think of to describe yourself when you're living in unconfessed sin, or do you tend to see yourself in terms that are less derogatory such as: "I make my share of mistakes"; "I struggle with always doing the right thing"; or maybe "I'm not perfect, but nobody is"?

3. How might it help us to get more serious about our sin if we thought and spoke about our sin as willful rebellion against God, rather than the gentler descriptions we're prone to use for ourselves?

4. Can you remember a time when you received a gift from somebody where it didn't seem as if there was any meaningful thought put into it? Maybe they regifted something they had received and didn't want; maybe it was given to you as a formality (everybody in the office gets each other something). In what way (if any) did this gift impact you?

5. Have you ever scheduled a block of time to prayerfully consider any areas of sin to repent of, either known or unknown? If so, how did it go? Did you find it meaningful and beneficial? Did you use any guides or checklists to help you be thorough in your prayer time? If so, what did you use?

Isaiah 1:21–31

EXEGETICAL IDEA
The Lord will replace Jerusalem's unjust, idolatrous leaders and populate the city with a godly remnant.

THEOLOGICAL FOCUS
When the Lord's covenant community is plagued by unjust and idolatrous leadership, he must purify it to bring his ideal to realization.

PREACHING IDEA
Leaders can make all the difference in the world.

PREACHING POINTERS
Between 1941 and 1945, Nazi Germany systematically murdered approximately six million Jews during what is now known as the Jewish Holocaust. It is arguably the darkest period of the last century. How is it that countless people sat by, either actively giving their consent or passively doing nothing, while so many horrific atrocities were being carried out against innocent people? While the answer to that question is undoubtedly complex and multifaceted, nobody can deny that a central component was the influential leadership of Adolf Hitler. This one man was instrumental in directing a nation's energies toward so much evil. And yet Hitler was only one man. He could never have accomplished all that he did without the support and consent of many otherwise normal German citizens.

Most people today look back and assume that, had they been living in Germany during this period of history, they would certainly have resisted and spoken out against this evil movement. And while a relative few would have strongly opposed Hitler's leadership had they lived through those horrific events, history is littered with political movements that resulted in large-scale brutality and carnage where a majority of citizens stood by and did nothing—or worse yet, actively participated. In reality, most people are followers. True leaders are a rare breed; virtuous leaders are even scarcer. In Isaiah 1, the prophet confronts Judah with her rebellion against Yahweh, particularly in the way that she dealt with and treated the weak and vulnerable. Isaiah 1:21–31 reveals that Judah wasn't always this way; she used to be a "faithful city," one known for its "righteousness" and "full of justice" for the oppressed (1:21). A central reason for this shift was the ungodly, self-serving leaders. Their influence evidently had a significantly negative impact—not only on the collective reputation of the nation, but also on the individual behavior of most of the people. This highlights emphatically how leaders can make all the difference in the world.

JUSTICE DEMANDS PURIFICATION (1:21–31)

LITERARY STRUCTURE AND THEMES (1:21–31)

This literary unit has the basic form of a judgment speech: there is a formal accusation (1:21–23), followed by an announcement of judgment (1:24–31). The accusation opens like a dirge as the prophet mourns Jerusalem's moral demise and, by implication, her imminent destruction. The first part of the announcement highlights the Lord's intervention in judgment by using six first-person verb forms (1:24–26a). The results of the Lord's intervention then follow (1:26b–31).

> **Dirge**
> The word אֵיכָה often has a simple interrogative force ("How?" or "Where?"), but it can also function as an interjection in rhetorical questions and introduce mourning songs (cf. Jer. 48:17; Lam. 1:1; 2:1; 4:1, 2), as it does here (see *HALOT* s.v. "אֵיכָה" 40; BDB s.v. "אֵיכָה" 32).

Isaiah 1:26–27, which in isolation resembles a salvation announcement, is a unique feature of this judgment speech. It appears to have a twofold purpose: (1) to bring hope to the remnant and (2) to pave the way for the portrayal of salvation in the next literary unit (2:2–4). Ironically, it complements the surrounding judgment message because the promise of the restoration of a remnant implies the doom of the unjust.

There are several verbal connections within 1:21–27 that point to the unity of these verses (cf. 1:22 and 25; 23a and 26a; 21a and 26b, 27; Liebreich 1956, 128–29). However, it is also apparent that 1:28–31, which correspond to 1:23b–24, has an important place in the structure of the unit:

A Verse 21: Zion described (note third-person feminine singular forms)
B Verses 22–23a: Zion addressed (note second-person feminine singular forms)
C Verses 23b–24: Zion's rebels described (note masculine singular and plural forms)
B Verses 25–26: Zion addressed (note second-person feminine singular forms)
A Verse 27: Zion described (note third-person feminine singular forms)
C Verses 28–29a: Zion's rebels described (note third-person masculine plural forms)
C Verses 29b–30: Zion's rebels addressed (note second-person masculine plural forms)
C Verse 31: Zion's rebels described (note masculine singular and plural forms)

- *What Jerusalem Had Become (1:21–23)*
- *Purifying What Is Corrupt (1:24–27)*
- *The Plight of the Rebels (1:28–31)*

EXPOSITION (1:21–31)

What Jerusalem Had Become (1:21–23)
Jerusalem, once characterized by covenant loyalty and justice, was now filled with disloyal leaders who profited from injustice.

1:21. The prophet laments that Jerusalem (= Zion, 1:27) has become corrupt. She was once a center for justice and fairness, but those days are now over. There is probably an allusion here to the era of David and Solomon, who became famous for his ability to make wise, just decisions (1 Kings 3:7–12, 16–28; 10:9), and to the time of Jehoshaphat, who promoted justice throughout the land and in Jerusalem (2 Chron. 19:5–10).

The personified city, which stands here for her rulers, is compared to a prostitute. This image is often used elsewhere of idolatry, which may possibly be in view here (cf. 1:29; see Erlandsson 1980, 101–2). However, the underlying reality may be covenant disloyalty in general, which found expression in injustice (1:23) and idolatry (1:29; Jones 1968, 322).

The reference to "murderers" at the end of the verse suggests this. The *piel* of רָצַח is rare, but in each of its other uses it refers to cold-blooded murder (2 Kings 6:32; Ps. 94:6; Hos. 6:9). In Psalm 94:6 the verb is used of exploitation of the vulnerable, including the widow and fatherless. This may be the case in Isaiah 1, where oppression of the widow and fatherless is denounced (1:23). If so, injustice is likened to murder (cf. 1:15). By depriving the poor and destitute of proper legal recourse and adequate access to the economic system, the oppressors had, for all intents and purposes, murdered their victims by subjecting them to abject poverty, hunger, and exploitation.

1:22. To depict the perversion of justice, Isaiah uses two metaphors, in which justice is compared to silver and wine. Zion's (note the second-person feminine singular suffix) silver has become impure dross, the substance separated from the silver during the refining process. Her wine (again note the second-person feminine singular suffix) has been diluted by water, losing its full, natural flavor.

1:23. The officials of the city had become calloused. The term סָרַר means "be stubborn, rebellious." It is used of a stubborn, disobedient son (Deut. 21:18.20) and often describes God's people as rejecting his moral will and rebelling against him (Neh. 9:29; Ps. 78:8; Isa. 30:1; 65:2; Jer. 5:23; 6:28; Hos. 4:16; 9:15; Zech. 7:11). It is possible that allusion is made to the Deuteronomic law regarding the rebellious son, especially if there is an allusion to it in Isaiah 1:19 (see comment above). The two terms used to characterize such a son (מָרָה and סָרַר) both appear in this context (מָרָה in 1:19, סָרַר in 1:23).

These officials were nothing more than thieves (the text literally reads, "companions of thieves"). Companionship implies likeness of character (cf. Ps. 119:63; Prov. 28:24; and see BDB s.v. "חָבֵר" mng. 2.f, 288). Rather than promoting justice, they exploited the system for profit.

The verbs highlight their greed. Both אָהֵב, "love," and רֹדֵף, "pursue," are participles, which characterize the leaders as greedy and as obsessed with financial gain. The individuals in view here were not capitalists in the modern sense of the term. They were members of the royal bureaucracy who held judicial positions. They accepted bribes and payoffs to rule in favor of those able to pay the price they demanded. Because they had no financial leverage, the poor and needy were at the mercy of such judges, who were more than willing to aid the rich in their efforts to take away the property of the common people through excessive taxation and interest rates. For a judge to accept a bribe (שֹׁחַד) was in direct violation of the covenant stipulations (Exod. 23:8; Deut. 16:19; cf. Deut. 10:17; 1 Sam. 8:3; 2 Chron. 19:7; Mic. 3:11).

Williamson points out that "virtually the whole of the second half of the Decalogue is alluded to in this passage" (2006, 139). As he observes, the prophet directly accuses the people of murder (Isa. 1:21; cf. Exod. 20:13) and theft (Isa. 1:23; cf. Exod. 20:15), and implies they are also guilty of false witness and coveting (Isa. 1:23; cf. Exod. 20:16–17). Furthermore, he compares their sin to adultery (Isa. 1:21; cf. Exod. 20:14) and to disobedience to parents (Isa. 1:23; cf. Exod. 20:12).

Purifying What Is Corrupt (1:24–27)

The Lord will remove the rebellious leaders and replace them with new, just rulers so that Jerusalem will once again be a center of loyalty and justice.

1:24. If the leaders of Jerusalem persisted in their oppression of the vulnerable (Isa. 1:23) and would not obey the Lord's command to promote justice (cf. 1:17), then the Sovereign Lord himself would intervene. The prophet highlights the Lord's sovereignty. He calls him "the Lord" (הָאָדוֹן), "LORD Almighty" (literally, "LORD of Armies"; cf. 1:9), and "Mighty One of Israel." Isaiah uses the title הָאָדוֹן five times; each time it appears before the title "LORD of Armies" (see Isa. 1:24; 3:1; 10:16, 33; 19:4) and depicts God in his role as the sovereign king who leads armies and brings judgment against evildoers. By placing the definite article on the title, the prophet emphasizes that the God of Israel is "the Lord," or "Master," par excellence. The term אֲבִיר depicts God as powerful; it sometimes refers to mighty warriors (Jer. 46:15; Lam. 1:15), angelic powers (Ps. 78:25), or strong animals such as bulls (Pss. 50:13; 68:30 [HB 31]; Isa. 34:7) and warhorses (Jer. 8:16; 47:3; 50:11). The precise form of the title "Mighty One of Israel" occurs only here, though the title "Mighty One of Jacob" does appear elsewhere (Gen. 49:24; Ps. 132:2, 5; Isa. 49:26; 60:16).

The sovereign king would come to dispense justice. Both verbs used in 1:24b indicate this. The first (*niphal* of נָחַם) speaks of the Lord consoling himself through administering justice, while the second (נָקַם), when used, as here, in the *niphal* stem, refers to getting revenge on one's enemies (see Judg. 15:7; 16:28; 1 Sam. 14:24; 18:25; Esther 8:13; Jer. 15:15; 46:10; 50:15; Ezek. 25:12, 15). As a just king, the Lord identified with the oppressed and regarded their oppressors as his personal enemies, against whom he would seek retribution.

It is shocking to hear the Lord refer to his own people as his adversaries/enemies (cf. Isa. 63:10; Lam. 2:4–5). This is the antithesis of the promise contained in the protection clause of the covenant (Exod. 23:22; cf. Deut. 30:7), yet it is consistent with the general principle that the Lord seeks vengeance against his enemies, especially those who oppress the needy (Ps. 94:1–7; Nah. 1:2).

TRANSLATION ANALYSIS 1:24
The translations display variety in their treatment of the verb נָחַם: KJV, "I will rid myself from"; ESV, "I will get relief from"; NIV, "I will vent my wrath on"; NRSV, "I will pour out my wrath on"; HCSB, "I will gain satisfaction against" (cf. *Tanakh*, "I will get satisfaction from"); NLT, "I will take revenge on." The KJV/ESV depict the Lord getting relief, NIV/NRSV picture him releasing his anger, and HCSB/*Tanakh*/NLT convey the notion of gaining revenge. *HALOT* (s.v. "נחם" 688) gives three categories for the verb in this stem (*niphal*): (1) to regret, (2) to be sorry, (3) to console oneself. They place Isaiah 1:24 under the third category, offering the gloss "to gain one's satisfaction, gratify oneself against," pointing to the parallel verb (נָקַם) for support. It is used in the sense of "console oneself, be consoled" (cf. *HALOT*'s third category) nine times. Apart from Isaiah 1:24 it refers to someone being consoled after a difficult emotional experience (Gen. 24:67; 38:12; 2 Sam. 13:39; Ps. 77:3 [Eng. 2]; Jer. 31:15; Ezek. 14:22; 31:16), in one case through the satisfaction of seeing revenge carried out (Ezek. 32:31). In Isaiah 1:24, where the verb is collocated with the preposition מִן, "from," the basic notion of being consoled is present, but, parallel to the verb נָקַם, the idea is that consolation is achieved through gaining revenge. The KJV and ESV do well in reflecting the preposition, but HCSB, *Tanakh*, and NLT come closest to expressing the illocutionary force. For fuller discussion of the verb נָחַם, see Parunak 1975, 512–32; and for a shorter summary, see Chisholm 1995, 388–89.

1:25–26. Addressing personified Zion again (Isa. 1:25–26; cf. 1:22–23a), the Lord announces he will attack her, but not for the purpose of destruction. Justice had become corrupted, but the Lord's intervention will purify the city by establishing judges and royal advisers who will champion what is just and fair.

> **Purify**
> In 1:25 the Hebrew reads, "I will refine your dross like lye." On the use of the preposition -כְּ here ("as with"), see GKC, 376 §118w. The noun בֹּר, used only here and in Job 9:30, refers to potash, or lye, an "alkali obtained from the ash of wood and plants, chemically K2CO3" (*HALOT* s.v. "בֹּר II" 153). (*HALOT* erroneously lists Job 24:19 as another passage where this word occurs.) Commenting on Job 9:30, David Clines (1989, 220) identifies it as "an alkaline solution made from the ashes of wood or vegetable matter (pot ashes); chemically it is caustic potash." Job 9:30 indicates it was used to wash the hands. The metaphor may be mixed in Isaiah 1:25, but it is more likely that the substance in view here was used as a flux, or cleaning agent, in the refining process (see *HALOT* s.v. "סִיג" 750).

Word repetition is used to correlate divine intervention (cause) and purification (effect). Isaiah 1:25 and 1:26 begin with the same verb form ("and I will cause to return"), used with different nuances. In 1:25a it is used of the Lord turning his hand against Zion for the purpose of purification (1:25b). In 1:26 it is used of the Lord restoring righteous judges and advisers.

> *TRANSLATION ANALYSIS 1:26*
> In 1:26a the Hebrew text reads, "I will restore your judges as in the first, and your advisers as in the beginning." Some translations render this in a word-for-word manner: KJV, "I will restore thy judges as at the first, and thy counselors as at the beginning"; ESV, "I will restore your judges as at the first, and your counselors as at the beginning"; NRSV, "I will restore your judges as at the first, and your counselors as at the beginning"; *Tanakh*, "I will restore your magistrates as of old, And your counselors as of yore"; HCSB, "I will restore your judges to what they once were, and your advisers to their former state." NLT is more paraphrastic in handling the temporal clauses and in clarifying that the statement envisions the restoration of the office, not the actual individuals: "I will give you good judges again and wise counselors like you used to have." NIV interprets the terms "judges" and "advisers" as referring more generally to leaders: "I will restore your leaders as in days of old, your rulers as at the beginning." However, in this context, where the legal corruption of the royal bureaucracy is in view (1:23), it is probable that the judges are those who made legal decisions in the courts and the advisers were those who established economic policies.

1:27. Isaiah 1:27a envisions Zion being "redeemed." The verb פָּדָה refers here to the city's being freed from its ethical impurity through the implementation of a new era of justice. In legal contexts this verb often refers to paying a price to release an object from one who has a claim upon it (see Exod. 13:13, 15; 21:8; 34:20; Lev. 19:20; 27:27, 29; Num. 18:15–17; Job 6:23). It is even used of paying a ransom to release one from captivity (Job 6:22–23; Ps. 49:8 [HB 9]). The verb describes how the Lord "redeemed" his people from Egypt. In this case they are viewed as slaves who were purchased by their new owner, the Lord (Deut. 7:8; 9:26; 13:5; 24:18).

In Isaiah 1:27b the city's purified are identified more specifically as, literally, "her returning ones." The verb "return" sometimes refers to a return from bondage (cf. Isa. 10:21; 35:10; 51:11), a nuance that might be suggested by the presence of פָּדָה, "redeem," in the parallel line. In this case the future exiles are in view. However, in Isaiah the verb more often refers to returning to the Lord in repentance (6:10; 9:12 [Eng. 13]; 19:22; 31:6; 44:22; 55:7; 59:20). In this case the referent is

Zion's repentant ones (cf. 1:19–20), who are described in 59:20 as the beneficiaries of the Lord's restoration of the city. Perhaps both nuances are intended.

> **Returning Ones**
>
> J. Alec Motyer (1993, 51) detects a wordplay here between "returning ones" and the first-person verb forms of שׁוּב, "return," that begin 1:25–26. He suggests that the literary device here gives "primacy to the divine acts which make the human response possible and meaningful."

How would the city be freed by justice and fairness? In this context the Lord restores justice through his intervention in judgment, which culminates in the reestablishment of human judges and advisers who promote justice and are faithful to the Lord. The Lord's intervention is the catalyst for this change, but it is implemented by his human instruments who are part of the group called Zion's "penitent ones" (see NIV11). So, the justice/fairness derives from the Lord, but it is implemented through his human servants (Wildberger 1991, 72; Williamson 2006, 158).

Some identify the justice/righteousness here as the Lord's just judgment that distinguishes sinners from the repentant (cf. Isa. 5:16; 28:17; see Blenkinsopp 2000, 187; Gray 1912, 37). This interpretation is possible, since the passage depicts purifying judgment. However, in this context the terms refer to justice in the courts (cf. 1:21) and depict the renewal of justice in the city in the aftermath of judgment (1:26).

The Plight of the Rebels (1:28–31)
The rebels will perish before the Lord's destructive judgment and will be ashamed of their idols.

1:28. The perpetrators of injustice and oppression (cf. 1:23) are characterized as "rebels," "sinners," and "those who forsake the LORD." The use of these three verbs links this literary unit with the preceding speech, where all three were used to describe Israel (cf. 1:2, 4).

1:29. According to 1:29, injustice is not their only sin. They are also guilty of idolatry. The use of the verbs חָמַד, "desire," and בָּחַר, "choose," in 1:29 highlights their freedom of choice and indicates that they were "fully responsible for their own fate" (Williamson 2006, 160).

The trees mentioned here were associated with fertility rites that involved child sacrifices (see Isa. 57:5) and the orchards were the site of pagan worship practices (Isa. 65:3; 66:17). According to Othmar Keel (1998, 46), Iron Age tree cults in the ancient Near East stressed "the age old Near Eastern concept of the tree as a symbol and signal of the presence of a divine power, namely of prosperity and blessing, which ultimately resides in the earth."

The prophet alludes to the second half of the Decalogue in his earlier accusation (cf. 1:21–23); here he completes the indictment by accusing the people of violating the first part of the Decalogue, which prohibits false worship and idolatry (cf. Exod. 20:2–7). The only commandment of the Decalogue to which allusion is not made in this speech is the one regarding the Sabbath, but the Lord has already denounced their hypocrisy in this respect in the prior speech (cf. Isa. 1:13).

In the day of judgment, the people's idolatry, rather than bringing them blessing, will be a source of shame. The idols cannot insulate them from judgment. On the contrary, idolatry is one of the reasons that judgment is imminent. Experiencing shame certainly involves feeling humiliation (cf. Isa. 54:4), but it also has the connotation of being impotent or helpless (cf. Isa. 24:23) and is often associated with defeat. Kirsten Nielsen (1989, 221) observes that the verb בּוֹשׁ "refers not only to the emotion that grips the disappointed but also to the impotence." She cites several psalms where this is the case; the same appears to be true in Isaiah.[1]

1:30. The "tree" mentioned here (אֵלָה) is associated elsewhere with idolatry (Ezek. 6:13) and fertility rites (Hos. 4:12–13). So, the metaphor, in which the idolatrous people (note the plural verbs) are likened to a tree and an orchard, highlights the theme of poetic justice. Those who worship under sacred trees in sacred orchards will themselves become like a withering tree and an unwatered orchard (Miller 1982, 40–41). The punishment mirrors and fits the crime.

1:31. Isaiah depicts the sinners as "mighty." It is tempting in this context (cf. Isa. 1:30) to see the metaphor of a tree here, in which case a mighty tree is depicted as being reduced to a mere fiber of flax that is burned up (cf. Nielsen 1989, 209; Wildberger 1991, 78). The adjective חָסֹן occurs in only one other passage, where it is associated with oaks (Amos 2:9). Depicting the sinners as a strong tree makes sense in the light of 1:29, for the people would have desired and chosen the best trees.

The noun פֹּעַל in the parallel line normally refers to an action or deed. It could refer to their idolatrous behavior in general (Wildberger 1991, 78), but perhaps the idols themselves are in view (Motyer 1993, 52). The noun can be used of something that is made (cf. Isa. 45:9, 11). In either case, the metaphor of the tree does not extend to this line, for פֹּעַל is never used elsewhere of the produce of a tree.

The comparison of the sinners' work to a spark suggests their actions are self-destructive (cf. Young 1965, 93). The noun נִיצוֹץ is used only here in the Old Testament, though it does appear in Sirach 11:32, where it refers to a spark that ignites coals (*HALOT* s.v. "נִיצוֹץ" 696). It is related to the verb נָצַץ, "to sparkle" (Ezek. 1:7; *HALOT* s.v. "נצץ" 717). Used in association with בָּעַר, "burn," it refers in 1:31 to a spark that ignites a fire. The sinners' idolatrous actions or the idols themselves are the spark that ignites their destruction. The image of fire suggests that destruction will be swift and complete. This is emphasized by the observation that no one would extinguish it. This same image of rebels being destroyed by unquenched fire appears again at the very end of Isaiah (66:24).

THEOLOGICAL FOCUS

The theological focus of this speech can be stated as follows: When the Lord's covenant community is plagued by unjust and idolatrous leadership, he must purify it to bring his ideal to realization. As the prophet develops this theological theme, a few emphases emerge:

1. The Lord's commitment to justice

Zion's perversion of justice prompts this speech and the Lord's intervention in judgment. He expects Zion to be a center of justice and does not tolerate the corruption he sees there. The Lord sides with the disadvantaged and oppressed. His judgment is an act of retribution against the oppressors, whom he regards as enemies. But this judgment is not strictly punitive; it is designed to achieve the ideal of justice and restore just leadership to the city.

2. The purification of the covenant community

As noted above, the Lord does not intend to destroy his covenant community. Judgment is necessary because of the community's ethical and cultic corruption, but its purpose is to purify and establish the Lord's ideal for it.

3. The folly of false worship

It is not surprising that disregard for the Lord's ethical standards goes hand in hand

---

1 See 19:9; 20:5; 23:4; 24:23; 26:11; 29:22; 30:5; 37:27; 41:11; 42:17; 44:9, 11; 45:16–17, 24; 49:23; 50:7; 54:4; 65:13; 66:5.

with pagan religious practices. In addition to their ethical sins, Zion's rebels engage in pagan fertility rites designed to bring them blessings. But their paganism will disappoint them in the day of judgment. Like their objects of worship (sacred trees), they are not immune to the fire of divine judgment; in fact, their practices are the spark that ignites their own destruction.

PREACHING AND TEACHING STRATEGIES

Exegetical and Theological Synthesis

The prophet Isaiah begins this section by issuing a prophetic judgment against the city of Jerusalem. However, he obviously wasn't concerned with the city itself (brick and mortar), nor were his comments directed primarily toward the inhabitants generally who lived within the city limits. The context would indicate that it was Israel's political leadership who were in the prophet's crosshairs. When people today refer to "the corruption of Washington, DC," we understand that Washington is being used as a figure of speech, a metonymy whereby the city has been substituted for the political leaders who live and work there.[2] In fact, we would typically understand "Washington, DC" here to include an entire system of leadership—elected officials, political appointees, lobbyists, and others who do business with them. In similar fashion, Zion (Jerusalem) here is representative of the political leadership of Israel who lived and worked in Zion.[3] In fact, God's very name (reputation) was tied to the city of Jerusalem. It was understood that God was Israel's true king, but he entrusted ruling authority to human descendants of David who were to function as God's representative "sons" from the time of Solomon onward (1 Kings 11:36; 2 Chron. 7:16).[4] It was their responsibility and calling to embody God's character and ideals before the people as his visible, flesh-and-bone representatives. This included the protection of and care for the most helpless and weak, and the punishment of those who attempted to take advantage of them. These kingly ideals are expressed clearly in Psalm 10:14–18:

> The victims commit themselves to you; you are the helper of the fatherless. Break the arm of the wicked man; call the evildoer to account for his wickedness that would not otherwise be found out. The LORD is King for ever and ever; the nations will perish from his land. You, LORD, hear the desire of the afflicted; you encourage them, and you listen to their cry, defending the fatherless and the oppressed, so that mere earthly mortals will never again strike terror.

As Israel's leaders, they are primarily the ones responsible for the nation's shift away from justice and righteousness into a place known instead for injustice and oppression of the most vulnerable (Isa. 1:21–23). As in the previous section (1:2–20), the prophet employs provocative language and imagery to confront

---

2 "Metonymy is a figure of speech where the word or phrase is substituted for another that is closely associated with it. For example, in the statement, 'The White House said today,' the phrase 'White House' stands by metonymy for 'the president' or 'the President's office speaking with his authority'" (Chisholm 1998b, 35).

3 Note the various synonyms confronting the leadership of Israel in Isaiah ch. 1: "you *rulers* of Sodom" (1:10), "your *princes* are rebels and companions of thieves" (1:23), and "I will restore your *judges* as at the first" (1:26).

4 For the descendants of David as being God's representative "sons," see 2 Sam. 7:8–16; 1 Chron. 17:3–15; and Ps. 2:6–7. For Davidic kings intended to function as God's representative leaders (his right-hand men) to carry out his righteous rule, and even probably to serve as priests on behalf of the people after the order of Melchizedek, see 2 Sam. 8:18, Pss. 45:6–7 [HB 7–8]; 110:1–4. See also Armerding 1975, 75–86; Bateman 1992.

his target audience's sinful behavior. He likens them to "a prostitute" (1:21), "rebels" (1:23), as well as "foes" and "enemies" of God (1:24). They have compromised the integrity of their leadership positions in exchange for cheap bribes (1:23) and callously neglected the needs of the fatherless and widows who depended on them.

Therefore, God declares he will purge the city of its wicked leaders (1:24–26). The leaders must heed the prophet's warnings and repent (1:27), or God will purge them out of the city in judgment (1:28). Either way, he is going to restore the city to its former condition as a place known for carrying out righteousness and justice for all (1:26).

In addition to their crimes of corruption and injustice toward the poor and vulnerable, the prophet alludes further to the leaders' participation in idolatry. The oak trees and the gardens (1:29) were places associated with pagan worship practices and fertility rites that even included the detestable practice of child sacrifice. In poetic fashion, God likens these wicked leaders to the oak trees under which they worshipped idols (1:30). While they may be strong and powerful now like a tall oak tree, God would reduce them to tinder that would easily be consumed by the fire of his judgment with no one available to come to their rescue (1:31).

Preaching Idea
Leaders can make all the difference in the world.

Contemporary Connections

What does it mean?
"An army of sheep led by a lion is better than an army of lions led by a sheep."[5] So said Alexander the Great, one of the most effective military leaders of all time. His point is simple: the qualities of the leader have a bigger impact on the success or failure of the group than the qualities of the individual members of that group.

To say that leaders can make all the difference in the world is to acknowledge that in school, the right teachers are often the difference between whether a student grows to love or to hate a particular subject and whether they excel or struggle academically. It is to say that the difference between a mature and well-adjusted child and one who is not is largely a reflection of their parents. To affirm that leaders can make all the difference in the world is to observe that churches rarely thrive without committed and gifted pastors casting a ministry vision and regularly communicating truth in impactful ways to their congregation. It recognizes how necessary it is for businesses, however small or large, to have a dedicated and intelligent leader, often with many competent department heads and team leaders managing many of the day-to-day operations. To declare that leaders can make all the difference in the world is to recognize that perpetually winning sports teams are almost always led by capable managers and coaching staffs. In a nutshell, when groups of people need to be mobilized in a united effort, whatever the cause, leadership is almost always an integral component. Leaders tend to shape the narratives that drive the behaviors of those under their authority. They have a significant impact on forming the goals, ideals, and ethics of the broader group that they lead.

Is it true?
Some might argue that God does not need human leaders to accomplish anything. The fact that he chooses to use them does not make them essential. This is true in one sense. The

---

5 "Alexander the Great as quoted in *The British Battle Fleet: Its Inception and Growth Throughout the Centuries to the Present Day* (1915) by Frederick Thomas Jane, but many variants of similar statements exist which have been attributed to others"; https://en.wikiquote.org/wiki/Alexander_the_Great.

Bible does teach that all people will have to one day stand before God and give an accounting of their lives to him (Rom. 14:10–12; 2 Cor. 5:10; Heb. 9:27; 1 Peter 4:3–5). In that day, nobody will be able to blame their parents, teachers, political leaders, or pastors for the decisions they made or their inaction on other occasions. We are all individuals with a free will to make moral decisions. As such, we are individually responsible for the decisions we make.

Nonetheless, it is also true that no person is an island. Our ideas, thoughts, judgments, and decisions are impacted by the influences around us. Leaders are important. They are often the catalysts to get people to do what they otherwise wouldn't do. The Old Testament is filled with examples of how, when God wanted to mobilize a group of people toward a noble cause, he would raise up a leader. Consider how, when God chose to deliver Israel from the oppressive arm of Pharaoh and the Egyptians, he raised up Moses. When he chose to lead them out of the wilderness and into the Promised Land, God commissioned Joshua for that task. When Jerusalem was in shambles and in need of repair following the Babylonian exile, not only for the sake of the people who lived there but also for the reputation of God himself whose temple lay in ruins he called on men like Nehemiah and Ezra.

The power of leaders to sway and impact entire populations of people for either good or bad is vividly on display in the books of Samuel, Kings, and Chronicles. Here we read about various kings—some righteous, most not—ruling over the nations of Israel and Judah. Almost without exception, the character of the king determined the character and direction of the nation. When Judah's king feared Yahweh, the nation followed suit. However, as soon as that king was succeeded by a compromising king who participated in idolatry, the nation quickly followed suit. This is similarly the case throughout the book of Judges. God would raise up a leader who would initiate a military victory against Israel's oppressive enemies, often accompanied by a religious revival. But as soon as that judge died, his or her influence was lost, and the nation would return to its previous dysfunction, resulting in more oppression.

Now what?
Because of the significant impact leaders can have on those under their care, they must remember that God will hold them to a higher standard of responsibility in judgment. Hebrews 13:17 says, "Obey your leaders and submit to them, for they are keeping watch over your souls and will give an account for their work." James 3:1 warns, "Not many of you should become teachers, my brothers and sisters, because you know that we will be judged more strictly." Thus, leaders must view their roles soberly and not be slack in their responsibility to watch out for those under their care. This applies to pastors, husbands, employers, politicians, teachers, parents, coaches, and more. Most people will hold some form of leadership position(s) in their lifetime. As such, they must consider seriously just how important their role is, and the potential they have to impact the lives of those under their care. Their words and actions will be scrutinized and emulated more than they realize by their followers.

Not only must believers today consider the impact of their own leadership in the lives of others, but they must also recognize how impactful the leaders in their own lives are. Much of who we are, what we value, and how we act is a direct result of the leaders we have listened to and emulated. This can be cause for gratitude and celebration when we are blessed to have Christian parents, an employer who is conscientious of our Christian beliefs, or a youth pastor who invests heavily into our teenager's life. However, it should also cause us to pause and consider, "Whom are we allowing to impact and influence us? Whose voices are we following? Whose examples are we imitating, consciously or unconsciously?" There are lots of people who are speaking into our lives each day. Many of them are well meaning and sincere. But this doesn't mean that they are leading us in the direction of loving God and others more.

Finally, this passage offers hope to Christ-followers who suffer under oppressive and corrupt leaders. As Gary Smith observes, "A day will soon come when God will transform this world, remove all sin, replace all evil leaders, and rule his kingdom in righteousness and justice" (2007, 114). This truth should encourage believers who live under the iron fist of God-hating leaders. They will not have the last word, and their cruel and domineering rule will not persist forever. God will intervene, and those who love and serve God will be ushered into a glorious kingdom. All the persecution, oppression, and hardships they faced during their lifetime will become a thing of the past.

Creativity in Presentation

In many parts of the world, police officers are known to be corrupt. In some places, police officers are paid by drug cartels or mafia organizations to look the other way or to tip off the criminals to impending sting operations. In other places, police officers will pull people over and demand a bribe to let them go, when no wrong has been committed.As a result, many people no longer trust the police to do their job and to protect them from evil people. Even more, there is nobody left to hold powerful drug cartels, mafia organizations, or gangs in check. Business owners are forced to pay mafia fees to remain in business. Journalists are threatened into silence rather than risk investigating and reporting about cartel operations. And everyday citizens are left living in communities with much higher crime rates and very little trust in the authorities to do the right thing. This illustrates the sort of political environment that Isaiah was confronting, where leaders were accepting bribes from the wealthy and powerful in exchange for neglecting justice on behalf of the common, decent citizens, particularly the most vulnerable in society.[6]

To illustrate the anger and frustration caused to victims and their families when judges fail to adequately punish perpetrators of violence or injustice, consider the example of Riverside County, California, Superior Court Judge Roger Luebs, who presided over a case involving two teenage boys who bullied a fellow classmate for years. In 2019, video showed the two boys confront Diego Stolz, a significantly smaller, thirteen-year-old classmate. Unprovoked, the first boy punched Stolz in the face, followed by the other boy punching him in the back. Diego fell to the ground and hit his head on the concrete. He never regained consciousness and later died from his injuries. After the perpetrators pled guilty to involuntary manslaughter, the judge sentenced them to only 150 hours of community service with no incarceration time whatsoever.[7]

Another example is found in the senseless and brutal murder of Sarah Halimi. A former kindergarten director, sixty-five-year-old Halimi was beaten for twenty to thirty minutes and then thrown off a balcony to her death. The motive for this violent, despicable assault was simply because the victim was of Jewish descent while her attacker, Kobili Traoré, was a Muslim. Despite the fact he was quoting verses from the Koran and shouting "Allahu Akbar" throughout the attack, the judges on France's highest court determined that Traoré was undergoing a "psychotic episode" at the time of

---

6 The documentary *Cartels and Police Corruption: Inside Mexico's Drug War* (Gaytan 2009) provides an example of this sort of culture of corruption in the city of Juarez, Mexico, between the drug cartels and the local police.
7 https://www.foxnews.com/us/california-diego-stolz-no-prison-time.

the attack and was thus unable to discern what he was doing. As such, they determined that he was unfit to stand trial and be held accountable for his actions.[8]

On a more positive note, the movie *Stand and Deliver* is based on the true story of Jaime Escalante, a math teacher in a rough Hispanic neighborhood in East Los Angeles in the 1970s and 1980s. He motivated students to overcome the obstacles in their lives and do great things. Despite the fact they came from challenging circumstances, his students consistently scored higher than average on the advanced placement calculus exam. Several of his students went on to excel, getting accepted at places like MIT, Harvard, and Berkeley, and landing jobs at places like NASA, the US Securities and Exchange Commission, and professorships at major universities. His story illustrates the reality that leaders can make all the difference in the world.

- God wants us to be careful whom we are granting influence over us (1:21–23).

- God wants to convert us into godly influencers over others (1:24–31).

DISCUSSION QUESTIONS

1. Who are the leaders in your life who have made the biggest impact on you?

2. What was it about those leaders that impacted you the most? The things they said or taught? Their lifestyle? Their genuine love for you and others? Their humility and transparency about their own struggles?

3. Share about a time in your life when God used you in a leadership role to impact others for his kingdom.

4. Who has God given you a leadership role over at the present time?

5. Are there ways you could better maximize your leadership impact on these people?

---

8   https://www.bbc.com/news/world-europe-56929040.

Isaiah 2:1–5

EXEGETICAL IDEA
Since all nations will someday recognize the Lord's authority, Isaiah urges God's people to obey the Lord in the here and now.

THEOLOGICAL FOCUS
Since all nations will seek the Lord's guidance and submit to his rule of peace, his people should preview that era by obeying his revealed moral will.

PREACHING IDEA
In the light of God's promise of a future kingdom, the best is yet to come!

PREACHING POINTERS
Global warming. Political corruption scandals. Skyrocketing national debt. Nuclear weapons proliferation. Mass shootings becoming commonplace. Riots and protests in the streets. Inner-city crime on the rise. Islamic terrorism. Growing rates of depression and mental illness. The breakdown of the nuclear family. A worldwide health pandemic. Human trafficking. The growing secularization of society. Everywhere we look, there seems to be justification for pessimism, anxiety, and hopelessness. Are there really solutions to all these problems? Even if there were, do we really trust the world's politicians to responsibly do the right thing?

The book of Isaiah begins with a similarly gloomy and negative view of life in Judah. Everywhere the prophet looked, there was reason for anger, skepticism, and feelings of futility: political corruption, religious compromise, oppression of the poor, cities burned and overrun by foreigners. We are inclined in our day to echo the sentiment of the prophet who longed for the good old days of the past (Isa. 1:21) as he contemplated the present plight of Jerusalem. It is precisely amid such pessimism and hopelessness that the message of Isaiah 2:1–5 strikes a stark, contrasting chord, inspiring optimism and hope. While so much is presently wrong with the world, all is not lost. The end of the story has not yet been written. Be reassured, the best is yet to come.

FUTURE TRANSFORMATION (2:1–5)

LITERARY STRUCTURE AND THEMES (2:1–5)

Jerusalem will become the seat of world government. The Lord will instruct the nations and ensure worldwide peace by judging their disputes. Since the nations will someday recognize the Lord's authority and seek his counsel, the prophet urges the covenant community to live by the Lord's standards in the here and now.

This short unit portrays a coming age of peace when the nations will recognize and submit to the Lord's authority. It has two main literary units—a description of the future age (2:2–4) followed by an exhortation to the prophet's contemporaries (2:5). While verbal links with 2:3 show that 2:5 relates to what precedes, the reference to the "house of Jacob" links it with what follows as well (cf. 2:6).[1] Perhaps it is transitional, concluding the preceding speech and, with 2:22, forming a hortatory frame around 2:6–21 (Bartelt 1996, 203, 231).

- *Heading and Jerusalem's Glorious Destiny (2:1–2a)*
- *Recognition of the Lord's Authority (2:2b–3)*
- *Ain't Gonna Study War No More (2:4)*
- *Previewing the Age to Come (2:5)*

EXPOSITION (2:1–5)

Heading and Jerusalem's Glorious Destiny (2:1–2a)

Isaiah envisions a time when Jerusalem will be elevated to prominence among the nations.[2]

2:2a. The phrase "end of days" occurs thirteen times in the Old Testament. It often refers to the future in a general way (see Gen. 49:1; Num. 24:14; Deut. 31:29; Jer. 23:20; 30:24; 48:47; 49:39). On other occasions, it appears to refer more specifically to the culminating period in Israel's history when God destroys his enemies and vindicates his people (see Deut. 4:30; Ezek. 38:16; Dan. 10:14; Hos. 3:5; Mic. 4:1; Oswalt 1986, 116).

In Isaiah 2:2–4 the situation described is the result of the purifying judgment and restoration announced in 1:26–27. The radical reversal in the nations' relationship to the Lord and his people (cf. 2:2–4 with 1:7) suggests that 2:2–4 depicts a culminating era. If so, the phrase "end of days" may be given an eschatological nuance in this context (Wildberger 1991, 88). Even so, John T. Willis is probably correct in arguing that the expression refers to "an indeterminate future" and is not a technical term for the eschatological age. While it sometimes refers to the eschatological age, this must be determined based on contextual factors, not the mere appearance of the expression "end of days" (see Willis 1979, 69; cf. Williamson 2006, 180–81).

TRANSLATION ANALYSIS 2:2
Most translations understand the expression בְּאַחֲרִית הַיָּמִים, "in the end of days," as referring to an eschatological era (cf. "in the latter days" in ESV, and "in the last days" in HCSB, KJV, NIV, and NLT). The NRSV ("in days to come") and *Tanakh* ("in the days to come") take the expression as referring to the future in general.

---

[1] Childs 2001, 31; Gray 1912, 48. For a contrary opinion, see Sweeney 1988, 135–36. For a critique of Sweeney, see Smith 2007, 127.
[2] The language used in 2:2a depicts the literal elevation of Zion. See Sailhamer 1992, 88–89.

Recognition of the Lord's Authority (2:2b–3)

In Isaiah's vision all nations submit to the Lord's authority and recognize Jerusalem as the center of his worldwide government.

The nations will come to Jerusalem willingly to learn from the Lord, the God of Jacob. This vision stands in stark contrast to the reality of Isaiah's time, when the people refused the Lord's instruction (Isa. 6:9–10).

> **God of Jacob**
>
> The title "God of Jacob" occurs only here in Isaiah (cf. Mic. 4:2 as well). Of its fifteen appearances in the Old Testament, nine occur in the Psalms. Four of these are in psalms that, like Isaiah's vision, celebrate the Lord's presence in Zion (cf. Pss. 46:8, 12 [Eng. 7, 11]; 76:7 [Eng. 6]; 84:9 [Eng. 8]). For further discussion, see Tull 2010, 84; Williamson 2006, 183; and especially Willis 1997, 300.

2:2b. The verb נָהַר (2:2b; cf. Jer. 31:12?; 51:44?; Mic. 4:1), "stream towards" (*HALOT* s.v. "נהר I" 676), pictures the nations flowing like a stream or river to Zion. (Note the related noun נָהָר, "river, stream.") Some (e.g., *Tanakh*) prefer to read here the homonymic נָהַר, "shine, be radiant (with joy)" (cf. Ps. 34:6 [Eng. 5]; Isa. 60:5; Jer. 31:12?; 51:44?). But as Williamson (2006, 169) points out, the parallel line (see Isa. 2:3a), which depicts movement to Zion, favors the reading "stream, flow." It is significant that the nations do not merely come or walk to Zion. The verb used, by comparing them to a stream or river, suggests swift, uninterrupted movement in unison.

> **Homonymic**
>
> J. J. M. Roberts (1992, 46–48; see also 2015, 41) suggests a double entendre here, in which case the prophet exploited the meaning of both of the homonyms: "It is probable that the prophet was purposely playing on the ambiguity between the two homonymous roots, *nhr* (1) and *nhr* (2), in order to express both joyous recognition of and movement toward God's exalted house" (1992, 48).

2:3. The prophet pictures the nations as learning the Lord's "ways" so they can walk in his "paths." The Lord's "ways" are sometimes his commandments, as embodied in his law (Deut. 8:6; Isa. 42:24; 58:2). However, in this context these terms appear to refer more generally to the instruction and just decisions the Lord will give to the nations when he establishes his kingdom on earth. These "ways/paths" comprise the Lord's תּוֹרָה, or instruction, to the nations (cf. Isa. 51:4).

TRANSLATION ANALYSIS 2:3
The translations differ in their handling of תּוֹרָה here. The ESV, KJV, and NIV have "the law"; HCSB, *Tanakh*, and NRSV opt for "instruction"; and NLT reads "teaching." As in 1:10, the word does not refer here to the law of Moses (cf. 5:24; 42:21, 24; 51:7), but more generally to the Lord's moral and ethical instruction, in this case given to the nations during the culminating era described here. Roberts (2015, 41) observes that "'law' is not a totally misleading translation," because "while Yahweh's instruction of the nations is obtained by prophetic or priestly oracles, once issued it would have the force of imperial law." John Sailhamer (1992, 91) emphasizes that the "law" in view here is "a revelation of divine wisdom, the means for becoming a wise and understanding people."

Ain't Gonna Study War No More (2:4)

The Lord will instruct the nations and ensure worldwide peace by judging their disputes.

There will be no need for weapons because the nations will submit their disputes to the Lord. Throughout human history nations have often resorted to war to settle their differences, but in this coming age they will look to the Lord to adjudicate their disputes. The expression "settle cases" (*hiphil* of יָכַח + preposition -לְ) refers elsewhere to defending the cause of someone (Job 16:21; Isa. 11:4) or to rebuking one in need of correction and guidance (Prov. 9:7–8; 15:12; 19:25). In his role as royal adjudicator for the nations (cf. "judge between" in the previous line), the Lord will defend the just cause of many nations. His wise and fair decisions will make it unnecessary for the nations to go to war to defend or promote their interests. They will transform their weapons into agricultural implements and will no longer train for battle.

Previewing the Age to Come (2:5)

Since the nations will someday submit to the Lord, the Lord's people should obey the Lord now.

The prophet is not content to simply depict this future age of peace. He draws an application for his contemporaries. If the nations will someday come all the way to Jerusalem to seek the Lord's instruction, then surely the Lord's covenant people (called here the "house," or family, of Jacob) should follow his teaching in the present (Oswalt 1986, 118–19; Young 1965, 114). In so doing they preview the future age. Judah appears to be the primary referent here (cf. Mic. 3:9–11), representing the entire covenant community (cf. Isa. 46:3; 48:1).

The "light" of the Lord is here the moral and ethical guidance he provides through his commandments and instruction. For Israel this includes the commandments of the law, but it also encompasses prophetic instruction, such as that given in the previous chapter. The imagery is that of walking in correct pathways (cf. 2:3) with the aid of a light that guides the way.

THEOLOGICAL FOCUS

The theological focus of this passage can be stated as follows: since all nations will seek the Lord's guidance and submit to his rule of peace, his people should preview that era by obeying his revealed moral will. As the prophet develops this theological theme, a few emphases emerge:

1. The Lord's relationship to the nations

According to Isaiah, Israel's God exercises dominion over all the nations (Isa. 40:15–17; 41:2) and has a plan for them (14:26). These nations are hostile toward God and his people (29:7–8), prompting God to react in angry judgment (34:2). He will reveal his glory and power in their sight (52:10; 61:11; 66:18), demonstrating his incomparability to them (43:9). Ultimately, as depicted in Isaiah 2:2–4, these nations will recognize the Lord's royal authority, become worshippers of the one true God (cf. 19:23–25), and experience his blessings, including deliverance from the horrors of death, which has shrouded the world throughout human history (25:7).[3]

2. The impact of the eschatological hope on present behavior

The future reality of worldwide peace should impact the way the Lord's people live in the present. If the nations will one day look to the Lord for guidance, then the covenant community can preview that era by living in accordance with his revealed will in the present.

3. The prominence of Zion

In the three opening speeches of the book, the prophet presents a short history of Zion, viewed from the prophet's eighth-century-B.C. perspective. The opening speech depicts Zion's present isolation and vulnerability (1:8). The second speech recalls what Zion once was (a center of justice), laments what she has become (1:21–23), and announces her purification and redemption (1:25–27). This third speech looks beyond redemption and portrays what Zion will someday be.

---

3 For a defense of reading Isaiah 2:1–5 from a premillennial perspective, see Sailhamer 1992.

PREACHING AND TEACHING STRATEGIES

Exegetical and Theological Synthesis
This section begins with an abrupt change of tone from the previous two units (Isa. 1:2–20, 21–31). Bright optimism replaces doom and gloom. The effect on the reader is one of surprise, even "shock" (Oswalt 2003, 88). Not only does Jerusalem appear in a positive light (2:3), having evidently corrected the issues that plagued it, but even the Gentile nations stream to Zion to hear from God so they can walk in his ways (2:2–3). These nations will look to Yahweh to judge international disputes rather than attempt to settle their differences by going to war with each other. As a result, there will no longer be any need for armies or weapons (2:4). In the light of this glorious future, the present people of God (house of Jacob) should walk according to these ideals here and now while they await the consummation of these promises (2:5).

Preaching Idea
In the light of God's promise of a future kingdom, the best is yet to come!

Contemporary Connections

What does it mean?
To say that the best is yet to come assumes that the current state of affairs in this world is less than optimal. This goes without saying. We all know intuitively that this world is not all that it could or should be. There is an anxious unrest within the human soul that longs for something better. We recoil in anger at the many injustices that occur on a far-too-regular basis. We grieve in the aftermath of a natural disaster or a fatal automobile accident. There is a general distrust (and in many cases, dislike) of earthly governments. People are skeptical at best of political policies and the motivations of the politicians who promote them. Our minds try to comprehend why so many around the world are forced to live in abject poverty while others have far more wealth than they could ever spend in multiple lifetimes. We wrestle with what it all means when a loved one is diagnosed with an inoperable brain tumor, or a child is born with Down syndrome or a crippling defect. The world is plagued by conflict and blood-stained by destructive wars. While there is much disagreement on what the root causes are behind this world's problems, and likewise on what the best solutions to those problems are, there seems to be universal acceptance of the reality that all is not yet right.

Despite the many undesirable realities that plague our present world, there is reason for hope that brighter days await us at some point in the future. The prophet Isaiah described an unspecified time in the future when the world will become a place where righteousness reigns, as everyone from every nation will make it their commitment to walk according to the law of the Lord God. Conflict and wars will cease because the Lord himself will judge disputes between the nations and perfect justice will prevail. This will eliminate the felt need by nations to claw for power and control over each other, or to defend against attacks by rival states and nations. Thus, all wars and geopolitical conflicts will come to an end for a time of unprecedented global peace.

Is it true?
The biblical narrative of redemption begins with God's creation of a perfect world (Gen. 1–2). Man and woman were the apex of this creation as they bore the very image of God (Gen. 1:26–27; 5:1). As such, they were able to commune with him as friends and learn from him as children would from their father. The rest of creation became a source of many pleasures for them (Gen. 1:29; 2:9–14). It also provided a place for meaningful work

and responsibility as humankind was charged with filling up and ruling over God's new creation (Gen. 1:28; 2:15).

God established his relationship with those first humans based on trust evidenced by their total obedience to him. God warned Adam and Eve not to eat of one tree in the garden of Eden, the Tree of Knowledge of Good and Evil. Should they choose to disobey him, the consequences of their actions would be severe; they would die (Gen. 2:16–17). As the story goes, Satan tempted Eve along with her husband, and the two of them made the decision to sin (Gen. 3:1–6). They believed Satan's lie that God had deceived them in a quest to keep something better from them. What followed that day was far worse than Adam or Eve could ever have imagined. Not only did Adam and Eve suffer the sentence of death upon themselves, but every descendant of theirs for all time would similarly become mortal and face the realities of sickness, aging, and eventual death. Additionally, their descendants would be born with the effects of a sin nature, the results of which would multiply pain and suffering in untold ways. This was highlighted almost immediately when Adam and Eve's son Cain murdered his own brother in a fit of selfish rage (Gen. 4:8).

The effects and consequences of sin would not be limited to the human race. Both the serpent (Gen. 3:14) and the ground (Gen. 3:17–18) were cursed. The apostle Paul describes the present physical world as "subjected to futility" and put in "the bondage of decay." It "groans and suffers" because of Adam's sin (Rom. 8:20–22). Furthermore, when Adam chose to obey Satan by sinning against God, he forfeited humanity's ruling authority over creation to Satan, and the world became subjugated to the oppressive rule of the Evil One (1 John 5:19; cf. John 12:31; 14:30; 16:11; 2 Cor. 4:4; Eph. 2:2; 6:12). All that is wrong with this world, whether interpersonal or geopolitical conflicts, crime and injustice, natural disasters, sickness, or death, can be traced back to that one act of rebellion in the garden (Rom. 5:12, 19; 1 Cor. 15:21–22).

Nevertheless, God promised that sin would not ultimately prevail; Satan would not get the last word. God would provide a savior. The New Testament teaches plainly that Jesus of Nazareth was Israel's long-awaited Messiah (John 3:17; Gal. 4:4–5). When he died on the cross and then rose again from the dead, Jesus not only secured salvation for all who would trust in him, he also defeated Satan and ensured that the days of Satan's rule over this world were numbered. Thus, those who trust in Jesus now not only obtain salvation from coming judgment (1 Thess. 1:10). They are also transferred out of Satan's kingdom into the kingdom of Jesus Christ (Col. 1:13–14; Heb. 2:14–15). Additionally, Jesus's death on the cross paid the ransom price to redeem this world away from Satan to be a kingdom ruled by Jesus (Rom. 8:18–25; Rev. 5:9–13). As a result, Jesus will one day return to this earth as the rightful ruler. In so doing, he will usher in a new creation, a worldwide kingdom founded upon righteousness, where sin and death and sorrow will be no more (2 Peter 3:13; Rev. 11:15; 21:1–7). The curse will be fully removed from the earth in that day (Rev. 22:3). For those who have embraced salvation in Jesus, the best is yet to come!

Now what?

The prophet Isaiah called on the people of God in his own day to "walk [now] in the light of the Lord" (2:5). In other words, God's people shouldn't wait until the Lord's future kingdom is fully established to begin living according to his righteous kingdom ethics. They should commit now to live out these ideals as a testimony to nonbelievers of the goodness of God's coming kingdom (2 Peter 3:11–14).

One important way for Christians today to live out the ideals of God's coming kingdom is by their acknowledgment of and commitment to God's Word as the absolute standard for truth and moral goodness. Isaiah here predicts that in God's coming kingdom, the whole world will look to God to teach them his ways to walk according to his paths (Isa. 2:3). In other words, everyone will accept that ultimate truth is defined by "the word of the Lord," and that objective standards for morality and righteousness are found exclusively in God's "law." (2:4).

The world today is mostly lost on questions of truth and morality. Postmodernism has been an influential force in most academic institutions, and really in all segments of society, for the past fifty-plus years. Postmodernism tends to resist any clear definition of itself. But at its core, it is the denial of any absolute standard or source of objective truth. Rather, "truth" is thought of as a personal and subjective concept that will differ from one individual or culture to the next. The eventual outcome of this philosophy on society is that people lack any foundational basis upon which to argue something to be true or false and morally right or wrong. Those who have grown up under this philosophy unsurprisingly place a lot of value in their own gut feelings and opinions about moral issues, and conversely have little to no regard for what a book like the Bible says or what an institution like the church has to say about those same issues.

Attacks on truth are nothing new. As the god of this present world system, one of Satan's primary tactics is to deceive people, blinding them to the truth (Matt. 13:19; John 8:44; 2 Cor. 3:14; 4:4; 1 Tim. 2:14; Rev. 12:9; 20:3, 10). Postmodernism's attack on objective truth is just one of the more recent chapters in Satan's long history of deceiving and blinding the world from recognizing and accepting God as the ultimate source of truth (Num. 23:19; Isa. 65:16; John 1:14; 3:33; 7:28; Titus 1:2; Heb. 6:18; 1 John 5:20) and his word as a revelation of that truth (Ps. 19:7–11 [HB 8–12]; John 17:17; Eph. 1:13; 1 Thess. 2:13; 2 Tim. 2:15; James 1:18). Just as light shines the brightest in the darkest places, so too Christians have an opportunity to provide a stark contrast to those who are groping in darkness looking for truth. As countercultural as it may be, Christians today must reject relativism and unashamedly affirm and promote God's Word as the ultimate and unfailing source of truth.

Christ-followers today can also live out the ethics of God's coming kingdom by their commitment to love and unity within the church (both local and universal). Isaiah 2:4 highlights the theme of harmony and peace that will define people in God's future kingdom. It shouldn't surprise us then that Jesus similarly emphasized how unity and love for each other should be a characterizing mark of the present iteration of God's kingdom people—the church. Jesus's primary prayer request to the Father for his followers (including all his future ones) was that they would practice unity with each other in the same way that the Father, Son, and Holy Spirit practice unity within the Godhead (John 17:11, 20–26). Our love for fellow Christians would be the indicator of our genuine faith in Jesus (1 John 2:9–10; 3:10–23; 4:20–21).[4] In fact, the church's love for each other as brothers and sisters would be a primary incentive for the lost to want to become followers of Jesus (Mark 9:50; John 13:34–35; 17:21).

We can set the tone and refuse to engage in the same sort of angry rhetoric or ad

---

4   For additional passages pertinent to God's call for unity within the church, see Ps. 133:1–3; Prov. 6:16–19; Acts 4:32–35; Rom. 12:3–18; 14:1–15:7; 1 Cor. 1:10–17; 12:12–27; 2 Cor. 13:11–12; Eph. 2:11–21; 4:1–16; Phil. 1:27; 2:1–11; 1 Peter 3:8–12.

hominem attacks that have become so commonplace in societal discourse today. We should take to heart the words of the apostle Peter:

> For it is commendable if someone bears up under the pain of unjust suffering because they are conscious of God. But how is it to your credit if you receive a beating for doing wrong and endure it? But if you suffer for doing good and you endure it, this is commendable before God. To this you were called, because Christ suffered for you, leaving you an example, that you should follow in his steps. . . . When they hurled their insults at him, he did not retaliate; when he suffered, he made no threats. Instead, he entrusted himself to him who judges justly. (1 Peter 2:19–21, 23)

Finally, Christians must remember that the true utopian society will never be brought about by human governments, political parties, or modern-day social movements. Each new generation tends to be critical of the ones before it, assuming they have the answers that eluded their parents and grandparents. Yet the problems that have plagued this world ever since Adam and Eve ate the forbidden fruit will continue to afflict humankind until all is brought back under the all-wise, all-benevolent rule of the Creator God. Thus, we must be careful how much of ourselves we are willing to devote to political parties or movements. No human politician is going to be the savior of our nation in the truest sense. While nations would suffer greatly if Christians removed themselves entirely from the political discourse, it is equally true that believers must not allow political movements to detract from the primary goal of promoting a kingdom that is not of this world. "For here we do not have an enduring city, but we are looking for the city that is to come" (Heb. 13:14).

Creativity in Presentation

It would not be hard to pull a few headlines from the most recent news reports which highlight the brokenness of the world and the prevalence of destructive wars. To explain why God calls believers, living in this war-torn world, to live out the ideals of his future kingdom, consider describing it in terms of a movie trailer. Movie trailers are previews of upcoming attractions that are soon to be released. Usually, a preview will show some of the best scenes, the funniest lines, and the most awe-inspiring special effects from the movie. They provide just a snapshot of what the film will be about, without revealing how it ends or giving away any spoilers. If they are done right, they will whet the appetite of viewers, so they leave wanting to see that movie in its fullness once it arrives at the theater. This is the role of believers today. Our lives lived out in devotion to God according to a set of ideals and morals that stand in stark contrast to those of the secular, conflict-ridden world around us should whet the appetites of nonbelievers who see our lives so that they want to be a part of God's coming kingdom of justice and peace once it arrives (cf. Matt. 5:14–16; Phil. 2:15; 1 Peter 2:12). Our lives serve to illustrate to a lost world that, in the light of God's promise of a future kingdom, the best is yet to come!

- God's coming kingdom will be a time of unparalleled righteousness (2:1–3).

- God's coming kingdom will be a time of unparalleled justice (2:4a).

- God's coming kingdom will be a time of unparalled unity (2:4b).

- An invitation for God's people to live out these kingdom ideals now (2:5).

DISCUSSION QUESTIONS

1. Why does a person's view of truth matter so much?

2. In what ways have you noticed that our society downplays the reality or importance of truth?

3. How you have seen Satan try to cause division within the church?

4. What are some ways we could foster unity in our nation, particularly between fellow believers?

5. In what ways does a Christian's hope that the best is yet to come impact how we live now?

FOR FURTHER READING

Goldsworthy, Graeme. "Regeneration." *NDBT*, 720–23.

Guinness, Os. 2000. *Time for Truth: Living Free in a World of Lies, Hype, and Spin*. Grand Rapids: Baker.

Johnston, Graham. 2004. *Preaching to a Postmodern World: A Guide to Reaching Twenty-first-century Listeners*. Grand Rapids: Baker.

Osborn, L. H. "Creation." *NDBT*, 429–35.

Isaiah 2:6–22

EXEGETICAL IDEA
Isaiah urges Israel not to trust in weak humans because the Lord is ready to bring devastating judgment, through which he will exalt himself and humiliate the proud.

THEOLOGICAL FOCUS
The Lord's people should trust in the Sovereign Lord, not in human beings or man-made gods, for the Lord will annihilate arrogant men and their false gods as he exalts himself through judgment.

PREACHING IDEA
God will judge the proud and destroy every idol.

PREACHING POINTERS
Some forms of pride are rather easy to detect – like the cruel classmate who publicly makes fun of another student's appearance, or the know-it-all coworker who routinely speaks to others in a condescending way, or the professional athlete who declares himself the greatest of all time during a press conference immediately following an impressive victory. Most people find behaviors such as these objectionable and even repulsive. This is especially true if we are the student whose appearance is being belittled by our classmate or if we are a member of the athletic team whose defeat is being rubbed in by the pompous athlete on the opposing team.

Pride takes other forms besides bragging and gloating over others. Many of these are more subtle, and thus are easier to overlook. One wise Christian writer defined pride as "the stubborn refusal to let God be God, with the corresponding ambition to take his place. It is the attempt to dethrone God and enthrone ourselves. . . . [Pride is] the pretense that we can manage without God or rival God" (Stott 1992, 111–12).

This definition aptly describes how Judah was behaving when the prophet confronted them with the message recorded in Isaiah 2:6–22. They were attempting to live independently of the Lord. Rather than look to him for guidance and direction, they had begun to turn to fortune tellers and mediums. Rather than trust in Yahweh for security and protection, Judah placed their hope in accumulated wealth, human armies, and fortified walls. They attempted to replace God with idols of their own making. In the same way that we take offense when arrogant people demean and belittle us, God is even more offended—and righteously so, when people he created live in ways that belittle his importance or dismiss their need of him. Thus God opposes the proud, and there is coming a day when he will judge the haughty and arrogant along with their false idols.

THE DEMISE OF HUMAN PRIDE (2:6–22)

LITERARY STRUCTURE AND THEMES (2:6–22)

Having given a glimpse of the Lord's coming kingdom (2:1–5), Isaiah announces the coming day of the Lord, in which he will unleash terrifying and destructive judgment. The Lord will destroy mortal human beings and everything in which they place their trust, including the human-made idols they worship. In the process he will exalt himself as rightful king and the only genuine source of security. Consequently, the Lord's people must cease placing their trust in human beings.

As noted above, 2:5, which forms a fitting conclusion to the preceding speech, has a dual function in the structure of chapter 2. While verbal links with 2:3 connect 2:5 to what precedes, the reference to the "house of Jacob" also links it with what follows (cf. 2:6). It is transitional, concluding the preceding speech and, with 2:22, forming a hortatory frame around 2:6–21. In 2:5 the prophet encourages the people to look to the Lord for guidance, while in 2:22 he urges them not to trust in mere human beings for security. The exhortations reflect two sides of the same coin. Isaiah 2:22, like 2:5, also has a transitional function in the macrostructure of this section (see the discussion below of the structure of 3:1–15).

Isaiah 2:6–9 is in the form of a prayer, in which the prophet addresses the Lord. He observes that the Lord has abandoned the people, removing his protection from them (2:6a). Several reasons are given for the Lord's abandoning the people. They have embraced foreign, pagan practices such as divination and idolatry (2:6b, 9a). The nation has accumulated wealth, used to form alliances with other nations, and horses and chariots essential for any army in the prophet's day (2:7–8). The prophet concludes his prayer by urging the Lord not to forgive the rebellious people (2:9b).

The prophet then turns to the people, warning them to run for their lives before the Lord's terrifying judgment (2:10). Isaiah 2:11–17 expands on this announcement of judgment. The passage is marked out by an *inclusio* describing how proud men will be humiliated and the Lord alone will be exalted (2:11, 17; Williamson 2006, 227). Isaiah 2:12–16 identifies the objects of this judgment, using a series of metaphors for the high and mighty.

Isaiah 2:18–21 describes the people doing what the prophet urges them to do in 2:10. These verses develop in further detail the themes of 2:6–10, as the many verbal links between the two sections indicate:

silver and gold (vv. 7, 20)
idols (אֱלִילִים) (vv. 8, 18, 20)
bow down (vv. 8, 20)
make (vv. 8, 20)
rocky cliffs (vv. 10, 19, 21)
go into (vv. 10, 19, 21)
dust (vv. 10, 19)
from the terror of the Lord and his royal splendor (vv. 10, 19, 21)

Within the section there is a refrain (2:19b, 21b), which divides it into two subunits. The single line in 2:18 may seem unduly short, as if a corresponding line has been omitted. However, the truncation appears to be deliberate when one examines the structure of 2:18–21. The first subunit simply makes the point that idols will disappear (2:18), as their worshippers hide in the caves (2:19a) from the Lord's royal splendor (2:19b). The second subunit provides more detail. The worshippers will throw their idols to the rodents and bats (2:20) as they seek shelter (2:21a) from the Lord's royal splendor (2:21b). The technique of repetition with supplementation in paneled structures is a common rhetorical device in Hebrew narrative and poetry.

- *Denouncing Pagan Influences (2:6–9)*
- *A Stern Warning (2:10)*
- *The Day of the Lord (2:11–17)*
- *Idolaters Run for Cover (2:18–21)*
- *Wise Advice (2:22)*

EXPOSITION (2:6–22)

Denouncing Pagan Influences (2:6–9)
The Lord has removed his protection from his people because they have embraced paganism by trusting in divination, wealth, military might, and idols for security.

2:6. Having given a glimpse of what Zion would one day become and having urged the "house of Jacob" to live accordingly, the prophet turns to the Lord. He observes that the Lord has abandoned his own people, the house of Jacob (2:6).

> **House of Jacob**
> R. Davidson (1966, 1–7) argues that "house of Jacob" in 2:6 refers to the northern kingdom. His conclusions are based on speculation regarding the background of the oracle derived from a questionable diachronic critical method. The focus of the first five chapters of Isaiah is Jerusalem/Zion and Judah; see 1:8, 21, 26–27; 2:1, 2–4; 3:1, 8, 16–17; 4:3–5; 5:3, 7, 14. In the text's canonical form "the house of Jacob" most likely has the same referent in 2:6 as in 2:5, and the appeal of 2:5 is most naturally understood as directed to the residents of Judah/Zion (cf. 2:1).

The collocation of נָטַשׁ, "abandon," and "people" is rare. It occurs in 1 Samuel 12:22 and Psalm 94:14. In both texts the speaker affirms the Lord will not abandon his people. In both cases כִּי appears before the negated verb. One wonders if the prophet intentionally and ironically echoed Samuel's promise to the nation, using כִּי as a cue to draw attention to the link. In this context, divine abandonment entails the removal of his protection, promised in exchange for loyalty (cf. Isa. 1:19–20, as well as Judg. 6:13; 1 Kings 8:57–61; 2 Kings 21:12–15; Jer. 7:28–29; 12:7–8). The prophet knows exactly why (note כִּי in Isa. 2:6b) the Lord has abandoned his people (2:6b–9a). They depend on omens, wealth, military power, and idols for security. So the Lord has withdrawn his protective hand and, as Williamson (2006, 213) observes, "left them to their own devices."

The Mosaic Law prohibited divination in Israel (Deut. 18:10), but in the ancient Near East it was a popular form of discerning the divine will and receiving guidance for life (cf. Deut. 18:14). As John Walton shows, the divination outlawed in Deuteronomy 18 is a specific type. There were two main categories of "divination" in the ancient world—inspired and deductive: (1) "Inspired divination is initiated in the divine realm and uses a human intermediary" (Walton 2006, 240). This type of divination took the forms of official and informal prophecy, as well as dreams. (2) "Deductive divination" also originates in the divine realm, "but its revelation is communicated through events and phenomena that can be observed." It is this deductive type of divination that the law prohibited. The Lord communicated directly through prophecy and dreams, but he did not authorize the deductive methods so popular in the culture (Walton 2006, 249). Deductive divination involved the interpretation of omens, which could be active (provoked) or passive (unprovoked). Active omens included examining the internal organs of animals and casting lots, as well as other methods. Passive omens came in celestial, terrestrial, and physiognomic forms.[1] Omen reading was essentially an attempt to manipulate one's destiny. Once the (hypothetical) future was known, one could then seek to avoid disaster by using magic. Walton explains: "While divination is concerned with gaining knowledge, magic involves exercising power." Magic involved the use of incantations and rituals designed "to manipulate cosmic forces in pursuit of self-interest" and to ward off the danger associated with bad omens (Walton 2006, 265).

2:7. Accumulating wealth and building a chariot force were also violations of the Mosaic law. Knowing the people would eventually ask for a king as the nations had, Moses made it clear that they could not have such a king. The kings of the nations accumulated wealth and built armies, but Israel's king was not to do so (Deut. 17:16–17). Silver and gold would elevate a king's pride and self-sufficiency (2 Kings 20:13; Isa. 39:2) and could be used as tribute in an attempt to form alliances and make the nation secure (1 Kings 15:18–19; 20:3–7; 2 Kings 14:14; 16:8; 18:14; 23:33–35). Such wealth easily became a source of false security for the kings of Israel and Judah and a substitute for the Lord's protective power.

The same was true of horses and chariots. In the second millennium B.C. warrior-kings of Near Eastern armies began to use horse-drawn chariots as a vital part of their military arsenal. The Old Testament frequently describes powerful armies—including those of Egypt, Assyria, and Babylon—as containing horses and chariots (Exod. 14:9, 23; Josh. 11:4; 1 Kings 20:1; 2 Kings 6:14–15; Isa. 5:28; Jer. 4:13; 46:9; Ezek. 26:10–11; Nah. 3:2; Zech. 9:10). The horse was a symbol of military might, and its very appearance and mannerisms struck fear into the heart of those being attacked (Jer. 8:16; Hab. 1:8). Because of its military importance, the horse was viewed as a guarantee of security (cf. Isa. 30:16) and an object of trust (Ps. 20:7 [HB 8]). In the Phoenician Karatepe inscription Azitawaddu boasts that he "acquired horse upon horse" with the aid of Baal and the gods (*COS* 2.31:149).

However, Yahweh, the covenant God of Israel, wanted his people to trust in his ability to protect and deliver, not in horses and chariots. From the very beginning of Israel's history, the Lord demonstrated his superiority to the chariot forces of the nations (Exod. 14–15; Josh. 11; Judg. 4–5) and he expected his people to trust in his power for military victory. After all, horses are made of mere flesh (Isa. 31:3) and are no match for the Lord, whose supernatural enablement is the true key to success in battle (Pss. 20:7 [HB 8]; 33:17–20; 76:5–7 [HB 6–8]; 147:10–11; Prov. 21:31; Isa. 30:15–16; 31:3; Hos. 14:3). But Solomon began to accumulate horses and chariots (1 Kings 10:26–29) and by Isaiah's time they were an essential part of Judah's military (see *NIDOTTE* 3:234–36).

2:8–9a. To make matters even worse, the people were worshipping worthless idols. The term אֱלִילִים is usually translated simply "idols," but the word highlights the worthless nature of these objects of worship. The adjective אֱלִיל is used elsewhere of worthless, ineffective physicians (Job 13:4), shepherds (Zech. 11:17), and divination practices (Jer. 14:14 *qere*). When applied to idols, the term is a derogatory epithet that highlights their inability to help those who trust in them.

In bowing before idols, the people engaged in a form of self-abasement that foreshadowed their impending judgment. Most of the translations interpret Isaiah 2:9a as if judgment is in view: HCSB, NIV, NLT, NRSV, *Tanakh* all use "humbled" and "brought low" or "brought low" and "humbled." Contrary to these, KJV ("boweth down" and "humbleth himself") understands this as a reference to worship. The

---

[1] This summary of deductive divination is based on Walton 2006, 249–63.

verbs are used of the effects of judgment in 2:11 and 17, but this does not seem to be the case here. In 2:11 (וְשָׁפֵל וְשַׁח) and 2:17 (וְשַׁח . . .) they appear in the *weqatal* form, as one expects in predictive discourse. But in 2:9 they are used in the *wayyiqtol* form, which is consistent with the narrative pattern of 2:7–8. It is preferable then to interpret them as part of the prophet's accusation, not the announcement of judgment, which begins in 2:10 with the prophet's exhortation to the people to run and hide. If part of the accusation, the verbs could be taken as describing their worship of idols (cf. 2:8). However, the verbs שָׁחַח and שָׁפֵל are not used elsewhere in this way, though שָׁחַח is used of bowing in submission in Isaiah 60:6. Perhaps they are used ironically. In bowing down to idols (the verb in 2:8 is חָוָה) the people had consequently become abased (Motyer 1993, 56; Williamson 2006, 217). The verbs also point ahead to the impending judgment, in which their self-abasement would be mirrored by divine judgment. Marvin Sweeney (1988, 176) observes, "the point of the whole oracle" is "that man's desire to lower himself with false gods (v. 6–9) leads to YHWH's lowering man." There is poetic justice here.

2:9b. Often prophets, following the example set by Moses, assumed the role of intercessor for the people, praying the Lord would show mercy and delay or postpone judgment (see Exod. 32:11–13; Jer. 14:7–9, 13, 19–22; Ezek. 22:30; Amos 7:1–9). However, rather than interceding and trying to convince God not to judge the people, Isaiah urges him not to forgive their sin. The appeal, which uses the verb נָשָׂא, "lift up," used here in the sense of "forgive," has a sarcastic tone. The people bowed low before their idols and shamefully abased themselves (Isa. 2:8–9a), so the prophet asks the Lord not to "lift them up." This may express the prophet's disgust at what he saw all around him. But in the light of his exhortations to proper behavior and repentance (cf. 1:16–20; 2:5, 22), it may be rhetorical. At the illocutionary level, it affirms divine justice and the people's guilt. From a purely objective perspective, they deserve to be punished.

A Stern Warning (2:10)
To signal impending doom, the prophet dramatically urges the people to hide from the Lord's terrifying presence.

The prophet depicts the Lord in terms familiar in the culture. The motif of a mighty warrior-king's enemies fleeing for shelter in caves and high places (see also 2:19, 21) is a theme that appears in the Neo-Assyrian royal annals and in Egyptian royal texts. For example, the Assyrian king Tiglath-pileser I described himself as a warrior "whose fierce battle all princes of the (four) quarters dreaded and took to hiding places like bats and scurried off to inaccessible regions" (Grayson 1976, 2:26). In a poetic account of Pharaoh Thutmose III's victory over his enemies, it is stated that "they hid in holes" when they heard the king's battle cry (Lichtheim 1976, 36). The motif also appears in the Ugaritic myths, where Baal's thunderous voice causes his enemies to flee to the forests and mountains (*COS* 1.86:262–63). One also finds the image of the warrior-king's terrifying splendor in ancient Near Eastern texts. In the Assyrian royal inscriptions, the king's *melammu*, "radiance" (cf. *CAD* 10.2 s.v. "melammu" 9–12), sometimes has a debilitating effect on the enemy. For example, Sennacherib boasted: "He, Hezekiah, was overwhelmed by the awesome splendor [*melammu*] of my lordship" (*COS* 2.119B:303).

The Day of the Lord (2:11–17)
In his day of battle the Lord will bring down all who are proud and will elevate himself.

2:11, 17. The Lord will direct his judgment against human pride (2:11, 17). Isaiah 2:11 mentions the proud look (cf. "eyes") of man being brought low, while in 2:17 man himself is brought down. Both verses declare that the

Lord will be exalted through judgment. Perhaps the most striking element in the description is לְבַדּוֹ, "alone." The following verses describe the Lord striking down all that is high and mighty; he alone will be recognized as king in the aftermath of the judgment. This theme has already appeared in the preceding literary unit, where the nations are pictured streaming to the Lord's temple as they seek his royal decrees (2:2–4), and it will be highlighted in subsequent passages (cf. 5:15–16), especially in Isaiah's vision of "the King" seated high on his throne (6:1–5). Here we see that the Lord establishes his kingship on earth through military might directed against proud forces that oppose him.

2:12. Isaiah 2:11 and 17 speak of judgment arriving "in that day." Isaiah 2:12 elaborates on the nature of this day. It belongs, as it were, to the Lord of Armies—a title that depicts, at least in this context, the Lord as a warrior who leads armies into battle (see comments above on 1:9). As already indicated in 2:11, it is directed against the proud, but 2:12 adds "all," emphasizing its thorough nature. None of the proud will escape. (For a fuller discussion of the theme of "day of the Lord," see below under "Theological Focus.")

2:13–16. In these verses the prophet uses four metaphors that aptly describe the proud: tall and strong trees, high mountains and hills, a strongly defended city, and merchant ships (Oswalt 1986, 126). At the same time, Judah and its leaders would have taken pride in all these things (Smith 2007, 140). It appears that the literal and symbolic are combined here.

Michael Barré (2003, 525) observes a chiastic pattern in 2:13–17: The first two sets are natural entities, while the last two sets are man-made things. The first set (trees) is a natural entity made of wood, while the fourth set (ships) is a man-made item composed of wood. The second set (mountains) is a natural entity composed of earth and stone, while the third set (a fortified walled city) is a man-made thing composed of earth and stone.

The cedars of Lebanon were well known for their height (2 Kings 19:23 = Isa. 37:24; Ps. 92:13 [Eng. 12]; Ezek. 27:5; 31:3); they could grow as high as thirty-five meters (approximately 115 ft.; King and Stager 2001, 25). Along with the strong oaks of Bashan, they are an appropriate symbol for the high and mighty because they were the most impressive trees known to ancient Israelites. David and Solomon used them to construct beautiful buildings that became a source of human pride (2 Sam. 5:11; 1 Kings 5:20–24 [Eng. 6–10]). During Solomon's reign, many buildings in Jerusalem were constructed from cedar (1 Kings 10:27). In the Lord's speech against Sennacherib, he compared Judah and Jerusalem to the cedars of Lebanon (Isa. 37:24).

High mountains and hills also symbolize the proud. They rise above the surrounding terrain, as if ruling over the landscape. They also seem stable and unmovable (Gen. 49:26; Deut. 33:15; Pss. 65:7 [Eng. 6]; 68:16–17 [Eng. 15–16]; 76:5 [Eng. 4]; Hab. 3:6). Judah is described as a land of mountains (Isa. 14:25; cf. Ps. 125:2) and Jerusalem/Zion was situated on a mountain/hill (cf. Isa. 10:32; 31:4), so this announcement of an assault against the mountains/hills was ominous.

Towers and walls defended Judah's cities, giving their inhabitants a sense of security. Consequently, the announcement that the Lord was targeting them in the day of judgment would have disturbed Isaiah's audience. The image of a well-fortified city, like that of the cedar and oak, combines the ideas of height and strength. The city tower looked down on all that was around it and was a place of refuge (Judg. 9:51; Ps. 61:4 [Eng. 3]; Prov. 18:10), while the fortified wall made the city seemingly impenetrable and secure (Deut. 3:5; Isa. 26:1; Jer. 15:20). They are apt symbols for self-secure proud humans.

The ships are linked structurally and conceptually with the trees, for the wood of the cedar and oak was used in the construction of ships and oars (cf. Ezek. 27:5–6).

The ships mentioned here, though small by modern standards, were seagoing vessels that were the finest of their time. The "ships of Tarshish" were so-called because they could make the long journey to Tarshish (1 Kings 10:22; 22:49 [Eng. 48]; 2 Chron. 9:21; Isa. 60:9; Lessing 2004, 140). The precise location of Tarshish is uncertain, the most likely options being Tartessus in Spain or Tarsus in modern Turkey. Philip King and Lawrence Stager (2001, 184) observe that these ships "are frequently associated with both maritime trade and metals" (cf. Isa. 23:1–3; Ezek. 27:25). In 1999 archaeologists discovered two Phoenician ships that were wrecked at sea sometime between 750 and 700 B.C. Each was transporting more than twelve tons of wine at the time it sank. The ships were about sixteen meters (approximately fifty-three feet) long and six meters (approximately twenty feet) wide. Reliefs from Sennacherib's palace depict such ships leaving the harbor at Tyre (King and Stager 2001, 178–85). These ships make an appropriate symbol of the proud because they were the finest of their class. They were also a product of human ingenuity and skill, designed to make cities and nations rich and powerful through trade.

> **Ships**
> The term שְׂכִיּוֹת (a plural form of שְׂכִיָּה) in 2:16b occurs only here (see HALOT s.v. "שְׂכִיָּה" 1327), but we can identify it as referring to some type of ship based on the parallelism within the verse and a Ugaritic cognate. Usage in Ugaritic suggests that אֳנִיָּה is a generic term for a ship, while שְׂכִיָּה refers to a specific type of ship. See Cohen 1978, 41–42. As the Hebrew text of 2:16 stands, הַחֶמְדָּה, "desire," is a genitive of attribute, indicating the quality of these ships.

Idolaters Run for Cover (2:18–21)
As they flee in panic from the Lord's terrifying presence, idolaters will discard their worthless, human-made images.

2:18, 20. The point is clear—these idols can provide no protection from the Lord's judgment (2:18, cf. 2:8). The verb used to describe their disappearance (חָלַף) contributes to the derogatory portrayal of the idols in this speech. It is used elsewhere of things that appear but then quickly move on or disappear (Job 9:26 [reed boats floating down a river]; Ps. 90:5–6 [grass]; Song 2:11 [rain]; Isa. 21:1; and Hab. 1:11 [wind]; HALOT s.v. "חלף I" 321). Throwing the idols to the rodents and bats (Isa. 2:20) suggests that in the end the worshippers realize that their man-made images are of no value and belong with the unclean animals that inhabit holes and dark places. Though they are made of silver and gold, they provide no protection (see Oswalt 1986, 128).

2:19, 21. The refrain of 2:19, expanded in 2:21, echoes 2:10, but with the additional image of the Lord rising to terrify the land. Most translate אֶרֶץ as "earth." The imagery of 2:12–16 does have a cosmic flavor about it, but אֶרֶץ is better taken here as referring to the land of Judah, the primary object of the Lord's judgment in this speech (cf. 2:7–8). The text describes the fearful response of those who witness the Lord's arrival; here it specifically makes the point that he intervenes for the very purpose of terrifying the objects of his judgment.

Wise Advice (2:22)
The prophet exhorts the people to stop putting their trust in mortal human beings.

At the beginning of 2:22 the Hebrew text has simply, "cease for yourselves from man." It does not state specifically what they are to cease doing. Most likely "cease from" carries the notion "cease being concerned about," as in 1 Samuel 9:5, where it can be translated "stop thinking about" (NIV) or "cease to be concerned about" (NASB). As noted above, the concluding exhortation combines with Isaiah 2:5 to form a frame for this speech. People should look for guidance to the Lord, not mortal human beings.

If even the highest and mightiest of men will be brought low by God's judgment, then it makes little sense to put one's trust in human alliances or human-made images.

THEOLOGICAL FOCUS

The theological focus of this passage can be stated as follows: the Lord's people should trust in the Sovereign Lord, not in human beings or human-made gods, for the Lord will annihilate arrogant people and their false gods as he exalts himself through judgment. As the prophet develops this theological theme, a few emphases emerge:

1. The Lord's sovereign power, in contrast to proud, but frail human beings

The Lord's sovereign power is the central theme of this speech. He is the Lord who leads armies (2:12) and is exalted in judgment (2:11). His mere appearance causes the objects of his judgment to flee in terror (2:10, 19, 21). Human beings, by way of contrast, are described as proud but, despite their hubris, are really frail (2:22) and destined for humiliation and defeat (2:11, 17), because they abase themselves by worshipping worthless idols (2:9, 20).

2. The folly of worshipping idols and trusting in human beings for security

Human beings seek security through divination, idolatry, alliances, and military might, but in the end none of these can insulate them from the Lord's terrifying judgment. The idols are the worthless product of human hands (2:8, 20). Those who willingly abase themselves and bow down before such images rather than the sovereign God and King end up running for their lives and seeking shelter in dark places that were created for rodents and bats, not human beings, to live (2:9, 19, 21). The human creators of the idols are mortal, sustained by the mere breath in their nostrils (2:22) that was imparted at creation (Gen. 2:7; Isa. 42:5). If God withdrew this breath of life, all human beings would die instantly (Job 34:14–15). In fact, Isaiah later observes that God tempers his judgment with mercy because otherwise frail human beings would perish (Isa. 57:16).

3. The day of the Lord as a day of divine self-revelation in judgment

Isaiah 2:12 speaks of the day of the Lord of Armies; it is a time of terrifying judgment in which he exalts himself. The theme of the day of the Lord is an important element in the Old Testament's portrayal of him as divine warrior. According to Douglas Stuart (1976, 159), the expression may be derived from a "widespread ancient Near Eastern tradition" that a mighty warrior-king "could complete a military campaign, or even an entire war of conquest against his enemies in a single day."[2] Generally speaking, the day of the Lord is an idiom used to highlight the Lord's "universal power and authority," which "insure that his victory will be accomplished swiftly and suddenly" (p. 163). In the Old Testament it may refer to either a particular historical judgment on a specific nation or to a culminating eschatological battle.

Sometimes it is a day of judgment against the Lord's own people, including the northern kingdom of Israel (at the hands of the Assyrians, Amos 5:18, 20), Judah (at the hands of the Babylonians, Lam. 1:12; 2:1, 21–22; Ezek. 7:19; 13:5; Zeph. 2:2–3), and the postexilic community (Joel 1:15; 2:1–2, 11; this judgment was averted when God had compassion on his

---

2 Stuart's thirteen supporting examples from the ancient Near East come from Sumerian, Assyrian, Syrian, Hittite, Canaanite, Egyptian, and Moabite texts, and span a time period from roughly 2000 B.C. to 830 B.C. The motif appears to be a common one, not restricted to a particular time or place. Citing Stuart's work favorably, Aster (2007, 259) argues that this motif of the sovereign's day of conquest "provides the most appropriate comparative context with which to analyze" Isaiah 2:5–22.

people, Joel 2:18). Sometimes the judgment of God's people appears in a cosmic framework (Zeph. 1:18). This judgment will bring both intense suffering (Zech. 14:1–3) and restoration (Isa. 61:2; Mal. 4:5) for Israel.

At other times the day of the Lord involves judgment on foreign nations (Joel 3:14 [HB 4:14]), including Babylon (at the hands of the Medes, Isa. 13:17–19; cf. 13:6, 9), Egypt (at the hands of the Babylonians, Jer. 46:10; Ezek. 30:3), Edom (Isa. 34:8–9; Obad. 15), and a northern coalition headed by Gog (Ezek. 39:8). In some cases, these ancient historical nations appear to be archetypes of the Lord's eschatological foes, as the cosmic elements in Isaiah 13 and Obadiah suggest.

To summarize, the day of the Lord encompasses several specific historical "days" or events, including among others the defeat of the northern kingdom, the Babylonian exile, Babylon's conquest of Egypt, and the fall of Babylon.[3] These examples of the Lord's intervention in history foreshadow and preview that final time period when he will annihilate his enemies on a cosmic scale.

PREACHING AND TEACHING STRATEGIES

Exegetical and Theological Synthesis

The prophet begins by expressing how the Lord has rejected his people Judah (house of Jacob; Isa. 2:6). He explains why in the verses that follow: it is because Judah has rejected him in exchange for other false gods/idols. Rather than looking to the Lord for guidance and direction, the people of Judah elected instead to turn to diviners and omen-readers like the pagans around them (2:6). Instead of relying on the Lord for their well-being and protection, God's people took comfort in their accumulated wealth and in the size and strength of their army (2:7). They even filled their land with the idols that the surrounding peoples worshipped. They chose to bow down to them in hopes of currying favor with these imaginary gods (2:8).

In the verses that follow, God warned the people that a day of judgment was coming, at which time he would humble those who have lifted themselves up against him in pride. Four distinct times the prediction is made that the proud and lofty ones will be brought low (2:9, 11, 12, and 17). The proud here are poetically likened to various things—the cedars of Lebanon and the oak trees of Bashan (2:13), the lofty mountains or uplifted hills (2:14), the high towers and fortified walls that surrounded strong cities (2:15), and the merchant ships used to carry out international trade (2:16). These were fitting metaphors for the proud for at least two reasons. First, these objects were themselves large or elevated in size. Thus, they illustrated the exalted posture of the proud ones. Additionally, most of these objects were literally used by the proud to gain or maintain their sense of security, and thus their lack of felt need for the Lord. The cedars and oak trees would have been used to build things like gates and merchant ships. The high towers and fortified walls, along with horses and chariots, provided a false sense of safety and security from foreign invaders. The lofty mountains and uplifted hills upon which cities such as Jerusalem were built added to the sense of protection and well-being in the event of a war. Finally, the ships provided a source of ongoing income in their accumulation of wealth. As such, the proud and arrogant people of Judah were closely associated with these objects.

This passage continues with a twofold prediction, warning Judah about a coming "day" of judgment (2:11, 12, 17, 20). Both aspects of this prediction are repeated for emphasis. The first part of the prediction is that all the worthless idols that these people have made and elevated against the true God will

---

3   See further Everson 1974, 329–37.

be utterly destroyed on that day of judgment (2:18, 20). In fact, the people themselves will cast away the very idols they had made for themselves (2:20). Evidently, it will become apparent to them in the day of God's wrath just how useless and impotent they are to provide salvation. Second, the people themselves will run to the caves on that day, trying their best to hide "from the fearful presence of the Lord" and "from the splendor of his majesty" (2:19, 21).

Isaiah 2 concludes with a stern word of advice to "stop regarding man" so highly. After all, "of what account is he?" (2:22 ESV).

Preaching Idea
God will judge the proud and destroy every idol.

Contemporary Connections

What does it mean?
First, this statement asserts that God will one day judge the proud and humble them before him. The Bible teaches that God hates pride (Ps. 5:4–5 [HB 5–6]; Prov. 6:16–17; 8:13; 16:5), and that he actively opposes those who are proud and arrogant (James 4:6; 1 Peter 5:5). For this reason, there is a day coming when the wicked will stand before their creator to give an account of their lives (Eccl. 11:9; 12:14; Matt. 16:27; 25:31–46; John 5:27–29; Acts 17:31; Rom. 2:5–9; 14:10; 1 Cor. 4:5; 2 Cor. 5:10; 2 Tim. 4:1; Heb. 6:2; Jude 14–15; Rev. 20:11–15). On that day, wicked people who thumbed their nose at God will be put in their rightful position. In fact, they will be forced to bow their knees low in humility before Jesus in recognition of his lordship and preeminence over all (Isa. 45:23; Rom. 14:11; 1 Cor. 15:24–25; Phil. 2:10–11).

Second, this statement affirms that every idol will be exposed by God to be artificial and impotent to satisfy the needs of humanity. But this raises the question, "What constitutes an idol?" Modern people might be inclined to assume that a warning about idols doesn't pertain to them. An idol may seem like an outdated concept from at least as far back as the ancient Greco-Roman world. However, an idol is anything other than the true God that people look to for ultimate joy, security, acceptance, peace, life purpose, and the rest. It is anything that a person wants so badly because they believe it is necessary for their life to be meaningful or satisfying (Eph. 5:5; Col. 3:5). Thus, one is often willing to sacrifice just about anything to obtain or maintain it.

As one author succinctly puts it,

> Each culture is dominated by its own set of idols. Each has its "priesthoods," its totems and rituals. Each one has its shrines—whether office towers, spas and gyms, studios, or stadiums—where sacrifices must be made in order to procure the blessings of the good life and ward off disaster. (Keller 2009, xi–xii)

Is it true?
Why would God single out the sin of pride over and above every other sin? What makes it such a serious offense in his eyes? Every sin is rooted, at some level, in a spirit of pride. Pride assumes I know better than God, and thus my ways are superior to his. Likewise, pride causes one to adopt an exalted posture of self-sufficiency and independence from God. As one author writes, "[Every] temptation is an enticement to live independently of God" (Anderson 2000, 146).

God designed humans to have all their basic needs and desires met by him. For example, our need for love and acceptance wasn't intended to be fulfilled by a romantic relationship with a significant other or by the shallow approval of other people. Rather, this need would be fulfilled in the perfect love of God for us and his acceptance of those who identify with Jesus through faith. Similarly, humanity's deep desire to find meaning and purpose in life was not to be found exclusively in a career, earthly accomplishments, financial success, or even in something as noble as raising responsible children. While those things can be meaningful in one sense, apart from God they are lacking in eternal significance. Only God can infuse these and other human pursuits with lasting meaning. It is pride then that drives one to craft their own gods/idols to meet their most basic needs and desires. The result of these efforts is that God is robbed of the worship and glory he deserves. C. J. Mahaney summarizes this well:

> Pride takes innumerable forms but has only one end: self-glorification. That's the motive and ultimate purpose of pride—to rob God of legitimate glory and to pursue self-glorification, contending for supremacy with Him. The proud person seeks to glorify himself and not God, thereby attempting in effect to deprive God of something only He is worthy to receive. No wonder God opposes pride. No wonder He *hates* pride. (2005, 32, emphasis original)

Now what?
The only appropriate response to pride in one's life is to willingly humble oneself before God (Lev. 26:41–42; 1 Kings 21:29; 2 Kings 22:19; 2 Chron. 7:14; 12:7; Prov. 3:34; 29:23; Dan. 10:12; Matt. 18:4; 23:12; Luke 14:11; James 4:6–10; 1 Peter 5:6). But what does humility actually look like? There is a tendency among many to substitute modesty for humility. That is to say, most human efforts at humility amount to superficial attempts to *appear* humble in the eyes of others. For example, rather than saying "Thank you" when someone pays us a compliment, we might say, "Praise God," or "I'm just happy to have been used by God." Many will even espouse some form of self-deprecation, insisting that their efforts were nothing significant or that others would have done a much better job than they did had they been given the opportunity. Some may even go so far as to portray a "woe is me" or an "I'm no good" persona in an attempt to convey a deeply contrite spirit. Rarely are these expressions of humility a sincere reflection of what is in one's heart, though. They are mostly just attempts at *appearing* humble before others. Ironically, the desire to appear humble may actually be an expression of pride.

It is important for us to recognize, however, that true humility is not expressed in self-loathing or a diminishing of one's potential to do meaningful things well. Jesus's life was the purest example of humility from start to finish. And yet Jesus didn't go around minimizing his own worth or abilities or downplaying his potential to make a meaningful impact on the world. Instead, Jesus demonstrated his humility first in his willingness to submit his own will to that of the Father (Matt. 6:10; 26:39, 42; Luke 22:42; John 5:30, 43; 6:38; 12:28; 14:31; Rom. 15:3), and secondly in his willingness to assume the posture of a servant toward others (Matt. 11:29; 20:26–28; Mark 10:45; Luke 22:7; John 13:14–15; Phil. 2:5–8).

True humility then is expressed first and foremost in recognizing the supremacy of God and intentionally living for his glory rather than our own. This means that we are always seeking to submit our will to his will. When we are confronted by the reality of our own sinful rebellion, our response is to confess to God that we have done wrong and to repent in our hearts. This leads to change, so that we can align ourselves moving forward with what God wants. Not surprisingly, many of the times when the Scriptures affirm that someone acted in humility is when they have walked according to God's laws (Deut. 8:2; 2 Sam. 22:26–28; Pss. 18:25–27 [HB 26–28]; 25:8–10; Isa. 66:2; Mic. 6:8; Zeph. 2:3; 3:11–13) or when they repented before God of their sins (Lev. 26:41; 1 Kings 21:29; 2 Kings 22:19; 2 Chron. 7:14; 12:1–7; 36:12; Ps. 55:19 [HB 20]; Jer. 44:10; Dan. 4:37; 5:22; 10:12).

Additionally, humility accepts the fact that we desperately need God, that it is in him that "we live and move and have our being; for we are indeed his offspring" (Acts 17:28; cf. Deut.

8:3; Ezra 8:21; Ps. 34:1–3 [HB 2–4]; Zeph. 3:12). Thus, we continually look to the Lord to meet all our basic needs for love, acceptance, purpose, security, peace, happiness, hope, and more.

Finally, humility involves actively working to serve the needs of others. In the same way that Jesus practiced his humility by willingly serving humankind, so too we are called to serve others as an act of humility. Jesus taught his disciples that whoever would aspire to greatness among them would need to volunteer to be last, that is, to be a servant of all (Mark 9:33–35). Similarly, Paul urged the believers in Philippi, out of humility, to consider the needs of others as more significant than their own (Phil. 2:3–4). He pointed to Jesus's example of humility as the paradigm after which Christians were to pattern their own humility. Thus, we can see that a humble person is not one who goes around with their head hung low feeling that they are less important than everybody else. That person probably wouldn't accomplish much of anything for God. Rather, it is a person who looks for opportunities to actively set aside his/her own desires and needs to serve others in the name and power of Jesus.

Finally, this passage should serve as a warning for believers to examine their own lives for any cultural idols they may have erected to meet needs or wants that can only legitimately be met in Jesus. Kyle Idleman's book *Gods at War* (2013) does an excellent job of surveying the most common idols in American culture today. He explores how our culture looks to food, sex, entertainment, success, money, achievement, romance, family, and "me" to obtain our basic needs for pleasure, power, and love. All too often, Christians drift from simply enjoying these things as wonderful gifts from God into viewing them as ultimate things (idols) that sadly become a substitute for God. The result is that these idols distract us from truly pursuing God the way he intended. In the same way that Judah had placed their full trust in things like silver and gold, horses and chariots, and ships and city walls as substitutes for trusting in God (Isa. 2:7–8, 15–16), so too many modern believers place their hopes and dreams in the things of this world to bring them security, peace of mind, and happiness. We must ask the Holy Spirit to help us identify the idols in our own lives, and look instead to God as the source of all that we need. We must be prepared to make changes in our thinking and behavior to reorient our lives wholly around Jesus Christ rather than whatever idols God reveals to us.

Creativity in Presentation

The people confronted by Isaiah in this passage were placing their trust in the military technology of their day. Things like chariots and fortified walls were effective from a human perspective in providing a sense of security from the military threats of the day. The preacher/teacher might consider beginning their message by describing some examples of modern or up-and-coming military technology that provides powerful nations today with a sense of security and superiority over military threats from geopolitical enemies. For example, a 2016 article in *Kiplinger* magazine (online) surveys eight amazing new military technologies. One new invention is a self-steering bullet. "Packed with tiny sensors," this .50-caliber bullet "can change course rapidly in midair, potentially giving even a mediocre shooter sniper-like accuracy, with the ability to hit moving targets with ease." Another invention this article highlights is a "satellite melter." The plan would be to send a satellite into orbit that would have the ability to reflect rays from the sun onto an enemy's satellite. Over the course of a couple weeks, the heat from the sun's rays will heat the satellite just enough to cause it to fall out of orbit and burn up on reentry into the upper stratosphere.[4]

Timothy Keller illustrates the nature and power of the modern-day idol of wealth in

---

4   https://www.kiplinger.com/slideshow/business/t057-s010-amazing-military-technologies/index.html.

the opening paragraphs of his book *Counterfeit Gods* (2009). In the immediate aftermath of the global economic collapse in 2008, there was a string of suicides by people who had formerly been extremely wealthy but had lost much of their wealth overnight. The CEO of Sheldon Good, a leading US real estate auction firm, shot himself while sitting behind the wheel of his Jaguar. Another man, a money manager who had lost $1.4 billion of his clients' money in Bernie Madoff's Ponzi scheme, took his life by slitting his wrists in his New York City office. Keller lists several other examples of extraordinarily wealthy and successful people who apparently felt they had nothing left to live for once they had lost all their money. Their lives so revolved around their image as wealthy and successful people, not to mention the creature comforts they had grown accustomed to, that their lives were essentially over the moment it was gone.

Proverbs 16:18 says, "Pride goes before destruction, a haughty spirit before a fall." I used to play a game with my daughters when they were younger using jumbo Lego® blocks. We would see how tall of a tower we could build before it would fall over. We would try to build the bottom of the structure wide and strong to give it a firm base. But to make it tall, we eventually had to stack one block upon another upon another. This made for a very weak and wobbly structure the higher we built. Eventually, it would inevitably come crashing down, and the two of us would laugh. Then we would try again to see if we could get it higher than the last time. In the same way that a Lego® tower gets weaker and more wobbly the higher we exalt the structure, so too the more one exalts himself/herself in pride, the more likely and susceptible they are to come crashing down to earth. If you have access to some large Lego® blocks, you may consider building a structure and then adding pieces to it during the sermon/lesson to illustrate the pride others display when they exalt themselves inappropriately. You may even write descriptions on the sides of different blocks, of various types of pride people exhibit in their life. One block might say "boasting about accomplishments." Another might say "social media" to refer to times when some use their social media posts to brag about themselves to others. Other blocks might say "prayerlessness," "unforgiveness," "a critical spirit," "rebellion against authority," "gossip," "self-righteousness," "talking too much," "inconsiderate of others," "failure to seek counsel," "vanity" (about your appearance), "stubbornness," "unrepentant sin," and more. The goal would be to stack these blocks one on top of the other until the tower comes crashing down onto the stage. This illustration would serve as a visual reminder that God will ultimately judge the proud and destroy every idol exalted over him.

- Idols were the reason for coming judgment (2:6–8).
  - The idol of acceptance (6)
  - The idol of comfort (7a)
  - The idol of security (7b)
  - The idol of accomplishment (8)
- Idols are an indicator of human pride (2:9–17).
- Idols will be revealed as ultimately ineffectual (2:18–22).

The Demise of Human Pride (2:6–22)

DISCUSSION QUESTIONS

1. In what ways is our culture similar to Judah's, as described by the prophet in Isaiah 2:6–8?

2. Satan's original sin was born out of pride. How might this impact his strategy in our lives today?

3. What are some ways that Christians today dethrone God, or live our lives as though we are trying to manage without him?

4. What are the prominent "idols" in our culture, and how do they function to replace God in our lives?

FOR FURTHER READING

Idleman, Kyle. 2013. *Gods at War: Defeating the Idols That Battle for Your Heart*. Grand Rapids: Zondervan.

Keller, Timothy. 2009. *Counterfeit Gods: The Empty Promises of Money, Sex, and Power, and the Only Hope That Matters*. New York: Penguin.

Mahaney, C. J. 2005. *Humility: True Greatness*. Sisters, OR: Multnomah.

Isaiah 3:1–4:6

EXEGETICAL IDEA
The Lord's judgment targets Judah's unjust leaders, vindicates the righteous, and humiliates the proud women of Jerusalem. Following his purifying judgment, a remnant will experience agricultural blessing and the Lord's protection.

THEOLOGICAL FOCUS
The Lord punishes leaders who refuse to guide his people in his ways and take pride in status acquired at the expense of others. Yet his purifying judgment leads to the restoration of his blessing and protection.

PREACHING IDEA
Sin results in devastation. Nevertheless, God still offers hope.

PREACHING POINTERS
On the evening of December 10, 2021, a tornado system moved through Western Kentucky, leaving several towns with significant damage. One of the hardest-hit communities was the town of Mayfield. Among the establishments destroyed that night was Mayfield Consumer Products, a candle factory where 110 employees were working at that time. The storm caused the factory's roof to collapse, killing eight employees while injuring many others. In the aftermath of the storm, twenty-two people lost their lives in Mayfield alone, with hundreds more injured. In addition to the lives lost that day, many of the survivors lost their homes or businesses. As a result, many residents lost their jobs as well. In the aftermath of a disaster like this, people are left wondering: "How could this happen?" "Is there any reason at this point for hope?"

The imagery in Isaiah 3 records a similar sort of devastation like that after a natural disaster. It describes the city of Jerusalem immediately following a major military defeat, probably following a long siege. As a result, much of the city's walls and infrastructure have been demolished. Any wealth or valuables have been looted and stolen. Worst of all, most of the young men have either been killed or captured and deported by the enemy. Those left behind are forced to figure out how to carry on without anyone qualified to lead them. Isaiah reveals that this horrible outcome would come upon Judah because of the people's sin and God's subsequent judgment. They would be reaping what they had sown (3:9, 11). Nonetheless, God assures those who remain faithful to him, the righteous ones, that it would ultimately be well with them (3:10). The unit ends with imagery of hope as the righteous remnant of Israel is beautiful and glorious once again. The God who brought judgment will be the same one who purifies and restores his people. He will again become their savior and protector, a refuge and shelter from the storm and rain.

RETRIBUTION, VINDICATION, HUMILIATION, AND RESTORATION (3:1–4:6)

LITERARY STRUCTURE AND THEMES (3:1–4:6)

The Lord will judge Judah for its stubborn rebellion, and shatter the stability of society. This just judgment targets the unjust leaders of the Lord's covenant community. The Lord will humiliate the women of Jerusalem, whose demeanor and dress reflect their pride in their status, which was achieved at the expense of the oppressed. The death in battle of the city's men leaves the women mourning and desperately competing for husbands. The righteous remnant that survives judgment will take delight in the Lord's abundant blessings and enjoy special status as his covenant people. The Lord will purify his covenant community through judgment and then restore his protective presence in a manner reminiscent of the days of Moses.

This literary unit contains two closely related judgment speeches (3:1–15; 3:16–4:1), followed by a salvation portrayal (4:2–6).

The literary device of *inclusio* marks out the first judgment speech; the divine title "Sovereign LORD of Armies" appears at the beginning and end (3:1, 15; Motyer 1993, 59; Sweeney 1996, 148). The divine warrior-king is the source of the chaos described in the speech.

The first speech begins with a formal announcement of judgment that first describes the Lord's intervention (3:1–4; note "the Lord . . . is about to take," [3:1] and "I will make" [3:4]) and then its consequences (3:5–7). A summary of the coming judgment (3:8a) is followed by an accusation (3:8b–9a; note כִּי, "for," at the beginning of 3:8b), spoken by the prophet, that provides the basis for judgment. It is supported by two laments linked together by the key words גָּמַל and רָעָה/רַע (3:9b, 11). Tucked in between these laments is a brief word of assurance to the righteous (3:10), whose deeds (מַעַלְלֵיהֶם) stand in stark contrast to the actions of the rebels (cf. מַעַלְלֵיהֶם in 3:8b). The prophet's accusation continues in 3:12 (cf. 3:8b–9a), with the focus becoming the corrupt leadership of the Lord's covenant community. The speech concludes with a description of the Lord confronting these leaders and pronouncing his formal accusation against them (3:13–15).

While the speech is marked out as a distinct unit, the introductory כִּי, "for," links it to the preceding exhortation (2:22; Sweeney 1996, 148; Young 1965, 135), which, like 2:5, has a transitional function in the macrostructure of this section. The imminent judgment upon Judah's human power structures (3:1–15) should motivate a positive response to the exhortation. While one could treat כִּי as asseverative ("surely, indeed"; Bartelt 1996, 210; Smith 2007, 145), usage of the expression כִּי הִנֵּה (cf. 3:1), "for look," elsewhere in Isaiah indicates that כִּי connects logically to what precedes. Especially instructive are those texts where כִּי הִנֵּה follows an exhortation, providing a reason why one should take heed (cf. Isa. 26:20–21; 60:1–2; 65:18).

The second judgment speech contains an accusation (basis for judgment) in 3:16, followed by an announcement of judgment (3:17–4:1). There are three references to the Lord's intervention (3:17–18a) and a detailed description of the effects of that intervention (3:24–4:1). Since 3:16 is incomplete by itself, the Lord's speech must extend through 3:17, even though he refers to himself in the third person (cf. 8:5–7, as well as 1 Kings 13:21). Isaiah 3:18 begins a new subunit (note "in that day"), apparently spoken by the prophet.

The concluding speech portrays the future age of salvation and restoration beyond the purifying judgment, which is mentioned in 4:4. Isaiah 4:2–3 describes how the Lord will renew his relationship with his covenant community, bestowing his blessings and restoring them to a special position as his "holy" people. Isaiah 4:4–6 focuses on the restoration of the Lord's protective presence following his purifying judgment. A temporal clause, introduced by אִם, "when" (see BDB s.v. "אִם" mng. 1.b[4], 50), describes the purifying judgment of the immediate future (4:4); while the *weqatal* clause at the beginning of 4:5 (note וּבָרָא, "and [the Lord] will create") introduces a description of the transformation that occurs in the aftermath of this judgment (4:5–6).

- *Instability and Anarchy (3:1–7)*
- *Rebellion, Guilt, and Innocence (3:8–11)*
- *Moral Incompetence at the Top (3:12)*
- *The Judge Speaks (3:13–15)*
- *Pride Personified and Punished (3:16–17)*
- *Makeover in Reverse (3:18–24)*
- *Security Gone (3:25–4:1)*
- *Blessing Restored (4:2–3)*
- *Purification and Presence (4:4–6)*

EXPOSITION (3:1–4:6)

Instability and Anarchy (3:1–7)
The Lord's removal of Judah's sources of physical sustenance and national security, as well as its leadership, results in anarchy.

3:1–3. The nation's loss of stability is the outworking of the Lord's vengeance and the result of his purifying judgment. This judgment eliminates all that makes a society secure, including the essentials of life (food and water), military strength, and those responsible for maintaining law and order and for providing spiritual leadership.

Included in the list are experts in magic and divination (3:2–3), which was prohibited by the Lord (cf. Deut. 18:10, 14 and note the remarks on Isa. 2:6 above). The list of leaders thus reflects the perspective of the people, who regarded diviners as indispensable (Gray 1912, 63). Divination was a means of knowing and controlling the future, but it is useless before the Sovereign Lord of Armies, who alone controls a nation's destiny and refuses to be manipulated by pagan ritual.

> **Magic**
> It is likely that חֲרָשִׁים in 3:3 refers to "magic" (so *HALOT* s.v. "חרשׁ I" 358) or to "magical arts." Note the reference to incantations that immediately follows. The proposed noun is otherwise unattested in Hebrew, though the root appears in Ugaritic (*HALOT* s.v. "חרשׁ III"; "חֹרֶשׁ" 358) and Aramaic (*HALOT* s.v. "חרשׁ I" 358). A less likely option is to understand the form as the plural of חָרָשׁ, "craftsman" (*HALOT* s.v. "חָרָשׁ" 358). English translations are divided: See KJV ("cunning artificer"), NIV ("skilled craftsman"), and NLT ("skilled craftsmen"), as opposed to ESV/NRSV ("skillful magician"), *Tanakh* ("expert enchanter"), and *HCSB* ("cunning magician").

3:4–5. With the breakdown in leadership at all levels, civil disorder prevails. Unqualified youths attempt to fill the void, but chaos prevails. The use of the verb נָגַשׂ, "oppress," to describe the oppression within society (3:5) is tragically ironic, for it is used elsewhere of foreign oppressors (Exod. 3:7; Isa. 9:3 [Eng. 4]; 14:2, 4; Williamson 2006, 249). Society is turned on its head as youths attack the elderly, and despised riffraff assault respectable people.

> **Youths**
> Hebrew תַּעֲלוּלִים in the second line of 3:4 may be an abstract plural ("ill treatment," cf. Isa. 66:4) or a numerical plural ("acts of mischief"; cf. *HALOT* s.v. "תַּעֲלוּלִים" 1768). In either case it does not appear to be a suitable subject for the following verb "rule" or a suitable parallel to the preceding "youths." If retained, it could be understood as metonymic for the youngsters who are characterized by such actions or taken as an adverbial accusative (see Williamson [2006, 231], who translates the line, "and they will rule over them in a childish manner"). In the light of the parallelism, an emendation to עוֹלְלִים, "children" (*HALOT* s.v. "עוֹלֵל" 798) is tempting, but it is difficult to account for the presence of the *tav* in the Hebrew text in this case. Nevertheless, several English translations seem to assume such a reading: KJV/NRSV/*Tanakh* ("babes"), ESV ("infants"), NIV ("children"), NLT ("toddlers"). The HCSB ("the unstable") appears to interpret the Hebrew text as it stands.

3:6–7. Those unfit to rule challenge traditional authority, leaving a leadership void that people desperately try to fill. Mere possession of a coat would not normally qualify one to rule, yet in the aftermath of a judgment that leaves people poverty-stricken, it apparently set one apart from others. But the one targeted for leadership refuses the offer, denying any special status. After all, what honor is there in ruling over a "heap of ruins"? The statement that reads literally, "I will not be a doctor" (חֹבֵשׁ, "binder" [of wounds]) is an ironic intertextual link to 1:6, where the nation was described as having wounds that were "not bound" (cf. חֻבָּשׁוּ; Williamson 2006, 251; Young 1965, 148).

> *TRANSLATION ANALYSIS 3:8–9*
> If the perfect verbal forms in lines 1 and 2 of 3:8 refer to the coming judgment (cf. 3:1), then they are rhetorical, indicating the certitude of Jerusalem and Judah's demise (cf. this use of the perfect in 2:11). There is no clear way of indicating this in English translation apart from using the future tense (cf. NLT). However, if the terms describe Jerusalem and Judah's moral decline prior to the judgment, then they may be translated with the English present (KJV, NIV) or present perfect (ESV, HCSB, NRSV, *Tanakh*).
>
> When the interjection אוֹי, "woe," is collocated with the preposition -לְ (as in the last line of 3:9), it indicates that the object of the preposition is in dire straits and/or that disaster is imminent or already being experienced (cf. Num. 21:29; 1 Sam. 4:7–8; Isa. 3:11; 6:5; 24:16; Jer. 4:13; 10:19; 15:10; 48:46; Ezek. 16:23; Hos. 7:13; 9:12). Consequently, it is typically translated as a noun, "woe" (cf. Prov. 23:29). Though paraphrastic, NLT brings out the force of the construction: "they are doomed."

Rebellion, Guilt, and Innocence (3:8–11)
The nation experiences disaster because of its open rebellion against its king. Both the guilty and the innocent receive justice.

3:8–9. The doom of Jerusalem and Judah was certain because they opposed the Lord and rebelled against his authority (Isa. 3:8). At the end of 3:8, the Hebrew text reads, "rebelling (against) the eyes of his glory." The reference to eyes indicates awareness, suggesting their rebellion occurs right in the Lord's very presence. (Note NLT: "they provoke him to his face.") Both their words and their deeds testify to their guilt; they even boast about their sinful deeds (3:9a). Once again the prophet compares the people to Sodom (cf. 1:10), for they flaunt their sin. Their sinful behavior is self-destructive (3:9b).

3:10–11. But the Lord's judgment, however inevitable and severe, discriminates between the righteous and the wicked. The "righteous" remain faithful to God (Isa. 57:1), despite being deprived of justice in the courts (5:23) and being falsely accused of wrongdoing (29:21). The Lord assures the righteous they will be vindicated and receive the reward they deserve (3:10). These rewards are compared to fruit because they are the natural product of their actions (cf. Jer. 17:10; 21:14; 32:19; Mic. 7:19).

The wicked will also get what they deserve (Isa. 3:11). The wicked have rejected God's moral and ethical standards and opposed both God and his people. In contrast to the righteous, whom they persecute (cf. 5:23), the wicked will be overtaken by divine judgment. God is patient with the wicked (26:10) and urges them to repent (55:7), but he eventually must punish them for their deeds (13:11; 14:5).

> **The Wicked**
>
> In the first line of 3:11, the adjective רַע, "evil," appears to modify רָשָׁע, "wicked." This collocation does not occur elsewhere, though the expression "evil of the wicked" appears in Psalm 7:10 [Eng. 9]. Perhaps the expression, though unique, emphasizes the depth of their sin. Tighter parallelism is achieved if one assumes ellipsis of כִּי (cf. Isa. 3:10) and takes רַע as a verb, "for he is evil." However, this proposal works better if one assumes the reading אַשְׁרֵי, "happy are," at the beginning of 3:10. See Williamson 2006, 258.

Moral Incompetence at the Top (3:12)

Oppression and unfit leadership plague the covenant community.

It is not entirely clear who is speaking in 3:12. Since the Lord is referred to in the third person in 3:13, it is possible that the prophet speaks in 3:12. However, this could be a quotation from the Lord himself without a formal introduction, as in 3:4. In favor of this is the fact that the Lord refers to the covenant community as "my people" in 3:15 (cf. 1:3).

In a context where the wicked dominate society, the Lord's people are economically oppressed (3:12a). There may be an allusion here to Israel's experience in Egypt, where Egyptian taskmasters afflicted them (cf. the use of the participle of נָגַשׂ, "oppress," to describe these taskmasters in Exod. 3:7; 5:6, 10, 13–14). If so, then these oppressors are cast in an especially negative light. Ironically, they have reenslaved God's covenant community.

In the face of such oppression, one would hope that strong leaders, like Moses, might emerge to promote justice and intervene on behalf of the oppressed. But the leaders of the community are unfit to rule (cf. Isa. 3:4) and misguide the people (3:12b). The verb used here (*hiphil* תָּעָה) means, "to cause to wander, mislead." It is used of leading an animal by a bit placed in the mouth (Isa. 30:28) and of shepherds leading their flocks astray (Jer. 50:6). It also describes the effects of intoxicants that make people stagger and stumble (Isa. 19:13–14). Here it refers to leaders misleading the people morally and spiritually (see 9:16, as well as 2 Kings 21:9; Jer. 23:13, 32; Mic. 3:5).

TRANSLATION ANALYSIS 3:12

The Hebrew text of the first line in Isaiah 3:12 reads, "My people, his oppressors deal severely." The singular participle מְעוֹלֵל, "deals severely," lacks agreement with the plural "his oppressors." Perhaps we should (1) emend נֹגְשָׂיו, "his oppressors," to נֹגְשִׂים, "oppressors," dropping the *waw* as virtually dittographic with the preceding *yod* and moving the initial *mem* of מְעוֹלֵל to the end of the preceding form; and (2) emend מְעוֹלֵל to עֹלְלוּ, understanding the *mem* as the ending of the preceding word and assuming haplography of *waw* (note the *waw* at the beginning of the following word, וְנָשִׁים, "and women"; see Williamson 2006, 261). This would yield a translation, "Oppressors treat my people cruelly." The NIV has "youths oppress my people." This reading apparently assumes an emendation of מְעוֹלֵל to עוֹלְלִים, "children" (for this term, see *HALOT* s.v. "עוֹלֵל" 798). Isaiah 3:4 may provide contextual support for this reading. See as well ESV, HCSB, KJV, NLT, NRSV, and *Tanakh*. The Hebrew text reads "women" in the second line of 3:12, but the parallelism is tighter if we read נֹשִׁים, "creditors" (cf. Isa. 24:2), rather than נָשִׁים, "women." This reading has support from several ancient versions (see Williamson 2006, 262).

The verb used in the final line of 3:12 (בִּלֵּעוּ), if from בָּלַע, "swallow, engulf" (cf. ESV), depicts the leaders as destroying (cf. KJV) the pathways of the people. But it is possible, in light of the parallelism (note "misguide"), that בָּלַע is a homonym, meaning, "confuse" (see *HALOT* s.v. "בלע III" 135; cf. HCSB, NASB, NLT, NRSV, *Tanakh*).

The Judge Speaks (3:13–15)
The Lord confronts the guilty in court and presents his formal accusation against them.

3:13–14. The courts of the land were corrupt (cf. 1:17, 21–23), but the Lord was ready to rectify the situation by intervening as the righteous judge (3:13) and bringing the culprits before his bar of justice (3:14a). His accusation is clear and direct: the leaders of the people have enriched themselves at the expense of the people (3:14b). The Lord compares the community to a vineyard that has been plundered. The background for the metaphor may be Exodus 22:4 (Eng. 5), which describes the penalty for letting one's animal loose in another man's field or vineyard. The verb בָּעַר is used here in the *piel* stem with the connotation "graze destructively."[1] It is likely a homonym of בָּעַר, "burn" (see *HALOT* s.v. "בער II" 146).

3:15. The Lord uses violent language to describe the oppressors' actions—they have crushed the poor and ground their faces (3:15a). No wonder the speech ends with a reference to the Lord as the one who leads armies (3:15b). His power would overwhelm the might of the oppressors, who have attacked the Lord's people (note "*my* people" in 3:15).

Pride Personified and Punished (3:16–17)
Having denounced the oppressive leaders of his covenant community (3:12–15), the Lord now turns to their wives, who are beneficiaries of their husbands' misdeeds. Patricia Tull (2010, 104–5), who appropriately cites Isaiah 32:7–10 and Amos 4:1–3 as conceptual parallels, comments on Isaiah 3:16: "To be the beneficiaries of riches that are not rightfully one's own, to provide someone else the pretext for dishonesty, to be willfully unaware of who is being harmed for the sake of one's baubles is to become guilty as well." These women display a proud, self-centered demeanor (3:16), but that will change in the coming judgment. Despite their arrogance and self-glorification, the Lord, called here the Sovereign Master (אֲדֹנָי, 3:17, see also 3:18), is the master of their destiny. He will mar their beauty, afflicting them with a humiliating skin disease right on their foreheads where it will be fully visible (3:17).

> **Afflicting**
> The Hebrew verb in the first line of 3:17 (שִׂפַּח) occurs only here. The root may be a by-form of ספח, from which is derived the noun סַפַּחַת, "scabs, flaking skin" (see *HALOT* s.v. "שׂפח" 1348). Another option is that the verb means, "strip bare," which creates tighter parallelism with the following line. In either case their foreheads are a source of embarrassment to them. The meaning of the rare Hebrew word פֹּת (cf. the suffixed form פָּתְהֵן in the second line of 3:17) is not entirely certain. Based on an Akkadian cognate, it may be seen as a reference to the forehead (cf. *HALOT* s.v. "פֹּת" 983; Williamson 2006, 277), which fits the parallelism nicely.

Makeover in Reverse (3:18–24)
The Lord will appropriately judge these proud women.

3:18–23. The Sovereign Master will take away all their fine clothing and jewelry (3:18–23). The use of the verb "remove" (*hiphil* סור) links this judgment with that of the previous speech, where the same Hebrew verb appears at the very beginning of the announcement of judgment

---

1 Some suggest the meaning "depasture" here. See Dearman 1988, 38; Gray 1912, 69; and Young 1965, 158.

(cf. 3:1). The long list of items in 3:18–23 has the rhetorical effect of highlighting the women's obsession with material wealth and physical beauty, as well as the loss they will experience. There are twenty-one items listed after תִּפְאֶרֶת, "beauty of."[2] As a multiple of seven (symbolic of what is full or complete; cf. 4:1; 11:15; 30:26) this twenty-one-fold list suggests gross excess far beyond what is necessary or appropriate (for a fuller discussion, see Tull 2010, 106). It is as if they have three complete wardrobes.

3:24. Judgment will bring a reversal in their circumstances (3:24): With their spices taken away and their pampered lifestyle over, their bodies will stink as the result of festering, untreated wounds (cf. Ps. 38:6 [Eng. 5]; Zech. 14:12). Their fine clothes will be replaced by sackcloth and a rope belt, and their braided hair by baldness (caused by the skin affliction mentioned in 3:17?). Prior to this, their striking beauty caught one's eye, but now a brand mars that beauty, for they are prisoners bound for exile. The punishment fits the crime. As Miller (1982, 42) states, "The manifestation of their sin will become the locus of judgment." The style changes in the final line in the list of 3:24, with the replacement item coming at the beginning of the clause and the item to be replaced coming at the end. This terminal deviation may signal closure and be for rhetorical effect (cf. Motyer 1993, 64; Williamson 2006, 285–86).

Security Gone (3:25–4:1)
With the men of the city killed in battle, these once proud women will have to beg the few men left to marry them and take away the reproach of widowhood.

3:25–26. In 3:25–26 the prophet shifts his focus from the women of the city to the city itself, which he addresses with the second-person feminine singular in 3:25 before describing her in the third person in 3:26. With her source of security lying dead in battle, she falls to the ground, mourning and lamenting her fate. This image of personified Jerusalem depicts the destiny of each of the women described prior to this. Since they share the same fate, the prophet can describe the entire city as a destitute woman.

4:1. A few men, perhaps older, weaker ones (cf. 3:25), will survive the defeat. Desperate to escape shame, several women grab hold of these men and beg to be married, even agreeing to provide for their own basic physical needs (4:1). The Hebrew reads, "but let your name be called over us," an idiom for ownership (cf. 2 Sam. 12:28; 2 Chron. 7:14; Jer. 7:10; 15:16; Amos 9:12; Roberts 2015, 65). In this male-dominated culture, virtually all women were married; their primary task in life was to build up their husband's family by having children and to contribute to the welfare of their family economically (cf. Prov. 31:10–31). In return the husband was responsible for providing for the woman's material needs. To be unmarried and/or childless was considered a disgrace (see Gen. 30:23; Isa. 54:4). Though this image stirs one's pity, the scene should not be viewed in isolation. These are the same proud women described earlier—arrogant, self-centered materialists whose wealth came at the expense of the poor.

Blessing Restored (4:2–3)
The righteous remnant that survives judgment (cf. Isa. 3:10) will take delight in the Lord's abundant blessings and enjoy special status as his covenant people.

4:2. The introductory phrase "in that day" refers to the time following the Lord's purifying judgment (cf. 4:4). The use of the phrase to introduce a salvation portrayal marks an abrupt shift from the preceding context, where it refers to a day of divine judgment

---

2 For a thorough lexical analysis of the items in the list, see Roberts 2015, 62–64.

(cf. 2:11, 17, 20; 3:7, 18; 4:1). This is consistent with the theme of reversal of judgment that highlights this speech. The future planned by God for his covenant community includes both purifying judgment and restoration of blessing. In fact, the former is a means to achieving the latter.

Isaiah 4:2 depicts the restoration of the Lord's agricultural blessing. The phrase צֶמַח יְהוָה has been traditionally understood as a messianic title, "branch of the Lord," here.[3] The prophets Jeremiah and Zechariah, who wrote later than Isaiah, use the word צֶמַח as a royal title, but in each case there are clear contextual indicators that the term is being used in this metaphorical manner. In Jeremiah 23:5 and 33:15 the term is preceded by "to David"; in Zechariah 3:8 it is appositional to "my servant"; and in Zechariah 6:12 it is appositional to "a man." But here in Isaiah 4:2 it is more likely that the word refers to literal agricultural growth, which the Lord will restore as a sign of his renewed favor (see Isa. 1:19; 30:23–24; 32:20; cf. Deut. 30:9). In the majority of its occurrences elsewhere the word refers to vegetation and crops (Gen. 19:25; Ps. 65:11 [Eng. 10]; Isa. 61:11; Ezek. 16:7; 17:9–10; Hos. 8:7). In Psalm 65:11 (HB 12) it is the Lord who is the source of the crops. The parallelism in Isaiah 4:2 also favors this view, for the corresponding phrase "fruit of the land" is used literally in the other passages in which it appears (Num. 13:20, 26; Deut. 1:25; see as well Ps. 104:13). In the complementary parallelism the ultimate source of the agricultural abundance (the Lord) is given in the first line, while the immediate source (the land) is mentioned in the second line.

The reference to the "*fruit* of the land" may form an intertextual link with the promise given to the righteous in Isaiah 3:10, where the Lord assures them that they will eat the *fruit* of their deeds. Correlating the two texts, we see that the fruit eaten by the righteous will take the form of the Lord's renewed blessing upon the remnant, as depicted in 4:2 (Abernethy 2014, 71–72).

The abundance of the land will become a source of admiration and honor to the remnant. The terms צְבִי, "splendor," and כָּבוֹד, "glory," refer not so much to the remnant's response, but to the impact that God's rich blessing will have on outside observers. As Williamson (2006, 309) states: "The point, then, is that from a situation of devastation and shame, the land will once again assume a position of universal recognition and honour."

The next pair of terms, גָּאוֹן, "pride," and תִּפְאֶרֶת, "beauty," probably refers to the impact of God's blessing on the remnant. The land's agricultural abundance will become a source of pride and delight to the remnant. This also marks a reversal of the false pride described earlier (Williamson 2006, 309–10). In 3:18 the word תִּפְאֶרֶת, "beauty," is used of the jewelry of Zion's women, in which they took great pride (cf. 3:16). But in 4:2 the same word refers to the rich vegetation that the Lord will cause to grow in the fields. The repetition of the word with different referents highlights the ironic change in perspective that occurs among the people once the Lord's purifying judgment

---

3   Most English translations reflect this traditional understanding of צֶמַח as a messianic title by translating "branch" (ESV, KJV, NIV, NLT, NRSV) or "Branch" (HCSB). *Tanakh* has "radiance," which the *Jewish Study Bible* understands in a royal sense (p. 792). For a defense of the traditional view, see Baldwin 1964, 93–97. She argues that the shoot of Yahweh of 4:2 is associated with the priestly washing of 4:4. Noting that the shoot of Yahweh is associated with the protection of Zion in 4:6, she correlates this passage with 32:1–2, where a human king shelters the people from harm. Roberts (2000, 20–27) identifies צֶמַח as the ideal king, and "the fruit of the land" as "the burgeoning population of the land." But how can "the burgeoning population of the land" be a source of pride to the remnant? After all, the burgeoning population is the remnant. For a thorough lexical study of צֶמַח and its related verb, see Rose 2000, 91–106. Rose regards the messianic view in Isaiah 4:2 as "implausible."

has done its work. In Isaiah's day the rich women of Zion took pride in their own appearance; in the future the blessing of the Lord will be the remnant's source of pride. Later in Isaiah the word is used to describe the pride of cities, nations, and human kings (10:12; 13:19; 28:1, 4; 44:13), all of which will be humbled by divine judgment. Glory belongs only to the Lord, who will impart it to his city, his temple, and his people (28:5; 46:13; 52:1; 60:7, 19; 62:3; 63:15).

Despite God's devastating judgment upon Judah, the Lord will preserve a remnant that will experience his renewed blessings (see Isa. 37:4, 31–32; and 46:3, where a different Hebrew root is used). The preservation of a remnant is already hinted at earlier, when the Lord assures the righteous that they will be rewarded (3:10), even though devastating judgment will come upon the land. The remnant motif becomes an important reminder that God's judgment, despite its severity, is designed to purify, not destroy, the people to whom he has committed himself through the covenant.

4:3. This remnant will be called holy. Elsewhere Isaiah uses this term of God, but here he applies it to the remnant that populates the restored Jerusalem of the future. They will be called "holy" (or, "set apart") because the Lord's purifying work will cleanse them from their sins (see 4:4) and enable them to live in the presence of the Holy One of Israel. In Isaiah 62:12 the prophet anticipates a day when the exiles will return to Jerusalem and will be called "the Holy People," as they were in the days of Moses (Deut. 7:6; 14:12, 21; 26:19; 28:9).

In Isaiah 4:3b this remnant is referred to as "all who are destined to live." The Hebrew reads, "everyone written for life in Jerusalem." This apparently refers to a register in which the Lord has recorded the names of those appointed to live (cf. Exod. 32:32; Ps. 69:28 [HB 29]; Dan. 12:1). The background for the image may be a citizenry register, attested in Ezekiel 13:9 and at Ugarit (cf. Ringgren 1980, 340).

Purification and Presence (4:4–6)
The Lord will purify his covenant community through judgment and then restore his protective presence.

4:4. Isaiah pictures the cleansing of the daughters of Zion and of Jerusalem, whose destiny is controlled by the Sovereign Master (אֲדֹנָי, see 3:17–18). The women of the city are pictured as stained by excrement (צֹאָה), a term used elsewhere of vomit (28:8) and feces (36:12 *qere*). The description is highly ironic, for their outward beauty is highlighted in 3:18–23. But here we see God's perspective, as he likens their ethical/spiritual condition to something putrid and disgusting. The reference to the shed blood of Jerusalem forms an intertextual link with 1:15, where God mentions the bloodstained hands of the city's people. There is also irony in the prophet's use of the divine title Sovereign Master. Earlier it is the Sovereign Master who judges (3:15, 17–18), but now he is the one who cleanses his people.

The instrument of cleansing will be "a spirit of justice and a spirit of burning [or destruction?]." The word רוּחַ can refer to a wind (Isa. 7:2; 17:13; 32:2; 41:16; 57:13), the personal Spirit of God (Isa. 30:1; 42:1; 48:16; 63:10), or a disposition (see Isa. 19:14; 29:10; 37:7). Since wind is sometimes associated with judgment, it is possible the term is used here in a metaphorical sense for the destructive but purifying judgment depicted in this context. However, the image of wind does not fit well with the metaphor of rinsing used in the first half of the verse. Another option is that the personal Spirit of God is in view, but elsewhere in Isaiah God's personal Spirit is not cast in the role of judge. Furthermore, the Lord's Spirit is viewed as definite elsewhere in Isaiah (רוּחַ is modified by "the LORD" or by a pronoun), but here the term is indefinite ("a spirit of judgment and a spirit of fire").[4] Perhaps it is best to see the term as referring to the disposition or attitude God brings to the task of judgment. In Isaiah 28:6 the phrase "spirit of justice" is used of the disposition to do justice that God gives to judges when he renews Israelite society. The nuance of the word בָּעֵר is uncertain. It could have the meaning "burning," in which case it depicts the judgment as being through fire (cf. 1:31). But it may refer more generally to destruction (cf. *HALOT* s.v. "בער II" 146) that will accompany the judgment (as perhaps is the case in 3:14).

4:5. This judgment will bring transformation. The word בָּרָא, "create," is used of the Lord's work. The word has the primary meaning "to bring about a new condition," whether from a nonexistent or preexisting state. In the latter case the word carries the nuance "renew, transform" (see Isa. 41:20). In 4:5 the Lord brings about a new situation as he creates a cloud, smoke, and a flame of fire to serve as tangible reminders of his protective presence. The imagery evokes memories of Israel's early history. During the exodus, God used a cloud and fire to protect his people from the Egyptians (Exod. 13:21–22; 14:19, 24; Num. 9:15–23; 10:34; 14:14). By utilizing these images from the past in a symbolic manner, the prophet emphasizes that Jerusalem will experience God's protective presence in the same vivid way as the exodus generation. The image of the Lord's presence hovering over the city's convocations marks a reversal in the Lord's attitude toward their worship. In Isaiah's day the sinful people's convocations disgusted the Lord (Isa. 1:13), but in the future he will honor them with his presence.

The Hebrew of the final clause of 4:5 reads, "over all of the glory (there will be) a canopy." Isaiah 62:2 speaks of the glory of restored Zion, but it would be odd to refer to Jerusalem as "all of the glory." It is better to (1) read כֹּל, "all," rather than כָּל, "all of," (2) take "glory" as the subject, understanding it as a metonymy for the manifestation of the divine presence, and (3) interpret "canopy" as a predicate nominative (Williamson 2006, 304, 314). This yields a translation: "over everything glory will be a canopy."

The term כָּבוֹד likely refers to the Lord's glory that overshadows all Zion like a canopy. The noun חֻפָּה, "canopy," is used in only two other passages, in both cases in the context of a wedding (Ps. 19:6 [Eng. 5]; Joel 2:16). There is nothing in this speech that suggests such a connotation, but perhaps the image is preparing us for the aborted love song in Isaiah 5:1–2 (see below). If so, the tragedy of what has happened in the Lord's vineyard is heightened by way of contrast with the future reality, which reflects the Lord's ideal for his relationship with his people.

4:6. If the divine glory is equated with the canopy in 4:5, then it may also be the reality behind the image of the סֻכָּה, "hut, shelter," in 4:6. At the level of locution, this hut provides shade for the city by day, protecting it from the intense heat of the sun's rays. It also shelters the city from the rain. At the end of 4:6 the Hebrew reads, "from cloudburst and from rain." Two different phenomena may be in view—a heavy storm (cf. the association of זֶרֶם, "cloudburst," with hail in Isa. 28:2; 30:30) and normal rainfall (cf. Pss. 72:6; 147:8; Isa. 30:23). But מָטָר, "rain," can also refer to a thunderstorm (cf. Ps. 135:7; Jer. 10:13; Zech. 10:1), so it is possible that the terms are roughly synonymous and are paired to depict a heavy downpour. In Isaiah 25:4–5 it is the Lord himself who protects his people from heat and rain, which symbolize would-be oppressors (cf. 32:1–2, where the imagery is used of leaders that the Lord provides to protect his people). It is important to note that elements (heat, storm)

---

[4] In Isaiah 32:15 some translate רוּחַ as "the Spirit" (see NIV), even though there is no indication of definiteness in the Hebrew text. The term is better understood as referring to life-giving strength or capacity in that passage.

appearing elsewhere as instruments of divine judgment or as covenantal curses (cf. Deut. 28:22; Isa. 28:2) against Israel cannot harm the restored covenant community of the future. The Lord protects his people, not only from outside enemies but also from his own wrath.

If the Lord stands behind the image of the hut, then the language may also connote kingship at the deeper, illocutionary level. The term "shade" (צֵל) is used elsewhere of a ruler's protective sovereignty, both in the Bible (cf. Judg. 9:7–15; Isa. 30:1–3; Ezek. 31:6, 12, 17) and in Akkadian literature. The parallel term "safety" (מַחְסֶה, "place of refuge") can also refer to the protective responsibility of a superior party in a covenantal relationship (cf. Isa. 28:15). The related verb חָסָה, "take refuge," is often used in covenant contexts (cf. Isa. 30:2) to refer to an action that, by its very nature, is a demonstration of loyalty obligating the superior party to fulfill his responsibility to provide protection. Those who take refuge in the Lord are often contrasted with rebels (Pss. 2:10–12; 5:10–12 [HB 11–13]; 31:18–20 [HB 19–21]; 34:22 [HB 23]; Isa. 57:13; Zeph. 3:11–13). The act of taking refuge is closely associated with a verbal affirmation of loyalty (cf. Pss. 16:1–4; 31:2, 7 [HB 3, 8]; 71:1, 5–6; 91:4, 14–16; 141:1–8). Taking refuge in the Lord also serves as a basis for a request for protection (Pss. 16:1; 25:20; 37:40; 57:2), suggesting it is the significance of the action as an expression of loyalty, not the act itself, that is primary. This explains why the action prompts divine loyal love and loyalty (cf. Pss. 17:7; 36:8 [HB 9]; 57:2, 4 [HB 3, 5]; Nah. 1:7).

THEOLOGICAL FOCUS

The theological focus of this passage can be stated as follows: the Lord punishes leaders who refuse to guide his people in his ways, ignore the well-being of the covenant community, and take pride in wealth acquired at the expense of others. Yet the Lord's purifying judgment leads to the restoration of his blessing and protective presence. As the prophet develops this theological message, the following emphases emerge:

1. The Lord's commitment to justice guarantees retribution.

The prophet pictures the Lord taking his position as judge and confronting those who have oppressed his covenant people. His commitment to justice is readily apparent as he holds accountable those who have abused their position of leadership. The guilty will receive just punishment for their deeds.

Old Testament theologians have debated the dynamics of retribution. Some favor the judicial model, where God intervenes directly in judgment, while others support an act-consequence model, where God is involved indirectly, or providentially, in assuring that actions bring self-destructive consequences.[5] In Isaiah 3 the evildoers' actions are self-destructive (cf. 3:9, 11). However, this does not necessarily mean those actions have inherent within them the seeds of destruction. Rather, they are self-destructive because they activate God's intervention as judge. The Lord himself removes stability from society (3:1, 4); and he takes his position as judge and pronounces sentence upon the guilty (3:13–15).

2. Divine retribution is discriminatory.

A corollary of the retribution principle is the Lord's vindication of his innocent, loyal followers (3:10). Though the righteous may experience the collateral damage of divine judgment (cf. Hab. 3:16–19), the Lord is committed to them and promises to reward them for their good deeds. In their case this is compared to eating the fruit of their actions. The expression "fruit of one's deeds" (Isa. 3:10) is used elsewhere of evil actions, which are punished accordingly (Jer. 17:10; 21:14; 32:19; Mic. 7:13). Only here is the phrase used of good deeds, and only here is the "fruit" eaten. The picture of

---

5   See Chisholm 2012, 675–76.

eating fruit is an appealing one, suggesting that the righteous will eventually derive pleasure and nourishment from their godly behavior.

3. The Lord's judgment brings reversal as he humiliates proud oppressors.

The hard-hitting judgment speech in Isaiah 3:16–4:1 causes one to wince at the severity of the punishment depicted. But the key to appreciating its severity is the first descriptive statement of 3:16: the women of Zion were proud (גָּבְהוּ). According to Proverbs 16:5, every proud heart is an abomination to the Lord and destined for judgment (cf. Prov. 16:18; 18:12). The judgment upon these women is just one element in the broader judgment announced in Isaiah 2, which targets all the proud (2:11, 15, 17; Smith 2007, 151; Williamson 2006, 289). Divine judgment typically brings about a reversal of situation, humiliating the proud (2:17) while elevating and vindicating the oppressed (3:10; cf. 1 Sam. 2:3–9). When viewed in this way, the humiliation of Zion's women becomes a vivid illustration of God's commitment to justice (see Isa. 3:13).

4. The objects of divine judgment get what they deserve.

The principle of poetic justice is apparent in this description of divine judgment. The women take pride in the wealth gained through their husbands' exploitation of the poor (3:14–15) and apparently show no concern for the oppressed widows of society (cf. 1:17, 23). So, it is appropriate that they would lose their husbands and sons, and that they would be reduced to poverty and widowhood.

5. The purifying nature of divine judgment

In this speech the prophet again depicts the purification of Zion (cf. 1:25–27). In his earlier description of the city's purification, he focuses on the restoration of honest judges and justice. Here the focus is on purification from sin (4:4). Judgment will eliminate the outward signs of pride and greed, as well as the evidence of moral guilt.

6. The reversal of judgment

In earlier speeches divine judgment reverses the circumstances of proud sinners as it humiliates them (2:11, 17; 3:24). But here the reversal goes in the other direction, transforming judgment into blessing as the Lord restores his blessings, transforms his people, and relates to them as protector, rather than judge and warrior.

7. The restoration of the Lord's covenant relationship with his people

In the aftermath of judgment, the Lord restores his people to a holy position, and he reveals his protective presence. He shelters them from harm, as he did in the time of Moses, and he restores the crops that were ruined in the judgment (cf. 3:1).

PREACHING AND TEACHING STRATEGIES

Exegetical and Theological Synthesis

Isaiah 3 describes the devastation following a military defeat in Jerusalem. Isaiah 3:1–7 showcases the extent of this devastation as Jerusalem is now utterly lacking in supplies (3:1), probably resulting from the siege. Much of the infrastructure has been reduced to ruins (3:6), and all the men who would have been considered leadership material have either been killed or deported (3:2–7; cf. Dan. 1:3–4). The ultimate cause of this devastation is God (Isa. 3:1, 4, 13–14). However, from a human perspective, this judgment will take the form of foreign oppressors. As a result, Judah would be forced to make children (those with no experience or leadership skill; 3:4), and those who feel utterly unqualified to serve, their leaders (3:6–7).

Isaiah 3:8–11 provides the basis for coming judgment. It is structured in the form of a simple A-B-A' chiasm:

    A. Woe to Judah for her wickedness. She has invited this evil back onto herself because of how she has treated God and others (3:8–9).
      B. The righteous have no reason for concern. It will be well with them, as they too will eat of the fruit of their actions (3:10).
    A'. Woe to Judah for her wickedness. What she has done to others will be done to her (3:11).

This section shows that God's judgment is not indiscriminate. He will deal with people based on their individual actions. The people will reap the rewards/consequences of their own behavior. The chiasm specifically highlights the righteous who choose not to go along with the wickedness of the broader culture and how they will not face judgment along with the rest. While they will still be impacted by the natural consequences of the nation's sins, they will not directly be targeted by God in judgment (3:10), and they have reason for great hope in the future kingdom (4:2–6).

In 3:12–15 the prophet specifically focuses in on Israel's corrupt leaders as the primary target of God's judgment. They are indicted for misleading the people (3:12), and for robbing from and oppressing the poor (3:14–15). Isaiah 3:16–4:1 continues this focus by confronting the leaders' wives who knowingly profited from their husbands' corruption and oppression. These pompous, wealthy, extravagantly dressed women would suffer a divine reversal. The accessories of beauty and status that had come to distinguish them would be replaced with symbols of poverty, ugliness, and shame (3:17–24). This reversal would be brought about by the large-scale removal of young adult men from their midst, many of whom would die in battle (3:25). Times will become so desperate for these women that seven of them would fight over a single man—one who won't even have the financial resources to provide for her basic needs (4:1).

As is often the case throughout Isaiah after a message of judgment, the Lord follows it up with a message of hope for the future. Despite the devastation described in Isaiah 3, one day in the future Jerusalem will once again be made beautiful and glorious (4:2). Those who remain will be called holy, as the Lord will have washed away their filth and cleansed them (4:3–4). He will be a savior to them. His relationship with them is described in images reminiscent of the exodus—a protective cloud by day and an illuminating fire by night (4:5).

Preaching Idea
Sin results in devastation. Nevertheless, God still offers hope.

Contemporary Connections

What does it mean?
To say that sin results in devastation is to acknowledge that sin is destructive by nature; it results in judgment from God. Those who choose to rebel against God's laws and instructions for life will reap devastating consequences. It isn't a matter of "if," but "when" and "How severe?" This principle is stated throughout Scripture. One of the most direct statements to this effect is found in Galatians 6:7–8a: "Do not be deceived: God cannot be mocked. A man reaps what he sows. Whoever sows to please their flesh, from the flesh will reap corruption." James 1:15 expresses this same principle this way: "Then, after desire has conceived, it gives birth to sin; and sin, when it is full-grown, gives birth to death."

Romans 1 ties the degenerative effects of sin in a person's life to the judgment or wrath of God "against all the godlessness and wickedness of people" (1:18). The degression begins when people suppress the truth about God, choosing to deny his existence or his right to be worshipped as God (1:21, 25). As a result of their disregard for God and his laws, their hearts become further darkened to truth and common sense, and they become fools to reality (1:21–22). God eventually gives them over to their sinful desires to do the things they insist on doing until those desires ultimately consume and control them (1:24, 26, 28). In the end people are so overcome by sinful lusts that they are defined by shameful, dishonorable, and degrading behaviors (1:26). Thus, they now receive in their bodies the due penalty for their sin (1:27).

Romans 1 reveals that a significant element of God's judgment against sin is simply to allow people to experience the natural consequences associated with their sin. As God's laws have been given as a gift to help us navigate life well, the way that it was intended by the Creator, disobedience to these laws will naturally result in destructive realities. It produces a judgment by way of the innate consequences of sin and rebellion in this life. Isaiah 3 describes God's people as going down the path of rebellion. Although they knew God, they no longer honored him as God in their daily obedience or worship (cf. Rom. 1:21). Therefore, God removed his hand of protection and blessing from them, allowing them to become vulnerable to attacks from surrounding nations. The "judgment" that they would experience would be the natural consequences of war and geopolitical conflicts with a more powerful, evil nation.

In addition to the natural consequences of human behavior lies the reality of God's future judgment. He who sees and knows all things promises to one day carry out vengeance for all wrongs committed against him (2 Thess. 1:6–10) and to reward obedience and integrity (Rev. 11:18). Isaiah 4:2–6 looked beyond Israel's immediate realities to a future kingdom where evildoers would be purged out of Jerusalem for good, and God's people would be cleansed of their filth. Whereas God would allow Israel to see just how vulnerable they were without his hand of protection (Isa. 3), Isaiah 4 describes him once again as Judah's protector and provider. He would be like a cloud by day protecting her from the heat of the sun, and a pillar of fire by night, providing her with warmth and light. Thus, while the immediate future looked bleak, even for the righteous few in Judah, there was still hope for them that their faithful commitment to God would not be overlooked. It would ultimately be well with the righteous, and they would eventually eat the fruit of their deeds (Isa. 3:10).

Is it true?

There are many examples where we can observe the natural consequences of sin in people's lives. Most sins produce feelings of guilt, shame, and regret that weigh heavily on a person because of an offended conscience. Unresolved guilt and shame may even lead to feelings of depression. Consider a sin like drunkenness. It often results in any number of natural consequences such as addiction, broken homes, child or spousal abuse, personal embarrassment, and an inability to maintain a consistent job, which further results in financial hardships (Prov. 20:1; 23:29–35). Sins such as anger, impatience, and bitterness will usually lead to a loss of peace and joy, not to mention arguments and fights that leave behind a trail of strained or broken relationships (Prov. 15:1; 29:8). Gluttony gives way to obesity, which carries with it an array of complicating health issues such as strokes, heart disease, sleep apnea, and osteoarthritis, just to name a few.[6] Fornication and adultery may result in broken marriages (Prov. 6:26–29), sexually transmitted diseases, or unplanned pregnancies. The Bible warns about the natural consequences of laziness, as it will often lead to hardship (Prov. 15:19; 18:9; Matt. 25:26–30) and poverty (Prov. 6:6–11; 13:4; 19:15; 20:4; 21:25; 24:30–34). Just about every sin that could be named will carry with it its own array of natural consequences.

---

6 https://www.mayoclinic.org/diseases-conditions/obesity/symptoms-causes/syc-20375742.

One of the unfortunate realities of "natural consequences" is that they almost always result in collateral damage. That is, they tend to negatively impact people beyond those who sinned. A man who commits adultery is not the only person who suffers the consequences of that sin; his wife and children will be deeply impacted too. Likewise, the woman who abuses intoxicants will negatively impact her family and friends as well. This was the case in Israel. When God removed his protective presence from Judah because of the rebellion of most of the inhabitants, even the righteous who lived there experienced all the same natural consequences. They likely wondered if this meant that it didn't pay to remain faithful to God. After all, they were experiencing God's judgment along with everyone else. However, God assured them that, even though they were indirectly suffering the natural consequences of sin now, they would ultimately avoid God's judgment in the future kingdom (Isa. 4:2–6).

Now what?
The primary application of this passage seems to be that one must be willing to pursue righteousness even when the cultural pressures around them pull in the directions of self-centeredness, arrogance, and rebellion against God's Word. The chiastic structure of Isaiah 3:8–11 draws the reader's focus to 3:10, which promises that God will *not* judge the righteous minority along with the wicked majority. Those who resist the cultural trends toward sinful and selfish living now will be rewarded later for their sacrifice, even if it isn't apparent at the present time.

The passage refers to several of the cultural trends that a righteous person must resist to maintain a God-honoring lifestyle. It shouldn't surprise the reader that the sinful realities described in Isaiah's time mirror many of the cultural trends today. Some of the sinful behaviors that invited God's judgment included oppressing others for self-advancement (3:5, 14–15), showing disrespect for those in authority (3:5), and flaunting one's sin before God like the ancient civilization of Sodom (3:8–9). Additionally, the description of the proud women in 3:18–23 would seem to indicate misplaced values such as materialistic greed and the vanity of an overemphasis on outward beauty. These all provide the preacher/teacher of this passage with specific points of application for modern audiences, as these continue to be sins that manifest themselves regularly within our own culture. In fact, the apostle Paul warned Timothy:

> But mark this: There will be terrible times in the last days. People will be lovers of themselves, lovers of money, boastful, proud, abusive, disobedient to their parents, ungrateful, unholy, without love, unforgiving, slanderous, without self-control, brutal, not lovers of the good, treacherous, rash, conceited, lovers of pleasure rather than lovers of God. (2 Tim. 3:1–4)

The parallels between Isaiah's day, the "last days," and our own culture today are striking.

Finally, this passage should serve as a message of hope for all, regardless of how big a mess they have made of their lives. Despite the complete devastation in Jerusalem due to sin and the resulting judgment, the prophet offers hope for a future where all would again be beautiful and glorious. This is because, while God does allow for devastation as judgment against sin, he is also a God who redeems and purifies those who turn to him in repentance and faith. Isaiah 4:2–6 uses the language of salvation and redemption throughout: "will be called holy" (4:3), "all who are recorded among the living," "the Lord will wash away the filth" (4:4). These descriptions invite the modern preacher to call on those in his audience who have made a mess of their life because of sin to turn in faith to God for cleansing, to be made whole, and to have their lives recorded for eternity in God's Book of Life.

Creativity in Presentation

Consider opening your lesson/sermon with a story like the one in the Preaching Pointers section above about a community ravished by a natural disaster such as a tornado. Additionally, you might download aerial drone footage of the aftermath of the disaster and play it as a powerful visual while you describe those events to help your audience identify with the emotions of the survivors left in Jerusalem at the time of the events described in Isaiah 3. As a follow-up, you might end the message by showing some before-and-after photos that show places that have been rebuilt after a natural disaster. Isaiah 4:2–6 provides an image of hope for the future—that what was presently a "heap of ruins" (3:6) would in the future be beautiful and glorious again (4:2).[7]

This passage highlights how Judah's leaders had failed the people and had led them astray. Specifically, Isaiah 3:12 states that their guides had misled them. On June 23, 2018, twelve members of a youth soccer team (ages 11–16) in Thailand became trapped in a cave they had entered to explore when heavy rainfall flooded parts of the cave. The flooding blocked their escape and forced them to hunker down further inside. Nine days passed before the group was discovered by some British divers. Another full week would pass before rescuers would be able to get them out safely. That day, the boys were under the supervision of a twenty-five-year-old coach. The coach failed to heed a sign at the cave's entrance that warned against entering the cave during the rainy season due to the danger of flooding. His negligence almost cost the lives of the entire team. In similar fashion, Judah's guides had ignored God's instructions in his law and from the prophets. As a result, many of God's people were led astray.

A friend of mine tells the true story of when he was trying to start a lawn years ago. He was pleasantly surprised to find several pounds of cheap grass seed at a private sale. Not having much money, he decided to buy enough to plant his lawn. Several weeks later, as the grass began to peek through the soil around his house, he began to wonder what type of grass he had actually planted because it didn't look the way he had envisioned. As the lawn began to grow, it soon became apparent that he hadn't planted grass seed at all. He had bought and planted thistle throughout what was supposed to be his lawn. Thistles are a thorny, invasive weed. You can imagine how discouraged and frustrated my friend was (not to mention a bit embarrassed) that moment when he realized his costly mistake.

The Bible warns that people must not deceive themselves into thinking that they will somehow avoid reaping what they sow (Gal. 6:7–9). Isaiah 3 confronts the wicked people of Judah, warning that those who spent their lives pridefully exalting themselves, pursuing their own selfish agendas at the expense of anyone who got in their way, would ultimately reap the consequences of their actions. Like my friend's lawn filled with thistle, the wicked can't expect to reap good things when they have sown the equivalent of thistle throughout their lives. They too will be sorely disappointed and embarrassed when the harvest of their life is revealed for all to see. While the righteous will "enjoy the [good] fruit of their deeds" (Isa. 3:10), it will not be so for the wicked. Rather, "they will be paid back for what their hands have done" (Isa. 3:11). It will become apparent that sin results in devastation. Nevertheless, God still offers hope as this passage also reveals.

- Sin brings devastation (3:1–4:1).
- God brings restoration (4:2–6).

---

7 Here is a website with some before-and-after photos showing the immediate aftermath of a tornado in Illinois, along with photos from one year later, after the rubble had been cleared and several homes had been rebuilt. https://petapixel.com/2014/12/22/now-photos-capture-illinois-tornado-victims-rebuilding-lives.

DISCUSSION QUESTIONS

1. What are some examples from your own life where you have experienced the principle of reaping what you have sown? (You may suggest examples to the group, such as choosing not to study for a test and getting a failing grade, consistently overeating leading to poor health, or materialistic spending patterns that led to credit card debt.)

2. Isaiah 3:4 says that part of God's judgment would include removing qualified leaders from their midst and replacing them with "children" and those who weren't qualified. Share some examples of good and bad leaders that you have observed or served under in the past. What character traits made them good or bad leaders in your opinion, and how significant was the impact of their leadership as a result?

3. In Isaiah 3:16–4:1, the wives of the corrupt leaders are confronted by God for their involvement in their husbands' corruption. What are some ways that Christians today need to be careful not to enable others' sins? While we may not be directly responsible for their actions, are there ways in which our inaction or support of others might make us guilty before God?

4. Can you remember a time in your life when things were so bleak that life seemed at some level to be over (perhaps after the loss of a close friend or family member, a divorce or break-up with a girlfriend/boyfriend, a serious medical diagnosis, etc.)? As you look back now, can you give testimony to how God provided for you, helping you to get through that time? What advice might you give to somebody who is going through a situation that appears hopeless now?

Isaiah 5:1–30

EXEGETICAL IDEA
The nation will be left desolate because it has failed to realize the Sovereign Lord's expectations and, despite his kindness, has violated his ethical standards by accumulating wealth through unjust means.

THEOLOGICAL FOCUS
The Lord powerfully intervenes and punishes his proud people with purifying judgment when they challenge his sovereignty by rejecting his word and perverting his standards of justice.

PREACHING IDEA
When people become wise in their own eyes and reject God's word, the consequences are painful and inevitable.

PREACHING POINTERS
We have all had an experience where we have uncovered spoiled food. Maybe it has begun to grow green mold or developed a putrid odor. Worse yet, maybe we didn't detect anything was wrong until we put some into our mouths and had a rude awakening on our taste buds. Yuck! Once it is discovered, there is only one thing to do with rotten food: throw it out.

Isaiah 5 compares Israel to a vineyard that Yahweh planted and tended. All along, his desire and expectation for his vineyard was that it would produce delicious grapes. However, when God went to check on the fruit, he discovered a harvest of sour grapes (5:2, 4). These grapes were totally unfit to eat. The reason for this was that Israel had embraced corrupt, unjust practices (5:7). They were acting in ways that seemed wise in their own eyes but showed disregard for God's laws (5:20–21, 24). In the process, they had replaced all that God called good and sweet with that which was evil and bitter (5:20). As a result, they had become sour to God, and he was about to spew them out of his mouth.

A VINEYARD IN RUINS AND DEATH IS IMMINENT (5:1–30)

LITERARY STRUCTURE AND THEMES (5:1–30)

The Lord did everything possible to make his vineyard fruitful, but the vineyard failed to produce good fruit. The Lord urges each member of the covenant community to consider the facts of the case and then announces he will destroy the vineyard because the verdict is clear: Israel, the Lord's vineyard, has produced injustice, not justice. The Lord will punish the proud men who have violated his ethical standards and accumulated wealth through unjust means. In response to their challenge, the Lord will demonstrate his sovereignty by using death, in the form of a mighty foreign army, as his instrument of judgment.

This literary unit contains two closely related speeches (5:1–7, 8–30). The first of these begins like a love song, which quickly goes sour and is transformed into a formal accusation. The Lord accuses his vineyard of failing to produce good grapes and announces he will destroy it. The final verse explains the realities behind the imagery of the song.

The speaker in 5:1–2 could be the prophet, in which case יָדִיד and דּוֹד (5:1) would mean "friend" (Williamson 2006, 332, 334). This proposal has the advantage of maintaining one speaker throughout 5:1–2. But דּוֹד is used in Song of Songs of the woman's lover. So it seems more likely that Israel (cf. 5:7) is the speaker here and is depicting herself as the Lord's bride using the figure of a vineyard.

But the love song does not end in sweet consummation of marriage; someone else (the Lord?) abruptly interrupts and finishes the song in the last line of 5:2 by observing that this vineyard did not produce for its lover. The Lord is the speaker in 5:3–6, and the prophet appears to supply the interpretation of the imagery in 5:7. Isaiah 5:3–6 displays the basic elements of a judgment speech: accusation (5:3–4) and formal announcement of judgment (5:5–6).

The second speech, from a form-critical perspective, contains six oracles, each introduced by הוֹי, "woe" (5:8–10, 11–17, 18–19, 20, 21, 22–30).[1] The interjection הוֹי contributes powerfully to the rhetoric of the speech. As noted earlier (see 1:4), this term was used in funeral laments (see 1 Kings 13:30; Jer. 22:18–19; 34:5; Amos 5:16). When used in prophetic judgment speeches, it carries the connotation of death and would certainly grab an audience's attention and convey a notion of urgency. By prefacing the formal accusation with this word, the prophet acts out Israel's funeral in advance, emphasizing that death is imminent.

A closer examination reveals some structural peculiarities. Woes 1, 2, and 6 have both an accusation of guilt and an announcement of impending judgment, but woes 3–5 have only the accusation:

Woe	Accusation	Announcement
1	v. 8	vv. 9–10
2	vv. 11–12	vv. 13–17
3	vv. 18–19	omitted
4	v. 20	omitted
5	v. 21	omitted
6	vv. 22–23, 24b	vv. 24a, 25–30

---

1 The discussion that follows is based on Chisholm 1986, 49–50.

Some form critics speculate that the missing announcements after woes 3–5 fell out of the text during its transmission (Clements 1980, 64–65) or that the announcements attached to the other woes were added later (Kaiser 1972, 96–109). Such explanations are, at best, unconvincing and, at worst, painfully pedestrian. Explaining the lack of structural symmetry by utilizing diachronic criticism shows insensitivity to the prophet's rhetorical creativity. The omission of the announcements after woes 3–5 is by design. If woes 3–6 are combined, they form a powerful accusation, culminating in an overwhelming announcement of judgment:

Woe(s)	Accusation	Announcement
1	v. 8	vv. 9–10
2	vv. 11–12	vv. 13–17
3–6	vv. 18–23, 24b	vv. 24a, 25–30

The clustering of woes 3–6 with no intervening announcement heightens the accusatory tone of the speech. They are like a series of hammer blows driving home the reality of the people's guilt. Based on the pattern established in woes 1–2, one anticipates an announcement, but the delay creates a foreboding mood. One expects that when the announcement does come, it will be terrifying in the extreme, and the final announcement meets expectations and then some.

Furthermore, as one can see from the outline above, the prophet creates a snowballing effect. The accusations increase in length from two lines of text in woe 1 (5:8, using the arrangement of lines in *BHS*) to four lines in woe 2 (5:11–12) and then ten in the final subunit (5:18–23, 24b). In similar fashion, the announcements increase in length from three lines in woe 1 (5:9–10) to seven lines in woe 2 (5:13–17) and finally fifteen in the third subunit (5:24a, 25–30). Through this technique the prophet impresses upon the listener two facts: the people are indeed guilty, and their punishment will indeed be overwhelming.

One apparent oddity is the structure of 5:24, which begins the final, long-awaited announcement (note the introductory לָכֵן, "therefore"), but then seemingly aborts it by returning to an accusatory tone (note כִּי, "because," at the beginning of 5:24b). But this too reflects careful rhetorical design. As the prophet finally begins to describe the coming judgment on these rebels, he stops and gets in one more parting shot, as it were, characterizing the sins he has just outlined as covenantal rebellion against the Holy One of Israel. Having erased any lingering question of the rebels' guilt, he resumes the final announcement (note עַל־כֵּן, "therefore," at the beginning of 5:25; Chisholm 1986, 53).

Moving beyond form criticism, we can detect several concentric structures within this speech.[2] The accusations, for the most part, are arranged in a chiasm, except for 5:20–21 and 24b, which are outside the basic structure by design in order to grab the audience's attention.

A Accusation: injustice (5:8; woe 1)
   Announcement of judgment (5:9–10)
  B Accusation: carousing (5:11–12a; woe 2)
    C Accusation: failure to recognize the Lord's work (5:12b; woe 2)
     Announcement of judgment (5:13–17)
    C' Accusation: failure to recognize the Lord's work (5:18–19; woe 3)
     D Accusation: perversity of morality and pride (5:20–21; woes 4–5)
  B' Accusation: carousing (5:22; woe 6)
A' Accusation: injustice (5:23; woe 6)
   Announcement of judgment (5:24a, 25–30)
   with embedded expanded accusation (5:24b)
     D+ Rejection of God's authority (5:24b)

Isaiah 5:8 describes the accumulation of property, which was accomplished through

---

2 What follows is a summary of Chisholm 1986, 50–52, with some modifications, esp. regarding 5:20–21.

pseudolegal means (cf. Mic. 2:1–2), such as the practice described in 5:23. The images of carousing obviously go hand in hand, and the key word "work" (מַעֲשֶׂה, 5:12, 19) coupled with רָאָה, "see," links the C sections of the outline.

It is important to note that the second C section is expanded (5:20–21, which I have labeled "D") by a denunciation of the sinners' moral perversity and pride. As noted above, these two woes (4 and 5) come where one expects the announcement for woe 3. This oddity, coupled with the disruption of the basic chiastic structure (A-B-C-C'-B'-A'), grabs one's attention and causes one to focus on the underlying problem in their thinking that spawns the specific sins highlighted in the other accusations.[3]

It is also significant that the prophet includes one more expansion of his indictment in 5:24b, which gives the basis for the preceding announcement (5:24a) and lies outside the series of accusatory woes. In the D section in 5:20–21, the prophet zeroes in on the perversity and pride that underlie specific sins. In 5:24b, which I label D+, he probes even deeper. Behind the perversity and pride lies a rejection of God's word, which is an expression of the authority of the Holy One of Israel.

The prophet also uses concentricity in the structure of 5:11–17. Isaiah 5:11–13 exhibit the following structure:

A Carousing condemned (5:11–12a)
  B Insensitivity to the Lord's work condemned (5:12b)
  B' Insensitivity to the Lord's work punished (5:13a)
A' Carousing punished (5:13b)[4]

Isaiah 5:14–17, which expand the theme of the punishment of the carousers (see commentary below), also display a concentric structure:

A Sheol eats the sinners (5:14)
  B The self-exalting sinners are humbled (5:15)
  B' The Lord exalts himself through judgment (5:16)
A' Sheep eat on the ruins of the sinners' houses (5:17)

- ***The Lord's Kindness and Israel's Ingratitude (5:1–2)***
- ***The Lord Announces Judgment (5:3–6)***
- ***The Prophet Interprets the Imagery (5:7)***
- ***Images of Death, Part One (5:8–10)***
  - *Accusation (5:8)*
  - *Announcement of Judgment (5:9–10)*
- ***Images of Death, Part Two (5:11–17)***
  - *Accusation (5:11–12)*
  - *Announcement of Judgment (5:13–17)*
- ***Images of Death, Part Three (5:18–30)***
  - *Accusation (5:18–23, 24b)*
  - *Announcement of Judgment (5:24a, 25–30)*

EXPOSITION (5:1–30)

The Lord's Kindness and Israel's Ingratitude (5:1–2)

The Lord did everything possible to make his vineyard fruitful, but the vineyard failed to produce good fruit.

---

[3] I owe this insight to Julie Dykes, who made this point in her 2020 Evangelical Theological Society (Virtual) Annual Meeting presentation, "Inverting Good and Evil: Thematic Chiasm in the Woes of Isaiah 5." Though I disagree with her proposed alternative chiastic structure, she is right to highlight 5:20–21 as surfacing deeper, fundamental problems that are the source of the sins denounced.

[4] The reference to hunger and thirst in 5:13b conceptually links the statement with the image of carousing in 5:11–12a.

5:1. This speech begins as a love song directed from the bride to the groom. As in the Song of Songs, she speaks of the groom as her love (דּוֹד); she also pictures herself as his vineyard, located on a fertile hill.[5] The Hebrew reads, "on a horn, a son of oil." "Horn" may refer here to the horn-shaped peak of a hill (cf. BDB s.v. "קֶרֶן" mng. 4, 902). "Son of oil" associates the hill with olive trees, but it may be an idiom suggesting fertility (BDB s.v. "שֶׁמֶן" mng. 1, 1032). At any rate, the point seems to be that it is a prime location for a vineyard. In Song of Songs the image of a vineyard is used of the young woman's body (cf. Song 1:6; 8:12). Within the framework of the love song, the grapes are the anticipated children.

5:2. The series of five verbs in 5:2a highlights the groom's effort to make his vineyard productive. He broke up its soil, removed the stones, planted a vine, and built a watchtower, used for observation and storage of equipment and wine (Walsh 2000, 128–42). Hopeful that the vineyard would yield a return, he constructed a winepress and then waited patiently in anticipation of a yield. After vines were planted, one had to wait four years or more for them to produce (Borowski 1987, 110).

> **Broke Up Its Soil**
> On the meaning of the verb עָזַק, used only here in the Old Testament, see *HALOT* s.v. "עזק" 810, which cites an Arabic cognate meaning "break up the soil." The verb appears in later Hebrew, meaning "to break clods and level the ground, to break ground, to till" (Jastrow 1967, 1062). Borowski (1987, 104) assumes a strictly chronological verbal sequence and argues that the verb cannot mean "dig, hoe" here, since one would first have to clear away the stones. He relates the word to the Arabic name of a bush (*'ajjaq*) and suggests that the verb refers to uprooting these bushes from the field prior to clearing it of stone. However, to remove stones from a field, one must break up soil to loosen and dig up the rocks. Perhaps this is what is described here.

However, the love song gets aborted, for 5:2b describes the vineyard as unproductive. As noted above, the Lord, who is the speaker in 5:3–6, probably speaks here. Despite his efforts to provide an environment where the vineyard could produce good grapes, it instead produced sour grapes. Rotten, diseased grapes are in view (Williamson 2006, 319–20, 338). Oded Borowski (1987, 161) argues that black rot is the disease in view here.

The Lord Announces Judgment (5:3–6)

The Lord urges each member of the covenant community to consider the facts of the case and then announces that he will destroy the vineyard.

5:3. At this point the underlying image of love and marriage recedes as the song takes on a legal and accusatory tone and is transformed into a judgment speech. The Lord directly addresses the residents of Jerusalem and men of Judah, who stand behind the image of the vineyard, and ironically casts them in the role of judges (5:3). To allow the defendant to serve as judge, one must be absolutely confident that the evidence is overwhelming!

Though one might understand the addressees as the people in general, it seems more likely that the leaders, primarily those in the royal bureaucracy, are in view here. As Marvin Chaney (1999, 110–11) points out, the woe oracle that immediately follows (5:8–10) favors this. Chaney argues that the phrase "dwellers in Jerusalem" in 5:3 "refers to the ruling elite of Jerusalem and/or to the Davidic king" (pp. 112–16). He understands

---

5   For דּוֹד, see Song 1:13–14, 16; 2:3, 8–10, 16–17; 4:16; 5:2, 4–6, 8–10, 16; 6:1–3; 7:10–12, 14; 8:5, 14.

the parallel phrase "people [literally, "men"] of Judah" as roughly synonymous, "referring either to the ruling dynasty of Judah or to its military aristocracy" (p. 116).

5:4–5. The Lord did everything in his power to assure that the vineyard would be productive (5:4a; cf. 5:2), yet the sour grapes were incontrovertible evidence of the vineyard's failure (5:4b). Having used thought-provoking rhetorical questions to establish the vineyard's failure, the Lord next announces its destruction (5:5a). He would remove its hedge (5:5b; cf. 5:2), allowing wild animals (a metaphor for an invading army) to overrun it. A hedge was made of thorny bushes and a wall was constructed from stones removed from the field (Borowski 1987, 105–6).

Isaiah 5:4–5 use wordplay to good effect. The verb עָשָׂה, "do, make," is a key word (Williamson 2006, 339–40). It is used to describe the production of grapes (5:2, 4b), the Lord's efforts to make the vineyard fruitful (5:4a), and the Lord's acts of judgment (5:5; Korpel 1996, 70–71). The repetition highlights poetic justice: the vineyard that produced sour grapes becomes the object of divine judgmental action. It also highlights the reversal in the Lord's attitude toward the vineyard: positive, supportive effort is turned into negative, destructive action. In this regard it is noteworthy that the song begins with the Lord pictured as a bridegroom and lover, but then ends with him being called Lord of Armies, as in earlier judgment speeches (Isa. 2:12; 3:1, 15).

5:6. The Lord will leave the vineyard uncultivated (5:6a) and deprive it of rain (5:6b), turning it into a weed-infested wasteland. The reference to the withholding of rain may echo the covenant curse language of Deuteronomy 11:11–17 (see esp. 11:14, 17), since violation of covenant is the underlying reality (see comments on Isa. 5:7 below).

The Prophet Interprets the Imagery (5:7)
The anticipated good grapes stand for justice and righteousness, while the sour grapes represent oppressive injustice.

It is obvious that the focus of the speech is covenant violation involving the perversion of the Lord's moral and ethical standards. The wordplay in 5:7 mirrors the perversion of the Lord's expectations: he expected מִשְׁפָּט, "justice," but instead the vineyard produced מִשְׂפָּח, "bloodshed." The two words share the same syllabic structure, the same prefixed *mem*, sibilants as their first root letter, and *pe* as their second root letter. But the difference in the third root letter produces a virtual antonym of מִשְׁפָּט, when one recognizes that מִשְׂפָּח is an effect of injustice. Likewise, the Lord expected צְדָקָה, "fairness, righteousness," but instead the vineyard produced צְעָקָה, used here of the painful cries of the oppressed or mistreated (cf. Gen. 19:13; 27:34; Exod. 3:7, 9; 22:23; 1 Sam. 9:16; Neh. 5:1; Job 27:9; 34:28; Ps. 9:12 [HB 13]). Again, the two words are similar in sound; they share the same syllabic structure and feminine ending, as well as the initial *tsade* and third root letter *qop*. But the substitution of *ayin* for *dalet* in the second root position produces a virtual antonym of צְדָקָה.

The use of the vineyard image for Israel provides an intertextual link with Isaiah 3:14, where the Lord accuses the leaders of the people of ruining (note בִּעַרְתֶּם, "you have ruined") the vineyard (the covenant community) by their robbery and oppression. In 5:1–7 the vineyard, identified as the house of Israel/the people of Judah (cf. 5:3, 7), becomes the object of divine judgment, which leaves the vineyard in ruins (5:5, לְבָעֵר). Correlating the two texts, we see two complementary truths. Corrupt leaders ruined the covenant community by producing, as it were, the sour grapes of injustice. Now the ethically ruined community they commandeered will be ruined by divine judgment, in the sense that

God will withhold his covenantal protection and blessing, subjecting it to invasion.

> **The House of Israel/the People of Judah**
> Chaney (1999, 116–17) regards the phrase "house of Israel" in 5:7 as referring to the "dynastic house" of the northern kingdom of Israel. The expression occurs only four other times in Isaiah (cf. 8:14; 14:2 [referring to the exiles who will return from Babylon]; 46:3; 63:7). In 8:14 the prophet refers to Israel and Judah as "the two houses [plural] of Israel," suggesting that the phrase "house of Israel" may refer to either. In 46:3 the parallelism may be synonymous (house of Jacob = house of Israel) or it could indicate a distinction between the two exilic communities. Contrary to Chaney's claim, the context suggests that Judah is the referent in 5:7. Those addressed in 5:3 are most naturally understood as the referent of "house of Israel" in 5:7, where the parallelism is best taken as synonymous. See Hans Wildberger 1991, 184. Gary Williams (1985, 462) shows that the use of "house of Israel" for Judah here contributes to the prophet's rhetoric in an effective way.

Images of Death, Part One (5:8–10)

Destruction is imminent for those who accumulate property. The Lord, the mighty warrior, announces they will be exiled, and their land will become unproductive.

Accusation (5:8)

The accumulation of landed property was a practice that violated the covenant stipulations (see Mic. 2:12), which emphasized that the Lord was the sole owner of the land (Lev. 25:23–28; Deut. 19:14). The Lord allowed his people to reside in his land and gave it to individual tribes as their inheritance. He established various laws to maintain socioeconomic equilibrium. But by Isaiah's time a royal military and judicial bureaucracy had developed, just as Samuel had warned (1 Sam. 8). As government expanded, it acquired more and more land and commandeered the economy and legal system. At various administrative levels, it invited bribery, graft, and other dishonest practices. The common people outside the urban administrative centers, through confiscatory taxation, conscription, excessive interest rates, and other oppressive measures, were gradually disenfranchised and lost their landed property and, with it, their rights as citizens.

The expression קֶרֶב הָאָרֶץ, literally "the middle of the land," is rare. Of its twelve uses, only six refer to the middle of the land of Israel (or Judah).[6] Three of these appear in Deuteronomy in texts that speak of the covenant community's responsibility to obey the Lord in the "middle of the land" (Deut. 4:5), of the need for generosity to the poor who will always be present in the "middle of the land" (15:11), and of the Lord's prohibition of murder in the "middle of the land" (19:10). Against this background, the image of the rich living alone in "the middle of the land" is ironic, for the actions that enabled them to do so (cf. Isa. 1:15, 21; 4:4) violated in principle all three of the Deuteronomic stipulations where the phrase occurs. It is not surprising that Isaiah later associates the phrase with judgment that will overtake the "middle of the land" (6:12; 7:22; cf. 10:23, which refers to the "middle of all the land").

Announcement of Judgment (5:9–10)

5:9. The punishment will be appropriate for the crimes committed. Those who have accumulated houses will see those houses destroyed and left uninhabited. The fields they have acquired will yield only a fraction of their potential (Chisholm 1986, 54). Miller (1982, 43) points

---

6 In the other six uses the referent of "land" is Egypt (Gen. 45:6; Exod. 8:22) or the earth in a broad sense (Gen. 48:16; Ps. 74:12; Isa. 19:24; 24:13).

out that the "correspondence is one of result or frustration of result." In the case of the houses, the rich owners will be deprived of that which they have greedily taken. Regarding the fields, Miller explains: "The intention of such land acquisition is to enlarge one's productive property and thereby one's wealth. But the judgment on those who commit this sin is that the object of their sinful greed will leave them poverty stricken."

5:10. One may detect an echo of the covenantal curses in 5:10 (Wildberger 1991, 199). Indeed, Deuteronomy 28:38 warns that the disobedient people will plant much seed but have little harvest due to an invasion of devouring locusts. Likewise, Deuteronomy 28:39 warns that the people will plant vineyards but enjoy no harvest because of worms.

Images of Death, Part Two (5:11–17)

Destruction is imminent for those who spend their days carousing and pay no attention to the Lord's activities. Those who disregard the Lord will be swept away by his righteous judgment, which will bring exile, death, and desolation upon the nation.

Accusation (5:11–12)

5:11. Isaiah once more uses irony for rhetorical effect (Roberts 1992, 41–43). In the first line of 5:11 the carousers pursue wine; in the second line wine chases them! The passage has a wisdom flavor. In Proverbs 23:29–35 those who linger (the *piel* of the verb אָחַר is used in 23:30, as in Isa. 5:11) over wine end up being its victim because the wine dulls their senses to what is going on around them.

> **Wine**
>
> Hebrew שֵׁכָר (5:11a) is usually understood as referring to beer, but in an Israelite context it is more likely that date-palm wine is in view. See Carey Walsh 2000, 200–202. Williamson (2006, 370) prefers to see שֵׁכָר as referring to any fermented intoxicating beverage other than grape wine, including the product of dates, honey, and raisins. He agrees with Walsh that beer is an "unlikely" referent. For a contrary view, see Roberts 2015, 80.

5:12. Music was an important part of the carousers' festivities (5:12a). Four instruments are listed, followed by still another reference to wine (cf. 5:11b). Williamson (2006, 358) points out that the first four items in the list are paired (harps and lyres, pipes and timbrels), while the fifth and final noun (wine) "is unpaired." This gives it "a certain emphasis, which seems suitable: 'and of course, especially wine.'" Terminal deviation is often used as a structural and rhetorical device in Hebrew poetry.

Overcome by wine, the carousers are desensitized to the purposes of the Lord (see also 5:19–22). The verbs of perception in 5:12b do not refer here to merely seeing, but to seeing with interest and understanding. The "knowledge" mentioned in 5:13a is most naturally understood as this lack of perception described in 5:12b.

In this context the work of the Lord is his impending judgment. The "deeds" of the Lord can encompass a variety of divine activities (Deut. 32:4; Job 36:24), including his victories over Israel's enemies and his deliverance of his people (Pss. 44:1 [HB 2]; 64:9 [HB 10]; 77:12 [HB 13]; 92:4 [HB 5]; 95:9; 111:3; 143:5; Hab. 3:2). But here his "deeds" (פֹּעַל) are the judgments on his people (cf. Hab. 1:5). The "work" (מַעֲשֶׂה) of God's "hands" can be his creation, including his people (see Pss. 8:6 [HB 7]; 19:1 [HB 2]; 138:8; Isa. 29:23; 60:21; 64:8), or his acts of justice (Pss. 28:4–5; 92:4 [HB 5]). Here the Lord's "deeds" and the "work of his hands" refer to the judgment about to come upon the wicked (see Isa. 5:19 [cf. 5:26]; cf. 10:12; 28:21; Hab. 1:5). The noun מַעֲשֶׂה, "work" (see also Isa. 5:19), provides an intertextual link with 5:5, where the related verb עָשָׂה, "do, make," is used of divine judgment (cf. Korpel 1996, 71).

A Vineyard in Ruins and Death Is Imminent (5:1–30)

Announcement of Judgment (5:13–17)
5:13–14, 17. The irony heightens in this announcement of judgment. The people are bound for exile (5:13a). Those who spend their days eating and drinking (5:11–12) will be deprived of food and drink (5:13b). But others will eat. Sheol will open its mouth wide and devour these carousing leaders (5:14), while sheep will graze on the ruins of the homes where the leaders once caroused (5:17).

> *TRANSLATION ANALYSIS 5:17B*
> The Hebrew text of 5:17b reads, "and ruins, fatlings, resident aliens will eat." חָרְבוֹת, "ruins," is best understood as an adverbial accusative of place. מֵחִים, "fatlings," is used only here and in Psalm 66:15, where it refers to sacrificial animals. גָּרִים, "resident aliens," is a substantival participle from גּוּר, "to live temporarily." A reference to resident aliens would make sense in the context, if they were pastoral nomads grazing their flocks among the ruins of the now uninhabited towns. However, tighter parallelism is achieved if we emend the form to גְּדָיִם (resh-dalet confusion), "young sheep," a reading supported by the LXX. In this case גְּדָיִם is appositional to the preceding מֵחִים. The translations are divided: HCSB/KJV/*Tanakh* ("strangers") and ESV ("nomads") follow MT in reading גָּרִים, while NIV ("lambs"), NRSV ("kids"), and NLT ("young goats") follow the LXX. The NRSV ("fatlings") and NLT ("fattened sheep") take מֵחִים as a reference to sheep as well, while NIV (like ESV, HCSB, and KJV) sees the referent of מֵחִים as the rich (note "the ruins of the rich"). I propose a translation: "and well-fed young sheep will eat among the ruins."

The image of Sheol as a devourer with a large mouth and throat is reminiscent of the description of Mot, the god of death, in the Ugaritic myths (Roberts 2015, 81). Mot boasts that his throat (*npš*, cf. Isa. 5:14) is like that of "the lion in the wasteland" (*COS* 1.86:265). He shovels "seven portions" into his throat with both hands (*COS* 1.86:265). When Mot opens his mouth, one lip reaches the earth, the other the heavens, and his tongue extends to the stars (*COS* 1.86:266). Baal is described as descending (*yrd*, cf. Isa. 5:14) into his throat (*COS* 1.86:266). Isaiah does not deify Sheol, which is treated as feminine in the Hebrew text (note the two feminine verbs in 5:14a), in contrast to the myths, where Mot is masculine. Sheol sometimes refers to the realm of the dead, located beneath the earth in ancient cosmology (Deut. 32:22; Isa. 14:9). But it is more than just a geographical location. As we see in Isaiah 5:14, Sheol is often viewed as personal and as having a voracious appetite (Prov. 1:12; 27:20; 30:16; Isa. 28:15; Hab. 2:5). While modern Western readers of the Bible might be inclined to dismiss this portrait as mere poetic personification, it is likely that ancient Israel had a more dynamic notion of death. Orthodox Israelite theology did not deify death, yet it may have viewed it as a demonic power opposed to God and his people (see Ps. 18:4–5 [HB 5–6]; Isa. 25:7–8; cf. Heb. 2:14–15). Even so, the Lord is ultimately sovereign over death (Pss. 16:10; 49:15 [HB 16]) and can even use it as his instrument of judgment, as in Isaiah 5:14.

5:15–16. The prophet uses wordplay in 5:15–16 to highlight the contrasting consequences of the coming judgment. Judgment will bring down proud men and their haughty demeanor (note esp. "eyes of the arrogant" [literally, "exalted"]; גְּבֹהִים), while the Lord would be "exalted" (note וַיִּגְבַּה) through judgment (cf. 2:11, 17). The *niphal* participle נִקְדָּשׁ is best taken as reflexive, "will set himself apart." Parallel to גָּבַהּ, it refers to elevating himself, but the underlying reality depicted by the spatial idiom is that he demonstrates his sovereign authority and power. He does this through his just judgment, which tangibly displays his "righteousness," or commitment to what is right. It is ironic that the Lord's "righteousness" (NIV11 "righteous acts") in judgment will be directed against those who perverted "righteousness" (5:7).

> **Through Judgment**
> It is noteworthy that the first line speaks of the Lord of Armies being exalted "in/by *the* judgment," while the second says the Holy God will elevate himself in/by "righteousness." The article is present in בַּמִּשְׁפָּט, "in/by the judgment," but absent in בִּצְדָקָה, "in/by righteousness." This variation does not occur elsewhere in Isaiah where the word pair appears. Note especially uses where both words have a prepositional prefix, as in 5:16: 1:27; 5:7; 9:7 (HB 6); the terms, though in proximity, are not truly juxtaposed in 54:17. Without a prepositional prefix, the terms are anarthrous when juxtaposed: 28:17; 32:16; 33:5; 56:1; 58:2; 59:9, 14. The definite form in 5:16 may indicate that an event, "the judgment," is envisioned, while the anarthrous parallel form characterizes this event. R. W. L. Moberly (2001, 67–68) entertains this possibility for the first line, though he suspects the Masoretic pointing does not reflect the original meaning but is instead "a reconstrual of the text."

The titles of the Lord are significant. The first, Lord of Armies (יְהוָה צְבָאוֹת), depicts him as the one who commands armies as his instrument of judgment (see 1:9). The second (הָאֵל הַקָּדוֹשׁ, "the holy God") is unique to this context.[7] It pictures God as the exalted, transcendent ruler of the world who exhibits his sovereignty and justice through his judgments, thereby demonstrating that proud men cannot challenge his rule. The title, though unique, is related conceptually to "the Holy One of Israel" (see 1:4), which appears twice later in this speech (5:19, 24) and paves the way literarily for the prophet's vision of the holy, exalted divine king in the next chapter.

Images of Death, Part Three (5:18–30)

Destruction is imminent for those who persist in sin, challenge the Lord to intervene, exhibit hubris, pursue pleasure, pervert justice, and reject the Lord's authority as their covenant God. His angry judgment will destroy these rebels through the instrument of a powerful, unrelenting, ruthless foreign army.

Accusation (5:18–23, 24b)

5:18–19. The prophet pictures sinners strenuously pulling their sin like a load. The image depicts their strong attachment to their sin, as well as its burdensome nature. Hebrew שָׁוְא, "emptiness," may describe the ropes as unreliable (see *HALOT* s.v. "שָׁוְא" mng. 2b, 1426), perhaps indicating they are frayed and weak. However, metaphor and reality may be mixed here, with שָׁוְא having an ethical nuance, "deceit." The fact that they are pulling iniquity and sin favors this. In this case deceit is viewed as an instrument used to facilitate sin.

In the chiastic structure of the accusations (see above), 5:19 corresponds thematically to 5:12b, which accuses these sinners of insensitivity to the Lord's purposes. Here they urge the Lord to accomplish his work quickly and to bring his plan to fruition so they can see what it entails. Their words reveal their spiritual ignorance, for the Lord's "work" is his impending judgment (see our comment on 5:12b above). This is, as Andrew Davies (2000, 113) observes, "their supreme folly," for "the work that they are urging him to hasten will result in their own destruction." The parallel line refers to this divine work as "the plan of the Holy One of Israel." This is the first time the title "Holy One of Israel" has appeared since 1:4, ironically here on the lips of those who will be punished by their sovereign king, who possesses moral authority over them. Though the sinners speak sarcastically here, the Holy One really does have a "plan" for his people and the nations (see as well Isa. 14:24–27; 19:17; 23:8–9; 25:1; 28:29). That plan includes judgment for their sinful rebellion against his authority (see 1:4; 5:24).

---

7   A similar expression, "this Holy God," occurs in 1 Samuel 6:20, but the more common title Elohim is used there.

5:20–21. Indeed, their entire view of morality is perverted. They look at evil, compared here to darkness and what is bitter, and have the audacity to call it good, compared here to light and what is sweet (5:20). Despite their warped sense of right and wrong, they view themselves as wise and discerning (5:21). Isaiah's characterization of his sinful contemporaries is consistent with the wisdom tradition, which denounces those who set their own standards for proper behavior, rather than following God's revealed moral standards (see Prov. 3:7; 26:5, 12, 16; 28:11). As noted earlier, this D section, which expands the second C section of the chiastic structure (see above), highlights their perverted, proud attitude as the root cause of the sins denounced in the concentrically arranged accusations. Their pride, in particular, will be the special target of divine judgment, according to 5:15–16.

5:22–23. In the chiastic structure of the accusations (see above), 5:22 and 23 correspond thematically to 5:8 and 11–12a. Like 5:11–12a, 5:22 denounces the sinners' carousing at the expense of their victims. The prophet sarcastically compares the carousers to courageous warriors when it comes to boldly drinking their mixed concoctions. The image may seem strange, but it ominously paves the way for the description of real warriors in the accusation that follows (5:25–30).

Isaiah 5:23, like 5:8, focuses on injustice. Isaiah 5:8 denounces the rich oppressors for accumulating landed property. Isaiah 5:23 reveals one of the ways they accomplished this; they commandeered the legal system and rigged it to their advantage. In their courts, justice is ignored (literally, "turned aside").

Announcement of Judgment
(5:24a, 25–30)

5:24a. The announcement of judgment uses metaphorical language to emphasize the swift and thorough destruction that will overtake the sinners (5:24a). They are like a plant that has an insufficient root system; the root rots and the blossoms dry up and blow away as if they were dust. Their demise will happen as swiftly as when fire devours straw or dry grass. They will be helpless before the Lord's judgment.

5:24b. Before the prophet elaborates on this impending judgment, he identifies the basis for judgment one more time (5:24b). The sinful people rejected and spurned (see 1:4 and our comments on this verb) God's word, which came to them in the form of corrective instruction. (See 1:10 and our comments there on the meaning of תּוֹרָה in this context.) In the D section (see above), the prophet zeroes in on the perversity and pride that give rise to specific sins. Here he probes even deeper. Behind the perversity and pride lies a rejection of God's word, which is an expression of the authority of the Holy One of Israel.

Divine titles used earlier in the speech reappear here. "LORD of Armies" (see 5:16, as well as 1:9) depicts the Lord as a mighty warrior-king who commands armies as he comes to punish the disobedient people. "Holy One of Israel" (see 5:19, as well as 1:4) pictures the Lord as the highly exalted king who possesses moral authority over his covenant community. The Lord has both the power and the authority to deal with his people decisively.

5:25. The earlier announcements of judgment, for the most part, describe the consequences of the impending judgment (see 5:8–10, 11–17). Only 5:16 directly mentions the Lord's involvement. Isaiah 5:25 focuses on the Lord's intervention as it describes his anger flaring up against his people (cf. Deut. 31:17) and his hand striking them. The expression "he will lift his hand" pictures a warrior extending his hand in battle to strike down his enemies (note the following statement, "and strike them"). It becomes part of the recurring judgment refrain in Isaiah 9:12, 17, 21; and 10:4.[8] When the Lord raises his hand to do battle, his enemies' destiny is sealed (23:11; 31:3) and no one can thwart him (14:26–27). The Lord's powerful intervention causes the normally stable mountains to shake and leaves corpses lying in the streets.

The imagery is well attested in the battle annals of ancient Near Eastern kings. Ramses III's loud battle cry caused the mountains to shake, and several Assyrian warrior-kings boast that the cosmos shook at their appearance (see Chisholm 1983, 161–62). Victorious kings also describe how they left the battlefield littered with corpses (see *ARAB* 2 §§253–254; Lichtheim 1976, 69–70; and *COS* 2.5A:36–38). The Assyrian parallels are especially ironic, since the Lord's instrument of destruction, described in detail in the following verses, was none other than the Assyrian army.

5:26. The Lord's sovereignty over this army is apparent. He lifts a signal flag and summons his army with a whistle. The army's response is immediate and swift (5:26). The use of מְהֵרָה, "hurriedly," and יָבוֹא, "comes," links 5:26 with 5:19, where the sinners urge the Lord to "hurry" (יְמַהֵר) and ask for his plan to "come" (וְתָבוֹאָה). The Lord will indeed hurry; his plan will indeed arrive, embodied in the powerful army described in 5:26–30. As I have stated elsewhere, "The proud rebels would get just what they scoffingly requested" (Chisholm 1986, 54). The reference to the army's origin in the "distant regions of the earth" may echo the covenant curse of Deuteronomy 28:49, which describes the Lord empowering a distant nation to invade and devastate Israel.

5:27–30. The Lord's approaching army is terrifying. Gorän Eidevall (2009, 25) points out "the consistent use" of singular verb forms and pronominal suffixes in Isaiah 5:26–30 to describe the army: "The collective is described as if it were one individual. As a consequence, the notion of each soldier's individuality—and fallibility!—is entirely suppressed." The use of the collective emphasizes the united effort of the army. It advances as a single, unified force ready to steamroll any who oppose it. The army's foreignness, highlighted by its origin in a distant land (5:26), is inherently fear-provoking. It advances relentlessly, not stopping to rest (5:27). The warriors are ready for battle, the horses are fully capable of making the long trip, and the chariots move swiftly forward (5:28). The invaders are like a powerful lion focused on its prey, which it rips to shreds (5:29).

As the "lion" growls loudly, the sound rivals the waves of the surging sea in volume (5:30a). Isaiah frequently uses darkness as a symbol of the distress that judgment brings (9:2; 29:18; 42:7; 45:7; 47:5; 49:9; 59:9; 60:2) and light as a symbol for divine deliverance and renewed blessing (9:2; 30:26; 42:6, 16; 45:7; 49:6; 51:4; 58:8; 60:1, 3, 19–20). The symbolism is ironic here, for darkness in 5:20 signifies moral evil, while light stands for what is fair and right. Those who confuse God's moral standards and change good (light) into evil (darkness) will be judged appropriately by God, who will change their light (sphere of life) into darkness (death and destruction; Chisholm 1986, 54). Dense darkness descends upon the land (5:30b) as clouds swallow up the light (5:30c).

The imagery of 5:29–30 reflects the way Assyrian kings describe themselves in their royal annals (see Chisholm 1986, 55–56; and

---

8 But here in 5:25 the statement is not a refrain. Isaiah 5:25–30 fits well in its present context and should not be relocated as part of some complex redactional scheme. Brown (1990, 442) states "there is not sufficient reason to consider 5:25b as a legitimate refrain, while it is obvious that the four repeated lines from 9:7 to 10:4 are just that, refrains. Consequently, there is no reason to claim that 5:25–30 originally belonged anywhere other than its present location." See as well, Irvine 1992, 221.

Johnston 2001, 287–307). For example, Sargon, who invaded the west during Isaiah's time, compared himself to a lion: "In the anger of my heart I mustered the masses of Assur's troops and, raging like a lion, I set my face to conquer those lands" (*ARAB* 2:27 §56). The image of loud growling (5:29–30a) may reflect siege warfare, which Sargon describes as follows: "Over that city I made the loud noise of my army resound like Adad, and the inhabitants . . . his people, the old men and old women, went up on the roofs of their houses and wept bitterly" (*ARAB* 2:94 §171). The dark clouds may allude to an invading army, described by Sargon in this way: "As with a dense cloud of the night, I covered that province, and all of its great cities" (*ARAB* 2:89 §163). Sargon's successor, Sennacherib, also used the image of a cloud to depict invading forces: "Like the onset of the locust swarms of the springtime they kept steadily coming on against me to offer battle. With the dust of their feet covering the wide heavens, like a mighty storm with (its) masses of dense clouds, they drew up in battle array" (*ARAB* 2:126 §252).

The Verb Forms in the Announcements of Judgment

5:9–10: As expected in predictive discourse, this announcement of judgment uses three *yiqtol* forms to describe the impact of the coming judgment.

5:13–17: This announcement uses an assortment of verbs to describe the coming judgment: (1) *qatal* (perfect) in 5:13, 14a; (2) *weqatal* (perfect with *waw*-consecutive) in 5:14a, 14b, 17a; (3) *wayyiqtol* (preterite with *waw*-consecutive) in 5:15a (two), 16; (4) *yiqtol* (imperfect) in 5:15b, 17b. The three *weqatal* forms and two *yiqtol* forms are expected in predictive discourse. The two *qatal* forms and three *wayyiqtol* forms are not. These narrative discourse forms describe future events as if they had already taken place. This rhetorical use of these forms fits in a woe oracle, which mimics a lament over one already deceased.

There is a pattern to the distribution of the forms: (1) two narrative discourse (rhetorical) forms in 5:13–14a, followed by two predictive discourse forms in 5:14a–b; (2) two narrative discourse (rhetorical) forms in 5:15a, followed by a predictive discourse form in 5:15b; (3) one narrative discourse (rhetorical) form in 5:16, followed by two predictive discourse forms in 5:17. By mixing verb forms like this, the prophet reminds his audience that judgment, while as good as done, is still future. This leaves a window of opportunity for a proper response to the prophet's exhortations (cf. 1:16–20; 2:5, 22). Despite the rhetoric of certitude, judgment remains contingent.

5:24a: As expected in predictive discourse, this announcement of judgment uses three *yiqtol* forms to describe the impact of the coming judgment (as in 5:9–10).

5:25–30: This announcement uses an assortment of verbs to describe the coming judgment: (1) *qatal* (perfect) in 5:25a, 25b, 30b; (2) *weqatal* (perfect with *waw*-consecutive) in 5:26a (two), 29b, 30b; (3) *wayyiqtol* (preterite with *waw*-consecutive) in 5:15a (four); (4) *yiqtol* (imperfect) in 5:24a (three), 26b, 27 (two); (5) *weyiqtol* (imperfect with *waw*-conjunctive): 29b (three), 30a.[9] The four *weqatal* forms, six *yiqtol* forms, and four *weyiqtol* forms are expected in predictive discourse. The three *qatal* forms and four *wayyiqtol* forms are not. As in the previous announcement (5:13–17), these narrative discourse forms describe future events as if they had already taken place. This rhetorical use of these forms fits in a woe oracle, which mimics a lament over one already deceased.

There is a pattern to the distribution of the forms: (1) six narrative discourse (rhetorical) forms in 5:25, followed by five predictive discourse forms in 5:26–27a; (2) three narrative discourse (rhetorical) forms in 5:27b–28, followed by six predictive discourse forms in 5:29–30a; (3) one narrative discourse (rhetorical) form in 5:30b, signaling closure through terminal deviation. Once again, by mixing verb forms like this, the prophet reminds his audience that judgment, while as good as done, is still future. There is a window of opportunity to respond positively to the prophet's exhortations (cf. 1:16–20; 2:5, 22). Judgment remains contingent.

THEOLOGICAL FOCUS

The theological focus of this passage can be stated as follows: the Lord powerfully intervenes and punishes his proud people with purifying judgment when they challenge his sovereignty by rejecting his word and perverting his standards of justice. As the prophet develops this theological theme, the following emphases emerge:

1. The Lord's commitment to justice

As in earlier speeches (cf. 1:21–31; 3:1–15), the Lord's commitment to justice is a central theme in this literary unit. He invested a great deal of energy in establishing his covenant community (see 5:2). His primary purpose in doing so was to create a community that would model his moral and ethical standards (5:7). This is consistent with the words of Moses, who told Israel that the Lord wanted the covenant community to be a showcase of his wisdom and justice to the surrounding nations (Deut. 4:5–8). By perverting justice, Israel perverted the Lord's purpose for his covenant community, requiring him to implement radical discipline. The Lord puts his commitment to justice on full display when he brings proud sinners down (Isa. 5:15–16). Poetic justice and irony permeate 5:8–30. The sinners who robbed others of their homes will not live in them (5:8–9). The fields they have stolen will not yield crops for them (5:10). Those who love to eat and drink will become the main course at Sheol's banquet (5:11–14), leaving only the sheep to eat on the ruins of the banqueting halls (5:17). Those who turn moral light to moral darkness (5:20) will be overwhelmed by the darkness of judgment (5:30).

2. The perversion of justice deprives God's people of a vibrant relationship with him.

In the song in Isaiah 5:1–7 the Lord compares his covenantal relationship to Israel to marriage and suggests, through love language, that he intends his people to enjoy intimacy with him. But

---

9   Robar (2015, 140) points out that the four *weyiqtol* forms in vv. 29b–30a occur in "an extended metaphor of the army as a young lion" embedded within the larger framework that describes the army.

their perversion of the relationship shatters this ideal and robs the community of intimacy with God. Fortunately, the image of the vineyard's destruction (5:5–6) is not the end of Israel's story. When the Lord destroys his enemies once and for all (27:1), he will transform his people into a productive vineyard (27:2–3), where the briers and thorns that once overran the vineyard (5:6) are removed (27:4) and the community becomes fruitful (27:6; see Story 2009, 184–86).

> **Intimacy with God**
>
> In this regard, Hubert Irsigler (1997, 55) detects a tone of lamentation in 5:1b–2 and 7. He observes: "The lamentations in verses 1b–2 and in verse 7 surround the scenery of legal dispute in verses 3–6, framing the discourse and completing it. The decisive intentional attitude of the speaker can be inferred from this: His major concern is neither the announcement of inevitable disaster, nor first and foremost the addressee's accusation, though he insists emphatically that his listeners should realise their true situation. Rather, the speaker fundamentally starts from the disappointment and lamentation about Judah's inexplicable and mysterious behaviour, as the favourite planting of YHWH."

3. The Lord's sovereign authority over crops, death, and the nations

The Lord's sovereign authority is apparent throughout 5:8–30. He can prevent the vines and fields from producing (5:10). Death itself is at his disposal and becomes his instrument of judgment (5:14). Even the mighty Assyrian army is at his beck and call. All he need do is whistle and it comes charging headlong to its assigned destination (5:26). The Lord does indeed have a plan he will carry out (5:19); he will cause the darkness of judgment to overwhelm the light (5:30), in effect reversing creation in Israel's land.

4. The primacy of the Lord's word

In chapter 5 the Lord denounces the perversion of his moral standards (see esp. 5:5 and 20). His proud people are wise in their own eyes (5:21), having rejected the Lord's word due to their failure to acknowledge him as the Holy One of Israel who possesses absolute moral authority (5:24; cf. 1:4). When people become wise in their own eyes and reject the Lord's authority, the consequences are inevitably abase. Such proud rebellion produces moral perversity, which brings injustice and pain in its wake. Ultimately, such rebellion is self-destructive, for it demands divine punishment. We see the pattern throughout the Bible, beginning in Eden, where the man and woman disobey God's command and pay the heavy price. It is especially apparent in the epilogue to the book of Judges, where people do what is right in their own eyes, resulting in horrible crimes being committed, including idolatry, theft, rape, murder, and civil war.

PREACHING AND TEACHING STRATEGIES

Exegetical and Theological Synthesis

Isaiah 5 begins as a "love song" (5:1) about unrequited love. Despite God's sincere and consistent overtures of love toward his people Israel (metaphorically described in the opening verses as a vineyard), they have consistently produced sinful, self-serving, even violent fruit (5:7), which is likened to "wild grapes" (5:2, 4, 7). In response to Israel's persistent rejection of God's laws and admonitions toward equitable and righteous living, the Lord is left with no other option but to bring severe judgment upon them. He would remove its hedge/wall, which would lead to it being trampled down and devoured (5:5). He would no longer prune or hoe it, allowing it to be overrun by briers and thorns, and he would withhold the rain from falling upon it (5:6).

This is followed by a series of six "woes" against Israel, particularly against those within the nation who are guilty of various evils (5:8, 11, 18, 20, 21, 22). Each woe serves as a warning of coming judgment by God upon them for their sin. The first woe (5:8–10) confronted the injustice of those who accumulated wealth in the form of houses and fields. It is implied by the broader context that the accumulated wealth was accompanied by corrupt and unjust practices as well as a lack of generosity toward the poor (5:23; cf. 1:4, 17, 21, 23; 3:14–15). When God judges Judah by means of an invading army followed by exile from the land (5:13, 26), these once beautiful houses will simply lie vacant. Furthermore, God will see to it that their farmland will yield very little produce.

Next, the prophet confronts those given to excessive partying and drunken revelry (5:11–17). They are described as running after strong drink from first thing in the morning until late into the evening (5:11). Their feasts reveal that they will spare no expense when it comes to food, wine, and all forms of musical entertainment. Yet they have invested nothing of themselves in the Lord's work. In response, they will be taken into exile where they will not be free to party any longer. Rather than feasting with sumptuous food and delicious wine, these formerly wealthy noblemen and women will be forced to go hungry and thirsty (5:13). Rather than opening their mouths wide to eat and drink, they will be swallowed up by Sheol when it opens its mouth and consumes them with its insatiable appetite (5:14). Even the sheep will eat as they graze on the pastures of the wealthy who are off in exile (5:17).

Isaiah 5:18–19 addresses those who are so deceived; they fail to see how their iniquities are like heavy loads that they carry with them. In their arrogance, they sarcastically mock God by daring him to quickly come and make himself known to them. The irony is that God's counsel will come speedily to pass upon them in the form of his judgment.

At this point in the passage, the woes begin to flow very quickly, one after the next with only a brief description of the behaviors being confronted. Isaiah 5:20 highlights how many in Judah have not only ignored God's law but have actually turned it on its head. They have begun to call evil good and good evil. They have substituted what was light for that which was darkness and that which was sweet for that which was bitter (both metaphors for right and wrong). The reason for this is that they have substituted God's laws and commands as the basis for their morality with simply doing whatever seems right and wise in their own eyes (5:21). In somewhat mocking fashion, God describes these partiers as those who are "heroes at drinking wine, and valiant men in mixing strong drink." Whereas actual heroes would have fought for the rights of the innocent, these people knowingly acquit the guilty and deprive the innocent of justice for their own financial gain while they callously pass their time inebriated and oblivious to the responsibility that accompanies those blessed with great wealth and power (5:22–23).

Isaiah 5:24 provides something of a summary statement of God's coming judgment as well as the reason for his righteous wrath. First, he likens the swift judgment that is coming on them to fire quickly consuming dry grass. Next, he summarizes Israel's sin. They have "rejected the law" of the Lord of Hosts and "spurned the word of the Holy One of Israel."

This chapter ends with a description of the harsh judgment that God promises to inflict on Judah. The human agent of this judgment will be the armies of foreign nations (5:26) with their arrows and chariots (5:28). However, these armies are simply doing the Lord's bidding. From a heavenly perspective, they come because God will stretch out his hand against his people to strike them down (5:25). Similarly, God is the one who will signal for the nations to come. He will whistle for them from the ends of the earth (5:26). These enemy armies will come with ferocity like a roaring lion chasing down its prey. Just as Israel's corrupt leaders have brought spiritual "darkness" (5:20) upon the land by their willful disregard of God's law (5:24), so too God will bring "darkness and distress" (5:30) upon their land when he punishes them.

Preaching Idea
When people become wise in their own eyes and reject God's Word, the consequences are painful and inevitable.

Contemporary Connections

What does it mean?
On various occasions throughout the Old Testament, God warned the Israelites to hold tightly onto his laws and commands and not to pursue that which was right in their own eyes. Numbers 15:37–39 reads,

> The LORD said to Moses, "Speak to the Israelites, and say to them: 'Throughout the generations to come you are to make tassels on the corners of your garments, with a blue cord on each tassel. You will have these tassels to look at and so you will remember all the commands of the LORD, that you may obey them and not prostitute yourselves by chasing after the lusts of your own hearts and eyes.'"

Similarly, Deuteronomy 11 reminds the Israelites to love the Lord their God and keep all his commandments when they enter the land (Deut. 11:1, 8, 13, 16, 22, 27–28, 32). They must make it their priority to teach their children daily the laws of the Lord their God to ensure that his commands remain constantly on their hearts and minds (Deut. 11:18–20). To the contrary, God goes on a little later to warn that they must not continue acting as they had been, "everyone doing what they see fit [literally, what is right in his own eyes]" (Deut. 12:8).

Thus, to say that people are wise in their own eyes means that they arrogantly believe that they know what is best or right for themselves. Specifically, it involves people who brazenly dismiss God's laws or instructions and replace them with ones of their own making.

We see this phenomenon now with people who identify as atheists, denying the existence of any god to whom they are accountable. While only a relative few would overtly identify themselves as atheists, [10] even professing Christians need to be careful to examine our own hearts regularly in regards to whether or not we are actively doing our best to live under the Lordship of Jesus. If we are not careful, we can fall into the trap of obeying Jesus's teachings that come natural to us or that are emphasized within our particular Christian community, but fail to pay as much attention to the commands that would require the most change from us. For some Christians, this could involve maintaining a commitment to biblical sexual ethics while ignoring the call to actively care for the poor. For others, it might be the exact opposite. Despite a commitment to regularly advocate for the poor and disadvantaged, they may lack concern for the Bible's clear teaching about avoiding all forms of sexual activity outside of a biblical marriage between a man and a woman. Some professing Christians might even go so far as to embrace the culture's lie that morality is subjective and that each person should do whatever is right in their own eyes.

For those who reject God's Word in favor of doing what is right in their own eyes, the consequences are always painful and inevitable. These consequences include both the natural, negative effects of sin as well as the consequences that result from God's judgment against sinners.

Is it true?
There are plenty of examples in Scripture where God's people abandoned his law to do what was right in their own eyes. Probably the most

---

10 According to Pew Research Center surveys conducted in 2018 and 2019, only about 4 percent of US adults identify themselves as atheists, and an additional 5 percent identify as agnostics. https://www.pewforum.org/2019/10/17/in-u-s-decline-of-christianity-continues-at-rapid-pace.

well-known of these took place in the very beginning, shortly after creation. God created Adam and Eve in his own image (Gen. 1:26–27; 9:6; James 3:9) in order that they would reflect his glory throughout the world as they lived in fellowship with him. To fulfill this high and privileged calling, it would be necessary for humanity to walk in obedience to the Lord's commands. However, Adam and Eve decided to spurn God's warning not to eat from the Tree of Knowledge of Good and Evil lest they die (Gen. 2:16–17; 3:1–7). Instead, they ate of the fruit that was pleasant in their own eyes (Gen. 3:6). This one rebellious act led to all sorts of unpleasant consequences including relational turmoil (Gen. 3:16), physical pain (Gen. 3:16–17), and the introduction of weeds and thorns into the world (Gen. 3:17–18). Worst of all, their rejection of God's command so they could do that which looked good to them led to both physical death (Gen. 3:19) and estrangement from their Creator God (Gen. 3:23–24). The entire human race has been suffering the consequences of their rebellion ever since (Rom. 5:12–19).

Other vivid examples of the severe consequences of choosing to do what is right in one's own eyes, rather than obeying God, can be found throughout the book of Judges. That book's message is aptly summed up in Judges 17:6: "In those days Israel had no king; everyone did as they saw fit [literally, what was right in his own eyes]" (cf. Judg. 14:3, 7; 21:25). Throughout the book, the reader is horrified by the resulting degradation throughout Israel as they replaced God's moral code with their own. The reader is forced to endure stories of God's people perpetually turning away from God to idols. There is a story involving human sacrifice by one of Israel's own leaders. The reader encounters a judge who fornicates with pagans and flaunts his disregard of his Nazirite vows. The book includes an account of an Israelite priest who, in order to protect himself from harm, throws his concubine to a group of violent men who gang-rape and eventually kill her. The book ends with a coordinated plan for Israelite men to kidnap and wed unsuspecting virgins against their will to negate the effects of their own foolish vow. Throughout the book, Israel suffers severe consequences for their sinful actions. God's people are repeatedly oppressed and enslaved by their pagan neighbors. Jephthah is bereaved of his daughter. Samson has his eyes gouged out and is made a laughingstock for Israel's enemies. Women are exploited and abused rather than cherished and protected. Civil war breaks out between some of the tribes. Israelite society progressively degenerates and spirals downward as the people suffer the consequences of their rejection of God's standards and moral laws in order to pursue that which was right in their own eyes.

Western civilization increasingly rejects God's laws and attempts to erase every facet of Judeo-Christian ethics that were once a bedrock of the United States and many European countries' societal codes of conduct. Those who would attempt to promote a Christian ethic of sexuality are labeled old-fashioned and out-of-touch. Worse yet, they are demonized by many of the world's leaders and trendsetters as haters or fear-mongers. The same is true for all who would speak in defense of the unborn. We are living in a time where there is a wholesale attempt to redefine morality through narratives that call evil "good" and good "evil."

But there are other "evils" that even many Christians are prone to call "good" that might not be as obvious as others. Consider for example the love of money and rampant materialism that is so much a part of many wealthier nations. Isaiah 5:8 specifically confronted the Israelites who were accumulating houses and wealth without regard for the poor around them. Many Christians in nations like America are guilty of this sin too.

Another form of evil that Westerners tend to overlook or even call "good" is the tendency to be "me-centered." In Isaiah 5, this attitude surfaced in those who would rise early in the morning to begin partying that extended well into the evening (vv. 11, 22). They would surround themselves with various sorts of entertainment and pleasure (v. 12). Their focus was completely on themselves, pursuing their own pleasure without devoting themselves to the needs or concerns of others.

While every culture throughout history has been guilty of self-centeredness, modern Americans seem to glorify it as a virtue. We emphasize "pursuing your dream" and "following your heart" as though that is the most noble thing one can do. Many of us have gotten used to most of our preferences being catered to in our consumeristic society. Companies tailor products to everyone's specific desires. At some point, all of this would seem to be antithetical to the attitudes of servanthood, deference toward others, and selfless love to which Jesus calls his followers (Jn 13:34, 15:12, 17; 1 Jn 3:23, 4:21). Instead, it promotes a sort of "everything's about me" attitude.

Now what?
The New Testament offers some helpful commentary on Isaiah 5 that is instructive for believers today. Jesus alludes to Isaiah 5 in his parable of the tenants in Mark 12 (cf. Matt. 21:33–46; Luke 20:9–19). In the parable, a man planted a vineyard and built a fence around it. He also built a tower and a winepress in the middle of the vineyard. Jesus is clearly picking up on the imagery from the prophet Isaiah, which his Jewish audience would have recognized. But Jesus adds that this vineyard was leased to tenants while the owner went into another country. When the time came to collect the lease payment (which in that day would have likely been paid by a portion of the fruit produced in the vineyard), the tenants refused to pay. Instead, they assaulted the rent collector and sent him away empty-handed. Again and again the owner of the vineyard sent servants to confront the tenants and collect payment, but every time they harassed and even killed the messengers. Finally, the owner decided to send his beloved son, assuming that they would certainly respect him. But the tenants rejected and killed even the son.

The parable was told by Jesus to confront the religious hierarchy in his day. They were part of a long history of Israel's leaders that had shunned God's Word to do their own thing. Time and again, God graciously sent his prophets as messengers to call Israel to repent and embrace God's righteous rules. But Israel's leaders consistently rejected, and at times even killed, God's prophets. Finally, God sent not just another prophet, but his own incarnate Son to be a revelation of his word to them. In fact, John describes Jesus as the Word of God who became flesh (John 1:1, 14). But the nation of Israel would ultimately crucify the Son of God in their rejection of God's Word.

Jesus warned at the end of his parable, "What then will the owner of the vineyard do? He will come and destroy those tenants" (Mark 12:9). In other words, when people become wise in their own eyes and reject God's Word, the consequences will be painful and inevitable. The most obvious way that people today reject God's Word is in their rejection of Jesus Christ, the incarnate Word of God to us.

In John 15:1, Jesus says, "I am the true vine." While the correlation isn't as clear as in the parable of the tenants, Jesus may again be making a connection with Isaiah 5. Both passages use the metaphor of a grapevine to emphasize the importance of bearing good fruit (Isa. 5:2, 4, 7; John 15:2, 4–5, 8, 16) to demonstrate that one is truly part of the people of God. Those who fail to bear good fruit will be gathered and thrown into the fire (John 15:6).

According to Jesus, the key to bearing good fruit is to abide in him (John 15:4–7). We are unable to produce righteousness on our own apart from the power of Jesus working in and through us (John 15:5). What Jesus promotes is not just a form of religion where one reforms his/her life to do good works. Rather, Jesus offers to come and dwell within us, renewing us from the inside out, when we surrender our lives to him in faith. He works from within to produce good fruit.

The role of the believer is to remain faithful to Jesus's teaching as presented in God's Word. It is "the word" spoken by Jesus that makes us clean (John 15:3). We abide in Jesus as we allow his words to abide in us (15:7). We further abide in Jesus's love when we keep his commandments, just as Jesus obeyed his Father's commandments (15:10). We continue to act as Jesus's friends only as we continue to do what he commands (15:14).

Thus, Christians today must find ways to abide in God's Word. This is a central way that we abide in Jesus, by continually saturating our minds with his Word so that it overflows into our thoughts and actions and keeps us from merely doing that which is right in our own eyes. This will require that Christians prioritize time out of their busy lives to read and meditate on Scripture. There are many helpful Bible reading plans or Bible apps that provide a Scripture for the day or a daily, Bible-based devotional reading. There are also apps and computer programs that will read the Bible to you. Christians today can take advantage of any number of cheap or free tools such as these in their pursuit of abiding in God's Word.

Additionally, believers must search out and connect themselves to a Christian church where the Bible is faithfully proclaimed and taught. In addition to large worship gatherings, they should look for a small group where they have opportunities to discuss and flesh out the meaning of God's Word in their everyday lives. The author of Hebrews highlights the importance of other Christians whose admonition and teaching help to protect us against developing a hard heart of unbelief toward the things of God brought about by the deceitfulness of the sinful world around us (Heb. 3:12–13). There are no substitutes for godly friends and acquaintances who know us and speak into our lives on a regular basis.

Creativity in Presentation

To illustrate God's repulsion toward Israel's "sour grapes," bring a piece of ripe, delicious fruit with you and begin by taking a few small bites of it. (Be careful to use something that is easy to chew, and don't take big bites. You'll want to be able to talk while you are eating.) If you bring a banana, ask the audience who else enjoys eating bananas. Ask someone who raises their hand to come up on stage with you. Then hand them a rotten piece of fruit and encourage them to enjoy it. They will likely cringe and resist taking it. Ask them why they are hesitant and insist that it isn't that bad. After they insist on not eating it, you can draw the comparison between their repulsion to the idea of eating a rotten piece of fruit to God's reaction toward the "fruit" being produced by Israel.

The 2005 animated movie *Hoodwinked!* retells the familiar story of Little Red Riding Hood. The story begins to play out in a way that anyone familiar with the classic children's story would recognize. Little Red arrives at her Granny's house with a basket of food. But she finds the wolf in bed disguised as Granny, who is later found tied up in the closet. When the police arrive to arrest the wolf shortly thereafter, he insists he is innocent. After interviewing each of the main characters in the plot, it becomes evident that the wolf wasn't a villain after all, and his actions were understandable once we heard his side of the story. In fact, the true villain is discovered to be a loveable, friendly looking bunny that appeared off and on throughout the movie. The movie takes a classic, well-known story with clearly defined "good guys" and a clearly defined "villain" and rewrites the script in such a way that the villain is no longer bad. It is quite illustrative of the way our society in general likes to create narratives that rewrite the script in order to present that which historically was known and accepted as evil, and portray it in a positive light so that it appears good. Similarly, those who were historically thought of as noble and good are often portrayed in ways to make them appear evil. As such, our culture is able to make that which is good appear evil and that which is evil appear good.

To demonstrate the culture's growing moral relativity, consider the story of Kay Haugaard, a college professor in Southern California as recounted by Os Guinness in his book *Time for Truth: Living Free in a World of Lies, Hype, and Spin* (2000). Each year, she had her students read and discuss *The Lottery* by Shirley Jackson. The story takes place in a rural American town. The townspeople have come together in what feels like a family-oriented, community gathering in the town square. The main event is a lottery, but the reader isn't told yet what exactly this event entails. Each year, one person is randomly selected as each community member draws a slip of paper. The one who draws the slip with the black dot is the "winner." This year, it is drawn by Tessie Hutchinson, a young wife and mother. It soon becomes evident that the lottery is to see whose life would be sacrificed that year. The whole town, including her own young kids, participate in stoning her to death.

When this story first appeared in *The New Yorker* in 1948, there was considerable public outrage over it. Throughout the 1970s and 80s, Haugaard noticed a gradual decline in her students' sense of moral outrage over this story's plot. Then it happened one year in the 1990s: not one student in a class of more than twenty could say that random human sacrifice was evil. One student thought the ending was "neat." Another student seemed indifferent. Another argued that it was "their ritual"—not right or wrong, just something they did. One young man even suggested that a certain amount of societal bloodshed seemed necessary. A nurse in her fifties explained that she taught a hospital course in multicultural understanding. She said, "If it's a part of a person's culture, we are taught not to judge, and if it has worked for them. . . ." At this point, Haugaard gave up. She said, "No one in the whole class of more than twenty ostensibly intelligent individuals would go out on a limb and take a stand against human sacrifice" (Guinness 2000, 21–23).

According to two concurrent surveys conducted by Barna Research in 2002 (one of adults and one of teenagers), Americans overwhelmingly indicated their conviction that truth is relative. Only 22 percent of adults surveyed indicated belief in moral absolutes. Among teenagers asked the same question, only 6 percent expressed a belief in moral absolutes. One might assume that those who identify as born-again Christians would be more likely to believe in moral absolutes. However, even among born-again Christians, only 32 percent of adults indicated a belief in moral absolutes while a mere 9 percent of born-again teenagers believe in absolute moral truths. The respondents were asked to indicate the basis upon which they make moral and ethical decisions. "By far the most common basis for moral decision-making was doing whatever feels right or comfortable in a situation" (whatever seems right in their own eyes). "Nearly four out of ten teens (38%) and three out of ten adults (31%) described that as their primary consideration."[11] Considering that this study is already more than twenty years old, these teenagers are now in their thirties, and the trend away from belief in absolute truth has almost certainly gotten worse. It shouldn't surprise us then when we see so much confusion and brokenness in the world, because when people become wise in their own eyes and reject God's Word, the consequences are painful and inevitable.

- God's pursuit of his people (5:1–2).
- God's dispute with his people (5:3–7).
- The fruit of God's people (5:8–23).
  - Greed (5:8–10).
  - Licentiousness (5:11–17).

---

11 https://www.barna.com/research/americans-are-most-likely-to-base-truth-on-feelings.

- - Deceitfulness (5:18–19).
  - Perversion (5:20).
  - Pride (5:21).
  - Injustice (5:22–23).
- God will uproot his people (5:24–30).

DISCUSSION QUESTIONS

1. What are some areas in your life where you have had to wrestle with whether something was right or wrong? What process did you go through in your mind to resolve this moral quandary? On what basis did you eventually determine that it was either acceptable or not acceptable?

2. What are some examples you have witnessed of a moral drift in society, where things that used to be considered right or wrong are no longer thought of in the same way? What influences do you think have contributed to these things no longer being thought of in the same way as they once were?

3. What tools or practices do you use, or have you experimented with, to keep your Bible reading time consistent and fresh? As this is typically a struggle for many, don't be afraid to share about your own struggles to make this a consistent practice. Brainstorm together some small steps that one could take to make this a more regular habit.

FOR FURTHER READING

Guinness, Os. 2000. *Time for Truth: Living Free in a World of Lies, Hype, and Spin*. Grand Rapids: Baker.

Isaiah 6:1–13

EXEGETICAL IDEA
Overwhelmed by God's holiness, Isaiah confessed his sinfulness, yet the Lord cleansed him and commissioned him to confront stubborn Israel with its sin.

THEOLOGICAL FOCUS
Recognizing God's holiness prompts one to confess sin and experiencing spiritual cleansing prompts one to carry out God's commission.

PREACHING IDEA
An encounter with the holy, sovereign God should lead us to repent of sin and humbly submit to God, resulting in our transformation.

PREACHING POINTERS
Metamorphic—in science, the word denotes rock that has undergone transformation by heat, pressure, or other natural agencies. However, the word can also denote some life-altering, transformative experience. On occasion, people will experience something so impactful it alters how they think or behave from that point forward. It could be a close call with death like a car accident or a heart attack that makes the brevity and uncertainty of life real. Maybe the birth of a child brings about a new sense of responsibility or purpose. Others may point to some religious or spiritual awakening within them that sparked a new and better direction for their lives. Whatever the experience, when its impact on an individual is a transformed life, we can rightly refer to it as a metamorphic event.

There may be no better word to describe the prophet's vision in Isaiah 6. Isaiah saw the Lord God, high and exalted in his temple. Angels surrounding him were declaring, "Holy, holy, holy is the Lord Almighty; the whole earth is full of his glory!" (6:3). One can only imagine the transformative impact such an experience would have on a person, to come face to face with the sovereign, holy creator of the universe. Understandably, Isaiah was overcome with a sense of his own sinfulness and unworthiness to be looking upon one so perfect and glorious. But his vision was accompanied by a calling. God sent him to go and speak on his behalf to the stubborn people of Israel. Despite assurances from God that his words would mostly fall on deaf ears, Isaiah nonetheless humbled himself before God and submitted to carry out the charge that he had been given.

A VISION OF THE KING (6:1–13)

Isaiah's vision of the holy God enthroned in his temple prompted him to confess his sinfulness, but the Lord cleansed the prophet and commissioned him to confront stubborn Israel with its sin until devastating judgment had overwhelmed the land.

LITERARY STRUCTURE AND THEMES (6:1–13)

Form critics label Isaiah 6 a "call narrative" (see Habel 1965, 297–323). Call narratives vary in their content and structure. In one type, the Lord confronts an individual and gives them a commission. The individual protests, but the Lord provides reassurance (see Exod. 3:1–4:17; Judg. 6:11–24; Jer. 1:4–10). Isaiah 6 differs. Here the prophet received a vision and volunteered to carry out a divine commission that was initially vague and not directed to him specifically. As Paul House (1993, 213) points out, Isaiah offered no objection and received no word of reassurance. Once he volunteered, he was told what to say and informed that his message would receive a negative response. In a similar way, Ezekiel received a vision of God as a prelude to the divine commission that required him to preach to a stubborn nation (Ezek. 1:1–3:11). There are also similarities between Isaiah 6 and the narrative in 1 Kings 22:19–22, where Micaiah sees a vision of the Lord seated in his heavenly assembly. As in Isaiah's case (see Isa. 6:8), the Lord asked for a volunteer to carry out his commission (in this case, the deception of Ahab; 1 Kings 22:21). Like Isaiah, "the spirit" responded positively (Wildberger 1991, 252). However, there are also some marked differences between Isaiah 6 and 1 Kings 22:19–22 (Kaiser 1972, 122). Only the seraphim, not the whole assembly, are specifically mentioned in Isaiah 6 and the question asked by the Lord is simply, "Whom shall I send? And who will go for us?" as opposed to 1 Kings 22, where the question has the nature of the mission embedded within it, "Who will deceive?" Furthermore, in 1 Kings 22 "the spirit" is not a prophet. Micaiah, who was a prophet, listened in on what was transpiring in the heavenly assembly, but he did not volunteer for service. Presumably he was given access to the deliberations of the assembly so he would understand God's agenda regarding Ahab and speak accordingly (see 22:14–15).

The narrative in Isaiah 6 is autobiographical, with first-person verbs spoken by the prophet providing the backbone of the narrative: Isaiah saw a vision of the Lord (6:1), spoke (6:5), heard (6:8a), spoke once more (6:8b), and then spoke a third time (6:11). Interspersed with Isaiah's words one hears other voices, including the seraphim (6:3), an individual seraph (6:7), and the Lord himself (6:8a, 9–10, 11b–13). As the narrative progresses, there is movement from seeing to hearing.

- *Isaiah's Vision (6:1–4)*
- *Isaiah's Response (6:5)*
- *Isaiah's Purification (6:6–7)*
- *Isaiah's Commission (6:8–13)*

EXPOSITION (6:1–13)

Isaiah's Vision (6:1–4)
Isaiah saw the Lord in his royal splendor, attended by fiery creatures that loudly proclaimed his sovereignty.

6:1. In the year of King Uzziah's death (740 B.C.), Isaiah saw a vision of the real king (cf. 6:5) sitting on his throne.[1] The Lord's sovereignty is highlighted by his elevated position (note the pairing of "high and exalted," for emphasis), the sheer size of his royal robe, which fills the temple, and the use of the title אֲדֹנָי, "Sovereign Master."

Interpreters debate the identity of the "temple" (6:1), called literally "the house" in 6:4. Did Isaiah see a vision of the heavenly royal court, comparable to Micaiah's vision (1 Kings 22:19–22), or was this a vision experienced in the Jerusalem temple (so Williamson 2018, 42–43)? We cannot be certain. Perhaps the question assumes a distinction that an ancient Israelite would not make. As Wildberger (1991, 263) says, "God dwells in heaven, but he is also present in the sanctuary" (see also Knierim 1968, 51–52).

6:2. Fiery creatures attended the Lord's presence. The term "seraphim" appears to derive from the verb שָׂרַף, "to burn." If so, these "burning ones" may have been so named because they had a fiery appearance, like the messengers of Yam in the Baal myth (see *COS* 1.86:246). Each creature used four of its six wings to cover its face and "feet" out of reverence for the King. They used the other two to fly.

6:3. The seraphs proclaimed the Lord's holiness. The threefold appearance of the word "holy" draws attention to the Lord's absolute sovereignty.[2] The repetition is for emphasis.[3] For example, in Isaiah 26:3 the word "peace" (שָׁלוֹם) is repeated to emphasize the degree of security God provides those who trust in him. The passage may be translated, "You will keep in perfect peace (literally, "peace, peace") the one who is firm in purpose." Threefold repetition, though rare, is a particularly forceful way of drawing attention to an idea.[4] For example, in Ezekiel 21:27 [HB 32] the Lord announces he will make Jerusalem "a ruin, a ruin, a ruin," meaning he will reduce the city to a pile of rubble and debris. In Jeremiah 7:4 the people, convinced they are safe, repeat "the temple of Yahweh, the temple of Yahweh, the temple of Yahweh" to emphasize why they believe they are secure. In Jeremiah 22:29 the prophet says "(O) land, land, land" in the preface to his message from the Lord. The repetition, by drawing attention to the addressee, stresses the urgency of listening.

As noted earlier (see 1:4), God's holiness in this context refers first and foremost to his sovereignty over the world that he rules. At the same time his holiness encompasses his moral authority, which derives from his royal position. This position is highlighted by the title יְהוָה צְבָאוֹת, traditionally, "Lord of Hosts." As noted above (see 1:9), this title depicts Yahweh as enthroned in the middle of his heavenly assembly. Sometimes it has a military connotation and can be translated "Lord of Armies,"

---

[1] It is not clear if the king's death preceded or followed the vision. No one can see God in his very essence (John 1:18; 1 Tim. 6:16), but humans can see "a manifestation of the glory of God in human form, adapted to the capabilities of the finite creature" (Young 1965, 235). Regarding Isaiah's experience, Smith (2007, 187) observes: "This was a limited manifestation that was adapted to finite mental comprehension and human observation, probably in a vision."

[2] 1QIs[a] has the adjective repeated just once, in conformity to the more common pattern. The LXX, however, has a threefold "holy" (Ziegler 1983, 142). Wildberger (1991, 249) points out that Psalm 99 includes a threefold declaration of the Lord's holiness (99:3, 5, 9).

[3] See *IBHS*, 233 n. 15; GKC, 431–32 §133k; Smith 2007, 190; Williamson 2006, 18. For an attempt to provide a more nuanced discussion of the triplet in Isaiah 6:3, as well as the other examples listed below, see Reimer 2012.

[4] For a discussion of the Christian view that the threefold repetition is a hint of the Trinity, see Young 1965, 243–44. He quotes Calvin as saying, "the passage is not as clear as might be . . . to deduce the Trinity from this passage would only be to give occasion to the unbelievers to boast." Oswalt (1986, 181) states, "There is nothing in the context to cause us to take this as a reference to the Trinity as the church fathers did."

a nuance that would be fitting in this context, where judgment is announced (6:11–13).

> **Sovereignty**
>
> John Oswalt (1986, 180) rightly points out, "holiness is distinctness, the distinctness of the divine from all other things." Wildberger (1991, 266) aptly identifies God's holiness here as "his absolute will, his kingly majesty in the midst of his people." Peter Gentry (2013, 400–417) challenges the idea that God's holiness is fundamentally his sovereign transcendence. He argues that God is holy in the sense that he is "consecrated" or "devoted" (p. 417). Regarding Isaiah 6, he attempts to validate his claim from the use of the verb in Isaiah 5:16 (p. 413). But in the parallelism of that verse נִקְדָּשׁ, literally "show himself holy," corresponds to וַיִּגְבַּהּ, "exalted," which refers to his transcendence. The statement in 5:16 is not about God's commitment to justice per se. It makes the point that his sovereign transcendence will be apparent to all when he unleashes his righteous judgment upon the evildoers denounced in Isaiah 5.

The seraphim also declared that the Lord's royal splendor fills the entire earth. The term כָּבוֹד, traditionally "glory," is often used by Isaiah of visible beauty or attractiveness (see Isa. 10:18; 11:10; 16:14; 17:4; 22:23–24; 35:2; 60:13; 61:6; 66:11). When describing earthly kings or kingdoms, it refers to their "pomp" or majestic splendor (8:7; 10:16; 21:16). When applied to the Lord, as here, it refers to the outward display or manifestation of his royal position (3:8; 24:23; 40:5; 58:8; 59:19; 60:1–2; 66:18–19; see Smith 2007, 190) that is visible to all and deserves praise (42:8, 12). It is also used of the splendor associated with God's rich eschatological blessings (4:2; 35:2) and with his ideal human ruler (11:10). According to Isaiah, God's glory will be revealed in an especially awesome manner when he establishes his kingdom on earth after defeating his enemies and restoring his people to Zion (24:23; 40:5; 59:19; 60:1–2; 66:18–19).

The seraphim are probably referring to God's present glory as seen in creation (Pss. 8:1, 9 [HB 2, 10]; 19:1 [HB 2]; 97:6; see Wildberger 1991, 267), which reveals certain divine attributes (Young 1965, 245; see Ps. 19:1–2 [HB 2–3]; Rom. 1:19–20). However, some prefer to see the seraphim's declaration as anticipating an eschatological revelation of divine glory (Ps. 72:19; see Kaiser 1972, 127; Smith 2007, 191) and/or as encompassing the revelation of his glory in judgment (Knierim 1968, 56; Oswalt 1986, 181–82).

6:4. The voice of the seraphim must have been exceedingly loud, for it shook the doors of the temple, which also was filling up with smoke. The language recalls the Sinai theophany, when the people of Israel stood before the smoking mountain and shook at the sound of the ram's horn (Exod. 20:18). Only in Exodus 20:18 and Isaiah 6:4 do the verb נוּעַ, "shake," and the root עשׁן appear in proximity. Since there is thematic correlation between these texts, it is possible that Isaiah intended an allusion to the Sinai theophany. If so, the point is this: The God of Sinai was alive and well, ruling over his world and still expecting the loyalty of his covenant people.

Isaiah's Response (6:5)

Isaiah saw the real King (Isa. 6:5), who is immortal and not bound by time.[5] Realizing his sinful condition, Isaiah anticipated being destroyed because he had viewed the King in his splendor.

Human kings, like Uzziah (see 6:1), come and go, but the Lord is the sovereign ruler of the world who has authority over his creation

---

5 The object of the verb ("the king") is placed first in the clause for emphasis (see *DHS*, 155 §110).

(see Oswalt 1986, 183). Under the umbrella of his universal rule, the Lord is Israel's king in a special sense (see Isa. 33:22; 41:21; 43:15; 44:6). Out of all the nations of the earth he chose Israel to be his covenant people.

Isaiah was certain that seeing the king in his glory would bring disaster down upon him. When the interjection אוֹי is combined with the preposition -לְ (as in 6:5; cf. 3:9), it indicates that the object of the preposition is in dire straits and/or that disaster is imminent or already being experienced.[6] Consequently, it can be translated as a noun, "woe" (cf. Prov. 23:29). A good way to indicate this is to translate as "disaster is upon me."

The perfect verb form (נִדְמֵיתִי) is used here rhetorically to indicate certitude. Though the action is imminent, the prophet uses the perfect to depict the action as already completed, indicating that it is as good as done.[7] The precise meaning of the verb דָּמָה in this context is uncertain. One could translate, "for I am destroyed" (see BDB s.v. "דָּמָה II" 198), a nuance well attested elsewhere for the *niphal* stem (see, e.g., Isa. 15:1).

The particle כִּי, "for," frequently follows the collocation אוֹי + -לְ, "woe to," and invariably has an explanatory or causal sense.[8] If דָּמָה means "destroyed" in Isaiah 6:5, then the explanatory statement seems synonymous with what precedes, as if cause and effect are the same. There may have been a subtle distinction in the mind of the prophet or perhaps he uses repetition rhetorically for emphasis. A parallel occurs in Jeremiah 4:13, where the prophet cries out, "Disaster is upon us" (אוֹי לָנוּ), and then explains, "for we are ruined" (כִּי שֻׁדָּדְנוּ), using a perfect of certitude rhetorically to emphasize their demise is certain.

HALOT, while acknowledging the possibility that דָּמָה means "destroyed" here (HALOT s.v. "דָּמָה III" 225), lists another option, דָּמָה II, "be silent," which they translate "be obliged to be silent" for Isaiah 6:5 (cf. Kaiser 1972, 128). In this case the logic would be as follows: "Disaster is imminent because I am incapable of offering praise, due to the fact that I am sinful. Since I, a sinful man, have seen the Sovereign King and am incapable of offering him the praise he deserves, I will be destroyed." However, this nuance of the *niphal* is rare (see Jer. 47:5).

Isaiah lamented that his lips were unclean. The term "unclean" often refers to that which is ritually defiled, but it can also have a moral or ethical connotation. Here the term has a ritual nuance on the surface, but it becomes apparent that moral impurity is the root problem (see Isa. 6:7b). Isaiah's uncleanness stands in stark contrast to God's holiness. The focus is the prophet's unclean lips because the appropriate response to God's holy presence is verbal praise (see Isa. 6:1–3; cf. Beuken 2004, 74). However, the prophet was sinful, and he lived among a community of sinners, making his lips unfit to offer praise. The principle of corporate solidarity is assumed here.

Isaiah's Purification (6:6–7)
One of the fiery creatures touched a hot coal to Isaiah's unclean lips and removed his impurity.

Both terms used for sin in 6:7 have been used in earlier chapters to describe the sin of the people, with whom Isaiah identifies here (see 1:4 and 5:18 for עָוֺן and 3:9 for חַטָּאת). The derivation of the verb כִּפֶּר (cf. תְּכֻפָּר) is debated, but usage indicates it refers to ritual cleansing (Lev. 5:6; 12:8; 14:19; 16:6, 11; Num. 28:22; 29:5) and/or to forgiveness of sin (Exod. 32:30; Ps. 79:9; Jer. 18:23). Here it refers to the forgiveness of sin, symbolized by the purification of Isaiah's lips.

---

6 See Num. 21:29; 1 Sam. 4:7–8; Isa. 3:11; 24:16; Jer. 4:13; 10:19; 15:10; 48:46; Ezek. 16:23; Hos. 7:13; 9:12.
7 See GKC, 312 §106n; *DHS*, 61 §41a; Joüon, 363 §112g.
8 See 1 Sam. 4:7; Isa. 3:9, 11; Jer. 4:13, 31; 6:4; 15:10; 45:3; Lam. 5:16; Hos. 7:13.

A Vision of the King (6:1–13)

> **Purification of Isaiah's Lips**
> Victor Hurowitz (1989, 39–89) compares the purification of Isaiah's lips to the mouth purification rituals known from ancient Mesopotamia. His attempt to see the latter as the background for Isaiah 6 is unconvincing. There are parallels, to be sure, but the marked differences between Isaiah 6 and the alleged parallel texts outweigh any superficial similarities and make the proposal less than compelling. The purification of Isaiah's lips appears to be an ad hoc event accommodated to a specific historical situation. By Hurowitz's own admission (p. 50), Akkadian sources speak of impurity of the *mouth* and (one text) of *pure* lips, but Isaiah does not use these expressions. Conversely, Hurowitz is not aware of any Akkadian text that uses Isaiah's phrase "*impure* lips."

TRANSLATION ANALYSIS 6:7
In 6:7 ESV, HCSB, and NIV translate תְּכֻפָּר with the somewhat archaic "atoned for." The NRSV's "blotted out" misses the semantic notion of the verb. The KJV "purged" (cf. *Tanakh*, "purged away") reflects the concept of physical purification suggested by the application of the hot coal to Isaiah's lips. The NLT's "forgiven" eliminates the purification image and simply brings out the metonymic concept present here. Perhaps "purified" is the best way to translate the verb here (understanding the prefixed form as preterite), since it retains the image of purification while also suggesting the idea of forgiveness, or removal (note the parallel verb וְסָר, "and has removed"; see BDB s.v. "סוּר" 693–94), of sin and its effect.

Isaiah's Commission (6:8–13)
Isaiah volunteered to be the Lord's prophetic spokesman. His message would harden the people's hearts until devastating judgment swept over the land.

6:8. When the Lord asked for someone to serve as a messenger on behalf of the heavenly royal court (note "for us"), Isaiah quickly volunteered. The first-person plural pronoun likely refers in this context to the Lord and the seraphim, though the entire heavenly court may be in view. The scene is reminiscent of 1 Kings 22:19–22, where the Lord says to his heavenly assembly: "Who will entice Ahab?" (22:20; cf. Blenkinsopp 2000, 226; Oswalt 1986, 185). With Isaiah's lips now purified, he was no longer inhibited by his sense of unworthiness and was eager to do the bidding of the Sovereign Master (אֲדֹנָי).

6:9. Isaiah was to tell the people to keep on listening and looking. But at the same time he was to exhort them not to truly understand or perceive. Isaiah did not literally proclaim these exact words, at least as far as we know. The Hebrew imperatival forms "are employed rhetorically in anticipation of the response" to Isaiah's prophetic ministry, which would expose their sin and call them to repentance. Though seemingly giving commands, they are sarcastic and can be paraphrased: "You continually hear, but never understand; you continually see, but never perceive." As I have observed, "Isaiah might as well have commanded them to be spiritually insensitive, because, as the preceding and following chapters make clear, the people were bent on that anyway" (see esp. Isa. 5:12, 19–21; Chisholm 1996, 431).

6:10. Having given the content of the message, the Lord explained to Isaiah the nature of the commission (6:10). His job was to desensitize the people, thereby preventing them from repenting and being healed. The verb שׁוּב, "return," is used here of turning back to God. This entails confession of sin, renewed allegiance to God, and obedience to his commands (Isa. 31:6; 44:22; 55:7; 59:20). The idiom is prominent in the Deuteronomic vision of Israel's future repentance and restoration (Deut. 4:30; 30:2, 8, 10). The use of "heal" implies that Israel's sinful condition was like a physical illness, robbing them of vitality and depriving them of God's blessings. A day would come when the Lord would heal his people's wounds and restore his favor (Isa. 30:26; 57:18–19). This healing would be made possible through the suffering of God's special servant, whose punishment at the hand of God would open the door for national restoration (Isa. 53:5). However, Israel's situation would get worse before it got better. In the immediate future God's judgment would leave Israel battered and bruised (Isa. 1:5–6) in the wake of a devastating invasion and exile (6:11–13; see 1:7–9).[9]

It looks as if the Lord was commanding Isaiah to harden the people. But as the surrounding chapters clearly reveal, the people were hardly ready or willing to repent. Therefore, Isaiah's preaching was not needed to prevent repentance! As in 6:9, the imperatives are sarcastic and "reflect the people's attitude." We can paraphrase: "Otherwise, they might see with their eyes, hear with their ears, understand with their mind, repent, and be restored, and they certainly wouldn't want that, would they?" Indeed, "from the outset" of the prophet's ministry, "the Lord may as well have commanded Isaiah to harden the people, because his preaching would end up having that effect" (Chisholm 1996, 431–32). Motyer (1993, 79) observes: "The imperatives of these verses must, therefore, be seen as expressing the inevitable outcome of Isaiah's ministry" (see also Gentry 2013, 415).

Even if we make allowance for the rhetorical dimension of the commission, there is a sense in which Isaiah's ministry would have a genuine hardening effect on those who heard it (Chisholm 1996, 432). God did not need to send the prophet to the people, who were already traveling the road to destruction. As Isaiah 3:9 declares, they had brought about their own demise. But Isaiah's preaching, which confronted them with their sin and warned them of impending judgment, would make them even more calloused as they refused to heed it.[10] Indeed, this hardening of the people through prophetic preaching would expedite the coming judgment, which in turn would bring at least some to the point where they were ready to take God's demands seriously. By 701 B.C., almost four decades after Isaiah's commission, the land was overrun by the Assyrians (1:4–9) and Hezekiah turned to the Lord for mercy and deliverance (Isa. 36–39; see Jer. 26:18–19).

6:11–12. The nature of the commission disturbed Isaiah emotionally, as indicated by his question "How long?" (Isa. 6:11a). This expression does not merely seek information (as suggested by Young 1965, 261 n. 48). It is used elsewhere to express strong emotion, often lament. (See Oswalt 1986, 190; Smith 2007, 196; Wildberger 1991, 273 all of whom cite Blank 1956, 81–83.) Yet, despite the emotional impact the message had upon him, Isaiah recognized

---

9   For a discussion of how 6:9–10 was handled in ancient textual witnesses, see Evans 1989, 53–80. Evans shows that in 1QIs[a] there is a "complete transformation" of the text so that the prophet is to exhort "the righteous (the Qumran sectaries) to take heed during the troubled times that lie ahead" (p. 60). The ancient versions soften the Hebrew text by shifting responsibility from God's decree to human sin. Evans concludes: "In a broad sense, then, there exists unanimity among these versions in that obduracy is viewed as the responsibility of the people, and can never be thought of as God's intention with respect to his own people" (p. 80).

10 Motyer (1993, 79) observes that Isaiah "faced the preacher's dilemma: if hearers are resistant to the truth, the only recourse is to tell them the truth yet again, more clearly than before. But to do this is to expose them to the risk of rejecting the truth yet again and, therefore, of increased hardness of heart. It could even be that the next rejection will prove to be the point at which the heart is hardened beyond recovery." Robinson (1998, 186) states correctly that the divine hardening in view here "ought not be understood in decretal terms, whereby God establishes this condition in his people as part of a preordained purpose." He explains further: "The primary theological context in which divinely imposed blindness and deafness occurs is reactive judgment upon human sin, not demonstration of decretal sovereignty."

the Lord's sovereignty, addressing him as "Lord" (better, "Sovereign Master": אֲדֹנָי).

Isaiah understood the implications of the commission, both for himself (his task would be difficult) and for the nation (such a stubborn response would necessitate judgment). Yet he was to persist in his ministry until judgment destroyed the cities, widespread ruin devastated the land, and the Lord sent the people into exile (6:11b–12). The devastation would be thorough, reaching the very middle of the land (note קֶרֶב הָאָרֶץ). As noted earlier (see comments on 5:8), the punishment was appropriate, for the middle of the land was inhabited by those who had taken property from others by dishonest means, in violation of the Deuteronomic stipulations that prohibited murder and called for obedience and generosity in the middle of the land (Deut. 4:5; 15:11; 19:11). When judgment swept through, the rich would be gone, leaving a meager remnant to try to eke out a living off the land (Isa. 7:22–25).

Exile

Wildberger (1991, 258) sees the "announcement that human beings will be carried off" (6:12) as being "at odds" with 6:11, which speaks of cities and houses as unpopulated. But surely 6:11 gives the effect, while 6:12 provides, at least in part, the cause. See Smith 2007, 197. Wildberger (1991, 258) also sees the reference to Yahweh, in a statement addressed by Yahweh to the prophet, as proof that "this verse must be a later interpretation inserted by a redactor" (see also Blenkinsopp 2000, 223; Kaiser 1972, 123). He seems to assume that Yahweh would not refer to himself by his name. But if so, why would an editor add something so incongruous? There is a better solution than what diachronic criticism, with its assumption of sloppy editorial work, can provide. When Yahweh uses his name or a title in an address to his prophet, or when he uses both the first and third person, there is a rhetorical purpose for doing so. In this case, the use of the name highlights the ironic and tragic truth that it is *Yahweh*, Israel's covenant Lord (6:1, 8, 11), who would remove the people from the land.

The prophecy was fulfilled in stages (see Seitz 1993, 58). Within the next decade the Assyrians reduced the territory of the northern kingdom and made it a puppet state. By 722 B.C. they had invaded Samaria, made it a province, and deported most of the people to Mesopotamia (2 Kings 18:9–11). In 701 Sennacherib invaded Judah, conquered dozens of cities (he gives the number as forty-six), took captive a huge number of people (he gives the number as 200,150), and isolated Jerusalem like a caged bird (*COS* 2.119B:303; 2 Kings 18:13, 17). In the aftermath of the Assyrian invasion the land was devastated (Isa. 1:7), just as the Lord had announced to Isaiah almost forty years before (note שְׁמָמָה in both 1:7 and 6:11).

6:13. Isaiah 6:13 emphasizes both the severity and appropriateness of the devastating judgment. The meaning of the first half of the verse seems clear—even if only a tenth of the land (its population is probably in view) survived, it would be subjected to another round of destruction.

The meaning of the second half of the verse is greatly debated. (For a discussion of different views, see Emerton 1982, 85–118.) As the text stands, it reads, "like a terebinth and like an oak that in the throwing down a pillar in them; a holy offspring, its pillar." If correct, it is unclear what it means. English translations typically understand מַצֶּבֶת as referring to a stump that is left when a tree is cut down (שַׁלֶּכֶת is understood as referring to the "felling" of a tree; see *HALOT* s.v. "שַׁלֶּכֶת" 1530). The "holy offspring," as a remnant that survives the coming judgment, is then compared to a stump that is left when a tree is chopped down and from which new growth may spring (see Job 14:7–9). If one follows this traditional interpretation, then there is a ray of hope here. Though the land would be chopped down like a tree, the Lord would leave a stump in the ground, as it were, from which a remnant, called "holy seed [i.e., offspring]," could sprout. In this case, the passage contributes to the theme of a remnant that would survive the judgment and through whom God would renew his covenant community (Isa. 1:27; 3:10; 4:2–6; 11:11–16). (For a defense of the traditional view, see Evans 1986; Hasel 1972, 244–48.) Within the context of chapter 6, the reference to holy offspring gives hope that a holy remnant will replace the corrupt nation, which stands condemned before the One who is holy (6:5; see Beuken 2004, 78, 83–84).

However, there is another less optimistic, interpretive option. The noun מַצֶּבֶת, in its only other use, refers to a memorial pillar (2 Sam. 18:18), like the more common מַצֵּבָה, which often refers to an idolatrous pillar (*HALOT* s.v. "מַצֵּבָה" 620–21; see also Iwry 1957, 227, who surveys usage of cognates). But would such an image make sense in this context? Both of the trees mentioned, the terebinth (אֵלָה) and oak (אַלּוֹן), are associated with idolatrous shrines elsewhere (Ezek. 6:13; Hos. 4:13). The phrase בָּם, "in them," appears as *bmh* in 1QIsᵃ, possibly referring to a בָּמָה, or high place, which is associated with a מַצֵּבָה elsewhere (1 Kings 14:23; 2 Kings 18:4). Finally, the relative pronoun אֲשֶׁר could conceivably be a corruption of an original אֲשֵׁרָה, "Asherah," understood as appositional to or as a gloss on the preceding אֵלָה, "terebinth," and/or אַלּוֹן, "oak." In some contexts an אֲשֵׁרָה appears to be a man-made object, perhaps a stylized tree (see, e.g., 2 Kings 17:16), but in Deuteronomy 16:21 it seems to refer to a living tree that is planted. (For discussion of different views on the identity of an אֲשֵׁרָה, see Day 2000, 52–59.) These trees, whether stylized or living, are associated elsewhere with sacred pillars (Exod. 34:13; Deut. 7:5; 12:3; 2 Kings 17:10; 18:4) and high places (2 Kings 18:4; 21:3; 23:15). Understanding מַצֶּבֶת as a sacred pillar and reading בָּמָה (for בָּם) and אֲשֵׁרָה (for אֲשֶׁר), one may translate Isaiah 6:13b: "like a terebinth or like an oak (an Asherah) when a pillar on a high place is thrown down. Holy offspring are its pillar."

In this case the verse does not end with a glimmer of hope, as in the traditional interpretation.[11] Rather, 6:13b understands the coming judgment as comparable to the destruction of an idolatrous high place. As the sacred pillar is thrown down (cf. שַׁלֶּכֶת) from the high place, the sacred trees are burnt up. The land would experience the same fiery destiny as the trees, and the "holy offspring," a sarcastic reference to the nation, would be thrown down like the sacred pillar. The people had been set apart by God as "holy offspring" (see Ezra 9:2, as well as Exod. 22:31; Isa. 62:12; 63:18), but they had become "offspring who do wrong" (Isa. 1:4; see further Beale 1991, 270). The comparison to an idolatrous cult is appropriate, for the people were worshipping at such sites. (See the commentary on 1:29–31, and Beale 1991, 259–61, 264–65, 269, 271 on the intertextual connection between 6:9–13 and 1:29–31.) If there is indeed idolatrous cult imagery in 6:13, then this may shed additional light on the language of 6:9–10, which anticipates the insensitivity of the people in response to Isaiah's preaching (see commentary above). Gregory Beale (1991, 258–59) points to similar language used in the idol polemic in Psalm 135:15–18 (cf. Ps. 115:4–8), where those who worship lifeless idols end up like those same idols. If Israel's idolatry is in view in Isaiah 6:13 (cf. 1:29–31), then there is an element of retributive justice in the description of 6:9–10. To add to the irony, Israel would be destroyed along with its idolatrous shrines (6:13). Beale (1991, 277) states that the people "would be punished for their idolatry by being judged in

---

11 For a defense of a "cultic" reading of the text along the lines suggested here, see Beale 1991, 257–78; as well as Iwry 1957, 225–32.

the same manner as their idols. Both the idols and the people would undergo destruction." He adds: "This pronouncement of judgment may also include an indictment that the idolaters had begun to resemble the nature of their idols."

THEOLOGICAL FOCUS

The theological focus of this passage can be stated as follows: recognizing God's holiness prompts one to confess sin. However, experiencing spiritual cleansing prompts one to carry out God's commission. As the prophet develops this theological theme, the following emphases emerge:

1. The Lord's holiness and sovereignty

Every element in Isaiah's vision reflects the Lord's holiness and sovereignty. He is seated on his throne in his temple and his royal splendor fills the earth (6:4). He is called the Sovereign Master (6:1, 8, אֲדֹנָי) and "the King" (6:5), as well as יְהוָה צְבָאוֹת (6:3, 5), a title that depicts him as enthroned in the middle of his heavenly assembly and sometimes as leading his armies into battle. This may well be the case in Isaiah 6, which describes Yahweh's devastating judgment upon the land (6:11–13). His attendants declare him "holy," using the term three times. In this context Yahweh's holiness is fundamentally his sovereign transcendence, but also includes his moral authority.

2. Human sinfulness in the presence of the holy God

Isaiah's response to the holy God was appropriate. He was very much aware of his own sinfulness and of the sinfulness of the community in which he lived. Praise was the order of the day, but sinful Isaiah, whose lips were impure, was incapable of offering praise. He realized that sinful human beings are not qualified to praise God. His response also indicates that sinful human beings are doomed in the presence of the holy God. He knew that it was inappropriate for sinners to see God, and he expected to be destroyed immediately.

3. Divine cleansing from sin and the appropriate response

Isaiah was not destroyed, even though he deserved to be. Instead, Isaiah was cleansed from his sin, as symbolized by the application of the purifying hot coal to his impure lips. Now free to speak, Isaiah did not join the seraphim in praise, but in response to the King's question volunteered to serve by carrying the prophetic message to the covenant community.

4. Human stubbornness and its devastating consequences

Isaiah's commission was to harden the community through preaching. The ironic rhetoric of 6:9–10 makes it clear the people would reject his message, which would confront them with their sin and warn them of judgment. As Isaiah continued to proclaim the prophetic word, the people would grow more stubborn. God's prophetic word is never neutral—it either draws repentant sinners to God or pushes rebels away from him. Their rejection of the truth both reveals and intensifies their hardness of heart. This passage illustrates the biblical doctrine that human beings are bent on rebellion and resist the prophetic word (John 1:10–11; Rom. 1:18–32; 3:9–18; 2 Cor. 4:3–4; Eph. 2:1–3; Col. 3:5–9; Titus 3:3). In Isaiah's day, even the covenant community was susceptible to such blatant rebellion (Isa. 1:2–3), necessitating God's purifying judgment (4:2–6).

PREACHING AND TEACHING STRATEGIES

Exegetical and Theological Synthesis

Isaiah 6 functions as the prophet's commission to preach to the nation of Israel. Its placement in the book initially seems odd. Why would

Isaiah's inaugural call not be placed at the very beginning of the book?[12] Maybe the simplest answer to this question is that chapters 1–5 provide somewhat of a general introduction to the book as they deal with the broad theme of Israel's sin and corruption leading to certain coming judgment. Isaiah 6 begins to provide the means by which the nation must and will ultimately obtain the wonderful promises laid out for a bright future. Israel/Judah will need to experience the Lord their God in the same way that Isaiah does here. They must see him as holy and exalted over them. They must likewise come to see themselves as sinners in need of cleansing by God. Finally, they must realize their own calling to be God's special and chosen people who will humbly carry his words to the nations around them.

Isaiah 6:1–4 begins with a description of what the prophet saw and heard. In his vision, he is transported either into the holy of holies in the temple, or possibly into God's heavenly throne room. He sees the Lord himself sitting on an elevated throne and wearing a very long robe (6:1). God is surrounded by winged, angelic beings (seraphim) proclaiming to one another the majesty of the Lord, "Holy, holy, holy is the Lord Almighty; the whole earth is full of his glory" (6:2–3). The awesomeness of God's presence is further highlighted as Isaiah states that the very foundations of the temple shook as the angels called out their praise. Additionally, the room was filled with smoke, probably from the altar of incense located in the holy place (6:6; cf. Exod. 30:1–10, 40:5, Lev. 16:12–13; 1 Chron. 28:18; Ezek. 41:21–22).[13]

In Isaiah 6:5, the reader discovers what Isaiah was thinking as he encountered this amazing vision of God. He responds first by saying, "Woe is me!" The implication of the word "woe" is that one is in dire straits because some disaster is imminent, usually divine judgment due to sin. It was often necessary for a prophet of God to pronounce a "woe" upon people whom he was called to confront because of their sin. However, Isaiah is here compelled to pronounce a woe upon himself. He goes on to say, "For I am lost" (ESV, NRSV), or "destroyed" (NET) or "ruined" (HCSB, NASB, NIV). The NLT's "I am doomed" might be closest to how a modern English speaker would say it. Isaiah's reason for feeling this way is explained: "I am a man of unclean lips, and I live among a people of unclean lips, and my eyes have seen the King, the Lord Almighty!" The sight of the Holy and Sovereign God confronted him with the stark contrast to his own sinfulness and that of the nation to which he belongs, Israel. It became abundantly clear to him that there was no way a sinner such as himself could remain standing in the presence of one so righteous and pure. As such, he was doomed to be destroyed because of his unrighteousness.

Thankfully, for his sake as well as for our own, Isaiah's encounter with God does not end with 6:5. As the prophet recoils at the realization of his own sinfulness, God draws toward him in a clear gesture of mercy and grace. One of the angels takes a burning coal from off the altar of incense with a set of tongs and places it against the prophet's mouth. The angel then tells him that his guilt has been taken away and his sin has been atoned for. Rather than destroying the prophet because of his sin, God instead provides atonement for Isaiah to cleanse him of sin and the associating guilt (6:6–7).

This passage ends with God's commission for the purified prophet. God asks whom he should send on behalf of himself and the entire

---

[12] "The experience described in the chapter is of such power and immediacy that it is hard to imagine it as anything other than inaugural" (Oswalt 1986, 172). See too Goldingay 2001, 58; McKenna 1993, 105–6.

[13] Hebrews 9:3–4 refers to the altar of incense (the golden altar) as located behind the second curtain in the most holy place. Revelation 8:3–5 likewise seems to describe a similar altar of incense located in God's heavenly throne room.

heavenly court. Isaiah wastes no time in volunteering to be the one. It is likely that God's question was rhetorical; Isaiah understood that he was being asked to go and bear God's message to the people. His response was not to ask for more details first so that he could make a more informed decision. (God doesn't appear to give him any information about what he is being called to do until after Isaiah has agreed to go.) Likewise, the prophet does not offer up excuses for why he shouldn't go as Moses did when he was commissioned to go to Egypt and deliver God's message to Pharaoh (Exod. 3:1–4:17). He doesn't run in the opposite direction as Jonah had upon receiving his call to preach to Nineveh (Jonah 1:1–3). He does not even ask for time to think about it. Instead, he immediately and unconditionally volunteers to be God's messenger.

Finally, God reveals to him what his mission will entail (Isa. 6:9–13). Unfortunately for Isaiah, he will not be very successful in changing the hearts and minds of the people of Israel. They have become hardened in their sin and their rejection of God's law. All that the prophet's warnings will do is harden them further in their opposition to Yahweh, which will ultimately make them more deserving of the predicted coming judgment against them. The judgment will result in many people being deported from the land (6:12) until cities lie waste without any inhabitants (6:11). Only a fraction of the nation's population will be left in the end. They will be like a mighty tree that has been cut down, leaving behind only a stump in its place (6:13).

Preaching Idea

An encounter with the holy, sovereign God should lead us to repent of sins and humbly submit to God, resulting in our transformation.

Contemporary Connections

What does it mean?

One of the most iconic movie scenes of all time is when Dorothy, the Scarecrow, the Tin Man, and the Cowardly Lion first meet the great and powerful Wizard of Oz. As the four characters cautiously make their way into the room to finally see the wizard, they encounter an awesome and terrifying being (at least he appears as such). His presence is accompanied by pillars of fire, colorful smoke, and sounds of thunder. The wizard's giant face appears to be floating in front of them as he speaks to them one at a time. Its transparent form gives the appearance that he is a spirit-like being without a physical body, something totally different from them. They are filled with both awe and trepidation in the presence of one who seems so distinct from them and appears to have supernatural power to destroy them if he so desires. I imagine this cinematic scene illustrates something of what it would have meant for Isaiah to stand in the very throne room of the sovereign, omnipotent, holy God of the universe. It would have been awe-inspiring and terrifying at the same time. He must have felt so weak and small against the backdrop of one who possesses all power and is immeasurably great.

God's power and greatness had a very significant effect on Isaiah. However, it was God's holiness that most impacted the prophet. "Holy, holy, holy" is how the Lord is described by the seraphim attending his presence. The holiness of God refers to that which sets him apart from his creation, particularly regarding his completely righteous and perfect nature. When people encounter the holiness of God, it is both a convicting and a frightening experience. One cannot help but sense their own guilt and shame on account of their many sins and imperfections that appear in stark contrast to God's righteous character. Realizations that one deserves severe judgment flood the mind of all who gaze upon the holiness of God.

The only proper response is for the person to humbly confess their guilt and express repentance before the Lord. In repentance, one admits that God's ways alone are true and right and pure, whereas their own attitudes and behaviors that conflict with God's are wrong in every sense of the word. As such, a repentant person will choose to submit themselves in obedience to the ways of God, resulting in a changed life. This is the only appropriate response when one encounters the holy, sovereign God.

Is it true?

There are several examples in Scripture of God revealing himself personally to people by way of a theophany. In almost every instance, the person to whom he appeared responded with amazement and fear, often to the point of fearing they would die. These events likewise often resulted in some form of repentance and/or submission by the person(s) to do whatever God demanded of them. Probably the most obvious example of this is when God appeared to the Israelites at Mt. Sinai. He warned the people ahead of time not to come too close to the mountain lest they die (Exod. 19:12–13, 21–22, 24). Here is how the people experienced God's presence that day:

> On the morning of the third day there was thunder and lightning, with a thick cloud over the mountain, and a very loud trumpet blast. Everyone in the camp trembled. Then Moses led the people out of the camp to meet with God, and they stood at the foot of the mountain. Mount Sinai was covered with smoke, because the LORD descended on it in fire. The smoke billowed up from it like smoke from a furnace, and the whole mountain trembled violently. (Exod. 19:16–18)

Notice how "everyone in the camp trembled" in fear at the awesome presence of God in their midst that day. In fact, the story goes on to record that "the people trembled in fear" and "stayed at a distance and said to Moses, 'Speak to us yourself and we will listen. But do not have God speak to us or we will die'" (Exod. 20:18–19). Their fear of God influenced their willingness to submit to whatever he said for them. Their request for Moses to speak and their professed willingness to listen implies more than just hearing Moses speak. It was the equivalent of their consent to obey whatever Moses said as the spokesperson for God.[14]

But what about people today? God does not seem to be revealing himself to people in the way that he occasionally did during Bible times. However, we today have something that none of the Old Testament saints had: we have the revelation of God in the person of Jesus Christ. Jesus "is the image of the invisible God" (Col. 1:15), "for God was pleased to have all his fullness dwell in him" (Col. 1:19). "The Son is the radiance of God's glory and the exact representation of his being" (Heb. 1:3). Thus, Jesus was able to say to his disciples while on earth, "Anyone who has seen me has seen the Father" (John 14:9; cf. John 1:1, 14; 10:30, 38; 12:45; 14:7–10; 17:5, 21). In fact, prior to Jesus's coming, nobody had fully seen the Father, only glimpses of his glory. In Jesus, though, the fullness of God's character was on display for more than three decades. They witnessed God's supernatural power over disease, nature, and the demonic realm. They witnessed his supernatural knowledge of all things including the private thoughts and intentions of people's hearts. They witnessed his holy character that Jesus lived out daily in the most practical of ways. Maybe most important of all, they witnessed the loving heart of the Father for his created people, rebellious though they be, as Jesus voluntarily submitted to the tortures of the cross, taking our sins on

---

14   Other similar examples in Scripture of people experiencing some form of an encounter with God resulting in them feeling great fear, often to the point of death, followed by their repentance/submission to God include Moses (Exod. 3:1–6; 33:20), Gideon (Judg. 6:22–23), Manoah and his wife (Judg. 13:3–20), Daniel (Dan. 8:15–18; 10:2–19), Saul who later became Paul (Acts 9:3–18), and the apostle John (Rev. 1:12–18).

himself. John 1:18 says, "No one has ever seen God; but the one and only Son, who is himself God and is in closest relationship with the Father, has made him known." In other words, only Jesus has fully revealed God to humanity when he himself became a human being and stepped into this world.

People today continue to encounter Jesus through his words and teachings which have been preserved and passed down in the pages of the New Testament. Our encounters with Jesus should cause us to be struck with humility at the reality of sin and judgment. In the same way that Isaiah trembled fearfully in the presence of the holy, sovereign God, we too should have a similar response to the judgment of eternal death in hell that looms over every rebellious, unrepentant sinner. Our response should be, "Woe to me! I am ruined. For I am a man [or woman] of unclean lips [and actions], and I live among a people of unclean lips [and actions]." In other words, the holy, selfless, God-exalting life that Jesus lived should serve as a stark contrast to the unholy, self-serving, self-exalting lives that we have lived. But just as Isaiah's impure lips were cleansed and his guilt was taken away by a gracious act of God, so too can the ones who bow in humble submission at the feet of Jesus find that same cleansing and forgiveness through the atoning work of Jesus on the cross. Their lives will be forever changed.

In fact, the apostle Paul likened the ministry of the Holy Spirit bringing about change in the life of a believer to when Moses saw the glory of the Lord and it caused his face to glow. Moses had to put a veil over his face so as not to blind the people who saw the temporary but glorious change in his appearance. Paul wrote of believers in Christ, "And we all, who with unveiled faces contemplate the Lord's glory, are being transformed into his image with ever-increasing glory, which comes from the Lord, who is the Spirit" (2 Cor. 3:18). In other words, when we encounter God today through the person of Jesus Christ and the ministry of the Holy Spirit, we can expect a glorious change in us that far exceeds the one that Moses experienced (2 Cor. 3:7–11).

Now what?

Human tendency is always to downplay our own sinfulness. We usually accomplish this in one of two ways. First, we compare ourselves with those who are worse than we are. Someone might say, "I know I shouldn't have browsed those internet sites, but it's only once in a while, and I'm staying away from any hardcore pornography. Plus, I would never act on any of those fantasies." Or, "I know I had a little too much to drink last night, but I'm not an alcoholic, and I'm careful to stay away from any illegal drugs." The not-so-subtle implication of those kinds of thoughts or statements is that, while we know what we did was wrong, there are lots of people who engage in far worse things than what we just did. So we can't be too bad, can we?

Another way that folks manage to downplay their sin is to define it in terms of a hard-fought battle where they simply came up short. Thus, when speaking about their sin, they may say things like, "I've made plenty of *mistakes* over the years," or "Hey, I'm not perfect." Additionally, they refer to sinful habits as a "struggle" or "battle" with this or that bad habit. While these sorts of admissions may appear noble on the surface, it's not hard to see through the façade that I am basically a good person who tries my best to do the right thing but, unfortunately, don't always get it right. We end up describing ourselves like a runner in a race who gave it his best shot but, unfortunately, wasn't the fastest person on the track that day. There's nothing to be ashamed of for trying hard and failing, right?

The problem with these sorts of descriptions or definitions of sin is that they are far too generous. If we are honest with ourselves and others, our sin has often not involved much of a struggle or battle at all. We just wanted to do what we wanted to do, and we didn't care who was hurt in the process. Our only battle came after the fact as we wrestled internally with how to posture ourselves or frame the narrative so as not to look too bad in the eyes of those who would find out. Rather than describing ourselves as "mistake-makers," "less than perfect," "strugglers/battlers against evil," wouldn't it be more accurate to use descriptions like "rebellious," "disobedient to God," "self-absorbed," and somebody who runs hard after "sordid" and "perverted" desires? Nobody likes to think (much less speak) of themselves in these ways, and thus we tend to posture and position ourselves into a better light through unwarranted comparisons with others and semantic sleights of hand.

However, none of this is possible when a person has an encounter with the holy, sovereign God of the universe. As soon as our sin is shown in the light of his holiness, rather than in comparison with those who are more sinful than we are, we are left with no place to hide. There is no longer any reasonable way to posture our actions other than to say, "Woe to me. I am ruined." Not only does the holiness of God put the sinner's selfish, perverted, rebellious heart into crystal-clear focus, but the omniscient, sovereign God is not fooled by delicate, semantic arguments designed to make us look better than we really are. God sees more than just our outward actions. His penetrating eyes see through to the thoughts, attitudes, and motives of our hearts. No pretense or posturing can fool him. The author of Hebrews said it best: "Nothing in all creation is hidden from God's sight. Everything is uncovered and laid bare before the eyes of him to whom we must give account" (Heb. 4:13).

As such, we are left with the uncomfortable but ultimately beneficial option of simply admitting our guilt and acknowledging just how wicked our actions have been. In humility, we must agree with God that we have brazenly and arrogantly rebelled against his holy laws which are written in his Word as well as on our God-given conscience. The Bible assures us that when we respond in this way, the Lord will cleanse us from all our unrighteousness and will invite us into the mission of impacting our world with truth and righteousness.

For those who have experienced the life-changing work of the Holy Spirit through salvation and forgiveness of sins, we must remember that, like Isaiah, we have been called to be the voice of God to a culture that is made up of people of unclean lips and actions. Therefore, we too must anticipate that many people will reject the message of God that our life declares. We should expect that people will often spurn our invitation to accompany us to church. They will often laugh at our conviction that the Bible should be obeyed. Many will ignore and resist our warnings about a God in heaven who is watching everything we do and to whom we must all one day give an accounting for our lives. They may even get angry with us when we resist and push back against the world's self-centered ideologies that suggest that people should be free to do what they want or be who they want to be. None of this should surprise us, nor should it deter us from faithfully standing with God and declaring his Word. In the same way that God warned Isaiah that his own people would reject him, Jesus warned his followers that they too would be persecuted, mocked, and even killed.[15]

To take this one step further, it is important for Christ-followers to recognize that ministry is rarely convenient. There was nothing convenient about taking an unpopular message about sin and coming judgment to a bunch of people stubbornly bent on resisting it. It must have seemed like

---

15 For Scriptures detailing how Christians are to anticipate rejection and suffering, see Matt. 5:10–12; 10:16–18, 22–25; John 15:19–21; 16:2; 17:14; Acts 14:22; 1 Cor. 4:11–13; 2 Cor. 4:8–11; 6:4–10; 1 Thess. 3:3–4; 2 Tim. 2:3; 3:12–15; 1 Peter 2:20–21; 4:12–14; Rev. 2:10–11.

such a waste of time and energy for Isaiah to be God's faithful prophet to these hard-headed folks. Nonetheless, God called him to be faithful still. I think that many in the church today mistakenly expect ministry to be convenient. They look for ways to serve God that don't take up too much of their time or that don't create scheduling conflicts for them. But the reality of ministry is that it is rarely convenient or easy. Helping a poor widow in our congregation or our neighborhood requires far more than just reposting something on our Facebook page about the plight of poverty or sending out the hashtag "#I-Stand-with-Widows" on Instagram. Caring for widows will likely involve writing some checks to widows in need or giving up half of my Saturday to scrape paint off second-story windows at her house. Serving Jesus will force us to do far more than simply talk about things that are popular with most in our culture, such as our love for the poor and marginalized or our opposition to racism. If we're honest, those are messages that are essentially safe for us to hold. They probably endear us to our culture more than put us at risk. But what about those messages that are biblical but deeply unpopular to express? Are we willing to trumpet these on our social media platforms and in our conversations around the water cooler at work? Are we really willing to risk being hated and misunderstood for the cause of Christ? Or do we prefer a version of following Jesus that will by and large be accepted by our non-Christian friends and family? Jesus has called his followers to real sacrifice and suffering. It will cost us dearly to serve God, but it will also be eternally rewarding.

Creativity in Presentation

Tornadoes are among the most powerful and destructive phenomena in nature. They have leveled entire towns. In an average year, they are responsible for some eighty human deaths and 1,500 injuries. And yet, despite the risk these storms pose for humans, some individuals are drawn toward them. People known as storm chasers will risk their lives for the opportunity to see and experience a twister up close. There is just something awesome and captivating about seeing the massive power of a tornado that can tear a roof off a house in seconds, pick up an automobile and fling it hundreds of feet, and snap electric poles like they were toothpicks. I imagine this must have been something of what it was like to be in the very presence of the all-powerful God of the universe. Isaiah was both captivated and amazed by God's power and beauty while at the same time struck by the danger and destructive nature of his holiness upon a sinful one such as he.

Les Misérables is a well-known book that was turned into a hit Broadway musical and at least a couple of movies. The story centers around the main character, Jean Valjean who had just been released from prison after spending nearly twenty years there for stealing a loaf of bread and then trying to escape capture. He is now jaded and angry at the world and seems resolved to continue living a life of crime in order to survive. After all, who would be willing to hire a convicted felon like him? Early in the story, a kind priest invites Jean Valjean to have supper and spend the night at the church residence where he lives. Despite the priest's generosity toward him, Valjean makes the selfish decision to steal several valuable silver pieces early the next morning before leaving. However, he is caught and returned for the priest to retrieve his valuables and to confirm that Valjean had in fact stolen them from the church. To everyone's surprise, the priest claimed that he had given those pieces to him, and even asserted that Valjean had inadvertently forgotten to take the most valuable pieces, two silver candlesticks, which he then gave to him. He insisted that the police release him immediately. As soon as the policemen leave, Valjean asks the priest why he just did that. The priest responded by telling Valjean to take those silver pieces and use them to become an honest man.

Valjean does just that. He apparently uses some of the money from the silver to buy a factory by which he is able to become a wealthy and prominent man in his town. He then uses this wealth to show kindness to the poor and disadvantaged and refuses to take advantage of people. First he helps Fantine who had worked in his factory by day, but who also worked the streets at night out of desperation to care for her daughter. After Fantine's untimely death, he fulfills a promise to her by adopting and caring for her young child Cosette, whom he raises as his own daughter. Most striking of all is the way that Valjean refuses to take revenge on a mean, overzealous inspector who has a vendetta against Valjean and tries at every turn to force him back into prison. At one point, Valjean has the perfect opportunity to murder the inspector, but lets him go free instead.

The moral of the story is that a person who has been the recipient of extravagant, undeserved grace should not be able to remain the same type of person. Grace has a way of changing us to reflect the character of the one who first showed us grace. In the same way, when Isaiah encountered the holy but gracious God, it spurred him toward repentance of his sin and a willingness to submit himself to serving God and others.

The song "Shine, Jesus Shine" reveals a wonderful message about how Jesus functions as the light of the world to shine his truth into a dark and corrupt world. Verses 2 and 3 are especially relevant as they unpack the truth that for the light and message of Jesus to penetrate our world today, it will have to happen through his human representatives (Christians) who represent him to a lost world (much like the ministry to which Isaiah was commissioned). However, for us to do this well, it requires that we have had our own personal encounter with Jesus, and that this encounter has changed us in noticeable ways, such that we now reflect the character of Jesus to others. The preacher might consider reading the lyrics of this classic worship chorus to reinforce the truth that an encounter with the holy, sovereign God should lead us to repent of sin and humbly submit to God, resulting in our transformation.

- Isaiah's vision (6:1–4).
- Isaiah's condition (6:5).
- God's provision (6:6–7).
- Isaiah's commission (6:8–10).
- Israel's decision (6:11–13).

DISCUSSION QUESTIONS

1. What thoughts come to your mind when you hear the word "holiness," particularly as it relates to holy people? Does this word elicit positive or negative feelings?

2. In what ways does our secular culture respond to the notion of holiness or holy people?

3. Have you ever felt a call by God to serve him in a particular way? What events or factors did God use in your life to bring you to a place of sensing his call and leading toward ministry?

4. Share some examples of how ministry can often be inconvenient. What are some ways that you find it challenging to embrace a heart of ministry due to various risks or inconveniences?

5. How should the image of God seated high upon his throne impact us this week? (Consider issues such as the world's disasters and our worries, our goals and priorities, our politics, and how we go about our daily work.)

FOR FURTHER READING

DeYoung, Kevin. 2014. *The Hole in Our Holiness: Filling the Gap Between Gospel Passion and the Pursuit of Godliness*. Wheaton, IL: Crossway.

Isaiah 7:1–8:10

EXEGETICAL IDEA
Isaiah made it clear that the covenant community should place their trust in the Lord's faithful promise of his protective presence, for a refusal to believe would turn potential blessing into divine discipline and tragic suffering.

THEOLOGICAL FOCUS
The Lord's people should place their trust in the Lord's faithful promise of his protective presence, for a refusal to believe can turn potential blessing into divine discipline and tragic suffering.

PREACHING IDEA
It is always wise to trust in God, for ultimate security is found only in him.

PREACHING POINTERS
When my wife was pregnant with our first child, a baby girl, we spent months thinking about what name we would give her. We considered several factors: Did we like the name? Did we like the shortened forms of her name that people would inevitably call her? How many other people did we know who shared that name? Would we name her after somebody in the family, or maybe somebody in the Bible? It didn't help that my wife and I had very different ideas of what names we liked and didn't like. At one point, we bought a book of possible names and just began to read through it together. Whenever a name seemed like a possibility, we highlighted it to consider for later. One name ended up sticking out to us both: Elliana. In addition to passing all the criteria we had set up ahead of time, the meaning of this name held significance to us. In Hebrew it means, "God has answered." We had been praying and trying to have a baby for a few years. We were beginning to wonder whether we were able to have children or not. Thus, this seemed the perfect name for our first baby girl.

Names are important. But few baby names were ever quite as consequential as the ones we encounter in Isaiah 7:1–8:10. This passage revolves around three different child names, each one intended to serve as an important message from God. The children themselves would serve as "signs" or object lessons to the nation of Judah that God's promises were sure, and that his word could be trusted regardless of the circumstances or the political climate of the day. While there was a significant temptation by the people of Judah and their king to look elsewhere for a sense of security and stability, God alone had the power to save and to protect. That truth is just as relevant today as it was more than 2,700 years ago. In a climate where there is much political turmoil, economic instability, and at times even religious hostility, it is always wise to trust in God, for ultimate security is found only in him.

A SIGN CHILD AND FORFEITED BLESSING (7:1–8:10)

In the face of the Israelite-Aramean coalition, the Lord challenged King Ahaz to trust in his promise of protection. But, when invited to seek a sign from the Lord to buttress his weak faith, Ahaz rejected the offer. In response the Lord gave the king a sign that he would be present with his people, both to deliver and to discipline. A young woman known to the royal court would give birth to a son and name him Immanuel, "God (is) with us." This child would eventually eat milk and honey, an experience that would give him moral insight. Before that day arrived, the northern coalition feared by Ahaz would be defeated, proving the Lord's ability to protect his people. But then the Lord would transform blessing into judgment through the Assyrians, who would conquer Judah and devastate the land, forcing people to survive on sour milk and honey. The Lord then instructed Isaiah to give his newborn son a name symbolizing the imminent defeat of the coalition. The Lord again warned that he would use the Assyrians to punish Judah, yet the prophet celebrated the fact that the Lord would destroy all invaders, proving again that he is the protector of his people.

LITERARY STRUCTURE AND THEMES (7:1–8:10)

Isaiah 7 is a narrative, introduced by וַיְהִי, "and it was," and a temporal clause ("in the days of"). Isaiah 7:1 is a summary statement, informing the reader that the Israelite-Aramean coalition was unable to conquer Jerusalem. Isaiah 7:2 begins a more detailed account of what happened as it flashes back chronologically to the beginning of the crisis, when Israel and the Arameans formed an alliance. In response to Ahaz's and Judah's fear at the news of the alliance, the Lord commissioned Isaiah to assure the king that he would thwart the coalition's plot to overthrow the Davidic dynasty. But Ahaz needed to trust in the Lord as his protector (7:3–9).

There is no narrative account of Isaiah delivering this message to Ahaz, but 7:10, which returns to the mainline of the narrative (see 7:3), assumes that he did (Hayes and Irvine 1987, 130). Isaiah 7:10–11 is an expansion of the previous message, as the offer of a sign serves to support the warning of 7:9. Ahaz's rejection of the offer (7:12) prompted a negative response from Isaiah in which he rebuked the king (7:13) and announced that the Lord would give the reluctant king a sign, whether he wanted one or not. The sign involved the timing of events, which would prove that God was indeed with his people to deliver them from the northern threat but also, ironically, to discipline the land for Ahaz's unbelief (7:14–17).

Isaiah 7:18–25 describes in detail this coming judgment. The section is divided into three subunits, each of which is introduced by וְהָיָה, "and it will be," and a temporal phrase ("in that day"; 7:18–20, 21–22, 23–25).

The chronologically awkward transition from the commissioning account in 7:3–9 to the narrative of the prophet's audience with the king (7:10) requires additional comment. As noted above, the narrative does not record the delivery of the prophet's initial message to the king (7:3–9), but it assumes it with the use of וַיּוֹסֶף . . . דַּבֵּר, "and he again . . . spoke," at the beginning of 7:10. Should we assume that 7:10 is simply a continuation of the implied speech, or does it constitute a new scene? To answer this, we must look at the precise wording of 7:10. The *hiphil* form וַיּוֹסֶף is collocated with the infinitive דַּבֵּר in only three other passages:

(1) Genesis 18:29: וַיֹּסֶף עוֹד לְדַבֵּר. The construction is used in a virtually repeated statement in the third panel of a six-paneled sequence (18:23–32). There is no change in scene, and one could translate the expression, "he continued to speak."

(2) Judges 9:37: וַיֹּסֶף עוֹד . . . לְדַבֵּר. The construction is used in a virtually repeated statement in the second panel of a sequence. There is no change in scene, and one could translate, "he continued to speak."

(3) Isaiah 8:5: וַיֹּסֶף . . . דַּבֵּר . . . עוֹד. The construction introduces a judgment speech that further develops the explanation given for the child's name in 8:3–4. It is not clear if this is a new scene (chronologically) or not, but one could conceivably translate it "he continued to speak."

The adverb עוֹד appears to be a continuity marker in texts (1) and (2), where it seems to have the force of "yet again." If עוֹד is a continuity marker, then it is unlikely that Isaiah 8:5 provides a parallel to Isaiah 7:10, because the latter omits עוֹד. The preceding context of Isaiah 7:10 also differs significantly from the above texts. The Lord speaks directly to Ahaz in 7:10–11, in contrast to 7:3–9 where the Lord commissions Isaiah to meet Ahaz and preach to him the message recorded in 7:4–9, including the divine oracle of 7:7–9. But there is no narrative of Isaiah doing this; it is assumed. The dialogue recorded in 7:10–25 may have occurred after the implied encounter between 7:9–10 (in this case, it is a new scene), or it could have been an extension of the speech delivered by Isaiah on that occasion. We simply do not know. However, the use of וַיֹּסֶף indicates that what follows is distinct in some way from the oracle to Ahaz that appears in 7:4–9. Indeed, in a case where the narrator leaves a gap in the account, inclusion of וַיֹּסֶף becomes an efficient way of advancing the story, and the omission of עוֹד helps us to see that the discourse of 7:4–9 has been broken off and that we have returned to the story line. In short, the syntax and context of Isaiah 7:10 are unique. The absence of עוֹד suggests that it does mark a pericope break, especially when one observes that, literally speaking, there is no speech made directly to Ahaz prior to this, only instructions regarding what the prophet is to say to Ahaz. It is also possible that the absence of עוֹד indicates that this incident occurred sometime after the initial message was delivered (see Num. 22:19).

The narrative continues in Isaiah 8, as the Lord instructed Isaiah to prepare for the birth of a sign child (8:1–2). Isaiah, using an autobiographical style (see ch. 6), then reported the birth of the child (8:3a). The Lord instructed Isaiah to name the child Maher-shalal-hash-baz as a portent of the imminent defeat of the northern coalition (8:3b–4). The Lord then expanded the message, announcing to Isaiah the Assyrian invasion of Judah (8:5–8). This expansion ends with a statement addressed to Immanuel, presumably the child whose birth was announced in 7:14. (On the significance of the introductory עוֹד . . . דַּבֵּר . . . וַיֹּסֶף as indicating continuity with what precedes, see above.) But the tone changes in 8:9–10, which address the invading nations in highly rhetorical fashion, taunting them and affirming God's presence with his people. The style of 8:10b suggests that Isaiah is speaking here.

There are several literary links between 8:1–10 and chapter 7. The appearance of "Immanuel" in 8:8 (as a proper name) and 8:10 (in a causal clause) links this speech with the sign of Immanuel (7:14). The report of the sign child's birth in 8:1–3 could be understood as the fulfillment of the birth prediction in 7:14, especially since the defeat of the northern coalition is associated with his growth and experience (cf. 8:4 with 7:16) and the ominous prediction of an Assyrian invasion follows the good news of deliverance (cf. 8:5–8 with 7:17–25). If Maher-shalal-hash-baz is not one and the same as Immanuel, then he is certainly a parallel sign child. (For fuller discussion of this possibility, see below.) The threefold appearance of the verb חָתַת (cf. חֹתּוּ) in 8:9 forms an intertextual link to 7:8, where the verb is used (note יֵחַת) of Ephraim's demise.

- *Prologue-Summary (7:1)*
- *The Lord's Challenge to Fearful Ahaz (7:2–9)*
- *Ahaz's Rejection of a Confirming Sign (7:10–12)*
- *The Lord Gives Ahaz a Confirming Sign (7:13–17)*
- *The Lord Explains the Sign (7:18–25)*
- *The Lord Reiterates the Sign (8:1–8)*
- *A Glimmer of Hope (8:9–10)*

EXPOSITION (7:1–8:10)

Prologue-Summary (7:1)

In 735 B.C., five years after Isaiah's prophetic commission, the northern kingdom of Israel formed an anti-Assyrian alliance with the Arameans of Damascus that ultimately failed.

When Judah refused to join the coalition, the alliance invaded Judah and attacked Jerusalem, hoping to replace King Ahaz with a puppet ruler. However, their attempt to take Jerusalem and remove Ahaz from the throne failed (Isa. 7:1; cf. 2 Kings 16:5), even though they did win a substantial victory over the armies of Judah (2 Chron. 28:5–8). Second Kings 16:7–9 informs us that Ahaz turned to Assyria for help, handing over treasure from the temple and royal palace as tribute. The Assyrian king, Tiglath-pileser III, marched against Aram and defeated Damascus. But Assyrian intervention was not the real reason why Judah escaped the threat of the northern alliance, as Isaiah 7 makes clear. Speaking through his prophet Isaiah, the Lord assured Ahaz that he would deliver Judah from the alliance's threat (7:7, 16; see as well 8:4), which he did. However, he also warned the king that refusal to trust in the Lord's protective power would bring grave consequences, a warning that proved to be true when Ahaz refused to embrace the Lord's promise and decided instead to trust in Assyria (7:17–25; see as well 8:5–8).

The Lord's Challenge to Fearful Ahaz (7:2–9)

The Lord challenged Ahaz to trust him to protect Judah from the threat of the northern coalition.

7:2. Having stated at the outset that the northern alliance's invasion failed, the narrator returns to the time when the "house of David" first heard the news of the threat (7:2; Clements 1980, 82; Hayes and Irvine 1987, 120). The report received by the house of David is stated simply: "Aram has rested upon Ephraim" (7:2). The verb נָחָה is probably from the root נוּחַ, "rest," collocated here with "upon" to indicate reliance within a treaty agreement. Aram "rested upon" Ephraim in the sense that they had Israel's military support. In this context, the "house of David" is Judah's royal court at the time of the event, headed up by King Ahaz. The narrator's use of the phrase reflects how the prophet addressed the royal court in the midst of the crisis (see 7:13). The phrase is rhetorically significant, for it is a reminder that Ahaz possessed a legacy and a promise from the Lord (2 Sam. 7). The alliance was threatening to end the Davidic dynasty (Isa. 7:6), but Ahaz could find assurance in his relationship with the Lord (7:9). Yet Ahaz, who was very young (cf. 2 Kings 16:2), was emotionally shaken by news of the alliance, as were his people (Isa. 7:2).[1] They were like trees, swaying before a powerful wind, in danger of being snapped or uprooted.

---

1 According to 2 Kings 16:2, Ahaz was twenty when he began to reign and ruled for sixteen years. But the chronology of Ahaz's reign is difficult to determine. See the commentary on 14:28 below for a discussion of the problem.

7:3. The Lord sent Isaiah out, accompanied by his son Shear-jashub, to meet the king while he was inspecting the city's water supply in anticipation of a siege. The prophet understood that both he and his children were signs (or object lessons) to the people in that their names carried symbolic significance (see 8:18). Isaiah's name means "the Lord delivers," and Shear-jashub's name means "a remnant will return." Their very presence should have reminded the king that the Lord was fully capable of delivering his people and decimating the enemy, so that only a remnant of the defeated invading forces would return home (see 7:4–9; Clements 1980, 83; Williamson 2018, 122). The verb שׁוּב is used here in the sense "turn back (in defeat), retreat" (see Pss. 9:4 [Eng. 3]; 74:21). The implication is that most of the enemy would fall in battle, leaving a mere remnant to retreat to home.[2] Of course, this great victory did not happen. Ahaz's failure to trust the Lord compromised the promise (see fuller discussion below).

> **Water Supply**
> On the location of the Upper Pool, see Smith 2007, 207; and Wildberger 1991, 295. Since enemy armies attacked the city from the north, this pool may have been on the northern side of the city. However, Millar Burrows (1958, 221–27) argues that the pool must have been in the lower Kidron Valley, for only there would fullers find enough water to conduct their occupation. En Rogel, the spring of the fuller (עֵין רֹגֵל, literally "spring of treading," referring to the treading that is done by fullers, see Wildberger 1991, 295), was in the Kidron Valley (Josh. 18:16). For a discussion of ancient Jerusalem's water supply and Hezekiah's projects in this regard, see King and Stager 2001, 213–23.

7:4. The prophet's message to the king was one of reassurance. The king was to get a grip on himself (note the reflexive *niphal* הִשָּׁמֵר, "watch yourself") and display calm confidence (the *hiphil* הַשְׁקֵט is exhibitive here, indicating the outward display of an inner quality). The verb שָׁקַט has the basic idea "be at rest, be quiet" (see Isa. 14:7; 57:20; 62:1). Here it connotes more than simply emotional calmness. In Isaiah 30:15 it is paired with "trust" (cf. also 32:17); keeping calm would be the product of faith in God's promises to the Davidic dynasty and in his ability to defeat any enemies who threatened Judah. The king must not let fear overpower his already swaying heart (7:2). The verb רָכַךְ (note the negated jussive יֵרַךְ) means "be soft, weak." Here it refers to emotional weakness in the face of danger that tends to incapacitate (Deut. 20:3; Jer. 51:46). Proper perspective was necessary. The anger of the alliance's leaders was raging against Judah, but their threats lacked real substance. They were more like what is left when a bonfire is dying out—smoking remnants of logs that are almost burned up (see Amos 4:11; Zech. 3:2). After all, they were just Rezin, Aram, and the son of Remaliah. The Lord avoids the Israelite king's name (Pekah; Isa. 7:1) and instead simply calls him the "son of Remaliah." Unlike the house of David, the "son of Remaliah" had no legacy or promise from the Lord. Therefore, David's offspring need not fear him or his foreign ally (Motyer 1993, 82).

7:5–6. The enemy had a clear-cut plan. They boasted they would attack, create widespread fear, and sweep through the land in victory. Then they would replace the Davidic dynasty with a puppet king, simply called "the son of Tabeel," perhaps a member of a Judahite family

---

2   Interpreters have offered various explanations for the significance of the name Shear-jashub in this context. For a summary, see Smith 2007, 208 n. 261. Smith correctly observes: "It seems that his name must have a positive meaning in this context."

that lived in Gilead (see Aharoni 1979, 370).³ But once again, this was just the "son of Remaliah" (7:5) talking about the "son of Tabeel."

TRANSLATION ANALYSIS 7:6 (NOTE 1)
Some translations understand the hiphil of קוץ in the sense of "frighten" (see KJV "vex" and ESV "terrify") or "terrorize" (see HCSB). This verb is well attested in the *qal* stem with a meaning of "to feel disgust, repugnance" or "to dread" (*HALOT* s.v. "קוץ I" 1089). The *hiphil*, which is not attested elsewhere, would have a causative nuance ("to frighten, horrify") that fits the context nicely. NIV ("tear it apart") and NRSV ("cut off") appear to understand the verb as derived from קָצָה or קָצַץ, both of which have the idea of "cutting off" (see *HALOT* s.vv. "קצה I" 1120; "קצץ I" 1125). However, both express this idea with the *piel* stem; neither occurs in the *hiphil*. *HALOT* (s.v. "קוץ II" 1090) offers a homonymic root as an option, which it understands as a by-form of קָצַץ and glosses as "demolish." But this alleged homonym occurs in only one other passage, Job 14:12, where it is intransitive, not transitive as in Isaiah 7:6. For further discussion, see Wildberger 1991, 284; and Williamson 2018, 99–100.

TRANSLATION ANALYSIS 7:6 (NOTE 2)
Translations differ in their treatment of the *hiphil* of בָּקַע. The basic idea of the verb is "to split" (*HALOT* s.v. "בקע" 149–50). NIV translates "divide" here (consistent with the way in which it understands the preceding verb), as if it describes splitting up territory once it has been subdued. But the verb often carries the notion of breaking through a barrier. In fact, the *hiphil* is used in only one other passage, 2 Kings 3:26, where it describes the Moabite king's attempt to break through the enemy's line. The KJV reflects this idea in Isaiah 7:6: "make a breach." The kings are probably referring to breaking through and invading Judah's borders, that is, to conquering it (note the more interpretive "capture" in NLT and "conquer" in ESV, HCSB, NRSV, and *Tanakh* [which has "invade" for the preceding verb]). The translation "invade" would nicely reflect the concept of breaking through, though it does not necessarily convey the idea of victory that the kings are assuming (note the following reference to placing the son of Tabeel on the throne of Judah). John Hayes and Stuart Irvine (1987, 126–27) argue that the verb describes a rapid invasion aimed at Jerusalem, not a prolonged campaign designed to subdue the entire country.

7:7–9. David's offspring did not need to fear their plot, for the "Sovereign LORD," who rules over all (6:1), was fully capable of thwarting the enemy's plan (7:7). In the end, Rezin, king of Aram, and the son of Remaliah, king of the northern rival state, could not defeat the Lord's chosen dynasty. Nor could the head of Damascus and the head of Samaria bring down the one who ruled from the Lord's chosen city, Jerusalem, for which he had such lofty plans (7:8–9a; see Isa. 2:1–4; 4:2–6; Hayes and Irvine 1987, 128; Wildberger 1991, 301). Isaiah 7:8–9 gives an explanation why the plot would fail. Damascus, led by Rezin, and Samaria, led by the son of Remaliah, were insignificant in comparison to the house of David and would be thwarted by the Lord.

In this address to Ahaz, the Lord uses the name Ephraim in referring to the northern kingdom (7:5, 9). At first, one might assume that Ephraim is simply a synonym for Israel, which is used by the narrator in identifying Pekah (7:1). Ephraim appears to be so used in the initial report that came to Ahaz (7:2) and in the following speech (see 7:17). However, one wonders if the Lord's choice of terms may be rhetorical in this context, where the legitimacy

---

3 For a discussion of options offered by interpreters, see Dearman 1996, 33–47; Smith 2007, 209 n. 266; and Williamson 2018, 128–30. An Assyrian inscription dating to 738 B.C. mentions Tubail, king of Tyre; some identify him as the individual in view here (Hayes and Irvine 1987, 127).

of the Davidic dynasty is in view, in contrast to the son of Remaliah (see below). In 8:14 (see also 8:18) the Lord refers to the "two houses of Israel," that is, the northern kingdom and Judah. So, while the narrator refers to Pekah by his official title ("king of Israel"), the Lord chooses to refer to the northern kingdom as simply Ephraim (or Samaria, 7:9; see 8:4) to avoid any implication of legitimacy. It is the Davidic dynasty that is destined to rule over a united *Israel* under the authority of the Holy One of Israel. It is also possible that the use of Ephraim hints at the defeat of the northern kingdom, prophesied in 7:16 and 8:4. By 732 B.C. Tiglath-pileser III had annexed much of the northern kingdom as provinces, reducing Ephraim/Samaria to a puppet state (2 Kings 15:29), a situation alluded to in Isaiah 9:1 (see Seitz 1993, 76).

In response to the Lord's assuring promise, Ahaz and his people must respond in faith. Otherwise, they would not be secure (7:9b). The verbal forms in 7:9b are plural, indicating that the king, the royal court, and the people are in view (see 7:2, 17). Their options are highlighted through wordplay. The *hiphil* of אָמַן carries the idea "regard as reliable," that is, "have faith, believe, trust." The object, though not stated here, is implied from the context. Ahaz must trust in God's promise and, more fundamentally, in God's ability to fulfill his promise (Williamson 2018, 134–35). The *niphal* of the same verb carries the nuance "be secure, established, upheld" (see 2 Chron. 20:20). The repetition of the verb, albeit in a different verbal stem, draws attention to the prophet's warning. Faith in the reliability of God's promise and character was the key to the nation's security.

How did it all play out? Unfortunately, Ahaz's refusal to trust in the Lord and his prophetic word compromised the promise inherent in Shear-jashub's name which, like so many promises in the Old Testament, proved to be conditional. Ironically, instead of the enemy being decimated, Aram and Israel won a devastating victory over Judah and carried many of its people away as captives (2 Chron. 28:5–8). Yet despite Ahaz's failure, the Lord remained faithful to the house of David. He prevented the alliance from taking Jerusalem (Isa. 7:1; cf. 2 Kings 16:5) and replacing Ahaz, just as he had promised (Isa. 7:7). Furthermore, his subsequent promise of the demise of Aram and Israel (see 7:16; 8:4) was fulfilled within three years' time. Sadly, in the aftermath of his crushing defeat, Ahaz turned for help to the Assyrians (2 Kings 16:7), who brought immediate relief (2 Kings 16:9), but only at a high price (2 Kings 16:8; 2 Chron. 28:20–21). Ahaz's decision to trust in Assyria rather than the Lord backfired, as it turned potential blessing into hardship and humiliation as Isaiah prophesied (see Isa. 7:17–25; 8:6–7).

Isaiah 7:8b reads: "Within sixty-five years Ephraim will be shattered from a nation." This has puzzled interpreters for at least three reasons: (1) it disturbs the parallelism that exists between 7:8a and 7:9a; (2) it is unclear what event is in view; and (3) such a long-range development would hardly be assuring to Judah in the immediate crisis—a lot could happen in sixty-five years! It is possibly a gloss (albeit relatively early) that seeks to correlate subsequent events with the prophecy to demonstrate its fulfillment.

However, the statement may not be as structurally intrusive as it first appears. Smith (2007, 210) detects a paneled structure here: (A) a prediction of the alliance's failure (7:7), (B) the weakness of Aram (7:8a), (A') a prediction of Ephraim's demise (7:8b), (B') the weakness of Ephraim (7:9a).[4] In this case the parallelism would be more balanced and symmetrical if "within sixty-five years" is taken as a gloss. However, if 7:8b were

---

4 Smith understands Syria as the subject of the third feminine singular verbs in 7:7 and takes כִּי at the beginning of 7:8 as concessive, "even though."

original, one would expect כִּי to follow the prediction, as in 7:8a. The *waw* at the beginning of 7:9 makes better sense if understood as a continuation of 7:8a.

Another option is to exclude 7:7 from and include 7:9b in the structure as follows (Motyer 1993, 82): (A) the head of Aram is Damascus (7:8a), (B) the head of Damascus is Rezin (7:8b), (C) Ephraim's demise is certain (7:8c), (A') the head of Ephraim is Samaria (7:9a), (B') the head of Samaria is the son of Remaliah (7:9b), (C') Judah must make the right decision to avoid ending up like Ephraim (7:9c). In this case 7:8c is a warning that supports the appeal of 7:9c. As Motyer explains: "Ephraim chose the path of human collective security by its alliance with Aram and thus sealed its doom." He adds: "To reject the way of faith for the collective security of an alliance with Assyria would likewise spell the end for Judah." The logic of the first half is clear: Ephraim's reliance upon weak Aram/Rezin would prove destructive. However, the logic of the second half is not as clear, for Ahaz was trusting in Assyria, not Ephraim/son of Remaliah. The structure lacks symmetry. However, if one supposes that Ahaz was considering capitulating to the pressure and joining the alliance, Motyer's proposed structure would make better sense. If Ahaz trusted in Ephraim, as Ephraim had trusted in Aram, then Judah would fall along with the alliance.

The reference to sixty-five years is problematic. If the prophecy was given in 735 B.C., then the date in view would be 670 B.C. But Israel had ceased to be a nation long before this in 722, when the Assyrians conquered Samaria and deported a large portion of the population (2 Kings 17:6). One suggestion is that this refers to the policy to settle foreign peoples in former Israelite territory, implemented by the Assyrian rulers Esarhaddon (681–669) and his successor Ashurbanipal (Gray 1912, 120; Wildberger 1991, 301–2). Once these foreigners settled in the land, any lingering Israelite claim to the territory was terminated.

Ahaz's Rejection of a Confirming Sign (7:10–12)

The prophet challenged Ahaz to ask for a confirming sign, but the king refused to do so.

7:10–11. Having presumably delivered the message recorded in 7:4–9, Isaiah followed up with a challenge. The Lord offered Ahaz the opportunity to ask for a sign confirming the promise of 7:7. He could ask for anything; Sheol below and the sky above were the limits. The word אוֹת, "sign," does not necessarily refer to something extraordinary or miraculous (see the fuller discussion below), but it can sometimes do so (see Isa. 38:7–8, 22) and such a sign is certainly within the scope of Isaiah's invitation in 7:11 (Hayes and Irvine 1987, 131; Williamson 2018, 147–48).

7:12. But Ahaz refused to ask for a sign, justifying his reply with a pious sounding statement about not testing the Lord. The verb נָסָה (used here in the *piel*) has the primary meaning, "to try out, test." In some cases, it is used of trying God's patience by questioning his wisdom and/or promise, as the Israelites did in the wilderness (Exod. 17:2, 7; Num. 14:22; Deut. 6:16). But the Lord is not above giving a sign to one who has weak faith (see Judg. 6:17) or even subjecting himself to a test in order to strengthen the fainthearted (Judg. 6:39). Indeed, Ahaz's response to the northern threat showed that his faith was deficient and needed a boost (see Isa. 7:2). Ahaz's objection sounds pious, as if he believed he was being tested and wanted to make it clear that God's promise was sufficient. However, Isaiah's response (7:13) shows this was not case. Ahaz's refusal, rather than being prompted by faith, was symptomatic of his lack of trust in the Lord (see Smith 2007, 212; Young 1965, 279–80). The king may have already decided to form an alliance with Assyria (see 2 Kings 16:7–8).

The Lord Gives Ahaz a Confirming Sign (7:13–17)

The Lord gave Ahaz a sign confirming that he would be with his people to deliver and to discipline them.

7:13. In his reply Isaiah switches from speaking specifically to Ahaz (7:11) to addressing the "house of David" (note the second-person plural verbal and pronominal forms in 7:13–14). In this context the "house of David" refers to Ahaz's royal court (7:2, 17). The use of the phrase may reflect the fact that a king, especially one like the youthful Ahaz, would consult his court advisers on important decisions, like how to respond to the threat posed by the northern alliance. But the phrase is also a reminder of Ahaz's privileged position and the Lord's promise (see the comments above on 7:4–9; Clements 1980, 87). The use of the plural is a continuation of 7:9, indicating that the prophet's reply relates to his earlier warning (7:9b).

Ironically Ahaz's refusal to "test" God tried God's patience. The verb לָאָה has the primary meaning "be weary, exhausted," especially emotionally (see Isa. 1:14.) When used in the *hiphil* (causative) verbal stem, as here, it means, "to tire one out" (Jer. 12:5; Mic. 6:3). In this case it refers to how Judah's royal house (Ahaz and his royal court) were exhausting both Isaiah's and God's patience by their failure to trust in the prophetic promise. In this regard, the switch from "your [singular, Ahaz's] God" (7:11) to "my [Isaiah's] God" (7:13) is telling. Isaiah was sure about his own loyalty, but not so sure about Ahaz and his court.

7:14–17. If Ahaz refused to seek a sign, then the Lord would give him one (7:14a). Isaiah calls God the "Lord," that is, Sovereign Master (אֲדֹנָי) as a reminder that he is sovereign over the affairs of nations and kings (see Isa. 6:1). The use of this title also links the announcement of the sign with the earlier promise and warning (7:7–9), which were given to the king by the Sovereign Master (note 7:7). By refusing to ask for a sign, Ahaz had failed to embrace the promise in faith. This was unfortunate, for his lack of trust would cause him and Judah to forfeit the full blessing that could have been theirs, as the explanation of the sign (7:15–25) makes clear. The promise would turn into a threat (Clements 1980, 87).

The confirming sign is outlined in 7:14b–17:

(1) A young woman known to the royal court would give birth to a child and name him Immanuel, "God (is) with us."

(2) This child would eventually eat milk (or possibly butter) and honey, an experience that would give him moral insight and facilitate his choosing what is right over what is wrong.

(3) However, before that day arrived, the northern coalition feared by Ahaz would be defeated.

(4) In conjunction with the defeat of the coalition, the Lord would bring upon Judah a time unlike anything they had experienced since the division of Israel into two kingdoms almost two hundred years before, namely Assyrian rule.

Isaiah 7:18–25 then elaborates on the sign: (1) both Assyria and Egypt would put pressure on Judah, but Assyria would be the more menacing of the two and conquer Judah (7:18–20); (2) because of the devastation to the land, people would be forced to survive on milk from their livestock and honey from the fields, which would be overrun with weeds and reduced to pastureland (7:21–25). (For a fuller discussion of these verses, see the commentary below.)

So, the sign involves the timing of events in relation to the child Immanuel's growth. Before the child ate a diet of milk and honey, the threat from the north would be eliminated, as God had promised (7:7–8). But his diet of milk and honey would be the result of God's judgment in the form of the Assyrian invasion, which would follow the defeat of the coalition. The unfolding of these events according to the timetable given by the prophet would be confirmation that God was indeed "with" his people.

This understanding of the sign as referring to God's providential, rather than miraculous, intervention is consistent with the use of the term אוֹת in Isaiah. The word can refer to a miraculous intervention (Isa. 38:7–8, 22; and see remarks on 7:11 above), but more frequently it is used of an event, object, or person that is vested with special significance and serves as an object lesson or reminder (8:18; 19:20; 20:3; 37:30; 55:13; 66:19). The "sign" outlined in Isaiah 37:30, like the one here in Isaiah 7:14–17, involves the timing of events in accordance with a prophetic prediction.

There has been much discussion about the identity and status of the young woman. Though some have understood the definite article to be a generic reference to the typical young woman about to conceive and bear a child, there is nothing in the context that requires or even suggests such an interpretation. It is more likely the article is used because the woman is present or at least definite in the prophet's mind (GKC, 407–8 §126r). Perhaps she was a member of the royal court, possibly even Ahaz's queen (Wildberger 1991, 310–12). Some identify her with the prophetess mentioned in 8:3. Indeed, if the verbal form קָרָאת (7:14) is taken as second person, which seems likely, then the woman is clearly present. Most assume that the verb קָרָאת is third-person feminine singular since "young woman" appears to be the subject. In this case, the form retains the older *tav* ending, as we see in the homonym קְרָא, "to meet, encounter," in Deuteronomy 31:29 and Jeremiah 44:23 (see GKC, 206 §74g). However, it is possible that the prophet addresses the young woman at this point and that the form should be understood as second-person feminine singular (cf. the LXX, which has a second-person singular form here). The article on עַלְמָה suggests the young woman was present, a proposal that is consistent with the royal court being addressed in Isaiah 7:13–14. Furthermore, in the three other occurrences of the third-person feminine singular perfect of קְרָא, "to call, name," the form is קָרְאָה, not קָרָאת (Gen. 29:35; 30:26; 1 Chron. 4:9). When the form קָרָאת appears, it is second person (Gen. 16:11; Isa. 60:18; Jer. 3:4 [*qere*]). If the woman is addressed, it is not clear if she is a member of the court, or the prophetess mentioned in Isaiah 8:3.

Because of Matthew's use of Isaiah 7:14 in relation to the virgin conception and birth of Jesus, many have assumed that עַלְמָה has the meaning "virgin." However, an examination of its usage does not support this assumption. The word can certainly *refer* to a virgin (Gen. 24:43; cf. 24:16), but we must not confuse referent and meaning. The limited usage in the Old Testament is ambiguous (Exod. 2:8; Ps. 68:25 [HB 26]; Prov. 30:19; Song 1:3; 6:8); it is not clear what extent of romantic involvement is in view in Proverbs 30:19. The form is the feminine derivative of עֶלֶם, "young man," which refers to age, not sexual experience (1 Sam. 17:56; 20:22), and the related noun עֲלוּמִים, "youth," refers to age. The Aramaic cognate is used in the targum of Judges of a woman (the Levite's concubine, Judg. 19:3–5) who was not a virgin. The evidence favors translating the word as indicating age, "young woman." The term may refer to a virgin, but this does not appear to be its technical meaning.

> **Virgin**
> The Ugaritic evidence is ambiguous. In *CAT* 24, we read *ǵlmt tld b[n]*, "a young woman will bear a son." J. C. L. Gibson's translation (1978, 128) suggests this statement is made following consummation of the marriage, but David Marcus leaves the pertinent lines (4–5) untranslated (Parker 1997, 215). The following context speaks of the wedding as imminent, not consummated. This also appears to be the case in *CAT* 14:204, where an offer is made for the young woman Huray (Gibson 1978, 87). The phrase *bn ǵlmt* in *CAT* 8:7 is intriguing, especially if it means "son(s) of the young woman" (see Parker 1997, 179).

In the context of Isaiah 7 it may refer to a young woman who was already married (and perhaps even pregnant), or it could refer to one who was a virgin at the time the prophecy was given. The time frame of the predicate adjective הָרָה (7:14) is uncertain. (On the morphology of the adjective, see Young 1965, 285 n. 33.) It may anticipate the woman's conception ("is about to conceive") or it may refer to a present condition (in which case we can translate "is pregnant"; see Gray 1912, 127, 132). The adjective הָרָה, when used as a predicate elsewhere, refers to a past pregnancy (from a narrator's perspective, 1 Sam. 4:19) or a present condition (from a speaker's perspective, Gen. 16:11; 38:24; 2 Sam. 11:5). Most regard the use in Judges 13:5, 7 as anticipating conception, but a present condition may be in view (see Chisholm 2013b, 390–91). The uncertainty of the woman's identity in Isaiah 7 makes interpretation difficult. If the young woman was a member of the royal court, then either a present or future translation is possible. If the young woman is the prophetess mentioned in 8:3, then the adjective should be translated future since Isaiah appears to have had relations with her after this meeting with Ahaz.

At any rate, the woman's status and conception are not central ingredients in the sign. As noted above, the sign pertains to the timing of events in relation to the growth of the child who is conceived, born, and named "God is with us." (For a discussion of Matthew's usage of the passage, see the excursus below.)

The name Immanuel contributes to the irony of the prophecy, for it suggests God would be present in a positive way. This expectation seems to be reinforced by the reference to milk and honey in 7:15 and certainly by the announcement of the demise of the northern coalition in 7:16. But the prophet turns what appears to be (and could have been, had Ahaz believed) a salvation announcement into a judgment speech. Milk and honey could conceivably be understood as symbols of God's blessing (Deut. 32:13–14; Job 20:17; 29:6), but in this context they are images of deprivation (Isa. 7:21–25). Eventually Immanuel would eat milk and honey, not because of prosperity but because the crops would be destroyed. For him, eating milk and honey would be a tangible reminder of the negative consequences of sin and unbelief. As such, the experience would motivate him to choose what is right and reject what is wrong, in contrast to those who confused and perverted these moral categories (Isa. 5:20).

> **Moral Categories**
> One might initially understand sour milk and honey to be the first food consumed by the child after he was weaned. Rejecting "evil" and choosing "good" would then refer to his discerning between tasty and distasteful food, something that would happen while he was still an infant (Clements 1980, 88). This view makes good sense, if one sees 7:15 strictly in connection with 7:16, which speaks of the imminent fall of the northern coalition. In other words, before the child was weaned and eating solid food, the enemy would be defeated. (In this case, the timing of the sign is very similar to what we see in 8:3–4.) However, 7:21–22 indicates that sour milk and honey would be the diet of everyone in the land in the aftermath of the Assyrian invasion

A Sign Child and Forfeited Blessing (7:1–8:10)

(7:17–20). As such they are signs of deprivation, not simply the contents of a newly weaned infant's diet. Perhaps the imagery has a double meaning—in relation to 7:16 and then 7:17–25. If so, then this is another example of irony in this prophecy.

Isaiah 7:16–25 tell us why (note the introductory כִּי) the child would be named Immanuel, why he would eat milk and honey, and why this diet would motivate him to make correct moral decisions. As noted above, God would demonstrate his presence through the events that would unfold in the immediate future. He would first fulfill his promise to protect Judah from the northern alliance, proving that he was worthy to be trusted, despite Ahaz's hesitancy. Aram and Israel, whom Ahaz (note the second-person masculine singular pronoun in 7:16) feared so much (7:2), would be abandoned. The singular הָאֲדָמָה, "the land" (7:16), depicts the Aramean-Israelite coalition as unified. The verb קוּץ means "abhor, loathe," but it can carry the additional nuance of "fear, dread" when used, as here, with "from the face of" (see Exod. 1:12; Num. 22:3). The *niphal* of עָזַב, "abandoned," pictures the land as being deserted (Lev. 26:43; Isa. 27:10; 62:12). The Assyrians would take the people of Aram and Israel into exile. If the young woman were a member of the royal court, perhaps a queen, then this would also contribute to the positive dimension of the prophecy. The northern coalition was threatening to end Ahaz's dynasty and replace him with the son of Tabeel. As Hayes and Irvine (1987, 135–36) point out, this would entail exterminating the royal family. But if the young woman was a queen, clearly the northern coalition's plot would fail, for her son would not be killed, but would grow up to eat sour milk and honey.

TRANSLATION ANALYSIS 7:15

As for the form לְדַעְתּוֹ (Isa. 7:15), most understand the preposition -לְ, prefixed to the infinitive construct of יָדַע, "know," in a temporal sense: ESV, NIV "when," HCSB, NLT, NRSV, *Tanakh,* "by the time." Generally speaking, the preposition -לְ can have a temporal force when used with an infinitive construct, but this is rare. See BDB s.v. "לְ" 7, 517; *HALOT* s.v. "לְ," 508. Indeed, in the other uses of -לְ with the infinitive construct of יָדַע, the preposition is never temporal. Most often, as one expects, it indicates purpose or result (see KJV, "that he may know"). The latter makes good sense here: Immanuel would eat a steady diet of milk and honey and *as a result*, having literally tasted the consequences of sin, he would be motivated to make correct moral and ethical decisions. The Septuagint favors the temporal view here, but Symmachus, Theodotion, and the Vulgate understand the construction as indicating purpose/result (see Wildberger 1991, 286).

Having proven the reliability of his promise, the Lord would then be present with Judah in judgment (7:17). Initially, the reference to unprecedented times might be hopeful, especially following the announcement of the northern coalition's demise. But the reference to the division of the kingdom is ominous since it recalls a time when Judah was greatly weakened. The expression "bring on" usually has a negative connotation, though it can be used in a positive sense (Gen. 18:19). In the only other passage where "day" (יוֹם) is the object of the verb, the nuance is negative, but "day" is modified there by "evil" (Jer. 17:18). Yet any hope we may have is dashed when "the king of Assyria" appears at the end of Isaiah 7:17, in apposition to "days." The syntax seems somewhat awkward, leading some to delete the phrase as a later interpretive gloss (see *BHS*; Balogh 2014, 523–24; Roberts 2015, 120). However, the oddity is more semantic than syntactical (on the surface, "days" and "king" are a peculiar match) and may be a rhetorical device designed to grab the audience's attention (Watts 1985, 106). Indeed, by placing "king of Assyria" at the end of the sentence, the prophet enhances its rhetorical impact (Oswalt 1986, 214). These coming "days" would be unprecedented because they would be dominated by the ominous figure of the Assyrian king, who would bring calamity upon Judah unlike anything since the division of the kingdom so long ago. As 7:18–25 makes crystal clear, Assyria, though perhaps viewed initially as a savior, would be a menacing presence and in the end Immanuel's diet of milk and honey would be a consequence of judgment, not blessing.

The Lord Explains the Sign (7:18–25)

The Lord explained that the Assyrians would conquer the land and destroy the crops, forcing people to survive on the milk produced by their livestock and the honey found in the fields.

7:18–19. The Lord himself would bring this calamity upon Judah. He is sovereign over the nations and all he had to do was "whistle" for them to do his bidding and they would arrive on the scene like swarming insects ready to make the land a nesting place and breeding ground (7:18–19; see 5:26). In this case, threatening enemies would come from both north and south. Coming from the south, Egypt would be like annoying flies as it sought to make Judah a buffer state against Assyrian aggression and invasion. Coming from the north, Assyria would seek to make Judah a launching pad for an invasion of Egypt. Assyria would be the more dangerous of the two, as the comparison to stinging bees indicates (see Deut. 1:44; Ps. 118:12).

7:20. Isaiah 7:20 focuses on Assyria as the one who would humiliate Judah, like a razor that shaves off the hair of the head, beard, and genitals. Having such hair is a sign of manhood, but Assyria would rob the men of Judah of their manly status and pride. But once again the Lord's sovereignty is highlighted, as indicated by the title Lord/Sovereign Master (אֲדֹנָי) and the reference to the king of Assyria as "hired." Though seemingly hired by Ahaz (2 Kings 16:7–9), Assyria was a mere tool in the hand of the real king (Isa. 6:1). The use of the title אֲדֹנָי links this portion of the judgment speech with its introduction (7:14) and with the earlier promise (7:7), the rejection of which prompted this speech.

7:21–25. As noted above, 7:21–25 clarifies the significance of the earlier reference to sour milk and honey (7:15). They would not be delicacies signifying blessing. On the contrary, the coming judgment would destroy the crops and turn the once cultivated fields into a wasteland overrun by thorns and briers. The people would have to live off the milk provided by their livestock and the honey they managed to find in the beehives in the thickets. The portrait coincides with the imagery of flies and bees in 7:18–19. Flies are attracted to milk, and bees produce honey. The Assyrian "bees" would devastate the land, producing conditions where honey would replace the usual grains in the diet of the people. The Egyptian "flies" would be attracted by the sour milk of Judah's deprivation and seek to exploit Judah's weakness.

Isaiah 7:23–25 focuses on the loss of vineyards, describing how once productive grape vines would be overrun by thorns and briers and transformed into pasturelands and hunting grounds. The imagery recalls earlier descriptions of a ruined vineyard. In 3:14 the Lord accuses the leaders of the people of ruining (cf. בִּעַרְתֶּם, "you ruined") the vineyard (the covenant community) by their robbery and oppression. In 5:1–7 the vineyard, identified as Israel/the people of Judah (cf. 5:3, 7), becomes the object of divine judgment that leaves it in ruins (cf. 5:5, לְבָעֵר, "to ruin"). As noted earlier, these texts, when correlated, indicate that corrupt leaders had ruined the covenant community by producing, as it were, the sour grapes of injustice. The ethically ruined community they had commandeered would in turn be devastated by divine judgment. There are several verbal links between 7:25 and 5:5–6: (1) שָׁמִיר/שַׁיִת, "thorns/briers" (used only in Isa. 5:6; 7:23–25; 9:17; 27:4); (2) עָדַר, "to hoe" (used only in Isa. 5:6 and 7:25);

and (3) מִרְמָס, "place of trampling." When we correlate 7:23–25 with 5:5–6, clearly the metaphor has become reality. As the Lord brings judgment on his ethically ruined "vineyard" (the covenant community), he devastates the literal vineyards that were ironically one of his gifts to the people (Deut. 6:11; 8:8).

How was the prophecy fulfilled? By 732 B.C. the Assyrians had conquered Aram (2 Kings 16:9) and divided much of the northern kingdom (Dor on the coast, Megiddo in the north, and Gilead in Transjordan) into provinces, fulfilling in part the prophecy of Isaiah 7:16. Samaria, reduced to a puppet state in 732, became a province in 722 (2 Kings 18:9–11), completing the prophesied demise of the northern coalition. The devastation of Judah, which resulted in Immanuel and his generation being forced to subsist on sour milk and honey, took place in 701, when Sennacherib invaded Judah (2 Kings 18:13; Isa. 1:7–9). By this time Immanuel was an adult, probably in his early to mid-thirties. The fact that Immanuel is called "the child" (הַנַּעַר) in Isaiah 7:16 does not mean that the eating of the milk and honey (7:15) had to take place during his youth. Though the sign would not reach its complete fulfillment for more than three decades, it would begin to unfold while Immanuel was still a child as the northern coalition met its demise (the event in view in 7:16). The term נַעַר is rather flexible in its range of usage. It can be used of an infant (Exod. 2:6), a seventeen-year-old (Gen. 37:2), and a full-grown youth capable of assuming the role of king (1 Sam. 16:11; 2 Sam. 18:5). So, Isaiah 7:15–16 could envision someone in his early twenties. If Immanuel was born around 735, then he was still a נַעַר in 715–710. Yet we must account for an additional ten years or so. As is often the case with prophecy, the sign outlined by the Lord does not give a precise timetable, only a relative one. This is consistent with the fact that the manner and timing of a prophecy are often contingent upon human factors. Perhaps the timing of the Assyrian devastation of Judah was impacted by such factors. Hezekiah's reform movement (ca. 715) may have prompted the Lord to delay his punishment of Judah. If so, the king's decision to pursue an anti-Assyrian alliance with Egypt likely prompted divine discipline through the instrumentality of the Assyrians. But this extended the fulfillment of the prophecy several years to a time when Immanuel would no longer technically be a נַעַר.

The Lord Reiterates the Sign (8:1–8)
The Lord instructed Isaiah to give his newborn son a name symbolizing the imminent defeat of the coalition. But he again warned that he would use the Assyrians to punish Judah.

8:1–4. Following Isaiah's prediction of the birth of the sign child Immanuel (7:14–25), a narrative of the birth of a sign child appears. The Lord instructed Isaiah to write the words Maher-shalal-hash-baz on a tablet and told the prophet he would summon two reliable witnesses (cf. Deut. 17:6; 19:15) to confirm what Isaiah had done (Isa. 8:1–2). Why the formality? Isaiah was about to father a child whom, as instructed by the Lord, he would name Maher-shalal-hash-baz (8:3). The precise syntax of the name is unclear, but the image of hurrying to the spoil and hastening to the plunder clearly refers to the aftermath of a battle in which one participant has been thoroughly defeated and is ripe for plundering. The Lord identifies that defeated participant as the northern coalition that was threatening Judah. In fact, before the child was old enough to verbally identify his father and mother, the Assyrian king would carry away the plunder of both Damascus, the capital of Aram, and Samaria, the capital of the northern kingdom (8:4). (On the fulfillment of the prophecy, see the discussion of 7:23–25 above.)

8:5–8. The northern kingdom, led by the "son of Remaliah," had the audacity to threaten the Davidic dynasty, rejecting the security that could have been theirs, symbolized by the gently flowing waters of Shiloah. Instead they placed their confidence in the leaders of the coalition (8:6). The Lord would bring the king of Assyria against them like a mighty flood that overwhelms everything in its path (8:7). This raging torrent would not stop at the border; it would pour into Judah and cover the land of Immanuel (8:8).

In both 7:14–16 and 8:3–4 the defeat of the northern coalition is related to the child's growth pattern, while in both 7:17–25 and 8:8 an Assyrian invasion of Judah follows the defeat of the coalition.[5] The obvious parallels between 8:1–8 and 7:14–25 invite the question: What is the relationship, if any, between Immanuel and Maher-shalal-hash-baz?

One can make a case for identifying the two. The discourse structure of the passage suggests this. A sign child's birth is predicted in 7:14, while a sign child's birth is described in 8:3. It makes sense to see the narrative as recording the fulfillment of the prediction. The child Immanuel is addressed in 8:8; this makes sense if his birth has just been described earlier in the passage. Later (see 8:18) Isaiah speaks of himself and his sons as signs (אֹתוֹת). Isaiah and Shear-jashub have signatory value by reason of the meaning of their names, and Maher-shalal-hash-baz's birth and naming are treated as signatory (note the writing of the name on the tablet and the presence of witnesses), but the only child who is specifically designated as a sign (אוֹת) is Immanuel.

While there are parallels between the two passages, there are also significant differences that make equating the two children problematic. Most obvious is the fact that the children have different names. In 7:14 the mother names the child, while Isaiah does the naming in 8:3. In 7:15 the event in Immanuel's experience that contributes to the sign, his eating sour milk and honey, appears to take place when he has reached adulthood, while Maher-shalal-hash-baz's addressing his father and mother takes place in infancy. If the "prophetess" (8:3) is the prophet's wife, which most assume, then she already had borne him a son, Shear-jashub. In that case it is unlikely the term עַלְמָה (7:14) would be applied to her.[6] If the sign children Immanuel and Maher-shalal-hash-baz are indeed distinct, then they function as parallel signs—one in the king's context, the other in the prophet's presumably more public context.

Of course, proponents of equating the two children can respond reasonably to these objections. There are other cases of dual naming in the Old Testament (see Gen. 35:18; 2 Sam. 12:24–25). It is possible that the mother named the child Immanuel, while Isaiah named him Maher-shalal-hash-baz. The names may be complementary. Immanuel's name is a reminder of God's presence, while Maher-shalal-hash-baz's name, which creates mental images of a battle and its aftermath, explains more specifically that God would reveal his presence in battle as he defeated Judah's enemies but then summoned the Assyrians to invade Judah. Immanuel's eating of sour milk and honey may have a dual meaning. Seen in connection with 7:16, it may initially pertain to the first food consumed by the child after he was weaned and refer to his discerning between tasty and distasteful food (Clements 1980, 88). If so, then this experience would coincide with the child's addressing his father and mother. (In its fuller meaning, in relation to 7:17–25, the diet of sour milk and honey, which is shared by all who are left in the land, is a sign of deprivation in the aftermath of the Assyrian invasion.)

As in 7:14–25, there is a tragic dimension to the prophecy in 8:4–8—a sense of loss as potential security is swallowed up by the reality of

---

5   For a chart showing the parallels between the two passages, see Blenkinsopp 2000, 239.
6   Wolf (1972, 449–56) argues that וָאֶקְרַב, "and I went near," suggests a first sexual encounter (cf. Deut. 22:14), indicating this was not Shear-jashub's mother, who had died. In this case, the prophetess was the prophet's new wife.

judgment. To highlight the contrast, the Lord uses the imagery of water—the gently flowing water of Shiloah and the flooding water of the Euphrates River (8:6–7). The symbolism behind the flooding Euphrates is identified as the king of Assyria, but who or what does the water of Shiloah represent? The name Shiloah occurs only here, but Nehemiah 3:15 mentions the Pool of Shelah (Siloam?), located near the royal garden in Jerusalem. Perhaps the water of Shiloah ran from the Gihon spring through an aqueduct into a pool that supplied the city with water (Wildberger 1991, 343). The presence of the modifier "gently" suggests that this water, in contrast to the flooding Euphrates, was not threatening but instead provided nourishment and symbolized peace and security. Since the reality behind the Euphrates is the king of Assyria, it is likely that the Lord himself is ultimately the reality behind the water of Shiloah. As noted above, if 8:6b refers to the northern kingdom's trust in its alliance with Aram, then 8:6a speaks of its rejection of the Davidic dynasty and ultimately the Lord who provides that dynasty with security. They could have found security in the Lord, but their rejection of the nourishing water of Shiloah, as it were, would bring upon them divine judgment through the instrumentality of the Assyrian king, symbolized by the flooding Euphrates. However, if 8:6b refers to Ahaz melting in fear before the northern coalition (or rejoicing over its defeat), then 8:6a speaks of the king's refusal to trust the Lord for security. Rejecting the nourishing water in his own backyard, as it were, he turned to Assyria for relief, but that decision would backfire, for the Assyrians, in contrast to the gently flowing water of Shiloah, would come like a destructive flood and inundate the land. Whether the northern kingdom or Judah is in view in 8:6, the prophecy has a tragic element, for potential security that is readily available (esp. if Judah is in view) is spurned, resulting in destruction. If Judah is in view, there is irony, for Ahaz looked to Assyria for relief and Judah would eventually get much more than it bargained for from that alliance.

The description of the Assyrian king, under the metaphor of the flood, is terrifying in its detail. The waters are described as "overwhelming and abundant." Both adjectives describe strength that comes from abundance; the pairing of the terms emphasizes the power of these waters. The adjective רַבִּים is often collocated with מַיִם. Frequently it is used of the abundant water found in a pool, sea, or large river, such as the Euphrates (Num. 20:11; 24:7; 2 Chron. 32:4; Pss. 77:19 [HB 20]; 107:23; Song 8:7; Isa. 23:3; Jer. 41:12; 51:13; Ezek. 17:5, 8; 19:10; 27:6; 31:5, 7, 15; 32:13). But apart from this literal use, there is often a more sinister connotation. The phrase "abundant waters" many times describes surging, roaring water (sometimes associated with death) that symbolizes hostile enemies who oppose God and threaten his people (Pss. 18:16 [HB 17 = 2 Sam. 22:17]; 29:3; 32:6; 77:19 [HB 20]; 93:4; 144:7; Isa. 17:13; Jer. 51:55; Ezek. 1:24; 43:2; Hab. 3:15). Of course, the irony in Isaiah 8:7 is that the threatening water is brought by God as his instrument of judgment.

The series of verbs used in 8:7–8 allows one to picture the devastating flood as it advances. The water rises (וְעָלָה) and flows over (וְהָלַךְ עַל) its banks. It moves into (וְחָלַף בְּ-) Judah, inundating (שָׁטַף) everything as it sweeps through (וְעָבַר) and threatens to drown everyone in its path (note "it will reach the neck"). As terrifying as the Assyrian flood was, ultimately the Lord, the Sovereign Master (note אֲדֹנָי), was orchestrating events (Aster 2018, 480). The Assyrian king was a mere instrument in his hand. The Assyrian flood was ready to rise (see וְעָלָה), but it was the Lord that was causing it to do so (see מַעֲלֶה).

The metaphor appears to shift in 8:8b, which depicts the king's outspread wings as covering the land. The mood remains ominous, however. Elsewhere the image of a bird's outstretched wings sometimes connotes divine protection (Pss. 17:8; 36:8 [Eng. 7]; 57:2 [Eng. 1]; 61:5 [Eng.

4]; 63:8 [Eng. 7]; 91:4]), but that is not the case here. Coupled with the metaphor of the flood, the image here is that of a predatory bird descending over the land as it zeroes in on its prey (Jer. 48:40; 49:22; cf. Motyer 1993, 92; Young 1965, 306–7). Oswalt (1986, 227) identifies the reality behind the metaphor and explains how this relates to the flood imagery: "An army fans out over the land like the fingers of a flood pouring through depressions and reaching up valleys. This spreading out of an army or flood suggests the spreading of wings, and that suggests a bird, in this case a bird of prey, extending its wings as it whistles down upon a victim." The reference to the Assyrian king's wings filling (note מְלֹא in 8:8) the entire width of the land is ironic, for in Isaiah's inaugural vision (6:3) it was the Lord's "glory" (or, "majestic splendor," כָּבוֹד) that filled (note מְלֹא) the earth. But now the Assyrian king's "pomp" (or "majestic splendor," כָּבוֹד, 8:7) would replace it in the vision of those under the Lord's judgment.

The vocative Immanuel at the end of 8:8 links this passage with the previous speech (7:14) and perhaps suggests that the child Maher-shalal-hash-baz is to be identified with Immanuel. At any rate, by addressing Immanuel, the prophet highlights the tragic irony associated with the name in the previous speech. God would be with his people, initially in deliverance but eventually in judgment. Immanuel, the tangible reminder of God's presence, would experience that reality in the form of the Assyrian invasion.

The reference to Immanuel's land (note "your land" in 8:8, addressed to Immanuel) might lead one to conclude that he was a royal child who would exercise authority over the land. The pronoun on "land" can sometimes refer to the king of the land (Num. 20:17; 21:22; Deut. 2:27; Judg. 11:17, 19; 2 Sam. 24:13; 1 Kings 11:22; Isa. 14:20), but it can also simply refer to one who is the native of a particular land (Gen. 12:1; 32:9; Jonah 1:8). This ambiguity is evident in Isaiah, where the pronoun can refer to a king (14:20 ["your land"]; 37:7 ["his land"]), or a native of a land (13:14 ["his land"]; see Chisholm 2002, 33).

A Glimmer of Hope (8:9–10)

The Lord would destroy all invading nations, proving he is the protector of his people.

While the appearance of the name Immanuel is ironic in 8:8 when associated with the Assyrian invasion, the very mention of the name triggers a reversal in mood (8:9–10; cf. Young 1965, 307). Suddenly the prophet turns to the invaders and taunts them with two rhetorical imperatives. The repetition of the rhetorical imperative, "be shattered" (חֹתּוּ, from חָתַת), highlights their coming demise. They would plot the fall of Jerusalem, but it would not happen, because God was with his people (כִּי עִמָּנוּ אֵל, 8:10b). The name Immanuel is embedded within the causal clause, now with a positive connotation explaining why the nations would not succeed. Though the Lord would turn from deliverer into judge, ultimately his presence would mean protection for his people and destruction for their enemies. As I have stated elsewhere (Chisholm 2002, 36): "When all was said and done, Judah's savior-turned-judge would reprise his role of deliverer and demonstrate his sovereignty over the raging nations that he had used as instruments of judgment."

Isaiah 8:9–10 is addressed to "nations," including "all" the "distant lands." The precise identity of these nations is uncertain. Since the defeat of the northern coalition has been announced (8:4, cf. 7:16), Aram and the northern kingdom may be in view (Hayes and Irvine 1987, 152). If so, the plural "nations" is readily explained. But coming on the heels of 8:7–8, which describes the Assyrian invasion of Judah (cf. 7:17–25), it is likely the Assyrians are the focal point, and the taunt foreshadows the events of 701, when the Lord devastated Sennacherib's army outside the walls of Jerusalem (cf. 10:5–34; 36:1–37:38). This proposal does not necessarily exclude the northern coalition, though the plural "nations" could reflect the fact that by the second half of the eighth century B.C. the Assyrian army included conscripts from several conquered nations (Seevers 2013, 216). When one faced the Assyrian hordes, one faced "nations," assembled under the Assyrian banner. The use of "distant lands" is consistent with Assyria being the referent, for Isaiah uses the root רחק of Assyria in the immediate context (5:26 [see the note there]; 6:12; 10:3). If 8:9–10 is addressed to Assyria, then it signals a major theme that emerges in the following chapters—the Lord's victory over Assyria once he has used them as an instrument of judgment (10:5–34) and his reversal of the devastation brought about by the Assyrians (9:1–7; 11:10–16).

TRANSLATION ANALYSIS 8:9–10
The verb רֹעוּ at the beginning of 8:9 is best translated "be broken." Several translations understand the verb as derived from the root רָעָה II, "get involved with, mixed up with" (*HALOT* s.v. "רעה II" 1262) and take this as a reference to banding together or uniting: HCSB/NRSV/Tanakh, "band together"; KJV, "associate yourselves"; NLT, "huddle together." However, the clearest examples of this root in the *qal* stem are participial and transitive (Prov. 13:20; 28:7; 29:3), not imperatival and intransitive. The NIV has "raise the war cry," from רוּעַ (*HALOT* s.v. "רוע" 1206), but this verb occurs elsewhere in the *hiphil*, *polal*, and *hitpolal* stems, not the *qal*. The ESV, "be broken," takes the root as רָעַע II (*HALOT* s.v. "רעע II" 1270–71), but the clearest examples of this verb in the *qal* are transitive ("break," Job 34:24; Ps. 2:9; Jer. 15:12). It is not certain if alleged examples of an intransitive/stative use ("be broken") in Proverbs 25:19 and Jeremiah 11:16 (see BDB s.v. "רעע II" mng. 2, 949) are valid; the root may be the homonymic רָעַע I, "be bad," in these texts. Oswalt (1986, 224) translates the verb "break forth," in the sense of "prepare for war" (p. 228). But the *qal* of רָעַע II, if it is used intransitively (there is some doubt about this), is stative ("be broken"), not fientive ("break forth"; see Prov. 25:19; Jer. 11:16). When fientive, it is transitive (Job 34:24; Ps. 2:9; Jer. 15:12), "break (something)." Other options include emending the text to דְּעוּ, "know" (Blenkinsopp 2000, 240; Kaiser 1972, 187 n. 1), with the support of the LXX (*dalet-resh* confusion would account for the corruption in MT), or understanding the root as רָעַע I, "be bad" (Young 1965, 307), but this verb is not attested elsewhere in the imperative. Though the evidence for the intransitive use of רָעַע, "break," is debated (see above), this reading is the best option here because it seems to be the least problematic syntactically and it coincides nicely with the following imperative of the synonym חָתַת. In this case both verbs are used rhetorically here with a taunting tone. They function as predictive, "you will be broken . . . you will be shattered." On the rhetorical use of the imperative (our passage not cited), see GKC, 324 §110c; *IBHS*, 572.

THEOLOGICAL FOCUS

The theological focus of this passage can be stated as follows: the Lord's people should place their trust in the Lord's faithful promise of his protective presence, for a refusal to believe can turn potential blessing into divine discipline and tragic suffering. As the prophet develops this theological theme, several emphases emerge:

1. The importance of faith as a basis for security

Hebrews 11:6 states, "without faith it is impossible to please God." We see this principle in Isaiah's initial message to Ahaz. In the face of a serious threat the Lord promised Ahaz and his people security (Isa. 7:7). However, they must do their part and trust in the Lord's ability to fulfill his promise (7:9). The wordplay in 7:9 highlights the relationship between faith and security. Without faith there can be no security. Without faith, divine blessing can be compromised and postponed.

2. Divine discipline

The Lord was fully capable of protecting his people and desired to do so. But Ahaz's failure to believe turned the Lord's promise of blessing into an announcement of judgment and deprived the king and his people of the Lord's blessings in the immediate future.

3. The Lord's reliable promises

Even in the face of the coming judgment, the reliability of the Lord's word is still evident. He kept his promise to thwart the plans of the northern coalition (7:7) and to bring about the demise of both Israel and Aram (7:16). In fulfillment of his ancient promise to David, the Lord preserved Ahaz and the Davidic dynasty, proving he is indeed "with" his people, fully capable of protecting them, but also ready to discipline them if need be. Once discipline had run its course, the Lord would defeat the enemy of his people, proving once again his commitment to them.

4. The Lord's sovereignty over the nations

The Lord is sovereign over the destiny of nations and uses them for his purposes. He would bring down the northern coalition while sparing, yet punishing, Judah. In carrying out his purposes for his covenant community, he would use the Egyptians and Assyrians. The image of God whistling for them to do his bidding highlights his absolute control over these powerful nations. They pose no threat to his sovereignty; they are mere instruments in his hand. Once he had used them for his purposes, he would destroy them.

Fulfillment of the Immanuel Prophecy According to Matthew

It is apparent from the analysis above that the child Immanuel was born and raised in Isaiah's time. As events unfolded according to the timetable given in Isaiah's prophecy, his name was a reminder to the people of Judah that God was indeed present with his people, initially delivering Judah from the threat posed by the northern coalition, but then bringing judgment upon the land because of the king's failure to trust his promises. Quite simply, for Immanuel to function as a sign he had to be present during the latter part of the eighth century B.C. when the prophesied events took place. Given the fact that a narrative of a sign child's birth follows Isaiah's prediction of a sign child's birth, it is possible that Maher-shalal-hash-baz and Immanuel should be identified.

However, Matthew understands Jesus's virgin birth as a fulfillment of Isaiah's Immanuel prophecy. After making the point that Jesus was conceived from the Holy Spirit, he states, "all this took place to fulfill what the Lord had said through the prophet," and then quotes Isaiah 7:14 (Matt. 1:22–23). Without reading Isaiah 7:14 in its literary and historical context, one might assume that Isaiah had predicted Jesus's virgin birth centuries before it took place and that the Immanuel prophecy pertains exclusively to Jesus. However, when Isaiah 7:14 is read in its context, Matthew's use of the passage appears to be problematic. This has led some to offer tortuous readings of Isaiah 7:14 in its context that disturb its plain meaning and violate its discourse structure.

A better approach sees the historical Immanuel of Isaiah's time as foreshadowing another child, a Davidic king through whom the Lord will bring salvation to his people and fulfill his promises to David (9:1–7).[7] Immanuel, whose name means "God is with us," is a type, or foreshadowing, of this greater child to come, who is given the title El Gibbor, "Mighty God," and who manifests God's presence in an even greater way (see the commentary below on Isa. 9:6). In the progress of revelation, Jesus fulfills Isaiah 9:1–7. He is the antitype toward whom Immanuel pointed and, as such, the prophetic prediction of Immanuel's birth can be applied to Jesus for Jesus's virgin birth fulfills, or fills out, the meaning of the original prediction when read in the literary context of Isaiah 7:1–9:7. To summarize, the sign child Immanuel was a reminder of God's presence with his people, initially in salvation (7:16), then in judgment (7:17–25; 8:8), but ultimately in salvation (8:9–10) through the greater child whom Immanuel foreshadows (9:1–7). Jesus's birth brings the full potential of the Immanuel prophecy to realization, so it is appropriate that Matthew sees his birth as its ultimate fulfillment. In the progress of revelation, it becomes apparent that the greater child's title El Gibbor is more than royal hyperbole. Jesus, via the virgin birth, is literally God in the flesh.

While this understanding of Matthew's use of Isaiah 7:14 may initially seem forced, it is consistent with Matthew's other uses of the Old Testament in chapters 1–2 and with his understanding of what constitutes fulfillment. When one examines his use of Hosea 11:1 (Matt. 2:15) and Jeremiah 31:15 (Matt. 2:18), as well as his understanding of Jesus's being called a Nazarene (Matt. 2:23), it is apparent that he does not understand fulfillment as a simple prediction of an event coming to pass. On the contrary, he uses both Hosea 11:1 and Jeremiah 31:15 in a typological or analogical manner, and he is quite creative in seeing Jesus's residing in Nazareth as fulfilling his role as God's Suffering Servant. We will now take a closer look at each of these three texts.

(1) Hosea 11:1/Matthew 2:15: Knowing that Herod intended to kill Jesus, the Lord warned Joseph to flee to Egypt. According to Matthew, this turn of events "fulfilled" Hosea 11:1, where God declared: "Out of Egypt I called my son." But Hosea's words are neither prophetic nor messianic. In the original context, God refers to how he brought the nation Israel out of Egypt in the time of Moses, only to have them rebel and turn to idols (11:2). How then can Jesus's descent into and return from Egypt fulfill Hosea's words? But we only have a problem if fulfillment must involve the realization of a prediction. That is not the case here. In this case fulfillment is the completion of a pattern that was established in the Old Testament and realized in full in Jesus. Matthew sees ancient Israel's history as a pattern for Jesus's experience. Just as Israel, God's "son," went down to Egypt and eventually returned to Canaan, so Jesus, God's greater Son, did the same. This repetition of history, as it were, highlights the fact that Jesus is the ideal Israel prophesied

---

7   In this regard, see Oswalt 1993, 232.

by Isaiah who would establish a new covenant community and succeed in carrying out God's purposes where the nation had failed (cf. Isa. 49:3–6). As the ideal Israel, Jesus faced testing in the wilderness (Matt. 4:1–11) in the form of physical hunger. In contrast to the historical Israel that grumbled, tested the Lord's patience, and even worshipped false gods, Jesus refused to let his hunger get the best of him and maintained his loyalty to God, even when offered the kingdoms of the world. Ironically, in combating Satan, he quoted from passages in Deuteronomy where Moses recalled Israel's failure in the wilderness (Deut. 6:13–16; 8:2–3).

(2) Jeremiah 31:15/Matthew 2:18: Enraged by the actions of the magi, Herod ordered the slaughter of all the boys in Bethlehem two years old or younger. This tragic event makes it clear that the arrival of the Messiah, which should have been welcomed by all with great joy, did not have a positive impact on the nation. Matthew sees the event as fulfilling Jeremiah 31:15, which refers to Rachel, representing mothers in Ramah (not Bethlehem), weeping for her children, who were being taken into exile by the Babylonians.[8] Once again, fulfillment involves the repetition of a pattern. Just as the mothers of Ramah wept over the fate of their babies, so the mothers in Bethlehem wept over the cruel treatment of their infants. This event, in which innocent children died because of the leaders' rejection of the Messiah, foreshadows the destruction that would come upon a future generation of Jewish children because of the leaders' rejection of Jesus (cf. Luke 23:28–29).

(3) Jesus the Nazarene (Matt. 2:23): Following Herod's death (in 4 B.C.), the Lord told Joseph to return to Israel, but Joseph settled in Nazareth (in Galilee), not Bethlehem. Matthew views this as fulfilling Scripture, though no Old Testament text says specifically that the Messiah would be called a Nazarene. Some see this as a subtle reference to Isaiah 11:1, which pictures the messianic king as a bud (Heb. נֵצֶר) that would spring from Jesse's roots (note NIV "Branch"). In this view "Nazarene" is a wordplay on the Hebrew term. However, rather than referring to any single verse in the Old Testament, it is more likely that Matthew refers to Isaiah's prophecy that Messiah would come as a humble and despised suffering servant (Isa. 53) and to the psalms in which a righteous sufferer laments being despised and persecuted by the enemies of

---

8   In Jeremiah 31:15 Rachel, the mother of Benjamin, represents the tribe of Benjamin, in whose territory Ramah was located (about four to seven miles north of Jerusalem). According to 1 Samuel 10:2, Rachel's tomb was in Benjaminite territory. However, according to Genesis 35:19 (cf. 48:7), Rachel was buried in Ephrath on the way to Bethlehem. This tradition associating Rachel with Bethlehem may have prompted Matthew to draw the connection between Jeremiah 31:15 and the slaughter of the infants in Bethlehem. For an attempt to harmonize the texts, see Tsumura 2007, 284. He identifies the northern Benjaminite site as the location of the tomb and observes that Rachel was buried on the *road* to Bethlehem, not in Bethlehem. Others identify Ephrath in Genesis 35:19 as a northern location (cf. Ps. 132:6), understanding Bethlehem as a later, erroneous gloss (see McCarter 1980, 181).

God (see, e.g., Pss. 22, 69).[9] Nathaniel's response in John 1:46 may suggest Nazareth had a bad reputation and its citizens were generally despised. At the very least, it suggests Nazareth was insignificant. The statement "he will be called a Nazarene" could be the same as saying, "he will be despised," or at least, "he will be insignificant." In other words, Nazareth was an appropriate hometown for Jesus because his association with it foreshadows his insignificant roots (from the human perspective, cf. Isa. 53:2) and ultimate rejection as the Suffering Servant of Isaiah 53 and as the righteous sufferer par excellence of the lament psalms.

To summarize:

(1) Jesus's exile to and return from Egypt highlights his role as the ideal Israel, who will succeed where the nation failed.

(2) Herod's slaughter of the infants is analogous to what Jeremiah 31:15 describes. It foreshadows Israel's rejection of Jesus and the even greater suffering that would overtake Jewish mothers and children in A.D. 70.

(3) Jesus's growing up in Nazareth foreshadows the fact that he would be despised and rejected. Bethlehem, the city of David the king, was the appropriate site for the adoring magi to worship the newborn king, but Nazareth was a more appropriate hometown for one who would be rejected and crucified.

In each instance Matthew sees fulfillment in a subtle manner. An underlying pattern is filled out more completely by an event in Jesus's experience. Fulfillment for Matthew is not simply a prediction coming to pass. The same is true with his use of Isaiah 7:14, which assures Ahaz of God's presence in the days ahead. This promise is filled out completely and ultimately through Jesus the virgin-born Messiah, who is "God with us" in the flesh, the one whom the Immanuel of the eighth century B.C. foreshadowed.

---

9 When Matthew cites a single prophetic text, he refers to the "prophet" (singular) and introduces the quotation with "saying" (cf. 1:22; 2:15, 17; 3:3; 4:14; 8:17; 12:17; 13:35; 21:4–5; 27:9). (The introductory "saying" is omitted in 24:15, but Daniel is referred to as a "prophet.") The structure in Matthew 2:23 is different. The reference is to "prophets" (plural) and "that," not "saying," introduces the citation. In 26:55–56, where Jesus refers to messianic prophecy in a general way, he also refers to the "prophets" (plural). The psalms are not part of the second section of the Hebrew Bible (the Prophets), but in Jesus's time one could refer to the entire Hebrew Bible as the Law and the Prophets (cf. Matt. 5:17; 7:12; 11:13 [the order is reversed here]; 22:40). Any passage not in the Torah (Pentateuch) was placed under the heading "Prophets." (A threefold division, Law-Prophets-Psalms, was known [cf. Luke 24:44], but it is mentioned just once in the New Testament.) For discussion of the problem, see Turner 2008, 100.

PREACHING AND TEACHING STRATEGIES

Exegetical and Theological Synthesis

The narrative here revolves around four kings. The reader is immediately introduced to three of them—Ahaz, king of Judah, Rezin, king of Syria, and Pekah, the king of Israel (7:1). Later in this section, we will encounter "the king of Assyria" (7:17, 18, 20; 8:4, 7). He is left unnamed throughout this passage, probably because the fulfillment of these prophecies extends throughout the reigns of multiple Assyrian kings. The specific referent to "the king of Assyria" in Isaiah 7:17–20 will be fulfilled by Tiglath-pileser (2 Kings 15:29; 16:7, 10; 2 Chron. 28:20) who ruled 745–727 B.C., whereas the references in Isaiah 8:4–8 would be fulfilled by Sennacherib who reigned 705–681 B.C. (2 Kings 18:13). In addition to four kings, this story will also highlight three children with prophetically significant names.

During this time Assyria was growing in power, and was increasingly becoming a threat to surrounding nations, particularly those in the west. Thus, Rezin (Syria) and Pekah (Israel/Ephraim) created an alliance with each other to better stand against Assyria if necessary (7:2). When they attempted to convince Ahaz (Judah) to join their coalition, he refused. Apparently, he had already decided to cozy up to the king of Assyria to appease him rather than risk trying to fight against him. This decision didn't sit well with Rezin and Pekah, and they joined forces and attacked Jerusalem (7:1; see also 2 Kings 15:37; 16:5; 2 Chron. 28:5–15). Their plan was to replace King Ahaz with another man, "the son of Tabeel" (7:5–6). They evidently knew that he would be a willing associate with them, unlike Ahaz.

Ahaz was an inexperienced twenty-year-old man who had just inherited the throne of Judah from his father Jotham (2 Kings 15:38–16:2). He was understandably frightened, along with the inhabitants of Jerusalem (Isa. 7:2). As a result of these attacks, a great number of Judah's military-age men were killed along with Ahaz's own son. Additionally, many of the wives and children of those killed were taken as captives.[10] Once Pekah and Rezin marched against Jerusalem (7:1), it must have seemed like only a matter of time before they too would be taken captive or killed.

Before this happened the Lord had sent Isaiah to reassure Ahaz that the Lord would protect him; he only needed to maintain trust in God. Isaiah encountered Ahaz at "the aqueduct of the Upper Pool," apparently inspecting the city's water supply to ascertain how long Jerusalem could expect to hold out against an Ephraimite/Syrian siege (7:3). Isaiah assures Ahaz that both Rezin and Pekah, two smoldering pieces of firewood (7:4), would be unsuccessful in their attempt to conquer Jerusalem. It is here that the reader encounters the first child with a prophetically significant name. It is the son of Isaiah who is named Shear-Jashub, which means "a remnant will return." His name should have served as a promise to Ahaz that only a remnant of the invading forces would return home, a sign of their defeat (see discussion above). However, for all to go well with Ahaz and Judah, he would need to place his full confidence and trust in Yahweh (7:7–9)—not in his own wisdom, not in other pagan nations (such as Assyria), and certainly not in any of the pagan gods/idols that Ahaz would eventually

---

10 Second Chronicles 28:6–8 states: "In one day Pekah son of Remaliah killed a hundred and twenty thousand soldiers in Judah—because Judah had forsaken the LORD, the God of their ancestors. Zikri, an Ephraimite warrior, killed Maaseiah the king's son, Azrikam the officer in charge of the palace, and Elkanah, second to the king. The men of Israel took captive from their fellow Israelites who were from Judah two hundred thousand wives, sons and daughters. They also took a great deal of plunder, which they carried back to Samaria."

come to worship (2 Kings 16:2–4; 2 Chron. 28:2–4, 23–25).

To bolster Ahaz's confidence in him, the Lord invited Ahaz to ask God for any sign at all, from the height of heaven to the depths of the earth (Isa. 7:10–11). God was apparently willing to do whatever Ahaz asked, as assurance to him that he could trust him to keep his promise so that Ahaz would no longer feel desperate. However, Ahaz declined to ask for a sign, and couched his refusal in a virtuous-sounding excuse: "I will not put the Lord to the test" (7:12; cf. Deut. 6:16). God was not fooled by his pious façade and recognized it for what it was. Ahaz had already determined in his heart that he was going to turn elsewhere for help. He lacked the faith to simply look to Yahweh for salvation. In his heart, he believed that the powerful nation of Assyria was a better bet than the God of Israel/Judah.

In response to Ahaz's rejection, the Lord nevertheless decided to provide him with a sign. The prophet Isaiah predicted that a young woman known to King Ahaz (probably a member of the royal court; see discussion above) would give birth to a son. This would be the second child with a prophetically significant name. The young mother was to call him Immanuel, which means "God is with us" (Isa. 7:14). Before this child was old enough to discern between good and evil, the lands of Israel and Syria would be deserted (7:16). In other words, both Rezin and Pekah would be defeated and their people would be deported out of their land. They would no longer be a threat to Judah.

However, it would not be all good news for Judah. God would also bring judgment upon Judah in the form of the king of Assyria (7:17). God would summon the nation of Assyria as his instrument of judgment against the people of Judah (7:17, 18, 20) for their sin (2 Chron. 28:19–20) and for Ahaz's refusal to trust in him alone (Isa. 7:9; cf. 2 Chron. 28:22–25). God is described here as having "hired" the king of Assyria (Isa. 7:20) to come up against his own people in judgment despite Ahaz having hired him to protect Judah from Israel and Syria (2 Kings 16:7–8; 2 Chron. 28:16, 21). Rather than be of any long-term help, Assyria would ultimately ravage Judah's land.

The effects of God's judgment on Judah via the nation of Assyria are highlighted in 7:20–25. The recurring phrase "in that day" (7:18, 20, 21, 23) anticipates the time when Assyria would invade the land of Judah (7:18) and the resulting effects of their occupation. First, the men of Judah would be emasculated and humiliated as indicated by the imagery of their head, facial, and pubic hair being shaved off (7:20). Additionally, their fields and vineyards would be devastated and overrun by "briers and thorns" (7:23–25), forcing the remaining inhabitants to live on curdled milk and honey (7:22) rather than a more robust diet with fruits, grains, and vegetables.

This outcome is rich with poetic irony. Ahaz refused to trust in Yahweh to deliver him, even though God had promised that he would save him and his people. Instead, he turned to the king of Assyria. In the end, the king of Assyria would come and oppress him and his people. It has been said that "this whole episode was like a mouse attacked by two rats, squeaking for the cat to come save him. The cat did. But the mouse ended up as dessert" (quoted in Ortlund 2005, 91). Ahaz's chosen savior would be no savior at all.

In Isaiah 8:1–4, the reader is introduced to the third child with a prophetically significant name. Isaiah is instructed by God to write "belonging to Maher-shalal-hash-baz" on a tablet in the presence of two recognizable witnesses, Uriah the priest and Zechariah. This would be the God-determined name of Isaiah's soon-to-be-conceived son. The meaning of the name indicated one who was hurrying to collect the plunder or spoil. Like the two previous children with prophetically significant names, this one too would serve as a sign from God indicating what was going to happen shortly. This tablet was evidently intended to serve as a formal document that would testify to the people of Judah of the coming military defeat of Syria (Damascus) and Israel (Samaria), the two kings they dreaded (7:16), by the king of Assyria (8:4).

Isaiah 8:5–10 uses the imagery of water to bring this section to a close. God's presence and protection are likened here to the gently flowing waters of Shiloah. In contrast, God uses the imagery of the rising flood waters of the Euphrates River to depict Assyria. Because Israel and Syria chose to place their trust in their own coalition rather than in God for help, they would ultimately be overcome by the army of Assyria which would pour into their nations like flood waters (8:8). However, these flood waters would overflow even into Judah's land as they too had chosen to reject the salvation that Yahweh offered them, and instead placed their trust in the military might of Assyria. The prophet returns to the name "Immanuel" (8:8, 10). In Isaiah 7:14, the name Immanuel served as a promise of God's protection. Here however, it appears to have a double meaning. Once again, the context points to God's salvation of Judah from the threat posed by Israel and Syria (8:6, 9–10). However, because this occurs within a context of judgment too (8:7–8), the promise that God is with us would seem to serve also as a warning about God's role as judge, even against his own people when they reject him and put their faith in false saviors.

Preaching Idea
It is always wise to trust in God, for ultimate security is found only in him.

Contemporary Connections

What does it mean?
To say that it is *always* wise to trust in God is to accept that God is always good and that he is always right. If he were not always good, then on what basis could we trust that obeying him would ultimately lead to that which is good for us and others? Similarly, if God were not always right, then how could we trust that he always knows what the best path is for our life? Maybe in this or that situation, God is mistaken. In that case, it might make sense to follow our own instincts.

The Bible is clear on both these points. The essence of God's nature is that he is good. Psalm 34:8 (HB 9) says, "Taste and see that the Lord is good; blessed is the one who takes refuge in him." Similarly, Psalm 145:9 says, "The Lord is good to all, he has compassion on all he has made." The prophet Isaiah himself witnessed the reality that God is perfect in holiness (Isa. 6:1–7; cf. Lev. 11:44–45; 1 Peter 1:15–16; Rev. 4:8; 6:10). Likewise, the Bible affirms that God is utterly wise and right in all that he says. The author of Hebrews said of God that no creature is hidden from his sight, but everything is naked and exposed to him (Heb. 4:13; cf. Ps. 139:1–6; Zech. 4:10; John 16:30; Col. 2:3). Additionally, the Bible asserts that God cannot lie (Num. 23:19; Titus 1:2). Thus, based on the nature and character of God, the apostle Paul assures his readers that they can "know that in all things God works for the good of those who love him, who have been called according to his purpose" (Rom. 8:28). This is why Hebrews 11:6 says, "And without faith it is impossible to please God, because anyone who comes to him must believe that he exists and that he rewards those who earnestly seek him." In other words, to please God, we must relate to him on the basis of faith, trusting in his good character as one who will reward those who pursue him in obedience.

This truth, that "it is always wise to trust in God; for ultimate security is found only in him," relates first to the entry point into a relationship with God. The salvation experience is founded upon this principle. It accepts by faith that eternal life (ultimate security) is found exclusively by placing one's trust in God through Jesus Christ. Humans are prone to look for other ways of achieving their own "salvation" from sin and guilt. This usually involves trying to earn a good standing before God or others by doing good things like trying hard to be a moral person or by making the world a better place through any number of noble causes like protecting endangered animals, saving the environment, or feeding the poor. While these are all good causes that should inspire Christians to action at some level, they cannot provide us with salvation. Apart from Christ, sinful humanity is lost and condemned to spend eternity separated from their Creator.

But what does this principle mean as it relates to those who have already trusted in Christ for salvation? The answer to this question should be obvious. In many respects, the entire Christian life is an exercise in whether we will walk by sight or by faith (Hab. 2:4; 2 Cor. 5:7; Gal. 3:11; Heb. 10:38). Will we act in ways that, humanly speaking, seem to be in our best interests for the moment, or will we trust that God's Word is true and that obedience to him is eternally in our best interest?

Is it true?
People are tempted to look for security in lots of places other than God. For many, money equals security. For them, the ability to pay the bills, put food on the table, and possibly to afford the nicer things in life results in them feeling safe. For others, security may be found in a romantic relationship or in a group of friends. As long as they have people who love and accept them, they feel that life will be worth living and are confident that they will be happy. Similarly, some may find solace in their talents, education, or IQ. This gives them confidence that whatever unknowns await them, they are prepared to tackle them head-on and find a way to manage.

Whatever it is that makes a person feel secure will likely become an avenue of temptation for them, particularly when access to that thing(s) appears to be blocked or limited. For example, if someone finds that they need friends to feel secure, they will be tempted to pursue friends regardless of the cost. Similarly, if a young person feels that they need a romantic partner in their life to feel loved or worthwhile, they may be tempted to compromise their morals to attract a person they like. Or they may be tempted to enter into a romantic relationship with someone who isn't even a believer in Jesus for fear that they won't be able to find somebody else as good as them. Likewise, a career-oriented person may be tempted to find their security in having money. This may result in being tempted to spend too much of their time and energy in their career to the neglect of their family and church or to compromise their ethics in the pursuit of a lucrative business deal. The need to feel secure and safe in life becomes a powerful motivator of human behavior.

Now what?
When I (Mike) was in the seventh grade, my family moved, and I began attending a new school. I remember having a difficult time making friends that first year and feeling nervous every day when I would go to lunch. Who would I sit with? Would anyone talk to me, or would I eat my lunch in silence? That experience affected me in the years that followed so that making friends became really important to me. There probably wasn't anything I feared more than returning to the days when almost nobody in my class knew me or cared much about me. Fast forward to my sophomore year in high school. By now, I had developed several good friends and a lot of friendly acquaintances. As a Christian attending a public school, I had learned how to ride the fence with my faith. I was able to avoid the serious and obvious sins that some of my unsaved friends were committing. At the same time, I was careful not to be too overt about my commitment to Jesus. After all, I didn't want to turn people off. In this way, I had figured out how to fit in and have friends without abandoning my Christian faith in the process. For

the most part, then, school had become enjoyable for me.

However, this all began to change one day. For reasons unknown to me, over the course of a couple of weeks, I noticed that several of the people I had been friendly with were becoming standoffish or just ignoring me. At first, I tried to brush this realization off with the consolation that I still had a core group of five to eight close friends, and this was sufficient. However, before long, even my close friends seemed to be far less interested in me. I hadn't done anything, and nobody had told me why this was happening, but those feelings of insecurity, anxiety, and loneliness that I experienced when I first attended this school began to flood back. My parents noticed that my countenance at home was affected. I became depressed most of the time.

It was at this time that I began to seriously contemplate my commitment to Jesus. I began to wonder if it was possible for me to be popular and well liked while at the same time identifying as a committed believer in Jesus. For weeks I wrestled with the question of whether I needed to fully embrace some of the lifestyle choices of my unsaved friends to be liked and accepted by them. Maybe this was the reason they no longer seemed interested in being my friend. Thankfully, as I contemplated this possibility, I knew that my faith in Jesus was in fact real, and that he was the most important relationship in my life. I couldn't just walk away from him to gain a better status in my public school or the acceptance of a few of my peers. One night while lying on my bed, I prayed to the Lord that instead of walking away from him to pursue my friends, I would do the opposite. I was going to commit to being bolder in my walk with Jesus. And if God decided that I wasn't to have another friend in high school, then I was going to trust him and be okay with that.

The very next day, it was as if a switch had been flipped. Friends who hadn't shown interest in me for weeks were suddenly coming up to me and asking how I was doing. One particularly important friend asked when we could hang out again. Looking back, I realize now that God took me through a valley, a test of sorts, to reveal to me how out of balance my desire for friends and peer acceptance had become. He wanted me to wrestle with who was more important to me: him, or my friends. To put it another way: Where was I finding my ultimate sense of security in life? Was I trusting in my friends to provide this for me, or was I walking by faith in God?

All of us will be tempted at times throughout our lives to allow fears, anxieties, and insecurities to drive us to do things that we know are wrong. In those moments, it will appear to us that we can solve our problems by choosing to sin. We must ask ourselves, "What does it look like for me to trust God in this situation?" and "What is it that I fear most—and do I fear God more than that?" Ultimately, our obedience or disobedience to God's Word will be the evidence of whether or not we trust him most for our ultimate security.

Creativity in Presentation

To illustrate the importance of and the nature of faith in God, consider inviting a young child (3-5 years old) to come up on stage. If possible, have your own child or grandchild participate, and offer them a word of explanation ahead of time about what you intend to do. Present them with a cheap toy that you are fairly certain they will want. Let them know they can have it as a gift for coming up and being part of your message. Give them a moment to soak in the fact that you have just offered them something for free. Then tell them that if they would prefer, they can have what appears to be a flat, empty brown bag (the sort that school lunches are sometimes put in) instead. More than likely, the child will look at you as though you are crazy and will say they want the toy. Reassure them that they can have the toy if that's what they choose. However, assure them that as someone who loves them and wants the best for them, you would recommend that they choose the brown bag instead because it's better than the toy. Once again, a young child will likely stick with the toy. After all, why would he/she be interested in a brown bag? At this point, thank the child and wish him/her well enjoying their new toy. Once they return to their seat, it's time to pull the $100 bill out of the brown bag that the child turned down. Of course, they couldn't see that the bag contained something so valuable. Challenge the audience to consider that this is what it means for us to live by faith in the word of God. Each day we have decisions to make, particularly when faced with temptation. Do we take the "cheap toy" now, or do we trust that what God offers us (the brown paper bag) really does contain something of much greater worth, and that one day we will come to experience that thing of greater value if only we will walk by faith and not by sight now. The pastor will want to be sure to handle this sort of illustration carefully so as not to make the child feel foolish for making the "wrong" choice. Avoid choosing a child that is known to be overly sensitive and reassure them and the audience that had any of us been a child, we would have certainly made the same choice, as this is how most young minds think.

Tell a story (or have somebody tell their own testimony) about what it would look like to trust God amid fearful and uncertain circumstances. Include how it would look for the person to put their trust in themselves or in things/people rather than God. For example, Vicki is a middle-aged Christian woman whose husband was controlling, mean, and verbally abusive. She eventually left him for her own safety and that of her children. She was forced to move with her kids into a small run-down rental property. As a single mother of three, Vicki struggles to pay her bills and meet her family's basic needs. In addition to her full-time, low-paying job, she has had to take on a second, part-time job a few evenings each week. She soon discovers that the place she is renting has a mold issue; this likely explains why her daughter's asthma issues have suddenly begun to affect her again. She is understandably frustrated and discouraged. One day, Vicki meets another man who is romantically interested in her. While he is not a Christian, he is much nicer than her former husband, and financially stable. After going out on a few dates with each other, he invites Vicki and her kids to move in with him. While she knows that this would be wrong, she can't help but think about all the ways this could fix her present problems. It would enable her to quit her second job. It would get her and her kids out of the rental, which will probably improve her daughter's health. She would again experience the joy of having a man in her life who would love her and care for her, not to mention a responsible male role model for her kids. From a human standpoint, this man appears to be her savior. And God doesn't appear to have answered her prayers regarding these issues yet. It just makes sense for her to move in with him. However, God has warned against immorality (Acts 15:20; 1 Cor. 5:11; 6:9, 18–20; Eph. 5:3–5), which this living arrangement would likely entail. Furthermore, the Bible warns against believers marrying unbelievers (Deut. 7:3–4; 1 Cor. 7:39; 2 Cor. 6:14–17). To walk by faith in this situation, then, would require Vicki to trust that God is at work in her situation even when her life is noticeably hard. It requires an act of obedience on her part, even though it appears on the surface that there is so much practically to be gained by her disobedience.

The movie *I Still Believe* (released March 2020) follows the college romance of singer and songwriter Jeremy Camp and his first wife, Melissa Lynn Henning. The two met and began dating while in college. Sadly, Melissa was diagnosed with cancer while the two were dating. After much prayer and cancer treatments, Melissa was miraculously healed and was given a clean bill of health. The two were happily married in October of 2000. However, Melissa discovered that her cancer had returned shortly after her marriage to Jeremy. Tragically, she died only three months after she was married at the age of twenty-one. Some of Jeremy Camp's songs reflect the emotions and struggles he faced during Melissa's sickness and eventual death. One of those songs entitled "I Will Walk by Faith" articulates the central message of this passage. The preacher might consider sharing this story along with the lyrics to the song "I Will Walk by Faith," which succinctly articulate the truth that it is always wise to trust in God, for ultimate security is found only in him.

- Child 1: Shear-jashuv—A Remnant Will Return (7:1–12).
- Child 2: Immanuel—God is with us (7:13–25).
- Child 3: Maher-shalal-hash-baz—Hurrying to Collect the Spoil (8:1–10).

DISCUSSION QUESTIONS

1. What are some things that people are tempted to look to for a sense of security in our uncertain world? (Perhaps money in the bank, a good job, friends, a strong military, their political party in power, a good family, a 401(k), etc.)

2. Share an example from your life where fear has tempted you to put your trust in people or things besides God for your ultimate security.

3. Read Matthew 28:19–20; John 14:18–20, 25–28; and Hebrews 13:5–6. How does the principle of "God with us" (Immanuel) still apply to believers today? In what ways do these passages assure us that God's abiding presence with us should serve as a source of peace and confidence?

Isaiah 8:11–9:7

EXEGETICAL IDEA
The righteous remnant within the covenant community must focus on the Lord as their source of security in an unsure world, for he will defeat Israel's enemies and establish a kingdom of justice and peace through a Davidic king.

THEOLOGICAL FOCUS
The Lord's people must focus on him when others are fearful and panicking, for the Lord controls his people's destiny and will establish a kingdom of justice and peace through the ideal Davidic king.

PREACHING IDEA
Amid political unrest, God's people must not fear but instead rest in the Lord and his promise of a glorious coming kingdom.

PREACHING POINTERS
One of our family's favorite home movies is one we recorded on the way back from a home improvement store. We had just purchased several plants for a landscaping project at our house. Among them was a small tree that we laid up the middle of the inside of our minivan. Our daughters at the time were five and two years old. For some reason, our two-year-old was terrified by the tree any time one of its branches moved. She had pushed her body away from the tree as far as she could in her car seat and looked out her window, refusing to look directly at the tree. But every ten seconds or so, she would turn her head just enough to glance at the tree with her peripheral vision. A branch would inevitably move, and she would cry out in fear with tears streaming down her eyes. Her older sister found this funny, and she laughed uncontrollably at her while my wife and I did everything we could to assure her that there was nothing to fear.

Whether it is a fear of plants, the dark, or maybe a harmless insect, children are prone to have misplaced fears. Isaiah 8:11–9:7 reveals that most adults similarly have misplaced fears. This can be especially true in the realm of politics. The people in Isaiah's day were afraid of the Israel-Syria coalition that threatened their livelihoods. God warned his people not to fear the things that the people in the broader culture feared. Rather, they were to fear the Lord alone above all else. If they would fear him, he would become a sanctuary for them from all the other things they were prone to fear. However, if they held onto their misplaced fears, God would be a stone of offense and a snare to them. In the end, only those whose hope and trust was anchored in Yahweh would experience the glorious, eternal government that the Lord's Messiah will ultimately set up at some point in the future.

A KING BRINGS THE LIGHT OF DELIVERANCE (8:11–9:7 [HB 6])

Having briefly addressed the hostile nations with a taunting and triumphant tone (cf. 8:9–10), the prophet returns to the present reality and the prospect of judgment. The future looked ominous, and many were fearful, but the Lord encouraged the righteous to keep their focus on him as their source of security in an unsure world. Isaiah declared his confidence in the Lord and urged the righteous to do the same when others panicked. Judgment would come, but then the Lord would dispel the darkness with the light of deliverance through the person of a Davidic warrior-king. Energized by the Lord, this king would defeat Israel's enemies and establish a kingdom of justice and peace.

LITERARY STRUCTURE AND THEMES (8:11–9:7 [HB 6])

The appearance of כִּי at the beginning of 8:11 gives the impression that there is a syntactical relationship between 8:10 and 11. However, 8:9–10 is addressed to the nations, while in 8:11 the prophet introduces a personal message that the Lord delivered to him. The כִּי is likely asseverative ("indeed"), not causal. The Lord's message to Isaiah was intended for not only the prophet but for other faithful followers of the Lord as well (see the reference to "my disciples" in 8:16), as the plural verbs and pronouns in 8:12–13 indicate.

Since the Lord is referred to by his title "Lord Almighty" (or "Lord of Armies") in 8:13, it is possible that his message is restricted to 8:12, in which case the prophet adds his words to the Lord's, beginning in 8:13. But if this is the case, the singular imperatives and the phrase "my disciples" in 8:16 are problematic. Isaiah 8:16 seems to be addressed to Isaiah by the Lord, so it is reasonable to assume that the Lord's speech, begun in 8:12, extends through 8:16. For other examples where the Lord uses a divine title to speak of himself, see 6:12 and 31:4–5. When the Lord speaks of himself in such a way in an address to his prophet, there is a rhetorical purpose for doing so. In this case, using his title "Lord Almighty" supports the preceding exhortation. The faithful, in contrast to the masses, must fear the mighty God who leads armies in judgment, not the people's false objects of fear.

The Lord's message contains an exhortation (8:12–13) followed by a motivating word of assurance and a warning (8:14–15). In 8:16 the Lord speaks directly to the prophet, as the singular imperatives indicate, and gives him special instructions. Isaiah's response to the Lord's message appears in 8:17–18, where he affirms his trust in the Lord and his role as the Lord's messenger.

> *TRANSLATION ANALYSIS 8:15–16*
> Most English translations end the quotation of the Lord's words with 8:15 and place 8:16 with 8:17–18 as part of the prophet's response (see ESV, HCSB, NIV, NLT). However, if the prophet is speaking in 8:16, it is not clear whom he is addressing with the singular imperatives. It makes better sense to understand 8:16 as the conclusion to the Lord's message. See *Tanakh*.

It is difficult to determine the speaker in 8:19–9:2 [HB 1]. The plural pronoun and imperative in 8:19a make it clear that a group is addressed. One option is that the Lord's message to Isaiah and his faithful followers resumes here, as the Lord again warns them not to think like the confused masses around them (cf. 8:12). However, if the Lord begins speaking again in 8:19, it is unclear where his speech ends and Isaiah's begins. (It is clear the prophet is speaking in 9:3 [HB 2], where he addresses the Lord.) The switch would seem to come before 9:1 (HB 8:23), where the Lord is the implied subject of the third-person verbs, but there is no formal indicator of a transition.

Another, perhaps better, option is that in 8:19 the prophet turns to the Lord's disciples and exhorts them to trust in the message (8:20) that has been delivered to them (cf. 8:16). The prophet speaks both before (8:17–18) and after this (9:3 [HB 2]), so, if we attribute 8:19–9:2 (HB 1) to him, we avoid the problems mentioned above. His speech contains an affirmation (8:17–18) and an exhortation (8:19–20), supported by a description of the destiny of those who will be judged (8:21–22a). There is a shift in mood at the end of 8:22 with the announcement that the darkness of judgment will be dispelled. This reversal of judgment is then described in 9:1–2 (HB 8:23–9:1), before the prophet speaks directly to the Lord and declares that his intervention for the nation has produced great joy (9:3 [HB 2]). Continuing to address the Lord (at least in 9:4 [HB 3]), Isaiah gives a series of three specific reasons for this joy, each of which is introduced with כִּי (9:4–7 [HB 3–6]; Kaiser 1972, 207). By the end of the unit, it appears the prophet is no longer directly addressing the Lord, but the use of the title "LORD Almighty" at the end of 9:7 [HB 6] does mirror the Lord's use of the title in his message to the faithful in 8:13.

To summarize, the speakers and addressees in 8:11–9:7 (HB 6) may be understood as follows:

8:11	*Isaiah* introduces the Lord's words:
8:12–15	The *Lord* warns his *disciples* (note second-person plural forms in 8:12–13)
8:16	The *Lord* gives *Isaiah* special instructions (note second-person singular forms)
8:17–18	*Isaiah* affirms his trust in the Lord
8:19–20	*Isaiah* urges the Lord's *disciples* to remain faithful
8:21–9:2 (HB 1)	*Isaiah* describes the judgment and deliverance to come
9:3–7a (HB 2–6a)	*Isaiah* addresses the *Lord*, praising him for his saving intervention
9:7b (HB 6b)	*Isaiah* affirms that the Lord will accomplish this deliverance

- *No Time for Fear (8:11–16)*
- *A Confident Prophet (8:17–21)*
- *A Time for Joy (8:22–9:7 [HB 6])*

EXPOSITION (8:11–9:7 [HB 6])

No Time for Fear (8:11–16)
The Lord warned his faithful followers not to fear but to keep their focus on him, their source of security.

8:11–13. Fear had swept over the land. In the northern kingdom there was concern over the menacing presence of Assyria. This prompted Israel to ally with Aram and then put pressure on Judah to join the alliance. This northern threat struck terror into the hearts of King Ahaz's royal court and the people of Judah (7:2). As people got caught up in panic, cries of "conspiracy" (קֶשֶׁר) could be heard (8:12). It is not clear what is in view here. (For a survey

A King Brings the Light of Deliverance (8:11–9:7 [HB 6])

of proposals, see Williamson 2018, 292.) Perhaps the northern alliance is in view (Gray 1912, 152), but the term usually refers to an internal conspiracy within a ruler's realm that threatens to topple him.[1] If that is the case here, 8:12 may refer to a conspiracy against Ahaz, perhaps by those wishing to join the northern alliance and to pursue an anti-Assyrian policy (Wildberger 1991, 358). Another option is that the "conspiracy" refers to Isaiah's warning of an Assyrian invasion (see Williamson 2018, 293) and/or his recommended policy of avoiding foreign alliances. This may have been viewed as treasonous by the royal court, which had decided on a pro-Assyrian policy (see Evans 1985, 112–13 and Young 1965, 310). Of course, in this case the second-person verb "do not say" would have to be directed to the Lord's disciples, not Isaiah, since the prophet would not be inclined to characterize his own message as conspiracy. Yet one gets the impression from 8:11 that the message of 8:12–15 is for Isaiah as well as the disciples. In any case, the reality (or rumor?) of conspiracy was causing widespread fear and terror.

In this context of fear and suspicion, the Lord clearly spoke a word of warning to Isaiah (8:11). Both the imagery of the Lord grabbing the prophet with his hand and the use of the verb יָסַר (וְיִסְּרֵנִי, if this is the correct reading) convey the gravity of the hour. This verb is often used of rebuking one who needs correction (see, e.g., Ps. 94:10; Prov. 9:7; Hos. 10:10), but this need not be the case here. The verb sometimes refers to teaching or training someone (Deut. 4:36; Job 4:3; Isa. 28:26; Hos. 7:15), which usually entails giving guidance and warnings, as a parent would do (Deut. 8:5; Prov. 31:1). In this case the Lord warned against walking "in the way of these people." The noun דֶּרֶךְ, "way," is used here, as it often is, of behavior. Their actions were not isolated; they had become a way of life. We know from other references to "these people" that they were insensitive to God's message (Isa.

6:9–10; cf. 29:9) because they were contaminated by sin (cf. 6:5), and their hearts, despite their professions of loyalty, were far from God (29:13–14). Without God as their anchor, they were overwhelmed with fear by the political intrigue going on around them.

With His Hand

The Hebrew reads, "like the grabbing of the hand." The form כְּחֶזְקַת (the prefixed preposition is -בְּ, "with," in some editions) consists of the preposition, functioning temporally, and an infinitive. חֶזְקַת is a construct form of חֶזְקָה, which is derived from חָזְקָה, a relatively rare infinitival pattern (GKC, 123 §45d). The following הַיָּד, "the hand," is a subjective genitive, apparently referring to the hand of God. Some see this as a reference to an ecstatic experience (Blenkinsopp 2000, 241; Gray 1912, 151; Wildberger 1991, 357), while others see it as referring to the power of God made evident to the prophet in a way beyond normal prophetic inspiration (Smith 2007, 225 n. 301; Young 1965, 309–10). Both interpretations may make more of the language than is warranted. The image is that of grabbing someone to get his attention with the purpose of giving guidance and direction.

The Lord instructed Isaiah and his other faithful followers (note the plural verbs in 8:12–13), whom he calls "my disciples" (8:16), not to get caught up in the accusations of conspiracy and not to fear what "these people" feared (8:12). Instead, they should keep their focus where it belonged, on him, "the LORD Almighty" (8:13). By placing the object first and then using the appositional pronoun (אֹתוֹ, "him") before the verb, the Lord draws attention to himself and highlights the contrast with the people's object of fear (see מוֹרָא, "his [i.e., the people's] fear [i.e., object of fear]" in 8:12, which also precedes the verb for emphasis). As noted above, it may seem odd that the Lord would refer to himself by his

---

[1] See 2 Sam. 15:12; 1 Kings 16:20; 2 Kings 11:14; 12:20; 14:19; 15:15, 30; 17:4.

title, rather than simply speaking in the first person, but he has a clear rhetorical purpose for doing so. The title "Lord Almighty" supports the preceding exhortation. The faithful, in contrast to the masses, must fear the one who leads armies in judgment, not the people's false objects of fear.

The Lord urged his followers to regard him as holy (8:13). The basic idea of the verb "be holy" is "to be set apart, different, unique." Here in the causative verbal stem (*hiphil*) the idea is "to make holy (in one's thinking)," in the sense of "treat as, regard as holy" (cf. *HALOT* s.v. "קדשׁ" mng. 4.a, 1074). Treating the Lord as holy entailed recognizing him for who he really is—the sovereign king who possessed the authority and power to protect his people. But it involves more than this, as 8:13b makes clear. The language used in 8:13b is quite strong—the people must treat the Lord as holy by making him their source of fear (מוֹרַאֲכֶם) and terror (מַעֲרִצְכֶם). The terms mirror the language of 8:12, where יָרֵא, "to fear" (תִּירְאוּ), the related noun מוֹרָא, "fear," and עָרַץ, "be terrified" (תַּעֲרִיצוּ) appear. But the language is not mere rhetorical hyperbole. The Lord's people should have a healthy fear of him for he is holy and unique, not common or ordinary. The verb עָרַץ appears with the *hiphil* of קדשׁ in Isaiah 29:23, which describes a time when the covenant community will stand in awe of God's greatness and give him the honor he deserves. But the term עָרַץ also has the notion of trembling in terror before God's majesty and power (Isa. 2:19–21). Rather than worrying about a "conspiracy," the people should have stood in terror before the holy God they had offended and all but disowned, for judgment was right around the corner. Isaiah and the faithful remnant must model the proper attitude.

8:14–15. The Lord attached a motivating statement to the exhortation (8:14–15) that begins positively: loyalty to the Lord would bring security. The word מִקְדָּשׁ, "holy place," refers to a sanctuary where the Lord is worshipped. If the righteous remnant continued to respect the Lord's holiness (8:13), he would become their holy place, as it were. While judgment fell all around them, the Lord would be a safe refuge for his loyal followers as they lived in his holy presence.

The mood suddenly becomes negative as the next four metaphors in the sequence suggest judgment, not security. The first two picture the Lord as a stone or rock over which the people trip and stumble. These metaphors are applied specifically to the two houses of Israel, a reference to the northern kingdom (Israel) and the southern kingdom (Judah). The next two metaphors come from the realm of hunting and picture the Lord as a trap or snare. These metaphors are applied specifically to the inhabitants of Jerusalem, the capital of the southern kingdom, which becomes the focal point of the prophet. Isaiah 8:15 develops the metaphors more fully, as it describes how "many" would stumble, fall, and be seriously injured (see 1 Sam. 4:18; Jer. 51:8 for the collocation of "fall" and "be broken"). Merging the second pair of metaphors with the first pair, the prophet also says they would be ensnared and captured.

Because of the apparent incongruity of the first metaphor in Isaiah 8:14, some prefer to emend מִקְדָּשׁ, "sanctuary." After all, the five metaphors are introduced by -לְ and collocated with וְהָיָה, "and it will be." The shift from a positive to negative image after the first, with no shift in predicate, seems awkward. Yet there is a clear structure and logic in the text as it stands: Isaiah 8:12 focuses on the perspective that Isaiah and the faithful were to avoid: the people had a false object of fear. Isaiah 8:13 then focuses on the perspective that the faithful should have: the Lord should be their object of fear. Isaiah 8:14a gives the positive benefits of such a perspective, while 8:14b–15 explains that those who failed to have the proper perspective would find the Lord to be an agent of judgment who would bring about their demise (Smith 2007, 227). The mood shift within the statement in 8:14, while not expected at the strictly grammatical level, is a highly effective attention-getting device that highlights the contrast that is so obvious in 8:12–13. The contrasting objects of fear are mirrored in the contrasting destinies of the people and the faithful. If one emends the text at the beginning of 8:14, the statement is still a powerful motivating argument, but one that is strictly negative: treat the Lord with respect or you will be destroyed by him along with the others. But retaining מִקְדָּשׁ, "sanctuary," preserves a verbal link with תַקְדִּישׁוּ, "you will regard as holy" (8:13). Those who sanctify the Lord find that he becomes their sanctuary.

8:16. Here the Lord speaks to the prophet (note the singular forms) and instructs him to preserve a written record of the "testimony" and "instruction" for the faithful remnant, called here the Lord's "disciples" (see Motyer 1993, 96). The "testimony," or legal confirmation (see Ruth 4:7), is probably the Lord's message delivered through the prophet, while the "instruction" (תּוֹרָה; cf. Isa. 1:10) refers specifically to the commands and warnings contained in the messages, such as we see in 8:12–15. Preserving the message would enable the faithful remnant to turn to it during times when the blinded majority sought prohibited means of discerning the future (8:20). When others were advocating seeking revelation from the spirits of the dead, the faithful would have a sure word from the Lord to guide them.

A Confident Prophet (8:17–21)

The prophet declared his confidence and urged the righteous to do the same when others were panicking.

8:17. In response to the Lord's message, Isaiah declared he would "wait" on the Lord. To wait (וְחִכִּיתִי) on the Lord is an expression of faith (cf. Isa. 30:18; 64:4). In a crisis the temptation is to turn to something tangible for help, such as one's own wits or someone who looks capable of providing protection or deliverance. Judah was guilty of this as they turned to surrounding nations like Egypt and Assyria for security amid a dangerous and hostile world. But Isaiah, speaking for the Lord's followers, affirmed that he would resist this temptation and wait for help from the Lord who had spoken to him, for he alone can give genuine security. He is unique in his ability to deliver those who wait on him (Isa. 64:4). Isaiah was able to maintain his faith even though he knew the Lord had hidden his face from the house of Jacob (see 2:5). He knew the Lord distinguishes between the righteous and the wicked. Indeed, those who fear the Lord and wait on him (cf. וְקִוֵּיתִי־לוֹ in 8:17) for deliverance (cf. Isa. 33:2, 6) are vindicated (Isa. 25:9).

The metaphor of hiding the face suggests angry disapproval and withdrawal of help. Rebellion prompts God to "hide his face" (Deut. 31:18; 32:20; Isa. 59:2; Jer. 33:5; Ezek. 39:24), which in turn leaves his sinful people vulnerable to their enemies (Deut. 31:17; Pss. 30:7 [HB 8]; 143:7; Ezek. 39:23). The expression also implies God was unresponsive to the suffering and prayers of his rebellious, sinful people (Isa. 64:7; Mic. 3:4). Though God may hide his face from his sinful people, he is predisposed to seek reconciliation with them. He hides his face for "a moment" but once they repent, he restores the relationship and extends his blessings (Isa. 54:8; cf. Ps. 30:5–7 [HB 6–8]). No wonder Isaiah's message quickly turns from doom to hope (see Isa. 8:21–9:6 [9:7]).

8:18. Isaiah understood his role as God's prophet. He declared that he and his sons were "signs and symbols" (or reminders and omens) commissioned by the Lord of Armies, who would intervene as a mighty warrior to deliver and judge. The word אוֹת, "sign," refers to a person, object, or event that is vested with special significance and supports or confirms a divine promise or warning (7:11, 14; 19:20; 20:3; 37:30; 55:13; 66:19). Isaiah and his sons were signs in that they possessed symbolic names designed to remind the people of God's ability and promise to deliver them: (1) Isaiah's name means "the LORD saves"; (2) Shear-Jashub means "a remnant will return," and assured the people that only a remnant of the invading army would leave Judah intact (see 7:3); (3) Maher-shalal-hash-baz, perhaps meaning "(one) hurries (to the) plunder, (one) hastens (to the) spoil," indicated that the Assyrian army would plunder the northern coalition (see 8:4). Their names also served as omens (מוֹפְתִים) in that they foreshadowed what would happen soon. Isaiah was also a "sign" and "omen" when he walked around half-naked for three years to illustrate God's approaching judgment upon Egypt and Cush (20:3).

Isaiah described the Lord of Armies as the one who "dwells on Mount Zion." This should have been encouraging to the faithful whom Isaiah addresses here (see 8:19), for it was a reminder that the mighty divine warrior-king lived among his people and would protect his dwelling place from hostile invaders, as indicated by the names of Isaiah and his sons (see Hayes and Irvine 1987, 165–66). The Lord's presence on Mount Zion sanctified it, making it safe from destruction, as the Assyrians painfully discovered (Isa. 37:32–35; cf. Joel 4:17 [Eng. 3:17]). Of course, this did not insulate the city from the Lord's disciplinary judgment (see Isa. 10:12). Furthermore, Zion was inviolable only for as long as the Lord resided there. Tragically, he eventually withdrew his presence from the temple and city (Ezek. 10–11), leaving it vulnerable to destruction (Ps. 74).

8:19–21. Having affirmed his own faith, Isaiah turned to the Lord's disciples and exhorted them to remain firm (8:19). He anticipated some would urge them to seek information about the future through the prohibited practice of consulting the spirits of the dead. But the faithful should reject this advice and look instead to the "instruction" and "testimony" that the prophet was to seal up for the disciples (8:20a, cf. 8:16).

Those promoting necromancy had darkened minds (8:20b) and would soon experience the darkness of judgment (see 8:22). The coming judgment would reduce them to the life of refugees, wandering about the land in desperate search of food (8:21a). Their hunger would incite them to angrily curse the king and the gods in whom they had placed their trust (8:21b).

TRANSLATION ANALYSIS 8:19
As noted above, 8:19 is spoken by the prophet to the Lord's disciples. I suggest the following translation: "When they say to you: 'Inquire of the mediums and the spiritists who chirp and mutter incantations. Should people not inquire of their gods by asking the dead about the destiny of the living?'" The subject of the plural verb "they say" is unstated; it may be the inhabitants of the city (see 8:14). Most English translations end the quotation of the people in the middle of the verse and understand the second half of the verse as Isaiah's response to their spiritism (see ESV, HCSB, KJV, NIV, NLT, NRSV). For example, ESV reads: "When they say to you . . . should not a people inquire of their God? Should they inquire of the dead on behalf of the living?" NIV has: "When someone tells you . . . should not a people inquire of their God? Why consult the dead on behalf of the living?" But the Hebrew text gives no indication there are two questions here with the first being negated and expecting a strong positive reply and the second being rhetorical. The syntax of 8:19b is better understood as a single question that continues the words of the people, as indicated in the suggested translation above (see *Tanakh*; Clements 1980, 102; Day 2000, 218; Hayes and Irvine 1987, 166–67; P. Johnston 2002, 146–47 ; Kaiser 1972, 199).

The Mosaic Law prohibited necromancy (Deut. 18:9–13), yet many sought to know the future by consulting the spirits of the dead. The first term used for the necromancers (אֹבוֹת, "mediums") appears to refer in 1 Samuel 28 to a pit used by a medium to conjure up the spirits of the dead.

Saul asked his servants to find "an owner of an אוֹב" (28:7), he told the medium, "conjure for me by (using) an אוֹב" (28:8), and Samuel is described as ascending from the ground (28:13; cf. 28:8, 14–15). By extension the word can refer to the spirit that is conjured up by use of the pit (see Lev. 20:27, which reads, literally, "a man or woman who has within them an אוֹב"; and Isa. 29:4, where we read, literally, "and your voice will be like an אוֹב from the ground"). However, in several other texts the term refers to the medium, especially when it is plural and paired with "spiritists" as in Isaiah 8:19 (יִדְּעֹנִים; see Lev. 19:31; 20:6; Deut. 18:11; 1 Sam. 28:3, 9; 2 Kings 21:6 = 2 Chron. 33:6 [in these two texts, "medium" is singular and "magician" plural]; 23:24; Isa. 19:3). In 1 Chronicles 10:13 (referring to Saul's visit to the medium) the word seems to refer to the medium. As in the case of the medium of Endor, these mediums attempted to conjure up the spirits of the dead, which would speak in a low voice from the pit (Isa. 29:4), perhaps even through the vocal apparatus of the conjurer (Lev. 20:27 may imply this).

The second term (יִדְּעֹנִים, "spiritist[s]") literally means "knowing one(s)." This may mean that the one so designated had special knowledge of how to conjure up the dead, but it is used at least once of the spirit, not the conjurer (Lev. 20:27). This suggests that special knowledge about the future through contact with the dead is in view. The word never appears in isolation; it is always paired with "medium," suggesting the phrase refers to a single person, a medium/spirit that is "in the know," as it were (see the discussion in Jeffers 1996, 171–72).

The mediums/spiritists are described as chirping and muttering. The first word (מְצַפְצְפִים, from צָפַף) is used of the chirping sound made by a bird (Isa. 10:14; 38:14), while the second (מַהְגִּים, from הָגָה) is used of the cooing of a dove (Isa. 38:14; 59:11). The latter is also used of humans speaking in an undertone, as when one is deep in thought (see *HALOT* s.v. "הגה I" 237). Perhaps the muttering of incantations, used to conjure up the dead, is in view here. The descriptive language, likening them to birds, is probably intended to be derogatory and to highlight the contrast with the clear prophetic word delivered to the prophet (8:20a, cf. 8:16).

> **Likening Them to Birds**
> Williamson (2018, 336) presents evidence from the ancient Near East that "the dead were thought to adopt a bird-like appearance and, indeed, to sound like them." See, as well, Karel van der Toorn 1988, 210–12.

One wonders how the people could turn to necromancy instead of the prophetic word, but 8:20b explains that their minds were unenlightened. The text literally reads, "there is no dawn to him." "Dawn," which connotes light dispelling darkness, is used here as a metaphor for understanding. They have no light of understanding, explaining why they encourage others to seek out the world of the dead for guidance. This imagery of the absence of dawn fits nicely with the description in 8:22 of darkness shrouding the land (Smith 2007, 231 n. 322).

The people wanted to know the future so they could attempt to ward off any predicted calamity. But their efforts would prove futile. According to 8:21, judgment would leave them homeless and hungry. They placed their faith in the king and their gods, but these false sources of security would let them down. Disillusioned, they would angrily curse both the king and the gods as they looked upward for deliverance that would not come.

A Time for Joy (8:22–9:7 [HB 6])
The light of deliverance would dispel the darkness of judgment as a Davidic warrior-king, empowered by the Lord, would defeat Israel's enemies, and establish a kingdom of justice and peace.

A King Brings the Light of Deliverance (8:11–9:7 [HB 6])

8:22. The darkness of judgment would overwhelm the land (8:22a), but then the darkness would be dispelled (8:22b–9:1 [HB 8:22b–23]). Isaiah 8:22 is typically understood in its entirety as portraying the darkness of judgment, with 9:1 (HB 8:23) then describing the dispelling of darkness. For example, NIV translates 8:22, "Then they will look toward the earth and see only distress and darkness and fearful gloom, and they will be thrust into utter darkness." The ESV reads, "And they will look to the earth, but behold, distress and darkness, the gloom of anguish. And they will be thrust into thick darkness." But it is more likely that the reversal comes in the final clause of 8:22. I prefer to translate the verse as follows: "When one looks out at the land, they will see distress and darkness, and gloom of affliction. But darkness will be driven away." Given the verse division, it appears that אֲפֵלָה מְנֻדָּח, literally "darkness, pushed," is a further description of what one sees when looking out over the land in the aftermath of judgment. But the verb נָדַח suggests the dispelling of darkness, the theme of the next verse, is in view. The verb, which occurs only here in the *pual* verbal stem, has the primary meaning "be scattered, driven away." The appearance of כִּי, "because," at the beginning of the next verse supports this, for the following clause explains why the darkness would be driven away. Granted, the transition seems abrupt and one might assume וַאֲפֵלָה, "and darkness," is paired with מְעוּף צוּקָה, "fearful gloom" (or "gloom of affliction") in parallel to צָרָה וַחֲשֵׁכָה, "distress and darkness," just before it (see Gray 1912, 161, 163). But the addition of מְנֻדָּח, "thrust into" (or "driven away"), quickly signals this is not the case. The abrupt and surprising shift in syntax mirrors the abrupt and radical change that is prophesied. Darkness, though overwhelming, would suddenly be dispelled as the light breaks through.

9:1 (HB 8:23). The Lord would drive away the gloom from the northern regions of the land. Speaking from a future perspective, beyond the coming judgment and the restoration to follow, the prophet recalls that the Lord "in the past" (or "at the former time") humiliated the land of Zebulun and the land of Naphtali. But then "in the future" (or "at the latter time") he transformed humiliation into honor for the regions called "Galilee of the nations," "the Way of the Sea," and "[the region] beyond the Jordan." The Assyrian king Tiglath-pileser III divided the northern kingdom into provinces when the Assyrians invaded the land in 734–732 B.C. "Galilee of the nations" may correspond to the province of Megiddo, located west of the Sea of Galilee. "The Way of the Sea" may refer to the province of Dor, located along the Mediterranean coast. "[The region] beyond the Jordan" refers to the region Gilead, situated east of the Jordan River, which may or may not have been a distinct province. (See Aharoni 1979, 374; as well as Otzen 1977–1978, 103; and Roberts 2015, 147–48.)

9:2 (HB 9:1). In place of deep darkness, which had enveloped the land, the people would see a bright (literally, "great") light. Darkness (חֹשֶׁךְ) here symbolizes the judgment that overwhelmed the northern kingdom (see the references to the northern tribes Zebulun and Naphtali in 9:1 [HB 8:23]) when the Assyrians invaded the land (see 8:22). Darkness often has this connotation in prophetic literature (Isa. 5:30; Ezek. 32:8; Joel 2:2, 31; Amos 5:18–20; Mic. 7:8; Nah. 1:8; Zeph. 1:15). In the parallel line, צַלְמָוֶת is used of this darkness. This word has been traditionally understood as a compound noun, meaning "shadow [צֵל] of death [מָוֶת]" (see Ps. 23:4). However, it is more likely that the term is an abstract noun meaning "deep darkness" (*HALOT* s.v. "צַלְמָוֶת" 1029; Williamson 2018, 364–66). It is frequently associated with darkness of night and contrasted with light or morning (Job 3:5; 10:21–22; 12:22; 24:17; 28:3; 34:22; Ps. 107:10, 14; Jer. 13:16; Amos 5:18). It is sometimes used metaphorically for the darkness of death (Job 10:21–22; 38:17), but this association with death is not part of the inherent meaning of the word.

A King Brings the Light of Deliverance (8:11–9:7 [HB 6])

Light contrasts here with the darkness of judgment and symbolizes the deliverance and resulting joy God would bring through his chosen king (see Isa. 9:3–7 [HB 2–6]). Isaiah frequently uses light as a symbol for divine deliverance and renewed blessing (30:26; 42:6, 16; 45:7; 49:6; 51:4; 58:8; 60:1, 3, 19–20). In Isaiah 42:6 the Lord's special servant brings light, symbolizing deliverance from bondage and oppression through the implementation of justice (cf. 49:6; 51:4–6), to the nations of the earth. In Isaiah 9 this light of deliverance comes to Israel in conjunction with the reign of an ideal Davidic king, whose commitment to justice (see Isa. 11:1–9) links him with the special servant of Isaiah's servant songs.

9:3 (HB 2). The Lord (addressed by Isaiah) would enlarge the nation and increase its joy. Those who once lived under the dark cloud of judgment would be delirious with joy, like farmers bringing in the harvest or warriors dividing the spoils of victory. The analogies are well chosen and not merely illustrative. They anticipate realities that would accompany the arrival of the light of deliverance (see Kaiser 1972, 208). The first illustration points to restored divine blessing (cf. 4:2); the second envisions the defeat of the nation's enemies (9:4–5 [HB 3–4]).

9:4 (HB 3). The prophet gives the first of three reasons (note כִּי, "for, because") for the increased joy of the people. The Lord, who is addressed, would shatter (הַחִתֹּתָ, from חָתַת) Israel's oppressors, compared here to a burdensome yoke that weighs down an animal and to a club (מַטֵּה) and rod (שֵׁבֶט) used to prod and beat it. The use of נֹגֵשׂ for the oppressor is an echo of Israel's oppression at the hand of the Egyptian slave drivers (see Exod. 3:7; 5:6, 10, 13–14). In Isaiah's historical context, the Assyrians, who decimated and eventually conquered the northern kingdom, are likely in view. In the next chapter they are compared to a rod that beats the Lord's people, though Judah, not the northern kingdom, is the victim there (Isa. 10:5, 24; both מַטֵּה and שֵׁבֶט are used). According to 30:31–32, the Lord's voice will shatter (חָתַת) the Assyrians when he beats them with his rod (שֵׁבֶט) and club (מַטֵּה).

The Lord's shattering of his enemies is compared to "the day of Midian's defeat" (literally, "the day of Midian"), an allusion to Gideon's victory over the Midianites (cf. Isa. 10:26, which makes this apparent). The allusion is particularly appropriate here, for it is the region of Zebulun and Naphtali that would be delivered (9:1 [HB 8:23]). Both of those tribes participated in Gideon's battle with the Midianites (Judg. 6:35). That battle was especially memorable because the Lord defeated the Midianite horde (Judg. 7:12) with just three hundred men (7:8). While Gideon's strategy ignited panic in the enemy, there was no doubt that the Lord's intervention determined the outcome (7:22). Prior to the battle, the Lord was concerned that he, not the boastful Israelites (7:2), should receive credit for the victory. By comparing the coming deliverance to the ancient defeat of Midian, Isaiah made it clear that the Lord's intervention would be decisive, and that Israel's God was still alive and well, just as he was in Gideon's time. Though subsequently he describes the Lord's instrument as a Davidic warrior-king (Isa. 9:6–7 [HB 5–6]), the Lord's empowerment of this ruler is evident in his royal titles (note esp. אֵל גִּבּוֹר, "Mighty God"; see discussion below).

9:5 (HB 4). The second reason for increased joy (note כִּי at the beginning of 9:5 [HB 4]) is closely related to the first (9:4 [HB 3]). The boots and bloodstained clothes of the enemy corpses would be burned up. The description of the boots as "marching [the *hapax legomenon* סֹאן is derived from the preceding noun סְאוֹן, "boot," see *HALOT* s.v. "סאן" 738] with shaking" (literal translation) recalls the numerical strength of the enemy, who shook the ground as they marched forward. But the fire and smoke of this bonfire would serve as a vivid reminder of the Lord's powerful intervention and his ability to reduce powerful enemies to rubble.

9:6–7 (HB 5–6). The third reason (note כִּי at the beginning of 9:6 [HB 5]) for increased joy is the arrival of an ideal Davidic king who would establish a kingdom of peace and justice. Isaiah describes him as follows (my translation):

9:6 (HB 5) For a child has been born to us,
a son has been given to us,
and the dominion is on his shoulder.
He has been given the name:
Extraordinary Strategist, Mighty God,
Everlasting Father, Prince of Peace.

9:7 (HB 6) Great will be the dominion and
there will be unending peace,
on David's throne and over his kingdom,
to establish it and to sustain it
with justice and righteousness,
from now until forevermore.
The zeal of the Sovereign Lord[2] will accomplish this.

It is not certain how the two *qatal* (perfect) forms and two *wayyiqtol* forms in 9:6 (HB 5) should be interpreted. One option is to understand them as rhetorical, expressing certitude, like the *qatal* forms in 9:1b–3 (HB 8:23–9:2). In this case they anticipate the birth and reign of an ideal Davidic king. Another option is that 9:6 (HB 5) speaks of the birth of a prince that has already occurred (Wildberger 1991, 401). In the historical context of Isaiah this would likely be Hezekiah. In this case the prophet looks forward to a time when this prince would take the throne of his ancestor David and the Lord would establish a kingdom of peace and justice through him. The *yiqtol* (imperfect) verb form at the end of 9:7 (HB 6) indicates this is indeed a future expectation. In defense of this view one can point to the use of שַׂר, "prince" (not מֶלֶךְ, "king") in the ruler's fourth title. This might suggest the ruler had not yet achieved full royal status. (For more on this, see the discussion of the title שַׂר שָׁלוֹם below.) Furthermore, Isaiah anticipated the Lord's defeat of Assyria outside Jerusalem (10:5–34) and Isaiah's contemporary Micah prophesied that a Davidic ruler would subdue and conquer Assyria (Mic. 5:5–6). Of course, if this hope were attached to Hezekiah, historical circumstances eventually made it clear that Hezekiah, at best, was a mere foreshadowing of another Davidic king who would establish this glorious kingdom. Furthermore, later prophets such as Jeremiah, Ezekiel, and Zechariah anticipate the arrival of an ideal Davidic king. This would not be the case if Hezekiah had already fulfilled the prophetic vision.

Interpreters debate how many titles the ruler is assigned. Some see as many as five, while others identify only one title (Prince of Peace). Several issues must be addressed:

(1) Does the verb וַיִּקְרָא, "and he called," have a stated subject here, or is the subject simply indefinite? If the former, then one or more of the following titles could be the subject with one or more being the object. If we assume for the moment that there are four titles, then the first three, all of which have an element pointing to deity, could be taken as appositional and understood as the subject. The fourth title would then be appositional or adverbial to the object, "his name": "Extraordinary Strategist, Mighty God, Everlasting Father called his name, Prince of Peace." Or, if the third title is understood as royal, given the fact that "father" can be a royal epithet and "everlasting" can be viewed as royal hyperbole (see below), one could translate: "Extraordinary Strategist, Mighty God called his name, Everlasting Father, Prince of Peace." However, it is not necessary for the *qal* of קָרָא,

---

2 Traditionally, "Lord of Hosts." See the commentary above on Isaiah 1:9.

"call," to have a stated subject. The subject may be indefinite, in which case it may be treated as passive in translation with the object(s) of the verb serving as subject(s): "One called his name Extraordinary Strategist, etc." There are several examples of קָרָא with an indefinite subject (see Gen. 25:26; 35:8; 38:29–20; Num. 11:3; 21:3; Josh. 5:9). So, the syntax of וַיִּקְרָא, due to its ambiguity, is not determinative when trying to decide how many titles are used. The issue must be settled based on other factors.

(2) Is there evidence of a fifth title at the beginning of Isaiah 9:7 (HB 6)? Some, based on Egyptian parallels, see a fifth title here. As the text stands, לְמַרְבֵּה הַמִּשְׂרָה, "to the increase of the dominion," makes for a good parallel with the following "to peace," but the final form of the *mem* in the *ketiv* of לְםַרְבֵּה makes the reading look suspiciously dittographic (note שָׁלוֹם at the end of 9:6 [HB 5]). There are at least a couple of emendations that would produce a fifth title (see Wildberger 1991, 387): (1) מַרְבֵּה הַמִּשְׂרָה, "the increase of the dominion," or, if a title, "one who increases dominion." But, if this were the original reading, it is difficult to account for the *lamed* in the present text, unless it was added to facilitate parallelism with "to peace." (2) רַב הַמִּשְׂרָה, "the great one of the dominion." (Wildberger [1991, 385, 405] prefers this reading, which he translates, "great in (his) sovereign authority.") In this case the initial *lamed-mem* on the first word is eliminated as dittographic, as is the final *he* (note the article on the following הַמִּשְׂרָה). But once we open the door to emendations, the most likely option is to read רַבָּה הַמִּשְׂרָה, "great will be the dominion," eliminating the initial *lamed-mem* as dittographic.

(3) Are the names theophoric? (See Gray [1912, 173], who attributes this view to Samuel David Luzzatto.) Such names, which were common in ancient Israel, would affirm something about God, not the ruler. In support of this approach, proponents emphasize that Mighty God (אֵל גִּבּוֹר) is a divine name in 10:21. William Holladay (1978, 108–9), who takes this approach, sees three names, the middle of which is theophoric: "Planner of Wonders, God the war hero (is) Father forever, prince of well-being." Paul Wegner (1992, 111) argues for two theophoric names, a proposal that produces better symmetry: "wonderful planner [is] the mighty God; the Father of eternity [is] a prince of peace." (See also Williamson 2018, 355, 398.) He explains that the two-part name "would be intended as a sign emphasizing God's greatness witnessed through his dealings with the nation of Israel, similar to how the names are used in the other sign oracles" in this context. However, as Wegner admits, applying the term שַׂר, "prince," to God is problematic (1992, 111–12). He suggests it is used in the general sense of ruler and chosen to set up a contrast with the human rulers "who are going to lead the nation into shame and defeat" (cf. 30:1–5; 31:1–3). Wegner calls this a "reasonable explanation" for שַׂר being applied to God, but the fact remains that it is more easily applied to a human ruler waiting to be enthroned or to one who is a שַׂר, "prince," in relation to God (see below). John Goldingay (1999, 241–42) understands all four expressions as describing God. He points to the use of אֵל גִּבּוֹר, "Mighty God," in 10:21 and father in 1:2–4, as well as God as planner in 28:29. He takes שַׂר in the military sense of commander, a divine function. Like Wegner, he prefers to arrange the names in two sentences: "One who plans a wonder is the warrior God; the father forever is a commander who brings peace."

Even if the names are theophoric, they must reflect to some degree what God accomplishes through the Davidic ruler. After all, the birth of this king prompts joy (note כִּי, "for," at the beginning of 9:6 [HB 5]) and is associated with the military victory described in the previous verses. Certainly, he is energized by God and as the instrument of divine victory he reflects in some way the characteristics described in the titles. Even if the titles do most naturally apply to God (and this is debatable with שַׂר שָׁלוֹם, "Prince of Peace"!), the divine attributes are embodied in the king who represents God and has been his instrument of victory over the enemy (see below). Since the focus is the (divinely empowered) king, it is best to see the titles applying to him.

There is strong contextual support for this: (1) Isaiah 9:7 (HB 6) focuses on the peace that will characterize the Davidic king's reign (cf. the title Prince of Peace). Isaiah 11, though not using שָׁלוֹם, "peace," develops this theme further. (2) The title אֵל גִּבּוֹר, "Mighty God," echoes the Gideon incident (see 9:4 [HB 3]), where Gideon was the instrument of divine victory (see Judg. 6:12, where גִּבּוֹר is used of Gideon). (3) Counselor (יוֹעֵץ) links with Isaiah 11:2, which refers to the spirit of counsel (עֵצָה) that the ideal king will possess. This will enable him to make wise and just decisions (cf. 9:7 [HB 6]). (4) Father (cf. Everlasting Father) is used in 22:21 of a coming leader who will be associated with the Davidic king.

It is best to see the names as titles describing the ideal Davidic king in his function as the Lord's representative. Symmetry is best achieved if we understand four titles, each of which has two components (see Gray 1912, 172; Smith 2007, 240; Young 1965, 333. All four relate to the king's function as a warrior.

Extraordinary Strategist. Within the immediate context, the first royal name is best understood as Extraordinary Strategist in a military sense. This title has traditionally been understood as two titles, "Wonderful, Counselor" (KJV). But the pattern of the following three titles, each of which has two elements, suggests the terms need to be combined into one title, literally "a wonder of a counselor," or "a wonder, that is, a counselor." The term פֶּלֶא, "wonder," refers to someone or something that is extraordinary. As one might expect, it is frequently used of God and his mighty deeds (Exod. 15:11; Pss. 77:11, 14 [HB 12, 15]; 89:5 [HB 6]; Isa. 25:1; 29:14). Here the term is qualified by יוֹעֵץ, "counselor," which is either genitival or appositional. In isolation one might think this word describes the king as one who gives wise advice in a general sense (cf. the use of the verb פָּלָא, "be extraordinary," with the noun עֵצָה, "counsel," in Isa. 28:29). But in this context, where the focus is the king's military prowess and success, the word probably refers specifically to the king's ability as a military strategist. In Isaiah 36:5 the noun עֵצָה, "counsel," is used of military strategy. So, this title depicts the king as one who can devise extraordinary military plans that allow him to defeat his enemies. As suggested by פֶּלֶא, "wonder," he can do so because the Lord Almighty energizes his every move (9:7 [HB 6]).

Mighty God. Since this title appears to refer to God in 10:21, applying it to the ideal king here might seem problematic. However, if the king is indeed God's representative, then it should not be surprising that a divine title is applied to him. In Psalm 45, a wedding song for a historical Davidic king on the occasion of his marriage to a princess, the psalmist addresses the king as "God" (45:6 [HB 7]), not because the Davidic king was viewed as actually divine but because he was God's chosen representative on earth. God supernaturally empowered him on the battlefield (45:5 [HB 6]), enabling him to conquer his enemies. As God's representative, the king was also responsible for promoting justice in his land (45:6–7 [Heb 7–8]). When people saw the Davidic king, they saw, as it were, God in the flesh. Ancient Near Eastern art and literature depict gods training and equipping kings for warfare and intervening in battle. In an Egyptian text, the Hittite enemy describes Ramses II as follows: "No man is he who is among us, It is Seth great-of-strength, Baal in person; Not deeds of man are these his doings, They are of one who is unique" (Lichtheim 1976, 67). The royal title Mighty God, when applied to the Davidic warrior-king, may well envision a similar response from those who see him (see Hayes and Irvine 1987, 181–82; Wildberger 1991, 404).

Of course, this idealistic image of the Davidic king was hardly reality in Israel's history, for many of the Davidic kings disobeyed God and the Davidic dynasty eventually fell to the Babylonians. In the progress of biblical revelation, we know that God's promise to David (see 2 Sam. 7; Ps. 89) is realized through Jesus. Since Jesus is the ultimate fulfillment of the vision of Isaiah 9:6, one might view this name as revealing his divine nature and as a proof text of his deity. However, in Isaiah's time the title would probably not have been understood in such a bold manner, but in a representative sense, as discussed above, and as hyperbolic. However, in its ultimate fulfillment in Jesus, it is notable that the title Mighty God is more than idealistic, royal hyperbole, for Jesus is God incarnate (see Roberts 2015, 153).

Everlasting Father. Isaiah uses the word "father" in an idiomatic manner that is attested in the ancient Near East. The title, when used of a prominent individual, especially a king, has the connotation "protector." Such a leader was responsible for protecting those dependent on his care.[3] In this context military protection is in view. In the original context the term "everlasting" would have been understood as royal hyperbole (see 1 Kings 1:31; Pss. 21:4–6 [HB 5–7]; 61:6–7 [HB 7–8]; 72:5, 17; cf. Wildberger 1991, 404). Of course, in the ultimate fulfillment of the prophecy the language is literally realized, for Jesus will reign eternally over his kingdom. Christians might be tempted to view this title in a Trinitarian sense and see it as alluding to Jesus's deity. However, to make this connection is theologically faulty, for Jesus, God's Son, is a distinct person from God the Father. Furthermore, to understand this title in a Trinitarian sense is anachronistic, for the doctrine of the Trinity was not clearly revealed until much later than Isaiah's day.

Prince of Peace. This title complements the preceding one nicely, for this king's fatherly protection of his realm will bring about an era of peace. "Peace" refers here to national security, which will be the primary benefit of his victories over the enemies of his people. Safe from the incursions of enemies, the people will be able to prosper (see also Isa. 26:3, 12; 32:17–18; 48:18; 52:7; 54:13 [cf. 54:14]; 60:17; 66:12). Ironically, genuine peace is realized through a mighty display of divine military power. Such is life in a fallen world where enemies oppose God and seek to destroy his people. We see this connection between military power and peace in Psalm 29 as well.

The use of שַׂר, "prince," rather than מֶלֶךְ, "king," is noteworthy. As stated above, if Hezekiah is the referent in Isaiah's eighth-century B.C. context (note "has been born" in 9:6 [HB 5]), this could point to the fact that he had not yet ascended the throne. However, there are other options: (1) R. A. Carlson (1974, 132–33), who sees an anti-Assyrian polemic in the names, understands this title as playing off the Akkadian word for king, *sharru*. (2) The term might point to the king as a שַׂר, or prince, in relation to Yahweh, the divine king (see Wildberger 1991, 402). (3) As suggested by Goldingay (see above), שַׂר may here be used in a militaristic sense to refer to a commander (cf. Gen. 21:22). (4) Wegner (see above) suggests it may play off the use of the term for Israel's flawed leaders for purposes of contrast (Isa. 30:1–5; 31:1–3).

Isaiah 9:7 (HB 6) specifies that this king would occupy David's throne and rule over his kingdom. Foundational to this vision of the revival of the Davidic dynasty's glory is God's irrevocable covenant with David, whereby he

---

3   For biblical examples of the idiom, see Isaiah 22:21 and Job 29:16. For examples in Northwest Semitic texts, see the inscriptions of Kilamuwa and Azitawadda in *COS* 2.30:147–50.

promised David and his descendants an enduring dynastic succession and universal dominion. This king would establish justice in his realm (cf. Isa. 11:1–9; see Goswell 2015, 109), in contrast to the corruption that characterized Jerusalem in Isaiah's day (see Isa. 1:17). Like David of old, he would establish "justice and righteousness" in his kingdom (cf. 2 Sam. 8:15).

The "zeal" of the Sovereign Lord would bring about the rule of this just king. On several occasions the Old Testament speaks of the Lord's zeal (the term is often translated "jealousy"). Sometimes God's zeal is associated with his anger against his enemies (Isa. 59:17), but on other occasions, as here, his zeal refers to his intense love for and commitment to his people. As Wildberger (1991, 407) says, "Where zeal is in action, there is no paralysis, no half-hearted lame effort." The Lord's zeal moves him to show compassion to (Joel 2:18; cf. Isa. 63:15), to seek reconciliation with (Zech. 8:2), to restore (Isa. 9:7; 37:32), and to protect and/or vindicate his people (Isa. 26:11; 42:13; Zech. 1:14). The word has a similar sense in Song of Songs 8:6, where it is used of human love. The Lord's passionate commitment to Israel and to the Davidic dynasty makes it certain that an ideal king will eventually rule from David's throne.

THEOLOGICAL FOCUS

The theological focus of this passage can be stated as follows: the Lord's people must focus on him when others are fearful and panicking, for the Lord controls his people's destiny and promises to establish a kingdom of justice and peace through the ideal Davidic king. As the prophet develops this theological theme, the following emphases emerge:

1. True security is found in the Lord.
This theme, which is prominent in Isaiah 7:1–8:10 (see above), continues in this passage. Judah's security was being threatened and people were fearful. Assyria's menacing presence was on the horizon, and closer to home the Israelite-Aramean alliance was pressuring Judah to join them. But Isaiah and the remnant of faith must trust in the Lord, for only in him can one find genuine security.

A corollary of this theme is that those who abandon faith in the Lord are doomed to fear, desperation, and disappointment. As judgment descended on Judah, those trusting in false sources of security would be swallowed up by panic and end up disillusioned as destruction swept over the land.

2. The reversal of judgment
Judgment would come on disobedient Judah, but it would not be final. The Lord would reverse his judgment upon the northern kingdom and replace the darkness with the light of deliverance. Salvation would come through a Davidic king empowered by the Lord.

3. The Lord's kingdom of justice and peace and the ideal Davidic king
The Lord would establish a kingdom of justice and peace through an ideal Davidic warrior-king who defeats Israel's enemies. A corollary of this theme is the Lord's faithfulness to his promise to David. The Lord chose David and his dynasty to rule his covenant people and he promised David and his descendants a special relationship with him (2 Sam. 7:14; Ps. 89:26–27 [HB 27–28]), an eternal dynasty (2 Sam. 7:11–16; Ps. 89:28–37 [HB 29–38]), and worldwide dominion (Pss. 2, 72). However, moral failure on the part of the king would bring divine discipline and postpone the full realization of the promises (2 Sam. 7:14; Ps. 89:38–51[HB 39–52]). Yet despite the failure of historical Davidic kings to live up to the ideal, the prophets make it clear that God would someday raise up a Davidic king through whom his promises would be realized.

PREACHING AND TEACHING STRATEGIES

Exegetical and Theological Synthesis

This unit begins (Isa. 8:11–13) with a strong warning from God not to fear what most of the people feared. It is unclear to what the conspiracy (8:12) refers (see discussion above). However, Isaiah 7 suggests it was political in nature. Similarly, the fear that was commonplace among many at this time was probably due to the geopolitical unrest caused by the Syrian-Israelite alliance against Judah and/or the potential ramifications of Judah's alliance with Assyria. Instead of fearing the potential consequences of a foreign invasion or a coup to replace their king, the people should have feared the Lord alone. After all, he is sovereign over any king or foreign nation. Yahweh would become a sanctuary for those who chose to put their confidence in him. However, putting their trust in political leaders and/or alliances with foreign powers would backfire on them. That decision would become a stumbling block or a "snare" (8:14–15).

Isaiah 8:16–22 lays out a stark contrast between those who walk by faith and those who walk by sight. Those who put their faith in the Lord and who feared him would look to God's Word and put confidence in his promises. They must bind up the testimony of God and seal his teachings in their hearts (8:16). Specifically, this included the promises God had given to Ahaz and Judah through the children who served as "signs and symbols" of things to come (8:18; cf. Isa. 7:4–16; 8:1–4, 9–10). It also included the promises of a bright future for Judah's inhabitants after God's judgment passed, particularly for those who remained faithful to the Lord (Isa. 9:1–7 [HB 8:23–9:6]; cf. 1:18–19, 24–27; 2:1–5, 10–17; 3:10; 4:2–6).

Those who rejected the Lord and his promises and chose instead to trust in political leaders, movements, and foreign nations would have a different destiny. People desperately needed guidance, and they wanted reassurance about their future. But when they rejected God's revelation as Ahaz did, to what sources of information could they turn? They were forced to inquire from "mediums and spiritists," hoping that the spirits of the dead could communicate with them (8:19). Unfortunately for them, any revelation they received would only lead to more darkness, not light. They would have no dawn (8:20). Instead, they would experience distress and hunger, both for food (7:21–23) and for answers to their problems (8:21). Rather than bow before God in humility, seeking wisdom from him, they looked to the earth for answers, which would leave them groping in utter darkness without truth (8:22).

This passage concludes (9:1–7 [HB 8:23–9:6]) with a promise for the people who remained faithful to God. For them, the gloom and sadness would give way to light and celebration. This future is described in terms that present a stark contrast to all who anchored their hope in earthly political leaders and coalitions rather than in the Lord. Whereas their futures would be marked by distress, anguish, gloom, and darkness (8:22), the coming future kingdom of God would be a time of "no more gloom" (9:1 [HB 8:23]), of "light" (twice; 9:2 [HB 1]), joy, gladness, and rejoicing (9:3 [HB 2]). This would happen when God breaks "the bar across their shoulders" and the "rod of their oppressor" (9:4 [HB 3]).

This would all be made possible by yet another "son" who would providentially be born (9:6–7 [HB 5–6]; cf. 7:3, 14–16; 8:1–4). Here a victorious king is in view. Consider how many words in these two verses associate this child with ruling authority: "government," "prince," "throne," and "kingdom." This child will become a great ruler whose government will bring about everlasting peace (9:7 [HB 6]). It will also be a kingdom in which righteousness and justice reign supreme. Previous chapters have confronted Israel's leaders for their oppression and injustice (1:17, 21, 23; 3:5, 14–15; 5:7, 23). This will all be eliminated in the coming kingdom ruled by a future Davidic heir.

Four distinct names used to describe this king accentuate his mastery as a military leader. First, he will be called a "Wonderful Counselor" or an "Extraordinary Strategist." This term likely points to his wisdom as a war strategist. He will also be known as a "Mighty God." This title may seem out of place for what would have been expected to be a mere mortal. However, it wasn't unprecedented to describe a human king in divine language, as kings were often viewed as representatives of God/gods. This king will be mighty in battle as he is empowered by God to be his representative to defeat Israel's enemies. A third title for this king will be "Everlasting Father." "Father" wouldn't have been understood by the original audience in a Trinitarian sense. Rather, the description of him as a father would have implied his role as a protector. Additionally, the term "everlasting" would have probably been thought of as hyperbole. Finally, this coming leader would be described as a "Prince of Peace." The result of his military victory(ies) will be peace for the kingdom over which he ruled. As a result, the citizens of this coming kingdom will be free to pursue a worship of God and their own happiness in a context of righteousness and safety.

Preaching Idea

Amid political unrest, God's people must not fear but instead rest in the Lord and his promise of a glorious coming kingdom.

Contemporary Connections

What does it mean?
For the people of Judah during the reign of King Ahaz, there was significant political unrest. Assyria was growing in power and influence and was quickly becoming a legitimate threat to attack smaller nations such as Judah. For this reason, Israel and Syria joined together as a coalition to be better positioned to resist Assyria should it attack. Pekah and Rezin, the kings of Israel and Syria, approached Ahaz with a demand that Judah join their coalition. However, Ahaz refused, choosing rather to align his people with the king of Assyria, the nation that Pekah and Rezin were attempting to hold off. In response, Israel and Syria attacked several towns in Judah, resulting in 200,000 people from Judah along with much spoil being carried off to Damascus (2 Chron. 28:5, 8). Additionally, Pekah slaughtered about 120,000 Judean people in a single day (2 Chron. 28:6).

It is quite understandable why the remaining people in Judah would have been frightened by all the political unrest in their day. The implications were nothing less than life-altering. Would their existing king remain in power, or would he be replaced by someone who didn't represent their interests? Would they retain their rights as free people, or would they become slaves to a cruel tyrant? Would a new leader impose higher taxes on them, driving them further into poverty? Unsurprisingly, there was disagreement about how the current leadership should have responded to the present crises. Most seemed to agree with Ahaz's decision to turn to Assyria for help, ignoring Isaiah's warning to put his hope exclusively in the Lord. They may have even called Isaiah's warnings about a future attack by Assyria an unwarranted conspiracy theory (Isa. 8:12). Nevertheless, there were a few disciples of Isaiah (Isa. 8:16) who believed in the veracity of his warnings.

In the end, rather than turn to the Lord in his time of desperation, Ahaz chose to call on the nation of Assyria for help (2 Kings 16:7–8). Initially, this must have seemed prudent to most in Judah, as Tiglath-pileser, king of Assyria, responded favorably to Ahaz. He sent his army to attack Damascus, the capital city of Syria, and carried off many of those people (Judah's enemies) as captives, killing King Rezin in the process (2 Kings 16:9). This would have felt like validation to all who were dismissive of Isaiah's warnings. However, in the end, this decision proved to be foolish and costly, as the Assyrians were no friend to Judah. Rather than act as Judah's deliverer and protector, the Lord would instead summon Assyria into Judah to invade it, humiliating the people and devastating their land (Isa. 7:18–25; 8:5–10).

While the specific political issues and the geopolitical actors change over time, people in every age are forced to grapple with the same basic question: Who or what should we fear most? Will we fear God, or will we fear things like human leaders, geopolitical threats posed by foreign powers, or the impact of things like lost freedoms and higher taxes?

While it is true that political leaders and policies have the power to impact our lives and well-being for the immediate future, there are two realities that should infuse believers with peace and hope concerning their future. First, the reality that God is sovereign over every human leader reassures us that nothing can happen that he has not caused or at least allowed. Even more importantly, this sovereign God has revealed that every corrupt and oppressive government will one day be defeated and replaced by a perfect kingdom ruled by God himself in the person of Jesus Christ. His kingdom will be established and upheld with justice and righteousness forever and ever (Isa. 9:7 [HB 6]). These truths eliminate the need for fear and anxiety regardless of the political crises of the day.

Is it true?

It is true that politics can make a significant impact on a person's everyday life. Politics can impact people's freedom, as well as the economy. Politics can dictate how much of their own personal paychecks people get to keep. Will individuals be free to pursue their dreams or even to worship according to their conscience? Politics might affect a person's access to things like healthcare, food stamps, or affordable housing. Whether there is war or peace between rival nations often comes down to political decisions.

These are serious issues by anyone's estimation. Some of them could be the difference between life and death. We would be foolish to downplay them as trivial.

It is understandable, then, why people are prone to fear having the wrong political leaders in power and/or being forced to endure undesirable political outcomes. And yet Jesus urged his followers not to fear those who had the authority to take their lives. Rather, they were to fear God, who has the power to destroy both soul and body in hell (Matt. 10:28). The principle that Jesus warned about is very similar to what we see in Isaiah 8:12–13. Rather than fear the potential outcomes from all the political unrest in one's world, one should fear God instead.

But, is it really true that we need not fear the implications of the political unrest in the world around us? The answer to this is, "Yes, believers in God do not need to fear the implications of politics," for at least two important reasons:

(1) First, the Bible is clear that God is sovereign over all kingdoms and world politics. In Daniel 4:17, King Nebuchadnezzar rightly discerned that "the Most High is sovereign over all kingdoms on earth and gives them to anyone he wishes and sets over them the lowliest of people." Proverbs 21:1 similarly says, "In the LORD's hand the king's heart is a stream of water that he channels toward all who please him." In other words, it may seem that this world's politics are a mess and that there is no rhyme or reason to the foolish and even harmful decisions made by earthly leaders. However, in truth, everything is happening under the watchful and sovereign eyes of the Lord. In fact, the Bible makes it clear that God was the one superintending the various political events in the early days of King Ahaz.

For example, when the ruler of Syria, Rezin, along with Israel's King Pekah, decided to attack God's people in Judah, killing 120,000 of them and carrying off 200,000 women and children to Damascus along with much spoil (2 Chron. 28:6–8), this was ultimately initiated by God. Second Kings 15:37 says, "In those days the LORD began to send Rezin king of Aram and Pekah son of Remaliah against Judah." Notice how it was the Lord who sent Rezin and Pekah against Judah. Additionally, 2 Chronicles 28:5 says,

> Therefore the LORD his God delivered him [King Ahaz] into the hands of the king of Aram. The Arameans defeated him and took many of his people as prisoners and brought them to Damascus. He was also given into the hands of the king of Israel, who inflicted heavy casualties on him. (See as well 2 Chron. 28:9.)

Again, clearly God gave Ahaz into the hand of the kings of Syria and Israel. These events didn't just transpire haphazardly or randomly. Rather, God was directly and sovereignly involved in them. Second Chronicles 28:19 explains further why the Lord did this: "The LORD had humbled Judah because of Ahaz king of Israel, for he had promoted wickedness in Judah and had been most unfaithful to the LORD."

As mentioned above, in response to the attacks by Israel and Syria, Ahaz turned to Assyria for help. Tiglath-pileser obliged by sending his own troops to Damascus, killing King Rezin and taking many people there captive. It would seem from a human standpoint that God wasn't involved in this. After all, the prophet Isaiah had urged King Ahaz to simply trust in the Lord for deliverance, not the military strength of a foreign, pagan nation like Assyria. Nevertheless, Isaiah described the coming attack by Assyria against Syria in this way,

> Because this people has rejected the gently flowing waters of Shiloah, and rejoices over Rezin and the son of Remaliah, therefore the Lord is about to bring against them the mighty floodwaters of the Euphrates—the king of Assyria with all his pomp. (Isa. 8:6–7)

Once again, we are assured the Lord would bring the king of Assyria against King Rezin like a powerful, fast-flowing river. Politically speaking, things certainly appear at times to be happening outside of the control or oversight of a good and powerful God. However, appearances can be deceiving. For behind the scenes stands an ever-present, all-wise God who is working all things out for the eventual good of his people (Rom. 8:28).

(2) Above all else, though, followers of Jesus need not fear the political threats or uncertainties of our day because we know who will win in the end. As a devoted Penn State football fan, 2016 was a memorable year, as the Nittany Lions were ultimately crowned the Big Ten champions. However, the season didn't appear very promising after a 2–2 start including a blowout 49–10 loss to the Michigan Wolverines. One especially exciting game for Penn State fans was a week 7 matchup against their biggest rival, the Ohio State Buckeyes, who just happened to be undefeated that year and were ranked number 2 in the nation. After three quarters, Penn State was losing by two touchdowns, 21–7. In the fourth quarter, Penn State somehow narrowed the deficit to only four by scoring ten unanswered points. However, with just under five minutes left in the game, Ohio State was positioned inside the thirty-yard line to kick a forty-five-yard field goal to go up by seven points. This is where the improbable happened. A Penn State player blocked the field goal attempt, and another player was able to scoop the ball up and run it nearly seventy yards for a momentum-changing touchdown. Penn State was now leading the Buckeyes by three points, having erased the fourteen-point deficit it carried into the fourth quarter. Penn State's defense would carry that momentum into the final drive of the game, leading to a huge upset win.

As a fan, I have watched that game several times in the years since. Every time, I roll my eyes and shake my head at some of the sloppy plays and missed opportunities that plagued my team throughout the first half. However, while I'm frustrated with my team, I'm not scared or nervous about the outcome. Why? Because I already know the final score. The outcome is no longer in question. I know with complete confidence that all will work out for my team in the end. My team will be celebrating when the clock strikes zero, while the opposing team will exit the field frustrated and sad.

The same holds true in politics. While history has yet to record these events, God has revealed how the world's political scene will ultimately unfold. For a time, God will allow various world rulers to dominate and oppress his people. Things will often appear bleak and hopeless. It will appear to many that we are on the losing team. However, amid the gloom, a bright light of hope will eventually shine (Isa. 9:2 [HB 1]). Those who are sad and pessimistic about their political environment will have reason to break out into rejoicing (Isa. 9:3 [HB 2]). The king will break onto the world's scene and defeat every evil and corrupt political leader. In their place, he will establish an everlasting kingdom marked by righteousness and justice (Isa. 9:6–7 [HB 5–6]).

Now what?
How is it possible to tell someone to fear God alone? How are people supposed to stop being afraid of something potentially harmful or even deadly? Fears aren't usually thought of as things people can just turn on or off. Try telling a person who is deathly afraid of flying to just relax while on a plane. Or ask a person who is petrified of public speaking to deliver a speech in front of a large crowd and just choose not to be afraid. If it were that simple, people would just choose never to be afraid, but of course it isn't that simple. Most people can't simply choose to be afraid or not be afraid of things. Why then would God tell his people not to be afraid of the things most others feared, and to fear him instead?

It's important at this point to define what is meant by "fear." My friend Jason Alley, who is on our church's pastoral staff, developed a helpful, biblically based definition of fear while preparing for a sermon series on the topic. Here is what he concluded:

> Fear is an overwhelming psychological impulse to change our circumstances or behavior in response to an outside person or event. Because of this or that stimuli, we can't remain as we are. Fear drives us to act contrary to our desires or even our convictions. God alone claims the right to overwhelm our sense of who we are and what we think is right. When we submit to another object of fear in a way that we should only submit to God that is idolatry.

The key is to understand that when the Bible says we aren't to fear certain things, it isn't referring to feelings or impulses that are mostly beyond a person's control. Rather, God is speaking to the behaviors that we choose due to those impulses. A courageous person isn't one who doesn't ever feel frightened in the face of danger. Rather, he or she has the fortitude to do the right thing regardless of how difficult or potentially costly that action is. Thus, when God says that his people are not to fear things like political threats from powerful enemy kings, he isn't concerned with our feelings so much as he is our actions. Will the impulses of fear drive us to disobey God in favor of obeying the object of our fear? Or will we deny those impulses in favor of obedience to God? Practically, this is what it means for us to fear God. It is to choose obedience to him and to maintain confidence in him above all else, despite any and every other rival we may be tempted to fear.

Thus, we must ask ourselves, do we really believe that God is sovereign regardless of who rules our land? Do we believe that God is at work even when the "better" candidate loses? When bad laws and harmful policies are enacted is it a sign that God is failing? If the political system becomes broken because of corruption or cheating, does this mean that God is somehow limited in accomplishing his ultimate purposes?

Most Christians know what the right answers are to these questions. They would claim to believe that God is still sovereign and is actively at work, regardless of the current political environment. But just as James argued that a person's works prove they really have faith (James 2:14–26), isn't it also true that one's fears are an indication of where their faith really lies? If a person has significant anxiety and fear about the future depending on which political party is in power, this evidences that they are trusting in those political leaders (along with their policies) to bring them a good, safe, and meaningful life. But as believers, aren't we supposed to look to God alone for those things, at least in an ultimate sense? God can work through earthly governments to bring about a better or safer life. When he chooses to work in this way, his people should rejoice and be thankful. But what happens when he doesn't choose to work in this way? Are his promises to provide for our needs no longer binding? Are the hopes of his people suddenly dashed? Of course not! God is still on the throne. He maintains control even when evil tyrants or inept representatives are in power.

Thus, believers need to guard their attitudes and actions in relation to politics. We must not allow ourselves to get caught up in the fear and anger surrounding political discourse that is typical of our society. If we genuinely fear God above all else, and if we truly believe that the sovereign, righteous Lord is working out a plan that will culminate in the return of the Lord Jesus to rule over this world forever, then it will show itself in our calm and collected demeanor regardless of which human is in power at any given time.

Similarly, Christians need to seriously consider whether they have elevated politics to the level of a modern-day idol. Fear is often an indicator of whom or what a person worships. The phrase "to fear God" in the Bible essentially means "to worship God."[4] When we elevate anything besides God to the status of an ultimate thing, something we feel we must have, then we have essentially turned that person/thing into an idol. People might elevate the need for a career that holds a certain level of prestige into an ultimate thing. For some, it is being in a romantic relationship. For others, it might be maintaining a certain standard of living, or possibly just being liked by lots of people or being a part of the popular crowd at school. For many adults today, including many Christians, politics is an area that can easily evolve from simply being something that we think and care about into something that we view as an ultimate thing.

Tim Keller comments on this phenomenon in his book *Counterfeit Gods: The Empty Promises of Money, Sex, and Power, and the Only Hope that Matters*:

> One of the signs that an object is functioning as an idol is that fear becomes one of the chief characteristics of life. When we center our lives on the idol, we become dependent on it. If our counterfeit god is threatened in any way, our response is complete panic. We do not say, "What a shame, how difficult," but rather "This is the end! There's no hope!"

This may be a reason why so many people now respond to U.S. political trends in such an extreme way. When either party wins an election, a certain percentage of

---

4   Cf. Gen. 22:12; Job 1:1; Eccl. 12:13; Acts 10:2; 13:16, 26; 1 Peter 2:17; Rev. 11:18; 14:7; 15:4; 19:5.

the losing side talks openly about leaving the country. They become agitated and fearful for the future. They have put the kind of hope in their political leaders and policies that once was reserved for God and the work of the gospel. When their political leaders are out of power, they experience a death. They believe that if their policies and people are not in power, everything will fall apart. (2009, 98–99)

The apostle Peter's admonition to the people of his own day is fitting for believers today:

But even if you should suffer for what is right, you are blessed. "Do not fear their threats; do not be frightened." But in your hearts revere Christ as Lord. Always be prepared to give an answer to everyone who asks you to give the reason for the hope that you have. But do this with gentleness and respect, keeping a clear conscience, so that those who speak maliciously against your good behavior in Christ may be ashamed of their slander. For it is better, if it is God's will, to suffer for doing good than for doing evil. (1 Peter 3:14–17)

When Peter wrote his epistle, Nero was the emperor of the Roman Empire. Nero was a wicked man who hated Christians. Yet Peter urged his readers to have no fear of those who would persecute them. Rather, they were to honor Christ the Lord as holy. In other words, they needed to remember that Jesus is the true Lord, and he alone is to be regarded as holy. Additionally, they needed to always be ready to explain their reason for hope and optimism to the lost and unbelieving world around them who wouldn't understand their faith and confidence in Jesus in the midst of such persecution. If they were called to suffer because of their Christian faith, they were to count this as part of God's will for their lives.

There is much here that we can take to heart in our own day as well. We must remember that if evil people get into power, the world is not over; God is still at work. If we ultimately lose our rights and religious freedoms, even our very lives, it is most important for us to remember that an unbelieving world is watching our response. For our brothers and sisters in some parts of the world, this sort of persecution and suffering is not merely a possible reality in the future. Their experience as a committed believer involves some painful and sad realities of mistreatment and injustice. Their courage in the midst of such hardship is a testament to their love for and faith in Jesus which he promises to reward greatly on the day of judgment. We must all remember Jesus's promise, "Blessed are those who are persecuted for righteousness' sake, for theirs is the kingdom of heaven" (Mt. 5:10).

Creativity in Presentation

Campaign Slogans

When politicians run for office, they typically adopt a campaign slogan meant to summarize what they hope to accomplish if elected to rally supporters around their candidacy. Consider opening the sermon with campaign slogans from past elections. Talk about the issues to which those slogans were alluding. What emotions were these slogans attempting to tap into? Some examples might include, "Free Soil, Free Labor, Free Speech, Free Men, Fremont," by John Fremont in 1856, who was highlighting the antislavery views of his party. Another was "Vote yourself a farm and horses," by Abraham Lincoln in 1860, referring to his party's support for a law that would grant homesteads on the American frontier. Still another was "I am for Wilson and an 8-hour day," by Woodrow Wilson in 1912, highlighting his support for laws regulating the length of a working day to prevent excesses and abuses against working-class folk. In 1916 Wilson used "War in the East, Peace in the West, Thank God for Woodrow Wilson," highlighting his commitment to keep America out of World War I. In 1920 Warren Harding used "Return to Normalcy," appealing to the desire of most to return to better times of peace following World War I.

Isaiah 9:6–7 (HB 5–6) essentially provides us with a "campaign slogan" for the greatest leader who will ever rule. He will be the Extraordinary Strategist, Mighty God, Everlasting Father, and Prince of Peace. His rule will bring about justice, righteousness, and peace for all people forevermore. All the things that prior kings and politicians hoped and promised to provide will actually and finally be fulfilled in this one ruler for all time.

Statistics on Fear

According to the Chapman University Survey of American Fears conducted in 2021, the top thing that people fear more than anything else is the threat of corrupt government officials. Four out of every five of those who participated in the survey indicated they fear corrupt government officials.

The top ten fears of which Americans reported being "Afraid" or "Very Afraid" include:

Top Ten Fears of 2020/2021	% Very Afraid or Afraid
1. Corrupt government officials	79.6%
2. People I love dying	58.5%
3. A loved one contracting the coronavirus (COVID-19)	58%
4. People I love becoming seriously ill	57.3%
5. Widespread civil unrest	56.5%
6. A pandemic or a major epidemic	55.8%
7. Economic/financial collapse	54.8%
8. Cyberterrorism	51%
9. Pollution of oceans, rivers, and lakes	50.8%
10. Biological warfare	49.3%

Most of the things on this list are closely related to issues of American and global politics. Americans are evidently far more fearful of the negative impact government can have on their lives than they are of many of the things more often thought of as common fears.[5]

Movie

In the movie *Back to the Future Part II*, Biff (played by Thomas Wilson) discovers a sports almanac that Marty McFly (played by Michael J. Fox) brought back with him from the future. With it, Biff was able to amass a huge fortune and acquire unmatched power in very short order by confidently gambling on numerous sporting events. With his wealth comes immense power and influence in society, which he selfishly uses for evil. This illustrates the power that would come to anyone who could confidently predict the future. It

---

5 https://www.chapman.edu/wilkinson/research-centers/babbie-center/_files/Babbie%20center%20fear2021/blogpost-americas-top-fears-2020_-21-final.pdf.

explains why people in Isaiah's time would be tempted to inquire of necromancers and mediums to discover and control the future. It likewise illustrates the appeal that psychic readings or horoscopes provide people still today. However, it also highlights the value of God's revealed Word and the testimony about his coming kingdom. The prophetic promises contained within God's Word have significant power to guide believers into wise choices in the present as they invest themselves in the things that will ultimately last. In the same way that Biff was able to confidently invest his money in the winning team time and time again, so too God's people who rely on his revelation can confidently invest themselves in God's promises even when they appear to be failing. Amid political unrest, God's people must not fear but instead rest in the Lord and his promise of a glorious, coming kingdom.

- When tempted with political fears, actively fear God instead (8:13–15).
- When tempted with political fears, cling to God's word (8:16–22).
- When tempted with political fears, remember who wins in the end (9:1–7).

DISCUSSION QUESTIONS

1. Why do politics hold so much sway over the hearts and minds of people?

2. Describe the ideal politician. What character traits would they have? What skills would they possess? How would they interact with people?

3. As you think about your answers to number 2 above: In what ways did Jesus exemplify those ideals, character traits, and skills during his time on earth?

4. How should the image of Jesus in Isaiah 9:6–7 and the promise of a glorious kingdom impact your perspective on political issues today?

5. What does it mean to fear God? How does a fear of God relate to other common fears that people often hold?

FOR FURTHER READING

Keller, Timothy. 2009. *Counterfeit Gods: The Empty Promises of Money, Sex, and Power, and the Only Hope That Matters*. New York: Penguin.

Isaiah 9:8 (HB 7)–10:4

EXEGETICAL IDEA
Culminating, devastating judgment was ready to fall on the northern kingdom (9:8–9 [HB 7–8]; 10:1–4) because the people had persisted in evil, despite the Lord's attempts to bring them to repentance.

THEOLOGICAL FOCUS
The Lord designs judgment to bring his people to repentance, but when they respond defiantly and persist in rebellion he must intensify his judgment.

PREACHING IDEA
Only by repentance will God's wrath be appeased.

PREACHING POINTERS
The eighteenth-century pastor and theologian Jonathan Edwards preached his most famous sermon, "Sinners in the Hands of an Angry God," about God's wrath and imminent hellfire judgment against the unrepentant. Responses to that message have unsurprisingly been mixed. While many praise it for its passion and vivid imagery, others have criticized Edwards's view of God as overly cruel and angry as he stands ready to unleash his fury against sinners. One such critic was the satirical author Phyllis McGinley, who wrote a poem mocking the now-famous sermon titled "The Theology of Jonathan Edwards."[1]

It isn't popular to speak about God's wrath today, and it probably never has been. Even in the church, people would much rather hear sermons about God's love, mercy, and patience than to hear about his wrath and judgment. Many mistakenly assume that sermons about God's wrath and the reality of eternal hellfire is more of an invention by morbid or controlling preachers than an authentic biblical doctrine. However, passages like Isaiah 9:8 (HB 7)–10:4 reveal that God's wrath against sin and his coming judgment against sinners is a reality that needs to be embraced and responded to by people in every generation. For it is only when people repent of their sins that God's wrath will be appeased.

---

1 The poem can be read in its entirety online: http://www.amerlit.com/poems/POEMS%20McGinley,%20Phyllis%20The%20Theology%20of%20Jonathan%20Edwards%20(1957)%20wit.pdf.

"HIS HAND IS STILL UPRAISED": PERSISTENT JUDGMENT ON PERSISTENT SIN (9:8 [HB 7]–10:4)

Culminating, devastating judgment was ready to fall on the northern kingdom (9:8–9 [HB 7–8]; 10:1–4) because the people had persisted in evil, despite the Lord's attempts to bring them to repentance. Prior to the forming of the Israelite-Aramean alliance, the Lord punished Israel through the Arameans and Philistines (9:10–12 [HB 9–11]). Yet Israel responded defiantly and refused to repent (9:13 [HB 12]), prompting a second round of judgment (9:14–17 [HB 13–16]). Throughout this period, both before and after the Aramean alliance, evil swept like fire through the land (9:18 [HB 17]) as internal dissension threatened the covenant community (9:19–21 [HB 18–20]). But the nation responded to judgment with false confidence (9:10 [HB 9]) as its leaders continued to act unjustly (10:1–2).

LITERARY STRUCTURE AND THEMES (9:8 [HB 7]–10:4)

The structure of this literary unit is clearly marked by a recurring refrain, "Yet for all this, his anger is not turned away, his hand is still upraised" (9:12, 17, 21 [HB 11, 16, 20]; 10:4). The unit begins with an announcement that the Lord had spoken a word of judgment that would fall upon the northern kingdom (9:8–9 [HB 7–8]). The following verses (9:10–21 [HB 9–20]) explain why this judgment was necessary. Contrary to some translations, which understand 9:10–21 (HB 9–20) as predominately prophetic (cf. KJV, NIV11; Gray 1912, 177, 181) or descriptive of the present (cf. NASB), these verses are best understood, for the most part, as historical. Past judgment had not prompted the people to repent and do what is right, so a culminating judgment was about to bring death to the northern kingdom (10:1–4). The structure of the unit may be outlined as follows. (For a defense of underlying exegetical decisions, see the commentary.)

Part One (9:8–12 [HB 7–11])

A   Announcement of impending judgment upon the northern kingdom (9:8–9a [HB 7–8a])

B   Accusation: A proud, defiant response to prior judgment (9:9b–10 [HB 8b–9])

C   Description of the first round of judgment (9:11–12a [HB 10–11a])

D   Refrain: The necessity of more judgment (9:12b [HB 11b])

Part Two (9:13–17 [HB 12–16])

A   Accusation: The people's response to prior (that is, the first wave of) judgment (9:13 [HB 12])

B   Description of the second round of judgment and its aftermath (9:14–16 [HB 13–15])

C   Description of the Lord's current attitude toward the people (9:17a [HB 16a])

D   Refrain: The necessity of more judgment (9:17b [HB 16b])

Part Three (9:18–21 [HB 17–20])

A   Accusation: Widespread evil ravaged the land (9:18 [HB 17])

B   Description of prior judgment (9:19a [HB 18a])

C   Accusation: Internal dissension that caused prior judgment (9:19b–21a [HB 18b–20a])

D   Refrain: The necessity of more judgment (9:21b [HB 20b])

"His Hand Is Still Upraised": Persistent Judgment on Persistent Sin (9:8 [HB 7]–10:4)

Part Four (10:1–4)

A Accusation: Widespread injustice (10:1–2)
B Announcement of impending judgment (10:3–4a)
C Refrain: The necessity of more judgment (10:4b)

There are some structural patterns that deserve comment: (1) The first and third panels focus on the people in general (9:9, 19 [HB 8, 18]), while the second and fourth panels focus on the leaders of the nation (9:14–16 [HB 13–15]; 10:1). (2) The first and third panels mention Ephraim (9:9, 21 [HB 8, 20]) and include a "devouring" motif (9:12, 20–21 [HB 11, 19–20]). (3) The second and fourth panels refer to widows and the fatherless (9:17 [HB 16]; 10:2).

- *False Confidence During the Aftermath of Judgment (9:8–12 [HB 7–11])*
- *Failure to Repent (9:13–17 [HB 12–16])*
- *Internal Dissension (9:18–21 [HB 17–20])*
- *Imminent Death (10:1–4)*

EXPOSITION (9:8 [HB 7]–10:4)

The prophet announced impending, culminating judgment (9:8–9 [HB 7–8]; cf. 10:1–4). This anticipates the Assyrian victory over the northern kingdom in 722 B.C. The Lord had already punished his people, but they had responded to judgment with smug, false confidence (9:10 [HB 9]). The prophet traced the history of recent judgment. There was a first phase when Aram and Philistia attacked the northern kingdom (9:11–12a [HB 10–11a]). This predated the alliance between Israel under Pekah and Aram under Rezin. More judgment was needed (9:12b [HB 11b]) because the people refused to repent (9:13 [HB 12]). The Lord brought a second round through the Assyrian king Tiglath-pileser III in 734–732, targeting the leaders who had misled the people (9:14–16 [HB 13–15]). But sin persisted, further alienating the Lord from the nation and making more judgment necessary (9:17 [HB 16]). The prophet surveyed the recent past, recalling how wickedness had swept through the land, prompting the Lord's wrath (9:18–19 [HB 17–18]). The underlying sin of the nation was greed (9:20), which manifested itself in the internal dissension that characterized the northern kingdom and then, when Israel allied with Aram, threatened Judah (9:21a [HB 20a]). This greed had produced rampant injustice within society (10:1–2), making more judgment necessary (9:21b [HB 20b]; 10:3–4).

False Confidence During the Aftermath of Judgment (9:8–12 [HB 7–11])

Israel's defiant response to judgment necessitated more judgment.

9:8–9 (HB 7–8). This new literary unit opens with the declaration that the Sovereign Master (אֲדֹנָי) "has sent a message against Jacob." The title אֲדֹנָי highlights the Lord's sovereign authority over his people (cf. 3:15, 17–18; 4:4; 6:1, 8, 11; 7:7, 14, 20; 8:7). The expression "send against" (שָׁלַח בְּ-) indicates this is a message (literally, "word") of judgment. This message would "fall on" Israel. The expression "fall upon" (נָפַל בְּ-) views the message as hostile, like an army that attacks its enemy (cf. Josh. 11:7). The prophecy of judgment has been proclaimed; it awaits fulfillment. If we understand this opening declaration as forming an *inclusio* with the woe oracle in 10:1–4, then it is likely that the judgment yet to fall is the Assyrian conquest of the northern kingdom in 722–721 B.C. The identity of the referent of "Jacob/Israel" is unclear in 9:8 (HB 7), but 9:9 (HB 8) specifies that Ephraim and Samaria (i.e., the northern kingdom) are in view.

This judgment would be evident to everyone (literally, "they will know, the people, all of them") in the northern kingdom (9:9 [HB 8]). Ephraim is singled out because of its prominent place among the northern tribes, and Samaria is mentioned because it was the

"His Hand Is Still Upraised": Persistent Judgment on Persistent Sin (9:8 [HB 7]–10:4)

capital. The prophet then gives us the first hint of why judgment would fall. The people of the northern kingdom are characterized by pride and arrogance of heart. Human pride is consistently depicted in a negative light; the Lord denounces and opposes the proud, who eventually fall from their lofty position (cf. Isa. 13:11; 16:6; 25:11).

9:10 (HB 9). This pride is evident in the words of the people. They had experienced two waves of the Lord's judgment (the details of which are given in 9:11–12a, 14–15, 19a [HB 10–11a, 13–14, 18a]), but they had not responded properly. Rather than repenting (see 9:13 [HB 12]), they defiantly boasted that they would rebuild their walls and houses and make them even more impressive than before. Where sunbaked bricks had once been used, the people would now use hewn stone (cf. Amos 5:11). They had formerly used sycamore-fig trees for lumber, but now, they boasted, they would replace their roofs with expensive cedar wood.

9:11–12 (HB 10–11). The prophet goes back in time and begins a review of prior judgments that brought about the destruction alluded to in 9:10 (HB 9). The verb forms (note the *wayyiqtol* forms in 9:11a and 12a [HB 10a, 11a]) point to the past. The Lord had "raised up [cf. NIV11, 'strengthened'] adversaries of Rezin" against his people and "spurred on" (the form יְסַכְסֵךְ is the *pilpel* of סוּךְ, "provoke"; cf. Isa. 19:2) their enemies. Rezin was the Aramean king who later made an alliance with King Pekah of Israel (cf. 7:1–8; 8:6) to counter the Assyrian threat in the west. One might think that the "adversaries of Rezin" would then be the Assyrians. However, it is apparent in 9:12 (HB 11) that the Arameans were attacking Israel from the east, as the Philistines attacked from the west, and devouring them as it were. So, the adversaries here are not Rezin's enemies but rather adversaries sent from Rezin (genitive of source). This must refer to a period before the Israelite-Aramean alliance, when the Arameans were enemies of Israel whom the Lord used to punish his people. Prior to the rise of Pekah to Israel's throne, Menahem had adopted a pro-Assyrian policy (2 Kings 15:19–20) that brought him into conflict with other western states that preferred to resist Assyria (Bright 1981, 272). When Pekah came to the throne, he shifted allegiance from Assyria to the neighboring states, one of which was Aram.

This earlier judgment (as well as an additional round of judgment that followed, see 9:14–17 [HB 13–16]) did not have a positive effect on the people (see 9:10, 13 [HB 9, 12]). Consequently, the Lord's anger had not subsided (literally, "returned") and his hand was still upraised (literally, "stretched out"). The imagery of the outstretched hand pictures the Lord as a warrior who has not yet completed his task of defeating his enemies but continues to brandish his weapon in his hand (cf. Josh. 8:26; 1 Chron. 21:16; Jer. 21:5).

Failure to Repent (9:13–17 [HB 12–16])
Israel's failure to repent necessitated more judgment.

9:13 (HB 12). The people had not "returned" to the Lord, who had struck them, or "sought" the "Lord Almighty" (literally, Lord of Armies). There is wordplay in the first line of the Hebrew text. The Lord's anger was "not turned away" (cf. 9:12 [HB 11], לֹא שָׁב) because the people had "not returned" (9:13a [HB 12a], לֹא שָׁב again) to the Lord by repenting of their sins. The repetition of the negated verb שׁוּב, "return," draws attention to the fact that the Lord's attitude toward them was an appropriate response to their sin. The verb "sought" (דָרְשׁוּ) conveys the idea of an active, volitional search. It is often used of seeking the divine will through formal means (cf. Isa. 58:2), but here, in parallelism with "return," it refers to seeking the Lord in repentance (see Isa. 55:6, as well as Deut. 4:29–30). The appearance

"His Hand Is Still Upraised": Persistent Judgment on Persistent Sin (9:8 [HB 7]–10:4)

of the divine title Lord of Armies (see the note on Isa. 1:9 above) is appropriate because it is in his role of warrior-king that Israel was experiencing the Lord.

This description of the people's response to judgment may, like 9:10 (HB 9), be current. But in the sequence of the historical review begun in 9:11 (HB 10), it may describe their failure to repent after the first wave of judgment came upon them (cf. 9:11–12 [HB 10–11]), which in turn prompted a second round of judgment (9:14–16 [HB 13–15]; see Smith 2007, 247–48).

9:14–16 (HB 13–15). Israel's failure to respond prompted the Lord to bring a second round of judgment upon them. The *wayyiqtol* forms in 9:14 and 16 (HB 13, 15) are best understood as preterites, referring to past judgment. Since 9:17 (HB 16) describes the Lord's current attitude toward the people, it is best to see 9:14–16 (HB 13–15) as referring to the Assyrian invasion of 734–732 B.C., which resulted in the territory of the northern kingdom being drastically reduced (Isa. 9:1 [HB 8:23]; cf. 2 Kings 15:29; see Blenkinsopp 2000, 219). This was the second wave of judgment after the Aramean–Philistine threat prior to the Aramean alliance (9:11–12a [HB 10–11a]).

Suddenly (note "in a single day"; cf. Isa. 10:17; 47:9), the Lord cut off both "head and tail" and "palm branch and reed" (i.e., both the branches and the stalk; 9:14 [HB 13]). The reference to the Lord acting decisively in "a single day" may reflect the "day of the Lord" theme (cf. 2:6–22), which, according to Stuart (1976, 159), is derived from a "widespread ancient Near Eastern tradition" that a mighty warrior-king "could complete a military campaign, or even an entire war of conquest against his enemies in a single day." It highlights the Lord's "universal power and authority," which "insure that his victory will be accomplished swiftly and suddenly" (p. 163).

The prophet identifies the reality underlying the imagery (9:15 [HB 14]). The "head" is "the elders and dignitaries," probably referring to civil/judicial leaders, and the "tail" is the prophets. Both groups led the people astray, so that the misled people were "led astray" (literally, "swallowed up," or perhaps, "confused"; 9:16 [HB 15]). (On the terminology used here, see the commentary on 3:12, where the same language is used for what was happening in Judah.)

9:17 (HB 16). In the aftermath of judgment on the leaders of the northern kingdom, the unrepentant people (cf. 9:10 [HB 9]) had become more corrupt. Isaiah 9:17 (HB 16) begins with עַל־כֵּן, "therefore," suggesting there is a logical connection between the historical review that precedes (note the *wayyiqtol* forms in 9:14, 16 [HB 13, 15]) and the description of the Lord's current attitude in 9:17 (HB 16; note the imperfects). Isaiah 9:16 (HB 15) describes how the leaders who were cut off by judgment (9:14–15 [HB 13–14]) had led the people astray. Isaiah 9:17 (HB 16) seems to assume their bad influence had persisted beyond the judgment and into the present. Indeed, the attitude expressed by the current generation in 9:10 (HB 9) is consistent with this. The misled people had become thoroughly corrupt.

The prophet singles out two groups. Normally robust young men are the pride and joy of their families and communities, for they are the warriors who make the nation secure. But the situation was so bad in Israel that the Lord (his title אֲדֹנָי, Sovereign Master, is used again, cf. 9:8 [HB 7]) did not derive joy from them, implying they were guilty (note "everyone" shortly after this) and he would not support them in battle (cf. Amos 4:10; Kaiser 1972, 225). Their defeat would leave the nation defenseless (Oswalt 1986, 255). Normally the Lord takes pity on the vulnerable members of society, epitomized by the fatherless and the widow; but in this case he had no compassion on them, for even they were corrupt.

"His Hand Is Still Upraised": Persistent Judgment on Persistent Sin (9:8 [HB 7]–10:4)

The verb רָחַם (יְרַחֵם) means "to have compassion, pity." The capacity to show compassion is one of God's fundamental attributes (Exod. 34:6). In Isaiah's time the Lord was predisposed to be compassionate to Israel (Isa. 30:18; cf. 49:15), but the people's rebellion forced him to withhold his compassion and punish them (27:11). Eventually, however, he would extend his compassion again and restore them to his favor (14:1; 49:10, 13; 54:8, 10; 55:7; 60:10). The statement in 9:17 (HB 16) is startling, for the Lord is depicted elsewhere as the champion of the fatherless and widows (see 1:17). Yet all the people, including the needy, had sinned, necessitating divine judgment. While the Lord is on the side of the poor, their poverty alone does not make them exempt from obeying the Lord's standards, nor does it insulate them from punishment if they, like their oppressors, violate his moral standards.

Strong language is used to describe the corrupt people ("ungodly and wicked"). The term translated "ungodly" (חָנֵף) is derived from a verbal root meaning, "be polluted, defiled." When applied to sinners, it refers to those who violate God's moral and ethical standards. An examination of passages where the word and its related terms are used indicates that such people ignore, resent, and misrepresent God (Job 8:13; 36:13; Isa. 32:6). They speak abusively of and to others (note the parallel line in 9:17 [HB 16], as well as Ps. 35:16; Prov. 11:9) and have no sympathy for the needy (Isa. 32:6). Despite their defiance of God, they are eventually destroyed by his angry judgment (Job 8:13; 15:34; 20:5; 27:8; Isa. 33:14). "Wicked" (*hiphil* רָעַע) is used in Isaiah 1:4, 16 of those who had spurned the Lord and were guilty of injustice.

Their wicked character was evident in their words—they spoke "folly." This term (נְבָלָה) is related to a verb meaning "be foolish" (cf. as well נָבָל, "fool"). It describes "folly, foolishness" and can refer to disgraceful crimes, such as rape and theft (Gen. 34:7; Josh. 7:15; 2 Sam. 13:12). Folly, as one might expect, characterizes the speech of fools (Isa. 32:6; cf. 1 Sam. 25:25). The term does not refer simply to that which is foolish, silly, or stupid. It has a moral connotation and refers to hostile and evil words and actions that are offensive to God (see Young 1965, 352).

Since the people had not repented, but had become thoroughly corrupt, more judgment was necessary. The Lord's anger had not subsided, and his hand remained outstretched (see 9:12 [HB 11] above).

Internal Dissension (9:18–21 [HB 17–20])
Israel's dissension necessitated more judgment.

The prophet's review of Israel's recent history continues, as the perfect (9:17a, 18a, 19a [HB 16a, 17a, 18a]) and *wayyiqtol* (9:17b, 18b, 19a [HB 16b, 17b, 18a]) verb forms indicate. The prefixed verb forms that are interspersed (9:17a, 18b, 19b [HB 16a, 17b, 18b]) are either preterites or imperfects used in a customary sense, describing continual or repeated action in the past ("was devouring," "were not taking pity," "were devouring").

9:18 (HB 17). More judgment was necessary (cf. 9:17 [HB 16]) because (cf. כִּי) throughout this period wickedness had overrun the land, like a brush fire that spreads to the forest (9:18 [HB 17]). "Wickedness" (רִשְׁעָה) refers to wicked behavior and speech that violates God's moral and ethical standards. The term is used of the native Canaanite people displaced by Israel (Deut. 9:4–5). In Ezekiel 18:20, 27 it refers to a person who is guilty of such sinful deeds as idolatry, adultery, injustice, robbery, and usury (see Isa. 9:10–13 [HB 9–12]).

9:19–20 (HB 18–19). Such wicked deeds prompted the "wrath" of the Lord of Armies (9:19a [HB 18a]). When used of human beings, "wrath" (עֶבְרָה) has the basic meaning "rage, fury" and is sometimes used of inappropriate outbursts of anger characterized by cruelty (see Gen. 49:7; Prov. 14:35; 22:8; Isa. 14:6; Amos 1:11). The term is often used of divine judgment; such fury characterizes the day of the Lord (see, e.g., Isa. 13:9, 13). The Lord's rage is stirred up by human sin, particularly pride, idolatry, and injustice (Isa. 10:6; Jer. 7:29; Hos. 5:10; 13:11). Yahweh's wrath devastated the land. The precise meaning of the verb נֶעְתַּם (*niphal* perfect third-person masculine singular of עָתַם) is uncertain since it occurs only here. (For various options, including proposed emendations, see *HALOT* s.v. "עתם" 904.) Perhaps it is related to an Arabic cognate, meaning, "be dark," but if so, the masculine form does not agree with its feminine subject ("land"). However, such lack of agreement sometimes occurs when the verb precedes the subject (see Kaiser 1972, 220 n. 8, who appeals to GKC, 465 §145o).

In addition to prompting Yahweh's wrath, the widespread wickedness was self-destructive (9:19b [HB 18b]). People were like fuel for the fire; they were showing no pity for one another. Overcome by greed, they devoured on the right and left but, like fire, were never satisfied (9:20a [HB 19a]). Their ravenous appetite is illustrated hyperbolically through a word picture of them eating the flesh of their own arm—or perhaps, even more gruesomely, the flesh of their own offspring (9:20b [HB 19b]).

The verb אָכַל, "eat, devour," is a key term in the prophet's rhetoric that serves to link sin and punishment. The wickedness of the people was like a fire that devours (9:18 [HB 17]). They greedily tried to "eat" everything (9:20 [HB 19]). But in the end, this backfired, for they themselves became "food" for the fire of the Lord's judgment (9:19 [HB 18]) as he allowed enemies to "devour" them (9:12 [HB 11]).

9:21 (HB 20). The reality behind the imagery is the internal dissension that divided the nation during this period. The prophet first mentions conflict between Ephraim and Manasseh, the two subtribal groups within the tribe of Joseph. Roberts (2015, 162) sees the conflict between Pekah and Shallum the Gileadite as the background here (2 Kings 15:8–25; cf. Hayes and Irvine 1987, 188; Wildberger 1991, 237–38). Not only were the northern tribes at odds with one another, they even attacked Judah (cf. Isa. 7:1–9).

The greed of the northern kingdom had prompted the Lord's judgment, which had no effect on the unrepentant people. Their greed had persisted to the point where the poor and vulnerable were now their victims (10:1–2). This necessitated another, more devastating round of judgment (9:21b [HB 20b]; cf. 10:3–4).

Imminent Death (10:1–4)
Israel's injustice demanded a day of reckoning.

10:1. With the introduction of הוֹי, "woe," Isaiah signals that the historical review is over. He returns to where he began this speech, as he announces the message (literally, "word") sent by the Sovereign Master that would fall on Israel (cf. 9:8 [HB 7]). As noted above (see 1:4; 5:8), the interjection הוֹי, "woe," was used in funeral laments (see 1 Kings 13:30; Jer. 22:18–19; 34:5; Amos 5:16). When used in prophetic judgment speeches, it carries the connotation of death and would grab an audience's attention and convey urgency. By prefacing the formal accusation with this word, followed by "those who make unjust laws," the prophet was acting out the addressees' funeral in advance, emphasizing that death was inevitable.

Many understand this woe oracle as addressed to Judah (see, e.g., Smith 2007, 251). If "my people" (Isa. 10:2) are the prophet's people, then Judah is in view (cf. 22:4; 26:20; 32:13, 18). But sometimes "my people" refers to the Lord's people (see 1:3; 3:15; 10:24; 19:25), in which case Israel and/or Judah can be the referent. (The referent of "my" in 3:12 and 5:13 is unclear.) In 10:24 the Lord refers to "my people who live in Zion," but no such qualifier appears in 10:2. If 10:1–4 is the culminating subunit of the speech begun in 9:8, then the northern kingdom is at least the primary referent here. Indeed, it appears this woe oracle is the prophetic word against Ephraim and Samaria mentioned in 9:8–9. However, it is possible that the prophet, while speaking primarily to the northern kingdom, also has Judah in mind, since Judah was guilty of injustice as well and would be threatened by Assyria.

The prophet focuses on the oppression and injustice dished out by the leaders of the northern kingdom. The noun אָוֶן, literally, "evil," in the first line characterizes their oppressive decrees, while the corresponding noun in the second line, עָמָל, literally, "trouble," may focus on the consequence for the victim (cf. Young 1965, 355 n. 16). When the words are paired elsewhere, they usually appear to be purely synonymous (see Num. 23:21; Job 4:8; 5:6; Pss. 7:14 [HB 15]; 10:7; 55:10 [HB 11]; 90:10; Hab. 1:3), but on a couple of occasions it is clear that אָוֶן precedes and results in עָמָל. For example, in Isaiah 59:4 sinners conceive אָוֶן and then give birth to עָמָל (see also Job 15:35).

10:2. The infinitives construct in 10:2a identify the purpose ("in order to") or result ("so that consequently") of their decrees, which deprive the poor of fair treatment and rob the needy of justice. The expression (לְהַטּוֹת מִן נָטָה), literally "to extend from," is used of thrusting someone away (cf. Job 24:4), while (לִגְזֹל גָּזַל), literally "rob," pictures the culprits grabbing what does not belong to them. The language of theft then gets more intense in 10:2b. Widows become their plunder (שְׁלָלָם) as they loot (יָבֹזּוּ, from בָּזַז) the fatherless. Now the picture is that of warriors pillaging their victims (cf. 8:4; 9:3; 10:6; 11:14; 17:14; 33:4; 42:22, 24; 53:12; see Roberts 2015, 86).

J. Andrew Dearman (1988, 43) points out that the expression translated "who issue . . . decrees" (literally, "who make/write . . . statutes") does not refer to "the making of laws in the modern sense," but rather "the recording of decisions and rulings brought for arbitration to judges," probably on behalf of the king. He explains that people were being deprived of their property rights in a system that brought material benefit to those administrating it. He adds (p. 44): "the statutes themselves almost certainly dealt with such things as the sale and transfer of property, foreclosure and confiscation of collateral, and conditions for servitude/debt slavery." Widows and the fatherless were particularly vulnerable.

In Isaiah 1–39 the synonymous expressions "poor" (דַּלִּים) and "oppressed" (עֲנִיִּים) almost always refer to those whom rich royal bureaucrats had deprived of justice and the necessities of life (3:14–15; 32:7 [*qere*]). Widows and fatherless children epitomized these victims of injustice dished out by big government (10:2). The Lord identifies with the poor, calling them his people (3:15), providing refuge for them (25:4), and promising to someday vindicate them (26:6). The ideal Davidic king envisioned by Isaiah will be their champion and make sure they are treated fairly and insulated from powerful oppressors (11:4).

10:3–4. Isaiah begins the formal announcement of judgment with a series of rhetorical questions. He mentions a "day of reckoning" that would come upon the oppressors. The term "reckoning" (פְּקֻדָּה) is derived from a verb (פָּקַד) that often describes God arriving on the scene for the purpose of judgment (see Isa. 10:12). When combined with terms designating time, such as "day(s), year, time," the noun refers to a time when God intervenes and punishes evildoers for their crimes (cf. Jer. 8:12; 10:15; 11:23; 23:12; 46:21; 48:44; Hos. 9:7; Mic. 7:4). When using the expression, the prophets do not envision one culminating event at the end of time, but rather a time when God intervenes in the course of history to deal with the specific evildoer(s) addressed in the context. The prophet also mentions disaster coming from afar on this day of reckoning. The reality behind this disaster is the Assyrian army (see Isa. 5:26), which invaded and defeated the northern kingdom in 722–721 B.C. and took most of the people into exile

(Clements 1980, 62; Motyer 1993, 111; Roberts 2015, 86; Wildberger 1991, 215).

When the Lord unleashes his judgment, there is no one to turn to for help, for no one can resist his invincible power. This theme recurs in Isaiah 20:6; 30:5, 7; 31:1–3. Only the Lord can provide genuine help (Isa. 41:10, 13–14; 44:2; 49:8; 50:7, 9). On that day, their "riches" (literally, "their glory"; Williamson 2018, 478) would be of no help, so the prophet sarcastically asks where they would leave (or perhaps, "abandon") their wealth (10:3b). They would either cower among the captives or fall among the slain (10:4a). The use of the verb "fall" (נָפַל) here is ironic. This literary unit began with the announcement that the Lord's prophetic word of judgment would "fall" on Israel (9:8). Now, at the end of the unit, the prophet warns that many would "fall" slain. (See Motyer [1993, 112], who speaks of an *inclusio*.)

The images of death in this woe oracle suggest this is the culmination of the judgment depicted in this literary unit—the final wave of judgment, as it were. So, it is surprising to hear the refrain once more, informing us that the Lord's anger has not subsided, and his hand remains outstretched (10:4b). This suggests another round of judgment, as if what the woe oracle describes would not exhaust divine punishment. The refrain may be hyperbolic at this point, suggesting judgment would follow Israel into exile and into the grave. But the refrain sets us up for a surprise, a plot twist as it were. A woe oracle against Assyria, the Lord's instrument of judgment, follows. Indeed, the Lord's anger is not yet exhausted. He still must deal with his arrogant instrument of judgment!

THEOLOGICAL FOCUS

The theological focus of this passage can be stated as follows: the Lord designs judgment to bring his people to repentance, but when they respond defiantly and persist in rebellion, he must intensify his judgment. As the prophet develops this theological theme, the following emphases emerge:

1. Persistent sinful rebellion prompts persistent judgment.

Sin has consequences. The Lord matched Israel's persistence in sin with judgment. The people refused to repent when punished and even defiantly boasted they would rebuild what the Lord had destroyed. So the Lord brought judgment in waves, culminating in exile and death. The truth is simple: sinners cannot escape the anger of God.

2. The Lord's anger is stirred when his covenant community is corrupted by dissension and oppression.

The Lord values peace and justice. In fact, peace and justice will characterize his kingdom (cf. 11:1–9). The northern kingdom experienced the Lord's anger because they promoted dissension in the covenant community and denied justice to the needy.

PREACHING AND TEACHING STRATEGIES

Exegetical and Theological Synthesis

This passage is neatly divided into four similar sections, each ending with the refrain, "Yet for all this, his anger is not turned away, his hand is still upraised" (9:12, 17, 21; 10:4). Each unit indicts the nation of Israel for some aspect of their persistent and unrepentant sin. Because of this, God's anger has been directed toward Israel, and he warns that future judgment will come.

The first unit (9:8–12 [HB 7–11]) confronts the people for their stubborn pride, demonstrated by their refusal to respond to God's prior acts of judgment against them. The prophet looks back to a time prior to the Israel-Syria alliance when the two nations were enemies. At that time, both Syria to the east and the Philistines to the west had come into military conflict with Israel (9:12 [HB 11]). According to Isaiah, these conflicts had been initiated by God as an act of judgment against his people in response to their sin (9:11 [HB 10]).

The result of this previous judgment was destruction throughout the land of Israel. Infrastructure such as city walls and houses were evidently destroyed, and fields and vineyards were ravaged. However, instead of looking to the Lord for help in humble acknowledgment of their sin, Israel acted in stubborn defiance. They pridefully boasted in their commitment to rebuild their broken-down structures bigger and better. When they rebuild, the bricks would be replaced with chiseled stones and the sycamore trees would be replaced with larger and more luxurious cedar trees (9:10 [HB 9]).

Next, the prophet indicts all the people for their godless actions, from the powerful, influential leaders (9:16 [HB 15]) all the way down to weak and vulnerable orphans and widows (9:17 [HB 16]). Throughout history, when God would judge Israel by raising up foreign adversaries to oppress them, they would often respond by crying out to him for help. This would force them to admit their sin and rid their land of false gods. However, nobody turned to the Lord or inquired of him this time (9:13 [HB 12]). As a result, God warned that he would cut off Israel's head (its leaders) as well as its tail (those who follow the leaders; 9:14–15 [HB 13–14]).

In the third section (9:18–21 [HB 17–20]), the land of Israel is described as ablaze with the fire from the people's wickedness (9:18 [HB 17]). The fire describes God's judgment against them for their sin as they themselves become the "fuel" that feeds the flames (9:19 [HB 18]). David McKenna writes:

> It is one thing to see the resources of the land burned up in judgment; it is quite another thing to see the relationships of blood relatives become the fuel for the fire. When the bonds of heredity and love that hold these relationships together are destroyed, civilization itself breaks down. Civil war leads to anarchy and anarchy bottoms out in cannibalism. (1993, 143)

Isaiah 10:1–4 completes this unit by taking aim at those who oppress the poor and vulnerable in society, specifically those corrupt leaders who use their political power to benefit themselves at the expense of the poor. Rather than use their governmental powers to protect the weak and help the poor, legislators were writing laws that legalized oppression (10:1) and judges were unfairly adjudicating cases at the expense of the poor, apparently by accepting bribes from those wealthy enough to pay them.

The prophet rhetorically asks what they will do on the day of judgment, referring to the coming Assyrian invasion which would result in death and deportation (10:3). To whom will they turn for help, and what good will their ill-gotten wealth do for them then? Their only option will be to die or to crouch in fear along with the rest of the captives. There is some irony as those who made the poor their prey (10:2) will themselves become both poor and prey at the hands of the Assyrians.

Preaching Idea
Only by repentance will God's wrath be appeased.

Contemporary Connections

What does it mean?
Israel was God's chosen people. As such, they were called to be set apart from the nations around them by their holy lifestyle and devotion to Yahweh alone. But they often failed in this respect. As a result, God had to confront Israel for her perpetual sin, including things like stubborn pride (9:8–10 [HB 7–9]; cf. 2:11–17; 3:16; 5:15), a failure to trust him (9:13 [HB 12]; cf. 2:6–8, 18–20; 7:1–13; 8:6–8, 12–13), a lack of civility toward one another (9:19–21 [HB 18–20]; cf. 1:15; 5:7), and oppression of the poor and vulnerable by corrupt leaders (10:1–2; cf. 1:17, 23; 3:14–15; 5:8, 23).

Thus, God brought initial judgment upon Israel in the form of military invasions from the

Syrians and the Philistines (9:11–12 [HB 10–11]). This was intended to be a wake-up call providing them an opportunity to repent and turn back to God. Instead, they chose to stubbornly and pridefully persist in sin rather than humble themselves before God. As a result, God warned them that a day was coming when an even more severe judgment would be brought against them in the form of an Assyrian invasion resulting in the destruction of their property and deportation (10:3–4).

In many respects, Israel's story is the story of all humanity. We were originally created to be God's people, created in his image to reflect his glory throughout the world. As was the case for Israel, though, humanity's sin complicated God's design. Because of Adam and Eve's initial rebellion (Gen. 3:1–7), all of their offspring have been born with a nature bent toward sin (Gen. 8:21; Pss. 51:5 [HB 6]; 58:3 [HB 4]; Rom. 5:12; Eph. 2:1–3), and all have likewise made the choice to sin against God in practice (Ps. 14:2–3; Eccl. 7:20; Rom. 1:28–32; 3:10–23; 5:12; 1 John 1:8, 10). Consequently, God's wrath abides on all people, and a day is coming when his judgment will be poured out upon the earth to punish all evildoers. Hebrews 10:26–27, 30–31 warns:

> If we deliberately keep on sinning after we have received the knowledge of the truth, no sacrifice for sins is left, but only a fearful expectation of judgment and of raging fire that will consume the enemies of God. . . . For we know him who said, "It is mine to avenge; I will repay," and again, "The Lord will judge his people." It is a dreadful thing to fall into the hands of the living God.[2]

Similarly, Paul wrote:

> All this is evidence that God's judgment is right. . . . This will happen when the Lord Jesus is revealed from heaven in blazing fire with his powerful angels. He will punish those who do not know God and do not obey the gospel of our Lord Jesus. They will be punished with everlasting destruction and shut out from the presence of the Lord and from the glory of his might. (2 Thess. 1:5a, 7b–9)

But there is good news as well. As the above Preaching Idea also affirms, God's coming wrath against sin and rebellious humanity can be appeased through repentance. This is why Jesus was sent to earth in human form: to live a sinless life and then die as a sacrifice on the cross so that he could absorb the wrath of God directed at sinful man in himself, thus becoming our substitute. Paul wrote in 2 Corinthians 5:21 that "God made him who had no sin to be sin for us, so that in him we might become the righteousness of God." The apostle Peter likewise described Jesus's suffering and death as the righteous one suffering on behalf of the unrighteous ones to reconcile lost humanity to God (1 Peter 3:18).

However, for anyone to benefit personally from Jesus's substitutionary sacrifice, God requires them to receive this gift through faith by humbly turning to God in repentance away from sin. Anyone who refuses to turn to Jesus from sin will remain under the wrath of God and face future judgment after they die. John 3:36 says, "Whoever believes in the Son has eternal life, but whoever rejects the Son will not see life, for God's wrath remains on them" (see also Rom. 2:2–5; Heb. 10:29–31).

Israel ignored God's initial acts of judgment against their sins. Rather than repent when God brought the Syrian and Philistine armies against them, they defiantly proclaimed they would simply rebuild (Isa. 9:8–13 [HB 7–12]). In similar fashion, many in the world today ignore God's warnings against their sin. Despite experiencing God's

---

2 See Matt. 3:7; Rom. 1:18; 2:5–9; Eph. 5:3–6; Col. 3:5–6; Jude 14–16; Rev. 6:15–17; 11:18.

"His Hand Is Still Upraised": Persistent Judgment on Persistent Sin (9:8 [HB 7]–10:4)

judgment firsthand through the destructive consequences of their sins, many defiantly persist in sinful choices. Even many who have heard how God poured out his wrath on Jesus to provide salvation choose to reject this offer. Like Israel, if they persist in rebellion, they will eventually face the frightening reality of God's judgment and wrath. To paraphrase the words of the prophet in Isaiah 10:3–4, "What will they do on the day of punishment, in the ruin that will come upon them? To whom will they turn for help? What good will the wealth they accumulated in this life be to them when they stand before God? Nothing remains then but to crouch among the rest of humanity who ignored God's warnings to repent."

Is it true?

Isaiah's prophetic warnings against Israel about a coming Assyrian military invasion (10:3–4; cf. 5:26–30; 8:3–4) did in fact come to pass. In 735–733 B.C., Assyria conquered parts of the northern kingdom of Israel (1 Chron. 5:26, 2 Kings 15:29). In 725 B.C., Shalmaneser V besieged Samaria, the ruling city of the northern kingdom. Three years later, in 722 B.C., Sargon completed the job and carried away the city's populace into exile (2 Kings 17:3–6; 18:11–12). Because of the degree of brutality carried out by the Assyrians on their captured enemies, this judgment would have been felt as especially severe (see sidebar below on Assyrian brutality).

Assyrian Brutality

The Assyrian army was known for its brutality. Their mistreatment of their captured foes was extreme even by ancient standards. The Assyrians purposely put their cruelty on public display to advertise their brutality as a sort of psychological warfare. Because the Assyrians were so widely known for their cruel torture, it instilled terror in the hearts of their enemies, often leading them to surrender without even putting up a fight. They were known to impale their victims en masse on large stakes. The stake would be driven into the body under the ribs. The victim's weight would cause the spike to slowly protrude deeper and deeper into the body until the person died. Assyrians were also fond of flaying enemy leaders alive. Beginning at the buttocks, thighs, or lower legs, they would cut the skin off their vic-

Impaled victims in Assyrian relief of attack on an enemy town during the reign of Tiglath-Pileser III 737–720 BCE from his palace at Kalhu (Nimrud).

tims in strips. They would then hang the strips of skin in a visible place for the rest of the people to see. Soldiers would routinely decapitate their defeated enemies en masse and then display the heads publicly. They would stack them into pyramids or hang them on tree branches. In one account, the Assyrians even made a necklace out of severed heads.

Other times, they would dismember their victims, and then leave them to roam around in agony until they died. They would gouge out their eyes, cut off legs, arms, noses, tongues, ears, and/or testicles. They would burn people alive, including even small children.[3]

Relief of Assyrian kings having rebels flayed as a warning to troublesome subjects

Biblical history is full of examples where God's warnings of judgment came to pass as prophesied. This historical track record serves as a precedent and a strong apologetic for the certainty that God will likewise one day pour out his eschatological wrath against sin just as he promised. Probably the most well-known example of this is the ancient story of the flood (Gen. 6–8). God prophesied through Noah that he was going to destroy the entire earth with a flood because of the rampant wickedness throughout the earth. Noah was told to build an ark to serve as a vessel of salvation for his family and any others willing to believe his message and repent.[4] However, only Noah's family responded to God's warning. Peter pointed back to the story of the flood as evidence that God's predicted judgments eventually come to pass, even if he is patient with sinful humanity in the meantime (2 Peter 3:3–7).

The historical evidence is clear that God will follow through on his warnings of judgment against sin. However, the realities of God's wrath and coming judgment must not overshadow the realities of his mercy and grace. In the same way that the Bible affirms God's hatred of sin and his need to judge it, the invitation to repent of sin and experience God's grace has been extended to all.

When Moses desired to see God upon the mountain, and the Lord agreed to have his glory proclaimed before him as he passed by, this is what Moses heard: "The Lord, the Lord, the compassionate and gracious God, slow to anger, abounding in love and faithfulness, maintaining love to thousands, and forgiving wickedness, rebellion and sin. Yet he does not leave the guilty unpunished; he punishes the children and their children for the sin of the parents to the third and fourth generation" (Exod. 34:6–7). Similar descriptions of God as full of grace and mercy standing ready to forgive sinners are reiterated often throughout Scripture.[5]

The essence of God's glory requires him to judge sin; he cannot simply clear the guilty of

---

3 https://medium.com/lessons-from-history/assyrians-torture-60fabb7a9642.
4 While the Bible nowhere says that the people in Noah's day outside of his own family were warned of their sin and given the opportunity to repent, this is assumed by many. Second Peter 2:5 describes Noah as a "herald of righteousness," which likely points to his role as a preacher among the ungodly people of his day. Additionally, 1 Peter 3:20 refers to God's patience in the days of Noah. This likely points to his patience with sinful humanity while he gave them ample time to repent. Furthermore, the story of Noah and the flood is regularly used in Scripture as a typological event foreshadowing the eschatological judgment that will destroy the earth by fire. A major point of comparison between the days of the flood and the future judgment includes the rejection and/or willful ignorance by the world's populace of that judgment such that when it comes, they are utterly surprised (Matt. 24:36–39; Luke 17:24–27; 1 Peter 3:18–22; 2 Peter 3:3–13).
5 See Num. 14:17–19; 2 Chron. 30:9; Neh. 9:17; Pss. 25:6; 86:5, 15; 103:8–14; 111:4; 112:4; 116:5; 145:8; Lam. 3:22; Isa. 30:18; Jer. 3:12–13; Dan. 9:9; Joel 2:13; Jonah 4:2; Mic. 7:18.

their offenses and ignore the wrongs they have done. However, the traits that God emphasizes most when defining his own character are mercy and grace, being one who is slow to anger and abounding in love for humanity. This is the basis for his willingness to forgive sins.

One of the clearest examples of this truth is found in the book of Jonah. God called his prophet to preach to the people of Nineveh, a major city of the Assyrians, who were known for their wickedness and their cruel and violent treatment of their enemies (see sidebar above on Assyrian brutality). God was understandably angry with them, and they were unarguably deserving of his judgment. And yet, Jonah initially refused to go and instead ran in the opposite direction. We might assume that his reticence was due to fear of how the Assyrians would treat a foreigner claiming to speak for God, telling them they were wicked and were about to be destroyed. While this may have factored into Jonah's thinking, his real motivation is revealed later in the book. Eventually Jonah goes to Nineveh and tells the city that God is planning to destroy them because of their sin. Surprisingly, the people respond in humility with repentance before God. As a result, God relents of the disaster he had intended to unleash upon them.

This didn't please Jonah one bit, as he desired to see God punish those wicked enemies of Israel. "He prayed to the LORD: 'Isn't this what I said, LORD, when I was still at home? That is what I tried to forestall by fleeing to Tarshish. I knew that you are a gracious and compassionate God, slow to anger and abounding in love, a God who relents from sending calamity'" (Jonah 4:2).

Jonah knew that God is always predisposed to show grace and mercy, even toward the worst of sinners. He desires for people to repent and experience forgiveness more than he wishes to execute wrath against them (2 Peter 3:9). But God does not force anyone to repent. Rather, he graciously extends the offer for sinners to admit the error of their ways and yield their lives to him.

Now what?

On September 11, 2001, the United States of America was attacked by various Islamic jihadists who hijacked commercial jets and crashed them into the Pentagon, the World Trade Center towers, and a field in Pennsylvania. In all, 2,996 people were killed that day. In the immediate aftermath of these events, as Americans were looking for answers to why and how this could happen, Christian leaders Pat Robertson and Jerry Falwell attributed them to God's judgment on America for sins like abortion, materialism, homosexuality, and pornography (Goodstein 2001). This was just the beginning, they said, if America didn't repent and change its ways.

However, most Christian leaders were quick to point out that nobody knows which events should be attributed to God's direct intervention. The United States is not Israel. As a nation, we are not in a covenant relationship with God. It is mere speculation on the part of those who declare that modern events are God's judgment against sin. While passages such as Isaiah 9:8–10:4 demonstrate that God can and does judge sinful nations with tragedies at times, we shouldn't assume that every tragedy points to God's judgment on sin.

Nonetheless, everyone has a God-given conscience that convicts them of wrongdoing (Rom. 2:14–15; 1 Tim. 1:19; Titus 1:15). Even those who have never heard the name of Jesus have intuition that there is a Creator God who made them and expects them to live and act according to the moral-code compass he placed within them (Rom. 1:19–20, 32). Those who deny this reality have suppressed the truth to pursue their sinful lusts (Rom. 1:21–31). As a result, they are without excuse and stand condemned, awaiting future judgment (Rom. 1:18).

The message of Isaiah 9:8 [HB 7]–10:4 should serve as a strong warning then to all who have never repented of their sins nor turned to Jesus for forgiveness and salvation. The gospel message invites them to turn to God and escape the destructive force of God's future wrath against sin. Sinners must not confuse God's patience and long-suffering toward sin with indifference or obliviousness about sin. God is acutely aware of the evil that each person does, and he cares deeply about the pain and destruction it causes. Sinners must understand that God's "kindness, forbearance and patience" are "intended to lead" sinners "to repentance" (Rom. 2:4).

For believers, we have the Holy Spirit who uses the Word of God to convict us of sin and lead us into righteousness (John 16:8; Eph. 6:17). Passages like Isaiah 9:8 [HB 7]–10:4 are warnings not to stubbornly persist in sin. We must be careful not to quench the Spirit's activity in our hearts by ignoring his promptings and conviction (1 Thess. 5:19). The author of Hebrews warned his readers not to become hardened by the deceitfulness of sin leading them to fall away from the living God (Heb. 3:12–13).

Christians who aren't careful and who persist in sinful habits face the very real possibility of becoming hardened to the realities of sin in their life. As a result, they can slip further and further away from a Spirit-led, fruitful, and meaningful life. Before long, they are left asking themselves if they are even children of God as their lives begin to look more like that of nonbelievers than lives exhibiting genuine faith in God.

As such, Christians should routinely take some time to examine themselves before God. They must invite God's Spirit to search out their hearts and reveal any areas of pride or stubborn rebellion against God (2 Cor. 13:5; 2 Peter 1:10). It is important to remember that repentance is more an act of one's will than it is an emotion. Often, believers wait until they feel like repenting to act. The problem with this is that sin often leads to a hardening of the heart, where one loses sensitivity to conviction. It is important to remember that God wants people to make the right choices. Doing the right thing often requires denying our feelings or impulses as an act of our Spirit-empowered will. Repentance is no different.

Finally, believers should respond to a passage such as this with gratitude toward Jesus for being the one who willingly absorbed the wrath of God for us. In a passage that highlights God's judgment against sinners, it is important to remember that, as recipients of grace and mercy, this is only possible because God poured out his wrath on Jesus while he hung on the cross. God's sense of justice demands payment for sin. Apart from Jesus's selfless, sacrificial act on our behalf, God would have no other option but to pour out the full fury of his wrath on us.

Creativity in Presentation

Movie

In the 1960 Disney movie *Pollyanna*, there is an extended scene where Rev. Paul Ford (played by Karl Malden) is preaching a fiery sermon to his congregation about fire and brimstone for the unconverted. He uses a very loud, angry, and harsh tone in his delivery. Throughout this scene, the chandelier can be seen shaking at the forcefulness of the preacher's delivery. Various congregants are shown to be deeply uncomfortable by the scowls on their faces and the way they shift in their seats. Pollyanna (played by Hayley Mills) is a young girl in the congregation who is listening to the sermon that day.

In a later scene, Pollyanna encounters Rev. Ford outside preparing for another of his sermons. She mentions to him how her father used to be a minister, and how he struggled at times because he was unable to get through to his congregation. The preacher asked her, "Did your father ever solve the problem?" She said that he read something one day that helped him. It was a quote from President Abraham Lincoln: "When you look for the bad in mankind, expecting to find it, you surely will." This caused her father to begin looking for the good in people. That was when he started looking through the Bible for the "happy passages." He discovered that there are more than eight hundred of them in the Scripture. The implication was that the preacher should stop preaching about sad and unpleasant things like sin, hell, and judgment. Instead, he should focus on happy things that don't make people uncomfortable. This movie was filmed decades ago, yet it illustrates the spirit of our day and how many people find messages about sin and coming judgment to be out of touch and unnecessarily offensive.

News Story
In September of 2021, Isaac and Lehua Kalua called the police to report that their six-year-old adopted daughter Isabella had gone missing. According to Lehua, the last time she had seen her daughter was just after supper the previous night when she put Isabella to bed. In the morning, she found her daughter's bed empty.

However, upon further investigation, Isabella's biological sister, also adopted by the Kaluas, reported to police that the last time she had seen her sister was two months earlier when she discovered her in a dog cage with duct tape bound around her mouth and nose. Supposedly, this was a common punishment inflicted upon little Isabella when she was caught sneaking into the kitchen at night to try to eat. Apparently, she was often deprived of food as well. On that night, her sister told police that, when she was found unresponsive in the cage, her adoptive mother Lehua placed the little girl in a bathtub filled with water in an unsuccessful attempt to revive her. According to the unnamed older sister, her adoptive parents asked her to keep this a secret.[6]

When we hear about tragic stories such as this one where a vulnerable person is neglected and abused in such horrific ways, our souls cry out with righteous indignation for judgment and accountability for those parents. In the same way that we are moved to anger and insist that judgment be meted out on people who commit such despicable acts, how much more is it appropriate for a holy God to react in anger and judgment when sinful humans commit acts of oppression and corruption against others.

How Calluses Form
I remember when I first started learning to play the guitar. My fingers weren't used to pushing down the strings to form chords. As a result, they would get really sore whenever I would practice. My teacher told me this was normal, and that I would have to push through the pain to grow calluses on my fingertips. As a result, it would become easier to play, not only because it would no longer hurt, but also because it takes less resistance to push down the strings with hardened fingertips.

Calluses form by repeated injury to the epidermis, resulting in a buildup of a hardened, thickened pad of dead skin cells at the surface layer of the skin.[7] The development of calluses on one's fingers illustrates the process involved in the hardening of one's heart. Initially, a person's fingers are soft and sensitive to pain. However, the more a person engages in the painful, damaging activity, the harder the skin gets until it becomes resistant to the pain of that activity. Similarly, a person's heart and conscience are initially sensitive to the pain of sin. When they engage in the painful, damaging activity of sin, their heart feels the pain of guilt and shame. However, the more a person chooses to ignore and push through the pain of their sensitive conscience, their heart grows callous and becomes resistant to

---

6   https://www.nbcnews.com/news/us-news/sister-told-police-parents-accused-murdering-daughter-6-kept-girl-cage-rcna5500.
7   https://www.britannica.com/science/callus-dermatology.

"His Hand Is Still Upraised": Persistent Judgment on Persistent Sin (9:8 [HB 7]–10:4)

the pain. After a while, the same activities that used to result in guilt and shame can now be undertaken without feeling much guilt at all. This is what the Bible means when it warns against allowing one's heart to become hardened by sin.

Only by repentance will God's wrath be appeased.

- The arrogant will be recipients of God's judgment (9:8–12).
- The rulers will be recipients of God's judgment (9:13–16a; 10:1–4).
- The subordinates will be recipients of God's judgment (9:16b–17a).
- Even the oppressed will be recipients of God's judgment (9:17b).

DISCUSSION QUESTIONS

1. What are some ways in which the sin of pride contributes to a stubborn persistence in sin?

2. Read Isaiah 10:3–4. How does the reality of future, divine judgment impact the present appeal of material wealth?

3. How does this passage impact your view of geopolitical conflicts and wars? Do you believe that God predetermines the outcome of every war? Do you think God uses foreign wars or national tragedies as a form of judgment on sin today as he did in the Old Testament times?

Isaiah 10:5–34

EXEGETICAL IDEA
The Lord would judge the arrogant Assyrians, because they did not acknowledge the Sovereign Lord but proudly attributed their success to their own strength.

THEOLOGICAL FOCUS
The Sovereign Lord sometimes uses proud nations to punish his people, but when these nations fail to acknowledge the Lord's sovereignty, the Lord judges them.

PREACHING IDEA
God opposes the proud but gives grace to the humble.

PREACHING POINTERS
Do you have many friends but not enough time to spend with all of them? If so, maybe it's time for you to make a few enemies. Consider the following advice:

Step 1: Work at being critical of others to their face. Better yet, be overly complimentary to people, but then scorch them behind their backs. Be sure to criticize them to enough people that you can be sure word will get back to them.
Step 2: Routinely ask people if they've gained weight recently.
Step 3: Ignore personal hygiene. Taking showers, using deodorant, and brushing your teeth are unnecessary. Remember, people throughout most of human history were unable to take advantage of these practices; there's no need for you to bother with them either.
Step 4: Routinely invade people's personal space. Be sure to stand no further than ten inches away from people when you talk to them. If you see them take a step back to create some room, be sure to step closer. This is especially effective when combined with step 3 above.

Nobody wants to make enemies. Only a fool would go out of their way to make other people not like them. Even worse is to make oneself an enemy of God. The quickest way to make oneself God's enemy is by acting in arrogant pride. James 4:6 says, "God opposes the proud." Isaiah indicted Israel for its pride (9:8–10:4, see esp. 9:9). Next, God confronts Assyria for its arrogant pride, which arouses his anger and prompted him to be the Assyrians' enemy (10:5–34, see esp. vv. 12, 15, 33). As a result of God's discipline against them, a remnant from Judah will turn back to God in humility (10:20–22), prompting him to surround them once again with his grace (10:23–34). Thus we see that not only does God oppose the proud but he also gives grace to the humble (James 4:6; cf. Ps. 138:6; Prov. 3:34; Dan. 5:20–21; Luke 1:52; 1 Peter 5:5).

THE LORD BRINGS DOWN THE PROUD ASSYRIANS (10:5–34)

The Lord's judgment would not stop with Israel. He would also bring judgment upon the arrogant Assyrians. The Assyrians did not acknowledge their role as the Sovereign Lord's instrument of punishment, but proudly attributed their success to their own strength, so the Lord would devastate the Assyrian army and bring down their pride. He would reverse the circumstances of the northern kingdom, restoring his relationship with them, and deliver Jerusalem from the Assyrian assault.

LITERARY STRUCTURE AND THEMES (10:5–34)

This literary unit focuses on the Lord's judgment on Assyria, his instrument in bringing punishment upon Israel and Judah. It begins with a lengthy woe (הוֹי) oracle, which includes the standard elements of a judgment speech: namely, an accusation (the basis for judgment) and a formal announcement of judgment. In this woe oracle, there are two panels:

A	10:5–11	Pronouncement of woe with accompanying accusation
B	10:12	Formal announcement of judgment (introduced by וְהָיָה, "and it will be")
A	10:13–15	Additional accusation (introduced by כִּי, "for")
B	10:16–19	Expansion of formal announcement of judgment (introduced by לָכֵן, "therefore")

The initial announcement of judgment speaks of divine intervention (10:12); the expansion includes a reference to divine intervention (10:16–17), followed by a description of its results (10:18–19).

The statement וְהָיָה בַּיּוֹם הַהוּא, literally "and it will be in that day," marks a shift in focus to the remnant of Israel that would survive the Lord's judgment (10:20), carried out through Assyria. Isaiah 10:20–23 is best classified as a salvation announcement, though 10:22–23 alludes to the judgment upon Israel that would necessitate salvation.

The appearance of לָכֵן, "therefore," followed by the messenger formula (literally, "thus says the Lord"), marks another shift within the literary unit (10:24a). In form-critical terms the following speech is a salvation (note "do not be afraid") oracle directed to those living in Zion (10:24a), though the content is a judgment speech against Assyria (10:24b–34). The dramatic description of the enemy's advance toward Jerusalem (10:28–32) is a unique feature of this speech.

- *Death to Assyria (10:5–19)*
- *Hope for the Remnant (10:20–23)*
- *Good News for Zion (10:24–34)*

EXPOSITION (10:5–34)

Death to Assyria (10:5–19)

Assyria's death was imminent because of its arrogance, which would prompt the Lord's severe judgment.

10:5. As noted above, the refrain at the end of the preceding woe oracle against Israel (10:4) suggests another round of judgment upon Israel, as if the death pronounced in the woe oracle does not exhaust divine punishment. But the refrain sets us up for a surprising shift in divine focus. A woe oracle against Assyria suddenly appears. Indeed, the Lord's anger is not yet exhausted. He still must deal with his arrogant instrument of judgment! As noted earlier, the interjection הוֹי, "woe," was used in funeral laments (see 1 Kings 13:30; Jer. 22:18–19; 34:5; Amos 5:16). When used in prophetic judgment speeches, it carries the connotation of death.

The Lord immediately highlights Assyria's role as his agent (Isa. 10:5b) because it is the abuse of that role that forms the basis for the coming judgment. In the Lord's hand, Assyria was a rod and a club used to beat the object of his anger. However, roles would soon be reversed, as the Lord would redirect his anger from his people to Assyria (10:24–25) and beat the Assyrians with a rod and club (10:31–32).

10:6. The Lord summarizes his commission to Assyria. He emphasizes his sovereignty; he is the one who sends and commands Assyria. (NIV "dispatch" translates the Hebrew צָוָה, "command" [אֲצַוֶּנּוּ, literally, "I will command him"].) He calls the object of his judgment "a godless nation" and "a people who anger me." The adjective חָנֵף, "godless," describes the nation as defiled or corrupted, as when the earth is polluted by shed blood (cf. Num. 35:33; Ps. 106:38; Isa. 24:5). The phrase עַם עֶבְרָתִי, literally "people of my anger," may refer to the people angering the Lord (cf. NIV11), but it is more likely describing the people as the objects of his anger (cf. ESV, "the people of my wrath"), that is, those who experience the outpouring of his wrath (cf. Isa. 9:18 [HB 19]; 13:9, 11, 13; 14:6). The Lord authorized Assyria to pillage and "trample." The image of trampling Israel like clay pictures the invader overrunning and conquering the land (cf. Isa. 41:25; Mic. 7:10).

The identity of the nation/people mentioned in Isaiah 10:6 is debated. Three factors favor Judah being the referent. The reference in 10:9 to the fall of Carchemish as a past event suggests that this prophetic oracle originates after 717 B.C., when the Assyrians conquered it. In this case the northern kingdom (Israel) had already been defeated (722–721), leaving only Judah. The verbs in 10:6 are imperfect, suggesting that the sending is underway or future. Finally, 10:11 makes it clear that Jerusalem is the target of the Assyrian onslaught. Assyria talks about dealing with Jerusalem (using an imperfect verb form) as they have dealt with Samaria (using a perfect verb form).

10:7. However, the Lord did not give Assyria free rein. They were his agent of punishment, but they intended to do far more. As G. B. Gray (1912, 196–97) says, "Assyria is guided not by the will of Yahweh, but by its own cruel lust; consequently, it exceeds its commission" (see also Wildberger 1991, 417–18). As Eidevall (2009, 43) says, 10:5–15 "can be regarded as a refutation of the Assyrian interpretation of the mandate given them" by the Lord. The Assyrians came with the intent to destroy and to cut off nations. The collocation of the verbs שָׁמַד (לְהַשְׁמִיד), "destroy," and כָּרַת (לְהַכְרִית), "cut off," refers to severe destruction that eliminates an individual or nation (cf. 1 Sam. 24:21 [HB 22]; Ps. 37:38; Isa. 48:19; Ezek. 25:7). The Assyrian royal annals attest to their ruthless treatment of victims, as well as their policy of removing entire populations from their native lands, as they did to Israel in 722–721 B.C. (cf. 2 Kings 17:23). The Lord sent Assyria to punish his people severely, but he did not intend for them to annihilate them. He promised to spare a remnant, so Assyria's boasting "threatens God's remnant promises" (Seitz 1993, 92).

10:8. The proud Assyrians bragged about their triumphs and boasted they would destroy Jerusalem, just as they had done Samaria. Even the Assyrian officers had a royal aura about them that exceeded the royal splendor of defeated kings (see Clements 1980, 111). There is a subtle wordplay here. Hebrew שָׂרַי, "my commanders," is cognate with the Akkadian word for king,

The Lord Brings Down the Proud Assyrians (10:5–34)

sharru (Machinist 1983, 734–35; Roberts 2015, 165; Young 1965, 361 n. 36).

10:9. Between 740 and 717 B.C. the Assyrian army conquered several city-states, including Samaria and its ally, Damascus. Assyria conquered Carchemish in 717, Calno (that is, Calneh, in northern Syria, cf. Amos 6:2) in 738, Arpad in 740 and again in 720, Hamath in 738 and 720, Damascus in 732, and Samaria in 722–721. (See Roberts 2015, 166; Wildberger 1991, 419–20. For a map showing these various sites, see Aharoni and Avi-Yonah 1977, 93, map 146.) The progression in the text, which is geographical rather than chronological, is ominous (see Gray 1912, 197). It reads, literally: "Is not like Carchemish, Calno? Or not like Arpad, Hamath? Or not like Damascus, Samaria?" In each pairing, the second site named is closer to Jerusalem than the first. The list starts in the far north (Carchemish), moves southward to Calno and Arpad (which were close to each other), and then progresses southward to Hamath, Damascus, and finally Samaria.

> **Conquered**
> Most assume that Isaiah 10:9 describes a series of past conquests, but Smith (2007, 257–58) prefers a combination of past and present. The fall of Carchemish (which he dates to 742 B.C.), Arpad, and Damascus were past, while the fall of Calno, Hamath, and Samaria were future. The reference in 10:7 to the conquest of "many nations," as something envisioned by Assyria might favor this view. However, 10:7 may simply summarize Assyrian policy. The use of the perfect in 10:10 to describe how Assyria conquered "the kingdoms of the idols" and again in 10:11 to describe the conquest of Samaria suggests these city-states had already been conquered (cf. 10:13–14). Assyria was now focused on a "godless nation" (10:6), namely Judah and its capital Jerusalem, the conquest of which was future (note the imperfect in the final line of 10:11).

10:10–11. The idol-gods of these states had not been able to protect their worshippers from Assyria and, from the Assyrian perspective, the idols of Samaria and Judah were inferior (10:10). The idols of Judah would fare no better than the idols of Samaria (10:11). This boast is a commentary on both Assyria and the Lord's covenant community. From the Assyrians' polytheistic perspective, idol-gods defended nations and the Assyrians were confident in the superiority of their gods, particularly Assur. Their boast also reflects the tragic reality that Israel and Judah were idolatrous and trusting in their false gods for national security (cf. Isa. 1:29–31; 2:8, 18, 20; 17:7–8, 10–11; 27:9; 30:22; 31:6).

10:12. Having established Assyria's pride as the basis for judgment, the prophet formally announces the Sovereign Lord's (the title אֲדֹנָי appears) intervention in judgment. The Lord had to complete his "work" of judgment against Jerusalem (cf. 5:12, 19), using the Assyrians as his agent. Then he would turn his attention to the king of Assyria. At this point the prophet quotes the Lord directly, as the switch to the first-person singular verb indicates ("I will punish"). "Punish" translates the Hebrew idiom "visit upon" (פָּקַד עַל). In several passages this expression refers to a retributive act. Often the one toward whom retribution is directed is identified after the preposition, while the reason for retribution (wrongdoing) is the object of the verb, sometimes being identified with the accusative sign (cf. Jer. 23:2). However, on other occasions, as here, the preposition simply introduces the object of punishment.

In Isaiah 10:12 the compound object has inherent within it the reason for judgment. It reads literally, "the fruit of the greatness of the heart of the king of Assyria and the beauty of the height of his eyes." The reference to "fruit" suggests the image of a tree, especially when collocated with גֹּדֶל, "greatness," which is used of the height of a tree in Ezekiel 31:7. In this case the fruit is the proud boasting (Isa. 10:8–11, 13–14; cf. Young

1965, 364) produced by the king's heart, which elevates itself with pride. In the parallel line, תִּפְאֶרֶת, "beauty," is used of that in which Assyria takes pride (cf. Isa. 4:2; 13:19; 20:5). Here it refers to the king's self-perception as he raises his eyes in pride. The shift from heart to eyes accurately reflects how arrogance develops. The pride rooted in one's heart surfaces in one's condescending look (cf. Motyer 1993, 115).

There are two significant intertextual links between this verse and the preceding literary unit: (1) The Lord speaks literally of the "fruit of the greatness of heart" of the Assyrian king, referring to the boastful words that his proud heart spews out. The expression "greatness of heart" (גֹּדֶל לֵבָב) also appears in 9:9 (HB 8), where it describes the pride of the northern kingdom as they boasted about rebuilding in the aftermath of divine judgment. The Lord had to punish the pride of his people, but the Assyrians were also proud and would become the targets of divine justice. (2) In 10:12 the Lord announced he would "punish" (פָּקַד) Assyria for its pride, just as he had warned his sinful people of a day of punishment (10:3; יוֹם פְּקֻדָּה). Punishment comes upon all who deserve it—both the Lord's covenant community and the Assyrians.

10:13. Prior to the announcement of judgment, the prophet used Assyria's own words to illustrate their arrogance and to condemn them (see Seitz 1993, 93). Now, having issued the official announcement of judgment, he expands upon the accusation (note כִּי, "for," at the beginning of 10:13) as he quotes the king of Assyria. The Assyrian king boasts of his strong hand and wisdom that have enabled him to take away the territory and wealth of nations. As Wildberger (1991, 421) points out, removing boundaries entails more than simply conquering an area. It alludes to the Assyrian practice of taking people into exile and then resettling others in their territory. Wildberger argues that such a practice was especially wicked because it violated the boundaries established by God (cf. Deut. 32:8).

As "a mighty one," the Assyrian king brings down those who stand in his way (literally, "those who sit"). The referent of the substantival participle יוֹשְׁבִים, "those who sit," is uncertain. It could refer to the inhabitants of the conquered lands (cf. Ps. 56:7 [HB 8]; see Gray 1912, 199). Another option is that the participle refers to those who sit on thrones, namely, kings (see BDB s.v. "יָשַׁב" mng. 1a, 442; *HALOT* s.v. "ישׁב" mng. 2, 444). In this case, the Assyrian king brings them down from their elevated positions as he establishes his rule over their lands.

The verbal forms used in Isaiah 10:13b have puzzled some. In 10:13a the Assyrian king begins with a perfect ("I have done"), suggesting that a historical review will follow. Isaiah 10:14 favors this, for the *wayyiqtol* at the beginning of the verse (literally, "my hand found"), followed by the perfect ("I gathered"), refer to accomplished deeds. In 10:13b there are three first-person verb forms. One is clearly perfect (שׁוֹשֵׂתִי, "I plundered"), but the other two first-person forms appear to be imperfects with so-called simple (or conjunctive) *waw*. Most repoint the conjunctions as consecutive (*wa-*) and read the forms as preterite, literally, "I removed ... I brought down," which easily solves the problem and produces a consistency of perspective for 10:13–14 (Blenkinsopp 2000, 252; Gray 1912, 202; Roberts 2015, 165; see as well as HCSB, NASB, NIV11).

But is this solution too easy? Perhaps the variation is intended. Various explanations are possible, all of which enhance the boast rhetorically: (1) The Assyrian king, in boasting of his past accomplishments, may blend the past and the present, since his imperialism is a continuing reality. In this case, the imperfects have a present progressive nuance: "I am removing ... I plundered ... I am bringing down." (2) As he speaks of the past, he may briefly generalize, with the imperfects having a habitual nuance: "I (always) remove ... I plundered ... I (always) bring down." (3) As he describes his accomplishments in factual terms, he may briefly lapse into a more dramatic mode, inviting the listener to watch the removal of boundaries and subduing of victims. In this case, the imperfects have a past progressive or, better, rhetorical (historical) present nuance. (The translation would be the same as number 1 above.) (4) Finally, he may, in describing his exploits, want to emphasize that his victories were typical, using the imperfects in a customary manner: "I would (typically) remove . . . I plundered . . . I would (typically) bring down."

10:14. The proud king illustrates how easy his conquests were. Taking the wealth of nations was as easy as gathering eggs from a nest that has been abandoned by the mother bird. He simply reached into the nest, as it were, and gathered up "all the countries [literally, earth]." There were no flapping wings or chirping. In other words, he encountered no real resistance or objections. "All the earth," while certainly boastful, accurately reflects the widespread conquests of the Assyrian kings, who extended their empire in all directions and boasted of their exploits. (For a striking example of such boasting from Sargon, the conqueror of Samaria, see Roberts 2015, 167.)

10:15. The prophet illustrates the absurdity of the Assyrian king's arrogance. The Lord chose the Assyrians as his agent of judgment, but they did not recognize his sovereignty. They were like an ax, saw, rod, or club in his hand, subject to his will. For the Assyrian king to boast as he did was as ridiculous as one of these weapons or implements trying to swing its owner around. The Assyrians would soon discover that the Lord controls them, not vice versa. As Gray (1912, 199) says, "history is the revelation of Yahweh's purpose, not of Assyria's might." Wildberger (1991, 422) suggests the illustration also indicates the Assyrians had violated the natural order of the world. God takes such violations very seriously. He states, "World order does not rest within itself. It is established by God, and whoever collides with it must deal with Yahweh."

10:16–17. Because of Assyria's hubris, the Lord would judge them (note לָכֵן, "therefore," at the beginning of 10:16). The prophet now expands his earlier announcement of judgment, drawing attention to the Lord's sovereignty by calling him, literally, "the Lord, the Lord of Armies." Isaiah uses the title הָאָדוֹן, "the Lord," five times; each time it appears before the title "Lord of Armies" (see Isa. 1:24; 3:1; 10:16, 33; 19:4) and depicts God in his role as the sovereign king who leads armies and brings judgment against evildoers. By placing the definite article on the title, the prophet emphasizes that the God of Israel is "the Lord," or "Master," par excellence. Of course, there is irony here, for earlier "the Master, the Lord of Armies" came in judgment against his people (1:24; 3:1), but now he attacks their enemy.

The Lord sent Assyria as his agent of judgment (10:6; אֲשַׁלְּחֶנּוּ, "I send him,"); now he would send (יְשַׁלַּח, "will send") a wasting disease against the Assyrian king's "sturdy warriors" (10:16a; cf. Smith 2007, 260). The term translated "sturdy warriors" pictures well-fed, healthy men. But the Lord would afflict them with a "wasting disease" that would rob them of their physical strength. The term translated "wasting disease" (רָזוֹן) refers to physical leanness; the noun is derived from a verbal root (רָזָה) meaning "decrease, dwindle." The image is one of strong warriors being reduced to skin and bones. The prophecy anticipates the destruction of Sennacherib's Assyrian army by the angel of the Lord in 701 B.C. (Isa. 37:36).

By destroying the Assyrian army, the Lord would also destroy the Assyrian king's "pomp" (כָּבוֹד, "glory, splendor"), which refers here to his pompous pride and self-exaltation (cf. Isa. 8:7). The Lord would ignite it with fire (10:16b). Indeed, the Lord himself would be this fire (10:17a). He is called the "Light of Israel," a divine title that occurs only here. Light is associated elsewhere with God's ability to save his people (Ps. 27:1; Mic. 7:8) and to guide the nations with his wise and just decisions (Isa. 2:5). But here, ironically, this light becomes a destructive fire that consumes the arrogant Assyrians (Wildberger 1991, 431–32). The Lord is also called Israel's Holy One, a title that reflects his sovereign position (see commentary on Isa. 1:4 above). Here the Holy One becomes a devouring flame.

In the path of the divine fire the Assyrians would be like thorns and briers that are swiftly consumed (10:17b, note "in a single day"). The imagery of thorns and briers is ironic, for the prophet used it earlier to describe the aftermath of the Lord's judgment on Judah (5:6; 7:23) and the self-destructive effect of Israel's sin that the Lord allows to consume the nation (9:18–19 [HB 17–18]). But now the Assyrians would be the object of divine judgment. The phrase "a single day" is also ironic since the prophet used it earlier to describe the Lord's judgment on Israel (cf. 9:14 [HB 13]). Assyria would now experience a sudden demise.

10:18. Of course, the Assyrians did not view themselves as thorns and briers—more like an impressive forest and a fruitful land (or, better, orchard). The fire of the Lord would thoroughly burn the forest and orchard (10:18a). The text reads literally, "and the glory of his forest and his orchard, from breath to flesh, he will destroy." The expression "breath to flesh" indicates the totality of one's being, encompassing both the immaterial (breath) and material (flesh) components.

This reference to breath and flesh marks a transition in images as the prophet pictures Assyria as a sick person who wastes away (10:18b; cf. 10:16a). The text reads literally, "like (the) melting of one who is sick (or staggers)" (כִּמְסֹס נֹסֵס). The repetition of the letter *samekh* (four times in the span of five consonants) draws attention to the statement. The form כִּמְסֹס comprises the comparative preposition -כְּ and the infinitive construct of מָסַס, which means "to dissolve, melt." Here it pictures an individual wasting away. The form נֹסֵס is a substantival participle from נָסַס, which occurs only here. Based on cognate evidence, a meaning "be sick" (cf. Syriac) or "shake, tremble" (cf. Akkadian) seems likely (see Wildberger 1991, 428).

10:19. The prophet returns to the primary metaphor of fire. The Lord's fire would devastate the Assyrian forest, leaving only a few trees standing—so few, in fact, that even a child who knows just a few numbers would be able to count them (10:19). The meager number of trees is referred to literally as "the remnant of the trees of his forest." The reference to a "remnant" (שְׁאָר) sets up a transition to the next literary unit, which focuses on the remnant (שְׁאָר) of Israel (Smith 2007, 261 n. 392).

Hope for the Remnant (10:20–23)
The Lord would preserve a remnant of Israel.

10:20. The statement וְהָיָה בַּיּוֹם הַהוּא, "and it will be in that day," marks a shift to the next literary unit within the speech. The prophet has just mentioned how the Lord's judgment would reduce Assyria to a remnant (cf. 10:19). Now he focuses on the remnant of Israel/Jacob as he envisions a time when the Lord would reverse his judgment on his people. The referent of Israel/Jacob is not clear. It includes the northern kingdom since 10:21 states that "a remnant will return." This is a play on Isaiah's son's name (Shear-jashub), which was a reminder that the Lord would defeat the northern kingdom (cf. 7:3). But Judah may be in view as well, since the prophet says the remnant would no longer rely on the one who struck them (10:20a). In this context this seems to refer to Judah's alliance with Assyria, which backfired on them in the end (cf. 7:17–25; 8:7–8). Assyria reduced both the northern kingdom and Judah to a remnant. In 722–721 B.C. the Assyrians took most of the population in the north into exile, and in 701 Sennacherib took a large number of people from Judah into exile. He boasted that he took 200,150 captives, along with numerous livestock, and that he conquered several towns, leaving Jerusalem isolated.

A day was coming when the Lord's people would no longer rely on such an unreliable nation. Instead, they would shift their allegiance to where it belongs—the Holy One of Israel, who is sovereign over nations (10:20b). There is irony here, for earlier the prophet accused Israel of spurning the Holy One of Israel and his word (1:4; 5:24). Those who did so would pay the consequences, but the remnant would place genuine faith in him. This verb translated "rely" has a concrete meaning, "to lean on for support" (Judg. 16:26; 2 Sam. 1:6; 2 Kings 5:8). When used metaphorically it refers to relying on an object for help and protection. Israel had relied on its own schemes and policies (Isa. 30:12) and its foreign alliances (Isa. 31:1). They gave lip service to the Lord (cf. 1:11–15), but their words were insincere, for they worshipped other gods and trusted in foreign alliances. However, a day would come when they would sincerely trust the Lord for security. The word translated "truly" (literally, "in truth") means "sincerely, honestly" (cf. Josh. 24:14; Judg. 9:15; 1 Sam. 12:24; 1 Kings 2:24; 3:6; 2 Kings 20:3 = Isa. 38:3; Isa. 48:1), "fairly" (Judg. 9:16, 19; Isa. 16:5; 61:8; Jer. 4:2), or "truly, faithfully" (Jer. 26:15; 28:9; 32:41).

10:21. Drawing on his own son's name (Isa. 7:3), the prophet announces that "a remnant will return." When Isaiah met Ahaz, he took his son with him. Their names were meant to encourage the weak king. Isaiah's name ("salvation is the Lord") was a reminder that the Lord is fully capable of saving his people, while Shearjashub's name ("a remnant will return") assured the king that only a remnant of the Aramean-Israelite coalition's army would return home once the Lord had defeated them. Of course, Ahaz's lack of faith compromised this promise (see the commentary above on 7:5–9). In the end, both the northern kingdom and Judah suffered terribly.

But now a reversal would take place. A remnant of Jacob would return to the Mighty God. "Return" may have a double meaning here: the remnant would "return" spiritually; they would repent of their sin and put their trust in the Lord (10:20; cf. the use of שׁוּב in 1:27; 6:10; 9:13 [HB 12]; 19:22; 31:6). But the term may also refer to their physical restoration from exile (cf. 35:10).

The title "Mighty God" (אֵל גִּבּוֹר) occurs only here and in Isaiah 9:6, where it is a royal title of the coming king, attesting to his God-given power as a warrior. This king is a possible referent here, in which case the prophet pictures Israel renewing its allegiance to both the Lord ("the Holy One of Israel," cf. 10:20) and the Davidic king (cf. Hos. 3:5; cf. Hayes and Irvine 1987, 202). However, it seems more likely that the "Mighty God" and "the Holy One of Israel" are one and the same here. A similar title is used of God in Deuteronomy 10:17; Jeremiah 32:18; and Nehemiah 9:32.

10:22. The announcement about a remnant returning to the Mighty God is a positive statement about Israel's future, but there is also inherent in it a negative aspect. The mere mention of a *remnant* implies that judgment would drastically reduce the population of the covenant community. The prophet envisions a situation where the nation is as numerous as the sand on the sea(shore). Even in that case, only a remnant would return. The imagery of sand upon the seashore is used elsewhere for a large number (cf. Gen. 41:49; Josh. 11:4; Judg. 7:12; 1 Sam. 13:5). It recalls the patriarchal promise that God would make Abraham's descendants as numerous as the granules of sand on the seashore (Gen. 22:17; 32:12). Usually the expression is "like the sand which is upon the sea" or "like the sand which is upon the shore of the sea," but the abbreviated "sand of the sea," which appears in Isaiah 10:22, also occurs. The words are ironic; the hypothetical formulation hints at the reality. Israel had indeed grown to be a great nation (2 Sam. 17:11; 1 Kings 4:20) in fulfillment of God's promise to the patriarchs. But judgment, prompted by Israel's rebellion, reduced the population to a mere remnant. (For further discussion, see below under Theological Focus.)

The prophet characterizes the coming judgment as thorough. He uses a rare word to refer to it (כִּלָּיוֹן). This word is used in only one other passage (Deut. 28:65), where it describes failing eyesight. The term is derived from the verb כָּלָה, "be finished" (used of God's judgment on Assyria in Isa. 10:18), and is related to the noun כָּלָה, "destruction," used in 10:23. It pictures judgment as thorough.

Judgment was also certain; it had been decreed (חָרוּץ, passive participle of חָרַץ). This word appears to have a primary meaning of "cut, carve" (cf. Lev. 22:22, as well as its derivatives). When used in an abstract manner, it means "to fix, determine, decide" (*HALOT* s.v. "חָרַץ I" 356). In 2 Kings 20:40 it refers to a formal, official royal decree. In Daniel it is used of God's fixed plan for Israel's future (9:26–27; 11:36). Here in Isaiah, God's coming judgment upon Israel is fixed or decreed (cf. 10:23, as well as 28:22, where judgment is directed against the "whole land"). The basic meaning of the term (an indelible mark is suggested) and usage elsewhere indicate a formal, irrevocable decree is in view. However, this did not mean the Lord would abandon his people. Though inevitable, judgment was designed to purify, and the Lord promised that a remnant of the exiles would be restored and reunited with the people of Judah under one king (cf. Isa. 11).

This judgment would also be entirely deserved. The prophet characterizes it literally as "overflowing [שׁוֹטֵף] (with) righteousness." The verb שָׁטַף, "overflow," has a frightening connotation; it is used in 8:8 of the Assyrian invasion, which is likened to a flood. Judgment would flood the land, but it would be an overwhelming expression of divine righteousness (צְדָקָה). Earlier Isaiah used this word of the justice demanded by God (1:27; 5:7, 23). Here it refers to the outworking of God's justice against those who have violated his standards (cf. 5:16). Those who refuse to promote justice among God's covenant community face the prospect of being on the receiving end of his retributive justice against the unjust.

10:23. Isaiah formally identifies the judge as the Sovereign Master (אֲדֹנָי) and the Lord of Armies as he reiterates that judgment is certain and would be thorough. He refers to the judgment literally as "destruction and that which is decreed." This is a hendiadys (cf. Young 1965, 370 n. 54), where two words are combined with the second modifying the first. We can paraphrase, "certain [that is, decreed, cf. 10:22] destruction." This judgment, which was imminent, would penetrate to the very heart of the land (the Hebrew reads literally, "in the midst of all the land").

Good News for Zion (10:24–34)
The Lord would deliver Jerusalem from the Assyrian assault.

10:24. The prophet returns to his positive message of salvation. At first, the use of לָכֵן, "therefore," at the beginning of 10:24 is puzzling, since judgment is the theme of the immediately preceding verses (10:22–23). How could the reality of impending judgment be the logical basis for not fearing? But לָכֵן must be understood in relation to the positive message of 10:20–21, with 10:22–23 being a parenthesis of sorts. The Lord has assured his people that he will preserve a remnant. Consequently, his people need not fear.

This formal salvation oracle, marked out by the formula "do not be afraid," comes from the Sovereign Master, the Lord of Armies. These are the same titles used in the previous verse to describe the one who would bring judgment upon the land. Ironically, this same God now assures his people. By using "my people," he assures them that he has not severed his relationship with them (cf. Motyer 1993, 118; Smith 2007, 263; Wildberger 1991, 442; Young 1965, 371). More specifically, the exhortation is addressed to those who live in Zion (Jerusalem) and are facing the Assyrian menace. Like Egypt of old, the Assyrians were already beating them with a rod and brandishing a club against them, or they would soon be doing so.

10:25. The Lord assures his people that his anger (זַעַם) at them (cf. 10:5 [note זַעַם], 22b–23) would come to an end very soon. He would then turn his wrath (אַף) against Assyria. Earlier the Lord directed his wrath at his own people in an unrelenting manner (cf. 5:25; 9:11, 16, 20 [HB 10, 15, 19]). In 10:4, after this judgment seems to reach its climax, we again read that the Lord's wrath had not subsided. A woe oracle against Assyria immediately follows (10:5), indicating that the Lord's wrath would turn against the arrogant instrument of his judgment. Here in 10:25, this theme is further developed.

10:26. The Lord of Armies would direct his wrath at Assyria with great vigor, as the imagery of 10:26 reveals. He would lash them with a whip, as violently as when he struck down Midian at the rock of Oreb. The prophet alludes to Gideon's battle with Midian, when the Ephraimites executed the Midianite general Oreb at a rock subsequently named for him as reminder of the Israelite victory (Judg. 7:25). This is the second time Isaiah alludes to Gideon's victory over Midian to describe the Lord's future victory over Assyria (cf. Isa. 9:4 [HB 3]). The analogy is appropriate because both foreign powers come against Israel with an overwhelming manpower advantage, only to be devastated by the Lord.

The second half of 10:26 reads literally, "and his staff (will be) over the sea, and he will lift it in the way of Egypt." If the text is retained, "the sea" alludes to the exodus. Since the next clause mentions the Lord raising his staff "as he did in Egypt" (literally, "in the way [or manner?] of Egypt") this reading fits the context. God instructed Moses to raise his staff (Exod. 14:16) and stretch out his hand over the sea, first to divide the waters so Israel could escape (14:21–22) and then to cause the waters to return so Pharaoh's army would be destroyed (14:26–28). The point of the allusion, as in the first half of the verse, is that Israel's God would intervene in miraculous power against Assyria just as he had in Israel's early history. The language also contributes to Isaiah's development of a second exodus theme, where the future deliverance of the people from exile is described in terms of the exodus from Egypt in Moses's day (cf. Isa. 11:15–16; 51:9–10).

The "sea" is an apt symbol for Assyria. In two lament psalms the sea symbolizes the primordial chaos that opposed the Lord's creative work (Pss. 74:13–14; 89:9–10 [HB 10–11]). Psalms of praise historicize the image by applying it to hostile nations that oppose the Lord and his people (Pss. 18:14–18 [HB 15–19]; 29:3, 10–11; 46:2–3, 6 [HB 3–4, 7]; 65:7 [HB 8]; 77:13–20 [HB 14–21]; 93:1–4; Chisholm 2013a, 75–84). In Isaiah 5:30 the prophet uses the image of the sea in his description of the Assyrian army. By using the sea to symbolize Assyria, the prophet acknowledges the enemy's apparent power, but he also reminds his Israelite audience that the Lord has always overcome the sea, from the time of creation throughout history.

Isaiah 10:26 highlights the reversal that would occur as the Lord turns his anger away from his people and directs it toward Assyria. Assyria was the club (מַטֶּה) of the Lord's anger (10:5), directed against Israel (10:6). The Assyrians lifted (נָשָׂא) their club (מַטֶּה) against the Lord's people, as Egypt had done long ago (10:24). But now the Lord would lift (נָשָׂא) his staff (מַטֶּה) over "the sea," as Moses did when the Egyptians tried to destroy Israel and met their demise in the waters of the Red Sea. Assyria's fate would be the same as Egypt's. Assyria struck (נָכָה) the Lord's people (10:24), but now the Lord would destroy

Assyria, as when he struck down Midian (10:26; note כְּמַכַּת, literally, "like the striking down").

10:27. When the Lord defeats Assyria, the burden placed on the Lord's people by the Assyrians would be removed (cf. 9:4 [HB 3]; 14:25). The image is that of an ox weighed down by a burdensome yoke. In 10:27b the Hebrew text reads, "and (the) yoke will be removed [or perhaps, broken] because of fat." If the reading is retained, this would refer to the yoke being removed or broken because the ox's neck has grown so large, suggesting it has been well fed. This would allude to the Lord's blessing (see Oswalt 1986, 273). However, the image is problematic, for earlier (cf. 9:4) Isaiah pictures the Lord shattering the Assyrian yoke, which is consistent with the imagery in 10:26. This sudden, violent removal of the Assyrian yoke seems inconsistent with the image in 10:27b, which implies that the Lord's blessing would be concurrent with Assyrian oppression. This seems to run counter to the immediate context, where the defeat of Assyria appears to precede the restoration of divine blessing. This apparent incongruity has led to some rather radical emendations of the text (see Wildberger 1991, 439–40). However, Smith (2007, 265) has proposed that "fat," rather than referring to restored blessing, alludes to Assyria's wealth, acquired in part through their oppressive taxation of Judah. As Smith points out, earlier in this speech "fatness" is associated with the Assyrians (10:16) and the image of a person wasting away is used to describe their demise (10:16, 18). So, in 10:27b "fat" alludes to Assyrian oppression, which is the basis for the Lord's judgment (10:26).

10:28–32. The prophet now shifts gears as he describes Assyria's assault upon Zion (cf. 10:24). The Assyrian army approaches from the north, passing through Aiath, Migron, and Michmash, where they store supplies (10:28). They camp at Geba, striking fear in the hearts of nearby Ramah and Gibeah (10:29). The prophet dramatically addresses Gallim, Laishah, and Anathoth (10:30) and observes that the people of Madmenah and Gebim are seeking cover (10:31). The Assyrian army arrives at Nob, just northeast of Jerusalem, and defiantly shakes its fist (literally, "waves its hand") at Jerusalem, called "Daughter Zion," perhaps to highlight her vulnerability.

Isaiah seems to be describing Sennacherib's assault on Jerusalem in 701 B.C., which ended in humiliating defeat for the Assyrian army (see 10:26, 33–34; cf. 8:9–10). However, historical records indicate Sennacherib approached Jerusalem from the southwest, not the north. This has given rise to a variety of interpretations of 10:28–32 (see Clements 1980, 117–18, for a survey). Hayes and Irvine (1987, 209–10; cf. also Roberts 2015, 174–75), for example, understand the passage as a description of the Israelite-Aramean invasion of Judah in Ahaz's day (ca. 735–733; cf. Isa. 7:1). But the context clearly has Assyria in view (10:5, 12, 24) and the speech postdates the fall of both Aram and Israel (10:9–11). Some suggest this invasion of Judah occurred during one of Sargon's western campaigns, either in 720 (Sweeney 1994, 457–70) or in 713–711 (Wildberger 1991, 451), but external support is lacking. (However, see Aster 2007, 254 n. 25.) Another option is that Sennacherib's forces approached Jerusalem from two directions, but again this is speculative. It is probably best to see the description as rhetorical. While it reflects how one might expect Assyria to invade, they did not in fact take this route when the event unfolded. The prophet's purpose, writing prior to the event, was to evoke the dramatic effect of a fast-approaching, intimidating invader, not to provide precise details. (See Motyer 1993, 119; Oswalt 1986, 274–75; Young 1965, 374.)

10:33–34. As the Assyrian invader taunts Daughter Zion, the prophet suddenly draws attention (note הִנֵּה) to the Lord (הָאָדוֹן), the LORD of Armies (cf. 10:16). He would chop down the

Assyrians, compared in their pride to large trees (cf. 2:12–14 for the imagery). They would fall with a mighty crash. Though the Assyrians were like a great forest (cf. 10:18–19), the Lord would topple them. Assyria may have been as impressive as the great Lebanon forest, yet it would fall. Ironically, just as the Lord's people would fall in the coming judgment (cf. 10:4), so their enemy, the Lord's instrument of judgment, would eventually fall as well.

The precise meaning of the final line is unclear. The Hebrew text reads, "and the Lebanon, as/by a mighty one, will fall." Lebanon, known for its great trees, is obviously a symbol of the Assyrians (cf. Ezek. 31:3). This is ironic, for the Assyrians boasted of cutting down cedars in the Lebanon forest. The adjective אַדִּיר is used substantively as a title, "Mighty One."

TRANSLATION ANALYSIS 10:34

How do we interpret the prefixed preposition -בְּ prefixed to אַדִּיר? It could be used in the sense of "in the capacity of" (the so-called bet of identity), in which case Assyria is the mighty one (see Williamson 2018, 640–41). We can paraphrase, "Lebanon will fall *as* a mighty one," that is, despite its being so mighty. See HCSB, "Lebanon with its majesty will fall"; *Tanakh*, "Lebanon trees shall fall in their majesty"; NRSV, "Lebanon with its majestic trees will fall." Another option is to take the preposition as introducing the agent, in which case the Lord is the Mighty One (cf. Isa. 33:21; see Motyer 1993, 120; Young 1965, 375): "Lebanon will fall *by* the Mighty One." The following translations support this interpretation: NIV11, "Lebanon will fall before the Mighty One"; ESV, "Lebanon will fall by the Majestic One"; NASB, "Lebanon will fall by the Mighty One."

THEOLOGICAL FOCUS

The theological focus of this passage can be stated as follows: the Sovereign Lord sometimes uses proud nations to punish his people, but when these nations fail to acknowledge the Lord's sovereignty and boast of their own strength, the Lord judges them, for he hates and opposes human pride. As the prophet develops this theological theme, the following emphases emerge:

1. The Sovereign Lord opposes the proud.

The Sovereign Lord opposes the proud and unleashes his power against them in judgment. The proud challenge the Lord's authority, which prompts him to demonstrate his sovereignty. This passage highlights the Lord's sovereignty, not only in its description of his judgment upon the proud Assyrians but also through the divine titles that appear. The Lord is called the Sovereign Master (אֲדֹנָי; 10:12, 23–24), the Lord (הָאָדוֹן; 10:16, 33), the Lord of Armies (10:16, 23–24, 26, 33), Israel's "Holy One" (10:17, 20), Mighty God (10:21), and Mighty One (depending on how one understands the syntax in 10:34; see above).

The Assyrians' pride was evident in their estimation of their own power and in their boasting. The Lord intended to use them as his agent of punishment. The punishment was designed to be severe (10:6), but the Assyrians were excessive. Rather than merely defeating Israel and robbing it of its wealth, they intended to destroy many nations (10:7). They attributed their success to their own strength and wisdom (10:13) and boasted of the ease with which they conquered nations (10:14). They were like an ax trying to wield the woodsman (10:15) as they defiantly shook their fist at Jerusalem (10:32). The Lord would bring down their pride, much like a fire that burns down a forest (10:16–18) or a woodsman who chops down great trees with his ax (10:33–34).

2. The Sovereign Lord spares a remnant.

The Sovereign Lord must sometimes punish his sinful people. Indeed, justice demands it. The prophet describes the Lord's judgment on Israel as (literally) "overflowing (with) righteousness" (10:22). But even when such an outpouring of retribution is necessary, the Lord mercifully spares a remnant and restores his relationship with them (10:20–21) because of his commitment to his people.

The Lord promised Abraham and Jacob that he would make their descendants as numerous as the granules of sand on the seashore (Gen. 22:17; 32:12). In fulfillment of this promise, Israel grew to be a great nation (2 Sam. 17:11; 1 Kings 4:20). But the Lord's judgment would reduce the nation to a mere remnant (Isa. 10:20–21). This does not negate the Lord's promise, however. The Lord's irrevocable promises are sure, but the timing of their fulfillment is often contingent upon human factors as divine sovereignty and human responsibility are held in delicate balance. In Israel's case, human sin undid the Lord's work, causing his people to forfeit the enjoyment of divine blessings that could have been theirs and postponing the ultimate fulfillment of the Abrahamic covenant (cf. Isa. 48:19). (See Oswalt 1986, 271.) But another eighth-century prophet, Hosea, assures Israel that the promise will be fulfilled (Hos. 1:10 [HB 2:1]).

PREACHING AND TEACHING STRATEGIES

Exegetical and Theological Synthesis

Isaiah 10:5–34 focuses on the theme of God's judgment against Assyria. Central to the rationale for this judgment is Assyria's pretentious pride. Isaiah 10:12 serves as a summary statement for the chapter: "When the LORD has finished all his work against Mount Zion and Jerusalem, he will say, 'I will punish the king of Assyria for the willful pride of his heart and the haughty look in his eyes.'" A parallel idea that runs throughout this passage is God's judgment against Israel/Judah. She too had exhibited pride (9:8 [HB 7]) in her relationship toward God, resulting in severe judgment. Ironically, the agent of God's judgment against prideful Israel is none other than arrogant Assyria. However, as soon as God is finished using Assyria as his agent of judgment, he will turn his wrath against her too.

While both Assyria and Israel/Judah are guilty of pride before God, only Judah will repent and turn back to him. Thus, Judah stands in contrast to Assyria in this passage. Whereas both nations receive judgment from Yahweh in response to their pride, a remnant in Israel will ultimately be the recipients of God's grace and protection when they posture themselves in humility before him and repent of their sinful pride.

From a homiletical standpoint, this passage can be divided into three sections based on two forms of pride exhibited by Assyria (10:5–11 and 12–19) and a third form of pride exhibited (but repented of) by Judah (20–22).

The first expression of pride that Isaiah confronts is the sin of self-centeredness in Assyria. The Assyrian leaders completely ignored God's purposes for them and brazenly attempted to be and do whatever they wanted. In 10:5–6, the prophet highlights how God was propping up Assyria to use them as a tool of judgment against rebellious Israel. Assyria was "the rod" of God's "anger" wielded by him against Israel (10:5). However, Assyria refused to consider God's role in their dominance on the world stage, nor did they care about what God's will was for them. Whereas 10:5–6 express the Lord's intention to use Assyria for his purposes, 10:7 says: "But this is not what he intends, this is not what he has in mind; his purpose is to destroy, to put an end to many nations."

God had a limited role for Assyria to play, but they didn't care. They overestimated their own greatness and assumed they were free to pursue whatever they wanted. Assyria pompously boasted, "Are not my commanders all kings?" (10:8). In other words, their military leaders were so dominant that they could do whatever they pleased. The Lord did not intend to have Assyria completely conquer Israel; he determined instead to preserve a remnant in

The Lord Brings Down the Proud Assyrians (10:5–34)

Judah. However, the king of Assyria gave no thought whatsoever to what God's will was. He cared only about his own self-centered ambitions. Just as Assyria had exerted its will on cities like Calno, Carchemish, Hamath, Arpad, Samaria, and Damascus, he imagined that he would do the same to Jerusalem (10:9). He further asserted that Jerusalem's and Samaria's gods (idols) were no match for him (10:10–11). In other words, he couldn't care less what Israel's/Judah's gods thought about his conquest into their land, for in his mind he was far superior in power to them.

As mentioned above, 10:12 serves as a summary statement of God's rationale for judging Assyria for his arrogant heart and boastful countenance. It also serves as a transition between 10:5–11 and 13–19. It summarizes 10:5–11, where the prophet confronted Assyria's pride of self-centeredness in their pursuit of their own interests over the Lord's. It also introduces 10:13–19, which highlight a second form of pride exhibited by the Assyrians: self-exaltation. If the pride of self-centeredness equates to an unwillingness to search out and follow the Lord's will for one's life, self-exaltation replaces a person's responsibility to exalt and worship God with the misguided notion of their own greatness and the desire to celebrate themselves.

Assyria evaluated all that God had empowered them to do militarily on the world stage, and rather than humbly worship God and credit him with those accomplishments Assyria chose to boast in their own perceived greatness:

> By the strength of my hand I have done this,
>   and by my wisdom, because I have
>   understanding.
> I removed the boundaries of nations,
>   I plundered their treasures;
>   like a mighty one I subdued their kings.
> As one reaches into a nest,
>   so my hand reached for the wealth of the
>   nations;
> as people gather abandoned eggs,
>   so I gathered all the countries;
> not one flapped a wing,
>   or opened its mouth to chirp. (10:13–14)

Assyria's boastful speech in these verses is all about what they have accomplished on their own. Notice all the uses of personal pronouns: "*my* hand," "*I* have done this," "by *my* wisdom," "*I* have understanding," "*I* removed the boundaries," "*I* plundered their treasures," "*I* subdued their kings," "*my* hand reached," and "*I* gathered." Not once does the king of Assyria pause to give the Lord credit for any of his accomplishments. His prideful boasting exalts himself exclusively. He is oblivious to reality, though, because God is the one who has sovereignly decided that Assyria would rule over their rival nations. God is even the one who granted the Assyrians military success over the Lord's own people Israel. Thus, God asks, "Does the ax raise itself above the person who swings it, or the saw boast against the one who uses it?" (10:15). How ridiculous that an ax would take credit for chopping down trees while failing to credit the one who wielded it!

Because the ax has boasted against the one who wielded it in the chopping down of various trees (other cities and nations), God will metaphorically chop down the forest that is the Assyrian military. The prophet predicts that Israel, God's holy nation, would become a fire that would burn and devour thorns and briers (= Assyria, 10:17). The Lord's fire would destroy "the splendor of his forests and fertile fields" (10:18; cf. 10:33–34). As a result, "the remaining trees of his forests will be so few that a child could write them down" (10:19). He would do this by sending "a wasting disease upon his sturdy warriors" (10:16). This defeat of Assyria's military warriors will happen "in a single day" (10:17).

The prophecy now shifts over to the remnant of Israel (10:20–34). The prophet says, "In that day the remnant of Israel, the survivors of Jacob, will no longer rely on him who struck them down but will truly rely on the Lord, the Holy

One of Israel" (10:20). If Assyria demonstrated pride against the Lord by their self-centeredness and their self-exaltation, Israel displayed pride against God by their self-sufficiency and failure to depend upon him for protection and salvation (Isa. 7:10–13; 8:5–8, 13–14, 17, 19; 9:13 [HB 12]). Up until this point, God's people had rejected any dependence upon God. Instead, they tried to create their own saviors through questionable alliances with foreign nations like Syria (Isa. 7:1–9; 8:5–6) and Assyria (Isa. 7:20). Worse yet, Israel/Judah was worshipping idols and looking to these false gods for protection and help while spurning help from Yahweh (10:10–11; cf. 1:29–31; 2:8, 18, 20; 17:7–8, 10–11; 27:9; 30:22; 31:6). Even when the Lord instructed King Ahaz not to fear foreign adversaries but to trust in the Lord—even promising him a sign of the king's own choosing as confirmation—Ahaz rejected God's invitation in exchange for his own plan (Isa. 7:1–13).

However, because of God's discipline and judgment against them, Judah would come to its senses and humbly turn back to God (10:21–23). For this reason, Isaiah assured them that they need not fear the military threats by Assyria (10:24), for God's anger would be directed away from them and onto the Assyrians (10:25). In the same way that God miraculously and providentially defeated some of Israel's enemies in the past (Midian under the leadership of Gideon and Egypt under the leadership of Moses) despite God's people being vastly outnumbered, so too can they trust him in their present crisis with Assyria (10:26–27). Isaiah 10:28–31 pictures the Assyrian army progressively making their way toward Jerusalem. They march from city to city, getting closer and closer. In 10:32, they finally arrive and defiantly shake their fist in the direction of Jerusalem. However, it will be at this moment that God will exercise terrifying power and chop down Assyria's mighty army like a forest being leveled to the ground (10:33). The nation of Assyria that God once used as his own ax will now have God's ax of judgment used against it with overwhelming force (10:34).

Preaching Idea

God opposes the proud but gives grace to the humble.

Contemporary Connections

What does it mean?

Pride takes many forms. But at its core, pride is the cult of "me-ism." As the sovereign creator, God deserves to be preeminent in all things (Col. 1:16–18; 3:23). He created us to be dependent on him for every aspect of life (Acts 17:28; Eph. 6:13–17). Furthermore, God understandably expects us to acknowledge him for who he is and for all that he does for us with daily gratitude, love, and worship (Matt. 22:36–38; 1 Cor. 10:31; Col. 3:17). When people fail in any of these areas, whether they realize it or not, they have postured themselves in direct opposition to God. Naturally, God does not respond passively. He actively opposes those who choose pride rather than humility.

Isaiah 10:5–34 illustrates at least three different forms of pride by Assyria or Israel. People in every age are susceptible to these same prideful attitudes—believers and nonbelievers alike. First, there is the all-too-common pride of self-centeredness. The Assyrians refused to consider what God's will and desires were for them; they only cared about what they wanted and what they stood to gain from additional military conquests. Eventually, God was finished using them to discipline and judge his people, but in their own minds the Assyrians were just getting started. They wanted to conquer the world, to plunder and seize all that they could for themselves. The last thing they cared about was whether the Lord had other plans for them. They didn't realize it yet, but they were setting up an eventual standoff with God as they prepared to march against Jerusalem, the capital city of his people.

Additionally, the Assyrians failed to give the Lord the credit he deserved for their victories. They arrogantly assumed that they alone were responsible for their greatness and success on the world stage. They boasted, "By the strength of my hand I have done this, and by my wisdom, because I have understanding" (10:13). As such, they stole the credit and the glory that belonged only to Yahweh. But God does not share his glory with anyone (Isa. 42:8; 48:11).

Years ago, a friend of mine worked as an administrator at a public university. Because of his prominent position at the university, I was surprised he didn't have a doctorate. One day I asked him if he had ever considered pursuing one. What he shared with me was heartbreaking. Years earlier he had in fact completed all the coursework for a doctorate. Additionally, he had finished much of the research for his dissertation. However, at some point while working on his dissertation, my friend's doctoral advisor stole his research and published much of it as his own. My friend was so devastated by this experience that he just gave up on completing the degree. He didn't have the motivation to develop a new thesis and begin his research all over again. In the same way that any of us would be deeply offended and angered if somebody else stole the credit for our work, so too is God when we rob him of his glory for what he has done.

One final example of pride in this passage is Israel's refusal to depend on God for his gracious protection. Like an adulterous wife who showers her love and affection on another, looking to him for her sense of security and love, Israel had turned to pagan nations and to idols rather than God. In the same way that a betrayed lover's anger will be aroused against their unfaithful spouse, so too God becomes righteously angry when his people fail to depend on him to meet their daily needs and run instead into the arms of other "lovers" of their own making to have those needs met. When Israel pridefully pushed God away in exchange for their own inferior protectors, they cut themselves off from his grace and simultaneously postured themselves along with their substitute gods in competition against the Lord.

God's nature predisposes him to prefer grace and mercy over anger and wrath. However, he will not force people to accept his overtures of grace and kindness. Thankfully for Israel's sake, they learned the lesson that pride provokes a fight with God (which we are always destined to lose), whereas humility, shown through repentance and submission, will always invite his grace. Israel learned to lean no longer on substitute saviors and returned to the Lord. Thus, God once again covered them with his grace and diverted his wrath away from them and onto their enemies.

Is it true?

History reveals that the prophecies in Isaiah 10:4–35 were fulfilled. If they were fulfilled when Sennacherib invaded Jerusalem in 701 B.C., the account of these events in 2 Kings 18–19 details exactly how God opposed the powerful and proud Assyrian army while showing grace to the remnant of his people in Judah under the contrite leadership of King Hezekiah.

King Hezekiah led Israel to repent of its idolatry and return to the Lord. As such, the remnant of Israel would "no longer rely on him who struck them down [Assyria]" but would "rely on the LORD" (Isa. 10:20). Hezekiah "removed the high places, smashed the sacred stones," "cut down the Asherah poles," and "broke into pieces the bronze snake Moses had made" to which Israel had made offerings (2 Kings 18:4). Additionally, "he trusted in the LORD" and "held fast" to him"; "he did not stop following him and "kept" his commands (2 Kings 18:5–6).

Hezekiah rebelled against Assyrian rule and refused to serve the Assyrian king any longer (2 Kings 18:7). As a result, the Assyrian army led by King Sennacherib advanced against the cities of Judah (2 Kings 18:13), including Jerusalem (2 Kings 18:17). A representative of Sennacherib proceeded to mock Jerusalem's inhabitants and boasted in his ability to destroy them. He taunted them, saying that their God was no match for his army, just as other cities' gods were no match for the overwhelming force of the Assyrians (2 Kings 18:19–25; cf. Isa. 10:8–11; 2 Kings 18:33–35; 19:9–13).

In response to these threats, Hezekiah tore his clothes and fell on his face in the temple before the Lord (2 Kings 19:1; 14–19). Unlike his father Ahaz (Isa. 7:10–13), Hezekiah put all his hope for salvation in Yahweh, asking the prophet Isaiah to pray for the remnant of Israel (2 Kings 19:2–4). Isaiah assured him that the Lord would be their savior. He would orchestrate events so that, upon hearing a troubling rumor, Sennacherib would promptly return to his own land where he would eventually be murdered (2 Kings 19:6–7, 28). Additionally, God promised that Assyria would be unable to enter Jerusalem or build a siege mound against it, because he would defend the city and save it for his own name's sake (2 Kings 19:32–34). This is exactly what happened.

> That night the angel of the LORD went out and put to death a hundred and eighty-five thousand in the Assyrian camp. When the people got up the next morning—there were all the dead bodies! So Sennacherib king of Assyria broke camp and withdrew. He returned to Nineveh and stayed there. One day, while he was worshiping in the temple of his god Nisrok, his sons Adrammelek and Sharezer killed him with the sword, and they escaped to the land of Ararat. And Esarhaddon his son succeeded him as king. (2 Kings 19:35–37)

The dramatic fulfillment of the prophecies of Isaiah 10:4–35 is one of the clearest examples of God's opposition to the proud while extending grace to the humble. This principle holds true today as much as it did in the days of Isaiah. As such, Christians and non-Christians alike must be careful to avoid the tendencies toward self-centeredness, self-exaltation, and self-sufficiency. A person who lives primarily for oneself or who attempts to function by their own strength alone is destined to encounter opposition from God in the form of discipline or judgment. On the other hand, God stands ready to help and defend all who humbly submit themselves to his gracious will and protection.

Now what?
Unfortunately, it is all too easy to slip into a lifestyle that revolves primarily around oneself. Temptations toward self-centered living abound. Sins such as gluttony, pornography, excessive entertainment, materialism, and laziness naturally appeal to our flesh. Our culture further markets these sins to us as though they were our birthright as privileged, twenty-first-century Americans. Whether it's the newest fast-food menu item, the next must-see Netflix series on which to binge, a sexually provocative video suggestion on YouTube, or the newest iPhone model, our eyes and ears are constantly being bombarded with invitations to live with self on the throne.

Additionally, we are also taught to pursue our own exaltation as though this were the primary purpose of our lives. Success is defined in terms of achieving the next promotion, earning a bigger paycheck, or acquiring the next degree. Other people can easily be viewed as obstacles to overcome or opponents to compete against. In the process of trying to maximize our own potential or ascend the ladder of success, biblical admonitions to humbly serve others or to put their interests ahead of our own seem strangely out of place. The apostle Paul pointed to the example of Jesus, the humble servant, in his admonition to the Philippians regarding prideful attitudes and behaviors that had crept into their midst. Those words may be even more relevant today.

> Instead of being motivated by selfish ambition or vanity, each of you should, in humility, be moved to treat one another as more important than yourself. Each of you should be concerned not only about your own interests, but about the interests of others as well. You should have the same attitude toward one another that Christ Jesus had, who though he existed in the form of God did not regard equality with God as something to be grasped, but emptied himself by taking on the form of a slave, by looking like other men, and by sharing in human nature. He humbled himself, by becoming obedient to the point of death—even death on a cross! (Phil. 2:3–8)

Years ago, while preaching through the book of Revelation, I was particularly struck by the imagery of Babylon. The description of that great city seems to describe the secular, worldly mindset in any age in contrast to those who live faithful and committed Christian lives. There seems to be a strong contrast between the followers of Christ, described as "the new Jerusalem" (Rev. 3:12) and a pure bride (Rev. 21:2, 9–10), and "Babylon the Great" who is the "Mother of prostitutes" (Rev. 17:5). As I considered this important literary contrast, I was struck by how much the imagery of Babylon in Revelation 18 mirrors American culture today. She is full of all kinds of sexual immorality (Rev. 14:8, 18:3, 9), rampant materialism and consumerism (Rev. 18:3, 11–13), inordinate wealth and luxury (Rev. 18:3, 7, 9, 14–17), and excessive comfort and entertainment (Rev. 18:14, 22). Additionally, Babylon has an elevated opinion of herself and her own importance. She "exalted herself" and "told herself, 'I rule as queen and am no widow'" (Rev. 18:7).

Babylon describes a society in which people are all about themselves and their own creature comforts. There is no consideration of living one's life for God or for others. Naturally, the admonition to the people of God as it relates to Babylon in Revelation is, "Come out of her, my people, so you will not take part in her sins" (Rev. 18:4).

How then can Christians, living in the heart of modern-day "Babylon," keep themselves separate from the prideful, me-centered attitudes that pervade every facet of twenty-first-century Western civilization?

We must remember that selfishness isn't overcome simply by denying ourselves. Proud behavior must be replaced with new behavior that is directed toward God and done for the good of others. For example, Paul urged those who were prone toward laziness and stealing to not only put off those wrong behaviors, but to replace them with a commitment to work hard and to begin giving generously (Eph. 4:28). Likewise, the person who was pridefully using his words to tear others down was not only to put an end to such destructive speech but replace it with words that encourage and offer grace (Eph. 4:29). Whatever prideful or self-centered practices one desires to weed out of their life, they must consider what positive actions and behaviors would serve to counteract those prideful tendencies.

Creativity in Presentation

Making Enemies
Consider opening the sermon with a skit or homemade video centered around the theme of "How to make enemies." Use the Preaching Pointers section above for some simple ideas. The more absurd the suggestions, the better. The more your audience considers how ridiculous it would be for people to go out of their

way to make enemies with others, the better it drives home the truth that a person who acts pridefully makes God their enemy and is behaving in a way that is antithetical to their own best interests.

Stealing the Glory
Everyone was surprised when Rosie Ruiz, a previously unknown athlete, won the Boston Marathon in 1980 with a near-record time of 2 hours, 31 minutes, and 56 seconds. This was the third fastest marathon time ever recorded by a woman. Ruiz was a secretary at a commodity trading firm in Manhattan at the time. According to her post-race interview, this was only the second time she had ever competed in a marathon. The prior year, she ran in the New York Marathon; amazingly, she had managed to trim nearly twenty-five minutes off her New York Marathon time.

It didn't take long before suspicions began to mount about Rosie's supposed victory. Eventually, race officials concluded that she had cheated, and they nullified her win. One witness came forward reporting that they had seen Ruiz jump out of the crowd and begin running about one mile from the finish line. Jacqueline Gareau, who initially appeared to come in second, was the actual winner. Ruiz refused to return her medal though, and so a new one was made for Gareau. She held onto it for thirty-nine years until her death in 2019, maintaining that she was the rightful winner. However, in 1996, another witness came forward revealing that Rosie had admitted to him that she had in fact cheated.[1]

Rosie Ruiz was not only guilty of cheating but was also guilty of attempting to steal the accolades and glory from Jacqueline Gareau, the rightful winner of the race. Had Rosie not been caught, Gareau would never have been able to bask in the excitement and glory rightfully belonging only to the woman who won the Boston Marathon. Every one of us is guilty of this very same offense whenever we try to take credit for what God has done through us. Rather than allow him to receive the credit for what he has accomplished, we selfishly and unfairly steal the glory that is due to him. Is it any wonder that God is so offended by our pride?

Competing Against the Best
Magnus Carlsen is a Norwegian chess player and five-time world champion. He became a grandmaster at the age of thirteen. He once played three games simultaneously against separate opponents, all while blindfolded. This meant that he had to remember each move and each of his opponents' moves without ever seeing the boards. He also had to be able to picture all three boards as he strategized each successive move in each match. And the games were timed. Thus, Magnus had limited time to think about each move. In the end, he won all three matches rather easily.

What would it look like if you were forced to compete head-to-head in a game of chess with the person who is the best? Even worse, what if our lives were at stake in the outcome of that competition? This would be a terrifying and hopeless feeling. And yet this is exactly what pride does to us. It puts us in direct competition with the almighty God of the universe. Pride makes us enemies with God.

Now, imagine if, instead of competing against the person who is the best, you were able to have that person join your team and play alongside you. Rather than knowing that you have absolutely no chance to win, you now know that you can't lose. What a confidence booster that would be! This is exactly what God offers to those who humbly ask for his help. He showers his grace upon them to accomplish what they could never do on their own. In the same way that Israel was rescued

---

1 https://www.nytimes.com/2019/08/08/sports/rosie-ruiz-boston-marathon-dead.html.

from the powerful Assyrian army because the hand of God was with them, so too we can experience God's protective power when we choose to humbly rely upon him.

God resists the proud, but gives grace to the humble.

- Pride confronted (10:5–20).
  - Assyria's pride of self-centeredness confronted (10:5–11).
  - Assyria's pride of self-exaltation confronted (10:12–19).
  - Judah's pride of self-sufficiency confronted (10:20–34).
- Pride dealt with (10:20–34).
  - God will show restraint on Judah due to their repentance (10:20–22a).
  - God will bring destruction against Assyria due to their defiance (10:22b–34).

DISCUSSION QUESTIONS

1. What are some behaviors that are motivated by pride that people may not immediately recognize as such (e.g., outbursts of anger when one doesn't get their way)?

2. How should the imagery of the ax and the logger in Isaiah 10:15 impact how we view and approach our own past accomplishments as well as our future goals?

3. Read 2 Kings 19:32–37. How should this account of the angel of the Lord striking down 185,000 Assyrian soldiers impact how you think about potential obstacles or barriers to accomplishing God's will in your life?

4. We live during a time when many within the secular culture around us boast in their rejection of God's Word. They arrogantly proclaim their superior belief in science and human philosophies. How does this passage impact how Christians should feel and respond to people like this?

Isaiah 11:1–12:6

EXEGETICAL IDEA
The Lord would establish a kingdom of peace through a new David and restore his exiled people from bondage, demonstrating his power through a new exodus.

THEOLOGICAL FOCUS
The Sovereign Lord, who is committed to fulfilling his covenant promises, will establish his rule on earth through an ideal Davidic king, deliver his people from exile, and renew his relationship with them.

PREACHING IDEA
Only Jesus will usher in the world in which everybody wants to live.

PREACHING POINTERS
I recently saw a marketing campaign advertising vacation destinations in Mexico with the slogan "Best day ever!" The advertisement included a video loop that contained people involved in all sorts of fun and appealing activities. There was a family sitting together on a beautiful beach watching the sunset. A person was receiving a relaxing massage in another clip. There were images of beautiful wildlife. In other clips, people could be seen swimming in a large, resort-style pool or cruising through the ocean on a WaveRunner®. A family was enjoying a delicious meal at an outdoor restaurant while being serenaded with live music. Every scene was designed to arouse within the viewer a sense of longing to be somewhere other than where they currently were. The goal was that those who saw the advertisement would develop a vision of what could be, by way of their next vacation, in hopes that they would subsequently buy into this opportunity soon.

In many ways, this is the prophet's goal in Isaiah 11:1–12:6. He describes a world to his audience that is much better than the one they currently inhabit. What he describes to them, should they be among those who experience it, would be their "best day ever." Like the marketers of the ad campaign, God wants his people to recognize that their present reality is far from ideal. The reason for this is because of how sin has cursed their world and ruined their society. However, there is coming a day when God's Messiah will arrive. He will usher in a new world where all that is wrong will be judged and made right. Only those who buy into this future world now will have a place at the table when that time comes. Thus, God's people must remain faithful to him and committed to his promise of a coming kingdom age.

JUSTICE, PEACE, AND RENEWAL (11:1–12:6)

The Lord would raise up a new David, who, energized by the Lord's Spirit, would establish a kingdom of justice and peace. The Lord would restore his exiled people from bondage, demonstrating his power as he did at the time of the exodus. His people would praise him as their savior and declare the majesty of their Sovereign Lord to the nations.

LITERARY STRUCTURE AND THEMES (11:1–12:6)

This literary unit contains a vision of what the Lord will accomplish for his people and for the nations. The prophet begins with a salvation portrayal that includes a utopia-like vision of a kingdom of justice and peace where even the animal kingdom is radically transformed. The Lord's instrument in establishing this kingdom will be a new David, viewed as originating in the root stock of Jesse.

A structural oddity occurs in 11:10–11, where the phrase וְהָיָה בַּיּוֹם הַהוּא, literally "and it will be in that day," occurs in successive statements. This phrase appears several times in Isaiah. There are no instances of it introducing an entirely new speech. It typically introduces a new unit within a larger speech (7:18; 10:20, 27; 14:3; 17:4; 22:20; 23:15; 24:21) or, in two cases, a subunit (7:21, 23). Occasionally, it introduces the final unit of the speech (10:27; 22:20; 23:15; 24:21; 27:12). In 27:12–13, where it appears in successive verses, the juxtaposed statements are thematically related and conclude the speech. This is not the case in 11:10–11, where 11:12–16 develops 11:11 in more detail. One could make a case for 11:10–11 being a double introduction of a new unit within the larger speech, since the nations are in view in both 11:10 and 11. But there are also links between 11:10 and what precedes, the primary one being the reference to Jesse (cf. 11:1), which could be understood as forming an *inclusio* for the first unit within the larger speech (see Motyer 1993, 121).[1] However, if 11:10 marks the introduction to a new unit within the larger speech, the repetition could be explained differently. In this case, references to the king's relationship with Jesse serve to introduce successive units. Nevertheless, I prefer to see a structural break between 11:10 and 11 since the king is the focus in 11:1–10, while the Sovereign Master/the Lord takes center stage in 11:11–16. This shift in subject is determinative to the structural analysis. Though the use of the phrase "and it will be in that day" in 11:10–11 does not correspond to 27:12–13 in function, its use in 11:10–11 is consistent with the general use of the phrase in Isaiah (see above), where it sometimes marks a conclusion (cf. 11:10) and at other times an introduction (cf. 11:11).

Moving in reverse chronological order (see Ortlund 2010, 211–12), the prophet next includes a salvation announcement, which describes how the Lord will inaugurate this kingdom of peace by delivering his people from exile in a grand new exodus (11:11–16). As is typical in such announcements, the focus is on the Lord's intervention (see 11:11–12, 15). The appearance of a remnant (note "the remnant of his people who are left from Assyria" [literal reading] in both 11:11 and 16) forms an *inclusio* for the announcement (Goswell 2017, 125)

This deliverance prompts praise from the Lord's people. This final subunit (12:1–6) contains two short praise songs that exhibit the following structure:

---

[1] Goswell (2017, 125) sees 11:10 as transitional in the structure of Isaiah 11.

I. First praise cycle (12:1–3)
   A. Prediction of praise (12:1a, "In that day you will say")
   B. Declarative praise (12:1b–d)
      1. Declaration of intent to praise (12:1b)
      2. Recalling the time of need (12:1c)
      3. Report of deliverance (12:1d)
   C. Affirmation of trust (12:2)
   D. Prediction of joy (12:3)

II. Second praise cycle (12:4–6)
   A. Prediction of praise (12:4a, "In that day you will say")
   B. Descriptive praise (12:4b–6)
      1. Call to praise (12:4b–5a)
      2. Reason for praise: the Lord's deeds (12:5b)
      3. Renewed call to praise (12:6a)
      4. Reason for praise: the Lord's majesty (12:6b)

A prediction of praise, "In that day you will say," introduces each of the songs. In the first, the prophet uses the singular form of the verb (וְאָמַרְתָּ, "you [singular] will say"), addressing the nation collectively as a unified community (12:1). Israel responds with the singular (note "I," "me," and "my" in 12:1–2). However, in the prediction of joy (12:3), Isaiah switches to the plural (וּשְׁאַבְתֶּם, "you [plural] will draw"), addressing the people as a group of distinct individuals. He continues with the plural in the second prediction of praise (12:4a; cf. וַאֲמַרְתֶּם, "you [plural] will say") and the following call to praise (12:4–5). However, the renewed call to praise (12:6), which is addressed to the "inhabitant [feminine singular] of Zion" [literal translation], switches to feminine singular imperatives. The feminine singular is used here as a collective (see NIV "people of Zion"), referring to the entire population of Zion (see GKC, 394 §122s; cf. Smith 2007, 283–84 n. 450).

- *A Kingdom of Justice and Peace (11:1–10)*
- *Second Exodus and Conquest (11:11–16)*
- *Celebrating Salvation (12:1–6)*

EXPOSITION (11:1–12:6)

A Kingdom of Justice and Peace (11:1–10)
The Lord will establish a kingdom of justice and peace through a new David.

11:1. The Lord will raise up a king from Jesse's line, which is pictured as a stock or stump that possesses roots. The term גֵּזַע, "root stock," appears only two other times. In Job 14:8 it refers to the stump of a tree that has been cut down (cf. 14:7) but is still able to produce new growth (cf. 14:9). In Isaiah 40:24 it refers to the root stock of a plant that grows from the ground, only to shrivel up when the hot wind blows on it. It is not certain if the use of the word in Isaiah 11:1 implies the line of Jesse has been chopped down, perhaps alluding to some diminishing of the Davidic dynasty. While usage in Job 14:8 would favor this, Isaiah 40:24 does not use the term of a stump but of a plant that grows from the ground.

The coming king is described as a branch or shoot (חֹטֶר, נֵצֶר) that grows out of the stump (or root stock) and produces fruit. This image contrasts sharply with that of the Assyrians in 10:33–34. The Assyrians would be chopped down like large trees in a forest, but the Lord would bring new growth to Jesse (Young 1965, 378–79).

It is significant that Jesse, not David, is the source of this growth. Rather than picturing the coming king as a descendant of David (cf. 9:7), the prophet goes back one generation on the genealogical tree to Jesse, David's father. Perhaps in this way he suggests the king will be a new or ideal David (see Motyer 1993, 121; Roberts 2015, 179; Schibler 1995, 102). Elsewhere in the prophets the ideal king to come is sometimes described as originating in David (cf. Jer. 23:5; 33:15, 21). On other occasions the king is depicted as a new David and simply called by that name (Jer. 30:9; Ezek. 34:23–24; 37:24–25; Hos. 3:5). Perhaps this distances the king, at least literally, from the disappointing descendants of the Davidic line and depicts him as David who, at least when idealized, was superior to those who followed in his line (see Sumner 2018, 643–59). Micah 5:2 (HB 1) may engage in this kind of idealizing, for it describes the coming king as one who emerges from Bethlehem, not Jerusalem, and whose "goings forth" (either his activities or origin) are rooted in Israel's distant past (see Wildberger 1991, 470).

11:2. The Lord's Spirit will rest upon the king, as one would expect with a new David (cf. 1 Sam. 16:13; 2 Sam. 23:2). The phrase "spirit of the Lord" occurs twenty-five times in the Old Testament, including five times in Isaiah. In the Old Testament it is sometimes used of the wind, viewed as the Lord's breath (Isa. 40:7; 59:19), or of the Lord's mind (Isa. 40:13), but it usually refers to the Lord's personal Spirit who cares for his people (Isa. 63:14) and empowers his chosen leaders.[2] When the Lord's Spirit left Saul and came upon David (1 Sam. 16:13–14), it was apparent David had replaced Saul as God's chosen king, for a ruler needs the divine Spirit to reign effectively.

In only one other passage is the Lord's Spirit described as resting (נוּחַ) on someone. In Numbers 11:25–26 the Lord takes some of the Spirit that rests upon Moses and gives it to the seventy elders. When the Spirit rests upon them, they prophesy. The Spirit referred to here is the Lord's Spirit (cf. 11:29). The capacity to prophesy is not mentioned in Isaiah 11, but the Spirit does provide supernatural enablement to rule wisely and justly.

The Spirit's enablement of the king is described through three genitival constructions that identify specific qualities the Spirit would impart to the king: "a spirit of wisdom and of understanding," "of counsel and of might," and "of the knowledge and fear of the Lord." The term רוּחַ may refer directly to the Lord's Spirit as one who imparts these qualities or to a Spirit-imparted "spirit" or disposition that is characterized by the qualities.[3] In either case, the Spirit enables the king to exhibit these qualities. (See Gray 1912, 216; Roberts 2015, 179; Wildberger 1991, 471; Young 1965, 381–82.)

The first word pair, "wisdom" and "understanding," combines synonyms to emphasize the degree of wisdom the Spirit will impart to the king (cf. Deut. 4:6). The king needs this extraordinary wisdom to assess legal claims accurately and to make just decisions (Isa. 11:3–5; cf. 1 Kings 3:9–12, 28; and see Williamson 2018, 648–49).

The second pair, "counsel" and "might," combines concepts that are closely related. The word "counsel" ordinarily refers to instruction or advice imparted by one party to another, but it can also be used of a proposal or plan (cf. Isa. 14:26, as well as Pss. 14:6; 20:4 [HB 5]; 33:10 [HB 11]; Jer. 49:30). "Might" refers to physical strength or military power (cf. Isa. 28:6; 33:13; 63:15). Apart from this passage, the terms are joined only in Isaiah 36:5 (= 2 Kings 18:20), where they refer to the ability to plan and execute an effective military strategy against an enemy. In Isaiah's earlier description of the ideal king (9:6 [HB 5]), two of the king's titles point to his ability to formulate strategy (cf. פֶּלֶא יוֹעֵץ, "a wonder, a counselor" (i.e., an extraordinary strategist) and to defeat opposition (אֵל גִּבּוֹר, "Mighty God"). In that context, the titles point to military prowess as a strategist and warrior. The warrior motif

---

2 See Judg. 3:10; 6:34; 11:29; 13:25; 14:6, 19; 15:14; 1 Sam. 10:6; 16:13–14; 2 Sam. 23:2; 1 Kings 18:12; 22:24 [= 2 Chron. 18:23]; 2 Kings 2:16; 2 Chron. 20:14; Ezek. 11:5; 37:1; Mic. 2:7; 3:8 (cf. Isa. 61:1).

3 Exodus 28:3 speaks of a "spirit [or disposition] of wisdom" that was imparted to the Aaronic priests, while Deuteronomy 34:9 speaks of Joshua possessing a "spirit [or disposition] of wisdom."

may be present in chapter 11 (cf. 11:4b) but, if so, it is secondary (see Wildberger 1991, 472). In this context the king's capacity to implement justice in his kingdom is the primary theme, so "counsel" probably refers to the capacity to discern what is a wise and just decision in any given case (cf. 11:3b–4a), while "might" refers to the ability to execute that decision (11:4b; see Motyer 1993, 122; Young 1965, 382).

The third pair, "knowledge and fear of the LORD," combines closely related expressions that refer to the king's loyalty to the Lord. "Fear of the LORD" refers here to a respect for the Lord's authority that motivates one to obey the Lord (Kaiser 1972, 256). In this context this means promoting God's standards of justice (cf. 11:3). Paired with "fear of the LORD," the term "knowledge" has the connotation "recognition, acknowledgment." It is not simply an awareness of facts. It entails recognizing the Lord's authority in a practical manner by submitting to his will. This meaning of the term is perhaps best illustrated in Jeremiah 22:16, where the Lord commends Josiah for his just royal acts and then asks: "Is that not what it means to know me?" Josiah demonstrated his recognition of the Lord's authority by promoting justice in his realm.

11:3. The prophet reiterates that the king will fear the Lord. The first line reads literally, "and his smelling (will be) in the fear of the LORD." The form וַהֲרִיחוֹ comprises the conjunction, a *hiphil* infinitive construct from the verb רוּחַ, which in the *hiphil* stem means "to smell" (*HALOT* s.v. "רוח" 1196), and a pronominal suffix. Sometimes the verb in this stem has the nuance "smell with delight" (cf. Lev. 26:31; Amos 5:21). In Isaiah 11:3 the idea may be that the king derives pleasure from fearing the Lord (Motyer 1993, 123). Another option would be that he "smells by the fear of the LORD," meaning that his fear of the Lord motivates him to "sniff out the truth" (Roberts 2015, 178; cf. Shifman 2012, 249). This proposal fits nicely with what follows (see 11:3b–4; Roberts 2015, 179). However, some prefer to delete the statement as corrupt.

Because he fears the Lord, the king will be thoroughly committed to justice (cf. Isa. 9:7). Human beings are often influenced by mere appearances or by hearsay. But this king can discern the truth and make just legal decisions. Of course, as Edward Young (1965, 384) observes, "for absolute justice, there must be absolute knowledge." In this king's case, the Spirit of the Lord supplies this supernatural knowledge (11:2; Wildberger 1991, 475).

11:4. The king will defend the just legal cause of the needy and poor. The "needy" are those whom royal bureaucrats deprived of justice and the necessities of life. Widows and fatherless children epitomized these victims of injustice (10:2). The Lord provides refuge for the needy (25:4) and promises to vindicate them (14:30; 26:6). This portrait of the king defending the needy reverses the situation described earlier (10:2), where they were denied justice and deprived of their possessions (see Smith 2007, 273).

It is not clear if אֶרֶץ refers here to the "land" or more broadly to the "earth" (cf. NIV11). The reference to the Lord's "holy mountain" in 11:9 suggests the land is in view (see commentary below), but 11:10 envisions a kingdom that encompasses the nations. It is best to see the king's rule as being worldwide, though centered in Jerusalem on his "holy mountain" (cf. Isa. 2:2–4).

The king will not only protect the needy from their oppressors; he will actively oppose the oppressors and eliminate the wicked from his kingdom. The "rod" (שֵׁבֶט) refers to the king's royal scepter, symbolizing his authority (see Marlow 2011, 228). The phrases "his mouth" and "the breath of his lips" indicate that a royal decree proceeding from his mouth/lips is in view. By royal decree he will order the wicked to be executed. This need not imply that the destruction of the wicked is supernatural and immediate (as Kaiser [1972, 258] and Young

[1965, 385] argue). It simply means that his decree, once issued, is certain of fulfillment, for the Spirit gives him the ability (גְּבוּרָה) to execute his decisions (cf. 11:2).

11:5. The prophet describes the king as wearing righteousness and faithfulness. Here, as elsewhere (cf. Isa. 59:17), clothing is associated with characteristics of the person. As Motyer (1993, 123) explains, "the garments express the inherent realities and capacities of a person and the purposes to which he commits himself (Isa. 59:16–17; 61:10; Ps. 132:9, 16, 18)." The term אֵזוֹר, usually translated "belt," refers to a waistcloth worn for support. "Righteousness" (צֶדֶק) refers in this context (cf. Isa. 11:3–4) to fairness or justice (cf. Isa. 1:21). "Faithfulness" (אֱמוּנָה) could refer to the king's allegiance to God (cf. 11:2) but, coming immediately after a description of the king's just rule, it is probably his commitment to justice or the integrity that characterizes his just decisions. The term is used elsewhere of integrity or honesty in a legal setting (cf. Prov. 12:17; Isa. 59:4). As Wildberger (1991, 479) points out, the judge's faithfulness "is the absolute reliability which a person might count on when in need of help in obtaining justice."

11:6–8. When the king implements justice, this radical change in human society will be mirrored by a radical transformation of the animal kingdom. Predators, symbolizing powerful oppressors in the human realm, will no longer prey on livestock, symbolizing the victims of injustice in the human realm. Wolves will no longer live in packs, isolated from the domesticated animals they seek to devour. Instead, they will settle down in peace with lambs. Likewise, leopards will lie down and rest with young goats, while oxen, young lions, and fatted livestock will live peacefully together. A "young lion" (Hebrew כְּפִיר) is a nomadic, subadult lion that is particularly ferocious, like the one that attacked Samson (Judg. 14:5–6; Strawn 2009, 150–58). Yet it will become tame and harmless. A small child, normally vulnerable to the attack of predators and incapable of controlling livestock, will be able to lead all these animals along, for their hostile and willful spirits will be tamed.

Isaiah's idyllic portrait continues as he pictures cows and bears grazing together. Normally a mother bear is highly protective of her young, but her cubs lie down with the calves. One already suspects that the diet of the former predators will be radically changed. The final line of 11:7 makes this explicit, as the prophet says the lion will eat straw, just as cattle do. To emphasize further the transformation that will occur, the prophet pictures an infant (literally, "suckling") playing on the hole of a snake and a toddler (literally, "weaned one") placing his hand on a serpent's nest. Both of the snakes referred to are poisonous.

Given the context, with its emphasis on the transformation of human society (see 11:3–5), one might conclude that this vision of the animal kingdom is strictly metaphorical, with the predators symbolizing human oppressors and the livestock (prey) symbolizing the victims of oppression. But in its larger canonical context, it is much more likely that the vision is to be taken literally. In his initial speech to Job, God reminds Job that the animal kingdom, as created, is truly a wild kingdom filled with conflict (Job 38:39–39:30). Predators stay alive by killing and eating other animals. Perhaps God created it so to mirror the cosmic conflict between God and the enemy that existed at the time of creation and is reflected in the prologue to the book of Job. This may be hinted at in the Genesis 1 creation account. The primordial deep and darkness are not eliminated as God creates and orders the world as we know it. They are integrated into the created order. Though this order is pronounced good, it is not ideal. In the new creation seen by John, darkness and the sea, the very elements of the created order that remind us there is cosmic opposition to God, are eliminated (Rev. 21:1, 25). Indeed, Psalms 74 and 89 tell us that God had to overcome a proud, fearsome enemy just to create this world. Paul writes this about the created order:

> For the creation waits in eager expectation for the children of God to be revealed. For the creation was subjected to frustration, not by its own choice, but by the will of the one who subjected it, in hope that the creation itself will be liberated from its bondage to decay and brought into the freedom and glory of the children of God. We know that the whole creation has been groaning as in the pains of childbirth right up to the present time. (Rom. 8:19–22)

The subjection of the creation to frustration includes the violence of the animal kingdom portrayed in Job and played out every day in the wild. But Isaiah envisions a time when all of that will change. The ideal king will transform human society so that justice and peace prevail, and this transformation will be mirrored in the environment as the animal kingdom is also radically changed.

11:9. Peace will prevail throughout the king's worldwide dominion. The verbs (both in the *hiphil* stem) in the first poetic line are typically understood in their well-attested senses of "harm" (see *HALOT* s.v. "רעע" 1270) and "destroy" (see *HALOT* s.v. "שחת" 1470). The unstated plural subject is naturally understood as the formerly fierce predators that will be tamed (11:6–8). However, there may be a subtle allusion to human oppressors as well (11:4) since the predators symbolize them. The verbs רָעַע and שָׁחַת (in their *hiphil* form) are also collocated in 1:4, where they are used of the sinful people of Judah and Jerusalem who are guilty of injustice (cf. 1:16–17). "On all my holy mountain" refers to Jerusalem (Zion), as usage of "holy mountain" elsewhere demonstrates.[4] In Isaiah 65:25b, which is almost identical to Isaiah 11:9a, the Lord's "holy mountain" is Jerusalem (cf. 11:18–19).

The peace depicted here will extend beyond Jerusalem. The "knowledge of the LORD," which produces the peace described in 11:9 (note כִּי, "for"), will fill the "earth" (אֶרֶץ), just as the water covers the sea. The perfect verbal form (מָלְאָה, "fill") is a future perfect or stative here, describing a condition that will prevail prior to the cessation of harm and will produce peace. In this context "knowledge of the LORD" probably has the same connotation as in 11:2 (see above), where it refers to allegiance to the Lord, not simply to awareness of the Lord or knowledge about him. This supports the subtle dual referent in the first half of 11:9. One might conceive of animals "knowing" the Lord, but this more naturally refers to an attitude that humans would display (cf. Gray 1912, 224, who, however, rejects the connection with 11:4).

As in 11:4 (see above), it is not clear if אֶרֶץ refers here to the "land" of Judah (or Israel) or more broadly to the "earth." The use of "holy mountain" in 11:9 might favor the land as referent, but 11:10 envisions a kingdom that encompasses the nations, suggesting the "earth," understood as the known world, is in view here. The king's rule will be worldwide, though centered in Jerusalem on his "holy mountain" (cf. Isa. 2:2–4; see Roberts 2015, 182). Allegiance to the Lord will produce peace in the king's royal city and then extend from there throughout the kingdom. Likewise, in the conclusion to Isaiah, peace-producing allegiance to the Lord is localized in Jerusalem (65:25, cf. 65:18–19), but within the broader context of a new creation (65:17) and worldwide recognition of the Lord's

---

4 See Pss. 2:6; 3:4 [HB 5]; 15:1; 43:3; 48:1 [HB 2]; 99:9; Isa. 27:13; 56:7; 57:13; 65:11, 25; 66:20; Jer. 31:23; Dan. 9:16, 20; Joel 2:1; 3:27 [HB 4:17]; Obad. 1:16; Zeph. 3:11; Zech. 8:3. On one occasion the phrase refers more broadly to the land of Israel (Ezek. 20:40; cf. Exod. 15:17, where the Lord's "mountain of . . . inheritance" appears to be the land of Israel).

royal splendor (cf. 66:19). Furthermore, in Habakkuk 2:14, where recognition of the Lord's glory fills the earth like the water of the sea, אֶרֶץ has a broader referent.

11:10. After describing the peace that will characterize the king's rule, the prophet returns to where he started, forming an *inclusio* for this first portion of his speech (Motyer 1993, 125). As in Isaiah 11:1, he speaks of the king's relationship to Jesse. Earlier the king was pictured as a shoot that came from Jesse's roots. But here the wording is different. The king appears to be a root in his own right. Considering usage elsewhere in the Bible and in West Semitic texts, "Root of Jesse" (שֹׁרֶשׁ) probably refers to Jesse's offspring (Stromberg 2008, 663–64). As such, it is likely synonymous with the "shoot . . . of Jesse" and the "Branch" that comes "from his [Jesse's] roots" in 11:1 (so Stromberg 2008, 665).

The king's dominion will be worldwide. Like a signal flag (cf. Isa. 30:17) used to rally troops or assemble people, the king will summon nations, who respond positively by seeking him. His dwelling place—either his palace or city, Jerusalem (cf. Kaiser 1972, 263)—would reflect his royal majesty (כָּבוֹד, "glory"). The picture is reminiscent of the vision in 2:2–4, where nations stream to Jerusalem to seek instruction, knowing they will receive just legal decisions from the Lord. Isaiah 11:10 makes it clear the Lord will provide this instruction and justice through his chosen king, the new David (cf. Roberts 2015, 182).

Second Exodus and Conquest (11:11–16)
The Lord will deliver his people from exile and make them secure in their land.

11:11–12. A shift in stated subject from the "Root of Jesse" (11:10) to the Sovereign Master (אֲדֹנָי) marks the transition to this new unit within the larger speech. Mention of nations facilitates continuity. However, there is a shift in perspective. In 11:10 the nations rally to the signal flag of the new David, while 11:11–12 focuses on the Sovereign Master's deliverance of his exiled people from among the nations.

The use of the title Sovereign Master (אֲדֹנָי; cf. 6:1) is appropriate in a context where the Lord's sovereign control over nations is envisioned (cf. 7:7, 20; 8:7; 10:12, 16, 24, 33). Yet there is also irony. Earlier the Sovereign Master appears as the judge of his sinful covenant people (3:15, 17–18; 6:8, 11; 7:14; 9:8, 17 [HB 7, 16]; 10:12, 23), but now he reverses the effects of judgment as he restores his people to their land (cf. 4:4).

The Hebrew text of 11:11a appears to be elliptical and perhaps textually corrupt. As it stands it reads literally: "And it will be in that day the Master will add a second time his hand to acquire the remnant of his people." One expects another verb to complement the *hiphil* of יָסַף, "add," which is typically collocated with a second verb to indicate that an action is repeated or continued.[5] In this case, with "his hand" following, a verb such as "lift" might be expected. (Cf. Isa. 49:22; see Gray [1912, 228], who reads שְׂאֵת, from נָשָׂא, "lift up.") Some propose solving the problem by emending שֵׁנִית, "second," to a verb, שַׁנּוֹת, "to lift," derived from a root שָׁנָה meaning "be high, elevated." If retained, שֵׁנִית, "second," alludes to the exodus event, which serves as the paradigm for the prophesied deliverance (see 11:15–16). In this case, a verb that collocates with "his hand" as accusative must be understood by ellipsis.

The purpose for the Lord's intervention in power (symbolized by his "hand") is to deliver his people from exile. The verb קָנָה (cf. לִקְנוֹת) often refers to buying an object, but that nuance does not appear to be contextually supported. Sometimes the verb means simply to "acquire," in the sense of "take possession of." That would seem to be the case here, in which case the focus is on the Lord's ownership of his people. The

---
5   See Isa. 1:13; 7:10; 8:5; 10:20; 23:10; 24:20; 29:14; 51:22; 52:1.

people are called a "remnant," alluding to the fact that judgment has fallen on the covenant community with only some being preserved (cf. 10:20–22).

The Lord will reclaim his people from various locations, representing the "four quarters of the earth" (cf. 11:12). The list includes eight different locations for the sake of completeness (the symbolic seven plus one for good measure). Between the reference to Assyria in the distant northeast and the islands/coastlands of the (Mediterranean) Sea in the distant west, he includes two triads (Blenkinsopp 2000, 267–68). The first, which includes Egypt, Pathros (Upper Egypt, that is the southern region of Egypt), and Cush (Nubia), moves from north to south, while the second, which includes Elam (east of Babylon), Shinar (Babylon), and Hamath (located north of Damascus), moves from southeast to northwest.

A widespread exile is assumed, but this need not mean the passage, at least at its core, comes from a later date (as Gray [1912, 225] argues; see also Clements 1980, 126; Kaiser 1972, 264; Wildberger 1991, 492). Assyria took the northern kingdom into exile in 722 B.C. (2 Kings 17:6; 18:11) and deported many from Judah in 701 B.C.[6] Isaiah predicted the Babylonian exile (cf. Isa. 39:6–7), and he foresaw exiles being in Egypt (cf. 27:12). It is possible that exiles from Israel were resettled by the Assyrians in Hamath and Babylon and that some from Israel and Judah migrated to Egypt, Pathros, and Cush during this period (see Roberts [2015, 188–89], who for other reasons sees 11:11 as a later expansion).

Though his exiled people would be scattered throughout the nations (cf. Isa. 11:11), the Lord would gather them from the four quarters of the earth. Totality is emphasized in two ways: (1) the references to Israel and Judah indicate that the reclamation will include both kingdoms; (2) the terms used for the "scattered" exiles are masculine (נִדְחֵי) and feminine (נְפֻצוֹת), respectively, suggesting that both males and females would return (cf. Gray 1912, 226).

The picture of the Lord lifting a signal flag is ironic and marks a reversal in his dealings with his people. Earlier he lifted a signal flag to summon a distant nation (Assyria) to judge his covenant people (5:26), but now he lifts a signal flag to beckon them to return home. Isaiah uses the imagery again in 49:22 where, in response to the raising of the Lord's signal flag, the nations transport the exiles home (cf. Wildberger 1991, 493).

11:13–14. The returning exiles will be unified as one nation, in contrast to the situation in Isaiah's time. Long ago Ephraim (representing the northern kingdom) had separated from Judah (7:17). Ephraim had fought against Judah (9:21), most recently in the Syro-Ephraimitic war, when the northern kingdom allied with Aram and threatened Judah (7:1–6). But this will all change. The jealousy Ephraim felt toward Judah will cease, and Judah's hostility toward Ephraim will come to an end. Reunited Israel and Judah will then extend the borders of their territory, attacking the Philistines to the west and defeating the inhabitants of the desert regions to the east. They will make the neighboring Transjordanian states of Edom, Moab, and Ammon their subjects (cf. Amos 9:12). This depiction of Israel's relationship to the nations differs significantly from the vision of Isaiah 2:2–4, where the nations recognize Yahweh's authority and willingly come to Jerusalem to seek his guidance. Perhaps Isaiah envisions here a prelude to the kingdom of peace described earlier. The description of the revived united kingdom's conquests is reminiscent of David's exploits, when he extended his rule over the neighboring peoples and nations through military might (2 Sam.

---

6   Sennacherib boasted that he took captive a huge number of people (he gives the number as 200,150), and isolated Jerusalem like a caged bird (*COS* 2.119B:303; 2 Kings 18:13, 17).

8:12). (See Gray 1912, 227; Hayes and Irvine 1987, 218; Motyer 1993, 126; Oswalt 1986, 288; Roberts 2015, 186–87; Wildberger 1991, 495–96.) An allusion to the greatness and power of the Davidic empire is not surprising in a context where the reign of a new David is anticipated (see Smith 2007, 277). The references to the Philistines, Edom, and Moab are also reminiscent of Exodus 15:14–15, where the Lord, having defeated Egypt at the Sea, leads his people to their dwelling place in Canaan, much to the chagrin of the people who live in the region. An allusion to the exodus-conquest period is not surprising here, since Isaiah depicts a new exodus in the following verses (Isa. 11:15–16). Furthermore, in 12:2 he uses the language of Exodus 15 (v. 2) to describe the joy that will characterize those who experience this new exodus.

11:15–16. In the previous verses Isaiah describes how the Lord will reclaim his exiled people from among the nations (11:11–12). The Lord's reunified covenant people will then extend their borders and become secure in their land (11:13–14). The prophet now returns to the starting point of this process and zeroes in on one important aspect of it—the reclamation of exiles from Assyria. As noted above, the Assyrians took most of the people of the northern kingdom of Israel into exile in 722–721 B.C. and they deported many residents of Judah in 701. But the Lord will reverse this through a grand new exodus.

Isaiah declares that the Lord will eliminate the obstacles that stand in the way of the exiles' return (cf. Motyer 1993, 126). The Lord will "destroy the gulf of the Egyptian Sea" (i.e., the Red Sea) and sweep his hand over the Euphrates River, reducing it to seven dry streams. This suggests that the prophet envisions a return of exiles from both Egypt (cf. 11:11) and Mesopotamia, but 11:16 specifically speaks of a remnant returning from Assyria in northern Mesopotamia. So it may be that the Egyptian Sea is symbolic here, facilitating the allusion to the exodus. The Lord will overcome the Euphrates River, just as he did the Red Sea.

> **The Red Sea**
> Another possibility, mentioned by Gray (1912, 227) and Smith (2007, 277), is that "the river" is the Nile. In this case, we have two options: (1) Isaiah 11:15 could be describing a return from Egypt, with 11:16 then focusing on a return from Assyria (cf. 11:11); (2) both the Egyptian Sea and the (Nile) river are symbolic for obstacles faced by the exiles as they return from Assyria (cf. 11:16).

There is some debate over the correct reading of the verb in the first line of 11:15. The Hebrew text has הֶחֱרִים, from חָרַם, "to put under the ban, devote to destruction" (cf. ESV, KJV, and NASB, "utterly destroy"). However, the LXX reads "dry up" here, prompting some to emend the Hebrew text to הֶחֱרִיב, from חָרַב, "to dry up" (cf. Isa. 50:2; 51:15; see NIV11). Another option (see *HALOT* s.v. "חרם II" 354) is to understand a homonym, חָרַם, meaning "divide." In any case, the Lord is eliminating the sea as an obstacle to his people's return.

The Lord sweeps his hand over "the Euphrates River" (literally, "the River") with his destructive wind. The idiom "sweeping the hand over" expresses judgment (cf. Isa. 19:16; Zech. 2:13). The Lord's רוּחַ refers here to either his breath (revealed in the wind) or to a wind that he controls. The meaning of the noun that appears before רוּחַ (בַּעְיָם, which comprises the preposition בְּ- and a noun, probably עַיִם) is uncertain, since it occurs only here. Some, based on an apparent Arabic cognate, take it to mean "heat," but others prefer an emendation to עֹצֶם, "strength." (For discussion of the issue, see Roberts 2015, 185; Wildberger 1991, 488; and Williamson 2018, 682–84.) In any case, the Lord strikes the river with his wind and turns it into seven streams (suggesting the totality of the transformation). The word "streams" (נְחָלִים)

probably refers here to seasonal wadis, which can be easily crossed when dry or shallow.

After clearing the obstacles to the exiles' return, the Lord will provide a "highway for the remnant of his people" leaving Assyria, just as he did for Israel when they left Egypt. The term מְסִלָּה, "highway," refers to a road that facilitates travel. The word is not used in the Pentateuch for Israel's route out of Egypt, but the point seems to be that the Lord guided his people (cf. Exod. 13:18, 20–22; 14:29; 17:1).

Celebrating Salvation (12:1–6)
The people will praise the Lord as their savior and king.

12:1. After Israel passed through the Red Sea safely and saw the Lord destroy the Egyptian army (Exod. 14), they sang a song of praise (Exod. 15:1–21). They will do so again following the new exodus (see Isa. 11:15–16; cf. Motyer 1993, 127; Young 1965, 401). Isaiah recites two short praise songs that Israel will sing when they experience deliverance from exile. Both are introduced with the formula, "In that day you will say" (12:1a, 4a). An echo of the original Song of the Sea can be heard in Israel's praise (see 12:2; cf. Exod. 15:2).

In the first song Israel begins with declarative praise, thanking the Lord for turning away from his anger and providing comfort in its place. Israel states its intention to give thanks (אוֹדְךָ, from יָדָה) and then gives the reason (כִּי) for this. The Lord was angry with Israel. The verb אָנַף, "be angry," is used exclusively for divine anger.[7] We know from the immediate context that the Lord expressed this anger by sending Israel into exile and reducing the nation to a remnant (cf. Isa. 11:11–12, 16). But when the Lord turns away from his anger and replaces it with comfort, the people will have reason to express their thanks.

The reference to the Lord's anger turning away (שׁוּב) marks a reversal from earlier judgment. Five times before this Isaiah has emphasized the extent of God's judgment by saying, "his anger is not turned away" (5:25; 9:12, 17, 21; 10:4). Finally, his anger will subside. The basic idea of the verb נָחַם in the *piel* verbal stem is "comfort, console, encourage" in the aftermath of hardship or tragedy. In this case God's exiled people have experienced his angry judgment and its effects, but the Lord comforts them by restoring them to their land. This theme of God's comfort to the downtrodden exiles becomes a recurring motif in Isaiah 40–66 (cf. 40:1; 49:13; 51:3, 12, 19; 52:9; 57:18; 61:2; 66:13).

The verb forms in 12:1b require comment. The form יָשֹׁב (from שׁוּב, "return") looks like a jussive (note the "shortened" form; the imperfect would be יָשׁוּב), but a prayer ("may he return") would not fit here, where Israel is explaining the reason for their thanksgiving (see Gray 1912, 230). The form, if retained, is best understood as an asyndetic (no prefixed conjunction) preterite, which overlaps morphologically with the jussive when it does not have a prefixed *waw*. The LXX, which uses the aorist here, supports this. However, the LXX also has a conjunction (note *kai*). It is likely the Hebrew form originally had a *waw*-consecutive (וַיָּשֹׁב, "and he returned," as one might expect here within a sequence of verbs. In this case the loss of the prefixed *waw* can be explained as virtual haplography, since *waw* and *yod* can be easily confused in a later script phase. The next verb (וּתְנַחֲמֵנִי) appears to be an imperfect (or jussive) with conjunctive *waw* ("and you will console me") but it is better to understand it as preterite ("and you consoled me"; cf. the LXX, which has an aorist form), since the comfort of salvation has already been experienced (cf. 11:15–16; 12:2). "In that day" (12:1, cf. 12:4) refers to the time when the

---

7   See Deut. 1:37; 4:21; 9:8, 20; 1 Kings 8:46; 11:9; 2 Kings 17:18; 2 Chron. 6:36; Ezra 9:14; Pss. 2:12; 60:1 [HB 3]; 79:5; 85:5 [HB 6]. The Moabite cognate is used in the Mesha inscription (Moabite Stone), line 5, of the anger of the Moabite god Chemosh.

Lord delivers his people in a grand new exodus (11:15–16). Perhaps we should revocalize the *waw* as consecutive (וַתְּנַחֲמֵנִי, "and you consoled me"), though this is not necessary in poetic style.

12:2. Israel next declares that God (אֵל) is their salvation, meaning (by metonymy) he is the author or source of their salvation (Young 1965, 403). This prompts them to affirm their trust in him and their refusal to fear (12:2a). The choice of אֵל as a divine title echoes the Song of the Sea, where Israel affirms of the Lord: "He is my God" (אֵלִי; Exod. 15:2). The term "salvation" (יְשׁוּעָה), which is used three times in Isaiah 12:2–3, refers to the physical deliverance of the exiles (cf. 11:11, 15–16). It echoes the prophet's name, which was a sign to the people of the Lord's ability to deliver his people (see Oswalt 1986, 290 n. 5; Seitz 1993, 112–13). Israel's decision to "trust" (בָּטַח) God is significant. During Isaiah's time, Israel trusted in their own schemes (Isa. 30:12) and in alliances with other nations (31:1; 36:6, 9), but only the Lord is worthy of his people's trust, for he alone can provide security and prosperity (26:3–4; 50:10; cf. 30:15).

The affirmation in 12:2b, "the Lord, the Lord himself, is my strength and my defense; he has become my salvation," echoes the Song of the Sea as well (cf. Exod. 15:2). The juxtaposition of יָהּ יְהוָה (Yah, Yahweh) occurs only here and in Isaiah 26:4, prompting some to delete יְהוָה as dittographic (in addition to יָהּ preceding it, וַיְהִי—consonantal ויהי—immediately follows it; Wildberger 1991, 500). This proposal finds support from Exodus 15:2, which has only יָהּ after זִמְרָת (see as well Ps. 118:14), and from the LXX, which has simply *kurios*, "Lord" (Gray 1912, 231). The form זִמְרָת should be emended to זִמְרָתִי, "*my* defense" (a suffixed form of זִמְרָה); the *yod* has been accidentally omitted by haplography (note the following יָהּ) in Exodus 15:2 with the error being perpetuated in the two texts that allude to it (Isa. 12:2 and Ps. 118:14). The meaning of the word is uncertain in this context.

TRANSLATION ANALYSIS 12:2
Some understand the noun as זִמְרָה, "strength" (by metonymy, "defense"; see NIV11; HALOT s.v. "זִמְרָה II" 274; Blenkinsopp 2000, 269; Wildberger 1991, 500; and the discussion in Williamson 2018, 708–10), which fits nicely with the preceding עֻזִּי, "my strength." The joining of synonyms would emphasize the concept of strength. Others take the noun as זִמְרָה, "song" (see ESV, HCSB, KJV, ESV; Motyer 1993, 129; Oswalt 1986, 290 n. 6). The verb זָמַר, "sing," appears in Isaiah 12:5. In this case, the Lord is the source of the singer's praise, for his protection is what prompts it.

12:3. After Israel crossed the Red Sea and sang praise to the Lord, they began their trek into the wilderness. No drinking water was available, so the people complained. At Marah Moses miraculously turned the bitter water into water fit to drink (Exod. 15:22–26). The people then came to an oasis at Elim, where they drank from twelve springs (Exod. 15:27). This sequence (minus the grumbling scene) is mirrored in Isaiah 12:1–3, where the prophet envisions the day when the returning exiles will praise the Lord (12:1–2) and will then draw water in joy from springs of salvation (12:3; see Motyer 1993, 129). The water and springs may be metaphorical here, referring to the refreshing joy experienced by those who are the recipients of the Lord's deliverance. But possibly the physical provision of water is envisioned as something that accompanies deliverance, as at Elim after the exodus (cf. Isa. 35:7; 41:18).

TRANSLATION ANALYSIS 12:3
The term מַעַיְנֵי (construct plural of מַעְיָן, "spring") is sometimes translated "wells" (ESV, KJV, NIV11), but the word refers to springs that gush up from the ground, not to man-made wells (cf. "springs" in HCSB, NASB). See HALOT (s.v. "מַעְיָן" 612), as well as Josh. 15:9; 18:15; 1 Kings 18:5; 2 Kings 3:19, 25; 2 Chron. 32:4; Pss. 104:10; 114:8.

Such springs were viewed as the handiwork of God (Ps. 104:10).

12:4. The second song takes the form of descriptive (or hymnic) praise, focusing on the character of the Lord as revealed through his mighty deeds. It displays the usual pattern—a call to praise followed by the basis (or reason) for praise (Isa. 12:4–5). A renewed call to praise follows (12:6a), accompanied by an additional reason for praise (12:6b).

The initial call to praise uses plural imperatives ("give praise," "proclaim," "make known," "proclaim," "sing"). Israel is speaking here (note "in that day you will say"), so one might think the nations are addressed. But the addressees are to proclaim the Lord's greatness "among the nations," which suggests they are distinct from them. It is likely the members of the restored remnant of Israel are envisioned here as exhorting one another to declare the Lord's greatness (cf. Clements 1980, 129; Motyer 1993, 129; Roberts 2015, 193; Smith 2007, 283). This concern that the nations know of the Lord's greatness is consistent with the Lord's goal of establishing his worldwide rule (2:2–4; cf. Smith 2007, 283).

The people are to make known the Lord's mighty deeds and proclaim (literally, bring to remembrance) that (כִּי) his name is exalted. The term used here for the Lord's deeds (עֲלִילוֹת, singular עֲלִילָה), which refers in several psalms to the Lord's mighty acts in conjunction with the exodus (Pss. 66:5; 77:12 [HB 13]; 78:11; 103:7; cf. Motyer 1993, 130), is appropriate in the context of a new exodus. The people have in mind, first and foremost, the mighty deliverance they have experienced. The Lord's name stands for his character and reputation, as revealed through his acts (Oswalt 1986, 294–95). It is exalted in the sense that it is superior to all other names, for the bearer of the name is superior to all other gods. The use of נִשְׂגָּב ("exalted") is ironic. Earlier Isaiah envisioned a day of judgment against the idolatrous people when the Lord alone will be exalted (Isa. 2:11, 17). But a day will come when the Lord will be exalted through his deliverance of his people (see Motyer 1993, 130).

12:5. The formal reason why the people should praise the Lord is stated concisely: "He has done glorious [literally, 'great'] things" (12:5a). This truth must be made known in all the earth (12:5b). The term translated "great things" (גֵּאוּת) alludes to the Song of the Sea, which declares the Lord is "highly exalted" (גָּאֹה גָּאָה, Exod. 15:1, 21). (The verb גָּאָה is the root of גֵּאוּת, the term translated "glorious things" in Isa. 12:5.) The verbal allusion drives home the point that the God of Moses is alive and well and capable of intervening in power for his people in a new exodus, just as he did at the Red Sea. According to Psalm 93:1, the Lord is robed in "majesty" (גֵּאוּת) as he is enthroned over the unruly water of the sea (93:3–4). However, the wicked refuse to see the Lord's "majesty" (גֵּאוּת), persist in evil, and experience God's judgment (Isa. 26:9–11).

12:6. A renewed call to praise is directed to the people of Zion, addressed collectively with a feminine singular form (see above). They should shout joyfully because the Holy One of Israel is great in their midst (12:6). This is not a mere abstraction—he has demonstrated his greatness through his mighty acts (12:4–5), the first and foremost of which is his deliverance of his people from exile through a new exodus (11:15–12:3).

The use of the title Holy One of Israel here marks a reversal in the Lord's relationship with his people. Earlier Isaiah accused Israel of spurning the Holy One of Israel and his word (1:4; 5:24). But then he foresaw a time when the Lord's people would again rely upon him as their sole source of security (10:20). This renewed relationship will culminate with the Holy One of Israel demonstrating his sovereign power among his people.

THEOLOGICAL FOCUS

The theological focus of this passage can be stated as follows: the Sovereign Lord, who is committed to fulfilling his covenant promises, will establish his rule on earth through an ideal Davidic king, deliver his people from exile, and renew his relationship with them. As the prophet develops this theological theme, the following emphases emerge:

1. The new David's kingdom of justice and peace

A new David will arise from the root stock of Jesse. Enabled by the Spirit of the Lord, he will establish a kingdom of justice and peace in which the wicked no longer oppress the vulnerable. Preserving order and justice was a chief responsibility of kings in the ancient Near East. Egyptian royal names from the Twelfth Dynasty often contain the elements *ma'at*, "justice," or *ma'a*, "just." Mesopotamian kings referred to justice in their royal year formulas and sometimes proclaimed a release of debts as proof of their commitment to justice. Kings were responsible for helping the weak and destitute of society, including widows, the fatherless, and the poor. (For a study of kingship and justice in the ancient Near East and the Bible, see Weinfeld 1995, esp. chs. 1–3.)

The transformation of human society brought about by the new David will be mirrored by a radical transformation of the animal kingdom. The categories predator-prey will become obsolete and fierce animals will no longer be a threat to humans.

All the world will recognize the Lord's authority, and nations will come to his chosen king, the new David, for guidance. The words of the Lord's Prayer, "your kingdom come, your will be done, on earth as it is in heaven" (Matt. 6:10) will become a reality. Human society strives for peace and justice, but inevitably fails in its quest. Wars rage over the globe and justice is rarely realized and often perverted. Only when the whole world recognizes the authority of the Lord and his king will true peace and justice come to earth (see Oswalt 1986, 284).

2. The restoration of Israel through a new exodus

The arrival of the new David's kingdom will bring the restoration of the Lord's covenant community. The Lord will restore his people through a new exodus, prompting them to become a worshipping community that praises him as the great and exalted God who delivers and protects his people. Exiles will return from all over the world, and Israel, once torn by conflict, will be reunified and secure within its borders.

Fulfillment

Questions regarding the fulfillment of Isaiah's vision naturally arise. A return from Assyrian exile never took place in Israel's history. Those who returned from Babylonian exile in the sixth to fifth centuries B.C. were mostly from the tribes of Judah, Benjamin, and Levi. The twelve tribes were not reunited in the postexilic period under the rule of a new David. Present geopolitical realities would suggest that Isaiah's vision cannot be realized, at least literally, for the exiles who never returned were assimilated into their new lands.

Hyperliteral interpreters nevertheless propose that God will resurrect, as it were, the entire geopolitical context of ancient Israel. That means that long-gone nations like Edom,

Ammon, Moab, Egypt of the pharaohs, Assyria, and Babylon, among others, must return. Proponents of this position point out that if God can resurrect Israel, he can do the same with these others. But there is a problem with such reasoning. The prophets predicted the resurrection of Israel (through its return from exile), but they assumed the continuation of the geopolitical context of ancient Israel. Yet that context has disappeared and before it did, the return from exile never reached the magnitude envisioned by the prophets.

For this reason, many resignify the vision, proposing that it will be fulfilled in a spiritual sense in and through the church. But in Romans 9–11 Paul teaches that God will restore Israel in accordance with his ancient promises and he clearly distinguishes Israel from the church.

There is a better way to resolve the problem, when one recognizes that the prophets' promises were often contingent, and their messages contextualized. As I have stated elsewhere:

> The complete fulfillment of the prophetic vision was contingent upon the mass repentance of God's exiled people, something that has not happened. But human failure is not a dead end, only a detour, in God's program. While human failure does not negate God's irrevocable promises, it has pushed the time of fulfillment beyond the prophets' ancient geopolitical context. The omniscient God knew this would happen, but he still contextualized the prophetic vision within the prophets' time so that it would be understandable to Israel and have integrity as a genuine incentive to the people to respond positively to God's call to repentance. Even though we are well beyond that ancient setting, we can anticipate the prophetic vision to materialize in its essence without expecting every literal detail to be realized. (Chisholm 2014, 66)

For a fuller discussion of the problem and of the solution proposed here, see Chisholm 2014, 53–68.

PREACHING AND TEACHING STRATEGIES

Exegetical and Theological Synthesis

The previous unit ends with the picture of a chopped-down forest depicting God's judgment against Assyria and its army (Isa. 10:33–34, cf. 10:18–19). Isaiah 11 begins with the imagery of new growth from a root stock or stump depicting the rejuvenation of the Davidic dynasty. Judah's place within the world had been significantly reduced because of God's judgment. However, the Lord would cause a branch to grow from the root stock (11:1).

This coming Davidic king possesses the Lord's Spirit (11:2). As such, he alone is qualified to usher in a kingdom of complete and unparalleled righteousness. The Lord's Spirit enables him to judge accurately and wisely, ensuring that peace and justice will prevail in his kingdom (11:2–5).

The animal kingdom will mirror the radical transformation of human society and the arrival of peace. Isaiah 11:6–9 describes the king's rule as marked by the unprecedented removal of predatory behavior. The animal kingdom will no longer be ruled by a dog-eat-dog mentality. Instead, there will be peace and harmony where there used to be predators and prey. Wolves will dwell with lambs and leopards lie next to goats. Carnivores like lions and bears will now graze alongside cows and oxen and be led along by a child. It will be safe for infants to play with once-deadly snakes. Predatory behavior, whether among humans or animals, will be terminated under this king's rule. The animal kingdom and human society will be guided by the knowledge of God and his laws. The result will be a world in which all people and every animal experience unparalleled safety.

This coming king will make Israel great among the nations, as in David's day. People from around the world will acknowledge the majesty of the new Davidic king. He will initiate a "second exodus" of God's oppressed people from the surrounding nations and restore them to their land (11:10–16). Israel and Judah will be reunited as they were during the reign of the original King David. A reunited covenant community will exercise political and military dominance over those nations that had previously oppressed them, as they leave their lands of bondage.

Isaiah 12 concludes this larger unit with two songs of praise and celebration to God. He is the one responsible for restoring his people. Though he had been angry with them because of their rebellion, he now gives them comfort and extends his kindness to them (12:1). As in the days of the original exodus out of Egypt, God has again become "salvation" for his people (12:2–3). The prophet urges them to proclaim the Lord's great name among the nations (12:4–6).

Preaching Idea

Only Jesus will usher in the world in which everybody wants to live.

Contemporary Connections

What does it mean?

This world is broken. We all know and feel it. There is oppression and injustice everywhere. Predatory behavior characterizes human society, as well as the animal kingdom. We all long for a world where these realities are no longer present. We desire a world where every animal is tame, where righteousness is always rewarded, and mistreatment of others is never tolerated. This is the world into which Jesus, the Lord's chosen king, will usher his people one day.

It almost goes without saying that this would be a world in which everybody wants to live. Nobody wants to be cheated or deceived by others. Weak, poor, and vulnerable citizens want to know that others are looking out for them, not looking to take advantage of them. Nobody wants to feel unsafe. Every parent wishes they could send their children out to play and not have to worry whether they will be preyed upon by an evil person or attacked by an animal.

I was recently in Mexico by myself. On my final day there, I decided to take a bus into town to get some souvenirs for my kids. Because I had to check out of my hotel that morning, I had to lug my suitcase and backpack with me. Consequently, it was obvious to all that I was in the process of traveling to or from the airport. Because of this, multiple taxi drivers stopped to see if I wanted a ride either to the airport or to my hotel. At one point, a random man noticed me and asked if I needed a ride to the airport. He pointed to his car and offered to drive me there for only 200 pesos (about $10). He seemed like a normal man and his car was nicer than most of the taxis. I was pretty sure he was just looking for a way to make some quick money from a "wealthy" US tourist. However, I knew that my wife would want me to stick with actual taxi drivers. After all, how did I know that this random stranger wouldn't attempt to kidnap or rob me? In the end, I decided to just take a taxi, but it pained me that I had to be suspicious of this stranger rather than accept his seemingly generous offer.

Unfortunately, there are predators in this world who look to prey on vulnerable people, and it forces us to take extra precautions and to be suspicious of those we don't know at times. This likely prevents us at times from making new friends or from receiving generosity from others. As such, everyone desires to live in a world where criminals are a thing of the past, where there is no need to be suspicious of anyone, and where even the animal kingdom is completely tame and safe.

Is it true?

People in every age have attempted to bring about a better world in which everybody would prefer to live. They pass laws and advocate for more just policies. People elect leaders, hire police forces, and appoint judges to enforce those laws and hold criminals accountable. They build schools to educate the next generation. Entrepreneurs invent new products designed to improve people's lives and create businesses that provide jobs and income for many. Yet in the end the world remains broken, ravaged by poverty, drug addiction, mental illness, crime, sickness, and more. People's best efforts are unable to usher in the sort of world in which everybody wants to live. In fact, despite progress on many fronts, it often seems as though the world is getting worse, not better.

The stark reality is that this world's problems are simply far too complex for people to solve on their own. Consider, for example, poverty. The United States of America is arguably the wealthiest civilization in the history of the world. And yet by some estimates, there are still approximately thirty-four million people, or about 11 percent of the US population, who live in relative poverty.[8] Why have we not been able to solve this problem with all the resources and energy that have been focused on this issue over the past century? If we're honest, one of the reasons is that we simply don't know how to solve this issue. The problem is more complex than simply redistributing resources from those who have more to those who have less. Solving the problem of poverty entails more than just finding people better jobs. Many jobs require a higher level of education or training that make it difficult for some. Additionally, there are simply some people who can't work. In some cases their addictions or medical issues prevent them from maintaining a job.

Many argue that the answer lies in providing people equal opportunities but then holding them accountable for their decisions when their life choices result in poverty. This is easy to say for people whose circumstances provided a decent school to attend, a relatively safe community with low crime in which to grow up, and a stable home with two responsible parents to give them an example of how to live life responsibly. But what about kids who have grown up without a responsible parent or parents to guide them? What about kids whose parents are in jail or are drug addicts? What about people whose lives have been severely impacted by serious physical illness? What about people whose families have been devastated by the untimely death of a young husband and father who was the sole breadwinner in that family? The answers to these questions are just as complex as the problems themselves.

The solution to something as complex as poverty ultimately requires God's transformation of human society as depicted in Isaiah 11. Before that day comes, God expects his people to be generous, not greedy (Ps. 112:5; Prov. 11:25; Luke 6:30, 38; 2 Cor. 9:11; Eph. 4:28;

---

8   https://www.debt.org/faqs/americans-in-debt/poverty-united-states.

1 Tim. 5:3–10; 6:17–19). But even so, as Jesus said, poverty will always stain the fallen world (Matt. 26:11). But that will all change when the Lord's chosen king, Jesus, empowered by the Lord's Spirit, establishes his kingdom on earth. He will possess the wisdom to judge equitably and righteously on behalf of the poor and the rich (Isa. 11:4).

The solution to wealth inequality requires more than redistributing wealth. It also requires significant heart change within everyone—including the poor. Heart transformation will happen when the earth is "filled with the knowledge of the LORD as the waters cover the sea" (Isa. 11:9). Then and only then will poverty finally go away.

Now what?
As we anticipate the day in which Messiah ushers in his kingdom, it's important to realize that the coming transformation will be fundamentally moral in nature as people live according to God's laws and principles. Isaiah 11:9 says that in Messiah's kingdom, "The earth will be filled with the knowledge of the Lord." People will recognize and submit to the Lord's authority. This means that nobody will bear false witness against another person. Nobody will slander or steal from their neighbor. No parents will feel the pain of a disrespectful child. No man or woman will have to deal with the suspicion that their spouse is having an extramarital affair. Conversely, everybody will look out for each other. There will be no poor people in part because everyone will be kind and generous. In fact, all citizens will love other people with the same concern they have for themselves. As the apostle Paul succinctly summed up Jesus's teaching, "For the whole law is fulfilled in one word: 'Love your neighbor as yourself'" (Gal. 5:14; cf. Matt. 22:34–40).

As we consider how great it would be to live in a world where everyone behaved in this way in accordance with God's laws, it should motivate us to live this way now. Sometimes we are inclined to argue against God's standards. After all, what is so wrong about two people of the same gender getting married? Why does it really matter if a couple waits until marriage to be sexually intimate with each other? Is it always wrong to steal, especially if a person uses what they take to help the poor? It shouldn't surprise us when the secular culture argues against God's revealed wisdom. However, if we're honest, many of us believers probably find ourselves questioning and even doubting the wisdom of God's laws at times. The arguments from the culture around us sound convincing, and we may be embarrassed or bothered by certain "outdated" biblical instructions.

When Christians are tempted to doubt that God's laws are best, we must remember how great the world will be when everyone embraces *all* of God's laws. Imagine if everyone waited until marriage to become sexually active, and then remained permanently faithful to their spouse. How much pain and suffering would be averted in the world? Imagine a world where nobody ever lied for any reason. Despite the argument that lying can be pragmatic, it also means that people always wonder if the other person is telling them the truth or not. It erodes trust and creates suspicion of others. The bottom line is: God's laws are always best, and Christians who commit to obeying them now will contribute to better homes, churches, workplaces, and communities—the sort that people desire.

Creativity in Presentation

Snakes Defanged
Isaiah 11:8 says, "The infant will play near the cobra's den, and the young child will put its hand into the viper's nest." There are various videos on YouTube where young children in India are shown playing with or lying next to venomous cobras. At first glance, this appears to be the epitome of parents acting foolishly and recklessly with their children's lives. However, things aren't as dangerous as they appear.

Snake charming is a centuries-old tradition in India. As part of their practice, charmers will commonly remove the snakes' fangs to ensure that they are unable to bite and inject their victims with venom. Others will remove the venom sac so that if they are bitten, they won't be in any danger. In the same way that these snake charmers have rendered otherwise deadly animals harmless, God will one day thoroughly and permanently "defang" the entire animal kingdom, rendering all animals safe even for infants.[9]

News Story
On January 3, 2022, Willie Stokes walked out of prison after serving thirty-seven years of a life sentence for a murder conviction given in 1984. Stokes was released after recent revelations surfaced that the district attorney's office at the time of Stokes's prosecution suppressed evidence that would have raised serious doubts about his guilt. The key witness in the case, Franklin Lee, testified at the time that Stokes confessed to him that he had committed the murder. Though Lee changed his testimony at the trial and denied that Stokes had ever made such a confession, the jury still found Stokes guilty, and he was sentenced to life in prison. However, it was recently discovered why Lee testified against Stokes in the first place. Two homicide detectives who were working the case approached Lee while he was in prison for unrelated crimes and solicited him to make a false statement that would indict Stokes for the murder. To elicit this false accusation, they bribed him with access to drugs and sex while in prison.

Philadelphia district attorney Larry Krassner acknowledged that Stokes's unfortunate case was part of a bigger culture of police and prosecutorial malpractice which was pervasive during the so-called tough-on-crime era of the 1980s and 1990s. This story illustrates how flawed even the best of criminal justice systems are when they are run by dishonest and corrupt people. Only when Jesus ushers in his future kingdom will these sorts of miscarriages of justice be a thing of the past once and for all.[10]

Book
In the book *The Art of Neighboring*, Dave Runyon, a pastor in the Denver area, tells about a time when he invited the mayor of Denver to speak to local pastors about how their churches could meet some of the community's biggest needs. The mayor spoke of elderly people who needed folks to check in on them to make sure they were eating well and being cared for, single moms in need of help with childcare, at-risk kids needing adults to take an interest in them, and people with drug/alcohol addictions or mental health issues. Then he said the following: "The majority of the issues that our community is facing would be eliminated or drastically reduced if we could just figure out a way to become a community of great neighbors." Suddenly, Dave had an epiphany. Wasn't Jesus the one who said the greatest command in all of Scripture was to love God and the second to love our neighbors? Could it be that when Jesus commanded his followers to love their neighbors, he meant to include the people who live right around them (Pathak and Runyon 2012, 18–20)? The rest of the book explores how Christians can impact their neighborhoods and lead people into a relationship with Jesus through the art of being good neighbors.

However, Christians cannot produce the kind of world Isaiah describes. God will do that through Jesus the Messiah when he establishes his rule on earth. Yet Christians can be good neighbors by advocating for justice, reconciliation, and peace in the name of Jesus. When they do so, they provide a glimpse now into what life will be like in Jesus's kingdom

---

9   https://www.insider.com/photos-snake-charmers-in-india-defy-local-laws-2019-10.
10 https://www.washingtonpost.com/nation/2022/01/04/man-freed-37-years-philadelphia-murder.

and whet the appetite of sinners to want to be a part of that world, one in which everyone wants to live. Only Jesus will usher in the world in which everybody wants to live.

- Jesus will usher in a world where injustice is eradicated (11:1–5).
- Jesus will usher in a world where predators are domesticated (11:6–9a).
- Jesus will usher in a world where Jesus is venerated (11:9b–10).
- Jesus will usher in a world where hostility is eliminated (11:11–16).
- Jesus will usher in a world where God's salvation is celebrated (12:1–6).

DISCUSSION QUESTIONS

1. As you reflect on the present fallen world, what aspects of the coming kingdom of God excite you the most? Take some time to discuss various specific ways that the coming kingdom will be different from the present world.

2. Has there been a time when you were a victim of somebody else's predatory behavior (you were stolen from, humiliated, taken advantage of, attacked, etc.)? If so, how has that experience impacted you? Has it made you more aware of the impact of your own behavior on others?

3. Who in your life comes to mind when you think about people who are good neighbors by demonstrating God's concern for justice and peace? What is it about their sacrifices or interactions with others that communicates Jesus's love so well? In what way(s) do you aspire to be more like them in that regard?

THE LORD REVEALS HIS SOVEREIGNTY THROUGH WORLDWIDE JUDGMENT (ISAIAH 13–27)

The next major unit of Isaiah's prophecy focuses on the Lord's sovereignty over the nations, a theme already introduced in chapters 1–12 (see esp. 2:2–4 and 11:1–9). This theme of the Lord's worldwide sovereignty both begins and ends this section. The unit opens with an oracle against Babylon (13:1), but before zeroing in on this Mesopotamian power, the prophet depicts the day of the Lord as a time of judgment upon all proud nations (13:2–16; cf. 14:26–27). This theme pops up briefly in the woe oracle of 17:12–14 and then is fully developed in chapters 24–27, the so-called Little Apocalypse, which describes culminating events through which the Lord establishes his kingdom on earth. The opening oracle against Babylon (13:1–14:27) and the following oracles (14:28–23:18) describe the Lord's judgment on various nations of Isaiah's time. This is the prelude to the worldwide judgment depicted in chapters 24–27.

Within chapters 13–23 are thirteen distinct oracles. Two of the oracles are הוֹי, or "woe," oracles (17:12–14; 18:1–7), while one has no formal genre indicator (20:1–6) and appears to be a report of a prophetic "sign" or object lesson (cf. 20:3). Ten of the oracles are introduced by מַשָּׂא, a term derived from the verb, נָשָׂא, "lift," and that elsewhere refers to a burden or load that must be carried. Perhaps it was originally used of a prophetic judgment oracle because of the nature of the "heavy" message that must be borne by the prophet and then unloaded upon his audience. Another option is that the term, when used of prophetic oracles, reflects the idiom "lift up [נָשָׂא] the voice," in which case it merely refers to a prophetic pronouncement (see *HALOT* s.v. "מַשָּׂא II" 639). (For discussion of the options, see Cook 2011, 27–29.) These oracles appear in this order:

Oracle (מַשָּׂא) concerning Babylon (13:1–14:27)
Oracle (מַשָּׂא) concerning the Philistines (14:28–32)
Oracle (מַשָּׂא) concerning Moab (15:1–16:14)
Oracle (מַשָּׂא) concerning Damascus (17:1–11)
Woe oracle (הוֹי) concerning the nations (17:12–14)
Woe oracle (הוֹי) concerning Cush (18:1–7)
Oracle (מַשָּׂא) concerning Egypt (19:1–25)
Prophecy/sign report concerning Egypt and Cush (20:1–6)
Oracle (מַשָּׂא) concerning Babylon (21:1–10)
Oracle (מַשָּׂא) concerning Dumah (21:11–12)
Oracle (מַשָּׂא) concerning Arabia (21:13–17)
Oracle (מַשָּׂא) concerning Jerusalem (22:1–25)
Oracle (מַשָּׂא) concerning Tyre (23:1–18)

For homiletical purposes, we have divided the oracles up into two preaching units, since many pastors will not want, for whatever reason(s), to preach separate messages on the individual oracles or oracle units of 14:28–23:18: (1) World Judgment Focused on Babylon (13:1–14:27), (2) Oracles Concerning Various Nations (14:28–23:18).

Isaiah 13:1–14:27

EXEGETICAL IDEA
The Lord will judge the world for its sin and arrogance, annihilating proud Babylon and restoring exiled Israel to its homeland.

THEOLOGICAL FOCUS
The Lord demonstrates his sovereignty over the world as he judges the arrogant king of Babylon, releases his people from exile, and restores them to their land.

PREACHING IDEA
At his appointed time, the sovereign God will deliver his people from the world's oppressive tyrants.

PREACHING POINTERS
Just wait! Those are two words that no child likes to hear. In truth, none of us like to be told to wait. It is often said that we live in an age of instant gratification. There aren't many things we have to wait on. We can cook a meal in minutes in the microwave. Voice assistant devices answer most of our questions in seconds. Mobile phones mean we must rarely wait to talk to most people. Amazon Prime has spoiled us to expect online orders to arrive in two days or less. We rarely even have to wait to watch most television shows or movies; many of them can be streamed whenever it's convenient for us. With smartphones and tablets, we don't even have to wait until we get home to binge-watch the next season of our favorite show.

Unfortunately for us, God's timetable of events often doesn't align with ours. We typically prefer God to intervene on our behalf *right now*. But often that just doesn't happen. This can be particularly frustrating as it relates to wicked world leaders who oppress and persecute God's followers. Those who are forced to endure persecution at the hands of tyrants such as Kim Jong-Un of North Korea or terrorist groups like al-Qaeda, al-Shabaab, or ISIS long to see God intervene in judgment to deliver them from their suffering. Together, believers across the world echo the question of the martyrs in Revelation 6:10: "How long, Sovereign Lord . . . until you judge the inhabitants of the earth and avenge our blood?" The answer to this question is found in Isaiah 13–14. While it does not provide a specific timetable, it does assure God's people that the Sovereign Lord has in fact purposed a day when he will judge every evil tyrant throughout every nation, resulting in the salvation of his people.

WORLDWIDE JUDGMENT FOCUSED ON BABYLON (13:1–14:27)

The Lord summons his army as he prepares to judge the world for its sin and arrogance. This day of the Lord will bring devastating, inescapable destruction. The Lord will annihilate proud Babylon, reducing it to a heap of uninhabitable ruins. Babylon's fall will enable exiled Israel to return to their homeland. The exiles will taunt Babylon's proud king, who will suffer a humiliating death.

LITERARY STRUCTURE AND THEMES (13:1–14:27)

This oracle against Babylon opens with a vision of worldwide judgment (13:2–16). The Lord summons his army (13:2–3), which the prophet describes as assembling for battle (13:4–5). He urges his audience to wail, for the day of the Lord is near, when everyone will be overcome by fear as the heavenly lights turn dark (13:6–10). The Lord then speaks, announcing he will intervene against the wicked and proud with devastating consequences (13:11–16). The Lord is clearly speaking in 13:11–13a, but the prophet may interject in 13:13b–16 to describe the terrifying effects of the Lord's intervention (note the third-person reference to the Lord in 13:13b).

The oracle now takes on greater specificity as the Lord announces he will stir up the Medes as his instrument of judgment (13:17–18). The primary target of divine judgment will be proud Babylon, which will be reduced to ruins (13:19–22). It is not clear if the Lord or the prophet is speaking at this point. The Lord speaks in 13:17 (note "I will stir up"), but by 14:1 the prophet is speaking (note "the LORD will have compassion"). "God" is mentioned in the third person in 13:19, so the transition in speakers appears to occur before that point.

Judgment gives way to a salvation announcement in 14:1–2, where the prophet announces the Lord will show compassion to his exiled people and restore them to their land. But the theme of judgment emerges again as the prophet recites a lengthy taunt song that Israel will sing over Babylon in the day of vindication (13:3–21). Within this song there is embedded discourse as the trees (13:8b), deceased kings (13:10–15), and all observers (13:16b–17) address the humiliated king of Babylon. The words of the kings are a taunt within the taunt song that includes an embedded lament (13:12) and the king of Babylon's former boast (13:13–14).

Identifying the speakers in 13:11–17 is challenging. The spirits of the dead kings speak in 13:10, but where do their words end? It is likely that 13:10–15 is the dead kings' taunt since the focus is the Babylonian king's descent into Sheol in both 13:10 and 15. Isaiah 13:16b–17 is spoken by those who observe the king's death (13:16a), but it is conceivable that the dead kings are still speaking and quoting what observers say. In this case 13:9 and 18, both of which speak of the dead kings in the third person, form an *inclusio* around the dead kings' taunt.

The Lord speaks again in 14:22–23, as he once more announces (cf. 13:17–22) he will intervene in judgment against Babylon. His words round off the central core of the speech that focuses on Babylon's demise (13:17–14:23). In the same way, the Lord's statement concerning worldwide judgment (14:26), coupled with the prophet's assertion that the Lord's plan cannot be thwarted (14:27), rounds off the entire speech, which begins with the theme of worldwide judgment (13:2–16) before zeroing in on Babylon. As Smith (2007, 321) observes,

"14:26–27 serves as a fitting conclusion to 13:1–14:25 and as an introduction to the rest of God's plans in 15:1–23:18. In these verses the prophet relates God's plans to use his powerful outstretched hand . . . which will carry out his designs for the nations."

Before moving from localized judgment against Babylon (14:22–23) to more general judgment against the world (14:26–27), the Lord interjects an oath and announces he will intervene in judgment against Assyria (14:24–25). The wording echoes 10:27 and serves to link the Babylon oracle with that earlier judgment speech. However, the reference to Assyria does not seem to fit in an oracle focusing on Babylon. This has given rise to various explanations for its appearance here. See the commentary on 14:24–25 below.

- *Heading (13:1)*
- *The Approaching Day of the Lord (13:2–16)*
- *The Devastation of Babylon (I) (13:17–22)*
- *The Lord's Compassion for His People (14:1–21)*
- *The Devastation of Babylon (II) (14:22–23)*
- *The Defeat of Assyria (14:24–25)*
- *The Lord's Plan for All Nations (14:26–27)*

EXPOSITION (13:1–14:27)

Heading (13:1)

The oracle is directed against Babylon because the Lord's judgment focuses on that proud kingdom.[1]

As noted above, the day of the Lord brings judgment on a worldwide scale, but Babylon is the primary target. Babylon epitomizes the pride of the nations, which were dispersed from Babylon when God confused the tongues of humanity (Gen. 11:1–9).

The Approaching Day of the Lord (13:2–16)

The Lord is ready to bring devastating judgment on the whole world.

13:2–3. The oracle proper begins with the Lord summoning his army for the purpose of invading royal cities (note "gates of the nobles," 13:2). The Lord commands his soldiers, who are hand-picked (13:3a). The term מְקֻדָּשַׁי, literally "my consecrated ones" (cf. NIV11, "those I prepared for battle"), describes them as "set apart" (the basic meaning of "holy") for this special task of implementing his angry judgment (cf. Oswalt 1986, 302). They are instruments through which the Lord will vent his anger (13:3b). He calls them עַלִּיזֵי גַּאֲוָתִי, the precise meaning of which is not clear (13:3c, NIV11, "who rejoice in my triumph"). The term גַּאֲוָה may refer to the Lord's royal eminence (cf. Deut. 33:26; Ps. 68:34 [HB 35]), in which case these soldiers are boasting in the royal authority of their commander, the Lord (cf. *HALOT* s.v. "גַּאֲוָה" 168, "who boast in my eminence"; see Smith 2007, 299; Wildberger 1997, 6). Another option is to understand גַּאֲוָה as referring to the pride of the warriors themselves. They are proud, exulting ones who belong to the Lord (cf. ESV, "my proudly exulting ones"). In this case the pronominal suffix refers to the entire expression, "exulting ones of pride," not simply the second word (see GKC, 440 §135n). Motyer (1993, 137) states that the Lord "calls them *my* not because he approves their arrogance, but because in all their arrogance, he owns them and directs the overflowings of their arrogance to his own ends."

13:4–5. As the Lord musters the army for battle, a loud noise can be heard, for the army

---

1   On the meaning and significance of מַשָּׂא, "oracle," see the introduction to Isaiah 13–27 above. On the precise identity of Babylon in this oracle, see the commentary below on 13:19.

is large and multinational (13:4). The divine title יְהוָה צְבָאוֹת, "Lord of Armies," (NIV11, "Lord Almighty") is appropriate in this militaristic context (see the commentary on 1:9). The army comes from a long distance away, led by the Lord (13:5a). The soldiers are his instruments of anger, on a mission to bring ruin to all the world (13:5b). The phrase כָּל־הָאָרֶץ, which can be used of a particular land, here refers to the entire world.

> TRANSLATION ANALYSIS OF כָּל־הָאָרֶץ IN 13:5
> See *Tanakh*, which translates "ravage all the earth," as well as Joseph Blenkinsopp (2000, 276); Brevard Childs (2000, 124); Seth Erlandsson (1970, 115); Motyer (1993, 137); Roberts (2015, 197). Several translations see the referent as more localized. See ESV and NASB, "to destroy *the whole land*"; NIV11, "to destroy *the whole country*"; as well as Hayes and Irvine (1987, 225). The oracle does focus on the judgment of Babylon later (13:19), but the use of תֵּבֵל, "world," in 13:11 indicates that a more worldwide judgment is in view in the first part of the oracle. Wildberger (1997, 21) sees the referent as including both Babylon and the whole earth.

13:6. The prophet dramatically urges his audience to wail, for the day of the Lord is near (13:6a). The implication is that there is nothing else that can be done. Doom is certain, so wailing is appropriate. Generally, "the day of the Lord" is an idiom used to emphasize the swift and decisive nature of the Lord's victory over his enemies on any given occasion. In the Old Testament it may refer to either a particular historical judgment on a specific nation or to a culminating end-time battle; see the discussion under Theological Focus below. Here in Isaiah 13, it has a cosmic dimension that is the framework for the Lord's judgment upon Babylon.

The day of the Lord will come "like destruction from the Almighty [literally, Shaddai]" (13:6b). The preposition -כְּ, "like," is used here in the sense of "in every respect like," indicating that the coming day will indeed be one of destruction sent from Shaddai. (On this use of the preposition, see GKC, 376 §118x.) The divine title Shaddai is probably used, at least in part, because it sounds like שֹׁד, "destruction." The repetition of the sounds *sh* and *d* draw attention to the statement. This title depicts God as the sovereign king and judge of the world who possesses the authority both to give and take life. The derivation and meaning of the name are uncertain. The most likely proposal is that the title means "one of the mountain," and portrays God as a royal judge who, in Canaanite style (cf. Isa. 14:13; Ezek. 28:14, 16), dispenses justice from his sacred mountain. The compound title El Shaddai (cf. Exod. 6:3) occurs in the patriarchal accounts of Genesis, where God is the source of life and fertility (Gen. 17:1; 28:3; 35:11; 48:3; 49:25). The title Shaddai is prominent in Job, where it is associated with God's rule (cf. Job 11:7). Here in Isaiah 13:6 it is used of God in his role of warrior-king as he brings destruction upon his enemies (cf. also Ps. 68:14 [HB 15]; Joel 1:15).

13:7–8. The prophet describes the physical effects the approaching day will have on those who experience its devastation. Their hands will fall limp and their hearts will melt, as it were. The idiom of a melting heart depicts one being overcome with fear so that any courage one might have drains out, leaving one incapacitated (cf. Deut. 1:28; Josh. 2:11; 5:1; 7:5; 2 Sam. 17:10; Ps. 22:14 [HB 15]; Isa. 19:1; Ezek. 21:7; Nah. 2:1[HB 2]). Panic-stricken, they cramp up in pain, like a woman in labor. They will stare at one another in confusion and their faces will become flushed as they tense up in fear, not knowing what to do. The final line of Isaiah 13:8 vividly depicts their panic; it reads literally, "faces of flames (will be) their faces."

13:9. The prophet now pictures the day of the Lord coming closer. In 13:6 he says it is "near," but now he pictures it as moving (note the participle בָּא, "coming"). The day is marked by cruelty, rage, and burning anger. Of the four terms used to characterize the day, three come from the semantic field for anger. This heaping-up of synonyms emphasizes the degree of divine anger that will be unleashed (Wildberger 1997, 24). The Lord's purpose (note לָשׂוּם, "to make") in bringing this rage-filled day to pass is to make the earth desolate and destroy the sinners who live upon it (cf. 13:11–12).

13:10. Terrifying sights in the heavens will accompany the day of the Lord. The luminaries (stars, sun, moon) will not shine, causing darkness to envelop the earth. Darkness connotes judgment, perhaps picturing dark clouds descending on the earth (Clements 1980, 136; Kaiser 1974, 17; cf. Isa. 5:30). Smith (2007, 301) suggests the darkening of the luminaries is caused by the smoke from the fire accompanying the destruction. In this context of cosmic judgment, the darkening of the luminaries may also depict at least a partial reversal of creation, where humans become scarce and the cosmos is shaken loose from its moorings (cf. 13:12–13; see Zeph. 1:2–18; and Young 1965, 423).

13:11–12. The Lord will judge the world, punishing the wicked for their sin and bringing down the arrogant. The use of the term תֵּבֵל, "world," indicates the judgment is cosmic in scope and not simply localized (note its use in Isa. 14:17, 21; 18:3; 24:4; 26:9, 18; 27:6; 34:1). The Hebrew text reads literally, "I will visit evil upon the world, and their sin upon the wicked." The point of the idiom "visit upon" is that the coming destructive judgment is the appropriate retributive consequence of their evil deeds and an expression of God's justice. They receive from him what they deserve. In Isaiah the objects of the Lord's punishment include Israel's oppressors (Isa. 10:12; 26:14), the entire sinful world (13:11; 26:21), and the heavenly-earthly coalition that opposes his rule (24:21–22; 27:1).

The Lord's judgment will be thorough, reducing humanity to a mere remnant. In fact, survivors will be as rare as pure gold (13:12). The implication is clear: since the judgment targets arrogant sinners (13:11), most must fall into that category (see Roberts 2015, 198).

13:13–14. The judgment will be so severe that it will shake the very structure of the cosmos (13:13). As the Lord of Armies unleashes his anger, he will shake the heavens above. The earth below will shake loose from its foundation. These cosmic disturbances will produce fear and panic (13:14). Those who survive the destruction will run like a hunted gazelle and scatter like sheep that have no shepherd. They are pictured running to their respective homelands, as if they are currently living in foreign lands. Perhaps merchants are in view. At this point the prophet may be starting to focus on Babylon (cf. 13:19), since many foreigners resided there (see Wildberger 1997, 27; and Young 1965, 425 n. 37, who describes Babylon as "a melting pot of the ancient world"), but there were also many displaced peoples under Assyrian rule (Erlandsson 1970, 117). Kaiser (1974, 18) sees the "vagueness of the statement" as encompassing any capital city where foreigners ("courtiers, merchants, warriors and slaves") are found in large numbers.

13:15–16. The invading army will be ruthless. They will stab to death everyone they find (13:15). Not even children and women will be spared. Babies will be dashed to the ground, houses looted, and women raped (13:16). The description reflects the realities of ancient warfare (cf. 13:18; Ps. 137:9; Lam. 5:11), as well as the principle of corporate solidarity and responsibility. A man's children and wives were viewed as his property (note how infants, houses, and wives are mentioned together in Isa. 13:16) and it was considered appropriate for judgment to impact adversely all that the sinner owned (see Num. 16:27, 32; Josh. 7:24–25; Ps. 109:9–14).

The Devastation of Babylon (I) (13:17–22)

The Lord would reduce Babylon to a pile of ruins.

13:17–18. The judgment announcement now takes on greater specificity. The Lord announces he is stirring up the Medes (Hebrew מָדַי) as his instrument of punishment (Isa. 13:17a). The verb "stir up" (*hiphil* of עוּר) is frequently used of God prompting people to accomplish his will; these texts testify to his sovereignty over nations and kings (cf. Isa. 41:2, 25; 45:13; Jer. 50:9; 51:1, 11; Joel 3:7, 9; Hag. 1:14).

Madai, the ancestor of the Medes, was a son of Japheth (Gen. 10:2; 1 Chron. 1:5). The Medes settled in the mountainous terrain northeast of Babylon. They were allies of the Babylonians when the latter defeated Assyria in the late seventh century B.C. Cyrus later made the Medes a part of his Medo-Persian empire, which conquered Babylon in 539 B.C.

The Medes will be single-minded in their quest for empire. They will not be bought off with silver or gold (Isa. 13:17b; Motyer 1993, 140; Wildberger 1997, 28). They will be driven by the bloodlust that accompanies conquest, showing no compassion or pity, not even for children (13:18).

13:19–22. The primary target of the Lord's judgment is now revealed—Babylon, the splendor of kingdoms and the source of the Chaldeans' pride (13:19a). The Chaldeans were a group of tribes living in southern Mesopotamia as early as the ninth century B.C. They vied with the Assyrians for control of Babylon in the eighth and seventh centuries. In 731 the Assyrian ruler Tiglath-pileser III took control of Babylon, giving himself the Babylonian throne name Pulu (2 Kings 15:19). Merodach-baladan regained the throne for the Chaldeans in 721 and retained it until 710, when the Assyrian king Sargon took it. The Assyrian king Sennacherib put down rebellions led by Merodach-baladan in 703 and 700. The Chaldean Mushezib-Marduk regained the throne in 693, but Sennacherib destroyed the city in 689. The Assyrian king Esarhaddon rebuilt it in 681. The Assyrians continued to control Babylon until 626 or shortly thereafter, when Nabopolassar regained it. Nebuchadnezzar was the most famous of the Chaldean kings (605–562). He established a powerful, far-reaching empire, but it did not last long after his death. Cyrus and his Medo-Persian forces took the city in 539.

Because of the reference to the Medes in 13:17, it is likely that 13:19 is referring to Cyrus's conquest of the city and the Chaldean empire in 539. However, historical records do not indicate that the Medes ravaged the city as described here (13:18; cf. 13:15–16) or that Babylon was reduced to ruins (see 13:20–22). Consequently, some prefer to understand 13:19 as referring to Sennacherib's invasion of the city in 689. (For further discussion of how the oracle is fulfilled, see below.)

Despite its great splendor, Babylon will not survive. In fact, it will experience devastation comparable to what God did to Sodom and Gomorrah (13:19b). The implication is that God is also the driving force behind Babylon's destruction, as 13:17 has already indicated (see Motyer 1993, 141). Human habitation of Babylon will end; nomadic people and shepherds will even avoid it (13:20). A variety of wild animals will occupy the ruins of the houses, fortresses, and palaces (13:21–22).

The Lord's Compassion for His People (14:1–21)

The Lord will deliver his people from exile and vindicate them before their oppressors.

14:1–2. Babylon's demise will mean renewal and restoration for Israel. The Lord will show compassion to his people. The capacity to show compassion is one of God's fundamental attributes (Exod. 34:6). In Isaiah's time the Lord was predisposed to be compassionate to Israel (Isa. 30:18; cf. 49:15), but the people's rebellion forced him to withhold his compassion and punish them (9:17; 27:11). Eventually, however, he will extend his compassion again (49:10, 13; 54:8, 10; 55:7; 60:10) by restoring his people to their land and making them secure. God's compassion toward his people stands in stark contrast to the Medes' treatment of Babylon's infants (cf. 13:18).

The exile alienates Israel from the Lord, but he will again choose Israel to be the object of his special favor. He chose the patriarch Jacob to be the recipient of his promises to Abraham and Isaac and, in conjunction with this promise, he selected Jacob's descendants to be his covenantal people. This theme of divine election is prominent in Isaiah 40–55, where God reminds Israel of their favored, chosen status (cf. 41:8–9; 43:10; 44:1–2; 45:4; 49:7). The notion of the Lord "again" choosing Israel reflects the perspective of the people. He had chosen them once and for all when he made his covenant with Abraham. But the exile seemingly ended the relationship, so the language of election is used to emphasize the Lord's renewed relationship with Israel at a practical level.

Israel's restoration will impact foreigners. Some will choose to reside in Israel and join themselves to the covenant community (14:1b). Foreign nations will transport the exiles back to the Lord's land, where they will become Israel's servants (14:2a; cf. Isa. 49:22–23). It will be a time of great reversal, for Israel will rule over those who once ruled them and oppressed them (14:2b; cf. Isa. 11:14).

14:3. Israel will experience relief from the suffering, anxiety, and hard labor of exile. The reference to "harsh labor" is an echo of Israel's experience as slaves in Egypt. The expression הָעֲבֹדָה הַקָּשָׁה, "hard labor," refers in Exodus 1:14; 6:9 and Deuteronomy 26:6 to the harsh treatment Israel endured at the hands of the Egyptians. Its use here in Isaiah 14:3 pictures the exile as a time of renewed slavery, which becomes the backdrop for the new exodus (cf. Isa. 11:10–16).

14:4. When relief comes, Israel will taunt their former oppressor, the king of Babylon. (On the identity of the king of Babylon, see the discussion of the fulfillment of the prophecy below.) They will declare sarcastically that the cessation of the oppressor's activities has brought about the cessation of hostile aggression. The word נֹגֵשׂ, "oppressor," is another echo of the Egyptian bondage, for the term was used of Israel's Egyptian oppressors (cf. Exod. 3:7; 5:6, 10, 13–14; see Erlandsson 1970, 121; Roberts 2015, 203; Wildberger 1997, 50; Young 1965, 434–35). But the disappearance of the oppressor means the disappearance of hostility.

The Hebrew term מַדְהֵבָה (NIV11, "fury") occurs only here and its root (דהב) is unattested elsewhere in Biblical Hebrew. 1QIs[a] reads מרהבה, which is also unattested elsewhere in Biblical Hebrew, but can be derived from the root רהב, which means "storm, assault, press" (cf. *HALOT* s.v. "רהב" 1192). *HALOT* (s.v. "מַרְהֵבָה" 633) accordingly offers the meaning "onslaught." (For discussion of the problem, see Erlandsson 1970, 29–32; Roberts 2015, 205; Wildberger 1997, 43.)

14:5–6. Israel attributes the fall of the Babylonian king directly to the Lord, who has broken the "rod of the wicked" and the "scepter of the rulers" (14:5). The rod (or club) and scepter symbolize the king's oppressive rule, which was experienced by nations (14:6). The breaking of the club and scepter symbolizes the cessation of their rule. The plural forms "wicked" and "rulers" (14:5) probably refer to the succession of Babylonian rulers who implemented the harsh policies described here (see Kaiser 1974, 34; Motyer 1993, 143). Their violence and ferocity are highlighted, using terms for striking (note מַכַּת . . . . מַכֵּה, literally, "striking . . . with striking"), anger (note עֶבְרָה and אַף), and lack of restraint (note בִּלְתִּי סָרָה, literally "without turning aside," and בְּלִי חָשָׂךְ, literally "without restraint").

The language used in 14:5–6 echoes 10:24, where the Assyrian oppressor is described with similar terms, specifically the verb נָכָה, "beat, strike down," and the nouns שֵׁבֶט, "scepter," and מַטֶּה, " rod (or club)," referring to the weapon used to beat the Lord's people. The allusion is significant, for it links the Babylonian and Assyrian oppressors. (For further discussion, see the commentary on 14:24–25 below.)

14:7–8. The fall of Babylon and its king will be cause for widespread celebration. All the earth will enjoy relief from Babylonian oppression and break into song (14:7). Even the trees will celebrate (14:8). Babylonian kings used wood from the Lebanon forest in building projects, so the trees are pictured here rejoicing that the woodsman no longer cuts them down. But there is likely an underlying reality here. The trees probably represent the city states and nations that are released from Babylon's exploitation (see 14:6, 16–17; cf. Ezek. 31:16–17).

14:9–10. The king of Babylon descends into Sheol, the underworld residence of the spirits of the dead (רְפָאִים; Isa. 14:9). Sheol shakes with excitement as it prepares to meet the king. It rouses the spirits of all the dead kings and makes them rise from their thrones. Their situation in Sheol, where they occupy thrones, mirrors their royal status while alive. They are called literally "rams of the earth" (עַתּוּדֵי אָרֶץ; NIV11, "leaders in the world"), a metaphor depicting them as leaders (cf. Jer. 50:8, where עַתּוּד is used of rams that lead their flocks). They respond in unison (note "they will all") to the king's presence and begin to taunt him, pointing out that he has become weak like them (Isa. 14:10).

14:11. His pomp has been brought down to Sheol, along with the music of his harps (played in the royal palace; 14:11a; cf. Erlandsson 1970, 123; Wildberger 1997, 62; Young 1965, 39). In place of all his splendor are a bed of maggots and a blanket of worms (14:11b), referring to the king's decaying corpse (cf. 14:19–20). The term גָּאוֹן, "pomp," refers here to the Babylonian king's majesty, which was an outward expression of his arrogance. Isaiah depicts the Lord bringing down human pomp and pride (Isa. 13:11, 19; 16:6; 23:9) and displaying his own majesty (2:10, 19, 21; 24:14). He alone is king (Isa. 6:5), and the pride of human kings is an affront to his sovereignty.

14:12–15. The Babylonian king had conquered nations (14:12b). In fact, many of these departed kings undoubtedly had been his victims (cf. 14:8, 16–17). But now he has been "cast down" (NIV11) to the earth. The language may reflect the first half of 14:12, where the ambitious Helel falls from the sky (cf. 14:13–15). However, many prefer to translate נִגְדַּעְתָּ, "cut down" (cf. ESV, HCSB, KJV, NASB), as if the king is a tree that has been chopped down (cf. the metaphorical use of the verb גָּדַע in relation to trees in Isa. 9:10 [HB 9]; 10:33). (See Young 1965, 440 n. 77; Gray [1912, 256] points out that the verb "does not necessarily imply the figure of a tree.") In this case, the mythological metaphor begun in 14:12a is suspended briefly in 14:12b, before being developed fully in 14:13–15. The image of the king being chopped down like a tree would be ironic considering 14:8, where he is depicted as one who cuts down (the verb there is כָּרַת, not גָּדַע, however) the trees of Lebanon.

The deceased rulers appear to mourn the demise of the Babylonian king. The word אֵיךְ, "how," at the beginning of 14:12 introduces a formal lament (cf. 2 Sam. 1:19; Ezek. 26:17); but in this case, as the immediate context demonstrates, the kings are not really sorrowful over Babylon's demise. At the functional (or illocutionary) level, the lament contributes to the taunt by highlighting the fact that the Babylonian king, despite his great hubris (cf. Isa. 14:13–14), is dead.

The dead kings use stylized and elevated imagery to depict the Babylonian king's hubris and humiliation. They address him as Helel (meaning "Shining One") son of Shachar (or "Dawn"), most likely the morning star Venus (see Day 2000, 167–71). This Helel was thrown down from heaven (14:12a) after an aborted attempt to elevate his status and to make himself like the high god. He boasted he would ascend into the heavens and set up his throne above the "stars of God [El]" on Zaphon, a name used of Baal's dwelling place in Ugaritic myth and of Zion in Psalm 48:1–2 (HB 2–3; Isa. 14:13). He intended to ascend to the tops (literally, "high places, backs") of the clouds and be like Elyon (NIV11, "the Most High"; 14:14). It is not clear if this means usurping Elyon's position or simply ruling alongside him. Either way, his ambitious plan is thwarted as he is brought down to Sheol (14:15a). He intended to set his throne on the "utmost heights" (יַרְכְּתֵי, 'remotest parts') of Zaphon, but ironically he instead ends up in the "depths" (יַרְכְּתֵי, "remotest parts") of the pit," a metaphor for Sheol (14:15b; cf. *HALOT* s.v. "בּוֹר" 116). Like Helel son of Shachar, the Babylonian king has delusions of grandeur that will be shattered (cf. 14:16–21). In fact, if Zaphon symbolizes Zion (cf. Ps. 48:1–2 [HB 2–3]), Helel's attempted coup may envision the Babylonian assault on Jerusalem, while his fall anticipates the end of the Babylonian Empire in 539 B.C.

What is the background for the imagery used in Isaiah 14:12–15? A close reading of these verses suggests Isaiah may be drawing on the imagery of West Semitic mythology.[2] Several elements point in this direction: (1) Helel is called the son of Shachar, a god whose birth is described in the Ugaritic mythological text, "The Birth of the Gracious Gods" (see Parker 1997, 205–14). (2) The "mount of assembly" alludes to a divine council, likely referred to as the "stars of God [literally, El]." In a Ugaritic text the gods are referred to as the assembly of the stars (Parker 1997, 182). (3) Zaphon was the dwelling place of the god Baal (Day 2000, 170), who was called the rider of the clouds, an epithet perhaps alluded to in 14:13 in the expression "tops [literally, 'high places'] of a cloud." (4) The title Elyon (NIV11, "the Most High") may echo one of Baal's titles (*'ly*; Heiser 2001, 359), though Elyon is not attested in Ugaritic literature. It would make good literary sense for Isaiah to depict these deceased foreign kings using imagery from their own mythological traditions to taunt another foreign king (see Young 1965, 441 n. 78). There is evidence the prophet was familiar with such traditions (see Isa. 25:6–8 and esp. 27:1).

Scholars have not been able to locate a mythological story that corresponds in all details to what is described in Isaiah 14:12–15. Most see Helel as attempting to usurp the high god El's position, but there are problems with this proposal. Michael Heiser (2001, 354–69) argues that the mythological account of Athtar's attempt to become Baal's replacement after the latter's death provides the background. However, John Day (2000, 171–74) contends that the differences between the depiction of Helel in Isaiah 14:12–15 and of Athtar in the myth are too great to support identifying them. It is possible that Isaiah's rendition of Helel's attempted coup is an adaptation of the earlier Ugaritic myth (see Roberts 2015, 209–10). Wildberger (1997, 63) proposes that Isaiah's account of Helel historicizes the mythical background. Day (2000, 174) acknowledges that "both provide variations on the theme of Athtar's inability to ascend the divine throne on Mt. Zaphon, and so there is probably some ultimate connection between them."

On the other hand, one could argue that Isaiah 14:13–14, rather than drawing on myth, pertains to a challenge against the authority of Israel's God. Both El and Elyon are titles of Israel's God, the "morning stars" are associated with the "sons of God" (NIV11, "angels") in conjunction with God's creative work (Job 38:7), and

---

2   Studies of the mythological background of the passage include, among others, Craigie 1973, 223–25; Day 2000, 166–84; Heiser 2001, 354–69; McKay 1970, 451–64; O'Connell 1988, 406–18; Page 1996, 120–40; Poirier 1999, 371–89; Prinsloo 1981, 432–38; Van Leeuwen 1980, 173–84; Wyatt 2009, 161–84.

Zaphon is identified as Zion in Psalm 48:1–2 [HB 2–3]. Furthermore, Psalm 82 pictures Israel's God standing in "the assembly of El" (82:1, NIV11, "great assembly"), where he identifies the "gods" as "sons of the Most High" (82:6).

If Isaiah alludes to a rebellion against Israel's God, who then is Helel? The Old Testament knows of no attempted coup against Israel's God by an entity named Helel. Since Venus's morning ascent in the sky is an apt illustration of the Babylonian king's attempt to elevate himself beyond his status as a mere human king, Helel could simply be a metaphor for the Babylonian king, whose assault on Jerusalem (symbolized by Zaphon) is described in a highly poetic fashion that reflects Israel's understanding of Yahweh and his heavenly council. In other words, Isaiah created this description of the Babylonian king's arrogance and placed it on the lips of the deceased kings. It is literarily unique and ad hoc.

Does Isaiah 14:12–15 Describe Satan's Fall?

Christian theologians have traditionally identified Helel with Satan, calling him Lucifer based on the Latin translation of the verse. They see here a description of Satan's original fall or final defeat, but this line of interpretation is problematic considering the immediate literary context. The king of Babylon is the addressee of both the larger and embedded taunts (14:4, 9–11) and the immediately following context depicts him as human. He is called "the man" (14:16), has conquered nations (14:16–17), and possesses a human body that does not receive a proper burial (14:19–20; cf. 14:11). Because of these contextual considerations, some commentators argue that Isaiah did not have Satan in view. John Calvin rejected the idea that these verses refer to Satan, calling the view "useless" and attributing it to "very gross ignorance" and lack of attention to the surrounding context.[3]

To support the idea that Satan's fall is in view in Isaiah 14:12–15, some have appealed to Ezekiel 28:11–19 as being a parallel text that also depicts Satan's fall. According to this view, the arrogant king of Tyre (28:12) is compared to a cherub who lived in Eden and was given special status by God before being expelled from Eden due to his pride and sin. However, this interpretation is problematic for several reasons: (1) Genesis 3:24 speaks of guardian cherubim placed at the entrance of Eden following Adam's expulsion from the garden, but it knows of no anointed cherub. In the traditional interpretation of Genesis 3, Satan is the reality behind the serpent and does not appear as a cherub. So, if Ezekiel 28 is alluding to Genesis 3, it must be utilizing an extrabiblical tradition that was known to Ezekiel. (2) The pronoun at the beginning of Ezekiel 28:14, which is addressed to the king of Tyre, is feminine singular (אַתְּ, "you"). But throughout this context the masculine singular is used when addressing the king of Tyre (see esp. the masculine pronoun אַתָּה in 28:12 and 15 and the three second-person masculine forms in 28:14b). Perhaps אַתְּ is a rare alternate form of the masculine pronoun (cf. Num. 11:5; Deut. 5:24;; and see GKC, 106 §32h) or should be repointed as a defectively written form of the masculine pronoun (cf. 1 Sam. 24:19; Neh. 9:6; Job 1:10; Ps. 6:3 [HB 4]; Eccl. 7:22). But a better option is to emend אַתְּ to אֶת, the preposition "with," as the LXX does. (See Allen 1990, 91; Day 2000, 176; Zimmerli 1983, 85.) One may then translate: "With an anointed cherub I placed you." The king of Tyre is compared to the first man, not a cherub, and 28:15–16 goes on to describe his creation, sin, and expulsion from the garden.

There are still elements in the description that are not present in Genesis 3, such as the first man being covered in jewels, possessing great wisdom, and being thrown down from the mountain of God. But all of these can be explained

---

3 See Calvin 1999, 7:442; as well as Oswalt 1986, 320; Smith 2007, 314 n. 94; Young 1965, 441.

in the light of intertextual links with other biblical texts and/or ancient Near Eastern motifs. A Neo-Babylonian myth contains a parallel to the king's/first man's physical beauty (Block 1998, 119). Job 15:7–8 implies that the first man had special access to divine wisdom (see Allen 1990, 94; Day 2000, 177–78). In Canaanite myth the high god El (perhaps referred to in Ezek. 28:2) lived on a mountain "at the source of the rivers," much like the biblical Eden, which is the source of four rivers and seems to be located in the mountainous area of Armenia (Gen. 2:10–14; see Day 2000, 28–32).

14:16–17. All who see the Babylonian king contemplate his demise (Isa. 14:16a). They ask sarcastically, "Is this the man who shook the earth and made kingdoms tremble, the man who made the world a wilderness, who overthrew its cities and would not let his captives go home?" (14:16b–17). There is great irony in the question. The king, as if he were divine, wants to ascend to the heights reserved for the Most High, but in reality he is merely "the man"—human and susceptible to death. He once "shook" (*hiphil* of רָגַז) the earth as he conquered kingdoms, but now all Sheol is stirred up over his arrival in the land of the dead (cf. רָגְזָה in 14:9). He has been brought down by the Lord (14:5), who shakes the sky and earth (13:13).

14:18–20. The king of Babylon will be humiliated in his death. The kings of the nations are buried in splendor, each in his own tomb (literally, "house," cf. Eccl. 12:5; Isa. 14:18). But not so the king of Babylon! Earlier he was pictured descending into Sheol and being greeted with a taunt by the deceased kings who reside there (Isa. 14:10–15). But now he is "cast out" from his grave, an idiom for being cast aside and not receiving a proper burial (cf. Isa. 34:3). The point is that he will not be buried at all (see Young 1965, 445). He is like a shoot that grows out of a root stock (cf. 11:1) but is viewed as insignificant, even abhorrent, the implication being that it is cut off and discarded (14:19a). A similar picture occurs in Isaiah 18:5–6, where the farmer prunes his vines and leaves the discarded branches for the birds and wild animals (see Erlandsson 1970, 37). The king will experience the same humiliation as his soldiers (14:19b). His dead body will be covered up (literally, "clothed") by a pile of lacerated corpses that are headed for the grave and treated with disrespect (note "trampled underfoot"). But while these others are at least buried, the king will be deprived of a proper burial (14:20a).

> **The Grave**
> The text reads literally, "to the stones of the pit." Many prefer to emend "stones," but this is unnecessary. The word translated "pit" refers to a cistern and is used in poetic texts as a metaphor for the entrance to the grave (see *HALOT* s.v. "בּוֹר" 116). Cisterns, used to catch runoff water, were usually cut out of bedrock and then plastered over (see King and Stager 2001, 126–27). Large cisterns could be used for mass burials (cf. Jer. 41:9). Invariably, sediment and stones would accumulate at the bottom of a cistern.

The reason given for this is the king's treatment of his own land, which he destroyed, and his own people, whom he killed. He did not do this directly, but indirectly. By arrogantly overextending his reach and treating other nations cruelly, he invited the wrath of his enemies, who did not spare his land or his people. As Wildberger (1997, 72) observes, "his single-minded arrogant lust for power was carried out at the expense of both land and people" (see as well Oswalt 1986, 324; Smith 2007, 318). For a modern parallel, one thinks of Hitler, whose quest for empire ended in devastation for Germany and the German people. In the end, he proved to be the greatest enemy of his own land and people.

In proverbial fashion the speakers observe that the offspring of evildoers are forgotten (Isa. 14:20b). The text reads literally, "the offspring of evildoers never will be/are called," apparently meaning their names are never again mentioned (*HALOT* s.v. "קרא" nif. 3, 1130). Some translations interpret this as a prayer (see NIV11, "Let the offspring of the wicked never be mentioned again," cf. ESV, NASB), but one would expect the negative particle אַל in this case. The presence of לֹא suggests the following prefixed verb has a habitual nuance, describing what is typical. The use of the plural מְרֵעִים, "wicked," is consistent with this.

14:20–21. The proverb would play itself out in the experience of the Babylonian king, whose dynasty will come to an end. The speakers issue a command that the king's offspring be executed for the sins of their fathers, referring to the kings of the Babylonian Empire (14:21a; see Clements 1980, 144). The penalty might seem unfair. Why should sons be punished for something their fathers had done? But the second half of the verse suggests a reason. The adage "like father, like son" would prove to be true in their case. They would inherit the Babylonian Empire and undoubtedly arrogantly perpetuate its policies. So, they must not be allowed to do what their fathers had done—conquering kingdoms and building new cities to extend their sovereign control of lands and people (14:21b). Oswalt (1986, 320 n. 10) suggests garrison cities, where military forces would live, are in view here.

Does God Punish Children for the Sins of Their Fathers?

Isaiah 14:20–22 appears to endorse the idea that a sinner's children be punished for the father's sin(s). As noted above, the elimination of the offspring would have the practical effect of terminating Babylonian imperialism and oppression, for the children would certainly seek to carry on their fathers' legacy.

But the notion of children being punished for the sins of their parents is still problematic in the light of the law of God, which prohibits punishing a child for a parent's sin (Deut. 24:16; see the implementation of this in 2 Kings 14:6). Furthermore, Ezekiel 18, addressed to the exiles, indicates that God follows the principle of individual responsibility and judges based on each one's personal behavior, not that of one's father.

Nevertheless, there is no doubt that God does sometimes punish children for their father's sin(s). The Lord warned his enemies that their sin would have negative consequences in their families throughout their lifetime (Exod. 20:5; 34:7; Num. 14:18). There are several incidents where God's punishment included the sinner's children. For example, the earth swallowed up the children of Dathan and Abiram when God judged their rebellious parents (Num. 16:27, 32). Achan's children were executed along with their disobedient father (Josh. 7:24). In accordance with David's self-imposed punishment, the Lord took the lives of four of his children because of his sin against Uriah (2 Sam. 12:5–6, 10; see 12:14–15; 13:28–29; 18:15; 1 Kings 2:25). With the Lord's approval, David turned seven of Saul's descendants over to the Gibeonites for execution because of Saul's sins against that city (2 Sam. 21:1–9).

So how does one resolve the tension? Before attempting to solve the dilemma, it is important to remember that God is the source of human fertility and that he gives children as a blessing (Gen. 1:28; Deut. 28:11; Ps. 127:3). He is within his rights to withhold or take away children from those who forfeit his blessing by their rebellious behavior. God's status as the Sovereign Lord and source of life implies that he can take away life when he deems it appropriate.

In this regard, Robert Stewart (2013, 274) speaks of the principle of "relevant difference," according to which "there can be no greater difference than that between the Creator and the created." He elaborates: "It is wrong for human beings to take another human's life without divine permission because humans, being made in the image of God, are equal to one another in terms of worth and dignity. But God is the ontological ground of all creation; no creaturely life exists apart from the will of God. As such God has the right to do as he sees fit with any or all of his creation."

When one carefully examines the passages mentioned above, it becomes clear that God sometimes punishes a sinner's children when the sinner rebels against him in a way that blatantly mocks his authority. God is not bound to a universal principle that always limits punishment strictly to the individual sinner. On the contrary, since children are a blessing the Lord bestows, he sometimes chooses to withdraw this blessing as he exacts retribution upon those who have forfeited divine favor. At the same time, God does not allow human judges to follow this corporate principle when implementing justice. It is restricted to situations where God himself is the offended party or is the guarantor of a treaty agreement. Ezekiel 18 describes God's merciful response to his people's sin in a specific situation. It does not state a universal principle; the generalized statements made by the prophet are limited by their context.

In the case of Isaiah 14:20–22, the punishment of the Babylonian king's offspring fits the pattern. The Babylonian king has oppressed the Lord's covenant people (14:3) and has arrogantly elevated himself, as if he were the Most High (14:12–14). From the Lord's perspective, the Babylonian king's hubris is a personal affront to his sovereignty and must be dealt with accordingly. (For a fuller discussion of this issue, see Chisholm 2018.)

The Devastation of Babylon (II) (14:22–23)

The Lord reiterates his intention to judge Babylon.

The taunt song ends and the Lord, in his role of commander of armies (note יְהוָה צְבָאוֹת, traditionally, "Lord of Hosts"; cf. 13:4), again states that he will intervene in judgment against Babylon (cf. 13:17). He will attack the offspring of Babylon's king (note "them"; 14:22a). In fact, he will cut off from Babylon all offspring and leave no survivors (14:22b), reducing the city to a swamp inhabited by wild animals (14:23a). He will, as it were, sweep Babylon away with a "broom of destruction" (14:23b).

The Defeat of Assyria (14:24–25)

The Lord would also judge the Assyrians.

The Lord of Armies interjects an oath into the oracle at this point. He vows that he will bring his plan to realization (14:24) by breaking (NIV11, "I will crush") the Assyrian invader in the land of Judah (14:25a, cf. "my land"). This will bring relief to his oppressed people (14:25b).

The language of 14:25b echoes 10:27, where the prophet tells the people that the Lord will turn aside (cf. NIV11, "lifted") the Assyrian "burden . . . from your shoulders" and their "yoke from your neck." Four terms from 10:27 appear here: "turn aside" (סוּר), "yoke" (עֹל), "burden" (סֹבֶל), and "shoulder" (שְׁכֶם). In both contexts, relief from Assyrian oppression is in view. In 14:25b the pronominal suffixes (note מֵעֲלֵיהֶם, "from upon *them*" and שִׁכְמוֹ, "*his* shoulder") have no antecedent earlier in the oath. In the light of 10:27, the Lord's people (cf. "my people who live in Zion" in 10:24) most certainly are the referent of the pronouns (the singular suffix being collective). This suggests the Lord is alluding to and adapting the prophecy of 10:27, altering it from direct address to third-person description. The absence of a grammatical antecedent in 14:25 is not problematic once one detects the allusion to 10:27. In fact, the elliptical style may even indicate there is an allusion.

This reference to the Assyrians' demise serves an important role in the prophet's overall rhetorical strategy. It may seem surprising to see a judgment speech against Assyria in this oracle against Babylon. In fact, some understand this as an interpretive key for 13:1–14:27 and identify the king of Babylon in the earlier verses of the oracle as an Assyrian ruler (see Hayes and Irvine 1987, 235). However, it is preferable to understand Assyria and Babylon as distinct. The oracle against Babylon (13:1–14:23) was fulfilled in 539–538 B.C., while this brief judgment speech of Assyria's demise in the land of Judah was realized in 701 B.C., when the Lord decimated Sennacherib's army. (For further discussion of the fulfillment of the oracle, see below.) By referring to the latter, albeit briefly, the Lord links the destruction of both Mesopotamian powers (Childs 2000, 127), just as the prophet earlier used an allusion to link their oppressive ways (see the commentary on 14:5–6 above; cf. 10:24). Smith (2007, 319) insightfully explains the relevance of the Assyrian insertion for Isaiah's contemporaries. During Hezekiah's reign, Judah allied with Babylon (the Chaldeans) against Assyria (see Isa. 39). But the oracle in 13:1–14:27 shows the folly of this. The Lord will eventually destroy Babylon (see esp. 13:17–22; 14:23–24), so Judah should not be making alliances with the Chaldeans. Indeed, an alliance was unnecessary, for the Lord himself will destroy the Assyrians.

The Lord's Plan for All Nations (14:26–27)

The Lord's plan of judgment encompasses all nations.

This plan begins with Judah, whom the Lord punishes for covenantal violations (cf. 5:12, 19). It is then extended to Assyria and finally to all nations (including Babylon; see Clements 1980, 146–47). The reference to the Lord's outstretched hand in 14:26–27 serves to link the final phase of the Lord's plan (worldwide judgment) with its earlier phases, which are the focus in chapters 1–12. The prophet uses the image of the outstretched hand in 5:25; 9:12, 17, 21 to describe the Lord's unrelenting judgment upon Judah, and then again in 10:4, as he makes the transition to a judgment speech against Assyria. By using it once more in 14:26–27, he links the oracle of Babylon (which includes the theme of worldwide judgment that is further developed in chs. 13–27) with chapters 1–12. In so doing, he makes it clear that the immediate judgment upon Judah and Assyria should not be viewed in isolation. It is the beginning of a divine plan encompassing all nations.

The word "plan" (עֵצָה) sometimes refers to instruction or advice imparted by one party to another, but it is also used, as here, of a proposal or plan (cf. Pss. 14:6; 20:4 [HB 5]; 33:10;

Isa. 5:19; Jer. 49:30). In Isaiah 44:26 the term is used of God's prophetic word, which announces his plans for the nations and his people. In contrast to the pagan diviners, whose attempts to control history are thwarted by God (47:13), the Lord brings his announced plans to realization, demonstrating his sovereignty over history. Here in 14:26 the Lord declares he has a plan for the nations. The language testifies to divine involvement in and sovereignty over history, yet it should not be interpreted in a fatalistic manner. God's plan takes account of human decisions and responses as well. As the Westminster Confession observes (V, 2), God's providential work in human history makes room for second causes, which operate necessarily, freely, or contingently. In the case of Assyria and the other nations, their pride and rebellion prompted God to decree (cf. "has sworn" in 14:24) their punishment.[4]

No one can "thwart" the purpose of the Sovereign Lord of Armies (14:27). The basic meaning of the verb פָּרַר is "break, frustrate, make ineffective." Once the Lord has decreed (cf. "has sworn" in 14:24) a course of action, no one can thwart his plan. However, he can thwart the strategies and purposes of the rebellious and proud nations (cf. Isa. 8:10; 44:25).

> **The Fulfillment of the Oracle**
> The oracle describes divine judgment in three phases: (1) the defeat of the invading Assyrian army (14:24–25), (2) the devastation of Babylon (13:17–14:23), and (3) worldwide judgment (13:2–16; 14:26–27). All three phases are part of the Lord's overarching plan for the nations (14:26–27), which is executed in conjunction with the day of the Lord. From Isaiah's perspective, it encompasses the immediate future and culminating events that usher in the kingdom of God (see Isa. 24–27).
>
> The judgment of Assyria described in 14:24–25 occurred in 701 B.C., when the Lord decimated Sennacherib's invading army (cf. Isa. 36–37). The worldwide, culminating judgment depicted in 13:2–16 and 14:26–27 still awaits complete fulfillment. The judgment of Babylon, which is the focal point of the oracle (cf. 13:1; 13:17–14:23) was fulfilled in 539–538 B.C., when Cyrus, king of the Medo-Persian Empire, conquered Babylon and subsequently allowed the Lord's exiled people to return to their homeland (cf. 14:1–2).
>
> However, there is no scholarly unanimity regarding the fall of Babylon. Some argue that Isaiah's prophecy regarding Babylon must pertain to events that occurred during or shortly after the prophet's ministry. They prefer to see the fulfillment of the oracle in 689 B.C., when Sennacherib devastated Babylon, an event Isaiah refers to in a later oracle (cf. 23:13). They identify the king of Babylon (14:3) as one of the conquering Assyrian kings (Tiglath-pileser III, Sargon, or Sennacherib). After all, the Assyrians, not the Babylonians, were the scourge of Israel and Judah in Isaiah's time, and the Assyrian kings ruled Babylon for much of this time (see the commentary above on 13:19). Tiglath-pileser III even took a Babylonian throne name, Pulu (a name that appears in 2 Kings 15:19; see esp. Erlandsson 1970).
>
> As attractive as this proposal may be in certain respects, its flaws outweigh its strengths. It is more likely that Isaiah's vision of Babylon's fall was realized in 539–538 B.C. and that the king of Babylon should be identified as a Chaldean, not Assyrian, ruler. Consider the following:
>
> 1. The fall of Babylon in 689 B.C. did not result in a release of Israelite exiles, as depicted in 14:1–2. On the other hand, when Cyrus conquered Babylon, he allowed the Israelite

---

[4] For further observations on the theme of God's "plan," see Albrektson 1967, 68–97, esp. 69–74; and Conrad 1991, 52–82.

exiles to return home (2 Chron. 36:22–23; Ezra 1:1–4).
2. The Medes, mentioned as conquerors of Babylon in 13:17, participated in Cyrus's campaign against Babylon (see as well, Jer. 51:11, 28).[5] Once absorbed into the Persian Empire, the Medes played a subordinate role (see Yamauchi 1997, 57). Isaiah and Jeremiah probably mention them, rather than the Persians, because in their day the Medes were still the more dominant of the two groups.[6]
3. Assyrian kings did indeed conquer Babylon, and Tiglath-pileser III took the Babylonian throne name Pulu. But in 2 Kings 15:19–20, which speaks of this, he is still called the "king of Assyria," not the "king of Babylon" (see also 2 Kings 15:29). In Isaiah 13:19 Babylon is the pride of the Chaldeans, a people distinct from the Assyrians. Indeed, in Isaiah 39:1 the prophet uses the title "king of Babylon" for Merodach-baladan, who opposed the Assyrian king and controlled the throne of Babylon from 721 to 710 B.C. It is true that Merodach-baladan and other Chaldeans contemporary with Isaiah were hardly world rulers, as depicted in Isaiah 14:16–17, but Nebuchadnezzar, the conqueror of Jerusalem, certainly ruled a vast empire. Isaiah spoke of the fall of Jerusalem and referred to Nebuchadnezzar, though not by name, in 39:7, calling him "king of Babylon." Of course, Nebuchadnezzar, who died in 562 B.C., had successors. Nabonidus was the ruler (with Belshazzar as his vice-regent; cf. Dan. 5:1) at the time Babylon fell to Cyrus. But we need not identify the "king of Babylon" in 14:3 with him or any specific individual. "The king of Babylon" symbolizes Chaldean pride and glory, as manifested in Nebuchadnezzar and his successors.

If 13:1–14:23 is a prophecy of Babylon's fall to Cyrus's Medo-Persian army, then the description of Babylon's fall in 13:14–22 and 14:22–23 is problematic. According to Isaiah, Babylon's fall would be exceedingly violent and final. But Cyrus's takeover of Babylon, while preceded by a military campaign, was relatively peaceful and even welcomed by some (cf. Roux 1966, 351–53). One faces this same problem with Jeremiah's prophecy of Babylon's fall (chs. 50–51); he too depicts it as violent and permanent. The problem has been resolved in various ways: (1) The downfall of Babylon involved a long process (cf. Grogan 1986, 103). In this regard, one could argue that the prophet merges the near and the far in his portrayal of Babylon's fall, mixing images from 689 B.C. with those of 539–538 B.C. (see the discussion of the fulfillment of 21:1–10 below). (2) The prophecy will be fulfilled in conjunction with a future Babylon of the end times (cf. Allen 1976, 19–27). This Babylon could be understood as literal (Allen's view) or archetypal. (3) The language in these verses is stylized and hyperbolic, being stereotypically used of the downfall of cities and kingdoms. In this case, the description reflects the judgment idiom of the Bible and the ancient Near East.[7] While the language used to describe Babylon's fall may seem excessive, it was essentially fulfilled, for the Babylonian Empire ended with the conquest of Cyrus.

---

5 Those arguing that the oracle pertains to the Assyrians' destruction of Babylon in 689 B.C. face a challenge explaining the reference to the Medes. It is true that Assyria controlled "towns of the Medes" at this earlier time (2 Kings 17:6; 18:11), but it would be odd for the prophet to single out a group that, at best, served as mere mercenaries in the Assyrian army.

6 Yamauchi (1997, 23) observes that the Medes "dominated the Persians until the rise of Cyrus" around 550 B.C. The first biblical reference to the Persians is in Ezekiel's prophecy (27:10; 38:5).

7 For biblical examples, see Isa. 34:11–15; Jer. 50:39–40 (used of Babylon); 51:36–37 (used of Babylon); Zeph. 2:13–15. For ancient Near Eastern examples, see the Sefire treaty (*COS* 2.82:214) and Ashurbanipal's description

THEOLOGICAL FOCUS

The theological focus of this passage can be stated as follows: the Lord demonstrates his sovereignty over the world as he judges the arrogant king of Babylon, releases his people from exile, and restores them to their land. As the prophet develops this theological theme, the following emphases emerge:

1. The Lord's sovereignty over the nations

Israel's God is no mere national deity. He has a plan for judgment that encompasses all nations (14:26–27), especially the arrogant ones—mighty Assyria (14:24–25) and its eventual successor on the world stage, the Babylonian Empire (13:17–22; 14:22–23). The Lord counters the hubris of the king of Babylon, who viewed himself as the ruler (or perhaps coruler) of the world. He humiliates this arrogant king by demonstrating to all that he is nothing but a frail human destined to die.

2. The deliverance of the Lord's covenant people

The Lord's judgment of nations has a goal—the deliverance of his covenant people. He defeats the Assyrian invader to release his people from their oppressive rule (14:25). He brings down the Babylonian Empire so his exiled people can return to their land (14:1–2).

PREACHING AND TEACHING STRATEGIES

Exegetical and Theological Synthesis

This literary unit is a prophetic oracle against Babylon (13:1). The theme of God's sovereignty is displayed from the outset as the Lord describes himself as the one consecrating and summoning his army to come and do battle against Babylon (13:2–5). This time when God brings judgment upon Babylon is described as "the day of the LORD" (13:6, 9). This day will elicit emotions of immense fear from those encountering God's wrath. Hands will become feeble; hearts will melt (13:7). Pangs of agony will seize them. They will experience anguish like a woman going through the excruciating pains of childbirth. The looks of terror on their faces reveal their utter horror on that day (13:8).

In 13:9–11 the prophet begins to extend this prophecy beyond just Babylon to encompass the entire world. He says that the day of the Lord "is coming . . . to make the land desolate and destroy the sinners within it." In context, "the land" refers to the entire earth, as 13:10–11 makes clear. Isaiah 13:10 describes the judgment as cosmic in scope, and in 13:11 the Lord says, "I will punish *the world* for its evil, the wicked for their sins." This is the first clue within the broader pericope that this prophecy had both local (Babylon) and global implications. The ultimate day of the Lord would bring judgment to all sinners throughout the whole world and would put an end to all the arrogant ones who had lifted themselves up in pride against God (13:11). In that day, sinners will be rarer than gold (13:12).

Next, we are informed that nobody will be safe from God's wrath in that day. While all attempt to flee to their own land, anyone who is caught will be killed (13:15). Even infants will be killed, and women will become victims of the cruel wrath meted out by the foreign army that God has summoned to exact judgment against Babylon. Isaiah 13:17 predicts it will specifically be the Medes who carry out the defeat of the Babylonians, making them their captives. Once again, the prophet reiterates that not only will the young men be slaughtered by this army, but even the young children will become their prey (13:18).

---

of the destruction of Elam (*ARAB* 2:310–11). For a discussion of the prophets' hyperbolic use of "destruction" language, see Heater 1998, 23–43.

The prophet goes on to predict that the city of Babylon would never again be inhabited by humans (13:20). Only wild animals like ostriches, wild goats, hyenas, and jackals would populate these ruins (13:21–22). As such, God's judgment against this once powerful empire would extend in perpetuity throughout the future.

At the beginning of chapter 14, there is a change in theme from the judgment of Babylon and the pagan nations to the deliverance of God's people Israel. They would be rescued out of the land that had enslaved them for decades and be restored to their own land of Israel (14:1). There will also be a reversal of fortunes for the people of God, as their former captors will now be their captives and will become their slaves. As a result of God's salvation, Israel will find relief from their pain and turmoil that they experienced while serving as captives in Babylon (14:3). They will use the opportunity to gloat over their former oppressors (14:4).

Their taunt against Babylon will exalt the Lord as the one who has broken the rod of the wicked tyrants. They used their scepter, symbolizing their authority, to oppress and persecute God's people, but now the entire earth is at rest (14:6–7). Even the trees join in the celebration and taunt the king of Babylon, for he will no longer be able to cut them down for his building projects (14:8).

In 14:9–20, the taunt continues with a focus on the theme of death and Sheol. The once mighty king of Babylon is mocked by those who have gone down into Sheol before him. He has now become just like them, totally weak and vulnerable, as death is the great equalizer (14:9–10). Hyperbole is used here to describe Babylon as the greatest of earthly kingdoms whose king(s) fancied himself as being like the Most High (14:14). It was as if he had attempted to ascend into heaven itself to set his throne even above the angels (14:13). Nonetheless, in ironic fashion, Babylon's king has been cut down and has fallen into the deepest depths of Sheol (14:12, 15). And whereas other nations' kings are honored by their people upon their death with their own royal tomb, not so with Babylon's king(s) (14:18–20). He will be loathed in death and treated like an enemy slain in battle whose body is discarded along with all the rest in a mass grave, because he will be responsible for the destruction of his own people and their land.

As an additional consequence the king's sons and grandsons will be destroyed. They will never rise back to power and restore any of their father's glory (14:20–21). Once again, the Lord declares this will ultimately be his own doing; it will be an extension of his sovereign, predetermined judgment against the nations (14:22–23). Isaiah 14:24–27 reveals that God's plans to judge Babylon are part of his broader plan to judge all the nations who have opposed God and have attempted to rival him rather than serve him. In addition to Babylon, God will similarly deal with the more imminent and pressing threat of the nation of Assyria. Assyria's judgment, like Babylon's, will be carried out according to the sovereign plans and purposes of God (14:24). As the prophet says, "This is the plan determined for the whole world; this is the hand stretched out over all nations. For the LORD Almighty has purposed, and who can thwart him? His hand is stretched out, and who can turn it back?" (14:26–27).

Preaching Idea

At his appointed time, the sovereign God will deliver his people from the world's oppressive tyrants.

Contemporary Connections

What does it mean?

Rulers tend to gravitate more and more toward a self-serving, oppressive, tyrannical form of rule. It is one of the reasons why God warned Israel against choosing a king to rule over them like the nations (1 Sam. 8:10–18). The prophet Samuel warned that a king would very quickly begin to oppress them by taking their sons and daughters as his servants, and their crops and flocks for his use. Selfish human pride is prone to abuse power and exploit others. This is magnified when godless leaders gain power. They have no fear of God and dismiss any notion of accountability to him. In fact, the worst godless rulers consider themselves worthy of their people's worship, adoration, and praise. Anything less than complete, unquestioning obedience to their commands is met with harsh mistreatment.

Throughout history tyrants have targeted Christians and worshippers of God for at least two reasons. First, Satan, as the ruler of this present world (John 12:31; 14:30; 16:11; Eph. 2:2; 1 John 5:19), inspires its leaders to oppress worshippers of God to intimidate and discourage others from becoming believers. Second, leaders who expect submission to their laws and demands cannot tolerate competing loyalties. True worshippers of God have always understood that he is their ultimate authority. As such, they must obey God over earthly rulers when the two are in conflict. For these reasons, tyrannical leaders often suppress or strictly regulate religious expression and worship.

Inevitably then, God's people throughout history have often suffered severe oppression. Isaiah 13:1–14:27 addresses the people of God as ones oppressed by one such wicked tyrant— the king of Babylon. This powerful world ruler considered himself to be so powerful and important, it was as if he himself were God with his throne exalted into heaven above even the angelic beings (14:13–14). He used his power to abuse and persecute the people of God (14:4–6).

Nonetheless, God showed himself to be the true sovereign king, the Most High. Just as the king of Babylon was brought back "down to earth" upon his death, so too every evil tyrant will eventually have to face his own mortality. In the afterlife, these kings will experience a dramatic reversal of the privilege and power they enjoyed during their lifetime. Even more sobering than this is the reality that they will have to stand before God and give an account of their lives. Evil tyrants will be forced to experience the punishment of God as he will put an end to their pride and arrogance once and for all (13:11).

In contrast to this, God's people will ultimately experience God's salvation. In his compassion, he will deliver them from their oppressors (14:1, 3)—if not in their lifetime, then after this life in eternity. God will accomplish all of this at his appointed time according to his sovereign plan (14:24, 26–27).

Is it true?

History bears out that the prophecies of Isaiah 13:1–14:27 have come to pass. In 612 B.C., Nineveh, the capital of Assyria, was sacked and burned by a joint attack of the Babylonians and the Medes. This lifted the yoke of the Assyrians off the neck and shoulders of Judah just as God predicted (Isa. 14:24–25).

Shortly after, Babylon attacked and conquered Judah just as Isaiah prophesied (14:2–6). In 597 B.C. Nebuchadnezzar, king of Babylon, captured Jerusalem, and over the next ten years he deported many Hebrews to Babylon. Isaiah predicted further that the king of Babylon would be a man of tremendous pride who would even exalt himself against the God of heaven (14:13–14).

The prophet Daniel records how Nebuchadnezzar's great pride against God resulted in judgment. God caused him to become like a beast who lived out in the fields and ate grass like an animal for seven years (Dan. 4:4–33). Both Isaiah and Daniel compare God's humbling of the proud king of Babylon to a once tall tree being cut down (Isa. 14:12; Dan. 4:10–15). Only at the end of this humiliating experience did Nebuchadnezzar finally acknowledge the Lord alone to be sovereign over every kingdom on earth (Dan. 4:34–37).

Worldwide Judgment Focused on Babylon (13:1–14:27)

Nebuchadnezzar was not the only Babylonian king who displayed great arrogance against the Lord. Belshazzar followed in the prideful footsteps of his predecessors. One evening while partying, he ordered the golden vessels that Nebuchadnezzar had looted from the Jerusalem temple to be brought to him so he and his concubines could drink from them as they worshipped their idols (Dan. 5:2–4). Little did he know that the Most High God was about to intervene in judgment against Babylon. A human hand appeared in Belshazzar's banqueting hall that evening and mysteriously wrote a message on the wall. Daniel was called to interpret the meaning of the message, "Mene, Mene, Tekel, Parsin" (Dan. 5:25):

Here is what these words mean:

Mene: God has numbered the days of your reign and brought it to an end.
Tekel: You have been weighed on the scales and found wanting.
Peres: Your kingdom is divided and given to the Medes and Persians. (Dan. 5:26–28)

Belshazzar likely still felt invincible, even though his own army had suffered a major defeat shortly before this at the hands of King Cyrus's advancing Medo-Persian army. After all, the city of Babylon had a massive outer wall, a smaller inner wall, and a wide moat surrounding the outer wall. Additionally, the city had a constant water supply from the Euphrates River that flowed under the walls and through the city. As such, Babylon was prepared to endure a very long siege, if necessary.[8] However, Cyrus's men diverted the flow of the Euphrates River enough that his soldiers were able to march through the riverbed into the city and surprise the Babylonians. Just as Isaiah predicted, in 539 B.C. the Medes (along with the Persians) were victorious and rose to power in place of the Babylonians (Isa. 13:17; Dan. 5:30–31). The king of Babylon was brought down to the grave that very night along with his arrogant hubris against the Most High God (Isa. 14:11–12, 15). Shortly after the defeat of Babylon, King Cyrus decreed that the exiles from Judah could return to their homeland and rebuild the city of Jerusalem, along with its walls and its temple, just as Isaiah prophesied (14:1).

There are sufficient indicators throughout this prophetic oracle to demonstrate that these prophecies pointed beyond the eventual judgment and destruction of Assyria and Babylon. The prophet described the eventual judgment of *all* worldly tyrants opposed to God and his people and the ultimate deliverance of *all* God's people from oppressive rulers (Isa. 13:9–11; 14:5–7, 26–27). In the same way that God's promises were fulfilled against Babylon and Assyria in the century or so that followed Isaiah, we can be certain that his broader global promises to judge all oppressive tyrants and to save all of his people from those who mistreat and abuse them will likewise be fulfilled at God's appointed time.

Now what?

Passages such as this one call for patience and perseverance from God's people. For believers who are being mistreated by leadership or unjust governments, it can be easy to become restless and impatient with God. Why isn't he doing anything? Is he really listening to my prayers for him to intervene on my behalf? Does he even care about what I'm going through? We must remember that God allowed Babylon to dominate and rule his people

---

8   Herodotus (an ancient historian) describes Cyrus's capture of Babylon as follows: "[The Babylonians] withdrew within their defenses. Here they shut themselves up, and made light of his siege, having laid in a store of provisions for many years in preparation against this attack." https://www.livius.org/sources/content/herodotus/cyrus-takes-babylon.

for nearly sixty years before intervening in judgment. Isaiah assured the people that God was not simply acting arbitrarily or without forethought. Rather, his actions against Babylon and Assyria, as well as every tyrannical government throughout history, have been planned out and purposed according to God's sovereign and wise providence (Isa. 14:24–27). Part of what it means to live by faith is that we trust that God will intervene on behalf of those who are his people, and that this intervention will happen at just the right time. In the meantime, God has called us to patiently endure suffering for his name's sake in this evil world (Matt. 5:10–12; 10:16–18, 22–25; 16:24; John 15:19–21; 2 Cor. 4:8–11; 1 Thess. 3:3; 2 Tim. 2:3; 3:12–13). We can take comfort in the words of the psalmist: "The wicked plot against the righteous and gnash their teeth at them; but the Lord laughs at the wicked, for he knows their day is coming" (Ps. 37:12–13).

Also, we must remember to pray for those who are in authority over us, including the ones who hate and mistreat us. First Timothy 2:1–4 says:

> I urge, then, first of all, that petitions, prayers, intercession and thanksgiving be made for all people—for kings and all those in authority, that we may live peaceful and quiet lives in all godliness and holiness. This is good, and pleases God our Savior, who wants all people to be saved and to come to a knowledge of the truth.

When we have leaders who mistreat us, our first inclination is probably to complain about them to others or even to confront them. We may be tempted to lash out in anger toward them if we are given the opportunity. It is an American pastime to complain about political leaders who advocate policies we consider to be unwise, unfair, or even evil. We may even curse these leaders to others or at least in the privacy of our own mind. But a question to ask ourselves is this, "Can I honestly say that I have prayed for those leaders?" The Scripture passage above tells us that one of the reasons God commands us to pray for our leaders is because he desires that all people come to a saving knowledge of the truth. God doesn't hate these wicked rulers; he sees them as deceived. He loves them and wants them to repent. Prayer helps us to protect our own emotions and attitudes toward oppressive leaders so that rather than hating them, we too will desire to see them come to a saving knowledge of Jesus.

Not only must we pray to the sovereign God about oppressive leaders who persecute us, but we must also remember to pray for our persecuted brothers and sisters around the world. Chances are, no matter how dysfunctional or corrupt the government you live under is, there are people in other parts of the world who are experiencing far more severe persecution because of their faith in Jesus. Hebrews 13:3 urges us to "Continue to remember those in prison, as if you were together with them in prison, and those who are mistreated as if you yourselves were suffering." One simple step pastors can take in helping their congregations to remember this is to recognize the International Day of Prayer for the Persecuted Church which falls on the first Sunday in November. There are various sites like The Voice of the Martyrs (www.persecution.com) or Open Doors USA (www.opendoorsusa.org) that put out videos that can be shown during a church service or at a small group meeting. Something else we do at my church is pass out information sheets about different parts of the world where there is significant risk of persecution. We ask each Sunday school or small group leader to dedicate at least fifteen minutes of their group time that Sunday to pray for believers in that part of the world. We also include a short paragraph in our church's monthly prayer promptings list about a specific person or family who has endured persecution and encourage our people to pray for them. These stories can similarly be found and shared from websites devoted to remembering the persecuted church.

Creativity in Presentation

Statistics

"The persecution of Christians is now 'worse than at any time in history.'"[9] Here are some sobering statistics based on a report released in January 2021 by Open Doors, surveying the period from October 2019 through September 2020.

- More than 340 million Christians are living in countries where they are at risk of suffering *high* levels of persecution because of their faith.
- There are 309 million Christians living in countries where they are at risk of suffering *very high* or *extreme* levels of persecution.
- One in eight Christians worldwide live in countries where they are at high risk of suffering severe persecution for their faith.
- On average, thirteen Christians are killed every day for their faith (4,761 in total).
- On average, twelve churches or Christian buildings are attacked every day (4,488 in total).
- On average, twelve Christians are unjustly arrested, detained, or imprisoned every day (4,277 in total).
- On average, five Christians are abducted for their faith every day (1,710 in total).
- North Korea tops the list of the most dangerous nations for Christians to live for the twentieth consecutive year. Christians there are either killed or sent to prison camps where the conditions are almost unlivable. Some 50,000–70,000 Christians are estimated to be presently imprisoned in North Korean prison camps.[10]

News

While the persecution of Christians in places like the United States isn't nearly as severe as in North Korea, Pakistan, or China, there is still a need to be prepared to suffer for the name of Christ. Parents should prepare their children for the prospect that they will be forced to suffer for their faith. There is a growing hostility against Christianity within Western nations, which indicates that more severe persecution is likely not too far away. With this in mind, the preacher might want to find a recent example of this sort of anti-Christian sentiment in the news and share that story. For example, in Finland, a member of Parliament, Päivi Räsänen, is facing charges of "ethnic agitation" for publicly expressing her personal Christian view about homosexuality. Räsänen's charges came after she questioned her church's sponsorship of an LGBTQ pride event in 2009 in a tweet with a link to her social media page that quoted Romans 1:24–27. During their closing arguments, the prosecution argued that the use of the word "sin" could be "harmful." Essentially, the prosecution had argued that it was only acceptable to quote or reference the Bible if what was said wasn't deemed upsetting or offensive to others. If convicted of this "crime," Päivi could face fines and time in prison.[11]

In 1983 Saddam Hussein began rebuilding the city of Babylon, portraying himself as the successor to King Nebuchadnezzar. He had bricks inscribed with his name on them, just

---

9 https://www.christianpost.com/news/christian-persecution-all-time-high-worldwide-report.html.
10 https://www.forbes.com/sites/ewelinaochab/2021/01/13/one-in-eight-christians-worldwide-live-in-countries-where-they-would-be-persecuted/?sh=1a4649005016.
11 https://www.foxnews.com/media/lawmaker-trial-europe-religion-free-speech-cautionary-tale.

as Nebuchadnezzar once did. He minted coins with his own face alongside Nebuchadnezzar's. He even posted signs throughout the city which read, "This was built by Saddam Hussein, son of Nebuchadnezzar." It is sadly ironic that Saddam Hussein modeled his life's ambitions after a man whose rule was interrupted by a seven-year bout with insanity that God used to humble him, and whose death was in part a result of God's predicted judgment for living in arrogant self-exaltation against the one true God. Saddam Hussein was ultimately captured and executed by hanging after being found guilty of crimes against humanity, including the mass murder of his own Iraqi citizens. It is estimated that he murdered more than a quarter of a million of his own people during his rule.[12] On the day of his death, spontaneous celebrations broke out across Iraq as people rejoiced over this evil tyrant's demise.[13] In the same way that it was said the king of Babylon would be taunted in death (14:4–21), so too was Saddam Hussein's death met with celebration. Isaiah 14:19–20 could apply to Saddam as much as the king he so emulated:

> But you are cast out of your tomb like a rejected branch; you are covered with the slain, with those pierced by the sword, those who descend to the stones of the pit. Like a corpse trampled underfoot, you will not join them in burial, for you have destroyed your land and killed your people. Let the offspring of the wicked never be mentioned again.

One day believers everywhere will cheer and celebrate as every wicked tyrant is destroyed once and for all and this world is ruled by the King of Kings and Lord of Lords. At his appointed time, the sovereign God will deliver his people from the world's oppressive tyrants.

- Judgment results in the destruction of Babylon (13:1–22).
- Judgment results in the deliverance of believers (14:1–7).
- Judgment results in the demotion of all boasters (14:8–27).

DISCUSSION QUESTIONS

1. Share about a time when you suffered directly or indirectly in some way for your faith in Christ, or because you took a stand against something sinful.

2. What are some things for which we should be praying regularly for those in authority over us?

3. After reading Matthew 5:2–12, how many of the Beatitudes relate to believers who suffer well for their faith? Why do you think this theme was so important for Jesus to teach to his disciples?

4. Hebrews 13:3 says, "Continue to remember those in prison, as if you were together with them in prison, and those who are mistreated as if you yourselves were suffering." Discuss how you would feel if you were in prison right now because of your faith in Jesus. What things would you long for most from your brothers and sisters in Christ on the outside?

---

12 https://en.wikipedia.org/wiki/Human_rights_in_Saddam_Hussein%27s_Iraq#:~:text=The%20total%20number%20of%20deaths,uprisings%20in%20Iraq%20in%201991.

13 https://web.archive.org/web/20070120145502/http://www.cnn.com/2006/WORLD/meast/12/30/hussein.iraq.reax.

Isaiah 14:28–23:18

EXEGETICAL IDEA
The Lord would demonstrate his sovereignty over the nations by judging Philistia, Moab, Aram, Cush, Babylon, Dumah, Arabia, and Tyre. He would also punish Israel for trusting in an alliance with Aram, and Judah, whose arrogant royal official Shebna epitomized the nation's pride. However, someday the Lord will make Jerusalem secure through a just Davidic king.

THEOLOGICAL FOCUS
The Lord would judge the proud, idolatrous nations, as well as his covenant people Israel and Judah. God's people should look to him for security and blessing. Someday the Lord will make a descendant of David his king. This ideal Davidic ruler will establish a kingdom of justice and peace that will encompass the whole earth.

PREACHING IDEA
Though God must judge all nations for their sin and rejection of him, there is hope because of God's love for all and his promise to establish a worldwide kingdom.

PREACHING POINTERS
What comes to your mind when you hear the term "shock jock"? The term is generally applied to a broadcaster who is prone to push the limits of communication by saying things they know will be startling and offensive. It may not be an exaggeration to suggest that the prophet Isaiah was the very first shock jock—albeit a righteous one! Not only did he say many provocative things, but for three of those years Isaiah walked naked through the streets of Jerusalem as he loudly proclaimed the judgment that was coming upon Egypt and Cush (Isa. 20:2–4). Can you imagine the shock this would have caused to visitors who stumbled upon Isaiah for the first time? They must have been even more surprised, probably horrified, to discover that he was a well-known prophet of God.

In a very real way, God did intend to shock his people through the ministry of Isaiah. Over time, the inhabitants of Judah had come to admire the strength and wealth of some of their regional neighbors like Assyria and Egypt. As such, many assumed it was in their best interests to link their fortunes and future security to those nations. God wanted to wake his people up to the following realities concerning the nations: (1) All of these nations would eventually face judgment from God. (2) As such, it makes no sense for God's people to put their hope and confidence in human nations and groups. (3) Finally, Judah and Israel's great hope is the same as that of all the nations of the world. One day God will send a descendant of David who will establish a kingdom founded upon justice and righteousness for all.

ORACLES CONCERNING VARIOUS NATIONS (14:28–23:18)

LITERARY STRUCTURE AND THEMES (14:28–23:18)

Within this section there are twelve distinct oracles. Two of the oracles are הוֹי, or "woe," oracles (17:12–14; 18:1–7), while one has no formal genre indicator (20:1–6). It appears to be a report of a prophetic "sign," or object lesson (cf. 20:3). Nine of the oracles are introduced by מַשָּׂא, a term that is derived from the verb נָשָׂא, "lift," and elsewhere refers to a burden or load that must be carried. For a listing of the oracles and a discussion of their arrangement, see the introduction to chapters 13–27 above, and more specifically the overview of chapters 13–23.

It is unlikely that the nations addressed in these oracles, except for Judah and perhaps Israel, heard these messages. The oracles probably had a twofold purpose. By affirming the Lord was sovereign over all nations, the oracles reminded Judah and its leaders that they need not fear foreign nations and served as a warning not to seek security through alliances with them. For Isaiah and other followers of the Lord, the oracles would encourage and strengthen their faith. They lived in tumultuous times, but their God was in control of the world and was worthy of their continued trust. He was working out his plan for the nations and would eventually establish his kingdom, centered in Jerusalem.

- *Judgment on Neighboring States to the East and West (14:28–16:14)*
- *Judgment on the Northern Coalition and the Nations (17:1–14)*
- *Judgment on Cush and Egypt (18:1–20:6)*
- *Judgment on Peoples to the East (21:1–17)*
- *Judgment on Judah (22:1–25)*
- *Judgment on Tyre (23:1–18)*

EXPOSITION (14:28–23:18)

Judgment on Neighboring States to the East and West (14:28–16:14)

14:28. Determining the chronology of Ahaz's reign is difficult. The historical records in 2 Kings provide information that is difficult to harmonize. According to 2 Kings 17:1, Hoshea took the throne of Israel (732 B.C.) in Ahaz's twelfth year. This suggests Ahaz's reign began in 744. Second Kings 16:1 says Ahaz began to reign in Pekah of Israel's seventeenth year (735). Second Kings 16:2 then tells us he was twenty years old when he took the throne and ruled for sixteen years, which would seemingly mean that his rule ended in 719. However, Sennacherib's invasion (701) took place in the fourteenth year of the reign of Ahaz's son Hezekiah (2 Kings 18:13), which means Hezekiah took the throne, at least as sole ruler, in 715. This in turn implies that Ahaz died in that year, which means his reign would have began in 731.

So, we seem to have three different dates for the beginning of Ahaz's reign: 744, 735, and 731, and consequently three different dates for the end of his reign: 728, 719, and 715. Eugene Merrill (1987, 402–4) proposes that Ahaz became a vice-regent under Jotham in 744 (2 Kings 17:1), a coregent with Jotham in 735, and primary ruler in 731 when Jotham died. But Merrill states that Ahaz was twenty in 735

(2 Kings 16:2) and that Hezekiah was born in 740, when Ahaz was fifteen (p. 404). In this view, "when he became king" in 2 Kings 16:2 refers to his becoming coregent in 735, while "he reigned in Jerusalem sixteen years" must cover the period from 731–715. However, making this four-year jump within the verse is problematic. The most natural way of reading 2 Kings 16:2 suggests Ahaz ruled sixteen years after beginning his reign at the age of twenty. This would mean that "when he became king" in 2 Kings 16:2 refers to his becoming primary ruler in 731. But this would also mean he was only seven when he became vice-regent in 744 and only eleven when Hezekiah was born in 740, which seems highly unlikely. Though questions remain concerning the chronology of Ahaz's reign as presented in 2 Kings, the simplest approach to Isaiah 14:28 is to assume that the year of Ahaz's death coincided with the first year of Hezekiah's reign as sole ruler (he had been a vice-regent under Ahaz prior to this), namely 715, fourteen years before Sennacherib's invasion in 701 (cf. 2 Kings 18:13). (See the discussion and conclusion in Roberts 2015, 221–23.)

14:29–31. The speaker (probably the Lord, cf. 14:30b) exhorts the Philistines not to rejoice over the fall of one called "the rod that struck you." The demise of this "snake" will not bring relief for the Philistines, for a viper will grow out of its root (14:29). While the poor and needy will find provision and safety, the Lord will destroy the root of the Philistines through a famine (14:30). This was not a time for rejoicing. In fact, the Philistines should wail in fear for a northern invader will come, bringing destruction (cf. the reference to smoke, probably the smoke of burning towns, cf. Clements 1980, 150) in its wake (14:31). The reference to the "famine" may be metaphorical, since the Philistines' "root" is the object of the judgment. However, it is more likely this refers to the aftermath of an invasion that will bring confiscation and destruction of crops, resulting in widespread hunger. The reference to "your survivors" dying from hunger is consistent with this.

The identity of the rulers referred to metaphorically in 14:29 is not clear. One option is that Assyrian rulers are in view since they had controlled Philistine territory since 734 B.C. The warning of judgment (14:31) fits well with Sargon's invasion of Philistia in 712. He put down a rebellion instigated by the king of Ashdod and made the Ashdod region into a province. But by 715, the date of the oracle, Sargon had been ruling Assyria for seven years and would not be succeeded by Sennacherib for another ten years. So, the change in rule implied in 14:29 does not coincide well with Assyrian history. However, some date the death of Ahaz to 727 (Wildberger 1997, 93; Young 1965, 450), the same year that Tiglath-pileser III died. In this case, Tiglath-pileser can be the rod/snake and his successors the viper (see Gray [1912, 266–67] for discussion of this option).

Another proposal is that the rod/snake is Ahaz, with the viper being his successor Hezekiah. This would explain why the oracle was delivered in the year of Ahaz's death, depicted as the breaking of a rod, or royal scepter. However, this proposal is problematic. Ahaz did not conquer the Philistines; in fact, the Philistines took territory from Ahaz early in his reign (2 Chron. 28:18). Hezekiah defeated the Philistines (2 Kings 18:8), but he would have invaded Philistine territory from the east, not the north (see Oswalt 1986, 331).

However, Roberts (2015, 221–27) makes a good case for this proposal. He contends Ahaz would have, despite some setbacks, attempted to recover territory taken by the Philistines and would have cooperated with the Assyrians when they attacked Philistia in 720 (pp. 224–25). He concludes "there is no substantive basis to deny categorically that Ahaz ever smote the Philistines" (p. 225). He also argues Hezekiah is the viper who succeeds the serpent (Ahaz). He demonstrates that Judean seals from the period use serpent symbolism, supporting "the identification of the two rulers as the Judean kings Ahaz and Hezekiah" (p. 226). Furthermore, Hezekiah did attack and defeat the Philistines (2 Kings 18:8) and probably supported the Assyrians when they invaded Ashdod in 712–711 (p. 227). He rebelled against Assyrian rule after this. As for the smoke from the north (14:31), Roberts acknowledges that it would have to refer to Assyria (p. 227). But of course, the northern invader need not be equated with the viper of 14:29. It is enough that the viper (Hezekiah) and the Assyrians were allies.

A third option blends these two views (Chisholm 2002, 54–55). It seems likely 14:29 does allude to Ahaz's death, especially in the light of the oracle being dated to that year. In this case, he is the rod/snake. Granted, he did not conquer or oppress the Philistines, but he was pro-Assyrian and invited the Assyrians to give him relief from Philistine military attacks (cf. 2 Chron. 28:16–18). To the anti-Assyrian faction in Philistia, this Assyrian ally may have symbolized Assyrian oppression. They must have blamed him for allowing, indeed inviting, the Assyrians to establish such a strong presence in the region. Furthermore, as Roberts argues, he may have supported Assyrian military efforts against the Philistines. With Ahaz's death, the anti-Assyrian faction in Philistia probably hoped his son Hezekiah would immediately abandon Ahaz's allegiance to Assyria and join them in an anti-Assyrian alliance (see Sweeney 1996, 234). Indeed, 14:32a may refer to Philistine envoys seeking such an alliance (see Childs 2000, 128; Clements 1980, 150). The Lord corrects their false hope. Ahaz's death will not be the dawning of a new day for them. In fact, as noted above, the Assyrian ruler Sargon squashed their rebellion in 712, as did Sennacherib in 701. In this case, Sargon, or perhaps Assyrian royal power more generally (see Oswalt 1986, 332), may well be the viper that succeeds Ahaz. Of course, the Lord himself is the sovereign king who wields the Assyrians as his instrument of judgment (note, "I will destroy" in 14:30; cf. 10:5, 15).

14:32. The Lord's judgment devastates Philistia, but he preserves his own people. This is hinted at in 14:30a, where he says the poor and needy will find pasture and safety. The identity of these poor and needy is not clear, but they are distinct from "all you Philistines" (14:29), who are addressed in 14:29–31 with feminine singular forms and are contrasted with the poor and needy (14:30b). Isaiah 14:32 brings clarification, as the Lord tells (Philistine?) envoys that his afflicted people will find security in Zion (Jerusalem), for he has established it. This anticipates the events of 701 B.C., when Sennacherib's invasion came to a screeching halt outside the walls of Jerusalem (cf. Isa. 37:36–37).

15:1–4. Moab's devastation is described in great detail. Eight different locations are mentioned in 15:1–2, 4, emphasizing the destruction is thorough and widespread. The movement is from south to north. Ar and Kir (-Hareseth) (15:1) were located south of the Arnon (see Roberts 2015, 234; Wildberger 1997, 131). The rest of the towns singled out were located north of it. Dibon was just a few miles north of the Arnon, while Nebo and Medeba were much farther north (15:2). Heshbon and Elealeh were located even farther north, while Jahaz was to the southeast of them (15:4).

Repetition is used to depict the sudden and devastating nature of the catastrophe. The phrase "in a night" (בְּלֵיל) and the verbs שֻׁדַּד, "ruined," and נִדְמָה, "destroyed," each appear twice in 15:1. Terms for wailing and weeping dominate 15:2–3: בְּכִי, "to weep" (15:2)/"weeping" (15:3); יְיֵלִיל, "wails" (15:2)/"wail" (15:3), while sorrowful shouting echoes from 15:4 (וַתִּזְעַק, "cry out," and יָרִיעוּ, "cry out"), mirroring the dismay the people feel. There is sound play between יָרִיעוּ, "cry out," and יְרֵעָה, from יָרַע, an otherwise unattested verb meaning, "quiver, be apprehensive" (cf. *HALOT* s.v. "ירע" 440) [NIV11, "are faint"]. The shouts emanating from Heshbon and Elealeh are heard in Jahaz, located several miles to the southeast.

Of course, all this weeping is accompanied by the usual outward signs of inward sorrow, as the people devote themselves totally to mourning. Every head and beard is shaved (15:2). People wear sackcloth everywhere—on the rooftops and in the public squares (15:3).

The usual sources of national security prove to be of no help. Dibon goes up to its temple and high places (15:2), but there is no divine intervention (cf. 16:12). Moab's warriors ("armed men") provide no defense; all they can do is join the mourners and cry out in dismay (15:4). The use of the verb יָרִיעוּ (from רוּעַ) is striking. It is often used of raising a battle cry or shouting in triumph (see *HALOT* s.v. "רוּעַ" 3, 1207) but not here, where ironically it describes the desperate shouts of the defeated and suffering.

15:5–9. The speaker expresses his sorrow over the horrible plight of Moab's refugees, who lament the destruction that has come upon them (15:5). To make matters worse, they must flee through an arid region where there is no water or vegetation (15:6; Smith 2007, 331). They carry their moveable property with them as they seek a place of refuge (15:7). Their cries of distress echo throughout Moab because of shed blood, which is so abundant that it fills streams (15:8–9a).

It is not certain who is speaking here. It may be the prophet or the Lord who speaks in the first person in 15:9b. In either case, the speaker appears to be expressing genuine emotion for Moab, not taunting them. Terence Fretheim (1984, 132–33), who argues God is speaking here, sees this as a window into God's heart.[1] Though God "is the one who has occasioned the judgment in the first place," seeing the plight of the victims still grieves him and he joins in the mourning. Fretheim relates this to God's declaration in Ezekiel 18:32 (cf. 33:11) that he takes no delight in the death of the wicked: "What heart-rending distress God feels over what has happened to the people." Certainly, the Lord is a compassionate God, but one wonders if Fretheim sees more here than the passage warrants. It is possible the speaker (whether the prophet or the Lord) is simply assuming the perspective of one observing the Moabites' demise to emphasize how severe the judgment will be (see Kaiser 1974, 68). In other words, the expression of sorrow is for dramatic, rhetorical purposes and not necessarily a window into the heart of God or the prophet.

The Moabites have suffered terribly, but there is more to come (15:9b). The Lord (presumably the speaker in 15:9b) will bring additional calamity upon them. More specifically he will bring "a lion" against the Moabite fugitives and survivors. Though the reference to a lion may seem abrupt, the abrupt style mirrors the sudden attack of a lion. This makes the scene especially terrifying, for the Moabites are vulnerable and in no condition to fight off such a ferocious and powerful predator. This could refer to literal lion attacks faced by refugees in the wilderness (Young 1965, 460) or it may symbolize an enemy (cf. Isa. 5:29; see Smith 2007, 331; Wildberger 1997, 139), perhaps referring to raiders who will exploit the Moabites' defenseless condition. It may not be necessary to choose between these options. Double entendre may be at work; both literal and figurative lion attacks may be in view.

16:1–2. The speaker encourages the Moabites to send rams to the ruler of the land, who resides on Mount Zion (16:1). These rams would

---

1 See also Motyer 1993, 150–51, 154–55, commenting on 15:5 and 16:9, respectively. Young (1965, 458) sees the compassion of the prophet here: "How compassionate he is!" See also his comments on 16:11, pp. 466–67. See as well Oswalt 1986, 346, commenting on 16:9. He sees the prophet's concern as an expression of God's compassion.

be offered as gifts in exchange for asylum or perhaps as tribute by those seeking to become Judah's vassal (Roberts 2015, 237; Smith 2007, 332). This appeal may anticipate the rise of the just Davidic king mentioned in 16:5.

The plight of the Moabite refugees becomes the focus once more. As they cross the Arnon, Moab's women panic, flying around like a bird that has been forced from its nest (16:2). This portrait of vulnerable women, deprived of the domestic setting where they find stability, sets the stage for the appeal in 16:3–4 (cf. Hayes and Irvine 1987, 243; Oswalt 1986, 342). When one sees 16:2 as the basis for the following appeal, there is no need to argue, as Clements (1980, 154) does, that it is displaced and belongs with 15:8.

16:3–5. In 16:3–4a the prophet, perhaps in the role of a Moabite messenger to Judah, makes an appeal on behalf of the Moabite fugitives. The appeal is made with second-person feminine singular verb and pronominal forms. Apparently, the addressee is Daughter Zion, mentioned in 16:1 (Roberts 2015, 237). This is rhetorically effective considering 16:2, which describes the plight of the Moabite women. An appeal is made to Daughter Zion, because one expects, or at least hopes, she will have pity on her fellow women. Of course, the reality underlying Daughter Zion is the ruler of Jerusalem (16:1).

The speaker urges Daughter Zion to formulate and execute a plan on behalf of the Moabite refugees. She is urged to provide relief for the fugitives and to hide them from those who pursue them and seek to destroy them. The image of shade (16:3) symbolizes shelter, while the noonday heat represents the enemies of Moab. Comparing the shade to night depicts a dark shadow cast by a large tree that provides relief from the sun's heat.

The tone changes as the prophet confidently affirms the oppressor will be eliminated, along with the destruction he causes.

Those who trample on others will be removed from the earth (16:4b). As the oppressor falls, the throne of a just Davidic king will be established (16:5). The Hebrew text of 16:5 reads literally, "A throne will be established in loyalty and he will sit upon it in faithfulness in the tent of David, one who judges and seeks justice, and is skilled (in) righteousness." The word חֶסֶד (בְּחֶסֶד, "loyalty"; NIV11, "love") can be defined in one of the following ways: "loyalty, devotion, commitment, faithfulness, reliability." Here it describes the character and rule of a Davidic king, to whom the oppressed and defeated Moabites are urged to look for relief and protection (cf. 16:1). When חֶסֶד is combined with אֱמֶת, "faithfulness," as it is here (cf. the parallel poetic line), the word pair conveys the idea of kind and fair treatment that expresses one's devotion to another (cf. Gen. 24:27, 49; 32:10; 47:29; Josh. 2:14). The ideal Davidic king envisioned here will treat his subjects in such a benevolent and just manner. Indeed, he is described as one who seeks justice and is skilled in righteousness, in the sense of knowing how to make and execute fair decisions. His commitment to justice will solidify his royal position (cf. "a throne will be established"), because God, who expects his chosen king to promote justice (cf. Ps. 101; Isa. 11:3–5), rewards the one who is faithful to this commission (cf. Jer. 22:16). By offering Moab protection under this king, Moab's divine Judge (cf. Isa. 15:9; 16:10) demonstrates his mercy and compassion.

When and how was the vision of 16:4b–5 fulfilled? Isaiah 16:4b may anticipate the Lord's destruction of Sennacherib's army, which forced the Assyrian ruler to return to his home (cf. Isa. 36–37). Isaiah 16:5 would then envision Hezekiah's rise to prominence. But any fulfillment in Isaiah's time was a mere foretaste of a day when the ideal Davidic ruler establishes his kingdom of justice and peace on the earth (Isa. 9:7; 11:1–10; cf. 2:2–4).

16:6–8. A group speaks in 16:6 (note "*we* have heard"), perhaps the prophet representing Judah. Moab's great suffering again becomes the focus in 16:7, prompting another lament (cf. 16:9–11), but first the speakers offer a reminder of the reason why the Lord has brought judgment upon Moab, namely, Moab's pride, which is well known. Three different words (all from the root גָּאָה, "be high") describe this pride. The word עֶבְרָה is also used. This term normally refers to "anger," so angry outbursts, prompted by arrogance, may be in view (see Job 40:11; Prov. 21:24).

Yet Moab's boasting (the term used is בַּד; see *HALOT* s.v. "בַּד IV" 109) lacks substance (16:6b; the text literally reads, "not so [are] his boasts"). Judgment has fallen, leaving Moab wailing (16:7a) over its devastation, which includes the loss of delicacies such as raisin cakes (cf. 2 Sam. 6:19; Song 2:5) and the produce of the fields and vines (16:7b–8). The fields of Heshbon and the vines of Sibmah have dried up (cf. 15:6), apparently from drought. But invaders (called here "rulers [literally, 'lords'] of the nations") have also contributed to the loss of Moab's agricultural abundance. They have trampled the shoots of its vines, which once reached as far as Jazer to the north (of Heshbon) and the Dead Sea to the west. This depicts both the abundance of northern Moab's vines, but also the extent of the invasion. The poet pictures the horses of an invading army stomping on grape vines, but this is also an apt metaphor for an invading army appropriating Moab's agricultural abundance.

16:9–11. An individual speaker chimes in at this point. It is not clear if this is the prophet or the Lord (see discussion above). Witnessing Moab's loss prompts him to join Jazer in weeping over the loss of Sibmah's vines and to drench Heshbon and Elealeh with his tears (16:9a), for the joyful shouts of the harvesters have ceased (literally "fallen"; 16:9b). There is no more happiness in the orchards and vineyards, and no one treads any grapes in the wine vats (16:10a).

Ironically, it is the Lord himself who has brought this calamity upon Moab (16:10b), yet Moab's plight moves him emotionally (16:11; cf. 15:9 and the discussion in the commentary on how to interpret the language). His inner being (מֵעַי, "my intestines" [NIV11, "my heart"], and קִרְבִּי, "my insides" [NIV11, "my inmost being"]) moans (יֶהֱמוּ, from הָמָה, literally "is turbulent") like a harp. The point of the comparison is not clear. The harp is typically mentioned in conjunction with celebration, not mourning, which is characterized by the cessation of the harp (cf. Job 30:31; Ps. 137:1; Ezek. 26:13). Perhaps he compares the constant growling of his stomach to the repetitive strumming of a harp or the churning of his stomach to the throb of the harp strings. (See Oswalt [1986, 347] for a helpful discussion of the imagery.)

16:12. The once proud, boastful Moabites (cf. Isa. 16:6) are desperate. They go to their worship centers (cf. 15:2) and pray their hearts out, but all to no avail (16:12). No relief comes. Isaiah 16:12 reads literally: "And it will be when he appears, when Moab is weary upon the high place, and goes to his holy place (sanctuary) to pray, he will not prevail." The *niphal* of לָאָה (נִלְאָה) means "to be tired" (cf. Isa. 1:14); in this context it probably refers to wearying oneself in passionate prayer (note "to pray" later in the verse). Chemosh was the patron deity of Moab and most likely the recipient of Moab's petitions for deliverance (cf. Num. 21:29; Jer. 48:46, as well as the Moabite Stone; *COS* 2.23:137–38). In the Moabite Stone, King Mesha attributes Moab's past defeats to Chemosh's anger with his people. However, in this Isaianic oracle the Lord affirms that he, not Chemosh, is the sovereign ruler over Moab (cf. 15:9; 16:10). When he decided to judge Moab, Chemosh became a nonfactor in Moab's destiny. As Young (1965, 467) observes, "In times of distress, how tragic when one consults those that are not gods!"

16:13–14. The oracle ends with an official pronouncement concerning its timing as the Lord provides a timetable for the fulfillment of the preceding message. The judgment on Moab will come in three years, measured just as a servant bound by a contract would count them. In other words, Moab's fall will take place in precisely three years.

Unfortunately, we are not able to know when this occurred. As Roberts (2015, 229) points out, the oracle does not identify the enemy invader. It could have been an Assyrian ruler or an incursion by Arab tribes from the east (see also Smith 2007, 327). Wildberger (1997, 116–17) surveys what we know of Moabite history from the time of the Ashdod revolt in 713–711 on into the sixth century B.C. The extant literature for that period does not describe an event that corresponds to what we read in the oracle. But it is unwise to draw conclusions from the silence of ancient sources that provide at best a partial record of what transpired in the distant past. (In this regard, see Kaiser's [1974, 65] conclusion following his survey of Moabite history [pp. 60–65].) Perhaps it is better to look earlier in Isaiah's career. Hayes and Irvine (1987, 239–40) suggest Shalmaneser V (727–722) may have acted against Moab. They point out the proximity of the Moabite oracle to the oracle against Aram (and Israel) that follows in Isaiah 17.

A similar oracle appears in Jeremiah 48, yet this need not mean that the fulfillment of Isaiah's oracle did not occur until the late seventh or sixth century. In fact, the pronouncement in Isaiah 16:13–14, which does not appear in Jeremiah 48, suggests Isaiah's oracle was fulfilled sometime during his ministry. It may have served as a prototype for Jeremiah's, but the two prophecies anticipate distinct events. In this regard, it is important to observe that Isaiah does not predict the destruction of Moab—a remnant, however weak and small, will survive.

Judgment on the Northern Coalition and the Nations (17:1–14)

17:1–3. The prophet draws attention to the devastation that will soon overtake Damascus. Damascus will be reduced from a town to a heap of ruins. The towns of Aroer will be abandoned and become grazing pastures for herds. The referent here is not clear. There are three towns named Aroer in the Old Testament. One is in Moab near the Arnon, a second in Ammon, and a third in Judah (1 Sam. 30:28; see *HALOT* s.v. "עֲרוֹעֵר II" 883; Wildberger 1997, 156–57). It is possible that we have here a fourth Aroer, located near Damascus. But it is more likely that this is the Aroer located near the Arnon. Israel conquered this area (Josh. 12:2; 13:9, 16; Judg. 11:26) but Hazael the Aramean eventually took it from them (2 Kings 10:33).

Aram's treaty partner, Ephraim (= the northern kingdom of Israel), will also suffer. Their fortified towns, symbolizing security, will disappear, as will the kingdom of Damascus and the remnant of Aram. The Arameans' destiny will be the same as the Israelites' "glory," which will be greatly diminished (see Isa. 17:4). This may refer to the Israelites' lost wealth and strength as symbolized by the fortified cities that are no more. Young (1965, 470) sees "glory" as encompassing "everything which the natural man would boast in," including fortresses, leaders, troops, and weapons. Smith (2007, 343) thinks in terms of cities, gold, palaces, economy, and armies.

The prophecy, which comes from early in Isaiah's career, anticipates Tiglath-pileser III's invasion in 734–732 B.C. He defeated the northern coalition, making Damascus an Assyrian province and Israel a puppet state. But the formula at the end of 17:3 reminds us that it is ultimately the Lord who brings judgment. He is Yahweh who commands armies, as both Aram and Israel discovered. (See 1:9 above for a discussion of the title יְהוָה צְבָאוֹת.)

17:4–6. Isaiah elaborates on what will happen to Jacob's (Israel's) "glory" (cf. 17:3). He points out that Israel will be greatly diminished. The verb used in 17:4 (יִדַּל, from דָּלַל) means to "be tiny, small" (*HALOT*, s.v. "דָּלַל I" 223; NIV11, "will fade"). In Isaiah 19:6 it describes streams that grow dry.

The prophet illustrates Israel's diminished glory. Their strength will leave them, like a person whose body wastes away (from רָזָה) due to being undernourished (17:4; cf. the use of the related adjective רָזֶה to describe lean sheep in Ezek. 34:20). The population will be reduced to a mere remnant. He compares them to the Valley of Rephaim, located near Jerusalem, after the grain harvest; only a few ears of grain are left once the harvesters are finished (17:5). Survivors will be few, like the two or three olives left near the top of the tree, or the four or five remaining on the tree's most fruitful branches once the harvesters complete their work (17:6).

> **Valley of Rephaim**
> Wildberger (1997, 158) states: "One wonders why, at this particular point, mention is made of the Valley of Rephaim (located close to Jerusalem . . .), especially since the passage deals with the northern kingdom." He then discusses how some emend the reading (to Ephraim) or regard it as a gloss. But there is no need for such pedantry. Isaiah was from Jerusalem and was writing primarily for Judah, which would have been quite familiar with the Valley of Rephaim. Roberts (2015, 243) suggests that the Valley of Rephaim, because of its proximity to Jerusalem, was probably "thoroughly stripped by the harvesting and gleaning, because it is so convenient to a large and poor urban population."

17:7–8. The severe judgment that falls on Israel will have a positive effect on those who survive and/or observe it. People will look to their maker, the Holy One of Israel, for security, rather than to their man-made altars, Asherah idols, and incense altars. The people are not identified specifically, but it is likely that the survivors of the judgment, as well as the people of Judah, are in view. Perhaps generic אָדָם, "man," is used as a reminder that they are products of the Lord's creative work, since the Lord is called their "Maker." This could refer to the Lord as the one who has given them physical life, but if the covenant community is in view, it may view the Lord as the one who formed it (Isa. 27:11; 44:2; 51:13; see Motyer 1993, 158). As the creator of the covenant community, he is the Holy One of Israel who has the sovereign right to rule over it. (On the title Holy One of Israel, see the commentary on 1:4.)

The altars mentioned here are those used in idolatrous worship (cf. Lev. 26:30), since they are listed with the Asherah idols (cf. Exod. 34:13; Deut. 7:5; 12:3; Isa. 27:9). Asherah was a Canaanite goddess, who was represented by a tree (Deut. 16:21), whether living or stylized.

17:9. Having looked ahead to the positive aftermath of the coming judgment, the prophet shifts his focus back to what will take place in the immediate future. Israel's strong cities will be abandoned, just as the Amorites abandoned their territory when Israel invaded the land. The land will be left desolate (cf. Isa. 6:11).

The Hebrew text of 17:9 reads literally: "In that day the towns of his strong place [i.e., Jacob's strong cities] will be like the abandoned [place] of the forest and the [???], which they abandoned from before the sons of Israel, and it will be a desolation." The phrase הַחֹרֶשׁ וְהָאָמִיר, "the forest and the [???]," is problematic. The meaning of the word אָמִיר is uncertain. In 17:6 it appears as a genitive after רֹאשׁ, "top"; the phrase refers to the location of the few olives left after the tree is shaken. So perhaps אָמִיר means "branches" (see *HALOT* s.v. "אָמִיר" 63), with the phrase רֹאשׁ אָמִיר referring to the "top of the branches," that is, the topmost branches. But this makes little sense in 17:9, even though the preceding word חֹרֶשׁ refers to wooded heights. It is preferable to emend הַחֹרֶשׁ וְהָאָמִיר to חָרְשֵׁי הָאֱמֹרִי,

"wooded heights of the Amorite." The LXX supports this in part, though it reads, "the Amorites and Hivites." Reading "Amorites" provides a subject for the verb עָזְבוּ, "they abandoned," in the following relative clause. If this is correct, it becomes apparent that the prophet is comparing the coming destruction of Jacob's fortified cities (cf. 17:3) to the conquest of the land when Israel drove the Amorites out of the highlands. Jacob, ironically cast in the role of the ancient Amorites, will lose what it once conquered.

17:10–11. Using the typical judgment speech form, the prophet next gives the reason (כִּי) for the judgment he has just announced. In 17:10–11 he addresses the one who will be judged with second-person feminine singular verbal and pronominal forms. It appears that the judgment of the northern kingdom is in view, so it is the likely addressee. The northern kingdom is called Ephraim (17:3) and Jacob (17:4) in the immediate context, which does not readily explain the use of the feminine here. However, there may be a clue at the end of 17:9 to understanding the prophet's use of the feminine singular in 17:10–11. Using a *weqatal* verb form, he announces, "and it will be [וְהָיְתָה, feminine singular] a desolation [שְׁמָמָה, feminine singular]." Earlier in the verse, he spoke of Jacob's towns (plural) becoming like the abandoned place (כַּעֲזוּבַת, feminine singular participle) of the wooded regions of the Amorites (assuming the emendation discussed above). He uses the feminine singular at the end of verse, as if the cities had indeed become the (new) abandoned place. The feminine singular subject of הָיְתָה can thus be viewed as the (new) abandoned place (containing the once strong cities) that is now desolate. Having made this subtle switch, the prophet now addresses this abandoned place in 17:10–11. In short, the addressee in these verses would be the strong cities of the land that will become the new abandoned place that will be desolate. To emphasize their impending destruction, the prophet, in his accusation, addresses them with the feminine singular, echoing "abandoned" and "it will be desolate" in the preceding announcement. As such, the repeated second-person feminine forms in 17:10–11 (ten in all) become a constant reminder of where their sin will lead. We could paraphrase each second-person form in 17:10–11 as "you (soon-to-be abandoned and desolate one)."

Behind the rhetorical figure of the abandoned and desolate one lies the leadership and populace of the northern kingdom. Judgment will come upon them because they have forgotten the God of their salvation and have failed to remember the Rock who was their fortress (17:10a). In this context, "have forgotten" and "have not remembered" refer to their failure to maintain loyalty to their God as evidenced by their idolatry (cf. 17:8). The divine titles ("God your Savior" and "Rock, your fortress") reflect the nation's ingratitude and flight from reason. One would think they would remain loyal to one who saved and protected them. Furthermore, no one in their right mind would reject their source of security.

The divine title "Rock" (צוּר) refers to the Lord as the protector of his people. The word often refers to a rocky summit (cf. 1 Sam. 24:2; Isa. 2:10, 19; Jer. 18:14; 21:13), where one can find refuge from enemies. The term appears as a divine title in Deuteronomy 32:4 (cf. also 32:13, 15, 18), where it is used of Israel's faithful God who delivered, cared for, and protected his people (cf. 32:5–18), proving his superiority to the gods of the nations (32:30–31). Hannah also uses the title (1 Sam. 2:2) in her song celebrating the Lord's deliverance and justice. It is especially prominent in the Psalms, where it depicts the Lord as the protector of his faithful followers (Pss. 18:2, 31, 46 [HB 3, 33, 47]; 19:14 [HB 15]; 27:5; 28:1; 31:2 [HB 3]; 62:2, 6–7 [HB 3, 7–8]; 71:3; 78:35; 89:26 [HB 27]; 92:15 [HB 16]; 95:1; 144:1). In Isaiah's day God's people had abandoned their true Protector and were trusting in man-made idols for security (cf. Isa. 17:8). God's judgment will reveal the folly of such misplaced faith (cf. Isa. 2:18–21).

Israel's failure to remember their God opened the door to foreign pagan influences (17:10b). The causal relationship is expressed through עַל־כֵּן, "therefore." Human beings have a spiritual vacuum in their souls. If they refuse to allow the true God to fill it, they will inevitably fill it themselves with false substitutes.

Isaiah uses an illustration from horticulture to make this point. Israel cultivates beautiful plants and an imported vine, taking great pains to make them grow and flourish (17:10b–11a). The plants and vines of the metaphor stand for false gods. This is hinted at using זָר, "strange" [NIV11, "imported"] to describe the vine. This word refers to anything or anyone that is outside a boundary. For example, זָר is used of a man outside one's family (Deut. 25:5), of a woman other than one's wife (Prov. 5:20), and of a man other than a woman's husband (Prov. 5:17). It is used of foreigners (Isa. 1:7) and of false gods worshipped by foreigners (Deut. 32:16; Pss. 44:20 [HB 21]; 81:9 [HB 10]; Isa. 43:12). On the surface of the prophet's metaphor, one sees a "foreign" vine imported from outside Israel. But the deeper reality is a false god. The beautiful plants probably refer to idol-gods that were particularly appealing to their worshippers. The root *nʿm* is used of various gods and goddesses in the Ugaritic texts (cf. Wildberger 1997, 182).

Israel's efforts to grow their plants and vine prove futile in the end, for the harvest is destroyed by disease. Israel's idols, which end up like failed crops, cannot save them; only the Lord can save and protect. The second half of 17:11 reads literally, "a heap of harvest in a day of disease and incurable pain." This is problematic, for there is no apparent syntactical connection to what precedes, and no predicate is present. It makes better sense to emend נֵד, "heap," to נַד (or נָדַד, both being *qal* perfect 3ms from נָדַד), "[the harvest] has fled [in the day of disease]," or to נֹדֵד (*qal* active participle ms from נָדַד), "[the harvest] is about to flee [in the day of disease]."

17:12–14. The placement of this woe oracle against the nations after the Damascus oracle makes good sense. The prophet has just described how the Lord will devastate Aram and Israel. This happened between 734–721 B.C., as the Lord used the Assyrians as his instrument of judgment against the coalition that threatened Judah. Of course, the Assyrians, under Sennacherib, eventually overran Judah and threatened Jerusalem. The Lord miraculously delivered the city in 701 by devastating Sennacherib's army (Isa. 36–37). This woe oracle, though it mentions "many nations," anticipates this deliverance, as the prophecy in 8:9–10 does (see above). Isaiah 17:14 depicts the threat disappearing in the morning, which coincides nicely with what happened to Sennacherib's forces (see Isa. 37:36; cf. Smith 2007, 347).

But what of the reference to "many nations"? By the second half of the eighth century B.C. the Assyrian army included conscripts from several conquered nations (Seevers 2013, 216; Wildberger 1997, 197–98). When one faced the Assyrian hordes, one faced "many nations," assembled under the Assyrian banner. Of course, even if the defeat of Sennacherib is the immediate historical referent of the oracle, this event foreshadows the Lord's ultimate defeat of the nations as he establishes Jerusalem as the capital of his earthly kingdom (see Isa. 24–27).

The prophet uses repetition for dramatic effect in the first half of the oracle (17:12–13a). We may translate as follows: "Woe to the raging (army) of many nations—like the raging of the seas they rage! (Woe) to the roaring (army) of peoples—like the roaring of strong waters they roar! The nations, like the roaring of abundant waters, roar!" The verb הָמָה, "rage," appears twice along with the related noun הָמוֹן, "raging," while the verb שָׁאָה, "roar," occurs twice and the related noun שָׁאוֹן, "roaring," three times. The adjective רַבִּים, "many, abundant," appears twice. Indeed, in the Hebrew text, with one exception, no more than one word intervenes between these terms. In a sequence of seventeen forms, one of these forms appears ten times. The prophet impresses upon the listeners the gravity of the threat as he overwhelms them with the tumult of the raging and roaring armies of many nations, which sounds like the raging and roaring of abundant waters.

The use of the phrase מַיִם רַבִּים, "abundant waters," is particularly striking. This phrase can refer to literal water (cf. Num. 20:11; Jer. 41:12), including the waters of the Mediterranean Sea (Isa. 23:13; Ezek. 27:26). But it is often used symbolically of hostile enemies of God who seek to destroy his people (cf. Pss. 18:16 [HB 17]; 32:6; 77:19 [HB 20]; 144:7; Jer. 51:55; Hab. 3:15). The background for the imagery may be Canaanite myth where the sea (deified as the god Yam) and its unruly waters threatened to disrupt the order of the world and destroy humankind. The Old Testament historicizes the mythical imagery by applying it to nations. The Lord is sovereign over these raging waters/nations (see, e.g., Pss. 29:3; 93:4). They challenge his kingship, but he turns them back.

The Lord, who is not specifically mentioned, counters the threat of the raging, roaring nations with his powerful battle cry. He will shout at them, causing them to flee to a distant land. Their retreat will resemble chaff or rolling tumbleweeds being driven before a powerful wind. The prophet escalates the imagery when describing the nations' retreat. In the first line of Isaiah 17:13b, he speaks of chaff being driven before the wind (רוּחַ), but in the second line he changes the agent to a סוּפָה, "gale," which is stronger than a mere רוּחַ (see Hos. 8:7).

The verb גָּעַר, used of the Lord's battle cry, sometimes refers to a verbal rebuke (cf. Gen. 37:10; Ruth 2:16; Zech. 3:2), but in contexts where it describes an expression of God's anger in conjunction with battle and conflict, this translation is inadequate. In these passages the term describes a loud shout or battle cry that incapacitates the enemy (note Pss. 9:5 [HB 6]; 106:9 [HB 10]; Nah. 1:4; as well as the related noun גְּעָרָה, "rebuke, shout," in Job 26:11; Pss. 18:15 [HB 16]; 76:6 [HB 7]; 104:7; Isa. 50:2; 66:15). The strong adverse physical effects of the action suggest that something stronger than a mere verbal rebuke is in view. This motif of the loud battle cry contributes to the Old Testament's portrait of the Lord as a God of war. He strikes terror into the hearts of those who dare challenge his authority or threaten his people. God's battle cry is often directed against surging water, which symbolizes the powerful, destructive enemies of God that threaten the world order and his covenant community. But as we see in Isaiah 17:13, God's shout strikes fear into their hearts and causes them to flee (2 Sam. 18:16 = Ps. 18:17 [HB 18]; Ps. 104:7). This was particularly true at the Red Sea, where God's battle cry rolled back the waters of the sea (Isa. 50:2) and destroyed the Egyptian horses and chariots (Ps. 76:7 [HB 8]).

The elimination of the threat will be sudden. In the evening one sees (Isa. 17:14; note הִנֵּה, "look") its terrifying presence, but before morning arrives it is gone (literally, "he is not"). This is the destiny of those who loot and plunder the Lord's people, for whom the prophet speaks here as representative (note "those who loot *us*," "those who plunder *us*"). The use of חֵלֶק, "portion," is particularly ironic and sarcastic. This word sometimes refers to the portion of the plunder allocated (cf. the parallel term גּוֹרָל, "lot") to a victorious warrior (cf. Gen. 14:24; Num. 31:36; 1 Sam. 30:24). The enemy armies come looking for portions of the loot. Instead, defeat is the only portion they get.

Judgment on Cush and Egypt (18:1–20:6)

18:1–2. A woe is pronounced against a "land of whirring [or quivering] wings," identified as Cush, located directly south of Egypt. The point of calling Cush a land of "whirring wings" is unclear. Perhaps it alludes to the insects that fill the land of Cush or to the sails of the boats mentioned in 18:2a, where Cushite messengers are pictured traveling in papyrus boats. The messengers' destination and purpose are not revealed. Some conclude they are sent out to establish alliances with other nations (including Judah), perhaps against the Assyrians (see Blenkinsopp 2000, 310; Clements 1980, 164; Hayes and Irvine 1987, 253–54). Between 720 and 702 B.C. Cushite kings gained control of Egypt. They appear to have been at peace with Assyria until 701, when their king, Shebitku, opposed Sennacherib. (For a summary of this period, see Currid 1997, 239.)

In 18:2b the prophet addresses swift messengers and instructs them to go to a nation/people that is generally thought to be Cush. Hayes and Irvine (1987, 254–55), however, identify this land as Assyria (see also Clements 1980, 164). (For a critique of both the Cushite and Assyrian interpretations, see Oswalt 1986, 360–61.) This raises a difficult question: What is the relationship between the envoys (צִירִים) sent out *by* Cush (18:2a) and the messengers (מַלְאָכִים) addressed here and sent *to* Cush? Is the prophet sending the Cushite messengers back home (see Cook 2011, 59–60; Erlandsson 1970, 75; Gray 1912, 311; Kaiser 1974, 93; Roberts 2015, 249–50; Wildberger 1997, 217? Or is the Lord responding to Cush's quest for an alliance by sending messengers of his own to Cush (see Childs 2000, 138; Lavik 2007, 68–70; Sweeney 1996, 257)?

The description of the nation/people in 18:2b has challenged interpreters. The nation is said to be, literally, "stretched out" (מְמֻשָּׁךְ) and "smooth" (מוֹרָט < מְמֹרָט?). This may depict them as tall (cf. NIV11; *HALOT* s.v. "משׁך" pu. 2, 646) and smooth-skinned (cf. NIV11; *HALOT* s.v. "מרט" pu. 2, 635). Csaba Balogh (2011, 140) translates it "tall and bald" (for discussion, see pp. 147–49).

Next the prophet calls them a people that is feared, literally, "from it and beyond" (מִן־הוּא וָהָלְאָה). A phrase "from that day forward" (מֵהַיּוֹם הַהוּא וָהָלְאָה) appears in 1 Samuel 18:9 and in Ezekiel 39:22. However, the expression in Isaiah 18:2 (see also 18:7) is different due to the omission of "day." It is typically understood in a locative sense, "far and wide" (NIV11; *HALOT* s.v. "הָלְאָה" mng. 1d, 245). Perhaps it is equivalent to the phrase "from there and beyond" (cf. 1 Sam. 10:3).

The next descriptive expression is particularly obscure: קַו־קָו וּמְבוּסָה. Literally, it would seem to mean "a measuring line, a measuring line, trampling," which makes no sense in the context. The Dead Sea scroll 1QIsᵃ reads קַו־קַו as one word, *qwqw*, which, based on an alleged Arabic cognate, may mean "strong" (*HALOT* s.v. "קַו II" 1081; Wildberger 1997, 208; cf. ESV, "mighty," and NASB, "powerful"). Others appeal to Isaiah 28:10, 13, where some regard קַו (along with צַו) as apparent gibberish spoken by a foreign tongue. In 18:2 קַו would then refer to the Cushites' strange-sounding language (cf. NIV11, "strange speech," and HCSB, "strange language," *Tanakh*, "gibber and chatter").

The form מְבוּסָה, which occurs only here and in Isaiah 22:5, appears to be a noun related to the verb בּוּס, "to trample" (*HALOT* s.v. "מְבוּסָה" 541). In this context, where the nation is feared, this would refer to the Cushites trampling on, or subduing, other lands (cf. NIV11, "aggressive"; ESV, "conquering"; HCSB, "powerful"; NASB, "oppressive").

Finally, the relative clause at the end of the verse describes the nation as one whose land "is divided [?] by rivers." The verb בָּזְאוּ (from an otherwise unattested בָּזָא) is typically understood to mean "divide" based on alleged Syriac and Arabic cognates (see Lavik 2007, 56; cf. Wildberger 1997, 208). *HALOT* (s.v. "בזא" 117) suggests "wash away," based on an Arabic cognate. Roberts (2015, 250) sees this as referring "to the waters of the Nile and Atbarah sweeping away the soil of the highlands of Sudan rather than to these rivers dividing the country of Kush."

18:3. The scope of the oracle broadens as the prophet addresses all the residents of the world. He tells them they will see a signal flag and hear a trumpet, which are likely a call to congregate for battle (Jer. 4:21; 51:27; cf. Isa.

5:26; 13:2; 31:9; see Balogh 2011, 171; Kaiser 1974, 94; Wildberger 1997, 222–23). If so, it need not mean the nations will fight, but only that they will observe a battle. However, some do not see a military nuance here. Blenkinsopp (2000, 310, cf. also Clements 1980, 165) says the flag and trumpet simply summon the nations to hear the message to follow (see Isa. 11:10–12, where a signal flag is used to assemble the exiles; cf. 27:13; 49:22; 62:10).

18:4. The prophet then tells his audience what the Lord has said. The Lord declared he will wait patiently and watch from his dwelling place. He compares himself to the shimmering heat produced by the sunlight and to a cloud producing a mist in the heat of harvest time. The comparisons illustrate the continual presence of the watching God who waits for just the right time to intervene in world affairs. Just as glowing heat and a night mist were characteristic of the harvest season, facilitating ripening of the crops, so the Lord's presence was overseeing world events (see Gray 1912, 314; Kaiser 1974, 95; Motyer 1993, 162; Wildberger 1997, 219–20; Young 1965, 477). But as Smith (2007, 351) observes, "these analogies do not describe God as distant and uninvolved, but intensely present everywhere (like the heat and humidity) as he sovereignly watches over what is happening." As such, the imagery may create an ominous mood. Christopher Seitz (1993, 148) speaks of impending judgment falling like a cloud of dew (cf. Balogh 2011, 174).

18:5. Building on the image of the harvest in the comparisons of 18:4, the prophet uses an agricultural metaphor in 18:5 to describe the coming judgment. He appears to switch the time frame, however, from the harvest season per se to a time before (לִפְנֵי) the grain harvest (קָצִיר), when grapes are pruned. The grain harvest takes place in April–May. Many interpret line 6 of the Gezer Calendar as referring to the months of pruning grapes considering the use of *zmr*, which is used of pruning in Leviticus 25:3–4 and Isaiah 5:6. However, this is problematic, if לִפְנֵי in Isaiah 18:5 has a temporal sense, for the Gezer Calendar places this pruning after the grain harvest. For this reason, Wildberger (1997, 208–9) takes לִפְנֵי in the sense of "in the sight of, in the presence of," rather than "before," and argues that the pruning envisioned in 18:5 takes place at the time of or shortly after the grain harvest (221; see also Lavik 2007, 149–50). However, Borowski (1987, 36, 38) argues that line 6 of the Gezer Calendar is referring to the grape harvest. It uses *zmr* since a מַזְמֵרָה (mentioned in 18:5 in a plural form) was used for both pruning and harvesting. Borowski places pruning in February, before the grain harvest. This would explain the use of לִפְנֵי in 18:5 if it is understood temporally. Prior to the grain harvest, the vinedresser prunes his vines. So the Lord, at just the right time, will prune his vines, as it were. However, 18:5 seems to be referring to a time when the grapes are ripening. According to Wildberger (1997, 221), this would be the time of a second pruning, which in his opinion is in view in line 6 of the Gezer Calendar and in Isaiah 18:5. (For a critique, see Balogh 2011, 174.)

There may be a simpler solution to the interpretation of 18:5. Most assume that קָצִיר in 18:5 refers, as in 18:4, to the grain harvest, but Gray (1912, 315) argues this is not the case. He contends that קָצִיר is used in 18:5 of the grape harvest, in contrast to its use in 18:4. He appeals to the use of קָצִיר in Isaiah 16:9 and 17:11 (cf. 17:10), where a grape harvest does seem to be in view. In this case, 18:5 is simply describing how the vinedresser prunes his grape vines before harvesting them.

18:6. Isaiah 18:6 makes it readily apparent that the pruning described in 18:5 is an image of judgment, for it speaks of the pruned branches being left for the birds of prey and wild animals to eat. Since one would expect these birds to eat meat (cf. Gen. 15:11; Ezek. 39:4), not discarded shoots from the vines,

Wildberger (1997, 222) suggests "the prophet is mixing imagery with reality" at this point; cf. Oswalt 1986, 363). Young (1965, 478) goes further, stating that Isaiah suddenly "leaves the metaphorical expressions . . . and now speaks in somber, even macabre fashion of the reality that is before him." The reference to the birds and wild animals alludes to the aftermath of a battle, when scavengers devour soldiers' corpses (Roberts 2015, 250; Wildberger 1997, 222). (See Ezek. 39:4 [cf. Ps. 79:2] and the discussion and illustration in Keel 1997, 103–4.) The final lines, which speak of the scavengers living off the discarded branches during the summer and winter, allude to the large number of casualties. The identity of the pruned branches destined to be devoured is not given, but since this is an oracle concerning Cush, it is reasonable to assume the Cushites are in view here (Balogh 2011, 176; Roberts 2015, 250; Wildberger 1997, 219). The judgment is described more directly in 20:3–6. (On the historical fulfillment of this oracle against Cushite-led Egypt, see the commentary below on 20:3–6.)

18:7. But the news was not all bad. The prophet envisions a time when the Cushites (described once more as they were in 18:2) would bring their tribute to Zion, the city with which the Lord who commands armies has chosen to identify by making it his capital (cf. Isa. 24:23). The pattern of this oracle—judgment followed by recognition of the Lord's sovereignty—is repeated in the next oracle, where the themes of judgment (19:1–15) and eventual submission (19:16–25) are developed more fully. The Cushite pilgrimage to Zion is just part of the worldwide recognition of the Lord's sovereignty that will characterize the age to come (Smith 2007, 352; cf. Isa. 2:2–4; 11:10; 14:2).

The name of the Lord sometimes stands by metonymy for the Lord himself (note the poetic parallelism in Isa. 24:15; 26:8; 48:1; 50:10; 56:6; 59:19). In Isaiah 30:27 the "name" of the Lord comes in judgment, accompanied by smoke and fire. Here the "place" of the Lord's name is Zion, where the Lord himself rules.

19:1. This oracle begins with a theophany of the Lord riding a swiftly moving cloud toward Egypt. This is the only place where Lord rides a "cloud" (עָב), but there are similar descriptions in Psalm 68:4 [HB 5], where the Lord rides "clouds" (עֲרָבוֹת; cf. *HALOT* s.v. "עֲרָבָה" 879), Deuteronomy 33:26, where he rides the "sky" (שָׁמַיִם; cf. Ps. 68:33 [HB 34]), and 2 Samuel 22:11 (see as well Ps. 18:10 [HB 11]), where he rides a cherub that is associated with the wind (see Wildberger 1997, 240). Apart from the connection with the cloud, other storm theophany elements, such as thunder and lightning, are absent in Isaiah 19:1. The main thrust of the image is the swiftness with which judgment is about to strike. Furthermore, Egypt's natural defenses (sea and desert) would prove worthless against one who can invade their land via the clouds in the sky (Balogh 2011, 235).

The prophet anticipates the Lord's arrival having a powerful impact in Egypt. The idols of Egypt would shake before him (נָעוּ, from נוּעַ). This is not merely a picture of the physical idols shaking and toppling, perhaps due to an earthquake. It is a strong polemic against the supposed reality behind the idols, the gods of Egypt, who have met their match in the Lord and tremble in fear before him (Young 1969, 14–15; note the use of נוּעַ in Exod. 20:18; Isa. 7:2). The word אֱלִילִים, "idols," refers primarily to the physical image of a god (Lev. 19:4; 26:1; Pss. 96:5; 97:7; Isa. 2:8, 18, 20; 10:10–11; 31:7; Hab. 2:18), but worshippers of such idols believe there is a reality behind the image (cf. Isa. 19:3); and the author of Psalm 97, after denouncing idols, speaks of the gods (the reality behind the idols) worshipping the Lord. Like their gods, the Egyptians are overcome with fear. The text reads literally, "the heart of Egypt will melt within him." The land of Egypt, standing by metonymy for its inhabitants, is personified and pictured as one whose strength fails him (cf. Isa. 13:7, as well as Josh. 5:1; 7:5). This is, of course, to be expected when the Egyptians' gods, in whom they placed their trust, are exposed as unreliable and incapable of providing protection. They have proven worthless, which is the meaning of the word used for them here: אֱלִילִים (cf. Job 13:4).

19:2. The Lord speaks in Isaiah 19:2–4, explaining how he will judge Egypt. He will stir up civil strife within Egypt (19:2). Conflict will start within families (brother against brother) and then spread out in ever wider circles—neighbor against neighbor, city against city, and kingdom against kingdom (probably a reference to the various districts within the land). The broadest circle reflects the conflict between the Cushites and Egyptians that occurred at the end of the eighth century B.C., when the Cushites took control of Egypt. (See Currid [1997, 235–39], , and Roberts [2015, 255], Wildberger [1997, 242] for summaries of the political situation in Egypt at that time.)

19:3. Internal conflict will cause panic within Egypt. The first line of 19:3 reads literally, "the spirit of Egypt will be laid waste [וְנָבְקָה, *niphal* perfect, from בָּקַק] within it." The verb is used elsewhere of reducing a place to ruins (Isa. 24:1, 3; Jer. 51:2; Nah. 2:2 [HB 3]) or bringing one's strategy to nothing (Jer. 19:7). Here, with "the spirit of Egypt" as subject, it apparently refers metaphorically to the loss of emotional stability (cf. NIV11, "lose heart," and *HALOT* s.v. "בקק I" 150, "be disturbed").

The Lord will thwart Egypt's strategy. The verb used here (אֲבַלַּע), if from בָּלַע, "swallow, engulf," depicts the Lord destroying (cf. KJV) Egypt's plans. But many prefer to understand בָּלַע as a homonym here, meaning "confuse," which fits well with the object, "his strategy" (see *HALOT* s.v. "בלע III" 135; cf. NLT, ESV ["confound"], NASB ["confound"]). (See Balogh 2011, 209–10.) In either case the Lord "will bring their plans to nothing" (NIV11).

Isaiah 19:3b describes the Egyptians in their panic turning to their idols and the dark arts for guidance. It is not clear if this is a response to the Lord frustrating their strategy (19:3a) or the way in which the Lord will frustrate their strategy. After all, idols and dead spirits will prove no match for the Sovereign Lord who commands armies (cf. 19:4b).

Seeking idols probably refers to typical ways of seeking oracles and omens from the idol-gods to ascertain and to control the future. Of course, the word used for the idols (הָאֱלִילִם, literally, "worthless things") suggests they are incapable of providing guidance. Indeed, the prophet has already announced that the idols will shake with fear before the Lord (see 19:1).

In desperation the Egyptians will turn to other means of discerning and manipulating the future, namely, "the spirits of the dead." The word used (הָאִטִּים) occurs only here in the Old Testament; it appears to be an Akkadian loanword, *etimmu*, which refers to the ghost or spirit of a dead person (*HALOT* s.v. "אִטִּים" 37; Wildberger 1997, 229). The remaining two terms mentioned in 19:3 refer to practitioners of the dark arts who are skilled in conjuring up the spirits of the dead. Both words appear in Isaiah 8:19.

Elsewhere in the Old Testament, seeking information from mediums/spiritists is sometimes depicted as a last resort taken by desperate people. This is certainly the case with Saul, who was unable to receive revelation from the Lord through the usual means (1 Sam. 28:6), and in Isaiah 8:19, where the people were alarmed at recent political developments. Such a scenario fits well in Isaiah 19:3, where the Lord has thwarted Egyptian strategy in the face of impending doom.

19:4. The Lord will hand Egypt over to a cruel master, a strong king who will rule over them. The word "master" appears in the plural here (אֲדֹנִים), even though an individual is clearly in view, as indicated by the singular adjective modifying it (קָשָׁה, "cruel") and the parallel "king" (singular). This is an example of the so-called plural of majesty or honorific plural. The "plural of majesty" is a variation of the well-attested abstract plural (GKC, 396–97 §124a; 398 §124g). More specifically, it is a concretized abstract plural, where the abstract quality is applied to a specific concrete possessor of it. Joel Burnett (2001, 21–22) points out that abstract plural forms "can be used in reference to a single individual or object that is exemplary of the quality named and to which a corresponding status applies." In the context of Isaiah 19:4, this "master" will exercise absolute authority over Egypt. For the Egyptians this harsh conqueror will be "lordship personified or the epitome of authority." The use of the plural suggests a degree of rhetorical emphasis (cf. Judg. 19:11–12, 26–27; 1 Sam. 26:15–16).

The identity of this ruler is not certain. If Egypt per se is in view here, then the referent may be the Cushite ruler Shabaka (Currid 1997, 240), who conquered Egypt and became ruler over a unified Egypt-Cush around 712 B.C. (Currid 1997, 235). Balogh (2011, 294) finds this unlikely. If Cushite Egypt is in view, then the king is probably one of the Assyrian rulers (Esarhaddon and Ashurbanipal) who dominated Egypt in the seventh century (cf. Isa. 20:3–6).

The Lord is identified at the end of the announcement as "the Lord, the Lord who commands armies." The title הָאָדוֹן, "the Lord," stresses his sovereignty. Isaiah uses this title five times; each time it appears before the title "Lord of Armies" (see Isa. 1:24; 3:1; 10:16, 33) and depicts God in his role as the sovereign king who leads armies and brings judgment against evildoers. By placing the definite article on the title, the prophet emphasizes that the God of Israel is "the Lord," or "Master," par excellence. He is the Master who uses a harsh human master as his instrument of judgment. (For more detail on the significance of the title "Lord who commands armies," traditionally translated "Lord of Hosts," see the commentary above on Isa. 1:9.)

19:5–7. Having quoted the Lord's announcement of judgment, the prophet describes the impact of the judgment in detail. The inundation of the Nile was indispensable to Egypt's well-being (see Currid 1997, 240–44). But drought would overtake Egypt, as the "water from the sea" (literal reading, cf. NIV11, "water from the river," probably the Nile) and a river (clearly the Nile) dries up (19:5). The Nile is fed by rains falling farther to the south, so drought in that region would have repercussions in Egypt, which depended on the Nile for its agricultural life. Similar descriptions of the Nile drying up appear in the Prophecies of Neferti from roughly 1990 to 1960 B.C. and in the Famine Stele from the Ptolemaic period (see *COS* 1.45:108, 53.131; Balogh 2011, 242–43; Wildberger 1997, 244). With the Nile running dry, irrigation canals will stink as water becomes stagnant, plants rot, and fish die (Smith 2007, 357). The streams (the branches of the Nile in the delta) will also dry up. Reeds, rushes, and plants along the river will wither and the nearby fields will be reduced to dust that is blown away by the wind (19:6–7).

19:8–10. The drying up of the Nile will have a negative impact on Egyptian commerce (see Currid 1997, 245). Fishermen will lament because the fish in the river will die and rot (19:8). Those who make linen garments will grieve because the unirrigated, dried-up fields will not produce the flax essential to their industry (19:9–10).

19:11–12. As judgment ravages Egypt, the Egyptians will be helpless to combat it. The officials (or princes) of Zoan, who served as advisers to Pharaoh, will prove worthless, as if they were fools giving stupid advice (19:11a; cf. 19:3). Zoan (Tanis), located in the northeastern delta region, was a seat of government. The prophet taunts these advisers, asking how they can claim to be wise (19:11b). He then addresses Pharaoh himself, challenging the king's advisers to discern and reveal what the Lord of Armies has planned against Egypt (19:12). (Note the shift from the second-person plural in 19:11, "how can *you say*," to the second-person singular in 19:12a, "*your* wise men," "to *you*.") The implication is clear: if they cannot understand his strategy, they cannot thwart him.

19:13–15. After once again declaring the officials of Zoan to be fools, the prophet turns on the officials (or princes) of Noph (Memphis), another important city in Lower Egypt (19:13). People relied upon them, as if they were cornerstones. But these officials were deceived and led Egypt astray. In fact, the Lord himself was the source of their confusion (19:14a).

The word translated "deceived" (19:13; נִשְׁאוּ, from נָשָׁא) is used elsewhere of the snake deceiving Eve through half-truths and lies (Gen. 3:13), of a king or god instilling his people with false confidence (2 Kings 18:29 = 2 Chron. 32:15 = Isa. 36:14; 2 Kings 37:10 = Isa. 37:10; Jer. 4:10), of an ally deceiving a treaty partner (Obad. 7), of false prophets giving their audience false hope (Jer. 29:8), and of proud complacency producing self-deception (Jer. 37:9; 49:16; Obad. 3). Here it describes how the Egyptian leaders were deceived or misled. The use of the passive verbal form (*niphal* stem) indicates that an outside agent was involved. Isaiah 19:14 identifies the Lord as Egypt's deceiver. Though popular Christian theology shies away from associating God with any kind of deception, the Bible provides ample evidence that God sometimes uses lies and deception to expedite judgment against sinners (see Chisholm 1998a, 11–28).

As a result of their divinely induced deception, the officials of Egypt were causing their people to stagger in confusion, just as a drunken man staggers around in his vomit (19:14b). Egypt will be helpless before the Lord's judgment (19:15). The imagery of "head or tail, palm branch or reed" suggests totality. The prophet uses the same metaphor in 9:14–15, where the head represents the leaders of Israel, and the tail represents the prophets. The palm branch and reed are not identified specifically. They probably correspond to the head and tail. The metaphor functions similarly here in Isaiah 19. The head represents Pharaoh (cf. 19:11) while the tail represents the advisers (cf. 19:11–14), who are comparable to the prophets of 9:14–15. The palm branch and reed probably correspond to Pharaoh and his advisers.

19:16–17. In the discussion of the oracle's structure, 19:16–17 is transitional (Oswalt 1986, 375). Viewed in isolation, it appears to be an extension of the preceding judgment speech, for it announces Egypt's coming subjugation to Judah. (Childs [2000, 144] speaks of 19:16–17 summarizing the preceding verses.) But the introductory "in that day" links them with the four literary subunits that follow, each of which begins with the same formula, "in that day." Subjugation to Judah would appear to be something negative from Egypt's perspective, but it would culminate in the Egyptians worshipping the Lord and becoming his people. As is often the case in prophetic literature (and in the Bible in general!), judgment is ironically the prelude to reclamation and a bright future (Oswalt 1986, 375).

The judgment described in the first part of the oracle (19:1–15) will leave Egypt confused and helpless. Before the upraised hand of the Lord of Armies, they will tremble in fear (19:16). The prophet compares them to women in this regard. In this ancient cultural context men were trained to fight in hand-to-hand combat, while women's roles were domestic in nature. Furthermore, women's smaller physical size placed them at a disadvantage, making them aware of their vulnerability and prone to react with fear before invading warriors. The prophet emphasizes Egypt's fearful response by combining the synonyms חָרַד, "tremble," and פָּחַד, "shake with fear" (cf. NIV11, "shudder with fear"). The Lord's hand is a warrior motif here, as suggested by the divine title to which it is attached, Lord of Armies. The verb translated "uplifted" (cf. NIV11) pictures the Lord brandishing a weapon against Egypt.

Judah will become dominant over Egypt. The mere mention of the land of Judah will cause fear in Egypt (19:17a). The first line reads literally, "And the land of Judah will become a (cause of) confusion [or shame] for Egypt." The point seems to be that the kingdom of Judah (the reference to the land of Judah is metonymic) will become a cause of confusion/shame (again metonymy is at work as the effect is put for the cause) for Egypt by conquering the latter and making it a vassal state (19:18–25). Egypt will realize that the Lord of Armies has a plan that necessitates its subjugation (19:17b; cf. 19:12). The Lord's plan (עֵצָה) has been mentioned before by the prophet. It encompasses judgment upon his own people (Isa. 5:19), Assyria (14:24), and all the nations of the world (14:26–27), including Egypt (19:12). In the process he thwarts the plan(s) of those who oppose him (8:10; 19:3). (For more on the "plan" of the Lord, see the commentary above on 14:26–27.)

19:18. In that day Egypt will be subject to the Lord (Balogh 2011, 255–56). "Five cities" in Egypt will speak "the language of Canaan"—that is, Hebrew—and make oaths to the Lord of Armies, probably referring to swearing allegiance in a treaty context (cf. Isa. 45:23). Why the prophet says "five," rather than "all" or "seven," symbolizing completeness, is not clear. He is likely referring to five prominent cities known at his time which, by synecdoche, stand for the remainder of the towns. He has mentioned two cities earlier in the oracle: Zoan (Tanis, associated with the Twenty-second Dynasty) and Noph (Memphis). Since there were four competing factions in Egypt at this time (see Currid 1997, 233–40; Wildberger 1997, 254), it is possible that he has Leontopolis (associated with Dynasty Twenty-three) and Sais (associated with the Twenty-fourth Dynasty) in mind as well. Napata, the capital of Cush (Nubia), may have been too far south to be included within the prophet's purview, but he has mentioned Cush already (18:1) and includes Cush and Egypt within the scope of the next oracle (20:3).

One of the five cities would be given a new name, a practice that was common when a city was conquered (cf. Judg. 1:17; 2 Sam. 12:26–28). However, the meaning of the name is uncertain. The Hebrew text reads עִיר הַהֶרֶס, meaning "the city of ruin," if we assume the noun הֶרֶס is related to הָרַס, "to ruin." Dead Sea scroll 1QIsᵃ and several versions (though not the LXX, which has "righteousness") support an emendation to חֶרֶס, a rare word for the sun (see Job 9:7, where it is mentioned with the stars). Most suggest this is the Egyptian city of On, later named Heliopolis by the Greeks, but one wonders why a town conquered by Yahweh/Judah would receive a name with such pagan overtones (the Egyptians worshipped the sun god Re). The name given in the Hebrew text might seem unduly negative in this context, but the judgment of Egypt has just been described in detail (19:1–17) and 19:22 refers to the Lord both striking and healing Egypt. Since 19:19–20 speaks of a monument serving as a sign and witness to the Lord in Egypt, perhaps a renamed city could do so as well. One called "The City of Ruin" would be a reminder of Yahweh's capacity to destroy, which in turn would give incentive to remain loyal to him (in this regard, cf. Zech. 14:18–19).

19:19. Fear (Isa. 19:17) will lead to loyalty (19:18), which in turn will lead to worship (19:19). In the day of Egypt's submission to the one true God there will be a sacrificial altar (מִזְבֵּחַ) to the Lord in the very heart of Egypt (19:19a). There will also be a monument (מַצֵּבָה) dedicated to the Lord at the Egyptian border (19:19b). This word often refers to a sacred pillar set up for a pagan deity. Several passages denounce the religious use of these pillars and demand their destruction (Exod. 23:24; 34:13; Lev. 26:1; Deut. 7:5; 12:3; 16:22; 1 Kings 14:23; 2 Kings 17:10; 23:14; Hos. 10:1–2; Mic. 5:12). However, in several texts, especially in Genesis, the term carries a neutral or even positive connotation. It is used to describe a monument set up as a reminder of a treaty (Gen. 31:45, 51–52) or as a burial marker (Gen. 35:20). On occasion it refers to a pillar set up in conjunction with the worship of the Lord (Gen. 28:18, 22; 31:13; 35:14; Exod. 24:4). Here in Isaiah 19:19 the word is used of a legitimate monument placed at Egypt's border as a reminder of its status as the Lord's vassal (cf. Balogh 2011, 258–60).

19:20. The altar will serve as a tangible reminder ("sign and witness") of Egypt's allegiance to the Lord of Armies and of his commitment to protect the Egyptians (19:20). When the Egyptians cry out (יִצְעֲקוּ) to the Lord due to oppressors (לֹחֲצִים), he will send (וְיִשְׁלַח) a savior and defender and rescue them (וְהִצִּילָם). There is a strong echo here of Exodus 3:8–10, where the Lord tells Moses he has heard Israel's cry (צַעֲקַת בְּנֵי־יִשְׂרָאֵל) and has come down to rescue them (לְהַצִּילוֹ) from their Egyptian oppressors (לֹחֲצִים). He tells Moses he is sending him (וְאֶשְׁלָחֲךָ) as his instrument of deliverance (see Erlandsson 1970, 78; Wildberger 1997, 276; Young 1969, 39). The irony is rich. Having turned to the Lord, Egypt will experience deliverance from oppression through a savior sent by the Lord, just as Israel experienced deliverance from *Egyptian* oppression through Moses, the one whom the Lord sent to them. Wildberger (1997, 276) speaks of this deliverer as "a second Moses." When correlated with Isaiah 19:4, this prediction is significant. The Lord will hand Egypt over to a cruel master, but eventually the Lord will bring them relief (Roberts 2015, 263).

Egypt will learn that the Lord is the only one able to provide genuine deliverance. Foreign alliances, divination, and idols are incapable of rescuing (נָצַל) the victims of divine judgment (Isa. 20:6; 47:14; 57:13). The Assyrian king Sennacherib boasted that no one, not even Israel's God, could deliver (נָצַל) Jerusalem from his armies (Isa. 36:18–20; 37:11–12), but the Lord demonstrated his power to the Assyrian king by annihilating his armies (Isa. 38:6; cf. 31:5).

19:21. The Lord will make himself known to the Egyptians (19:21a). The construction נוֹדַע with לְ־, "make himself known to," which occurs only here in Isaiah, refers to God's self-revelation to the Egyptians. Ezekiel uses the expression of God's self-revelation to Israel through Moses (Ezek. 20:5) and to all the nations in the eschaton (38:23). In the latter case this self-revelation is accomplished through a display of God's power in judgment (cf. 38:21–22). But in Isaiah 19:21 divine self-revelation comes in the form of his intervention on behalf of the Egyptians in response to their prayers for help (cf. 19:20; see Wildberger 1997, 276).

As one might expect, divine self-revelation brings knowledge to its recipients. Egypt will "know the Lord" in the sense that they will recognize and acknowledge him as their king. We see this same nuance for the verb יָדַע, "know," in 1 Samuel 2:12, which says that Eli's wicked sons "did not know" the Lord; they refused to acknowledge his moral authority over their behavior. King Josiah, on the other hand, did "know" the Lord; he acknowledged the Lord's authority by obeying his policies regarding justice (Jer. 22:16).

There is irony here when one recalls the exodus account, where the Lord reveals his divine power so that Pharaoh and the Egyptians will "know" him (see, e.g., Exod. 7:5; 14:4, 18). They will recognize, through the judgment they experience, that Israel's God is Yahweh, the one who is Israel's ever-present deliverer. Here in Isaiah 19:21, however, the Egyptians experience his saving presence like Israel of old, and commit to worshipping, not just fearing, him (Clements 1980, 172; Oswalt 1986, 380).

Once the Egyptians recognize the Lord's authority over them, they serve him by presenting sacrifices and offerings to him and by fulfilling the vows they make to him (19:21b).

As Young (1969, 40) points out there is a "gradation" in the description of Egypt's "conversion" to the Lord. We read of an altar in the middle of the land (19:19) and of the Egyptians crying out to the Lord (19:20). As the Lord reveals himself, the Egyptians recognize his authority (19:21a) and serve him through worship (19:21b).

19:22. Isaiah 19:22 pictures the Lord striking Egypt and then, in response to the Egyptians' prayerful repentance, healing them. It is possible this anticipates a judgment beyond the one described in 19:1–17 (cf. Zech. 14:18–19), but it is more likely the prophet is summarizing. The striking of Egypt is the judgment announced in Isaiah 19:1–17 (cf. Balogh 2011, 263), while the healing corresponds to 19:18–21, where Egypt recognizes the Lord's sovereignty, looks to him in their distress, experiences his deliverance, and worships him.

The language is reminiscent of the exodus account, which tells how God struck Egypt with plagues to deliver his people from bondage (Exod. 8:2 [HB 7:27]; 12:23, 27; Josh. 24:5). The allusion highlights the reversal that will take place in the Lord's relationship with Egypt. Once again, he will strike Egypt (Isa. 19:1–17), but this time judgment will be the prelude to a new era in which the Egyptians are healed and become worshippers of the one true God (Smith 2007, 362–63; Young 1969, 42). The verb "to heal" is used metaphorically here of restoration. It is an apt metaphor because divine judgment, like a physical injury or illness, wounds and threatens life. Because he is a merciful God, the Lord often offers healing to those whom he has been forced to punish (Isa. 30:26; 57:18–19; Jer. 30:17; 33:6). According to Isaiah's fourth Servant Song, Israel's healing is made possible by the servant's willingness to suffer on behalf of his people (Isa. 53:5).

19:23. To this point the prophet has focused on the transformation that will take place within Egypt. He now broadens the scope. When Egypt becomes a loyal subject of the Lord, it will experience peace. There will be a highway connecting Egypt and Assyria, and the residents of the two nations will visit one another and be at peace. Some interpreters see a fulfillment of this prophecy in the late eighth century B.C., when Sargon promoted trade with Egypt, but this approach is unconvincing (Hayes and Irvine 1987, 266; Niccacci 1998, 217–24; Roberts 2015, 264). Sargon's gesture of peace was short-lived. Sennacherib, Sargon's successor, was in conflict with Egypt, as were subsequent Assyrian kings. Furthermore, Egypt and Assyria never joined with Israel in the worship of the one true God (see 19:24–25). The prophet's vision is utopian and eschatological.

19:24. Isaiah's vision of Egypt's future transformation culminates with a truly remarkable prophecy in which Israel, Egypt, and Assyria join as a threesome to serve the Lord. This was a radical reversal of the political situation of Isaiah's time. Erlandsson (1970, 79) comments, "Conflict between Assyria and Egypt with Israel as a pawn in the game shall one day be transformed into a peaceful community founded on Yahweh's blessing."

According to 19:24, all three will be a "blessing." In this context this term (בְּרָכָה) envisions the three nations as recipients of divine blessing (cf. 19:25). In the case of Israel, there may be an allusion to the Abrahamic covenant in which the Lord promised to bless the patriarch and make his offspring into a great nation (Gen. 12:2; 22:17). (Balogh [2011, 266] considers the intertextual link obvious.) Genesis 12:2 anticipates a time when Abram (Abraham) would "be a blessing," that is, become a paradigm of what it means to be blessed by God. This in turn would result in Abraham's name being used in formal blessings (cf. Gen. 22:18; 26:4). It is possible that such a formalized blessing is in view here in Isaiah 19:24 (cf. *HALOT* s.v. "בְּרָכָה I" 161). In Zechariah 8:13 the Lord promises that his people, though presently a curse word among the nations, would become a blessing—that is, a recipient and prime example of a nation blessed by God—resulting in their name being used in formalized blessings rather than in curses. For examples of formal blessings utilizing names in a paradigmatic manner, see Genesis 48:20 and Ruth 4:11 (Balogh 2011, 267–68).

19:25. The blessing of the Sovereign Lord (note Lord of Armies) will extend to the whole earth, including Egypt and Assyria (19:25). In pronouncing blessing on Egypt, the Lord will call them "my people, Egypt." The phrase "my people" is followed by a proper name twenty-nine times in the Old Testament. In every other case the name Israel follows, so the inclusion of the name Egypt after "my people" must have been shocking to Isaiah's ancient Israelite audience. Yet it draws attention to the Lord's concern for the world, not just his chosen people, and to his intention to extend his beneficent rule to all the world (cf. Isa. 2:2–4).

In pronouncing blessing on Assyria, the Lord calls them "the work of my hands." Elsewhere the "work" of the Lord's "hands" can be his acts of justice and judgment (Pss. 28:4–5; 92:4 [HB 5]; Isa. 5:12; 10:12) or his works of creation (Pss. 8:6 [HB 7]; 19:1 [HB 2]), including his people (see Isa. 29:23; 60:21; 64:8). Only in two other texts does the Lord himself use the phrase "the work of my hands"; in both cases he refers to the Israelite exiles whom he would restore to the land (Isa. 29:23; 60:21). So, it would have been shocking for Israel to hear Assyria identified in this way. Yet, as in the case of Egypt, the language highlights God's concern for the world, not just one people.

In extending his blessing to Israel, the Lord calls them "my inheritance." The Lord uses these words on nine other occasions. Each time he refers to either Israel (cf. 2 Kings 21:14; Isa. 47:6; Jer. 12:7–9; Joel 3:2) or the land he has given to Israel (Jer. 2:7; 16:18; 50:11). Here the Lord compares his people to landed property one would inherit from his ancestors and pass down to his descendants. The value of such property would have been inestimable. By using this idiom, the Lord emphasizes how important Israel is to him. In Isaiah 63:17 the people appeal to this fact as they ask the Lord to withdraw his punishment and restore his people to his favor.

There was no historical fulfillment of this prophetic vision. Its realization lies in the future. Since the Assyrian and the ancient Egyptian empires have long since passed into history, one should expect an essential, not hyperliteral, fulfillment of Isaiah's utopian vision. Someday the powerful, Assyria-like and Egypt-like nations of the world will join in worshipping the one true God in his kingdom of peace (cf. Isa. 2:2–4). For a fuller discussion of essential fulfillment of historically contextualized prophecy, see Chisholm 2014, 53–68.

20:1. Having described Egypt's ultimate destiny, the prophet returns to the immediate future. The Egyptians will someday become worshippers of the one true God, but before that happens, they will experience judgment. The message is dated specifically to the year (712 or 711 B.C.) in which the Assyrian king Sargon II sent his army on a campaign against the Philistine city of Ashdod (20:1). (For the historical background, see Currid 1997, 238–40; Hayes and Irvine 1987, 267–70; Roberts 2015, 269–70.)

20:2. The Lord instructed Isaiah to perform a symbolic action, which he dutifully carried out. The prophet removed the sackcloth from his body and the sandals from his feet and walked about "naked" and barefoot. The Hebrew term עֲרוֹם can often refer to "nakedness" (Gen. 2:25; Job 1:21; Eccl. 5:15 [HB 14]). Roberts (2015, 270) argues that the prophet did indeed expose his nakedness to observers. Isaiah's actions were an object lesson of what would happen to the Egyptian and Cushite captives, who would be publicly shamed by having their nakedness exposed (cf. 20:4). (See also Balogh 2011, 312.)

He observes, however, that this need not mean the prophet remained unclothed twenty-four hours a day. He appeared naked only when publicly making his point (see also Smith 2007, 366). Others contend it is unlikely that Isaiah would have exposed his nakedness. In this view the term עָרוֹם refers hyperbolically to stripping down to his undergarments (cf. *HALOT* s.v. "עָרוֹם" mng. 2, 883; Wildberger 1997, 293–94).

It is noteworthy that Isaiah was already wearing sackcloth when given these instructions. This suggests he was already in mourning, perhaps for Judah's impending judgment. If so, as Wildberger (1997, 294) says, removing the sackcloth would "elevate, still another notch, his desire to depict this mourning." There may be irony in the language. In Psalm 30:11 [HB 12] the psalmist says to God, "you removed [literally, 'opened'] my sackcloth." "Opening" one's sackcloth indicates the cessation of mourning and the arrival of joy; but in Isaiah's case, removing the sackcloth and replacing it with nothing signified the coming defeat and humiliation of the Egyptians and Cushites.

20:3–4. It is unclear how the reference to "three years" in Isaiah 20:3 relates to Isaiah's symbolic act. Most take it with what precedes, indicating that Isaiah walked about naked and barefoot for three years. In this case, it appears the Lord did not provide an explanation for the prophet's behavior until three years after he started performing the symbolic act. While this might seem unlikely, people knew Isaiah was a prophet and would have realized such a bizarre act must have some significance. They would have waited in suspense for an explanation (see Motyer 1993, 171). However, the accentuation of the Masoretic Text understands "three years" with what follows. In this case, we may paraphrase: "Just as my servant Isaiah has walked about naked and barefoot—for three years this will be a sign and portent against Egypt and Cush—so the king of Assyria will lead away . . .". In this case, this might mean that after Isaiah had begun acting out the sign for an unspecified time period, the Lord explained its significance and announced the prophet would continue to perform the ritual for three more years. Or it could mean the prophet performed the symbolic act on one occasion and that this action would serve as a sign for three years. (See Balogh 2011, 308–9, 314–15, following ancient Jewish commentators.)

Isaiah's action is called a "sign and portent" (20:3). In 8:18 the expression "signs and symbols" [or, "portents"] is used of Isaiah and his children, whose names had great symbolic significance (see the note there). Several times in Deuteronomy the phrase describes the miraculous judgments God brought upon Egypt to force Pharaoh to release his people from slavery (Deut. 4:34; 6:22; 7:19; 26:8; 29:2; 34:11; cf. Neh. 9:10; Pss. 78:43; 105:27; 135:9; Jer. 32:20–21). The covenant curses would serve as a "sign and a wonder" ["portent"] to wayward Israel (Deut. 28:46). Here in Isaiah 20:3, where the phrase is followed by the preposition "against" (עַל), it has an ominous quality. Isaiah acted out in advance what would happen to the people of Egypt and Cush. The king of Assyria would defeat them and lead captives away "stripped and barefoot." Both young and old would be humiliated, as their nakedness would be exposed for all to see (20:4).

20:5–6. The prophet drew out the implication for the Lord's covenant community. Those who trusted in the Egyptians and Cushites for security would be disappointed (20:5). Those living on the coast, probably Egypt's Philistine allies, would lament the demise of their source of security and express their despair (20:6). Consequently, it made no sense for Judah to seek security through an alliance with the Egyptians and Cushites (see Oswalt 1986, 386; Smith 2007, 368).

The prophecy was fulfilled in the following decades. Sennacherib defeated an Egyptian-led coalition in 701 B.C. at Eltekeh. His successors

Esarhaddon (681–669) and Ashurbanipal (668–627) defeated the Cushites and conquered Egypt.

Judgment on Peoples to the East (21:1–17)

21:1. This oracle concerns "the desert by the sea" (מִדְבַּר־יָם), which apparently refers to Babylon (21:9). The Assyrians called southern Mesopotamia the Sealand because of its proximity to the Persian Gulf. Merodach-baladan, called the "king of Babylon" in Isaiah 39:1, ruled over the marshy Sealand and vied with the Assyrians for control of Babylon. So, it may be that "desert by the sea" refers to Merodach-baladan's territory (see Childs 2000, 151–52; Smith 2007, 371; Sweeney 1996, 28–81). It is also noteworthy that Jeremiah 51:36 speaks of Babylon having a "sea" (Blenkinsopp 2000, 324). If so, as Sweeney argues, מִדְבָּר does not refer to an arid region, but simply to a "marginal or border" area. One wonders, however, if מִדְבַּר־יָם is a deliberate alteration of the Akkadian *mat tamti*, "land of the sea," highlighting the fact that judgment would devastate the region, leaving it a מִדְבָּר, or unpopulated wasteland. If so, this is ironic, since earlier the king of Babylon was described as one who reduced the world to a wasteland (מִדְבָּר) as he overthrew cities (cf. 14:27).

This highly dramatized oracle begins with a vivid description of an approaching invader. Like windstorms sweeping through the south of Israel (the Negev), an invader comes from the desert, from a land that is feared. The windstorms in view could reach "gale force, producing dust storms which may reduce visibility to less than fifty yards" (Stadelmann 1970, 106).

21:2. The prophet reports that he has received a distressing message (literally, "a hard vision"): the betrayer betrays, and the destroyer destroys (cf. Isa. 33:1). The identity of the betrayer and destroyer is not given. Is he the object (Babylon?) or instrument of divine judgment? (See Wildberger 1997, 316.)

Elam is commanded to rise, and Media is told to lay siege, though an object is not identified. Apparently, they are to attack the object of judgment. This might lead one to believe they are the betrayer/destroyer. However, both Elam and Media are addressed as feminine (note the feminine singular imperative forms, עֲלִי, "rise up," and צוּרִי, "besiege"), while the betrayer/destroyer is masculine (note the masculine singular participial forms הַבּוֹגֵד, "the betrayer" [NIV11, "the traitor"] and הַשּׁוֹדֵד, "the destroyer" [NIV11, "the looter"]).

The speaker, perhaps the Lord (see Wildberger 1997, 317; but Erlandsson [1970, 83] disagrees), announces he has put an end to all her groaning. The identity of "her" is not provided, but Babylon is probably in view (see 21:9, where Babylon is depicted as feminine). If so, then "her groaning" could allude to the pain she has caused others (see NIV11, "all the groaning she caused"). If the judgment is viewed as future, the perfect verbal form is rhetorical, emphasizing the action is as good as done. The preceding commands to Elam and Media to involve themselves in the conflict suggest this is the case.

21:3–4. The prophet experiences emotional and physical distress because of this "hard vision" (NIV 11, "dire vision"). His midsection cramps up, like a woman during childbirth. He is bent over by the news and horrified by the sights of the vision. His heart staggers (תָּעָה), perhaps referring to an irregular or rapid heartbeat, and he is overcome by fear. Normally he enjoys twilight time (when work is finished), but it has become a time of terror for him. Perhaps this suggests he received the "hard vision" at twilight, but it may mean no rest is possible, even at the end of the day, for one who has experienced this vision (see Young 1969, 66). The prophet's response does not imply that he has any special sympathy for Babylon. It may simply highlight the severity of the judgment. Being human, Isaiah is naturally affected emotionally by the horror of what he sees (cf. Oswalt 1986, 393). Smith (2007, 372), who sees the prophecy as referring to the Assyrian destruction of Babylon in 689 B.C., suggests the prophet's anguish is not over Babylon's fall but over its implications for Judah, which would be robbed of an ally (see also Childs 2000, 152). (See the discussion of the fulfillment of the oracle below.)

21:5–7. Isaiah 21:5–7 dramatically highlights the urgency of the situation. The prophet addresses military officers, pointing out, perhaps sarcastically, that this is no time for feasting (21:5a). They must prepare their shields for battle (21:5b) because, according to the Lord, conflict is on the horizon. In fact, the Lord instructed Isaiah to post a lookout, who must stay very alert and keep his eyes open for messengers (21:6–7). One definitely senses trouble brewing.

TRANSLATION ANALYSIS 21:5
The four infinitives absolute in Isaiah 21:5a are substituted for finite verbs, but it is unclear what mood should be understood. Some translators understand them as imperatival (HCSB, KJV), while others treat them as indicative/descriptive (ESV, NASB, NIV11). The latter seems preferable in this context where war is imminent and battle preparations are more appropriate than eating and drinking. If taken as imperatival, they would need to be understood sarcastically, mocking the addressees for their lack of readiness for battle.

21:8–9. The lookout then gives his report. He faithfully manned his post by day and night (21:8). Then a messenger, driving a chariot, brought the news: Babylon has fallen, and all its idols are shattered (21:9). From the perspective of the messenger, the perfect verbal forms in the quotation treat Babylon's fall as accomplished, even though it is still future from the perspective of the prophecy (cf. 21:2, 5–6). When calamity falls on idol-worshippers, their man-made idol-gods are inevitably exposed as weak and unworthy of worship (cf. Isa. 30:22; 40:19–20; 42:17; 44:9–10; 45:20), for the Lord refuses to give to others any of the glory and praise that he alone deserves (Isa. 42:8; 48:5).

21:10. The relationship between 21:10 and what precedes is problematic. Isaiah 21:10a presents special challenges that can only be resolved once one understands what is being said in the second half of the verse. The prophet concludes by once again addressing the military officers. Isaiah 21:10b reads literally: "That which I have heard from the Lord of Armies, the God of Israel, I have declared to you." The addressee is plural, as the form לָכֶם, "to you," at the end of the verse indicates. "That which I have heard from the Lord" corresponds to "for this is what the Lord says to me" in 21:6a. The content of the Lord's message appears in 21:6b–9. So, it is likely that the plural addressee in 21:10b is to be identified with the plural addressee of 21:5 (the military officers). In 21:10b he tells them he has faithfully reported to them the message introduced in 21:6a.

Isaiah 21:10a reads literally, "my trampled one and the son of my threshing floor." The form מְדֻשָׁתִי, "my trampled one," consists of a noun (מְדֻשָׁה) that occurs only here and a suffixed first-person singular pronoun. The noun is related to the verb דּוּשׁ, "to trample" (in threshing; cf. Deut. 25:4; 1 Chron. 21:20; Isa. 28:28; Hos. 10:11). The expression "son of my threshing floor" (or "my son of a threshing floor," since the pronominal suffix can be understood with the phrase) occurs only here; the idiom associates the trampled one with the threshing floor where such trampling takes place. The point seems to be that the one so addressed has been trampled, as it were, like grain stalks on the threshing floor.

But who is speaking and who is being addressed? Typically, Isaiah 21:10a is taken with what follows, with "my trampled one, son of my threshing floor" being vocative. Since the Lord is spoken of in the third person in 21:10b, it is likely that the prophet is speaking. If so, he is identifying with the trampled one; this is consistent with his emotional reaction in 21:3–4. The "trampled one" would seem to be equivalent to the group addressed by "to you" in 21:10b, namely, the military officers addressed in 21:5. If so, this would suggest the military officers are doomed, being depicted proleptically as trampled in conjunction with the fall of Babylon (21:9).

Interpreters have reached no consensus regarding the time frame of the oracle's fulfillment. Several prefer to see the prophesied events unfolding in Isaiah's time. In this case, an Assyrian attack on Babylon is in view. Sargon conquered Babylon in 710 B.C., while Sennacherib took it in 703. Both times Merodach-baladan fled from the city. Sennacherib defeated Merodach-baladan in 700 and he conquered and destroyed Babylon in 689 (see Erlandsson 1970, 89–91; Sweeney 1996, 279–80). Sweeney (1996, 280) understands the fulfillment of the oracle in conjunction with Sennacherib's destruction of Babylon in 689 (see also Roberts 2015, 278; Smith 2007, 370); Erlandsson (1970, 92) prefers 700; while Hayes and Irvine (1987, 272–74) relate it to Sargon's victory in 710. Proponents of this late-eighth/early-seventh-century date of fulfillment usually understand Elam and Media in 21:2 as Babylonian allies, which they were at that time (see Erlandsson 1970, 89–91). In this case, one may understand the verb צוּרִי in 21:2 in the sense of "barricade" or simply "attack" (see Sweeney 1996, 281; and the discussion of 21:2 above), or take the verb as a battle cry to attack Assyria (so Erlandsson 1970, 92; cf. Roberts 2015, 277). Regarding the latter approach, Smith (2007, 371) says, "Babylon's neighbors are being encouraged to attack the Assyrian invading forces (21:2) to divert their attention from Babylon." Hayes and Irvine (1987, 274) take a different angle—they understand Elam and Media as "probably a reference to troops from regions dominated by the Assyrians who had been commandeered into the Assyrian army" (cf. Isa. 22:6).

Other interpreters prefer to see the oracle being fulfilled much later, in 539–538 B.C. in conjunction with Cyrus's conquest of Babylon. In this view Elam and Media attack Babylon (21:2). The reference to Media certainly fits this period (cf. Isa. 13:17), but Elam had ceased to be an independent nation after the mid-seventh century (Sweeney 1996, 279). However, Wildberger (1997, 379) points out that the Elamites did not disappear from the historical stage at that time; they remained a force in the region and were eventually assimilated into the Persian Empire and served in Cyrus's army (see also Blenkinsopp 2000, 326). Wildberger says, "In a sense the Persians were the heirs of Elam." Kaiser (1974, 124) regards Elam and Media as "paraphrases for the Persian kingdom." Young (1969, 63) sees Isaiah's message as contextualized. He states: "Later writers spoke of Persia, but Isaiah mentions Elam, for in his day such a designation would be better understood by the Jews."

A few interpreters prefer to see the message as layered, with some elements of it reflecting the fall of Babylon in Isaiah's day and others pointing to Cyrus' conquest of the city in the sixth century. A. A. Macintosh (1980) proposes that the text is a "palimpsest," with an early prophecy "overwritten" by a later hand. However, rather than proposing multiple authorship we could simply argue that Isaiah, writing under inspiration, merged the near and the far into his portrayal of Babylon's demise (in this regard, see Motyer 1993, 175). The biblical prophets frequently do this. Sometimes prophecies are fulfilled progressively (see, e.g., 1 Kings 13:1–3; 14:10–16; see Chisholm 2014, 62–63). Jesus's Olivet Discourse, especially in the Lukan version (Luke 21:5–28), blends near and far as he predicts the fall of Jerusalem in A.D. 70 and also speaks of culminating realities.

21:11–12. This next oracle is the shortest of the messages contained in Isaiah 13–23. It pertains to Dumah, the precise identity of which is uncertain. The noun דּוּמָה means "silence" (cf. Pss. 94:17; 115:17), but most, based on the analogy with the other oracles in these chapters, take it as a proper name. There was an Israelite town Dumah, located near Hebron (Josh. 15:52) but, as Wildberger (1997, 331) observes, it "would not have been important enough to be the subject of this oracle." The LXX identifies Dumah as Idumaea, that is, Edom, and some see the Edomites as the focus of the oracle (Blenkinsopp 2000, 329; Young 1969, 76). The fact that the inquiring voice comes from Seir (Edomite territory) might favor this interpretation. In Genesis 25:14 (cf. 1 Chron. 1:30) the name Dumah appears as one of Ishmael's sons, suggesting it may be the name of an Arabian site to the east. The name appears in a list that also includes Kedar (Gen. 25:13) and Tema (Gen. 25:15), both of which are mentioned in the oracle that immediately follows (cf. Isa. 21:14, 16–17). Perhaps Dumah was an oasis in Arabia (Smith 2007, 376). The proximity of the Dumah oracle to the preceding oracle concerning Babylon, located to the east, and to the following oracle concerning Arabia, again located to the east, is consistent with this interpretation. (For discussion see Wildberger 1997, 328–29, 331.) Wildberger, (1997, 331) who prefers Arabian Dumah as the referent, associates it with Akkadian *adummatu*, mentioned by Sennacherib (cf. Roberts 2015, 280; Sweeney 1996, 285). The Assyrian kings Sargon, Sennacherib, Esarhaddon, and Ashurbanipal made military expeditions against the Arabians. Sennacherib is said to have conquered *adummatu* (Dumah?). Later, the Neo-Babylonians under Nebuchadnezzar also campaigned in Arabia; Nabonidus made Tema his home for a lengthy period. (See the historical survey in Wildberger 1997, 332–33, as well as his map on 334.)

The prophet hears someone calling to him from Seir, located in Edom. Though the voice calls from Edom, we are not given details about who exactly is calling. Perhaps the Edomites are concerned about Dumah's destiny because of economic considerations (Oswalt 1986, 398), or refugees from Dumah who have migrated to Edom express concern about the future of their home. Roberts (2015, 280) speculates that "an Edomite trader" or "Qedarite kinsman residing in Seir" is the speaker.

The voice from Seir asks the watchman (prophet), "What is left of the night?" All the watchman can say is, "Morning has come, and also night." Some translations understand אָתָה, "has come," a perfect verbal form, in a present (ESV, KJV, NASB) or future (cf. NIV11) sense, but it is more naturally understood in a past sense (see Wildberger 1997, 337). The watchman's point is that morning did come but was then followed by night. His failure to answer the question suggests he is not certain when the present darkness of night will end. He simply invites the questioner to ask again, if he so desires, at some point in the future. It is likely that night symbolizes military defeat (cf. Kaiser 1974, 131; Wildberger 1997, 337). Roberts (2015, 280) observes that the watchman's (i.e., prophet's) response "is not reassuring" because it suggests God has not answered his inquiry: "A deity's refusal to respond to an oracular request in such a fashion, even if it is simply to delay responding, has negative overtones and suggests the oracle, if it ever comes, will not be good news (cf. 1 Sam. 14:37; 28:6; Amos 8:11–12; Mic. 3:6–7)." Since the watchman (prophet) in the oracle provides no definitive answer to the question addressed to him (see below), it is possible that irony is at work here (cf. Motyer 1993, 177). It is an oracle concerning Dumah, but ironically it is an "oracle of silence" as well.

The historical setting of this oracle is not certain. As with the preceding oracle concerning Babylon, some associate it with Assyrian incursions into Arabia in Isaiah's time (Roberts 2015, 282; Sweeney 1996, 285). If the oracle is a companion of the one that follows, this would be the case, since the following oracle concerning Arabia was to be fulfilled within a year (see 21:16).

Others place the setting much later, in the sixth century B.C., in conjunction with Neo-Babylonian control of the area (Clements 1980, 180).

21:13–17. The next oracle pertains to Arabia (Hebrew עֲרָב), a region located southeast of Edom (see the map in Wildberger 1997, 334). The phrase בַּעְרָב after מַשָּׂא does not mean "an oracle concerning Arabia," but rather, "an oracle in the steppe." The phrase is taken from the first line of the oracle (note בַּיַּעַר בַּעְרָב, literally "in the thicket, in the steppe"). (See Roberts 2015, 281; Wildberger 1997, 339–40.) The "steppe" refers here to the region we know as northern Arabia. Three specific places within the region are referred to in the oracle (Dedan, Tema, and Kedar). Tema and Kedar were sons of Ishmael (see Gen. 25:13, 15).

The prophet addresses the Dedanite caravans, which spend the night in the steppe, and then describes how they have brought (or perhaps urges them to bring) water for the thirsty (21:13–14a). At this point, we do not know the identity of the thirsty. He then tells how the residents of Tema have met (or urges them to meet) the fugitives with food (21:14b). We discover that the thirsty are refugees, but we do not yet know from what they are fleeing. The prophet provides greater specificity, as he explains that they are fleeing from the sword, the bow, and the weight of battle (21:15). Finally, in 21:16–17 the prophet identifies the refugees as the defeated warriors of Kedar. The defeat assumed and dramatized in 21:13–15 actually lies in the immediate future, for we discover that Kedar's demise will take place exactly one year from the time the prophecy was delivered. This chronological notation places the oracle in Isaiah's time. It probably alludes to Assyrian attacks on this region (see Erlandsson 1970, 94–95; Kaiser 1974, 134–35; Roberts 2015, 282; Sweeney 1996, 287).

Judgment on Judah (22:1–25)

22:1a. The Valley of Vision is mentioned in 22:5 as the focal point of the judgment sent by the Master, the Lord of Armies. It is associated with Jerusalem (22:9–10), so perhaps the Tyropoean Valley, Kidron Valley, or Hinnom Valley is in view. (Sweeney 1996, 299–300, argues that the Kidron Valley is the referent.) It is not clear why it is called the "Valley of Vision." Perhaps the prophet received the oracle there in a vision, or it is so named because the valley is the focal point of the prophetic vision (22:5). Another option is that the valley is the primary target of the judgment—perhaps, if the Hinnom Valley is in view, because Molech worship occurred there (Wildberger 1997, 358–59).

22:1b–3. The prophet addresses the noisy city mentioned in 22:2. He uses second-person feminine singular forms, consistent with the fact that the city (עִיר)/town (קִרְיָה), described in 22:2a is the addressee. He wants to know why the entire city (cf. כֻּלָּךְ, "all of you") has gone up to the rooftops (22:1b). He identifies and describes the addressee as follows: "(With) shouts a noisy city is full, a rejoicing town" (22:2a, literal translation). The verbal root of the adjective עַלִּיזָה, "rejoicing," means "to rejoice, shout" (see 2 Sam. 1:20; Pss. 28:7; 96:12; 149:5; Prov. 23:16; Jer. 50:11; 51:39; Hab. 3:18; Zeph. 3:14). As usage indicates, the verb does not necessarily have a negative connotation; on the contrary, it is often used of the joy that accompanies worship. However, when the adjectival derivative is used of cities, it consistently has a negative connotation. It depicts cities as places of revelry and commotion (Isa. 23:7; 24:8; 32:13; Zeph. 2:15). Such cities are characterized by a proud attitude of self-sufficiency that eventually prompts divine judgment. Elsewhere the rooftop (cf. גַּגּוֹת) is associated with mourning (Isa. 15:3; Jer. 48:38), but that does not seem to be the case here (Wildberger 1997, 361). The town is apparently celebrating (Isa. 22:2a; cf. 22:13), even though it has experienced death and captivity. People lie dead, but they have not been killed by the sword or in battle (22:2b). This probably alludes to a siege, during which some have died of starvation. Leaders abandoned the city, but they were captured without the use of weapons, even when they fled far away (22:3).

22:4. Because of (עַל־כֵּן, "therefore") these tragic circumstances, the prophet addresses any who would try to console him, saying (literally), "Look away [note the masculine plural form שְׁעוּ] from me! I will weep bitterly. Do not insist on comforting me over the destruction of the daughter of my people!" In light of what has transpired, lamentation, not celebration, is appropriate.

22:5. According to the prophet (22:4), the death and captivity that have overtaken the community (cf. 22:2b–3) should prompt mourning, not celebration (22:1b–2a). Now he elaborates on why (כִּי) mourning is appropriate (22:5). It is evident the community has experienced judgment sent from "the Master, Yahweh of Armies" (NIV11, "the Lord, the LORD Almighty"). Israel's sovereign covenant Lord, who leads armies into battle, has brought a "day" of disaster upon the "Valley of Vision"—a day of tumult (מְהוּמָה), trampling (מְבוּסָה), and terror (מְבוּכָה). The syntactical structure and the sound-play (note the initial *mem* and the same vocalic pattern in all three nouns) create a mood of intensity and suggest the judgment has come in overwhelming waves. The three coordinated genitives modify a single construct noun ("day"). This is relatively rare and suggests the genitives "form one closely connected whole" (GKC, 414, 128a n. 3). The first noun (מְהוּמָה, "tumult") may even be an echo of the covenant curse in Deuteronomy 28:20. This "day" of judgment was marked by great destruction, as walls were battered down. There was widespread panic, as people cried to הָהָר, literally "the mountain," in hopes that relief would come there.

22:6. The invading army included Elamite archers and chariots, as well as soldiers from Kir. In Isaiah's time the Elamites were allies of the Babylonians, but if Isaiah is describing an invasion that took place in his day (see the discussion of the oracle's setting below), then Elamite soldiers fighting in the Assyrian army may be in view (see Hayes and Irvine 1987, 281; Sweeney 1996, 295). We know little about Kir, which is mentioned elsewhere in 2 Kings 16:9, where we are told that the Assyrian king (Tiglath-pileser III) settled conquered Arameans there, and in Amos (1:5; 9:7). It is possible the soldiers of Elam and Kir are singled out because of their foreignness. It is human nature to be afraid of that which is foreign, and both Elam and Kir were, from the Israelite perspective, distant lands, located on the far end of the world as it were.

22:7. Enemy chariots filled the valleys and chariot teams were posted right outside the city gate. Introductory וַיְהִי, "and it was," indicates the prophet is describing what has happened, as do the two *qatal* (perfect) verbal forms. This is consistent with Isaiah 22:3 and 6, which also use *qatal* (perfect) verbal forms to describe what has transpired. This narratival style continues in 22:8–12, where the prophet uses a mixture of five *wayyiqtol* (22:8–10, 12) and six *qatal* (22:9–11) verbal forms to review what has taken place leading up to the present moment of crisis.

The prophet uses a second-person feminine singular pronominal form in his address (note עֲמָקַיִךְ, "your valleys"). Most likely, he is addressing the "noisy city," as he does in 22:1b–3. If Jerusalem is in view (cf. 22:10), this probably refers to the valleys of Judah. Since Jerusalem is the central city of Judah, the valleys can be viewed as belonging to her. The noun used here, עֵמֶק, "valley," refers to broad plains where chariots can function effectively (Wildberger 1997, 365–66), not to the ravines near Jerusalem (as Young [1969, 96] proposes).

22:8. The crisis began to unfold when Judah's security was removed (22:8a, which reads literally, "he uncovered the covering of Judah"). The referent of Judah's "covering" is unclear. The term is obviously metaphorical; the underlying reality may be the border defenses or the outlying towns (on the latter, see Smith 2007, 386).

At that time, the nation began to prepare for an invasion. They checked the weapons arsenal located in the "House [NIV11, 'Palace'] of the Forest" (22:8b), perhaps a reference to the royal armory, called the "House of the Forest of Lebanon" (1 Kings 7:2; 10:17, 21; see Wildberger 1997, 367). The prophet uses a second-person masculine singular verbal form in his address (וַתַּבֵּט; "you looked"), but the referent is unclear. Since he has just mentioned Judah, perhaps he addresses the personified nation at this point. Roberts (2015, 288) understands the addressee as the king of Judah. Perhaps we should emend the form to masculine plural (וַתַּבִּיטוּ) considering the prophet's use of seven second-person masculine plural verbal forms in Isaiah 22:9–11.

22:9–11. As the people prepared for the worst, they noticed many breaches in the "walls of the City of David" (22:9a). This prompted them to tear down some of the city's houses to make the (weakened parts of the) wall inaccessible (22:10b). The verb בָּצַר, often translated "to strengthen" (NIV11) or "to fortify" (ESV, HCSB, KJV, NASB), means "be inaccessible" in the *qal* stem. So here, in the *piel* stem, it likely means "make inaccessible" (*HALOT* s.v. "בצר III" 148; Wildberger 1997, 369). To what does this refer? Perhaps they used debris from the demolished houses to plug the gaps (cf. Gray 1912, 371). In conjunction with this demolition operation, it was necessary to count the houses in the city (22:10a). When houses were torn down, their residents would need to be relocated. Counting the number of houses would help those planning the operation since, as Wildberger (1997, 369) points out, the dislodged "would need some place to stay." Another option (Kaiser 1974, 145) is that houses were counted to help plan the relocation of refugees arriving from outside the city.

Water would be essential during a siege. Consequently, the people stored up water in the Lower Pool (22:9b) and built a reservoir between two walls to contain water from the Old Pool (22:11a). King and Stager (2001, 221) suggest this reservoir is the Pool of Siloam. The location of the Lower Pool is uncertain (Wildberger 1997, 368). Roberts (2015, 289) thinks it is the Pool of Siloam. The Old Pool may be the same as the Upper Pool mentioned in 7:3, if the latter is located at the lower end of the Kidron Valley (Wildberger 1997, 370; cf. the commentary on 7:3 above).

All their efforts to provide for their security were shortsighted, for they failed to look in faith to the one who made the Old Pool long ago (22:11b). The third feminine suffixes on עֹשֶׂיהָ, "the one who made *it*," and יֹצְרָהּ, "the one who formed *it*," most naturally refer to the feminine noun בְּרֵכָה, "pool," in the previous clause. However, since a pool (בְּרֵכָה) is man-made, in what sense did the Lord "make" and "form" the Old Pool long ago? Obviously, indirectly, through those whom he enabled providentially to build it many years before. In fact, it is likely the pool is viewed metonymically here. The pool was built to hold water provided by the Lord. It was now serving as the source of the water being collected in the reservoir. The real point is this: the people were working hard to make sure they had life-sustaining water; their focus was on the reservoir fed by the Old Pool, but it should have been on the one who provides the water that led to the Old Pool being constructed in the first place. Another option, if the Old Pool is the antecedent of the suffixes, is that the pool simply stands by synecdoche for the city (cf. 22:10). The people were frantically trying to preserve the city through their own efforts, when they should have looked to the one who built the city long before this, working through human instruments. In any case, ultimately the city's safety did not lie in its defense system and water supply, but in the Lord.

22:12–14. At the time when the people recognized their vulnerability (cf. 22:7–8), the Lord, through his prophet, called upon them to mourn (22:12), probably in conjunction with repentance (cf. Joel 2:12). (See Motyer 1993, 185; Wildberger 1997, 372; Young 1969, 102) Instead, they adopted a fatalistic "eat, drink, and be merry, for tomorrow we die" attitude and enjoyed a feast (Isa. 22:13; cf. 22:2). Though they had tried to strengthen the city's defenses, deep down they were pessimistic about their future. As Smith (2007, 388) points out, they should have been preserving their food and wine for the siege ahead. Their failure to do so suggests they believed the city would be taken and they would die. This pessimism was the result of their mindset. They were trusting in their own efforts, which they regarded as inadequate, rather than in the Lord (Motyer 1993, 185).

The Lord considered the people's response sinful. Speaking as the Master, the Lord of Armies (NIV11, "the Lord, the LORD Almighty"), he solemnly announces that this sin would not be atoned for until they died. In other words, death was inevitable (Young 1969, 104). Ironically, however, the Lord in his great mercy did deliver the city. However, before elaborating, we must first look at the historical setting of this prophecy.

A close reading of the passage strongly suggests this message was given during the siege of Jerusalem after Sennacherib's invasion of Judah in 701 B.C., but before the Lord miraculously delivered the city (see Isa. 37–38). A review of the details is in order:

1. The people of Jerusalem were carousing, as if celebrating a victory (22:1b–2a, 13a). But this was not because the Assyrians had left or been defeated. No, the people were convinced their doom was inevitable, so they decided to adopt the "eat, drink, and be merry, for tomorrow we die" attitude (22:13b). The irony of 22:1b, where the people are carousing on rooftops, now comes into focus. Elsewhere, lamentation occurs on rooftops (Isa. 15:3; Jer. 48:38). That did not seem to be the case in Jerusalem, but the carousing was just a poor substitute for genuine lamentation.

2. An enemy invader, with soldiers that came from distant foreign places (Isa. 22:6), invaded the land with their chariots and captured cities (22:5, 7a). The prophet's description reflects Sennacherib's invasion of Judah (cf. Isa. 1:7–8). In his account of the invasion, Sennacherib boasted that he "besieged forty-six" of Hezekiah's "walled cities and surrounding smaller towns, which were without number." He describes how he breached the walls, conquered the cities, and took 200,150 people captive, along with numerous livestock (*COS* 2.119B:303).

3. With their outer defenses gone (22:8a), the people knew Jerusalem was vulnerable, so they frantically tried to shore up the city's defenses and water supply (22:8b–11a).

4. But the enemy advanced to the very gate of the city (22:7b) and began the siege. Many died from starvation (22:2b) and those leaders who tried to escape were captured (22:3).

5. It was a time for lamentation and repentance (22:4, 12), but the people were looking only to their paltry efforts at self-defense, which they knew would fail. Consequently, the Lord gave them over to judgment, for he regarded their failure to turn to him as sin (22:14).

As one can readily see from the details, the passage fits very well in the context of Sennacherib's siege in 701 B.C. As such, it appears to come from the same time as Isaiah 1:2–20 (see above).

So, how did all of this turn out? Ironically, despite the people's faithless, sinful response to the Assyrian crisis, the Lord delivered the city from Sennacherib, forcing the Assyrian king to retreat to his homeland (see Isa. 37:36–38). Hezekiah humbled himself before the Lord, prompting the Lord to show mercy. Despite the oath he took (22:14), the Lord did not bring destruction on the city, at least at this time. This indicates that the oath, despite sounding like an unconditional verdict of judgment, was implicitly conditional. Yes, if the situation stayed unchanged, judgment would inevitably fall. But repentance could prompt the Lord to alter his plan and extend mercy (cf. Jer. 18:1–8). Micah, Isaiah's contemporary, announced around this same time that Jerusalem would become a heap of ruins, resembling a plowed field (Mic. 3:12). Yet the leaders of Judah in Jeremiah's time recalled that Hezekiah's humble intercession prompted the Lord to relent from judgment (Jer. 26:17–19).

22:15. The second literary unit within the oracle begins with the Lord commissioning the prophet to deliver a message to Shebna, a royal official.

The use of the title "the Master, the Lord of Armies" (NIV11, "the Lord, the LORD Almighty") facilitates the transition from the preceding unit. Shebna is a called a "steward" and described as being "over the house [palace]" (see NIV11, "the palace administrator"). The term סֹכֵן, "steward," is well-attested in cognate languages, where it is used of a prefect, overseer, or administrator (see *HALOT* s.v. "סֹכֵן" 755; Wildberger 1997, 384). The personal name Shebna is attested outside the Old Testament (see *HALOT* s.v. "שֶׁבְנָא" 1395) and appears in 2 Kings 18:18, 37; 19:2; and Isaiah 36:3, 22; 37:2, where it is used of a governmental scribe during Hezekiah's time. It is not certain if this is the same individual mentioned in Isaiah 22:15.

22:16. The message proper begins, as the preceding literary unit did, with a question challenging Shebna's behavior.

The force of the initial questions (literally, "What to you here? Who to you here?") appears to be: What right do you have to be here? Shebna had apparently constructed an impressive grave for himself, hewed and chiseled out of rock, as a sign of his status in the royal court. Interpreters wrestle with the reason for Isaiah's condemnation of Shebna, but it seems apparent that Shebna's pride of position is the reason for the prophet's denunciation (see 22:18; cf. Motyer 1993, 187). His pride, furthermore, epitomized what was wrong with the nation. Young (1969, 105) states that Isaiah "gives an example of the self-centeredness and luxury-loving attitude of the people as it is exemplified in a single individual, and that an individual of responsibility."

22:17–19. The prophet, after making sure he has Shebna's attention (note הִנֵּה, "look"), addresses him as a "man (in his strength)" (see *HALOT* s.v. "גֶּבֶר" 175; cf. NIV11, "mighty man"), probably with a sarcastic tone intended (see Motyer 1993, 188; Smith 2007, 391). He tells Shebna that the Lord is ready to remove him from his position. He uses a great deal of verbal repetition to highlight the official's punishment (22:17–18a). This is best demonstrated through the following literal translations:

(1) "The Lord is about to hurl you away (with) hurling" (the *pilpel* participle of טוּל, "throw," followed by an otherwise unattested noun, טַלְטֵלָה, related to the verb טוּל).

(2) "And (he) is about to wrap you, wrapping" (*qal* participle from עָטָה, "wrap," followed by the *qal* infinitive absolute of the same verb,

used for emphasis). Roberts (2015, 294) explains that the verb, in light of the imagery of throwing, "conveys the sense of wrapping or wadding up a garment tightly so that one is able to throw it away. In this case, it would imply that Yahweh was discarding Shebna as a piece of used and useless old clothing."

(3) "Winding he will wind you up (with) winding" (the *qal* infinitive absolute of צָנַף, "wind up," followed by the *qal* imperfect of the same verb and an otherwise unattested noun, צְנֵפָה, related to the verb צָנַף). However, in this third clause, there appears to be an ellipsis, with the verb used in a pregnant sense, "will wind you up (and throw you)." *HALOT* (s.vv. "צָנַף I, II" 1039) offers two options for the verb צָנַף: "wind up," or "sling." "Wind up" fits well with the second line ("wrap"), but "sling" makes for a good parallel with the first line ("hurl"). Either verb works with "like a ball," but "sling" fits better with "to a wide land." Roberts (2015, 292, 294) may be correct in seeing both homonyms here: "Wadding you up, he will sling you away energetically [with a slinging]." In this case, the arrangement of verbs within 22:17–18a is chiastic: throw-wrap-wrap-throw.

In any event, Shebna will be sent off into exile, along with the chariots that brought him so much prestige (כָּבוֹד, "glory"), and die there (22:18b). This is appropriate for one who brings disgrace to the royal family (cf. "your master's house") through his arrogant actions and/or his miserable end. For rhetorical impact, the Lord then speaks directly to Shebna, stating he will personally remove (note the first-person form of הָדַף, literally, "push away") the official from his position in the royal court (22:19). He will be torn down from his office.

22:20–22. The Lord, speaking in the first person (cf. 22:19a) informs Shebna: "I will summon my servant, Eliakim son of Hilkiah" (22:20). The Lord will take Shebna's robe and belt, symbols of his authority, and put them on Eliakim as he transfers authority to him (22:21a). Eliakim will become a "father" to the residents of Jerusalem and Judah (22:21b). "Father" is used metaphorically here for a leader, representing the king, who protects those under his authority, as a father protects his children (see Job 29:16; Isa. 9:6 [HB 7]; see Young 1969, 113–14). The Lord will place on Eliakim's shoulder the "key to the house of David," to which he will have the authority to give or withhold access (22:22). As Roberts (2015, 295) points out, the key in view was "a large key that locked and unlocked the lockable doors in the palace complex." Roberts explains that attaching the key to his shoulder was probably "a sign of authority" as well as "a convenient way to keep track of the tool."

Eliakim son of Hilkiah and Shebna are mentioned together elsewhere in conjunction with Sennacherib's siege of Jerusalem in 701 B.C. In these texts Eliakim is said to be עַל הַבָּיִת, "over the house," while Shebna is listed as a scribe (see 2 Kings 18:18, 26, 37; 19:2 = Isa. 36:3, 11, 22; 37:2). Consequently, this prophecy concerning Eliakim must have been given prior to this event. If Shebna the scribe is the same individual addressed in Isaiah 22:15–25, then his demotion is apparent (see Roberts 2015, 292). There is no reference, however, to his humiliating exile (cf. Isa. 22:17–19). It is possible that Shebna the scribe was a different individual than the Shebna the steward, who was over the palace before Eliakim (Seitz 1993, 160).

22:23–24. The Lord states he will give Eliakim stability and honor. He will be secure, like a peg driven into a solid wall (22:23a), and bring honor to his father's family (22:23b). His relatives, compared to growth from the ground or a plant (22:24a), will benefit from his high status, though they are undeserving of such positions and prestige. They are compared to small, or ordinary, bowls and jars hanging from the secure peg (22:24b; see Wildberger 1997, 400).

This likely alludes to nepotism, where unqualified persons receive positions simply because of whom they know, not because of their skill (Roberts 2015, 295; Young 1969, 117). Another option is that 22:24 describes how the people will lean on this official for stability, when they should be leaning on the Lord. Human leaders, no matter how commendable, are not capable of bearing such weight (see Clements 1980, 191; Motyer 1993, 188). However, it is unclear why, in this case, the people would be compared to shoots and leaves that are closely connected to Eliakim's father's house (22:24a).

Oswalt (1986, 423) prefers to see 22:24 more positively. Eliakim is such a reliable person that others, even the insignificant, find stability in him. But Oswalt must admit that the announcement of Eliakim's fall in 22:25 is abrupt in this case. If 22:24 is transitional in the way explained above, the abruptness disappears. Smith (2007, 393) argues similarly, stating 22:24 is "simply saying that everything and everyone will depend on" Eliakim. He contends that "in that day" at the beginning of 22:25 marks a structural boundary and that 22:25 is a "separate oracle" (see also Childs 2000, 162). He must admit, however, that in this case "no reason is given to explain why this peg will fall to the ground." The phrase "in that day," while highlighting the judgment and marking it as structurally distinct, does not necessarily signal a new oracle. Conceptually the phrase links what follows with what precedes, as is evident by the continuation of the imagery of the peg driven into a solid place.

22:25. No matter how one understands 22:24, it is apparent Eliakim's success will not last (22:25). The peg driven into the wall (cf. 22:23) will break off due to the sheer weight of the many bowls and jars hanging from it. Everything crashes to the floor below. This apparently refers to a time when Eliakim, and those benefitting from their relationship to him, will lose their positions in the royal court.

Some regard 22:24–25 as a later addition. For example, Roberts (2015, 295) states: "It is unlikely that in an oracle of judgment against Shebna, Isaiah would promise his office to Eliakim and then, in the same oracle, announce the collapse of Eliakim's office." But if 22:24 refers to nepotism, as Roberts argues, then, contrary to Roberts's assumption, this is not so much an oracle against Shebna as it is an oracle against the self-serving pride of leaders. This attitude is exhibited by Shebna for sure, but Isaiah also anticipates it in Eliakim. The real point is that the royal court of Judah had become corrupt. The Lord will, in turn, deal with the proud leaders of the covenant community, in the immediate future and beyond.

Judgment on Tyre (23:1–18)

23:1. Following the heading, which identifies Tyre as the focal point of the oracle, the prophet addresses the ships of Tarshish (cf. Isa. 2:16). King and Stager (2001, 184) observe that the ships of Tarshish are "associated with both maritime trade and metals" (cf. Isa. 23:1–3; Ezek. 27:25). These ships could make long journeys (1 Kings 10:22; 22:48 [HB 49]; 2 Chron. 9:21; Isa. 60:9). Most likely they are called "ships of Tarshish" here and in Ezekiel 27:25 because they were capable of sailing there (Lessing 2004, 140). The precise location of Tarshish is uncertain, the most likely options being Tartessus in Spain or Tarsus in modern Turkey. In 1999 archaeologists discovered two Phoenician ships that were wrecked at sea sometime between 750 and 700 B.C. Each was transporting over twelve tons of wine at the time it sank. The ships were about sixteen meters (approximately fifty-three feet) long and six meters (approximately twenty feet) wide. Reliefs from Sennacherib's palace depict such ships leaving the harbor at Tyre (King and Stager 2001, 178–85).

The prophet tells the ships to wail because the harbor of Tyre would be destroyed and no longer available to them. The syntax is difficult. The text reads literally, "for it is destroyed from a house, from entering." Perhaps the *mem* prefixed to "house" (cf. מִבַּיִת) was originally enclitic and suffixed to the preceding verb. In this case, one can read "house" as the masculine singular subject of the masculine singular verb "destroyed, devastated." Otherwise, there is no stated subject; it is unlikely that Tyre, mentioned in the heading, is the subject, since Tyre is portrayed as feminine throughout the following oracle. It is unclear why Tyre would be referred to as a "house." Apparently, "house" is metaphorical here, perhaps depicting Tyre as a haven for the trading ships that travel the sea. The מִן on בּוֹא, "entering," here indicates negative consequence, "so as not to enter" (see GKC, 382 §119y). Tyre is thus depicted as a ruined house that no one can even enter anymore.

The final line of Isaiah 23:1b reads literally, "from the land of Kittim it has been revealed to them." The land of Kittim is Cyprus, from which a message came regarding the fall of Tyre. But what is the antecedent of the third-person masculine plural suffix (cf. לָמוֹ, "to them")? Apparently it is the "ships," which have been addressed with a masculine plural imperative earlier in the verse. As noted earlier, this incongruity in gender may be due to the prophet envisioning the "ships" metonymically; it is the sailors or merchants who are called to lament when the bad news reaches them from Cyprus (Lessing 2004, 142).

23:2–3. Isaiah next addresses the residents of the coast and the merchants of Sidon, located north of Tyre. The "coast" (אִי) probably refers here to the Mediterranean coast north (as suggested by the reference to Sidon) and perhaps even south (cf. Isa. 20:6) of Tyre, though some translate as "island" and understand Tyre as the addressee.

The prophet calls them to lament. The verb דֹּמּוּ (from דָּמַם) has traditionally been understood to mean, "be silent" (cf. ESV, KJV, NASB, NIV11), as a sign of sorrow. However, some propose here a homonymic דָּמַם, meaning "wail, lament" (*HALOT* s.v. "דמם II" 226; cf. HCSB), which would correspond conceptually to "wail" in 23:1b and in 23:6, where the residents of the coast are addressed, as in 23:2. (For a defense of this reading, see Wildberger 1997, 406; Oswalt 1986, 430. For a defense of the reading "be silent," see Gray 1912, 387, 389; Lessing 2004, 142.)

The last form in 23:2 (מִלְאוּךְ) has generated discussion. As it stands, it reads, "they have filled you [feminine singular]." But who are the subject and the addressee, and how does the verb relate syntactically to what precedes? One option is to read "Merchant(s) of Sidon, (who) pass over (the) sea, have filled you (with merchandise)." In this case one can either (1) take the singular forms סֹחֵר and עֹבֵר as collective with the plural verb bringing out the implied plurality of the collective subject (Young 1969, 123 n. 5), or (2) emend סֹחֵר to סֹחֲרֵי (plural construct) and עֹבֵר to עֹבְרֵי (plural construct) or to עֹבְרִים (assuming haplography of the *yod-mem* sequence in MT; note the following יָם, "sea"). In either case, the addressee would seemingly be Tyre, which has not been specifically mentioned thus far, apart from the heading. This is problematic because it entails an abrupt shift in addressee from the residents of the coast (23:2a) to Tyre in 23:2b. Furthermore, it appears Tyre is then referred to in the third person in 23:3.

There are still other options, if one retains the verb at the end of 23:2: (1) "Merchant(s) of Sidon (and) those who pass over the sea have filled you." In this case, סֹחֵר and עֹבֵר, rather than being appositional, are distinct entities, and can serve as the compound subject of the plural verb. (2) "Merchants of Sidon crossed the sea [reading the perfect עָבְרוּ; cf. 1QIs[a] and 4Q55 (4QIs[a]); see Roberts 2015, 299], they filled you." But the problem of the feminine addressee remains in either case.

Dead Sea scroll 1QIs[a] reads "your messengers" at the end of 23:2. If we follow this lead, it is preferable to emend the text to מַלְאָכָו, "his messengers" (with a defectively written form of the third-person masculine singular suffix). This would entail understanding a metathesis of *waw* and *kaph* or eliminating the *waw* before *kaph* and taking the initial *waw* from the beginning of the next form. One can then collocate the resulting form with the prepositional phrase at the beginning of 23:3 and read, "his messengers (are) on abundant waters." (For a discussion of other proposals made by interpreters, see Wildberger 1997, 406.)

If one retains the traditional verse division, 23:3a would read, "and on abundant waters the seed of Shihor, the harvest of the Nile, (is) her yield." Shihor probably refers to one of the eastern branches of the Nile or to a lake in the eastern delta. In parallel with יְאוֹר, "the Nile," it may refer (through a part for whole style) to the Nile (cf. Jer. 2:18). (See the discussion in *HALOT* s.v. "שִׁחוֹר" 1457). At any rate, the Egyptians shipped their grain via the sea to Tyre and sold it there.

The third-person feminine singular suffix on "yield" (תְּבוּאָתָהּ) probably refers to Tyre, which has not been specifically mentioned yet, apart from the heading. If Tyre is the referent, then the city is also the subject of the third-person feminine singular verb in 23:3b (וַתְּהִי, "and she was"), which identifies it as "the trading profit" [or "merchandise"] of the nations. (NIV11 has "marketplace.") "Trading profit" (סַחַר) stands by metonymy for the city where traders from various nations buy and sell for a profit.

R. Reed Lessing (2004, 214) summarizes 23:1–3 as follows: "Taking vv 1–3 together, the idea is that the ships of Tarshish, the most honored ships in the known world, were transporting the most famous crop (wheat) from the most famous land (Egypt) and placing it in the most desired harbor in the Mediterranean world, the island of Tyre. No better situation could exist for the Phoenicians. But this would collapse because soon there would be no more harbor."

23:4–5. Having mentioned the merchant(s) of Sidon (cf. 23:2), the prophet now addresses the personified city of Sidon, urging her to "be ashamed." A reason is then given. The text reads, literally, "for (the) sea, the fortress of the sea, has said, saying" (23:4a). The syntax is problematic: Is "fortress of the sea" in apposition to "sea" or is it adverbial, "(to) the fortress of the sea"? Furthermore, the identity of the "fortress of the sea" is uncertain. Is it Tyre? (See Young 1969, 125.)

The content and meaning of the quotation is cryptic (23:4b). It reads, literally, "I have not been in labor and have not given birth and have not raised young men (and) have (not) brought up young women" (the negative particle is omitted by ellipsis in the second line). The speaker appears to be lamenting the fact she has not given birth and, consequently, has not had the opportunity to raise children. But what is the point and how is this a cause of shame to Sidon? Perhaps the sea (or the fortress of the sea = Tyre?), by comparing itself to an unproductive barren woman, is lamenting it can no longer produce merchandise for Sidon and others.[2] Consequently, Sidon will no longer enjoy the reputation and wealth it has achieved, making it ashamed of its diminished status (see Wildberger 1997, 425–26). This makes excellent sense if Tyre is speaking as the "fortress of the sea," or is addressed by the personified sea, since Tyre was the city to and through whom the wealth of nations flowed over the sea.

Isaiah 23:5 is a bit more straightforward. When the report of Tyre's fall reaches Egypt, the Egyptians will "be in labor" (NIV11, "be in anguish") at the news. In other words, the bad news, with its economic implications, will cause the Egyptians to writhe in their distress, much like a woman giving labor. The metaphor emphasizes the severe negative emotional impact the report will have. The use of the verb יָחִילוּ (from חִיל) plays off חַלְתִּי (from חִיל), "I have (not) been in labor," in the previous verse (see Young

---

2 Lessing (2004, 214) understands the children as colonies.

1969, 126). Though the details are not entirely clear, it appears that the failure of the sea (or fortress of the sea) to be in labor and produce children will, ironically, cause the Egyptians to go into labor as it were (Lessing 2004, 216).

23:6–7. The prophet again addresses the residents of the coast (cf. 23:2), urging them to travel to Tarshish and wail (23:6). Perhaps this means they are to join Tarshish (cf. 23:10) in lamenting Tyre's fall, but it may be a warning to flee far away (Young 1969, 127), for Tyre's fate will extend to the entire region of Canaan (Phoenicia; see 23:11). The residents of the coast are asked rhetorically if this is the city in which they rejoice (23:7a). The city is then described as ancient and as having a vast scope of economic influence (23:7b).

23:8–9. The prophet now asks and then answers a question. He asks who has planned the downfall of Tyre. Before answering, he describes Tyre's widespread influence. She has a royal aura about her, as one who wears (or perhaps, bestows) crowns. Her merchants are princes, and her traders are honored in the earth. The prophet now answers his question: the Lord of Armies (NIV11, 'Lord Almighty') has planned Tyre's downfall. He has done so to dishonor Tyre's pride and bring low all who are honored in the earth (identified as Tyre's traders in 23:8).

23:10–11. The prophet has addressed the ships of Tarshish (23:1); he now speaks to personified "Daughter Tarshish" herself. It is not clear exactly what the prophet says, let alone means, in 23:10. The Hebrew text reads literally, "Cross over, your land, like the Nile, daughter of Tarshish, there is no longer a waist belt." If the verb "cross over" (עִבְרִי) is retained, perhaps the prophet urges Tarshish to overflow her own land, as the Nile does in Egypt. The second half of the verse then makes the point there is nothing restraining her (the restraint is likened to a belt) from doing so. Translators following this line of interpretation include ESV ("cross over your land like the Nile, O daughter of Tarshish; there is no restraint anymore"), HCSB, and NASB. But what would be the point of Tarshish overflowing her own land? Furthermore, what is the reality behind the restraint that has been removed? And how would this exhortation relate to the theme of the oracle, Tyre's fall?

Young (1969, 131) understands this to mean that Tarshish, and all of Tyre's colonies, are now free from her "restraining hand" (see also Motyer 1993, 191–92). But this makes Tyre's fall something to celebrate. This is contrary to the mood of the context, where Tyre's fall affects the nations negatively (see 23:11).

The LXX and 1QIs^a read "work" (= Hebrew עִבְדִי) at the beginning of 23:10. (*Dalet-resh* confusion would explain MT.) The point may be that Tarshish should now engage in agriculture, just as the Egyptians do along the Nile. Why? Perhaps because with Tyre fallen, Tarshish can no longer trade for Egyptian produce formerly sold in Tyre. If one follows this reading, then מֵזַח, "belt," in 23:10b should probably be emended to מָחוֹז, "harbor" (see Ps. 107:30 and *HALOT* s.v. "מָחוֹזָה" 568; an error of transposition would explain MT) or understood as an Egyptian loanword referring here to ship construction (see *HALOT* s.v. "מֵזַח" 565). The NIV11 reflects this interpretation: "Till your land as they do along the Nile, Daughter Tarshish, for you no longer have a harbor." If one retains מֵזַח with the meaning "belt," it may be Tyre is viewed as a source of defense. As Gray (1912, 391) points out, in Job 12:21 removing the belt (מְזִיחַ, not מֵזַח) causes one to be disarmed and defenseless (see Smith 2007, 401–2).

The meaning of Isaiah 23:11 is clearer: someone (presumably the Lord, mentioned in 23:11b and in 23:9) has stretched his hand over the sea (the Mediterranean is in view) and caused kingdoms to tremble. How has he done this? By issuing a command that the fortresses of Canaan (= Phoenicia, which includes first and foremost Tyre) be destroyed. (The prepositional phrase אֶל־כְּנַעַן after צִוָּה, "command," here does not mean "to Canaan" but rather "regarding Canaan.") The destruction of Phoenicia will have a negative economic impact upon the nations, explaining why they will tremble when Canaan is destroyed.

23:12–13. With the scope of the judgment broadened to include the entire Phoenician coast (23:11), it is natural that Sidon, located north of Tyre, would again be addressed (cf. 23:4–5). Addressing her, literally, as "the oppressed one, Virgin Daughter Sidon," the Lord informs the city she will no longer exult. He sarcastically urges her to arise and cross over to Cyprus (Kittim), but then states she will find no rest there.

He next draws her attention to the land of the Chaldeans. The Assyrians attacked it and reduced it to a pile of ruins, inhabited by wild animals. This may refer to Sennacherib's destruction of Babylon in 689 B.C. (Oswalt 1986, 434–35). However, since the *land* of the Chaldeans is mentioned, it could refer to an earlier Assyrian invasion of the region (Roberts 2015, 302; Smith 2007, 396). (For a discussion of the setting of the oracle, see below.) At any rate, the Phoenician coast awaits the same destiny as the land of the Chaldeans.

The text of 23:13 poses several problems. As it stands, it reads: "Look (at) the land of the Chaldeans! This, the people, was not. Assur founded it [feminine] for desert animals. They raised his siege towers. They laid bare its [feminine] fortresses. He made it [feminine] into a ruin." The second line should probably be translated: "This (is) the people (that) is not," referring to the fact the Chaldeans have lost their status as a people. The negated perfect (לֹא הָיָה) can refer to a present reality (cf. Isa. 15:6). The verb "founded" (יְסָדָהּ, NIV11, "made it") normally refers to building and establishing a place. Here it is used sarcastically; the Assyrians have "founded," as it were, a place for the desert animals to live, ironically by making the land (the antecedent of the feminine singular suffix on the verb) no longer habitable for people (see Roberts 2015, 302).

The variation between masculine singular and plural is particularly puzzling. The statement "they raised up his siege towers" seems awkward; one would expect agreement between the verb and pronominal suffix in number (either "they raised up their siege towers" [cf. NIV11] or "he raised up his siege towers"), and some emend the text accordingly. As it stands, the plural subject would probably be the Assyrian soldiers (not specifically mentioned prior to this) who carry out the campaign of Assur (the antecedent of the third-person masculine singular pronoun on "siege towers"), viewed as a collective entity. (For a similar variation between singular references to Assur and a plural apparently referring to Assur's soldiers, see Isa. 10:24.) It is possible that behind Assur, the name of Assyria, is the Assyrian king (Roberts 2015, 302) or, more likely, the Assyrian god who is so named. A Neo-Assyrian seal shows Assur as a winged warrior who shoots a bow above the king's chariot as the king directs an attack on a walled city (*ANEP*, no. 536 with commentary on p. 314). There is actually an alternating pattern in the text as it stands: "*Ashur* founded it . . . *they* raised *his* siege towers. *They* laid bare. . . . *He* [Ashur] made it into a ruin."

23:14. This first literary unit ends as it began, with the prophet calling upon the personified ships of Tarshish to wail (cf. 23:1). The reason for weeping is stated more directly than in 23:1; quite simply, the ships should wail because their fortress has been destroyed. In this context the "fortress" probably refers to Tyre (cf. 23:4), viewed as a haven for the trading ships. Lessing (2004, 221) argues the *inclusio* highlights the oracle's main theme—Tyre's demise. Furthermore, he proposes that the addition of "your fortress" in 23:14 focuses "attention on what Tyre had lost, namely the fortress that protected her vast fleet of ships," which in turn "were the symbol of her strength, glory, and honor." He adds, "The rhetorical effect is that Tyre's greatest asset will be impotent and useless."

23:15–16. Following Tyre's destruction (cf. 23:14), it will be forgotten for seventy years, measured precisely just as the "days" of a typical king would be. The comparison to a "king's days" (NIV11, "king's life") suggests specificity, for the events of a king's "days" were carefully recorded in royal annals (cf. 1 Kings 14:29; see Motyer 1993, 193). The point is not that a king typically lived or reigned for seventy years, but rather, the prophesied seventy years would be carefully recorded and measured just as the typical king's days would be. Yet following this lengthy period Tyre will experience a revival. The prophet compares the city to a prostitute, probably because she was, as a trading center, involved with so many foreign nations in her effort to gain material wealth (Young 1969, 138). Isaiah refers to "the song of the prostitute," perhaps a well-known song that urges a prostitute who has been forgotten to take up her harp and sing some songs to regain the attention of people (including potential clients, one would presume).

23:17–18. When Tyre's time of judgment has ended, the Lord himself will intervene on her behalf. Though it may be offensive to modern ears, the prophet extends the metaphor of the prostitute. Tyre will be like a prostitute who returns to her lucrative profession. The reality behind the image is the restoration of Tyre as a trading port where "all the kingdoms on the face of the earth" come to buy and sell. But Tyre will not be allowed to hoard her wealth. Her profits will be set apart to the Lord, who in turn passes on the wealth to those who live (or sit) in his presence (cf. Judg. 20:26; 2 Sam. 7:18; as well as 1 Sam. 1:22; Ezek. 44:3). Perhaps this refers to priests (Wildberger 1997, 437), though all the citizens of Jerusalem (cf. Isa. 4:2; see Hayes and Irvine 1987, 293; Kaiser 1974, 172; Motyer 1993, 194) or even the entire nation of Israel (cf. Isa. 61:6; cf. Gray 1912, 396) may be in view. This seems to presuppose Tyre will become a vassal state to Judah.

> **Set Apart to the Lord**
>
> Various things are described as "set apart" (i.e., holy; cf. קֹדֶשׁ לַיהוָה) for the Lord, including the Sabbath (Exod. 16:23; 31:15), the priest's breastplate (Exod. 28:36; 39:30), private property (such as a house or field; Lev. 27:14, 21, 23), and tithes of produce or animals (Lev. 27:30, 32). Here Tyre's economic profits are set apart to the Lord, meaning they will be offered as tribute to him. The imagery of a prostitute's profits being set apart to the Lord as holy is a bit shocking, especially considering Deuteronomy 23:18, which prohibits the earnings of a prostitute being offered to the Lord. However, the prophet is speaking metaphorically here (Tyre's economic profit being compared to a prostitute's wages), not literally. Though the metaphor seems to cast the Lord in an unsavory role, the point is clear: Tyre will become a subject in the Lord's kingdom and her economic wealth will be devoted to positive ends. See Oswalt 1986, 437; Young 1969, 140.

Scholars have reached no consensus on the background of this oracle. Oswalt (1986, 428) points out that "Tyre came under attack five different times from Isaiah's time to 332 B.C." These include Sennacherib (701), Esarhaddon (679–671), Nebuchadnezzar (585–573), Artaxerxes III Ochus (343), and Alexander the Great (332). If one assumes the prophecy depicts the destruction of Tyre and insists on a literal fulfillment of it, then we must look to Alexander's conquest, for only he leveled the city (see Motyer 1993, 192). However, one wonders if such an interpretation is required. The focus of the oracle is Tyre's loss of status and influence as a commercial center. References to destruction may be taken as hyperbolic. Though some have argued that the attack of Nebuchadnezzar (see Seitz 1993, 168–69, who draws parallels between the oracle and Ezek. 26–28) or that of Artaxerxes III Ochus (Kaiser 1974, 162) are in view, it is better to place the oracle in Isaiah's time, if at all possible.

Sennacherib brought the Phoenician coast under his control and besieged Tyre for five years. The Sidonian king Lulli fled to Cyprus (cf. Isa. 23:12; see *COS* 2119B:302). The Assyrians dominated the area until around 630 B.C. Esarhaddon forced the king of Tyre, Baal, to submit to a vassal treaty (*ANET*, 533–41; for a summary of Esarhaddon's dealings with Tyre, see Wildberger 1997, 418–19). Eventually Tyre gained its independence, approximately seventy years (cf. 23:17) after Sennacherib established Assyrian control over the city and region. (See Erlandsson 1970, 101–2; Lessing 2004, 169–97; Motyer 1993, 193; Roberts 2015, 301–3; Sweeney 1996, 307–10.) Some reject Isaianic authorship of the oracle and prefer to date it to the time of Esarhaddon rather than Sennacherib. (See Clements 1980, 191–92; Wildberger 1997, 417–19. For a refutation of this view, see Sweeney 1996, 308–9.)

If the final prophecy depicts a time when Tyre becomes subject to Judah, it moves beyond Isaiah's time. Tyre was an ally of Judah under Josiah, but the latter did not rule it. Indeed, before too long, the Babylonians would move in and fill the vacuum left by Assyria. It is likely then, that the portrait of the Lord's rule over Tyre moves ahead to a time when the Lord reigns over the nations (see chs. 24–27; cf. 19:23–25). "Tyre" is retained for purposes of contextualizing the prophecy for Isaiah and his contemporaries. But the main point here is that the great commercial centers of the earth will one day be subject to the Lord's rule over the world (see Childs 2000, 166–67, 169).

THEOLOGICAL FOCUS

The Lord judges the enemies of his people and makes the covenant community secure as he establishes Jerusalem and installs a just Davidic king. The Holy One of Israel will demonstrate his sovereignty over the nations by defeating them. It makes no sense for his covenant people to worship foreign gods, to trust in alliances with nations, or to fear powerful multinational empires. Judgment will remind the Lord's covenant community that he alone is their creator, savior, and protector. The Lord's people should trust in the Lord for security, for he will someday rule the nations from Jerusalem and even powerful archenemies will join Israel in worshipping the one true God. As the prophet develops this theological theme, the following emphases emerge:

The Lord's sovereignty over the nations

The Lord's sovereignty extends over the neighboring states to the west (Philistia) and east (Moab), who had a false sense of security (cf. 14:28; 16:6). He will attack both countries, using a powerful invader as his instrument of punishment (cf. 14:29–31; 15:9; 16:11). The Moabites will turn to their god for deliverance but end up disappointed (15:2; 16:12), for the Lord alone controls the destiny of nations. The Lord demonstrates his sovereignty over the nations by judging the Cushites and Egyptians. The divine name and title Yahweh of Armies appears nine times in these chapters, stressing Yahweh's military power and kingship (18:7; 19:4, 12, 16–18, 20, 25). Judgment is severe, but as is often the case in the prophetic oracles it is followed by restoration. Beyond judgment, the Lord eventually makes Cush, Egypt, and even Assyria his loyal subjects. The distant Cushites will bring tribute to the Lord (18:7) and the Egyptians will recognize the Lord as their king and bring him offerings (19:18–22). A day will come when archenemies Egypt and Assyria will join with Israel in serving the Lord, the one true God (19:23–25).

The Lord of Armies determines the destiny of nations. He planned Tyre's downfall, yet he would eventually restore Tyre and exercise authority over it (23:17–18). The theme of the Lord's "planning" the destiny of nations was introduced earlier in the oracles concerning Babylon and Egypt. The Lord planned the demise of Assyria (14:24, cf. 14:25–26) as part of a larger plan for the nations (14:26–27). This plan encompassed Egypt (19:12, 17) and Tyre (23:8). As we have seen so often in these oracles, the Lord abhors pride and opposes those who view themselves as high and mighty. He planned Tyre's downfall to bring low the pride of the city and its trading partners (23:8–9).

The deliverance of the Lord's covenant people

The Lord will bring an invader against Judah's neighbors, but he will protect his covenant people. He made Jerusalem secure so his needy, oppressed people could find refuge there (14:32; cf. 14:30a). Indeed, Moab's only hope was to seek refuge in Zion's ruler (16:1), for the Lord will bring down the oppressive destroyer in conjunction with establishing a Davidic ruler's kingdom of justice (16:4b–5). The Master, the Sovereign Lord of Armies, expects his covenant people to repent of sin in response to his discipline. When discipline comes, the Lord's people sometimes look to their own strength and ingenuity for security. But such attempts at self-preservation are doomed. When they fail, the Lord's people must not become pessimistic about their future but turn instead to the only one who can deliver them.

The Lord as savior and protector of his people

The Lord alone is the creator, savior, and protector of his covenant community. He judges Israel because they have sought security in an alliance with Aram, forgetting that the Lord is their savior and protector (rock). But when judgment has fallen, survivors will reject their idols and trust in the one who created the covenant community and exercises sovereign control over it. He demonstrates his ability to protect his people by turning back the raging nations. Since the Lord will judge Egypt and Cush in the immediate future, the Lord's people should not place their trust in these nations. Rather than looking to nations for security, the covenant community should trust in the Lord, for he is sovereign over the nations and will eventually receive their worship (see esp. 20:5–6). The Lord is the sole source of true blessing and security (19:23–25). Consequently, rather than fearing or trusting in alliances with nations for security, the Lord's people should trust in the Sovereign Lord who determines the destiny of nations.

PREACHING AND TEACHING STRATEGIES

Exegetical and Theological Synthesis

Due to the length of this preaching unit (nine chapters), the preacher/teacher will likely have to make some difficult decisions about which passages/verses to address directly and which to leave out due to time constraints. There will almost certainly be chapters or sections that you will not even be able to read, much less explain. Instead, we suggest that you provide more of a ten-thousand-foot view for most of this section, and strategically unpack a few of the pericopes in more detail. Additionally, the preacher/teacher will want to determine which themes to focus on when constructing the sermon/lesson, as there are various directions one could take with a passage this large.

We feel that it would be best to focus on the places where the theme of God's future worldwide, messianic kingdom is highlighted. While this section's predominant theme is that of judgment against the nations of the world (including God's own people Israel and Judah), many of these judgment oracles include hopeful statements predicting or alluding to the nations' future involvement in God's messianic kingdom. As such, we see that God's judgments here are redemptive, not merely punitive in nature. They set out to correct sinful behavior, not merely to condemn it. The result of God's judgments against the nations (including Israel and Judah) will be to reclaim these groups for himself. God will create converts and worshippers from among these nations that he judges.

Our analysis of this passage will provide a brief summary of each of the separate units within the broader unit, giving particular attention to those verses where God's redemption of the nations in his future worldwide kingdom is in view.

Isaiah 14:28–32: Judgment predicted against Philistia

King Ahaz of Judah had cooperated with Assyria to afflict Philistia. Thus, the Philistines rejoiced when they heard of Ahaz's death. They likely hoped that his successor would be friendlier to them. However, the prophet warned Philistia that their rejoicing was premature, for their situation would get worse. Philistia would be ravaged by a military invasion and defeat (14:31), accompanied by famine (14:30) leading to widespread death as God judged them.

Nonetheless, this oracle ends with a sentiment of hope as the poor and needy (cf. 14:30), whom the prophet refers to as "the afflicted of his [the Lord's] people," namely Judah, will find refuge and safety in Zion (Jerusalem; 14:32). This likely anticipates God's deliverance of Jerusalem in 701 B.C. from Sennacherib through his miraculous intervention.

Isaiah 15–16: Judgment predicted against Moab

This oracle depicts the aftermath of a military invasion where Moab's cities have been destroyed (15:1–4), their men humiliated (15:2), their land devastated (15:6), and their wealth plundered (15:7). This is understandably accompanied by widespread mourning (15:3–4, 8). If all of this isn't bad enough, God threatens to bring even more judgment upon the Moabite refugees who escape the initial attacks. He will bring a "lion" (possibly symbolic of an enemy attack) to prey upon them in their weak and helpless condition (15:9).

Sprinkled throughout this oracle are possible expressions of compassion by God for the Moabite people. In Isaiah 15:5 the prophet says, "My heart cries out over Moab." Later he exclaims, "I weep as Jazer weeps" (16:9). Then he writes, "My heart laments for Moab like a harp, my inmost being for Kir Hareseth" (16:11). Conversely, it is possible that these expressions of sorrow are simply rhetorical, included for dramatic effect rather than revealing something about God's emotions toward the Moabite people (see fuller discussion above).

Whichever the case, God does seem to express genuine concern for the Moabite refugees in Isaiah 16:3–5. Despite having just predicted judgment upon them, the prophet encourages the Moabites to send rams to the ruler who resides on Mount Zion as a gift in exchange for asylum there (16:3). He additionally encourages Judah to provide shelter and protection for them (16:4). The prophet then anticipates a time when Moab's oppressors are no more and when the ravages of war and the need to flee as refugees are distant memories. In their place will be a descendant of David who reigns, apparently over them. He will judge in righteousness and justice. In the immediate future Isaiah anticipates God's deliverance of Jerusalem in 701 B.C. from Sennacherib through his miraculous intervention. Additionally, this prophecy likely anticipates the future messianic kingdom that will extend beyond Judah/Israel to include even former idol-worshipping (16:12) Gentile nations like Moab (House 2019, 440–41).

Isaiah 17:1–14: Judgment predicted against Syria and Israel

God is no respecter of persons, as his judgments against the nations will include even his own covenant people. In Isaiah 17 God warns of judgment against both Syria (Damascus) and Israel (Ephraim), the nations that aligned themselves together to attack Judah as part of a larger strategy to ward off future Assyrian offensives (Isa. 7:1–8:10).

Israel will be judged for having foolishly put their trust in another nation rather than in the Lord. Additionally, God will judge Israel for their reliance on false gods and idols (17:7–8). Israel had forgotten about their covenant God, the one who desired to be their "rock" and "fortress" (17:10). As a result of their misplaced faith, God will bring upon them many nations (17:12–13) who will devour their land and steal their produce (17:10–11). These foreign invaders will likewise plunder and loot their wealth (17:14).

As with most of the other oracles, there is an element of hope expressed here. One of the anticipated results of God's judgment in that day will be that "people will look to their Maker and turn their eyes to the Holy One of Israel" (17:7). No longer will they look to the idols that their own hands have made (17:8). As such, God's judgment here is shown to not merely be punitive in its intent, but corrective. God intends to inspire change among the people of Israel as part of his broader purpose to reclaim these nations as future worshippers.

Isaiah 18:1–7: Judgment predicted against Cush

The opening six verses of this oracle contain a description of God's coming judgment against the people of Cush. The imagery of pruning is used as the bad fruit is cut off and left for the birds and scavenger animals to eat (18:5–6). Additionally, the imagery of the birds and wild animals feeding on the discarded branches alludes to the aftermath of a battlefield where the birds and scavengers feed off the dead bodies of the fallen soldiers (18:6).

Somewhat abruptly, the prophet switches gears and predicts a time when the inhabitants of Cush will bring tribute to the Lord in Zion. This contributes nicely to the theme of God's goal of redeeming worshippers for himself from all the nations of the world.

Isaiah 19:1–25: Judgment predicted against Egypt (and Assyria)

God is portrayed in dramatic fashion in this passage as the one who will deliver judgment against Egypt and its idols. He is described as riding on a swift cloud as he comes quickly in judgment (19:1). God is the one who stirs up the Egyptians against each other (19:2), the one confounding the thinking of Egypt's counselors (19:3, 11–15), and the one who turns the Egyptians over to a hard master and a fierce king (19:4). The reader is left to conclude that the severe drought that leads to a famine will likewise be caused by the hand of God. This drought will have wide-ranging effects on the land and the Nile River, not to mention the farming and fishing industries (19:5–9). In that day, Egypt will become like terrified, vulnerable women as they are made subject to the land of Judah. As before, this will be the Lord's doing as he attacks them (19:16) according to his plan (19:17).

That plan apparently includes integrating Egypt into the people of God. Specifically, the prophet predicted there would be five cities in the land of Egypt where the people would swear their allegiance to the Lord of Armies (19:18). Additionally, there would be an altar dedicated to the Lord in the heart of Egypt and a monument devoted to him at the border (19:19) as symbols of their commitment to worship and serve the Lord. Not only will Egypt be a place devoted to the one true God, but he will likewise be committed to them. When they cry out to him because of oppressors, he will respond by sending them a savior (19:20). God will make himself known to the Egyptians in that day, and they in turn will worship him (19:21). He will "strike" them (an allusion to judgment) and "heal" them (19:22). Their healing would come about as the people of Egypt returned to the Lord with humble pleas for mercy.

In that day, the Assyrians too will be part of the cohort of God-fearing nations (19:23–24). God will call Egypt "my people," Assyria "my handiwork," and Israel "my inheritance" (19:25).

This passage combines many of the important themes throughout this broader unit, including its central focus on God's reclamation of the nations. Included in this passage are at least the following themes:

(1) God's judgment against sinful people (19:1–17)

(2) God's salvific grace extended to Egypt and Assyria: He will send a savior to them when they cry out to him (19:20). He will make himself known to them (19:21) and bring healing to them in response to their pleas for mercy as they return to him (19:22).

(3) The Gentile nations becoming worshippers of the Lord (19:18–19, 21, 23)

(4) A future kingdom in which Gentile nations are integrated into God's people (19:25)

The preacher/teacher may want to consider using this passage as the primary text, drawing main points from it, and then supporting those points with references to other oracles in 14:28–23:18.

Isaiah 20:1–6: Judgment predicted against Egypt and Cush

This oracle is unique within the broader pericope (Isa. 14:28–23:18) in that Isaiah was not simply given words to speak against a nation. Here, God commanded Isaiah to walk around naked and barefoot (20:2) for three years as a sign to foreshadow the judgment that would befall Egypt and Cush. This was meant to dramatize how the king of Assyria would eventually lead away Egyptians and Cushites, both young and old, naked with their buttocks uncovered (20:3–4). In that day, the people of Judah would be ashamed of the way they had placed their hope in Egypt and Cush for their protection rather than in God (20:5–6).

Isaiah 21:1–10: Judgment predicted against Babylon

Once again Isaiah foretells judgment and destruction upon Babylon (cf. Isa. 13:1–14:23). In the day of Babylon's destruction, God will demonstrate just how powerless Babylon's false idol-gods would be to deliver her (21:9). As such, God will demonstrate to Babylon and the watching nations that he alone is sovereign and worthy of their worship.

Isaiah 21:11–17: Judgment predicted against Dumah and Arabia

These oracles are very short. Nonetheless, there are several exegetical issues, particularly in the first couple verses about Dumah, that must first be resolved for this section to be understood. The imagery likely points to a military attack that would result in defeat for the people of Dumah (see commentary above; 21:11–12). The following oracle against Arabia is a little more straightforward. It describes refugees from Kedar (21:16–17) following a military attack (21:15) that has left them homeless and hungry (21:14). Given the timetable provided (21:16), we can safely conclude that these judgments were fulfilled through the Assyrian attacks during Isaiah's day.

Isaiah 22:1–25: Judgment predicted against Jerusalem (and Shebna)

We saw earlier how God did not exempt the people of Israel from the same sorts of judgments predicted against the surrounding, Gentile nations (see Isa. 17:1–14). Now we see that even Jerusalem, Judah's capital and home to Mount Zion and God's temple, is also vulnerable to God's judgments when his own people persist in rebellion and sin like the surrounding nations. This oracle begins by describing the people of Jerusalem during a siege. Oddly and to the puzzlement of the prophet, the people are feasting on their rooftops (22:1–2). This made no sense considering that people lay dead within the city, not because of war but due to starvation (22:2). Their senseless celebration is likely due to their abandonment of hope. They want to enjoy what little time they have left (22:13). Additionally, the people in the city have done all that they can to resist the enemy that has besieged them. They have even dismantled houses to shore up breaches in the city's walls and have diverted waters from the Gihon Spring to points within the city's outer walls (22:9–10).

However, the prophet confronts the inhabitants of Jerusalem for failing to do the most basic of things when confronted with an attack from a foreign enemy: Why haven't they turned to the Lord for help? Rather than partying away what could be their final days on earth in reckless jubilation, they should have called for weeping and mourning as a sign of repentance before the Lord their God. In addition to making every effort to solidify their water supply and to fortify their wall, they should have begged God to come to their aid and depended upon him for deliverance (22:11–12). For this reason, Jerusalem's inhabitants should assume that their iniquity would not be atoned for and that they would die at the hands of their enemies.

We are reminded nonetheless that despite God's commitment to judge sin, these are still God's precious, chosen people. As such, it pains him (or at least it pains the prophet Isaiah) to watch them flounder in their sin and rebellion and then reap the consequences of their actions (22:4). (See commentary above for a discussion about how this prophecy was likely fulfilled in surprising fashion in 701 B.C.)

The latter half of Isaiah 22 is unique within the broader pericope (Isa. 14:28–23:18) in that it is an oracle against an individual, Shebna. He was a palace administrator (22:15) and had standing and wealth within Judean society. The prophet asks rhetorically what business he has hewing out a tomb for himself in Jerusalem (22:16). It seems that Shebna's pride and ambition were the basis for the prophet's harsh words against him. It is likely that, from God's perspective, this man and his sin served as a prime example of what was wrong with Jerusalem as a whole. The people had become proud and were given to pursuing their own glory and advancement rather than glorifying God or serving him.

In the same way that Shebna served as a case study for much of what was wrong with God's people at that time, so too he would become an example of what God would do by way of judgment to the people of Jerusalem. God uses the imagery of someone wadding up cloth and hurling it far away (22:17–18). This picture likely points to the harsh realities of deportation, whereby many of God's people, particularly those of noble ranks, would be ripped from their homeland and exported into distant places where many of them would die, never to return home again. Shebna's position of authority and honor would be taken from him and given to another, Eliakim (22:19–23). However, Eliakim's success would also be temporary. For reasons left unstated by the prophet, Eliakim would metaphorically be like a peg fastened to the wall that would eventually give way. All that was hanging from it would then fall to the ground, signaling that his term as a leader would end in failure (22:23–25).

Isaiah 23:1–18: Judgment predicted against Tyre and Sidon

Tyre and Sidon were the two most important Phoenician cities. Being port cities with harbors, they were important for their maritime trade. This judgment oracle anticipates the destruction of their harbors (23:1) and the resulting financial impact this would have on the merchants and traders who had come to rely on them for doing business (23:2–3, 5), including many of the wealthy and powerful people of the world (23:8).

Like other places destined for judgment, the Lord is explicitly credited with bringing about the judgment upon Tyre and Sidon (23:8–9, 11–12). He does so in response to their arrogance and to the pride of those who depended upon them for business (23:9).

However, after seventy years, the Lord will restore Tyre to her place among the nations as a place of trade and commerce. He poetically and somewhat surprisingly likens her to a prostitute who will once again do business with the kingdoms of the world. In that day, though, her merchandise and wages will be holy to the Lord. She will supply goods (food and clothing) to those who dwell before the Lord (23:17–18). Once again, then, this oracle contributes to the theme that God's judgment against the nations would ultimately result in the Lord's redemption of those nations. It anticipates a time when all nations of the earth will be set apart for the Lord as they humbly submit themselves under the rule of King Messiah.

Preaching Idea
Though God must judge all nations for their sin and rejection of him, there is hope because of God's love for all and his promise to establish a worldwide kingdom.

Contemporary Connections

What does it mean?
If we have learned anything in the book of Isaiah thus far, it is that God will judge sin wherever he encounters it. In fact, he must judge sin because he is holy and cannot tolerate evil forever. However, the doctrine of God's wrath and judgment must not negate in our minds the equal truth that God loves the people of this world that he created. These two realities converge at the very heart of the gospel message: that human sin necessitates divine judgment. But God's love for those whom he must ultimately judge also motivates a desire within him to show mercy. Thus, a solution was devised, one so profound and yet so unlikely that it could only have been conceived by God. God's son would become a human being to voluntarily absorb God's wrath on sin in his own body, as a substitute for all humankind (2 Cor. 5:21; 1 Peter 3:18). In this way, the penalty of sin would be paid for in full and God could extend mercy to all.

Therein lies the great hope of the world. But for this hope to be realized, God's Son could not remain dead. He must rise again, victorious over sin and death. He will then return to earth to become the ultimate, conquering ruler. In his role as supreme king, he will rule over the whole world in truth, with righteousness and justice for all. Isaiah's audience wasn't as fortunate as we are today to be able to see how the initial phase of God's plan would play out through the life, death, resurrection, and ascension of Jesus. Still, they must have been intrigued by the imagery of hope in Isaiah's prophecies, which envisioned a future in which all the nations of the world would one day be reclaimed as God's people (cf. 19:25), ruled by an ideal descendant of King David (Isa. 16:5). They would faithfully worship the Lord alone, not the idols that were so prevalent throughout the pagan lands (Isa. 17:7–8; 18:7; 19:18–25; 21:9; 23:17–18). In the Lord, all the nations of the earth would find shelter from their oppressors as they became connected to God's chosen people Israel (Isa. 14:32; 16:1–5; 18:7; 19:24–25).

Thus, while God's judgment against sin and those who reject his rule is a predominant theme throughout these chapters, it is also evident that such judgment is purposeful beyond just punishing sin. Somehow God will use this judgment to turn the hearts of some throughout Israel and the Gentile nations to him. These converts will no longer perpetuate a tradition of rebellion against the Lord. He will raise up some who will recognize him as the good, gracious, and sovereign God he is. And so it will be that the Lord will establish a multinational kingdom in the earth one day composed of all who recognize and embrace God's Messiah as their Lord and sovereign king.

Is it true?
The doctrine of the coming judgment of God against sin is pervasive throughout the Bible.

The author of Hebrews describes this coming judgment:

> For if we deliberately keep on sinning after receiving the knowledge of the truth, no further sacrifice for sins is left for us, but only a certain fearful expectation of judgment and a fury of fire that will consume God's enemies.... It is a terrifying thing to fall into the hands of the living God. (Heb. 10:26–27, 31 NET)

Consider too what Paul wrote in Romans 2:5 (NET):

> But because of your stubbornness and your unrepentant heart, you are storing up wrath for yourselves in the day of wrath, when God's righteous judgment is revealed!

Passages such as these exemplify the wrath and fury of God which he will one day pour out on sinners who have never repented and turned to God.

At the same time, the Bible teaches plainly that God loves the entire world (John 3:16) and that he "is patient" about exercising judgment against sinful humanity, "not wanting anyone to perish, but everyone to come to repentance" (2 Peter 3:9). Luke records how Jesus, when he approached Jerusalem in the week leading up to his passion, wept over that city because of their ignorance concerning what would bring them peace (probably referring to their acceptance of him as their Messiah). He then goes on to foretell judgment that would be coming upon them instead (Luke 19:41–44).

God's love for even society's most despised people was on display throughout Jesus's ministry. The very people considered the most unworthy of love or acceptance were often the people to whom Jesus was most drawn. Jesus chose to eat dinner with Matthew's tax collector friends, much to the chagrin of the religious leaders (Matt. 9:9–13; Mark 2:14–22; Luke 5:27–38). When asked why he chose to eat with such sinners, Jesus replied, "It is not the healthy who need a doctor, but the sick. I have not come to call the righteous, but sinners." When Jesus came through Jericho, a large crowd surrounded him. What a surprise it must have been to everyone when Jesus singled out the least-liked man there that day to have lunch with him: Zacchaeus the tax collector, a known traitor and thief (Luke 19:1–10). Plenty of other examples of Jesus's love for the people most deserving of divine judgment abound. There is the story of the woman caught in adultery (John 8:2–11), the healing of the Gadarene demoniac(s) (Matt. 8:28–9:1; Mark 5:1–20; Luke 8:26–40), and the thief on the cross (Luke 23:39–43) who earlier that day had been taunting Jesus (Matt. 27:44; Mark 15:32). Even Saul of Tarsus (later known as the apostle Paul), a vehement critic of Jesus who persecuted and murdered some of Jesus's followers, was specifically targeted by Jesus to be a recipient of mercy (Acts 9:1–6).

Now what?
We shouldn't be surprised when we read prophecies about people being redeemed out of the pagan nations and being included among God's people. God truly loves those the world deems to be unlovable. He offers another chance to those who seem to have exhausted all their chances. If Jesus healed and cleansed a naked, demon-possessed man who was out of his mind, then he is able and willing to save an arrogant, blasphemous, skeptical college professor. If Jesus had compassion on greedy, dishonest tax collectors who took advantage of the poor, then his heart is similarly moved for the plight of the rebellious young woman who steals from others to support a destructive drug addiction. The Lord delights in reclaiming and redeeming men and women who have been deceived and trapped by Satan, and transforming them into purified, grateful worshippers of God.

If a sinless God loves even the worst of humanity, how much more should we be willing to open our hearts to the least desirable of society. If Jesus had compassion and showed mercy toward those like the thief on the cross who arrogantly rejected him and mocked him right up until the very end of his life, then we too should humble ourselves enough to forgive those who sin against us and even pray for them to experience the awesome grace and forgiveness of Jesus.

Creativity in Presentation

"Give Me Your Tired . . . ."

The United States of America is a land made up mostly of immigrants. From 1892 to 1954, about 12 million people from all over the world immigrated into America, passing through the Port of New York and New Jersey at Ellis Island. Many of these people were fleeing situations where they had little hope for a safe or prosperous life. The Statue of Liberty serves as a symbol of the United States' welcome to all who desire to come and integrate into this great country. Towering more than three hundred feet into the air, the sight of the statue would have been a recognizable landmark alerting the passengers on those ships that they had arrived. The following message is engraved on the pedestal of the statue: "Give me your tired, your poor, your huddled masses yearning to breathe free." The United States of America represented a land of hope, a place where people could expect freedom and justice for all. It was a place that welcomed anybody, including the poor and helpless of the world.

In many ways, this serves as an illustration of God's future kingdom, one that will welcome in people from any and every nation. It will include those who were poor and needy, those oppressed by others. Isaiah pictures the refugees and outcasts from Moab asking the people of Zion to open their borders and offer them protection and shelter from their oppressors (16:1–4). In response to this, the prophet anticipates the future messianic kingdom in which refugees from all nations will be welcomed to come under the protective shadow of King Jesus (16:5).

A Story of Redemption

Jeffrey Dahmer was one of the most notorious serial killers in American history. After being caught, Dahmer confessed to crimes of kidnapping, rape, murder, dismemberment, and even cannibalism involving seventeen men and boys between 1978 and 1991. In a 1994 *Dateline* interview with Stone Phillips, only eight months before being murdered himself by a prison inmate, Dahmer shared how his father had sent him books about creation science while in prison. These opened his eyes to the fallacy of atheism and the reality that he, along with everyone else, would one day have to give an account to God. According to Dahmer, he became convinced that evolution is a complete lie, and that the Lord Jesus Christ is the true Creator. Most importantly, he confessed that he had personally accepted Jesus as his Lord and Savior.[3]

In his book *Dark Journey, Deep Grace: Jeffrey Dahmer's Story of Faith* (2015), Roy Ratcliff writes about the day he received a call from Dahmer. Ratcliff was a pastor in the community where Dahmer was incarcerated. The person on the other end of the line said that Jeffrey wanted to know if Roy would baptize him. His first thought was that this must be a joke. However, after being assured that it wasn't and that Dahmer was serious, he obliged. Ratcliff ended up developing a discipleship relationship with Jeffrey, meeting weekly to study the Bible with him. Ratcliff recounts how another Christian who knew about his relationship with the infamous inmate once remarked, "If Jeffrey Dahmer is going to heaven, then I don't want to be there." Later, when Ratcliffe heard about this comment, he thought, "How can a Christian hold

---

3   https://www.youtube.com/watch?v=6tSxuyM93Js.

that viewpoint? I don't understand it. . . . Is forgiveness limited to those who are not very bad after all?" (2015, ch. 7).

Mom Turns in Her Own Son for Murder
In October of 2021, a Mississippi woman called the police to turn in her own son, eighteen-year-old Jordan Glasper, after he confessed to the shooting death of Michael Cross-Clay in an apartment in Memphis, Tennessee. Commenting on the mother's courage to do the right thing, one local pastor was quoted as saying, "Now that mother, she went a long way. I admire what she did but that would be tough for most mothers to do." Stories such as this demonstrate how one can love another person and yet still turn them over for judgment. Rather than serving as evidence that this mother didn't love her son, her willingness to expose him to judgment for his crime was likely motivated by a sense of justice for the victim and his family. In the same way, God's judgment of unrepentant sinners is not evidence of his hatred toward them. On the contrary, God loves even hardened sinners and desires to see them repent. But his commitment to holiness and justice for the victims demands that he also be a God who judges sin.[4] However, even though God must judge all nations for their sin and rejection of him, there is also hope because of God's love for all and his promise to establish a worldwide kingdom for all who repent of their sinful ways.

As suggested earlier, one approach to covering such a large unit in one sermon would be to anchor the sermon around Isaiah 19:1–25, and then highlighting shorter sections from other passages throughout the broader pericope that support these main points.

- God's holiness means judgment is coming (19:1–17).
- God's love means there is hope (19:18–25).

DISCUSSION QUESTIONS

1. Why do you think God would have asked his prophet to publicly walk around naked for three years (Isa. 20:1–6)? As "object lessons" go, doesn't this seem a bit excessive, even over the line? How do you think people responded to this?

2. Share about a time when you were shocked to hear of someone who became a follower of Jesus. What was it about their lifestyle or personality that made you assume there was very little hope of them becoming a new creation in Christ?

3. Read 1 Corinthians 10:6–13. According to this passage, what are some ways that God's judgment against sinners can have a redemptive and refining purpose in the big picture of how God is working in the world?

4. Read Isaiah 16:3–5. As you imagine what it will be like when Jesus rules over the world in the coming messianic kingdom, what new realities are you most excited about? Consider some of the ways that life will change as a result of Jesus's rule.

FOR FURTHER READING

Ratcliff, Roy. 2006. *Dark Journey, Deep Grace: Jeffrey Dahmer's Story of Faith*. Abilene, TX: Leafwood.

---

4 https://wreg.com/news/local/mom-turns-in-son-who-confessed-to-memphis-shooting.

Isaiah 24:1–23

EXEGETICAL IDEA
The Lord will judge the entire earth because of its violation of the "everlasting covenant," defeat all opposition, and establish his reign on Mount Zion.

THEOLOGICAL FOCUS
The Lord judges the nations when they break the everlasting covenant and then extends his rule to the entire earth.

PREACHING IDEA
God ushers in a glorious new world for his people by destroying the present corrupt earth, judging wicked humanity, and establishing his rule over the earth.

PREACHING POINTERS
Over the centuries, one of the tougher questions with which Christian theologians have wrestled is, "How can God send people to hell who reject him, but who have never had a chance to hear the gospel?" This is particularly troubling for those who live in regions of the world where there is no gospel witness at all. Basic fairness and justice would seem to require that a person only be held accountable for laws or standards of which they are aware. While aspects of this question remain difficult to answer, the Bible does teach universal accountability for sin based on general revelation, to which everyone has access (Ps. 19:1–6 [HB 2–7]; Rom. 1:18–20). All people should be able to deduce certain truths about God's existence and character from creation. Additionally, everyone has been hardwired with a conscience that informs them about God's righteous demands and their moral accountability before him (Rom. 2:12–16). Thus, the Scriptures teach that all humanity will be without excuse when they someday stand before God to give an account of their lives (Rom. 1:20).

Isaiah 24 contributes to the biblical doctrine of general accountability for sin. The prophet describes all humanity as having broken "the everlasting covenant" between them and God (Isa. 24:5). As such, they are guilty and deserving of judgment. In language reminiscent of the worldwide flood in the days of Noah, Isaiah warns of similar eschatological judgment against the world that will destroy the earth in its present corrupt form. God's judgment will pave the way for him to usher in his kingdom over a new, regenerated earth populated by the righteous.

WORLDWIDE JUDGMENT (24:1–23)

The Lord will judge the entire earth because of its violation of the everlasting covenant. He will defeat the heavenly-earthly coalition arrayed against him and establish his reign on Mount Zion.

LITERARY STRUCTURE AND THEMES (24:1–23)

The particle הִנֵּה, "see," followed by two participles, introduces an announcement of imminent judgment. The focus is on the future, as indicated by the prophet's use of *weqatal* (24:1b–2) and *yiqtol* (24:3a) verb forms, the standard forms employed in predictive discourse. A prophetic speech formula ("the LORD has spoken this word") concludes this opening subunit (24:3b).

In 24:4 the prophet's rhetorical perspective changes, as he speaks of judgment as completed. *Qatal* and *wayyiqtol* verb forms predominate in 24:4–12, but the *yiqtol* form in 24:13 ("so *it will be* on the earth") indicates that the judgment just described is, in reality, yet in the future (Roberts 2015, 313).

Isaiah 24:14–16a is an interlude in the prophet's announcement of judgment. An unidentified speaker describes voices from the west praising the Lord (24:14) and then calls upon those in the east to join in (24:15). We discover that the speaker is a group (24:16a, note "*we* hear"), not the prophet, who instead laments the unfolding judgment and the sin that produces it (24:16b, note "but *I* said"). On the relationship of 24:16a (the nations' praise) and 24:16b (the prophet's lament), see the commentary below.

The prophet continues his description of the coming judgment in 24:17–20, combining rhetorical perspectives. He uses the standard forms for predictive discourse (*weqatal* and *yiqtol* forms) in 24:18a and 20, but also employs *qatal* forms and a *wayyiqtol* form in 24:18b–19. Perhaps he speaks as one seeing the judgment unfold. Judgment has already been initiated (24:18b–19) and the devastating consequences are ready to occur (24:17–18a, 20).

A temporal expression (literally, "and it will be in that day") introduces the final subunit (24:21–23) within this judgment speech. In 24:21–23a the prophet speaks of what will transpire, as indicated by his exclusive use of predictive discourse verb forms (*yiqtol* and *weqatal*); in the aftermath of the Lord establishing his rule (24:23b), he describes the inauguration of the Lord's rule as having happened (note the *qatal* form מָלַךְ, literally, "has become king").

- **Thorough Judgment Is Imminent (24:1–3)**
- **A Covenant Curse Overtakes the Earth (24:4–13)**
- **An Interlude of Praise (24:14–16a)**
- **Inescapable, Violent Judgment Overwhelms the Earth (24:16b–20)**
- **Enemies Fall and the King Rules from Zion (24:21–23)**

EXPOSITION (24:1–23)

Thorough Judgment Is Imminent (24:1–3)
The Lord's judgment will devastate the earth.

24:1. The prophet draws attention (הִנֵּה, "see") to the Lord's imminent judgment, which will devastate the earth (24:1a). The noun אֶרֶץ can refer to a specific land or, more broadly, to the "earth" (i.e., the known world of the prophet's time). The subsequent context shows that the latter is in view here (see esp. 24:4, 13, 18, 21; as well as Chisholm 1993, 240 n. 13; Roberts 2015,

313; Young 1969, 149). For rhetorical purposes (attention-getting sound play) he uses two relatively rare verbs (בָּקַק and בָּלַק) that sound alike (note *bet* and *qoph* in both roots). Both verbs mean "to lay waste" (*HALOT* s.vv. "בלק" 135, "בקק I" 150). This devastation will entail distorting the earth's surface and scattering its inhabitants (24:1b).

There may be an allusion here to Genesis 11, which describes how God scattered the people of Babel for their hubris in attempting to build a tower into the heavens (note esp. Gen. 11:4, 8–9, where this same verb, פּוּץ, appears; and see Chisholm 1993, 242; Young 1969, 149). Three of the verbs used in Isaiah 24:1, 4 to describe the coming judgment have *b* and *l* sounds and echo the name Babel (בָּבֶל): בּוֹלְקָהּ, "devastate it" (24:1); אָבְלָה, "dries up" (24:4); and נָבְלָה, "withers" (24:4). The judgment of Babylon is prominent in the preceding oracles against the nations (Isa. 13–14; 21). Furthermore Isaiah 13:1–16 and Isaiah 24, both of which describe cosmic judgment, form an *inclusio* around these oracles. Since Babylon is prominent in chapter 13, it would not be surprising to find allusions to it in chapter 24. If there is an allusion intended, then it likely draws attention to the cosmic scale of God's judgment. Just as the judgment at Babel had a profound and lasting impact on the world, so the outpouring of divine anger described in chapter 24 will mark a new era in world history.

24:2. The judgment will be thorough and will not discriminate between the high and the low. Socioeconomic status will be irrelevant. The judgment will negatively impact priests and common people, masters and servants, honored ladies and their servants, sellers as well as buyers, borrowers and lenders, creditors and debtors.

24:3. The prophet highlights the devastation by emphatic constructions (24:3a): The earth will surely (or perhaps completely) be laid waste (הִבּוֹק תִּבּוֹק) and will surely (or perhaps completely) be plundered (הִבּוֹז תִּבּוֹז). The prophet's certainty is based on the fact (כִּי, "for") the Lord has spoken (24:3b). His word is reliable and activates judgment (Young 1969, 153).

A Covenant Curse Overtakes the Earth (24:4–13)
The coming judgment is due to covenant violations.

24:4. The prophet's rhetorical perspective changes here as he views the judgment as completed. Using perfect (*qatal*) verbal forms, he describes the earth/world as dried up, withered, and shriveled. Again, no one is exempt. Even the high and mighty among the people of the earth have shriveled up.

The noun תֵּבֵל, "world," appears here, parallel to אֶרֶץ, "earth." This word pair clearly refers to the earth/world, as opposed to a specific land, in several texts. In other contexts a broader worldwide scope is not as obvious, but still makes adequate, if not excellent sense. Used apart from אֶרֶץ, תֵּבֵל refers to the world in several passages. According to Luis Stadelmann (1970, 130), תֵּבֵל designates "the habitable part of the world."

24:5. The prophet now reveals the basis for the judgment: the earth has been defiled under the burden of its inhabitants (Wildberger 1997, 471). More specifically, the people of the earth have transgressed laws, violated a statute, and broken a permanent covenant.

Which covenant is in view here, and which laws and statute does the prophet have in mind? Interpreters have answered this question in different ways: (1) some propose this is a creation covenant made between the Lord and humankind at the time of creation (Dumbrell 1984, 74; Young 1969, 158); (2) many identify it as the Noachian mandate (Blenkinsopp 2000, 351–52; Childs 2000, 179; Gray 1912, 411; Hayes and Irvine 1987, 300–301; Hibbard 2006, 56–68; Kaiser 1974, 183; Sweeney 1996, 332; Seitz 1993, 180–82);

Vogels 1986, 32; (3) still others see this as the Sinaitic or Mosaic covenant between God and Israel (Gowan 1986, 77; Johnson 1988, 27–29).

A survey of the key terms is in order. The plural תּוֹרֹת, "laws," almost always refers to the laws of the Mosaic covenant.[1] In Genesis 26:5 it refers to the laws given by the Lord to Abraham, but one senses the patriarch is here being held up as a model for his descendants, with the narrator using legal language anachronistically for rhetorical reasons. As for חֹק, "statute," it can sometimes refer to the Mosaic Law (see Ezra 7:10), but it has a much broader range of usage and can refer to various human and divine decrees.[2] The phrase "permanent covenant" (בְּרִית עוֹלָם) has nine different referents in the Old Testament: (1) God's promise to Noah after the flood (Gen. 9:16); (2) God's promise to give Abraham numerous descendants and permanent possession of the land (Gen. 17:7, 19; cf. 1 Chron. 16:16–17; Ps. 105:9–10); (3) a permanent "obligation" (a nuance בְּרִית can have) placed on Abraham and his offspring (Gen. 17:13); (4) the obligation of keeping the Sabbath (Exod. 31:16); (5) the obligation of placing the bread of the presence before the Lord on the Sabbath (Lev. 24:8); (6) the priests' share of Israel's offerings (Num. 18:19); (7) God's promise to give Phinehas a priestly dynasty (Num. 25:13); (8) God's promise to David (2 Sam. 23:5); and (9) God's future covenant with Israel, guaranteeing their blessing (Isa. 55:3; 61:8; Jer. 32:40; 50:5; Ezek. 16:60; 37:26). It is noteworthy that the phrase is never used of the Mosaic covenant, only of various specific elements within it.

How should we assess the three main proposals?

(1) The cosmic context of Isaiah 24 (note אֶרֶץ/תֵּבֵל) might suggest that a creation covenant is in view. However, there is one major obstacle to this proposal: the creation account contains no covenant-making scene, and no such covenant is mentioned in the Old Testament. Some see an allusion to such a covenant in Hosea 6:7 ("Like Adam, they have broken the covenant," NIV84), but in this context אָדָם may refer to humankind generically ("like human beings [typically do], they have broken the covenant"). Another option is that אָדָם is a place name (cf. Josh. 3:16), as suggested by שָׁם, "there," in the following line. In this case an emendation of -כְּ, "like," to -בְּ, "at," would allow us to translate it, "as at Adam they have broken the covenant" (NIV11).

(2) Since the expression בְּרִית עוֹלָם, "permanent covenant," is used in Genesis 9:16 of God's promise to Noah, the Noachian mandate would seem to be an option, especially when one considers the allusion to the Noachian flood in Isaiah 24:18 (see Clements 1980, 205). However, Genesis 9:16 does not use the phrase of the Noachian mandate per se, but rather of the promise not to destroy again the world by water (see 9:11, 15). Isaiah 24:5 speaks of the covenant being broken. How can a unilateral promise by God be broken by human beings?

As I have suggested elsewhere,

Isaiah's penchant for irony must be recognized. It would seem that the prophet transfers the phrase from the promise to the mandate in order to emphasize that the promise, no matter how unconditional, does not exempt humankind from fulfilling the mandate or provide immunity from divine judgment if those obligations are neglected or perverted. In other words, the obligation inherent in the mandate is just as perpetually binding on humankind as

---

1 Exod. 16:28; 18:16, 20; Lev. 26:46; Ps. 105:45; Ezek. 43:11; 44:5, 24; Dan. 9:10.
2 Gen. 47:22, 26; Exod. 15:25; 1 Sam. 30:25; Ps. 2:7.

the promise is on God. Furthermore, the prophet may also be suggesting that humankind, by violating the mandate, has, for all intents and purposes, made the promise ineffectual. Even though the promise guarantees that God will never again devastate the world to the degree he did in Noah's day, God is not beyond severely judging his rebellious world in a way that resembles the Flood. In short, by giving the phrase "the everlasting covenant" a new twist, Isaiah is saying that the mandate is every bit as important as the promise and that violation of the mandate emasculates the promise of its practical value for humankind. (Chisholm 1993, 247)

Admittedly, this rhetorical explanation comes close to acknowledging that Isaiah bound the mandate and promise together as a covenant. This in turn would seem to imply that the promise was implicitly contingent on obedience to the mandate.

Steven Mason (2007, 177–98) argues that the Noachian covenant is conditional and that the violation of the mandate results in abrogation of the promise. According to Mason, the juxtaposition of וְאַתֶּם, "as for you" (Gen. 9:7) and וַאֲנִי הִנְנִי, "as for me, behold I" (Gen. 9:9) points to the two related dimensions of the covenant and indicates its conditional nature. The fulfillment of the promise depends on obedience to the mandate. The mandate, of course, requires human beings to be fruitful and multiply. In this regard, they are not to kill one another, since this would violate the image of God possessed by all humanity and would be counter to the mandate.

In this case, one may see the verb "defile" (חָנֵף) in Isaiah 24:5 as referring to bloodshed. This verb is used sometimes of the defilement of the land by adultery (viewed as a metaphor for idolatry; cf. Jer. 3:1–2), but it can also refer to the defilement caused by bloodshed (Num. 35:33–34; Ps. 106:38). In this context the latter is in view. Isaiah 26:21 announces the Lord is coming to judge the world for its sins; the earth (cf. הָאָרֶץ both here and in 24:5) will expose the blood that has been shed on its surface. This implies that the primary sin being judged is murder on a mass scale. According to Numbers 35:33–34, bloodshed defiles the land (הָאָרֶץ); atonement can be made for the land only by shedding the blood of the murderer. Isaiah pictures such a scenario on a cosmic level. Mass slaughter of human life has polluted the earth (24:5; 26:21); the Lord comes to make atonement for the earth by judging those who have perpetrated the crime.

Isaiah 54:9–10 is a potential roadblock to seeing the "permanent covenant" as the Noachian mandate, for this text appears to view the Noachian promise as unconditional and not dependent for its fulfillment on keeping the mandate. However, it is possible there is implicit contingency here and that this passage is speaking of the Lord's commitment to his side of the bargain, as it were. If so, it is possible that the phrase הָקִים בְּרִית, "establish/institute a covenant," in Genesis 6:18 and 9:9, 11, 17 refers to a renewal of the original mandate to Adam to be fruitful and multiply (Gen. 1:28–30). However, since Genesis 1 does not refer to the mandate as a covenant per se, Isaiah's "everlasting covenant" could be referring solely to the renewed mandate of Genesis 9:1–7, now elevated to covenant status and confirmed by the promise (albeit an implicitly contingent one) of Genesis 9:8–17.

(3) The appearance of תּוֹרֹת, "laws," certainly makes one think of the Mosaic covenant (see above), but the cosmic tone of the chapter seems to preclude this (see תֵּבֵל, "world," in 24:4, as well as "peoples" in 24:13; cf. 24:18, 21). How can the nations of the earth be held accountable for breaking the Mosaic Law, which, strictly speaking, governed Israel?

I have suggested elsewhere that a combination of the second and third proposals is preferable (Chisholm 1993, 245–49; 2002, 65–66).

With respect to the nations, the "permanent covenant" is best understood as the Noachian mandate, which was foundational to the fulfillment of the specific promise to which the phrase is applied in Genesis 9:16. For Israel and Judah, both of whom are included in the previous judgment oracles against the nations (see Isa. 17 and 22), the "permanent covenant" is the Mosaic Law. The Mosaic prohibitions against murder and bloodshed (Exod. 20:13; Num. 35:6–34) can be viewed as an extension of the Noachian mandate specifically applied to Israel/Judah. Indeed, prior to this Isaiah has denounced the covenant community for murder and bloodshed (Isa. 1:16–17, 21; 4:4; see Chisholm 1993, 248). We may find a parallel to this in Amos's oracles against the nations in chapters 1–2 of his prophecy. The nations' rebellious deeds (פֶּשַׁע) are best seen as covenantal violations. For the nations, their lack of respect for their fellow humans violates the Noachian mandate, at least in spirit, while Israel and Judah have broken the stipulations of the Mosaic covenant (Chisholm 2002, 381).

24:6. The violation of the permanent covenant has brought severe consequences. A "curse" (אָלָה) has consumed the earth. The earth's inhabitants have paid the penalty for their guilt and been reduced to a mere remnant. The term אָלָה, "curse," refers primarily to an oath taken in a legal or covenantal context. Covenants sometimes contained an itemized list of judgments that would fall on one who violated the agreement. These judgments could be called *curses* (אָלוֹת the plural form of אָלָה; Deut. 29:21 [HB 20]) because the agreement, complete with its threatened judgments, would be sealed by an oath (cf. Deut. 29:12 [HB 11]). By extension the word can refer, as it does in Isaiah 24:6, to the threatened punishment in its realized form. Biblical covenants (cf. Lev. 26:20; Deut. 28:17–18, 22–23, 38–42) and ancient Near Eastern treaties typically threatened agricultural infertility as a curse or judgment for violating the agreement.

Ancient Near Eastern examples can be found in the Treaties of Esarhaddon (§64; *ANET*, 539) and the Aramaic Sefire Treaty (stele 1A; *ANET*, 660). It comes as no surprise then to see references to agricultural infertility in Isaiah's description of cosmic judgment (cf. Isa. 24:4, 7–11).

24:7–9. Crop failure, a sign of an accursed condition, has indeed occurred. The new wine has dried up, as it were, and the vines have shriveled up (24:7a). The term תִּירוֹשׁ refers to fresh wine as it ferments in the wine press (cf. Prov. 3:10; Hos. 9:2; Joel 2:24). Perhaps the image here is of empty wine vats. With no grape harvest to pile into them, they appear to have dried up. Those who enjoyed drinking new wine (called here literally, "all the joyful of heart" [NIV11, "all the merrymakers"]) are reduced to groaning over their loss (Isa. 24:7b). The sounds of celebrations—musical instruments and revelry—have ceased (24:8). There is no more merriment, characterized by singing and wine drinking (24:9a). Other intoxicants taste bitter in the mouths of those who drink them (24:9b).

Fresh Wine
On the alcoholic, intoxicating nature of תִּירוֹשׁ, see Roberts 2015, 314. On wine production in ancient Israel, see Walsh 2000, 187–247. Once harvested, grapes were taken to the treading floor. When the skins of grapes are broken, the juice interacts with yeasts that are found naturally on the grapes' skins; this process converts the sugar in the juice into alcohol. Six to twelve hours after treading of the grapes, the fermentation process reaches its peak and then continues at a slower pace for two to five days. The alcohol kills the yeast cells, which die off once the alcoholic content reaches 14 percent. Walsh concludes: "Hence, the naturally produced wine of ancient Israel did not get higher than 14 percent alcohol" (p. 188). During fermentation, carbon dioxide is released and drives oxygen from the surface of the juice, facilitating the conversion of sugar to alcohol. The juice bubbles, or "boils," at this

> stage. The juice must be exposed to the air long enough for the carbon dioxide to escape, but if exposed to the air for too long, the juice will turn to vinegar. The surface juice was stirred to prevent it from turning to vinegar. In ancient Israel fermentation began while the grapes were still in the treading floor, but the juice was typically transferred to collecting vats or storage jars.

24:10–13. The prophet next depicts a ruined town where the entrance to every house is closed (24:10). The qualifying term תֹּהוּ, "ruined," occurs in several other passages. Sometimes it is used to describe a desert (Deut. 32:10; Job 6:8; 12:24; Ps. 107:40) or some other uninhabited place (Isa. 45:18). Often it stands parallel to a term meaning "nothing, emptiness, futility" and indicates lack of substance (see Job 26:7; Isa. 40:17, 23; 41:29; 49:4). This nuance fits well in Genesis 1:2, where the earth is submerged by the deep and has not yet appeared. In Isaiah 24:10 the term characterizes the city as empty or uninhabited (i.e., ruined) as the result of the devastating judgment depicted in the context (cf. 24:12).

Why were all the houses "closed"? Possibly this refers to their being closed off, as it were, by the debris of the destruction, but the verb סֻגַּר, "barred," suggests the residents have intentionally locked the doors to prevent entry (cf. Josh. 6:1; Eccl. 12:4). Perhaps people have fled the town, locking the doors of their homes behind them to prevent theft and looting, with the hope they might be able to return in the future. Some suggest the few survivors of the devastation are in view (see Oswalt 1986, 449; Roberts 2015, 315). In this case the reference to "every" house being shut up is problematic, unless we assume this refers to every house left standing. (For a discussion of the interpretation of Isa. 24:10b, see Young 1969, 164.)

Interpreters debate the identity of this ruined town, which is also mentioned in 25:2; 26:5–6; and 27:10. (Wildberger [1997, 485–86] distinguishes the city of 24:10–12 from those mentioned in chs. 25–27. However, see the discussion below.) Since the fall of the town occurs in the context of worldwide disaster (see esp. 24:11, 13), some conclude it is a typical city, symbolizing proud, rebellious human society. For example, Clements (1980, 202) writes: "The *city of chaos* . . . must either be taken here as typical of the situation that will befall any city at that time, or, more probably, possesses some kind of typical or representative function. There is a complete lack of any specific national reference, and none of the activities which are pursued within the city differentiate it in any special way. It can best be understood, therefore, as a pictorial description of the body of organized human society, a type of 'Vanity Fair,' which is to be subjected to divine judgment" (emphasis original; see also Childs 2000, 179; Oswalt 1986, 448–49).

However, the context does appear to refer to specific representatives of this town, including Moab, Babylon, Jerusalem, and Samaria (see Chisholm 2002, 66; and a more detailed study in Chisholm 1993, 241–44). There are verbal links between 24:7–12 and the earlier Moabite oracle (cf. 16:8–10), and between the Moabite oracle of 25:10–12 and other descriptions of the ruined town (cf. 25:2, 5; 26:5). Babylon is a possible referent, since the larger unit in which the prophecy appears (chs. 13–27) begins with an oracle against Babylon that depicts worldwide judgment (cf. 13:9–13). In 25:2 the ruined town is called "the foreigners' stronghold" and is described in a manner that is fitting if Babylon is the referent (see Johnson 1988, 59). Furthermore, there may be echoes of the Babel account in 24:1–4. But one may also hear echoes of Jerusalem and/or Samaria. Dan Johnson (1988, 29–35), who distinguishes the town of 24:10–12 from the hostile, ruined (foreign) town of chapters 25–26, argues Jerusalem is in view. Verbal links between 24:8–9 and Isaiah 5:11–14, where Judah's wealthy carousers are denounced, support this. (For a detailed refutation of Johnson's attempt to make Jerusalem the *exclusive* referent in 24:10–12, see Chisholm 1993, 250–52.) Samaria is a possibility as well, especially if the ruined, fortified town of 27:10 alludes to Samaria, as Paul Redditt (1986, 332) proposes. Both Jerusalem and Samaria are referred to as fortified in earlier oracles (see 17:3; 22:5, 8–11) and there are verbal links between 27:9 and 17:8 (cf. also 24:13 with 17:6; see Johnson 1988, 88–91).

I have argued elsewhere that it is best to understand the prophet's description of the ruined city in chapters 24–27 as intentionally ambiguous (Chisholm 1993, 250):

> The universal, generalized language draws attention to the common character of the destiny of the rebellious cities/powers of the world, while at the same time making it possible to see behind the imagery any number of specific cities that epitomize such rebellion. The description of the city is accompanied in chap. 24 by allusion to specific cities and is more directly associated in chaps. 25–27 with tangible historical manifestations of this city. Recognizing Isaiah's use of ambiguity allows one to harmonize the various passages referring to a city while preserving differences in emphasis and focus.

The images of 24:7–10 are repeated in 24:11–12. People lament in the streets over the loss of wine (24:11a; cf. 24:7, 9) and joyful celebrations cease on earth (24:11b; cf. 24:10). The town has been reduced to ruins and rubble (24:12; cf. 24:10).

In 24:13 the prophet switches back from his postjudgment rhetorical perspective to the present and speaks of the judgment as future (note the *yiqtol* form יִהְיֶה; see Oswalt 1986, 449; Roberts 2015, 315). Through an agricultural metaphor, he again emphasizes how devastating the judgment will be. The people left will be as few (cf. 24:6) as the olives and grapes when the harvesters go through.

An Interlude of Praise (24:14–16a)
Judgment will culminate in the nations praising the Lord.

A change in mood occurs in 24:14, as "they"—probably the nations mentioned in 24:13 (Roberts 2015, 315; Smith 2007, 421; Young 1969, 168)—lift their voices and rejoice in the majesty of the Lord. These shouts come from the west (literally, "from the sea"). An unidentified speaker, which is a group (note "we hear" in 24:16a) turns to those in the east and urges them to honor the Lord (26:15a) along with those in the west (note "in the islands [or perhaps coasts] of the sea"). The name (that is, reputation) of the Lord God of Israel is the focal point of this praise (24:15b). From the extremities of the earth the group hears songs praising the Righteous One for his splendor (24:16a). The title Righteous One is used here of the Lord (cf. 24:14–15). In this context it depicts the Lord as the just judge of the world who has appropriately punished those who have violated his standards (see as well Deut. 32:4; Pss. 7:9, 11 [HB 10, 12]; 11:7; Isa. 45:21; Jer. 12:1; Zeph. 3:5).

It seems appropriate that the nations praise the Lord, whose sovereign power is the focus of the preceding verses. But how does this interlude of praise fit the surrounding context, where judgment is the focus? There appear to be two options:

(1) This chorus of praise follows the coming judgment, as suggested by the *yiqtol* verb forms in Isaiah 24:14a, which can be taken as future (cf. 24:13). If they are understood as progressive present, then the speaker could be assuming a rhetorical stance beyond the judgment. In this case, the rhetorical perspective continues in 24:14b–16a, where the group speaking uses two *qatal* forms (צָהֲלוּ, literally, "they have rejoiced," and שָׁמַעְנוּ, literally, "we have heard") as well as an imperative. In this interpretation, 24:16b, where the prophet does not join the nations in praise, but instead laments

the coming judgment, must mark the beginning of a new subunit. If the nations are praising the Lord following the judgment, then it may be "that the world's experience of God's worldwide judgment has persuaded the surviving remnant that Yahweh is indeed the God of the whole world" (Roberts 2015, 315). Kaiser (1974, 187–88) sees "redeemed Jews" speaking to the nations in 24:15–16a.

(2) This chorus of praise may be occurring in the present, prior to the coming judgment. In this case, the prophet counters the nations in 24:16b, making it clear their praise is premature and inappropriate, for the nations are destined for judgment. (See Sweeney 1996, 328–29, who classifies 24:14–23 as a disputation speech.) But this raises the question: Why would nations that honor and respect the Lord be subjected to judgment? Perhaps their praise is shallow and insincere, but there is no indication of this in their words. The main support for this would be the prophet's words in 24:16b, if taken as a counterresponse. But if 24:16b simply goes back to the present situation of the prophet, who is anticipating the coming judgment, then his words are not countering those of the nations.

When the evidence is weighed and the options considered, it is better to interpret 24:14–16a as genuine praise from the (remnant of) nations that follows the coming judgment. This is an eschatological song of praise that corresponds to the songs recorded in 25:1–5, 9; and 26:1–6. The prophet's lament in 24:16b marks a shift in perspective, back to the present (cf. Smith 2007, 422), and begins a new subunit.

Inescapable, Violent Judgment Overwhelms the Earth (24:16b–20)
Returning to the present, the prophet reiterates that judgment is certain.

24:16b. With the words "but I said," the prophet abruptly returns from the distant future, when nations will recognize the Lord's sovereignty, to the present. In fact, "but I said" can be understood as the prophet's response to the statement in 24:3b, "for the Lord has spoken this word." Granted, in this case 24:4–16a is a lengthy parenthesis, but these verses are bound together by the fact the prophet, for the most part, takes a rhetorical stance beyond the coming judgment. Both he and the remnant of nations speak from that perspective (24:4–12, 14b–16a), with only a few brief lines reminding us that all this is still future (24:13–14a).

As the prophet contemplates the coming judgment, he is distraught (24:16b). He anticipates personal ruin when he declares "woe to me" (אוֹי לִי). When the interjection אוֹי is collocated with the preposition לְ-, it indicates the object of the preposition is in dire straits and/or that disaster is imminent or already being experienced (cf. Num. 21:29; 1 Sam. 4:7–8; Isa. 3:9, 11; 6:5; 24:16; Jer. 4:13; 10:19; 15:10; 48:46; Ezek. 16:23; Hos. 7:13; 9:12). Consequently, it can be translated as a noun, "woe" (cf. Prov. 23:29). A good way to indicate this is to translate: "disaster is upon me." Just before this, he cries out רָזִי־לִי twice, but the meaning of רָזִי is uncertain. Interpreters offer various options (see *HALOT* s.v. "רָזִי" 1210), but most likely רָזִי is a noun related to the verb רָזָה, "to dwindle, disappear" (*HALOT* s.v. "רזה" 1209; cf. Roberts 2015, 316). In this case, the prophet anticipates being diminished in strength or swept away altogether.

What is the reason for the prophet's pessimism? Possibly he is identifying with the victims of the coming disaster and speaking for them rhetorically. Very few will survive the coming judgment. However, another explanation seems more likely. Following the cry "woe to me," he describes how betrayers continue to betray. The sheer repetition (literally, "betrayers have betrayed, [with] betrayal betrayers have betrayed") draws attention to his lament. The betrayers, who are unfaithful and violent, are the objects of the coming judgment. They are described in 24:5–6 as violating the permanent covenant and defiling the earth by shedding blood. It is possible the prophet speaks as an innocent victim of these evildoers and anticipates persecution and even death at their hands.

24:17–18. The prophet announces that terror (פַּחַד), pit (פַּחַת), and snare (פַּח) will overwhelm the inhabitants of the earth (24:17). All three nouns share the *pe-khet* consonantal tandem. The nouns פַּחַד and פַּחַת also share dental consonants in the third root letter position (*dalet* and *tav*). Furthermore, the vowel sound "a" is repeated throughout. The sound play draws attention to the fact that these three will be the Lord's allies against the people of the world, conspiring to capture and destroy them (24:18a). Those who flee from the sound of terror will fall into the pit. Those who happen to climb out of the pit will be taken captive by the snare. The effect of the metaphor is clear: judgment will be inescapable, implying it will be overwhelming.

Indeed, the coming judgment will be cosmic in scope (24:18b), like Noah's flood, to which allusion is made here. The particle כִּי, "for," at the beginning of 24:18b indicates the cosmic scope of the judgment is the reason why the objects of judgment will be unable to escape it. The prophet again moves from the present and takes a rhetorical stance in the future (cf. 24:4–12, 14b–16a), as indicated by his use of *qatal* and *wayyiqtol* verbal forms. The windows (אֲרֻבּוֹת) in the sky have opened and poured water from the heavenly ocean upon the earth, as in the days of Noah (Gen. 7:11; cf. 8:2). This precise collocation (literally, "the floodgates from the height") occurs only here, but it is like the expression "the floodgates of the heavens" (Gen. 7:11; 8:2; 2 Kings 7:2, 19; Mal. 3:10). In several texts מָרוֹם, "height," is a synonym for שָׁמַיִם, "heavens."[3] In ancient Near Eastern and Israelite prescientific cosmology there was a heavenly ocean or reservoir of water (cf. Gen. 1:6–7; Pss. 104:13; 148:4). To bring abundant rainfall, God released water from the heavenly reservoir by opening the windows or floodgates of the heavens (cf. 2 Kings 7:2, 19; Mal. 3:10). In the time of Noah, he inundated the earth with water from above to wipe out the sinful inhabitants of the world (Gen. 7:11; 8:2). As noted above, Isaiah 24:18, which also depicts universal judgment, may well allude to the Noachian account. Humankind's violation of the Noachian mandate (cf. Isa. 24:5; 26:21), which prohibited bloodshed (cf. Gen. 9:7), jeopardized the Noachian promise (Gen. 9:16) and will bring a flood-like judgment upon the earth once more. Zephaniah also depicted divine judgment in flood-like terms (cf. Zeph. 1:2–3 with Gen. 6:7; 7:4, 23).

> **Heavenly Ocean or Reservoir of Water**
> According to Genesis 1:6–7, the sky separates the waters below it and above it. The waters below were eventually confined to one place and called "seas" (1:10); this allowed the dry land to appear. A heavenly ocean is located above the sky and therefore above the sun, moon, and stars, which are placed in the sky (see Gen. 1:14–19). One also finds this cosmological structure depicted in ancient Near Eastern literature and art. See Stadelmann 1970, 46–47. This cosmological structure is assumed in the flood account. According to Genesis 7:11 (cf. 8:2), "all the springs of the great deep

---

3 The appearance of אֲרֻבּוֹת, "windows," and the *niphal* of פָּתַח (נִפְתָּחוּ), "open," establishes the likelihood of a literary allusion here. However, מִמָּרוֹם, "from the height," is used in Isaiah 24:18 instead of "the heavens" (as in Gen. 7:11; 8:2; Mal. 3:10) or "in the heavens" (as in 2 Kings 7:2, 19). The noun מָרוֹם, "height," is a synonym for heaven, the dwelling place of God (cf. Isa. 24:21; 33:5, 16; 57:15). See BDB s.v. "מָרוֹם" 928–29.

burst forth and the floodgates of the heavens were opened." One of the sources of the flood is the heavenly ocean. For those tempted to identify this heavenly ocean with an alleged antediluvian water vapor canopy that supposedly ceased to exist after the flood, note that in biblical cosmology this heavenly ocean is still in existence *after* the flood (see 2 Kings 7:2, 19; Pss. 104:13; 148:4; Isa. 24:18; Mal. 3:10; and possibly Ps. 29:10). Furthermore, Genesis 8:2 does not suggest the heavenly ocean ceased to exist after the flood. On the contrary, it simply states the floodgates, or windows, of heaven were closed. Texts depicting a postdiluvian situation refer to them being opened in conjunction with God sending rain in abundance as a sign of his blessing (2 Kings 7:2, 19; Ps. 104:13; Mal. 3:10). Isaiah 24:18 pictures them being opened in conjunction with a culminating cosmic flood-like judgment.

The judgment shakes the earth (cf. Isa. 13:13) to its very foundations, which are equated elsewhere with the subterranean regions of the earth (cf. Deut. 32:22; Pss. 18:7 [HB 8]; 82:5; Prov. 8:29; Jer. 31:37). The motif of the shaking (רָעַשׁ, "shake") earth often appears, as here, in theophanic contexts (see Judg. 5:4; 2 Sam. 22:8 [= Ps. 18:7 (HB 8)]; Pss. 68:8 [HB 9]; 77:18 [HB 19]; Isa. 13:13; Jer. 10:10; cf. Wildberger 1997, 500).

24:19–20. In Isaiah 24:19 the prophet continues to view the judgment from the vantage point of the future as he uses three *qatal* verbal forms to describe the devastation. In each case he uses an infinitive absolute before the finite verbal form for emphasis. This combination of verbs pictures a violent earthquake.

In 24:20, the prophet makes another abrupt shift in perspective, returning to the present and viewing the judgment as future. The verb sequence is what we expect in predictive discourse: *yiqtol*, followed by three *weqatal* forms, and then a negated *yiqtol*. There is a chiastic structure:

A The earth indeed staggers (*yiqtol* with emphatic infinitive preceding) . . .
  B and (the earth) sways (*weqatal*) . . .
    C and its rebellion is heavy (*weqatal*) . . .
  B' and (the earth) falls (*weqatal*)
A' and (the earth) does not rise (*yiqtol* with negative particle preceding and infinitive following)

As in 24:19, an infinitive absolute appears with the first verb (נוּעַ) for emphasis. Comparisons are used in the first two clauses: the earth staggers like a drunkard and sways like a hut (presumably in the wind). The negated construction in the final clause is a case of terminal deviation for stylistic purposes; it creates a sense of finality. The variation in subject (from "the earth" to "its rebellion") in C highlights the clause as the centerpiece of the chiasmus. It is thematically foundational, for it gives the reason for the destruction described in the A and B clauses.

The Hebrew term פֶּשַׁע has the primary meaning "rebellious act, rebellion," but by metonymy the word can connote the consequence of rebellion, namely, guilt. (NIV11, "guilt of its rebellion," attempts to reflect both the primary meaning and the contextual connotation.) In its secular (nontheological) use the related verb (פָּשַׁע) refers to a subordinate party rebelling against a ruling authority (1 Kings 12:19; 2 Kings 1:1; 3:5, 7; 8:20, 22). The term is appropriate in Isaiah 24:20, for the inhabitants of the earth have rebelled against God's royal authority by violating the "everlasting covenant" (24:5).

Enemies Fall and the King Rules from Zion (24:21–23)

The Lord of Armies will defeat a heavenly-earthly coalition of enemies and establish his rule on Mount Zion (24:21–23).

24:21–22. This final subunit is formally introduced with וְהָיָה, "and it will be," followed by "in that day." The Lord will punish a cosmic coalition comprising the army of heaven and the kings of the earth. The collocation פָּקַד עַל is used here in its well-attested sense of "visit upon, punish." In this case the object of punishment follows the preposition, but the reason for punishment is not specified, probably because the preceding context makes the basis for punishment clear (see 24:20; cf. 24:5, 16b). The heavenly-earthly coalition will be first rounded up and imprisoned for "many days," after which they will be punished.

The precise phrase "host of the height" (NIV11, "powers in the heavens above"; צְבָא הַמָּרוֹם) occurs only here in the Old Testament, but it is likely an equivalent of צְבָא הַשָּׁמַיִם, "the host of the heavens," a phrase that refers to the sun, moon, and stars (cf. Deut. 4:19). The heavenly lights were objects of worship in the ancient Near East (cf. Deut. 17:13); in the Old Testament they are depicted as members of God's royal court (1 Kings 22:19) who surround his throne, answer his summons, and do his bidding (cf. Isa. 40:26). They are also called "sons of God" (Gen. 6:2, 4; Job 1:6; 2:1; 38:7; Pss. 29:1; 89:6 [HB 7]), "morning stars" (Job 38:7), "stars" (Judg. 5:20), and "holy ones" (Ps. 89:5, 7 [HB 6, 8]). God delegated to them authority over the nations (Deut. 32:8 [LXX]), but many have rebelled against God (Ps. 82; cf. Gen. 6:1–4; 2 Peter 2:4; Jude 6) and oppose his rule by energizing human kings to resist his will (note "kings on the earth" in Isa. 24:21b and see Dan. 10:13, 20). The New Testament reveals the identity of their leader, Satan (cf. Rev. 20:2–3). Isaiah 24:21–22 envisions a day when this hostile coalition of heavenly and earthly powers will be subdued, imprisoned, and executed. In Isaiah 34:4 their demise is depicted in metaphorical terms: the stars dissolve, roll up like a scroll, and wither away. The apocalyptic literature (Daniel and Revelation) provides more detailed descriptions of this eschatological war and God's culminating victory (see esp. Rev. 20:1–3, 7–10).

24:23. The judgment will be accompanied by the dimming (or perhaps darkening) of the moon and sun. The verbs translated "dismayed" (חָפְרָה) and "ashamed" (בוֹשָׁה) appear together in eight other texts. With one exception (Prov. 19:26), the tandem describes the humiliation and shame that follow military defeat and/or divine judgment (Pss. 35:26; 40:14 [HB 15]; 70:2 [HB 3]; 71:24; Jer. 15:9; 50:12; Mic. 3:7). Such is the case here, where the Lord defeats and imprisons the heavenly host (Isa. 24:21–22), whose humiliation and shame are expressed outwardly by their being dimmed. The specific reason given (כִּי) for the shame of the heavenly luminaries is not just their defeat but the Lord's exaltation as king, which is accompanied by the display of his "glory," that is, royal splendor, in Zion. Appropriately, he is called the Lord of Armies, for he has defeated his enemies in battle prior to taking his rightful throne in Jerusalem. There is, of course, great irony here, for the Lord of Armies (צְבָאוֹת) has defeated the host (or army, צְבָא) of heaven (24:21). The elders who witness his glory must be the leaders of the covenant community. There may be an echo here of what happened at Sinai, where seventy of the elders of Israel witnessed the splendor of the Lord and enjoyed a meal in his presence (Exod. 24:9–11). (See Clements 1980, 208; Gray 1912, 424; Young 1969, 182. This marks a reversal of the judgment that comes upon corrupt elders earlier in the prophecy (cf. Isa. 3:14; 9:15; see Oswalt 1986, 456).

THEOLOGICAL FOCUS

The theological focus of this passage can be stated as follows: the Lord judges the nations when they break the everlasting covenant and then extends his rule to the entire earth. As the prophet develops this theological theme, the following emphases emerge:

1. The kingship of the Lord
The kingship of the Lord is the central theme of this judgment speech. The entire earth is

subject to his rule and responsible for keeping his laws and statutes (24:5). In the aftermath of judgment, the nations will recognize and praise his royal splendor (24:14–15). As the mighty warrior-king, the Lord of Armies, he will defeat the heavenly-earthly coalition arrayed against him and establish his rule on Mount Zion (24:21–23).

2. The permanent covenant

All nations are in a covenantal relationship with the Lord, who holds them accountable for violating it. The "permanent covenant" is best understood as the Noachian mandate, which prohibits wholesale bloodshed. Genesis 9:16 uses the phrase *permanent covenant* of the Lord's promise, but obedience to the accompanying mandate is essential for the promise to be fully realized. For Israel and Judah, the permanent covenant is the Mosaic Law, which prohibits murder and bloodshed (Exod. 20:13; Num. 35:6–34) and, in this regard, is an extension of the Noachian mandate. Violation of this covenant brings a "curse" (Isa. 24:6) upon the earth that deprives the world of fertility (24:4, 7–9).

PREACHING AND TEACHING STRATEGIES

Exegetical and Theological Synthesis

Isaiah 24 serves as a transition between the previous judgment oracles against various nations (Isa. 13–23) and the present section dealing with a culminating worldwide judgment (Isa. 24–27). Whereas the judgments prophesied against Babylon, Egypt, Moab, Tyre, and so on pointed implicitly to the reality that all nations will eventually be judged by God, Isaiah 24 explicitly makes this point (24:1, 3–6, 13, 17, 19–21). Additionally, this passage introduces the theme of God's coming worldwide rule and the resulting celebration among his people (24:14–16).

The passage begins with a statement that God will make the entire earth desolate through his judgment (24:1). Oswalt (2003, 281) points out the significance of this theme as seen by the prophet's repeated use of the word "earth" in this chapter—sixteen times in only twenty-three verses. The prophet shows the *worldwide extent* of the coming judgment in 24:2–3 through his list of contrasting groups of people, none of which will escape God's hand of punishment for sin. Religious leaders will be treated the same as all the rest of the people. Class distinctions between the powerful and the vulnerable will not make any difference to God either. Those who are wealthy will not be able to avoid accountability for their actions through bribery. They too will be judged by the same criteria as those who are poor. Because of this, the highest people of the earth, those whose privilege has often exempted them from having to answer for their corruption, will languish and mourn (24:4).

In 24:4–6, the prophet lays out the *basis* for God's worldwide judgment. The earth itself is defiled (24:5), lying under a curse (24:6). This is due to the sins committed throughout by its inhabitants. They have transgressed God's laws and violated his statutes (24:5). While only Israel and Judah had been directly given God's law (Torah), the New Testament argues that all people have God's laws written on their hearts, that is, consciences (Rom. 2:14–16). Additionally, this passage describes the world's inhabitants as being guilty of violating "the everlasting covenant" (24:5). This is most likely an allusion to the covenant God made with Noah and humankind immediately following the flood (Gen. 9:16). Whereas God promised Noah and his descendants that he wouldn't destroy the entire earth in judgment again as he did with the flood, there was an implied stipulation that humankind would show respect for the dignity of human life through their actions. They were commanded to be fruitful and multiply, producing children to repopulate the earth with God's image (Gen. 9:1, 7; cf. Gen. 1:27–28). Additionally, God warned them that he would require the life of anyone (or any animal) who shed the blood of innocent people (Gen. 9:5–6). Isaiah 26:21 specifically highlights sins involving murder and bloodshed as a primary basis for God's coming judgment upon the world. This ties the world's population at the end of time to the covenant God made with humanity immediately following the flood.

Isaiah 24:7–13 reveals the *result* of God's coming judgment: the world's happiness and celebrations will immediately end; their party will be over. The merry-hearted now sigh (24:7) and all gladness is banished from the earth (24:11) as their music is stopped (24:8–9; cf. 25:5). The wine that accompanied their joyous feasts is mostly gone (24:7, 9, 11), and what does remain has become bitter to those who drink it (24:9). Their city is broken down (24:10) and left in ruins (24:12). The "city" here is likely a generic city symbolizing cities throughout the world. This theme of the "city" being left in ruins due to God's judgment will continue in the coming chapters (cf. Isa. 25:2, 12; 26:5; 27:10). It contrasts with the opposite reality of the people of God who will be protected within the confines of their own fortified city of Zion/Jerusalem (Isa. 24:23; 25:4; 26:1–2, 20; 27:13). Finally, 24:13 uses a metaphor from harvest to show that God's judgment will leave only a relatively few of the earth's inhabitants, similar to the olives or grapes left after the harvest.

There is a radical shift in tone in 24:14. This shift happens so quickly that initially it seems out of place and confusing. Whereas the passage up to this point has conveyed the judgment upon the unbelieving world and their subsequent response, 24:14–16a describes people shouting for joy and praising God from the ends of the earth. Most likely, the prophet is contrasting the pain and weeping of the wicked who are experiencing judgment from God with the rejoicing of believers around the world who are experiencing vindication and deliverance from their suffering. Their deliverance has come precisely because many of the wicked kings and tyrants who persecuted them have now been judged. Whereas the songs of the wicked have been silenced in the preceding verses (24:8–9), the righteous break forth in spontaneous songs of praise and rejoicing (24:14, 16; cf. 26:1, 19; 27:2).

Isaiah 24:17–23 portrays the *certainty* of God's judgment against the wicked world with several vivid poetic images. First, God's judgment is described as a "pit" into which the wicked are sure to fall (24:17, 18, 22). If one tries to evade it by crawling out of the pit, they will become entrapped instead in a "snare" (24:17, 18). Next, the eschatological judgment is conveyed with imagery reminiscent of Noah's flood (24:18–19). The windows of heaven will be opened, pouring down judgment like rain upon the earth, and the foundations of the earth will be violently shaken and split apart, flooding the land with judgment from the reservoirs under the earth's surface (Gen. 7:11; 8:2). In Isaiah 24:20, the earth is likened to an inebriated man, staggering around in the drunkenness of his sin. In the end, he eventually falls to the ground, illustrating how he suffers the consequences of his own foolish actions. This passage ends by poetically likening the rulers of this world to the heavenly luminaries (sun, moon, and stars) exalted high above the earth. They will apparently cease to shine on the day of judgment as God locks them up in a prison. In their place, the Lord of hosts alone will reign on Mount Zion in Jerusalem. His glory will outshine the brightest of the stars in the sky.

Preaching Idea
God ushers in a glorious new world for his people by destroying the present corrupt earth, judging wicked humanity, and establishing his rule over the earth.

Contemporary Connections

What does it mean?
The entire world is ripe for judgment. Certainly, those who have grown up hearing God's Word

taught but who have rejected that teaching stand guilty before God and are deserving of his judgment. However, what about those who have never read the Bible or heard the name of Jesus? How can they be deserving of judgment? While this is not a simple question in some regards, the Bible does seem to indicate that people will be judged based on the revelation they have received (Matt. 10:15; 11:22; Luke 12:45–48; Heb. 10:26–31). Furthermore, all people have access to certain aspects of general revelation from God. For example, all people can see from creation that there must be a God—a grand designer and creator of all things (Ps. 19:1–4 [HB 2–5]; Rom. 1:18–23). Additionally, all people have been programmed from birth with a moral code of conduct we call a conscience. This predisposes everyone to intuitively realize that things such as murder, theft, rape, and lying are wrong (Rom. 2:14–16; 1 Tim. 4:2; Titus 1:15). Finally, there are aspects of God's dealings with humanity from history that provide all people with a basis for understanding that they will be held accountable to God for their actions. Most notably in this regard is the historical reality of the worldwide flood (Gen. 6–8) which exemplifies God's resolve to judge sinners and call them to account for their choices.

While God's love predisposes him to be patient and merciful toward all (Exod. 34:6; Ps. 86:15; Isa. 30:18; Rom. 2:4; 1 Tim. 2:4; 2 Peter 3:9), his holiness and his love for victims of sin require him to judge sinners and cleanse the world of wickedness (Isa. 59:18; Rom. 12:19; 2 Peter 3:10; Heb. 10:30; Rev. 6:10–11). When that day of judgment comes, the party will be over for unrepentant sinners. The Bible describes the destination of rebellious sinners as a place of extreme torment and punishment (Matt. 25:46; Luke 16:23; Rom. 2:8–9; 2 Thess. 1:9). The most common description of this torment is that of fire (Matt. 13:40–42, 50; 25:41; Mark 9:43–44, 48; Luke 3:17; 16:24; 2 Thess. 1:8; Jude 7). It is also described as a place of darkness where there will be weeping and gnashing of teeth (Matt. 8:12; 13:42, 50; 22:13; 24:51; 25:30; Luke 13:28; 2 Peter 2:17; Jude 13).

As terrible as this judgment will be, it isn't inevitable for all. According to the Bible, when Jesus died on a cross, he absorbed God's judgment against sin for anyone and everyone who will repent in faith and accept his free offer of salvation. During the present age, God patiently withholds judgment to give ample time for sinners to hear about and respond to the gracious and glorious invitation of the gospel (Rom. 2:4–5; 2 Peter 3:9, 15). At some point, though, he will carry out vengeance against those who have rejected him, thereby removing them permanently from this world. He will then create a new heaven and a new earth that will be populated only by those who have identified themselves with God in this life. In so doing, he will usher in a glorious, eternal kingdom on earth.

Is it true?
The world today flaunts its sin and wickedness. At the time of my writing this chapter, the news each day is dominated by stories about Russian president Vladimir Putin and his military's daily, violent, unprovoked assaults against Ukrainian civilians. Western nations like the United States seem to be ever growing in their widespread acceptance and celebration of any and every form of sexual perversion. Recently, a State University of New York at Fredonia professor made the news when video clips surfaced on social media of him defending pedophilia. In the video, he claimed that it wasn't self-evident to him that nonconsensual, sexual contact between an adult man and a child would be objectively wrong, even with one as young as an infant.[4] According to the World Health Organization, around 73 million unborn children on

---

4   https://www.foxnews.com/us/suny-professor-under-review-for-reprehensible-video-defending-pedophilia.

average are murdered by abortion every year.[5] In 2016, the International Labour Organization reported that an estimated 40.3 million people were trapped in some form of forced labor, and another 15.4 million trapped in forced marriage.[6] There is simply no shortage of evidence that this world is full of violence, corruption, and every form of evil. For sure, then, this world is deserving of God's righteous condemnation.

The Bible teaches that all people know intuitively, at some level at least, that they will have to give an account of their lives to their Creator after they die. God's wrath against all unrighteousness has been revealed to all people, but this truth is often suppressed by sinful humanity (Rom. 1:18). We don't like the idea of being accountable to somebody else for our actions. We want to be autonomous and independent. We want to call our own shots and make our own decisions based on our own ideas. Thus, some choose to dismiss the reality of God altogether, or at least his right to rule over their lives. While most people at least acknowledge the existence of God, many choose to craft or conceive of him in a way that they like—a way that fits their own imaginations (Rom. 1:23).

In addition to our intuitive awareness of coming judgment, humanity also knows from history that God is likely to judge the world because of sin. We know this because long ago, God demonstrated his commitment to judge sinners through a worldwide flood that destroyed the world, including all but eight people and a handful of animals (Gen. 6:9–22; cf. 1 Peter 3:20; 2 Peter 2:4–5, 9–10). However, the secular world today, as well as some Christians, have suppressed the historical truth of a worldwide flood. Peter wrote in his day that they "deliberately forget" how the earth was deluged by a flood (2 Peter 3:3–6). I once heard someone explain that to "deliberately forget" something is like "being stupid on purpose." Why would people deliberately forget this historic reality? Peter explains that "by the same word the present heavens and earth are reserved for fire, being kept for the day of judgment and destruction of the ungodly" (2 Peter 3:7). In other words, if people admit that God judged the whole world long ago because of sin, then it follows that he could and probably will do it again in the future. Thus, people don't primarily reject the historical reality of the flood because it is unscientific or unsupported by the objective evidence, but rather because it is uncomfortable and inconvenient.

As noted in the commentary above, the flood story likely provides the background behind the everlasting covenant that Isaiah mentions (Isa. 24:5) which was broken by humankind. Thus, it is the basis of God's future judgment. As such, while many people today mock the notion of divine intervention and judgment, they do so to their own peril. Though God used the flood initially to punish the sinners in Noah's day who had utterly rejected him by fully giving themselves over to sin, his covenant after the flood was an act of mercy and kindness. God established this covenant to protect the dignity and value of human life, encouraging marriage and reproduction and warning them against any form of murder (Gen. 9:5–7). Additionally, God made the rainbow a promise to them and their descendants that he would not destroy the earth in this manner ever again. As such, it served as an ongoing symbol of his mercy and grace.

Now what?

Seeing how this passage serves as a strong warning that God will judge sinners one day, the appropriate response for everyone should be to repent of their sin and humble themselves before Jesus. Isaiah 24 describes nonbelievers at the time of God's judgment as ones who are partying and reveling in

---

5 https://www.who.int/news-room/fact-sheets/detail/abortion.
6 http://www.ilo.org/global/topics/forced-labour/lang--en/index.htm.

their sin. They are drinking their booze while dancing and frolicking to their festive music with laughter and jubilation (24:7–9). However, when judgment strikes, their partying will immediately end as their alcoholic drinks will suddenly taste bitter and their music will be abruptly stopped. Elsewhere, the Bible describes God's judgment day with the analogy of a person who is sound asleep, oblivious to the thief that is about to break into their home and plunder all their belongings (Matt. 24:43; 1 Thess. 5:2–4; 2 Peter 3:10; Rev. 16:15). Jesus was the first to use this analogy (Matt. 24:43), when he drew a connection between the targets of judgment in the days of Noah's flood and those who would be alive on the final day of the Lord. He said,

> For in the days before the flood, people were eating and drinking, marrying and giving in marriage, up to the day Noah entered the ark; and they knew nothing about what would happen until the flood came and took them all away. That is how it will be at the coming of the Son of Man. (Matt. 24:38–39)

His point was that the people in Noah's day were oblivious to the flood waters that were shortly to come upon them. They were going about their daily lives as usual. When judgment came, it completely surprised them. But that didn't have to be the case. The people at that time had Noah preaching to them (2 Peter 2:5), presumably warning them about the coming judgment. At the very least, he was likely explaining why he was building a huge boat and collecting pairs of animals for so many years. The time that it took for Noah and his sons to construct the ark (the lag time between God's prediction and the actual judgment itself) was an expression of God's patience toward them. It afforded them an opportunity to repent and turn to God for mercy and salvation (1 Peter 3:20).

It is easy for those in the world to assume that God is never going to judge them. After all, they have routinely committed selfish and wicked acts, without being struck by lightning or having the ground swallow them whole. Furthermore, countless men and women who lived before them didn't encounter some form of divine punishment in their lifetime. Thus, many foolishly assume that they can live as they please, even blaspheming and cursing God, and expect no retribution from him at any point. They fail to realize that what they interpret as proof of God's ambivalence toward how they choose to live, or worse yet, proof that he doesn't exist at all, is really evidence of his love and patience toward sinners (2 Peter 3:3–9).

The same admonition of preparedness and alertness applies to believers today as well. In his second epistle, Peter reminds believers how the day of the Lord would come like a thief, exposing the earth and every action committed in it to judgment (2 Peter 3:10). He goes on to say,

> Since everything will be destroyed in this way, what kind of people ought you to be? You ought to live holy and godly lives as you look forward to the day of God and speed its coming. That day will bring about the destruction of the heavens by fire, and the elements will melt in the heat. But in keeping with his promise we are looking forward to a new heaven and a new earth, where righteousness dwells. (2 Peter 3:11–13)

In other words, Christians must live now in expectation of the kingdom that Jesus will establish at his coming. We are eagerly awaiting a kingdom in which righteousness dwells. Thus, we should be devoting our life to righteousness as an expression of our commitment to Jesus and his kingdom. We must avoid the lure of this world and the temptation to assume that Jesus will delay his return indefinitely, so therefore it doesn't matter how we live. While the believer's eternal destiny may no longer be at stake, we should be motivated to remain diligent so that when he does return, we will be found without spot or blemish and living at peace regardless of our circumstances (2 Peter 3:14).

Creativity in Presentation

The Party's Over

For many in our culture, college is a time for raucous parties with loud music and lots of booze. Inebriated students are unfortunately not uncommon among college students, even though most have yet to reach the legal drinking age. Partiers must always be alert, because a disgruntled neighbor might report to the authorities their unlawful activities. Whether in real life or just on television, we've probably all seen the police break up wild parties. A knock on the door, a man with a badge3, and suddenly the partygoers begin to scatter in every direction. In a matter of moments, the laughter and music stop. In similar fashion, Isaiah 24 describes the people of this world reveling in their sin like a bunch of partygoers. When God shows up in judgment, the party will be over for the evildoers of the earth.

Deserving of Judgment

For an illustration of the large-scale problem of sin within society, consider the following. According to the New York State Metropolitan Transportation Authority, recent studies revealed that nearly 30 percent of New York City bus riders and 8 percent of subway users dodge paying their fares. In 2019, former New York governor Andrew Cuomo launched a joint NYPD-MTA task force to address the issue of fare evaders. But the program made very little impact on the problem, despite its high cost; in fact, the money lost from unpaid fares jumped from an estimated $150 million in 2017 to more than $300 million in 2019. The current trend is said to be unsustainable for the MTA if something isn't done to curb this problem.[7]

Evidence for a Worldwide Flood

A vast number of ancient flood "myths" in almost every civilization around the world supports the historicity of the biblical flood. John D. Morris of the Institute for Creation Research writes:

> One of the strongest evidences for the global flood which annihilated all people on Earth except for Noah and his family, has been the ubiquitous presence of flood legends in the folklore of people groups from around the world. And the stories are all so similar. Local geography and cultural aspects may be present but they all seem to be telling the same story.[8]

Morris goes on to list various facets of the biblical flood account that align with most of the more than two hundred flood stories from people groups all over the world. Those similarities include the following:

1. Eighty-eight percent of the stories featured a favored family.

2. In 66 percent of the myths, that family was forewarned about the coming flood.

3. In 66 percent of the stories, the flood was due to the sinfulness of humanity on earth.

4. In 95 percent of the accounts, the flood was global in scope, not local.

---

7   https://www.foxnews.com/us/nyc-fare-evasion-bus-subway-taxpayers-millions.
8   https://www.icr.org/article/why-does-nearly-every-culture-have-tradition-globa.

5. Seventy percent of the flood legends included survival by means of a boat.

6. In 67 percent of stories, animals were also saved/preserved in addition to humans.

7. In 57 percent of the accounts, the survivors landed on the top of a mountain.

8. In 35 percent of the flood stories, birds were sent out.

9. Seven percent of the stories mention the rainbow.

10. Thirteen percent of the accounts included the survivors offering a sacrifice to the gods.

11. In 9 percent of the legends, exactly eight people were saved from the flood.

In addition to sharing some of the above details, the preacher/teacher might want to pick one or two such flood myths and summarize them for their audience to show that, while different in some respects, they share many of the same basic elements. The following Wikipedia page includes hyperlinks to summaries of many of the flood myths in existence: https://en.wikipedia.org/wiki/List_of_flood_myths.

God ushers in a glorious new world for his people by destroying the present corrupt earth, judging wicked humanity, and establishing his rule over the earth.

- The reality of judgment—Judgment is coming (24:1–4, 17–23).
- The basis for judgment—Guilty as charged (24:5–6).
- The result of judgment—The party is over (24:7–13).
- In spite of judgment—A reason for celebration (24:14–16).

DISCUSSION QUESTIONS

1. Read Isaiah 24:4–6 and Romans 8:19–22. Both passages draw a clear connection between humanity's sin and corruption within creation. Why do you think the physical world has been impacted because of people's sin? Read Genesis 3:17–19. How do these verses further explain the relationship between the physical world's accursed condition and humanity's sin?

2. Atheism and secular humanism are on the rise within Western culture. In your opinion, what are the primary factors/reasons why people choose to reject God altogether?

3. Isaiah 24:5 presupposes that all the inhabitants of the world know about laws and statutes of God and understand the terms of a covenant between them and God. How is this possible with people who have never read the Bible and have never heard a gospel presentation?

4. As we considered above, New Testament passages that speak about the delay in God's future judgment highlight God's patience (1 Peter 3:20; 2 Peter 3:9). Do you see any irony in the fact that God's delaying judgment of the wicked is evidence of his patience, but becomes the basis for believers' impatience in wanting to see his judgment executed now?

Isaiah 25:1–27:13

EXEGETICAL IDEA
Judgment will dominate the immediate future, but the prophet looks beyond that as he focuses on Israel's restoration and the vindication of the righteous.

THEOLOGICAL FOCUS
The Lord will vindicate his covenant people by establishing his rule from Zion, defeating all enemies, reclaiming the exiles, and restoring his favor and blessing.

PREACHING IDEA
Believers celebrate their salvation as God defeats all their enemies, including death.

PREACHING POINTERS
Have you ever been to the funeral of a child or teenager who tragically died due to a natural disaster, some form of sickness, or a random act of violence? Maybe you knew a young serviceman or woman who died while serving our country in the prime of life. I (Mike) recently received word of some friends whose forty-year-old son just died from a brain tumor. Their only other child tragically died in infancy. One can only imagine the pain they are experiencing. At times like these, people inevitably begin to question God's goodness and his wisdom. Why would he allow this to happen? If he is all-loving and all-powerful, why wouldn't he do something to prevent these sorts of tragedies?

These are undeniably complex questions that require more than just a trite or simplistic answer, or worse yet, some shallow-sounding cliché. Nonetheless, the answer to these questions is addressed by God in these chapters. The deep longing of the human heart for the Lord to do something about the problem of death is provided here: "He will swallow up death forever. The Sovereign Lord will wipe away the tears from all faces" (Isa. 25:8). What a tremendous promise! Ever since the beginning of time, humanity has been suffering the anguish associated with sin in the form of sickness and eventual death. However, according to Isaiah, a time is coming when God will put an end to death forever. What's more, the bodies of those who have died long ago will be raised again as "the earth will give birth to her dead" (Isa. 26:19). The people of God will worship him and celebrate his salvation and gift of eternal life.

THE RESTORATION OF ISRAEL AND THE VINDICATION OF THE RIGHTEOUS (25:1–27:13)

The Lord will vindicate his covenant people as he establishes his rule from Zion and defeats those who oppose him—including death, the greatest enemy of all. He will restore his favor and blessing as he reclaims the exiles and brings them back to their homeland.

LITERARY STRUCTURE AND THEMES (25:1–27:13)

This second subunit within Isaiah 24–27 contains three distinct speeches. The first speech (25:1–12) begins with the prophet addressing the Lord, whom he praises as the victorious king who faithfully protects his people (25:1–5). The prophet then announces that the Lord of Armies will hold a banquet on Mount Zion and destroy death (25:6–8). There is a shift in style in 25:6 as the Lord is spoken of in the third person and a *weqatal* verb form introduces predictive discourse. Another *weqatal* form (25:7a) carries the discourse along. The verbs switch to a perfect, another *weqatal*, and an imperfect in 25:8 (see discussion below). A prophetic speech formula (25:8b, literally, "for the Lord has spoken") concludes this portion of the speech. In the final section of the speech, the people praise the Lord (25:9–12). The introductory formula (literally, "and one will say in that day") marks the transition and the people use the first-person plural as they praise the Lord. The particle כִּי, "for," links 25:10–12 with 25:9.

A heading (26:1a) introduces the second speech, which begins with a song that will be heard in Judah when the Lord vindicates his people and establishes his rule. The song appears to extend through 26:8; the first-person plural appears in 26:1b and 8. The song contains the following elements: an affirmation of confidence (26:1b), an exhortation to the gatekeepers to open the gates so the righteous nation may enter (26:2), a prayer to the Lord expressing confidence in his provision for those who trust him (26:3), an exhortation to trust in the Lord as the protector of his people (26:4) who brings down the proud (26:5–6), and a final prayer to the Lord, affirming his enablement of the righteous (26:7) and the people's commitment and faith (26:8).

A shift from the first-person plural (26:1b–8) to the singular in 26:9 indicates that an individual (most likely the prophet) now speaks on behalf of the people. He expresses his desire for the Lord's intervention against the wicked (26:9a), who persist in evil despite the Lord's patience and fail to recognize impending judgment (26:9b–11a). The prophet anticipates judgment coming upon these evildoers (26:11b). He seems to be speaking from the standpoint of the present, not the eschatological perspective of 26:1–8.

The shift back to the first-person plural in 26:12 indicates a transition to a new subunit within the speech, which extends through 26:15. Addressing the Lord, the people praise him for what he has done for the nation. The speakers here are living in the present, not the period of the future restoration (cf. 26:1–8).

A shift in mood occurs in 26:16–18. Though still addressing the Lord, the people recall the distress of the nation (26:16) and lament their inability to bring about deliverance (26:16b–18).

As earlier in the speech, an individual (probably the prophet) now speaks (26:19–27:1; cf. 26:9–11).[1] Identifying with the people (cf. "my people" in 26:20), he addresses them as a unified nation, using the second-person singular.[2] Switching to the second-person plural, he also addresses those who will rise from the dead (26:19b).

One might assume that "in that day" in 27:1 signals the beginning of a new subunit, but the theme of judgment is consistent with 26:21 (note the use of the verb פָּקַד, "punish," in both verses). The image of the Lord's victory over Leviathan fits better with what precedes than with the song of the vineyard that immediately follows (cf. 27:2–6). In 27:1 the phrase "in that day" marks the conclusion of the preceding subunit, as it does in 27:12–13.

The third and final speech of the subunit begins with "in that day" (27:2), linking it to the preceding speech (cf. "in that day" in 27:1). But there is an abrupt shift in focus here, as the prophet turns from the Lord's judgment of Leviathan to a song about a vineyard that the people are urged to sing (27:2–6). In this song the Lord speaks to his people, assuring them of his protection and renewed blessing. It may seem odd that the people would sing a song in which they quote the Lord speaking in the first person (see Young 1969, 237). But this appears to be the case, unless the point is that the people should compose and sing a song about the vineyard (27:2) because of the Lord's renewed favor (27:3–6). In this case, 27:3–6 would not be the words of the song per se, but simply the impetus for composing one.

The mood changes in 27:7–11 as the focus shifts back to the present reality. The nation has experienced severe judgment for its sin. The "fortified city" is desolate, but there is a ray of sunshine amid the darkness. Through judgment the Lord destroys the pagan altars and idols.

The speech concludes on a positive note (27:12–13) as the prophet tells how the Lord will one day bring his people back from exile in Assyria and Egypt. They will worship him on his holy mountain in Jerusalem. The twofold "and it will be in that day" (וְהָיָה בַּיּוֹם הַהוּא) once more shifts the focus on the future, where 27:6 leaves off.

- **Celebration of the Lord's Victory and His Vindication of His People (25:1–12)**
    - The Prophet Praises the Lord (25:1–5)[3]
    - An Announcement of the Lord's Banquet (25:6–8)[4]
    - The People Praise the Lord (25:9–12)[5]
- **Vindication Replaces Distress (26:1–27:1)**
    - A Future Generation Celebrates Its Vindication (26:1–8)[6]

---

1   One might initially think the Lord is speaking to his people (note "my people" in 26:20), but the third-person reference to the Lord in 26:21a suggests the prophet is speaking.
2   Note the second-person masculine singular forms in 26:19a ("your dead"), 19b ("your dew"), and 20a. He uses a second feminine singular form (note חֲבִי, "hide") in 26:20b.
3   The speaker (probably the prophet) uses the first-person singular as he addresses the Lord in praise.
4   There is a shift in style as the Lord is spoken of in the third person and a *weqatal* verb form introduces predictive discourse. A prophetic speech formula (25:8b, "the Lord has spoken") concludes the subunit.
5   The introductory formula (literally, "and one will say in that day") marks the transition and the people use the first-person plural as they praise the Lord. The particle כִּי, "for," links 25:10–12 with 25:9.
6   The heading marks the transition to a new subunit. It is not certain how far the song extends. I have extended it through 26:8, after which the communal first-person plural gives way to the singular.

- *The Prophet Anticipates the Lord's Judgment (26:9–11)*[7]
- *The People Recall the Lord's Provision (26:12–15)*[8]
- *The People Express Their Distress (26:16–18)*
- *The Prophet Assures the People of Their Vindication (26:19–27:1)*[9]

- **The Coming Salvation in Contrast to the Present Judgment (27:2–13)**
  - *The Lord Sings of a Fruitful Vineyard (27:2–6)*
  - *The Present Reality: Judgment on a Sinful People (27:7–11)*
  - *The Future Reality: Return from Exile and Renewed Worship (27:12–13)*

EXPOSITION (25:1–27:13)

Celebration of the Lord's Victory and His Vindication of His People (25:1–12)

The prophet praises God as his people's protector and anticipates a time when the Lord will defeat death and bring down the proud.

25:1. The prophet now addresses the Lord personally (note "my God") from a perspective beyond the judgment (cf. 25:2). The prayer begins like a thanksgiving song, with the prophet declaring his intention to exalt the Lord and praise his name (25:1a; cf. Exod. 15:2; Pss. 30:1 [HB 2]; 54:6 [HB 8]; 118:28; 138:2; 145:1). He then gives the basis for praise (note כִּי, "for"). The Lord is deserving of praise because he has performed with perfect faithfulness extraordinary deeds planned long ago (Isa. 25:1b).

Isaiah 25:1b reads literally, "for you have done an extraordinary (thing), plans from a distant (time) (with) faithfulness (and) trustworthiness." The term פֶּלֶא refers in its most basic sense to someone or something that is "extraordinary" (cf. Isa. 9:6). When it is collocated with the verb עָשָׂה, "to do," as it is here, the expression refers to God's mighty deeds.[10] In fact, according to the psalmists, God alone can perform such deeds (Pss. 72:18; 136:4). Isaiah refers specifically to God's powerful judgment (see Isa. 25:2–5).

The phrase מֵרָחוֹק, "from a distance," can be used in either a geographical (cf. Isa. 5:26) or temporal manner. When used in the latter sense, as it is here, it testifies to the fact that God has a plan for history that he works out both providentially and through direct intervention in human affairs. This plan encompasses the rise and fall of nations (cf. Isa. 22:11; 37:26). His power and wisdom make it certain that his plan will be realized. Therefore the Lord can declare the end from the beginning (cf. Isa. 46:10).

In speaking of the Lord's faithfulness in carrying out his plans, Isaiah combines two nouns, both derived from a root (אמן) meaning "be reliable, faithful," to emphasize the single concept. (NIV11's use of "perfect" is an attempt to reflect this emphasis. See also NASB. ESV chooses to translate both words: "faithful and sure.") The first word (אֱמוּנָה), when used literally, means "firmness, steadiness" (cf. Exod. 17:12). In its abstract use, it refers to honesty, integrity, reliability, or faithfulness (cf. Isa. 33:6). The second word (אֹמֶן) occurs only here in the

---

7   The shift from the first-person plural (26:1b–8) to the singular indicates that an individual (most likely the prophet) now speaks on behalf of the group.
8   The shift back to the first-person plural indicates a transition to a new subunit.
9   The appearance of "in that day" in 27:1 may signal the beginning of a new subunit, but the theme of judgment is consistent with 26:21 (note the use of the verb פָּקַד, "punish," in both verses). "In that day" here marks the conclusion of a subunit, as it does in 27:12–13.
10 Exod. 15:11; 34:10; Josh. 3:5; Job 5:9; Pss. 40:5 [HB 6]; 72:18; 77:14 [HB 15]; 78:12; 86:10; 88:10 [HB 11]; 111:4; 136:4; Joel 2:26.

The Restoration of Israel and the Vindication of the Righteous (25:1–27:13)

Old Testament. In this context the point seems to be that God has proven reliable. He planned events long ago and has been faithful to his stated intention.

25:2. The prophet expands the basis for praise (note כִּי, "for") by stating more specifically what the Lord has done. He has turned the city into a heap of ruins that will not be rebuilt. This city, also called a "fortified town," is not identified specifically, though it is called literally a "fortress of foreigners." It is probably the same city as the one described in 24:10–12 (and in 26:5–6 and 27:10). (See the commentary on 24:10–12 above.)

25:3. The destruction of the city is the prelude to the Lord receiving the respect he deserves. Because of judgment (note "therefore"), a strong people, probably representative of all such people groups (note the plural "nations" in the parallel line), will honor the Lord. The towns of violent nations will fear him. The primary meaning of the verb יָרֵא is "to fear," but in this context, where it is in poetic parallelism with "honor," the translation "respect" or "revere" (cf. NASB; NIV11) captures the idea nicely. Judah honored and revered the Lord in only a superficial, external manner (Isa. 29:13), but in the aftermath of judgment nations far and wide will give the Lord the respect and genuine worship he deserves (cf. Isa. 41:5; 59:19). As Kaiser (1974, 198) says, "This demonstration of Yahweh's power will open the eyes of the nations who now rely upon their own power, and they will become aware who the real lord of the nations is," prompting them to "recognize him, pay him due honour and fear him, abandoning for ever their own rule by force." (For insightful theological analyses, see Oswalt 1986, 461; and Smith 2007, 430.)

25:4. The prophet gives an additional reason (note כִּי, "for") why the Lord deserves praise. Through his judgment upon violent nations, the Lord has proven to be the protector of the poor and needy during their distress. This group is not specifically identified, but it must refer to those who were preserved from the threats of the violent. They are the ones who speak in 25:9, rejoicing that their trust in the Lord has been vindicated through his saving intervention (see also 26:1–8).

The prophet calls the Lord a stronghold and compares him to a shelter that protects one from a downpour. He also compares the Lord to shade that shields one from the heat of the sun. In Isaiah's day Judah looked to Egypt for the "shade" of protection (cf. Isa. 30:2–3), but the Lord alone can provide security and will do so in the time beyond judgment when he becomes Zion's shelter from the downpour and the heat (cf. Isa. 4:6).

Such shelter and shade are necessary, for the breath of violent oppressors (עָרִיצִים; cf. 25:3; 13:11) is like a cold downpour, on the one hand, and on the other, like heat in a dry land (25:5a). In either case one needs a shelter, for one cannot withstand in one's own strength the onslaught of such powerful natural forces. The imagery speaks volumes about the vulnerability of the Lord's people, the potentially overwhelming might of their enemies, and most importantly, the Lord's capacity to protect the vulnerable from the power unleashed against them (see Oswalt 1986, 462).

The Hebrew text reads כְּזֶרֶם קִיר, "like a downpour of a wall," at the end of 25:4. Presumably, this would refer to a downpour crashing against a wall (see Young 1969, 190, who develops the metaphor along these lines). But better parallelism is achieved if we read קֹר, "cold," referring to a cold downpour (Gray 1912, 427; Roberts 2015, 320; Wildberger 1997, 516). The references to both a cold rain and scorching desert heat, though contrastive at the surface level, complement each other and suggest the Lord can protect his people from the whole spectrum of dangers they may face.

25:5. The prophet concludes his address to the Lord by shifting his focus, as indicated by the shift to imperfect verbal forms. Perhaps the verbs state characteristic truths. The Lord's judgment, described in 25:1–4, is evidence of his ongoing sovereignty. He characteristically subdues unruly foreigners. Just as the shade of a cloud suppresses the heat, so the Lord overcomes the violent, silencing their song. Another option is that the prophet has shifted his rhetorical stance from beyond the judgment, which is described as completed in 25:1–4, to the present. In this case, the imperfects declare his confidence that the Lord will subdue the violent, unruly foreigners. In either case, the switch to the imperfect is an example of terminal deviation that signals closure to the prophet's prayer.

25:6. In 25:6–8 Isaiah delivers a prophetic message (note the formula "the Lord has spoken" at the end of 25:8). The use of a *weqatal* verb form at the beginning of 25:6 formally introduces the predictive discourse to follow.

The prophet envisions a day when the victorious Lord of Armies (NIV11, LORD Almighty) will hold a great banquet on "this mountain" for all peoples (25:6). This royal banquet, which inaugurates his rule (cf. 24:23), will consist of rich food prepared in oil and of aged wine that has been strained. The referent of "this mountain" (see also 25:7, 10) is Mount Zion, where the Lord of Armies will establish his earthly kingdom (Isa. 24:23). Isaiah envisions a glorious future for Zion once the king establishes his throne there. The nations will stream to it to receive instruction from the Lord (Isa. 2:2–4; 27:13), and the Lord's people will find shelter and security there (4:5).

25:7–8. The inauguration of the Lord's rule on earth will mean the death of death. Death is compared to a covering that covers all peoples and nations. In this context, the covering is probably a symbol of mourning, as suggested by the reference to tears in 25:8 (see 2 Sam. 15:30; 19:5; Esther 6:12; Jer. 14:3–4; and Wildberger 1997, 532; Young 1969, 194).

The Lord will "swallow up" death once and for all. The use of the verb "swallow" to describe the Lord's victory over death is ironic in a couple of ways. The Lord swallows up death, while the nations are enjoying the banquet (Isa. 25:6; see Roberts 2015, 323). Furthermore, death is pictured in both the Old Testament and ancient Near Eastern literature as having a voracious appetite (cf. Isa. 5:14, and esp. Prov. 1:12, which uses this verb to describe how death swallows up its victims). The Canaanite myths deify death and depict him as having a huge mouth and long tongue. Death boasts of its huge appetite for human flesh, comparing itself to a hungry lion (see Gibson 1978, 68–69). So while the nations eat their delicious meal, the Lord swallows up the great swallower himself, death.

As noted earlier (see the discussion of Sheol in Isa. 5:14), Death is often viewed as personal in the Old Testament. This portrait should not be reduced to mere poetic personification. Though orthodox Israelite theology did not deify death, it is likely that ancient Israel had a more dynamic notion of death (see Ps. 18:4–5 [HB 5–6]; cf. Heb. 2:14–15). Israel thought it could bargain with death and avoid disaster (Isa. 28:15, 18), but no mere human can stand up to its power. Only the Lord has the power to destroy it.

With death eliminated, the Lord, the Sovereign Master (אֲדֹנָי), will wipe away the tears of sorrow from every face. This refers to those who have been impacted negatively by death and have suffered the loss of loved ones. As Wildberger (1997, 533) observes, "mourning will be swallowed up, just as death itself."

To this point the prophet has described the worldwide effects of the death of death (cf. "all peoples" and "all nations" in Isa. 25:7, and "all faces" in 25:8a). But now he focuses on Israel, the Lord's people (note "his people," in 25:8b). The Lord will remove the disgrace of his people from all the earth. The Lord's victory over death brings deliverance to all

The Restoration of Israel and the Vindication of the Righteous (25:1–27:13)

peoples of the earth, but it would have special meaning for his covenant people who experienced the disgrace and humiliation of defeat and exile (see Isa. 30:7; 54:4), accompanied by death on a mass scale (see 26:19; cf. Dan. 12:1–2). But in conjunction with his victory over death, the Lord will restore his people to their land, delivering them from the tomb of exile (Isa. 27:12–13; cf. Ezek. 37:1–14). The promise is certain: "the Lord has spoken."

25:9. When the Lord vindicates his people, they will praise him. They waited for him, and he proved worthy of their trust by saving them (Isa. 25:9). The verb קָוָה, which appears twice in 25:9, has the basic idea of "wait in anticipation, expect, look for" (cf. Isa. 5:2, 4, 7; 59:9, 11; 64:3). When used with the Lord as the object, it can refer to trust or faith (cf. 8:17; 26:8; 33:2; 40:31). Here God's people celebrate the inauguration of his earthly kingdom; they affirm their faith has been rewarded for God has intervened to save them. Later Isaiah envisions a time when all the nations will "wait for" (that is, trust in) the Lord (cf. 51:5; 60:9).

The Lord appears in the role of savior throughout Isaiah. Recognition of his sovereignty and repentance are sometimes prerequisites to experiencing his saving work (Isa. 17:10; 30:15). This salvation takes the form of deliverance from distress, bondage, and exile; it is sometimes viewed as the outworking of divine justice in that the Lord delivers his oppressed people from those who have mistreated them (35:4). To save his people the Lord must often come as a warrior and annihilate his enemies (59:17; 63:1, 5; cf. 33:2–3). In the days of Moses, the Lord delivered his people from Egyptian bondage (63:8–9); in the same way he will deliver the exiles (12:2–3; 43:3, 12; 45:15; 49:25–26; 59:1; 60:16) and those who are oppressed by the wicked (Isa. 59:16). Zion is also a recipient of the Lord's saving intervention and supernatural protection, both in Isaiah's time (37:20, 35) and in the future (26:1; 33:6; 52:7, 10; 60:18; 62:1). Through his servant, the Lord extends his salvation to the nations (49:6; 51:6, 8). The Lord is concerned that all people recognize he alone is the savior; other so-called gods are incapable of providing the security for which human beings so desperately long (43:11; 45:22; 46:7; 47:13, 15).

25:10–12. Isaiah 25:10 gives the basis (כִּי) for the call to praise ("let us rejoice") in 25:9b. Two complementary reasons are given: The Lord's hand, symbolic here of his protective power, will rest on Mount Zion (25:10a), and he will bring down proud Moab (25:10b–12), which is representative of the hostile nations that oppose the Lord (Childs 2000, 185; Smith 2007, 435; Young 1969, 199). This reference to Moab's demise is consistent with Isaiah 11:14, which pictures restored Judah of the future defeating the Moabites in battle. While many powerful nations will worship the Lord (cf. 19:23–25), the Lord will still oppose the proud. Seitz (1993, 192) observes that 25:10–12 serves "the express purpose of offering a check on any simple view of universalism that would misunderstand the mystery of the prophet's proclamation of coming salvation for all nations. Any whiff of human pride or residue of national arrogance will be judged severely by the Lord of the nations."

The image of Moab's fall is a vivid one: Moab will be trampled like straw in manure. The metaphor is extended in 25:11a, as Moab is pictured spreading out its hands in the straw and manure, as if trying to swim. This humiliation is fitting, for Moab was proud (25:11b). The source of pride was Moab's impressive walls, which the Lord will surely bring down. Three perfect verbal forms are used in 25:12, perhaps indicating the prophet has once more shifted his rhetorical perspective to a time after the judgment. He also addresses Moab (note "your ... walls"), making the description more personal. Both these variations may be examples of terminal deviation, where stylistic shifts signal the conclusion of the literary unit.

The Restoration of Israel and the Vindication of the Righteous (25:1–27:13)

Vindication Replaces Distress (26:1–27:1)
The Lord will judge the wicked and vindicate his people.

26:1. The second speech within chapters 25–27 (see above) begins with a song that will be heard in the land of Judah at the time of deliverance and vindication (26:1a). The people declare they have a "strong city," which is most likely a reference to Zion (cf. 24:23; 25:10). This "strong city" stands in contrast to the ruined city depicted in the context (see 26:5–6; cf. 24:10–12; 25:2; 27:10). The city is strong because it experiences the Lord's deliverance, which is compared to a city's defensive walls and rampart (26:1b; cf. Isa. 60:11).

26:2. Next comes an exhortation to the gatekeepers to open the city's gates so a righteous, faithful nation may enter (26:2). The Lord's protection is not extended indiscriminately; there are moral qualifications. Only a loyal nation is allowed to enter the strong city and experience the protection it provides.

26:3. Foundational to this loyalty is a firm faith in the Lord (26:3). Isaiah 26:3 reads literally, "A firm purpose you will guard (with) peace, peace for in you (is its) confidence." The noun יֵצֶר (related to the verb יָצַר, "to form, shape") refers here to a purpose shaped in the mind. The form סָמוּךְ is a passive participle of the verb סָמַךְ, "to lean, support, uphold." Used here as an attributive adjective, it modifies יֵצֶר, "purpose," and refers to a purpose that is well-supported, or firm. In this context, the phrase is metonymic, for it refers to one who possesses a firm purpose. Addressing the Lord, the nation expresses its confidence that he protects one who displays a firm purpose. While this is a general principle, in this context the speakers have the righteous nation (cf. 26:2) in mind. The noun שָׁלוֹם, "peace," functions as an adverbial accusative here, indicating that the Lord's protection brings security. The noun is repeated for the sake of emphasis. The traditional translation "perfect peace" attempts to bring this out, though "absolute security" may come closer to the meaning. In this context, the national security of the righteous nation (cf. 26:2) is the focus, not emotional or psychological composure. The final causal clause makes it clear this security is a reward for those whose confidence is in the Lord. The form בָּטוּחַ here refers to "an inherent quality" of the subject (the firm purpose, i.e., one who possesses such a purpose); he is characterized by confidence (see GKC, 136 §50f).

26:4. A shift in addressee occurs in Isaiah 26:4. The people (note the plural imperative) are urged to trust in the Lord, for (כִּי) he is an enduring protector. The divine epithet Rock (צוּר) appears (see 17:10 and the comment there). The word refers to a rocky summit (cf. 1 Sam. 24:2; Isa. 2:10, 19; Jer. 18:14; 21:13) where one can find refuge from enemies. In Isaiah's day Israel had abandoned their true protector and people were trusting in man-made idols for security (cf. Isa. 2:8). God's judgment would reveal the folly of such misplaced faith (cf. Isa. 2:18–21). But in the day of restoration, they will see the importance of trusting in the only One who can provide genuine protection. The modifier עוֹלָמִים (the plural of עוֹלָם, "forever") emphasizes the enduring nature of this protection (cf. NIV11, "eternal").

26:5–6. The prophet expands the basis for praise (note כִּי, "for") by stating specifically that the Lord's protection of his people entails bringing down the proud city that opposes them. (See our earlier comments regarding the identity of this city; cf. 24:10–13.) As before in these chapters, rhetorical perspectives are mixed (as in 24:4, 13–16, 19–20; 25:1–4). Speaking from a standpoint beyond the coming judgment, the people state the Lord has brought down (note the perfect הֵשַׁח) those who live on high. But then they switch perspectives and speak of the Lord humbling the exalted town as a present

The Restoration of Israel and the Vindication of the Righteous (25:1–27:13)

or future event (note the two *hiphil* imperfect forms from שָׁפֵל, "be low"). Justice will be served when this city is humiliated, for the oppressed and poor will stomp on it (26:6; cf. 25:4).

26:7. The people again address the Lord in 26:7. After observing that the path of the righteous is level, they attribute this to the Lord. The "path of the righteous" refers to the daily activities and destiny of the righteous, compared to a road or path upon which one walks. The "righteous" are those who obey the Lord's commandments (cf. 26:8) and trust in his protection (cf. 26:2–4). Here they express their confidence that the Lord will make their way level and smooth, that is, prosperous and secure (cf. Prov. 2:20–22; 4:18).

The syntax of Isaiah 26:7b is problematic. Some interpreters understand יָשָׁר, "upright," as a divine title and take it as vocative, "Upright One" (cf. KJV, NASB, NIV11; see Motyer 1993, 215; Oswalt 1986, 474). There are at least two other options: (1) The form may be a textual corruption of the preceding מֵישָׁרִים, "level." It is omitted in the LXX. (2) It may be understood as an adverbial accusative in relation to the verb תְּפַלֵּס, "you will make level." "The path of the righteous" is the direct object of the verb (cf. מַעְגַּל, "path," in Prov. 4:26), so יָשָׁר, "smooth," would be an accusative of specification and/or product: "(as) a smooth (path), the path of the righteous you make level."

26:8. The people close their prayer by affirming their commitment to the Lord. They wait with anticipation for the Lord's judgments (26:8a). The plural form of מִשְׁפָּט often refers to the Lord's commandments, but here it is more likely that his acts of judgment upon the wicked are in view (26:9–11; cf. 26:5–6; see Young 1969, 213). The people desire judgment to fall because it will enhance the Lord's reputation (26:8b). The reference to the "way" (אֹרַח) of the Lord's judgments plays off the phrase "way of the righteous" in 26:7. In contrast to the way of the righteous, which the Lord makes level, the "way" of his judgments is directed toward the wicked.

26:9. The shift from the first-person plural (26:1b–8) to the singular in 26:9 indicates that an individual, most likely the prophet, is now speaking as the people's representative. He yearns to see the Lord unleash his judgment upon the wicked (26:9a), not because of some morbid desire to see people suffer but because of the way judgment vindicates the Lord. When judgment falls, the people of the world learn something about divine justice. The term used here, צֶדֶק, often refers to "righteousness"; but in this context, where judgment is the focus, justice is in view.

26:10–11. Unfortunately, when God mercifully withholds punishment, the wicked fail to learn about justice. Even in a land where uprightness is promoted, the wicked persist in their evil ways and ignore God's majesty (26:10). The Lord's hand is lifted, ready to strike in judgment, but the wicked fail to grasp what is about to happen (26:11a). It is only appropriate that they be humiliated and consumed by the Lord's fiery judgment (26:11b).

In 26:11b the referent of קִנְאַת־עָם, literally, "zeal of people," and its syntactical relationship to the preceding verbs are uncertain. One option is to understand the zeal as the Lord's anger directed toward people, specifically those among the "people of the world" (cf. 26:9) who are the objects of his judgment. Another option is that this refers to the Lord's zeal, or intense devotion, for his own people. (See Roberts 2015, 331; Smith 2007, 447; Wildberger 1997, 562; Young 1969, 217.) But in this case, one might expect to see "your people" as an indicator of the relationship. In either case, the phrase would seem to be the object of the verb "see" (NIV11, "regard") but this is awkward because "be ashamed" intervenes between the verb and its object. If "zeal" is the cause of the shame, one would expect to see a preposition before it (see *HALOT* s.v. "בוש" 116).

The final clause of 26:11b reads literally, "Also fire, your enemies, it will consume them." It would seem best to take the pronominal suffix on the verb as appositional to "your enemies," unless it is enclitic, in which case "your enemies" is the object of the verb. Another option is that "your enemies" is a genitive modifying "fire," that is, "fire (reserved for) your enemies will devour them" (cf. Oswalt 1986, 480; Roberts 2015, 326; Wildberger 1997, 551).

> *TRANSLATION ANALYSIS 26:11B*
> The mood of the three prefixed verb forms in 26:11b is unclear. They could be taken as imperfects, indicating confident expectation: "they will see, they will be ashamed . . . will consume them" (see HCSB, KJV; cf. NASB, which takes the first two as present and the third as future; see Motyer 1993, 216). Or, they may be taken as jussives, indicating prayer: "let them see, let them be ashamed . . . let it consume them" (see ESV, NIV11; cf. NLT, which takes the first and third as jussives; see Childs 2000, 187; Roberts 2015, 326. In either case, the speaker expresses his belief that judgment is appropriate and necessary.

26:12. The people speak in 26:12, addressing the Lord and praising him for his enablement. These are Isaiah's contemporaries (cf. 26:18), not the nation of the future (cf. 26:1). They are confident the Lord will establish (note the imperfect form תִּשְׁפֹּת) "peace" (שָׁלוֹם), that is, national security (cf. 26:3) for them (26:12a). This confidence comes from experience, for all the nation's accomplishments were made possible (note the perfect form פָּעַלְתָּ, "you have done") by the Lord (26:12b). As Wildberger (1997, 563) observes: "One might think of the victories of Israel described in the book of Judges, which are in fact depicted as Yahweh's victories; cf. also Exod. 14:14. Thus it had been in the past; why would it be any different in the future!"

26:13. Of course, Israel did not experience uninterrupted victory and blessing. Throughout their history, "lords" ruled over them (Isa. 26:13a), as depicted in Judges, which seems to be the primary focus here (see comments on Isa. 26:15 below). More recently, they had become subjects of the Assyrian Empire. But the people acknowledge (נַזְכִּיר, literally, "bring to remembrance") the Lord alone as their sovereign (26:13b). After all, a careful study of Israel's history, especially the Judges period, reveals that foreign conquerors were able to subdue Israel only because the Lord allowed them to do so, usually as punishment for his people's sin.

26:14. These "lords" eventually died; they will not live again or rise from the grave (26:14a). The Lord demonstrated his sovereignty over them by judging them; he destroyed them and "wiped out all memory [זֵכֶר, literally, 'remembrance'] of them" (26:14b). The contrast between God and these tyrants is stark. Israel brings to remembrance the Lord's name (26:13), but the remembrance of these defeated enemies is destroyed.

The first clause in 26:14 reads literally, "Dead ones do/will not live." Viewed in isolation, the statement sounds like a generalization about all the dead, in which case the imperfect verb form may be taken as generalizing and translated with the present tense (cf. HCSB). However, in this context it is more likely that the "lords" (foreign tyrants) mentioned in 26:13 are in view, at least primarily. (See Wildberger 1997, 564; Young 1969, 220. Roberts [2015, 331–32] sees an allusion here to the Assyrian ruler and correlates this text with 14:4–21.) Isaiah 26:14b, which speaks of the dead as objects of the Lord's violent judgment, favors this as well. Indeed, the verb פָּקַדְתָּ, "you punished," is used elsewhere of the Lord's decisive judgment upon proud rulers (cf. 10:12; 13:11; 24:21). Of course, it may be that the prophet utilizes "a familiar quotation," reflecting a general truth, to make his point about the foreign masters. (See Wildberger 1997, 564.

The Restoration of Israel and the Vindication of the Righteous (25:1–27:13)

He cites biblical and extrabiblical evidence for the notion "that there is no return from death.")

The second clause in 26:14b uses the Hebrew noun רְפָאִים to describe the dead (cf. 14:9). This word is used several times of an ethnic group that lived east of the Jordan. In some texts they are depicted as tall (Deut. 2:20–21). The gigantic King Og of Bashan is called the last of the Rephaim (Josh. 12:4; 13:12), but certain Philistine giants are called "offspring of הָרָפָה" (see 2 Sam. 21:16–22; cf. esp. 1 Chron. 20:4). (For a survey of the ethnic use of the term, see P. Johnston 2002, 130–32.) There are also references to the Valley of Rephaim, located near Jerusalem (see P. Johnston 2002, 132). However, here in Isaiah 26:14 the word refers to those who are dead. As noted above, the referent may be specifically former kings who are now dead. This is clearly the case in Isaiah 14:9, where the Rephaim inhabit Sheol, occupy thrones, and are specifically called "all the kings of the earth." Yet other texts appear to identify the Rephaim as the dead in general (see Isa. 26:19, as well as Job 26:5; Ps. 88:10 [HB 11]; Prov. 2:18; 9:18; 21:16). It may be that "Rephaim" simply describes the dead; any greater specificity is indicated contextually, not by the term per se. (For a survey of usage of the term when used of the dead, see P. Johnston 2002, 128–30.)

Dead

The word *rp'um* appears in some Ugaritic texts and in a handful of inscriptions (Aramaic, Phoenician, Neo-Punic). It is beyond the scope of this commentary to discuss these. For a survey, see P. Johnston 2002, 134–42. Scholars debate the relationship, if any, between the extrabiblical and biblical references. As Johnston (p. 142) explains, the majority view is that the Rephaim in West Semitic texts are "dead ancestors who were seen as semidivine patrons or protectors." A minority view identifies the Semitic and biblical Rephaim as "an ancient people or warrior group, whose name came to be used of the heroic dead, and was later 'democratized' to include all the dead."

Johnston points out that "two features in the biblical texts are particularly noteworthy." First, the term "occurs with distinctly different meanings, without apparent confusion or need for explanation." Second, "the dead Rephaim are portrayed significantly differently from the Ugaritic *rpum*: they are lifeless and need rousing, tremble before God, they are not limited to heroes or kings, they are never individually named, they do not travel, participate at banquets or play any role vis-à-vis the living as protectors or patrons." He concludes: "Here as so often, the Israelite writers appear to have taken a general Semitic concept and adapted it significantly to fit their particular Yahwistic perspective." For additional discussions of the Rephaim, replete with references to literature on the subject, see Day 2000, 217–25; and Matthew McAffee 2016, 78–87. McAffee (2016, 87) suggests the prophet is polemicizing "against popular Judean beliefs similar to those embraced at Ugarit earlier, namely, that departed monarchs acquire a quasi-divinized status and are somehow able to confer certain blessing on devotees."

The two halves of Isaiah 26:14 are connected by לָכֵן, which normally indicates a cause-effect relationship and is translated "therefore." But in this case, what is present (or future; note the imperfects in 26:14a) is not the cause of what has already taken place (note the perfect and two *wayyiqtol* forms in 26:14b). Rather, here לָכֵן introduces the cause (devastating judgment) with the effect (permanent death) preceding (note Roberts 2015, 326, who translates "because"). According to BDB (s.v. "כֵּן" mng. 3.d[*b*], 487), לָכֵן here infers "the cause from the effect" and develops "what is logically involved in a statement." In other words, 26:14b does not give a consequence of 26:14a, "but the development of what is implicit in it." ESV's translation, "to that end," attempts to bring this out. Another option is to see 26:14a as parenthetical, with לָכֵן making a logical connection to 26:13.

The Restoration of Israel and the Vindication of the Righteous (25:1–27:13)

26:15. While the Lord brought Israel's oppressive foreign lords down to the grave, he enlarged the nation and brought honor to himself by expanding the borders of the land. This does not refer to the situation in Isaiah's time. It seems to recall the time of the Davidic-Solomonic empire, when Israel conquered the surrounding nations and expanded its borders to unprecedented limits. If so, then 26:13 would have in mind primarily the Judges period that preceded David's conquests (see Wildberger 1997, 565). One might object that the people of Judah are speaking here (cf. 26:1). Even so, their perspective need not be limited to their own tribal history, especially when one considers that David, the Judahite, ruled all Israel. Furthermore, in the following context the scope broadens to include all Israel (cf. 27:6, 12).

26:16. The mood, which has been largely positive, changes in 26:16–18. Though the Lord did mighty things for the nation (26:12) and delivered them from oppressive tyrants (26:13–15), the nation experienced distress and was very much aware it had not realized its potential.

During this distress, the nation "visited" (פְּקָדוּךָ, "they visited you," NIV11, "they came to") the Lord and poured out prayers to him because of the divine discipline they were experiencing (26:16). The Hebrew text of 26:16 poses some special difficulties; it reads, literally: "O Lord, in the distress they visited you; they poured out an incantation, your discipline (was) to them." The use of the verb פָּקַד, "visit," here is peculiar, since the Lord is the object of the verb. Perhaps it has the nuance "seek" (with interest or desire), as in a handful of passages elsewhere. The verb צָקוּן (with paragogic *nun*), from צוּק, apparently means "pour out," though elsewhere it is not used of pouring out words, but rather molten metal (Job 28:2) or oil (Job 29:6). The object here, לַחַשׁ, refers elsewhere to an incantation (Isa. 3:3), such as one that a snake charmer might use (Eccl. 10:11; Jer. 8:17). So perhaps a prayer that is muttered with a whisper is in view.

The reference to the Lord's discipline (מוּסָר) makes it clear the distress mentioned earlier in the verse was sent by the Lord.

26:17–18. The people describe their distress with a metaphor (Isa. 26:17). They feel like a pregnant woman who is ready to give birth to her baby. She writhes and cries out as her labor pains overtake her. The Lord's discipline had produced similar pain and panic in the people. Yet it gets worse. As the people strained like a woman in labor, the baby did not come forth (26:18a).

They explain the metaphor in 26:18b: Despite their efforts, they are not able to produce salvation (the plural is used, referring to acts of salvation) in the earth. Nor do "the people of the world" fall. The switch to the imperfect in 26:18b, in contrast to the perfects in 26:18a, indicates that the reason for their distress persists into the present.

The phrase "people of the world" sounds very general, as if humankind were in view (as in 26:9). However, the context appears to be more focused at this point. Israel's distress is in view here (26:16), and 26:19 assures the nation that new life will burst on the scene. Indeed, Israel will someday fill the surface of the world (תֵּבֵל, as in 26:18) like the produce of a vineyard (27:6). If the birth metaphor continues in 26:18b, then the point would seem to be that Israel is not able to save itself or expand its population. Isaiah 26:19 is then a response, announcing that this situation will change.

Another option, preferred by many, understands "the people of the world" as foreign enemies who do not fall in battle (see Clements 1980, 216; Gray 1912, 445; Hayes and Irvine 1987, 313; Oswalt 1986, 485). They continue to threaten and oppress Israel. This would certainly reflect the reality of Isaiah's time. In favor of this view, one may point to 26:9, where the same expression refers to humankind in more general terms and to 13:11,

The Restoration of Israel and the Vindication of the Righteous (25:1–27:13)

where the "world" is characterized by evil and is the object of the Lord's cosmic judgment.

26:19. An individual now responds to the distressed people, addressing them as a unified nation (note the second-person singular forms in 26:19–20) with whom he identifies (note "my people," 26:20). Initially, one might think the Lord is speaking, but 26:21, which is formally connected to 26:20 (note כִּי), refers to the Lord in the third person. As in 26:9–11, the prophet is most likely speaking here.

He begins with a startling assertion, announcing that the nation's dead will live again and rise from the dust (26:19a). This is in stark contrast to the oppressive foreign lords mentioned earlier (26:14), who will not live or rise from the grave. The speaker then addresses the dead as those who dwell in the dust, urging them to wake up and shout for joy (26:19b) because of what they are about to experience. They will experience renewal, like plants drenched with the morning dew, for the land of the dead will yield its inhabitants.

Isaiah 26:19 poses several interpretive challenges. The first pertains to the syntax of 26:19a, which reads literally, "your dead will live; my corpse, they will rise." (For a discussion of various proposals, see McAffee 2016, 92–93.) One might think the prophet is anticipating his own resurrection, but the following third-person plural verb (יְקוּמוּן, "they will rise") does not agree with "my corpse" (נְבֵלָתִי) in gender or number. If he were speaking of himself rising, one would expect a singular verb form. One could eliminate the final *yod* on "my corpse" as dittographic (note the *yod* prefix on the following verb; cf. Gray 1912, 449) and vocalize the noun as feminine plural, but then there would be lack of agreement in gender between subject (feminine) and verb (masculine). One expects to see a second ("your corpse[s]") or third-person suffix on the noun ("their corpse[s]"; cf. ESV, NASB, NIV11), but it is difficult to see how either would have been accidentally omitted in this graphic environment. Philip Schmitz (2003, 147) takes the –*i* ending as gentilic and the entire form as an accusative of state. He translates, "as a corpse they shall rise" (p. 148). (Perhaps, to bring out the adjectival quality of the proposed gentilic, we should translate, "as a corpse-like one.") He cites Genesis 25:25 for support, "the first came out red" (note the –*i* ending on אַדְמוֹנִי, "red"). If the *yod* is a singular suffix, perhaps the prophet simply identifies with the dead of his people (cf. "my people" in Isa. 26:20). In this case, to account for the plural verb that follows, the singular "corpse" would have to be understood collectively (see GKC, 394 §122s; and cf. Ps. 79:2; Isa. 5:25; Jer. 7:33; 9:21; 16:4; 19:7; 34:20). (On the lack of gender and number agreement between collective feminine singular "corpse" and the plural masculine verb that follows, see GKC, 462–63 §145c.) Still another option is to understand "my corpse" as an adverbial accusative, with "your dead" being the subject of the following verb. The KJV understands the syntax in this way: "Thy dead men shall live, together with my dead body shall they arise."

The identity of the addressee(s) in the first half of Isaiah 26:19b poses another problem. The speaker addresses those who dwell in the dust (i.e., the dead) with second-person masculine plural imperatives, urging them to awake and rejoice. He then supports the exhortation with a reason (כִּי) for doing so. But within the causal clause, he returns to the second-person singular (note טַלֶּךָ, "your dew"), as if addressing the nation again (cf. 26:18–19a). He may now be speaking to the dead as unified (hence the collective singular), though he uses the plural (רְפָאִים) in the next line. It seems more likely that he dramatically shifts addressees, first speaking to the dead and then turning back to the nation. Certainly, by the next line, where the dead are referred to in the third person (note רְפָאִים), he is no longer addressing them. We could paraphrase: "Awake and rejoice, O dust dwellers. You (dust dwellers) should respond this way because your dew,

The Restoration of Israel and the Vindication of the Righteous (25:1–27:13)

O Israel, is like the life-giving dew that comes with the morning light" (see below).

A third issue concerns the meaning of the statement: "for dew of lights (is) your dew." In this context, dew, as is often the case, is a symbol of life and fertility. The plural "lights" (אוֹרֹת, from אוֹרָה, the feminine counterpart of אוֹר, see *HALOT* s.v. "אוֹרָה I" 25) probably indicates degree (cf. BDB s.v. "אוֹרָה I" mng. 2, 21), referring to a bright light, namely, the morning light that bursts forth brightly (Day 1978, 265–69). The point of the metaphor would be this: the nation's life-giving (divinely imparted) dew, as it were, will soak the dust of the ground, causing the corpses to spring up to new life, like plants sprouting from well-watered soil (see NET note).

The syntax of the final line poses a fourth problem. The text reads literally, "and (the) earth, (the) dead, will cause to fall." The syntax has been understood in a variety of ways (see P. Johnston 2002, 112–13): (1) The Lord is taken as subject of the verb תַּפִּיל, "cause to fall" (which is morphologically ambiguous and may be taken as second-person masculine singular or third-person feminine singular), with "dew" an implied object and "land of the dead" a secondary object: "you will cause (dew) to fall (on) the land of the dead." (2) The Lord is subject, "land" is object, and the verb "cause to fall" is used in a militaristic sense: "you will cause the land of the dead to fall" (i.e., you will defeat it, forcing it to release its dead). (3) The LXX takes "land" as the subject, reads "dead" (רְפָאִים) as "evildoers" (רְשָׁעִים), and understands the verb as intransitive (*qal*?): "the land of the ungodly will fall." (4) The "land of the dead" is taken as subject: "the land of the dead will give birth" (i.e., cause a baby to drop). (5) The "earth" is taken as subject and "dead" as object: "the earth will cause to fall (i.e., drop or surrender) the dead (within it)" (P. Johnston 2002, 113–14; Oswalt 1986, 476 n. 22). McAffee (2016, 93–94) prefers to take this in a negative light: "the earth [i.e., the underworld] will make the Rephaim fall," that is, "never to rise again." (6) Again, the "earth" is subject and "dead" the object, but the verb has a different sense: "the earth will cause to fall (i.e., give birth to) the dead" (see Roberts 2015, 332–33; Wildberger 1997, 551, 556; Young 1969, 2:229).

In response to options 1 and 2, the people, not the Lord, are addressed in 26:19–20. As for option 3, it requires emendation of two of the three forms. The fourth option (like the first three) requires, contrary to the accentuation, taking land as construct with the following noun. Either the fifth or sixth option is best. In either case, the earth, where the corpses presently reside, is giving up (like a conquered foe or, more positively, like a woman in labor) its dead (unless one opts for McAffee's interpretation).

Of course, once one addresses these technical details, a larger interpretive question remains. Is the resurrection of the dead described here to be understood literally, metaphorically, or perhaps in both ways?

The immediate context supports the notion of a literal resurrection of Israel's dead (Childs 2000, 191–92; Gray 1912, 446; Motyer 1993, 219; Oswalt 1986, 285; Smith 2007, 451–53; Young 1969, 226). According to 26:14, the oppressive foreign lords will not come back to life: "the dead [מֵתִים] will not live [בַּל־יִחְיוּ], the dead [רְפָאִים] will not rise [בַּל־יָקֻמוּ]." This same wording appears in 26:19, where the prophet assures the nation: "your dead [מֵתֶיךָ] will live [יִחְיוּ], my corpse(s) will rise [יְקוּמוּן]" as he announces that the land of the "dead" (רְפָאִים) will yield its inhabitants. Literal resurrection is in view in 26:14. The contrast between the destiny of the dead oppressors and the nation's dead is tighter if 26:19 is also understood as referring to literal resurrection. Further support comes from 25:7–8, where the Lord vanquishes death and its effects once and for all, and from Daniel 12:2, which uses the verb "awake" (יָקִיצוּ; cf. הָקִיצוּ in Isa. 26:19) of those sleeping in the dust who will come to life.

However, there is contextual support for a metaphorical resurrection (Clements 1980, 216;

Hayes and Irvine 1987, 314; Sweeney 1996, 343; Wildberger 1997, 567–68). In Isaiah 26:18 the nation laments the fact that it cannot produce deliverance on the earth, implying that it is in need of such and perhaps alluding to the reality that many have been exiled. The next speech ends with a description of the Lord gathering his people from all lands, including Assyria and Egypt, and bringing them back to their homeland to worship the Lord in Jerusalem (27:12–13). The idea of a metaphorical resurrection gets further support from Ezekiel 37 (see esp. 37:12–14), where resurrection imagery is used to depict the restoration of exiles from both Israel and Judah.

But it is unnecessary to choose between these two options, as if they were mutually exclusive. It is best to see both a literal and metaphorical resurrection, given the contextual support for both (P. Johnston 2002, 224–25; Roberts 2015, 333). This seems to be the case in Isaiah 25:6–8 (see the commentary above) and there is no reason why both literal resurrection and return from exile cannot be in view here as well. In short, the inauguration of the Lord's kingdom will bring victory over death in all its forms. Israel's dead will rise, and the nation will return from its tomb in exile.

26:20. Identifying with the nation (note "my people," cf. 22:4), the prophet urges them to hide from the wrath that will pass through. The judgment will not last long (note "for a little while"), but it will be severe. The noun זַעַם, "wrath," is used elsewhere in Isaiah of the Lord's judgment on his people through the Assyrians (10:5, 25), and, as in 26:20 (cf. 26:21), on all nations (13:5; 30:27). It causes great panic (13:7–8) and brings devastating destruction (Isa. 13:6, 9; 30:27–28).

26:21. The prophet elaborates on why (כִּי) it is necessary to seek refuge. The Lord himself is about to emerge from his dwelling place to punish the iniquity of those who live on the earth. The second half of the verse indicates the iniquity in view specifically involves bloodshed. Currently the earth covers the blood shed upon it and the victims of this violence. But when the Lord arrives for judgment, the earth, cast in the role of a witness against the perpetrators of iniquity, will disclose the blood shed upon it and the slain whom it currently covers. The evidence of the crimes committed by the earth's inhabitants will be visible to all and their guilt undeniable.

In the light of 24:5 (see commentary above) it appears this bloodshed by the nations violated a permanent covenant, most likely the Noachian prohibition against murder, as well as the accompanying mandate to be fruitful and multiply. According to 24:5, the earth is "defiled" (חָנְפָה) by its inhabitants because they have violated the stipulations of the covenant. The verb חָנֵף, "defiled," is used sometimes of defilement caused by bloodshed (Num. 35:33–34; Ps. 106:38). This correlates well with Isaiah 26:21, where mass killing on a worldwide scale appears to be in view.

27:1. When the Lord comes to judge, he will destroy the forces of evil as he wields his mighty sword against them. The enemy is called Leviathan and the "monster of the sea," and is described as "the gliding serpent" and the "coiling serpent." In this context this creature symbolizes the earthly-heavenly coalition that defies the Lord's rule (24:21–22; Motyer 1993, 221; Oswalt 1986, 491).

The name Leviathan is used elsewhere of a multiheaded mythical sea serpent that opposes God (cf. Ps. 74:14). This creature appears in Ugaritic mythology by the name Litanu (or Lotan), where it is said to have seven heads and is called the "wriggling" (Ugaritic *qltn*) serpent, as in Isaiah 27:1 (cf. NIV11, "coiling," which translates Heb. עֲקַלָּתוֹן = Ug. *qltn*).[11] In the myths Leviathan is closely associated with the sea god

---

11 See Gibson 1978, 50, 68; Parker 1997, 111, 141–42. For a thorough study of Leviathan traditions in the ancient Near East, see Barker 2014, 129–70.

Yam and is an enemy of the god Baal and his ally Anat. In the Old Testament the name appears in four other passages. In Psalm 74:14 it appears to be another name for the sea (cf. 74:13). The psalmist praises God because he defeated this creature. Certain elements in the context suggest the exodus is in view (cf. 74:15b, "you dried up the ever-flowing rivers"), but this divine victory also seems to be associated with God's creation of the world (74:16–17). Both God's original creative work and his deliverance of Israel at the sea are probably in view here. In Psalm 104:26 Leviathan appears to be a large marine creature made by God to "frolic" in the sea. There appears to be no mythological allusion here; Leviathan is simply one of the animals created by God (cf. 104:24–25). Leviathan is also mentioned twice in the book of Job. As Job curses the day of his birth, he refers to experts in incantations as "those who are ready to rouse Leviathan" (Job 3:8). Apparently in pronouncing formal curses they summoned the destructive Leviathan to make the curse a reality. In God's speech to Job, he gives a detailed description of Leviathan that appears to contain mythical elements (Job 41). Job's initial fatalism ("the LORD gave and the LORD has taken away," Job 1:21) was too simplistic and did not begin to explain his experience, nor did his later bitter accusations that God was unjust. As the reader knows from the references to the Adversary (Job 1:6–12; 2:1–7), there is cosmic evil in the world that challenges God's authority. In God's speech he reminds Job of this. Job has been victimized by evil; his only hope is to turn to the Sovereign Creator, who has the power to defeat the forces of evil and restore equilibrium to Job's world. To summarize, except for Psalm 104:26, Leviathan is a symbol of the evil cosmic forces that oppose God. God overcame Leviathan when he created the world and when he delivered his people from Egypt and created a new nation (Ps. 74:14). Leviathan continues to be a dangerous force in the world that has no equal on earth (Job 41:33) and rules "over all that are proud" (Job 41:34). Yet a day is coming, says Isaiah, when the Lord would destroy this archenemy of all that is good.[12]

This enemy is also called "the monster of the sea." The term תַּנִּין, "monster," is sometimes used of a literal snake (Exod. 7:9–10, 12; Deut. 32:33) or sea creature (Gen. 1:21; Ps. 148:7), but it can also refer to the mythological creature known as Leviathan or Rahab (cf. Ps. 74:13–14; Isa. 51:9). In Isaiah 51:9 it symbolizes Egypt (cf. Ezek. 29:3; 32:2), which was defeated at the exodus (cf. Isa. 51:10).

The Coming Salvation in Contrast to the Present Judgment (27:2–13)
The Lord will restore his people as his vineyard and reverse the effects of judgment.

27:2. This third speech of the subunit begins with an exhortation to sing "in that day." As the preceding context indicates, this is that future day when the Lord judges his enemies and vindicates his people. The exhortation is directed to an unidentified group; they are to sing about a fruitful vineyard that belongs to the Lord (see Isa. 27:3–6). This recalls an earlier song about the Lord's vineyard (5:1–7). But in that case, the Lord was forced to destroy the vineyard because it failed to produce good grapes. The reality behind the imagery was Israel's failure to produce a just and righteous society. But in this new song of the vineyard, the situation is reversed (cf. Skjoldal 1993, 170) as the Lord promises to protect his vineyard Israel and cause it to flourish. The Lord's original vision for his people is finally realized. Regarding the contrast between Isaiah 5:1–7 and 27:2–6, Todd Hibbard (2006, 181) stresses that "what is reversed is primarily

---

12 For a concise discussion of how the Old Testament appropriates the mythological motif of the battle with the sea (monster) and applies it to God's creative work, history, and eschatology, see Day 2000, 98–107. See also Chisholm 2013a, 75–84.

The Restoration of Israel and the Vindication of the Righteous (25:1–27:13)

YHWH's attitude and behavior toward the vineyard."

27:3–4. Speaking in the first person and from the perspective of "that day," the Lord affirms that he guards his vineyard and waters it (27:3a). The vineyard has his attention day and night, so no one can harm it (27:3b). Israel enjoys his protection and no longer experiences his anger (27:4a). Because of their sinful rebellion the Lord was forced to pour out his angry judgment upon his people (cf. Isa. 42:25; 51:17, 20), but the story does not end there. The Lord will withdraw his anger from his people (cf. Isa. 51:22) and direct it toward the hostile nations (cf. Isa. 34:2; 59:18; 63:3, 5–6).

> *TRANSLATION ANALYSIS 27:3A*
> In 27:3a the Hebrew text reads literally, "for moments I will water it." Some translate as if the watering is continual: ESV: "every moment I water it" (cf. KJV, NASB, NIV11). If this is the meaning of the expression, then the statement is hyperbolic, for vineyards received water only during the rainy season. It is possible that "for moments" refers to regular watering, that is, at the appropriate time of the year (cf. HCSB, "I water it regularly"). See Wildberger 1997, 585.

In fact, the Lord speaks as if he is eager to demonstrate his commitment to his vineyard (27:4b). He says, literally, "If only (there were) briers and thorns in the battle, I would stride against them, I would set them all on fire." Motyer (1993, 222) says: "Such is the Lord's zeal for his vineyard that he longs for a chance to prove how much he cares: just let a weed appear!" If the vineyard represents the Lord's people, then the briers and thorns symbolize the enemies that threaten to overrun the vineyard (Young 1969, 239–40). Stepping away from the metaphor, the Lord declares he is ready to engage these enemies in battle, confidently striding out to fight them. Returning to the metaphor of briers and thorns, he announces he would burn them up.

27:5. Yet this need not be their destiny. In 27:5 the Lord urges his enemies to look to him as their refuge. This would, of course, entail a radical change in attitude, but the Lord emphasizes they should make peace with him. A formal treaty arrangement is probably in view. In Joshua 9:15 the expression "make peace with" is used of a covenant sealed by an oath.

27:6. The focus shifts back to Israel. Days are coming when the nation will take root, bloom, and produce fruit (Isa. 27:6a). All the surface of the earth will be filled with produce (26:6b; cf. Ps. 80:9 [HB 10]; Hos. 14:5–7). The metaphor of Israel as a fruitful plant depicts a time when the nation will enjoy the Lord's blessing and have a positive impact on others. Roberts (2015, 338) sees the metaphor as referring more specifically to population increase (cf. Isa. 37:31).

27:7. Israel's future will be bright, in contrast to the present reality, which now becomes the prophet's focus. He begins with a question, the meaning of which is unclear. It reads literally, "Like the striking down of the one striking him down has he struck him down, or like the killing of his killed ones has he been killed?"

The identity of the "one striking him down" is difficult to determine. Earlier passages have spoken of both the Lord (5:25; 9:13 [HB 12]) and the Assyrians (10:20, 24) as striking down (נָכָה) Israel. A couple of options seem possible: Perhaps we could paraphrase: "Has the Lord struck down Israel in the same way the Assyrians struck down Israel?" In this case the prophet's point is that the Lord (the subject of "he struck") has not unleashed the same ruthless attack on Israel as the Assyrians ("the one striking him down") have done. But the Assyrians were the Lord's instrument of judgment, so a contrast between them seems artificial (Wildberger 1997, 594). A second option is that the Lord has not struck down Israel as he has done their enemies. We could paraphrase: "Has the Lord struck down Israel in the same way he, the Lord, struck down his enemies, who had struck down his people?" In this case "the one striking him down" is objective in relation to the preceding "striking down."

The identity of "his killed ones" in the second part of the question is also difficult to determine. If the first option is chosen above, then the point would be that the Lord has not struck Israel to the degree the Assyrians had done. In this case "his killed ones" refers to Assyria's victims. But, as noted above, a contrast between the Lord and his instrument, the Assyrians, seems artificial. If the second option is chosen above, then the point here is that the Lord has not unleashed his judgment upon Israel to the same degree he has upon his enemies. "His killed ones" would be other victims of the Lord's judgment. Motyer (1993, 224) suggests this recalls the destruction of the Egyptians at the Red Sea and the annihilation of Sennacherib's army outside Jerusalem (cf. Isa. 37:36).

So, even though judgment has fallen on the nation, the question forces them to consider their situation. It is not as bad as it could be. As Sweeney (1996, 347) observes, this "suggests a basis for hope and thereby leads to the proposition of restoration that follows." Or, as Childs (2000, 197) says, the prophet's goal is "didactic from the start by forcing a negative response to the query." He "raises the issue of God's purpose in his past acts of judgment by evoking the reflection of his addressees."

27:8. Nevertheless, the Lord has punished Israel. He has opposed her and, like a powerful windstorm, has driven her away. The first half of 27:8 is difficult; it reads literally, "with a shout (?), in sending her away, you contend with her." The meaning of the first word (בְּסַאסְּאָה) is unclear. An apparent Arabic cognate is used of gathering animals with a call, so perhaps a summons is in view, or a startling cry (see *HALOT* s.v. "סאסא" 738). The phrase "in sending her away" (בְּשַׁלְחָהּ) probably refers to the Lord expelling the nation as he contends with her. The *piel* of שָׁלַח is used elsewhere of a man divorcing his wife and the verb רִיב (cf. תְּרִיבֶנָּה in 27:8) is often used of legal disputes, so the metaphor may picture the Lord formally dissolving his marriage with his people. This would explain why the nation is referred to with the feminine singular pronoun here, as opposed to the masculine singular in 27:7, 9–10 (see Oswalt 1986, 498).

The Lord is addressed in 27:8a (note "you contend"), but he is described in the third person in the second half of the verse. The relatively rare verb הָגָה means "expel, remove." It is used elsewhere of removing dross from silver (Prov. 25:4) and of eliminating the wicked from the royal court (Prov. 25:5; see *HALOT* s.v. "הגה II" 237). Here it is used of the Lord's breath, compared to a strong east wind, blowing away something in its path (cf. Job 27:21), probably vegetation that it has dried up (cf. Gen. 41:6; Hos. 13:15; see Wildberger 1997, 595).

27:9. The prophet now appears to take a positive turn as he speaks of guilt being atoned for and sin being removed. However, as with Isaiah 27:7–8, there are interpretive challenges. The second line reads literally, "and this (is) all the fruit of removing his sin." The reference to removing sin corresponds to "the guilt of Jacob" being "atoned for" (or expiated) in the prior line. But it is unclear how the imagery of fruit is functioning in this context. It could refer to the product or result of sin being removed, as specified in 27:9b. (See Roberts [2015, 339], who translates, "and this will be the full expression [of repentance] for the removal of his sin.") Yet the reading "all the fruit" (כָּל־פְּרִי), draws suspicion, especially after יְכֻפַּר ("will be expiated") in the previous line. One wonders if it is a corruption of לְכַפֵּר, "to expiate." In this case, the following הָסֵר, "removing," would stand in apposition to לְכַפֵּר, making one wonder if לְכַפֵּר is a gloss on הָסֵר (see *BHS* textual note). Eliminating לְכַפֵּר as such, one may translate, "and (by) this (there will be) a removal of his sin."

The Restoration of Israel and the Vindication of the Righteous (25:1–27:13)

Another interpretive issue concerns the referent of "this" in 27:9a. Does it look back or forward? If back, then it refers to the judgment described in 27:8 (see Hayes and Irvine 1987, 317; Seitz 1993, 199; Sweeney 1996, 348; ; Young 1969, 245–46). In this case, there may be a note of sarcasm in that atonement, rather than prevention of judgment, is realized through Jacob paying the penalty for his sin. Another option is that "this" anticipates 27:9b, in which case 27:9b may have a hortatory nuance. Atonement is available to the people, if they destroy their idols (see Roberts 2015, 339). This may imply that sin's consequences can be avoided, or it may refer to the means of reconciliation with God following judgment (see Smith 2007, 463). In this reading, Jacob would be the antecedent of the third-person suffix on בְּשׂוּמוֹ, "when he makes." However, if God, who is addressed in 27:8a, is the subject, then the point would be that his judgment would purify the nation by destroying its idols (for discussion of the Asherah idols, see 17:8). In other words, judgment has an atoning function.

27:10–11. The prophet next describes the judgment that has overtaken the nation (cf. 27:8). A fortified city has been deserted and reduced to a pasture for cattle. Fortified cities had thick walls and defense towers to protect them from the onslaught of invaders. In this context this city is associated with Israel/Jacob (cf. 27:6, 9, 12), a nation that lacks spiritual discernment (27:11; cf. Hos. 4:14). The city likely depicts Samaria and/or Jerusalem (see the comments on Isa. 24:10–13 above). (See Roberts 2015, 340; Sweeney 1996, 348; Wildberger 1997, 596–97; Young 1969, 247–49.) However, others (Childs 2000, 198; Oswalt 1986, 499; Seitz 1993, 198–99; Smith 2007, 464) prefer to see the city as symbolizing Judah's enemies. Though fortified cities are impressive to human eyes (cf. Num. 13:28; Deut. 1:28), they are unable to withstand the fury of God's attack (Deut. 3:5–6; 9:1–3; Josh. 14:12; Hos. 8:14; Zeph. 1:16).

In the last line of Isaiah 27:10 the prophet depicts the city as a plant stripped bare by cattle. Perhaps the city's orchards and vineyards are in view (cf. Roberts 2015, 340). He extends the metaphor in 27:11a. Devoid of foliage, the branches become brittle and break off. Women gather them up as kindling for cooking fires. The reality behind the imagery is the nation that has no understanding. Tragically, their creator withholds compassion and grace from them (27:11b; cf. Hos. 1:6; 2:4 [HB 6]). The second of these divine titles (יֹצֵר, literally, "one who forms") is used of a potter (cf. Isa. 29:16; 41:25; 45:9; 64:7). The Lord withholds compassion from the people he has made, but later in Isaiah his sentiments change as he assures Israel he is committed to their well-being because they are the work of his hands (43:1; 44:2, 24; 45:11; 49:5; cf. 64:7).

27:12–13. The prophet shifts back to the future (cf. 27:2–6), as he announces what will take place "in that day." The Lord will gather his people from distant lands, all the way from the Euphrates River in Mesopotamia to the stream of Egypt, located on the border of Egypt (27:12). A large ram's horn will be blown, summoning exiles from the regions of Assyria and Egypt. They will congregate on the holy mountain in Jerusalem and worship the Lord (27:13).

Isaiah 27:12 speaks of the Lord beating out (יַחְבֹּט), as one would grain (Judg. 6:11; Ruth 2:17; Isa. 28:27) or olive trees (Deut. 24:20), though no object is expressed. The latter may be in view here since the imagery of a tree has just been used in Isaiah 27:10–11. In this case the Israelites are depicted as olives that are gathered up one by one. The noun שִׁבֹּלֶת can refer to ears of grain (Ruth 2:2; Job 24:24; Isa. 17:5) or to olive branches (Zech. 4:12), but, followed by הַנָּהָר, "the River," it may be understood as the homonymic "flood" (of waters; cf. Ps. 69:2, 15 [HB 3, 16]). Roberts (2015, 340) proposes double entendre here. The reference to Assyria reflects the reality

The Restoration of Israel and the Vindication of the Righteous (25:1–27:13)

of Isaiah's time. The northern kingdom had been taken captive by the Assyrians, as had many in Judah (see Roberts 2015, 340).

THEOLOGICAL FOCUS

The theological focus of this passage can be stated as follows: the Lord will vindicate his covenant people by establishing his rule from Zion, defeating all enemies, reclaiming the exiles, and restoring his favor and blessing. As the prophet develops this theological theme, the following emphases emerge:

1. The restoration of the covenant community

The dominant theme of this literary unit is the Lord's restoration of his covenant people. Beyond the judgment that lies in the immediate future, he will deliver them from exile (27:12–13) and establish the Zion ideal. He will dwell among his people in Zion, protecting them from danger and bestowing his blessings upon them. Nations will come to Zion and join the covenant community in worship. This is vividly portrayed in 25:6–8 through the vision of the eschatological banquet. Jesus spoke of this banquet as inaugurating the kingdom of God/heaven on earth (Matt. 8:11; Luke 13:29; 14:15; 22:16–18) and mentioned the patriarchs (Matt. 8:11), all the prophets (Luke 13:28), and peoples from all corners of the earth (Luke 13:29) as participants.

2. The death of death and Leviathan

A main feature of the vision of the eschatological banquet is the death of death, whom the Lord will swallow up once and for all (Isa. 25:7–8a). For Israel in particular, the inauguration of the Lord's kingdom will bring victory over death both literally and metaphorically. Israel's dead will rise from their graves and the nation will return from its tomb in exile (26:19). The Lord will also destroy Leviathan, once and for all (27:1). In this context, Leviathan, a hideous sea monster known in West Semitic myth, symbolizes the heavenly-earthly coalition that opposes the Lord (cf. 24:21).

PREACHING AND TEACHING STRATEGIES

Exegetical and Theological Synthesis

Isaiah 25–27 focuses on a few interrelated themes, some of which were introduced in chapter 24. First among them is the theme of celebratory worship by the people of God in response to his judgment against sinners (cf. Isa. 24:14–16), particularly those who used their clout and influence to oppress and persecute them while on earth. Isaiah 25:1 begins with a direct expression of praise to God for the wonderful things he has done. It goes on to describe those wonderful things in terms of destroying the fortified city and making it a heap of ruins (25:2). This develops another theme from chapter 24 (vv. 10, 12). As explained previously, the "city" in view here isn't a particular city, but symbolizes the secular world's cities or civilizations in general. Isaiah 25:3 makes this clear when it says "cities of ruthless nations will revere [God]" (cf. 25:5) as a result of his judgment against them. God's final judgment on them will result in their destruction with no hope of rebuilding.

Isaiah 25:4–5 describes God's protection and salvation of his own people with various colorful analogies. He is like a stronghold, or a secure shelter where one would be safe during a dangerous storm. The prophet also compares him to a cloud that provides shade on a very hot day. The land of Israel can get oppressively hot, especially in the desert. In many areas, there are very few if any shade trees. Thus, a cloud that offered shade to a traveler on a hot day would have been a major blessing. These metaphors effectively communicate how God had protected his people from their enemies who were out to hurt them. His judgment against their adversaries resulted in their protection, salvation, and thus their celebration. This celebration is formalized

The Restoration of Israel and the Vindication of the Righteous (25:1–27:13)

by the Lord himself as he throws a lavish feast for them (25:6). It will be a feast which includes the best meats and perfectly aged wine.

Isaiah 25:7–8 introduces one of the most amazing prophecies in the entire book of Isaiah. It tells how God will defeat humanity's greatest enemy, death (cf. Isa. 26:19). In 25:7, death is described as "the shroud that enfolds all peoples," and "the sheet that covers all nations." By this, he means that death is a dark reality that will eventually touch the life of every person in every nation. However, the Lord promises that he will "swallow up death forever." In so doing, he will "wipe away the tears from all faces," and "remove his people's disgrace from all the earth."

In response to this, God's people will rejoice in his salvation (25:9). The same salvation that raises God's people from the dead will simultaneously sentence their enemies to humiliation and destruction (25:10–12). Moab serves as an example of one such enemy of Israel whom God in his wrath will trample like straw in manure. He will "bring down" Moab's "pride," along with their fortified cities. To be brought down to the dust (cf. Isa. 26:5) is likely a reference here to death (Gen. 3:19; Job 17:13–16; 34:15; Pss. 22:29 [HB 30]; 104:29; Eccl. 3:20; 12:7), which stands in stark contrast to the people of God who will rise from the dust (Isa. 26:19).

In contrast to the people of this world who reject God and watch as he demolishes their fortified cities (25:12; 26:5–6), the people of God praise him in song because they "have a strong city" with secure walls that protect them from their enemies (26:1). God is their "rock eternal," who keeps them in a state of "perfect peace" as they continually trust in him (26:3–4).

God's people rejoice over his judgment of the wicked because it ultimately brings about righteousness throughout the earth (26:7–12). God's followers recognize that righteous living results in security and prosperity (a level path; 26:7). This is more than a mere moralistic lifestyle; it involves a life devoted to God and his ways. Thus, his people wait for and desire God above all else (26:8–9a). When his judgment against sin is revealed throughout the earth, people learn the importance of righteous living (26:9b). Ironically, when sinners continue to get away with their unrighteous, immoral behavior without suffering God's judgment, they come to regard God and his ways as optional and unimportant at best (26:10). Thus, the prophet prays that the world's inhabitants would recognize God's zeal to protect his people by judging their enemies before it is too late (26:11). God's people praise God for providing them with "peace" (security and prosperity). They acknowledge that God made all of the nation's past accomplishments possible (26:12).

The prophet continues to draw out contrasting realities between God's people and their oppressors in 26:13–15. Israel has had many lords who have ruled over them throughout their long history, but only one is worthy of their remembrance and praise (26:13). Why? Because all their earthly oppressors will eventually be a thing of the past. They will die, never to rise again. Thus, while God is worthy of the people's *remembrance*, he will wipe away the *remembrance* of Israel's enemies (26:14). Whereas these enemy nations along with their wicked tyrant leaders have been or will be destroyed, the people of God and their borders will be enlarged (26:15).

Isaiah 26:16–18 would seem to switch gears suddenly to describe Israel in its present state. In the immediately preceding context, the prophet looks forward to when all Israel's enemies will be judged by God, leading to Israel's blessing and expansion. In the present, though, God's people have experienced the distress of his discipline upon them in the form of these oppressive enemies. In their distress, they whispered a prayer to God for his intervention and help (26:16). They compare this oppression to the pain of childbirth (26:17–18). Prior to their crying out to God, they had been trying on their own to bring about deliverance from their affliction. However, they were unable to accomplish

The Restoration of Israel and the Vindication of the Righteous (25:1–27:13)

salvation on their own. Their enemies did not fall due to their own efforts.

Nonetheless, what Israel could not do for itself, God will accomplish on their behalf. He will come "out of his dwelling to punish the people of the earth" (26:21) who have rebelled against him and simultaneously oppressed his people. In the meantime, God encourages his people to enter their rooms and hide themselves from God's wrath until his judgment is over (26:20). The imagery of them hiding in their homes until God's fury is past is a poetic way of describing how God's people must wait patiently for him to enact his judgment on the earth. In the meantime, regardless of whatever circumstantial danger they face, God's people are protected by their faith in God. For even if they should die before God's judgment against their enemies is complete, they can have confidence in their eventual resurrection from the dead (26:19). Furthermore, the imagery of God's people finding safety within the confines of their chambers likely contributes to the theme of God's people possessing a city that offers them protection and security (Isa. 25:4; 26:1–2, 4) in contrast to the people of this world whose city will be destroyed and whose strongholds are no match for God's judgment when it comes (Isa. 24:10, 12; 25:2–3, 12; 26:5; 27:10).

In the day when God comes to judge this world, he will defeat Israel's earthly enemies such as Babylon, Assyria, Moab, and every other oppressive nation. However, God's judgment will also strike at the cosmic source of all evil in the world. He will punish Leviathan, the ancient serpent of the sea (27:1). As mentioned above, Leviathan serves as a symbol of the evil cosmic forces that oppose God and, by extension, the people of God. Satan, called "the ancient serpent" and "the dragon" (Rev. 12:3–17; 20:2; cf. Gen. 3:1), is the reality behind the metaphor, along with those who align themselves with Satan in opposition to God. Thus, when God enacts this final judgment, it will universally defeat every enemy of God's people.

In Isaiah 27:2–6, God looks beyond the day when his worldwide judgment has been completed. In that day, Israel will be like a well-tended, fruitful vineyard (27:2). Why will this be? Because God will be the keeper of the vineyard. He will faithfully water it day and night (27:3). He will go to battle against the thorns and briers that would dare to grow and threaten his precious vines (27:4). As a result, Jacob will take root and produce fruit that will fill the entire earth (27:6). This corresponds to the earlier imagery of Israel increasing as a nation and expanding her borders throughout the entire earth (Isa. 26:15).

As such, God's present discipline of Israel is not like his eventual judgment against the nations (27:8–9). While God contended with Israel by sending them into exile, he contended with Israel's enemies by means of his fierce breath by which he removed them all together. As such, God's action against his own people was to discipline them in a way that would remove their sin. They would repent of their idolatry, destroying their idolatrous altars and removing their incense altars and Asherah poles.

Isaiah 27:10–11 describes the aftermath of a civilization that has been judged by God. Here, the prophet seems to be describing Israel and/or Samaria. As such, it is a continuation of the prior verses that explained how God would discipline his people through exile to bring about a repentant heart in them. During exile, their towns were abandoned and their streets overgrown, resembling a place where animals could graze (27:10). The city is further likened to a dead tree with dried-up branches that are only good for firewood. This judgment came because God's people foolishly turned their back on the Lord in favor of false gods. For this reason, God will not show mercy on them when he enacts judgment (27:11).

Finally, 27:12–13 emphasizes that God's judgment against Israel would not entail permanent destruction or abandonment. While he will not have compassion on them nor show them mercy during their time of exile (Isa. 27:8), he will nonetheless show them mercy and kindness in the future. In that day, when God judges the world and removes Israel's enemies, he will bring his people back to their land, where they will again "worship the Lord on the holy mountain in Jerusalem" (27:13).

Preaching Idea
Believers celebrate their salvation as God defeats all their enemies, including death.

Contemporary Connections

What does it mean?
God would judge Israel's geopolitical enemies, demolishing their cities (25:2–3, 10–12; 26:5) and destroying their people. By extension, God will remove from this world all ruthless and wicked people, many of whom have persecuted believers in some form or another, with his fiery judgment (25:3, 5; 26:11, 14) in preparation for his coming kingdom. He will wipe away once and for all the tears and reproach of his followers (25:8). As a result, his people will rejoice and celebrate (25:6–9; 26:19; 27:13).

The world's evil despots have been responsible for innumerable deaths and immense suffering throughout history. In the last century alone, Mao Zedong, Joseph Stalin, and Adolf Hitler were responsible for the collective murder of as many as 118 million people.[13] Additionally, nations such as Afghanistan, North Korea, Nigeria, and India are just a few of the places where being a Christian makes one a target of significant persecution. While it is almost impossible to obtain accurate numbers on how many Christians have been martyred or persecuted for their faith in the last century, the number has certainly been growing. It isn't hard to understand why Christians, especially those who live under the cruel tyranny of an evil, God-hating dictator, will celebrate God's judgment against their enemies. Persecuted believers today identify intimately with the prayers of the souls of those who have been martyred for their Christian testimony, "How long, Sovereign Lord, holy and true, until you judge the inhabitants of the earth and avenge our blood?" (Rev. 6:10).

However, the greatest enemy that Christians face today is not North Korea, Iran, China, India, or any of their authoritarian leaders. Neither would it be accurate to think of any of the Islamic terrorist groups such as al-Qaeda, Boko Haram, or ISIS as Christianity's worst enemy. Rather, Christianity's most pernicious enemy (as well as that of all humanity) is none other than death itself. The apostle Paul referred to death as humanity's "last enemy" (1 Cor. 15:26). It affects all people in every age without exception.

Immediately after the creation of humankind, God warned Adam and Eve that if they disobeyed him by eating the forbidden fruit, they would certainly die (Gen. 2:17; 3:1–3). Believing the serpent's lie that she would not actually die, Eve ate the fruit and then offered some to her husband and he too ate (Gen. 3:4–6). God proved truthful and the devil a liar as Adam and Eve were expelled from the garden and cut off from the tree of life. Ever since sin entered into the world, humans have suffered the daily assault of death pulling them ever closer to the grave (Rom. 5:12–14; 6:23; 1 Cor. 15:22).

Thus, when the prophet predicted that God's salvation of his people would ultimately include victory over death and the grave (Isa. 25:8–9; 26:19), this promise extended hope to everyone, including those who had already died. Furthermore, it was a promise that generated hope for all eternity. No wonder this prophecy elicited such rejoicing and worship.

---

13 https://www.jcpe.tv/top-ten-most-evil-dictators-of-all-time-in-order-of-kill-count.

The Restoration of Israel and the Vindication of the Righteous (25:1–27:13)

Is it true?
Is death humanity's greatest enemy? Consider the following excerpt from a published sermon I wrote a few years back from John 11 on death and resurrection.

> Humans spend much effort in life trying to postpone death. In fact, the entire medical industry is devoted to fighting and postponing death as long as possible. According to a recent *Forbes* article, the average family of four spent nearly $21,000 on healthcare in 2012. The US government spent an additional $8,600 per person on average on healthcare. That's almost $14,000 per person each year Americans spend primarily trying to postpone death. This doesn't include the time and money invested in things like exercise equipment, healthy foods, antiaging skin creams, cosmetics, hair dyes, and any number of things we use to postpone or cover up the effects of aging. Yet despite all that money and energy, death is an inevitable reality. One author wrote, "We may postpone it, we may tame its violence, but death is still there waiting for us . . . Death spares none." (Hontz 2013, 144)

Death is inevitable for all. It is impervious to any human attempt at preventing it. The strong cannot overcome it with willpower or physical might. Neither can death be bribed by the wealthy to pass them up. It cannot be bargained with by the wise or crafty. Likewise, death will not be intimidated by the most powerful and influential of leaders. The discreet and inconspicuous cannot hide from the pervasive eyes of death. Humanly speaking, death is inescapable for all. It does not discriminate; it is truly no respecter of persons. Unsurprisingly then, even wealthy, powerful people must grapple with a fear of their own mortality. In a *Time* magazine article, the author writes that for billionaire Ted Turner, "life has been a struggle to master what he calls his 'greatest' fear—the fear of death" (Painton 1992).

There could have been no greater news for the people in Isaiah's day than to hear that God would conquer death once and for all at some point in the future. The same continues to be true for people today. With the elimination of death, all tears and sadness will be a thing of the past. The death of death will be accompanied by a resurrection of the righteous who had previously died. For the readers of Isaiah's prophecy, it wouldn't become evident for another seven hundred years that the resurrection of saints would only be made possible through the death and resurrection of Jesus the Messiah. In fact, Paul directly ties God's promise to swallow up death forever (Isa. 25:8) with the resurrection of Jesus in 1 Corinthians 15:54. Earlier in that chapter, Paul established the connection between our future resurrection and Jesus's when he said,

> And if Christ has not been raised, your faith is futile; you are still in your sins. Then those also who have fallen asleep in Christ are lost. If only for this life we have hope in Christ, we are of all people most to be pitied. But Christ has indeed been raised from the dead, the firstfruits of those who have fallen asleep. For since death came through a man, the resurrection of the dead comes also through a man. For as in Adam all die, so in Christ all will be made alive. (1 Cor. 15:17–22)

Paul here describes Jesus as the "firstfruits" of our resurrection. Firstfruits was a Jewish feast held in the early spring at the beginning of the grain harvest. The Jews were required to bring the firstfruits of their harvest to God in thanksgiving for the crops still to come (Lev. 23:9–11). Their willingness to give of their firstfruits required faith that God would later provide a full harvest. The Feast of Firstfruits also coincided with the Feasts of Passover and Unleavened Bread (Exod. 12:1–20). Because Jesus died on a Friday (Mark 15:42; John 19:31), the same day that the Passover meal was eaten, this means that Jesus would have risen from the dead on Sunday (Matt. 28:1; Mark 16:1–2; Luke 24:1; John 20:1), the morning of the Feast of Firstfruits.[14] This is significant, for it shows that Jesus's resurrection was the "firstfruit" of a much greater harvest to come. In John 12:23–24, Jesus predicted his coming death in this way:

> The hour has come for the Son of Man to be glorified. Very truly I tell you, unless a kernel of wheat falls to the ground and dies, it remains only a single seed. But if it dies, it produces many seeds.

Jesus saw his own death and burial as the planting of a seed, one that would bring forth much fruit or a much greater harvest. Therefore, Paul referred to Jesus's resurrection as the "firstfruits" in 1 Corinthians 15:20, because as he will go on to say, "For as in Adam all die, so in Christ all will be made alive" (15:22). In his death on the cross, Jesus paid for sin in full. But it was in his resurrection that Jesus conquered death, paving the way for a future harvest of resurrections by all who have trusted in him. Thus, Paul can declare that Jesus "must reign until he has put all his enemies under his feet. The last enemy to be destroyed is death" (15:25–26). Once all this has taken place, and Christ's followers have been clothed in their new resurrection bodies, "then the saying that is written will come true: 'Death has been swallowed up in victory'" (15:54; see Isa. 25:8).

This salvation is cause for celebration now and for eternity. In fact, Paul ends his long treatise on resurrection in 1 Corinthians 15 with a celebratory taunt to death, "Where, O death, is your victory? Where, O death, is your sting?" (15:55). One can picture the underdog victors after a war celebrating together in mocking fashion of their now-defeated enemies with fists raised defiantly, "Where is your victory? Where is your sting?" But this celebration is ultimately an expression of worship and gratitude toward God as the one who accomplished this victory on our behalf. Thus, Paul writes, "But thanks be to God! He gives us the victory through our Lord Jesus Christ" (15:57).

Now what?
If you've ever been to the funeral of a close family member or friend who died early in life, you have no doubt wrestled with questions such as, "Where was God when this happened?" "Why did God allow him/her to die so young?" or "If God really loved them, why didn't he intervene to prevent his/her death?" A natural tendency is to become angry and bitter toward God for not doing anything. In that moment, one struggles to understand why God didn't do more to prevent our loved one's untimely death.

It is important during times like these to remember that God *did* do something to save that person from death. In fact, God did everything necessary to deliver them from death itself, rather than simply from that one incident that caused their death. God sometimes does

---

14 Whereas we tend to think of a new day beginning at sunrise, the Jewish day began at sundown or twilight the previous evening. Jesus and his disciples ate the Passover meal after sundown on the night before he was betrayed and crucified. Firstfruits was celebrated the day after the Sabbath following the beginning of the Feast of Unleavened Bread, which began on the Day of Passover (Exod. 12:1–20; Lev. 23:11; Num. 28:16–31; Deut. 16:1–12). For the chronology of the Jewish feasts in relation to the death and resurrection of Jesus, Brad Gray from *Walking the Text* offers a helpful explanation and teaching at https://walkingthetext.com/bread-of-life-pt-7.

intervene to heal people of cancer or protect people who have been a victim of a serious car accident caused by a drunk driver. When he does things like these, we rightfully rejoice and express our gratitude to him. However, these interventions by themselves are only temporary prolongments of a person's life. They don't deliver the person from death itself. However, in Jesus's work on the cross and through his resurrection, God has conquered death itself for all who identify themselves with Christ. For this reason, Jesus said to Martha in John 11:25–26, "I am the resurrection and the life. The one who believes in me will live, even though they die; and whoever lives by believing in me will never die." Don't miss what Jesus says here about those who die. Because he is the resurrection and the life, those who seemingly die really don't. Rather, they continue to live eternally while they await the resurrection of their bodies in the future.

This truth is not meant to trivialize the pain associated with the tragedy of a parent who loses a child to leukemia or a husband whose wife is tragically killed by a random act of violence. But it does provide a completely different perspective, a hopeful one, for those who are left to deal with the aftermath of death. Paul said it well in his first letter to the Thessalonian congregation:

> Brothers and sisters, we do not want you to be uninformed about those who sleep in death, so that you do not grieve like the rest of mankind, who have no hope. For we believe that Jesus died and rose again, and so we believe that God will bring with Jesus those who have fallen asleep in him. (1 Thess. 4:13–14)

Because Jesus provides resurrection hope to all those who identify with him by faith, the appropriate response is gratitude and worship. Even during deep pain at the loss of a friend or close relative, the doctrine of a future resurrection provides genuine peace and comfort for those who are in Christ. This calls for regular worship and celebration of the one who provides us with such a great salvation.

Every Sunday provides believers with a fresh opportunity to celebrate our new life in Jesus. It is generally accepted that believers transitioned away from Saturdays to worship on Sundays (Acts 20:7; 1 Cor. 16:1–2) because it commemorated the day on which Jesus rose again. As such, the start of every week provides believers with a new opportunity to reflect on and remember Jesus's sacrificial death and victorious resurrection. It should infuse us with joy and optimism regardless of our circumstances. After all, every sad or difficult event is but a brief and temporary obstacle on the road to our destination of eternal life in God's coming kingdom.

Creativity in Presentation

Grave Robber

In 2011, Anatoly Moskvin, a Russian professor, was arrested by the police who were investigating a series of crimes involving graves that had been vandalized and desecrated in cemeteries in and around Nizhny Novgorod, a city in Russia. Moskvin himself was extremely intelligent and highly educated; he was considered an expert in cemeteries. Local authorities originally reached out to him for help in their investigation of these crimes. However, when they visited his home, investigators discovered what appeared to be life-sized dolls that Moskvin had dressed in brightly colored clothing. They sat on shelves or around tables throughout his cluttered home. However, on closer inspection, it turned out that these were the mummified bodies of girls who had died between the ages of three and fifteen. Moskvin had dug up the remains of these children in order to preserve them in his home.

It was initially assumed that this demented individual must have had some form of a sexual fetish toward these dead bodies, but that turned out not to be the case. Rather, Moskvin held the irrational belief that if he could take these children out of their graves, he could bring them back to life, and by so doing he could save them from their premature deaths. While this man obviously suffered from some form of strange and delusional thinking, his desire to find a way to overcome the grave by giving life back to those who had died is innate to all people. The human soul longs for a solution to the age-old enemy that is death. What Anatoly Moskvin unsuccessfully attempted to do for those children, the Lord Jesus Christ has triumphantly accomplished through the cross and resurrection.[15]

Delivered from Death

Sol Gringlas was born to a Jewish couple in Ostrowiec, Poland, on August 22, 1919. His family called him by his Jewish name, Shaul Meir. In 1939, Nazi soldiers invaded his hometown. As a Jew, he was forced to work for them and live separated from his family in a barracks until 1943, when he was shipped in a crowded train car for days until he arrived at his destination, the Auschwitz concentration camp. Upon his arrival, he was greeted by the sight of children's shoes and clothing heaped into huge piles. These had belonged to people who had been murdered. Someone turned to him and said, "Shaul, this is the end."

A few days later, Sol was moved again, this time to the Nordhausen concentration camp in Germany. This would be his home for the next two years where he would be forced to fight for survival, as most of the other prisoners there would eventually be killed. However, on April 11, 1945, Sol received the news that the Americans had arrived and that he had been liberated. Sol would live to be one hundred years old, but he never forgot the day of his liberation. He celebrated that day every year as his "second birthday," the day when his life started all over again. This story illustrates the celebratory emotions felt by one who has just been delivered from what seemed like certain death. The people of God have even greater reason to celebrate for God has defeated death itself and given them eternal life.

Life Below the Surface

When I was in kindergarten, our class planted sunflower seeds in small pots to learn about how plants grow. We watered them and set them on the windowsill in our classroom while we waited for them to bloom. Each morning when I came into my classroom, I would go over to my pot and look to see if anything was growing. Days passed, and still there was no evidence of a plant growing. I began to grow frustrated and impatient. Will this thing ever start to grow? Then it happened one morning—another student's plant had begun to sprout above the soil. I hoped this meant that mine would be next. The next morning, a couple other students had a sprout growing in their pot too, but not me. By the next morning, most of the students could point to the plant growing in their pot, and I wondered, "Is mine a dud? Maybe mine is never going to grow." Able to wait no longer, I took my finger and began to dig away at the soil. Sure enough, just below the surface, there was my sprout. If I had been more patient, it would certainly have introduced itself to me on its own in another day or two. In truth, the seed that had been planted had begun to germinate life long before I was able to see it. That life was below the surface, so it was out of sight. But its life was just as real as when it began to sprout out of the soil for me to see it.

The New Testament teaches that when a person identifies with Jesus through faith, they are given eternal life. That life is not

---

15 https://en.wikipedia.org/wiki/Anatoly_Moskvin.

something they will only receive at some point in the future. Rather, it is something they possess now, at the point of their faith in Jesus. John 5:24 says, "Whoever hears my word and believes him who sent me *has* eternal life and will not be judged but has crossed over from death to life" (emphasis added). For those who are followers of Jesus, eternal life is something they already possess. They have already passed from death to life.

Like that germinated plant that had yet to sprout, our eternal life exists below the surface. One day, at the resurrection, we will be clothed with new bodies. At that point, the life that has been below the surface will sprout into view for us and for all to see. Until then, we live by faith, knowing that because Jesus rose again as our firstfruits, we too will one day rise again.

For the above illustration, consider bringing two pots with you as an object lesson. In one of them, have a growing plant of some type that is evident for all to see. In the other, have a plant that has not yet sprouted. Ask the group which one represents life. The unexpected answer will be that both are equally symbols of life, even though we can only see the life in the one because the life in the other plant remains below the surface.

Believers celebrate their salvation as God defeats all their enemies, including death.

One option for this section is for the preacher to move thematically through the passage rather than in a linear fashion from beginning to end.

- God destroys the world's "cities" in judgment against the enemies of his people (25:2; 25:12; 26:5; 27:10).
- God surrounds his people with their own strong "city" in protection from their enemies (26:1–4).
- God defeats the ultimate enemy of his people—death (25:8; 26:19).

DISCUSSION QUESTIONS

1. Isaiah uses the metaphor of a "city" to describe the unbelieving people of this world who will be the recipients of God's future judgment. In what ways does a city serve as a fitting metaphor for the world's system that stands in opposition to God? (If you have time, read Revelation 18, which similarly describes God's future judgment against this world metaphorically as judgment against the city of Babylon. In what ways does Babylon resemble some of the sinful attributes that are especially present in modern cities around the world today?)

2. Discuss the ways in which you have wrestled with a fear of dying. Were there periods of your life where this fear was more pronounced than others? Were there events in your life that triggered these fears?

3. As you understand it, what is the significance of Jesus's resurrection to the gospel message? Could God have granted salvation to people simply based on Jesus's substitutionary death on the cross without also raising Jesus from the dead? Why or why not?

4. Read Isaiah 25:4–5 and 26:1–4. What are some of the vivid metaphors with which the prophet describes God's protection of his own people who are poor and needy?

FOR FURTHER READING

Bayly, Joseph. 1973. *The Last Thing We Talk About*. Elgin, IL: Cook.

JUDGMENT GIVES WAY TO SALVATION (ISAIAH 28–35)

This next major literary unit mirrors the two prior literary units (chs. 1–12, 13–27) in its movement and emphases. Isaiah 28–33 contains messages pertaining to the covenant community. Images of judgment predominate in 28:1–30:17 (fifty-six of seventy verses focus on judgment), but the theme of salvation predominates in 30:18–33:24 (sixty of sixty-nine verses have a positive focus). As in chapters 1–12, the emphasis shifts from judgment in the first part of the section (see chs. 1–9) to salvation in the second part (see chs. 10–12). Additionally, the Lord's deliverance of Jerusalem from the Assyrian threat is an important theme (29:5–8; 30:27–33; 31:4–9; 33:1, 12, 19; cf. 8:9–10; 10:5–34), as is the spiritual transformation of the covenant community (29:17–24; 32:1–8, 15–20; 33:15–16; cf. 1:25–27; 2:2–4; 4:2–6; 9:6–7 [HB 5–6]; 11:1–9). The theme of chapter 34 is the Lord's judgment upon the nations, particularly Edom, which serves as an archetype for the enemies of the Lord and his people. This more worldwide focus mirrors chapters 13–23 and the culminating Little Apocalypse of chapters 24–27. This section ends in chapter 35 with the Lord leading the exiles home—a theme that concludes the Little Apocalypse (27:12–13) as well as chapters 1–12 (see 11:10–12:6). The focus on the return from exile at the end of each of the three major literary units in chapters 1–35 (11:10–12:6; 27:12–13; 35:1–10) paves the way for the book's interlude (chs. 36–39), which ends with a prediction of exile (39:6–8), and for chapters 40–55, which address the future exiles with a promise of deliverance and restoration.

The internal structure of chapters 28–33 exhibits six panels, each of which begins with a woe oracle, followed by a positive message of salvation for the covenant community. Additional messages of judgment conclude panels 1 and 2 (28:7–29; 29:9–14), while panel 5 has an additional judgment + salvation sequence (32:9–14, 15–20). The conclusion to the section exhibits the judgment + salvation pattern (34:1–17; 35:1–10). The structure of the section may be outlined as follows:[1]

Panel One (28:1–29)
Woe Oracle Against Samaria (28:1–4)
Salvation (28:5–6)
Judgment Speech (28:7–29)

Panel Two (29:1–14)
Woe Oracle Against Jerusalem (29:1–4)
Deliverance of Jerusalem (29:5–8)
Judgment Speech (29:9–14)

---

1   For a very similar outline of the structure of Isaiah 28–33, see Stansell 1996, 71. Stansell labels 28:23–29 as a salvation unit, omits 30:27–33, places 31:4 with 31:1–3, and treats 32:9–20 as a distinct panel, even though it is not introduced by הוֹי, "woe."

Panel Three (29:15–24)
Woe Oracle Against Those Who Devise Secret Plans (29:15–16)
Salvation (29:17–24)

Panel Four (30:1–33)
Woe Oracle Against Those Who Seek Foreign Alliances (30:1–17)
Salvation (30:18–33)

Panel Five (31:1–32:20)
Woe Oracle Against Those Who Seek Foreign Alliances (31:1–3)
Salvation (31:4–32:8)
Judgment (32:9–14)
Salvation (32:15–20)

Panel Six (33:1–24)
Woe Oracle Against the "Destroyer" (33:1)
Prayer (33:2–9)
Salvation (33:10–24)

Conclusion (34:1–35:10)
Judgment Upon Nations, Particularly Edom (34:1–17)
Salvation (35:1–10)

In the first two panels salvation is mentioned only briefly, before a judgment speech fills out the panel. In panel 5, as in panels 1–2, a judgment speech follows the message of salvation, but in this case another round of salvation then appears. The change in emphasis from panels 1–2 is obvious. Panel 6 differs significantly from the preceding panels. The woe oracle is addressed to an enemy, not the covenant community. A prayer follows, which is answered by an oracle of salvation to which the prophet responds with a message of salvation. The theme of judgment against enemies is expanded in the first part of the conclusion, as the nations are summoned to hear of their impending doom. The concluding message of salvation begins with a call to nature to rejoice, followed by a portrait of the exiles' return to Zion.

For proclamation purposes, we have divided this literary unit into six expositional/preaching sections: (1) 28:1–29; (2) 29:1–24; (3) 30:1–33; (4) 31:1–32:20; (5) 33:1–24; (6) 34:1–35:10.

Isaiah 28:1–29

EXEGETICAL IDEA
The Lord's destructive judgment upon both Samaria and Judah will remove the covenant community's corrupt leaders and replace them with those who promote justice.

THEOLOGICAL FOCUS
The Lord, the people's only genuine source of security, judges corrupt leaders to establish justice in his covenant community.

PREACHING IDEA
The Lord alone can provide genuine security.

PREACHING POINTERS
In a 1943 paper entitled "A Theory of Human Motivation," Abraham Maslow (1943, 370–96) proposed a hierarchy of human needs. According to Maslow, the most basic of human needs are physiological—things such as breathing, food, water, and sleep. These things are necessary for life. Only one level above this on his proposed pyramid of needs are those related to human safety and security. While just a theory, Maslow's hierarchy of needs assumes that the more basic or essential a need is believed to be by an individual, the more it will likely impact their behavior. In other words, because food and water are needed to live, most people will do almost anything to get or maintain food and water. Similarly, because issues of safety and security are also very high on the spectrum of human needs, they too will naturally have a significant impact on many people's actions. Most people will go to great lengths in their life in order to feel safe and secure.

Isaiah 28 focuses on this issue of security. The prophet confronts the leaders of Israel and Judah regarding their misplaced faith as it related to whom/what they were trusting in for security. While Israel was trusting primarily in their capital city of Samaria to protect them in the event of a military attack, Judah's sense of security was tied to their "covenant with death," as the prophet referred to it. This was likely a reference to their alliance with Egypt. In reality, neither strong cities nor powerful military allies can provide ultimate protection, especially in the event that God decides to act in judgment against a people. As such, this passage explores the issue of security, including false sources of security. It reveals how, in the ultimate sense, the Lord alone provides genuine security.

JUDGMENT OVERWHELMS THE ENTIRE LAND (28:1–29)

The Lord's destructive judgment will overwhelm both Samaria and Judah, despite their confidence in false sources of security. Security can be found in the Lord alone, whose wisdom is evident even in judgment as he removes the covenant community's corrupt leaders and replaces them with those who promote justice.

LITERARY STRUCTURE AND THEMES (28:1–29)

This first panel of chapters 28–35 (see above) begins with a woe oracle directed against Samaria, called "that wreath, the pride of Ephraim's drunkards," and "that fading flower." As is typical, an accusation is embedded within the woe pronouncement as Ephraim's people are depicted as "drunkards" whose pride is misplaced in a city (28:1), rather than in the Lord (cf. 28:5–6). An announcement of judgment follows, as the Lord intervenes powerfully (28:2) with devastating results (28:3–4).

In a brief interlude the prophet reminds his audience that salvation is the end result of the coming judgment, which will culminate with the Lord becoming the "beautiful wreath" of the remnant that survives (28:5) and the source of renewed stability and security (28:6).

The prophet expands the judgment speech as he focuses on the priests and prophets, whose spiritual dullness makes them incapable of leading as they should (28:7–9). For this reason, judgment will come upon them in the form of a foreign invader speaking a strange language (28:10–13).

There is an important lesson for Jerusalem and its mocking leaders in all of this. The prophet turns to them as he calls them to attention (28:14) and accuses them of misplaced confidence (28:15). For this reason, the Lord announces he will intervene in judgment (28:17–22) against those who have rejected the security he provides (28:16). This subunit is marked out by an *inclusio*, with mockers being addressed at the beginning and end (28:14, 22).

The speech ends in a unique manner. After a call to hear (28:23), a series of rhetorical questions pertaining to plowing and planting appears (28:24–25). The prophet affirms that God instructs the farmer regarding these matters (28:26). He then speaks of the proper techniques of threshing (28:27–28), before again affirming that the Lord is the source of wisdom in this regard (28:29). On the surface, this section of the speech seems intrusive and unrelated to the preceding judgment speech. But we must assume it contributes to the message in some way. Indeed, just as divinely imparted wisdom characterizes the work of the farmer, so it is evident in God's dealings with his wayward people.

- ***Woe Oracle Against Samaria: Destructive Judgment Overwhelms Samaria (28:1–4)***
- ***Salvation: Transformation Beyond Judgment (28:5–6)***
- ***Judgment Speech (28:7–29)***
  - *Destructive Judgment Overwhelms the People and Their Leaders (28:7–13)*
  - *Destructive Judgment Overwhelms Jerusalem and Its Leaders (28:14–22)*
  - *The Wisdom of God Evident in Judgment (28:23–29)*

Judgment Overwhelms the Entire Land (28:1–29)

EXPOSITION (28:1–29)

Woe Oracle Against Samaria: Destructive Judgment Overwhelms Samaria (28:1–4)
The Lord will judge Samaria.

28:1. The prophet's use of "woe" (הוֹי) suggests death is imminent. He anticipates the demise of Samaria, whom he depicts as a wreath (or perhaps, crown) and a flower. The imagery reflects the city's prominence, both topographically (located at the head of a fertile valley) and politically. It was a great source of pride to the drunkards of Ephraim (the northern kingdom of Israel) who delighted in its beauty.

The identity of these "drunkards" is not clear. If the language is taken literally, the prophet may be depicting the people at large as given to the abuse of wine, indicating they had lost their moral compass and were on the brink of destruction. Perhaps he has in mind the rich residents of the city that comprise a royal bureaucracy prone to carousing and frivolity (see Amos 6:6; as well as Isa. 5:11–12, 22; see Smith 2007, 476). The use of "Ephraim" suggests a broader focus unless the phrase is understood to refer to the rich drunkards within Ephraim. In Isaiah 28:7 he pictures the spiritual leadership (priests and prophets) as being drunk, but the phrase "these also" (or perhaps, "even these") at the beginning of the verse indicates they are part of a larger group of drunkards, most likely those mentioned in 28:1. Perhaps the prophet is using drunkenness metaphorically to describe how spiritually insensitive and misguided the people are. This seems to be the case with the priests and prophets (28:7–9). Yet literal drunkenness may also be in view.

In addition to the introductory "woe" (הוֹי), there are other ominous signs in 28:1. Samaria may be a beautiful flower in the eyes of Ephraim's drunkards, but their vision is obviously blurred. The prophet calls the city a "fading" flower, anticipating its demise. Flowers are known for their outward beauty, but in Isaiah they symbolize that which is temporary and soon fades—Samaria's splendor, as well as human beings and their promises, in contrast to the reliable Word of God (cf. 40:6–8). The reference to "pride" is also foreboding, for the Lord's day of judgment targets the proud (cf. 2:12). The final phrase in the verse, "laid low by wine" (הֲלוּמֵי יָיִן), also has a negative connotation. The verb הָלַם, "to strike, beat" (*HALOT* s.v. "הלם" 249), is used in Proverbs 23:35 of drunkards who feel no pain when they are beaten by others. The drunkard is vulnerable to attack and oblivious to an assault, perhaps by those wanting to rob him. In Isaiah 28:1 it is (by metonymy) the wine itself that does the beating, for it is the wine that makes the drunkard defenseless. Whether literal or figurative drunkenness is in view here (could it be both?), Ephraim's drunkards are victimized by that which intoxicates them and robs them of their senses.

28:2. The prophet draws attention (note הִנֵּה, "see") to the Lord's agent of judgment, called here "one who is powerful and strong" (28:2a). This likely refers to the Assyrians. The Lord's sovereignty over his agent is highlighted by the title אֲדֹנָי, Sovereign Master (NIV11, Lord; cf. 3:15, 17–18; 6:8, 11; 7:14; 9:8, 17 [HB 7, 16]; 10:12, 23–24, 33; 11:11; 22:5, 12, 14–15; 25:8), along with the possessive idiom to describe his ownership of the agent. The text reads literally, "(there is) a powerful and strong (one) (belonging) to the Sovereign Master." Vivid imagery is used to describe the devastating power of this strong agent (28:2b). He is like a hailstorm accompanied by destructive winds. This storm produces a flash flood of raging water, capable of knocking everything in its path to the ground.

28:3–4. The power of this agent of judgment is unleashed on Samaria. The beautiful wreath, in which Ephraim's drunkards take such pride (cf. 28:1), is trampled underfoot (28:3). The fading flower (cf. 28:1), like an early fig discovered prior to the harvest, is, as it were, devoured quickly (28:4).

Salvation: Transformation Beyond Judgment (28:5–6)

The Lord will preserve a remnant and restore national security.

Before expanding the judgment speech (see 28:7–13), the prophet stops to make the point that judgment will not destroy the nation (see Motyer 1993, 230). In the aftermath of judgment, the Lord becomes the "wreath" of the remnant of his people (28:5), suggesting they will delight in him, rather than in Samaria, or any other false source of hope for that matter. To highlight the contrast between the present and the future, the prophet uses language from 28:1 and 28:4 to describe how the Lord will become a beautiful wreath (צְבִי עֲטֶרֶת) and an attractive (תִּפְאָרָה) crown to "the remnant of his people" (28:5). He will provide internal stability through righteous judges and national security through divinely energized warriors. He will become (i.e., impart) a "spirit of justice" to those responsible for making legal decisions (28:6a; cf. 11:2–5) and strength to those responsible for defending the gate against would-be invaders (28:6b).

Judgment Speech (28:7–29)

Destructive Judgment Overwhelms the People and Their Leaders (28:7–13)

The Lord's judgment will target the leaders of Israel and Judah.

In 28:7–13 the prophet resumes the judgment speech of 28:1–4 as he denounces the priests and prophets for their drunken behavior (Oswalt 1986, 509). But whose priests and prophets are in view here—Israel's or Judah's? In favor of Israel as the referent, note: (1) the words "and also these" appear to link 28:7 with what precedes, as does the motif of drunkenness (cf. 28:1); and (2) Isaiah 28:7 appears to expand on 28:1 by pointing out that even the religious leaders of Ephraim (priests and prophets) are drunkards. However, Smith (2007, 479), who understands 28:7–13 as pertaining to leaders in Judah, observes that the transitional "and also these" and the reference to drunkenness do not necessarily mean that Samaria remains the focus. He sees a transition here to the leadership of Judah, whose behavior is analogous to the corrupt leaders in the north (see also Roberts 2015, 350). In favor of Judah as the referent, consider the presence of "therefore" in 28:14, which indicates a logical relationship between the denunciation of 28:7–13 and the behavior of the rulers of Jerusalem, who are addressed in 28:14. Perhaps it is unnecessary to choose between Israel and Judah. Sweeney (1996, 362–63) identifies 28:7–13 as a judgment speech against the leaders of Ephraim, but he then suggests that "the Judean leadership" is included within the scope of the speech as well.

28:7–8. Isaiah's vivid description of the drunken priests and prophets is facilitated by repetition. Six times he uses the synonymous שָׁגָה (thrice), תָּעָה (twice), or פּוּק (once) to describe how they "stagger" (note NIV11, "stagger, reel, stumble,") about because of being thoroughly intoxicated.[1] Oswalt (1986, 510) suggests that the repetition "seems to imitate the stumblings and gigglings of the drunk." The *niphal* of בָּלַע, if meaning "swallowed" (cf. ESV, KJV), would be ironic, given the large amount of wine they have imbibed. But it seems more likely, considering the parallelism, that this is a homonym, meaning "confused" (*HALOT* s.v. "בלע III" 135;

---

[1] Hebrew שֵׁכָר (cf. 5:11) is usually understood as referring to beer, but in an Israelite context it is more likely that date palm wine is in view. See Walsh 2000, 200–202. For a modification of this view, see Williamson's (2006, 370) comments on Isaiah 5:11. He prefers to see שֵׁכָר as referring to any fermented intoxicating beverage other than grape wine, including the product of dates, honey, and raisins. He agrees, however, that beer is an "unlikely" referent.

cf. NIV11, "befuddled," and NASB; contrary to Irwin 1977, 16–18).

In their inebriated condition the prophets are not fit to reveal prophetic visions and the priests are unable to make correct decisions pertaining to the application of the law (Smith 2007, 480). All that comes from their mouths is vomit (again, synonyms are used in the description), which completely covers (note "there is not a spot") all the tables. In the case of the priests, their intoxication is in direct violation of the Mosaic law (see Lev. 10:8–10; Ezek. 44:21; cf. Roberts 2015, 350; Smith 2007, 479).

As Wildberger (2002, 22) points out, the failure of prophets and priests to maintain sobriety could have a devastating impact on the nation: "False information being provided by a prophet could pitch a country into utter disaster and a faulty decision on the part of a priest could defame someone who was innocent, could even cost that person's life. They thus could carry out the responsibilities of their office only with great presence of mind and could hold sway only with wisdom." Hayes and Irvine (1987, 324) understand the language of Isaiah 28:7–8 as metaphorical, while Young (1969, 271–73) insists on a literal interpretation. But is it necessary to choose between these options as though they were mutually exclusive? Perhaps the language depicts their literal drunkenness, which is a symptom of their spiritual insensitivity.

28:9. Despite the Lord's attempts to communicate to his people, they have failed to respond. They are as incapable of understanding spiritual truth as infants just weaned from their mothers' breasts. There is some debate as to the meaning of 28:9a, which reads literally, "To whom is he teaching knowledge? Whom is he making to understand what is heard?" The subject of the verbs is not specified. Perhaps this is what the people say about the Lord's prophet, Isaiah. In this case, the verse could be paraphrased: "Who does he [the Lord's prophet] think he is talking to—infants?" (See Blenkinsopp 2000, 389; Clements 1980, 227; Motyer 1993, 231–32; Oswalt 1986, 511–12; Roberts 2015, 351; Wildberger 2002, 22–23; Young 1969, 274–75.) But it seems more likely that Isaiah is asking the questions and that the Lord is the subject of the verbs (cf. Exum 1982, 120). In this case, the prophet answers the questions in the second half of the verse. Isaiah 28:12 supports this, for it recalls how God invited his people to find refuge in him, only to be rejected by them.

28:10. The relationship of 28:10 to 28:9 (note the linking כִּי, "for, indeed") is not entirely clear. If the people are being quoted, then they may be mocking the prophet as one who tries to dictate laws and rules to them. In this case, צַו could be understood as a noun meaning "command" (related to the verb צִוָּה, "to command") and קַו might mean "measuring line" (that is, "rule"), a term used in 28:17. They complain that the prophet speaks to them as if they were infants in need of constant instruction and correction. But if, in response to the questions of 28:9a, the prophet is characterizing the people in 28:9b, a different interpretation of 28:10 may be preferable. Since they are incapable of understanding the truth, the Lord will judge them accordingly. He will speak to them through incomprehensible baby talk. In this case the terms צַו and קַו have no literal meaning—they are simply monosyllabic sounds that mimic the sounds they will hear.[2] The final statement, literally "a little there, a little there," refers to the short syllabic structure of the preceding babbling sounds.

---

2   For a brief survey of the different ways the passage has been interpreted, see Noegel (2021, 198–200), who discusses eight proposals and observes that "the passage leaves us spinning in contemplation." He concludes: "We must consider multiple options while deciding upon none."

28:11–13. Isaiah 28:11–13 favors this latter interpretation and is best understood as an elaboration on 28:10. In this case, כִּי at the beginning of 28:10 is best translated "indeed," with the כִּי at the beginning of 28:11 introducing an explanation ("for") of the meaning of 28:10. The Lord will speak to his people through foreigners (28:11). He once invited his people to find rest and security in him, but they were unwilling to listen to him (28:12). So now the word of the Lord would be transformed into the babbling sounds of a foreign tongue (28:13a; cf. 28:10). Without divine guidance and with only this gibberish of judgment ringing in their ears, the people will stumble, suffer injury, and be captured (28:13b). The punishment fits the sin (Miller 1982, 47–48). The form לְמַעַן could simply point to the result ("so that") of the Lord's decision to speak to them through a foreign tongue, but it can just as easily indicate the Lord's purpose ("in order that") in doing so. In this case, his decision to substitute foreign gibberish for his kind invitation is designed specifically to lead to the people's downfall.

Destructive Judgment Overwhelms Jerusalem and Its Leaders (28:14–22)

The Lord's judgment will eliminate Jerusalem's false sources of security.

28:14. The prophet now shifts his focus to Jerusalem and its leadership, who are characterized as boastful men. The prophet calls them אַנְשֵׁי לָצוֹן, "men of boasting" (NIV11, "scoffers"). The noun לָצוֹן, "boasting," is related to the verb לִיץ, which usually refers to scoffing or deriding. In this context the noun appears to refer to their boastful claim that their covenant with death insulates them from harm (cf. 28:15), as does the *hithpolel* verb form of לִיץ in 28:22. The phrase "men of boasting" occurs in Proverbs 29:8, where this group is contrasted with the wise.

The inclusion of לָכֵן, "therefore," at the beginning of 28:14 indicates a logical relationship between what precedes and what follows. The prophet has just announced that judgment is coming in the form of a foreign invader (28:10–13). Considering this approaching reality, it is important for Jerusalem's leaders to listen to the Lord's prophetic word that follows (28:14). They think they have insulated themselves from destruction, but the coming devastation will reach them as well as Samaria (Oswalt 1986, 516).

28:15. These leaders are confident they have struck a deal with death that gives them security. Some prefer a cultic interpretation here, arguing that the leaders made, through cultic ritual, an actual treaty with the god of the underworld. More likely, death (as well as the parallel Sheol) is used by metonymy here for Egypt, with whom the leaders had entered into an anti-Assyrian alliance (30:1–7; 31:1–3; cf. Clements 1980, 230; Dekker 2007, 120–23; Oswalt 1986, 517; Roberts 2015, 353; Smith 2007, 486; Young 1969, 284). They believed Egypt could protect them against the Assyrians and consequently national death, as it were. In other words, their treaty with Egypt was as good as making an agreement with death itself since, in their view, it provided assurance that death would not overtake them. Nathan Mastnjak (2014, 465–83) has recently argued that the covenant with death is made with Assyria. He explains (p. 481) that "the scoffers of v. 15 claim that they will not suffer destruction when the Assyrians invade since they have a covenant with Assyria. It is not that 'Death' is going to protect them from the coming Assyrians, but that 'Death' is Assyria. They will avoid the flood coming on Ephraim because they are on the flood's side.... To trust in a treaty with an entity with the strength and appetite of Death/Sheol is, according to the prophet, to trust in a lie and a falsehood."

Assyria is alluded to here as an "overwhelming scourge" that "sweeps by." The meaning of שׁוֹט (*qere* reading; cf. 1QIsᵃ) is debated. A noun שׁוֹט, meaning "scourge, whip" is attested (see BDB s.v. "שׁוֹט" mng. 2, 1002; cf. Isa.

10:26). But here it is combined with שֶׁטֶף, "overflow, flood" (*HALOT* s.v. "שׁטף" 1475; cf. Isa. 8:8), suggesting the noun might be a homonym referring to water. (This option is discussed in *HALOT* s.v. "שׁוֹט II" 1441, which concludes it is a "questionable lexeme." But see Wildberger 2002, 30.) Young (1969, 283, 290) suggests there is a mixed metaphor, perhaps utilized to create "a striking assonance" (see also Hom 2012, 101–2; Motyer 1993, 233; Oswalt 1986, 517).

The leaders are quoted as saying they have made "a lie" their refuge and "falsehood" their hiding place. Obviously, they would not have used these words to describe the covenant they made with death (see Exum 1982, 125; Young 1969, 284). The prophet sarcastically substitutes "lie" and "falsehood" for the treaty itself to taunt them and to emphasize their self-delusion (Clements 1980, 231; Oswalt 1986, 517; Roberts 2015, 353).

28:16. In response to their arrogant boasting, the Lord announces his plan for Zion. Hebrew לָכֵן, "therefore," at the beginning of 28:16 indicates a logical relationship between the rulers' boast in 28:15 and the Lord's announcement. Indeed, their boast prompts the announcement (Oswalt 1986, 517). Speaking as the Sovereign Master (note the title אֲדֹנָי combined with the divine name Yahweh), he announces on a positive note that he will make Zion secure (28:16–17a). But he will also sweep away the current leadership, whose supposed covenant with death will prove worthless (cf. 28:17b–18). In contrast to these self-deluded, doomed leaders, the one who places his trust in the Lord remains stable (28:16b). The text reads literally, "the one who believes will not hurry," that is, will not panic in the face of the coming judgment.

The image of a cornerstone and a sure foundation suggests stability and reliability. The referent of the metaphor is not entirely clear, but it is likely that the stone is the Lord's chosen ruler(s), who administers his justice fairly (cf. 28:6, 17a; 32:1), in contrast to the morally incompetent rulers addressed here (cf. 28:14). Perhaps, in Isaiah's historical context, the contrast is between Hezekiah and those who opposed him (see Hayes and Irvine 1987, 327–30).

Cornerstone

Isaiah 28:16b reads literally, "a tested [i.e., by metonymy, 'approved'] stone, a cornerstone of preciousness of a foundation (that is) founded." There is no consensus on the meaning of בֹּחַן. Benjamin Noonan (2013, 314–19) surveys five options, offers objections to the traditional reading "tested," and understands the term as an Egyptian loanword referring to "greywacke," a type of gray sandstone, a suggestion that would fit well, as Noonan points out, in the Egyptian context of this passage. GKC (422 §130f n. 4) paraphrases, "a precious corner stone of surest foundation." Hayes and Irvine (1987, 328) see Hezekiah as the referent, while Young (1969, 286–87) interprets the passage as messianic. Wildberger (2002, 42) prefers to identify the cornerstone as faith, while Clements (1980, 231) identifies it as God himself (see also Smith 2007, 487–88). For a survey of the various interpretations that have been offered, see Kaiser 1974, 253; and Oswalt 1986, 518. For a fuller study of the history of interpretation, see Dekker 2007, 9–64.

28:17–19. In conjunction with establishing a sure foundation in Zion, the Lord will "make justice the measuring line and righteousness the plumb line" (28:17a). The language is consistent with the building imagery of 28:16 (Oswalt 1986, 519; Smith 2007, 488; Young 1969, 288). His intent is to make Zion a center for justice (cf. 1:27; 33:5), where his righteous standards are acknowledged and implemented. Failure to meet his demand for justice (cf. 5:7) prompts his righteous judgment (5:16), which purifies the city of its sinful leaders (28:17b; cf. 1:28). He will then administer justice through his chosen leaders (cf. 28:6), particularly a Davidic king (9:7; 11:4; cf. 32:1; see Wildberger 2002, 42).

The Lord's justice demands the removal of the current leadership. Their "refuge" and "hiding place," namely, their covenant with death, will prove to be a false source of security (a "lie"; 28:17b–18, see comments above on 28:15). Hail (cf. 28:2) will sweep it away and a flood will overwhelm it. The leaders' covenant with death will be annulled as devastation sweeps through. They will become a trampled place (מִרְמָס; cf. 5:5), as it were (see 28:3). The devastation will be relentless as it sweeps through every day, from morning until night (28:19a). Some see the repetitive nature of the devastation as indicating a move from a specific situation (the Assyrian invasion) to a generalization (Clements 1980, 231–32), but more likely this refers to Assyria's growing presence in the region in the latter part of the eighth century B.C. (Hayes and Irvine 1987, 329; Oswalt 1986, 519–20; Smith 2007, 489). Naturally, when the import of this announcement is fully grasped, it will produce terror (28:19b). The inclusion of רַק, "only, nothing but," emphasizes the extent of terror—it will be all encompassing.

Terror

The Hebrew text reads literally, "and it will be nothing but terror, explaining what is heard," that is, once the message is understood it will produce nothing but terror. The noun זְוָעָה, "terror," is related to the verb זוּעַ, "to tremble" (see *HALOT* s.v. "זְוָעָה" 267). The *hiphil* of בִּין is often interpreted here to mean "understand," but in 28:9, where it is also used with שְׁמוּעָה, "what is heard," it has a causative sense, "to make understand, explain." It is likely 28:19 is playing off the earlier use, which is best understood as the prophet describing the Lord's unsuccessful attempts to communicate to his drunken people (see comments above). But as the judgment unfolds, they realize the import, albeit too late, of the Lord's warning of disaster. See Roberts 2015, 355; Smith 2007, 489; Young 1969, 291.

28:20. The prophet illustrates their misplaced faith through the metaphor of a bed that is too short and a blanket that is too small (28:20). The bed and blanket represent these leaders' false sense of security in their covenant with death. The bed and blanket seemingly offer rest and protection from the cold. But this bed disappoints the one who tries to get some sleep on it because it is so short one cannot stretch out on it. Furthermore, the blanket does not provide adequate protection from the cold because it is too small to wrap around oneself.

28:21. To this point the focus has been on the Lord's instrument of judgment (cf. 28:2, 11, 17–19), but now the prophet makes it clear the Lord himself will intervene (28:21). The prophet alludes to two events in Israel's past in which the Lord supernaturally intervened in battle to defeat his enemies. At Perazim the Lord "broke out" (פֶּרֶץ) against the Philistines, allowing David to win the battle (2 Sam. 5:17–21; 1 Chron. 14:8–12). Shortly thereafter David again defeated the Philistines as he charged into battle behind the Lord's army, which he heard marching through the trees above him (2 Sam. 5:22–25). Second Samuel 5 locates this second battle in the Valley of Rephaim (5:22) and says David pursued the defeated enemy from Geba to Gezer (5:25). But the Chronicler's version mentions simply "the valley" (1 Chron. 14:13) and describes David's pursuit as extending from *Gibeon* to Gezer (14:16; cf. Dekker 2007, 162; Irwin 1977, 35–36; Motyer 1993, 234; Roberts 2015, 355; Smith 2007, 489; Wildberger 2002, 44). So, the reference to Gibeon may be an allusion to David's second victory over the Philistines as recorded by the Chronicler. Another option, given the reference to hail in Isaiah 28:17, is that the prophet refers to Joshua's victory over the Canaanite forces, when the Lord hurled great hailstones down upon the enemy, allowing Joshua's army to prevail (Josh. 10:10–11; cf. Blenkinsopp 2000,

394–95; Clements 1980, 232; Hayes and Irvine 1987, 329–30; Kaiser 1974, 255; Oswalt 1986, 520; Seitz 1993, 210; Young 1969, 292;).

The Lord's judgment is here called his "strange work" (זָר מַעֲשֵׂהוּ, literally, "strange is his work") and his "alien task" (נָכְרִיָּה עֲבֹדָתוֹ, literally, "alien is his task"). It is "strange/alien" in two related ways. First, it is strange/alien in its object. In the theophanies mentioned in 28:21a, the Lord attacked foreigners—the Philistines. Now he reveals his theophanic splendor and power again, but this time, ironically, his own people are the target of his anger. There may be an allusion here to Exodus 34:10, where the anticipated destruction of the Canaanites (cf. 34:11) is called "the work of the Lord" (מַעֲשֵׂה יְהוָה). But now the Lord must intervene against his own covenant people, the earlier beneficiaries of his mighty "work." Second, the Lord's work is strange/alien in that it is contrary to his ideal for his people and to the mercy he typically shows them (cf. Dekker 2007, 162–63). The Lord longs to be his people's protector (see 28:16) and delights in extending mercy to them (cf. Exod. 34:6–7). Indeed, throughout Isaiah his mercy inevitably prevails over his wrath (Kinzer 2017). But now there will be a radical departure from the norm. At least temporarily, he must attack his people. Even so, in due time, beyond judgment, he will establish his ideal for his people (28:5–6, 16–17a) and reveal his theophanic splendor as he turns his might against the Assyrians (cf. 29:6; 30:27–33).

28:22. The prophet addresses the leaders and urges them not to persist in their boasting (28:22; cf. 28:14). He warns them that refusal to heed his exhortation will make their already dire situation even worse. He compares them to prisoners bound in chains and declares that continued boasting would make those chains tight (literally, "strong"). The reality behind the chains is likely the obligations demanded by their covenant with their overlord, death. Ironically, these obligations prove to be shackles (Irwin 1977, 37). They must take heed because the message is one of certain, widespread judgment originating with the Sovereign Master (אֲדֹנָי), who is the Lord of Armies (יְהוָה צְבָאוֹת).

The language used here is very similar to an earlier judgment announcement (cf. 10:23; see Roberts 2015, 355). Isaiah refers to the judgment as literally, "destruction and what is decreed." This is a hendiadys (cf. Young 1965, 370 n. 54, on Isa. 10:23), where two words are combined, with the second modifying the first. We can paraphrase, "certain [i.e., decreed] destruction." As in 10:23, the prophet formally identifies the Judge as the Sovereign Master and the Lord of Armies. The statement regarding the extent of judgment is slightly different. In 10:23 judgment extends to literally the "middle of the whole land," while in 28:22 it is said to be "against the whole land."

The Wisdom of God Evident in Judgment (28:23–29)

The timing and extent of the coming judgment will reveal the Lord's wisdom.

Isaiah begins the conclusion to this speech with an appeal to listen carefully (28:23). This complements nicely the exhortation not to boast (28:22). This is a time for rapt attention, not arrogance, for the Lord's wisdom is about to be revealed (cf. 28:29).

The prophet draws a lesson from agriculture. A farmer does not simply keep on plowing a field. Once the field is plowed, he plants his crops in appropriate locations (28:24–25). He learns to do this from God who, by establishing the laws and patterns of nature, makes it clear when plowing and planting should occur (28:26). (Roberts 2015, 359, speaks of "natural revelation" mediated through observation. See also Young 1969, 298.) When harvest time arrives, the farmer utilizes the proper techniques, beating caraway seed and cumin with a stick, while threshing the grain (28:27–28). He does his threshing for just the right amount of time and not in excess. Once more, the farmer's insight comes from the Lord of Armies, who imparts his counsel and wisdom (28:29).

In 28:29b the Hebrew text reads literally, "he has made counsel wonderful; he has made wisdom great." When used in the *hiphil* stem the verb פָּלָא can mean "make hard, difficult" (cf. Lev. 27:2; Num. 6:2) or "do something exceptional, unique" (cf. Judg. 13:19; Ps. 31:21 [HB 22]; Joel 2:26). Here, in combination with "counsel," it refers to the extraordinary wisdom that God imparts to farmers that allows them to grow and harvest food in accordance with the divinely ordained seasons of nature (cf. 28:24–28). The noun עֵצָה often refers to advice, counsel, or guidance. This meaning fits well here where the referent is the guidance God gives to farmers as they plant and harvest. The parallel term, תּוּשִׁיָּה, can refer to wisdom or to the success that wisdom brings (cf. BDB s.v. "תּוּשִׁיָּה" 444). The two synonyms are paired only here and in Proverbs 8:14, where personified Lady Wisdom declares she possesses both. When kings appropriate the wisdom that she makes available, they can rule justly and effectively. As the source of all wisdom the Lord rules justly over his worldwide dominion, including his covenant people Israel.

What is the significance of the illustration in this context? Within this discourse the prophet has announced that severe judgment is coming. But however strange and alien it may seem (cf. 28:21), it will be administered at just the right time and in just the right measure, because the same wisdom God imparts to farmers will characterize his intervention in his people's experience. Destruction, pictured in the plowing, beating, and threshing, is coming. It appears to be as inevitable as the agricultural season, with its sequence of plowing, planting, and harvesting. But the prophet has also held out a glimmer of hope for those who survive the judgment (28:5–6, 16). The plowing will not last forever and the harvesting will be done in proper measure, not in excess. In the end the process will yield fruit. Sweeney (1996, 366) says it well:

The farmer's activities are essentially destructive, but the destruction is temporary and leads to a positive result. He plows, harrows, and overturns the earth, but it is of limited duration. Because his purpose is to provide food, he plants seeds and orders his land so that cummin [*sic*] and the various grains will grow. Likewise, when he harvests his crops, his actions are essentially destructive, but again they are not thoroughly destructive in that they lead to a positive result. Cummin [*sic*] is not completely threshed with a threshing sledge, but beaten with a stick until it is ready. Grain is not thoroughly crushed, but is only crushed enough to prepare it as food. In this manner, the actions of the farmer are compared to those of the coming invader. There will be destruction and hardship, but the result will be the reestablishment of YHWH's glory and justice once the incompetent leadership is removed.

Likewise, Childs (2000, 211) observes that "even as the farmer's activity seems strange and incoherent as he first tears open the ground before sowing his seed, so also Yahweh's apparently violent acts of judgment also follow a wise purpose. In his own time and according to his own counsel he will also bring forth suitable fruits from his creation" (see also Clements 1980, 233; Motyer 1993, 235; Roberts 2015, 359; Young 1969, 297).

Smith (2007, 491) disagrees with this line of interpretation: "The farmer's activity should not be allegorically applied to God's activity of judging and saving." For Smith, the point is simply that God provides wise instruction and counsel, as is evident from watching the farmer. He adds, "The wise farmer hears God's instruction and is successful because he follows God's wise counsel. Should not the spiritual and political leaders of Judah do the same?" In other words, these verses are essentially hortatory: "Now the prophet's audience must listen to what God has said about Israel's mistakes, the false instructions of the prophets and priests, and the deceptive covenant with death in 28:1–22. If they will listen to God's wisdom and respond the right way, they can avoid the disasters that Isaiah has predicted in 28:7–22" (p. 493; cf. Oswalt 1986, 521–24).

Perhaps the illustration operates at two levels. As Smith argues, it has a hortatory dimension: The covenant community must recognize and embrace the wisdom that comes from God. This is their only hope of avoiding the announced judgment. At the same time, if judgment is unleashed (and the leaders' obstinance makes it appear that this is inevitable), it will be wisely administered in proper measure and with a positive goal in view. This should encourage the godly, for they could rest assured the Lord will eventually establish his kingdom of justice (28:5–6, 16). The lesson from the farmer also reminds them God's wisdom must be embraced if one is to survive the coming destruction.

THEOLOGICAL FOCUS

The theological focus of this passage can be stated as follows: the Lord, the people's only genuine source of security, judges corrupt leaders to establish justice in his covenant community. As the prophet develops this theological theme, the following emphases emerge:

1. False sources of security

The corrupt leaders of the northern kingdom placed their faith in their capital city Samaria, while the equally corrupt leaders of Judah were confident that their alliance with "death" (probably a treaty with Egypt) would insulate them from destruction. But the Lord will overwhelm them with judgment, which is compared to a powerful storm accompanied by raging flood waters that sweep away everything in their path. This is viewed as his strange and alien work because he comes as a warrior in theophanic splendor to punish, not protect, his people and causes them to experience his judgment, rather than the mercy that has always characterized his relationship with them.

2. The only true source of security

Images of judgment dominate this speech, but more fundamentally it addresses the theme of security. Both the northern kingdom and Judah will discover the hard way that genuine security is found only in the Lord, who imparts wisdom to humans and values justice. The Lord alone is the covenant community's source of security, for he holds their destiny in his hands. Just as the farmer utilizes the wisdom imparted from God to grow and harvest his crops, so the people should respond positively to the Lord's wisdom as revealed through his prophet. But because they reject the message, they will hear instead the incomprehensible language of foreign conquerors, who are the reality behind the overwhelming flood sent by the Lord.

3. The wisdom and goal of judgment

If judgment must indeed come, it will reveal God's wisdom, for he will execute it appropriately and in correct measure. Just as the seemingly violent actions of the farmer, such as plowing and threshing, have a positive end, so the Lord's judgment has a positive goal. It removes the covenant community's corrupt leaders and replaces them with leaders who will promote what the Lord truly values—justice.

PREACHING AND TEACHING STRATEGIES

Exegetical and Theological Synthesis

This chapter begins with the prophet confronting the people of Israel for their pride and misplaced confidence in their capital city, Samaria (28:1–13). The city itself appeared beautiful and prosperous as it was situated at the head of a fertile valley (28:1, 4). As such, the city was like a glorious crown/wreath of flowers (28:1–3) that one would wear on their head. However, just like the flowers' beauty, God warned that

Samaria's glory would not last (28:4). Rather, God would come upon them in his judgment like a raging storm, resulting in the destruction of their prized city (28:2–3).

Only the Lord himself deserved to be a "glorious crown" for his people (28:5) as he alone could provide them with the just judges and strong warriors for which they longed (28:6). Because Israel's leaders had placed their hope for security in their impressive city rather than in God, the prophet describes them repeatedly as a bunch of confused, staggering drunkards (28:1, 3, 7–8). Rather than exhibiting sensible judgment and wisdom, Israel's priests and prophets have displayed clouded vision leading them to stumble in giving judgments (28:7). They are thus likened to infants, apparently too young to comprehend God's words to them since they have rejected him (28:9). Since they apparently can't comprehend the words of the prophet who had called them to trust in God alone (28:12), God will instead get their attention by speaking to them in what will sound like the gibberish of baby talk (28:10, 13). Of course, this is fitting since they have shown themselves to be mere infants in their understanding. However, this will be the gibberish of foreigners whose language they don't understand when they come to conquer them. They will "fall backward" and "be injured and snared and captured" (28:13).

The prophet next shifts his attention from Israel and its leadership in Samaria to Judah and its corrupt leaders in Jerusalem (28:14–22). Like the leaders in Israel, they too were looking for their security in the wrong place. Unlike Israel, though, their misplaced sense of security was not in one of their cities, but rather in a covenant with one of their allies, probably Egypt. The prophet described this pact as "a covenant with death." Isaiah warned that these people had foolishly made lies their refuge and had taken shelter in falsehood (28:15).

God reminded them that it was he who had laid the cornerstone as a foundation in Zion. Furthermore, he alone is the one who would one day establish justice and righteousness in their land (28:16–17). As such, their covenant with Egypt would not amount to anything. It would be swept away as though in a storm, and the waters would destroy the façade of protection that they had erected as their shelter (28:17–18). The Assyrian forces would move through Judah like an overwhelming scourge that beats them down a little at a time as their cities would fall one by one, day after day, producing terror throughout (28:18–19).

Their decision to make a treaty with another country rather than simply look to the Lord for protection and help will be like someone whose bed is too short and whose blanket is too small (28:20). What that person assumed would be a source of comfort and warmth is shown to be insufficient. A short bed can't provide comfort to one who is tall, neither can a small blanket that doesn't cover one's body provide warmth on a cold night. In the same way, the nation of Egypt would not be able to protect Judah from the overwhelming forces of the Assyrian army.

But it will not just be the Assyrians that the Judean people should fear. Because of their choice to spurn their covenant with the Lord in favor of a covenant with death, the Lord himself will break out in judgment against his own people. The prophet likens this to another incident in Judah/Israel's past soon after David had been anointed king over Israel. Upon hearing of this, the Philistines assembled for battle to try to defeat David and the Israelite army. David wisely looked to the Lord for his security, asking God if he should march up against the Philistines at that time. The Lord assured him that he should, and in a series of battles the Lord defeated David's enemies on Mt. Perazim and in the Valley of Gibeon (28:21; cf. 2 Sam. 5:17–25; 1 Chron. 14:8–17). In similar fashion, God was going to break out again, only this time it would be against his own people of Judah in judgment. As such, it would be a "strange" and "alien" work of God (Isa. 28:21). God warns them not to scoff or boast in their situation, lest their present bonds be made worse. Their covenant with Egypt functioned like chains of enslavement, rather than the liberating force they had assumed it would be. In truth, anytime God's people choose to trust in something other than him as their primary source of security, they become enslaved to rather than liberated by that person or thing. They are ultimately forced to serve its demands so they can acquire and maintain it without ever actually reaping the benefits they imagined it would provide them. It will always be an insufficient source of true security (28:22).

Isaiah 28:23–29 may appear confusing at first glance. What is the prophet's point in discussing the wisdom behind farming techniques here in this context? There may be two points of application intended from this closing admonition. First, it seems that Isaiah is likening God's painful but purposeful judgment of his people to the processes of a farmer in sowing and reaping. Just as the farmer's activities involve the violent actions of plowing up the ground and later of threshing, beating, and crushing grains (28:24, 27), so too God's actions in disciplinary judgment appear violent and harsh. However, the farmer's actions are ultimately wise (28:26, 29), as they are necessary to produce and harvest beneficial crops (grains/spices). Similarly, God's judgment against his own people may appear at first to be unnecessarily harsh, even strange and out of character (28:21). Nonetheless it too is ultimately purposeful, with the goal of cultivating the fruit of repentance and purification within the hearts of his people. Second, in the same way that a farmer needs to listen to the wisdom that God gives him to navigate the process of sowing and reaping, so too God's people must listen to the wisdom of God through the prophet's warnings (28:23). In this way they can avoid aspects of coming judgment and bear precious fruit instead of the fruit that prompted God's judgment.

Preaching Idea
The Lord alone can provide genuine security.

Contemporary Connections

What does it mean?
To understand what it means to say that the Lord alone will provide genuine security, it is important to first consider what it doesn't mean. Nik Ripken, author of the book *The Insanity of God*, wrestles with this very question. He writes,

> I am not sure if I ever heard it said out loud, but I . . . picked up the idea that obedience to God's call would result in a life of safety and security. . . . "The safest place to be," I was told more than once, "is right in the center of God's will." And that sounded both true and reassuring. . . . It might, in fact, be safe to be in the center of God's will—but we would be wise to stop and think about what it means to be safe. (2013, xxviii)

To be secure in God does *not* mean that one will always be safe from physical harm. In fact, Jesus himself said that following him required being willing to take up one's cross daily (Luke 9:23–24; cf. Matt. 10:38–39; 16:24–26; Mark 8:34–35; Luke 14:27). Additionally, the security that God provides does not guarantee financial stability via a healthy savings account or 401(k) nor a surplus of food. Divinely provided security is not an assurance that God will provide each person with the man or woman of their dreams or with enough friends that one never experiences the pain of loneliness. While these desires flow out of the basic longings that all of us would like to have met, the Bible does not promise that God's people will always experience all these blessings in their lives. Many of God's faithful servants had to endure hardships like beatings, imprisonment, hunger, shipwrecks, betrayal and abandonment from friends, and even martyrdom (Acts 5:40; 12:3–6; 16:22–23; 20:23; 21:13, 32; 27:27–44; 1 Cor. 4:11; 2 Cor. 11:23–27; Phil. 1:7, 13–17; 4:12; 2 Tim. 4:10; Rev. 7:14–16).

God does guarantee his followers peace and comfort in the midst of life's hardships and dangers (Isa. 28:12; cf. Isa. 25:4–5; 26:3–4, 12). This peace comes from the basic knowledge that we are destined for God's eternal kingdom. The most we stand to lose in this life is our life itself, but honor, vindication, and eternal joy await in the world to come (Isa. 28:5; cf. Isa. 25:6–9; 26:1–2; 27:13). At that time, every noble human desire will be ours to enjoy. Most importantly in the context of Isaiah 28, though, the believer is promised protection against God's wrath (Isa. 28:16–19; cf. Isa. 12:2; 25:9; 26:20–21). When his judgment falls upon the world, those who have aligned themselves with Jesus through faith can rest assured that their futures are secure in him.

Is it true?

Security is a big deal. There is so much we do to bolster our sense of security against any number of threats. People install home security systems to deter thieves from breaking into their homes. Some purchase safes or pay to secure their valuables in safety deposit boxes at a local bank. All sorts of insurance plans offer people security against possible threats such as expensive medical emergencies, automobile accidents, or unforeseen disasters like house fires or floods. Business owners hire lawyers to craft contracts ensuring others will live up to their commitments and to protect themselves against lawsuits. Seat belts, football helmets, safety glasses, cans of mace, EpiPens, sunscreen—the list of items used to offer us better protection from life's mishaps is all but endless. At a deeper level, though, there are things that people assume will provide them security from a meaningless or second-rate life. These are the things that many believe, "Without this, I won't be happy or feel fulfilled in life." This list includes things like financial wealth, a positive standing within society, a group of close-knit friends, a romantic lover, a meaningful career, a healthy and attractive body, and more.

While many of the above things can deliver limited protection, circumstantial peace of mind, or even enjoyment, none of these can provide the sense of meaning or purpose in life for which we all ultimately long. Only God can offer eternal life. Only a life lived for him will produce the sort of fruit or enjoyment that lasts forever. Even more, only God can offer security from coming judgment, which is why Jesus warned, "Do not be afraid of those who kill the body but cannot kill the soul. Rather, be afraid of the One who can destroy both soul and body in hell" (Matt. 10:28). The knowledge of life after death for those who are in Christ has the power to infuse the righteous with comfort, hope, and courage regardless of their circumstances. This security is unmatched by any this world has to offer.

This truth is aptly illustrated by Jesus in one of his parables. In response to a request for him to speak with a man's brother to tell him to share their father's inheritance, Jesus warns the man against the danger of covetousness. Jesus then talks about a rich man whose land had produced plentifully. That man decided to tear down his barns and build bigger ones in which to store all his excess produce. Upon completion of this project, the man finally feels secure. He is comforted by all that he has stored up for himself and plans to relax and enjoy many more years of his life without worry or the need for strenuous labor. Little did he know, however, that he would die that very night. Not only would he not be able to enjoy anything he had laid up for himself, but worse than this he would have to stand in judgment before God. According to Jesus, this man gained the whole world but he ultimately lost his eternal soul (Luke 12:13–21).

The apostle Paul learned a thing or two about perspective as it relates to security in this life. Despite suffering great hardships, Paul was able to write the following:

> Rather, as servants of God we commend ourselves in every way: in great endurance; in troubles, hardships and distresses; in beatings, imprisonments and riots; in hard work, sleepless nights and hunger . . .

through glory and dishonor, bad report and good report; genuine, yet regarded as impostors; known, yet regarded as unknown; dying, and yet we live on; beaten, and yet not killed; sorrowful, yet always rejoicing; poor, yet making many rich; having nothing, and yet possessing everything. (2 Cor. 6:4–5, 8–10)

Elsewhere, Paul likewise wrote,

Who shall separate us from the love of Christ? Shall trouble or hardship or persecution or famine or nakedness or danger or sword? As it is written: "For your sake we face death all day long; we are considered as sheep to be slaughtered." No, in all these things we are more than conquerors through him who loved us. For I am convinced that neither death nor life, neither angels nor demons, neither the present nor the future, nor any powers, neither height nor depth, nor anything else in all creation, will be able to separate us from the love of God that is in Christ Jesus our Lord. (Rom. 8:35–39)

Paul understood well that when a person is joined in a relationship with God in Christ, no earthly danger or discomfort can make them insecure. His own sense of security wasn't tied to the comforts or pleasures of this life, nor to his own physical safety. Rather, Paul's sense of well-being and security were bound up in God's eternal purposes for his life and the assurance that he had in his eternal salvation.

Now what?
It is sadly ironic that all the energy and resources many spend trying to make themselves secure end up distracting them from pursuing the only source of genuine security. Our access to so many things that claim to provide security too often desensitizes us to our need for the security found only in God. Thus, we must be sure that our hope and peace are anchored in God and his promises, not in the fleeting things provided by the world. We must consider seriously whether our affluent American lifestyle has become a hindrance to our daily pursuit of God in any significant ways. Specifically, where are we failing to trust Jesus for our security? Are we seeking security in other things? Do we take great comfort in consistent paychecks afforded by stable jobs, a house that is paid off, friends or family members who are always there for us when we need them, or even just our own intelligence and resourcefulness? While all of these can be good things, it is important to remember that they are all gifts from God. He is the source of all our earthly provisions. These are merely how he sometimes blesses us to provide for our needs.

Additionally, it is essential to remember that missional living involves risk. God never promised his followers that they would experience safety from all the threats in this life. On the contrary, he warned that we would be persecuted by the world and betrayed by the members of our own families. It could be easy to assume that a life devoted to serving Jesus should result in material blessings and physical comfort. Then, when those things don't transpire, resentment may begin to build, and abandoning Christ may seem like the logical decision to make. It is essential then to recognize and accept that serving God requires a commitment to embrace the risk and potential hardships involved in ministry and service.

My (Mike's) wife's childhood pastor worked in a large inner-city ministry that catered to the needs of homeless men, many of whom were trying to recover from years of alcoholism or drug addiction. After completing a months-long residential program at the ministry, these men would be left looking for a place to live and a way to make the transition back into normal life while hopefully avoiding the pitfalls and temptations that previously got them into their mess. On many occasions, this pastor would open up his own home as a temporary place for these men to live, often for months at a time. Understandably, this involved risks to him and his family. Would these men steal from him? Would these men secretly bring drugs into his home? Would this put him and/or his family in greater danger? Some looked at the choices this pastor made and concluded that he and his wife were foolish or naïve to do what they did. But it is important for all of us to remember that the Christian life was never supposed to be free of danger or risk. While we are called to be wise and to be sure that we are being led by the Holy Spirit, this isn't the same as avoiding any danger or risk to our personal safety.

Finally, we must be careful not to worship God out of a false assumption that to do so will make our life safe from harm. While God presents himself as our rock amid hardships (Isa. 17:10; 26:4; 30:29; 44:8) and as our savior and deliverer from coming judgment (Isa. 12:2; 26:1–2, 20–21; 27:9; 45:17; 61:10), he never presents himself as a divine vending machine to provide us with everything we want.

In the novel *Safely Home*, Randy Alcorn tells the story of a wealthy Christian businessman, Ben Fielding, who travels to China to visit his old college roommate. While both men were professing believers at one time, Ben hasn't practiced his faith ever since his son tragically died in a drowning accident. Ben has blamed God for not intervening to save his son. Ben's old friend Li Quan has also faced much suffering in his life, but approached it from a very different perspective. At one point in the book, the two of them have a particularly powerful interaction, where Ben reveals this tragic part of his life's story to his friend and the anger he has harbored toward God.

Quan: "I know something of suffering, Ben Fielding. I have learned God is not my servant. Did you think he was like the story of Aladdin? That he was your genie? That he is safe and tame, at your call to do tricks to entertain you? That is an American way to think, perhaps. But it is not true to Shengjing [Chinese word for the Bible]. You cannot rub a magic lamp and command God to do your will. You accepted blessing from his hand, and still you do—yet you reject him because of adversity?"

Ben: "He was my only son."

Quan: "Yes. And my grandfather lost his only son. Li Quan lost his only father in prison. And my only mother in an earthquake . . . and two cousins, several friends. Some nights I long to see my parents. But I can see Father's eyes and Mother's smile only in my dreams. Yes, your old roommate knows a little of suffering, though far less than many. Are we not the clay and God the potter? When he refuses to conform to our wills, do we discard him? If you are looking for a religion centered around yourself, Ben, I must agree that Christianity is a poor choice."

Ben: "He had no right."

Quan: "He has the right to strike us down as we sit. Why do you cling to rights that are not yours? Where did he promise you would not suffer? I can quote many Scriptures where he promised we *would* suffer. Is it God you have rejected? Or have you turned from a false god created in your own image?" (Alcorn 2011, 109)

This interaction between Ben and Li Quan illustrates the misguided perspective of far too many American Christians. We surmise that any God who would allow us to suffer has trampled upon our sacred rights, that he has wronged us in some way. Nothing could be further from the truth. Often God lovingly allows us to suffer to purify and refine us. Many times, God allows us to suffer by removing the false objects we depend upon for our sense of security. He does this to make us refocus our gaze on him. But whatever his reasons, God does not owe us a comfortable life, nor has he promised us this. Instead, God has promised to be our Savior from coming judgment and to comfort us with his presence as he walks with us through whatever trials and persecutions we encounter during this life.

The City Gate

Isaiah 28:5–6 states: "In that day the Lord Almighty will be a glorious crown, and a beautiful wreath for the remnant of his people. He will be a spirit of justice to the one who sits in judgment, and a source of strength to those who turn back the battle at the gate."

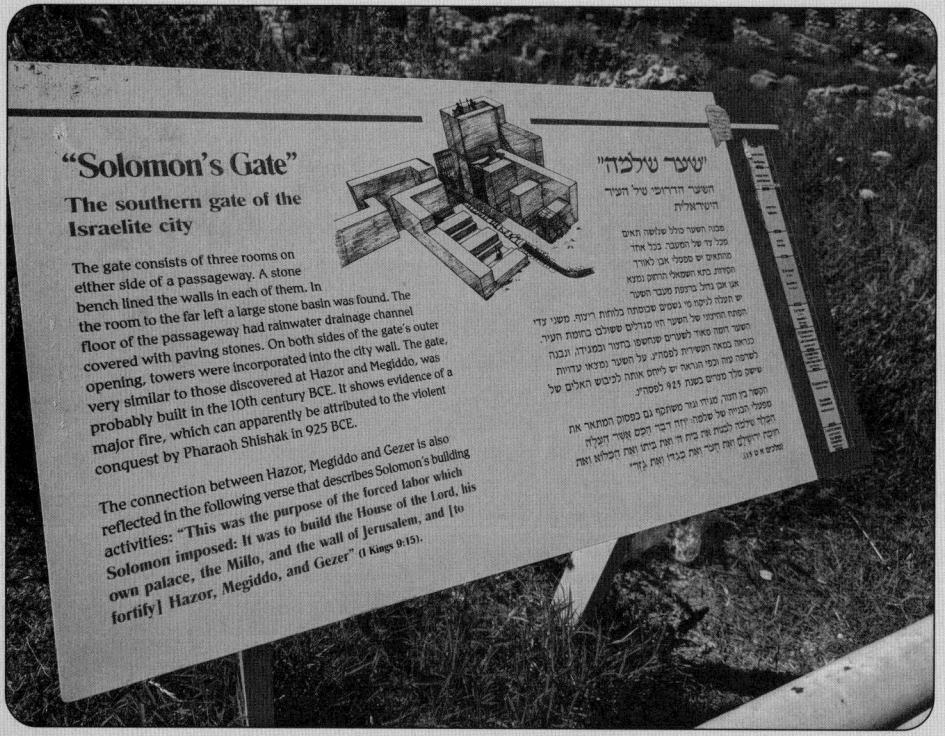

Sign describing "Solomon's Gate" in Gezer.

As one would enter through a city gate in the ancient world, there would typically be small rooms on both sides of the road leading into the city. These rooms were primarily occupied by the city's elders who would sit to hear legal disputes from the people of the town (Deut. 21:19; 22:15–21, 24; 25:7–10; Josh. 20:4; Ruth 4:1–11;

2 Sam. 15:2–6; Job 29:7–17; Prov. 31:23). Even the king would sometimes set up his throne by the city gate to consider legal matters (2 Sam. 19:8; 1 Kings 22:10; 2 Chron. 18:9). Thus, the city gates were important places that became associated with justice and righteousness (Isa. 29:20–21; cf. Prov. 22:22–23; Amos 5:10, 12, 15; Zech. 8:16).

However, a city's gates would become a strategic defense point during wartime. As such, the inner rooms would no longer be occupied by elders adjudicating legal disputes. Instead, they would be filled with soldiers standing ready to defend against invading enemy combatants (Isa. 22:7; 28:6; cf. 2 Sam. 10:8; 2 Chron. 32:6). Whoever controlled the city gate, effectively controlled the city. Thus, to "possess the gate" became a figure of speech akin to having dominance over those people (cf. Gen. 22:17; 24:60).

Photograph of Gezer city gate and inner rooms

Isaiah 28:5–6 highlights both of these important functions of the city gate when emphasizing how God was ultimately the one behind the granting of justice to the oppressed and vulnerable as well as providing protection via the soldiers within the city gate. He is said to be "the spirit of justice to the one who sits in judgment (in the city gate)" and "strength to those who turn back the battle *at the gate.*"

Creativity in Presentation

The Danger of Drunkenness

Isaiah 28 repeatedly describes the leaders of Israel as intoxicated with wine and strong drink (28:1, 3, 7–8). There are plenty of stories from the news that illustrate the dangers associated with drunkenness. For example, five people were tragically killed over Memorial Day weekend in 2022 when two boats collided on the Georgia River in Savannah, Georgia. The driver of the boat who caused the accident survived the crash but was arrested for driving under the influence of alcohol. Among the five who died were a husband and wife along with their two sons.[3]

To operate a boat or a motor vehicle assumes a high level of responsibility by the driver. When they grow careless about their responsibility and engage in foolish behavior such as consuming intoxicants, the consequences on others can be deadly. The same is true of Christian leaders. Those who accept roles as spiritual leaders assume a higher level of responsibility. Their actions or inactions don't simply affect their own lives; they negatively impact the lives of those under their leadership as well. As such, God promises to hold leaders to a stricter judgment, and warns them not to enter their roles without considering the weight of responsibility and accountability associated with this calling (James 3:1).

Misplaced Confidence

Franz Reichelt tried to invent a wearable parachute that would protect pilots in the event of an airplane crash. Despite several failed attempts to demonstrate that his prototype would work using dummies, Franz was convinced that his invention would be successful if deployed from a higher altitude where the chute would have more time to catch the wind. To prove his theory, Reichelt decided to perform a demonstration in front of friends and journalists at the Eiffel Tower in Paris. So confident was he that instead of using a dummy as before, Franz surprised everyone when he decided to jump himself while wearing his parachute. Those present tried earnestly to dissuade him from jumping. Undeterred, Reichelt boldly leaped off a platform part of the way up the tower, about two hundred feet off the ground. Sadly, his confidence in his own parachute was misplaced as he plummeted like a rock to the hard ground below, dying on impact.[4]

In similar fashion, many people today have chosen to stake their lives and even their eternal souls in misplaced, insufficient sources of security. Unfortunately, these substitute saviors will fail people on the day of judgment as they are wholly insufficient at delivering from God's judgment.

Risky Business

On May 12, 2020, Mission Aviation Fellowship pilot Joyce Lin died when the plane she was flying crashed into Lake Sentani in Indonesia shortly after takeoff. Mission Aviation Fellowship is a mission organization that desires to see isolated people changed by the love of Jesus Christ. Joyce was in the process of transporting rapid COVID-19 test kits and other essential supplies to a remote village in Indonesia the day of her accident; she was only forty years old. By many accounts, Joyce was a very brilliant and multitalented person. In addition to her training as a pilot, she held two master's degrees from the Massachusetts Institute of Technology (MIT). From the world's perspective, they might be tempted to look at her life as a waste. Somebody with her intelligence could have done so many other "important" things. Why did she risk her life flying an airplane into remote locations to take the gospel of Jesus Christ to people? Whereas the secular world can't

---

3   https://nypost.com/2022/05/30/5-dead-in-georgia-boat-crash-on-memorial-day-weekend.
4   https://allthatsinteresting.com/franz-reichelt.

understand why somebody with her credentials would "waste" their life flying an airplane into the jungle to convert people from a remote, backward country to her religion, Christians ask a different question: they want to know how God could allow somebody who had dedicated her life serving him to die so young.[5]

This story illustrates two significant points. First, the world's value system is not compatible with the kingdom of God. The world is inclined to assume that people should generally live their lives based on the principle of how to get the most out of it for themselves. This is the "safest" way to live. When a person could work a job that would give them a large paycheck, great benefits, and societal clout, why would they trade all of that to be a missionary? Their view of security fails to consider eternity. But second, many Christians too struggle with a false view of security. They assume that God will protect them from danger if they serve him with their life. The story of Joyce Lin illustrates that serving God is risky business, but it is also an eternally rewarding business. In the final analysis of life and eternity, the Lord alone can provide genuine security.

- Israel's misplaced hope (28:1–13).
- Jerusalem's misplaced hope (28:14–15).
- The Lord alone is a sure foundation for hope (28:16–29).

DISCUSSION QUESTIONS

1. Think about some times in your life recently when you felt vulnerable, insecure, or unsafe. What were the factors that caused you to feel this way? How should the reality of one's relationship to God overcome or put those feelings into a proper perspective?

2. What are some examples of things that you are prone to look to for security other than Jesus?

3. God accused the leaders of Ephraim of being drunk (28:1, 3, 7–8) which caused them to stagger in their vision and stumble in giving judgment. What are some things in our culture today that cause many Christians to stagger in their vision or stumble in their judgment, as it relates to decisions about where their security is found?

4. Isaiah 28:22 describes the people of Judah as being in chains because they had unwisely placed their hope for salvation in a covenant with death rather than in God. In what ways do people become servants to whatever things they choose to depend upon for their security?

FOR FURTHER READING

Alcorn, Randy C. 2011. *Safely Home*. Carol Stream, IL: Tyndale.

Ripken, Nik. 2013. *The Insanity of God: A True Story of Faith Resurrected*. Nashville: B&H.

---

5 https://www.washingtonpost.com/nation/2020/05/18/missionary-pilot-death-coronavirus.

Isaiah 29:1–24

EXEGETICAL IDEA
The Lord will bring a powerful army against Jerusalem, but then deliver the city from its attackers, demonstrating that he alone controls the city's destiny and is deserving of its trust. The Lord will restore his exiled people, prompting them to acknowledge his sovereignty as their spiritual vision is restored.

THEOLOGICAL FOCUS
The Lord demonstrates his sovereignty over the destiny of his people first by bringing a powerful army against Jerusalem, and then by mightily delivering the city from its attackers. Divine judgment has a positive goal: the spiritual transformation of the covenant community and their recognition of the Lord's sovereignty.

PREACHING IDEA
God directs hardships and discipline in his people's lives to bring about spiritual renewal and to demonstrate his trustworthiness.

PREACHING POINTERS
Mysterious. Unpredictable. Transcendent. Ineffable. These are just some of the words that come to mind when trying to describe the ways of God sometimes. The apostle Paul declares, "Oh, the depth of the riches of the wisdom and knowledge of God! How unsearchable his judgments, and his paths beyond tracing out!" (Rom. 11:33). There are many times when God's actions or inactions do not make much sense to us. We have all wrestled at times with thoughts such as, "If I were God, I would do this or that." For some who are skeptical or even cynical of Christianity, this is often a reason they give for withholding faith in him. If God is really loving and all-powerful, then why does he allow wicked people to carry out their nefarious plans?

While the answer to questions such as this are admittedly complex and elusive much of the time, passages such as Isaiah 29 confirm that God orchestrates some of the hardship in the world to accomplish his own sovereign plans. The existence of pain and suffering in the world does not serve as an indication that God is not in control of the world. Rather, pain and suffering function at some level as part of his sovereign plan. While on the surface it might appear strange that God would describe himself as the force behind the evil Assyrian army besieging and encircling his own people (29:2–3), in the end he will demonstrate himself to be both wise and loving even in this. God's sovereign actions will result in the just judgment of the Lord's enemies (29:20–21) as well as the salvation and spiritual renewal of his own people (29:17–19, 22–24).

JERUSALEM'S COMING CRISIS AND TRANSFORMATION (29:1–24)

The Lord will bring an army against Jerusalem, for the city's residents do not truly honor him, but trust instead in their own wisdom. The siege will prompt great mourning and confusion among the spiritually insensitive people. But then the Lord intervenes in great power and delivers the city from its attackers, demonstrating he alone controls the city's destiny and is deserving of its trust. Despite the leaders' failure to submit their plans to the Lord, the Lord will transform the covenant community. He will judge oppressors, giving the needy cause to rejoice. He will restore the exiles, prompting his people to acknowledge his sovereignty as their spiritual vision is restored.

LITERARY STRUCTURE AND THEMES (29:1–24)

In this second expositional/preaching unit of chapters 28–35, we deal with panels two and three (see above):

The second panel of chapters 28–35 (29:1–14) begins with a woe oracle against Zion (cf. 29:8), called here Ariel. After speaking of Ariel in the third person (29:1a, 2), the Lord directly addresses the personified city (29:3–4), using the feminine singular. Despite her religious festivals, the city will be besieged and humiliated. Isaiah 29:2–3 highlights the Lord's intervention—four first-person verbs appear. Isaiah 29:4 focuses on the impact this intervention would have on the city.

As in the preceding panel, there is an interlude that tempers the message of judgment (29:5–8; cf. 28:5–6). An attacking army will threaten Zion, but the Lord will spare the city by defeating the invaders. A theophanic description of Yahweh of Armies is thematically central to this unit (29:6). Paired וְהָיָה, "and it will be," clauses appear both before (29:5) and after (29:7–8) it. Three of these four clauses contain similes (29:5a, 7–8), while the other stresses the suddenness of the judgment (29:5b). The similes in 29:5 and 7 use the preposition -כְּ with a noun (note "like fine dust" and "as . . . with a dream," respectively) after וְהָיָה. The style changes in 29:8, where כַּאֲשֶׁר, "just as," follows וְהָיָה. The structure of 29:8a is symmetrical. It reads literally:

And it will be [וְהָיָה] as when [כַּאֲשֶׁר] the hungry one dreams [יַחֲלֹם] and look, [וְהִנֵּה] he eats, but he awakens [וְהֵקִיץ] and his throat [נַפְשׁוֹ] is empty,

or as when [וְכַאֲשֶׁר] the thirsty one dreams [יַחֲלֹם] and look [וְהִנֵּה] he drinks, but he awakens [וְהֵקִיץ] and look [וְהִנֵּה] (he is) weak and his throat [נַפְשׁוֹ] is longing (for water).

In 29:8b, כֵּן, "so," with the imperfect (יִהְיֶה, "it will be") completes the preceding comparative (כַּאֲשֶׁר) statements, reading literally, "and it will be as when . . . or as when . . . so it will be . . ."

As the prophet resumes the judgment speech, he addresses the people (note "these people" in 29:13–14 and the second-person plural forms in 29:9–11a). The Lord describes their divinely induced spiritual insensitivity, which prevents them from understanding Isaiah's message to them (29:9–12). The reason for this judgment is their failure to fear the Lord (29:13). They speak as if they are loyal to the Lord, but their hearts are far from him. Consequently (note לָכֵן), the Lord will intervene and thwart the supposedly wise (29:14).

The third panel of chapters 28–35 (29:15–24) begins with a woe oracle against those who hide their plans from the Lord (29:15). The prophet illustrates the absurdity of this (29:16). By not consulting the Lord's guidance, they are like a pot that insults its creator, the potter.

One expects an announcement of judgment to follow this denunciation, which is inherently accusatory. There is an element of judgment in 29:20–21, but the mood of the next unit (29:17–24) is primarily positive. The prophet announces that a great reversal will occur (29:17), bringing with it renewed spiritual vision (29:18). The oppressed will rejoice in the Lord (29:19), for his justice will prevail and be evident to all (29:20–21).

The Lord himself, designated the one who redeemed Abraham, speaks to Jacob (29:22–24). He announces that their shame will be removed (29:22). When they see the rejuvenation of the covenant community, they will acknowledge his sovereignty (29:23). Furthermore, those who have been spiritually wayward will gain understanding and submit to the Lord's guidance (29:24).

- *Jerusalem Attacked (29:1–4)*
- *Jerusalem Spared (29:5–8)*
- *Jerusalem's Spiritual Insensitivity (29:9–14)*
- *Denunciation of Those Who Make Secret Plans (29:15–16)*
- *Transformation and Reversal (29:17–24)*

EXPOSITION (29:1–24)

Jerusalem Attacked (29:1–4)
The Lord will attack and besiege Jerusalem.

29:1. The Lord pronounces a woe against Ariel, used here as a poetic name for Zion (see 29:8). The meaning of the name is uncertain. If a compound noun, it would seem to be a title, meaning "lion of God." In 29:2 the word is used in a simile, in which "lion of God" makes no sense as a point of comparison. A word אֲרִיאֵל appears in Ezekiel 43:15, where it refers to an altar hearth. If this is the term used in Isaiah 29:2, the simile suggests Zion, when assaulted by the enemy, will be like an altar hearth, which contains smoldering coals and sacrificial fires. The image suggests fire, which in turn suggests destruction. In this regard, Roberts (2015, 363) writes: "To say that Jerusalem will be like an altar hearth suggests to me a city scorched and blackened by fire, just like the base of an altar long used for repeated burnt offerings."

Ariel is called literally a "town (where) David encamped." Some interpret the verb חָנָה to mean "settled" (cf. NIV11) or "dwelt" (KJV), but more likely it refers here to besieging the town, as in 29:3. In this case it recalls David's attack on the Jebusite stronghold at Jerusalem (2 Sam. 5:6; see Clements 1980, 235).

In the second half of Isaiah 29:1 the Lord sarcastically urges Ariel's people: "Add year upon year, let festivals recur" (literal translation). Apparently, he is referring sarcastically to their obsession with religious ritual designed to gain the Lord's favor (see Isa. 1:11–15, cf. Motyer 1993, 237; Oswalt 1986, 527; Smith 2007, 496).

29:2–4. The Lord announces he will intervene in battle against Ariel (29:2–3). He will press hard against Ariel by encircling her with troops and erecting siege works. The verb חָנָה, "encamp," is used here of launching a siege against Ariel. The simile כַּדּוּר, "like a circle," pictures the Lord's army encircling the town. The meaning of מֻצָּב (a *hophal* participle from נָצַב, which in the *hiphil* means "to place in position") is uncertain. Collocated with the verb צַרְתִּי (from צוּר, "besiege"), and in parallelism with מְצֻרֹת, "fortifications" (NIV11, "siege works") it may refer to siege towers. Or it might refer collectively to troops positioned around the city.

The prophecy anticipates Sennacherib's siege of Jerusalem in 701 B.C. Sennacherib tells how he besieged and conquered forty-six of Judah's fortified cities by "using packed-down ramps and applying battering rams, infantry attacks by mines, breeches, and siege machines." He then boasts that he "locked up" Hezekiah "within Jerusalem, his royal city, like a bird in a cage," and "surrounded him with earthworks," making "it unthinkable for him to exit by the city gate" (*COS* 2.119B:303).

The siege will cause great sorrow (29:2b). To emphasize the emotional impact, two similar sounding nouns (תַּאֲנִיָּה and אֲנִיָּה), both related to the verb אָנָה, "to lament" (cf. Isa. 3:26; 19:8), are joined (cf. Lam. 2:5; see Young 1969, 307). Ariel (addressed with the feminine singular) will be so overcome with sorrow she will barely be able to talk (29:4). She is pictured as lying on the ground (note וְשָׁפַלְתְּ, "and you will be low") and speaking in low tones, like a spirit conjured up by a medium from the grave below. As noted earlier (see comments on 8:19), the word אוֹב appears to refer in 1 Samuel 28 to a pit used by a medium to conjure up the spirits of the dead. Saul asked his servants to find "an owner of an אוֹב" (28:7), he told the medium, "conjure for me by (using) an אוֹב" (28:8), and Samuel is described as ascending from the ground (28:13; cf. 28:8, 14–15). By extension the word can refer to the spirit that is conjured up by use of the pit and speaks "from the ground," as it were. Its words sound like the chirping of a bird (note צָפַף; cf. Isa. 10:14; 38:14). The comparison of Ariel's voice to that of an underworld spirit connotes death, which appears to be her destiny. As Roberts (2015, 364) observes, "If Jerusalem was not dead yet, the best one could say for her was that she already had one foot in the grave."

> **Siege Works**
>
> "I will . . . encircle you with towers and set up my siege works against you" (Isa. 29:3). This verse predicts how Sennacherib and his Assyrian army would besiege Jerusalem in 701 B.C. It references "siege works," which referred to anything an invading army would build as part of their siege to gain an advantage against the inhabitants of a walled city. This would have included things like siege ramps, towers, and battering rams.
>
> Siege ramps (2 Sam. 10:15; 2 Kings 25:1; Jer. 6:6; 32:24; Ezek. 4:2) were made from trees, rocks, or gravel from the surrounding area. They enabled invading soldiers to quickly climb over the wall.
>
>
>
> Relief of Assyrian Attack on a Town
>
> Battering rams (Ezek. 4:2; 21:22; 26:9) were machines with wheels and a large log suspended from ropes. The attacking army would wheel the battering ram right up to the city gate or wall. Later designs incorporated a roof or barrier that would shield soldiers from arrows shot by archers on top of the city wall. This provided cover for soldiers as they swung the suspended log into the wall or gate. The force of the hits from the log would weaken the structure causing it to crack and eventually crumble.
>
> A siege or breaching tower (Isa. 29:3; 30:25; Nah. 2:5) was an elevated platform built to be at least as tall as the city wall. These machines were also built with wheels to maneuver them into a strategic location near the wall. Soldiers would use this platform to defend their comrades attempting to scale the city wall. Most towers incorporated a drawbridge that would lower on top of the enemy's wall allowing soldiers to quickly enter the city. Because these

towers were vulnerable to fire, they were often covered in a flameproof material such as iron or animal skins.

Jerusalem Spared (29:5–8)
The Lord will spare Jerusalem and defeat the invader.

29:5–6. Jerusalem was on the verge of destruction, but the Lord would turn against the army he had prompted to besiege the city. Suddenly the horde of violent foreigners outside her walls will be reduced to fine dust and wind-blown chaff (Isa. 29:5). The prophet combines two similar-sounding synonyms (פֶּתַע פִּתְאֹם, "instantly, suddenly") to emphasize how swiftly the destruction will come. The judgment originates with the Lord of Armies, who will unleash devastating power against the enemy (29:6). The judgment takes the form of thunder, earthquake, a loud noise (or perhaps shout, קוֹל גָּדוֹל), a windstorm, a strong gale, and a consuming fire.

29:7. The threat to the city will prove to be like a dream or night vision that seems so real but then vanishes when one awakens. Roberts (2015, 364–65) says: "The host of enemies attacking Mount Zion will prove to be just as insubstantial and transient as such vividly experienced yet soon forgotten dreams of the night" (cf. Kaiser 1974, 268; Young 1969, 311). It is perhaps more than coincidental that the Lord's angel destroyed the Assyrian army in the night and that their corpses were visible in the morning (2 Kings 19:35; Isa. 37:36).

29:8. The expectations of the attacking foreign horde will go unsatisfied. Just when victory seems imminent, the invaders will be overwhelmed. They will be like a hungry, thirsty dreamer who imagines himself eating and drinking, but then wakes up to find he is still hungry and thirsty (see Kaiser 1974, 268; Motyer 1993, 238; Young 1969, 312–13). Smith (2007, 497) understands both Isaiah 29:7 and 29:8 as describing how the Assyrians' desire for conquest will go unfulfilled. Oswalt (1986, 529) takes both verses as referring to the transient nature of the threat. But it is best to see 29:7 as focusing on the transience of the threat, with 29:8 then highlighting the disappointment of the Assyrians.

The prophecy anticipates the defeat of Sennacherib's army, when the Lord's death angel wiped out a vast number of the Assyrian army in a single night, forcing Sennacherib to break off his campaign and return to Nineveh without conquering Jerusalem (2 Kings 19:35–36; Isa. 37:36–37).

Jerusalem's Spiritual Insensitivity (29:9–14)
The Lord denounces the people's spiritual insensitivity.

29:9. The prophet resumes the judgment speech with two pairs of rhetorical imperatives addressed to the people (29:9a). Repetition draws attention to them and highlights the action envisioned. We may translate literally: "Act amazed and be amazed! Act blind and be blind!" The imperatival mood is rhetorical. The commands indicate what is true or anticipate what will happen. The Lord is not encouraging or condoning sin here. The people had already blinded themselves by rejecting God and his prophet. The command is sarcastic and expresses the Lord's frustration with his people (cf. Amos 4:4). In Isaiah 6:10 the Lord uses the verb שָׁעַע, "be blind," in commissioning Isaiah; he urges the prophet to make the people blind. In that passage the command is also sarcastic; it announces the effect that Isaiah's preaching will have on the people. However, once judgment runs its course and accomplishes its purifying work (Isa. 29:17–24), spiritual insight and sensitivity will be restored within the covenant community (29:18, 24).

The Hebrew text of 29:9b switches from the imperative to perfective forms, describing how "they" are drunken and stagger, though not from literal intoxicants. The third-person perfective forms are problematic after the imperatives in 29:9a. Even more problematic is the following explanatory (כִּי) clause (29:10), which appears to address the ones described in 29:9b. To achieve consistency, some revocalize the perfects in 29:9b as imperatives: שִׁכְרוּ, "be drunk," and נָעוּ, "stagger." (See ESV, NIV11, NLT; Wildberger, 81.) Like the preceding commands, these would be rhetorical, describing present behavior or anticipating what would happen.

However, the perfects in 29:9b can be retained, if they are introducing asyndetic relative clauses that are vocative (so Irwin 1977, 56, and Roberts 2015, 366) or if the subject is understood as the prophets and seers mentioned in 29:10b. In the latter case, 29:10a gives the formal reason (note כִּי) for the condition described in 29:9a: the people are astonished and blind because the Lord has put a deep sleep upon them. 29:9b is parenthetical; it corresponds to 29:10b. One would expect prophets to counteract the blindness described in 29:9a, but they are drunken and staggering, as it were. Indeed, as 29:10b makes clear, the divinely imposed deep sleep is due to the Lord cutting off prophetic revelation from the people.

29:10. In any case, the imagery of 29:9 points metaphorically to spiritual insensitivity (see 29:10–14). The Lord has poured out (נָסַךְ) upon them, as it were, a disposition (רוּחַ) of deep sleep (תַּרְדֵּמָה) so that they are oblivious to the truth (29:10a). The reality behind the metaphor is revealed in 29:10b–12.

With rare exceptions (Isaiah, for example), the Lord no longer revealed himself through the spoken prophetic word (29:10b). Prophets are to be the people's spiritual eyes, but the Lord has shut them. Seers (another term for prophets) are to be the people's heads, but the Lord has covered them up. The covering of the head is probably synonymous with the shutting of the eyes. Covering the head (a hood may be envisioned; cf. Hayes and Irvine 1987, 334) would prevent one from seeing (see Wildberger 2002, 84). When people rejected the prophetic word, the Lord sometimes judged them and expedited their demise by withholding further revelation (cf. Amos 8:11–12; Mic. 3:5–7). As Roberts (2015, 368) points out, "the cessation of prophetic oracles" is a "recurring and well-known motif in prophetic literature." Yet the Lord's action is not arbitrary (Smith 2007, 499; Wildberger 2002, 83; Young 1969, 316). In fact, it is a response to the desire of the rebellious people themselves, who ordered the prophets and seers to "see no more visions" and to "give . . . no more visions of what is right" (cf. Isa. 30:10a). Instead, they demanded to hear "pleasant" messages, which in reality are "illusions" (30:10b).

29:11–12. Nevertheless, prophetic revelation had not completely ceased. After all, Isaiah was proclaiming the truth to them. Yet they were unresponsive to his message (29:11–12; cf. 6:9–10), as if a deep sleep had indeed been poured out upon them (cf. 29:10a). Isaiah's "whole vision" had no impact on the people. In illustrating the point, he compared it to a sealed scroll (29:11a). Isaiah divided the people into two categories. Those capable of reading could not access the words of the scroll because it was sealed (29:11b), while those unable to read were obviously incapable of knowing its contents, even if the seal were to be opened (29:12).

29:13. The Lord, designated the Sovereign Master (אֲדֹנָי), gives his assessment of the people's condition as a basis (note יַעַן כִּי, "because") for the announcement that follows (cf. 29:14, which begins with לָכֵן, "therefore"). They claim to be loyal to the Lord and even honor him with their words (literally, "lips"), but their hearts are far from him (29:13a). In this context the "heart" represents the inner person, where one's true feelings and passion reside. It stands in contrast to the mouth and lips, which represent mere words that may or may not accurately reflect what is on the inside. The words of the godly are a true reflection of their inner motives and commitment (Ps. 19:14 [HB 15]), but evildoers often disguise their inner character with deceptive words (Ps. 55:21 [HB 22]; Prov. 26:23; Ezek. 33:31). Because of their corrupt hearts, the people's words were meaningless. As Isaiah himself confessed, he lived among a people of unclean lips (Isa. 6:5). Any "fear" (NIV11, "their worship") of the Lord on their part was superficial, expressed through adherence to man-made commands they had been taught (29:13b). Perhaps this is why the Lord calls them "these people," rather than "my people." Isaiah consistently uses the phrase "this/these people" in a derogatory sense (6:9–10; 8:6, 11; 9:16 [HB 15]; 28:11, 14; see Blenkinsopp 2000, 406).

29:14. One expects an announcement of judgment after the accusatory statement of 29:13. Indeed, the spiritual insensitivity of the people will prompt the Lord to intervene mightily (29:14a). The text reads, literally, "Therefore look I—he will again [literally, "add"] do what is extraordinary with this people, doing what is extraordinary and an extraordinary thing." The threefold repetition of the root פלא draws attention to the extraordinary nature of the Lord's intervention. Wildberger (2002, 91) paraphrases the *hiphil* of פֶּלֶא in 29:14, "set unheard of things in motion." The form, though often used of the Lord's intervention on behalf of his people, can also refer to his judgment against them (see Deut. 28:59; see Kaiser 1974, 273). Isaiah 29:14b seems to imply judgment as it speaks of the wisdom of the wise being destroyed and hidden. Clements (1980, 239) sees irony here. In the past, God intervened mightily to save his people, but that "is now entirely turned round by the prophet to affirm its opposite effect." He adds, "God will act, but instead of leading to Israel's deliverance and freedom from the yoke of Assyria, it will lead to their destruction and further submission to it."

But one wonders if the Lord's intervention is fundamentally negative here. The next speech, after denouncing those who hide their plans from the Lord (29:15–16), describes how the Lord will transform the covenant community (29:17–24) as he eliminates their blindness (29:18) and gives them understanding (29:24). So, in addition to exposing human wisdom as inadequate, the Lord's extraordinary intervention will deliver the people from their spiritual insensitivity. Young (1969, 321) points out that the intervention, by demonstrating that human wisdom is foolish, may prompt people to "turn to the Lord, the only source of true wisdom and perception." Of course, this speech has already made it clear the Lord will bring a great deliverance during threatening judgment (see 29:1–8). As Smith (2007, 501) points out, this miraculous intervention will "confound the king's wise advisors who guided the king to make an alliance with Egypt in order to save Judah from Assyria (chaps. 30–31). They act contrary to the wise instructions of God. There will be no wisdom found in all the shrewd political scheming of the so-called 'intelligentsia.'"

There is another textual indicator that 29:14 envisions something positive beyond mere judgment. The Lord announces he will "again" (יוֹסִף) do what is extraordinary. To what prior extraordinary act is he alluding? The *hiphil* of פֶּלֶא also appears in 28:29, prompting Roberts (2015, 369) to see an allusion to that passage. But that text generalizes about the imparting of divine wisdom to farmers and does not refer to some prior event. The use of פֶּלֶא with the verb points one in the direction of the Lord's mighty deeds in the distant past, particularly the exodus (cf. Exod. 15:11; Ps. 77:11, 14 [HB 12, 15]; 78:12; cf. Kaiser 1974, 274). If so, the Lord is speaking here of doing something on a par with the exodus event, when he miraculously delivered his people from an overwhelming military enemy. Such a deliverance has already been depicted in Isaiah 29:5–8. Of course, the irony should not be missed. Judah was trusting in an alliance with Egypt to protect them against the Assyrians. But long ago the Lord had demonstrated his sovereign power over Egypt. So why would his people now place their faith in Egypt, rather than in the one who annihilated Egypt?

Denunciation of Those Who Make Secret Plans (29:15–16)

The people's attempt to ensure their security will fail.

29:15. The third woe in the series of woes in chapters 28–35 (cf. 28:1; 29:1) is directed against those who think they can hide their plan (לַסְתִּר עֵצָה, "to hide counsel") and activities from the Lord. As their rhetorical questions indicate, they believe no one will see or recognize them. The text describes them as, literally, "those who make deep, from the Lord to hide counsel; and their deeds are in darkness" (29:15a). After the participle "make deep," some understand the preposition מִן (note מֵיהוָה, "from the Lord") as indicating that the deep plans are "too deep" for the Lord (Blenkinsopp 2000, 406; Irwin 1977, 60–61). William Henry Irwin cites Psalm 88:6 (HB 7) as a text where Sheol appears to be beyond the Lord's awareness. However, if that is the notion here, then it would reflect the people's faulty concept, for the Old Testament makes it clear that even Sheol is within the Lord's jurisdiction and ultimate control (cf. Job 26:6; Ps. 139:8; Prov. 15:11; Amos 9:2). It is more likely the preposition has the force of "away from," indicating that they made their deep plans apart from consulting the Lord (cf. 28:15; Wildberger 2002, 98). But perhaps it is best to take "from the Lord" with "to hide," since the preposition מִן, "from," is so often collocated with the *hiphil* of סָתַר, "hide" (cf. BDB s.v. "סָתַר" 711; see NASB, NIV11).

The immediate context does not specifically identify the plan and actions, but the broader context suggests the plan is their alliance with Egypt (cf. Blenkinsopp 2000, 408; Roberts 2015, 374; Smith 2007, 503), which is depicted as a covenant with death because they believed it insulated them from disaster (cf. 28:15 [which also uses the verb סָתַר, "hide"] and 30:1 [which uses עֵצָה, "plan"]). The references to deepness and darkness fit well, for this covenant would have been transacted, metaphorically speaking, in the deep, dark underground region of Sheol. The noun מַחְשָׁךְ, "darkness" (cf. 29:15) is used elsewhere of the realm of death (cf. Pss. 88:6 [HB 7]; 143:3; Lam. 3:6).

29:16. Such thinking was topsy-turvy. In fact, their questions prompt the prophet to exclaim literally, "O your perversity!" Their belief that they could shield their plan from the Lord and control their own destiny defied all common sense. It was as silly as mistaking the potter for the clay that he uses to form his pottery (29:16a). Indeed, it would be absurd for the pot to deny the potter had formed it or to insult the potter by saying he knows nothing (29:16b). To do so is to deny the very ground of the critic's own existence and, worse yet, to undermine the logical basis for his critique. After all, if the potter is incompetent, what does that say about the pot (see Young 1969, 325)! Yet this is what Judah's leaders were doing. By leaving the Lord out of their plan, they were essentially denying his authority and wisdom as their creator. Such hubris was doomed to fail (cf. 29:14). As Wildberger (2002, 99) observes, "one cannot carry out political decisions by ignoring the one who is in charge of historical events."

Transformation and Reversal (29:17–24)

The Lord will restore his people and remove their enemies.

29:17. In the faulty thinking of Judah's leaders, the clay was master of the potter. In response to this perverted reversal of the truth, the Lord does some reversing of his own (see Oswalt 1986, 537) "in a very short time." He will demonstrate his sovereignty by judging proud oppressors (cf. 29:20–21) and by giving the oppressed cause for joy (29:19). This transformation is illustrated in 29:17. The cedar forest of Lebanon (cf. 14:8; 40:16; 60:13), symbolizing the proud (cf. 2:13; 10:34), is reduced to a mere orchard in size (כַּרְמֶל, see *HALOT* s.v. "כַּרְמֶל I" 499), while the orchard, symbolizing the needy, expands to become a forest. (See Hayes and Irvine 1987, 335. Oswalt [1986, 538] understands a reversal to be in view here, as the "positions of the noble and the common" are transformed. However, he understands כַּרְמֶל to refer to a plowed field, rather than an orchard.)

Some do not see the parallelism of 29:17 as contrastive but as synonymous. In this case, both lines picture renewed fertility (Wildberger 2002, 110). Several take כַּרְמֶל in the first line as a common noun ("orchard" or "fruitful field") but understand the same term in the second line as a proper noun parallel to Lebanon (Irwin 1977, 62–63; Roberts 2015, 376; Wildberger 2002, 103–4). They also appeal to 32:15, where renewed fertility is depicted, as the desert (מִדְבָּר) becomes an orchard (כַּרְמֶל), and the orchard (כַּרְמֶל) is considered a forest (יַעַר).

In response to this view, the following points can be made: (1) It is more likely that כַּרְמֶל has the same meaning in the parallel lines. The parallelism is chiastic: Lebanon corresponds to forest (יַעַר; cf. 1 Kings 7:2; 10:17, 21), with כַּרְמֶל occupying the pivotal, central positions in the chiasmus. (2) The notion of Carmel becoming a forest as a sign of renewed fertility makes no sense, for Carmel was already viewed as majestic and was well known for its lush vegetation (see Song 7:5; Isa. 33:9; 35:2; Amos 1:2; Nah. 1:4). This interpretation can work only if Lebanon and Carmel are viewed as already desolate (cf. Isa. 33:9) and then "restored to former glory" (Irwin 1977, 63). (3) The transformation described in 32:15 is not the same as in 29:17. In 32:15, in conjunction with the outpouring of the Spirit, the *desert* is changed into an orchard, depicting renewed fertility. In this context, the second line depicts the expansion of an orchard into a lush forest—an orchard par excellence. In 29:17 a desert (מִדְבָּר) is not mentioned. Fertility is not the theme, but rather a reversal in prominence. This notion of reversal is supported by 29:19–21. In this context, the Lebanon forest is reduced *in size* to an orchard, and the orchard expands to the size of a forest.

29:18. The prophet uses an additional illustration to depict the coming transformation. The deaf hear the words of the scroll and the blind, now freed from gloom and darkness, see. In addition to picturing the concept of radical change, this illustration depicts the spiritual transformation of the covenant community (Oswalt 1986, 538; Roberts 2015, 378; Smith 2007, 505). The "deaf" have not been mentioned prior to this, but the phrase "words of a scroll" echoes 29:11, where the scroll is associated with Isaiah's prophetic vision. The gloom and darkness represent judgment (cf. Isa. 8:22), which will pass (cf. 29:22b–23a). The prophet alludes here to the destruction of the Assyrian horde, described vividly in 29:5–8. Though the precise terminology differs, the reference to the eyes of the blind conceptually echoes 29:9–10, which uses the metaphors of blindness and shutting the eyes to illustrate the spiritual insensitivity of the people and its consequences. When the Lord intervenes, a transformation will take place as many come to their senses. They will now hear and respond to prophetic revelation and, having witnessed the Lord's powerful intervention, will acknowledge his sovereignty, and gain renewed understanding (29:23–24).

29:19. The prophet now begins to describe the reality behind the metaphorical language of 29:17. The humble and needy will rejoice in the Lord, the Holy One of Israel. This corresponds to the image of an orchard growing to the proportions of a forest. The terms "humble" and "needy" refer here to the economically distressed who are oppressed by the rich and powerful (cf. Isa. 32:7; 61:1). In the future the Lord will bring them relief, prompting them to praise him (cf. 11:4).

29:20. This relief is now described. The oppressors of the humble and needy will disappear. This corresponds to the image of the forest being reduced in size to an orchard (cf. 29:17). These oppressors are characterized as ruthless mockers who watch for opportunities to do evil. "Ruthless" refers to their violent actions, while "mockers" points to their arrogant attitude. The phrase "watchers of evil" (NIV11, "all who have an eye for evil") depicts them as watching carefully for opportunities to do evil. But judgment will eliminate them and cut them off.

29:21. The prophet specifies their evil deeds. They falsely testify in court, depriving the innocent of justice. They are characterized literally as "those who make a man a sinner with a word." This refers to verbal testimony in which they accuse someone of wrongdoing. They lay traps for the one who seeks to mediate justice at the city gate, where legal issues were resolved. This refers to devious schemes that undermine efforts to ensure justice (Wildberger 2002, 114). With "emptiness" (תֹּהוּ, NIV11, "false testimony") they deprive the innocent of justice. The noun תֹּהוּ probably characterizes their lies, which lack any substance or correspondence to the truth (Young 1969, 329).

29:22–23. This literary unit culminates with the Lord speaking directly to the "house [i.e., family/offspring, cf. NIV11, 'descendants'] of Jacob." The Lord's speech is introduced with לָכֵן, "therefore," indicating a logical connection with what the prophet has just announced. The coming transformation, depicted in 29:17–21, has a positive effect on the covenant community in the ways described by the Lord.

In his introduction of the Lord, the prophet calls him the one "who redeemed Abraham." The verb translated "redeemed" (פָּדָה) is not used elsewhere of Abraham, so it is unclear what event in the patriarch's experience is in view. Perhaps this refers to the Lord delivering Abraham from the shame of childlessness by giving him a son. This then becomes an analogy for what the Lord will do for his covenant community (29:23). Since the verb is often used of the redemption of Israel from Egypt in the time of the exodus (Deut. 7:8; 9:26; 13:5; 15:15; 21:8; 24:18; 2 Sam. 7:23; Mic. 6:4), it is possible that Abraham here represents his descendants, the Israelites (Smith 2007, 505–6). In Isaiah 41:8 Jacob is identified as the offspring of Abraham, and in 51:2 Abraham is called the father of the Lord's people.

The coming transformation brings the cessation of Jacob's shame, which is evident in his very face (29:22b). As 29:23 suggests, this shame is the result of having lost his children, whom the Lord will restore. This probably refers to the return of the exiles (cf. 43:6). In 60:21–22 the Lord speaks of Zion's increased population in the eschaton as being "the work of my hands," a phrase used in 29:23. By referring to these children as the "work" of his hands, the Lord also reverses the alien "work" of 28:21.

Though the miraculous deliverance of Jerusalem was announced earlier (see 29:5–8), judgment will also overtake the land (cf. 28:1–4, 11, 13–15, 18–22) and an exile of the north and of many in Judah will occur (see Roberts 2015, 380; see the commentary on 10:20 above).

When Jacob sees his restored children, the people will show the Lord the respect he is due (29:23). The switch from the singular (the text reads literally, "when *he* sees *his* children, the work of my hands in *his* midst"), referring to Jacob, to the plural in the second half of the verse shows that the nation (called "the house of Jacob," 29:22) is the reality behind "Jacob." The people will sanctify the Lord's name, sanctify the Holy One of Jacob, and display a healthy fear (note NIV11, "stand in awe") of the God of Israel (note יַעֲרִיצוּ, from

עָרַץ, "to fear," see commentary on 8:13 above). The *hiphil* of קָדַשׁ appears twice. The usage is causative, but obviously this does not mean they are making the Lord holy in an ontological sense. After all, he already is holy (cf. 6:3) and reigns as the Holy One of Jacob, a variation on the title Holy One of Israel, which is used twenty-five times in Isaiah (cf. 29:19). The verb refers to the renewed perception of the people, who will set the Lord apart in their thinking. They will treat or consider him to be holy (cf. *HALOT* s.v. "קדשׁ" 1074), meaning they will acknowledge him as their king (cf. 8:13).

29:24. Many rebels will be judged and eliminated in the day of transformation (see 29:20–21), but some who had gone astray will be reclaimed (29:24). These are called "wayward in spirit" and "those who complain" (*qal* of רָגַן). Perhaps the use of תָּעָה, "go astray," alludes to 28:7, where the verb is used twice of priests and prophets. If so, a reversal is described here. Its use here also anticipates the confession in 53:6, where the people admit, "We all, like sheep, have gone astray." The verb רָגַן, "complain," appears in Deuteronomy 1:27 (see also Ps. 106:25), where it is used (in the *niphal* stem) of the Israelites grumbling in the wilderness. In this regard, it is noteworthy that the verb תָּעָה is also used of the wilderness generation, whose hearts wandered from the Lord (Ps. 95:10; see Wildberger 2002, 117). These former wandering complainers will, in the day of transformation, possess renewed understanding of the Lord (cf. Isa. 29:23).

THEOLOGICAL FOCUS

The theological focus of this passage can be stated as follows: the Lord demonstrates his sovereignty over the destiny of his people by first bringing a powerful army against Jerusalem and then by mightily delivering the city from its attackers. Divine judgment has a positive goal—the spiritual transformation of the covenant community and their recognition of the Lord's sovereignty. As the prophet develops this theological theme, the following emphases emerge:

1. Superficial loyalty, human wisdom, and divine discipline

The people give lip service to the Lord, but do not truly fear him. They trust in their own wisdom to provide for their security. But this wisdom will perish as the Lord threatens their security and leaves them debilitated from sorrow.

2. Divinely imposed blindness

The people rejected the Lord's prophetic word, so the Lord punished them appropriately. He imposed upon them a spiritual blindness that entailed a diminishing of prophetic revelation. Even when the Lord did speak, as he was doing through Isaiah, the people would be insensitive to the message. Their refusal to listen to the Lord's word meant they would be cut off from it.

3. Divine sovereignty on display in a surprising way

The Lord will impress upon the people the fact of his sovereignty through a two-part plan. He will shatter their false sense of security by bringing a terrifying army against Jerusalem, proving that alliances with other nations cannot provide lasting protection. But the Lord will then deliver the city through a remarkable intervention, comparable to the exodus. He will display his sovereign power over the hostile attackers, proving that his people should trust in him alone during crises.

4. Two facets of judgment

The coming judgment has two facets. On the one hand, it brings death (note הוֹי, "woe," in 29:15) upon those who exclude the Lord from their plans, and it eliminates the oppressors who deprive the innocent of justice (29:20–21). On the other hand, judgment brings relief for the needy (29:19). Some who are spiritually insensitive will now understand, as the Lord lifts the blindness he had imposed upon the nation (29:18, 24). As the exile is reversed, the covenant community's shame is removed (29:22–23a).

5. Contrasting attitudes toward the Sovereign Lord

Some will pay the consequences of rejecting their creator and the security that only he can provide (29:15–16). But others will rejoice in the Holy One of Israel (29:19) and recognize he is indeed the sovereign king of Israel (29:23b).

PREACHING AND TEACHING STRATEGIES

Exegetical and Theological Synthesis

Isaiah 28–33 contains a series of six "woe" oracles. Two of these (the two shortest) appear in chapter 29. For this reason, some may choose to preach/teach these units separately. Due to the relative brevity of these oracles and the thematic coherency between these two passages, we have chosen to treat them as one preaching unit. For those who wish to deal with them separately, they might consider focusing first on the theme of how God is sovereignly involved in the life of his people, both in judgment and in eventual salvation in Isaiah 29:1–14. Then, in Isaiah 29:15–24, one could focus on how God uses judgment and discipline to bring about spiritual renewal.

As mentioned above, chapter 29 emphasizes God's role in the events that were about to play out for Jerusalem. With the benefit of hindsight, we can confidently conclude that the prophet is foretelling how the Assyrian army would advance through Judah culminating in them besieging and threatening the city of Jerusalem in 701 B.C. (29:1–3). However, the prophet describes these events as being carried out by God. There's no mention of the foreign invader. Rather, God is described as the perpetrator of these events against Jerusalem, cryptically referred to as Ariel (29:1, 2, 7). In 29:2, God says, "I will besiege Ariel," resulting in moaning and lamentation. In 29:3, God will encamp around them, besiege them with towers, and raise siegeworks against them. An enemy army will carry out these events, but also the hand of God will directly orchestrate the army's actions. In the end, the people of Jerusalem will be brought low to the ground, with their voices emanating from the ground like a dead spirit. The imagery conveys the fact that the people of Zion would be as good as dead.

Whereas the first four verses of this chapter emphasize how God will bring a foreign army against Jerusalem resulting in their humiliation and apparent death, 29:5–8 presents a divine reversal of sorts. Here, the Lord suddenly turns in judgment on the very ones he had brought up against Jerusalem. "In an instant" (29:5), the Lord of Armies will visit Jerusalem's foreign foes with thunder, an earthquake, a whirlwind, and a devouring fire (29:6). These are all vivid metaphors for God's judgment. The result will be that the armies that had come up against Jerusalem will be like a bad dream. They seem very real and frightening for a time, until Jerusalem awakens from its dream and realizes there's nothing to fear (29:7). Similarly, from the perspective of the invaders themselves, their experience will be like that of a dreamer who is hungry and about to eat, or thirsty and about to drink, only to wake up and realize that the thing they were about to consume to quench their appetite or thirst was itself just a dream (29:8).

The final section in this chapter (29:9–24) highlights Jerusalem's callous attitude toward God. On the surface, they were a very devout people. Isaiah 29:1 sarcastically highlights the fact that the people of Jerusalem consistently celebrated their religious holidays and feasts year after year. However, 29:9–24 indicates that their hearts did not match up with their outward routines. The prophet confronts them directly when he says, "These people come near to me with their mouth and honor me with their lips, but their hearts are far from me. Their worship of me is based merely on human rules they have been taught" (29:13). In other words, these people had mastered the art of religion. They knew how to say the right things and stay active in their religious traditions, but their hearts were far from loyal to God.

The prophet accused them of being drunk with wine, such that they lacked the vision to walk straight (29:9; cf. Isa. 28:1, 3, 7–8). The prophet sarcastically told the people to be blind, to be drunk, and to stagger. His sarcasm points out what he knows is already happening and what will continue to happen soon. The sense is probably something akin to, "Since you are blind, go ahead then and be blind. Go ahead and stay drunk, and stagger around too—not just with alcohol, however, but with the confusion sent by God" (29:9–10). In the same way that the Lord was involved in the Assyrian invasion (29:2–3) and in the subsequent judgment against Assyria (29:5–6), so too God would be involved in the people's spiritual blindness. While 29:9 accuses the people of blinding themselves to the words of God (a reference to their dismissal of the prophets), 29:10 says that the Lord has poured out upon them a spirit of deep sleep, closing their eyes, and covering their heads to the spiritual realities around them. This seems to indicate that God has blinded them to his truth by cutting off the prophetic visions so that they are left in the dark. Since they have refused to heed the prophets' warnings, God will stop sending them prophets.

Isaiah 29:11–12, however, suggests that not all prophetic visions will be terminated. After all, these very words being told to the people were part of a prophetic vision from Isaiah. However, visions such as this would seem unintelligible to the people. It would be as if the prophets' messages were mere words on a page to one who is not able to read, or like a message in a scroll that is sealed and can't be opened to those who can read.

The reason for this is stated in 29:13. The people's devotion to the Lord was wholly insincere. They draw near to him with their words and rituals, but their hearts are far from him. Thus, the Lord will intervene, as he will again do wonderful things on their behalf (29:14). One would expect some threat of judgment or punishment. However, the evidence seems to indicate this would be a positive act of grace by God on behalf of his covenant people. He would *again* do some wonderful (29:14) thing on behalf of Judah. This is possibly a reference to God's mighty deliverance of Israel by means of miraculous plagues and the parting of the Red Sea at the exodus. In doing this, God would show how foolish Judah's wise men were. They had counseled their leaders to enter an alliance with Egypt rather than depend upon the Lord God to be their savior from the Assyrians. As pointed out in the commentary above, there is great irony in the fact that Judah had turned to Egypt for her salvation rather than to God. Egypt had at one time been their oppressor, and the Lord had shown himself superior in every way to the gods of Egypt as he miraculously rescued them out from Pharaoh's cruel and violent treatment. Why then would they think that Egypt was a more capable deliverer now when faced with the threat of Assyrian oppression? It made absolutely no sense.

Isaiah 29:15 introduces the second woe in this pericope. Here the prophet confronts those who were attempting to conceal their plans from the Lord. They believed God didn't know what they were doing. This likely refers to those in Jerusalem who were advising Judah's leaders to carry out plans they knew weren't from the Lord. They were aware of God's disapproval of his people making political alliances with pagan nations rather than depending upon him for help. The prophet Isaiah had made this fact abundantly clear to King Ahaz and the people at that time (Isa. 7–8). These advisers had turned everything upside down. Instead of putting their trust in the sovereign God, they staked their hope in the strength of a pagan nation. But this was not just any nation—this was Egypt. Israel's greatest story of deliverance from a ruthless oppressor involved Egypt as the antagonist. The exodus confirmed God's superiority to Egypt. As such, Judah's decision to spurn God in favor of Egypt was sadly ironic. It turned things upside down. By rejecting God's help in favor of their own scheme, it was like the pot declaring itself wiser than the potter (29:16).

Isaiah 29:17–24 predicts the reversal that will transpire because of God's judgment. This also seems to be related to God's promise to do "wonder upon wonder" with "these people," as he would make the wisdom of their wise men perish (29:14). Here too we are told how the ruthless and the mockers would come to nothing (29:20), while the humble and the oppressed needy will experience a renewal leading to fresh joy in the Lord (29:19). The ruthless proud bear false witness against the innocent in legal proceedings by the city gate (29:21). The prophet likens the proud oppressors to the lofty forests of Lebanon, whereas the humble are likened to an orchard (29:17; NIV11, "fertile field"). As a result of God's sovereign intervention, the proud will be brought low, while the humble are exalted. The forest will become a mere orchard, while the orchard grows into a great forest.

Whereas the ruthless proud are brought down to nothing (29:20), the house of Jacob will be exalted by the Lord who redeemed Abraham, as they will no more be ashamed (29:22). Removing the collective shame of one's group would have been very significant for people in an honor-shame culture. In his book *The 3D Gospel: Ministry in Guilt, Shame, and Fear Cultures*, Jayson Georges's (2014, 24) comments help us understand how important the promises by God to remove the shame of his people would have been to them:

> Managing shame is essential because a shamed person (unlike a guilty person) can do very little to repair the social damage. Correcting shame requires a sort of remaking or transformation of the self; one's identity must change. More often than not, a person of a higher status must publicly restore honor to the shamed.

God would serve as the "person" of higher status who would restore the honor of these people that had been eroded by the wicked in a society who had turned the innocent into offenders by their false witness.

Isaiah 29:23–24 completes this section by describing the spiritual renewal and transformation of Judah that God himself would orchestrate. Those who had formerly gone astray and those who murmured and complained about God would now appropriately view him as the object of their worship. They would sanctify his name as the Holy One of Jacob, and they would worship God as their sovereign and powerful king. He alone would be viewed as the source of their security.

Preaching Idea

God directs hardships and discipline in his people's lives to bring about spiritual renewal and to demonstrate his trustworthiness.

Contemporary Connections

What does it mean?

To say that God directs hardship in a believer's life does not mean that he is the direct source of *all* hardship in our lives. Just because the Bible credits God as sometimes initiating and orchestrating hardship in people's lives, it doesn't logically require that he always be the source behind bad things that happen. Additionally, to say that God directs hardship in a person's life is not a denial of human free will. We should not assume, for example, that the Assyrians had no choice in the matter when they besieged Jerusalem with the goal of killing, conquering, and subjugating God's people. It would be a mistake to understand this passage or similar ones to mean that God instigates humans to commit sinful acts against others. I do not pretend to understand exactly how God's sovereignty works regarding human free will. However, people are always held accountable before God for their own individual choices in Scripture (Eccl. 12:14; Matt. 12:36–37; Jude 14–15; Rev. 20:12–13). Furthermore, the Bible indicates that God never incites or tempts people to do wrong (James 1:13–15). On the contrary, God always provides a way of escape from temptation to ensure that nobody ever *has* to sin (1 Cor. 10:13–14).

To say that God directs hardships means that at a minimum, he *allows* bad things to happen to them. Certainly, a sovereign and omnipotent God can intervene to prevent any and every bad thing that happens. For him to direct those hardships for his own purposes means that at a minimum, he strategically chooses not to prevent them.

Furthermore, in such cases God chooses to use the bad actions to achieve a positive goal. For example, imagine a twelve-year-old boy who loves basketball. He can't imagine anything more fulfilling at this time in his life than to one day play on his high school's varsity team. And so naturally he tries out for the middle school boys' basketball team along with several of his friends. But to his great dismay, he doesn't make the cut. He is forced to endure the pain of not only missing out on playing basketball, but watching from the stands as his closest friends play the game he loves without him. Now this boy's father didn't cause his son to be cut after tryouts were over. In fact, he was rooting for his son to make the team. However, he wisely realized that this painful experience was an excellent growth opportunity for his son. So he challenged the son to accept this hardship as evidence that his pure talent alone wasn't enough to fulfill his desire to play varsity ball one day. He encouraged him to use this painful experience as motivation to discipline himself to practice each day between now and next year's tryouts.

While this boy's father did not *cause* his son's hardship, he did *use* this hardship to bring about good things for his son.

This passage presents God as the one directing the events of the Assyrian invasion into Judah. We know from Isaiah 10 that God didn't need to incite the Assyrians' hearts to want to act in violent aggression toward the Judeans. This was within the scope of their existing behavior toward other nations and something they clearly wanted to do. Also in Isaiah 10, God predicted that he would judge and punish the Assyrians for their insolent pride, despite him sending them as his instrument of judgment against his own people (10:5–6). Both Isaiah 10 and 29 anticipate God's judgment against Assyria in 701 B.C. Additionally, both chapters identify the Assyrian army as God's instrument to judge his people. In chapter 10, God makes it clear that Assyria was not innocent for what they did, even though God sovereignly used their actions to bring about his own purposes on behalf of his people. God holds Assyria accountable for their actions and judges them for their sins (10:12, 16–19). Thus, we can safely conclude that even though God poetically describes himself as the one distressing, besieging, and raising siegeworks against Jerusalem ("Ariel"), this should not be interpreted as God inciting Assyria to do these things against their own will. It is likely best to understand God as allowing Assyria to carry out its plans against Jerusalem to accomplish his own purposes. Some of God's purposes for allowing this hardship to come against his people are alluded to in this passage. By extension, these same realities also help to explain why God sometimes directs hardship in the lives of believers today.

First, *God uses hardship to display his power and grace to us.* The leaders of Jerusalem had chosen to spurn God's help in defending against the coming Assyrian onslaught. Instead, they chose to lean upon Egypt for their security. By allowing the Assyrians to march against Jerusalem and besiege the city, God revealed how vulnerable his people were without his help. Similarly, God revealed that Egypt was impotent to deliver them. This would lead Jerusalem to humbly turn to the Lord, providing him an opportunity to display his power and grace to them as he miraculously delivered them in a way only he could.

In similar fashion, hardship has a way of revealing to us today how our own idols or false sources of security are ultimately unable to provide us with ultimate meaning or purpose in life, not to mention salvation from future judgment. Thus, hardship tends to direct our attention back to God as the only one who can provide us with these essential things.

Second, this passage highlights how *God uses hardship to strengthen our commitment to and faith in him*. The people in Jerusalem were going through the external motions of faith in God and religion (29:1). However, their hearts were far from a pure devotion to him (29:13). They demonstrated the true nature of their hearts toward God by their unwillingness to fully trust him to be their savior and protector (29:9–10) despite promises and admonition by the prophets (29:11–12). Thus, God used the hardship of the Assyrian invasion, from which he delivered them, to deepen their commitment to him and strengthen their faith.

Similarly, God has a way of using hardship to deepen our faith and commitment to Jesus. Trials have a way of forcing us to trust Jesus rather than ourselves. This is particularly true when we have been walking in rebellion against God, or when we have minimized his role in our experience. God will often use hardships of various sorts to get our attention by not allowing us to enjoy life when it is being lived in devotion to false gods. Trials force us to reevaluate how we have been living and why it has become unfulfilling.

Third, *God uses hardships to remind us that our ultimate joy is found in God's salvation*. The prospect of losing one's freedom, one's wealth, and possibly one's life at the brutal hands of the Assyrian army would have been a very traumatic experience for the inhabitants of Jerusalem. How glorious it must have been for them when the Lord miraculously, without any help from the Egyptians, rescued them. This would have caused them to recognize in a fresh way the blessing that God was to them. In that moment, they would have experienced a fresh joy in the Lord that couldn't be reproduced by anything else. This is exactly what the prophet predicted would happen once God rescued them: "In that day . . . the humble will rejoice in the Lord; the needy will rejoice in the Holy One of Israel" (29:18–19). No longer would Jacob be ashamed of God (as seen in their earlier rejection of him as their source of security). Rather, they would stand in awe of him once they witnessed his salvation (29:22–23). Too often, humans become content in this world with lots of things other than God. Hardships have a way of removing the things that rival God for our affection to free us up to pursue him. As St. Augustine once said, "God wants to give us something, but cannot, because our hands are full—there's nowhere for Him to put it" (quoted in Lewis 2001, 94).

Is it true?

The reality of God directing and using hardship in the lives of believers is seen throughout Scripture. Paul famously prayed for his "thorn in the flesh" to be taken away. God responded by saying, "My grace is sufficient for you, for my power is made perfect in weakness" (2 Cor. 12:9). Paul went on to say he was content in hardships of various kinds because God's strength became more evident in his life when he was weak. Earlier in the same letter, Paul wrote that our afflictions lead to us receiving comfort from God so that we can comfort others with the same sort of comfort we have received (2 Cor. 1:3–4). He went on to imply that a reason why God allowed his people to be afflicted with hardship was so we could comfort others (2 Cor. 1:6–7). The writer of Hebrews says that Jesus himself was matured or perfected through suffering (Heb. 2:10). He clarified this statement a few chapters later when he wrote that Jesus "learned obedience from what he suffered," and in this way he was "made perfect" (Heb. 5:8–9).

Finally, consider one of the most treasured verses in all of Scripture, Romans 8:28: "And we know that in all things God works for the good of those who love him, who have been called according to his purpose." Christians have taken great comfort in this promise that all things, including suffering, will work out for their ultimate good one day. Romans 8:29 goes on to clarify what is meant by the believer's good. It says all believers have been predestined to be conformed to the image of Jesus Christ. In other words, hardship serves to mature us and build our character so that we ultimately resemble Jesus.

How does hardship mature us in Christlike character? One of the ways it does this is by driving us to depend upon God's strength and grace for our comfort and joy. In truth, we tend to forget God when life is good and things are easy. We drift toward apathy and self-sufficiency. We tend to neglect God because we fail to sense our need for him. This is what regularly happened throughout the book of Judges. Whenever God would provide Israel with safety and prosperity, the next generation would forget him and turn to idols. In response, God would raise up Israel's enemies against them (orchestrating hardship in their lives) to get their attention, often resulting in them calling on him for help. God would then graciously raise up a leader who would help restore Israel's worship of the Lord and help them gain political freedom from their enemies. However, once life became peaceful again and oppression was gone, usually after a few decades had passed, the nation would again forget God and worship idols.

Suffering is often God's necessary instrument to remind us how empty life is without him at the center. He reminds us that only in him can true purpose and joy be experienced. Suffering highlights how much we need God to handle life's biggest problems. On our own, we usually only make them worse.

Now what?

Understanding that God sovereignly directs hardships and salvation in a believer's life should impact how we view and feel about trials in general. Whereas many in the world today might feel the need to fall apart, drift into despair, or even take their own life when certain forms of hardship hit them, this shouldn't be the case for Christians. Not only do we have an eternal hope that transcends every trial, but we also know that God is at work amid every hardship. He is working to transform our lives to be more like Christ. Thus, there is always a silver lining to every hardship. I'm not suggesting that a Christian doesn't grieve or that they act as though they are immune to pain. Not even Jesus was immune to pain as he begged his Father to remove the cup of suffering from him as he neared the suffering of the cross (Matt. 26:36–46). However, Christians should be willing to accept suffering, not only as part of living in a fallen world, but better yet, as part of God's good purposes for their lives. The words of Job should ring in our ears, "Shall we accept good from God, and not trouble?" (Job 2:10). We can show that we accept suffering from God by our willingness to worship him in the very midst of our pain. This was the surprising posture that Job took when he discovered that he had lost much of his property and every one of his adult children all in the same day.

> At this, Job got up and tore his robe and shaved his head. Then he fell to the ground in worship and said: "Naked I came from my mother's womb, and naked I will depart. The Lord gave, and the Lord has taken away; may the name of the Lord be praised." (Job 1:20–21)

What an act of faith on the part of a believer when they choose to proclaim their devotion to God even when experiencing great heartache and pain. Isaiah predicted that the day would come when the inhabitants of Jerusalem would do this very thing. God said that "they will keep my name holy; they will acknowledge the holiness of the Holy One of Jacob, and will stand in awe of the God of Israel" (Isa. 29:23). Unfortunately, they had to experience God's salvation before they were able to recognize his worthiness to be worshipped.

As we consider the fact that God is working in our hardships to bring about his good purposes for our lives, we should remember that it is much easier to endure pain and suffering when we know that it is purposeful and ultimately beneficial for us. A woman will endure the agony of childbirth because she knows that a precious child is being brought into her life. A person recovering from surgery will endure weeks or months of painful rehabilitation sessions because they know that it is the only way for them to regain their mobility and the full use of their bodies. Medical students will endure years of tedious study and twenty-four-hour shifts as interns for the opportunity to mature into respected physicians. For this reason, James could tell Christians to "consider it pure joy" when they encountered hardships of various sorts (James 1:2–4). These trials would produce valuable character in them bringing about maturity.

I'm reminded of the Mastercard commercials from the 1990s that went like this: "Tickets: $28; 2 hot dogs, 2 popcorns, 2 sodas: $18; 1 autographed baseball: $45; real conversation with your eleven-year-old son: priceless!" Each commercial would end by saying, "There are some things money can't buy; for everything else, there's Mastercard." The father in that commercial couldn't look at the suffering he was enduring financially as though the bottom line was how much it was all costing him. Sure, a couple of hot dogs, some popcorn, and sodas would be a fraction of the cost at the local grocery store. Watching the same game on television would have been free. But the memories he was making and the bond he was deepening with his son was what made it all worth it. In the big picture, the hardship that his wallet endured that day was a valuable investment in his relationship with his beloved son. Similarly for the believer, the hardships we are forced to endure can be viewed as investments in our Christian maturity if we choose to respond to them with faith in God rather than with frustration, anger, and complaining. This is why Paul could write, "I consider that our present sufferings are not worth comparing with the glory that will be revealed in us" (Rom. 8:18). Said another way, what God is producing in us through the sufferings of this present time is, well, priceless.

Creativity in Presentation

Purpose in the Pain
Have you seen speed painters who perform their art in front of a live audience? They will create a masterpiece in only one to two minutes. They will typically have one or two brushes in both hands, often painting in bold colors on a black canvas. One common variation includes the artist painting their picture upside down making it much harder for the audience to figure out what if anything is the actual subject matter of their artwork. Inevitably, if the artist has done his or her job well, once they have finished their work, they will flip the piece around revealing somewhat of a hidden masterpiece that was in process all along unbeknownst to the audience who couldn't imagine what the finished product would look like until the very end.

I once watched an example of this type of performance on *Switzerland's Got Talent* (similar to *America's Got Talent*). The artist began by drawing what appeared at first to be a crude, cartoonish figure of one of the judges with chalk, black marker, and other mediums. This was followed by other somewhat indiscernible, seemingly random additions that made little sense to the audience or judges. The looks on their faces made it obvious they were unimpressed and somewhat confused by the artwork. One by one, the judges began to press their red buttons signifying their conclusion that her performance didn't measure up. Eventually, the fourth and final judge pressed his button signifying that she had failed. Undeterred, the artist added a few more quick touches before flipping the artwork over and splashing chalk onto the drawing. In that moment, the drawing suddenly reflected a masterpiece that had been looming all along. It had simply been undetectable to all except the artist.

This illustrates the work that God is often doing in the lives of his faithful servants as they are enduring hardship and suffering. To the watching world, it appears that God is either not paying any attention, or he has no idea what he is doing in their life. Humanly speaking, their life looks like a mess in many ways. However, beneath the surface, God is actually producing a masterpiece, one that will only be able to be fully appreciated in the end. For optimal effect, the preacher may consider finding and showing a short video clip illustrating one of these speed painting performances.

A Better Perspective on Pain
Clive Staples Lewis (better known as C. S. Lewis), the famous Oxford philosopher and professor, was a man who experienced more than his share of suffering in his life. He details this in his book, *Surprised by Joy* (1955). Lewis's mother passed away when he was only ten years old. His father then became so overcome with grief that he withdrew from life and sent Clive away to a boarding school. While there, Lewis was regularly bullied and picked on by the older boys. As a young man, he entered the army, which led to him having to fight in World War I. Lewis witnessed dozens of his friends and fellow soldiers killed in the prime of their lives. The images of their horribly smashed but still moving bodies was a traumatic sight. At one point, he himself was injured by shrapnel to the point that he almost lost his life. For years after the war, Clive suffered from nightmares and flashbacks from his time in combat; today this would be diagnosed as post-traumatic stress disorder. Another deep wound that Lewis carried with him throughout his adult life was his father's ongoing alienation from him. His father didn't approve of his choice to become a Christian, and thus he was never proud of his son's accomplishments as a Christian philosopher and writer. Not only did his father disapprove of his Christian beliefs, but so did most of Lewis's colleagues at Oxford. Though very popular with the students, he was never offered a full professorship because of how much the academy resented his Christian faith.

Despite all the hardship recounted above, none of it was as painful as the death of his wife Joy. Lewis married Joy later in life even though she had cancer and wasn't expected to live very long. However, her cancer went into remission, and suddenly the prospect of the two of them living out the remainder of their lives together became a reality. However, this quickly changed when Joy's cancer returned with a vengeance about two years later. Joy died soon thereafter, and Lewis described her death as the deepest pain that he endured in his lifetime. Twenty years before this, Lewis wrote the following in his book, *The Problem of Pain*:

> Now God, who has made us, knows what we are and that our happiness lies in Him. Yet we will not seek it in Him as long as He leaves us any other resort where it can even plausibly be looked for. While what we call "our own life" remains

agreeable we will not surrender it to Him. What then can God do in our interests but make "our own life" less agreeable to us, and take away the plausible source of false happiness? It is just here, where God's providence seems at first to be most cruel, that the Divine humility, the stooping down of the Highest, most deserves praise. (2001, 94)

God directs hardships and discipline in his people's lives to bring about spiritual renewal and to demonstrate his trustworthiness.

- God uses hardship to display his power and grace to us (29:1–8).
- God uses hardship to strengthen our commitment and faith (29:9–18).
- God uses hardship to remind us of our joy in God's salvation (29:19–24).

DISCUSSION QUESTIONS

1. When you consider the doctrine of the sovereignty of God in relation to hardships and suffering, do you find this to be troubling or comforting? How so?

2. In Isaiah 29:1–4, God directly connects himself with the actions taken by the Assyrian army against Jerusalem. God makes a similar connection between himself and the Assyrian army's conquests in Isaiah 10:5–19. In Isaiah 10, God also promises to punish the Assyrians for their sinful actions as soon as he is finished using them for his own purposes. How do you understand the relationship between God's sovereignty and human free will in these contexts? How can God use Assyria as his own instrument, and then turn around and punish them for their actions? (For a discussion of this issue, see the "What does it mean?" section above.)

3. Share about a time when hardship led to growth in your life. How might your life be different if you had never gone through that difficult experience?

4. Read Hebrews 12:5–11. What correlations exist between a parent who administers painful discipline to their children and God when he directs hardship into the life of one of his children?

FOR FURTHER READING

Lewis, C. S. 2001. *The Problem of Pain*. New York: HarperCollins.

Isaiah 30:1–33

EXEGETICAL IDEA
The Lord will punish those who seek help from Egypt and reject his authority, but he will extend his mercy to those who trust him as he defeats Assyria.

THEOLOGICAL FOCUS
The Sovereign Lord is the only source of security for his people.

PREACHING IDEA
The path of rebellion leads only to ruin, but repentance brings blessing and rejoicing.

PREACHING POINTERS
Every generation has a concept of what a rebel looks like. If one attended high school in the 1950s, they might imagine somebody in tight jeans with a white t-shirt, a black leather jacket, slicked back hair, and a cigarette behind his ear. If one was a child of the '60s, they may instead envision a marijuana-smoking hippie with long hair and a tie-dyed t-shirt. When I attended high school in the '90s, there was a subculture of people who identified themselves as goth and dressed in all black. Many of them dyed their hair black, wore black makeup, and embellished their faces and bodies with piercings and jewelry. These students personified rebellion in my day.

In Isaiah 30, the prophet confronts the "rebellious" (30:1, 9) people of Jerusalem. They chose to ignore his prophets' warnings against seeking help from foreign nations. Their refusal to trust in him was not just foolish but an act of rebellion. The people of Jerusalem thought they knew better than God and trusted their own wisdom more than his promises (30:12). Thus, God was going to have to judge them. However, because the Lord is such a patient and gracious God (30:18), he called on his people to repent, promising them that he waits expectantly for them to turn back to him (30:19). When they do, they would be greeted with salvation, blessings, and joy (30:15, 23–26, 29).

REBELLION AND MERCY (30:1–33)

The Lord is superior to even the most prominent of nations. Egypt will not be able to provide security for Judah. Only the Lord can defeat the Assyrians. Those who trust in Egypt and reject the Lord's authority face severe judgment. But the Lord is just and extends his mercy to those who trust in him.

LITERARY STRUCTURE AND THEMES (30:1–33)

This panel begins with a woe oracle against those who seek an alliance with Egypt. The Lord denounces his people for looking to worthless Egypt for security (30:1–5). In an oracle against "the animals in the Negev," he lampoons those who transport tribute to Egypt (30:6–7). He then instructs the prophet to record a message as evidence against the rebellious people, who tell the prophets not to speak of judgment. They make it clear they do not want to hear what the Holy One of Israel has to say (30:8–11). But the Holy One of Israel will not be silenced. In two formal judgment speeches against the people, he describes how they will be decimated by a foreign invader (30:12–14, 15–17).

The mood changes abruptly. The nation's weakened condition will prompt the Lord to be merciful toward those who wait for him (30:18). Jerusalem's sorrow will be transformed into blessing. The Lord will provide spiritual guidance that will result in the people rejecting their idols (30:19–22). He will restore their prosperity as he brings healing to them (30:23–26). Jerusalem's renewal will be accompanied by violent, devastating judgment upon the Assyrians (30:27–33). Assyria's defeat chronologically precedes the transformation and restoration depicted in 30:18–26 (Ortlund 2010, 214).

- *Denunciation of Those Who Seek Help from Egypt (30:1–17)*
- *God's Mercy Brings Blessing and Deliverance (30:18–33)*

EXPOSITION (30:1–33)

Denunciation of Those Who Seek Help from Egypt (30:1–17)

The Lord denounces Judah's foreign alliances, especially its treaty with Egypt.

30:1. The fourth literary panel of chapters 28–33 (see above) begins with a woe oracle directed against stubborn children. The verb סָרַר, "be stubborn" (סוֹרְרִים) is used with בֵּן (בָּנִים), "son," in only one other context: Deuteronomy 21:18, 20. There it describes a rebellious son who rejects the discipline of his parents and insists on pursuing a lifestyle characterized by gluttony and drunkenness. The men of the city are commanded to execute (by stoning) the rebellious son and thereby "purge the evil" from the community as a warning to the rest of the nation (21:21; Young [1969, 336] suggests an allusion to this text). A related noun סָרָה, "rebellion," is used in Isaiah 1:5 of sinful Israel, likened to rebellious children (cf. 1:2) who persist in self-destructive behavior. In Isaiah 30:1, the stubborn children rebel by rejecting the Lord's plan (עֵצָה, cf. 5:19; 28:29) and pursuing their own (see 29:15). Furthermore, they pour out a libation. The meaning of this statement is unclear, but 30:2 describes them traveling to Egypt to seek an alliance with Pharaoh (either Shabaka or his successor Shebitku). Apparently, the libation alludes to a ritual associated with ratifying a treaty (Hayes and Irvine 1987, 266; Wildberger 2002, 120, 124).

But this treaty-making is not the Lord's doing. He specifically says it does not originate with his Spirit. In this context the referent is the Lord's personal Spirit, probably viewed as the one who energizes the prophets. This strategy for security does not come from the Lord, who communicates his will through his prophets. The Lord's prophet, Isaiah, advised Ahaz to avoid entangling alliances and to trust in the Lord (cf. Isa. 7).

In seeking a foreign alliance, they added sin to sin (30:1b). The sins correspond formally to the two infinitival phrases. The text reads literally, "to make/do a plan, but not from me," and "to pour out a libation, but not (from) my spirit" (Motyer 1993, 245). They did not really trust the Lord, so they did not seek his guidance but instead made and executed their own plan. They acted in a manner that demonstrated their lack of trust. In short, the lack of faith in their heart was revealed by their actions.

30:2. The woe pronouncement is extended specifically to "those who walk [i.e., travel] to go down to Egypt" (literal translation) without consulting the Lord (30:2a). Their purpose in visiting Egypt is to find refuge in Pharaoh's stronghold and to seek shelter in Egypt's "shade" (30:2b). The Lord is the true "refuge" (מָעוֹז) of his people (Isa. 17:10; 25:4; 27:5), but they insist on walking by sight, not faith, and look elsewhere for protection. The expression לַחְסוֹת בְּצֵל, "to seek shelter in the shade," refers here to making a treaty with Pharaoh. Isaiah 30:6–7 describes Judah transporting tribute to their new lord to ensure his military protection (cf. 31:1–3). The expression also occurs in Judges 9:15, where the thorn bush (representing Abimelech), in response to the trees' request to be their king (9:14), urges them to "seek shelter in my shade." With these words, he accepts their appeal, but only if they recognize his authority. "To seek shelter" in someone is tantamount to a declaration of loyalty, for it reveals the object of one's trust. In Psalms those seeking shelter in the Lord are the same as those who love the Lord's name (5:11 [HB 12]), fear him (31:19 [HB 20]), and serve him (34:22 [HB 23]). Seeking shelter in the Lord is closely associated with a declaration of loyalty and repudiation of idols (Ps. 16:1–4). Those who seek shelter in the Lord are contrasted with rebels who are threatened with destruction if they fail to repent and to acknowledge the sovereignty of the Lord's chosen king (2:10–12).

30:3–5. Judah's treaty with Egypt will prove disappointing. Instead of the desired protection, Judah will experience only shame and humiliation (Isa. 30:3). Pharoah had officials in Zoan, located in the Egyptian delta, and Hanes, perhaps located east of Zoan (30:4). The officials in Zoan, eager to make the alliance with Judah, send messengers to Hanes to meet the Judahites there. Yet, in the end, everyone (note כֹּל, "all") will be shamed, because Egypt is a nation that can offer no genuine help but only disgrace (30:5).

> **Pharaoh Had Officials**
> The antecedent of the third-person masculine singular pronominal suffixes (30:4 reads literally "his officials and his messengers") must be Pharaoh. Interpreters typically identify the antecedent as Judah or the king of Judah, but neither is mentioned specifically in the preceding verses, which use plural forms to refer to those from Judah. To resolve this problem, Wildberger (2002, 121) follows the LXX by reading absolute plural forms ("leaders" and "messengers") without the pronouns, but this is the easier reading and, for that reason, an unlikely original. Wildberger (2002, 120) is driven to this reading by his belief that "an assertion stating that the pharaoh has princes in Zoan and sends messengers to Hanes makes no sense in this context." As Roberts (2015, 383) points out, the Nubian pharaoh at this time (somewhere between 705 and 701 B.C.) had his administrative center at either Thebes or Memphis,

not in the delta. Nevertheless, as 30:4 observes, he did have officials assigned to Zoan, in the delta (Roberts 2015, 383; Wildberger 2002, 127). In this case Pharaoh's messengers are sent there by his officials in Zoan, to meet those arriving from Judah (30:2a; cf. Roberts 2015, 383).

30:6–7. The short oracle in 30:6–7, designated a מַשָּׂא, concerns "the animals in the Negev," referring here to the donkeys and camels (cf. 30:6b) used by the Judahites to transport their tribute through the Negev to Egypt. The word מַשָּׂא is related to the verb נָשָׂא, "to lift," and means "load, burden." It is appropriate here, since the oracle depicts the donkeys and camels carrying (note the use of the verb נָשָׂא) loads of tribute (Irwin 1977, 76).

The description highlights the danger of the journey and the high value of the tribute. The land through which the tribute-bearers travel is one of "hardship and distress," filled with dangerous, deadly animals, such as lions and poisonous snakes. The donkeys and camels are loaded down with "riches" and "treasures." To risk such a trip and pay such a price shows Judah is desperate for security. But Egypt will prove to be a disappointment. Any "help" she might offer will be devoid of substance. The Hebrew texts reads, "Egypt, (with) futility and emptiness helps."

Therefore, the Lord gives her a name that sarcastically refers to her ineffectiveness. The meaning of the name, however, is unclear. The Hebrew text reads, literally, "Rahab [that is, 'Proud One'], they, sitting [הֵם שָׁבֶת]." But this makes little, if any sense, unless "sitting" refers to inactivity. This line of interpretation is reflected in some translations, including NIV11 ("Rahab the Do-Nothing") and ESV ("Rahab who sits still"). Perhaps הֵם should be revocalized הֹם, a qal participle from הום meaning, "one making noise." In this case, the text may be understood, "one who makes noise (while) sitting." It would point to Egypt's proud claims, as well as its failure to back them up. Another option is to emend the text to הַמָּשְׁבָּת, a *hophal* participle of שָׁבַת, "to rest" (*HALOT* s.v. "שׁבת" 1409). In the *hiphil* שָׁבַת can mean "put to an end, remove, cause to disappear," so the *hophal* would express the passive of one of these nuances. Perhaps "brought to an end" would fit here as a reference to Egypt's impending defeat and humiliation. One could then translate it as, "Rahab, the one brought to end" (cf. NASB, "Rahab who has been exterminated"). The title "Rahab," which is used of Egypt elsewhere (cf. Isa. 51:9; Ps. 87:4), means "Proud One," and highlights Egypt's inflated view of itself. In Job (9:13; 26:12) and in Psalm 89:10 (HB 11) Rahab is a name for the sea and/or the serpentine sea creature symbolic of chaos and evil. Isaiah 51:9 associates this creature with Egypt, which was defeated by the Lord at the exodus. In ancient myths and in the Old Testament the chaotic sea/sea monster threatens creation and the world order. Egypt became a tangible, historical manifestation of evil because it opposed God's creation of his covenant people.

30:8. The Lord instructs the prophet to record formally (on tablet and inscription) a message that will serve as an enduring witness against the Lord's people (30:8). This likely refers to the present speech. When their plan to find security in Egypt fails and judgment comes crashing down upon them, the formal record of the prophecy will serve as proof of the Lord's authority over them and their destiny.

30:9. Such formal proof is necessary because of (כִּי) the people's attitude toward the Lord and his prophets. They are a rebellious (מְרִי) nation, characterized by deceit and a refusal to obey the Lord's instructions (30:9). Long before this, Moses characterized Israel as rebellious (מְרִי) and stubborn (Deut. 31:27). After Saul blatantly disobeyed the Lord's command, Samuel informed the king that the sin of rebellion (מְרִי) was particularly wicked in the sight of the Lord, for it entails a refusal to obey the Lord's word (1 Sam. 15:23). Such was the case with Isaiah's generation. They claimed allegiance to the Lord but were not truly loyal to him. This appears to be the force of the adjective כֶּחָשִׁים, "deceitful," used here to modify "children." The related verb is used in Joshua 24:27 of those who prove to be disloyal to an earlier pledge of allegiance (see also Isa. 59:13; Jer. 5:12). When the Lord's instruction came to them, they refused to obey (literally, "listen," which is a metonymy of cause for effect here; cf. as well Isa. 28:12).

30:10. In this case, the Lord's "instruction" (30:9, תּוֹרָה) came through his prophets and took the form of correction (for this nuance of תּוֹרָה, see Isa. 1:10; 5:24; 8:16, 20). The prophets communicated to the people the content of their prophetic visions, which pertained to "what is right." The term נְכֹחָה literally refers to what is straight, and then, metaphorically, to what is honest or morally correct (cf. Isa. 26:10; 59:14; Amos 3:10). The plural form in Isaiah 30:10 can be understood as abstract ("what is right") or as numerical ("right things"). Either way the people told the prophets to cease this corrective instruction. Instead, they wanted to be told "pleasant [literally, 'smooth'] things" and "illusions." Of course, the people would not actually ask to be deluded; they simply wanted to hear positive messages (Motyer 1993, 248; Roberts 2015, 389). But the Lord here identifies what such messages really were—nothing but deceptive illusions—and sarcastically puts that word on the lips of the people.

30:11. As if it were not bad enough to dictate to the prophets what they should say, the people demanded they stop talking about "the Holy One of Israel." Comparing the prophets' message of condemnation and judgment to a road, the people urged them to turn aside and leave the road (Young 1969, 346–47). They capped their demand by saying, literally, "Cause to cease from our face the Holy One of Israel," meaning, "Put away from before us the Holy One of Israel." Their description of the Lord as the "Holy One of Israel" probably reflects the prophets' words to them. They obviously did not regard him as sovereign. By trying to control the prophets' messages, they were essentially claiming sovereignty over their own lives.

30:12. But the Holy One of Israel would not be silenced. He responds to the people's demand with a judgment speech that begins with a formal accusation (note יַעַן, "because"). The people have rejected the prophetic word (cf. 30:9–11) and instead placed their trust in oppression and deceit (30:12). In other words, they are self-reliant, thinking their own cruel and dishonest schemes give them prosperity and security, all at the expense of others. Since unjust practices are not otherwise mentioned in the immediate context, it may be the oppression and deceit are related in some way to the main theme of this section: Judah's alliance with Egypt. Perhaps oppressive and deceitful means were used to accumulate the wealth sent to Egypt as tribute (cf. 30:6). Roberts (2015, 390) suggests that leaders heavily taxed and exploited the people to acquire horses and chariots from Egypt and strengthen their defenses (see also Smith 2007, 515).

30:13–14. The formal announcement of judgment (note לָכֵן, "therefore" at the beginning of 30:13) follows. Their sin would result in swift and violent destruction. The Lord uses vivid imagery to depict this. Their sin will become like a high wall that develops a crack. The crack then turns into a bulge and the wall suddenly gives way and comes crashing to the ground. The crash is so violent the wall shatters into pieces like a broken pot. Sometimes one can salvage a broken pot by using some of the larger sherds to take coals from a hearth or to scoop water out of a cistern. But in this case the pot is reduced to tiny fragments that cannot be used for any positive purpose.

30:15. Another judgment speech follows. The Lord is introduced as both the Sovereign Master and the Holy One of Israel. The pairing of these titles, which occurs only here in the Old Testament, emphasizes the Lord's sovereignty.

He begins by reminding the people that deliverance was readily available to them. All they needed to do was repent and rest in the Lord. Strength to overcome the enemy was accessible to them if they calmly trusted in the Lord. But just as the people were unwilling to obey the Lord (30:9), so they were unwilling to place their trust in him (30:15; cf. 28:12). The two, of course, go hand in hand (see Roberts 2015, 390).

30:16–17. Their alliance with Egypt (30:1–2) bred confidence. Even in a worst-case scenario, which they probably regarded as unlikely, they were confident they could escape destruction. They boast they will flee on fast horses. The Lord counters their arrogance by announcing they will indeed flee. Poetic justice will be served, as the worst-case scenario comes to pass! (See Miller 1982, 56.) Their pursuers will match the speed of their horses and panic will overtake them (30:17). The battle cry of one enemy will put a thousand to flight, and the shout of five enemies will cause the people to run away in fear, until only a few remain, like an isolated flag on a hill. Wordplay draws attention to the description of judgment. The noun תֹּרֶן, "flagstaff," echoes the verb נוֹתַרְתֶּם, "you are left" (Wildberger 2002, 163), and the noun נֵס, "banner," echoes the verb תָּנֻסוּ, "you will flee." The image of one man putting a thousand to flight is a tragic reversal of the Israelite conquest of Canaan, when one Israelite chased a thousand of the enemy as the Lord fought for his people (Josh. 23:9–10). But now the opposite would be the case, for the Lord will not be fighting for his people (cf. Deut. 32:30).

God's Mercy Brings Blessing and Deliverance (30:18–33)
The Lord will reverse the circumstances of his people and defeat their enemies.

30:18–19. Suddenly there is a change in tone from judgment to salvation. Isaiah 30:18 begins with וְלָכֵן, "and therefore," indicating the situation described in the previous announcement of judgment prompts this change in attitude. As the Lord's people flee in terror from their enemies until only a few remain, the Lord's compassion is stirred. Judgment must run its course, but the Lord will patiently wait until he can extend favor to his people. Waiting will turn to action, as the people's condition prompts him to arise and show them compassion.

From the Lord's perspective it is a matter of justice (30:18b). His willingness to show favor and compassion is attributed to his just character (note כִּי, "for"). At first this is puzzling, since justice would seem to demand punishment of the rebels denounced in the preceding judgment speech. In other words, the situation described in 30:16–17 is the just punishment for rebels who refuse to listen to the Lord. But the following statement is the key to understanding the logic here. Among the people there are some, like Isaiah (cf. 8:17), who are waiting for the Lord. Unlike the rebels, they maintain trust in him. The just God does not indiscriminately implement justice, sweeping the faithful away with the rebels. As far as he is concerned, it is only fair that he extends his favor and compassion to those who wait for him.[1]

---

1 The verb חָנַן is often understood in terms of the theological concept of "grace," defined as unmerited favor. But this is not the case here, where divine favor is based on justice. One gets the impression this favor is deserved, for the recipients are waiting for the Lord in faith. One sees this as well with the expression "find favor in the eyes of," where favor is often prompted by the recipient's character and/or actions (see, e.g., Gen. 6:8 [cf. v. 9]; 39:4 [cf. v. 3]; Ruth 2:10 [cf. vv. 11–12]; 1 Sam. 16:22 [cf. v. 21]). It is best to define חָנַן as "show favor," without attaching to it the notion that the favor is unmerited unless, of course, the context dictates such an understanding.

(See the helpful discussion in Roberts 2015, 393–94.) This faithful remnant, forced to endure affliction, will end up "blessed." The form used here (אַשְׁרֵי) is an abstract plural referring to the results (security and happiness) that divine blessing produces (see Isa. 32:20; 56:2; as well as Pss. 1:3; 2:12; 34:8 [HB 9]; 41:1 [HB 2]; 65:4 [HB 5]; 84:12 [HB 13]; 89:15 [HB 16]; 106:3; 112:1; 127:5; 128:1; 144:15).

In the aftermath of judgment, a remnant inhabits Zion and experiences transformation (Isa. 30:19). Their weeping will certainly (note the infinitive absolute בָּכוֹ) come to an end, for the Lord will certainly (note the infinitive absolute חָנוֹן) extend his favor to them in response to their cry for help. Indeed, as soon as he hears them, he will answer.

30:20–21. The prophet briefly refers to the coming judgment (30:20a) before resuming the positive emphasis of 30:18–19 (30:20b). The Sovereign Master will bring difficult times upon the people. This is compared to providing them with food and water, but, in this case, the food will be adversity and the water affliction. Yet hardship often leads to spiritual sensitivity and, in turn, spiritual renewal. Indeed, when the weeping people cry out to him for help (30:19), the Lord will give them spiritual guidance.

Their "teachers," perhaps a reference to the prophets whom the rebels rejected and tried to silence (30:9–11; cf. Young 1969, 356–57), will no longer be hidden (or perhaps, hide themselves [*niphal*]), but will be visible (30:20b). The people will hear a voice behind them, apparently that of the teachers. Whether they are inclined to go to the right or to the left, the voice would identify the correct road upon which they must walk (30:21). This command to walk in the road (דֶּרֶךְ) counters what the rebels said earlier to the prophets, urging them to turn aside from the road (דֶּרֶךְ, cf. 30:11). By this they meant that they did not want to be confronted anymore with the Holy One of Israel or his prophetic messages.

There has been some discussion regarding the identity of the "teachers" in 30:20. Since the form appears to be plural, they should probably be identified with the prophets who receive visions from the Lord (30:10). Some prefer to see a more direct reference to the Lord here. The form could be taken as singular, referring to the Lord as the teacher of his people (cf. Job 36:22), or it could be understood as a plural indicating respect with the Lord as the referent.

30:22. In any case, the "road" is metaphorical, referring to the correct moral pathway. Isaiah 30:22 makes this apparent, for it describes how the people will reject idolatry. In fact, they will desecrate (*piel* of טָמֵא) their silver- and gold-plated idols, throwing them away as if they were menstrual rags and commanding each one to get out (cf. NIV11, "away with you"). All who trust in such man-made "gods" are inevitably disappointed (Isa. 42:17) for these idols lack power and cannot protect themselves, let alone others (21:9; 40:19–20; 44:9–20; 45:20). The Lord is unwilling to share his glory with such images (42:8; 48:5).

30:23–25. When the people throw away their idols, the Lord will restore his agricultural blessings. He will provide the rain that causes their seed to grow and they will have an abundance of crops (30:23a). The language echoes that of 30:20, which describes the Lord giving (note וְנָתַן at the beginning of 30:20 and 23) adversity as food (לֶחֶם). But eventually he will give them the abundant produce of the ground as their food (לֶחֶם again). In this day of renewed blessing their cattle will graze in wide pastures (30:23b) and have plenty of feed to eat (30:24). As a sign of the abundance of rain, streams of water (perhaps man-made ditches) will flow down all the hills (30:25a).

An unexpected statement interrupts this scene of abundant prosperity. This renewed blessing will occur "in the day of great slaughter, when towers fall" (30:25b). The statement is a reminder that judgment will occur in conjunction with renewal. But it is not certain whose judgment is in view. The reference may anticipate Assyria's fall, described in the following verses (30:27–33). Roberts (2015, 395) understands the Assyrian army's siege towers as the referent. Taking the language in this way does have the advantage of making the statement fit more easily into the portrait of salvation that the prophet is painting here. The only prior references to a "tower" (מִגְדָּל) occur much earlier (cf. 2:15 and 5:2). In 2:15 a "high tower," symbolizing security, is the object of the Lord's judgment on the day he punishes his people. It may be that Isaiah alludes to that day, in which case Judah is the object of judgment, as described earlier in this speech (30:12–17). Another possible link with Isaiah 2 is the reference to idols made of silver and gold in 2:22 (cf. 2:20, though a different term for "idols" is used there). The two passages may be harmonized as follows: The Lord will attack Judah's towers (2:15), which symbolize the nation's attempt to make itself secure, causing those towers to fall (30:25). Recognizing how useless gold and silver idols really are, people will discard them (2:20; 30:22). While many panic (2:19–21), a remnant turns to the Lord (30:19) and experiences his renewed blessing (30:23–25). In any case, it is clear true security and accompanying prosperity do not come from defense "towers," but from waiting on the Lord (30:18), acknowledging dependence on him (30:19), following his direction (30:20–21), and repudiating all false substitutes (30:22).

30:26. The prophet returns to his description of the time of renewed blessing. He depicts it as a time of dazzling light, when the moon shines like the sun and the sun shines seven times brighter, like the light of seven days (30:26a). The language is metaphorical and hyperbolic. Elsewhere (cf. 24:23; 60:19–20) the prophet, in speaking of this same time, says the moon and sun will disappear as the Lord becomes the light source for his people. Obviously, both scenarios cannot be literally true. In the passages where the moon and sun disappear, the prophet is emphasizing how great the Lord's royal splendor will be in the day of restoration. In 30:26, where he depicts the moon and sun growing brighter, he is emphasizing how overwhelming the Lord's blessings, symbolized by the bright light, will be.

That time will also be a day of healing (30:26b). The Lord will bind up (חָבַשׁ) the fracture (שֶׁבֶר, "break, fracture") of his people (fractured bones, in need of being set in proper place, are probably in view) and heal their wounds (מַכָּתוֹ, "his wound"). The appearance of שֶׁבֶר, "break, fracture," echoes the metaphors of 30:13–14, where the people are compared to a wall that collapses and shatters (note שִׁבְרָהּ, 30:13) suddenly (see Irwin 1977, 96; as well Young 1969, 362). This shattering (note שִׁבְרָהּ at the beginning of 30:14) would be like the shattering (שֶׁבֶר, 30:14) of a pot that is smashed to pieces.

This healing marks a reversal of the people's condition described at the beginning of the prophecy (1:6), when the prophet depicted them as having wounds (מַכָּה) that had not been bandaged (literally, "bound up," חֻבָּשׁוּ; cf. Roberts 2015, 395). In that passage, the reality behind the imagery was the devastation of invasion (1:7–9), which is also in the background in this speech (cf. 30:16–17). The Lord will heal the people's wounds by bringing prosperity where there was once ruin.

30:27. With הִנֵּה, "look" (NIV11, "see"), Isaiah shifts the focus back to judgment, but now the nations, especially Assyria, become the objects of divine punishment. For the Lord's people, this will be cause for celebration. The prophet begins by drawing attention to the approaching "Name of the LORD [i.e., Yahweh]," who comes from afar to unleash his burning anger like a blazing fire. The name of the Lord sometimes stands by metonymy for the Lord himself (note the poetic parallelism in Isa. 18:7; 24:15; 26:8;

48:1; 50:10; 56:6; 59:19). Whenever the "name of the LORD" is specifically mentioned, the Lord is revealing in a special way the character trait suggested by his personal name. The name Yahweh means "he is [with]," or perhaps better, "he will be [with]" (cf. Exod. 3:12–15). The name focuses on his protective presence with his people. In this context of judgment, the ever-present one comes to deliver them from their enemies and to vindicate them.

One wonders why the Lord's name comes "afar" (literally, "from a distant place"). After all, Solomon built the temple "for the Name of the LORD" (1 Kings 5:5 [HB 17]; 8:20) and the Lord responded by putting his name there (1 Kings 9:2, 7). Isaiah earlier speaks of the Lord dwelling on Zion (Isa. 8:18). One would think the Lord's "name" would simply emerge from the temple to defend his people. Roberts (2015, 398) suggests the Lord's coming from afar reflects the ancient motif of Yahweh coming from his dwelling place on Sinai to deliver his people (cf. Deut. 33:2, 26–29; Judg. 5:4–5; Ps. 68:8–9, 18 [HB 9–11, 19]; Hab. 3:3–15). He observes additionally that the prophet's audience "must have felt that Yahweh was somehow absent for these disasters to overtake Jerusalem." (On this last point, see as well Wildberger 2002, 196.) Along similar lines, Oswalt (1986, 566) says the idea of the Lord coming from afar may have been intended for the "deists" of Isaiah's day "who considered that God was too far away to be of any practical help." Of course, Solomon had acknowledged that the Lord could not really be confined to a temple, even though he said he would place his name there (1 Kings 8:27–29). Perhaps "from afar" is a reminder of this truth. The Lord really dwells in heaven and cannot be threatened by invading armies. (In this regard, note that Isaiah 31:4 describes the Lord coming down to do battle on Mount Zion.) Furthermore, the sinful people had created a rift in their relationship with the Lord. If they felt as if he was not present, there was good reason for that. For all intents and purposes, he was not dwelling among them.

Yahweh, the ever-present helper, was not functionally present; he had given the people over to judgment. But now his "name" was about to return.

There may be an ironic allusion to an earlier description of the Assyrian army. In Isaiah 5:26, which also begins with הִנֵּה, the Lord summons an army from a distant place, and it comes (יָבוֹא) to carry out his judgment against his sinful people. (On the text-critical issues in the passage, see the commentary on 5:26 above.) In the historical and literary context of that passage, Assyria is the reality behind this army. Here in 30:27, also introduced with הִנֵּה, the name of the Lord "comes" (בָּא) from a distant place to annihilate the Assyrians (see 30:31). The Lord reverses his earlier judgment and now directs his anger toward the arrogant instrument of judgment (cf. 10:5–34).

One can also detect allusion in the language used to describe the Lord's anger in 30:27. The prophet speaks of his "anger" (אַף) and "wrath" (זַעַם). Both terms are used in 10:5 in describing Assyria as the instrument of the Lord's anger. They appear again in 10:25, where the Lord says his wrath (זַעַם) toward his people will end and he will direct his anger (אַף) against Assyria. The appearance of both words in 30:27 reiterates this. At the end of 30:27, the Lord's tongue is compared to a fire that devours. This may be an echo of 10:17, where the Lord is depicted as a fire (אֵשׁ) that devours (אָכַל).

30:28. The references to the Lord's lips and tongue in 30:27 are at first puzzling, but 30:28, which refers to his "breath" (רוּחַ) provides clarification. The term רוּחַ sometimes refers to the breath that emanates from one's mouth and/or nose. Here it is the Lord's hot breath of judgment (cf. 30:27) that pursues his enemies. The Lord's breath is closely associated elsewhere with a hot wind that dries up or blows away all that lies in its path (Isa. 11:15; 27:8; 40:7; 59:19; see also the use of the synonym נְשָׁמָה, "breath," in Isa. 30:33; Ps. 18:15 [HB 16]). So here the lips and tongue are mentioned as those parts of the mouth through/over which the breath passes.

The Lord's breath is compared to a powerful, rushing stream that reaches one's neck. There may be an echo here of Isaiah 8:8, the only other passage in the Old Testament where the verb שָׁטַף is used of a torrent that reaches the neck. If so, then one can again detect a reversal. In 8:8 the Assyrians are the torrent that inundates Judah, but in 30:28 they are the targets of the rushing torrent that comes from the Lord's mouth (see Roberts 2015, 398; Seitz 1993, 220).

The purpose of the Lord's onslaught is described with another metaphor. The text reads literally, "for [the purpose of, note the preposition -לְ] shaking nations in a sieve [used to sift out] what is worthless." It is not clear if the nations in their entirety are chaff or if only some are viewed as such. Isaiah 30:31 focuses on Assyria, but the Assyrian army included soldiers from many of their vassal states (Roberts 2015, 399). When one faced the Assyrian army, one faced "nations" (see the commentary on 8:9–10 above).

The metaphor becomes more mixed in 30:28b, where the prophet compares the nations to animals that are led by reins or bits placed in their mouths (note "jaws"; on the meaning of רֶסֶן, "bit," see *HALOT*, s.v. "רֶסֶן I" 1249). The Lord will use reins or a bit, as it were, to lead the nations "astray." The image depicts the Sovereign Lord as the one who controls the nations and leads them to the destiny that he has determined for them, in this case, their demise.

30:29. The Lord's intervention will bring great joy to his people. They will sing as if celebrating a holy festival and rejoice like those who travel to the mountain of the Lord to the sound of music. The "mountain of the LORD" is the temple mount in Jerusalem (cf. Isa. 2:3; cf. Zech. 8:3). The representative worshipper described here is also said to go "to the Rock of Israel." The phrase occurs only here and in 2 Samuel 23:3, where it stands parallel to "the God of Israel." The divine title "Rock" refers to the Lord as the protector of his people (cf. Isa. 17:10; 26:4 and the comments there). The word refers to a rocky summit (cf. 1 Sam. 24:2; Isa. 2:10, 19; Jer. 18:14; 21:13) where one can find refuge from enemies. (See the helpful discussion in Wildberger 2002, 200.)

30:30. The prophet resumes his description of the Lord coming in judgment. The Lord will cause his majestic voice to be heard and the lowering of his arm to be seen (Isa. 30:30a). Powerful warriors were adept in hand-to-hand combat with the sword, spear, and/or bow. Consequently, a warrior's arm is symbolic of his strength and military prowess. In his role of warrior-king the Lord exerts his power against his enemies. When Isaiah refers to his "arm," it usually has this connotation (Isa. 40:10; 48:14; 51:5, 9; 52:10; 59:16; 62:8; 63:5, 12). On a few occasions, as here, it pictures the Lord as the protector of his people, who uses his powerful arm to defeat his enemies (cf. 33:2, where NIV "strength" is literally "arm").

The Lord's theophanic self-revelation is accompanied by intense anger (the combining of the synonyms אַף and זַעַף emphasizes the degree of anger), a consuming flame of fire (cf. 29:6), driving rain, and hailstones (30:30b). Unless the metaphors are mixed, the flame of fire is probably lightning in this context, where rain, hail, and thunder (cf. 30:31) are also mentioned. There is an ironic reversal involved in the references to rain (זֶרֶם) and hail (בָּרָד). In 28:2 they are used of the Lord's agent of judgment, probably Assyria, but now Assyria becomes the object of divine judgment (cf. 30:31), and the driving rain and hail are directed against it (Motyer 1993, 252–53).

30:31–32. Indeed (note כִּי at the beginning of 30:31) Assyria will be shattered (or perhaps, terrified; see Smith 2007, 526) by the Lord's powerful voice (cf. 8:9; 9:4) as the Lord strikes with his rod (30:31) and club (30:32a). The "voice" of the Lord is sometimes his audible spoken word

(Deut. 5:25; 18:16); by extension it can refer to the Lord's commands or instructions (in the idiom "hear the voice of the LORD"). However, in contexts like Isaiah 30:31, where the Lord appears as a warrior, his voice is usually associated with the elements of the storm. In such cases his voice is the thunder, viewed as a battle cry (see Pss. 18:13 [HB 14]; 29:3–9). There is an ironic reversal in the references to the Lord's rod (שֵׁבֶט) and club (מַטֶּה). In Isaiah 10:5, 24 the Lord uses Assyria as a rod and club to beat the object of his anger. But now roles are reversed, as the Lord redirects his anger toward Assyria (10:25) and beats them with his rod and club (Roberts 2015, 399; Seitz 1993, 220). The Lord's people will celebrate his attack on Assyria (30:32; cf. 30:29). Each blow against the enemy is accompanied by the music of celebration.

Isaiah 30:32b poses some interpretive challenges. It reads, literally, "and with battles, brandishing, he fights against it." The reading "battles" (מִלְחָמוֹת) fits the militaristic context, but it may be preferable to read it as וּבִמְחֹלוֹת, "and with dances" (from מְחֹלָה, "dance"; cf. HALOT s.v. "מְחֹלָה" 569), which fits with the references to musical instruments, and with what precedes. Such dances were sometimes performed in the aftermath of a military victory (cf. Exod. 15:20; Judg. 11:34; 1 Sam. 21:12; 29:5). The noun תְּנוּפָה, which usually refers to a sacrifice of some type, could allude to a celebratory ritual here (Wildberger 2002, 202). But since the following statement refers to fighting, it may carry the nuance "(with) brandishing," as in Isaiah 19:16 (see BDB s.v. "תְּנוּפָה" mng. 1, 632). The perfect verbal form (נִלְחַם) seems out of place in this predictive discourse. Perhaps it has a future perfect nuance here ("he will have fought"), since the fighting (and winning) logically precedes the celebration. If one reads with the *ketiv*, then the third-person feminine singular suffix on the preposition -בְּ (בָּהּ) probably refers to Assyria. But the *qere* reading, "against them," has the support of many Hebrew manuscripts, the targum, and the Vulgate. Both are problematic, however, since Assyria is referred to with the masculine singular earlier in the verse (עָלָיו, "upon him"). It may be preferable to read בֹּה, understanding the suffix as an archaic third-person masculine singular form (Roberts 2015, 397 n. p; cf. the *ketiv* בֹּה in Jer. 17:24).

30:33. The Lord's victory over Assyria culminates with the death of its king. Preparation has already been made for him in Topheth, where fire and wood are waiting for him. The Lord's fiery breath (cf. 30:28) is ready to ignite it. The fulfillment of this vision of judgment came in 701 B.C., when the Lord miraculously destroyed the Assyrian army and forced Sennacherib to retreat to his homeland (Isa. 37:36–37; 2 Kings 19:35–36). The king himself was not killed and cremated in Jerusalem, but the corpses of his dead soldiers had to be disposed of and many were probably burned. So, if we allow for metonymy (king standing for his army), we can detect a degree of literality in Isaiah 30:33 (see Smith 2007, 526; Wildberger 2002, 202). Furthermore, the biblical account of Sennacherib's humiliating defeat describes his death at the hands of his two sons, an event that occurred twenty years after his disastrous siege of Jerusalem (2 Kings 19:37; Isa. 37:38). It is obvious the language in Isaiah 30:27–33 is highly metaphorical, describing in very poetic terms the demise of the Assyrian army and eventual violent death of the king himself (see Hayes and Irvine 1987, 345).

THEOLOGICAL FOCUS

The theological focus of this passage can be stated as follows: the Sovereign Lord is the only source of security for his people. As the prophet develops this theological theme, the following emphases emerge:

1. The Lord's sovereignty over the nations

Judah was desperately seeking security in the face of the Assyrian threat. Many turned to Egypt for help and rejected the prophets' calls to repentance. But Egypt could not help. Only the Lord could defeat the Assyrians. He would come against them like a devastating storm and annihilate them, much to the delight of those among his people who were trusting him as their source of security.

2. Contrasting destinies and divine justice

Many had decided to walk by sight, not by faith. They looked to Egypt, not the Holy One of Israel, for safety. They did not want to hear about the Holy One of Israel and told the prophets to cease talking about him and his demands. But the Holy One of Israel cannot and would not be silenced. Those who refused to repent and place their trust in him would experience his judgment. Yet the Lord is just and shows mercy to those who maintain trust in him. He gives them spiritual guidance, restores his blessings, and devastates their menacing enemy, Assyria. Justice demanded that he discipline his people for their insistence upon trusting in Egypt for security, rather than in him. But his justice is finely tuned, for it also demands that he extend his favor and compassion to those who maintain loyalty and wait for him, as well as to those who repent and reject their idols.

PREACHING AND TEACHING STRATEGIES

Exegetical and Theological Synthesis

Rebellion (30:1–17)

This passage begins with the accusation that God's people were acting like "obstinate children" (30:1).[2] In 30:9 the prophet calls them "rebellious people" who are "unwilling to listen to the Lord's instruction." Isaiah 30:15 further accuses them of being unwilling to repent and return to the Lord when confronted by him. Instead, they defiantly said, "No" (30:16).

Isaiah 30:1 highlights their rebellious heart as they carry out their own plan, not the Lord's. Their plan is their alliance with Egypt, which the Lord says was "not by my Spirit." In their enthusiasm to carry out their own plan, they failed to consult with God for his direction (30:2). This was intentional, not simply an accidental oversight. The people were committed to pursue their own agenda. The Lord warns them that Egypt will not profit them one bit. The only thing that Egypt will provide them is shame and humiliation (30:3–5).

Isaiah 30:6–7 is an oracle about the "animals of the Negev." Here, the prophet highlighted the risks and sacrifices associated with the people's rebellion. The animals refer to the donkeys and camels that the envoys from Judah had loaded with treasures to buy protection from Pharaoh. However, the trip from Jerusalem to Egypt would be dangerous. They would have to travel "through a land of hardship and distress," where lions and venomous snakes were a real threat. This was a lot of trouble to go through just to acquire the help of one whom the prophet mockingly referred to as a proud "Do-Nothing."

The rebellious people who refused to consult God also dismissed God's words (30:9–11). God told Isaiah to write this indictment of the people on a tablet as a witness of their rebellion (30:8). This would serve as proof in the future that God had warned them regarding their defiance, but that they didn't listen. Their brazen rejection of God's word was tantamount to instructing the prophets to stop prophesying what was true or right. Instead, they wanted to only hear pleasant or smooth things, even if they were merely illusions (30:10). Specifically, they didn't want to hear anything more about "the Holy One of Israel" (30:11).

---

2 The ESV translates סוֹרְרִים as "stubborn," while the NIV11 translates it as "obstinate." Most English translations opt for "rebellious" (HCSB, KJV, NASB, NET, NKJV, NLT). In 30:9, the prophet uses a different Hebrew word, מְרִי, "rebellious."

Because these people had despised God's word (30:12), they set themselves up for an eventual collapse. Isaiah likens them to a high wall that has developed a crack in it. As such, the integrity of the structure has become compromised, and little by little the wall will begin to bulge until suddenly it collapses in ruin (30:13). Their destruction will be severe, like the smashing of a pottery jar that has been violently crushed until only the tiniest pieces are left (30:14).

In 30:15–17 the prophet offers more evidence of their rebellion. He highlights their refusal to repent of sin even after being confronted. God had offered them salvation if they would only rest confidently in him for their protection. In other words, they didn't have to do anything at all except to trust in the Lord for help, and he would have graciously delivered them. But they refused to repent of their plans and would not listen or turn to God. They assumed they would be able to flee from the Assyrians. God warned that they would indeed flee but would not be able to escape from his judgment. In panic they would run in terror for their lives.

Repentance (30:18–22)
Being the ever-merciful and gracious God that he is, the Lord still invited his people to repent. He was ready to be gracious to them (30:18). The prophet promised, "As soon as he hears, he will answer you" (30:19). Though the Lord has fed them hardship and adversity, he is ready to guide them when they cry out in repentance (30:20–22). They must destroy all their carved idols, saying to them, "Away with you!" God's voice will then once again be heard in their ears instructing them like a teacher to go this way or that (30:21; cf. Isa. 29:9–12, 18, 23–24).

Rejoicing (30:23–33)
The final portion of this chapter highlights the blessings that God will again pour out on his people once they have repented of their rebellion and idolatry. Isaiah 30:23 highlights the very basic blessing of rain that carried many important ramifications for their existence. Water was essential for growing crops. It was also necessary for producing the grass and hay that the livestock needed for grazing (30:23–24). Finally, the rain was needed to feed fresh-water springs and brooks that provided them with drinking water (30:25). Israel was a land that required consistent rainfall for people to be able to live there. Unlike Egypt, which enjoyed the Nile, or Babylon with its access to the Tigris and the Euphrates, Israel had very little by way of consistent sources of fresh water. The Promised Land was a place that was predominantly desert or wilderness. As such, it was a land that required the people to depend firmly on God's consistent provision of rain for their very survival.

Next, 30:26 highlights God's blessing in terms of his healing and restoration. The prophet metaphorically described God's blessing as brightness (30:26). This increased brightness will coincide with God's healing the wounds caused by his own judgment. Whereas God will protect and restore his own people, he will pour out his burning anger upon his enemies. It will be like a stream of fiery sulfur that flows up to their necks, leading to their swift destruction (30:27–28, 33). Similarly, his judgment against Judah's enemies will be like a harsh storm with fire and hail (30:30). If neither of these metaphors are foreboding enough, the prophet further predicts the Assyrians' defeat by depicting God beating them with repeated, furious blows from a rod in his hand (30:30–32). As a result, Israel will dwell in peace and safety in Zion once again. Their sadness would be replaced with gladness as they celebrate in song like they do during their religious feasts (30:29).

Preaching Idea
The path of rebellion leads only to ruin, but repentance brings blessing and rejoicing.

Contemporary Connections

What does it mean?

There is something about being a rebel that appeals to many of us at some level. Calling our own shots, doing whatever we want, making our own decisions—it all sounds adventurous, liberating and fun. There is much within popular culture over the past several decades that feeds our appetite for rebellion. Many of the lyrics to hit songs glorify rebellion in one way or another. Popular movies often script the main character as a rebel. Whether it's the cool kid in high school who's always getting in trouble, the teenager who proves somehow that she is smarter than her parents, or an old western movie with a cowboy who saves the day while playing by his own rules, Hollywood loves rebels, and so do many of us.

The truth is though, in the real world, it rarely pays to be a rebel. How many of the kids in high school who self-identified as a rebel did well academically or went on to do well in college? How many gang members ended up in prison, or worse yet, died prematurely? How many people in the workplace who routinely dismissed their boss's instructions received promotions or even kept their jobs very long? Our experience tells us that rebellion rarely results in good things. While it may be fun for a brief time, rebellion almost always catches up with a person and results in various forms of ruin.

Probably the most subtle form of rebellion, and yet the most dangerous, is the type found in Isaiah 30. It's when God's people defiantly resist obeying him in favor of doing their own thing. This form of rebellion can often be paired with a very respectable, religious lifestyle, going through the motions of religiosity, saying many of the right things, while refusing to truly obey some of God's clear instructions. Unfortunately, churches today are filled with these people. They are often nice and unassuming on the surface. They pray before meals, show up for church most Sundays, even teach a Sunday school class, volunteer as an usher, or sing on the worship team. But below the façade is a person who daily says "no" to God in one area of life or another.

There are countless reasons people may give to explain their disobedience. Some perpetually describe themselves as "struggling" in this or that area. But if they're honest, it goes well beyond just a struggle to do the right thing. They have simply determined that they enjoy certain sins and don't really desire to repent and change. They may give lip service to their desire to change, but deep down they are stubbornly content to continue doing their own thing. Others may see nothing wrong with doing their own thing. The version of "Christianity" that they have embraced is one in which they pick and choose the parts they like, maybe the one that fits their preferred political views, or the ones that align with their modern values and sensibilities, but they exclude the parts they find offensive or disagreeable.

This sort of rejection of God's Word, which is quite common today, is just another form of rebellion. Just like the people in Jerusalem at that time, many today draw near to Jesus with their lips, but their hearts are far from God. Their worship and devotion to him are driven more by the commandments and values taught by people (Isa. 29:13). However, this sort of religion does not bring God's blessings. Rather, it leads to judgment or discipline from God.

Is it true?

It's easy to think of certain groups of people as societal rebels. But the truth is, the rebels addressed by Isaiah were normal, even religious folks. They were continuing to keep their annual feasts (Isa. 29:1) and gave verbal assent to their devotion to God (Isa. 29:13). There weren't any significant external markers that identified them as "obstinate children" such as their dress or the music they listened to. Rather, theirs was just a subtle but very real commitment to do their own thing rather than submit their wills to God's on the issues over which they disagreed. Their obedience was a partial obedience rather than a commitment to fully obey God regardless of the cost. This was the crux of their rebellion as God viewed it. The same is so often common with believers today.

Human nature fights against absolute obedience to Jesus, or to anyone for that matter. There are many converging factors that contribute to this attitude. People have a natural desire to express their own opinions or to fight for their personal rights over and against what some authority figure may seek to impose on them. Additionally, there is a growing distrust in general of people in authority, and often for good reason. Whether it be politicians, judges, religious leaders, or police officers—individuals in authority have abused their power and have hurt the very people they are supposed to lead and protect. These and other factors contribute to an almost cynical attitude at times toward the idea that an educated and thinking person today would unconditionally and unquestioningly obey anyone, including God. Thus, for many today, there is a built-in skepticism and suspicion toward the idea of "complete obedience" to Jesus Christ.

However, is it accurate to refer to persons as "Christ-followers" who only obey *most* of Jesus's commands and only knowingly reject *some* of his teachings, namely, the ones they find objectionable? The answer to this question would seem to be "no."

People who obey an authority figure most of the time, but refuse their instructions on those rare occasions when they disagree with their given logic or rationale, are ultimately only being obedient to themselves. It just so happens that they agree much of the time with that authority figure in their life. While it would appear much of the time that they are living obediently, the real test of obedience is always whether one complies when they don't agree. Will they submit their own ideas, desires, plans, and logical reasoning to those of another? Will a teenager obey her parents' instruction that she not attend a party with her friends, even though she really wants to and believes it to be in her best interests? Will a company employee follow protocols she finds to be unnecessary and a waste of time? Will a student abide by his school's dress code in the parts that he finds unnecessary and pointless? The answer to these questions ultimately determines whether one is obedient or rebellious toward the authority figures in their lives, not whether they comply with the rules and wishes they already agree with. (To be clear, I'm not referring to those who consciously object to obeying an authority figure who is trying to compel them to do something immoral, illegal, or genuinely abusive.)

It becomes essential, then, that those of us who call Jesus our Lord embrace a form of obedience that attempts to be consistent and comprehensive. We mustn't approach the commands of Jesus as we would a grand buffet of options from which we pick and choose the ones we like most and disregard the rest (cf. Luke 6:46). As St. Augustine said centuries ago, "For to believe what you please, and not to believe what you please, is to believe yourselves, and not the gospel" (*Contra Faustum* 17.3).

Now what?
People today haven't changed all that much from those throughout history. As J. Daniel Baumann observed, "We are very much like the people of the ancient world. It is only in some superficial thoughts, rational beliefs, and mental moods that we are different. In all of the basic heart realities we are the same. . . . We are linked across the centuries by the realities and ambiguities of the human soul" (quoted in Robinson 2001, 91–92). The same temptations that led the Israelites to justify their rebellion against God's commands are often factors in the lives of Christians today. These same factors often result in Christians

failing to fully obey all that the Bible says we should be doing.

(1) Lack of trust in God. The primary contributing factor for Isaiah's audience's rebellion was their lack of trust in God for their security. People today struggle with this same desire for security, and it leads us to contemplate rebellion as well. What about the single man/woman in their late twenties whose friends are married and having children already, and who wonders whether he/she will ever find a godly spouse? Will they wait patiently for God to bring the right person along, or do they need to consider marrying someone who doesn't love Jesus to ensure that they don't remain alone for the rest of their life? What about the person who isn't earning a lot at their present job? They are making enough to live on, but there are so many things they wish they had that others can afford but they can't. Also, they are concerned about having enough on which to retire one day. Meanwhile, the Bible instructs us to give generously to the Lord and to the poor. But doing so will make it even less likely that they will be able to live as comfortably as they want. Do they trust that God will provide for their needs if they are generous with their finances, or do they assume it is up to them to figure out how to make the best of their situation, even if it means not giving anything to the Lord's work or to help the poor around the world? In such situations, will people trust God enough to obey him or will they rebel against him?

(2) Unholy alliances. Another factor that contributed to the people's rebellion in Isaiah's day was their desire to enter an unholy alliance with Egypt. This was driven by their lack of trust in God. However, there are other factors that often drive people into making unhealthy alliances that ultimately pressure them into some form of compromise as it relates to their commitment to God. While this partnership seemed advantageous to Judah, God knew that it would only serve to further dilute their faith in Yahweh. If their alliance would have succeeded, they would have naturally assumed that Egypt was responsible for their victory, not God. This may also have resulted in them eventually worshipping the gods of Egypt. After all, based on the worldview of people at that time, if Egypt was able to fend off the mighty Assyrian army, it was evidence that Egypt's gods were superior to those of Assyria. By extension, they would have assumed Egypt's gods were superior to the Lord as well.

Similarly, Christians today must wrestle with their own strategic partnerships, many of which will have a direct impact on their commitment to Christ, for better or for worse. Marriage companions, business partners, places of employment, close friendships, political affiliations, even denominational or church memberships—each of these poses the possibility that one's loyalty to Christ will be seriously tested (2 Cor. 6:14–18). Discretion requires that we seriously consider how our affiliations and alliances are likely to impact our commitment to obey all that Jesus commanded of us. For example, if a person has closely allied himself in business to a company or business partner, what sorts of expectations will then be placed upon him and how might these conflict with his commitment to Jesus Christ, particularly as it relates to loving and leading his family and to serving in his local church? Similarly, in what ways would the trajectory of a young Christian's life change if they decide to marry a person who isn't a Christ-follower? As Oswalt (2003, 348) has aptly warned, "We must ask ourselves why we are entering into dependent relations with people or institutions and what such people or institutions can really offer us."

(3) Fear. Finally, we see in this passage how fear became a strong impetus for the people's rebellion against God. They feared what would happen if God didn't perform a miracle on their behalf to deliver them from the Assyrians. Thus,

they were motivated to bolster their chances of resistance by aligning themselves with Egypt, even though God had warned them against this.

Fear can be a common factor in our disobedience today too. Will I lose friends or status if I share Christ faithfully with my classmates, coworkers, or neighbors? How will people react to my social media posts defending my Christian values? What sacrifices will I be forced to make if I fully commit my life to Jesus? Will I be financially disadvantaged if I regularly give generously to the poor or to any number of Christian organizations? There is a reason why Scripture often warns about the danger of being driven by fear, particularly a fear of people (cf. Prov. 29:25; Isa. 51:7; Matt. 10:28; John 12:42–43; Acts 4:29–31; Gal. 2:11–13). Complete obedience to Jesus today requires courage. It also requires confidence in our eternal hope that every sacrifice made in this life will be generously rewarded in the kingdom to come.

Creativity in Presentation

Song Lyrics

Rebellion is a common theme in every age, as evidenced by the lyrics of mainstream music that echo the attitudes of the culture. There are plenty of popular songs that glorify rebellion or take pride in being a rebel. The preacher/teacher might consider pulling excerpts from different songs from various decades and musical genres to illustrate the pervasive spirit of rebellion in the world. Some examples are:

> "I Did It My Way" by Frank Sinatra (released in 1969)

> "We're Not Gonna Take It" by Twisted Sister (released in 1984)

> "It's My Life" by Bon Jovi (released in 2000)

> "Rule Breaker" by Ashlee Simpson (released in 2008)

Unholy Alliances

To illustrate the risks associated with unwise alliances, consider finding a story about people with contrasting values or beliefs who entered into a partnership that ended poorly due to their irreconcilable differences. One real-life example involves a restaurant in my hometown that was started by two men. Initially, the business was a success. They outgrew their original location and expanded to a new, larger facility. Things seemed to be going well. However, behind the scenes, differences between the owners were beginning to brew. I first became aware of some problems when another pastor at my church and I met with the owners to discuss their involvement in a community event our church was hosting. We asked about whether the restaurant would be willing to provide food at a discounted rate in exchange for our mentioning them as cosponsors in our marketing campaign for the event. At one point in our conversation with them, one of the partners was called away to do something. As soon as he was out of earshot, the other partner whispered to us that he would have to work at convincing the other co-owner to give us a generous rate. He shared how he valued having their restaurant be used for charitable events in the community, but that his business partner was all about maximizing profits. He found a lot of personal fulfillment in being able to support the community, but his business partner didn't share this value. It wasn't a complete surprise to us when we discovered only a couple of months later that this restaurant was closing its doors due to the two owners having "a different vision for the restaurant."

Rebellion Leads to Ruin

In May 2022, four-year-old Xavier Rigney, a nonverbal boy with autism, somehow slipped unnoticed from his mother's sight and made his way outside and through the locked fence that surrounded the swimming pool at the apartment complex where he lived in Lawrence,

Kansas. Video surveillance captured the boy running toward and then into the pool. Immediately, his entire body became submerged and he began to drown. Thankfully, the story has a happy ending as a twelve-year-old neighbor witnessed Xavier drowning and ran to get his father, Tom Westerhouse, who was able to rescue the boy. Though Xavier was underwater for more than three minutes, Tom performed CPR and the boy coughed up water and was revived before paramedics even arrived on the scene.

Much like in this story, our Heavenly Father has put up fences in our life in the form of rules and warnings. Like that child, all that we can see is an impediment to our fun. What child doesn't enjoy swimming in a pool? In our foolishness, we brazenly forge through the barriers God has placed upon us, thinking it will lead to our happiness and fulfillment, only to eventually discover that our rebellion instead results in ruin. Thankfully, this doesn't have to be the end of the story. Like the neighbor in the story, God has come to rescue us from our own sinful rebellion. If we will embrace repentance, God is willing to restore his favor to us, resulting in spiritual renewal and rejoicing. While the path of rebellion leads only to ruin, repentance brings about blessing and rejoicing.

- Rebellion (30:1–17).
    - The road to rebellion ... (1–5, 8–11, 15).
        - ... involves a commitment to do what I want (1).
        - ... involves a failure to consult with God (2–5).
        - ... involves a dismissal of God's word (8–11).
        - ... involves a refusal to repent of sin (15–16).
    - The risks of rebellion (6–7).
    - The ruin of rebellion (12–14, 16–17).
- Repentance (30:18–22).
- Rejoicing (30:23–33).

DISCUSSION QUESTIONS

1. Our culture glorifies rebellion, particularly in its music and movies. Can you think of examples from movies where one of the main characters was a rebel presented in a positive light? Similarly, can you think of any hit songs from your generation that encouraged rebellion against authority?

2. What are some practical ways believers today struggle to trust God?

3. Read 2 Corinthians 6:14–18. What factors should believers consider before entering into an alliance with others? How should Christians determine the difference between an acceptable relationship and a foolish alliance? For example, when does a friendship with sinners cross the line into becoming a sinful alliance? Likewise, what is the difference between working for a secular company and being "unequally yoked" (to borrow the language of 2 Cor. 6) to a secular institution?

4. What are some ways that fear sometimes keeps you or others from obeying Jesus?

Isaiah 31:1–32:20

EXEGETICAL IDEA
After disciplining those who trusted in false sources of security, the Lord will deliver Zion from the Assyrian threat and provide just leadership, accompanied by renewed blessing and genuine security.

THEOLOGICAL FOCUS
The Lord protects and transforms his covenant community by defeating their enemy, establishing just leadership, and providing them with prosperity and security.

PREACHING IDEA
It is folly to trust in any saviors other than the Lord God.

PREACHING POINTERS
Government agencies generally don't have the best reputation for being quick, efficient, or reliable. This includes government agencies designed to respond immediately after a natural disaster or major crisis. Former president Ronald Reagan once humorously said, "The nine most terrifying words in the English language are: 'I'm from the government, and I'm here to help.'" Examples of this abound, such as the failures of both the local and federal governments leading up to and following the flooding of New Orleans when Hurricane Katrina struck in 2005.[1] Then there's the failed response by FEMA to the massive destruction across Puerto Rico caused by Hurricane Maria in 2017.[2] These are just two of the many examples that highlight how poor governments typically are at rescuing the people who depend upon them during times of crisis.

In Isaiah 31–32, the prophet confronts the people of Judah for their foolishness in trusting the government of Egypt to protect them from the looming disaster of an Assyrian invasion. In the same way that governments today so often fail their people in times of crises, so too God warned Judah that Egypt would utterly fail to provide them with security and peace. Egypt was a "false savior." This passage highlights three separate false saviors, none of which could deliver them from harm nor provide them with the security they desired. Rather, as the prophet indicated, only God is a wholly sufficient savior. He alone is worthy of our confidence and devotion.

---

1 https://www.politico.com/story/2012/10/10-facts-about-the-katrina-response-081957.
2 https://newrepublic.com/article/149899/troubling-failure-americas-disaster-response.

GENUINE SECURITY (31:1–32:20)

Genuine security comes from the Lord, not the Egyptians and their horses and chariots. He will deliver Zion from the Assyrian threat and give his people new, just leaders who will protect the community and not tolerate fools. Justice will be the foundation for the transformation the Lord will bring about.

LITERARY STRUCTURE AND THEMES (31:1–32:20)

The next literary panel of chapters 28–35, like the preceding one, begins with a woe oracle against those who trust in Egypt rather than in the Holy One of Israel (31:1–3; cf. 30:1–17). Judgment will come upon both the helper (Egypt) and those who expect to be helped (Judah).

Isaiah 31:4 appears to continue the judgment announcement of 31:3b. It is connected to it by כִּי, "for," and describes the Lord coming down like a lion to do battle. One would think this battle is directed against those who have not trusted him. The phrase צָבָא עַל suggests this, for elsewhere it means "fight against" (Num. 31:7; Isa. 29:7–8; Zech. 14:12), not "fight upon" (Roberts 2015, 404). Judgment against Zion is in view, but this is not the whole story. In 31:5, as in the previous panel (cf. 30:18), the prophet abruptly shifts from judgment to salvation, suggesting 31:4 is transitional in the structure of the speech. It concludes the preceding judgment announcement, but provides the contrastive lead-in for the following message of assurance. Once he has disciplined the city, the Lord will protect and deliver it (31:5). The description of the Lord's powerful intervention is briefly interrupted, as the prophet issues a call to repentance (31:6–7). He then resumes the message of assurance by describing the defeat of Assyria (31:8–9; cf. 30:27–33). The message is marked formally by introductory ("this is what the Lord has said to me," 31:4) and concluding ("this is what the Lord says," 31:9) messenger formulas.

The prophet continues the positive message in 32:1–8, but the focus now shifts from deliverance, the main theme of 31:4–9, to renewed security. A new, just king will lead the people (32:1–4) and fools will no longer be given undeserved respect (32:5–8).

Unlike previous literary panels, a second sequence of judgment and salvation appears in this panel. The prophet warns the complacent women that judgment is coming and with it the loss of the prosperity they enjoy (32:9–14). But this is not the end of the story. The Lord will rejuvenate the covenant community (32:15–20). Justice will prevail, bringing security and renewed prosperity.

- **The Futility of Trusting Egypt (31:1–3)**
- **Deliverance and Security (31:4–32:8)**
- **False Security and Renewed Blessing (32:9–20)**

EXPOSITION (31:1–32:20)

The Futility of Trusting Egypt (31:1–3)
Those who trust in Egypt will be disappointed.

31:1. The prophet pronounces a woe oracle against those who go down to Egypt for help (31:1a). The Egyptians had plenty of horse-drawn chariots, and Judah was convinced that relying on Egypt's military was the best way to combat the Assyrian threat. The oracle begins by referring to those who go down (participle; הַיֹּרְדִים) to Egypt and rely (*yiqtol*/imperfect; literally "lean," יִשָּׁעֵנוּ) upon horses. It then switches to a *wayyiqtol* verb form, which is best taken as perfective, "have trusted" (וַיִּבְטְחוּ). Their mental decision to trust in chariots and horses, coupled with their failure to look to/seek (note the negated *qatal* forms: וְלֹא שָׁעוּ, "they have not looked," and לֹא דָרָשׁוּ, "they have not sought") the Holy One of Israel/the Lord, has given rise to action (going down, relying). Motyer (1993, 254) observes, "Thus, act reveals character and expresses decision." By turning to Egypt, they failed to look to the Holy One of Israel and did not seek the Lord (31:1b). They thought their strategy was wise, but it was doomed to failure because they had rejected the source of genuine wisdom.

31:2–3. The prophet, apparently mimicking their claim to be wise (cf. Hayes and Irvine 1987, 347), sarcastically observes that the Lord too (note וְגַם, "but also") possesses wisdom (31:2a). He is implementing a wise plan of his own by confounding their strategy and thwarting their attempt to preserve themselves. In fact, the plan is already underway. The Lord has brought calamity through the menacing presence of Assyria and has, in the face of Judah's flagrant unbelief, refused to relent from his announced judgment. The expression "turn aside a word" (*hiphil* of סוּר + דָּבָר, "word") is used only here and in Joshua 11:15, where it means "to leave undone"; Joshua did not leave undone any of the commands Moses had passed on to him. Here the prophet affirms the Lord has not left undone—that is, failed to set in motion—the words of judgment he has pronounced against sinful Judah. He will rise against this nation (literally, "house") of evildoers and against the helper of these workers of iniquity, namely, the Egyptians to whom they looked for help (31:2b; cf. עֶזְרָה, "help," in both 31:1 and 2). The Lord will stretch out his hand, and the helper Egypt will stumble and fall—along with Judah, the one supposedly being helped. Together they will come to an end (31:3b). Ironically the Lord, who brought disaster (רַע) near, will finish off the "house of evildoers" (note מְרֵעִים, from רָעַע), referring to Egypt (Miller 1982, 58).

Egypt was totally incapable of helping Judah because they were men, not God, and their chariot horses were flesh, not spirit (31:3a). The prophet uses the divine title אֵל, "God," rather than the title אֱלֹהִים, "God," or the personal name Yahweh. He is not using the term in the sense of "a god," as if he were a polytheist, just as אָדָם here does not refer to "a man." Rather, אֵל has the nuance of "deity" here. In other words, the contrast does not concern personal identity, but essence. The Egyptians are human (the force of anarthrous אָדָם, "man") in nature, not deity (the force of anarthrous אֵל, "God"), like the Holy One of Israel/the Lord is (31:1, 3b). Being mere humans, the Egyptians would not be able to thwart God's purposes. Human beings and God are categorically different (cf. Num. 23:19; Ezek. 28:2, 9; Hos. 11:9). Because they are made of flesh, people are limited by physical boundaries and are mortal; God is of a spiritual essence and is not subject to human limitations. He is wiser and more powerful than human beings. In a conflict between the two, God will emerge the victor every time. Egypt relied on its chariotry to win battles, but the chariots were only as reliable as the horses that pulled them. Horses, like human beings, are made of flesh and are therefore susceptible to physical limitations. They can get tired, be injured, or die. God, on the other hand, is of a spiritual essence and not subject to such weakness. Judah should have been trusting in God, not flesh. After all, God is the source of the life-giving spirit that animates all flesh (Job 12:10; Ps. 104:29–30; Isa. 42:5). If he decides to remove the spirit, the flesh decays (Job 34:14–15; Pss. 78:39; 146:4). Because its horses, the keys to its success, were mere flesh, Egypt could not insulate Judah from God's punishment.

TRANSLATION ANALYSIS 31:2
Most translations understand the verbs in 31: 2a (וַיָּבֵא, "and he brought," and לֹא הֵסִיר, "he did not turn aside") as present (ESV, HCSB, NIV11), future (KJV, NLT), or a combination thereof (NASB). It is possible the forms are

rhetorical, describing future developments as if they were already unfolding or had already done so (see Young 1969, 374 n. 2). Motyer (1993, 254–55) takes the verbs as gnomic. However, the forms (a *wayyiqtol* [1QIsᵃ appears to read a *yiqtol* form here] and a negated *qatal*) are most naturally understood as perfective. See Hayes and Irvine (1987, 347), who see here an allusion "to some earlier calamity or evil state." They also observe, "God has not cancelled his words." They add, "the words of Yahweh still stand; they have not been cancelled or called back." See also Kaiser 1974, 313; and especially, Smith 2007, 531–32. In 31:2b the prophet switches to a *weqatal* verb form (וְקָם), which is typical of predictive discourse. While judgment has been set in motion (31:2a), its full implementation is yet future (31:2b).

Deliverance and Security (31:4–32:8)

The Lord will deliver his people and make them secure.

31:4. As noted above, 31:4 appears to continue the judgment announcement of 31:3b. The initial כִּי, "for," gives the impression that what follows expands upon the announcement that those who have trusted in Egypt will, together with Egypt, perish. The statement begins with a simile (כַּאֲשֶׁר; "*as* a lion growls"), which is interrupted by a description of this lion (אֲשֶׁר, "which") before the sentence is completed (כֵּן, "*so* he will come down, the Lord").

The lion in view is a "young lion" (כְּפִיר; cf. ESV, NASB, which is preferable to NIV11's "great lion"), a nomadic, subadult that is particularly ferocious, like the one that attacked Samson (Judg. 14:5–6). The parenthesis depicts such a lion as undeterred by a band of shepherds, who shout at it, trying to scare it off. With the same determination, the Lord, who is appropriately called by the title "Lord of Armies," will descend for battle. Perhaps there is irony here: Judah goes down (יָרַד) to Egypt for help (31:1), but the Lord comes down (יָרַד) to discipline and then defend his people (cf. 31:5; see Hayes and Irvine 1987, 349).

31:5. At this point, it does not bode well for the sinful people, but a surprising reversal occurs in 31:5. Using another simile, the prophet compares the Lord of Armies to birds that hover over a nest to protect their young (see Kaiser 1974, 317). As the Lord descends (cf. 31:4), he hovers, as it were, over the city to "shield" it. This verb (יָגֵן, from גָּנַן), to which the word "shield" (מָגֵן) is related, means "to cover, surround, defend" (BDB s.v. "גָּנַן" 170). It pictures the Lord protecting his people from danger. The word appears in God's promise to Hezekiah, "I will defend this city" (2 Kings 19:34; 20:6; Isa. 37:35; 38:6). God fulfilled his promise by destroying Sennacherib's army and delivering the city from the Assyrian threat (Isa. 37:36–37).

Shawn Zelig Aster (2017, 358) proposes that the prophet here "subverts" an "Assyrian image of power." The Assyrian royal inscriptions use the bird as a metaphor to describe a fleeing enemy or a defeated enemy, caged like a bird. But here the Lord is likened to birds hovering overhead to protect their young. The prophet takes an Assyrian metaphor, used to derogatorily describe an enemy, and turns it on its head as it were. The Lord is not a weak bird overwhelmed by Assyrian might. He is a bird with protective "power" that "is qualitatively superior to that of any human polity, including Assyria" (p. 359).

The Lord will deliver and rescue the city. In so doing, he will "pass over" it. This verb (פָּסַח) occurs only here and in Exodus 12 (vv. 13, 23, 27), which tells how God "passed over" the homes of the Israelites and did not kill their firstborn. The Passover sacrifice and festival (פֶּסַח) commemorated the event. By using this rare verb here, Isaiah appears to allude to this incident. (See Kaiser 1974, 317; Smith 2007, 533–34; Young 1969, 378–79. Wildberger [2002, 224] is hesitant, but open to the idea.) The limited distribution of the term (only in these two passages), as well as the appearance of the verb "deliver, spare" (*hiphil* of נָצַל) in both Isaiah 31:5 and Exodus 12:27, suggest a conscious literary connection. It is also noteworthy that in both instances God used a destructive agent to annihilate the enemy. Exodus 12:23 mentions "the destroyer" (identified in Ps. 78:49 as "destroying angels"), while Isaiah 37:36 speaks of the "angel of the LORD." It is likely then that 31:5 pictures the Lord supernaturally protecting his people from judgment, just as he did in Egypt in the days of Moses. As he unleashes his wrath on their enemies, he insulates them from harm.

31:6. As he describes the Lord's plan for Zion, the prophet stops to exhort people to repent (cf. 30:15). The text is syntactically awkward; it reads literally, "return to (the one against) whom the sons of Israel have made rebellion deep." The shift from direct address (note the initial imperative) to the third person is odd, but certainly not unique in Hebrew poetry (see GKC, 462 §144p). Perhaps it betrays Isaiah's expectation that only a few will respond positively (cf. 6:9–13) and separate themselves from the predominant behavior of the covenant community (see Young 1969, 379–80).

31:7. The motivating argument for the exhortation is based on what will happen when judgment falls: it makes sense to return to the Lord now, for the day will come when everyone in the covenant community rejects the idols they have made to worship (cf. 2:18–21; see Smith [2007, 535] for a helpful discussion). The switch back to the second person in the second half of the verse (literally, "which *your* hands have made for *yourselves*") indicates that those addressed at the beginning of 31:6 are idolaters. One sees a similar pattern in the preceding panel. A day will come when survivors of judgment cry out to the Lord for help (30:19). The Lord will respond positively and provide spiritual guidance (30:20–21). At that time, this remnant will discard their idols (30:22).

31:8–9. Isaiah now resumes the description of the Lord's intervention to deliver Jerusalem. (The *weqatal* verb form at the beginning of 31:8 resumes the predictive discourse of 31:5.) He will rescue the city by defeating Assyria. Isaiah 31:8a depicts the Lord's miraculous deliverance of the city from Sennacherib's army in 701 B.C. Assyria will fall by a sword, but not one made by human hands. Within the literary context, this serves as a reminder that Egypt (cf. 31:1–3) will not be the city's savior (see Kaiser 1974, 317; Roberts 2015, 405). The fulfillment of this prophecy came when the Lord's angel decimated Sennacherib's army, forcing him to retreat to Assyria (Isa. 37:36–37). Isaiah 31:8b–9a appears to extend beyond the events of 701. The prophet now depicts an Assyrian military defeat where soldiers flee and young men are captured and forced to be laborers. The Assyrian stronghold falls as an invader causes its commanders to panic. This part of the prophecy anticipates the demise of the Assyrian Empire, which took place during 612–609 B.C., and was later described in horrific detail by the prophet Nahum.

Isaiah 31:9a reads, literally, "his rocky cliff, from [i.e., because of] fear, will pass away and his commanders will be afraid from [i.e., because of] a banner." The first statement refers to an Assyrian "rocky cliff," or "stronghold" (NIV11). Perhaps Nineveh is in view, but it is more likely this refers metaphorically to Assyrian defenses, pictured as an inaccessible rocky cliff that provides security. The reality behind the metaphor is not just city defenses, but the army, led by the king and his commanders, that defends Assyria. (See Smith [2007, 535], who identifies the stronghold as the Assyrian king. This makes good sense, considering the parallelism with שָׂרָיו, "his commanders.") Assyria's army, led by its king, will "pass away" (יַעֲבוֹר; see NIV11, "fall"), in the sense of "perish" (see BDB s.v. "עָבַר" mng 6c, 718). This will be due to fear (מָגוֹר, cf. BDB s.v. "מָגוֹר II" 159), which will paralyze them. The second statement elaborates on the first. Assyrian commanders will be terrified

(וְחַתּוּ; cf. BDB s.v. "חָתַת" 369) by the invading army's banner and unable to defend themselves.

The conclusion of the Lord's speech, introduced in 31:4 ("this is what the Lord says to me"), is marked by the words "declares the Lord" (31:9b). The Lord is described as the one whose fire is in Zion and whose furnace is in Jerusalem. In this context the fire and the furnace, which also connotes fire, are symbols of the Lord's destructive judgment (cf. Ps. 21:9 [HB 10]; Mal. 4:1 [HB 3:19]). They serve as a reminder that the Lord will be the ultimate source of Assyria's demise (cf. Isa. 10:16–19; 30:27–33).

32:1. With the interjection הֵן, "see," Isaiah shifts the focus to "a king" who will rule according to righteousness. He will be joined by officials who rule according to justice. This king and his officials (שָׂרִים) stand in contrast to the Assyrian "rocky cliff" (NIV11, "stronghold," probably a metaphor for the Assyrian king and his army) and its commanders (שָׂרִים), whom the Lord will defeat (cf. 31:9).

The king is not identified, but it is reasonable to equate him with the ideal Davidic king described earlier (cf. 9:7). Like David of old (2 Sam. 8:15), this king promotes righteousness (צֶדֶק) and justice (מִשְׁפָּט) within his realm in accordance with the instructions of Moses (Deut. 16:18–20), who said that Israelite judges must "judge the people fairly" (16:18; literally, "[with] justice of righteousness" [מִשְׁפַּט־צֶדֶק]). The Lord gives higher priority to doing righteousness and justice than he does to offering sacrifices (Prov. 21:3). The Lord's goal is that all of Abraham's descendants "keep the way of the Lord by doing what is right and just" (Gen. 18:19). It is not surprising, then, that doing justice and righteousness becomes the standard for God's chosen kings (Jer. 22:2–3), one that is realized in the reign of the ideal Davidic king depicted by Isaiah and Jeremiah (Jer. 23:5–6; 33:15–16; see Smith 2007, 540; Wildberger 2002, 236).

32:2. Each one of the officials who rules over the Lord's people will be a protector and provider. They are compared to a shelter (literally, "hiding place") from the wind and a refuge from the storm (זֶרֶם, cf. Isa. 4:6). There is a contrast with the scene depicted in Isaiah 30:30, where the Lord attacks the Assyrians with a storm (זֶרֶם). These officials also provide nourishment and relief for the people, like streams of water in the desert or the shadow of a great rocky cliff in a sun-beaten dry land. Again, there is a contrast with an earlier image used of Assyria. In 31:9 the Assyrian "rocky cliff" (סֶלַע, probably the king and his army as the defense of Assyria) passes away due to the Lord's judgment, but here just rulers will be like a rocky cliff (סֶלַע) that provides relief from the scorching sun. (NIV11 uses "stronghold" in 31:9 and "rock" in 32:2.)

32:3–5. It will be a time of transformation. Impaired eyes and ears will now function as intended (32:3). The mind (literally, "heart") that typically acts hastily will take the time to discern the proper course of action (literally, "will discern in order to know"; 32:4a). The tongue(s) of stutterers will speak with ease (32:4b). But the meaning lies at a deeper level. Isaiah 32:5 speaks of fools no longer being given undeserved respect. Isaiah 32:6–8 then go on to denounce fools and contrast them with the noble. This suggests that 32:3–4 is talking about a moral and ethical change in perspective. Wisdom was currently lacking, accounting for fools being given respect. But during the just king's reign that will change. People will possess the basic characteristics of wisdom—the ability to observe accurately, the patience to discern the proper course of action, and the capacity to articulate what is wise.

32:6–7. The prophet gives the reason why (note כִּי, "because, for") fools will no longer be respected when the just king rules. What appears is essentially a character profile of the typical fool (note the use of the representative singular

נָבָל, "fool," as well as the third-person singular pronouns and verbs in both verses). The implications of this are significant. On the one hand, by giving fools respect, the covenant community tolerated, and perhaps in some cases even endorsed, the behavior described here. On the other hand, the future demotion of fools to their proper status means the covenant community, under the leadership of just rulers, will not endorse or tolerate such behavior. We may rightly assume, therefore, that the behavior depicted here is the antithesis of justice.

Before describing specifics, the prophet portrays the typical fool in more general terms. A fool (נָבָל) can be spotted by his speech, which is characterized as folly (נְבָלָה; cf. comments on 9:17 above). His words reflect his attitude, which is sinful (cf. 10:1). The text reads, literally, "his heart does sin," suggesting he acts out his sinful deeds in his mind before committing them. These sinful actions include violating God's standards (on the meaning of the verb חָנֵף, see the comments on the related adjective חָנֵף on 9:17 above), misrepresenting the Lord, and depriving the hungry and thirsty of needed relief. Armed with wicked weapons (32:7a; note כֵּלָיו, "his weapons"), probably referring here to words, a fool plans (יָעַץ) evil schemes, in order to destroy (or perhaps, "so that he destroys") the vulnerable with lying words, probably referring to false legal testimony. He does this even when the needy speak what is right, again probably in a legal context (32:7b).

32:8. Regarding such wicked people as "noble" (cf. 32:5) is a travesty, for a noble person, in contrast to a fool, plans (יָעַץ) noble things that give him moral and ethical stability (32:8). (Isaiah 32:8b reads literally, "and he stands upon noble things.") The term נָדִיב, "noble one," sometimes refers simply to one who occupies a noble position, but here the term has an ethical connotation (cf. Ps. 51:14 [HB 16]; Prov. 17:26; and see Motyer 1993, 259). The use of the term נָדִיב in Isaiah 32:5 and 8 probably indicates the prophet had the leaders of Judah in mind as the primary examples of the fools he describes.

False Security and Renewed Blessing (32:9–20)
Judgment will eliminate the people's false sources of security and restore God's blessings.

32:9. The prophet returns to the present as he urges the "complacent" women/daughters who "feel secure" to listen to his message. In this context, the term "complacent" (שַׁאֲנַנּוֹת) describes a proud attitude (cf. Ps. 123:4) that refuses to recognize impending doom (cf. Job 12:5). (See Young 1969, 392. For a contrary opinion, see Wildberger 2002, 250.) Though Zion is not specifically mentioned here, it is likely the women of Jerusalem are in view (cf. Isa. 31:4, 9, as well as 32:13–14). The prophet denounced the women of Jerusalem earlier for their pride and ostentatious demeanor (cf. 3:16–4:1).

32:10–14. Judgment was around the corner. Within a year's time these self-assured women would be trembling because of a failed summer fruit harvest (32:10), a harbinger of coming disaster (cf. 32:13–14). Anticipating the arrival of that day, the prophet exhorts these women to tremble and shudder. They should remove their clothes (cf. 3:18–23) and put on garments fit for mourning (32:11–12a). The reason for mourning is introduced by the threefold עַל, "on account of," in 32:12b–13a: mourning is appropriate because the pleasant fields, fruitful vines, and the people's land (cultivated land is in view) will not yield their produce (cf. 32:10b). Instead, the land will produce thorns and briers.

But the judgment will not be limited to the fields and crops. It will also extend to the towns and fortresses, for they will be abandoned and reduced to a perpetual ruin (32:13b–14). At this point, one realizes the judgment will culminate in an invasion. Even the stronghold will be abandoned, along with the once bustling town. The Ophel (an elevated area within Jerusalem, see *HALOT* s.v. "עֹפֶל II" 861) and watchtower will be reduced to a field, populated only by wild donkeys and flocks.

The Hebrew term עוֹלָם, used to emphasize the extent of the judgment, is often translated "forever, eternal" (cf. ESV, KJV, NASB, NIV11). Giving the word this nuance is appropriate when it applies to God's promises or character (cf. 40:8, 28). However, in other cases it refers to long periods of time within a temporal framework; its precise force must be determined from the context. Sometimes the term looks backward and refers to antiquity, to something that is ancient, or to a long period of time that extends from the distant past to the present (Isa. 42:14; 44:7; 46:9; 51:9; 57:11; 58:12; 61:4; 63:9, 11, 16, 19; 64:4–5). When it is forward-looking, it can refer, perhaps hyperbolically, to situations or entities that will continue perpetually or with no immediate end in sight (Isa. 9:7 [HB 6]; 14:20; 24:5; 25:2; 30:8; 32:14, 17; 33:14; 34:10, 17; 35:10; 45:17; 51:6, 8, 11; 54:8; 55:3, 13; 57:16; 59:21; 60:15, 19–21; 61:8). However, this need not mean the situation in view is envisioned as eternal. For example, Jerusalem's citadel and watchtower will be reduced to a perpetual, not an eternal, ruin (32:14), as the very next verse makes clear. This situation will end when the Lord renews the land (note "till," in 32:15).

Did This Prophecy "Fail"?

Jerusalem was not destroyed in this fashion by the Assyrians when they invaded Judah in 701 B.C. For this reason, some understand the prophecy as pertaining to the towns of Judah, many of which Sennacherib did destroy. But it is important to remember that Micah also prophesied Jerusalem would be reduced to ruins by the Assyrians (Mic. 3:12). Yet we discover that Hezekiah's repentant response to the prophetic warning resulted in the Lord relenting from full judgment and sparing the city (see Jer. 26:17–19). These prophecies of utter doom were implicitly conditional, designed to motivate a proper response so that judgment could be averted. Of course, the prophecy was not necessarily canceled. Later, when the nation returned to its sin, the prophecy was reactivated, and Jerusalem was thoroughly destroyed by the Babylonians in 586. (See Chisholm 2010, 566–67.)

32:15. The desolation described in Isaiah 32:13–14 is not permanent. It lasts only until "a spirit" (NIV11, "the Spirit") is revealed from on high (32:15a). Then a radical transformation will take place (32:15b–20).

The verb יֵעָרֶה (*niphal* from עָרָה, 32:15a) is usually translated here as "poured" (ESV, KJV, NASB, NIV11, NLT), a meaning that fits well with the prepositional phrases "upon us" and "from on high." However, the verb normally has the nuance "expose, uncover, reveal" (see *HALOT* s.v. "עָרָה" 881–82). Twice it is used of emptying a container of its contents: Rebekah empties her pitcher of water into a trough (Gen. 24:20) and officials empty a money chest of its contents (2 Chron. 24:12). The nuance is not exactly "pour out," since the object of the verb is the container from which the contents are poured, not the contents per se. Hence, "empty out" is a better gloss than "pour out." In Isaiah 32:15 the spirit in view would be the substance of what is poured out, not the container from which something else is poured. Perhaps it is best then to understand the usual nuance here, "reveal," but, in light of the prepositional phrases with which it is collocated, interpret it in a unique metonymic sense of "revealed and sent down."

The referent of רוּחַ, "spirit," is debated. Some translate "the Spirit," as if God's personal Spirit is in view (ESV, NASB, NIV11, NLT). However, there is no indication of definiteness in the Hebrew text, such as an article, pronominal suffix, or modifying genitive. The term is better understood as referring to a life-giving capacity (literally, "wind, breath") imparted from "on high," implying it derives from God (cf. NET, "new life"). This rejuvenating spirit transforms the once barren and desolate land (cf. 32:12–13a) so that it bears fruit and crops (32:15b). The prophet offers two word-pictures to depict this. The unpopulated and uncultivated desert (מִדְבָּר; cf. Isa. 14:17; 27:10), becomes an orchard (כַּרְמֶל; cf. Isa. 10:18; 16:10; 29:17), while the orchard expands into a forest (יַעַר).

32:16–20. This physical transformation mirrors the rejuvenation of society, which will now be characterized by justice, righteousness, and peace (32:16–20). Linking the portrait of 32:15b with the theme of societal renewal, the prophet states that justice (מִשְׁפָּט) would dwell in the desert and righteousness in the orchard (32:16). The implication is clear. It is the implementation of justice and righteousness, brought about by the impartation of a rejuvenating spirit (32:15a) that transforms the desert and orchard. This transformation in the physical realm is a tangible portrait of a more profound change that occurs in society. The byproduct (note מַעֲשֶׂה, "product," and עֲבֹדָה, "work") of righteousness is peace and lasting security (32:17), evident in renewed agricultural prosperity and in national security (32:18–20), both of which are signs of renewed covenantal blessing.

The prophet uses verbal repetition to highlight the reversal that take places (Roberts 2015, 417; Young 1969, 401–2). The term בֶּטַח, "confidence, security," in 32:17b echoes בֹּטְחוֹת, "feel secure," used in 32:9–11 of the complacent women confronted there. That unwarranted complacency would be replaced by genuine security, the byproduct of righteousness (see Wildberger 2002, 261–62). The prophet's use of the qualifier עַד־עוֹלָם, "lasting" (NIV11, "forever") in 32:17b echoes the use of the same phrase in 32:14. There it describes the seemingly lasting effects of the coming judgment, but lasting security now prevails. In 32:18 the prophet depicts the people living in "secure" (מִבְטַחִים) homes and "undisturbed" (שַׁאֲנַנּוֹת) places of rest. Both adjectives echo the terms that describe the complacent women in 32:9–11 (שַׁאֲנַנּוֹת and בֹּטְחוֹת). Again, as noted above, genuine security, produced by righteousness, replaces unwarranted complacency. The women described earlier had no reason to be complacent because their sinful society was on the brink of disaster and their sense of security was only imagined. But once God purifies and restores his covenant community, the people will truly be secure.

In 32:19 the prophet returns briefly to the present and anticipates the impending judgment announced earlier in the speech. The trees of the forest will fall down and the city (presumably Jerusalem) will topple, but those who survive the judgment will experience joy as they sow seed and graze their livestock (32:20). Another option is that 32:19 refers to the fall of Assyria, which was depicted earlier as a forest the Lord chops down (10:18–19; see Kaiser 1974, 335–36; Young 1969, 402–3). In this case, renewed blessing accompanies the Lord's victory over the menacing Assyrians (cf. 30:27–33; 31:4–9).

THEOLOGICAL FOCUS

The theological focus of this passage can be stated as follows: the Lord protects and transforms his covenant community by defeating their enemy, establishing just leadership, and providing them with prosperity and security. As the prophet develops this theological theme, the following emphases emerge:

1. The Lord's superiority to horses and chariots

In the face of the Assyrian threat, Judah's leaders decided to look to Egypt for security, with its horse-drawn chariots (31:1–3). The Old Testament frequently describes powerful armies—including those of Egypt, Assyria, and Babylon—as possessing horses and chariots (Exod. 14:9, 23; Josh. 11:4; 1 Kings 20:1; 2 Kings 6:14–15; Isa. 5:28; Jer. 4:13; 46:9; Ezek. 26:10–11; Nah. 3:2; Zech. 9:10). The horse was a symbol of military might, and its very appearance and mannerisms struck fear into the heart of those being attacked (Jer. 8:16; Hab. 1:8). Because of its military importance the horse was viewed as a guarantee of security (cf. Isa. 30:16) and an object of trust (Ps. 20:7 [HB 8]). In the Phoenician Karatepe inscription Azitawaddu boasts that he "acquired horse upon horse" with the aid of Baal and the gods (*COS* 2.31:149).

However, the Lord wanted his people to trust in his ability to protect and deliver. From the beginning of Israel's history, he demonstrated his superiority to the chariot forces of the nations (Exod. 14–15; Josh. 11; Judg. 4–5) and he expected his people to trust in his power for military victory. After all, horses are made of mere flesh (Isa. 31:3) and are no match for the Lord, whose enablement is the true key to success in battle (Pss. 20:7 [HB 8]; 33:17–20; 76:5–7 [HB 6–8]; 147:10–11; Prov. 21:31; Isa. 30:15–16; 31:3; Hos. 14:3).[3] The Lord would supernaturally deliver his people from Assyria (Isa. 31:8–9).

2. Justice and folly

The Lord will transform his covenant community and provide new leadership (32:1–2). These leaders will promote justice and righteousness. No longer will fools be regarded as noble, for their behavior is contrary to the standards of justice. Fools do not provide for those needing relief and they exploit the poor and needy (32:5–8). But once justice is firmly established through divine enablement, the community will experience renewed agricultural prosperity and national security (32:16–20).

PREACHING AND TEACHING STRATEGIES

Exegetical and Theological Synthesis

Isaiah 31–32 picks up and continues the themes and storyline begun in chapter 28. The setting remains the same as in the previous chapters. The threat of an assault against Jerusalem by the Assyrians is growing ever more likely. In response to this threat, the leaders of Judah have made the decision to send envoys to Egypt with significant financial resources to attempt to buy their help and protection. This strategic decision was coupled with the choice by Judah not to consult with the Lord God or trust him for help and security (31:1). The prophet specifically confronts the people about three false saviors in which they were trusting rather than God.

False Savior #1: Military Might (31:1–9)

This section begins with the fifth woe of the broader pericope (Isa. 28–33). This woe is directed toward those who go down to Egypt for help (31:1). Specifically, they were trusting that Egypt would provide them with horses and chariots, which were the ancient equivalent of tanks and fighter jets today. Horses provided soldiers with the ability to move more quickly on the battlefield without exerting much human energy. Thus, they could quickly overtake foot soldiers. Chariots would have typically been manned by both a driver and an archer. Likewise, this would have provided them much greater speed to get into position to attack and then retreat than archers on foot.

Egypt was famous for the number and quality of the horses bred there. When Solomon was king of Israel, he purchased horses and chariots from Egypt (2 Chron. 1:16–17; 9:28). Earlier God had expressly warned Israel's kings against accumulating many horses, at least in part because God did not want his people to return to Egypt to acquire them (Deut. 17:16). God had miraculously and powerfully delivered them out from Egypt. He did not want them returning to Egypt and groveling for help as though their God was somehow no longer able to provide for them or protect them from other threats. This in fact was the primary issue in Isaiah 31. By trusting in horses and chariots from Egypt, the people were refusing to trust in the Lord their God (31:1; cf. Ps. 20:7 [HB 8]).

---

[3] For a fuller discussion of this theme, see *NIDOTTE* 3:234–36.

Isaiah pointed out how foolish this decision was on the part of Judah's leaders. They evidently attributed wisdom to their counselors who promoted this plan. Thus, the prophet pushed back by saying, "Yet he [God] too is wise." This statement was full of sarcasm in that it was an obvious understatement. Did they really think their wisdom was superior to God's? Apparently they did, because they opted to reject God's counsel in favor of their own human counselors and advisors. God is not just simply wise, as some men are wise. Rather, God is eminently wiser than the wisest of humans. He is in fact the source of all wisdom (Job 28:20–28; Prov. 2:6–11; Dan. 2:21).

The Egyptians, along with Judah's counselors and leaders, are mere mortals, whereas God is spirit. Thus, only the Lord can craft a strategy that is sure to defeat Judah's enemies, the Assyrians. He promises to come down like a lion and fight on behalf of his people (Isa. 31:4). This reality makes the trek down to Egypt and any discussion about horses and chariots completely pointless. Thus, the prophet urges Judah to turn from their false savior of military might, and turn to the Lord, their only real protector (31:6). Even though so many in the nation have rebelled against him, yet many will return to him one day, abandoning and destroying their idols, once it becomes obvious that he has defeated their enemy (31:7). God will do this by "a sword, not of mortals." With this sword he will put the Assyrians to flight (31:8). What an amazing promise, and one that would be fulfilled quite literally when the angel of the Lord would carry out a great slaughter against the Assyrian army, apparently with an angelic or spiritual sword of some type (Isa. 37:36).

False Savior #2: Flawed Leaders (32:1–8)
Isaiah 32:1–8 highlights a second false savior in Judah: flawed leaders. The prophet begins by describing the chosen messianic king who will one day reign in righteousness (32:1). He will appoint princes or rulers under him who will govern justly. These rulers will provide security and peace for the people (32:2), especially the weak and vulnerable who were used to being overlooked and exploited by flawed leaders. Jesus's rule will be a welcomed sight and a comforting reality. It will be like a place of safety and shelter during a harsh storm. It will also be like streams of water and a source of shade in a dry and hot desert place (32:2).

The leaders and the people alike will be filled with understanding in that day (32:3–4). No longer will fools or wicked people be placed into government or religious leadership positions, resulting in all sorts of wickedness and false notions about God being taught (32:5–6). Similarly, under Messiah's rule, the leaders that are established will make sure that the poor do not go hungry and will see to it that they are not exploited by the wealthy in their courts (32:6–7).

All of this pointed to Judah's flawed leaders as one more example of false saviors. Most in Judah were aware of how crooked the political process was; they were certainly aware that many of their leaders were self-serving, dishonest, and corrupt. Nonetheless, they still looked to their leaders to make decisions on their behalf. They trusted that their leaders would make the best decisions to rescue them from the Assyrian threat. They placed their hope and security in these leaders, if for no other reason than that they didn't really have any other choice. These were the ones who were making decisions on their behalf, and thus they looked to them in the hope that they would make wise and sensible judgments.

However, the people needed to look to the Lord alone. When their politicians announced that they were going to turn to Egypt for help, the people needed to speak out in favor of the Lord their God. At the end of the day, when the current leadership has turned completely away from the Lord, God's people must ultimately look to the promises of the future kingdom for their hope and sense of peace and security rather than to the promises made by their present, flawed politicians.

False Savior #3: Economic Abundance (32:9–20)
This third section is addressed to the women of Jerusalem. It isn't clear why the prophet directs his comments toward them, or if he has a specific group of women in mind. However, it seems somewhat reminiscent of Isaiah 3:16–4:1 where the wives of the wealthy but corrupt leaders of Israel were confronted for their proud, ostentatious attitudes. They had been complicit in their husbands' corruption, enjoying the wealth and comfortable lifestyle afforded to them by their husbands' corrupt practices. Similarly, these women are accused of having grown complacent (32:9, 10, 11) because of their comfortable lifestyle. As stated in the commentary above, the word "complacent" here implies a proud attitude. Isaiah 3:24 also urged the women in that context to replace their rich robes with sackcloth to mourn their coming judgment. This is similar to the admonition given to the women in 32:11. This passage also follows a section that addressed the corrupt leaders who were taking advantage of the poor. Thus, these women could be the wives of those corrupt leaders.

Regardless of whether these women should be identified as the wives of the corrupt leaders and noblemen in Judah, they have evidently gotten used to having fruitful harvests with plenty to eat and drink (32:10, 12). Their abundance and ease of lifestyle (32:9, 11) have caused them to become complacent about the prospect of coming judgment. They seem oblivious to their own sin and the fact that it will eventually elicit judgment from God. This judgment will negatively impact their fruitful harvests (32:12) by replacing the fertile soil with thorns and briers. Additionally, the populated city with its palace and joyous houses will become deserted. It will instead become pastureland for donkeys and flocks (32:13–14).

However, the prophet indicates that there is hope beyond this judgment. God will send a wind/spirit from on high that will result in a divine reversal, whereby judgment gives way to blessing. The wilderness will be restored into a fruitful field, and the fruitful field will grow into a mighty forest (32:15). The imagery of the land's renewal describes more than just agronomics. As the prophet goes on to say, the cultivation of new plant life will coincide with the cultivation of justice and righteousness, resulting in peace, security, and rest for those who inhabit this renewed land (32:16–18). Thus, like the prior section (32:1–8), which described the coming messianic kingdom ruled by the righteous king, so too this section ends by looking ahead to that same time when God will restore and make all things new.

As such, the prophet seems to be confronting the false savior of economic abundance.

The wealthy and powerful in Judah had grown complacent toward God and the prospect of coming judgment. They were apparently unworried about having to give an account to God for how they were living or how they had treated the vulnerable. They trusted that the comfortable lifestyles afforded to them by their wealth would provide them with ongoing prosperity. As such, they hadn't accounted for the reality of future judgment. Therefore, the prophet harkens to a time in the future when their wealth would do them no good, as they wouldn't be able to purchase salvation from God. Only those who have been impacted with the life-giving wind/spirit from God, leading to a renewal of righteousness, will escape this judgment and be able to enjoy the time when God has made all things new.

Preaching Idea
It is folly to trust in any saviors other than the Lord God.

Contemporary Connections

What does it mean?
Everyone desires to feel safe in the world. They want to be able to relax, to be at peace so they can enjoy life. People need to have a reason for optimism about their future, to have hope that whatever lies ahead, it is as good or better than their present experience. At the same time, life is full of risks, danger, and misfortunes. People lose their job. Natural disasters unexpectedly strike. Spouses commit infidelity. Sickness, violent crime, societal upheaval, car accidents, house fires, relationship breakups, bankruptcies—life is full of painful, stressful, frustrating, even terrifying events. Not every hard or painful life experience can be as easily defined as these. For example, how does one quantify the feeling that their life doesn't have any ultimate purpose? Or what about the lingering feelings of depression that some people experience without any obvious circumstantial causes to explain it? What about the person who feels lonely despite having numerous friends and acquaintances? How about the man or woman who feels trapped in an unfulfilling marriage? There are many reasons that cause people to experience pain, sadness, loneliness, or to feel hopeless about their futures, some easier to explain or define than others.

But whatever the cause of a person's pain, it motivates them to look for something to ease it and inject hope into their situation. Whatever things people hope will give them the fortitude to press on and make their life seem worthwhile and meaningful can rightly be called a person's saviors.

However, the things that people assume will make their life more worthwhile, the sources to which they turn other than God to feel hopeful about their future, are ultimately insufficient. Rather than discovering something or someone that really has the power to "save" them, they embrace false saviors. False saviors appear on the surface to offer a remedy, to fill a void, or to enable them to cope well with the hardships and disappointments innate to living in a fallen world. However, these are just illusions. In fact, every potential savior other than the Lord Jesus is inadequate.

Is it true?
People look to a lot of different things to feel secure or hopeful about their future. They often assume that if only they had this or that thing, they would feel safe and their lives would be meaningful. People today are prone to mistakenly look to the same three false saviors that the people of Judah trusted.

Military might. People often assume that living in a powerful nation with a strong army makes them secure. Many nations that are smaller rely on political treaties or allies with stronger nations to guarantee their safety in the event of a military attack. Consider, for example, the North Atlantic Treaty Organization (NATO) with its thirty allied nations. The primary goal of this partnership is for the various nations to protect each other's safety and security, including by means of military action when necessary. This would seem on the surface to be a sound strategy. A strong military is usually an indication that the citizens of that nation need not worry much about foreign invasions. However, can military strength truly guarantee one's safety? Recent events tell us, "No." Those who perished on September 11, 2001 lived in a nation that is the lone world superpower, with the most sophisticated military in human history, but attackers were still able to take down two of the tallest towers in the world. Certainly, having a strong military is desirable, and I feel blessed to live in the United States for this reason among many others.

However, military strength is no guarantee of one's security. This is especially true when God decides to judge a nation.

In fact, the broader reality of judgment really exposes just how vulnerable humans are and how useless militaries are at providing security or safety from eternal accountability and judgment. All will have to stand before their Creator to give an account of their lives one day (Heb. 9:27). Therefore, if people are to truly have a sense of peace and hope for a long-term future, they must depend upon a savior who is able to address not only their present-day geopolitical enemies, but also one who addresses their alienation from God. Jesus came to earth for that very purpose. He alone is able to guarantee our salvation from coming judgment through his substitutionary death and triumphant resurrection from the grave (Eph. 2:13–17; Col. 1:12–13, 19–22; 1 John 4:9–10).

Flawed leaders. Another common "false savior" in modern society is flawed politicians. People tend to dislike politicians regardless of their party affiliation. Favorability polling in the United States for almost all politicians, whether presidents or members of Congress, is generally quite low. Often, these polls reflect that well under half of those polled have a favorable view of the person in office. And yet, many politicians are reelected election cycle after cycle. Why is this? The answer is certainly complex and multifaceted. At some level, many may feel as though they don't have much of a choice in who runs for office or in who has the clout to win a primary battle. Thus, they feel forced to vote for the better of two unlikable candidates. Anyone who lives in the United States throughout a major political season understands just how much collective money, time, and energy our society invests in getting the next person elected. During their campaigns, these politicians or wannabe politicians are heralded as the next great savior of our society. They proclaim all the wonderful things they will do once they are elected. Chances are, if the man or woman we supported ends up winning, we feel a great sense of relief. We feel hope and optimism that this or that issue will finally be addressed and solved. It isn't long, though, before we begin to realize that very little is likely to change for the better with them in office.

While there are many reasons why this is often the case, some not the fault of the politician, it still serves to highlight how undeserving flawed politicians are of the title *savior*. Most of us are guilty of placing far too much faith and confidence in politicians or political parties to make our world better, or to protect us from harm. The sense of security and optimism we tend to feel when our person or party is in office is largely unwarranted. Similarly, the sense of deep loss and anxiety we feel when the other party wins the election is likewise unnecessary. It isn't that politics don't matter or that one party isn't different from the next. It's just that our hope and peace in the world are not derived from flawed political leaders, but rather from the promises of God. Christian hope will not be realized by a political party. It will only be realized by King Jesus, who alone is able to save the world when he ushers in righteousness and justice for all (Isa. 32:1–5).

Economic abundance. Most people consider economic abundance to be a savior. Consider how affluence has become the definition of success in our culture. When we refer to someone as being successful in life, we almost always mean that they have made a lot of money and are thus able to afford a comfortable lifestyle. It is essentially hardwired into most of our minds as Westerners that the number-one measure of whether our lives were lived well is how much money we have made.

However, consider all the things that are viewed as relatively unimportant when considering whether to call somebody a success. Did they live with good character? Did they remain faithfully committed to their spouse? Were they loving and responsible parents who made time to raise their children well? Were they kind and generous toward others, and did it show in how they used or invested their money and time? What was the overall quality of that person's life, and how did this contribute to their overall physical and emotional health and happiness? One would think that these would all be pertinent questions to consider when assessing how successfully a person lived. And yet how many people are held up today as successful despite broken marriages, drug addictions, dysfunctional kids, and self-centered, narcissistic personalities that enable them to justify making life all about themselves much of the time? We could list plenty of professional athletes, Hollywood actors or actresses, politicians, or wealthy business tycoons who fit this description all too well. Despite what our culture has led us to believe, wealth and abundance are not the equivalent of a successful life—not even close.

Money likewise can't buy contentment, peace of mind, or genuine hope about one's future. Economic abundance, like military might and flawed politicians, is a false savior. It makes many promises about life but can't deliver. Far too many people have ruined their lives accumulating wealth (1 Tim. 6:9–10). In some cases, the very thing people believed would fix most or all of their problems contributed to the unraveling of their family and the compromise of their character, and multiplied the stress and anxiety in their lives many times over.

Our culture's list of false saviors is much longer than the three addressed in Isaiah 31–32 that have been highlighted above. Space does not allow for a lengthy discussion of many others, but here are some additional ones to consider:

Intoxicants. One of the ways people attempt to deal with their pain and disillusionment is through drugs and alcohol. Recent studies revealed that more than 25 percent of the adult population engages in binge drinking. Additionally, nearly fifteen million people in the United States suffer from alcohol use disorder.[4] More than one in five people over the age of twelve have either used illegal drugs or misused prescription drugs within the last year. Fifty percent of people twelve and over have used illicit drugs at some point in their lifetime.[5] As the statistics reveal, far too many turn to intoxicants to help them forget about their problems. However, this only adds one more problem and does nothing to alleviate their other issues.

Fame/popularity. There is a growing infatuation within the Western world with the idea of being famous. One 2012 study of ten-to-twelve-year-olds found that a desire for fame solely for the sake of being famous overshadowed every other goal, including financial success, achievement, or a sense of community. Researchers found that the two predominant motivators for fame were (1) the desire to be seen and valued, and (2) the desire to live an elite, high-status lifestyle.[6] Internet sites like YouTube and various social media sites provide a more natural outlet for young people to experiment, putting themselves out for a broader audience to potentially notice and affirm them. While there is nothing wrong with being famous in and of itself, for many it is just another false savior. They view it as a ticket out of their boring, second-class life into one that is envied by others. The prospect of fame gives them a sense of hope and optimism. However, only Jesus can provide people with the sense of importance and status for which they long. Only he provides his children with a meaningful cause to devote their lives to that will last for eternity.

---

4   https://www.niaaa.nih.gov/publications/brochures-and-fact-sheets/alcohol-facts-and-statistics.
5   https://drugabusestatistics.org.
6   https://blogs.scientificamerican.com/beautiful-minds/why-do-you-want-to-be-famous.

Good causes. A final example of a false savior is the pursuit of good causes, such as environmentalism, protecting endangered animals, political activism, drilling wells in third-world countries, rescuing people from human traffickers, and more. Of course, not everyone who devotes themselves to good causes is pursuing false saviors. Evangelism, feeding the poor, showing hospitality to strangers, and caring for widows and orphans are just a few examples of good causes that God has commanded Christians to pursue. However, these are not to be done as ends in themselves. These activities, while good, do not have salvific benefits to them. In other words, Christians do not engage in feeding the poor because this activity alone will merit them salvation (Eph. 2:8–9; 2 Tim. 1:9; Titus 3:5), or because this activity by itself will give significance to their otherwise meaningless life. Rather, we engage in these sorts of activities as an expression of love toward our Lord and Savior, Jesus Christ. Because Jesus loves the poor, widows, orphans, the unsaved, and all the rest, we engage in activities designed to help and bless them, knowing that it glorifies Jesus.

However, many today who have no relationship with Jesus at all assume that engaging in charitable activities or activism on behalf of others will somehow elevate their life's value and make it meaningful. But this is impossible. However good some of these endeavors might be, they still leave people comparing themselves with others and wondering, "How good is good enough?" They still feel guilty for all the things they could have done but failed to do. Most of all, nobody has the power to fill the void in their life caused by sin and rebellion against God. Attempts to simply be a better person lack the ability to atone for past sins and failures. Thus, those who expect good causes to infuse their lives with value and meaning are also grasping at false saviors rather than the one who alone has the power to redeem them and infuse their lives with true meaning and eternal purpose.

Now what?
It's important for Christians to identify potential false saviors in their lives. I'm reminded of the way every G.I. Joe cartoon episode ended when I was a kid. There was a short clip that ended with a G.I. Joe character giving advice to kids such as, "Don't get into a car with a stranger," or "Always tell the truth." The child in the clip would reply, "Now I know." Then G.I. Joe would say, "And knowing is half the battle." There is truth in the saying, "Knowing is half the battle." It's impossible to recalibrate our thinking about the false saviors in our lives until after we have first identified what those false saviors are.

One way to identify false saviors is to consider what you think about when trouble arrives and your future seems uncertain. For example, if a young person finds a sense of security in being popular and being accepted into a particular friend group, what do they turn to most often when popularity or peer acceptance is threatened? If they most easily find comfort by thinking about the fact that they have a great sense of humor and a likeable personality, or that they know several members of the opposite sex who would love to go out with them, then this probably indicates that they are viewing acceptance and friends as their savior. However, if that young person has learned to think instead about God's good character and the fact that he loves and accepts us in Christ, this is evidence that God, not friends, is their true savior. Similarly, when a retiree on a fixed income watches his retirement fund take a significant hit due to a sudden economic downturn, where do their thoughts turn to reassure themselves that things will be okay? Are they comforted by the reminder that God will supply all of their needs according to his riches in glory in Christ Jesus (Phil 4:19)? Or do they primarily console themselves with thoughts about how they are still healthy enough to get another job if necessary and have quite a bit of equity saved up in their home. While those things might be true, and are certainly part of the equation, it can nonetheless be instructive for Christians to ask themselves whether God or something else is their primary source of peace and comfort.

It is important to point out that God often meets our needs through the things we might be prone to trust in, such as our friends or access to a part-time job. Thus, one might ask why we would refer to these things as false saviors? The key is to distinguish between the Giver (God) and the gifts. James wrote that "every good gift and every perfect gift is from above," from the Father (James 1:17). It isn't wrong to enjoy these things, nor even to find a sense of security from them. But we must never confuse the blessings themselves with the God who provides those blessings. At the end of the day, it isn't friends or sources of additional income that guarantee us that things will be okay and that our futures are secure; it is the God who blessed us with those things. Should my savings run out before I find another job, my hope should remain just as firm as when I had a healthy retirement account. My thought process should be something akin to, "The same God who provided for my needs these past seventy years with money he enabled me to save will continue to meet my needs in some other way for the remaining years of my life."

What then do we do about those "false-savior" thought patterns that have become ingrained in our minds? It is one thing to recognize that popularity has become a false savior, and to admit that God alone is one's true source of acceptance. But it's much more difficult to renew our minds so we have faith in God when I'm feeling rejected by my peers or financially strapped.

I was recently at a discipleship-related conference where one of the speakers presented a seminar on what they called "stronghold busters." Mental strongholds are beliefs or patterns of thinking inconsistent with what God says is true that have developed into sinful behaviors. The term "stronghold busters" is based on 2 Corinthians 10:4-5:

"The weapons we fight with are not the weapons of the world. On the contrary, they have divine power to demolish strongholds. We demolish arguments and every pretension that sets itself up against the knowledge of God, and we take captive every thought to make it obedient to Christ." A stronghold buster, then, is a written statement that first identifies the lie that a person has believed, followed by a statement of truth. For example, the person who feels they need to be famous to feel validated as a person of importance might write a statement such as the following: "I renounce the lie that being famous enhances my actual value as a person or is evidence that my life is a success. I announce the truth that in Christ, I have already been accepted by God, and living for his glory rather than my own is the real key to a meaningful life." Finally, the person should commit to reading the stronghold buster statement out loud for the next forty days. Additionally, whenever those thoughts or feelings arise in their mind, they should reread the statement. Over time, one will begin to renew their mind according to God's truth (Rom. 12:2), which will result in new habits.[7]

Creativity in Presentation

Their Bark Is Worse Than Their Bite
A few years ago, I watched an episode of *Inside Edition*, a television news program devoted to investigative journalism. In this episode the show's producers decided to try

---

[7] The science of brain neuroplasticity supports this practice as a means of rewiring the brain and forming new habits in place of old ones. To read more about this, go to https://www.healthline.com/health/the-science-of-habit#4.

an experiment to see whether a homeowner's dog(s) would protect them in the event of a home invasion. The first homeowner had a five-year-old yellow Labrador retriever named Perry. The homeowner was fairly certain that her dog would come to her rescue if somebody broke into her home and began to attack her, but she was curious to find out. *Inside Edition* arranged with the homeowner to have a man burst into her home and act as though he was hurting her. When he did, to the owner's disappointment, Perry immediately ran toward the door. The same thing happened in the next home as well. This time the dog was a mix between a Labrador and a Pit Bull. This homeowner too had assumed his dog would attack any unwanted guests. While his dog briefly came to inspect what was happening when the supposed intruder was "attacking" the homeowner, this dog didn't try to protect her owner either. Finally, in the third home, a pair of small dogs attempted to protect their owner. One of them jumped between the attacker and his master and barked to try to scare the intruder away. None of these dogs were very ferocious, however, and I doubt any of them would have stopped an intruder set on hurting the homeowner.[8]

In each of the above examples, the homeowners assumed their dogs would act as their "savior" in the event of an attack by an intruder. Their dogs provided them a sense of security and made them feel safe inside their homes. However, they were disappointed to discover that in the moment of truth, their dogs let them down. Their dogs were false saviors. They weren't able or willing to save them as the owners assumed they would.

Awakenings

The 1990 movie *Awakenings* was based on the true story of people who were suffering from encephalitis lethargica, also known as sleeping sickness. This disease attacked the brain, mysteriously leaving some of them in catatonic states where they would sit like a statue, speechless and motionless. One neurologist, Oliver Sacks, wrote about people with this condition, "They neither conveyed nor felt the feeling of life; they were as insubstantial as ghosts, and as passive as zombies."[9]

Dr. Malcolm Sayer (played in the movie by Robin Williams) experimented with the drug L-Dopa after hearing about its success in treating patients with Parkinson's disease. Initially, the results appeared to be nothing short of a miracle. The patients fully awoke out of their catatonic states and were able to experience life and communicate like normal people. However, within a relatively short period of time, the patients began to exhibit facial and body tics corresponding to feelings of paranoia and agitation. The negative side effects grew worse, while the positive effects of the L-Dopa drug gradually stopped working. Sadly, these patients reverted to their previous catatonic states.

Just as the positive effects of the L-Dopa drug eventually wore off, so also the luster of false saviors eventually fades. Initially, such saviors appear to infuse people with joy and happiness, but in the course of time those same people experience the destructive effects of elevating things or other people over Jesus Christ as their source of joy, significance, meaning, status, and the rest. In the end, these "saviors" are never able to fulfill or deliver what they claim. They all prove to be false saviors.

A Green Desert

Isaiah 32:15 describes how God will transform the desert of Judah into a fruitful field. Much of Israel is dry, rocky land. In fact, about 60 percent of Israel's territory today is covered by

---

[8] The video of this episode can be seen here: https://www.youtube.com/watch?v=NZ74oFctP_g.
[9] https://en.wikipedia.org/wiki/Encephalitis_lethargica#cite_ref-10.

desert. Some areas of the Judean desert receive less than two inches of rain per year. Naturally, the terrain is covered in rocks and dirt with very little vegetation.

However, there is a rare phenomenon referred to as a "green desert" where the normally dry, barren land turns green with plant life. This happens right after a few days of rainfall, immediately followed by strong sunlight. The result is that green vegetation sprouts and covers the ground. A recent example of this took place in 2015 after record rainfalls were recorded in the region during the winter rainy season. Pictures of this event taken by Jewish photographer Nir Cohen can be found online.[10] The teacher/preacher may want to consider showing his audience before and after pictures of areas that have been transformed from brown desert into green pasture. While this phenomenon is somewhat rare and only lasts briefly, it offers a glimpse of what the Messiah's kingdom will look like after he transforms the earth, removing the curse once and for all.

It is folly to trust in any saviors other than the Lord God.

- False Savior #1: Military might (31:1–9).
- False Savior #2: Flawed leaders (32:1–8).
- False Savior #3: Economic abundance (32:9–20).

DISCUSSION QUESTIONS

1. In Isaiah 31:8, God predicted that the mighty Assyrian army would be defeated "by a sword, not of mortals." This anticipated when the Angel of the Lord would slaughter 185,000 Assyrian soldiers, providing a miraculous victory for God's people. Read Ephesians 6:10–13. What principles can be drawn from these passages about spiritual warfare and how they correlate with each other?

2. In Isaiah 32:1, the prophet predicts the future messianic reign of Jesus and the righteous leaders he will install into leadership positions. Read Isaiah 32:6–7. How do corrupt leaders function, both then and now? Can you think of specific examples of how these descriptions are playing out now in the world?

3. As you think about your own life, what are some "false saviors" you are sometimes tempted to trust? Why do you think this is? What is it about those things/people that make them appear to be a valid savior?

4. As you think about the potential "false saviors" in your own life, how should God be the one to fill the void or meet the need that those things appear to fill or meet for you? For example, for people tempted to believe that fame would provide genuine status and infuse life with meaning, it would be important to recognize that when God saved them and made them his children, this infused them with the greatest status available to anyone. Knowing that the King of Kings and Lord of Lords affirms them as his beloved friend and child should do far more for their sense of importance and value than the accolades of men.

---

10 https://www.greenprophet.com/2015/03/judean-desert-goes-spectacularly-green-in-wake-of-winter-storms-photos.

FOR FURTHER READING

For a more in-depth explanation about stronghold busters, the Stronghold Buster Seminar notes are available at https://www.ficm.org/wp-content/uploads/2021/03/2021-StrongholdBuster-1.pdf.

Isaiah 33:1–24

EXEGETICAL IDEA
In answer to prayer, the Lord will deliver and restore his favor to the covenant community, but only those who fear him and pursue righteousness will experience his blessings.

THEOLOGICAL FOCUS
The Lord, the mighty warrior-king, demonstrates his enduring commitment to those within the covenant community who fear and obey him.

PREACHING IDEA
God delivers those who appeal to him alone in faith based on his grace.

PREACHING POINTERS
People are naturally proud and want to be independent whenever possible. From an early age, children will often resist help from their parents, insisting they can do it themselves. Adults similarly take pride in their own work, especially when they can complete a task that most would have had to hire somebody else to do. Unfortunately, many people assume this same do-it-yourself, confident spirit of independence when it comes to things for which God has instructed us to trust in him alone. It is one thing to repair your own automobile or teach yourself to play a musical instrument without the help of a mechanic, tutor, or coach. It is altogether different when a person attempts to secure their own salvation apart from the Lord.

In Isaiah's time, this passage served to confirm God's gracious willingness to deliver his people from the threat of their enemy, the Assyrian king. However, Isaiah 33 becomes an ideal passage to preach about God's salvation from sin generally. In the same way that Hezekiah and the inhabitants of Jerusalem thought they could accomplish their own salvation apart from God, so too people throughout history have tried to accomplish their salvation on their own, usually through some form of moralism or good works. However, humans are utterly incapable of saving themselves from God's coming wrath against sin. It is only when people appeal to God alone in faith based on his grace that they will discover him to be their great deliverer.

THE MIGHTY WARRIOR-KING DELIVERS ZION
(33:1–24)

In response to their prayer for help, the Lord will come as a mighty warrior-king and deliver his people from their enemies. He will restore his favor to the covenant community, but only those who fear him and pursue a righteous lifestyle will experience his blessings.

LITERARY STRUCTURE AND THEMES (33:1–24)

This next panel within chapters 28–33 begins with a woe oracle against Zion's enemies (33:1). A prayer then appears (33:2–4), which contains a communal petition for the Lord to intervene and deliver (33:2), a declaration of confidence that the Lord will defeat the threatening nations (33:3), and a taunt against the fleeing enemies (33:4). Addressing the community, the prophet praises the Lord and gives assurance to those who fear him (33:5–6). A lament over the present situation, which prompted the earlier petition (33:2), takes us back to where this subunit began (33:7–9).

In response to the prayer, the Lord announces he will intervene against the enemy (33:10–13), whom he taunts (33:11). In 33:14–16 it is not clear if the Lord or the prophet is speaking. The Lord is still speaking in 33:13 (note "what I have done" and "acknowledge my power"), so these verses could be a continuation of the oracle. However, in these verses the speaker makes it clear only the righteous will benefit from the Lord's powerful intervention. This sounds like a continuation of the prophet's words in 33:6b, where he emphasizes the importance of fearing the Lord. Consequently, it is preferable to understand 33:14–16 as the prophet's response to the divine oracle and as the introduction to his announcement of salvation in 33:17–24. It seems clear the prophet is speaking in 33:17–24, addressing the community and then speaking on their behalf. He refers to the Lord in the third person in 33:21–22. The referent of "king" in 33:17 may be the Lord, since he is called "our king" in 33:22.

- *Impending Doom for the Enemy (33:1)*
- *Seeking Deliverance (33:2–9)*
- *Deliverance Is Coming (33:10–24)*

EXPOSITION (33:1–24)

Impending Doom for the Enemy (33:1)
The Lord will judge the enemies of his people.

33:1. Like the preceding panels, this panel begins with a woe oracle. However, this time it is directed at the enemy of the Lord's people, designated somewhat vaguely as "a destroyer" and "betrayer" (cf. 21:2). In 33:3, this enemy is identified as "nations," but in this context one naturally thinks of Assyria (cf. 30:31; 31:8; see Seitz 1993, 234–35). Though "nations" sounds quite general, it could reflect the fact that by the second half of the eighth century B.C. the Assyrian army included conscripts from several conquered nations (Seevers 2013, 216). When one faced the Assyrian hordes, one faced "nations," assembled under the Assyrian banner (see comments above on 17:12–14; and 30:27–33).

The designations "destroyer" and "betrayer" highlight the violence perpetrated by the enemy, as well as its unreliable character. The term בָּנַד, "betray," does not refer simply to deceit but to deceit in violation of a relationship of trust (see Wakely 1997, 582–95). In this context, treaty violations may be in view (cf. 33:8), but it is difficult to be more specific than this. If Assyria is in view, the treachery may be in relation to the Lord, for the Assyrians exceeded the bounds placed upon them by the Lord (cf. 10:5–15; see Erlandsson 1974, 473). Or perhaps this refers to Sennacherib's refusal to leave Judah, even after Hezekiah had paid him tribute (2 Kings 18:13–25). (See Motyer 1993, 263. For a helpful discussion of the chronological issues that complicate a reading of 2 Kings 18, see Roberts 2015, 425.) In any case, the enemy had not yet been the victim of violence and treachery, but that was about to change. When they had finished destroying and betraying, they in turn would be destroyed and betrayed. The talionic, retributive nature of the judgment is evident in the verbal repetition (Miller 1982, 58–59).

Seeking Deliverance (33:2–9)
The people lament their circumstances and look to the Lord for deliverance.

33:2. The people speak, petitioning the Lord to intervene on their behalf. They ask to receive his favor, pointing out that they are waiting for him. Their prayer sounds like a response to Isaiah's description of the Lord in Isaiah 30:18, where the prophet depicts him as ready to extend his favor to those who wait for him in faith. In 30:19 he emphasizes the Lord will indeed extend favor when he hears their cry for help. In this case, divine favor entails a show of strength, viewed metaphorically as an arm. The people ask the Lord to be their source of strength each morning and their source of deliverance in the time of distress.

33:3–4. They declare their confidence in the Lord's ability to rout the attacking nations (33:3). Speaking rhetorically from a vantage point following the Lord's intervention in response to their prayer, they declare that the nations have fled and scattered. The reason for the enemy's panic is the loud noise produced by the Lord himself as he reveals his majesty. The people then taunt the defeated nations, who are deprived of the plunder they accumulated (33:4). Others descend like swarms of locusts on their plunder and devour it.

33:5. Isaiah declares the Lord is exalted (cf. 2:11, 17), for he dwells in a high place (33:5a), a reference to his heavenly sanctuary (cf. Ps. 102:19 [HB 20]). Speaking from a vantage point beyond the Lord's deliverance of Zion, the prophet observes the Lord has filled (perfect of certitude) Zion with justice and righteousness (Isa. 33:5b, cf. 28:17; 32:16).

33:6. Looking ahead, he states the Lord will be (note the *weqatal* verb form) the community's source of stability (33:6a). The text reads literally, "he will be the steadiness of your times." The noun אֱמוּנָה, "faithfulness," has the primary meaning "steadiness" (cf. Exod. 17:12). Here it refers by metonymy to the Lord as the source of the community's steadiness, or stability. The prophet further identifies the Lord as "a rich store of salvation" (literally, "a treasure of acts of salvation"), as well as "wisdom and knowledge." The noun חֹסֶן, "treasure," is used of a stockpile of riches (cf. Prov. 15:6; 27:24; Jer. 20:5; Ezek. 22:25). Here the riches are, metaphorically speaking, the Lord's acts of deliverance (יְשׁוּעוֹת). He is also the community's source of wisdom and knowledge, which are evidence of his favor (Eccl. 2:26).

However, not just anyone experiences the stability and wisdom the Lord provides. To access the Lord's treasure, one must fear him (Isa. 33:6b). A different word for "treasure" is used here (אוֹצָר), but אוֹצָר and חֹסֶן are closely associated elsewhere (cf. Jer. 20:5). The fear of the Lord *is* the Lord's treasure in the sense that it is the means to access the treasure the Lord makes available. The "fear of the LORD" refers here to a respect for the Lord's authority that motivates one to obey him (see Isa. 11:2–3, as well as Pss. 34:11 [HB 12]; 111:10; Prov. 1:7, 29; 2:5;

8:13; 9:10; 16:6; 23:17; cf. Isa. 50:10). As Proverbs 1:7 teaches, this fear is the starting point for attaining genuine wisdom, which in turn brings stability and prosperity. Isaiah borrows from the wisdom tradition here, making it clear that God opens his treasure house of wisdom to those who fear (obey) him.

33:7–8. We now hear the lament that accompanies the earlier petition (Isa. 33:2). It gives a detailed account of why divine intervention is so needed. The sound of weeping is heard in the streets (33:7). It comes from messengers sent on peace missions. The background is unclear. Perhaps these are messengers sent to negotiate peace with an invading army (one thinks of the Assyrians in 701 B.C.), only to have failed in their mission (see Kaiser 1974, 345). Highways are deserted, suggesting there is danger (33:8a). This may reflect societal lawlessness, or it may be because an invading army has overrun the land, making travel risky and unwise (Oswalt 1986, 596; Smith 2007, 555; Young 1969, 411).

Isaiah 33:8b goes deeper than the descriptive language of 33:7–8a and gets to the core of the problem. A covenant has been broken. This could refer to a period of societal lawlessness, where people think nothing of breaking agreements. Another option is that this reflects the same situation as in 33:1, which denounces a destroyer and betrayer (probably the Assyrians). The broken covenant could refer to Sennacherib's refusal to withdraw from Judah once Hezekiah had paid him tribute (cf. 2 Kings 18:13–16; see Smith 2007, 555; Oswalt 1986, 596; Young 1969, 412).

How one interprets this breach of covenant will determine how one understands the next statement. If Sennacherib's invasion is the background, then one can retain the reading, "he has despised cities" (see Young 1969, 412 n. 18). However, if societal lawlessness is in view, it may be better to read "witnesses" (עֵדִים) for "cities" (עָרִים), as 1QIs^a does. In this case, a breakdown of the legal system has occurred, where agreements are violated and witnesses dismissed with disdain. In any event, a lack of regard for one's fellow human beings is evident.

33:9. The land itself appears to be shriveling up. It has dried up and withered. Personified Lebanon, which was famous for its forests and cedars, looks ashamed and is blackened with rot. The fertile plain of Sharon (cf. 35:2), located on the Mediterranean coast between Carmel to the north and the Yarkon River to the south, is dry like the desert. Bashan to the east and Carmel to the west, both well-known for their trees and vegetation (cf. 2:13; 35:2), look as if they are shaking off their leaves, as it were. The reality behind this scene is not entirely clear. Some see the language as metaphorical, reflecting the people's response to the Assyrians' presence and/or the actual devastation of the land (Clements 1980, 267; Oswalt 1986, 597; Roberts 2015, 427; Smith 2007, 555–56; Young 1969, 412–13). The picture of land and trees drying up appears to depict the effects of a drought (cf. 32:10–13; see Wildberger 2002, 284). If this is literally the case, this portrait of nature shriveling up suggests an accursed condition that is a harbinger of judgment to come (cf. 32:14; see also 24:4–13).

Deliverance Is Coming (33:10–24)
In response to the people's lament, the Lord will deliver them and make them secure.

33:10. In response to the people's lament, the Lord declares he will "arise," implying he will intervene on their behalf (33:10a; cf. Ps. 12:6 [Eng. 5], as well as Isa. 2:19, 21; 28:21). He reiterates his intention to get involved: "I will exalt myself and lift myself up" (literal translation; 33:10b). In Psalm 94:2 the psalmist implores the Lord, "lift yourself up" as he addresses the Lord as "Judge" and asks him to repay the proud for their evil deeds. This same notion of arising for judgment is present in Isaiah 33:10, as the following verses make clear.

33:11. Though the addressee is not specified in 33:11, it is likely the Lord (who is still speaking in 33:13) speaks here to the objects of his judgment, identified in 33:12 as the "peoples" (i.e., the hostile nations, cf. 33:3). He taunts them, comparing their plans to conceiving chaff and their actions to giving birth to straw (33:11a). Conceiving corresponds to their plans and giving birth to their attempts to implement those plans (see Young 1969, 414). He then compares their breath to a fire that will consume them (33:11b). The imagery suggests self-destruction. The fire from their own mouths ends up consuming their plans and efforts.

> **Hostile Nations**
> Smith (2007, 557) disagrees (see also Wildberger 2002, 286). He proposes that the people of Jerusalem/Judah are addressed in 33:11. Their efforts at self-preservation will prove unsuccessful. Isaiah 33:12 then describes the destruction of the Assyrians by the Lord, who proves to be the only source of genuine security. Smith emphasizes the switch from second person (33:11) to third person (33:12) to support seeing different referents. However, it is possible the Lord taunts the enemy (33:11) before turning to his people (33:12) and assuring them that the enemy will be destroyed when he arises in response to their prayer (33:2) and lament (33:7–9).

33:12. Isaiah 33:12 makes the self-destruction clear, as it pictures the hostile nations being burned to ashes and consumed by fire as thoroughly and quickly as if they were thorn bushes cut down for kindling. This differs from the earlier portrait of the Lord destroying the hostile nations with fire (29:6–7; 30:27–33). But, as Kaiser (1974, 346) observes, "there is no question as to who will bring this about." The Lord is the ultimate cause of their demise.

33:13. The Lord next addresses both those who are far off and those who are near. He urges those who are far off to hear about what he has done (33:13a). This implies his victory over the enemy will be so impressive that the news will travel to distant lands. He urges those who are near to acknowledge (literally, "know") his power (33:13b), which is evident in the judgment they have seen.

33:14. As noted above, it is not clear if the Lord or the prophet is speaking in 33:14–16. The thematic parallel with 33:6 makes the prophet a likely choice. He responds to the preceding oracle of salvation by first describing the reaction of sinners to the Lord's powerful intervention against his enemies. As the hostile nations go up in flames (cf. 33:12), the sinners in Zion do not celebrate. Instead, they are terrified (33:14a) and ask who can possibly dwell with such consuming, unquenchable (literally, enduring) fire (33:14b). They do not see fire as the Lord's instrument of deliverance, but instead as a threat to their very existence (Oswalt 1986, 599). Their words speak volumes, for it is apparent they feel alienated from God.

33:15–16. Their questions, which are probably intended as rhetorical, really do have a better answer than the expected "no one." A certain type of person can dwell safely with the God whose fire destroys the wicked. Earlier the prophet stated that the Lord gives genuine security to those who fear him (33:6). Here he unpacks this. The one who dwells with the Lord lives a righteous life and speaks uprightly (33:15a). He refuses to profit from dishonest gain, including bribes. He wants nothing to do with plots to murder or harm others (33:15b). This is the kind of person who lives in the heights and finds safety in mountain strongholds (33:16a). The language is metaphorical, depicting safety and security. The righteous will have all the food and water they need to sustain themselves (33:16b). Within the framework of the metaphor, one might legitimately ask, "Where would one find food and water in the heights and mountain strongholds?" The implication is that the Lord himself will provide for their needs.

The speaker's response (33:15–16) to the sinners' questions (33:14) resembles the so-called entrance liturgies of Psalms 15:1–5 and 24:3–6. In both instances the question focuses on who is given access to the Lord. The reply gives the moral and ethical qualifications, followed by an assertion that such people find security.

33:17–19. The prophet now addresses the righteous within the covenant community as a collective unity (cf. Isa. 33:6; see Young 1969, 421). He assures them their eyes will see a "king in his beauty" (33:17a). Initially, one thinks of the ideal Davidic ruler envisioned earlier (cf. Isa. 9:6–7; 11:1–9; 16:5; 32:1). However, in 33:22 the prophet, speaking for the community, affirms: "The Lord is our king" (cf. 6:5), making it possible that the Lord is the referent in 33:17 (cf. Irwin 1977, 153; Kaiser 1974, 347; Roberts 2015, 429; Smith 2007, 561; Wildberger 2002, 300–301). Applied to a king, the term "beauty" (cf. בְּיָפְיוֹ "in his beauty") probably refers to his royal splendor, as in Psalm 45:2 [HB 3], which attributes this quality to the Davidic king (the verb יָפָה appears there). Perhaps Isaiah 33:17 focuses on the ideal Davidic king (cf. 32:1), whose "splendor" can be seen with the eyes, while 33:22 is a reminder that ultimately the Lord is the king under whose authority the human king rules (cf. 6:5, cf. Young 1969, 421).

Beyond the coming judgment and deliverance, when the Lord establishes his rule through an ideal Davidic king, the people would also see "a land that stretches afar" (33:17b; literally, "a land of distances"). The invading Assyrians had overrun and taken control of the land, restricting travel (cf. 33:8) and hemming in the residents of Jerusalem. But now Judah would have extensive territory, because the Assyrians would be long gone (33:18–19; see Smith 2007, 561; Young 1969, 422). The people would recall how the Assyrians dominated their land, striking terror into their hearts. But now there would be no Assyrian officials calculating and collecting taxes (33:18). The people would no longer have to listen to an incomprehensible foreign tongue (33:19) as a reminder of God's judgment (cf. 28:11).

33:20–22. Speaking on behalf of the people, the prophet urges the community to look at Zion, a city where religious festivals are held (33:20a). With the Assyrian menace gone, the city is peaceful and secure, like a tent solidly anchored with stakes and ropes (33:20b). The reason for this is simple—the Lord's powerful presence (33:21a). The text reads literally, "Instead there (as) a mighty one the Lord (will be) for us." The title "Mighty One" (אַדִּיר) focuses on the Lord's royal majesty and power. Elsewhere the adjective modifies the waters of the sea (Exod. 15:10; Ps. 93:4), tall trees (Ezek. 17:23; Zech. 11:2), gods (1 Sam. 4:8; from the perspective of the Philistines), and kings (Ps. 136:18). The author of Psalm 8 declares the Lord's very name is majestic (8:1, 9 [HB 2, 10]), while Psalm 93:4 affirms his sovereignty over his enemies, symbolized by the raging waters of the sea. Some detect the title in Isaiah 10:34, where one could translate, "Lebanon will fall by (the agency of) the Mighty One." However, another option is to translate, "Lebanon [symbolizing Assyria] will fall as a mighty one." (See the commentary on 10:34 above.)

The prophet uses a metaphor to depict the stability the Lord will provide the city (33:20b). He pictures the city as a place where wide streams and rivers flow (cf. Ps. 46:4 [HB 5]). Water, so essential for life, is abundant. But one might think this will make the city vulnerable to attack; invaders could sail their ships right into the city via the broad rivers. But such attacks, if made at all, will not succeed, for the Lord will deliver the city (Isa. 33:22). Though the ships are envisioned as mighty (אַדִּיר), the presence of the

Lord, the Mighty One (אַדִּיר), will keep the city safe (cf. Ps. 48:7 [HB 8]; see Young 1969, 425).

Speaking for the people, the prophet describes the Lord as "our judge," "our lawgiver," and "our king" (Isa. 33:22). The first title depicts the Lord in a royal role. Kings could be called "judges" because they were responsible for making laws and maintaining justice in the courts (cf. 2 Sam. 15:4; 2 Kings 15:5; Prov. 29:14; Isa. 16:5; Mic. 5:1). The Lord is the judge of the whole earth who promotes justice within his dominion (Gen. 18:25; Judg. 11:27; Pss. 7:11 [HB 12]; 9:4 [HB 5]; 50:6; 75:7 [HB 8]; 94:2; Jer. 11:20). According to Isaiah 33:22, the Lord will, in his capacity as judge, defend his people's interests by delivering them from the foreigners who had oppressed them (cf. 33:18–19). The second title, "lawgiver," is related to the first. Ideally kings are to be wise and enact just laws (Prov. 8:15), but the civil authorities in Isaiah's day were morally corrupt and made unjust laws that were oppressive to the people (Isa. 10:1). However, the prophet envisioned a day when the Lord himself will rule over his people and issue just decrees. The third title, "king," is more general. It is in his role of king that the Lord promotes justice, the focus of the first two titles.

33:23. The prophet, rather abruptly, seems to address a ship, using a second-person feminine singular pronoun. This ship's rigging (literally, ropes) is slack, the sailors do not secure the mast, and they have not unfurled the sail (or perhaps the identifying flag). But what is the reality behind the imagery and how does it fit the context? Since a ship seems to be mentioned, perhaps the imagery should be understood in light of 33:21 where the prophet, speaking within a highly metaphorical framework, says enemy ships will not sail on Jerusalem's wide rivers. Perhaps here he addresses one of these hypothetical ships and depicts it as unable to sail (see Holmyard 1995, 273–78). In this case, 33:23b may refer to the looting of this vessel, presumably by the group referred to in 33:24 (the Lord's forgiven people, it would seem; see Kaiser 1974, 349; Roberts 2015, 430). However, the terms used for a ship in 33:21 are both masculine forms (אֳנִי and צִי), so it seems odd the prophet would address the ship as feminine in this context.

If enemies and/or nations are in view, then one expects a masculine form, whether singular (cf. 33:1) or plural (33:4, 11, 13a). Likewise, if the Lord's people are addressed, one expects a masculine form, either singular (for the collective community; see 33:6, 17–18, 20) or plural (addressed as an entity comprised of many individuals; see 33:13b).

The most likely antecedent for the second-person feminine singular form is Zion, mentioned in 33:20. In this case the prophet, playing off the nautical image of 33:21, depicts Zion as an unprepared ship. If so, 33:23b could depict a reversal in Zion's situation; she now loots her enemy (Motyer 1993, 268; Young 1969, 426). But it could also picture Zion, like a vulnerable ship that cannot sail, being looted by an enemy.

33:24. In any case, the condition of the city is viewed positively in 33:24. A resident (שֹׁכֵן; either a representative or collective singular) will not complain of illness. The people who live in the city (note the feminine singular pronominal suffix on בָּהּ, "in it") will experience forgiveness of sin. The idiom נָשָׂא עָוֹן, "lift up sin," often means to "incur, bear guilt," but it can also mean "remove, forgive sin," as it does here. In its theological creed Israel affirmed the Lord was by nature a forgiving God (Exod. 34:7; Num. 14:18; Mic. 7:18). Both individuals and the nation sought and received divine forgiveness (Pss. 32:5; 85:2 [HB 3]; Hos. 14:3). Based on the use of the idiom used here (which does not exhaust the semantic field for forgiveness in the Hebrew Bible), forgiveness sometimes means God removes, at least in part, the present and seemingly lasting consequences of past sins (Hos. 14:2; Mic. 7:18–19), no longer holds the offenders accountable for those past transgressions (Ps. 32:5 [cf. 32:1]), and restores them to renewed fellowship (Ps. 85:2 [HB 3; cf. 85:1 (HB 2)]).

> **Renewed Fellowship**
> At other times, God's forgiveness means he gives an offender a "reduced sentence." For example, the reference to forgiveness in Exodus 34:7 may allude to the events recorded in Exodus 32, where God relents from bringing the full consequences he had threatened, but nevertheless still severely punishes the primary offenders. Likewise, in Numbers 14:13–19 Moses asks the Lord to forgive the people for their rebellion (14:1–12). The Lord forgives them (14:20) in the sense that he does not totally and immediately destroy them as he threatened (14:12, 15). However, the Lord still severely punishes them for their actions by prohibiting them from entering the Promised Land (14:21–35).

THEOLOGICAL FOCUS

The theological focus of this passage can be stated as follows: the Lord, the mighty warrior-king, demonstrates his enduring commitment to those within the covenant community who fear and obey him. As the prophet develops this theological theme, the following emphases emerge:

1. The Lord's responsiveness to his people

In the face of the grave danger posed by the hostile nations, the people ask the Lord to show them his favor by saving them (Isa. 33:2). He responds to their plea, announcing he will intervene on their behalf (33:10). His willingness to save them is grounded in his royal justice, which prompts him to defend his subjects from those who would betray and destroy them (33:22; cf. 33:1).

2. The recipients of divine favor

The Lord is a just king who is determined to establish justice as foundational in his covenant community (33:5, 22). He will make his people secure, but there are conditions that must be met to become a recipient of his favor. Only those who fear the Lord will experience the security he promises (33:6). The sinners among his people, like the Lord's enemies, are rightly terrified of his fiery anger (33:14, cf. 33:3). But the righteous, who live in accordance with the just king's moral and ethical standards (33:15), find him to be a place of refuge (33:16)—which encompasses, in part, forgiveness of sin (33:24).

PREACHING AND TEACHING STRATEGIES

Exegetical and Theological Synthesis

What goes around comes around. Isaiah 33:1 begins with Isaiah's prediction that the Assyrian king would be betrayed and destroyed. The one who destroyed so many others, and who betrayed Judah after he agreed to leave them alone when they paid him a large sum of money, would himself be betrayed and destroyed (cf. Isa. 37:37–38).

This is followed by the people's prayer for God to deliver them from the coming crisis. It is particularly important to note that their request to God for his salvation is based on God's grace, not their own merit (33:2). Their prayer goes on to affirm their complete faith and confidence in him as they commit to wait for him to act (33:2). They believe that the Lord's voice will scatter their enemies before them (33:3–4) and that he will save them (33:6), filling Jerusalem with justice and righteousness (33:5).

In 33:7–9 the people express their desperation for God to come to their aid. Their own efforts to bring about their salvation apart from him have failed. The envoys of peace sent to negotiate with Sennacherib have returned dejected after the Assyrian king double-crossed them. In fear, the citizens of Jerusalem remain hidden within the city walls, leaving the outer streets and highways abandoned (33:8). The once fertile regions of Lebanon and Sharon have become like deserts—a metaphor describing how bleak things now appear to be in Judah (33:9).

Even though Judah is only now turning to the Lord as a last resort after their own efforts have failed, he nonetheless responds with the assurance of his salvation. Speaking in the first person, he taunts Judah's enemies with the news that he will be exalted over them (33:10). Their efforts to conquer and harm his people are like giving birth to chaff or stubble that will be burned up by their own breath (33:11–12). The metaphorical language in 33:11–12 likening God's judgment against Assyria to a consuming fire takes on a more worldwide tone in 33:13–14. Not only are the nations who make up the Assyrian army in view now, but all "sinners" and all who are "godless" tremble at the prospect of coming, fiery judgment. This even includes the unrepentant among the people of Zion (33:14). The prophet asks, "Who of *us* can dwell with the consuming fire" (emphasis added) or "dwell with everlasting burning?" The fire here correlates to God's holiness that will consume all sin and wickedness in judgment. In an indirect sense, the imagery here would similarly point to the realities of hell, the place of eternal judgment and torment reserved for unrepentant sinners.

In 33:15, the prophet answers the question he posed in 33:14. Who is it that can dwell with the consuming fire of God's holiness? It is the person who has repented of sin. As such, he lives righteously, refusing to participate in the oppression of the weak and vulnerable in order that he might profit financially. This person will dwell securely and will have his needs met by the Lord (33:16). That the promise in 33:16 would be realized in the coming resurrection (cf. Isa. 25:6–12; 26:19) and kingdom is made clear in the remainder of this chapter. The poetic descriptions in 33:17–24 anticipate the coming messianic kingdom.

These verses describe a literal place where the righteous followers of God would one day dwell. Four times the author explicitly describes things that people there will see with their eyes. First, their "eyes will see the king in his beauty" (33:17a). Hands down, the greatest aspect of heaven will be seeing Jesus, our creator, savior, and righteous king, face-to-face. Second, "they will view a land that stretches afar" (33:17b). We will enjoy a renewed earth where the curse of sin has been destroyed (cf. Isa. 30:23–25; 32:15–17; 35:1–2, 6–7). Third, the prophet comforts them with what they *won't* see any longer. No more will they see the insolent people (33:19) who oppressed them and whose speech they could not understand (cf. Isa. 28:10–11). As such, they will remember the terrors they felt when foreigners like the Assyrians threatened them with violence and poverty, but now these will all be merely a distant memory (33:18). Finally, the prophet predicts that in that day, their "eyes will see Jerusalem" as "a peaceful abode" (33:20). It is likened to a tent whose stakes will never be pulled up. It will be a place of complete security. There is no longer any reason to worry about what the future might hold. As such, all fear, anxiety, and worry will melt away. The Lord in his majesty will be there as their leader (33:21). The United States Constitution has wisely separated the three branches of government to limit too much power from residing in one person. The country's founders understood that power tends to corrupt human leaders, and ultimate power tends to corrupt absolutely. However, no such separation of power is needed when the ruler is the righteous Messiah, the Son of God. As such, Jesus will function as judge (judicial branch), lawgiver (legislative branch), and king (executive branch; 33:22).

Isaiah 33 concludes by describing the hypothetical enemies of God's people in that day. They will be like a broken-down ship that is unable to mount any sort of attack (33:23). Even a lame person would be able to carry away the spoil from that ship. The imagery here is rhetorical rather than literal, as there will be no lame people in the kingdom (Isa. 35:5–6). In fact, nobody there will even get sick at all (33:24a). Sickness and injuries were byproducts of sin and the resulting curse. However, that curse will be gone. Instead, "the sins of those who dwell there will be forgiven" (33:24b).

Preaching Idea
God delivers those who appeal to him alone in faith based on his grace.

Contemporary Connections

What does it mean?
Throughout the past five chapters (Isa. 28–32), the prophet confronted Judah for rejecting the Lord's admonition to trust in him alone (Isa. 28:16; 30:15, 18–19; 31:1). Instead, they had chosen to enter a costly covenant with Egypt in hopes that Egypt's military would deter the Assyrians against a military campaign into Jerusalem (Isa. 28:15; 30:1–2, 16; 31:1). But God had warned them that this covenant would not prove to be advantageous, as Egypt was entirely unable to do for them what only God could do (Isa. 28:18–20; 30:3–7; 31:4–5); he alone has the power to save. In Isaiah 33, it appears that the people of Judah have finally stopped trying to achieve their own salvation on their own terms. After Egypt proved to be an impotent partner (as God predicted), Judah tried one last-ditch effort to accomplish their salvation without God. In desperation, they attempted to pay off Sennacherib, king of Assyria, with the rest of their gold and silver (2 Kings 18:13–16). However, this too proved to be foolish and pointless, as Sennacherib accepted their ransom payment but then immediately betrayed their trust (Isa. 33:1, 7–8), sending his army to Jerusalem to demand their surrender (2 Kings 18:17–35). When it became clear that all of Judah's efforts to save itself had failed, they finally called out to the Lord in desperation (Isa. 33:2–6). In response to their prayer, the Lord graciously promised to save them from the Assyrians.

In its original context, this passage served to confirm God's gracious willingness to deliver his people from the threat of their geopolitical enemy, the Assyrian king. However, much of the passage takes on a more worldwide and eschatological tone as it predicts a time in the distant future when people would see the ideal, messianic king in all his beauty (33:17). It likewise describes the messianic kingdom as the ultimate hope for all of God's redeemed who place their trust in him alone (33:17–24). Furthermore, while the chapter begins with a "woe" against the king of Assyria (the likely referent of the "destroyer"), the prophet shifts gears in the middle of the chapter to indict all sinners, including those among the inhabitants of Zion (33:14). Thus, the objects of God's judgment in this passage are all sinners, not just the wicked Assyrians. Finally, the chapter ends with the timeless promise for all of God's redeemed that they will be forgiven for all their iniquities (33:24). Thus, modern preachers can correlate the principles from this passage related to God's salvation of Judah from Assyria in the eighth century B.C. to God's salvation of all who call on him through the work of Jesus on the cross.

Is it true?
A study of how the New Testament authors interpreted or used many of the Old Testament stories and prophecies shows it is appropriate to read the Old Testament through a typological lens, where historical people or events anticipate or point to future realities. This is especially true as it relates to stories that connect to the theme of God as a great deliverer or savior. Consider, for example, the story of Noah's ark from Genesis 6–8. The apostle Peter interprets this story as a type that pointed to New Testament believers' salvation from sin and eternal judgment. In 1 Peter 3, he specifically draws a connection between the waters of baptism and the flood waters of that day. The ESV translates 1 Peter 3:21, "Baptism, *which corresponds* to this" (emphasis added). "Which corresponds" translates the Greek word ἀντίτυπον (antitype), which described how believers' baptism relates to the

deliverance of Noah's family from the flood. In other words, Peter interpreted Noah's flood as a "type" of the waters of baptism whereby the baptismal water serves as a symbol for God's judgment against sin generally. In the same way that the ark provided salvation from that judgment, so too Jesus provides salvation from the coming judgment. As such, the New Testament shows the validity of a modern preacher using the story of Noah's ark to teach about Jesus's salvation of sinners today.

Another example can be found in 1 Corinthians 10:1–6. Paul here connected first-century Christians back to the wilderness generation in Moses's day by way of typology. He wrote that those Old Testament saints "ate the same spiritual food" and "drank the same spiritual drink" as believers today. This is a likely reference to the communion meal, by which Christians symbolize their partaking of the body and blood of Jesus. In the wilderness, they ate manna from heaven as their food (cf. John 6:31–35, 41–42, 47–58) and drank water from a rock that miraculously gushed water (Exod. 17:1–7). Paul makes the bold claim that this rock was Christ (1 Cor. 10:4). In what sense should that rock be identified as Jesus Christ? The answer is found in 10:6, which says, "Now these things occurred as examples to keep us from setting our hearts on evil things as they did." The Greek behind this translation says, ταῦτα δὲ τύποι ἡμῶν ἐγενήθησαν, literally, "But these happened as *types* [τύποι] for us" (emphasis added). In other words, Paul interpreted the exodus event and the wilderness wandering typologically as pointing to greater realities that were ultimately fulfilled in Jesus.

These examples should sufficiently demonstrate the appropriateness of reading Old Testament stories with an eye that looks for types. Just as it was acceptable for Peter and Paul to use stories that display God's salvation in the Old Testament, like Noah's ark and the exodus, to teach about his salvation of sinners through Jesus's death on the cross, so too modern readers shouldn't shy away from making similar connections between the story of Judah's miraculous salvation from Assyria in Isaiah 33–37 and our own salvation in Jesus. While a preacher may want to avoid referring to various elements in Isaiah 33 as "types" in the formal sense, the passage does lend itself to a typological treatment. As referenced above, the passage seems to intentionally point beyond the immediate situation to a more worldwide experience of sin, judgment, and salvation. These elements include:

- an indictment of all sinners, not just those in the immediate context (33:14).
- a promise of salvation based on God's grace through faith (33:2, 6, 10, 22).
- the futility of human effort to acquire or earn one's salvation (33:1, 7; cf. 28:15–19; 30:3–7).
- the eternal fiery judgment that will consume God's adversaries (33:11–12, 14).
- the future kingdom that awaits all the redeemed (33:17–24).
- all the redeemed being forgiven for their sins (33:24).

Now what?

This passage provides the preacher with an ideal opportunity to proclaim the plan of salvation. One may want to expound upon the contrasting destinations of heaven and hell for believers and nonbelievers, respectively. The preacher may want to incorporate some of the more than 160 references to hell in the New Testament. Isaiah 33:17–24, on the other hand, provides a rich description of the coming messianic kingdom of heaven. This provides an ideal opportunity for the preacher to lay out a biblical theology of heaven.[1]

---

[1] For a thorough treatment on the biblical promises of heaven and how many of those descriptions anticipate an earthly fulfillment, see Randy Alcorn, *Heaven* (2004).

The Mighty Warrior-King Delivers Zion (33:1–24)

This passage also gives insight into the nature of God's grace. It is amazing to consider that God sent his prophets to the people of Judah urging them to simply trust in him in exchange for his protection and salvation. And yet his people repeatedly rejected his kind offers to help them. Ahaz rejected God's deliverance from the Syrian-Israelite coalition. Instead, he opted for an alliance with Assyria (Isa. 7:1–13). Hezekiah spurned God's gracious invitation to trust him for salvation, choosing instead to rely on Egypt. It is only after every possible option had failed them that God's people finally looked to him in faith. They literally looked at the Lord as their last resort. Nevertheless, God's grace is so amazing that he is willing to save sinners even under those circumstances. The same is true for people today. There are many who heard about God as children growing up in church who choose to reject him and pursue their own sinful lusts. For some, it wasn't until after they tried everything but God, discovering that none of it truly satisfies or fulfills, that they finally turned to him in repentance and faith. God's mercy extends even to those individuals.

Lee Strobel is a well-known Christian author and apologist. But before he came to be a follower of Christ, he was an ardent skeptic. In fact, Strobel was an atheist journalist who thought the idea of an all-knowing, all-loving God was just plain stupid. One day his formerly agnostic wife told him that she had accepted Jesus as her savior. For Lee, this was the worst possible news. He was afraid of what this new belief system would do to her. He began to attend church with her, but not primarily because he was interested in having what she had; instead, he hoped to be able to use his training as a journalist to investigate the biblical claims about Jesus and refute them. He hoped to be able to dissuade his wife from remaining in the "cult" she had joined. However, during his investigations, to his surprise, he began to become convinced of the veracity of the claims about Jesus. After a twenty-one-month investigation, Strobel finally realized that his opposition to God and the gospel was completely unfounded, and he surrendered his life to Jesus.[2] One of the great truths of the gospel is that Jesus is willing to receive even the most ardent of skeptics or the worst of sinners when they simply humble themselves and embrace Jesus as Lord.

Finally, this chapter serves as an opportunity for Christians to celebrate their salvation in Christ. The preacher should challenge his listeners to imagine how fearful and hopeless the inhabitants of Jerusalem must have felt, and invite them to share those same emotions. What must it have been like to see the intimidating army of soldiers on the other side of the city wall, knowing how the Assyrians brutally treated their captives, and realizing that it was only a matter of time until that same fate befell them? The situation for believers was just as hopeless before God's intervention in their lives. An unbeliever's destiny—an eternity separated from God in hell—was an even worse prospect than the one those eighth-century B.C. Judeans faced. Conversely, God's people today should allow themselves to identify with the sense of wonder, joy, and excitement those same people would have experienced the morning they discovered 185,000 dead Assyrian soldiers lying on the ground (Isa. 37:36), the fulfillment of the salvation God promised in Isaiah 33:5–6 and 10–13. The miracle of our own salvation is no less miraculous or special. As such, this is an ideal passage to conclude with a celebration of the Lord's Supper.

---

2   For a succinct video of Strobel sharing his salvation testimony, see https://www.youtube.com/watch?v=E8IE9Y-4wudk. The 2017 movie *The Case for Christ* is similarly based upon the story of how Strobel went from critic to Christian apologist.

The Mighty Warrior-King Delivers Zion (33:1–24)

Creativity in Presentation

Who Can Dwell with the Consuming Fire?
On August 12, 2018, a wildfire raged through Glacier National Park in Montana. Two men, Justin Bilton and his father, attempted to escape by driving through an area where the fire had reached right up to the road on which they were traveling. The father recorded the event on his phone as his son drove. They decided to push forward and attempt to get through the area. Very quickly, though, they found themselves driving right through the middle of a raging forest fire. In the video, hot, burning trees can be seen on both sides of the road. Fear can be heard in the son's voice as he says, "Dad, this is insane! … The car is heating up! It's gonna explode!" He then begins to pray for God to please help them. Near the end of the video, the two drive up to a burning log that has fallen across the road, preventing them from going any further. The video ends with the two men anxiously considering their options. They appear to be trapped with no way out. The father suggests putting on some gloves, getting out of the vehicle, and trying to move the burning tree. Though not shown in the video, the duo ultimately drove in reverse back out of the fire. They were rescued by two park employees who were able to evacuate them in a boat, saving their lives.

This story illustrates the terror and the devastating effects of a consuming fire. Nobody can live amid such conditions. One can only imagine what it will be like for those souls who reject God and end up being cast into the consuming fire of hell. The story also highlights the futility of trying to rescue oneself, as the men briefly consider trying to move the burning log by hand in the middle of a raging forest fire. Finally, the story illustrates the relief one would feel upon being rescued from certain death. The preacher could show a clip from this video if there aren't young children in the room, as it could be traumatic for some.[3]

Testimony of God's Grace
As stated above (under "Now what?") one of the amazing realities of God's grace is his willingness to save anyone, including those who were ardent critics of him. One example of this is the testimony of Jeff Shot. After growing up in a Christian home, Jeff succumbed to the influences of some atheist friends as well as well-known skeptics like Richard Dawkins, Christopher Hitchens, and Sam Harris. Jeff had also become addicted to pornography, which became a motivating factor in his journey away from God. After deciding that he no longer believed in God, he turned instead to a life of hedonism, drugs, and "antitheism." In high school, Jeff even made the news after wearing a controversial, blasphemous costume of Jesus for the school's Fictional Character Day.

Despite his libertine lifestyle, Jeff knew that something was missing. After investigating pagan mythology, Jeff decided to invite Sobek—a hedonistic, Egyptian crocodile god—into his life as his patron deity during an occultic ceremony which he participated in by a creek near his house. Sobek was known as the god "who eats while he also mates." However, this did nothing to improve the emptiness he felt, and he began to speak openly about considering suicide if things didn't improve.

For the first time in years, Jeff decided to reconsider Christianity. He decided to ask God to reveal himself to him. He also began to read his Bible again. Over the next few months, he experienced a series of events that made it certain to him that God was out there and was pursuing him. Finally, in October of 2014, he prayed to receive Christ and asked God to forgive him of his sins. He also realized he needed to renounce Sobek as his patron deity. That night, Jeff had a very intense and vivid dream,

---

[3] The video from this event can be viewed here: https://www.youtube.com/watch?v=yXubO7VPow0.

unlike any he had had before. In his dream he was walking along a river. Suddenly, a large crocodile emerged and began to chase him. He tripped and fell. As he got up and looked behind him, he expected to see the reptile at his heels. Instead, it was retreating frantically into the water. As he got to his feet, he noticed an angelic figure at his side—the one who was evidently responsible for the crocodile's retreat. When he woke up, Jeff was astonished by the obvious symbolism in his dream. God used it to confirm that he had forgiven and accepted him as his son. What an amazing testimony of God's love and grace![4] This story serves to show how God delivers those who appeal to him alone in faith based on his grace.

- A prayer of desperation (33:1–9).
- A promise of salvation (33:10–13).
- The problem of judgment (33:14–19).
- A preview of heaven (33:17–24).

DISCUSSION QUESTIONS

1. What makes Isaiah 33:2 such a powerful prayer?

2. In 33:17–20, how many things will the people "see" in that day? Why is it significant for them to see these things with their own eyes?

3. Consider the various roles of God's kingship, administered through Christ (33:17), mentioned in 33:22. How do they correlate to the three branches of government? What implications does this have for Christ's rule in his coming messianic kingdom? How do these roles relate to the central tenets of the gospel?

4. Read 33:17–24. Consider the various descriptions of the kingdom and discuss the significance of each of them.

FOR FURTHER READING

Alcorn, Randy C. 2004. *Heaven*. Wheaton, IL: Tyndale.

Osborne, Grant R. 2010. "The Old Testament in the New Testament." In *The Hermeneutical Spiral: A Comprehensive Introduction to Biblical Interpretation*, 322–44. Downers Grove, IL: IVP Academic.

---

[4] https://chnetwork.org/story/from-mocking-jesus-to-worshipping-him/.

Isaiah 34:1–35:10

EXEGETICAL IDEA
The Lord's anger ignites devastating judgment, but he will lead the godly home on "the Way of Holiness," transforming the desert and healing the handicapped.

THEOLOGICAL FOCUS
The Lord will punish the hostile nations for mistreating his people; he is committed to restoring his covenant people, but only the godly are allowed to experience the joy of this great transformation.

PREACHING IDEA
God's people should be encouraged by the promise of coming judgment, as it will be a day of both vengeance and salvation.

PREACHING POINTERS
From 2011 to 2014, the National Geographic Channel aired a reality television show called *Doomsday Preppers*. The show featured individuals or families who were so concerned about the possibility of a future catastrophic event that they were devoted toward preparing for that day. The participants expressed fear about different doomsday scenarios such as solar flares or a natural disaster such as an earthquake or meteorite. Others feared a global health pandemic, a nuclear war, or even the eventual effects of global warming. The results, though, looked about the same for each. They attempted to prepare for these potential events by stocking up on food and ammunition, and by making sure they had the knowledge and means to produce their own food, filter clean drinking water, and protect themselves against various threats.

There is much we don't know about the future. Nonetheless, the Bible does warn about a coming doomsday of sorts. However, God will initiate this day. It will be a day of his vengeance and wrath upon the sinful world that has rejected his rule over them. Isaiah 34 describes this event as resulting in great destruction and "slaughter" (34:2, 6) where the mountains are left flowing with human blood as dead corpses lie everywhere (34:3, 7). The luminaries in the sky fall to the earth while the sky rolls up like a scroll (34:4). The streams and soil are turned into burning pitch and sulfur (34:9). This destruction will leave cities and entire civilizations desolate (34:10, 12).

As horrible as this day will be for those who have rejected God, Isaiah 35 describes a wonderful coming day of salvation and transformation for God's people. In fact, the positive effects of this day are described in images that directly contrast with the negative effects upon God's enemies in chapter 34. Together, these chapters warn people to prepare adequately for this coming time.

DEVASTATING JUDGMENT AND TRANSFORMATION (34:1–35:10)

The dominant image of Isaiah 34 is the Lord as warrior, but his justice is the underlying theme, for it is his desire for retribution that prompts him to do battle against the nations, and against Edom in particular. Isaiah 35 focuses on the Lord's transforming power. He comes to deliver and vindicate his people, restore them to their city Zion, and remove all sorrow. As if mirroring this restoration of the covenant community, he transforms the desert and heals the handicapped. But not everyone will participate in this joyful occasion; only the godly will travel the "Way of Holiness." The morally unclean and fools are excluded.

LITERARY STRUCTURE AND THEMES (34:1–35:10)

The announcement of judgment begins with a call to the nations to listen (34:1). Their attention is essential because the Lord is angry with the nations and is ready to destroy their armies (34:2–3). The judgment will have a cosmic scope; the stars in the sky will disappear (34:4).

Though he is not formally introduced, the Lord himself speaks in 34:5. He announces that Edom, the archetype for the hostile nations, will be the focal point of his violent judgment (note חַרְבִּי, "my sword," and חֶרְמִי, literally, "my destruction"). It is not clear if the introductory כִּי is explanatory ("for") or asseverative ("indeed, surely"). If explanatory, then 34:5a should probably be included with 34:4 in the outline (see above). It seems a bit odd, however, that the Lord would break into the prophet's description of judgment and complete the final sentence. If כִּי is asseverative, then 34:5a can be viewed as syntactically independent and as the introduction to the judgment announcement upon Edom. But even so, with its reference to the cosmic judgment announced in 34:4 (note "heavens" in both 34:4 and 5), it is conceptually linked to what precedes and is transitional. In any case, הִנֵּה עַל־אֱדוֹם, "look, upon Edom," sharpens the focus to Edom.

The speech is primarily an announcement of judgment, for there is no clear-cut formal accusation (but see the discussion of 34:8b below). The motif of divine intervention is prominent initially (note 34:5–6, 8), but then gives way to a lengthy description of the effects of judgment (34:9–17).

In the announcement of salvation Isaiah urges the dry regions to rejoice and blossom, for they are about to see the royal splendor of the Lord (35:1–2). He then turns to an unidentified group and urges them to strengthen those who are fearful, for the Lord is coming to vindicate and deliver them (35:3–4).

The prophet next describes the transformation that accompanies the Lord's arrival (35:5–10). This unit begins with a poetic couplet that is introduced with אָז, "then," collocated with an imperfect (35:5). The focus is on transformation in the human realm as the blind and deaf are healed. A second couplet is introduced in the same manner (35:6a), continuing the focus on physical healing. The lame and mute are joyful, but not simply because they have been healed. An explanatory (note כִּי) couplet attributes their joy to witnessing the transformation of the dry regions (35:6b). Starting with a וְהָיָה initiated clause ("and it will be"), the prophet fills out this vision of transformation in more detail (35:7). Isaiah 35:8–9a is juxtaposed structurally. The first clause in 35:8, וְהָיָה־שָׁם מַסְלוּל, "and a highway will be there," refers to a highway that will go through the transformed wilderness. It will be called the "Way of Holiness," for the ungodly and fools are prohibited from using it. Isaiah 35:9a begins with "no lion will be there" (לֹא־יִהְיֶה שָׁם אַרְיֵה) and ends with "and they [literally, it] will not be found there" (לֹא תִמָּצֵא שָׁם). Here the prophet informs us that dangerous predators will not threaten travelers on this highway. The speech ends with a portrait of the redeemed returning to Zion via this way and entering the city with shouts of joy (35:9b–10).

- **Announcement of Judgment (34:1–17)**
  ○ Worldwide, Cosmic Judgment (34:1–4)
  ○ The Lord's Blood-drenched Sword (34:5–17)
- **Announcement of Salvation (35:1–10)**
  ○ The Blossoming of the Desert (35:1–2)
  ○ The Lord's Arrival (35:3–4)
  ○ Transformation (35:5–10)

EXPOSITION (34:1–35:10)

Worldwide, Cosmic Judgment (34:1–4)
The Lord will annihilate the hostile nations.

34:1–2. The prophet calls the nations to draw near to hear his message (34:1a), which is for the whole world and all who live in it (34:1b). It is urgent that they listen, for the Lord is angry with all the nations and has turned his wrath against all their armies (34:2a). Destruction and slaughter await them (34:2b). The verb (*hiphil* חָרַם) translated "totally destroy" in NIV11 (cf. KJV and NASB, "utterly destroyed") often means "put under a ban, devote to destruction," as a religious act of holy war (cf. ESV, "has devoted them to destruction"; HCSB, "will set them apart for destruction"). The prophet's use of perfect verbal forms in 34:2b may suggest he refers to the Lord's decision, made prior to the battle, to devote the objects of his anger to destruction and slaughter (cf. ESV, "he has devoted them to destruction, has given them over to slaughter"). However, the *hiphil* of חָרַם typically describes the actual implementation of destruction (cf. NIV11, "will totally destroy"), not simply the formal decision to do so (see, e.g., Num. 21:2; Deut. 2:34; 3:6; 7:2; 13:16; 20:17; Josh. 2:10; 6:18, 21; 8:26; Judg. 1:17; 21:11; 1 Sam. 15:3, 8). If the event is in view, then the prophet assumes a rhetorical vantage point just beyond the judgment. The perfect verbal forms would emphasize the certitude of the coming judgment (Young 1969, 429). But within this rhetorical framework, the battle must have just ended, for 34:3 depicts its aftermath as still future (note the imperfect and *weqatal* verbal forms).

> **Religious Act of Holy War**
> As Israel prepared for the conquest of the Promised Land, Moses instructed them to exterminate the native populations of the land (Deut. 7:2; 20:17), just as they had destroyed the Amorites living in Transjordan (Deut. 2:34; 3:6; Josh. 2:10). The city of Jericho was put under the "ban" (חֵרֶם, a noun related to the verb חָרַם, that also appears in Isa. 34:5). All living things were to be killed, and the articles of gold, silver, bronze, and iron were to be placed in the Lord's treasury (Josh. 6:17–21). When Achan violated the rules pertaining to the ban, Israel was placed under the ban until the offender, whose deeds had made him liable to destruction, was executed (Josh. 7:1, 11–13). The Jericho incident is just one of several cases where the Lord implemented a ban against an enemy. Others include the following: (1) Numbers 21:2–3 tells how the Israelites, as they approached Arad, made a vow to the Lord to devote to destruction all the Canaanites living in that area in exchange for a victory. (2) Deuteronomy 13:12–18 contains a command that an idolatrous city must be devoted to destruction. All people and livestock must be killed, and all the loot burned along with the city as a whole offering (כָּלִיל) to the Lord, apparently to appease his anger (13:17). (3) Throughout their campaigns in Canaan, the Israelite army under Joshua devoted

the Canaanites and their cities to destruction (Josh. 8:26; 10:1, 28, 35, 37, 39–40; 11:11–12, 20–21). (4) The Lord commanded Saul to put the Amalekites under the ban (1 Sam. 15), a command he only partially obeyed. (5) First Kings 20:42 indicates Yahweh had devoted the Aramean king Ben-hadad to destruction, although in this case the king of Israel did not implement the divine will. (6) Several other prophetic texts, like Isaiah 34:2, 5, speak of the Lord devoting enemy nations to destruction (cf. Jer. 50:21, 26; 51:3; Mic. 4:13; Mal. 4:6 [HB 3:24]). Ironically, the Lord also speaks of subjecting his own people to the ban through the instrumentality of a foreign army (Isa. 43:28; Jer. 25:9), but Zechariah 14:11 envisions a time when he will no longer subject Jerusalem to such judgment. This concept of the ban is also attested in the Moabite Stone (Mesha inscription), where Mesha of Moab boasts that he devoted to his god Chemosh seven thousand Israelite captives (*COS* 2.23:137–38). For a detailed study of the concept of the ban in the Old Testament, see Niditch 1993, 28–77.

34:3. In the aftermath of the Lord's victory over the nations, corpses are left exposed and rotting on the battlefield (Isa. 34:3a). The text reads literally, "their slain will be thrown aside, and their corpses—their stench will ascend." The hills are saturated with their blood (34:3b). The text reads literally, "hills will melt from their blood." The verb מָסַס, "melt," is used elsewhere to describe wax melting into liquid (cf. Pss. 68:2 [HB 3]; 97:5; Mic. 1:4). Here the verb depicts the turf on the hills becoming so soaked with blood (note the causal מִן) that it becomes unstable and erodes, as if being turned into liquid form (cf. Motyer 1993, 270; Young 1969, 430).

34:4. The prophet depicts the judgment as cosmic in scope. The stars in the sky (literally, "the army of the sky") dissolve (literally, "rot"), as the sky rolls up like a scroll (34:4a). The stars wither up, like a leaf on a vine or a fig on a tree that dries up and falls off (34:4b). As noted earlier (see the commentary on 24:21 above), the phrase "army of the sky," (or traditionally, "the host of the heavens") refers elsewhere to the sun, moon, and stars (cf. Deut. 4:19). The heavenly lights were objects of worship in the ancient Near East and, unfortunately, in Israel (cf. Deut. 4:19; 17:13; 2 Kings 17:16; 21:3, 5; 23:4–5; Jer. 19:13; Zeph. 1:5). They are members of God's royal court (1 Kings 22:19; Neh. 9:6) who surround his throne and carry out his will (cf. Isa. 40:26). They are also called "sons of God" (Gen. 6:2, 4; Job 1:6; 2:1; 38:7; Pss. 29:1; 89:6 [HB 7]), "morning stars" (Job 38:7), "stars" (Judg. 5:20), and "holy ones" (Ps. 89:5, 7 [HB 6, 8]). God delegated to them authority over the nations (Deut. 32:8 [LXX]), but many have rebelled against God (see Ps. 82; cf. Gen. 6:1–4; 2 Peter 2:4; Jude 6) and oppose his rule by empowering human kings to disobey him (note "kings on the earth" in Isa. 24:21b; and see Dan. 10:13, 20). The New Testament reveals the identity of their leader as Satan (cf. Rev. 20:2–3). Isaiah 24:21–22 envisions a time of cosmic judgment when a coalition of heavenly and earthly powers are subdued, imprisoned, and executed. In similar fashion, Isaiah 34 depicts God's judgment upon the nations (34:1–3) and the heavenly forces (34:4–5a) that energize their wicked agenda (see Oswalt 1986, 609).

The Lord's Blood-drenched Sword (34:5–17)

The Lord will destroy Edom, which represents the enemies of God and his people.

34:5. As noted above, the Lord speaks in 34:5, though there is no formal introduction. If the introductory כִּי is explanatory ("for"), it indicates formally (not just conceptually) that the devastating work of the sword, now completed, is the reason why the stars will disappear. In this case, the perfect verbal form is best understood as future perfect in function: "for my sword will have drunk its fill in the sky." If one takes כִּי as asseverative, the perfect verbal form probably has a present perfect function: "Indeed, my sword has drunk its fill in the sky." When linked with 34:5b, this suggests the attack upon Edom follows the judgment upon the stars—the Lord's sword, having drunk its fill in the sky, now descends upon Edom to continue its destructive work. Smith (2007, 573) states, "After wielding its destructive power in the heavens, this sword will descend to earth on the representative nation Edom." But one might expect, as in Isaiah 13–27, worldwide, cosmic judgment to be the culmination of divine judgment upon specific nations, not the prelude to it. This might lead one to opt for an explanatory use of כִּי linking 34:5a with what precedes, rather than what follows. However, the use of the verb תֵּרֵד, "will descend," in 34:5b envisions movement of the sword from the sky to the earth (Edom in particular). This means the judgment in the sky is closely linked with the judgment of Edom and precedes it. (This is the case, even if כִּי is explanatory.) Perhaps in such a short literary unit as we have here, one should not expect chronological precision. Judgment in the near future (upon Edom) gets blended with culminating cosmic judgment.

Yet there may be a better explanation. If, as suggested above, the cosmic battle depicted in 34:4–5a refers metaphorically to judgment upon the heavenly powers that undergird the nations, then it is likely that historical judgments (actually, near future from the prophet's perspective), such as the punishment of Edom, have a cosmic dimension as well. This means the judgment on Edom encompasses spiritual forces, including those energizing Edom. For this reason, we need not restrict the worldwide, cosmic judgment described in 34:1–5a to the eschaton. In this regard, Oswalt (1986, 611) observes: "The figure is that when the divine sword has done all it can do to the heavenly host, the pantheon of national gods, then it will fall on the nations themselves as represented by Edom."

With הִנֵּה עַל־אֱדוֹם, "look upon Edom," Edom becomes the focal point of the Lord's judgment. Isaiah 34:2 speaks of the Lord devoting the armies of the nations to destruction (note the *hiphil* of חָרַם; see comment above). Here the related noun form חֵרֶם is applied to the Lord's judgment upon Edom. Isaiah 34:5b reads literally, "Look, upon Edom it [the Lord's sword, see 34:5a] will descend, and upon the people of my ban for judgment." One may paraphrase the second phrase, "even on the people I have devoted to destruction (it will descend) for judgment." Like its related verb, חָרַם, the noun חֵרֶם describes an object that has been put under the "ban"—that is, devoted to destruction by the Lord.

The Edomites were descended from Esau and eventually became enemies of Israel. David conquered Edom (2 Sam. 8:11–14), but the Edomites later freed themselves from Judah's domination (2 Kings 8:20–22). When the Babylonians conquered and destroyed Jerusalem in 586 B.C., the Edomites exploited the situation to their advantage, showing no compassion on Judah's refugees (Ps. 137:7; Lam. 4:21–22; Ezek. 25:12–14; 35:1–15; 36:5; Obad. 10–14). According to the Old Testament prophets, Edom will be an object of God's angry judgment (Isa. 63:1–6; Jer. 49:7–22; Ezek. 25:12–14; 32:29; 35:1–15; Amos 1:11–12; 9:12; Obad. 1). By the time of Malachi (fifth century B.C.) these prophecies were realized, at least in part (Mal. 1:2–4). Understandably, the focus on Edom leads some to conclude Isaiah 34 was written around the time of the Babylonian exile, when so many other prophets denounce Edom for its hostility to Judah and Jerusalem. In this regard, it is noteworthy that Isaiah's oracles against the nations exclude Edom (though Seir is mentioned briefly in 21:11). However, hostility between Edom and Israel began early on (Num. 20:14–21) and persisted throughout Israel's history (see Motyer 1993, 268–69). Ezekiel 35:10, though dating to the time of the exile, alludes to Edomite hostility against "two nations," referring to both Israel and Judah. This encompasses earlier historical periods, as well as the Edomite hostility at the time of Jerusalem's exile. There was conflict between Edom and David, Solomon, and other kings of Judah (2 Sam. 8:14; 1 Kings 11:14; 2 Kings 8:20–22; 14:7).

34:6–7. In response to the Lord's announcement that his sword will descend in judgment upon Edom (cf. Isa. 34:5b), the prophet anticipates the gory consequences (34:6). He sees a sword covered with the blood of lambs and goats and with fat from the kidneys of rams. We are then told the reason (כִּי) for this—there is a sacrifice in Bozrah (the Edomite capital) and a great slaughter in Edom. Isaiah 34:7 goes on to elaborate. In addition to the animals mentioned in 34:6a, wild oxen and bulls are slaughtered, drenching the land with their blood and covering it with their fat.

The sacrifice is said to be "to/for the Lord." One might think the phrase indicates the sacrifice is being offered to the Lord (cf. Jonah 1:16). However, when this is the case, the noun זֶבַח, "sacrifice," is collocated with a verb for sacrificing. No such verb occurs in Isaiah 34:6. In fact, within the metaphorical framework the Lord is the one slaughtering the animals with his sword for the purpose of making a sacrifice (cf. Jer. 46:10 as well).

34:8. Isaiah 34:8 reminds us of what we already know to be true—the prophet is not describing a literal sacrifice. Rather, he is depicting the judgment of the Edomites, the people whom the Lord has devoted to destruction (cf. 34:5b). The metaphor of a bloody sacrifice highlights the violent, devastating nature of the event.

But Edom's judgment, however gory, is deserved. The prophet calls it the Lord's "day of vengeance" (יוֹם נָקָם). This phrase occurs just four times in the Old Testament. In Proverbs 6:34 it refers to a legal day of reckoning, when a jealous husband gets revenge on the man who has slept with his wife. The other three references are in Isaiah. In 61:2 it is used of the time when the Lord frees the poor from oppression and judges their oppressors. Here in 34:8 and in 63:4 it refers to God's judgment upon the nations and Edom in particular. The noun נָקָם, "vengeance," when used of God, refers in most cases to his exacting just punishment upon those who have opposed him and harmed his people (cf. Deut. 32:43; Isa. 35:4; 47:3; 59:17; Ezek. 24:8; Mic. 5:15). Vengeance is a corollary of God's justice. From Israel's perspective, God's day of vengeance is a day of salvation. It is the year of the Lord's "favor" and brings comfort for those who mourn (Isa. 61:2). In Isaiah 63:4 the phrase "day of vengeance" stands in poetic parallelism with "year of my redemption" (NIV11, "the year for me to redeem") a phrase that focuses on this positive dimension of the judgment.

In 34:8 the prophet also calls Edom's time of judgment "a year of retribution." The rare noun שִׁלּוּמִים, "retribution," occurs only three times in the Old Testament. In Micah 7:3 it refers to bribes (compensation, payments) accepted by judges for making decisions favorable to the party offering the bribe. In Hosea 9:7 the word is used of God's punishment upon Israel as the compensation she receives for her sins. This same nuance is present in Isaiah 34:8, where God gives Edom what she deserves. The imagery of one's work being paid highlights God's justice and serves as a reminder that one's deeds do not go unnoticed by the divine Judge.

In this case, the Lord repays Edom for its hostility toward Zion. Isaiah 34:8b reads literally, "a year of retribution, for the cause (?) of Zion." This may mean the Lord is taking up Zion's just cause against Edom (cf. ESV, NIV11) or that he is judging Edom for its "strife with" or "hostility toward" Zion (cf. HCSB, NLT; note the use of רִיב in 2 Sam. 22:44 (= Ps. 18:43 [HB 44]); Ps. 55:9 [HB 10]). In either case, it is clear Edom has shown hostility to Zion and will now be punished for its actions.

34:9–10. The prophet next describes the devastating effects of the Lord's intervention in judgment. The description is hyperbolic, but the point is clear: Edom will become a burning wasteland, overrun by wild creatures and weeds. Edom as a nation will be no more.

Isaiah 34:9–10 depicts a burning wasteland that is not fit for human habitation. Edom's streams are turned into pitch and her soil into brimstone (34:9a). Her land becomes burning pitch (34:9b). It burns around the clock, with smoke continually ascending (34:10a). For generation after generation, it will "lie desolate" (literally, "be dried up") and no one will dare pass through it (34:10b). It will not be fit to sustain life.

34:11–15. Ironically, however, the land will have inhabitants, indicating the exaggerated nature of the language used in 34:9–10. People will not live there, but plenty of wild creatures will occupy Edom's ruins, including owls and other types of birds, as well as wild dogs and wild goats, among others (34:11a, 13b–15). The image of various wild creatures inhabiting ruins may be stereotypical, since it occurs in at least two other prophetic judgment texts (see Isa. 13:21–22; Jer. 50:39).

Isaiah 34:11b pictures someone, probably the Lord (cf. 34:8), stretching out a measuring line and plumb line over Edom, as if planning to construct something (cf. Isa. 44:13; see Oswalt 1986, 615; Roberts 2015, 436). But in this case, all that is measured is the territory given over to "chaos" (תֹהוּ) and "desolation" (בֹהוּ). The terms are not joined here, but nevertheless they remind one of the phrase תֹהוּ וָבֹהוּ used in Genesis 1:2, where it describes the primeval condition of the earth prior to God's creative work. The earth did not appear as we know it; it was covered by a great watery deep and shrouded in darkness. The phrase also appears in Jeremiah 4:23 to describe the devastating nature of God's judgment, which reverses creation. It causes the earth to revert to its primordial unformed, unpopulated condition and darkens the heavenly lights. The term בֹהוּ appears only in Genesis 1:2, Isaiah 34:11, and Jeremiah 4:23, always in conjunction with תֹהוּ. The word תֹהוּ occurs in isolation in several other passages, including Isaiah 45:18, which alludes to Genesis 1:2. On occasion it is parallel to a term meaning "nothing, emptiness, futility" and indicates lack of substance (Job 26:7; Isa. 40:17, 23; 41:29; 49:4). Sometimes it is used to describe a desert/wasteland (Deut. 32:10; Job 6:8; 12:24; Ps. 107:40) or a ruin that is uninhabited or fit only for wild animals (Isa. 24:10). Isaiah 34:11 envisions Edom becoming such a ruin. It does not go as far as Jeremiah 4:23 in depicting the devastation of judgment as encompassing heaven and earth, but the appearance of the word pair has a decidedly ominous connotation and suggests a reversal of creation, at least in Edomite territory.

Isaiah 34:12–13a sharpens the focus of divine judgment. Edom's nobles will have nothing left to call a kingdom (34:12a). In fact, they and the princes will be no more (34:12b). Her fortresses will be overgrown with thorns, and her fortified cities with nettles and brambles (34:13a).

Wild creatures will live there. Four were mentioned earlier (34:11a). In 34:13b–15, a second list of the future residents of Edom's ruins appears; it contains eight animals, twice as many as the prior list. The seventh animal in this second list (קִפּוֹז, a type of owl, 34:15a) is described in more detail than the others (note the use of four verbs to describe her activity), perhaps indicating the culmination of the list. But then an eighth animal is added for good measure (34:15b). If we understand seven as pointing to completeness, the addition of an eighth creature emphasizes that the ruins will be overrun by these animals.

34:16–17. The prophet urges his audience to examine "the scroll of the Lord" (34:16). This phrase occurs only here in the Old Testament. Apparently, it refers to a scroll upon which is written the divine decree of Edom's judgment (note "for it is his mouth that has given the order" later in the verse). Most likely, it refers to the announcement that has just been made (34:11–15) and is now expanded. The notion of an official order gives the prophecy a formal tone that suggests Edom's downfall is predetermined and certain. Within this scroll one finds the Lord's command that the animals will reside in Edom's ruins. Not one will be missing. His mouth has given the order and they will be assembled there. The Lord has even allotted Edom's territory to them, as if they were people receiving a land inheritance (34:17). They will possess the land of Edom and dwell there perpetually. In other words, Edom has ceased to exist as a nation (cf. Mal. 1:3).

The Blossoming of the Desert (35:1–2)
The Lord's arrival will transform the desert.

Employing personification, Isaiah exhorts the desert and the dry land to be glad, and the wilderness to rejoice and blossom like a flower (35:1). He urges it to richly blossom and to rejoice greatly. The glory of Lebanon, known for its trees, particularly cedars, has been given (or perhaps "assigned") to the wilderness, as well as the splendor of Carmel and Sharon (35:2a; cf. 33:9). This blossoming is accompanied by the arrival of the Lord (35:2b; cf. 35:4). The people (the likely referent of the masculine plural pronoun, "they"), who are addressed in the following verses, will see the royal splendor of the Lord, who is Israel's God.

The Lord's Arrival (35:3–4)
The Lord's arrival is imminent and will result in his people's deliverance.

The prophet addresses an unidentified group in 35:3–4. Since he urges them to strengthen the fearful, we can probably assume these addressees are loyal followers of the Lord who have maintained their faith and confidence in him (Smith 2007, 579). The prophet commands them to strengthen feeble hands and staggering knees (35:3). The language depicts the physical effects of intense fear (cf. 35:4a)—trembling hands and knocking knees. He tells the addressees to say to the faint of heart, "Be strong! Do not fear!"

This is an appropriate message because of what is about to take place. Drawing attention to the immediacy of the event (note הִנֵּה, "look"), they are to tell the fainthearted their God is coming with vengeance and retribution (35:4b). The reference to vengeance (נָקָם) links this passage with the preceding judgment speech, which announced the Lord's day of vengeance (נָקָם) against his enemies (34:8; Smith 2007, 579–80). For his people, this outpouring of judgment means deliverance (Roberts 2015, 441).

Transformation (35:5–10)
The Lord's arrival will bring radical transformation.

35:5. When the Lord arrives to deliver his people, there will be a radical transformation. The blind will see and the deaf hear (35:5). Usage of blind and deaf imagery elsewhere in Isaiah suggests spiritual transformation is fundamentally in view here (Oswalt 1986, 624; Roberts 2015, 441). The imagery is used of rebellious Israel of Isaiah's time (6:9–10; 29:18) and of the spiritually insensitive exiles of the future (42:18–20; 43:8). But a time is coming when the blind and deaf community will be spiritually transformed (29:18; 32:3–4) and released from bondage (43:19–21; cf. 35:8).

35:6–7. When the Lord arrives, the lame leap like a deer and the mute can shout for joy (35:6a). The images of physical healing continue the portrait of 35:5, but an explanatory clause (note כִּי) makes a transition to a related theme, the transformation of nature (35:6b). The lame and mute undoubtedly experience joy over their release from their physical handicaps, but they also rejoice at what they see happening around them. Water flows (literally, "bursts forth") in the desert and in the wilderness, enabling the lush growth and prompting the joy mentioned earlier (35:1–2). Where there was once just sand and parched ground, there are now pools and springs (35:7a). What was once the haunt of jackals is transformed into a place of lush vegetation (35:7b). The reference to jackals links this passage to the preceding judgment speech (cf. 34:13, see Roberts 2015, 441). There is a strong contrast between the positive transformation witnessed by the restored covenant community and what happens in Edom, where judgment turns the land into a ruin inhabited by jackals and other wild creatures.

35:8. Isaiah pictures a road leading from the land of exile to Zion (35:8; cf. Isa. 11:16; 43:19; 49:9–11). It is given the name "the Way of Holiness." This road is "holy" because it is set apart (or reserved) for those who have been delivered from exile (cf. 35:9–10). But there are also moral and ethical restrictions that make this highway "holy." No one who is "unclean" may travel on it, nor are "wicked fools" given access to it (35:8b). The term אֱוִילִים, "fools," can be used of those who give bad advice (Isa. 19:11) or who are deranged (Hos. 9:7), but in nearly all of its twenty-six occurrences it refers to those who are morally deficient and live contrary to God's moral principles (see, e.g., Ps. 107:17; Prov. 1:7; 14:9; 20:3; Jer. 4:22). In Isaiah 35:8 the term is associated with "unclean," suggesting this moral connotation is present. So understandably, one does not expect such fools to be traveling on the Way of Holiness.

35:9–10. In addition to being off limits to sinful people, the Way of Holiness is also free of lions and other dangerous animals. No such predators can be found there (35:9a). Isaiah identifies specifically the travelers on the road—the redeemed (35:9b–10a), who have been ransomed by the Lord. The terms come from the legal sphere. The first (גָּאַל, "redeem," 35:9b) originates in the Israelite social structure. A "redeemer" was a protector of the family interests. This family guardian could reclaim an individual from slavery (Lev. 25:48–49) or buy back property that the family had been forced to sell (Lev. 25:25–34). He also had the responsibility to avenge a family member who had been murdered (Num. 35:19). The book of Ruth indicates that a family protector could raise up offspring for a deceased relative. How much of this sociological background underlies Isaiah's use of the term is not entirely clear, but the prophet's use of the word as a divine title (see Isa. 41:14; 43:14; 44:6, 24; 47:4; 48:17; 49:7, 26; 54:5, 8; 59:20; 60:16; 63:16) may suggest the Lord viewed the exiled nation as his family and felt some responsibility to relieve their oppressed condition. As Israel's redeemer the Lord delivers the people from the bondage of exile (43:14; 48:20), but this redemption is not strictly physical, for it involves the forgiveness of sin (44:22–23; 59:20). The two facets of redemption are, of course, related, for it was Israel's sin that led to the exile.

In legal contexts the second verb (פָּדָה, "ransom," 35:10a) often refers to paying a price to release an object from one who has a claim upon it (see Exod. 13:13, 15; 21:8; 34:20; Lev. 19:20; 27:27, 29; Num. 18:15–17; Job 6:23); it can also refer to paying a ransom to release one from captivity (Job 6:22–23; Ps. 49:8 [HB 9]). The verb describes how the Lord "redeemed" his people from Egypt. In this case they are viewed as slaves who were purchased by their new owner, the Lord (Deut. 7:8; 9:26; 13:5; 24:18). It is noteworthy the deliverance depicted in Isaiah 35:10 is described in identical language in 51:11, which is in a second exodus context (cf. 51:9–10).

TRANSLATION ANALYSIS 35:8
The Hebrew text of 35:8b is especially difficult; it reads, literally, "An unclean (one) will not pass by (on) it, and it (is) for them/him; one who walks (on the) road, and fools will not stray." The MT places an *athnaq* with "for them/him," indicating "and it is for them/him" goes with

what precedes and "one who walks in the road" with what follows. The first clause seems fairly straightforward: the unclean will not be allowed on this holy road, for their unclean status is the antithesis of holiness. As for the remainder of the verse, ESV reads, "It shall belong to those who walk on the way; even if they are fools, they shall not go astray." KJV reads, "but it shall be for those: the wayfaring men, though fools, shall not err therein," and HCSB has, "but it will be for the one who walks the path. Even the fool will not go astray." For the meaning in this case, see Young 1969, 453–54. But why would fools be traveling on the road in the first place if it is holy and, as such, presumably reserved for the holy? "Fools" makes a good parallel with "unclean," and both are collocated with a negated imperfect. So, one would expect the final clause to be saying that fools, like their counterpart the unclean, would not travel the road (Oswalt 1986, 625). But in this case, how is the verb יִתְעוּ, "stray off" (from תָּעָה) being used here? Perhaps it means "stray into (it)" (cf. NET) or "wander about on (it)" (cf. NASB, "But it will be for him who walks that way, and fools will not wander on it," and NIV11, which shifts the order of the lines to facilitate the parallelism, "it will be for those who walk on that way. The unclean will not journey on it; wicked fools will not go about on it"). But even if we allow this somewhat strained nuance for תָּעָה, what do the words between the parallel lines mean? Perhaps if we ignore the *athnaq*, we can read, "But it (is) for him, one who walks (in the) way" (see the translations cited above, except for KJV), and understand the statement as a parenthetical comment contrasting the one who is allowed to travel the road with those who are forbidden to do so. (See NET, "it is reserved for those authorized to use it.") In this case, we may assume, based on the fact that the highway is called the Way of Holiness, that the one walking in the way is holy, in contrast to the unclean/fools. Yet one is forced to admit there is presently no completely satisfactory explanation for 35:8b.

The redeemed will return (presumably from exile; cf. Isa. 51:11) and enter Zion with a joyful shout and with enduring joy upon their heads (35:10a). The prophet uses irony here. The picture of joy being on the heads of the redeemed is an ironic twist on the description of mourners putting dirt or ashes on their heads. Happiness and joy will overtake them, while sorrow and sighing will flee (35:10b).

In 35:9–10 the travelers are the returning exiles, but the immediate context suggests that only those who are holy, godly, and wise will have access to the road (35:5, 8). This is consistent with Isaiah 33, which also makes a moral distinction between the righteous and sinners and makes it clear that only the godly will experience the restoration provided by the Lord (see comments above on 33:6, 15–16).

THEOLOGICAL FOCUS

The theological focus of this passage can be stated as follows: the Lord will punish the hostile nations for mistreating his people; he is committed to restoring his covenant people, but only the godly are allowed to experience the joy of this great transformation. As the prophet develops this theological theme, the following emphases emerge:

1. The Lord as warrior

Isaiah 34 portrays the Lord as a warrior who unleashes judgment upon the nations and their armies. This judgment is cosmic in its scope as the Lord judges the stars in the sky, which symbolize spiritual forces that energize the hostile nations. His sword descends to earth, with Edom being the focus of his judgment. He devastates Edom, leaving it a wasteland inhabited only by wild animals.

2. The Lord's justice

The Lord's judgment is not arbitrary. It is a day of vengeance in which he repays Edom for its hostility against Zion.

3. The Lord's transformative power

The Lord's transformative power heals the handicapped, turns the desert and wilderness into a well-watered region with lush vegetation, and rejuvenates his people by leading them back to Zion and restoring their joy. The healing of the blind and deaf, which can be taken literally, mirrors a spiritual transformation that will occur. The people of Isaiah's time were, by and large, spiritually insensitive, and depicted in terms of being blind and deaf (cf. 6:9–10; 29:18). The future exiles are depicted in the same way (42:18–20; 43:8). But the Lord will transform the covenant community in conjunction with restoring them from exile.

This passage in many ways defines Jesus's ministry. When John's disciples asked Jesus if he was indeed the Messiah, he did not answer with a simple "yes." Instead, he told them to report to John what they had seen, and he pronounced a blessing on those who persevere through persecution (Matt. 11:4–6). In addition to challenging John to persevere (11:6), Jesus's words assured John that the messianic age had arrived. He alluded to two passages, Isaiah 35:5–6a and 61:1a. When read in context, both texts bring comfort to those who are suffering and assure the downtrodden that vindication will ultimately come (see Isa. 35:3–4; 61:2–3). John needed to find strength in those promises. When Jesus healed the blind, deaf, lame, and mute (cf. Matt. 9:33; 11:5; 12:22; 15:14, 30; 21:14; Luke 7:21), the prophecy of Isaiah 35:5–6 was materializing before the very eyes of the people. Jesus's healing ministry was proof of his transformative power and a vivid object lesson of the spiritual healing he offered to sinners (cf. Matt. 9:1–8). After all, the physical illnesses that human beings experience are ultimately the effect of sin. As the Suffering Servant, Jesus had come to redeem sinners from the guilt and effects of sin (Isa. 53:4–6, 11; cf. Matt. 8:17).

4. Holiness as a prerequisite

The highway leading to Zion is named the Way of Holiness, signifying there is a moral requirement for participating in the coming restoration. Indeed, the ungodly and fools are excluded from traveling on the road.

PREACHING AND TEACHING STRATEGIES

Exegetical and Theological Synthesis

Isaiah 34–35 presents contrasting realities for the people of this world who have rejected God versus those who worship him when the final day of judgment arrives. Isaiah 34 focuses primarily on the negative realities of God's vengeance against the wicked, whereas chapter 35 looks at the positive transformation that will result for God's own children. There are three points of obvious contrast between these two groups of people.

(1) The first point of contrast involves the lives/bodies of the people of each group. In chapter 34, the wicked experience a mass destruction of life (34:2–7). Because they have been devoted to destruction by God (34:2, 5), their slain bodies will cover the land and the mountains will flow with their blood (34:3, 7). The righteous, on the other hand, will experience the opposite. Rather than destruction, their bodies will undergo healing and regeneration (35:5–6). Those with blind eyes will now see; those with deaf ears will now hear. The lame will leap for joy, and the tongue of the mute will be loosed to speak.

(2) A second important contrast involves the impact of that day on the land. In chapter 34, the land possessed by the wicked is transformed into an uninhabitable place. Streams are turned to pitch, and the soil becomes sulfur (34:9). Additionally, their towns/cities are overrun with thorns and thistles (34:13). Conversely, the land of the righteous will be like a desert that blossoms into a fertile place (35:1–2). Fresh water

will spring forth in the deserts, producing refreshing pools and lush vegetation (35:6–7).

(3) Finally, there is a third important contrast that emerges from these chapters. The wicked in chapter 34 are expelled from their land (34:10, 12). This is directly related to the transformation of their land into something uninhabitable that forces people out of their towns and cities. This theme is highlighted by the repeated mention that wild animals now inhabit those places where people used to dwell (34:11, 13–15). In Isaiah 35, the exact opposite is predicted for the righteous. There, the ransomed of God are free to return to their land as though back from exile (35:10). A highway is described as appearing in the desert paving a straight path back to Zion (35:8). No fools or wicked ones will be able to get in their way or cause them to go astray. Whereas the wild animals were described in Isaiah 34 as now inhabiting the dwelling places of the wicked, preventing them from living there, it will not be so with the righteous. The opposite is true for the people of God as no lions or wild animals will be able to impede their trek back to Zion (35:9).

As a result of all of this, the redeemed of the Lord are repeatedly described as rejoicing throughout Isaiah 35. The chapter begins with three poetic references to the wilderness rejoicing over its blossoming with new vegetation (35:1–2). Then, in 35:6, the lame leap for joy and the mute sing for joy as their bodies experience miraculous healing. Finally, the chapter ends with multiple references to the joy experienced by the ransomed of the Lord who return with singing to Zion (35:10). As such, Isaiah 35 begins and ends with an *inclusio* of joy and singing that surrounds this passage. That is a stark contrast to the tone of chapter 34. In fact, at each point of contrast between these two groups, rejoicing is explicitly mentioned—at the healing of their bodies (35:5–6), at the transformation of the land (35:1–2), and at the restoration back to their homeland (35:10).

The effect for the reader is the realization that God's coming day of vengeance and judgment will result in a stark reversal of fortunes. The wicked who had conquered, deported, and oppressed the people of God will get what is coming to them. The Edomites who were perpetual enemies of Israel (see commentary above under 34:5) become a type or example of the enemies and persecutors of God's people throughout human history. The destruction of the Edomites, which would take place in the relatively near future for Isaiah's audience, would be the eventual destiny for all the world's nations who oppose and persecute the people of God. They all will be "exiled" from their homes and slaughtered just as they deported and oppressed God's people. The righteous on the other hand will be made whole and restored to their land with great rejoicing and celebration. As such, they should long for and welcome that day with expectant joy, knowing it will result in their vindication, healing, and restoration.

Preaching Idea

God's people should be encouraged by the promise of coming judgment, as it will be a day of both vengeance and salvation.

Contemporary Connections

What does it mean?

At first glance, it is obvious that the theme of Isaiah 34 is God's judgment against rebellious sinners. It would appear then that the chapter has an overall negative vibe in contrast to the overwhelmingly positive tone in chapter 35, which focuses on the blessings that befall the righteous at the eschaton. However, on closer inspection, the judgment of the wicked is described as "vengeance . . . to uphold Zion's cause," or on behalf of God's people (34:8; 35:4). Furthermore, this vengeance is directly linked to God's salvation of his people (35:4). Thus, God's judgment of the wicked here is presented in a positive light, as far as it impacts the people of God. The overall tone of the broader passage (chapters 34–35) then is positive despite the imagery of death and bloodshed, because even this results in *the vindication of the righteous*. This becomes the first of four blessings associated with God's future salvation of his people in this passage.

A second such blessing is *the re-creation of the land*. Isaiah 35 begins with descriptions of how the formerly dry and barren wilderness will suddenly blossom with abundant foliage (35:1–2). A few verses later, the prophet predicts that springs of water will break forth in the wilderness leading to a dramatic, positive transformation throughout nature (35:6–7). In Genesis 3, Adam and Eve's sin in the garden of Eden resulted in the ground becoming cursed and producing thorns and thistles (Gen. 3:17–18). The same imagery of "thorns" and "thistles" growing up and infesting the land was used in Isaiah 34:13 in describing the consequences of God's judgment against Edom and the sinful world. As mentioned above, Isaiah 34 stands in contrast to chapter 35 regarding the land of the sinners versus the land that will be inhabited by God's people one day. As such, it becomes clear for the reader that God's transformation of the land on behalf of his ransomed is part of God's undoing of the consequences of sin and the curse.

There is another blessing associated with salvation in Isaiah 35, *the rejuvenation of our bodies*. The prophet predicts that at this time, "The eyes of the blind shall be opened, and the ears of the deaf unstopped; then will the lame man leap like a deer, and the tongue of the mute shout for joy" (35:5–6). These images describe the miraculous healing of all sorts of physical ailments and handicaps. The broader scriptural narrative informs us that these healings will transpire in relation to the resurrection of the dead to new life (Isa. 25:7–8; 26:19). In other words, it won't just be our spirits that are saved when Jesus returns, but our bodies too will be restored and made whole.

Isaiah 35 ends with a description of one final blessing that rounds out our understanding of God's salvation here. The prophet describes God's people as experiencing a *restoration to their homeland*. For the original audience this would have pointed to a return from exile, at least for those reading it after the Babylonian exile. It would have conveyed thoughts of political and religious liberation. It would have also indicated a sense of national pride and financial prosperity. For much of its history, Israel suffered from the realities of geopolitical domination and oppression. For this reason, when Israel's prophets spoke about the promise of salvation, it often carried political overtones that implied national freedom. For example, the story of the exodus, which serves as a type of salvation for the Jewish people throughout their Old Testament Scriptures, was predominantly a deliverance from slavery and oppression in Egypt into a land all their own. As such, when their prophets spoke about a coming messiah who would save/deliver them, Jewish minds thought primarily about a military leader who would free them from domineering political oppressors such as Rome in the first century.

God's people should be encouraged by the promise of coming judgment, as it will be a day of both vengeance and salvation. Salvation here means far more than just deliverance from sin or hell as Christians today are often prone to think. Rather, the meaning here in Isaiah was more earthly and political. It included a vindication of the righteous by the death of their enemies. It also included a re-creation of their land to which they would freely return. They would then live in that land with rejuvenated bodies that had been miraculously healed or raised back to life by God.

Is it true?
For God's salvation to be complete, it must involve a wholistic solution to the problem and consequences of sin. Christians have often

been accustomed to thinking about salvation exclusively through the lens of a person's relationship to God. Because of sin, people are born alienated from him. They rightly understand Jesus's death and resurrection as providing for their forgiveness and reconciliation back to God. The eternal consequence of hell is then replaced with the blessing of eternal life with God. While this is certainly central to the biblical teaching on salvation, it is an incomplete understanding of salvation. The salvation accomplished by Jesus results in far more than just personal forgiveness of sin and deliverance from hell. For it to be complete, it must address all the things affected in the beginning when sin first entered the world; it must undo all of the negative consequences associated with sin and the curse.

Thus, for starters, the fullness of God's salvation work would need to correct the negative effect of sin on the physical earth. In Genesis 3:17–19, God told Adam,

> Because you listened to your wife and ate fruit from the tree about which I commanded you, "You must not eat from it," cursed is the ground because of you; through painful toil you will eat food from it all the days of your life. It will produce thorns and thistles for you, and you will eat the plants of the field. By the sweat of your brow you will eat your food.

In response to humanity's sin, God cursed the physical creation with weeds, thorns, and thistles. To this we could add things like natural disasters, droughts, and famines. The world became a harder place to live, a less inhabitable place because of sin. However, Isaiah 35 describes a time in the future when those who experience God's salvation will inhabit an earth that has been transformed for their benefit. The deserts will once again blossom (35:1–2) as water breaks forth in the once barren wildernesses (35:6–7). Romans 8:19–23 connects this reality to the fulness of God's salvation for his people:

> For the creation waits in eager expectation for the children of God to be revealed. For the creation was subjected to frustration, not by its own choice, but by the will of the one who subjected it, in hope that the creation itself will be liberated from its bondage to decay and brought into the freedom and glory of the children of God. We know that the whole creation has been groaning as in the pains of childbirth right up to the present time. Not only so, but we ourselves, who have the firstfruits of the Spirit, groan inwardly as we wait eagerly for our adoption to sonship, the redemption of our bodies.

God's plan of salvation includes not only the redemption of our souls but also the redemption of his physical creation. It too must be set free from its "bondage to decay."

Not only must God's salvation repair the effects of sin upon the earth to be complete, but it also needs to address the negative impact sin has had on the human body. God said that sin would lead to death. More specifically, he warned Adam and Eve that they would die on the day they ate of the forbidden fruit (Gen. 2:17; cf. Rom. 5:12). The very day they ate of it, they were expelled from the garden and cut off from the tree of life. Their bodies began the gradual process of physical decline that would eventually result in death. Paul spoke of the ongoing process of death in the human body of living people: "Therefore we do not lose heart. Though *outwardly we are wasting away*, yet inwardly we are being renewed day by day" (2 Cor. 4:16, emphasis added). The outer self here is a reference to the physical body that is in process of "wasting away" or deteriorating. This ongoing process of decay leading to death is a direct result of sin.

Every person experiences these effects within their physical bodies differently. Some are blessed with relatively good health throughout their life. But even healthy people feel the decline that takes place as they age. There is a reason why even professional athletes only have a relatively short window of time when they can compete with the best in the world before they are forced to retire. Most people reach their physical peak in their mid-twenties, and then begin a noticeable decline sometime in their mid-thirties. At this point, their bodies begin to lose muscle mass, their metabolism often slows down leading to unwanted weight gain, and they notice a decrease in their overall flexibility, just to name a few of the negative impacts of aging on the body. Some experience this more directly than others such as the one diagnosed with cancer at a young age, the child born with Down syndrome or spina bifida, or even the person forced to go through life with a severe allergy to peanuts or gluten. For others, the normal hardships of aging are exacerbated by diagnoses such as Alzheimer's, diabetes, or Parkinson's disease. Like the thorns and thistles that grow up from the ground, these physical impairments are constant reminders of the destructive and painful consequences of sin. Every time a parent receives the sad news that their precious newborn baby has been born with a physical defect, or an accident victim is told that they will lose one or both of their legs because of the severity of their injuries, or a diabetic patient permanently loses their ability to see, they are reminded that the wage of sin is death.

In order then for God's salvation to be complete, it must include a solution to the problems associated with aging and death. It must eliminate every reminder of the curse in the human body. The promise in Isaiah 35:5–6 assures us of this very reality. Those who are among the saved or the "redeemed" (35:10) are promised that when their bodies are resurrected to new life, every physical ailment, deformity, or weakness experienced in this life will be transformed into something wholly better and more beautiful. This truth is succinctly captured by Paul in 1 Corinthians 15:42–44:

> So it will be with the resurrection of the dead. The body that is sown is perishable, it is raised imperishable; it is sown in dishonor, it is raised in glory; it is sown in weakness, it is raised in power; it is sown a natural body, it is raised a spiritual body.

We've just considered the significance of the re-creation of the world and of the rejuvenation of our physical bodies as part of God's broader salvation of his people. But what about the restoration of people to their homeland? On the surface, this applies to those who were in Babylonian exile and would return to the land of Israel. However, a bigger salvific principle is at play here. It is closely related to the themes of the re-creation or restoration of the earth in general and the vindication of the righteous discussed above. As a result of sin, this world has ceased being an ideal "homeland" for God's people. The wicked have corrupted all forms of leadership and government, leading to the neglect, suffering, and even oppression of those who are righteous. On an even broader scale, sin leads to a moral decline within every culture, making it uncomfortable for God's children to live here on this earth. Jesus said it this way:

> If the world hates you, keep in mind that it hated me first. If you belonged to the world, it would love you as its own. As it is, you do not belong to the world, but I have chosen you out of the world. That is why the world hates you. (John 15:18–19)

Paul made a similar point when he said, "But our citizenship is in heaven. And we eagerly await a Savior from there, the Lord Jesus Christ" (Phil. 3:20). Both were making a similar point. As long as this world is overrun with wicked people who are at enmity against God, they will treat God's people as their enemies and make their lives here difficult and uncomfortable.

Martin Heidegger, a twentieth-century German philosopher, argued that there is a sense or feeling within every person that wherever they live, there is something about the surrounding environment that makes it feel less than home.[1] Home is generally the place where a person is most able to relax. It is where they can be themselves, let down their guard, and not worry about how others will think about them. Home is the place where one is surrounded by family, those who love then unconditionally. It is a place that has been furnished and decorated according to one's own personal preferences. Ideally, then, it is the place of ultimate comfort and peace. On the contrary, anyone who has spent time in a foreign country understands how difficult and awkward life can feel. There are so many things that make one feel out of place and uncomfortable. They often speak a different language making communication very hard. They eat different foods and dress in different fashions. But at an even deeper level, foreigners often have very different values and think about life itself differently. One's homeland is the place that gives a person much of their sense of identity and belonging. The result for many who attempt to live in a foreign country for very long is that they experience significant anxiety and discomfort. They often feel as though nobody really understands or accepts them, and thus they are unable to live authentically. Heidegger argued that all people experience some level of this sense of not being at home, regardless of where or with whom they live.

The Bible teaches that this world in its present form is not home, in the deepest sense of that word, for Christians. The world's attitudes, values, and philosophies do not align with ours. Because of this, the world does not love us, and we do not feel as though we belong. In fact, whether they know it or not, the people of this world are under the influence of Satan, who is the god and ruler of this world (John 8:44; 12:31; 16:11; 2 Cor. 4:4; Eph. 2:2; 1 John 5:19; Rev. 12:9). This is why they don't understand or receive the ways of God, and in some cases why they hate and persecute God's children.

But the glorious truth of Isaiah 35 is that when God orchestrates his ultimate salvation, it will include a judgment and destruction of those who had rejected him and persecuted his people, vindicating his followers as having been right all along. Additionally, with the re-creation of this earth into a place of comfortable habitation, this earth will be transformed into a place that is quite literally heaven on earth. For the first time since Adam and Eve roamed the garden of Eden, God's people will feel completely at home on this earth. As such, all believers will experience a restoration to their homeland.

Now what?

Isaiah 34 speaks to those who have rejected God. It serves as a warning that a time is coming when judgment will rain down from God upon all sin. Some may shake their fist at God with impunity now, but this is only because of his great mercy and patience. This will not last forever, and those who have not repented of their sins and turned to God in faith should be warned that judgment day is approaching.

However, as stated above, this passage was intended primarily as a message of encouragement for God's people (35:3–4). Just like the prophet Isaiah in his own day, God's preachers and teachers today are to use these promises to "strengthen the feeble hands and steady the knees that give way." They are to tell those who have an anxious heart to be strong and not fear! In other words, this passage was intended to give hope and encouragement to God's people living amid hard circumstances. It was intended to direct people to feel a certain way as much as to think a certain way. People who read this

---

1 http://www.samvriti.com/2013/05/10/heidegger-the-unheimlich.

passage or who hear a sermon from these chapters should leave feeling hopeful and comforted, even if they came feeling anxious and fearful.

Take for example the sixty-one-year-old man who entered church with a walker and struggles to get to his seat because his Parkinson's disease has made it difficult for him to even walk. If that weren't bad enough, his debilitating condition has made it almost impossible for him to speak in a way that others can understand. This has resulted in people having very limited and only surface-level conversations with him, or just avoiding interaction with him altogether. He comes to church feeling lonely, abandoned, discouraged, and angry. The preacher should speak to him from this passage, because regardless of the ways in which the effects of sin have impacted his body and stolen his quality of life, this passage was meant to be a word of hope from God to him. There is coming a day when every physical limitation will be a thing of the past as he will be given a new body devoid of any problems. Hallelujah!

The preacher should likewise speak to the widow whose husband of thirty-five years suddenly passed away from a heart attack in recent weeks. As a result of that loss, her home now seems unbearably quiet. What used to be a place of joy and relaxation with the one person who knew all about her faults and yet loved her deeply nonetheless has become a place that reminds her daily of his absence. This passage was meant to remind her that this world now is not her ultimate home, but that there will be a homecoming in the future when she will be reunited with her husband and all believers who have passed away. That day will bring about a restoration of sorts to her homeland.

Additionally, the preacher should address the ones in the congregation who have experienced injustice recently, or those who have grown frustrated with the corruption in politics. These people should take comfort in the promise that God will one day vindicate the righteous and punish those who are wicked. The unrighteous who now seem to get away with their schemes and corrupt dealings will one day be fully exposed and judged. Their defeat will be on full display for the world to witness, whereas those who have aligned themselves with God will be publicly and eternally vindicated.

In many ways, then, Isaiah 34–35 serves as a message of hope and comfort to all of God's people. But it also serves as a reminder that this world remains a deeply flawed place because of sin. For those whose lives feel abundantly blessed and joyous in the present, great! They should thank God for these blessings and worship him for his kindness. However, we must all remember that the life still to come for believers in Christ is far better than anything this world has to offer. As such, we should regularly affirm the final prayer recorded in Scripture, "Come, Lord Jesus!" (Rev. 21:20).

Creativity in Presentation

Devastation and Depopulation

Isaiah 34 describes the mass destruction of human life resulting from God's judgment against Edom, descriptive of his broader judgment against sinners worldwide. As a result of this destruction, their once inhabitable cities and towns would become "a haunt for jackals" and other wild animals. Additionally, the cities and towns once occupied by people would now be overrun with weeds and thorns as they lie desolate (34:13–15). For an actual example of the sort of destruction and depopulation being described here, consider using the events surrounding the earthquake in Tohoku, Japan on March 11, 2011. On that day, a magnitude-9 earthquake shook the region in the early afternoon hours. It was the strongest earthquake on record ever to hit Japan. This was followed by a massive tsunami with waves up to 128 ft. high that traveled as far as six miles inland. It flooded an area of approximately 217 square miles, destroying more than 120,000 buildings and damaging a million-plus more. The tsunami also caused the cooling system at the Fukushima Daiichi nuclear power plant to fail, resulting in a level-7 nuclear meltdown and the release of radioactive materials. Once densely populated cities in Japan's Tohoku region were devastated and vacant for years following the tsunami. Consider showing before-and-after pictures of this area to illustrate the sort of devastation and depopulation predicted to occur at the end of time against the sinful world's population centers. Be sure to emphasize to your audience that you are not suggesting that this natural disaster was an act of God's judgment similar to the destruction of Edom in Isaiah's day. The point of this illustration would only be to help your audience enter into the overwhelming sense of despair and loss felt by the Edomites. It is also wise to consider your audience before using an illustration such as this as images showing this sort of devastation where there were significant lives lost could be disturbing to younger children or those who may have been impacted more closely by these events.

The Deaf Hear
Cochlear implants were introduced in the early 1960s and 1970s. With these devices people with inner ear damage can hear, when traditional hearing aids don't work. There are several emotionally stirring videos on YouTube of people who have been deaf receiving cochlear implants and hearing sounds clearly for the first time. In many of these videos, the look on the people's faces is priceless. The preacher/teacher might show some of these clips and encourage their audience with the truth that these reactions will be common throughout the world when Jesus returns. Parents and siblings will talk for the first time with their loved one who dealt his/her entire life with Down syndrome, now entirely whole. Amputees will be running and leaping for joy as they try out their new legs for the first time. There will be rejoicing all around as people experience new and vibrant bodies.

Never Been More Homesick
Tell a story about a time when you felt homesick. Explain the factors involved in your feelings of homesickness, such as that you didn't know many people or that your loved ones weren't with you. Maybe you were in a foreign culture and just felt out of place.

An example from my life was the summer I worked at a Christian camp before my sophomore year of college. Most of the other counselors and summer staff were students from the same Christian college; consequently, many of them knew each other. I, on the other hand, was the only student there from my college, so I basically didn't know anybody. In addition to this, I didn't have a vehicle, so I lacked the ability to drive into town to get away on our off days. And because it was a campsite, there wasn't any good place to just relax on a couch and watch TV. One can only get so comfortable hanging out by himself in a rustic cabin sitting on a wooden bunk. Finally, I realized that camp ministry wasn't a good fit for me because of my personality. As counselors, we were constantly expected to be enthusiastic and excited for the sake of our campers. My personality lends toward a more even-keeled disposition. I found it exhausting trying to manufacture a fake personality and be somebody I wasn't just to do my job. After a few weeks, I really began to long for home. I missed the camaraderie of hanging out with my closest friends and the comfort that comes from being with family. I missed the freedom of being able to get in my car and go where I wanted to go. And I missed the comforts of my own bedroom and my own living room where I could just relax. You can imagine how happy I was when the bus finally dropped me off at the end of the summer in my own hometown. I relished the opportunity to reunite with my friends and family and just be myself.

This, I imagine, is what it will be like when Jesus returns. It will be like finally being at home, reunited with friends and family who died before us, and finally surrounded by people who think like we do about the things that really matter.

God's people should be encouraged by the promise of coming judgment, as it will be a day of both vengeance and salvation.

- A warning to the world (34:1–17).
  - Sin ultimately leads to death (1–8).
  - Sin presently leads to destruction (9–17).
- Reassurance to the righteous (35:1–10).
  - We will experience a recreation of the world.
  - We will experience rejuvenation in our bodies.
  - We will experience a restoration to our homeland.

DISCUSSION QUESTIONS

1. Read Isaiah 34:1–2. Who will be the recipients of God's judgment according to these verses—the ones devoted to destruction? Now, read 34:5–6. Who are the ones here described as the recipients of judgment? What do you think the relationship is between the two groups in this passage, and how do they contribute to the broader meaning here?

2. Read Isaiah 34:6 and notice how it is filled with imagery of the Mosaic sacrificial system. What is the significance of this imagery for people who are the recipients of God's eschatological judgment?

3. Read Isaiah 35:3–4. What does this passage say about the purpose of the passage? What was the prophet trying to accomplish for his listeners?

4. What physical deficiencies are you most looking forward to seeing healed in the resurrection? What things are you most looking forward to doing that you are presently unable to do, because of your physical limitations?

5. Was there a time in your life when you experienced homesickness? What were the factors that caused you to feel that way? How do those same factors impact Christians living in a corrupt and sinful world?

THE LORD DISPLAYS HIS SOVEREIGN POWER (ISAIAH 36–39)

Except for Hezekiah's prayer (38:9–20), chapters 36–39 correspond to 2 Kings 18:17–20:19. In the literary context of Isaiah, they serve as a bridge between the book's two main sections (chapters 1–35 and 40–66). The resolution of the Assyrian crisis, described in chapters 36–37, fulfills Isaiah's prior prophecies about Assyria's demise and Jerusalem's deliverance. Isaiah's prophecy of the Babylonian exile (39:5–7) paves the way for the following chapters, in which the prophet assumes an exilic–postexilic rhetorical stance.

Within chapters 36–39 one finds three distinct literary units, the structure of which may be outlined as follows:

- (I) The Lord's Victory over the Assyrians (36:1–37:38)
- (II) Hezekiah's New Lease on Life (38:1–22)
- (III) Hezekiah Shows Off His Wealth (39:1–8)

THE CHRONOLOGY OF CHAPTERS 36–39

Sennacherib's siege of Jerusalem, described in chapters 36–37, occurred in 701 B.C. Isaiah 37:38 jumps forward to 681 B.C., the year in which Sennacherib was assassinated.) Hezekiah's healing from a terminal illness occurred before the deliverance of Jerusalem (38:6; cf. 37:35). The visit of the Babylonian envoys, sent by Merodach-baladan, took place sometime after his healing (39:1).

It is likely this visit took place after the deliverance of the city and Sennacherib's departure. Some have objected to this for the following reasons: (1) Merodach-baladan is called "king of Babylon" (39:1). He ruled Babylon from 721 to 710 B.C. and again from 705 to 703, but not after that. However, the reference to Merodach-baladan being king need not mean this visit occurred in 703 or before. Merodach-baladan continued to organize a rebellion against Assyria for three more years. He had been king of Babylon, and so the narrator, perhaps reflecting an anti-Assyrian attitude, gives him this title. It is like Americans still referring to former presidents by their title of "president," even years after they have been out of office. (2) Chapter 39 does not mention the deliverance of the city. This is an argument from silence. The reference to Hezekiah's recovery may imply the city's deliverance since both were mentioned together just before this (38:5–6). (3) Hezekiah possessed great riches at the time of the envoys' visit (39:2), which seems unlikely if he had already paid Sennacherib tribute (cf. 2 Kings 18:13–16). But this argument proves too much, since 39:6 says Hezekiah's wealth would be taken to Babylon (not Assyria) someday (cf. 2 Kings 24:10–17, esp. 24:13). If Hezekiah had not yet paid tribute to Sennacherib, how could this be the case? Perhaps 2 Kings 18:15 uses exaggerated language to describe Hezekiah's tribute payment and/or Hezekiah was able to hide some of his riches from Sennacherib and/or replenish his silver supply (cf. 2 Kings 18:14) following his tribute payment to Sennacherib.

Isaiah 36:1–37:38

EXEGETICAL IDEA
When the arrogant Assyrian king threatened Jerusalem, the Lord assured Hezekiah that he would deliver the city and humiliate the Assyrians.

THEOLOGICAL FOCUS
The Lord is sovereign over the destiny of nations and humiliates those who arrogantly challenge his authority.

PREACHING IDEA
God honors those who live for his glory, but those who defy his glory are doomed.

PREACHING POINTERS
People most naturally live for their own glory. Many of our daily actions are done out of concern to protect or enhance our own reputations. Our concern about what others think of us motivates much of what we do. We often calculate the things we say or don't say by whether it will make us look petty, arrogant, intelligent, whiny, cruel, or generous. It isn't uncommon at all to say something we don't really mean simply because it will make us look better than how we would be perceived if we were completely honest.

Many of the sins people struggle with are directly related to their desire to promote their own glory. Jealousy and covetousness flow out of a belief that I am as important or more important than that person. Lying is often viewed as a good option because we feel the need to protect our own honor by covering up some shameful truth about ourselves. Gossip is fueled by our desire to appear better than others. Yet we aren't nearly as tempted to speak ill of them in their presence because we don't want them to think ill of us. Many other examples could be offered to show that the default of all humans is to protect and promote their own glory and honor.

In contrast to this tendency is the Bible's admonition that we commit ourselves to live first and foremost for God's glory. In 1 Corinthians 10:31, believers are exhorted that in whatever they do, including when they eat and drink, they should live for God's glory. Thus, the calculus for our words and actions should always include how this will impact God's reputation. Isaiah 36–37 reveals just how important God's glory is to him. Just as Judah was at the brink of being conquered by the powerful Assyrian army, King Hezekiah appealed to the Lord for his help on the primary basis of God's own honor and reputation. In response to this, the Lord affirmed that he would act on Judah's behalf out of his concern for his own glory.

THE LORD'S VICTORY OVER THE ASSYRIANS (36:1–37:38)

When Sennacherib demanded that Judah surrender, the Lord reassured King Hezekiah that he would deliver the city from the Assyrian threat. When the Assyrian king arrogantly taunted Hezekiah, he insulted the Lord. Hezekiah appealed to the Lord, praying that the Lord would defend his honor by delivering Jerusalem. The Lord assured Hezekiah he would do just that, announcing he would humiliate the Assyrians and deliver the city. The narrator concludes by telling how the Lord annihilated the Assyrian army, forcing Sennacherib to retreat home, where he was eventually assassinated by his own sons.

LITERARY STRUCTURE AND THEMES (36:1–37:38)

Within the framework of chapters 36–39, this account of the Lord's victory over Sennacherib's Assyrian army is the first of three episodes. It includes six scenes.

The first scene (36:1–22) is introduced by וַיְהִי, "and it was," followed by a temporal indicator. A *qatal* verb form (עָלָה, "went up") initiates the story proper, which is carried along in typical fashion by a series of *wayyiqtol*-initiated clauses (36:1–3). The scene is predominantly discourse, including Sennacherib's message to Hezekiah (36:4–10), the reply of Hezekiah's officials (36:11), and the Assyrian official's response, which contains an additional message from Sennacherib (36:12–20). The scene closes with a description of the people's silent reaction to the Assyrian demand for surrender and the officials' report to Hezekiah of Sennacherib's message (36:21–22). The shift in location from the aqueduct (cf. 36:2) to Hezekiah's palace signals closure for the first scene and a transition to the next.

The next scene (37:1–7) begins with וַיְהִי, "and it was," followed by a temporal indicator (37:1a). An infinitive construct initiates the action ("when Hezekiah heard") and a series of *wayyiqtol*-initiated clauses carries the account along (37:1b–2). Once more discourse predominates, including the officials' report to Isaiah of Sennacherib's demand (37:3–4) and the Lord's response to Hezekiah through Isaiah (37:5–7).

The next three scenes are initiated by shifts in focus. A switch in focus to the Assyrian official introduces the third scene (37:8–13), the bulk of which is a discourse containing Sennacherib's message to Hezekiah (37:10–13). A switch in focus to Hezekiah signals the beginning of the fourth scene (37:14–20), which consists almost entirely of Hezekiah's prayer to the Lord (37:15–20). Another shift in focus, this time to the prophet Isaiah, marks the beginning of the fifth scene (37:21–35), which comprises the Lord's response to Hezekiah's prayer. It contains two parts—a taunt against the arrogant Sennacherib (37:21–29) and a promise to Hezekiah (37:30–35).

The final scene (37:36–38) describes how the Lord, through his angel (literally, "messenger") brought his word to pass by decimating Sennacherib's army, which caused the Assyrian ruler to retreat to his homeland (37:36–37). An epilogue to the scene and episode (introduced by וַיְהִי, "and it was") tells how Sennacherib was assassinated by his own sons (37:38).

The Lord's Victory over the Assyrians (36:1–37:38)

- *Sennacherib's Demand That Judah Surrender (36:1–22)*
- *Isaiah's Reassuring Word to Hezekiah (37:1–7)*
- *Sennacherib's Taunt of Hezekiah (37:8–13)*
- *Hezekiah's Prayer for Deliverance (37:14–20)*
- *The Lord's Response to Hezekiah (37:21–35)*
- *The Lord's Judgment of Sennacherib (37:36–38)*

EXPOSITION (36:1–37:38)

Sennacherib's Demand That Judah Surrender (36:1–22)

Sennacherib demanded that Hezekiah surrender—for no one, he boasted, could defeat the Assyrian army.

36:1. In King Hezekiah's fourteenth year (701 B.C.), the Assyrian king Sennacherib invaded Judah and captured all its fortified cities (36:1).[1] In his account of the invasion, Sennacherib boasted that he "besieged forty-six" of Hezekiah's "walled cities and surrounding smaller towns, which were without number." He breached the walls, conquered the cities, and took 200,150 people captives, along with numerous livestock (*COS* 2.119B:303). According to the Assyrian king's account, he trapped Hezekiah "like a caged bird" in Jerusalem.

36:2–3. Sennacherib sent one of his officials to Jerusalem from Lachish, a strongly fortified city located approximately thirty miles to the southwest of the capital. He brought with him a large army (חַיִל כָּבֵד) and met three of Hezekiah's officials at the aqueduct of the Upper Pool (see commentary on 7:3) on the road to the Launderer's Field. This was the same location where Isaiah and his son Shear-jashub met Hezekiah's father, King Ahaz, thirty-four years before (cf. 7:3). On that occasion, when confronted by the military threat of the Israelite-Aramean alliance, Ahaz rejected the prophetic word and turned to Assyria for help. Now, ironically, Hezekiah faced a military threat from Assyria. How would he respond? (See Young 1969, 458.)

36:4–6. The Assyrian official delivered a message from Sennacherib (36:4), whom he called "the great king." Sennacherib's message begins with a question: "On what are you basing this confidence of yours?" Before answering the question, he sarcastically asserts that Hezekiah's battle strategy is comprised of "empty words" (36:5a, literally, "a word of lips," a phrase used in Prov. 14:23 of mere talk in contrast to action). He then essentially repeats his earlier question, "On whom are you depending, that you rebel against me?" (36:5b), though in this case he makes the point Hezekiah is guilty of rebellion. Sennacherib answers his own question: Hezekiah has placed his trust in Pharaoh, king of Egypt. He speaks of the Egyptian ruler in disparaging terms, comparing him to a splintered reed staff that punctures the hand of anyone who leans on it for support (36:6). Ironically, the official's depiction of Pharaoh serves as additional confirmation of what Isaiah said about Egypt (cf. 30:1–7; 31:1–3).

---

[1] The invasion was precipitated when Hezekiah allied with the king of Sidon, the king of Ashkelon, and the leaders of Ekron to free themselves from Assyrian rule. See Borowski 1995, 148–55. The rebellion failed before the onslaught of the Assyrian army. The king of Sidon fled to Cyprus, while Sennacherib took the king of Ashkelon as a prisoner and executed the leaders of Ekron. The Assyrians invaded central Judah and captured several cities, including Lachish. See Na'aman 1979, 61–86; Ussishkin 1977, 28–60; 2013, 1–34. For a convenient summary of Sennacherib's invasion of Judah, see Keimer 2018, 299–301. For a detailed study of the Kings version of the invasion, see Evans 2009. See further Gallagher 1999; Kalimi and Richardson 2014; Ussishkin 2014; Young 2012.

36:7. Sennacherib anticipates another possible response. Perhaps Hezekiah would reply more theologically and assert he has placed his trust in Judah's God, the Lord. Such a response would be wrongheaded, he asserts, for Hezekiah has rebelled against the Lord by eliminating his worship sites throughout the land and centralizing Judah's worship in Jerusalem (36:7). Sennacherib reveals his lack of understanding of the significance of Hezekiah's reform. Hezekiah had indeed eliminated the high places—and the idols being worshipped there (2 Kings 18:4). Sennacherib, with his polytheistic, idolatrous mindset, thought these were cult centers authorized by the Lord. But the Lord disapproved of such worship (Deut. 16:21) and commanded Israel to destroy these idolatrous worship places (Num. 33:52; Deut. 12:3). Hezekiah obeyed what the Lord had commanded, and the Lord commended his actions (2 Kings 18:3, 5–7).

36:8–9. The Assyrian official interrupts the reading of Sennacherib's message with his own appeal to Hezekiah. Sennacherib has argued that Egypt is a false source of protection and that Hezekiah has angered his own God. Therefore, the official reasons, the only wise course of action is to capitulate to Sennacherib's demands. If Hezekiah does so, the Assyrian official will provide him with as many horses as he needs for his chariot force (36:8). Surely this makes more sense than trusting in Egypt (36:9). The official is probably assuming Hezekiah will be hesitant to surrender out of fear that capitulation to Assyria will incur the wrath of his Egyptian ally. But he assures Hezekiah he will give him what he needs to repel any Egyptian retaliatory attack.

36:10. The official returns to Sennacherib's message, which seeks to undermine Hezekiah's faith in the Lord. Sennacherib argues that Hezekiah has offended his own God (cf. 36:7). Furthermore, the Lord is on Sennacherib's side; he is the one who commissioned Sennacherib to destroy Judah (36:10). There is, of course, a degree of truth in this (cf. Isa. 5:25–30; 7:17–25; 8:7–8; and especially 10:5–6). But Sennacherib is wrong to think he has received a blank check from the Lord. He is a mere instrument of judgment in the Lord's hand whose arrogance the Lord will punish (cf. 10:5–19; 37:23, 28–29) in response to Hezekiah's prayer for deliverance.

36:11–12. The Assyrian official delivered Sennacherib's message in Hebrew (literally, "Judahite"). This disturbed Hezekiah's officials because there were people on the city wall who could hear it. They asked him to speak in Aramaic, the diplomatic language of the empire (36:11). But the Assyrian official refused to do so, pointing out his message was not for the king and his officials alone. On the contrary, it was for all the people because they too would suffer the consequences of rebellion. Sennacherib's siege of Jerusalem would eventually deplete the city's food and water supply, forcing its inhabitants to eat their own excrement and drink their own urine in a desperate effort to stay alive (36:12).

36:13–15. In arrogant defiance of Hezekiah's officials, the Assyrian called out loudly in Hebrew to those on the wall and urged them to hear the words of "the great king, the king of Assyria" (36:13). Sennacherib warns them not to be deceived by Hezekiah, for he is not able to deliver them from the Assyrian army (36:14). As earlier, Sennacherib also discounts trust in the Lord. He warns the people to resist any attempt by Hezekiah to generate trust in the Lord by claiming that the Lord will deliver the city (36:15). The king expands upon this in 36:18–20.

36:16–17. But before doing so, he takes a more positive approach. After telling them not to listen to Hezekiah (36:16a), he makes an attractive offer. He tells them to give him a token of submission and come out to him. If they do, he promises to give each man his very own vine, fig tree, and cistern (36:16b). Of course, this will only be temporary, for he has already decided to turn Judah into an Assyrian province and to relocate its people in another land which, he assures them, will be like Judah, a fertile source for grain and wine (36:17). Ironically, the language is reminiscent of the Solomonic era (cf. 1 Kings 4:25 [HB 5:5]). It is also reminiscent of God's promise to Israel in the conclusion to Moses's blessing of the tribes (Deut. 33:28). There the Lord promised to make Israel secure and prosperous in its own land, driving out their enemies and providing them with the rain needed to make their crops flourish. However, due to Judah's sin an enemy was now at Jerusalem's gates. The commander's offer echoes God's ancient promise, drawing attention to the tragic circumstances in which God's people now find themselves.

36:18–19. Returning to his earlier argument (cf. Isa. 36:15), he warns the people that Hezekiah is misleading them when he says the Lord will deliver them (36:18a). The particle פֶּן, "lest, otherwise," at the beginning of 36:18 should be understood in relation to the exhortation at the beginning of 36:16, "do not listen to Hezekiah." In the structure of 36:16–20, the introductory jussive is supported in two ways: by causal כִּי, which introduces a positive reason why they should ignore Hezekiah (36:16b–17), and by פֶּן, which introduces a negative reason why they should ignore him (36:18–20). In short, they should ignore Hezekiah because (1) the Assyrian king promises them security and prosperity if they surrender, and (2) Hezekiah's promise will prove to be deceptive when the Assyrian king conquers them.

Sennacherib appeals to the Assyrians' military accomplishments. None of the gods of the surrounding nations has been able to deliver his land from the king of Assyria (36:18b). He arrogantly asks where the gods of Hamath, Arpad, and Sepharvaim are, suggesting they have disappeared before Assyria's might (36:19a). Indeed (וְכִי), he asks, did Samaria's gods rescue it (36:19b)? The facts were on Sennacherib's side. The Assyrians had conquered Arpad in 741 B.C., Samaria in 722, and Hamath in 720. (The location of Sepharvaim is not known.)

36:20. In conclusion Sennacherib asks them to identify any gods that have rescued their lands from the Assyrians (36:20a). There are, of course, none, implying it is foolish for them to expect the Lord to deliver Jerusalem (36:20b). At this point, Sennacherib has crossed a line. Earlier he argued the Lord was angry with Hezekiah and had commissioned the Assyrians to invade Judah (36:7, 10). But now he claims the Lord is incapable of delivering Jerusalem, even if he desires to do so. From a limited human perspective the Assyrian army was invincible (cf. Isa. 5:29), but the Lord was sovereign over their every move. For the Assyrians to think they could defeat the Lord was like an ax or club trying to swing its owner (10:15). Assyria failed to realize it was a mere instrument in God's hand (10:5–6). The Lord would chop the proud Assyrians down to size, laying an ax to their roots and causing them to come crashing to the ground (10:33–34). Contrary to the commander's boast, the Lord was fully capable of delivering the city (31:5). This is a blasphemous insult (cf. 37:4) that dishonors the Lord and prompts a hard-hitting response (37:21–29).

36:21–22. No one replied to the Assyrian official, because Hezekiah had issued a royal command forbidding a response (36:21). Instead, the three officials mentioned earlier (cf. 36:3, 11) went to Hezekiah with their clothes torn as a sign of mourning (cf. Smith 2007, 608) and reported to the king what the Assyrian official had said (36:22).

Isaiah's Reassuring Word to Hezekiah (37:1–7)

The prophet assured Hezekiah that the Lord would deliver the city.

37:1–2. When Hezekiah heard the report, he tore his clothes, put on sackcloth as a sign of mourning (cf. Gen. 37:34; 2 Sam. 3:31; Esther 4:1), and went to the temple (Isa. 36:1). He sent officials and priests to Isaiah with a message; they too wore sackcloth (37:2).

37:3. Hezekiah describes the day as one of "distress and rebuke and disgrace" (37:3a). The first (צָרָה) and third (נְאָצָה) terms focus on the emotional impact of Sennacherib's words—they bring distress and disgrace to those who hear them. The middle word (תּוֹכֵחָה) characterizes Sennacherib's message as insulting.

Hezekiah compares the situation to that of a woman who lacks the strength to push a baby out of the birth canal (37:3b). The Assyrian insults robbed Hezekiah of his strength. But there may be an even more alarming connotation. In ancient times, prior to modern surgical advances in gynecology, a woman's inability to give birth to a baby meant death for mother and child (cf. Oswalt 1986, 645; Young 1969, 474). Hezekiah's metaphor suggests he is very much aware that the Assyrian threats mean death for him and his kingdom.

37:4. But Hezekiah did not capitulate to despair. He hoped (note אוּלַי, "perhaps") that the Lord, whom he identifies as Isaiah's God (note "your God"), would take notice of the Assyrian's blasphemous threat and hold him accountable for his insolent words (36:4a). Hezekiah accuses Sennacherib of sending his official for the purpose of defying (לְחָרֵף) the living God. According to Ernst Kutsch (1986, 211), the verb חָרַף has the meaning "abuse (verbally), blaspheme, scoff." He adds, "The one who scoffs at another seeks to denigrate the latter in significance, worth, and ability; he makes clear that he scorns and despises the other." There are several texts where the verb or its related noun חֶרְפָּה refer to a crime, sometimes of a verbal nature, that deserves and/or receives retribution (cf. 1 Sam. 25:39; Ps. 79:12; Isa. 65:7; Jer. 15:15; see Kutsch 1986, 212).

The title "living God" (אֱלֹהִים חַי) is unique to this context (see also 37:17 and the parallel in 2 Kings 19:4, 16). A closely related form of the title (אֱלֹהִים חַיִּים) occurs in Deuteronomy 5:26, where Moses recalls that Israel heard the voice of the "living God" speaking from the fire at Sinai and lived to talk about it. This title also appears in 1 Samuel 17:26, where David accuses Goliath of defying (חָרַף) the battle lines of the living God (cf. 17:10). Jeremiah uses this title when affirming the Lord's sovereignty over the nations and his incomparability to the pagan gods (Jer. 10:10–11). The Lord tells Jeremiah to warn the people not to misrepresent the words of the "living God," who rules over all (Jer. 23:36). Another form of the title (אֵל חַי) occurs in Joshua 3:10, where Joshua tells the people they will know the "living God" is among them when he drives out their enemies before them. (This form of the title also appears in Pss. 42:2 [HB 3]; 84:2 [HB 3]; and Hos. 1:10 [HB 2:1].) The title "living God" in its various forms is not simply affirming God is alive, as opposed to dead, or that he exists. The title is associated with God's sovereignty, powerful presence, and ongoing intervention in the experience of his people. He is the living God in the sense that he actively intervenes for his people. We see this especially in David's case, where he delivers (1 Sam. 17:37, 47) his servant and gives him the victory over the enemy.

Hezekiah hopes that hearing the Assyrian's words will prompt the Lord to intervene. He anticipates the Lord punishing them for what they have said. The verb יָכַח, in the *hiphil* stem (וְהוֹכִיחַ) sometimes by metonymy carries the nuance, "punish" (cf. 2 Sam. 7:14; Hab. 1:12; see *HALOT* s.v. "יָכַח," 410), which fits well in this context. The Lord will punish "the words" of the Assyrian king, meaning he will punish the speaker for what he says. Another option is that the verb refers here to a formal accusation and announcement of doom that serves as a prelude to divine judgment (see Job 22:4; Ps. 50:21; as well as Isa. 37:22–35).

Having described what might happen, Hezekiah urges the prophet to pray on behalf of those who remain (literally, "the remnant that is found"; 37:4b). The expression literally means "lift up a pray on behalf of." It also appears in Jeremiah 7:16 and 11:14, where the Lord tells the prophet Jeremiah not to pray for the idolatrous people. Both here and in Jeremiah the expression points to the intercessory role of God's prophets. In addition to proclaiming God's message to the people, they also spoke to God as the people's representatives. Like Moses of old, they interceded with God, asking him to withhold judgment (cf. Exod. 32:9–14; 1 Sam. 12:19; Jer. 15:1; Amos 7:1–9).

The second-person verb form ("you will lift up") appears to be in sequence with the third-person verbs that appear in Isaiah 37:4a. If so, it has a hortatory nuance, "so pray." As Hezekiah contemplates the possibility of divine intervention, he suddenly asks the prophet to pray that this will indeed be the case (cf. Roberts 2015, 456). Another possibility is that the second-person verb logically connects to 37:3a, after a long parenthesis: "A day of distress and insult and disgrace (is) this day . . . so lift up a prayer on behalf of the remnant that is found."

The Assyrian army had devastated the countryside of Judah and taken a huge number of captives (see 2 Kings 18:13, as well as the commentary on Isa. 36:1 above). Those left in Jerusalem were the "remnant" of Judah. Yet the Lord would deliver this remnant (Isa. 37:31–32) and restore them to his favor (cf. Isa. 4:2–3).

37:5–6. When Hezekiah's officials came to Isaiah (37:5), the prophet gave them a message from the Lord for the king (37:6a). The Lord told Hezekiah not to fear the insults of the Assyrian king, delivered through his underlings (37:6b; cf. 2 Kings 19:6). The Lord agreed with Hezekiah's assessment (cf. 37:4). The Assyrian king had indeed blasphemed the Lord. The verb used here (גִּדְּפוּ) is rare. In 37:23 (cf. 2 Kings 19:6, 22) it is used of defiantly raising one's voice and lifting one's eyes against the Lord, who is identified as the Holy (that is, Sovereign) One. In Numbers 15:30 and Ezekiel 20:27 the verb is used of blatant sin against the Lord. In Psalm 44:16 [HB 17] there is no stated object. The psalmist (Israel) may be the recipient of the enemy's insults.

37:7. The Lord assures Hezekiah that he does not tolerate such insolence. Drawing attention to his response (note הִנְנִי, "look, I"), he declares he is about to place (note the participle נוֹתֵן) within Sennacherib a "spirit" (רוּחַ) that will prompt him to return to his own land when he hears a report (וְשָׁמַע שְׁמוּעָה), about which specifics are withheld. It is not clear if this "spirit" is personal (cf. 1 Kings 22:19) or impersonal, that is, a disposition of fear (cf. Oswalt 1986, 647). After the king returns to his homeland, the Lord will cause him to fall by the sword there. Curiously, the Lord does not mention the devastation of Sennacherib's army (37:36) at this point.

Since the verb שָׁמַע, "hear," appears in 37:9, it is tempting to see the report given there as the referent of the report predicted in 37:7 (cf. Roberts 2015, 457). If so, the report does not have its intended effect, for when Sennacherib heard that Tirhakah had come out to fight him, he assured Hezekiah he would not break off the invasion (37:10–13) nor retreat to his homeland (see Smith 2007, 612). In this case, the account highlights Sennacherib's stubborn resistance to the Lord's attempt to prompt him to leave. However, even though he did not respond to the report as the Lord had anticipated and resisted the "spirit" placed within him, he only temporarily thwarted the Lord's purpose. The Lord's sovereign power prevailed in the end when he devastated Sennacherib's army (cf. 37:36) and forced him to retreat. Understanding the report of 37:7 in this way explains why no mention is made of the destruction of the Assyrian army. The Lord intended to scare off Sennacherib by the report of 37:9. When that did not happen due to Sennacherib's hubris, a more severe measure was needed. There are many examples in the Bible of the Lord's antecedent will being thwarted, as it were, necessitating implementation of an alternative plan, which we may label his consequential will. There are also examples of individuals, despite being influenced by a spirit sent from the Lord, acting counter to his moral will.[2]

Since the report of Isaiah 37:9 does not have the predicted effect on Sennacherib, it is possible that another report is in view, although there is no reference to it in the chapter. Perhaps it is implied between 37:36 and 37:37. Events could have unfolded as follows: The Assyrian official departed and joined Sennacherib at Libnah (37:8), but to prevent Hezekiah from escaping or being reinforced, he probably left outside Jerusalem at least some of the significant force that had accompanied him (cf. 36:2). When the Lord devastated this army (37:36), Sennacherib, who was now busy with Tirhakah (37:9), would have received the report of its defeat outside Jerusalem. This report, in conjunction with the "spirit" placed within him by the Lord, prompted him to return to Assyria (37:37). There he was subsequently assassinated (37:38), in fulfillment of the Lord's promise to Hezekiah (37:7). However, this scenario is unlikely if all or most of the army left Jerusalem with the Assyrian official (cf. 37:8) and/or the devastation described in 37:36 overtook the main Assyrian army. In this case, the report or rumor predicted in 37:7 may have come from Mesopotamia, prompting Sennacherib, his army now in ruins, to retreat.

Sennacherib's Taunt of Hezekiah (37:8–13)
Sennacherib boasted of his successes and warned Hezekiah that resistance would be futile.

37:8. The Assyrian official left Jerusalem and found that Sennacherib had departed from Lachish and was now fighting against Libnah (37:8). It is unclear if the official took the army (cf. 36:2) with him. As noted above, he probably left some forces there to prevent Hezekiah from escaping or being reinforced. But he may have taken the bulk of the army to support Sennacherib in his continuing campaign against the towns of Judah, in this case, Libnah.

37:9–10. At this point Sennacherib heard that Tirhakah, called here "the king of Cush" (i.e., Nubia), had marched out to fight against him (37:9a). Anticipating a battle, Sennacherib sent messengers to Hezekiah (37:9b) to tell him he should not get his hopes up by thinking the Lord had rescued the city from the Assyrians (37:10). The blasphemy continues as he speaks of Hezekiah's God, in whom he trusts, as deceiving the king by promising him deliverance. The verb for "deceit" (hiphil of נשׁא; cf. Isa. 19:13) is the same one used by the woman in Genesis 3:13, when she accuses the snake of deceiving her.

37:11–13. Sennacherib supports his argument, as he did earlier (cf. 36:18–20), by appealing to Assyria's track record. The kings of Assyria who preceded him defeated all the lands that resisted them (37:11), a partial list of which is included for good effect (37:12b–13). The answer to his boastful question (37:12a, literally, "Did the gods of the nations, which my fathers destroyed, rescue them?") is embedded within it. No, they did not rescue the nations. On the contrary, the Assyrian kings destroyed those nations. Consequently, what makes Hezekiah think he will be any different (cf. 37:11b)? No god, including Hezekiah's, can rescue his worshippers from the Assyrian war machine. For any god to claim such power is sheer deception. Sennacherib's point is clear: once he disposes of Tirhakah, he will return to Jerusalem and finish the job he

---

2 Gideon and Jephthah demonstrated lack of faith after receiving the Lord's spirit (cf. Judg. 6:34–40; 11:29–31); and Samson, Saul, and David, despite possessing the Lord's spirit, were all seriously flawed leaders.

started by adding Hezekiah and Judah to the list of Assyria's conquered foes.

The reference to Tirhakah is problematic for some interpreters. According to his military annals, Sennacherib defeated the Egyptian army at Eltekeh before besieging Jerusalem. Furthermore, Tirhakah did not become king until 690 B.C., eleven years later. However, Isaiah 37 does not actually say Sennacherib fought Tirhakah on this occasion. Though Tirhakah marched out to do battle, he may have turned back. Another option is that Sennacherib fought the Egyptians on two separate occasions and the battles are streamlined in the Assyrian record. As for the title "king of Cush," this simply reflects Tirhakah's status when this account was completed. The reference to Sennacherib's death in 37:38 indicates that the account in its final form postdated his assassination in 681. So, calling Tirhakah "king" is comparable to saying, "Queen Elizabeth (II) was born in 1926" (Kitchen 2003, 16).

Hezekiah's Prayer for Deliverance (37:14–20)
Hezekiah asked the Lord to deliver the city.

37:14–15. When Hezekiah read the message from Sennacherib, he went to the temple (literally, "house of the Lord"), spread the letter out before the Lord (37:14), and prayed (37:15). This was appropriate, for the Assyrian king had insulted the Lord by suggesting he was deceiving Hezekiah. In so doing, he was assuming the Lord was unable to deliver his people from the Assyrians.

37:16. Hezekiah begins by addressing the Lord as יְהוָה צְבָאוֹת, the one who leads armies (see the commentary on 1:9), and as the God of Israel who sits over the cherubim. The mentioning of the cherubim alludes to the ark of the covenant (cf. 1 Sam. 4:4; 2 Sam. 6:2), which was a tangible reminder of the Lord's presence (Num. 10:33–36), a place where he met with his people (Exod. 25:22) and from which he ruled over them (2 Sam. 6:2). According to 2 Samuel 6:2, the name/title Lord of Armies was invoked over the ark, indicating his ownership of it. The title suggests the ark was viewed as a portable throne for the Lord from which he would arise when doing battle with his enemies and to which he would return victoriously (Num. 10:35–36). By referring to the ark, Hezekiah attests to the fact that the Lord, though the ruler of all nations (cf. Isa. 37:16), dwells in a special way among his people in the Jerusalem temple (see Roberts 2015, 468).

Hezekiah affirms that the Lord alone is God over the kingdoms of the earth and that he created the heavens and earth. Isaiah 37:16b reads literally, "for you, you made the heavens and the earth." Hezekiah uses the second-person pronoun before the second-person finite verb for emphasis, as if to affirm, "you and no other made the heavens and the earth" (Young 1969, 484). The Lord is sovereign over all the nations by reason of being the creator of the world. If the Assyrians were able to conquer nations, it was only because the Lord allowed them to do so. The Sovereign Creator is also Israel's God, fully capable of protecting his covenant nation from the Assyrians.

37:17. Using strongly anthropomorphic language, Hezekiah urges the Lord to hear with his ears and to open his eyes and see (37:17a). He asks the Lord to listen to the words of Sennacherib, who has deliberately insulted (לְחָרֵף, "to insult") the living God (37:17b; cf. 37:4).

37:18–20. Hezekiah acknowledges the Assyrians have indeed destroyed all the lands (37:18) and burned their idol gods (37:19a). They were able to do so because these idols were, in contrast to the "living God" (cf. 37:17), not really gods at all, but human-made objects, formed from wood and stone and therefore easily destroyed (37:19b). Hezekiah appeals to "the LORD our God," the God of Israel and the only true God who rules all kingdoms (cf. 37:16). He asks the Lord to deliver Israel from Sennacherib's hand (37:20a), so that all the kingdoms of the earth might recognize the truth that the Lord is unique (37:20b). Hezekiah needs and desires deliverance, but his ultimate concern is the Lord's reputation (see Oswalt 1986, 655).

The final clause of 37:20, which reads literally, "for you, O Lord, you alone," appears to be elliptical (Roberts 2015, 463). Dead Sea scroll 1QIs^a and the parallel in 2 Kings 19:19 add "God," before "you alone," which conforms to the pattern in Isaiah 37:16. However, in Isaiah 45–46 the Lord declares, "I am God, and there is no other" (45:22; 46:9) and "I am the LORD, and there is no other" (45:5, 6, 18; 46:6–18; see Smith 2007, 621 n. 116; Wildberger 2002, 423). The statement in 37:20b seems to correspond conceptually to the latter of these. By substituting "LORD" for "the [only true] God" (cf. 37:16), Hezekiah identifies the Lord as this God (see Motyer 1993, 282).

The Lord's Response to Hezekiah (37:21–35)

The Lord responded to Hezekiah's prayer by sending the king a message through Isaiah (37:21). The response includes a taunt against the Assyrian king Sennacherib (37:22–29), followed by assuring words to Hezekiah (37:30–35).

37:21–22. As Oswalt (1986, 659) points out: "Sennacherib has spoken to Hezekiah concerning the Lord [cf. vv. 10–13]; Hezekiah has spoken to the Lord concerning Sennacherib [cf. vv. 16–20]; now the Lord speaks to Hezekiah concerning Sennacherib." As Oswalt observes, God has "the final word." In his word "against" (עַל) Sennacherib, the Lord directly addresses the Assyrian ruler. He pictures "Virgin Daughter Zion," seemingly vulnerable and at the mercy of the Assyrian king, despising and mocking him. She shakes her head, which was a mocking gesture (37:22; cf. Pss. 22:7 [HB 8]; 109:25; Lam. 2:15). The text reads literally, "after you, (her) head Daughter Jerusalem shakes." This suggests he has turned to flee (cf. NIV11, "as you flee") and she is following him (Young 1969, 488).

37:23–25. The Lord sarcastically asks the Assyrian king to identify the one whom he has blasphemed and insulted as he raised his voice and lifted his proud eyes. He then gives the answer to his questions: the Holy One of Israel, a title that points to the Lord's sovereignty and his relationship to his people (Isa. 37:23; cf. 1:4). Indeed, through his servants the Assyrian king blasphemed the Sovereign Master (אֲדֹנָי, 37:24a) another title highlighting the Lord's sovereign position and superiority to Sennacherib.

The Assyrian king boasts of his military exploits with a good dose of hyperbole, claiming, as Wildberger (2002, 427) points out, to accomplish "the impossible" (37:24–25). Typically, all or most of the verbs in 37:24–25 are translated as perfective, as if the king were claiming to have already done these things (cf. NIV11). However, it is preferable to translate the *qatal* forms as perfective ("I have ascended" [37:24]; "I have dug" [37:25]; "and drunk" [37:25]) and the *yiqtol* forms with prefixed *waw*-conjunctive (not consecutive) as anticipatory ("and I will cut down" [37:24]; "and I will enter" [37:24]; "and I will dry up" [37:25]). The king boasted of ascending Lebanon with his chariots and anticipated cutting down its trees and invading its remote regions and thick forests (37:24). He dug wells in the lands he conquered and anticipated invading Egypt, where he would dry up its streams with the soles of his feet (37:25). The imagery highlights the ease of the envisioned conquest (cf. Young 1969, 491).

37:26–27. He attributed his success to his own prowess, but the Lord informs him that his conquests were simply part of the Lord's sovereign plan, determined long ago and now being realized (37:26). The Lord decided cities would be reduced to ruins, leaving their inhabitants humiliated (37:26b–27a). The defeated people are shriveled up like vegetation in the fields or grass on rooftops when blasted by a hot wind from the east (37:27b). In his plan God determined beforehand that he would use the Assyrians for his purposes. He created/formed the blueprint for the Assyrian conquests in the distant past and, when the time was right, made it a reality. Their success was part of his plan; they were mere pawns in the hand of the Lord of history. It was absurd for the Assyrians to defy God, for he could and would turn their success into disaster (cf. 37:28–29). (For further discussion of the plan/decree of God, see the pertinent notes at Isa. 5:19; 10:22; 14:26; 31:2.)

37:28–29. The Lord is thoroughly aware of all the Assyrian king does, including his raging hubris (37:28). Because he has raged against the Lord and displayed an arrogant complacency that has reached the Lord's attention (the text reads literally, "and your complacency has come up into my ears"), the Lord will make him return the way he came (37:29). He will put a hook in his nose, like a conqueror does to a captive (cf. 2 Chron. 33:11, which reads, "and they seized Manasseh with hooks"; and Ezek. 19:4, 9, where the captive is compared to a captured lion, cf. 19:3), and a bit in his mouth, as one does to a stubborn horse or donkey (cf. Ps. 32:9; Prov. 26:3).

In the quotation of the Assyrian king's boast in Isaiah 37:24–25, he uses a first-person pronoun or verb ten times (in the Hebrew text). In 37:26, 28–29 the Lord does some boasting of his own, as he uses a first-person pronoun or verb eleven times, drowning out the arrogant king's bragging as he asserts that he, not Sennacherib, is the sovereign ruler.

37:30. The Lord now addresses Hezekiah. The text reads literally, "and this for you (is) the sign." Though Hezekiah's name is not mentioned (NIV11 supplies it), it is clear from what follows that he, not Sennacherib, is now being addressed. The introductory וְזֶה, "and this" corresponds to "this" at the beginning of 37:22, which is spoken to Hezekiah (cf. 37:21).

As discussed earlier (see commentary on 7:14–17), the word אוֹת, "sign," can refer to a miraculous intervention (cf. Isa. 38:7–8, 22), but more frequently it is used of an event, object, or person that is vested with special significance and serves as an object lesson or reminder (cf. 8:18; 19:20; 20:3; 55:13; 66:19). The "sign" outlined in Isaiah 37:30, like the one given in Isaiah 7:14–17, involves the timing of events in accordance with a prophetic prediction. In other words, the "sign" in this case pertains to God's providential, rather than strictly miraculous, intervention.

More specifically, the sign here relates to the agricultural timetable. Because of the Assyrian presence in Judah, normal agricultural activity was suspended. The Assyrians destroyed or consumed (cf. 1:7) the harvest of the present year. Hezekiah and the people would have to eat what grew on plants that had sprouted from seeds sown in prior years (cf. Lev. 25:5, 11). They would need to do the same in the coming (or "second") year. This indicates it would be too late to plant a crop in the coming year, typically done toward the beginning of the agricultural cycle in November–December (see Borowski 1987, 34). So the present year must have been almost over and the new year ready to begin. But the following (or "third") year Hezekiah and the people (note the plural imperatival forms in Isa. 37:30b) would be able to sow, reap, plant vineyards, and eat grapes according to the normal schedule, because the Assyrian menace would be gone. At that time people could recall the Lord's prediction and realize the fulfillment of the prophesied sequence was a tangible indicator, or "sign," of the Lord's protective presence. The restoration of crops and vineyards counters the promise of the Assyrian official (cf. 36:17; see Abernethy 2014, 112).

37:31–32. But there is more to the sign than this. Just as the harvest of the third year would replace the meager growth that preceded it, so the remnant of the people of Judah would take root and yield a harvest of fruit in the days ahead (37:31). Those left in Jerusalem would be able to leave the city once the Assyrian threat was eliminated (37:32a), presumably to repopulate the land. The zeal of the Lord of Armies would assure this (37:32b; cf. 9:7). On several occasions the Old Testament speaks of the Lord's zeal (the term קִנְאָה is often translated "jealousy"). Sometimes God's zeal is associated with his anger against his enemies (Isa. 59:17). At other times it refers to his intense love for and commitment to his people, which moves him to show compassion to (Joel 2:18; cf. Isa. 63:15), to seek reconciliation with (Zech. 8:2), to restore (Isa. 9:7), and to protect and/or vindicate his people (Isa. 26:11; 42:13; Zech. 1:14). Here in Isaiah 37:32 his zeal encompasses both his anger against the Assyrian king and his commitment to his people.

37:33–34. This divine zeal would prevent the Assyrian king from attacking Jerusalem (37:33). In fact, he would return the way he had come and would not set foot in the city (37:34). Five times in 37:33–34 the Lord declares what the Assyrian king will "not" do. Only once does he describe what Sennacherib will do—namely, return by the way he came (Smith 2007, 630).

37:35. The Lord would defend (וְגַנּוֹתִי, from גָּנַן; cf. 2 Kings 20:6; Isa. 31:5) the city in order to deliver it (Isa. 37:35a). The Lord had two primary motives for delivering the city. He desired to preserve his reputation in the face of the Assyrian king's insults and to demonstrate his faithfulness to his servant David, whose dynasty, embodied in Hezekiah at this time, had been placed in jeopardy by the king's hostility (37:35b). Though human opinion of God does not increase or diminish his royal status in any way, God desires to receive his proper due from his creatures (Isa. 48:11). This prompts him to intervene in human affairs, even when his people do not deserve his favor (cf. Isa. 43:25; Ezek. 36:22; Dan. 9:19). The reference to David as the Lord's "servant" is significant. The title is a reminder of God's covenant with David, whereby he promised him an enduring dynasty (2 Sam. 7; cf. 1 Kings 11:13, 34, 36, 38; Ps. 89:3, 20 [HB 4, 21]; Jer. 33:21–22). David made Jerusalem his capital city and moved the ark of God there. From that time forward the city became inextricably linked with God's covenantal promises to David. Because of his commitment to David, the Lord would rescue David's city, thereby assuring the continuance of his dynasty.

The Lord's Judgment of Sennacherib (37:36–38)

As he predicted, the Lord judged Sennacherib severely.

37:36. The Lord's taunt against Sennacherib was no idle threat. The angel (מַלְאָךְ, "messenger") of the Lord struck down 185,000 Assyrian soldiers (Isa. 37:36a).[3] There is irony here: Sennacherib sent "messengers" to intimidate Hezekiah (cf. 36:2; 39:9), but now the Lord sends a "messenger" of his own to do more than talk.

The attack by the angel happened during the night, for the corpses were discovered in the

---

3   It is not clear if the title refers to a particular angel. The phrase is definite, but it may simply refer to a definite angel in any given context without implying the same angel is always the referent. (See the use of the phrase "the servant of the LORD," which refers to a definite servant in each context but not the same servant in every passage.) Those who assume the same angel is in view in every passage debate this angel's precise identity. Some have argued he is God himself (or perhaps the second person of the Trinity in a preincarnate form), while others contend that the angel, though distinct from God, comes with divine authority and can therefore speak and be treated as God himself.

morning (37:36b). The text of 37:36b reads literally, "and they arose early in the morning, and, look, all of them (were) dead corpses." The subject of the verb, "they arose early," is not identified. It could be the people of Jerusalem, but only if the army that accompanied the Assyrian official is in view (cf. 36:2) and we assume he left a significant number there when he went to find Sennacherib. More likely, the subject is the remainder of Sennacherib's army, who awoke to find devastation in their camp.

The number given (185,000) seems unreasonably high.[4] It is possible the Hebrew term אֶלֶף, typically understood as "thousand," refers instead to a military contingent comprised of a much smaller number. Another option is that the number is intentionally exaggerated, a literary technique attested in military accounts from the ancient Near East.

It should come as no surprise that Sennacherib does not mention the death of his soldiers in his annals, given his well-attested propensity for falsifying history (see Laato 1995). It is perhaps more important to observe what he did not say; namely, he did not claim to conquer the city or to depose Hezekiah. (In this regard, see Roberts 2015, 472.)

According to a later tradition, preserved in Herodotus, Sennacherib had to break off his attack on the Egyptian delta when mice ate at the Assyrians' quivers, bowstrings, and shield grips. The reference to mice could be a clue to what happened. Perhaps a plague broke out in the Assyrian camp, killing many soldiers. However, Mordechai Cogan and Hayim Tadmor (1988, 250–51) raise several objections, arguing that Herodotus is not a reliable guide in this case. Nevertheless, apart from the Herodotus tradition, it is entirely possible that a plague could have been the instrument used by the angel of the Lord to decimate the Assyrians. Roberts (2015, 472) provides several examples of devastating plagues from ancient Near Eastern, including Assyrian, records.

37:37–38. With his army decimated, Sennacherib returned to Nineveh (37:37), where he was subsequently assassinated by two of his sons, who then fled to Ararat (Urartu, located north of Assyria; 37:38a). Esarhaddon replaced his father on the Assyrian throne (37:38b). The biblical text gives no exact time frame for this incident, but we know from Assyrian history that it occurred twenty years later in 681 B.C. Several ancient sources, including the Babylonian Chronicle, corroborate the biblical account, although they mention only one assassin, identified as Arda-milissu (called Adrammelech in 37:38). (See Cogan and Tadmor 1988, 239–40; and Parpola 1980, 171–82.) He was upset that Sennacherib had chosen a younger son, Esarhaddon, to succeed him. The biblical text informs us that Sennacherib was worshipping his god Nisroch at the time of the assassination. No such god is known in extant records from Mesopotamia. The name may be a corrupted form of the Mesopotamian god Nusku.

THEOLOGICAL FOCUS

The theological focus of this passage can be stated as follows: the Lord is sovereign over the destiny of nations and humiliates those who arrogantly challenge his authority. As the prophet develops this theological theme, the following emphases emerge:

---

4   For a helpful discussion of the issue of large numbers in the Old Testament, see Merrill, Rooker, and Grisanti 2011, 240–46 (see esp. the works cited in 244 n. 61). First Kings 20:30 clearly demonstrates that numbers were either sometimes inflated in military accounts or have been misunderstood by later interpreters. According to that text, after Israel had killed one hundred thousand Arameans in battle (20:29), the rest of the Aramean army fled to Aphek, where the town wall collapsed and killed twenty-seven thousand of them. That a falling wall in such a relatively small settlement could kill that many soldiers is unlikely.

1. The Lord's sovereignty over the destiny of his people

The Assyrian king Sennacherib boasted he would conquer Jerusalem and revealed his plan to relocate its people (cf. 36:17). He threatened Judah's very status as a nation. However, in response to Hezekiah's prayer, the Lord announced he would deliver the city (37:33–34). The Lord, not the Assyrian king, controlled the destiny of his people.

2. The Lord's opposition to arrogant human kings

The Assyrian king claimed correctly to be the Lord's instrument of judgment against Judah (36:10). But he pressed his argument way too far when he boasted that the Lord would not be able to deliver the city because the Assyrian army was undefeated and invincible (36:18–20; 37:11–13). He accused the Lord of misleading Hezekiah with empty promises (37:10). The Lord was offended by this hubris and considered it blasphemy (37:6, 23). He explained that the Assyrians' successes were by his decree and in accordance with his plan (37:26). He announced he would turn back the Assyrians and humiliate Sennacherib (37:7, 29, 33–34). This was no idle threat, for the Lord carried out this prediction by decimating Sennacherib's army, forcing him to return to Nineveh, where he was assassinated by his own sons (37:36–38). In this way the Lord demonstrated he is indeed the Living God who is active in the world, the Holy One of Israel who protects his people, and the Sovereign Master who controls the destiny of nations (37:4, 17, 23–24).

3. The Lord's superiority to the idol-gods of the nations

Sennacherib's fatal error was thinking the Lord was like the idol-gods of the nations the Assyrians had defeated. Hezekiah understood the vast difference between these so-called gods, which were the handiwork of men (מַעֲשֵׂה יְדֵי־אָדָם), constructed from wood and stone (37:19), and the Lord, who made (עָשָׂה) the heavens and earth and ruled all the earth's kingdoms (37:16). He knew the Lord was the only true God and consequently had the power to deliver his people, something the pagan gods were incapable of doing (37:20).

4. The Lord's concern for his own reputation

The Lord assured Hezekiah he would deliver Jerusalem for the sake of his own reputation (37:35). Indeed, Hezekiah had prayed for this when he asked the Lord to deliver the city so that all the kingdoms of the earth, which belong to the Lord (37:16), would recognize him as the only God (37:20).

5. The Lord's commitment to the Davidic dynasty

The Lord also assured Hezekiah he would deliver the city for the sake of his servant David (37:35). The Lord made promises to David that had ramifications for Israel (cf. 2 Sam. 7:9–16; Ps. 89:18–37 [HB 19–38]). The bearer of the promise at this time was David's descendant Hezekiah. By threatening Hezekiah and the royal city of Jerusalem, the Assyrian king was threatening the promise so the Lord would thwart his intentions.

PREACHING AND TEACHING STRATEGIES

Exegetical and Theological Synthesis

Isaiah 36:1 establishes the setting for this story as Hezekiah's fourteenth year as king. Assyria was engaged in a military invasion of Judah, and they were having success conquering the fortified cities and towns. As their army arrived at Jerusalem, the military commander of the Assyrian army met with a small contingent of Judean leaders to discuss possible terms of a surrender (36:3). The commander began the negotiation by representing his master as "the great king" (36:4). Throughout these chapters the king of Assyria views himself as the supreme

The Lord's Victory over the Assyrians (36:1–37:38)

ruler on earth. He or his spokesmen denigrate the God of heaven. On the other hand, Hezekiah, the king of Judah, humbles himself before God and seeks to magnify God's honor.

The commander engages in psychological warfare to convince Hezekiah to surrender quickly without putting up a fight or forcing Assyria to endure a long siege. His first line of reasoning is to attack their coalition with Egypt. Egypt would be of no value (36:5–6). This aligned with what God had said when he warned Judah not to put their trust in Egypt (Isa. 28:18–20; 30:1–7; 31:1). However, the commander goes from speaking truth about Egypt to speaking foolishness. He basically says, "If you think that your God will protect you, he won't." Why? Because Hezekiah destroyed the high places of worship throughout Judah years earlier when he became king, limiting their worship to the temple only (36:7). The commander misinterpreted these actions. Contrary to what he said, this endeared Hezekiah to the Lord as a righteous king, not the other way around (2 Kings 18:3–4; cf. Isa. 30:22, 31:7). The altars that he had destroyed were altars to idols and false gods. As such, Hezekiah's prior reforms helped demonstrate his acknowledgment that the Lord alone deserved to receive honor and glory in Israel.

The commander continued his attempt to intimidate Judah by saying, "I will give you two thousand horses—if you can put riders on them" (Isa. 36:8). This was the equivalent of trash-talking one's opponent by bragging about how much bigger and stronger your team is. Next, the Assyrian diplomat questions their trust in the Lord. After all, according to Israel's own prophets, he was the one who had sent Assyria against Judah as judgment against them. To some degree, this was true (cf. Isa. 5:25–30; 7:17–25; 8:7–8; 10:5–6). As such, it likely made the group of Judean delegates concerned that the citizens of Jerusalem would lose heart and side with the Rabshakeh. Thus, they ask him to speak in Aramaic, the diplomatic language at that time, rather than Hebrew. Unwilling to oblige their request, the commander turned his attention to the Judeans on the wall to appeal for them to surrender. He warns them that if they don't surrender, they will be forced to eat their own dung and drink their own urine in the event of a famine resulting from a long siege. Conversely, the commander promised that if the people surrender to him, he will deport them to a great land where each would have access to their own vine, their own fig tree, and their own cistern to eat and drink to their heart's desire (36:16).

Notably, the commander used this opportunity to praise the Assyrian king, once again calling him "the great king" (36:13). Meanwhile he insults the Lord by telling them not to trust in him to deliver them (36:15). (Later the king of Assyria sends a letter to Hezekiah that follows this same line of argument [Isa. 37:10–12].)

As we turn the page to Isaiah 37, we encounter Hezekiah's response to the Assyrian army's claims. However, he doesn't make his rebuttal to the commander or even to the king of Assyria. Rather, he makes his appeal to the Lord. He tears his clothes, puts on sackcloth as a sign of humility, and goes into the temple to pray (37:1). He then calls for a day of distress and repentance for the people's sins (37:3). Hezekiah then says to Isaiah, "It may be that the Lord your God will hear the words of the field commander, whom his master, the king of Assyria, has sent to ridicule the living God, and that he will rebuke him for the words that the Lord your God has heard" (37:4). Hezekiah draws attention to the way that the king of Assyria has mocked the living God. His hope is that God, who has certainly heard their words, would act on behalf of his people for the sake of his own reputation.

Later in the chapter, when Hezekiah receives the letter from the Assyrian king attempting to cast doubt on the Lord's ability to deliver, Hezekiah lays the letter before the Lord in the temple. It is as if he is saying, "O Lord, look at what the

Assyrian king has said about you. Look at how he has insulted you" (37:17). Hezekiah declares that God alone is the ruler over every nation on earth, not just Israel (37:16). He also declares that the Lord is "the living God" (37:4, 17). This title is likely meant to contrast the Lord with the lifeless, impotent idols of the pagan nations around them, particularly the ones from the nations Assyria was able to conquer. When the king of Assyria brags that he defeated the surrounding nations, and that their gods could not stop him, Hezekiah counters his argument by pointing out that it was because they were dead idols made of wood and stone (37:19).

Finally, Hezekiah prays, "Now, LORD our God, deliver us from his hand, so that all the kingdoms of the earth may know that you, LORD, are the only God" (37:20). The basis for his request is not anything that Judah has done to deserve deliverance, or the virtue of their identity as God's people. He doesn't even appeal to God's mercy and love for them. Instead, he asks for God to deliver Judah in order that all the nations of the earth might know that he alone is God. In other words, Hezekiah's expressed concern is for God's reputation, not his own well-being. Hezekiah cares about God's reputation and honor above that of the false gods. He is concerned that the people worship the Lord alone. Thus, this isn't simply empty talk by a man trying to manipulate God into doing what he wants him to do. Certainly, he was concerned for his own personal safety and legacy as a king, but he also genuinely cared about the Lord's reputation and honor too.

This passage began with *the Assyrian leaders insulting God's glory* (Isa. 36:1–22). This was followed by *Hezekiah's appeal to God's glory* in his prayer for rescue (Isa. 37:1–20). In the final section of this passage, we witness *God's defense and vindication of his own glory* (Isa. 37:21–29). In response to Hezekiah's prayer, the Lord sends the prophet to assure him that he will deliver his people. God affirms that while the Assyrians have despised and scorned the people of Jerusalem, the one whom they ultimately have insulted is the Lord himself (37:23–24). He then asserts his sovereign authority over Assyria. The Lord planned all their successes long ago (37:26–27). Furthermore, the Lord is aware of their blasphemous boasting against him (37:28). Because they rage against God, he promises to put his hook in their leader's nose and a bit in his mouth and force him back to his homeland (37:29).

After providing a promise that would serve as a sign to his people that they would ultimately be saved (37:30–34), God again says that the reason why he will defend Jerusalem is for his own sake, for his reputation and glory (37:35). The passage ends with one of the most amazing and overwhelming displays of God's sovereign force against his enemies in all of Scripture: the angel of the Lord went out and struck down 185,000 Assyrian warriors. Additionally, after the king returned to Assyria, he was struck down with the sword, and replaced by Esarhaddon his son (37:37–38).

Preaching Idea
God honors those who live for his glory, but those who defy his glory are doomed.

Contemporary Connections

What does it mean?
What does it mean to live for God's glory? This is a saying that gets thrown around by preachers quite often. But since we don't often speak about doing things for another person's glory in other contexts, we shouldn't assume that everyone knows what it means. "Glory" refers to anything that makes a person worthy of others' praise or admiration. For example, Proverbs 20:29 says, "The glory of young men is their strength." A young man's strength is recognized by others as a desirable trait, making those who possess it worthy of others' admiration. Similarly, Proverbs 16:31 describes an older person's

gray hair as a "crown of glory." Because our culture today values youth and beauty so much, we have a harder time appreciating how gray hair would be something desirable. However, the ancient Hebrew culture revered the aged for their wisdom. Thus, one's gray hair was an indication that they had experienced much in life, giving them an invaluable perspective on life from which to teach others. To live, then, for another person's glory means to live in such a way as to draw attention to and magnify the things about them that elicit praise and admiration from others. To say it more simply, it involves acting in ways that prioritize the reputation and status of another.

When the Bible says that we are to do all things for the glory of God (1 Cor. 10:31), it means that we are to consider how our words and actions reflect on his reputation. At times, this will mean choosing to sacrifice what others think about us as we seek to promote and exalt their opinion of God. For example, a financially successful Christian may choose to live much more modestly than others with similar incomes in order to invest generously in helping the needy and spreading the Gospel. In addition to giving up some additional comforts in life, they will also be sacrificing the glory and honor that would otherwise have been leveled their way by the watching world who would admire their worldly success. Or consider the person who chooses to love an enemy rather than engage in selfish ambition or even to pursue revenge. This person too may have to sacrifice their own reputation by appearing to some to be weak and unwilling to defend their own honor. However, the alternative would risk others having a diminished view of Christ and his church. After all, if they claim to be a Christian, but act with no more grace or love toward their enemies as the next person, would their example compel others to pursue Christianity? Christians must remember that God promises to honor these sorts of sacrifices in his eternal kingdom (Isa 40:10; 62:11; Matt 19:29; Lk 14:12-14; 1 Cor 3:12-15; Col 3:23-24; 2 Tim 4:7-8; Heb 10:32-36; Rev 22:12).

Is it true?
Genesis 1:27 teaches that human beings were created in the image of God. Genesis 1:28 then gives the creation mandate to "be fruitful and increase in number; fill the earth." The implication seems to be that God wanted his people to reproduce and multiply his image throughout the world he created. This same progression appears again in Genesis 9 in God's instructions to Noah and his family following the flood. After reaffirming that he had made them in his own image (9:6), he instructed them to "be fruitful and increase in number; multiply on the earth and increase upon it" (9:7).

Fast-forward to the life and ministry of Jesus. John's gospel tells us that Jesus was in the beginning with God. In fact, Jesus and the Father shared the same glory because Jesus was himself God (John 1:1). Jesus was sent to earth to be a tangible, visible revelation of God to humanity. In Jesus, God "became flesh and made his dwelling among us" so that we could see the glory of God with our own eyes (John 1:14, 18). Jesus was the perfect representation of what the ideal human should have been had Adam and his descendants never sinned. Jesus lived his life to perfectly showcase the attributes and character of God the Father. In everything Jesus did, he sought to accomplish his Father's will, not his own (Matt. 26:39; John 4:34; 5:30; 6:38; 14:31). As such, the apostle Paul was able to say of Jesus that he was the visible "image of the invisible God" (Col. 1:15; cf. 2 Cor. 4:4) and that "God was pleased to have all his fullness dwell in" Jesus (Col. 1:19). The writer of the book of Hebrews similarly described Jesus as "the radiance of God's glory and the exact representation of his being" (Heb. 1:3). God's ultimate mission in the redemption of humanity is to transform those who trust in Jesus into the very image of God by conforming them into the likeness of Jesus (Rom. 8:29; cf. Eph. 4:20–24; Col. 3:8–10).

This process is also described as glorification (Rom. 8:30), because through it we are made to reflect the very glory of God.

Just before Jesus ascended into heaven, he summarized the mission his followers were to pursue in his absence: "Therefore go and make disciples of all nations, baptizing them in the name of the Father and of the Son and of the Holy Spirit, and teaching them to obey everything I have commanded you" (Matt. 28:19–20). It is interesting to compare Jesus's mandate to his disciples with the one God gave to Adam and Eve at creation, and then again to Noah and his family mentioned above (Gen. 1:27–28; 9:6–7). In each instance, the command involved multiplying the image of God throughout the whole world. Jesus's followers were to multiply disciples of Jesus who would observe everything Jesus had commanded. As a disciple of Jesus committed to obeying him in everything, they would imitate the one who fully exemplified the image of God in his life and actions. As such, both the Old and the New Testament demonstrate God's overarching concern to have his glory spread throughout the earth through the character and behavior of his individual creatures.

Now what?

Charles Sheldon's classic book *In His Steps* (1898) popularized the now famous slogan, "What would Jesus do?" In the book, Rev. Henry Maxwell challenges his congregation one Sunday to commit to a year of constantly asking themselves the question "What would Jesus do?" and committing to act accordingly. This challenge was accepted by some of the members of his church and the trajectory of their lives was dramatically changed, as was the town in which they lived. It would be fair to point out that simply asking the question "What would Jesus do?" and committing to follow it doesn't guarantee that one will always do the right thing, because how can one always know what Jesus would do in each situation? Nonetheless, the principle behind this practice is both simple and profound. To the degree that one can discern how Jesus would act based upon what is known from the Scriptures about how he lived his life, it provides a blueprint for how we should act. God's overarching desire for our lives is for us to be conformed into the image of Christ, the one who radiated the glory of God and reflected his very image to us.

While we may not know for sure what Jesus would or wouldn't do, we can be certain of the essence of his character. We know, for example, that Jesus was humble and that he hated pretense and outward shows of piety that were disconnected from a genuine love of God. We know that Jesus was particularly compassionate toward those who were disliked by most, those considered outcasts. This included those who were shunned by religious people because of their sinful lifestyles. Jesus said that he came to earth to reach out to those who were spiritually sick and in need of a physician, not for those who appeared to have it all together (Mark 2:17). We know that Jesus often prioritized getting alone to pray even over ministry with the crowds. We also know that Jesus was fully committed to obeying his Father, regardless of the sacrifice it required of him. We could go on and on describing what Jesus was like. Chances are, there are some glaring ways that our lives differ from what we know about Jesus's life. If a person really wants to live for God's glory, then they should choose the most obvious area where their life is out of step and begin walking as Jesus walked. This is what it means to be Jesus's disciple.

Second, if one intends to live for God's glory, it will require that they routinely spend time with God in his Word, gazing upon the beauty of his character. Second Corinthians 3:18 says, "And we all, with unveiled face, beholding the glory of the Lord, are being transformed into the same image from one degree of glory to another." This passage teaches that one of the ways God transforms us into his image is by our gazing upon his glory. When we look deeply upon another and admire their glorious attributes and qualities, our hearts are naturally drawn to imitate them.[5] As a preacher, I will naturally begin to imitate and become more like the preachers I regularly listen to and whose styles I most admire. A teenage girl who is concerned about her appearance will naturally identify women she believes to be beautiful, whether it be some of the popular girls in her class at school, models in magazines, or actresses in movies she watches. She will then consciously or subconsciously imitate their fashions, hairstyles, makeup, and the rest and try to make them her own. Similarly, a teenage boy who aspires to be a great athlete will admiringly watch professional athletes who play at the highest level and will try to play the game the same way they do. This exemplifies the power of worship and how through worship and admiration, we become more and more like the objects of our praise and veneration.

Finally, we would be wise to consider the implication of God's glory in our own practice of prayer. In Isaiah 37, God responded affirmatively to Hezekiah's prayer demonstrating his willingness at times to conform his own will to ours in response to prayer. But what is striking about Hezekiah's prayer in this passage is how he appealed primarily to God's own glory. In 37:4, Hezekiah expressed hope that God would respond to his prayer because he had heard the insulting words of the Assyrian commander against the Lord. In 37:14–20, Hezekiah laid the letter he received from the king of Assyria before the Lord as if to say, "Look at what he said about you, God." He also described God as "the living God" (37:17) in contrast to the gods of the other nations the Assyrians were able to conquer, as they were no gods at all, but simply dead idols of wood and stone (37:19). In 37:21, God assured Hezekiah that he would act because Hezekiah chose to pray to him. He made it clear that a significant reason he chose to fight against the Assyrians was because they had raised their voice to mock and revile the Lord (37:23–24). His reason for intervening was different from what some might have expected. It wasn't primarily because of God's love for his people or because he is a God of mercy. Rather, God is shown to be passionate about defending his own honor and reputation, and this is presented as his primary motivation in this passage.

We see this principle that God will actively defend his honor elsewhere in Scripture. As Isaiah 48:11 says, "For my own sake, for my own sake, I do this. How can I let myself be defamed? I will not yield my glory to another." Similarly, as God said through the prophet Ezekiel, "It is not for your sake, people of Israel, that I am going to do these things, but for the sake of my holy name, which you have profaned among the nations where you have gone" (Ezek. 36:22). In both instances, God is motivated to action because his reputation was at stake.

In Exodus 32, after the Israelites fashioned a golden calf to worship, God expressed his intention to destroy the nation and begin again with Moses (32:10). However, Moses prayed for God to reconsider based upon what the Egyptians would say (32:12). Moses argued that they would assume God had evil intentions when he brought the people into the wilderness. This would reflect badly on his reputation. In response to Moses's appeal, the Lord relented of his plan to destroy Israel.

In Daniel 9, the prophet prayed on behalf of his countrymen. He prayed for forgiveness for the collective sins of his people and for God to show them mercy. As part of his prayer, he appealed to God based on his honor and reputation. Daniel 9:19 says, "Lord, listen! Lord, forgive! Lord, hear and act! For your sake, my God, do not delay, because your city and your people bear your Name." Here Daniel drew attention to the fact that Israel's destiny would ultimately

---

5   See G. K. Beale (2008) to further explore the connection between worship and personal formation.

reflect on God's own name. Once again, we see him act on behalf of his people.

What would it look like if all our prayers incorporated genuine concern for God's reputation? Would God be more sympathetic to our prayers if we showed concern for his glory and honor and sought to pray accordingly? Would some of the things we typically pray for have to be eliminated from our list of requests since they are only about us and what we want and have no connection at all to God's glory and praise? Would this infuse our prayer life with additional concerns and requests we wouldn't otherwise consider because of our new commitment to prioritize God's reputation and glory? Many of the things we already pray for would continue but would take on a different flavor. For example, our prayers against temptation would include our concern that our choice to sin would reflect poorly on God's character. Our prayers for a successful ministry endeavor wouldn't be about how we would look as the ones who planned or carried out the event, but how God's reputation would be enhanced because of our efforts. When we consider that God's overarching purpose for all our lives is for us to bring glory to him, there likely isn't a more practical emphasis for us to consider in our prayers than this: that God's reputation would be enhanced and defended in all that we do.

Creativity in Presentation

Personal Representative

Encourage your audience to imagine how they would feel and what it would be like if each of them had to choose another person to fully represent them in everything they would normally do each week. That person would assume your identity so that everybody in your life would see them and assume it was you. They would act as a parent to your children in your place. They would go to your place of work and represent you. They would hang out with your friends at school for the week. At the end of the week, your reputation would be completely linked to how they acted in your place. If that person loses their temper at work and says some mean things to your coworkers, it will permanently reflect on you. If they provide an unwholesome example to your children at home, your kids will assume it was you. If they acted immaturely at your school and alienated you from your normal group of friends, there's nothing you could do about it. If this person decides to break the law and gets arrested or receives a traffic citation, you are on the hook.

If this scenario were real, I am sure you and I would be very nervous about how the other person might act, and thus we would be extremely careful whom we chose to represent us. However, this is exactly what Jesus has chosen to do with us. The only visible reference points many people have for what Jesus is like is by watching us, his followers. Paul said that Christians are Jesus's ambassadors—that when we speak, it is as if God were speaking to people through us (2 Cor. 5:20). As such, God's glory and reputation are directly linked to our actions. We are his personal representatives. We live for God's glory when we remember this fact and accurately represent the holy character of God before the world.

A Good Name Is Better

Describe some scenarios (real or hypothetical) where a person's reputation has been unfairly tarnished and how it negatively impacted them. For example, have them consider a father whose soon-to-be-ex-wife fabricated a story about him abusing their child to keep him from sharing custody of the child. Or tell a story about a woman who saved her money for years to buy her first house. When the time came to apply for a loan, the bank informed her that somebody else had taken out a few loans in her name. She has been a victim of identity theft. As a result, her credit is shot and she is unable to purchase a house. Another option might be to have them imagine a business owner who develops a good reputation for doing good work and treating people well. However, unknown to him, one of his trusted employees has secretly been overcharging customers' accounts for work that was never done and pocketing the profits. After one of his customers finally discovers that they have been overcharged for work many times over, they make this revelation public. The owner of the business immediately fires the corrupt employee, but the damage has already been done. As word gets out, many of his regular customers grow uncomfortable doing business with him any longer.

All these stories illustrate the value of a person's reputation. Once it has become sullied, it is usually very difficult, if not impossible, to repair. And the impact on the person is usually significant. The same is true of God's reputation. When a Christian discredits God's good name, it generally has significant negative ramifications. This explains why God is so passionate about his glory.

Daring God

Tancredo Neves was a Brazilian politician who ran for president of his country in 1985. He famously declared that if he received five hundred thousand votes from his own party, not even God could prevent him from being president. He was in fact elected president on January 15, 1985. However, he tragically fell ill the day before he was inaugurated as president. He died five weeks later without ever becoming president.

Another similar story involves Thomas Andrews. Andrews was the managing director and the head of the drafting department at Harland and Wolff, a shipbuilding company in Belfast, Ireland. More importantly, he was the architect in charge of the great ocean liner known as the Titanic. When asked how safe the ship was, Thomas brazenly said that "even God himself couldn't sink the ship." Not only did the Titanic sink on its maiden voyage, but Thomas Andrews himself perished along with the more than 1,500 other passengers that fateful day in April of 1912.

It would be presumptuous to insist that either of these men died because of their arrogant, blasphemous comments. Only God knows if that was a factor or not. However, we do have clear precedent for this sort of action by God in the example of King Sennacherib in Isaiah 36–37. And we can know with certainty that one day, everyone will have to stand before God and give an account of every idle word they speak (Matt. 12:36–37). In light of that future day, we must remember that God honors those who live for his glory, but those who defy his glory are doomed.

- Sennacherib insults God's glory (36:1–22).
- Hezekiah appeals to God's glory (37:1–20).
- God defends his own glory (37:21–29).
- God vindicates his own glory (37:30–38).

Hezekiah's Reforms

Isaiah 36:7: "But if you say to me, 'We are depending on the LORD our God'—isn't he the one whose high places and altars Hezekiah removed, saying to Judah and Jerusalem, 'You must worship before this altar'?"

King Sennacherib referred to the religious reforms Hezekiah enacted soon after he became king, when he removed all the high places in Judah (see 2 Kings 18:3–4). Recent archaeological excavations provide some additional historical evidence for these reforms. Excavations by the Israel Antiquities Authority in 2016 at Tel-Lachish (Isa. 36:2; 37:8) unearthed a gate shrine dating to the eighth century B.C. The shrine consisted of two rooms. In one of them, a double altar was found with four horns. The horns on this altar had been intentionally broken off, and the room had been sealed off, evidencing a decision to cut off the worship at this site. Even more interesting was the discovery of a stone fashioned into the shape of a chair with a hole cut in the middle of it consistent with a latrine or toilet from that period. Tests on the toilet revealed that it had never actually been used, but rather was symbolic. According to 2 Kings 10:27, when Jehu destroyed a shrine to Baal in Samaria, "they demolished the pillar of Baal, and demolished the house of Baal, and made it a latrine to this day." This confirms the practice of installing a toilet in a shrine to desecrate it and ensure that it is no longer used as a site for worship. The shrine's desecration must have happened sometime before the city's destruction by Sennacherib in 701 B.C., most likely confirming the biblical record of Hezekiah's reforms a little more than a decade earlier.[6]

DISCUSSION QUESTIONS

1. Read through Isaiah 36. How many different arguments can you identify by the Assyrian commander as he seeks to convince the people to surrender to him? Are any of them based upon truths or partial truths? How do you think you would have responded to these arguments?

2. In what ways does the king of Assyria insult God's glory in his appeal for the inhabitants of Jerusalem to surrender (36:13–20; 37:9–13)? Conversely, in what ways does Hezekiah positively appeal to God based on his glory and honor (37:1–4, 14–20)? Finally, when God responds to Hezekiah to assure him that he will defend Jerusalem from Sennacherib, what are the reasons he gives for intervening (37:5–7, 21, 23–24, 28–29)?

3. Hezekiah refers to the Lord as "the living God" in Isaiah 37:4 and 17. What is the significance of this description of God, particularly considering the context of Isaiah 37:17–19?

4. How would your prayers change if all your requests involved some aspect of concern for God's reputation and glory? What are some examples of requests that would have to be eliminated from your prayers if you applied this filter to your prayer list? What are some examples of requests that might need to be added that you don't always think to include?

FOR FURTHER READING

Beale, G. K. 2008. *We Become What We Worship: A Biblical Theology of Idolatry.* Downers Grove, IL: IVP Academic.

Sheldon, Charles M. 1898. *In His Steps: What Would Jesus Do?* Chicago: Advance.

---

6 See https://www.heritagedaily.com/2016/10/gate-shrine-from-1st-temple-period-discovered-during-excavations-at-tel-lachish-national-park/112844; see also https://doi.org/10.1086/703343.

Isaiah 38:1–22

EXEGETICAL IDEA
Hezekiah's prayer prompts the Lord to give both the king and his royal city, Jerusalem, a reprieve. Hezekiah then thanks the Lord for sparing his life in response to his prayer.

THEOLOGICAL FOCUS
The Lord is willing to respond positively to the heartfelt petition of his people.

PREACHING IDEA
You are going to die, so turn to the Lord for salvation and set your house in order.

PREACHING POINTERS
Lately, you've not been feeling well. For the past six months or so, you've noticed that you have been fatigued more than usual. At first, you assumed it was just a matter of a busy schedule or just a sign that you're not as young as you used to be. You've always prided yourself on staying in shape, but having recently celebrated your forty-sixth birthday, you also realize that you're not twenty-five anymore either. However, when you begin to experience abdominal pain that you can't explain and that won't go away, you decide to have it checked out. The doctor runs a series of tests and schedules a follow-up appointment with you. When the diagnosis finally comes back a week later, it is even worse than you feared: you have stage four pancreatic cancer. Your options aren't promising. The doctor wants to begin an aggressive treatment immediately, but he also wants you to know that in all likelihood, your chances of surviving beyond six months are slim. As such, he urges you to set your house in order.

This is the scenario we encounter in Isaiah 38. King Hezekiah unexpectedly grew sick and was on the verge of death. When Isaiah the prophet came to visit with him, his message from the Lord was a solemn one: "Put your house in order, because you are going to die; you will not recover" (38:1). Like anyone else who experiences a moment like this, it likely engendered an array of negative emotions, including fear, anger, sadness, and regrets. Nonetheless, there is at least one significant blessing that results when one receives word that they are soon going to die. Unlike those who pass away from a heart attack or a car accident or some other totally unexpected occurrence, those who receive such news are provided the gift of knowing their time left on earth is short, and thus they can make whatever decisions are necessary to prepare themselves and their loved ones for their imminent passing. In a general sense, the realities of a relatively short life and a certain coming death are true of all people in every age. Because death is final and its implications are eternally impactful, it should motivate all of us to petition God for salvation and take to heart Isaiah's admonition to Hezekiah to put his house in order.

HEZEKIAH'S NEW LEASE ON LIFE (38:1–22)

Isaiah informed Hezekiah that he would soon die, prompting the king to petition the Lord to be healed. The Lord responded favorably to Hezekiah's request, promising to heal him and to deliver Jerusalem from the Assyrian threat. The king responded by offering a thanksgiving song, praising the Lord for his deliverance.

LITERARY STRUCTURE AND THEMES (38:1–22)

This literary unit has two main sections: the Lord's assuring response to Hezekiah's prayer (38:1–6, 21–22, 7–8) and the king's thanksgiving song in response to his healing (38:9–20). The account of Hezekiah's healing begins with a temporal phrase, "in those days," followed by a description of the king's terminal illness (38:1a). The prophet Isaiah's announcement of the king's impending death (38:1b), Hezekiah's prayer (38:2–3), and Isaiah's assuring message to the king (38:4–8) then follow. Isaiah 38:21–22, if original to Isaiah, appears to be misplaced. Hezekiah's request for a sign (38:22) logically precedes the prophet's announcement of one (38:7). Indeed, the parallel account in 2 Kings 20:7–8 places Hezekiah's words where one expects to see them.

Hezekiah's song of thanks, which has a formal introduction (Isa. 38:9), displays standard elements of the thanksgiving genre. Hezekiah recalls his time of need and quotes the lament and petition he offered to the Lord during the crisis (38:10–16). The mood turns to praise as the king thanks the Lord for healing him (38:17–20).

- **The Lord's Assuring Response to Hezekiah's Prayer (38:1–6, 21–22, 7–8)**
- **Hezekiah's Thanksgiving Song (38:9–20)**

EXPOSITION (38:1–22)

The Lord's Assuring Response to Hezekiah's Prayer (38:1–6, 21–22, 7–8)

The Lord decided to give Hezekiah additional years of life.

38:1. At some point during the Assyrian threat (note "in those days" and the reference to the king of Assyria in 38:6), Hezekiah became terminally ill (38:1a). Isaiah took him a message from the Lord, who instructed the king to put his house in order because he was about to die. As if to emphasize the point, the Lord added, "you will not recover" (38:1b). With the Assyrians threatening to conquer the city (cf. 38:6), this was a display of mercy on the Lord's part, for the Assyrians would undoubtedly subject Hezekiah to cruel torture while executing him for rebelling against their authority.

38:2–3. But Hezekiah did not accept the Lord's decision fatalistically. Turning his face to the wall (probably to gain some measure of privacy, cf. 38:3b), he prayed to the Lord (38:2). The prayer, as recorded in 38:3a, is brief and contains no formal petition for a reversal of the Lord's decision. We subsequently discover the king's prayer was more extensive than this (cf. 38:10–16). The king outwardly expressed his sorrow by weeping loudly (38:3b).

The king asks the Lord to "remember" his faithful service. An omniscient God does not literally forget or call to remembrance. When used of God, the verb "remember" is idiomatic and means "to give careful, special attention to." In Genesis 8:1, for example, we are told that God "remembered" Noah during the devastating flood. Shortly thereafter, God assured Noah he would remember his covenantal promise not to destroy the earth (Gen. 9:15–16). Later he remembered Abraham by delivering the patriarch's nephew, Lot, from Sodom before the annihilation of the city (Gen. 19:29). God remembered barren Rachel by giving her the capacity to bear a child (Gen. 30:22). (See also Exod. 2:24; 6:5; 32:13; Lev. 26:42, 45; Deut. 9:27; 1 Sam. 1:19.) Lamenting psalmists often asked God to remember them in their distress (Pss. 25:7; 74:2; 89:50 [HB 51]; 106:4; cf. as well Judg. 16:28; 1 Sam. 1:11). In Isaiah 43:25 God declares he will not remember the sins of his people, meaning he will no longer hold their sins against them.

Here Hezekiah asks the Lord to give him special consideration by rewarding his loyalty to God. He had served the Lord in faithfulness and integrity and accomplished what the Lord willed. The text reads literally, "Remember that I have walked about before you in truth and with a whole heart, and the good in your eyes I have done." The expression "walk about before" (*hithpael* of הָלַךְ + לִפְנֵי) is often an idiom for service (cf. Gen. 17:1; 24:40; 48:15; 1 Sam. 2:30, 35). It is used of Abraham and the patriarchs to describe the way in which they lived obediently before God (Gen. 17:1; 24:40; 48:15). By adding "faithfully" (literally, "in truth") to the statement, Hezekiah emphasized his loyal obedience to God's will as a basis for his request for extended life. The phrase means "sincerely, honestly" (see the comment on "truly" in Isa. 10:20). Solomon recalled that David had exhibited such sincerity (1 Kings 3:6), in accordance with the Lord's command to the king (1 Kings 2:4). The author of Psalm 26 affirmed he had walked faithfully before the Lord (Ps. 26:3), while the author of Psalm 86 recognized one needs special guidance from the Lord in order to demonstrate such loyalty (Ps. 86:11).

The expression "wholehearted" refers to a will that is sincerely committed or devoted to a person and/or task (cf. 1 Kings 8:61; 11:4; 15:3, 14; 1 Chron. 12:39; 28:9; 29:9, 19; 2 Chron. 16:9; 19:9; 25:2). The expression (literally, "with a complete heart") refers to Hezekiah's willingness to follow the Lord's commands. It focuses on one's inner motivation. In 1 Chronicles 28:9 David urges Solomon to serve the Lord with a "complete heart" (NIV11 "wholehearted devotion"), which he closely associates with a "willing mind." First Chronicles 29:9 tells how the people rejoiced over the generosity of their leaders, who contributed voluntarily to the temple building project with a "complete heart" (NIV11 "wholeheartedly"). An almost identical expression (used in 1 Kings 20:3, which is parallel to Isa. 38:3) refers to strong determination (1 Chron. 12:38) and is used to describe full commitment and devotion to the Lord and his commands (1 Kings 8:61; 1 Chron. 29:19; 2 Chron. 19:9). An aged Solomon allowed his foreign wives and their pagan gods to move him away from full commitment to the Lord (1 Kings 11:4). According to 2 Chronicles 25:2, King Amaziah carried out his royal duty before the Lord without being fully committed to him. On the other hand, King Asa, though he was not completely obedient, was nevertheless fully committed to the Lord (1 Kings 15:14). The Lord recognizes those who are fully committed to him and gives them special divine empowerment (2 Chron. 16:9).

The expression "good in your eyes" refers to the addressee's will or desire (Josh. 9:25; Judg. 19:24; 1 Sam. 14:36, 40; 2 Sam. 19:38 [HB 39]; 2 Kings 10:5). In Deuteronomy 6:18 Moses commands Israel to "do what is right and good" in the eyes of the Lord. According to 6:17, this entailed obeying the stipulations of the law. Utilizing wordplay, Moses promised the people that if they obeyed, it would "go well" for them in the "good" land to which the Lord was bringing them. According to Moses, behavior that was "good" in the Lord's "eyes" would bring a reward. Hezekiah exploits this logic in his lament, suggesting his good behavior should count for something. It comes as no surprise that the Lord responds favorably to Hezekiah's plea (cf. Isa. 38:5).

38:4–6. The Lord sent Isaiah back to the king with a new message (38:4–6). Identifying himself as the Lord, the God of Hezekiah's ancestor (literally, "father") David, he told him he had heard his prayer and seen his tears (38:5a). The reference to the God of David suggests the Lord's positive response to Hezekiah's prayer was grounded in God's covenantal commitment to David and his descendants. On more than one occasion God tempered his disciplinary judgment because of his commitment to David and his dynasty (1 Kings 11:34, 36; 15:4–5; 2 Kings 8:19). In Isaiah 37:35 the Lord promises to deliver Judah "for the sake of David" his "servant."

The reference to David in conjunction with prayer and tears is not coincidental. The terms "prayer" (תְּפִלָּה) and "tears" (דִּמְעָה) occur together only here (see also the parallel text in 2 Kings 20:5) and in the concluding petition of Psalm 39 (see vv. 12–13 [HB 13–14]), a penitential lament in which David reflects upon his mortality and the brevity of life (38:4–6 [HB 5–7]).

The Lord announced he would give Hezekiah fifteen additional years of life (Isa. 38:5b). Of course, this implied there would be relief from the Assyrian threat. In this regard, the Lord promised he would deliver both Hezekiah and the city from the Assyrian king (38:6). He would defend (גָּנַן; cf. 31:5) the city, for the sake of his own reputation and because of his promise to David (cf. 37:35). Hezekiah's new lease on life would mirror that of the covenant community in Jerusalem.

38:21–22, 7–8. The prophet instructed the king's attendants (note the plural verbs) to apply a poultice of figs to Hezekiah's deadly boil, assuring them the king would live (38:21; cf. 2 Kings 20:7). The final clause says simply, "and he will recover," a direct reversal of the Lord's earlier announcement, "you will not recover" (Isa. 38:1).

Hezekiah asked for a sign that he would indeed survive and be able to worship again in the temple (38:22; cf. 2 Kings 20:8). The prophet told him the shadow cast by the sun would go back ten steps, which it did (Isa. 38:7–8). This turning back of the clock, as it were, mirrors the promise of increased days for Hezekiah (Oswalt 1986, 678). The miracle took place, ironically, on the stairway of Ahaz, the one who had refused to seek a sign from the Lord when offered one during a crisis (cf. 7:11–12). In contrast to his father Ahaz, Hezekiah was eager to see a display of the Lord's sovereign power as a guarantee of his saving intervention.[1]

In Hezekiah's case the Lord did not bring to pass the initial prophetic message he spoke through Isaiah. Though the announcement of Hezekiah's death is stated emphatically (38:1b; "you are going to die; you will not recover") and there are no formal indicators of conditionality, the prophecy nevertheless proved to be contingent. Furthermore, its failure to come to pass did not cast Isaiah in the role of a false prophet. Hezekiah seemed to assume the Lord might relent and, sure enough, he did so. The passage is instructive for how prophecy works. Most prophecies were conditional, whether marked as such or not (see Chisholm 1995, 2010).

Hezekiah's Thanksgiving Song (38:9–20)
Hezekiah offers a thanksgiving song to the Lord in gratitude for his deliverance from death.

38:9–10. After his recovery from his terminal illness, Hezekiah prayed to the Lord (38:9). He begins by recalling the lament he offered before he was healed (note "I said," 38:10). He

---

1 On the contrast between Ahaz, as depicted in ch. 7, and Hezekiah, as depicted in chs. 36–38, see Conrad 1991, 41–45.

lamented he would die before his time and be forced to walk through the gates of Sheol into the dwelling place of the dead (38:10). In the Mesopotamian text The Descent of Ishtar seven gates close behind the one who enters the land of the dead (COS 1.108:382). We see this same imagery in the Old Testament, where only the sovereign power of God can rescue one from "the gates of death" (cf. Pss. 9:13 [HB 14]; 107:18–19) and the "bars" of the subterranean land of the dead (אֶרֶץ, "land," here, also called the "pit"; Jonah 2:6).

38:11. Hezekiah expressed regret that he would no longer see the Lord in the land of the living or look upon his fellow human beings (note collective אָדָם, "humankind") along with those dwelling in the world (38:11). According to Roberts (2015, 484), "seeing" the Lord "is an ancient idiom referring to participation in worship at the sanctuary" (see also Blenkinsopp 2000, 485). In the pagan context in which the idiom arose, a worshipper would see an image of the deity in the sanctuary. Roberts explains that the "idiom was initially continued in Hebrew despite the lack of divine images," but eventually it was altered from "seeing" (*qal* verbal form) to "appearing [*niphal*] before."

38:12–14. Hezekiah next used a series of comparisons to lament his plight (38:12–14). In the first of these, he spoke of his dwelling place being pulled out, or uprooted (נִסַּע), and then rolled up like a shepherd's tent (38:12a). Like a weaver, he rolled up his life, and God (the unstated, but implied subject) now cuts it off from the loom. Addressing God, he lamented, "from day until night you bring me to an end" (literal translation, 38:12b). In his nighttime desperation, he cried out until the next morning, but to no avail. With all the ferocity and strength of a lion, God (the implied but unstated subject of the verb) breaks all his bones (38:13a). The cycle continues, as God brings him to an end from day until morning (38:13b; cf. 38:12b). Hezekiah can muster only a little strength as he chirps like a bird and coos like a dove (38:14a). His eyes have grown weak looking upward for relief. Addressing God as the sovereign master (אֲדֹנָי), he asks for deliverance from the oppression that has overwhelmed him (38:14b).

The form עָרְבֵנִי literally means "stand surety for me," suggesting the metaphor is that of the Lord standing surety for one who is being economically exploited (Roberts 2015, 484). This verb is typically used in the economic sphere with the meaning "guarantee, stand surety for" (cf. *HALOT* s.v. "ערב I" 876). For example, in Genesis 43:9 Judah guarantees Benjamin's safety (cf. Gen. 44:32). Proverbs warns against standing surety for another (Prov. 6:1; 11:15; 17:18; 20:16; 22:26; 27:13). Speaking metaphorically, Hezekiah begs God to take responsibility for his well-being, just as a benefactor might do for a debtor (cf. Ps. 119:122). This metaphor fits well after the reference to oppression (Wildberger 2002, 460).

38:15–16. There was little else Hezekiah could say. The Lord (the implied subject) had spoken and acted (Isa. 38:15a), leaving the king in bitter distress (38:15b). But despair does not overtake him. Again addressing God as the sovereign master (38:16a; cf. 38:14b), he asks that his health be restored and his life preserved (38:16b). Though human beings are often described as letting others live (Gen. 47:25; Num. 31:18; Josh. 2:13; 6:25; 9:20; Judg. 8:19; 2 Sam. 8:2; 2 Kings 8:1, 5), it is ultimately the Lord alone who has power over death and possesses the authority to grant life (cf. 2 Kings 5:7).

In the final two clauses of Isaiah 38:16 an imperfect form (literally, "and you will restore me to health") is followed by an imperative ("and make me alive"). The sequence is unusual, tempting interpreters to emend one of the verbs to correspond to the other. As the text stands, the imperfect expresses a request or wish (Barré 2005, 164–65). Other examples of the sequence include Hosea 14:3 [Eng. 2]: "completely forgive [imperfect] iniquity and receive [imperative] (what is) good," and Job 17:10: "return [imperfect] and enter [imperative]." In both cases both verbs express a request or wish.

38:17. Introductory הִנֵּה, "look," marks a transition in Hezekiah's prayer. In 38:10–16 he recalls his time of need and his petition for divine help. Now he makes the transition to thanksgiving as he praises the Lord for healing him.

He begins by acknowledging that the distress he experienced turned out for his benefit (38:17a). He then explains what he means (38:17b). He experienced the Lord's saving power in a fresh way when he was delivered from death, called here "the pit of destruction." The phrase שַׁחַת בְּלִי is better translated "pit of oblivion," since the word בְּלִי has the primary meaning "without." It depicts the pit of death as a place where any meaningful existence ceases (Wildberger 2002, 462; see comments below on 38:18).

In addition to physical deliverance, Hezekiah experienced the Lord's forgiveness of sin, which is vividly depicted as the Lord throwing behind his back all the king's sins, where they would be, as it were, "out of sight, out of mind" (Barré 2005, 171). The idiomatic expression "put behind," or "put behind one's back," means to "reject." It is used elsewhere of Israel rejecting the Lord (1 Kings 14:9; Ezek. 23:35) or his commands (Neh. 9:26; Ps. 50:17). But here it is the Lord who mercifully puts Hezekiah's sins behind his "back," as if to declare they are no longer a barrier.

The king's confession, as well as his earlier observation that his suffering was designed for his benefit (Isa. 38:17a), suggest his close call with death was the result of divine discipline. Apparently, the life-threatening distress he suffered made him aware of personal sin and prompted him to confess it. In this way, his suffering contributed to his ultimate well-being, for one's spiritual condition is always God's top priority. Hezekiah's response to the announcement of his impending death contains a reference to his good deeds, but no confession of sin (cf. 38:3). Nor does his rehearsal of his lament include a penitential element (38:10–16). Nevertheless, here he mentions forgiveness of sins, implying he did see a connection between the trouble that came upon him and his sins. In this regard, Roberts (2015, 485) observes that Hezekiah's "former bitter suffering was for his own good and well-being (v. 17), presumably to turn him from his sins."

38:18. Hezekiah elaborates on his reference to death as the "pit of oblivion" (cf. 38:17). He explains that Sheol does not give thanks to the Lord, nor does death praise him (38:18a). Sheol and death stand by metonymy (container for contents) for the dead who dwell there, as 38:18b makes clear: those who descend into the pit (that is, "cistern") do not anticipate (literally, "wait for") the Lord's faithfulness. Depending on the context, the Hebrew term אֱמֶת can carry the idea of "trustworthiness, constancy, faithfulness, truth" (see *HALOT* s.v. "אֱמֶת" 68–69). When used of God, it often describes how he is faithful and true to his promises to his loyal followers; they can count on him being constant and reliable (cf. Isa. 61:8, as well as Pss. 25:10; 26:3; 40:10–11 [HB 11–12]; 43:3; 57:10; 86:15; 89:14; 146:6). His faithfulness prompts him to protect and save his people (Pss. 54:5; 57:3 [HB 4]; 61:7 [HB 8]; 91:4). But, from Hezekiah's perspective, it is too late for the dead to expect such divine intervention.

38:19. By way of contrast, the living can praise the Lord, just as Hezekiah was doing (Isa. 38:19a). In the land of the living, as opposed to the world of the dead, fathers can teach sons about the Lord's faithfulness (38:19b).

Hezekiah's highly negative depiction of death is by no means unique (cf. Pss. 6:5 [HB 6]; 30:9 [HB 10]; 88:10–12 [HB 11–13]; 115:17). In ancient Hebrew thought the realm of the dead was not a place of praise. The dead maintained a shadowy existence; they were no longer part of the worshipping community that witnessed and praised God's mighty acts. Living on this side of the resurrection, Christians recognize that the view expressed in these Old Testament laments is limited in scope and in need of fuller divine revelation (cf. Phil. 1:21–23).

38:20. Hezekiah declares that the Lord has saved him (Isa. 38:20a) and promises that the worshipping community will praise the Lord with music in his temple for the remainder of their lives (38:20b). This is only appropriate. Hezekiah asked the Lord to preserve his life (note 38:16, הַחֲיֵנִי, "Keep me alive," from the verb חיה). Now that the Lord has answered his petition, he will lead others in praise for the rest of their lives (cf. 38:20, חַיֵּינוּ, "our lives").

THEOLOGICAL FOCUS

The theological focus of this passage can be stated as follows: the Lord is willing to respond positively to the heartfelt petition of his people. As the prophet develops this theological theme, the following emphases emerge:

1. Petitionary prayer as the catalyst for divine favor

Hezekiah coupled his petition for prolonged life (cf. 38:16) with an affirmation of his faithfulness to the Lord (38:3). In so doing, he was apparently asking the Lord to reward his loyalty, and the Lord responded favorably (38:5). But this is not simply a matter of Hezekiah's personal relationship to the Lord. The Lord's reference to David at the beginning of his response suggests that the Lord viewed the deliverance within the context of his promise to David (cf. 37:35).

This passage is one of many throughout the Scriptures in which the Lord responds favorably to petitionary prayer. The psalms contain numerous thanksgiving songs, which, like this one, praise the Lord for a positive answer to the psalmist's petition. One must reject any notion of so-called divine impassibility articulated in such a way that it runs counter to the overwhelming abundance of biblical evidence.

2. The Lord's willingness to reverse a decision he has announced

It is noteworthy that in Hezekiah's case, the Lord announced the king would die but then reversed that decision in response to his prayer. Though the text does not actually say the Lord "relented," the passage provides one of many biblical examples of the Lord's willingness to alter a statement of intention within the context of his give-and-take with his people. Hezekiah's experience illustrates that the Lord often declares his intentions contingently, as if inviting humans to engage him through prayer (see Chisholm 1995).

3. The role of suffering in one's spiritual growth

Another factor in understanding the Lord's decision to prolong Hezekiah's life emerges in Hezekiah's statement about his suffering being for his benefit (38:17). As noted above, his subsequent reference to his sins being forgiven suggests the Lord's purpose in announcing the king's death pertained to his spiritual growth. The announcement was, as it were, a "wake-up call" for Hezekiah, which prompted the king to confront his own shortcomings. When he did so, the Lord rewarded the good that he had done, as well as his prior commitments to David.

4. The close relationship between the king and the covenant community

The Lord's deliverance of Hezekiah was not simply a personal matter. When the Lord announced he would prolong the king's life, he also promised he would deliver the city of Jerusalem (38:5–6). It is apparent that the destinies of the king and the nation were intertwined (cf. 1 Sam. 12:13–15, 20–25). The Lord's mercy to Hezekiah mirrored his mercy to the covenant community.

5. The Lord's sovereignty over life and death

This account also reminds the readers that the Lord is sovereign over life and death (cf. Isa. 25:8; 28:15–18). He alone determines the life span of individuals and decides the destiny of his covenant community. He can deliver one from "the gates of death" (38:10) and the "pit of destruction" [or "oblivion"] (38:17).

PREACHING AND TEACHING STRATEGIES

Exegetical and Theological Synthesis

This chapter begins with a historical account of King Hezekiah's sickness and miraculous recovery (38:1–8). This is followed by a first-person account from Hezekiah detailing how he personally felt throughout this ordeal. While the actual writing was done after God healed Hezekiah, it includes details about how he felt when he found out he was going to die and elements of his prayer to God concerning his diagnosis. One option would be for the preacher to outline his message around the narrative events in 38:1–8 and use the information from 38:9–22 to provide more details and substance about the various key events of the narrative.

The reader is informed immediately that Hezekiah has become deathly sick. This is confirmed by the prophet of God, who comes and tells him to set his house in order since he is going to die and not recover. We can only imagine how we would feel if we received this news while in the prime of our adult life as Hezekiah was. Elisabeth Kübler-Ross (1969) famously described the five stages of grief that most people experience when they receive news of their impending death. Contrary to what some assume, Kübler-Ross didn't say that all people go through all these stages, or even that they go through the stages in the same order. What she did conclude from her research was that most people go through most of these stages: denial, anger, bargaining, and depression, before reaching the final stage of acceptance. We discover throughout this chapter that Hezekiah seems to have experienced all these stages except the final one: acceptance. That is likely because God healed him before he would have worked through the necessary emotions to reach the stage of acceptance.

In 38:2–3, Hezekiah's immediate thought is to bargain with God. It is noteworthy that Hezekiah doesn't just pray and ask for healing or for mercy, but he appeals to God based on his own past righteousness: "Remember, LORD, how I have walked before you faithfully and with wholehearted devotion, and have done what is good in your eyes" (38:3). In other words, he bargains for God to heal him in exchange for the righteous things he has done throughout his life. He has given God something (his service), and he hopes to receive healing and more time to live in return. We further see in Hezekiah a second emotion: depression or sadness. Isaiah 38:3 concludes with the revelation that Hezekiah wept bitterly. Two more times in this chapter, reference is made to the king's bitterness or sadness (38:15, 17).

Finally, it appears there were elements of both denial and anger in Hezekiah's response. In 38:10, the king exclaims, "In the prime of my life must I go through the gates of death and be robbed of the rest of my years?" Hezekiah would have been thirty-nine years old at this time, well within the prime of his life. His statement here may carry an element of disbelief or a hint of unfairness. Of course, he knew that he would eventually die, but was this really going to happen in the middle of his days? He goes on to lament, "I said, 'I will not again see the Lord himself in the land of the living; no longer will I look on my fellow man, or be with those who now dwell in this world'" (38:11). This one line contains various possible elements of grief. He expresses sadness over the fact that he will no longer be able to worship the Lord in the temple. This may also carry an element of bargaining, as if to say, "God, if you allow me to live, I will continue to worship you and to lead this nation to worship you." It also carries an element of sadness and possibly anger that his death will prevent him from worshipping the God he loves and from seeing the people he loves. In 38:12–15, Hezekiah's frustration and anger with God appear. He argues that his life is like a tent that has just been plucked up and removed. Similarly, his life is like a piece of fabric that is being woven on a loom, but then it is suddenly and prematurely cut off before it has been finished (38:12). Finally, he likens himself to one who has been attacked and mauled to death by a lion (38:13). Hezekiah leaves no doubt that he blames God for this. Twice he refers to God in the third person: "He has cut me off from the loom," and "he broke all my bones." Twice he addresses the Lord directly in his prayer, saying, "You made an end of me" (38:12–13). Once more, in 38:15, Hezekiah says, "But what can I say? He has spoken to me, and he himself has done this."

These verses reveal to us that Hezekiah responded to the unexpected news of his impending death the same way any other human being would. He was depressed; he was angry. He was in disbelief. He even bargained with God to try to change things that were outside of his control. Ultimately, God listened to Hezekiah's prayer and chose to heal him, contrary to God's original assertion that Hezekiah would not recover. He even revealed that he would grant Hezekiah fifteen more years.

This was a major blessing in at least two ways. First, he was granted the blessing of restored health and additional years. This was an answer to prayer. In fact, God specifically referenced having heard Hezekiah's prayer as a reason for his healing (38:5). He followed this promise up with a sign to confirm the certainty of the promise (38:7–8). God would cause the sun to go back ten steps on the sun dial. Hezekiah's ten extra hours of daylight corresponded with the fifteen additional years of life that God also miraculously granted to him that day. Second, Hezekiah was given the knowledge of precisely how much time he had left before he would die. He now knew that he had exactly fifteen years, no more and no less. He had ample time to prepare for the inevitability of his death.

Hezekiah's close encounter with death had a meaningful impact on his life. It was ultimately for his own benefit that he suffered in this way (38:17). Appropriately, he committed himself to praise the Lord for his salvation (38:18–20).

This passage also makes clear that when God decided to heal Hezekiah, it involved a clear change in what would have otherwise happened as revealed by the prophet (38:5, cf. 38:1). Prayer is effective at times in influencing the will of God. This would seem to mitigate against the theory that God's will has been unalterably predetermined in eternity past. Otherwise, when God spoke through the prophet saying that Hezekiah would not recover from his sickness, one would have to conclude that God was lying. The natural implication from the story is that God had genuinely intended to allow Hezekiah to die at that point had it not been for his prayer asking for God to reconsider. It is also likely that God was moved by Hezekiah's repentance. Isaiah 38:17 seems to connect God's deliverance to his casting Hezekiah's sins behind his back. Thus, this story reveals not only the power of prayer but also the power of repentance in motivating God to reconsider what he would have otherwise done.

Hezekiah's New Lease on Life (38:1–22)

Preaching Idea
You are going to die, so turn to the Lord for salvation and set your house in order.

Contemporary Connections

What does it mean?
While most people who have fallen ill have not been told that they were about to die, all people are going to die sometime (unless of course Jesus returns first). And in the scope of time and eternity, death is much closer than most realize. The older people get, the more they realize how quickly time passes. When people are young, they tend to feel as though they have all the time in the world. But soon, a decade of life passes and then another. Before they know it, middle age has set in, and with it the reality of the brevity of life. Talk to just about anyone in their golden years, and they will probably tell you that it feels like just yesterday that they were young. Where did the time go? Even for those who are blessed to live a long and full life, death is ultimately not far off.

Another important reality to consider is that nobody knows for sure when their appointment with death has been scheduled. Most healthy people assume they will live into their eighties or nineties. Thus, a twenty-year-old assumes he still has sixty years or more of life ahead. But the hard reality is that we do not know how or when we will die. People die unexpectedly all the time. The world recently had a very poignant example of this with the COVID-19 pandemic. Most people know at least one person who was healthy and relatively young who contracted and died from that virus. A year earlier, few had ever even heard of coronaviruses. Nobody could have anticipated a global pandemic that would contribute to the death of millions of people including some in the prime of their life. Others die unexpectedly every day from things like heart attacks, automobile accidents, and acts of violence. As such, proper preparation for death is something one should always be thinking about, as none of us are guaranteed tomorrow (James 4:13–15).

What then did Isaiah mean when he urged Hezekiah to put his house in order? We can only speculate as to what the specific things were that he needed to do to order his life in preparation for death. It likely involved determining who would replace him as king and other logistical details related to the royal transition. It also likely involved personal issues, such as final conversations with close friends and family members and decisions he may have been putting off that now needed attention. The nonspecific nature of this admonition may indicate that it was an open-ended exhortation to use what time he had left to plan and prepare as best he could for death. In this respect, the admonition to Hezekiah becomes a practical one that every one of us should take to heart as well. Wisdom would dictate that we too should make proper preparations in the light of the inevitability of death.

While the admonition to put one's house in order will look different for everyone, it is essential for everyone to consider their standing before God. Hezekiah was already an Old Testament believer and worshipper of the Lord when he received the message predicting his impending death. Still, it seems that he reevaluated his standing before God, prompting him to repent of sin in his life (38:17). This likely contributed to God's delivering him from imminent death and granting him fifteen more years. Believers and nonbelievers alike should approach the reality and uncertainties of death with a priority to repent of sin to become right with God. While God doesn't promise to deliver everyone from physical death as he did Hezekiah, he has more importantly promised to save us from eternal death and judgment as a result of sin.

Is it true?
About a year after the US Constitution was ratified, Benjamin Franklin famously wrote the following in a letter to a friend: "Our new

Constitution is now established, everything seems to promise it will be durable; but, in this world, nothing is certain except death and taxes."[2] The reality is that people have attempted to avoid both death and taxes. I once knew a couple who owned quite a bit of land back in the woods out of view from any road. Over the course of a few years, the husband secretly worked at building a pole barn that he could use as a house for him and his wife. To avoid attention, he purposely didn't secure any permits or hire any outside help. When he was finished, the couple sold the main home on the property with some of the land, and quietly moved deeper into the woods into the place he had built. His hope was that if nobody officially knew he was living there, he could avoid paying taxes. Needless to say, the county eventually became aware of his situation, and he was forced to pay taxes like everybody else. There have probably been some crafty people throughout history who have found ways, legally or otherwise, to avoid paying their taxes. Death, however, is truly unavoidable. Many have tried to escape it or at least delay it, but everyone succumbs to it eventually.

Despite the inevitability of death, many procrastinate preparing for it. According to recent surveys, only 32 percent of Americans have a will. Unsurprisingly, the older people get, the more likely they are to have a will. But even among adults ages fifty to sixty-four, only 56 percent have a will.[3] Similarly, a 1995 survey of one thousand people found that 80 percent of respondents felt that prearranging one's funeral was a good idea. However, only 24 percent of respondents had done so.[4] There are many factors involved in why many have not yet made any meaningful plans for their death. Among them are the human tendency to just assume we've got plenty of time to make those plans and don't need to worry about dying any time soon.

Far more significant than failing to plan for physical death is a failure to prepare adequately for eternity. This group is harder to quantify numerically. Many have given considerable thought about and tried to make spiritual preparation for eternity based on their particular set of beliefs. This group is different from irreligious people. It wouldn't make much sense for many irreligious folks, particularly those who identify as atheists or agnostics, to prepare for an eternal destiny they don't believe even exists. But there is a significant number of people in our world today who believe in the existence of God and in the reality of heaven and hell, but who live from day to day without ever dealing with the issue of their sin and coming judgment. If one were to ask them how they think a person gets into heaven when they die, they may say something like, "I don't really know," or "I guess I hope my good works outweigh my bad ones." These answers reveal little more than wishful thinking rather than a serious pursuit of what God's Word really says about such matters.

Additionally, there are those who understand the basic tenets of Christianity, and who look back to a time when they prayed a prayer asking Jesus to come into their heart or raised a hand at the end of a sermon or even walked down an aisle to speak with a counselor at the end of a meeting. These people have made a clear decision to trust Christ at some point in their life. However, their lives don't much resemble the character traits of Jesus. In fact, they live their lives in a way that is almost indistinguishable from their nonbelieving friends and coworkers. As such, they are often plagued with doubts about the genuineness of their own

---

2 https://constitutioncenter.org/blog/benjamin-franklins-last-great-quote-and-the-constitution#:~:text=%E2%80%9COur%20new%20Constitution%20is%20now,and%20taxes%2C%E2%80%9D%20Franklin%20said.
3 https://www.legalzoom.com/articles/estate-planning-statistics.
4 https://iccfa.com/blog/overview-of-preneed.

commitment to Jesus and live with recurring fear about their eternal destiny.

Finally, there are others who have confidently trusted in Jesus for their salvation, and their lives bear the fruit of the one who loves them. Nevertheless, they too have areas in their life marked by frequent disobedience or indecision despite the Spirit's prodding and conviction. Maybe they refuse to step out of their comfort zone to invite an unsaved coworker to church or even to share Jesus with them. Possibly there is a besetting sin that they know they should talk to a Christian friend or counselor about, but they are too ashamed. For some, it may involve a broken relationship and resentment directed toward someone due to past sins against them. They know that Jesus would have them extend forgiveness and deal with their bitterness, but their hurts and their pride have stood in the way.

Chances are, most can identify with one of the above scenarios. In every example, Jesus invites people to put their proverbial houses in order—to repent and allow him to cleanse them of their sins and bring them into a restored relationship with him and with the Father. None of us wants to enter eternity with significant regrets about things we neglected to do or things we just put off indefinitely, especially as it relates to our relationship with God.

Now what?

We should all set aside time to reevaluate our lives and prayerfully reflect upon whether or not we are ready to die. If I was told by God that this was my last week on earth, what things would I be sure to accomplish? What conversations would I make it my priority to have? What relationships would I attempt to mend? Are there people I would want to thank for having made a major impact on my life? Conversely, what things would suddenly not matter to me? Why not have those conversations now and mend those broken relationships before an unexpected crisis hits? Why would we want to put important matters off when tomorrow is not guaranteed (James 4:13–17)?

This principle of getting our houses in order before we pass away is especially important for parents and grandparents. We have been given the awesome opportunity and responsibility to raise our children and influence our grandchildren to live successfully in this world. If you were to die unexpectedly tomorrow, your window of opportunity to impact your children and grandchildren would come to an end. Have you prepared them for the things that really matter? Have you taught them the important lessons of life? In Isaiah 38:19, Hezekiah reflects on the fact that only "the living . . . praise you, as I am doing today; parents tell their children about your faithfulness." In other words, there are important things for a father and mother to teach their children, but this is only possible while they are still living. Parents can thank God and testify to their children about God's faithfulness. Once they're gone that door will close. Whatever lessons one's parents failed to teach, their children will have to learn from somebody else. Once we are gone, who knows who will step into the role of influencers over our children or grandchildren.

Parents should consider making a list of topics and lessons you want to discuss with your children. It could be a running list that grows as the Lord lays on your heart a new lesson that you want to teach them. What is truth and how can they know it? How do we know the Bible is the Word of God? Who is Jesus and why does he matter? Does God care about us, and how can we know he does? What are strategies for coping with life's tragedies? What is God's design for men, women, and sex? If the love of money is the root of all evil, then how should they view earning money and how might that affect their future career plans? These are just a few examples of the sorts of conversations parents should be intentionally initiating with their children as they grow. Parents might consider using a list such as this for nightly dinner discussions or for weekly family devotions. Another suggestion might be for mom or dad to start a tradition of picking their kids up one day each week from school and taking them out somewhere to have discussions over coffee or soda. These are some practical ways to intentionally redeem the time you have with your kids or grandkids.

Additionally, we should create opportunities to learn from other Christians who know their time left on earth is short. When visiting folks in the nursing home, try asking them probing questions such as, "If there was something about your life that you wish you could do differently, what would it be?" "Were there things that were important to you as a younger man/woman that no longer seem important now?" "What are the two or three lessons that are most important for someone my age to take to heart?"

Finally, this chapter should serve to motivate God's people to be men and women who pray. In the same way that God was willing to alter the future because of Hezekiah's prayer, we too should expect that God does in fact hear every one of our prayers, and that sometimes he even changes what he had intended to do in response to those requests from his children. A righteous person's prayers really do have great power (James 5:16).

Creativity in Presentation

The Sands of Time
Purchase a large hourglass with sand that you uncover and reveal at the beginning of your sermon. Explain how the hourglass represents the time in a person's life. Find a way to hide or cover the remaining amount of sand in the top half of the hourglass from the audience's view, to make the point that nobody knows how much time they have left. When will their time run out? You can paint the glass on the upper portion or tape a piece of paper to cover it. Let the hourglass sit off to the side and continue to run throughout your message. There are multiple affordable options to purchase hourglasses online that last in increments of thirty, forty-five, or sixty minutes. It would be especially dramatic if the time expires right around the time your sermon is planned to be finished. When it does, you can point this out to your audience and make closing applications about why we must all be ready now and not put off getting our houses in order.

Unexpected Death
Find a couple of stories in the news of people who died unexpectedly. Read the headline and maybe give a detail or two about each one. It isn't difficult to find a recent story about a vehicle accident that took the life of a passenger, or a person who lost a battle with cancer, or some random act of violence that took the lives of people. Alternatively, you could look at the obituaries and find people who died unexpectedly of a heart attack or something similar. Point out how relatively common this sort of occurrence is and ask the congregation to imagine what those people were thinking about an hour or two before their deaths. List very common things like what their plans were for the coming weekend, a project they were working on around the house for which they needed to pick up supplies at the store, or what they were planning to buy as a birthday gift for a friend or family member. It is unlikely that any of them were thinking, "You know, I may not have many days left on earth. I had better put my house in order just in case."

Testimony
Find somebody in your church who is battling a serious disease or who recently recovered from a serious illness. Interview them in front of the congregation or ahead of time on camera about how their diagnosis and the prospect of likely death changed their thinking about life. How have their priorities changed? Do they have an increased appreciation for each day/month of life? How have their thoughts about heaven and

eternity increased, and what impact has this had on their daily activities and attitudes?

I recently interviewed a man in our congregation who has been battling cancer for the past two years. Because he is a father of three teenagers, I interviewed him on Father's Day and then used a few of the points he had shared with me ahead of time to form a short devotional challenge to close out the service. This man has outlived his doctors' initial estimate of how long he would probably live. Nonetheless, it is still likely that his cancer will eventually be the cause of his death. I asked him how this situation had impacted his life. One of the things that he shared had to do with his interaction with his children who still live at home. Because of his chemotherapy treatments, he often doesn't feel very well. As a result, it's very easy for him to want to say "no" or "not right now" when his kids want him to spend time with them. However, he also knows that he may not have very many opportunities left to say "yes" to them. Thus, the uncertainty of how much time he has left with them has caused him to prioritize saying "yes" whenever possible. Another nugget of wisdom he shared is that he has learned the importance of just being present with his family when he is at home rather than escaping into watching TV, playing games on his phone, or even reading a book. These simple lessons are things that all of us would be wise to listen to and reflect upon After all, we are going to die eventually, so we had better turn to the Lord for salvation and set our house in order.

- Hezekiah prepares for his impending death (38:1).
- Hezekiah prays for God to give him more time (38:2–8).
- Hezekiah praises God for his answered prayer (38:9–22).

DISCUSSION QUESTIONS

1. Hezekiah was thirty-nine years old when he received the promise that he would live fifteen more years. That means that for fifteen years leading up to his fifty-fourth birthday, he knew it would be his final one. What year do you plan to die? Which year will be your final birthday celebration? (Pause, and give some time for the obvious answer to settle in.) Of course, none of us knows when we will die. How then should we prepare for our death if we don't know when it is going to occur?

2. If you discovered that you had only a couple weeks left to live, what things would you do? Be specific. What conversations do you think you would want to have with your family? Are there broken relationships you would want to repair either by asking for or extending forgiveness? How would your daily routine change?

3. Hezekiah said that this painful ordeal was ultimately for his benefit (38:17), probably because it led him to a renewed love for the Lord who answered his prayer (38:19). Can you think of a time when you went through a very painful ordeal that in hindsight, God used for your own benefit?

Isaiah 39:1–8

EXEGETICAL IDEA
Hezekiah shows off his wealth to the Babylonian messengers, prompting Isaiah to announce the Babylonian exile.

THEOLOGICAL FOCUS
As illustrated by Hezekiah's actions, there is a fine line between faith and failure.

PREACHING IDEA
Beware of pride and self-centeredness, which easily grow in the soil of God's blessings and success.

PREACHING POINTERS
It is human nature to forget things. The challenge to remember important things is a daily struggle. How did people ever make do without smartphones to remind them about all their important events and meetings? In the same way that humans routinely do not remember important dates and events, we are also prone to forget the spiritual lessons we've learned in the past. This was the case with King Hezekiah. He was just coming off a dramatic spiritual success story of God answering his prayer for healing and blessing him with the gift of fifteen more years of life (38:5). This was accompanied by a miracle where God turned back the sundial ten steps as proof that he had directly acted on Hezekiah's behalf (38:7–8). This happened in the context of God also miraculously delivering the entire city of Jerusalem from the powerful Assyrian army when his angel struck down 185,000 of them in one night (38:6; cf. 37:36–37).

These events must have had a huge impact on Hezekiah. He would have learned how powerful God is and why it is essential to look to him for Judah's defense and protection. He would also have learned the futility of political alliances with pagan nations. None of those alliances had helped him in the past. Only the Lord was able to deliver. Finally, he would have learned a lesson about the importance of God's glory, and why it is essential to maintain a proper posture toward him of humility and praise.

Nevertheless, Hezekiah seems to have forgotten every one of these lessons when the Babylonian envoys paid him a visit with gifts and flattery. Hezekiah used this opportunity to show off his own glory rather than to magnify the Lord for what he had done for him. Additionally, Hezekiah yet again appears to be enamored with the allure of a political alliance, this time with Babylon, rather than trusting in the protection afforded by the Lord. As such, this story reveals the importance of remembering the lessons we have learned rather than repeating the failures from our past.

HEZEKIAH SHOWS OFF HIS WEALTH (39:1–8)

Hezekiah welcomes messengers from Babylon and shows them his wealth. The Lord uses this occasion, where the king's pride is evident, to announce the Babylonian exile.

LITERARY STRUCTURE AND THEMES (39:1–8)

This literary unit has two main sections: Babylonian messengers visit Hezekiah (39:1–2), and then Isaiah visits Hezekiah (39:3–8). Within the second unit, there are three movements: Isaiah's initial dialogue with Hezekiah (39:3–4), Isaiah's prophetic message to Hezekiah (39:5–7), and Hezekiah's response to the message (39:8).

- *Babylonian Messengers Visit Hezekiah (39:1–2)*
- *Isaiah Visits Hezekiah (39:3–8)*

EXPOSITION (39:1–8)

Babylonian Messengers Visit Hezekiah (39:1–2)

Following Hezekiah's recovery from his life-threatening illness, the Chaldean Merodach-baladan sent letters and a gift to him.

The Chaldeans were a group of tribes living in southern Mesopotamia as early as the ninth century B.C. They vied with the Assyrians for control of Babylon in the eighth through seventh centuries. In 731 the Assyrian ruler Tiglath-pileser III took control of Babylon, giving himself the Babylonian throne name Pulu (2 Kings 15:19). Merodach-baladan regained the throne for the Chaldeans in 721 and retained it until 710, when the Assyrian king Sargon took it. The Assyrian king Sennacherib put down rebellions led by Merodach-baladan in 703 and 700. Though Merodach-baladan was no longer "king of Babylon" (he had ruled Babylon from 721 to 710 and again from 705 to 703), the title is given to him here, since he had once ruled the city and was still hopeful of regaining control of it.

Hezekiah gladly received the bearers of the letters and gift. He showed them all the wealth of his palace and kingdom, including his storehouses of silver, gold, spices, olive oil, and weapons (39:2). Merodach-baladan was probably courting Hezekiah as a fellow anti-Assyrian ally. Perhaps flattered by the recognition, Hezekiah demonstrated to Merodach-baladan's messengers that he would indeed make a powerful ally.[1] But as Smith (2007, 658) points out, Hezekiah, having been granted an additional fifteen years to live, had no need to make an alliance with Babylon for the sake of security.

Isaiah Visits Hezekiah (39:3–8)

Isaiah confronted the king and used the occasion to announce God's judgment on the Davidic dynasty through the Babylonian exile.

The prophet Isaiah paid Hezekiah a visit and asked the king a series of questions (39:3–4). He wanted to know what the messengers had said and from where they had come. Hezekiah did not answer the first question (at least no answer is recorded in the text), but he did tell Isaiah that the men had come from the distant land of Babylon.

---

1 See Blenkinsopp 2000, 488; Motyer 1993, 296; Oswalt 1986, 695; Smith 2007, 657. Jang (2017, 130–35) sees a parallel between Hezekiah's action and Ahaz's hiring the Assyrians, alluded to in Isaiah 7:20. For a more positive view of Hezekiah's actions, see Goswell 2019, 91–92; Seitz 1993, 265–66.

Isaiah then asked what they had seen in the palace. Hezekiah readily acknowledged that they had seen everything in his palace, explaining that he had shown them everything in his storehouses.

Hezekiah's actions were evidence of a proud spirit, and Isaiah used the occasion to pronounce a judgment speech from the Lord against the royal house (39:5–7). The prophet began by urging the king to hear the word of the Lord of Armies. The title is appropriate here, for a future military defeat, orchestrated by the Lord, is described within the message. At some point in the future, the wealth Hezekiah and his ancestors had accumulated would be taken off to Babylon. Nothing would be left. To make matters worse, some of Hezekiah's royal descendants would be carried away to Babylon, where they would serve the Babylonian king as eunuchs, diminishing the strength of the Davidic dynasty (cf. 2 Kings 24:15).

Hezekiah's response, in contrast to his reaction when told earlier he was about to die (cf. Isa. 38:3), was very matter-of-fact (38:8). He replied that the Lord's word was "good," and then said (perhaps to himself), "For there will be peace and security in my lifetime." Greg Goswell (2019, 106) takes this positively; Hezekiah is content to rest in the Lord's "enduring kingship." Perhaps there is an admission of wrongdoing here that recognizes the Lord's mercy in delaying judgment. (See Seitz [1993, 262–63], as well as Young [1969, 538–39], who sees Hezekiah's response positively.) But then again, the response seems self-focused, possibly assuming the anti-Assyrian coalition would succeed (Roberts 2015, 489). Oswalt (1986, 697) concludes that "the picture here is essentially negative. Hezekiah is not the promised 'child'; he is not infallible." (Oswalt alludes here to the prophecy of 9:6–7; see as well, Motyer 1993, 297; and 2017, 117–35; Smith 2007, 659–60; and esp. Jang 2017.)

THEOLOGICAL FOCUS

The theological focus of this passage can be stated as follows: as illustrated by Hezekiah's actions, there is a fine line between faith and failure. As the prophet develops this theological theme, the following emphases emerge:

1. True security lies in the Lord.

Hezekiah had learned that true security lies in the Lord's power to protect and deliver. In response to Hezekiah's prayers, the Lord delivered Jerusalem from the Assyrian threat and healed Hezekiah from a terminal illness. But in this chapter Hezekiah flirts with the Babylonians, as if an alliance might be useful in assuring national security. The Lord uses the occasion to announce that Judah will eventually fall to the Babylonians.

2. Faith in the Lord's protective power must be sustained.

As he faced the Assyrian threat and the reality of premature death, Hezekiah exhibited faith in the Lord's power to deliver and restore. But when the crises ended, his faith lapsed as he courted Babylonian messengers and showed off his wealth and military power.

This is a pattern we see often in the Old Testament. Following a spiritual victory, an individual or the nation experiences a letdown where people decide to walk by sight rather than by faith. Examples abound, including: (1) Israel's grumbling right after being delivered at the Red Sea (Exod. 14–17); (2) Israel's demand for a king, right after trusting the Lord and experiencing his victory over the Philistines (1 Sam. 7–8); (3) David fleeing from Saul and putting his trust in Goliath's sword, not too long after defeating the Philistine champion through God's enablement (1 Sam. 17, 21); and (4) Elijah's fleeing in fear from Jezebel after confronting the prophets on Carmel and experiencing the intervention of God in power (1 Kings 18–19).

PREACHING AND TEACHING STRATEGIES

Exegetical and Theological Synthesis

Isaiah 39 begins by telling the reader that the king of Babylon had sent envoys to Judah to meet King Hezekiah to inquire about how he had miraculously recovered from his illness (39:1). The fame related to his recovery had been magnified by the celestial miracle that accompanied his healing. When the sun went back ten steps on the sundial (Isa. 38:8), apparently word quickly spread that Israel's God had performed this miracle as proof of his divine healing of King Hezekiah. Additionally, the fact that this miracle occurred right around the time that God also decimated a significant portion of the Assyrian army in one night would have doubly aroused the interest of foreign nations like Babylon. If Hezekiah's God was powerful enough to defeat the mighty Assyrians and make the sun move backward in the sky, then other nations would have wanted to align themselves with Judah, especially those who, like Judah, viewed Assyria as a major threat. As they say, "The enemy of my enemy is my friend."

So how did Hezekiah respond when these emissaries came to inquire about his healing? Did he remember the lesson about appealing to God's glory and reputation that he learned when he prayed to God for deliverance from the Assyrians (Isa. 36–37)? No. He seems to have forgotten this lesson. Rather than using the opportunity to testify to the greatness of God, he instead seems to bask in his own greatness and glory by showing off all his wealth (39:2). His behavior seems to imply a desire to impress them, probably because he wanted to solidify an anti-Assyrian alliance with them. If this was the case, then Hezekiah forgot another important lesson—one that he should have learned after his previous alliances with Egypt (Isa. 28:15–19; 30:1–7; 31:1) and Assyria (Isa. 33:1, 7–8; 36–37) failed to help him at all. He forgot that the only alliance that mattered for God's people was the one with Yahweh. He alone had the power to protect them.

After a brief exchange between Hezekiah and Isaiah (39:3–4), the prophet warned him that all the wealth he had just shown off to the Babylonian envoys would one day in the not-too-distant future be looted and carried away by the same Babylonians (39:5–6). Additionally, some of Hezekiah's own direct descendants would be carried off into exile to serve as eunuchs in the pagan king's palace (39:7). When Hezekiah responded to Isaiah's prophetic message to him, his comments seem almost dismissive of the future implications. He said that Isaiah's words seemed good to him since at least there would be peace in his days (39:8). He seems to be concerned only for himself and doesn't appear to show sorrow for his own children or grandchildren. One would have expected Hezekiah to repent of his foolish pride. After all, maybe God would have reconsidered his predicted judgment against Judah. There seems to be a stark contrast between how Hezekiah responded when the prophet predicted the king's imminent death in chapter 38 to how he responded here in chapter 39. In chapter 38, when he faced the prospect of his own death due in part to his sins, Hezekiah repented and asked for God to graciously reconsider his predicted judgment. Here, however, when the judgment would impact his descendants rather than him, Hezekiah treats it as a final word from God. It would seem he has forgotten that God responds to penitent prayers and may be willing to change his mind about coming judgment.

In all, this brief passage reveals a version of Hezekiah that is out of character to most of what we thought we knew about him. The lessons that Hezekiah seemed to learn along the way in the chapters leading up to this one have all apparently been forgotten. As such, the reader is left with a realistic view of a flawed, otherwise godly, leader. Hezekiah's forgetfulness is directly related to his recent success and the experience of God's blessing. Even though Judah's recent victory over Assyria was totally an act of God's power on his behalf, and despite that fact that his miraculous healing was a gesture of God's grace, Hezekiah seems to have allowed these blessings to go to his head. However good and devout Hezekiah was throughout much of his life, this final chapter of his life shows he was not the ideal, righteous king whom God had predicted would establish a kingdom of justice and peace (Isa. 32:1–8, 15–18; 33:17–24). Rather, they awaited another king, someone more noble and selfless than Hezekiah.

Preaching Idea
Beware of pride and self-centeredness, which easily grow in the soil of God's blessings and success.

Contemporary Connections

What does it mean?
There is something innate to humans that makes us prone to assume credit for the good things that happen to us. When we encounter success by way of our accomplishments, we are quick to think, "I did that," but often slow to recognize the many contributions made by others enabling us to achieve those things. If you ask an Olympian gold medalist what brought them to the moment of winning gold, their response will likely be about all their hard work and the sacrifices they endured. They will think about the many hours spent practicing, the money spent on coaches, all the junk food they avoided, and the exercise they did to keep their body in peak shape. Rarely will they think first about the fact that God created them with an ideal body type for their sport, or that he blessed them with good health. Do they consider further where their coordination and athletic aptitude came from, something with which most people simply are not born? Does it occur to them that had they been born in a place like North Korea, they wouldn't have had the freedom to pursue that sport at all. Similarly, had they been born in Haiti or Irian Jaya, they wouldn't have had the financial resources to afford coaches or training equipment. While hard work and personal sacrifice are often part of what it takes to be successful, there are always other significant factors outside a person's control that have contributed to their success. And yet, most people rarely stop to consider just how indebted to the Lord they are for the successes they have experienced in life.

King Hezekiah had just come through a great success story. From a human perspective, it would appear to others that he must have done something special to have utterly defeated the mighty Assyrian army that had advanced upon Jerusalem. This was especially unprecedented since his own army suffered zero casualties. Even more, Hezekiah miraculously recovered from an illness that should have taken his life. The accompanying miracle in the heavens caught the attention of the Babylonians, who came to sing his praises. After all, he must have been an amazing king to have impressed the gods, causing them to act in such a way on his behalf. We the readers know the truth behind these incidents. God didn't act on Hezekiah's behalf because he had done some amazing thing. Rather, God acted based on his own mercy and for his own name's sake. Hezekiah had no legitimate reason to brag or assume credit for anything that happened to him. Nonetheless, he seems to have gotten so caught up in all the praise and flattery heaped on him by the Babylonian envoys that he forgot it was the Lord's doing and not his own. He forgot to give credit where credit was due.

Is it true?
God warned the Israelites when they were about to enter Canaan that the blessings in that land would tempt them to forget that it was God who brought them out of captivity in Egypt (Deut. 8:14), through the barren wilderness, and into the land of prosperity. He urged them to "remember how the LORD your God

led you all the way in the wilderness these forty years" (8:2). God went on to inform his people that he used their forty years in the wilderness to humble them by teaching them the lesson that they needed to depend upon him for their very survival. We do not live by bread alone, but by the very words of God (8:3). He taught them this lesson by miraculously providing them with daily manna from heaven and by preserving their clothing and sandals for the entirety of that time (8:3–4). This was all about to change in one sense, though. The Promised Land would be a place of abundance and prosperity. It would be a good land with freshwater springs and fertile ground for flocks to graze and for growing all sorts of crops and fruit trees. Its hills would contain iron ore and copper. The people would no longer wander around in tents but would build houses to dwell in, and they would accumulate silver and gold (8:7–13). God thus warned them: "Be careful that you do not forget the Lord your God, failing to observe his commandments. . . . Otherwise, when you eat and are satisfied . . . then your heart will become proud and you will forget the Lord your God" (8:11–14).

The same reality is true for all of us. It's far easier to remember our desperate need for God when things are hard or when we have needs that we are unable to meet on our own—when our child is suffering from troubling symptoms but the doctors are baffled at the cause, or when we are unable to find work but have bills piling up that need to be paid, or when our spouse has grown distant or our teenager appears to be walking away from her faith. These are the sorts of situations that drive us to our knees in prayer and remind us how desperate we are for God's intervention in our lives. However, when those crises pass and we begin to experience the land of blessing and prosperity, our hearts are prone to forget God and all the lessons we learned when going through the valleys or when wandering in the wilderness.

This was exactly where Hezekiah found himself. He experienced two separate situations, both of which threatened to take his life. He and the people of Judah were surrounded by the powerful Assyrian army (Isa. 36–37), and then Hezekiah became deathly sick (Isa. 38). In both instances, the king humbled himself and cried out to God for help. He appealed to God's mercy and grace. God miraculously delivered and healed him. A short time later, Hezekiah moved into the land of prosperity. The Assyrians had returned home, his health was restored, and powerful foreign diplomats were lavishing him with gifts as they affirmed Hezekiah's importance and greatness. By all accounts, Hezekiah's response to them reveals he quickly forgot the lessons he had learned while walking through the wilderness when he was forced to depend on the Lord. He forgot how vulnerable he and his people had been without the Lord's sovereign provision and protection.

True learning requires remembering. If we can't remember something, did we ever truly learn it in the first place? Think back to high school or college days when you sometimes had to cram for a test. Often, this required you to memorize a list of things or a series of definitions. If you were like me you found creative ways with mnemonic devices to remember those facts just long enough to take the test. However, if it was a subject that you weren't planning to use again anytime soon, you probably chose to just store those facts in your short-term memory. The reality is, while you may have memorized those details for the test, you never actually learned them. They never became a part of you. They were simply extraneous facts that you placed into your short-term memory to pass that test.

The same is sadly true of many of the tests and lessons that God wants to teach us. In the moment of our crisis, we recognize our need for God, and we cry out to him. We experience his love and provision toward us. But once we are out of the crisis, we can quickly forget those lessons and revert to our former ways of thinking. Thus, the lessons never really take root in our hearts, and real learning never takes place.

Speaking about this situation in Hezekiah's life, 2 Chronicles 32:31 says, "But when envoys were sent by the rulers of Babylon to ask him about the miraculous sign that had occurred in the land, God left him to test him and to know everything that was in his heart." God used the envoys as a test to see if Hezekiah had learned the lessons from the previous chapters in his life. Sadly, he failed this test. Second Chronicles 32:25 says, "But Hezekiah's heart was proud and he did not respond to the kindness shown him; therefore the LORD's wrath was on him and on Judah and Jerusalem." In pride, Hezekiah showed off his God-given wealth and failed to return praise and worship back to the Lord in the presence of the Babylonian envoys.

Now what?
Stories such as this reveal that the Bible is true and trustworthy. If the Bible were just a collection of made-up or embellished myths about ideal characters that the authors of Scripture wanted others to emulate, then one would fully expect the text to always present Israel's heroes with ideal and noble character traits. The heroes would always do the right thing. Just think about how American folk tales and heroes are presented. Superman almost always does the right thing. He is always courageous, never selfish, never weak. Whenever he sees evil, he boldly takes it on and almost always comes out the winner. Stories about the Lone Ranger similarly present him as always honest and brave. Conversely, the villains in these stories are always selfish, dishonest, and cowardly in the end. As such, it is always easy to spot the good guys and the bad guys in works of fiction.

Unfortunately, real life isn't usually that straightforward. It isn't only the bad politicians in the "other" party who lie and accept bribes from special interest groups to help them get reelected. We also unfortunately discover sometimes that even beloved pastors are susceptible to moral failures. And even police officers who risk their lives to uphold justice for the innocent will sometimes accept bribes to turn a blind eye to wrongdoing. At times, it isn't clear who the good guys and the bad guys really are. The fact that the Bible presents even the heroes of Israel as deeply flawed people at times reinforces the conclusion that these stories are historically true. They aren't myths invented to serve as ideal examples after which people were to model their own behavior. Apologists refer to this as the criterion of embarrassment. The fact that the biblical writers were willing to include accounts that would have been embarrassing for even the heroes of their faith shows that they cared about preserving truth. David was a great king, but he took advantage of a woman, killed a man, and failed as a father. Peter was one of the leaders of the early church, and yet it's consistently recorded that he said a lot of wrong things at the wrong times, inviting the correction of Jesus. Samson was a divinely empowered deliverer of his people even though he had a weakness for women and violated his Nazirite status. So too Hezekiah was one of the greatest kings of Judah who, despite having a wicked father, led his nation through a spiritual revival. He eliminated idols and restored exclusive, Yahwistic worship in the temple. Nonetheless, in this story, the reader sees that he too was susceptible to pride and forgetfulness. He sounds immensely selfish when the prophet predicts that his own sons would be taken captive as eunuchs in the palace of Babylon. His response was that this word from God was good, because at least it wouldn't happen in his lifetime (Isa. 39:8).

This story would have driven home the point to Isaiah's audience that Hezekiah was not the righteous ideal king about whom Isaiah had prophesied. He was not the one who would usher in a kingdom of justice and peace. They would need to look for somebody else, who was in fact Jesus. This should serve as reassurance to God's people today who grow discouraged with their own lack of faithfulness to God. He does not ultimately accept us on the basis of our own righteousness, but because of the righteousness of Jesus.

Finally, it is important that we do not forget about our dependence on God, who abundantly provides for us and blesses us. We must remember that all our successes and accomplishments have been made possible by God's providence and blessings, not simply our own hard work, intelligence, or even just dumb luck.

There is an ancient Jewish tradition that goes back to before the time of Jesus, centered around remembering the Lord's blessings. When they entered the Promised Land with all its prosperity, they were to bless the Lord their God for the good land he had given them (cf. Deut. 8:10). The Jews developed a series of prayers designed to bless (that is, praise) God for all the blessings they received each day, including many of the otherwise mundane or routine ones. Eventually, they developed a standard format for these prayers whereby each one began with, "Blessed are you, O Lord our God, King of the universe." Upon waking up each morning, they would pray, "Blessed are you, O Lord our God, King of the universe, who opens the eyes of the blind," referring to God waking them up again. As they got dressed for the day, they would pray, "Blessed are you, O Lord our God, King of the universe, who clothes the naked." They would memorize and recite various prayers before eating bread, tasting fruit, or drinking wine. They would offer blessing to the Lord when seeing a pleasant sight or smelling a pleasant fragrance, acknowledging that it is his goodness that created the world with such good and appealing sights and smells. There is even a prayer blessing God for the relief that comes from using the bathroom. The point of this practice is to daily keep before one's mind the reality that God is the giver of every good gift.[2]

We probably won't embrace the full Jewish practice of daily reciting the many traditional blessing prayers. However, we would do well to at least implement the practice of regularly expressing thanksgiving to God for even the most basic of blessings. Consider setting a goal of thanking God for at least ten new things each day for a week. Consider keeping a journal of the things for which you have thanked God. It will surprise you how many things you had come to just take for granted that really are blessings from the Lord. Things like a hot shower, a garage that keeps your car windows from icing up, a friend who wants to have lunch with you, or technological advancements that make your life easier are examples of blessings God has made possible for us. Consciously thanking him for those things should cause one to remember his hand in our many blessings and thus avoid the tendency toward pride and self-centeredness that usually arises in those who experience prosperity and success.

Creativity in Presentation

Personal Story

Share a personal story about a time you forgot something important. A humorous example for me was when I forgot my anniversary until my wife and I both received a text from my mom that afternoon, wishing us a happy anniversary. Thankfully, I had the flexibility to quickly run to the store and buy a card and some gifts before my wife got home from work that evening. When she arrived, she was so proud of me that I had remembered. It turns out, she had forgotten too until she received the same text from my mom. I pretended to be indignant that she had forgotten our anniversary for a few minutes before confessing with a smile that I too had forgotten.

Other examples aren't as humorous, like the time (two times actually) I forgot to pick my daughter up from middle school, and she was left standing outside alone well after everyone else was picked up. There was the time when we

---

2 For a discussion on the Jewish tradition of blessing prayers, see Spangler and Tverberg 2009, 98–107.

forgot to pay our county taxes by the deadline and incurred a significant fine. Forgetfulness is a painful reality of life that often results in negative consequences to which everyone can relate. Use some examples from your own life to illustrate our tendency to forget the spiritual lessons that God has taught and the negative consequences we experience as a result.

Social Media Boasts
There have been various occasions when a bank robber has been caught after he/she brazenly and foolishly bragged about their criminal exploits on social media. In 2015, twenty-three-year-old Dominyk Alfonseca posted pictures and videos to his Instagram account of a bank teller in Virginia Beach, Virginia, stuffing a duffle bag with cash after he slipped her a note. He also posted a photo of the note requesting the money. Needless to say, the man was arrested a mere twenty-two minutes after leaving the bank.

In another incident, Ryan Homsley robbed a bank in Portland, Oregon, dressed in a striped shirt and horn-rimmed glasses that made him look to many like the character Waldo from the "Where's Waldo?" books. He was quickly dubbed by media outlets as the "Where's Waldo Bandit." One month later, Homsley robbed another bank in a nearby town. Soon after, Ryan boasted on his Facebook page that he was indeed "Waldo," along with bank surveillance photos from his robbery. Authorities were soon alerted to his posts, and he was arrested.[3]

Hezekiah too made the foolish decision to boast of his wealth to the envoys from the pagan nation of Babylon. By brazenly flaunting his wealth to these men, he was partially responsible for the plundering of Judah. His actions seem to have motivated and inspired them to return, this time with nefarious intentions to steal the very treasures Hezekiah showed them (Isa. 39:2–6).

Beware of pride and self-centeredness, which easily grow in the soil of God's blessings and success.

- Don't forget about the impact of God's provision (39:1–2).
    - In fear, Hezekiah again trusted in worldly alliances rather than God.
- Don't forget about the importance of God's glory (39:2–6).
    - In pride, Hezekiah accepted credit rather than give glory to God.
- Don't forget about the implications for future generations (39:7–8).
    - In selfishness, Hezekiah minimized the problems his descendants would have to face.

---

3   For these and other stories of people who were apprehended after boasting of their robberies on social media, see https://listverse.com/2022/09/10/10-status-updates-that-ruined-otherwise-successful-bank-robberies.

Hezekiah Shows Off His Wealth (39:1–8)

DISCUSSION QUESTIONS

1. Can you think of a time in your life when you felt profoundly moved by God to make some changes in your life, only to return to your previous way of living a short time later? What are some of the factors involved in this common experience, whereby we are so quick to forget the lessons God teaches us?

2. Which do you think poses the greater obstacle to one's spiritual growth—adversity or prosperity? Why might prosperity pose the bigger threat?

3. What strategies do you use in your everyday life to keep you from forgetting important things? Can you think of any similar things that might be helpful in preventing you from forgetting the lessons God has taught you in the past?

FOR FURTHER READING

Spangler, Ann, and Lois Tverberg. 2018. *Sitting at the Feet of Rabbi Jesus: How the Jewishness of Jesus Can Transform Your Faith*. Grand Rapids: Zondervan.

REFERENCES

Abernethy, Andrew T. 2014. *Eating in Isaiah: Approaching the Role of Food and Drink in Isaiah's Structure and Message*. BibInt 131. Leiden: Brill.

Aharoni, Yohanan. 1979. *The Land of the Bible: A Historical Geography*. Translated and edited by Anson F. Rainey. Rev. and enlarged ed. Philadelphia: Westminster.

Aharoni, Yohanan, and Michael Avi-Yonah. 1977. *The Macmillan Bible Atlas*. Rev. ed. New York: Macmillan.

Albrektson, Bertil. 1967. *History and the Gods: An Essay on the Idea of Historical Events as Divine Manifestations in the Ancient Near East and in Israel*. ConBOT 1. Lund: Gleerup.

Alcorn, Randy. 2004. *Heaven*. Wheaton, IL: Tyndale.

———. 2011. *Safely Home*. Carol Stream, IL: Tyndale.

Allen, Kenneth W. 1976. "The Rebuilding and Destruction of Babylon." *BSac* 133:19–27.

Allen, Leslie C. 1990. *Ezekiel 20–48*. WBC 29. Dallas: Word.

Amzallag, Nissim, and Mikhal Avriel. 2012. "The Cryptic Meaning of the Isaiah 14 *Māšāl*." *JBL* 131:643–62.

Anderson, Neil. 2000. *The Bondage Breaker: Overcoming Negative Thoughts, Irrational Feelings, Habitual Sins*. Updated and exp. ed. Eugene, OR: Harvest House.

Armerding, Carl E. 1975. "Were David's Sons Really Priests?" In *Current Issues in Biblical and Patristic Interpretation: Studies in Honor of Merrill C. Tenney Presented by His Former Students*, edited by Gerald F. Hawthorne, 75–86. Grand Rapids: Eerdmans.

Aster, Shawn Zelig. 2007. "The Image of Assyria in Isaiah 2:5–22: The Campaign Motif Reversed." *JAOS* 127:249–78.

———. 2017. "Isaiah 31 as a Response to Rebellions Against Assyria in Philistia." *JBL* 136:347–61.

———. 2018. "The Shock of Assyrian Imperial Ideology and the Responses of Biblical Authors in the Late Eighth Century." In *Archaeology and History of Eighth-century Judah*, edited by Zev I. Farber and Jacob L. Wright, 475–88. ANEM 23. Atlanta: SBL Press.

Baldwin, Joyce G. 1964. "Ṣemaḥ as a Technical Term in the Prophets." *VT* 14:93–97.

Balogh, Csaba. 2011. *The Stele of YHWH in Egypt: The Prophecies of Isaiah 18–20 Concerning Egypt and Kush*. OTS 60. Leiden: Brill.

———. 2014. "Historicising Interpolations in the Isaiah-Memoir." *VT* 64:519–38.

Barker, William D. 2014. *Isaiah's Kingship Polemic: An Exegetical Study of Isaiah 24–27*. FAT 2/70. Tubingen: Mohr Siebeck.

Barré, Michael L. 2003. "A Rhetorical-Critical Study of Isaiah 2:12–17." *CBQ* 65:522–34.

———. 2005. *The Lord Has Saved Me: A Study of the Psalm of Hezekiah (Isaiah 38:9–20)*. CBQMS 39. Washington, DC: Catholic Biblical Association of America.

Bartelt, Andrew H. 1996. *The Book around Immanuel: Style and Structure in Isaiah 2–12*. BJSUCSD 4. Winona Lake, IN: Eisenbrauns.

Bateman, Herbert, IV. 1992. "The Use of Psalm 110:1 in the New Testament." *BSac* 149:438–53.

Bayly, Joseph. 1973. *The Last Thing We Talk About*. Elgin, IL: Cook.

References

Beale, Gregory K. 1991. "Isaiah 6:9–13: A Retributive Taunt Against Idolatry." *VT* 41:257–78.

———. 2008. *We Become What We Worship: A Biblical Theology of Idolatry*. Downers Grove, IL: IVP Academic.

Bergey, Ronald. 2003. "The Song of Moses (Deuteronomy 32.1–43) and Isaianic Prophecies: A Case of Early Intertextuality?" *JSOT* 28:33–54.

Beuken, Willem A. M. 2004. "The Manifestation of Yahweh and the Commission of Isaiah: Isaiah 6 Read Against the Background of Isaiah 1." *CTJ* 39:72–87.

Blank, Sheldon H. 1956. "Traces of Prophetic Agony in Isaiah." *HUCA* 27:81–92.

Blenkinsopp, Joseph. 2000. *Isaiah 1–39: A New Translation with Introduction and Commentary*. AB 19. New York: Doubleday.

Block, Daniel I. 1998. *The Book of Ezekiel: Chapters 25–48*. NICOT. Grand Rapids: Eerdmans.

Block, Daniel I., and Richard L. Schultz, eds. 2015. *Bind Up the Testimony: Explorations in the Genesis of the Book of Isaiah*. Peabody, MA: Hendrickson.

Borowski, Oded. 1987. *Agriculture in Iron Age Israel*. Winona Lake, IN: Eisenbrauns.

———. 1995. "Hezekiah's Reforms and the Revolt Against Assyria." *BA* 58:148–55.

Bright, John. 1981. *A History of Israel*. 3rd ed. Philadelphia: Westminster.

Brown, William P. 1990. "The So-Called Refrain in Isaiah 5:25–30 and 9:7–10:4." *CBQ* 52:432–43.

Burnett, Joel S. 2001. *A Reassessment of Biblical Elohim*. SBLDS 183. Atlanta: Society of Biblical Literature.

Burrows, Millar. 1958. "The Conduit of the Upper Pool." *ZAW* 70:221–27.

Calvin, John. 1999. *Calvin's Commentaries*. Translated by W. Pringle. 22 vols. Repr., Grand Rapids: Baker.

Carlson, R. A. 1974. "The Anti-Assyrian Character of the Oracle in Is. IX 1–6." *VT* 24:130–35.

Chaney, Marvin L. 1999. "Whose Sour Grapes? The Addressees of Isaiah 5:1–7 in the Light of Political Economy." *Semeia* 87:105–22.

Childs, Brevard S. 2000. *Isaiah*. OTL. Louisville: Westminster John Knox.

Chisholm, Robert B., Jr. 1983. "An Exegetical and Theological Study of Psalm 18/2 Samuel 22." PhD diss., Dallas Theological Seminary.

———. 1986. "Structure, Style, and the Prophetic Message: An Analysis of Isaiah 5:8–30." *BSac* 143:46–60.

———. 1987. "Wordplay in the Eighth-Century Prophets." *BSac* 144:44–52.

———. 1991. "A Theology of Isaiah." In *A Biblical Theology of the Old Testament*, edited by Roy B. Zuck, 305–40. Chicago: Moody Press.

———. 1993. "The 'Everlasting Covenant' and the 'City of Chaos': Intentional Ambiguity and Irony in Isaiah 24." *CTR* 6:237–53.

———. 1995. "Does God 'Change His Mind'?" *BSac* 152:387–99.

———. 1996. "Divine Hardening in the Old Testament." *BSac* 153:410–34.

———. 1998a. "Does God Deceive?" *BSac* 155:11–28.

———. 1998b. *From Exegesis to Exposition: A Practical Guide to Using Biblical Hebrew*. Grand Rapids: Baker.

———. 2002. *Handbook on the Prophets: Isaiah, Jeremiah, Lamentations, Ezekiel, Daniel, Minor Prophets*. Grand Rapids: Baker Academic, 2002.

———. 2009. "How a Hermeneutical Virus Can Corrupt Theological Systems." *BSac* 166:259–70.

———. 2010. "When Prophecy Appears to Fail, Check Your Hermeneutic." *JETS* 53:561–77.

———. 2012. "Retribution." In *Dictionary of the Old Testament Prophets*, edited by Mark J. Boda and J. G. McConville, 671–76. Downers Grove, IL: IVP Academic.

———. 2013a. "Suppressing Myth: Yahweh and the Sea in the Praise Psalms." In *The Psalms: Language for All Seasons of the Soul*, edited by Andrew J. Schmutzer and David M. Howard Jr., 75–84. Chicago: Moody Press.

———. 2013b. *A Commentary on Judges and Ruth*. Kregel Exegetical Library. Grand Rapids: Kregel.

———. 2014. "Israel According to the Prophets." In *The People, the Land, and the Future of Israel: Israel and the Jewish People in the Plan of God*, edited by Darrell L. Bock and Mitch Glaser, 53–69. Grand Rapids: Kregel.

———. 2018. "Rizpah's Torment: When God Punishes the Children for the Sin of the Father." *BSac* 175:50–66.

Claassen, W. T. 1974. "Linguistic Arguments and the Dating of Isaiah 1:4–9." *JNSL* 3:1–18.

Clements, Ronald E. 1980. *Isaiah 1–39*. NCB. Grand Rapids: Eerdmans.

Clines, David J. A. 1989. *Job 1–20*. WBC 17. Waco, TX: Word.

Cogan, Mordechai, and Hayim Tadmor. 1988. *II Kings: A New Translation with Introduction and Commentary*. AB 11. New York: Doubleday.

Cohen, Harold R. (Chaim). 1978. *Biblical Hapax Legomena in the Light of Akkadian and Ugaritic*. SBLDS 37. Missoula, MT: Scholars Press.

Conrad, Edgar W. 1991. *Reading Isaiah*. OBT. Minneapolis: Fortress.

Cook, Paul M. 2011. *A Sign and a Wonder: The Redactional Formation of Isaiah 18–20*. VTSup 147. Leiden: Brill.

Craigie, Peter C. 1973. "Helel, Athtar, and Phaethon (Isa. 14:12–15)." *ZAW* 85:223–25.

Culver, Robert D. 1969. "Isaiah 1:18: Declaration, Exclamation or Interrogation?" *JETS* 12:133–41.

Currid, John D. 1997. *Ancient Egypt and the Old Testament*. Grand Rapids: Baker.

Davidson, R. 1966. "The Interpretation of Isaiah II 6 ff." *VT* 16 (1966):1–7.

Davies, Andrew. 2000. *Double Standards in Isaiah: Re-evaluating Prophetic Ethics and Divine Justice*. BibInt 46. Leiden: Brill, 2000.

Day, John. 1978. "טַל אוֹרֹת in Isaiah 26;19." *ZAW* 90:265–69.

———. 2000. *Yahweh and the Gods and Goddesses of Canaan*. JSOTSup 265. Sheffield: Sheffield Academic.

Dearman, J. Andrew. 1988. *Property Rights in the Eighth-Century Prophets: The Conflict and Its Background*. SBLDS 106. Atlanta: Scholars Press.

———. 1996. "The Son of Tabeel (Isaiah 7.6)." In *Prophets and Paradigms: Essays in Honor of Gene M. Tucker*, edited by Stephen Breck Reid, 33–47. JSOTSup 229. Sheffield: Sheffield Academic.

Dekker, Jaap. 2007. *Zion's Rock-solid Foundations: An Exegetical Study of the Zion Text in Isaiah 28:16*. OTS 54. Leiden: Brill.

DeYoung, Kevin. 2014. *The Hole in Our Holiness: Filling the Gap Between Gospel Passion and the Pursuit of Godliness*. Wheaton, IL: Crossway.

Dumbrell, William J. 1984. *Covenant and Creation*. Nashville: Nelson.

Dykes, Julie. 2020. "Inverting Good and Evil: Thematic Chiasm in the Woes of Isaiah 5." Paper presented at the (Virtual) Annual Meeting of the Evangelical Theological Society, November 20.

Eidevall, Gorän. 2009. *Prophecy and Propaganda: Images of Enemies in the Book of Isaiah*. ConBOT 56. Winona Lake, IN: Eisenbrauns.

Emerton, J. A. 1982. "The Translation and Interpretation of Isaiah vi. 13." In *Interpreting the Hebrew Bible: Essays in Honour of E. I. J. Rosenthal*, edited by J. A. Emerton and S. C. Reif, 85–118. Cambridge: Cambridge University Press.

Erlandsson, Seth. 1970. *The Burden of Babylon: A Study of Isaiah 13:2–14:23*. Translated by George J. Houser. ConBOT 4. Lund: Gleerup.

———. 1974. "בָּנָה." *TDOT* 1:470–73.

———. 1980. "זָנָה." *TDOT* 4:99–104.

Evans, Craig A. 1985. "An Interpretation of Isaiah 8 11–15 Unemended." *ZAW* 97:112–13.

———. 1986. "Isa 6:9–13 in the Context of Isaiah's Theology." *JETS* 29:139–46.

———. 1989. *To See and Not Perceive: Isaiah 6.9–10 in Early Jewish and Christian Interpretation*. JSOTSup 64. Sheffield: JSOT Press.

Evans, Paul. 2009. *The Invasion of Sennacherib in the Book of Kings: A Source-Critical and Rhetorical Study of 2 Kings 18–19*. VTSup 125. Leiden: Brill.

Everson, A. Joseph. 1974. "The Days of Yahweh." *JBL* 93:329–37.

Exum, J. Cheryl. 1982. "'Whom Will He Teach Knowledge?' A Literary Approach to Isaiah 28." In *Art and Meaning: Rhetoric in Biblical Literature*, edited by Alan J. Hauser, D. M. Gunn, and David J. A. Clines, 108–39. JSOTSup 19. Sheffield: JSOT Press.

Fretheim, Terence E. 1984. *The Suffering of God: An Old Testament Perspective*. OBT. Philadelphia: Fortress.

Gallagher, William R. 1999. *Sennacherib's Campaign to Judah: New Studies*. CHANE 18. Leiden: Brill.

Gayton, Theirry, dir. 2009. *Cartels and Police Corruption: Inside Mexico's Drug War*. France: Ligne de Front.

Gentry, Peter J. 2013. "The Meaning of 'Holy' in the Old Testament." *BSac* 170:400–417.

Georges, Jayson. 2014. *The 3D Gospel: Ministry in Guilt, Shame, and Fear Cultures*. N.p.: Timē Press.

Gibson, J. C. L. 1978. *Canaanite Myths and Legends*. 2nd ed. Edinburgh: T&T Clark.

Gitay, Yehoshua. 1983. "Reflections on the Study of the Prophetic Discourse: The Question of Isaiah I 2–20." *VT* 33:207–21.

Goldingay, John. 1999. "The Compound Name in Isaiah 9:5(6)." *CBQ* 61:239–44.

———. 2001. *Isaiah*. NIBCOT. Peabody, MA: Hendrickson.

Goldsworthy, Graeme. "Regeneration." *NDBT*, 720–23.

Goodstein, Laurie. 2001. "After the Attacks: Finding Fault; Falwell's Finger-Pointing Inappropriate, Bush Says." *The New York Times*, Sept. 15. https://www.nytimes.com/2001/09/15/us/after-attacks-finding-fault-falwell-s-finger-pointing-inappropriate-bush-says.html.

Goswell, Gregory. 2015. "The Shape of Messianism in Isaiah 9." *WTJ* 77:101–10.

———. 2017. "Messianic Expectation in Isaiah 11." *WTJ* 79:123–35.

———. 2019. "Farewell to Davidic Kingship: The Meaning and Significance of Isaiah 39." *ResQ* 61:87–106.

Gowan, Donald E. 1986. *Eschatology in the Old Testament*. Philadelphia: Fortress.

Gray, G. B. 1912. *A Critical and Exegetical Commentary on the Book of Isaiah I–XXVII*. ICC. Edinburgh: T&T Clark.

Grayson, A. Kirk. 1976. *Assyrian Royal Inscriptions*. Vol. 2: *From Tiglath-pileser I. to Ashur-nasir-apli II*. RANE. Wiesbaden: Harrassowitz.

Grayson, A. Kirk, and Jamie R. Novotny. 2012. *The Royal Inscriptions of Sennacherib, King of Assyria (704–681 BC), Part 1*. RINAP 3.1. Winona Lake, IN: Eisenbrauns.

———. 2014. *The Royal Inscriptions of Sennacherib, King of Assyria (704–681 BC), Part 2*. RINAP 3.2. Winona Lake, IN: Eisenbrauns.

Greenberg, Moshe. 1983. *Biblical Prose Prayer: As a Window to the Popular Religion of Ancient Israel*. Taubman Lectures in Jewish Studies. Berkeley: University of California Press.

Grisanti, Michael A. 2001. "Inspiration, Inerrancy, and the OT Canon: The Place of Textual Updating in an Inerrant View of Scripture." *JETS* 44:577–98.

References

Grogan, Geoffrey W. 1986. "Isaiah." In *The Expositor's Bible Commentary*, edited by Frank E. Gaebelein, 6:3–354. 12 vols. Grand Rapids: Zondervan.

Guinness, Os. 2000. *Time for Truth: Living Free in a World of Lies, Hype, and Spin*. Grand Rapids: Baker.

Habel, Norman C. 1965. "The Form and Significance of the Call Narratives." *ZAW* 77:297–323.

Hasel, Gerhard. 1972. *The Remnant: The History and Theology of the Remnant Idea from Genesis to Isaiah*. Berrien Springs, MI: Andrews University Press.

Hayes, John H., and Stuart A. Irvine. 1987. *Isaiah the Eighth Century Prophet: His Times and His Preaching*. Nashville: Abingdon.

Hays, Christopher B. 2011. "The Book of Isaiah in Contemporary Research." *Religion Compass* 5, no. 10:549–66.

Heater, Homer, Jr. 1998. "Do the Prophets Teach That Babylonia Will Be Rebuilt in the Eschaton?" *JETS* 41:23–43.

Heiser, Michael S. 2001. "The Mythological Provenance of Isa. XIV 12–15: A Reconsideration of the Ugaritic Material." *VT* 51:354–69.

Hibbard, J. Todd. 2006. *Intertextuality in Isaiah 24–27: The Reuse and Evocation of Earlier Texts and Traditions*. FAT 2/16. Tubingen: Mohr Siebeck.

Holladay, William L. 1978. *Isaiah: Scroll of a Prophetic Heritage*. Grand Rapids: Eerdmans.

Holmyard, Harold R., III. 1995. "Does Isaiah 33:23 Address Israel or Israel's Enemy?" *BSac* 152:273–78.

Hom, Mary Katherine Y. H. 2012. *The Characterization of the Assyrians in Isaiah: Synchronic and Diachronic Perspectives*. LHBOTS 559. London: T&T Clark.

Hontz, Michael. 2013. "The Universal Enemy." In *Glimpses of the Christ: Sermons from the Gospels*, edited by Jarl K. Waggoner, 144–59. Waxhaw, NC: Kainos Books.

House, Paul R. 1993. "Isaiah's Call and Its Context in Isaiah 1–6." *CTR* 6:207–22.

———. 2019. *Isaiah: A Mentor Commentary*. Mentor Commentary 1. Ross-shire: Mentor.

Hurowitz, Victor (Avigdor). 1989. "Isaiah's Impure Lips and Their Purification in Light of Akkadian Sources." *HUCA* 60:39–89.

Idleman, Kyle. 2013. *Gods at War: Defeating the Idols That Battle for Your Heart*. Grand Rapids: Zondervan.

Irsigler, Hubert. 1997. "Speech Acts and Intention in the 'Song of the Vineyard' Isaiah 5:1–7." *OTE* 10:39–68.

Irvine, Stuart A. 1992. "The Isaianic *Denkschrift*: Reconsidering an Old Hypothesis." *ZAW* 104:216–31.

Irwin, William Henry. 1977. *Isaiah 28–33: Translation with Philological Notes*. BibOr 30. Rome: Biblical Institute Press.

Iwry, Samuel. 1957. *Maṣṣēbāh* and *Bāmāh* in 1Q Isaiah[A] 6 13." *JBL* 76:225–32.

Jang, Sehoon. 2017. "Is Hezekiah a Success or a Failure? The Literary Function of Isaiah's Prediction at the End of the Royal Narratives in the Book of Isaiah." *JSOT* 42:117–35.

Janzen, Waldemar. 1972. *Mourning Cry and Woe Oracle*. BZAW 125. Berlin: de Gruyter.

Jastrow, Marcus. 1967. *A Dictionary of the Targumim, the Talmud Babli and Yerushalmi, and the Midrashic Literature*. 2 vols. Brooklyn: Shalom.

Jeffers, Ann. 1996. *Magic and Divination in Ancient Palestine and Syria*. SHCANE 8. Leiden: Brill.

Johnson, Dan G. 1988. *From Chaos to Restoration: An Integrative Reading of Isaiah 24–27*. JSOTSup 61. Sheffield: Sheffield Academic.

Johnston, Gordon H. 2001. "Nahum's Rhetorical Allusions to the Neo-Assyrian Lion Motif." *BSac* 158:287–307.

Johnston, Graham. 2004. *Preaching to a Postmodern World: A Guide to Reaching Twenty-first-century Listeners*. Grand Rapids: Baker.

Johnston, Philip S. 2002. *Shades of Sheol: Death and Afterlife in the Old Testament*. Downers Grove, IL: InterVarsity Press.

Jones, Douglas R. 1968. "Exposition of Isaiah Chapter One Verses Twenty One to the End." *SJT* 21:320–29.

Kaiser, Otto. 1972. *Isaiah 1–12*. Translated by John Bowden. Philadelphia: Westminster.

———. 1974. *Isaiah 13–39*. Translated by R. A. Wilson. OTL. Philadelphia: Westminster.

Kalimi, Isaac, and Seth Richardson, eds. 2014. *Sennacherib at the Gates of Jerusalem: Story, History and Historiography*. CHANE 71. Leiden: Brill.

Keel, Othmar. 1997. *The Symbolism of the Biblical World: Ancient Near Eastern Iconography and the Book of Psalms*. Translated by Timothy J. Hallett. Winona Lake, IN: Eisenbrauns.

———. 1998. *Goddesses and Trees, New Moon and Yahweh*. JSOTSup 261. Sheffield: Sheffield Academic.

Keimer, Kyle H. 2018. "Sennacherib's Invasion of Judah and Neo-Assyrian Expansion." In *Behind the Scenes of the Old Testament*, edited by J. S. Greer, J. W. Hilber, and John H. Walton, 299–305. Grand Rapids: Baker Academic.

Keller, Timothy. 2009. *Counterfeit Gods: The Empty Promises of Money, Sex, and Power, and the Only Hope That Matters*. New York: Penguin.

King, Philip J., and Lawrence E. Stager. 2001. *Life in Biblical Israel*. LAI. Louisville: Westminster John Knox.

Kinzer, Todd A. 2017. "The Strange and Foreign Work of Yahweh: An Emphasis on Divine Mercy in Isaiah 28:20–22." PhD diss., Dallas Theological Seminary.

Kitchen, Kenneth A. 2003. *On the Reliability of the Old Testament*. Grand Rapids: Eerdmans.

Knierim, Rolf. 1968. "The Vocation of Isaiah." *VT* 18:47–68.

Korpel, Marjo C. A. 1996. "Structural Analysis as a Tool for Redaction Criticism: The Example of Isaiah 5 and 10.1–6." *JSOT* 21:53–71.

Kübler-Ross, Elisabeth. 1969. *On Death and Dying: What the Dying Have to Teach Doctors, Nurses, Clergy, and Their Own Families*. New York: Macmillan.

Kutsch, Ernst. 1986. "חָרֵף II." *TDOT* 5:209–15.

Laato, Antti. 1995. "Assyrian Propaganda and the Falsification of History in the Royal Inscriptions of Sennacherib." *VT* 45:198–226.

Lavik, Marta H. 2007. *A People Tall and Smooth-Skinned: The Rhetoric of Isaiah 18*. VTSup 112. Leiden: Brill.

Lessing, R. Reed. 2004. *Interpreting Discontinuity: Isaiah's Tyre Oracle*. Winona Lake, IN: Eisenbrauns.

Lewis, C. S. 1955. *Surprised by Joy: The Shape of My Early Life*. New York: Harcourt, Brace & Co.

———. 2001. *The Problem of Pain*. New York: HarperCollins.

Lichtheim, Miriam. 1976. *Ancient Egyptian Literature: A Book of Readings*. Vol. 2: *The New Kingdom*. Berkeley: University of California.

Liebreich, Leon J. 1956. "The Compilation of the Book of Isaiah." *JQR* 47:114–38.

Machinist, Peter. 1983. "Assyria and Its Image in the First Isaiah." *JAOS* 103:719–37.

Macintosh, A. A. 1980. *Isaiah XXI: A Palimpsest*. Cambridge: Cambridge University Press.

Mahaney, C. J. 2005. *Humility: True Greatness*. Sisters, OR: Multnomah.

Marlow, Hilary. 2011. "The Spirit of Yahweh in Isaiah 11:1–9." In *Presence, Power and Promise: The Role of the Spirit of God in the Old Testament*, edited by David G. Firth and Paul D. Wegner, 220–32. Downers Grove, IL: IVP Academic.

Maslow, Abraham H. 1943. "A Theory of Human Motivation." *Psychological Review* 50:370–96.

References

Mason, Steven D. 2007. "Another Flood? Genesis 9 and Isaiah's Broken Eternal Covenant." *JSOT* 32:177–98.

Mastnjak, Nathan. 2014. "Judah's Covenant with Assyria in Isaiah 28." *VT* 64:465–83.

McAffee, Matthew. 2016. "Rephaim, Whisperers, and the Dead in Isaiah 26:13–19: A Ugaritic Parallel." *JBL* 135:77–94.

McCarter, P. Kyle, Jr. 1980. *I Samuel: A New Translation with Introduction and Commentary*. AB 8. New York: Doubleday.

McKay, J. W. 1970. "Helel and the Dawn-Goddess: A Re-examination of the Myth in Isaiah XIV 12–15." *VT* 20:451–64.

McKenna, David L. 1993. *Isaiah 1–39*. Preacher's Commentary 17. Nashville: Nelson.

Merrill, Eugene H. 1987. *Kingdom of Priests: A History of Old Testament Israel*. Grand Rapids: Baker.

Merrill, Eugene H., Mark F. Rooker, and Michael A. Grisanti. 2011. *The World and the Word: An Introduction to the Old Testament*. Nashville: B&H Academic.

Mettinger, Tryggve N. D. 1988. *In Search of God: The Meaning and Message of the Everlasting Names*. Translated by Frederick H. Cryer. Philadelphia: Fortress.

Milgrom, Jacob. 1964. "Did Isaiah Prophesy During the Reign of Uzziah?" *VT* 14:164–82.

Miller, Patrick D. 1982. *Sin and Judgment in the Prophets*. SBLMS 27. Chico, CA: Scholars.

Moberly, R. W. L. 2001. "Whose Justice? Which Righteousness? The Interpretation of Isaiah V 16." *VT* 51:55–68.

Motyer, J. Alec. 1993. *The Prophecy of Isaiah: An Introduction and Commentary*. TOTC 18. Downers Grove, IL: InterVarsity Press.

Na'aman, Nadav. 1979. "Sennacherib's Campaign to Judah and the Date of the *lmlk* Stamps." *VT* 29:61–86.

Niccacci, Alviero. 1998. "Isaiah XVIII–XX from an Egyptological Perspective." *VT* 48:217–24.

Niditch, Susan. 1993. *War in the Hebrew Bible*. New York: Oxford University Press.

Nielsen, Kirsten. 1989. *There Is Hope for a Tree: The Tree as Metaphor in Isaiah*. Translated by Christine and Frederick Crowley. JSOTSup 65. Sheffield: JSOT Press.

Noegel, Scott B. 2021. *"Wordplay" in Ancient Near Eastern Texts*. ANEM 26. Atlanta: SBL Press.

Noonan, Benjamin J. 2013. "Zion's Foundation: The Meaning of בֹּחַן in Isaiah 28,16." *ZAW* 125:314–19.

O'Connell, R. H. 1988. "Isaiah XIV 4B–23: Ironic Reversal Through Concentric Structure and Mythic Allusion." *VT* 38:406–18.

Ortlund, Eric. 2010. "Reversed (Chrono-)Logical Sequence in Isaiah 1–39: Some Implications for Theories of Redaction." *JSOT* 35:209–24.

Ortlund, Raymond C., Jr. 2005. *Isaiah: God Saves Sinners*. Preaching the Word. Wheaton, IL: Crossway.

Osborn, L. H. 2000. "Creation." *NDBT*, 429–35.

Osborne, Grant R. 2010. "The Old Testament in the New Testament." In *The Hermeneutical Spiral: A Comprehensive Introduction to Biblical Interpretation*, 322–44. Downers Grove, IL: IVP Academic.

Oswalt, John N. 1986. *The Book of Isaiah Chapters 1–39*. NICOT. Grand Rapids: Eerdmans.

———. 1993. "The Significance of the *'Almah* Prophecy in the Context of Isaiah 7–12." *CTR* 6, no. 2:223–35.

———. 2003. *Isaiah*. NIVAC. Grand Rapids: Zondervan.

Otzen, Benedikt. 1977–1978. "Israel Under the Assyrians: Reflections on Imperial Policy in Palestine." *ASTI* 11:96–110.

———. 1979. "Israel Under the Assyrians." In *Power and Propaganda: A Symposium on Ancient Empires*, edited by Mogens Trolle Larsen, 251–61. Mesopotamia 7. Copenhagen: Akademisk Forlag.

Page, Hugh R. 1996. *The Myth of Cosmic Rebellion: A Study of Its Reflexes in Ugaritic and Biblical Literature*. VTSup 65. Leiden: Brill.

Painton, Priscilla. 1992. "The Taming of Ted Turner." *Time*, January 6, 1992.

Parker, Simon, ed. 1997. *Ugaritic Narrative Poetry*. Edited by Mark S. Smith. WAW 9. Atlanta: Scholars Press.

Parpola, Simo. 1980. "The Murderer of Sennacherib." In *Death in Mesopotamia: Papers Read at the XXVIe Rencontre assyriologique international*, edited by Bendt Alster, 171–82. Mesopotamia 8. Copenhagen: Akademisk Forlag.

Parunak, H. Van Dyke. 1975. "A Semantic Survey of NḤM." *Bib* 56:512–32.

Pathak, Jay, and Dave Runyon. 2012. *The Art of Neighboring: Building Genuine Relationships Right Outside Your Door*. Grand Rapids: Baker.

Poirier, J. C. 1999. "An Illuminating Parallel to Isaiah XIV 12." *VT* 49:371–89.

Prinsloo, W. S. 1981. "Isaiah 14:12–15: Humiliation, Hubris, Humiliation." *ZAW* 93:432–38.

Ratcliff, Roy. 2006. *Dark Journey, Deep Grace: Jeffrey Dahmer's Story of Faith*. Abilene, TX: Leafwood.

Redditt, Paul L. 1986. "Once Again, the City in Isaiah 24–27." *HAR* 10:317–35.

Reimer, David J. 2012. "On Triplets in a Trio of Prophets." In *Let Us Go Up to Zion: Essays in Honour of H. G. M. Williamson on the Occasion of His Sixty-fifth Birthday*, edited by Iain Provan and Mark Boda, 203–17. VTSup 153. Leiden: Brill.

Ringgren, Helmer. 1980. "חָיָה." *TDOT* 4:324–44.

Ripken, Nik. 2013. *The Insanity of God: A True Story of Faith Resurrected*. Nashville: B&H.

Robar, Elizabeth. 2015. *The Verb and the Paragraph in Biblical Hebrew: A Cognitive-linguistic Approach*. Studies in Semitic Languages and Linguistics 78. Leiden: Brill.

Roberts, J. J. M. 1992. "Double Entendre in First Isaiah." *CBQ* 54:39–48.

———. 2000. "The Meaning of 'צמח חי' in Isaiah 4:2. *JBQ* 28:20–27.

———. 2015. *First Isaiah: A Commentary*. Hermeneia. Minneapolis: Fortress.

Robinson, Geoffrey D. 1998. "The Motif of Deafness and Blindness in Isaiah 6:9–10: A Contextual, Literary, and Theological Analysis." *BBR* 8:167–86.

Robinson, Haddon W. 2001. *Biblical Preaching: The Development and Delivery of Expository Messages*. 2nd ed. Grand Rapids: Baker.

Rose, Wolter H. 2000. *Zemah and Zerubbabel: Messianic Expectations in the Early Postexilic Period*. JSOTSup 304. Sheffield: Sheffield Academic.

Roux, Georges. 1966. *Ancient Iraq*. Middlesex: Penguin Books.

Sailhamer, John H. 1992. "Evidence from Isaiah 2." In *A Case for Premillennialism: A New Consensus*, edited by Donald K. Campbell and Jeffrey L. Townsend, 79–102. Chicago: Moody Press.

Schibler, Daniel. 1995. "Messianism and Messianic Prophecy in Isaiah 1–12 and 28–33." In *The Lord's Anointed: Interpretation of Old Testament Messianic Texts*, edited by P. E. Satterthwaite, Richard S. Hess, and Gordon J. Wenham, 87–104. Grand Rapids: Baker.

Schmitz, Philip C. 2003. "The Grammar of Resurrection in Isaiah 26:19a–c." *JBL* 122:145–49.

Schultz, Richard L. 2004. "How Many Isaiahs Were There and What Does It Matter? Prophetic Inspiration in Recent Evangelical Scholarship." In *Evangelicals & Scripture: Tradition, Authority and Hermeneutics*, edited by Vincent Bacote, Laura C. Miguélez, and Dennis L. Okholm, 150–70. Downers Grove, IL: InterVarsity Press.

———. 2012. "Isaiah, Isaiahs, and Current Scholarship." In *Do Historical Matters Matter to Faith? A Critical Appraisal of Modern and Postmodern Approaches to Scripture*, edited by James K. Hoffmeier and Dennis R. Magary, 243–61. Wheaton, IL: Crossway.

Seevers, Boyd. 2013. *Warfare in the Old Testament: The Organization, Weapons, and Tactics of Ancient Near Eastern Armies.* Grand Rapids: Kregel Academic.

Seitz, Christopher R. 1993. *Isaiah 1–39.* IBC. Louisville: Westminster John Knox.

Sheldon, Charles M. 1898. *In His Steps: What Would Jesus Do?* Chicago: Advance.

Shifman, Arie. 2012. "'A Scent' of the Spirit: Exegesis of an Enigmatic Verse (Isaiah 11:3)." *JBL* 131:241–49.

Skjoldal, Neil O. 1993. "The Function of Isaiah 24–27." *JETS* 36:163–72.

Smith, Gary V. 2007. *Isaiah 1–39.* NAC 15A. Nashville: Broadman & Holman.

Spangler, Ann, and Lois Tverberg. 2018. "For Everything a Blessing." In *Sitting at the Feet of Rabbi Jesus: How the Jewishness of Jesus Can Transform Your Faith,* 98–107. Grand Rapids: Zondervan.

Stadelmann, Luis I. J. 1970. *The Hebrew Conception of the World.* AnBib 39. Rome: Pontifical Biblical Institute.

Stansell, Gary. 1996. "Isaiah 28–33: Blest Be the Tie That Binds (Isaiah Together)." In *New Visions of Isaiah,* edited by Roy F. Melugin and Marvin A. Sweeney, 68–103. JSOTSup 214. Sheffield: Sheffield Academic.

Stassen, S. L. 1994. "Marriage (and Related) Metaphors in Isaiah 54:1–17." *Journal for Semitics* 6:57–73.

Stewart, Robert. 2013. "'Holy War,' Divine Action and the New Atheism: Philosophical Considerations." In *Holy War in the Bible: Christian Morality and an Old Testament Problem,* edited by Heath A. Thomas, Jeremy Evans, and Paul Copan, 265–84. Downers Grove, IL: IVP Academic.

Story, J. Lyle. 2009. "Hope in the Midst of Tragedy (Isa. 5:1–7; 27:2–6; Matt. 21:33–46 par.)." *HBT* 31:178–95.

Stott, John R. 1992. "Pride, Humility, and God." In *Alive to God: Studies in Spirituality,* edited by J. I. Packer and Loren Wilkinson, 111–21. Downers Grove, IL: InterVarsity Press.

Strawn, Brent A. 2009. "*kĕpîr 'ărāyôt* in Judges 14:5." *VT* 59:150–58.

Stromberg, Jacob. 2008. "The 'Root of Jesse' in Isaiah 11:10: Postexilic Judah, or Postexilic Davidic King?" *JBL* 127:655–69.

Stuart, Douglas. 1976. "The Sovereign's Day of Conquest." *BASOR* 221:159–64.

Sumner, Stephen T. 2018. "The Genealogy and Theology of Isaiah 11:1." *VT* 68:643–59.

Sweeney, Marvin A. 1988. *Isaiah 1–4 and the Post-exilic Understanding of the Isaianic Tradition.* BZAW 171. Berlin: de Gruyter.

———. 1994. "Sargon's Threat Against Jerusalem in Isaiah 10, 27–32." *Bib* 75:457–70.

———. 1996. *Isaiah 1–39 with an Introduction to Prophetic Literature.* FOTL 16. Grand Rapids: Eerdmans.

Tadmor, Hayim, and Shigeo Yamada. 2011. *The Royal Inscriptions of Tiglath-pileser III (744–727 BC) and Shalmaneser V (726–722 BC), Kings of Assyria.* RINAP 1. Winona Lake, IN: Eisenbrauns.

Toorn, Karel van der. 1988. "Echoes of Judean Necromancy in Isaiah 28,7–22." *ZAW* 100:199–217.

Tsumura, David Toshio. 2007. *The First Book of Samuel.* NICOT. Grand Rapids: Eerdmans.

Tull, Patricia K. 2010. *Isaiah 1–39.* SHBC. Macon, GA: Smyth & Helwys.

Turner, David L. 2008. *Matthew.* BECNT. Grand Rapids: Baker Academic.

Ussishkin, David. 1977. "The Destruction of Lachish by Sennacherib and the Dating of the Royal Judean Storage Jars." *TA* 4:28–60.

———. 2013. "Sennacherib's Campaign to Judah: The Events at Lachish and Jerusalem." In *Isaiah and Imperial Context: The Book of Isaiah in the Times of Empire,* edited by Andrew T. Abernethy, Mark G. Brett, Tim Bulkeley, and Tim Meadowcroft, 1–34. Eugene, OR: Pickwick.

_____. 2014. *Biblical Lachish: A Tale of Construction, Destruction, Excavation and Restoration.* Jerusalem: Israel Exploration Society.

Van Leeuwen, Raymond C. 1980. "Isa. 14:12, *ḥôlēš'al gwym* and Gilgamesh XI, 6." *JBL* 99, no. 2:173–84.

Vogels, Walter. 1986. *God's Universal Covenant.* 2nd ed. Ottawa: University of Ottawa Press.

Wakely, Robin. 1997. "בָּגַד" (#933). *NIDOTTE* 1:582–95.

Walsh, Carey Ellen. 2000. *The Fruit of the Vine: Viticulture in Ancient Israel.* HSM 60. Winona Lake, IN: Eisenbrauns.

Walton, John H. 2006. *Ancient Near Eastern Thought and the Old Testament: Introducing the Conceptual World of the Hebrew Bible.* Grand Rapids: Baker Academic.

Watts, John D. W. 1985. *Isaiah 1–33.* WBC 24. Waco, TX: Word.

Wegner, Paul D. 1992. "A Re-examination of Isaiah IX 1–6." *VT* 42:103–12.

Weinfeld, Moshe. 1995. *Social Justice in Ancient Israel and in the Ancient Near East.* Jerusalem: Magnes.

Westermann, Claus. 1963. "The Way of Promise Through the Old Testament." In *The Old Testament and Christian Faith: A Theological Discussion*, edited by Bernhard W. Anderson, 200–224. New York: Harper & Row.

_____. 1967. *Basic Forms of Prophetic Speech.* Translated by Hugh Clayton White. Philadelphia: Westminster.

_____. 1991. *Prophetic Oracles of Salvation in the Old Testament.* Translated by Keith Crim. Louisville: Westminster John Knox.

Wildberger, Hans. 1991. *Isaiah 1–12: A Commentary.* CC. Translated by Thomas H. Trapp. Minneapolis: Fortress.

_____. 1997. *Isaiah 13–27: A Commentary.* CC. Translated by Thomas H. Trapp. Minneapolis: Fortress.

_____. 2002. *Isaiah 28–39: A Commentary.* CC. Translated by Thomas H. Trapp. Minneapolis: Fortress.

Williams, Gary Roye. 1985. "Frustrated Expectations in Isaiah V 1–7: A Literary Interpretation." *VT* 35:459–65.

Williamson, H. G. M. 2006. *Isaiah 1–5: A Critical and Exegetical Commentary.* ICC. London: T&T Clark.

_____. 2009. "Recent Issues in the Study of Isaiah." In *Interpreting Isaiah: Issues and Approaches*, edited by David G. Firth and H. G. M. Williamson, 21–39. Downers Grove, IL: IVP Academic.

_____. 2018. *Isaiah 6–12: A Critical and Exegetical Commentary.* ICC. London: Bloomsbury T&T Clark.

Willis, John T. 1979. "The Expression *be'acharith hayyamin* [sic] in the Old Testament." *ResQ* 22:54–71.

_____. 1983. "On the Interpretation of Isaiah 1:18." *JSOT* 25:35–54.

_____. 1984. "The First Pericope in the Book of Isaiah." *VT* 34:63–77.

_____. 1997. "Isaiah 2:2–5 and the Psalms of Zion." In *Writing and Reading the Scroll of Isaiah*, edited by Craig C. Broyles and Craig A. Evans, 1:295–316. 2 vols. VTSup 70. Leiden: Brill.

Wolf, Herbert M. 1972. "A Solution to the Immanuel Prophecy in Isaiah 7:14–8:22." *JBL* 91:449–56.

Wyatt, N. 2009. "The Concept and Purpose of Hell: Its Nature and Development in West Semitic Thought." *Numen* 56:161–84.

Yamauchi, Edwin. 1997. *Persia and the Bible.* Grand Rapids: Baker.

Young, Edward J. 1965. *The Book of Isaiah: The English Text, with Introduction, Exposition and Notes.* Vol. 1: *Chapters 1–18.* NICOT. Grand Rapids: Eerdmans.

References

———. 1969. *The Book of Isaiah: The English Text, with Introduction, Exposition and Notes.* Vol. 2: *Chapters 19–39.* NICOT. Grand Rapids: Eerdmans.

Young, Robb Andrew. 2012. *Hezekiah in History and Tradition.* VTSup 155. Leiden: Brill.

Ziegler, Joseph, ed. 1983. *Isaias.* 3rd ed. SVTG 14. Göttingen: Vandenhoeck & Ruprecht.

Zimmerli, Walther. 1983. *Ezekiel 2: A Commentary on the Book of the Prophet Ezekiel.* Hermeneia. Philadelphia: Fortress.